Cisco IOS Bridging and IBM

Network Solutions

Cisco Systems, Inc.

Macmillan Technical Publishing
201 West 103rd Street
Indianapolis, IN 46290 USA

Printed in the United States of America 1 2 3 4 5 6 7 8 9 0

Library of Congress Cataloging-in-Publication:
98-84217

ISBN: 1-57870-051-5

Warning and Disclaimer

This book is designed to provide information about **Cisco IOS Bridging and IBM Network Solutions**. Every effort has been made to make this book as complete and as accurate as possible, but no warranty or fitness is implied.

The information is provided on an "as is" basis. The author, Macmillan Technical Publishing, and Cisco Systems, Inc. shall have neither liability nor responsibility to any person or entity with respect to any loss or damages arising from the information contained in this book or from the use of the discs or programs that may accompany it.

The opinions expressed in this book belong to the author and are not necessarily those of Cisco Systems, Inc.

Associate Publisher	Jim LeValley
Executive Editor	Julie Fairweather
Cisco Systems Program Manager	H. Kim Lew
Managing Editor	Caroline Roop
Acquisitions Editor	Tracy Hughes
Development Editor	Liz Green
Project Editor	Brian Sweany
Team Coordinator	Amy Lewis
Book Designer	Louisa Klucznik
Cover Designer	Karen Ruggles
Production Team	Kim Cofer
	Deb Kincaid
	Nicole Ritch
	Lisa Stumpf
Indexer	Tim Wright

Trademark
Acknowledgments

Acknowledgments

The Cisco IOS Reference Library is a result of collaborative efforts of many Cisco technical writers and editors over the years. This bookset represents the continuing development and integration of user documentation for the ever-increasing set of Cisco IOS networking features and functionality.

The current team of Cisco IOS technical writers and editors includes Katherine Anderson, Jennifer Bridges, Joelle Chapman, Christy Choate, Meredith Fisher, Tina Fox, Marie Godfrey, Dianna Johansen, Sheryl Kelly, Yvonne Kucher, Doug MacBeth, Lavanya Mandavilli, Mary Mangone, Spank McCoy, Greg McMillan, Madhu Mitra, Oralee Murillo, Vick Payne, Jane Phillips, George Powers, Teresa Oliver Schuetz, Wink Schuetz, Karen Shell, Grace Tai, and Bethann Watson.

This writing team wants to acknowledge the many engineering, customer support, and marketing subject-matter experts for their participation in reviewing draft documents and, in many cases, providing source material from which this bookset is developed.

Contents at a Glance

About the Cisco IOS Reference Library

Introduction Bridging and IBM Networking Overview

PART 1 BRIDGING

Chapter 1 Configuring Transparent Bridging

Chapter 2 Transparent Bridging Commands

Chapter 3 Configuring Source-Route Bridging

Chapter 4 Source-Route Bridging Commands

PART 2 IBM NETWORKING

Chapter 5 Configuring Remote Source-Route Bridging

Chapter 6 Remote Source-Route Bridging Commands

Chapter 7 Configuring Data-Link Switching Plus

Chapter 8 DLSw+ Configuration Commands

Chapter 9	Configuring Serial Tunnel and Block Serial Tunnel
Chapter 10	Serial Tunnel and Block Serial Tunnel Commands
Chapter 11	Configuring LLC2 and SDLC Parameters
Chapter 12	LLC2 and SDLC Commands
Chapter 13	Configuring IBM Network Media Translation
Chapter 14	IBM Network Media Translation Commands
Chapter 15	Configuring DSPU and SNA Service Point Support
Chapter 16	DSPU and SNA Service Point Configuration Commands
Chapter 17	Configuring SNA Frame Relay Access Support
Chapter 18	SNA Frame Relay Access Support Commands
Chapter 19	Configuring Advanced Peer-to-Peer Networking
Chapter 20	APPN Configuration Commands
Chapter 21	Configuring NCIA Client/Server Topologies
Chapter 22	NCIA Server Configuration Commands
Chapter 23	Configuring IBM Channel Attach
Chapter 24	IBM Channel Attach Commands
Appendix A	Ethernet Type Codes
	Index

Table of Contents

About the Cisco IOS Reference Library 1

Introduction Bridging and IBM Networking Overview 5

Cisco IOS Reference Library Organization 1

Other Books Available in the Cisco IOS Reference Library 1

Book Conventions 2

Transparent and Source-Route Transparent Bridging 5

Source-Route Bridging (SRB) 10

Remote Source-Route Bridging (RSRB) 12

Data-Link Switching Plus (DLSw+) 13

Serial Tunnel and Block Serial Tunnel 23

SDLC and LLC2 Parameters 27

IBM Network Media Translation 29

QLLC Conversion 32

Downstream Physical Unit and SNA Service Point 36

SNA Frame Relay Access Support 37
Advanced Peer-to-Peer Networking 40
Native Client Interface Architecture (NCIA) 52
IBM Channel Interface Processor 56

PART 1   **BRIDGING 59**

Chapter 1   **Configuring Transparent Bridging 61**
Transparent and SRT Bridging Configuration Task
    List 61
Configuring Transparent Bridging and SRT
    Bridging 62
Configuring Transparently Bridged Virtual LANs
    (VLANs) 63
Configuring Routing Between VLANs 65
Configuring Transparent Bridging over WANs 68
Configuring Concurrent Routing and Bridging 73
Configuring Integrated Routing and Bridging 74
Configuring Transparent Bridging Options 77
Filtering Transparently Bridged Packets 81
Adjusting Spanning-Tree Parameters 89
Tuning the Transparently Bridged Network 92
Monitoring and Maintaining the Transparent
    Bridge Network 94
Transparent and SRT Bridging Configuration
    Examples 95

Chapter 2   **Transparent Bridging Commands 117**
access-list (extended) 117
access-list (standard) 119
access-list (type-code) 120
bridge acquire 122
bridge address 123

bridge bridge 124

bridge circuit-group pause 125

bridge circuit-group source-based 126

bridge cmf 127

bridge crb 128

bridge domain 129

bridge forward-time 130

bridge-group 131

bridge-group aging-time 132

bridge-group cbus-bridging 133

bridge-group circuit-group 134

bridge-group input-address-list 135

bridge-group input-lat-service-deny 136

bridge-group input-lat-service-permit 137

bridge-group input-lsap-list 138

bridge-group input-pattern-list 139

bridge-group input-type-list 140

bridge-group lat-compression 141

bridge-group output-address-list 141

bridge-group output-lat-service-deny 142

bridge-group output-lat-service-permit 143

bridge-group output-lsap-list 144

bridge-group output-pattern-list 146

bridge-group output-type-list 146

bridge-group path-cost 147

bridge-group priority 148

bridge-group spanning-disabled 149

bridge-group sse 150

bridge hello-time 151

bridge irb 152

bridge lat-service-filtering 153

bridge max-age 153

bridge multicast-source 154

bridge priority 155

bridge protocol 156

bridge route 157

clear bridge 158

clear bridge multicast 158

clear sse 159

clear vlan statistics 160

encapsulation isl 161

encapsulation sde 161

ethernet-transit-oui 162

frame-relay map bridge broadcast 164

interface bvi 165

ip routing 166

show bridge 167

show bridge circuit-group 170

show bridge group 171

show bridge multicast 172

show bridge vlan 173

show interfaces crb 174

show interfaces irb 177

show span 178

show sse summary 180

show vlans 181

x25 map bridge 182

Chapter 3   **Configuring Source-Route Bridging 187**

SRB Configuration Task List 187

Configuring Source-Route Bridging 188

Configuring Bridging of Routed Protocols 196

Configuring Translation between SRB and
    Transparent Bridging Environments 199

Configuring NetBIOS Support 203

Configuring LAN Network Manager (LNM)
Support 208

Securing the SRB Network 215

Tuning the SRB Network 223

Establishing SRB Interoperability with Specific
Token Ring Implementations 227

Monitoring and Maintaining the SRB Network 229

SRB Configuration Examples 230

Chapter 4 **Source-Route Bridging Commands 251**

access-expression 251

access-list 253

bridge protocol ibm 255

clear netbios-cache 256

clear rif-cache 257

clear source-bridge 257

clear sse 258

ethernet-transit-oui 259

lnm alternate 261

lnm crs 262

lnm disabled 263

lnm loss-threshold 264

lnm password 265

lnm pathtrace-disabled 266

lnm rem 267

lnm rps 268

lnm snmp-only 269

lnm softerr 269

mac-address 270

multiring 271

netbios access-list bytes 273

netbios access-list host 275

netbios enable-name-cache 277

netbios input-access-filter bytes 277
netbios input-access-filter host 278
netbios name-cache 279
netbios name-cache name-len 280
netbios name-cache proxy-datagram 281
netbios name-cache query-timeout 282
netbios name-cache recognized-timeout 283
netbios name-cache timeout 283
netbios output-access-filter bytes 284
netbios output-access-filter host 285
rif 286
rif timeout 287
rif validate-age 288
rif validate-enable 289
rif validate-enable-age 290
rif validate-enable-route-cache 291
show controllers token 292
show interfaces tokenring 297
show lnm bridge 301
show lnm config 301
show lnm interface 303
show lnm ring 305
show lnm station 306
show netbios-cache 308
show rif 309
show source-bridge 310
show span 313
show sse summary 314
source-bridge 315
source-bridge connection-timeout 317
source-bridge enable-80d5 318
source-bridge explorer-dup-ARE-filter 320
source-bridge explorer-fastswitch 320

source-bridge explorer-maxrate 321

source-bridge explorerq-depth 322

source-bridge input-address-list 322

source-bridge input-lsap-list 323

source-bridge input-type-list 324

source-bridge max-hops 325

source-bridge max-in-hops 326

source-bridge max-out-hops 326

source-bridge output-address-list 327

source-bridge output-lsap-list 328

source-bridge output-type-list 329

sourcc-bridge proxy-explorer 330

source-bridge proxy-netbios-only 331

source-bridge ring-group 332

source-bridge route-cache 333

source-bridge route-cache cbus 334

source-bridge route-cache sse 335

source-bridge sap-80d5 336

source-bridge spanning (automatic) 337

source-bridge spanning (manual) 338

source-bridge transparent 339

source-bridge transparent fastswitch 341

PART 2   **IBM NETWORKING 343**

Chapter 5   **Configuring Remote Source-Route Bridging 345**

RSRB Configuration Task List 345

Configuring RSRB Using Direct Encapsulation 346

Configuring RSRB Using IP Encapsulation over an FST Connection 347

Configuring RSRB Using IP Encapsulation over a TCP Connection 350

Configuring RSRB Using IP Encapsulation over a
    Fast-Switched TCP Connection 351
Configuring RSRB Using TCP and LLC2 Local
    Acknowledgment 352
Configuring Direct Frame Relay Encapsulation
    Between RSRB Peers 357
Establishing SAP Prioritization 357
Tuning the RSRB Network 359
Monitoring and Maintaining the RSRB Network
    361
RSRB Configuration Examples 362

Chapter 6   **Remote Source-Route Bridging Commands
                   379**
                   locaddr-priority 379
                   locaddr-priority-list 380
                   priority-group 382
                   priority-list 382
                   rsrb remote-peer lsap-output-list 384
                   rsrb remote-peer netbios-output-list 385
                   sap-priority 386
                   sap-priority-list 387
                   show local-ack 388
                   source-bridge cos-enable 389
                   source-bridge fst-peername 390
                   source-bridge keepalive 391
                   source-bridge largest-frame 391
                   source-bridge passthrough 392
                   source-bridge remote-peer frame-relay (direct
                       encapsulation) 394
                   source-bridge remote-peer fst 395
                   source-bridge remote-peer ftcp 397

source-bridge remote-peer tcp 398
source-bridge tcp-queue-max 400

Chapter 7   **Configuring Data-Link Switching Plus 403**
DLSw+ Configuration Task List 403
Defining a Source-Bridge Ring Group for DLSw+
    404
Defining a DLSw+ Local Peer for the Router 404
Defining a DLSw+ Ring List or Port List 405
Defining a DLSw+ Bridge Group List 406
Defining DLSw+ Remote Peers 406
Enabling DLSw+ over Frame Relay 410
Enabling DLSw+ on a Token Ring or FDDI
    Interface 411
Enabling DLSw+ on an Ethernet Interface 411
Enabling DLSw+ on an SDLC Interface 412
Enabling DLSw+ over QLLC 413
Enabling NetBIOS Dial-on-Demand Routing 414
Tuning the DLSw+ Configuration 414
Monitoring and Maintaining the DLSw+ Network
    417
DLSw+ Configuration Examples 418

Chapter 8   **DLSw+ Configuration Commands 439**
clear dlsw circuit 439
clear dlsw reachability 440
clear dlsw statistics 440
dlsw allroute-netbios 441
dlsw allroute-sna 441
dlsw bgroup-list 442
dlsw bridge-group 443
dlsw disable 445
dlsw duplicate-path-bias 446

dlsw group-cache disable 446

dlsw group-cache max-entries 447

dlsw icannotreach saps 448

dlsw icanreach 449

dlsw llc2 nornr 450

dlsw local-peer 451

dlsw mac-addr 453

dlsw netbios-keepalive-filter 454

dlsw netbios-name 455

dlsw peer-on-demand-defaults 456

dlsw port-list 458

dlsw prom-peer-defaults 459

dlsw remote-peer frame relay 461

dlsw remote-peer fst 463

dlsw remote-peer interface 465

dlsw remote-peer tcp 467

dlsw ring-list 470

dlsw timer 471

dlsw udp-disable 473

qllc dlsw 474

sdlc dlsw 475

show dlsw capabilities 476

show dlsw circuits 478

show dlsw fastcache 480

show dlsw peers 481

show dlsw reachability 483

show dlsw statistics 486

Chapter 9   Configuring Serial Tunnel and Block Serial Tunnel 487

STUN Configuration Task List 488

Enabling STUN 488

Configuring SDLC Broadcast 488

Specifying STUN Protocol Group 489

Enabling STUN Interfaces 491

Establishing the Frame Encapsulation Method 491

Configuring STUN with Multilink Transmission
    Groups 496

Setting Up STUN Traffic Priorities 497

Monitoring STUN Network Activity 500

STUN Configuration Examples 500

Block Serial Tunneling (BSTUN) 509

Bisync Network Overview 510

Asynchronous Network Overview 512

Frame Sequencing 514

BSTUN Configuration Task List 516

Enabling BSTUN 516

Defining the Protocol Group 517

Enabling Frame Relay Encapsulation 518

Defining Mapping Between BSTUN and DLCI 518

Configuring BSTUN on the Serial Interface 518

Placing a Serial Interface in a BSTUN Group 519

Specifying How Frames are Forwarded 519

Setting Up BSTUN Traffic Priorities 520

Configuring Protocol Group Options on a Serial
    Interface 521

Configuring Direct Serial Encapsulation for
    Passthru Peers 523

Configuring Local Acknowledgment Peers 523

Monitoring the Status of BSTUN 523

BSTUN Configuration Examples 523

**Chapter 10   Serial Tunnel and Block Serial Tunnel
                Commands 539**

asp addr-offset 540

asp role 541

asp rx-ift 542

bsc char-set 543

bsc contention 543

bsc dial-contention 544

bsc host-timeout 545

bsc pause 546

bsc poll-timeout 546

bsc primary 547

bsc retries 548

bsc secondary 548

bsc servlim 549

bsc spec-poll 550

bstun group 551

bstun keepalive-count 551

bstun lisnsap 552

bstun peer-name 553

bstun protocol-group 554

bstun remote-peer-keepalive 555

bstun route 556

bstun route (Frame Relay) 557

encapsulation bstun 558

encapsulation stun 559

frame-relay map bstun 560

frame-relay map llc2 561

locaddr-priority-list 562

priority-group 563

priority-list protocol bstun 564

priority-list protocol ip tcp 565

priority-list stun address 566

queue-list protocol bstun 567

queue-list protocol ip tcp 568

sdlc virtual-multidrop 569

show bsc 570

show bstun 575

show stun 577

stun group 578

stun keepalive-count 579

stun peer-name 580

stun protocol-group 581

stun remote-peer-keepalive 582

stun route address interface dlci 583

stun route address interface serial 584

stun route address tcp 585

stun route all interface serial 586

stun route all tcp 587

stun schema offset length format 587

stun sdlc-role primary 588

stun sdlc-role secondary 589

Chapter 11   Configuring LLC2 and SDLC Parameters 591

LLC2 Configuration Task List 591

Controlling Transmission of I-Frames 591

Establishing Polling Level 594

Setting Up XID Transmissions 595

Monitoring LLC2 Stations 596

SDLC Configuration Task List 596

Enabling the Router as a Primary or a Secondary
    SDLC Station 597

Enabling SDLC Two-Way Simultaneous Mode 599

Determining the Use of Frame Rejects 600

Setting SDLC Timer and Retry Counts 600

Setting SDLC Frame and Window Sizes 601

Controlling the Buffer Size 601

Controlling Polling of Secondary Stations 602

Configuring an SDLC Interface for Half-Duplex
    Mode 603

Specifying the XID Value 603
Setting the Largest SDLC I-Frame Size 604
Monitoring SDLC Stations 604
Configuration Examples 605

Chapter 12   LLC2 and SDLC Commands 609

encapsulation sdlc 610
encapsulation sdlc-primary 611
encapsulation sdlc-secondary 612
llc2 ack-delay-time 613
llc2 ack-max 614
llc2 idle-time 615
llc2 local-window 616
llc2 n2 617
llc2 t1-time 618
llc2 tbusy-time 619
llc2 tpf-time 620
llc2 trej-time 621
llc2 xid-neg-val-time 622
llc2 xid-retry-time 623
sdlc address 624
sdlc address ff ack-mode 625
sdlc dlsw 626
sdlc dte-timeout 626
sdlc frmr-disable 627
sdlc holdq 628
sdlc k 629
sdlc line-speed 630
sdlc n1 631
sdlc n2 632
sdlc partner 632
sdlc poll-limit-value 633
sdlc poll-pause-timer 634

sdlc poll-wait-timeout 636

sdlc qllc-prtnr 637

sdlc role 638

sdlc sdlc-largest-frame 639

sdlc simultaneous 639

sdlc slow-poll 640

sdlc t1 641

sdlc test serial 642

sdlc vmac 644

sdlc xid 644

show interfaces 645

show llc2 648

Chapter 13   **Configuring IBM Network Media Translation 653**

SDLLC Configuration Task List 653

Configuring SDLLC with Direct Connection 653

Configuring SDLLC with Remote Source-Route
    Bridging (RSRB) 655

Configuring SDLLC with RSRB and Local
    Acknowledgment 657

Configuring SDLLC with Ethernet and
    Translational Bridging 657

Customizing SDLLC Media Translation 658

Monitoring SDLLC Media Translation 660

QLLC Conversion Configuration Task List 660

Enabling QLLC Conversion on a Serial Interface
    660

Customizing QLLC Conversion 663

Monitoring QLLC Conversion 665

SDLLC Configuration Examples 666

QLLC Conversion Configuration Examples 672

Chapter 14   **IBM Network Media Translation Commands 681**

qllc accept-all-calls 681

qllc largest-packet 682

qllc npsi-poll 684

qllc partner 685

qllc sap 686

qllc srb 687

qllc xid 689

sdllc partner 690

sdllc ring-largest-frame 692

sdllc sap 693

sdllc sdlc-largest-frame 694

sdllc traddr 695

sdllc xid 696

show interfaces 697

show qllc 700

show sdllc local-ack 703

source-bridge fst-peername 704

source-bridge qllc-local-ack 705

source-bridge remote-peer fst 706

source-bridge remote-peer interface 707

source-bridge remote-peer tcp 709

source-bridge ring-group 710

source-bridge sdllc-local-ack 712

x25 map qllc 713

x25 pvc qllc 716

Chapter 15   **Configuring DSPU and SNA Service Point Support 719**

DSPU Configuration Task List 719

Defining DSPU Upstream Hosts 719

Defining Downstream PUs 721

Defining DSPU LUs 723

Configuring DSPU to Use a Data-Link Control 724

Defining the Number of Outstanding, Unacknowledged Activation RUs 734

Configuring SNA Service Point Support 735

Monitoring DSPU and SNA Service Point Feature
Status 742

DSPU and SNA Service Point Configuration
Examples 742

Chapter 16 **DSPU and SNA Service Point Configuration
Commands 751**

dspu activation-window 751

dspu default-pu 752

dspu enable-host (Ethernet, Frame Relay, Token
Ring, FDDI) 753

dspu enable-host (QLLC) 754

dspu enable-host (SDLC) 755

dspu enable-pu (Ethernet, Frame Relay, Token
Ring, FDDI) 756

dspu enable-pu (QLLC) 756

dspu enable-pu (SDLC) 757

dspu host (Frame Relay) 758

dspu host (QLLC) 760

dspu host (SDLC) 761

dspu host (Token Ring, Ethernet, FDDI, RSRB,
VDLC) 763

dspu lu 765

dspu ncia 766

dspu ncia enable-pu 767

dspu notification-level 768

dspu pool 769

dspu pu (Frame Relay) 770

dspu pu (QLLC) 772

dspu pu (SDLC) 773

dspu pu (Token Ring, Ethernet, FDDI, RSRB, VDLC, NCIA) 774

dspu rsrb 777

dspu rsrb enable-host 779

dspu rsrb enable-pu 780

dspu rsrb start 781

dspu start 782

dspu vdlc 783

dspu vdlc enable-host 784

dspu vdlc enable-pu 786

dspu vdlc start 787

lan-name 789

location 789

show dspu 790

show sna 792

sna enable-host (QLLC) 793

sna enable-host (SDLC) 794

sna enable-host (Token Ring, Ethernet, Frame Relay, FDDI) 794

sna host (Frame Relay) 795

sna host (QLLC) 797

sna host (SDLC) 798

sna host (Token Ring, Ethernet, FDDI, RSRB, VDLC) 800

sna rsrb 802

sna rsrb enable-host 802

sna rsrb start 803

sna start 804

sna vdlc 805

sna vdlc enable-host 806

sna vdlc start 807

Chapter 17   Configuring SNA Frame Relay Access Support 809

SNA FRAS Configuration Task List 809
Configuring FRAS BNN Statically 810
Configuring FRAS BNN Dynamically 810
Configuring FRAS Boundary Access Node Support 811
Configuring SRB over Frame Relay 811
Configuring FRAS Congestion Management 812
Configuring FRAS DLCI Backup 812
Configuring Frame Relay RSRB Dial Backup 813
Configuring Frame Relay DLSw+ Dial Backup 813
Monitoring and Maintaining FRAS 815
FRAS Configuration Examples 815
FRAS Host Overview 824
FRAS Host Configuration Task List 827
FRAS Host Configuration Examples 828
FRAS MIB 832

Chapter 18   SNA Frame Relay Access Support Commands 833

frame-relay map llc2 833
frame-relay map rsrb 834
fras backup dlsw 834
fras ban 836
fras ddr-backup 837
fras-host ban 838
fras-host bnn 839
fras-host dlsw-local-ack 840
fras map llc 840
fras map sdlc 841
interface virtual-tokenring 842
llc2 dynwind 843

show fras 844

show fras-host 845

show fras map 847

source-bridge 847

Chapter 19   Configuring Advanced Peer-to-Peer Networking 851

APPN Command Modes 851

Completing APPN Definitions 852

Changing APPN Definitions 852

APPN Configuration Task List 852

Defining an APPN Control Point 853

Configuring Serial Interface Encapsulation 857

Defining an APPN Port 857

Defining an APPN Link Station 862

Defining an APPN Connection Network 868

Defining an APPN Class of Service 869

Defining an APPN Mode 871

Defining an APPN Partner LU Location 872

Starting the APPN Subsystem 874

Stopping the APPN Subsystem 874

Starting and Stopping APPN Ports and Link Stations 874

Tuning the APPN Network 875

Monitoring the APPN Network 876

APPN Configuration Examples 877

Chapter 20   APPN Configuration Commands 899

adjacent-cp-name 899

appn class-of-service 900

appn connection-network 901

appn control-point 902

appn link-station 904

appn mode 905

appn partner-lu-location 907

appn path-switch connection 908

appn port 908

appn routing 910

appn start 911

appn start link-station 911

appn start port 912

appn stop 913

appn stop link-station 914

appn stop port 915

atm-dest-address 915

backup-dlus (APPN control point) 916

backup-dlus (APPN link station) 917

buffer-percent 918

central-resource-registration 919

class-of-service 920

connect-at-startup 921

cost-per-byte (APPN link station) 922

cost-per-byte (APPN port) 923

cost-per-connect-time (APPN link station) 924

cost-per-connect-time (APPN port) 925

cp-cp-sessions-supported 926

desired-max-send-btu-size 927

dlur 928

dlur-dspu-name 928

dlus (APPN control point) 929

dlus (APPN link station) 930

effective-capacity (APPN link station) 931

effective-capacity (APPN port) 932

fr-dest-address 933

hpr (APPN control point) 934

hpr (APPN link station) 935

hpr (APPN port) 936

hpr max-sessions 937

hpr retries 937

hpr sap 938

hpr timers liveness 939

hpr timers path-switch 940

interrupt-switched 941

lan-dest-address 942

limited-resource (APPN link station) 943

limited-resource (APPN port) 944

link-queuing 944

local-sap 945

locate-queuing 946

max-cached-entries 947

max-cached-trees 948

maximum-memory 948

max-link-stations 949

max-rcv-btu-size 950

minimum-memory 951

negative-caching 952

node-row 953

null-xid-poll 955

owning-cp 956

port (APPN connection network) 957

port (APPN link station) 957

ppp-dest-address 958

propagation-delay (APPN link station) 959

propagation-delay (APPN port) 960

pu-type-20 961

reserved-inbound 962

reserved-outbound 963

retry-limit (APPN link station) 964

retry-limit (APPN port) 965

role (APPN link station) 966

role (APPN port) 967

route-additional-resistance 968

rsrb-virtual-station 968

safe-store-cycle 969

safe-store-host 970

safe-store-interval 971

sdlc-dest-address 972

sdlc-sec-addr 973

security (APPN link station) 973

security (APPN port) 974

service-any 975

serving-nn 976

show appn class-of-service 977

show appn connection-network 980

show appn directory 982

show appn dlur-lu 983

show appn dlur-pu 984

show appn dlus 986

show appn intermediate-session 988

show appn link-station 990

show appn mode 993

show appn node 994

show appn port 996

show appn rtp 999

show appn session 1001

show appn topology 1003

smds-dest-address 1007

tg-number 1007

tg-row 1008

transmission-priority 1010

user-defined-1 (APPN link station) 1011

user-defined-1 (APPN port) 1011

user-defined-2 (APPN link station) 1012

user-defined-2 (APPN port) 1013

user-defined-3 (APPN link station) 1014

user-defined-3 (APPN port) 1015

vdlc 1016

verify-adjacent-node-type 1017

wildcard 1018

x25-dest-address 1019

x25-subaddress 1020

xid-block-number 1021

xid-id-number 1021

Chapter 21   Configuring NCIA Client/Server Topologies 1023

NCIA Server Session to Local Token Ring Using DLSw+ Local Switch 1023

NCIA Server Session with DLSw+ 1025

NCIA Server Session with DSPU 1028

NCIA Server Session with RSRB 1030

Monitoring and Maintaining an NCIA Server Network 1033

NCIA Server Configuration Examples 1034

Chapter 22   NCIA Server Configuration Commands 1039

clear ncia circuit 1039

clear ncia client 1040

clear ncia client registered 1040

ncia 1041

ncia client 1042

ncia rsrb 1043

ncia server 1044

show ncia circuits 1046

show ncia client 1047

show ncia server 1049

Chapter 23   Configuring IBM Channel Attach 1051

Cisco's Implementation of the IBM Channel Attach
  Interface 1051

Interface Configuration Task List 1054

Loading the CIP Image 1055

Selecting the Interface 1056

Configuring IBM Channel Attach for TCP/IP
  CLAW Support 1057

Configuring IBM Channel Attach for TCP/IP
  Offload Support 1059

Configuring IBM Channel Attach for CSNA
  Support 1061

Selecting Host System Parameters 1064

Monitoring and Maintaining the Interface 1068

Configuring TN3270 on a Channel Interface
  Processor 1071

VTAM Host Configuration Considerations for
  Dynamic LU Allocation 1075

LU Address Mapping 1077

TN3270 Configuration Modes 1079

TN3270 Configuration Task List 1082

Cisco MultiPath Channel 1089

Requirements 1090

Configuration Overview 1090

Configuration Tasks 1091

Configuring the CIP Internal LAN for CMPC 1094

IBM Channel Attach Interface Configuration
  Examples 1096

CMPC Configuration Examples 1104

Chapter 24   IBM Channel Attach Commands 1119

adapter 1119

channel-protocol 1121

claw 1121

client (lu limit) 1123

client (lu nailing) 1124

cmpc 1126

csna 1127

dlur 1129

dlus-backup 1130

generic-pool 1131

idle-time 1132

interface channel 1133

ip precedence 1134

ip tos 1135

keepalive 1137

lan 1138

link 1139

lsap 1140

max-llc2-sessions 1142

maximum-lus 1142

name 1144

offload 1144

preferred-nnserver 1146

pu (DLUR) 1147

pu (direct) 1148

show extended channel cmpc 1150

show extended channel icmp-stack 1152

show extended channel ip-stack 1152

show extended channel llc2 1153

show extended channel statistics 1154

show extended channel subchannel 1158

show extended channel tcp-stack 1160

show extended channel tg 1161

show extended channel tn3270-server 1167

show extended channel tn3270-server client-ip-ad-
    dress 1170

show extended channel tn3270-server dlur 1173

show extended channel tn3270-server dlurlink
    1175

show extended channel tn3270-server nailed-ip
    1176

show extended channel tn3270-server pu 1178

show extended channel tn3270-server pu lu 1182

show extended channel udp-listeners 1185

show extended channel udp-stack 1186

show interfaces channel 1187

shutdown 1191

tcp-port 1192

tg 1193

tn3270-server 1194

timing-mark 1195

unbind-action 1196

vrn 1197

Appendix A   Ethernet Type Codes 1199

Index   1207

About the Cisco IOS Reference Library

The Cisco IOS Reference Library books are Cisco documentation that describe the tasks and commands necessary to configure and maintain your Cisco IOS network.

The Cisco IOS software bookset is intended primarily for users who configure and maintain access servers and routers, but are not necessarily familiar with the tasks, the relationship between tasks, or the commands necessary to perform particular tasks.

CISCO IOS REFERENCE LIBRARY ORGANIZATION

The Cisco IOS Reference library consists of eight books. Each book contains technology-specific configuration chapters with corresponding command reference chapters. Each configuration chapter describes Cisco's implementation of protocols and technologies, related configuration tasks, and contains comprehensive configuration examples. Each command reference chapter complements the organization of its corresponding configuration chapter and provides complete command syntax information.

OTHER BOOKS AVAILABLE IN THE CISCO IOS REFERENCE LIBRARY

- *Cisco IOS Configuration Fundamentals*. 1-57870-044-2; Currently available

  This comprehensive guide details Cisco IOS software configuration basics. Cisco IOS Configuration Fundamentals offers thorough coverage of router and access server configuration and maintenance techniques. In addition to hands-on implementation and task instruction, this book also presents the complete syntax for router and access server commands, and individual examples for each command. Learn to configure interfaces in addition to system management, file loading, AutoInstall, and set up functions.

1

- *Cisco IOS Dial Solutions,* 1-57870-055-8; Currently available

  This book provides readers with real-world solutions and how to implement them on a network. Customers interested in implementing dial solutions across their network environment include remote sites dialing in to a central office, Internet Service Providers (ISPs), ISP customers at home offices, and enterprise WAN system administrators implementing dial-on-demand routing (DDR).

- *Cisco IOS Wide Area Networking Solutions.* 1-57870-054-x; Currently available

  This book offers thorough, comprehensive coverage of internetworking technologies, particularly ATM, Frame Relay, SMDS, LAPB, and X.25, teaching the reader how to configure the technologies in a LAN/WAN environment.

- *Cisco IOS Switching Services.* 1-57870-053-1; Currently available

  This book is a comprehensive guide detailing available Cisco IOS switching alternatives. Cisco's switching services range from fast switching and Netflow switching to LAN Emulation.

- *Cisco IOS Soutions for Network Protocols,* Vol I: IP. 1-57870-049-3; Available April 1998

  This book is a comprehensive guide detailing available IP and IP routing alternatives. It describes how to implement IP addressing and IP services and how to configure support for a wide range of IP routing protocols including BGP for ISP networks and basic and advanced IP Multicast functionality.

- *Cisco IOS Networking Protocols,* Vol II: IPX, AppleTalk, and more. 1-57870-050-7; Available April 1998

  This book is a comprehensive guide detailing available network protocol alternatives. It describes how to implement various protocols in your network. This book includes documentation of the latest functionality for the IPX and AppleTalk desktop protocols as well as the following network protocols: Apollo Domain, Banyan VINES, DECNet, ISO CLNS, and XNS.

- *Cisco IOS Network Security.* 1-57870-057-4; Available May 1998

  This book documents security configuration from a remote site and for a central enterprise or service provider network. It describes AAA, Radius, TACACS+, and Kerberos network security features. It also explains how to encrypt data across enterprise networks. The book includes many illustrations that show configurations and functionality, along with a discussion of network security policy choices and some decision-making guidelines.

BOOK CONVENTIONS

Software and hardware documentation uses the following conventions:

- The caret character (^) represents the Control key.

  For example, the key combinations ^D and Ctrl-D are equivalent: Both mean hold down the Control key while you press the D key. Keys are indicated in capitals, but are not case-sensitive.

- A string is defined as a nonquoted set of characters.

  For example, when setting an SNMP community string to *public*, do not use quotation marks around the string; otherwise, the string will include the quotation marks.

Command descriptions use these conventions:

- Vertical bars (|) separate alternative, mutually exclusive, elements.
- Square brackets ([ ]) indicate optional elements.
- Braces ({ }) indicate a required choice.
- Braces within square brackets ([{ }]) indicate a required choice within an optional element.
- **Boldface** indicates commands and keywords that are entered literally as shown.
- *Italics* indicate arguments for which you supply values; in contexts that do not allow italics, arguments are enclosed in angle brackets (< >).

Examples use these conventions:

- Examples that contain system prompts denote interactive sessions, indicating that the user enters commands at the prompt. The system prompt indicates the current command mode. For example, the prompt `Router(config)#` indicates global configuration mode.
- Terminal sessions and information the system displays are in `screen` font.
- Information you enter is in `boldface screen` font.
- Nonprinting characters, such as passwords, are in angle brackets (< >).
- Default responses to system prompts are in square brackets ([ ]).
- Exclamation points (!) at the beginning of a line indicate a comment line. They are also displayed by the Cisco IOS software for certain processes.

CAUTION

Means *reader be careful*. In this situation, you might do something that could result in equipment damage or loss of data.

NOTES

Means *reader take note*. Notes contain helpful suggestions or references to materials not contained in this manual.

TIMESAVER

Means *the described action saves time*. You can save time by performing the action described in the paragraph.

Within the Cisco IOS Reference Library, the term *router* is used to refer to both access servers and routers. When a feature is supported on the access server only, the term *access server* is used. When a feature is supported on one or more specific router platforms (such as the Cisco 4500), but not on other platforms (such as the Cisco 2500), the text specifies the supported platforms.

Within examples, routers and access servers are alternately shown. These products are used only for example purposes—an example that shows one product does not indicate that the other product is not supported.

Bridging and IBM Networking Overview

Cisco IOS Bridging and IBM Network Solutions discusses the following software components:

- Transparent and Source-Route Transparent Bridging
- Source-Route Bridging (SRB)
- Remote Source-Route Bridging (RSRB)
- Data-Link Switching Plus (DLSw+)
- Serial Tunnel and Block Serial Tunnel
- SDLC and LLC2 Parameters
- IBM Network Media Translation
- Downstream Physical Unit and SNA Service Point
- SNA Frame Relay Access Support
- Advanced Peer-to-Peer Networking
- Native Client Interface Architecture (NCIA)
- IBM Channel Interface Processor

This overview chapter gives a high-level description of each technology. For configuration information, refer to the appropriate chapter in this publication.

TRANSPARENT AND SOURCE-ROUTE TRANSPARENT BRIDGING

Cisco IOS software supports transparent bridging for Ethernet, Fiber Distributed Data Interface (FDDI), and serial media, and supports source-route transparent (SRT) bridging for Token Ring media. In addition, Cisco supports all the mandatory Management Information Base (MIB) variables specified for transparent bridging in RFC 1286.

Transparent Bridging Features

Cisco's transparent bridging software implementation has the following features:

- Complies with the IEEE 802.1D standard.

- Provides the capability to logically segment a transparently bridged network into virtual local-area networks (LANs).

- Provides two Spanning-Tree Protocols—an older bridge protocol data unit (BPDU) format that is compatible with Digital and other LAN bridges for backward compatibility, and the IEEE standard bridge protocol data unit (BPDU) format. In addition to features standard with these Spanning-Tree Protocols, Cisco's proprietary software provides for multiple domains for spanning trees. The spanning-tree parameters are configurable.

- Allows frame filtering based on MAC address, protocol type, or the vendor code. Additionally, the bridging software can be configured to selectively filter local area transport (LAT) multicast service announcements.

- Provides deterministic load distribution while maintaining a loop-free spanning tree.

- Provides the capability to bridge over Asynchronous Transfer Mode (ATM), dial-on-demand routing (DDR), Fiber Distributed Data Interface (FDDI), Frame Relay, multiprotocol Link Access Procedure, Balanced (LAPB), Switched Multimegabit Data Service (SMDS), and X.25 networks.

- Provides concurrent routing and bridging, which is the ability to bridge a given protocol on some interfaces in a router and concurrently route that protocol on other interfaces in the same router.

- Provides integrated routing and bridging, which is the ability to route a given protocol between routed interfaces and bridge groups, or to route a given protocol between bridge groups.

- Provides fast-switched transparent bridging for Frame Relay encapsulated serial and High-Speed Serial Interface (HSSI) interfaces, according to the format specified in RFC 1490.

- Provides fast-switched transparent bridging for the ATM interface on the Cisco 7000, according to the format specified in RFC 1483.

- Provides for compression of LAT frames to reduce LAT traffic through the network.

- Provides both bridging and routing of virtual LANS (VLANs).

Cisco access servers and routers can be configured to serve as both multiprotocol routers and Media Access Control (MAC)-level bridges, bridging any traffic that cannot otherwise be routed. For example, a router routing the Internet Protocol (IP) can also bridge Digital's LAT protocol or NetBIOS traffic.

Cisco routers also support remote bridging over synchronous serial lines. As with frames received on all other media types, dynamic learning and configurable filtering applies to frames received on serial lines.

Transit bridging of Ethernet frames across FDDI media is also supported. The term *transit* refers to the fact that the source or destination of the frame cannot be on the FDDI media itself. This allows FDDI to act as a highly efficient backbone for the interconnection of many bridged networks. The configuration of FDDI transit bridging is identical to the configuration of transparent bridging on all other media types.

Integrated Routing and Bridging

While concurrent routing and bridging makes it possible to both route and bridge a specific protocol on separate interfaces within a router, the protocol is not switched between bridged and routed interfaces. Routed traffic is confined to the routed interfaces; bridged traffic is confined to bridged interfaces. A specified protocol may be either routed or bridged on a given interface, but not both.

Integrated routing and bridging makes it possible to route a specific protocol between routed interfaces and bridge groups, or route a specific protocol between bridge groups. Local, or unroutable, traffic can be bridged among the bridged interfaces in the same bridge group, while routable traffic can be routed to other routed interfaces or bridge groups. Figure I–1 illustrates how integrated routing and bridging in a router interconnects a bridged network with a routed network.

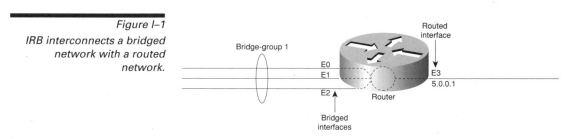

Figure I–1

IRB interconnects a bridged network with a routed network.

You can configure the Cisco IOS software to route a specific protocol between routed interfaces and bridge groups, or to route a specific protocol between bridge groups. Specifically, local or unroutable traffic is bridged among the bridged interfaces in the same bridge group, while routable traffic is routed to other routed interfaces or bridge groups. Using integrated routing and bridging, you can:

- Switch packets from a bridged interface to a routed interface
- Switch packets from a routed interface to a bridged interface
- Switch packets within the same bridge group

Bridge-Group Virtual Interface (BVI)

Because bridging operates in the data-link layer and routing operates in the network layer, they follow different protocol configuration models. Taking the basic IP model as an example, all bridged interfaces would belong to the same network, while each routed interface represents a distinct network.

In integrated routing and bridging, the BVI is introduced to avoid confusing the protocol configuration model when a specific protocol is both bridged and routed in a bridge group. Figure I–2 illustrates the BVI as a user-configured virtual interface residing within a router.

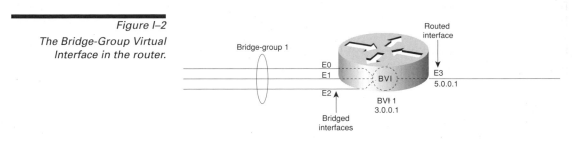

Figure I–2

The Bridge-Group Virtual Interface in the router.

The BVI is a normal routed interface that does not support bridging, but does represent its corresponding bridge group to the routed interface. It has all the network layer attributes (such as a network layer address and filters) that apply to the corresponding bridge group. The interface number assigned to this virtual interface corresponds to the bridge group that this virtual interface represents. This number is the link between the virtual interface and the bridge group.

When you enable routing for a given protocol on the BVI, packets coming from a routed interface, but destined for a host in a bridged domain, are routed to the BVI and are forwarded to the corresponding bridged interface. All traffic routed to the BVI is forwarded to the corresponding bridge group as bridged traffic. All routable traffic received on a bridged interface is routed to other routed interfaces as if it is coming directly from the BVI.

— **NOTES** ————————————————————————————————————

Because the BVI is a virtual routed interface, it has all the network layer attributes, such as a network address and the ability to perform filtering.

_____

To be able to receive routable packets arriving on a bridged interface, but destined for a routed interface, or to receive routed packets, the BVI must also have the appropriate addresses. MAC addresses and network addresses are assigned to the BVI as follows:

- The BVI "borrows" the MAC address of one of the bridged interfaces in the bridge group associated with the BVI.

- To route and bridge a given protocol in the same bridge group, you must configure the network layer attributes of the protocol on the BVI. No protocol attributes should be configured on the bridged interfaces, and no bridging attributes can be configured on the BVI.

Because there can be only one BVI representing a bridge group, and the bridge group can be made up of different media types configured for several different encapsulation methods, you might need to configure the BVI with the particular encapsulation methods required to switch packets correctly.

For example, the BVI has default data link and network layer encapsulations that are the same as those available on Ethernet interfaces, but you can configure the BVI with encapsulations that are not supported on an Ethernet interface. In some cases, the default encapsulations provide appropriate results; in other cases, they do not. For example, with default encapsulation, ARPA packets from the BVI are translated to SNAP when bridging IP to a Token Ring or FDDI bridged interface. But for IPX, Novell-ether encapsulation from the BVI is translated to raw-token or raw-FDDI when bridging IPX to a Token Ring or FDDI bridged interface. Because this behavior is usually not what you want, you must configure IPX SNAP or SAP encapsulation on the BVI.

Other Considerations

- Integrated routing and bridging is not supported on cBus platforms (AGS+ and Cisco 7000 series).
- Integrated routing and bridging is supported for transparent bridging, but not for source-route bridging.
- Integrated routing and bridging is supported on all media interfaces except X.25 and ISDN bridged interfaces.
- Integrated routing and bridging supports three protocols: IP, IPX, and AppleTalk in both fast-switching and process-switching modes.
- Integrated routing and bridging and concurrent routing and bridging cannot operate at the same time.

Source-Route Transparent (SRT) Bridging Features

Cisco routers support transparent bridging on Token Ring interfaces that support SRT bridging. Both transparent and SRT bridging are supported on all Token Ring interface cards that can be configured for either 4- or 16-MB transmission speeds.

As with other media, all the features that use **bridge-group** commands can be used on Token Ring interfaces. As with other interface types, the bridge group can be configured to run either the IEEE or Digital Spanning-Tree Protocols. When configured for the IEEE Spanning-Tree Protocol, the bridge cooperates with other SRT bridges and constructs a loop-free topology across the entire extended LAN.

You also can run the Digital Spanning-Tree Protocol over Token Ring. Use it when you have other non-IEEE bridges on other media and you do not have any SRT bridges on Token Ring. In this configuration, all the Token Ring transparent bridges must be Cisco routers. This is because the Digital Spanning-Tree Protocol has not been standardized on Token Ring.

As specified by the SRT bridging specification, only packets without a routing information field (RIF) (RII = 0 in the SA field) are transparently bridged. Packets with a RIF (RII = 1) are passed to the source-route bridging module for handling. An SRT-capable Token Ring interface can have both source-route bridging and transparent bridging enabled at the same time. However, with SRT bridging, frames that did not have a RIF when they were produced by their generating host never gain a RIF, and frames that did have a RIF when they were produced never lose that RIF.

Because bridges running only SRT bridging never add or remove RIFs from frames, they do not integrate source-route bridging with transparent bridging. A host connected to a source-route bridge that expects RIFs can *never* communicate with a device across a bridge that does not understand RIFs. SRT bridging cannot tie-in existing source-route bridges to a transparent bridged network. To tie-in existing bridges, you must use source-route translational bridging (SR/TLB) instead. SR/TLB is described in Chapter 3, "Configuring Source-Route Bridging."

Bridging between Token Ring and other media requires certain packet transformations. In all cases, the MAC addresses are bit-swapped because the bit ordering on Token Ring is different from that on other media. In addition, Token Ring supports one packet format, logical link control (LLC), while Ethernet supports two formats (LLC and Ethernet).

The transformation of LLC frames between media is simple. A length field is either created (when the frame is transmitted to non-Token Ring) or removed (when the frame is transmitted to Token Ring). When an Ethernet format frame is transmitted to Token Ring, the frame is translated into an LLC-1 Subnetwork Access Protocol (SNAP) packet. The destination service access point (DSAP) value is AA; the source service access point (SSAP) value is AA, and the organizational unique identifier (OUI) value is 0000F8. Likewise, when a packet in LLC-1 format is bridged onto Ethernet media, the packet is translated into Ethernet format.

Bridging between dissimilar media presents several problems that can prevent communication from occurring. These problems include bit-order translation (or using MAC addresses as data), maximum transmission unit (MTU) differences, frame status differences, and multicast address usage. Some or all of these problems might be present in a multimedia bridged LAN. Because of differences in the way end nodes implement Token Ring, these problems are most prevalent when bridging between Token Ring and Ethernet or between Ethernet and FDDI LANs.

Problems currently occur with the following protocols when bridged between Token Ring and other media: Novell IPX, DECnet Phase IV, AppleTalk, Banyan VINES, XNS, and IP. Further, problems can occur with the Novell IPX and XNS protocols when bridged between FDDI and other media. Cisco recommends that these protocols be routed whenever possible.

SOURCE-ROUTE BRIDGING (SRB)

Cisco bridging software includes SRB capability. A source-route bridge connects multiple physical Token Rings into one logical network segment. If the network segment bridges only Token Ring media to provide connectivity, the technology is termed source-route bridging. If the network bridges Token Ring, and non-Token Ring media is introduced into the bridged network segment, the technology is termed remote source-route bridging (RSRB).

Source-route bridging enables the routers to simultaneously act as a Level 3 router and a Level 2 source-route bridge. Thus, protocols such as Novell's Internetwork Packet Exchange (IPX) or Xerox Network Systems (XNS) can be routed on Token Rings, while other protocols such as Systems Network Architecture (SNA) or NetBIOS are source-route bridged.

Source-route bridging technology is a combination of bridging and routing functions. A source-route bridge can make routing decisions based on the contents of the MAC frame header. Keeping the routing function at the MAC, or Level 2, layer allows the higher-layer protocols to execute their tasks more efficiently and allows the LAN to be expanded without the knowledge of the higher-layer protocols.

As designed by IBM and the IEEE 802.5 committee, source-route bridges connect extended Token Ring LANs. A source-route bridge uses the RIF in the IEEE 802.5 MAC header of a datagram (see Figure I–3) to determine which rings or Token Ring network segments the packet must transit. The source station inserts the RIF into the MAC header immediately following the source address field in every frame, giving this style of bridging its name. The destination station reverses the routing field to reach the originating station.

Figure I–3
IEEE 802.5 Token Ring frame format.

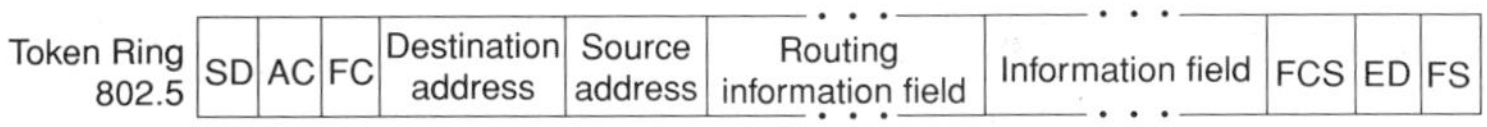

Token Ring 802.5	SD	AC	FC	Destination address	Source address	Routing information field	Information field	FCS	ED	FS

The information in a RIF is derived from explorer packets generated by the source node. These explorer packets traverse the entire source-route bridge network, gathering information on the possible paths the source node might use to send packets to the destination.

Transparent spanning-tree bridging requires time to recompute a topology in the event of a failure; source-route bridging, which maintains multiple paths, allows fast selection of alternate routes in the event of failure. Most importantly, source-route bridging allows the end stations to determine the routes the frames take.

Source-Route Bridging Features

Cisco's source-route bridging implementation has the following features:

- Provides configurable fast-switching software for source-route bridging.

- Provides for a local source-route bridge that connects two or more Token Ring networks.

- Provides *ring groups* to configure a source-route bridge with more than two network interfaces. A ring group is a collection of Token Ring interfaces in one or more routers that are collectively treated as a *virtual ring*.

- Provides two types of explorer packets to collect RIF information—an *all-routes* explorer packet, which follows all possible paths to a destination ring, and a *spanning-tree* explorer packet, which follows a statically configured limited route (spanning tree) when looking for paths.

- Provides a dynamically determined RIF cache based on the protocol. The software also allows you to add entries manually to the RIF cache.

- Provides for filtering by MAC address, link service access point (LSAP) header, and protocol type.

- Provides for filtering of NetBIOS frames either by station name or by a packet byte offset.

- Provides for translation into transparently bridged frames to allow source-route stations to communicate with nonsource-route stations (typically on Ethernet).

- Provides support for the SRB Management Information Base (MIB) variables as described in the IETF draft "Bridge MIB" document, "Definition of Managed Objects for Bridges," by E. Decker, P. Langille, A. Rijsinghani, and K. McCloghrie, June 1991. Only the SRB component of the Bridge MIB is supported.

- Provides support for the Token Ring MIB variables as described in RFC 1231, "IEEE 802.5 Token Ring MIB," by K. McCloghrie, R. Fox, and E. Decker, May 1991. Cisco implements the mandatory tables (Interface Table and Statistics Table), but not the optional table (Timer Table) of the Token Ring MIB. The Token Ring MIB has been implemented for the 4/16-Mb Token Ring cards that can be user adjusted for either 4- or 16-Mb transmission speeds (CSC-1R, CSC-2R, CSC-R16M, or CSC-C2CTR).

- Source-route bridging is supported over FDDI on Cisco 7200 series routers.

- Particle-based switching is supported (over FDDI and Token Ring) by default on Cisco 7200 series routers.

REMOTE SOURCE-ROUTE BRIDGING (RSRB)

In contrast to SRB, which involves bridging between Token Ring media only, RSRB is Cisco's first technique for connecting Token Ring networks over non-Token Ring network segments. (DLSw+ is Cisco's strategic method for providing this function.)

Cisco's RSRB software implementation includes the following features:

- Provides for multiple routers separated by non-Token Ring segments. Three options are available:

  - Encapsulate the Token Ring traffic inside IP datagrams passed over a Transmission Control Protocol (TCP) connection between two routers.

  - Use Fast-Sequenced Transport (FST) to transport RSRB packets to their peers without TCP or User Datagram Protocol (UDP) header or processor overhead.

  - Use data-link layer encapsulations over a single serial line, Ethernet, Token Ring, or FDDI ring connected between two routers attached to Token Ring networks.

- Provides for configurable limits to the size of the TCP backup queue.

Figure I–4 shows an RSRB topology. The virtual ring can extend across any non-Token Ring media supported by RSRB, such as serial, Ethernet, FDDI, and WANs. The type of media you select determines the way you set up RSRB.

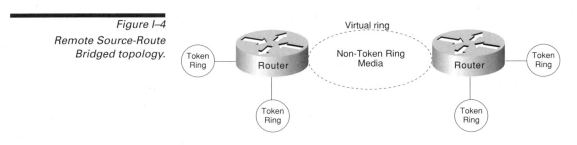

Figure I–4
Remote Source-Route Bridged topology.

NOTES

If you bridge across Token Ring media, it is recommended that you do not use RSRB. Use SRB instead. See Chapter 3 for more information.

DATA-LINK SWITCHING PLUS (DLSW+)

DLSw+ is a method of transporting SNA and NetBIOS. It complies with the DLSw standard documented in RFC 1795 as well as the DLSw Version 2 standard. DLSw+ is an alternative to RSRB that addresses several inherent problems that exist in RSRB, such as:

- SRB hop-count limits (SRB's limit is seven)
- Broadcast traffic (including SRB explorer frames or NetBIOS name queries)
- Unnecessary traffic (acknowledgments and keepalives)
- Data-link control timeouts

DLSw Standard

The DLSw standard, documented in RFC 1795, defines the switch-to-switch protocol between DLSw routers. The standard also defines a mechanism to terminate data-link control connections locally and multiplex the traffic from the data-link control connections to a TCP connection. The standard always calls for the transport protocol to be TCP and always requires that data-link control connections be locally terminated (the equivalent of the Cisco local acknowledgment option). The standard also requires that the SRB RIF be terminated at the DLSw router. The standard describes a means for prioritization and flow control and defines error-recovery procedures that ensure data-link control connections are appropriately disabled if any part of their associated circuits breaks.

The DLSw standard does not specify when to establish TCP connections. The capabilities exchange allows compliance to the standard, but at different levels of support. The standard does not specify how to cache learned information about MAC addresses, RIFs, or NetBIOS names. It also does not describe how to track both capable or preferred DLSw partners for either backup or load-balancing purposes. The standard does not provide the specifics of media conversion, but leaves the details up to the implementation. It does not define how to map switch congestion to the flow control for data-link control. Finally, the MIB is documented under a separate RFC.

DLSw Version 2 Standard

In the Version 1 standard, the network design was required to be fully meshed so that all peers were connected to every other peer. This design created unnecessary broadcast traffic because an explorer was sent to every peer for every broadcast.

DLSw Version 2 addresses this problem and improves scalability in DLSw networks with the following enhancements:

- UDP/IP Multicast Service
- Enhanced Peer-on-Demand Routing Feature
- Expedited TCP Connection

UDP/IP Multicast Service

IP multicast service reduces the amount of network overhead because it avoids the need to maintain TCP Switch-to-Switch Protocol (SSP) connections between two DLSw peers when no circuits are available and it ensures that each broadcast results in only a single explorer over every link. Furthermore, multicast service avoids duplication and excessive bandwidth of broadcast traffic because it replicates and propagates messages only as necessary to its multicast members. This functionality is a subset of Cisco's existing DLSw+ border peering feature. In a border peer network, address resolution packets are sent via the border peer network and can take advantage of border peer caching to minimize bandwidth usage. DLSw Version 2 is for customers who run a multicast IP network and do not need the advantages of border peering.

With UDP Unicast, explorer frames and unnumbered information frames are sent via UDP rather than TCP. This feature eliminates retransmission of explorers and unnumbered information frames that could occur during congestion. Cisco's DLSw+ introduced the UDP Unicast feature prior to the release of DLSw Version 2 in Cisco IOS Release 11.2(6)F. One difference between the two enhancements is that the Release 11.2(6)F UDP Unicast feature requires that a TCP connection exist before packets are sent via UDP. Because the TCP session is up and capabilities have been exchanged, the peers know exclusive reachability information which will permit them to further reduce the explorer load on the network. DLSw Version 2, on the other hand, sends UDP/IP multicast and unicast before the TCP connection exists. Although DLSw Version 2 employs IP multicast service when address resolution packets (CANUREACH_EX, NETBIOS_NQ_ex, NETBIOS_ANQ, and DATAFRAME) are sent to multiple destinations, the response frames (ICANREACH_ex and NAME_RECOGNIZED_ex), are sent via UDP unicast.

Enhanced Peer-on-Demand Routing Feature

DLSw Version 2 now establishes TCP connections only when necessary and the TCP connections are brought down when there are no circuits to a DLSw peer for a specified amount of time. This method, known as peer-on-demand routing, was recently introduced in DLSw Version 2, but has been implemented in Cisco DLSw+ border peer technology since Cisco IOS Release 10.3.

Expedited TCP Connection

DLSw Version 2 more efficiently establishes TCP connections. Previously, DLSw created two uni-directional TCP connections and then disconnected one after the capabilities exchange took place. With DLSw Version 2, a single bidirectional TCP connection is established if the associated peer is known to support DLSw Version 2.

DLSw+ Features

DLSw+ is Cisco's version of DLSw and it supports several additional features and enhancements. DLSw+ is fully compatible with any vendors RFC 1795 implementation and the following features are available when both peers are using DLSw+:

- Peer groups and border peers.
- Backup peers.
- Promiscuous and on-demand peers.
- Scalability enhancements through explorer firewalls and location learning.
- NetBIOS dial-on-demand routing feature support.
- UDP Unicast support.
- Border Peer caching and load balancing.
- Support for LLC1 circuits.
- Support for Multiple Bridge Groups.
- A choice of transport options, including TCP, FST, and direct encapsulation in High-Level Data Link Control (HDLC) or Frame Relay.
- SNA type of service feature support.
- Local acknowledgment for Ethernet-attached devices and media conversion for SNA PU 2.1 and PU 2.0 devices.
- Conversion between LLC2 to SDLC between PU 4 devices.
- Local or remote media conversion between LANs and either Synchronous Data Link Control (SDLC) Protocol or QLLC.
- SNA View, Blue Maps, and IBM's LAN Network Manager support.

- MIB enhancements that allow DLSw+ plus features to be managed by the CiscoWorks Blue products, SNA Maps, and SNA View. Also, new traps alert network management stations of peer or circuit failures.
- DLSw+ Enhancements

DLSw+ goes beyond the standard to include additional functionality in the following areas:

- Modes of Operation—Ability to determine the capabilities of the participating router and to operate according to those capabilities.
- Improved Scalability—Ability to construct IBM internetworks in a way that reduces the amount of broadcast traffic and therefore enhances their scalability.
- Improved Performance—Ability to offer higher-performance transport options when the line speeds and traffic conditions do not require local acknowledgment.
- Enhanced Availability—Overall availability of an end-to-end connection between a pair of SNA and NetBIOS end systems.

Modes of Operation

DLSw+ operates in two modes:

- Standards compliance mode—DLSw+ can automatically detect (through the DLSw+ capabilities exchange) that the participating router is manufactured by another vendor. DLSw+ then operates in DLSw standard mode.
- Enhanced mode—DLSw+ can automatically detect that the participating router is another DLSw+ router. DLSw+ then operates in enhanced mode, providing the additional features of DLSw+ to the SNA and NetBIOS end systems.

NOTES

DLSw+ does not interoperate with prestandard implementations such as RFC 1434.

Some enhanced DLSw+ features are also available when a Cisco router is operating in standards compliance mode with another vendor's router. In particular, enhancements that are locally controlled options on a router can be accessed even though the remote router does not have DLSw+. These include reachability caching, explorer firewalls, and media conversion.

Improved Scalability

One significant factor that limits the size of Token Ring internetworks is the amount of explorer traffic that traverses the WAN. DLSw+ includes the following features to reduce the number of explorers:

- Peer Groups—The large Token Ring internetworks that Cisco has helped to build over the last several years all have followed a similar structure. That structure is a hierarchical grouping of routers based upon the usual flow of broadcasts through the network. A cluster of routers in a region or a division of a company is combined into a peer group.

- Border Peers—Within a peer group, one or more routers are designated as border peers. When a DLSw+ router receives a test frame or NetBIOS name query, it sends a single explorer frame to its border peer. The border peer takes complete responsibility for forwarding the explorer on behalf of the peer-group member. This arrangement eliminates duplicate explorers on the access links and minimizes the processing required in access routers.

- On-Demand Peers—On-demand peers greatly reduce the number of peers that must be configured. As Figure I–5 shows, you can use on-demand peers to establish an end-to-end circuit even though the DLSw+ routers servicing the end systems have no specific configuration information about the peers. This configuration permits casual, any-to-any connection without the burden of configuring the connection in advance. It also allows any-to-any switching in large internetworks where persistent TCP connections would not be possible.

- Explorer Firewalls—An explorer firewall permits only a single explorer for a particular destination MAC address or NetBIOS name to be sent across the WAN. While an explorer is outstanding and awaiting a response from the destination, subsequent explorers for that MAC address or NetBIOS name are merely stored. When the explorer response is received at the originating DLSw+, all explorers receive an immediate local response. This eliminates the start-of-day explorer storm that many networks experience.

- NetBIOS Dial-on-Demand Routing—This feature allows you to transport NetBIOS in a dial-on-demand routing (DDR) environment by filtering NetBIOS Session Alive packets from the WAN. NetBIOS periodically sends Session Alive packets as LLC2 I-frames. These packets do not require a response and are superfluous to the function of proper data flow. Furthermore, these packets keep dial-on-demand interfaces up and this up time causes unwanted per-packet charges in DDR networks. By filtering these NetBIOS Session Alive packets, you reduce traffic on the WAN as well as some costs that are associated with Dial-on-Demand Routing.

- UDP Unicast Enhancement—The SSP address resolution packets are sent via UDP unicast service rather than TCP. SSP packets include: CANUREACH_EX, NETBIOS_NQ_ex, NETBIOS_ANQ, and DATAFRAME. UDP Unicast enhances the scalability of TCP peer networks because it allows DLSw+ to better control address resolution packets and unnumbered information frames during periods of congestion. Previously, these frames were carried over TCP. TCP retransmits frames that get lost or delayed in transit, and hence aggravate congestion. Because address resolution packets and unnumbered information frames are not sent on a reliable transport on the LAN, sending them reliably over the WAN is unnecessary. By using UDP for these frames, DLSw+ minimizes network congestion.

UDP Unicast Enhancement does not affect Fast-Sequenced Transport (FST) or direct peer encapsulations.

- Border Peer Caching—Border Peer Caching increases the scalability of DLSw+ by minimizing broadcast traffic, bandwidth requirements, and the requirement for border peers to replicate explorers. Previously, border peers did not learn reachability information from the broadcasts that they forwarded. Now, border peers learn reachability information based on relay responses and store it in their remote and group caches. After the first search when a peer is found, every subsequent explorer is forwarded to the known destination, rather than forwarded as a broadcast. As a result, the network has fewer broadcasts.

- LLC1 Circuits—Support for LLC1 circuits more efficiently transports LLC1 UI traffic across a DLSw+ cloud. With LLC1 circuit support, the LLC1 UI frames are no longer subject to input queuing and are guaranteed to traverse the same path for the duration of the flow. This feature improves transportation of LLC1 UI traffic because there is no longer the chance of having a specifically routed LLC1 UI frame broadcasted to all remote peers. The circuit establishment process has not changed except that the circuit is established as soon as the specifically routed LLC1 UI frame is received and the DLSw+ knows of reachability for the destination MAC address. Furthermore, the connection remains in the CIRCUIT_ESTABLISHED state (rather than proceeding to the CONNECT state) until there is no UI frame flow for a MAC/SAP pair for 10 minutes.

- Multiple Bridge Groups—This feature allows you to assign more than one bridge group for different physical ethernet segments. See the **dlsw bridge-group** command for more information.

Figure I–5
Scalability with DLSw+.

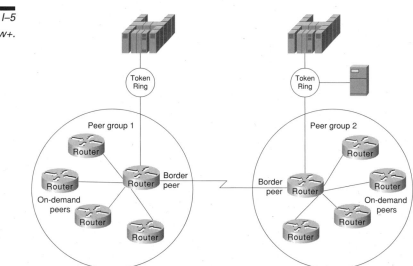

Improved Performance

DLSw+ improves performance by offering higher-performance transport options in the following areas:

- Transport Connection Type
- SNA Type of Service

Transport Connection Type

The transport connection between DLSw+ routers can vary according to the needs of the network and is not necessarily tied to TCP/IP as the DLSw standard is. Cisco supports three different transport protocols between DLSw+ devices:

- TCP for transport of SNA and NetBIOS traffic across WANs where bandwidth is limited and termination of data-link control sessions is required. This transport option is required when DLSw+ is operating in standards compliance mode.
- FST for transport across IP WANs with an arbitrary topology with sufficient bandwidth to accommodate SNA and NetBIOS.
- Direct encapsulation for transport across a point-to-point connection where the benefits of an arbitrary topology are not important.

SNA Type of Service

Performance is further enhanced with the SNA Type of Service feature. Although DLSw+ priority queuing provides prioritization on the output queue of the interface, the priority characteristics are lost once the packet leaves the DLSw+ router and traverses the network. SNA Type of Service sets IP precedence in all DLSw+ frames, either setting all DLSw+ to a high precedence, or building multiple pipes for different priority traffic and setting each one appropriately. Also, when running APPN over DLSw+, APPN Class of Service (COS) characteristics are lost once the packet is delivered to the DLSw+ router for bridging over an IP network. With the new DLSw+ SNA TOS feature, however, SNA TOS works in conjunction with weighted fair queuing to reduce the response time for SNA sessions and, therefore, ensures that DLSw+ gets more bandwidth. DLSw+ traffic is prioritized and APPN COS characteristics are preserved across the network.

With the SNA Type of Service feature, DLSw+ sets the precedence bits in the IP header of outbound DLSw+ packets. When DLSw+ is used in conjunction with APPN, SNA TOS maps APPN COS to IP TOS, and preserves SNA COS across an IP backbone. If priority queuing is not configured on DLSw+, the IP precedence value of "Network" is used for all DLSw+ packets. This default value ensures more bandwidth for DLSw+ packets than for other types of packets.

Table I–1 describes the various IP precedence values that map to the TCP ports.

When the **priority** option on the **dlsw remote-peer** command is configured, DLSw+ automatically activates four TCP ports to that remote peer (ports 2065, 1981, 1982, and 1983) and assigns traffic to specific ports according to the rules defined in Table I–2. Alternately, SAP prioritization, LOCADDR prioritization, or APPN COS can be used to customize how traffic is assigned to these ports.

Table I–1 *IP Precedence Values*

TCP Ports	Priority Queue Level	IP Precedence APPN Value	IP Precedence DLSw+ Value
2065	High	Network	Network control
1981	Medium	High	Internetwork control
1982	Normal	Medium	Critical
1983	Low	Low	Flash override

Table I–2 *Port Number Priority Values*

TCP Ports	DLSw+ Queue Priority	Type of Traffic (default)
2065	High	Circuit administration frames Peer keepalives Capabilities exchange
1981	Medium	None
1982	Normal	Information frames
1983	Low	Broadcast traffic

If the **priority** option is not configured in the **dlsw remote-peer** command, then all DLSw+ traffic defaults to port 2065 and is assigned IP precedence "network." The default TOS settings can be changed by using policy routing based on the TCP ports that the DLSw+ router uses.

For an example configuration of DLSw+ with policy routing, see the **dlsw remote-peer-tcp** command in Chapter 8, "DLSw+ Configuration Commands."

Please note the following design considerations with the SNA Type of Service feature:

- APPN COS-to-IP TOS mapping occurs only if DLSw+ and APPN are running in the same router and the **priority** keyword is specified on the remote peer statement.
- SNA TOS applies only to TCP or FST encapsulation types.
- When using FST encapsulation, SNA TOS marks all DLSw+ traffic with IP precedence "network."

Enhanced Availability

DLSw+ offers enhanced availability by caching a table of multiple paths to a given MAC address or NetBIOS name (where a path is either a remote peer or a local port). Furthermore, with the Border Peer Caching feature, border peers build an additional cache (group), which is checked before forwarding explorers for other routers.

Maintaining multiple paths per destination is especially attractive in SNA networks. A common technique used in the hierarchical SNA environment is assigning the same MAC address to different Token Ring interface couplers (TICs) on the IBM front-end processors (FEPs). DLSw+ ensures that duplicate TIC addresses are found, and, if multiple DLSw+ peers can be used to reach the FEPs, they are cached.

The way that multiple capable peers are handled with DLSw+ can be biased to meet either of the following network needs:

- Fault Tolerance—To rapidly reconnect if a data-link connection is lost. If load balancing is not enabled, the Cisco IOS software maintains a preferred path and one or more capable paths to each destination. The preferred peer is either the peer that responds first to an explorer frame or the peer with the least cost. The preferred port is always the port over which the first positive response to an explorer was received. If the preferred peer to a given destination is unavailable, the next available capable peer is promoted to the new preferred peer. No additional broadcasts are required, and recovery through an alternate peer is immediate. Maintaining multiple cache entries facilitates a timely reconnection after session outages.

- Load Balancing—To distribute the network traffic over multiple DLSw+ peers in the network. The Cisco IOS software can be configured to perform load balancing, in which case circuits are established in round-robin fashion using the list of capable routers. When used for load balancing, this technique improves overall SNA performance.

Figure I–6 shows a peer table of preferred (pref) and capable (cap) routes.

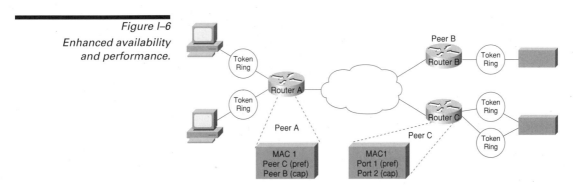

Figure I–6
Enhanced availability
and performance.

In addition to supporting multiple active peers, DLSw+ supports backup peers for all encapsulation types (including direct, FST, and TCP), which are connected only when the primary peer cannot be reached.

DLSw+ Support for Other SNA Features

DLSw+ can be used as a transport for SNA features such as LNM, DSPU, SNA service point, and APPN through a Cisco IOS feature called VDLC.

LNM over DLSw+ allows DLSw+ to be used in Token Ring networks that are managed by IBM's LNM software. Using this feature, LNM can be used to manage Token Ring LANs, control access units, and Token Ring-attached devices over a DLSw+ network. All management functions continue to operate as they would in a source-route bridged network or an RSRB network.

DSPU over DLSw+ allows Cisco's DSPU feature to operate in conjunction with DLSw+ in the same router. DLSw+ can be used either upstream (toward the mainframe) or downstream (away from the mainframe) of DSPU. DSPU concentration consolidates the appearance of multiple physical units (PUs) into a single PU appearance to VTAM, minimizing memory and cycles in central site resources (VTAM, NCP, and routers) and speeding network startup.

SNA service point over DLSw+ allows Cisco's SNA service point feature to be used in conjunction with DLSw+ in the same router. Using this feature, SNA service point can be configured in remote routers, and DLSw+ can provide the path for the remote service point PU to communicate with Net-View. This allows full management visibility of resources from a NetView 390 console, while concurrently offering the value-added features of DLSw+ in an SNA network.

APPN over DLSw+ allows Cisco's APPN feature to be used in conjunction with DLSw+ in the same router. With this feature, DLSw+ can be used to access an APPN backbone or APPN in the data center. DLSw+ also can be used as a transport for APPN, providing nondisruptive recovery from failures and high-speed intermediate routing. The DLSw+ network can appear as a connection network to the APPN network nodes.

To use DLSw+ as a transport for other Cisco IOS SNA features requires a feature called virtual data-link control. Cisco IOS data-link users (such as LNM, DSPU, SNA service point, and APPN) write to a virtual data-link control interface. DLSw+ then reads from this interface and sends out the traffic. Similarly, DLSw+ can receive traffic destined for one of these DLUS and write it to the virtual data-link control interface, from which the appropriate DLU will read it.

In Figure I–7, APPN and DLSw+ use Token Ring and Ethernet, respectively, as "real" data-link controls, and use virtual data-link control to communicate between themselves. When one of the high-layer protocols passes data to the virtual data-link control, the virtual data-link control must pass it to a higher-layer protocol; nothing leaves the virtual data-link control without going through a data-link user.

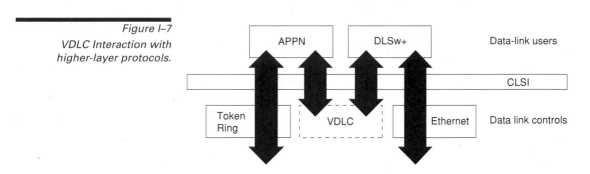

Figure I–7
VDLC Interaction with higher-layer protocols.

The higher-layer protocols make no distinction between the virtual data link control and any other data-link control, but they do identify the virtual data link control as a destination. In the example shown in Figure I–7, APPN has two ports: a physical port for Token Ring and a logical (virtual) port for the virtual data link control. In the case of the APPN virtual data link control port, when you define the APPN virtual data link control port, you can also specify the MAC address assigned to it. That means data going from DLSw+ to APPN by way of the virtual data link control is directed to the virtual data link control MAC address. The type of higher-layer protocol you use determines how the virtual data link control MAC address is assigned.

SERIAL TUNNEL AND BLOCK SERIAL TUNNEL

The Cisco IOS software supports serial tunnel (STUN) and block serial tunnel (BSTUN). The BSTUN implementation enhances Cisco series 2500, 4000, 4500, 4700, and 7200 routers to support devices that use the Binary Synchronous Communication (Bisync) datalink protocol and asynchronous security protocols that include Adplex, ADT Security Systems, Inc., Diebold, and asynchronous generic traffic. BSTUN implementation is also supported on the 4T network interface module (NIM) on the Cisco series 4000 and 4500. Support of the bisync protocol enables enterprises to transport Bisync traffic and SNA multiprotocol traffic over the same network.

STUN Networks

STUN operates in two modes: passthrough and local acknowledgment. Figure I–8 shows the difference between passthrough mode and local acknowledgment mode.

The upper half of Figure I–8 shows STUN configured in passthrough mode. In passthrough mode, the routers act as a wire and the SDLC session remains between the end stations. In this mode, STUN provides a straight pass-through of all SDLC traffic, including control frames.

The lower half of Figure I–8 shows STUN configured in local acknowledgment mode. In local acknowledgment mode, the routers terminate the SDLC sessions and send only data across the WAN. Control frames no longer travel the WAN backbone networks.

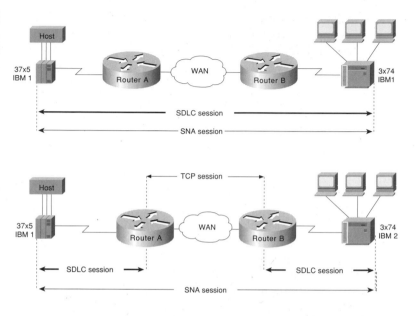

Figure I–8

Comparison of STUN in
passthrough mode and local
acknowledgment mode.

NOTES

To enable STUN local acknowledgment, you first enable the routers for STUN and configure them to appear on the network as primary or secondary SDLC nodes. TCP/IP encapsulation must be enabled. The STUN local acknowledgment feature also provides priority queuing for TCP-encapsulated frames.

Serial Tunnel

The STUN implementation provides the following features:

- Encapsulates SDLC frames in either the Transmission Control Protocol/Internet Protocol (TCP/IP) or the HDLC protocol.

- Allows two devices using SDLC- or HDLC-compliant protocols that are normally connected by a direct serial link to be connected through one or more Cisco routers, reducing leased-line costs.

  When you replace direct serial links with routers, serial frames can be propagated over arbitrary media and topologies to another router with a STUN link to an appropriate end point. The intervening network is not restricted to STUN traffic, but rather, is multiprotocol. For example, instead of running parallel backbones for DECnet and SNA/SDLC traffic, this traffic now can be integrated into an enterprise backbone network.

- Supports local acknowledgment for direct Frame Relay connectivity between routers, without TCP/IP required.

- Allows networks with IBM mainframes and communications controllers to share data using Cisco routers and existing network links. As an SDLC function, STUN fully supports the IBM SNA and allows IBM SDLC frames to be transmitted across the network media and shared serial links. Figure I–9 illustrates a typical network configuration without STUN and the same network configured with STUN.

- Encapsulates SDLC frame traffic packets and routes them over any of the supported network media (serial, FDDI, Ethernet, and Token Ring, X.25, SMDS, and T1/T3) using TCP/IP encapsulation. Because TCP/IP encapsulation is used, you can use any of the Cisco routing protocols to route the packets.

- Copies frames to destinations based on address. STUN in passthrough mode does not modify the frames in any way or participate in SDLC windowing or retransmission; these functions are left to the communicating hosts. However, STUN in local acknowledgment mode does participate in SDLC windowing and retransmission through local termination of the SDLC session.

- Ensures reliable data transmission across serial media having minimal or predictable time delays. With the advent of STUN and WAN backbones, serial links now can be separated by wide geographic distances spanning countries and continents. As a result, these serial links have time delays that are longer than SDLC allows for bidirectional communication between hosts. The STUN local acknowledgment feature addresses the problems of unpredictable time delays, multiple retransmissions, or loss of sessions.

- Allows for configuration of redundant links to provide transport paths in the event part of the network goes down.

Figure I–9
IBM network configuration
without STUN and with STUN.

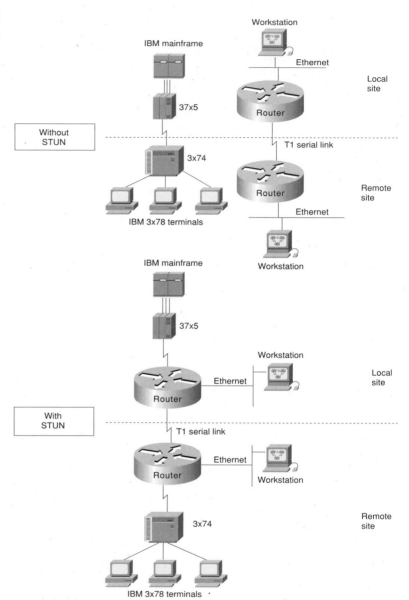

BSTUN Networks

The Bisync feature enables your Cisco 2500, 3600, 4000, 4500, or 7200 series router to support devices that use the Bisync datalink protocol. This protocol enables enterprises to transport Bisync traffic over the same network that supports their SNA and multiprotocol traffic, eliminating the need for separate Bisync facilities.

At the access router, traffic from the attached Bisync device is encapsulated in IP. The Bisync traffic can then be routed across arbitrary media to the host site where another router supporting Bisync will remove the IP encapsulation headers and present the Bisync traffic to the Bisync host or controller over a serial connection. HDLC can be used as an alternative encapsulation method for point-to-point links.

Block Serial Tunnel

Cisco's implementation of BSTUN provides the following features:

- Encapsulates Binary Synchronous Communications (Bisync), Adplex, ADT Security Systems, Inc., Diebold, asynchronous generic, and Monitor Dynamics Inc., traffic for transfer over router links. The tunneling of asynchronous security protocols feature (ASP) enables your Cisco 2500, 3600, 4000, 4500, or 7200 series router to support devices that use the following asynchronous security protocols:
  - adplex
  - adt-poll-select
  - adt-vari-poll
  - diebold
  - async-generic
  - mdi
- Provides a tunnel mechanism for BSTUN over Frame Relay, without using TCP/IP encapsulation.
- Supports legacy Bisync devices and host applications without modification.
- Uses standard synchronous serial interfaces on Cisco 2500 series and the 4T network interface module (NIM) on the Cisco 4000 series and Cisco 4500 series.
- Supports point-to-point, multidrop, and virtual multidrop configurations.

SDLC AND LLC2 PARAMETERS

The Logical Link Control, type 2 (LLC2) and SDLC protocols provide data-link-level support for higher-level network protocols and features such as SDLLC and RSRB with local acknowledgment. The features that are affected by LLC2 parameter settings are listed in the next section, "Cisco's Implementation of LLC2." The features that require SDLC configuration and use SDLC parameters are listed in the section "Cisco's Implementation of SDLC" later in this chapter.

LLC2 and SDLC package data in frames. LLC2 and SDLC stations require acknowledgments from receiving stations after a set amount of frames have been sent before sending further data. The tasks described in this chapter modify default settings regarding the control field of the data frames. By modifying the control field parameters, you can determine the number of acknowledgments sent for frames received and the level of polling used to determine available stations. In this manner, you can set the amount of resources used for frame checking and optimize the network load.

SDLC is used as the primary SNA link-layer protocol for WAN links. SDLC defines two types of network nodes: primary and secondary. Primary nodes poll secondary nodes in a predetermined order. Secondary nodes then transmit any outgoing data. When configured as primary and secondary nodes, Cisco software routers are established as SDLC stations.

Cisco's Implementation of LLC2

Cisco's LLC2 implementation supports the following features:

- Local acknowledgment for RSRB

  This feature is used in the implementation of RSRB as described in Chapter 3.

  Because LANs are now connected through RSRB and WAN backbones, the delays that occur are longer than LLC2 allows for bidirectional communication between hosts. Cisco's local acknowledgment feature addresses the problem of delays, retransmissions, and loss of user sessions.

- IBM LAN Network Manager (LNM) support

  Routers using 4- or 16-Mbps Token Ring interfaces configured for SRB support LNM and provide all IBM Bridge Program functions. With LNM, a router appears as an IBM source-route bridge, and can manage or monitor any connected Token Ring interface.

  LNM support is described in Chapter 3.

- SDLLC media translation

  The SDLLC feature provides media translation between the serial lines running SDLC and Token Rings running LLC2. SDLLC consolidates the IBM SNA networks running SDLC into a LAN-based, multiprotocol, multimedia backbone network.

  SDLLC is described in Chapter 13, "Configuring IBM Network Media Translation."

- ISO Connection-Mode Network Service (CMNS)

  CMNS implementation runs X.25 packets over LLC2 so that X.25 can be extended to Ethernet, FDDI, and Token Ring media.

Cisco's Implementation of SDLC

Cisco's SDLC implementation supports the following features:

- Frame Relay access support

  With the Frame Relay access support feature, a router functions as a Frame Relay Access Device (FRAD) for SDLC, Token Ring, and Ethernet-attached devices over a Frame Relay Boundary Network Node (BNN) link.

  Frame Relay access support is described in Chapter 17, "Configuring SNA Frame Relay Access Support."

- SDLLC media translation

  The SDLLC feature provides media translation between the serial lines running SDLC and Token Rings running LLC2. SDLLC consolidates the IBM SNA networks running SDLC into a LAN-based, multiprotocol, multimedia backbone network.

  SDLLC is described in Chapter 13.

- SDLC local acknowledgment

  SDLC local acknowledgment is used with SDLC serial tunnel (STUN). The Transmission Control Protocol/Internet Protocol (TCP/IP) must be enabled. With local acknowledgment, STUN SDLC connections can be terminated locally at the router, eliminating the need for acknowledgments to be sent across a WAN.

IBM NETWORK MEDIA TRANSLATION

The Cisco IOS software includes the following media translation features that enable network communications across heterogeneous media:

- SDLLC media translation enables a device on a Token Ring to communicate with a device on a serial link.
- QLLC conversion enables an IBM device to communicate with an X.25 network without having to install the X.25 software on local IBM equipment.

SDLLC is a Cisco Systems proprietary software feature that enables a device on a Token Ring to communicate with a device on a serial link by translating between LLC2 and SDLC at the link layer.

SNA uses SDLC and LLC2 as link-layer protocols to provide a reliable connection. The translation function between these industry-standard protocols takes place in the proprietary Cisco software.

Figure I–10 illustrates how SDLLC provides data-link layer support for SNA communication.

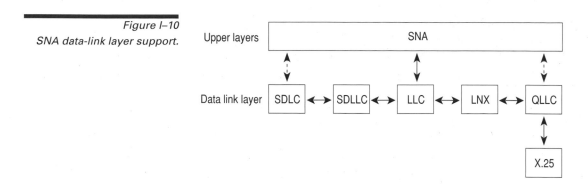

Figure I–10
SNA data-link layer support.

SDLLC Media Translation Features

The SDLLC software allows a physical unit (PU) 4, PU 2.1, or PU 2 to communicate with a PU 2 SDLC device as follows:

- SDLLC with Direct Connection—A 37x5 FEP on a Token Ring and the 3x74 cluster controller connected to a serial line are each connected to an interface on the same router configured with SDLLC.

- SDLLC with RSRB—A 37x5 FEP on a Token Ring and a 3x74 cluster controller connected to a serial line are connected to different routers. Only the device to which the 3x74 is connected is configured with SDLLC. The routers communicate via RSRB using direct encapsulation, RSRB over an FST connection, or RSRB over a TCP connection.

- SDLLC with RSRB and Local Acknowledgment—A 37x5 FEP on a Token Ring and a 3x74 cluster controller connected to a serial line are connected to different routers. Only the device to which the 3x74 is connected is configured with SDLLC. The routers communicate via RSRB over a TCP connection that has local acknowledgment enabled.

In all these topologies, each IBM end node (the FEP and cluster controller) has no indication that its counterpart is connected to a different medium running a different protocol. The 37x5 FEP responds as if the 3x74 cluster controller were communicating over a Token Ring, whereas the 3x74 responds as though the 37x5 FEP were communicating over a serial line. That is, the SDLLC software makes translation between the two media transparent to the end nodes.

Virtual Token Ring Concept

Central to Cisco's SDLLC feature is the concept of a virtual Token Ring device residing on a virtual Token Ring. Because the Token Ring device expects the node with which it is communicating also to be on a Token Ring, each SDLLC device on a serial line must be assigned an SDLLC virtual Token Ring address (SDLLC VTRA). Like real Token Ring addresses, SDLLC VTRAs must be unique across the network.

In addition to the SDLLC VTRA, an SDLLC virtual ring number (SDLLC VRN) must be assigned to each SDLLC device on a serial line. (The SDLLC VRN differs from the virtual ring group numbers that are used to configure RSRB and multiport bridging).

As part of its virtual telecommunications access method (VTAM) configuration, the IBM node on the Token Ring has knowledge of the SDLLC VTRA of the serial device with which it communicates. The SDLC VTRA and the SDLLC VRN are a part of the SDLLC configuration for the router's serial interface. When the Token Ring host sends out explorer packets with the SDLLC VTRA as the destination address in the MAC headers, the router configured with that SDLLC VTRA intercepts the frame, fills in the SDLLC VRNA and the bridge number in the RIF, then sends the response back to the Token Ring host. A route is then established between the Token Ring host and the router. After the Cisco IOS software performs the appropriate frame conversion, the system uses this route to forward frames to the serial device.

Resolving Differences in LLC2 and SDLC Frame Size

IBM nodes on Token Ring media normally use frame sizes greater than 1 KB, whereas the IBM nodes on serial lines normally limit frame sizes to 265 or 521 bytes. To reduce traffic on backbone networks and provide better performance, Token Ring nodes should send frames that are as large as possible. As part of the SDLLC configuration on the serial interface, the largest frame size the two media can support should be selected. The Cisco IOS software can fragment the frames it receives from the Token Ring device before forwarding them to the SDLC device, but it does not assemble the frames it receives from the serial device before forwarding them to the Token Ring device.

Maintaining a Dynamic RIF Cache

SDLLC maintains a dynamic RIF cache and caches the entire RIF; that is, the RIF from the source station to destination station. The cached entry is based on the best path at the time the session begins. SDLLC uses the RIF cache to maintain the LLC2 session between the router and the host FEP. SDLLC does not age these RIF entries. Instead, SDLLC places an entry in the RIF cache for a session when the session begins and flushes the cache when the session terminates. You cannot flush these RIFs because if you flush the RIF entries randomly, the Cisco IOS software cannot maintain the LLC2 session to the host FEP.

Other Considerations

- As part of Cisco's SDLC implementation, only modulus 8 Normal Response Mode (NRM) sessions are maintained for the SDLC session.
- SDLC sessions are always locally acknowledged. LLC2 sessions can be optionally configured for local acknowledgment.
- SDLLC does not apply to SNA subarea networks, such as 37x5 FEP-to-37x5 FEP communication.

- Parameters such as the maximum number of information frames (I-frames) outstanding before acknowledgment, frequency of polls, and response time to poll frames can be modified per interface. If local acknowledgment is not enabled, these parameters are modified on the SDLC interface. If local acknowledgment is enabled, these parameters are modified on the Token Ring interface.

- Local acknowledgment only applies when the remote peer is defined for RSRB using Internet Protocol (IP) encapsulation over a TCP connection. If no local acknowledgment is used, the remote peer can be defined for RSRB using direct encapsulation, RSRB using IP encapsulation over an FST connection, or RSRB using IP encapsulation over a TCP connection.

QLLC CONVERSION

Qualified Logical Link Control (QLLC) is a data-link protocol defined by IBM that allows SNA data to be transported across X.25 networks. (Although IBM has defined other protocols for transporting SNA traffic over an X.25 network, QLLC is the most widely used). Figure I–11 illustrates how QLLC conversion provides data-link layer support for SNA communication.

Figure I–11
SNA data-link layer support.

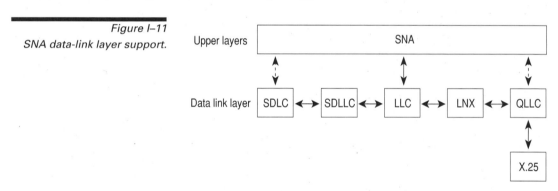

As shown in Figure I–12, any devices in the SNA communication path that use X.25, whether end systems or intermediate systems, require a QLLC implementation.

Figure I–12
SNA devices running QLLC.

As shown in Figure I–13, the QLLC conversion feature eliminates the need to install the X.25 software on local IBM equipment. A device attached locally to a Token Ring network can communicate through a router running the QLLC conversion feature with a remote device attached to an X.25

network using QLLC. Typically, the locally attached device is a front-end processor (FEP), an AS 400, or a PS/2, and the remote device is a terminal controller or a PS/2. In this case, only the remote device needs an X.25 interface and the FEP can communicate with the terminal controller as if it were directly attached via a Token Ring network.

Figure I–13
Router running QLLC
conversion feature.

More elaborate configurations are possible. The router that implements QLLC conversion need not be on the same Token Ring network as the FEP. As shown in Figure I–14, QLLC/LLC2 conversion is possible even when an intermediate IP WAN exists between the router connected to the X.25 network and the router connected to the Token Ring.

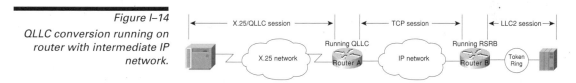

Figure I–14
QLLC conversion running on
router with intermediate IP
network.

Cisco's Implementation of QLLC Conversion

SNA uses QLLC and X.25 as link-layer protocols to provide a reliable connection. QLLC itself processes QLLC control packets. In a Token Ring environment, SNA uses LLC to provide a reliable connection. The LAN-to-X.25 (LNX) software provides a QLLC conversion function to translate between LLC and QLLC.

Figure I–15 shows the simplest QLLC conversion topology: a single Token Ring device (for example, a 37x5 FEP) communicates with a single remote X.25 device (in this case a 3x74 cluster controller). In this example, a router connects the Token Ring network to the X.25 network.

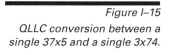
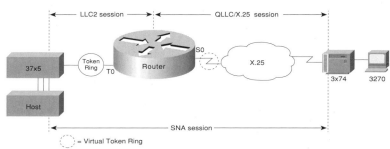

Figure I–15
QLLC conversion between a
single 37x5 and a single 3x74.

In Figure I–15, each IBM end node has no indication that its counterpart is connected to a different medium running a different protocol. The 37x5 FEP responds as if the 3x74 cluster controller were communicating over a Token Ring, whereas the 3x74 responds as though the 37x5 FEP were communicating over an X.25 network. This is accomplished by configuring the router's X.25 interface as a virtual Token Ring, so that the X.25 virtual circuit appears to the Token Ring device (and to the router itself) as if it were a Token Ring to which the remote X.25 device is attached.

Also in this figure, the LLC2 connection extends from the 37x5 FEP across the Token Ring network to the router. The QLLC/X.25 session extends from the router across the X.25 network to the 3x74 cluster controller. Only the SNA session extends across the Token Ring and X.25 networks to provide an end-to-end connection from the 37x5 FEP to the 3x74 cluster controller.

As Figure I–16 shows, a router need not directly connect the two IBM end nodes; instead, some type of backbone WAN can connect them. Here, RSRB transports packets between Router A and Router B, while Router B performs all conversions between the LLC2 and X.25 protocols. Only the router attached to the serial line (Router B) needs to be configured for QLLC conversion. Both Router A and Router B are configured for normal RSRB.

Figure I–16

QLLC conversion between a single 37x5 and multiple 3x74s across an arbitrary WAN.

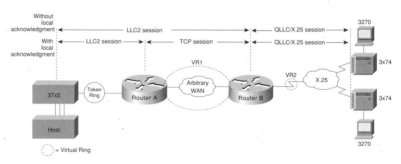

How communication sessions are established over the communication link varies depending on whether LLC2 local acknowledgment has been configured on Router A's Token Ring interface. In both cases, the SNA session extends end-to-end and the QLLC/X.25 session extends from Router B to the 3x74 cluster controller. If LLC2 local acknowledgment has not been configured, the LLC2 session extends from the 37x5 FEP across the Token Ring network and the arbitrary WAN to Router B. In contrast, when LLC2 local acknowledgment has been configured, the LLC2 session extends from the 37x5 FEP Router A, where it is locally terminated. A TCP session is then used across the arbitrary WAN to Router B.

Comparing QLLC Conversion to SDLLC

Although the procedures you use to configure QLLC are similar to those used to configure SDLLC, there are structural and philosophical differences between the point-to-point links that SDLC uses and the multiplexed virtual circuits that X.25 uses.

The most significant structural difference between QLLC conversion and SDLLC is the addressing. To allow a device to use LLC2 to transfer data, both SDLLC and QLLC provide virtual MAC addresses. In SDLLC, the actual MAC address is built by combining the defined virtual MAC (whose last byte is 0x00) with the secondary address used on the SDLC link; in this way, SDLLC supports multidrop. In QLLC conversion, multidrop is meaningless, so the virtual MAC address represents just one session and is defined as part of the X.25 configuration. Because one physical X.25 interface can support many simultaneous connections for many different remote devices, you only need one physical link to the X.25 network. The different connections on different virtual circuits all use the same physical link.

The most significant difference between QLLC conversion and SDLLC is the fact that a typical SDLC/SDLLC operation uses a leased line. In SDLC, dial-up connections are possible, but the maximum data rate is limited. In QLLC, both switched virtual circuits (SVCs) and permanent virtual circuits (PVCs) are available, but the favored use is SVC. While the router maintains a permanent connection to the X.25 network, a remote device can use each SVC for some bounded period of time and then relinquish it for use by another device. Using a PVC is very much like using a leased line.

Table I–3 shows how the QLLC commands correspond to the SDLLC commands.

Table I–3   *QLLC and SDLLC Command Comparison*

QLLC Command	Analogous SDLLC Command
qllc largest-packet	sdllc ring-largest-frame, sdllc sdlc-largest-frame
qllc partner	sdllc partner
qllc sap	sdllc sap
qllc srb, x25 map qllc, x25 pvc qllc	sdllc traddr
qllc xid	sdllc xid
source-bridge qllc-local-ack	source-bridge sdllc-local-ack

Other Implementation Considerations

Consider the following when implementing QLLC conversion:

- To use the QLLC conversion feature, a router must have a physical link to an X.25 public data network (PDN). It must also have an SRB/RSRB path to an IBM FEP. This link could be a Token Ring or Ethernet interface, or even FDDI, if RSRB is being used.

- QLLC conversion can run on any router with at least one serial interface configured for X.25 communication and at least one other interface configured for SRB or RSRB.

- QLLC conversion security depends upon access control in SRB/RSRB and X.25 and upon XID validation.

You can configure DLSw+ for QLLC connectivity, which enables the following scenarios:

- Remote LAN-attached devices (physical units) or SDLC-attached devices can access a front-end processor (FEP) or an AS/400 over an X.25 network.
- Remote X.25-attached SNA devices can access a FEP or an AS/400 over a Token Ring or over SDLC.

For information on configuring DLSw+ for QLLC conversion, see Chapter 7, "Configuring Data-Link Switching Plus."

You can configure DSPUs for QLLC. For more information on this configuration, see Chapter 15, "Configuring DSPU and SNA Service Point Support."

DOWNSTREAM PHYSICAL UNIT AND SNA SERVICE POINT

Downstream physical unit (DSPU) is a software feature that enables the router to function as a physical unit (PU) concentrator for SNA PU type 2 nodes. PU concentration at the device simplifies the task of PU definition at the upstream host while providing additional flexibility and mobility for downstream PU devices.

The DSPU feature allows you to define downstream PU type 2 devices in the Cisco IOS software. DSPU reduces the complexity of host configuration by letting you replace multiple PU definitions that represent each downstream device with one PU definition that represents the router.

Because you define the downstream PUs at the router rather than the host, you isolate the host from changes in the downstream network topology. Therefore, you can insert and remove downstream PUs from the network without making any changes on the host.

The concentration of downstream PUs at the router also reduces network traffic on the WAN by limiting the number of sessions that must be established and maintained with the host. The termination of downstream sessions at the router ensures that idle session traffic does not appear on the WAN.

SNA Service Point Support in the Cisco IOS software assumes that NetView or an equivalent product is available at the SNA host. The user interacts with the network management feature in the router and at the SNA host. In the Cisco IOS software, you can configure the host connection and show the status of this connection. At the SNA host, you can use the NetView operator's console to view alerts and to send and receive Cisco syntax commands to the Cisco device.

Figure I–17 shows a router functioning as a DSPU concentrator.

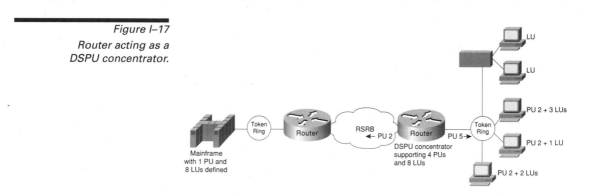

Figure I–17
Router acting as a
DSPU concentrator.

Typically, a router establishes one or more upstream connections with one or more hosts and many downstream connections with PU type 2 devices. From an SNA perspective, the router appears as a PU type 2 device to the upstream host and assumes the role of a system services control point (SSCP) appearing as a PU type 5 device to its downstream PUs.

The SSCP sessions established between the router and its upstream host are completely independent of the SSCP sessions established between the router and its downstream PUs. SNA traffic is routed at a logical unit (LU) level using a routing algorithm that maps downstream LUs onto upstream LUs.

Figure I–18 illustrates the SNA perspective of DSPU.

Figure I–18
SNA perspective of DSPU.

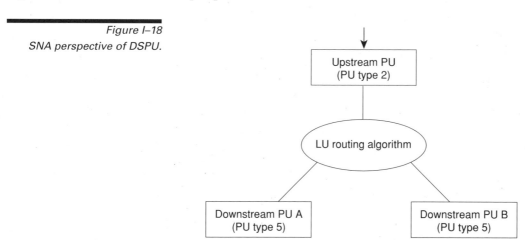

SNA FRAME RELAY ACCESS SUPPORT

Using Frame Relay Access Support (FRAS), the Cisco IOS software allows branch SNA devices to connect directly to a central site front-end processor over a Frame Relay network. FRAS converts

LAN or SDLC protocols to a Frame Relay format understood by the Network Control Program (NCP) that runs in a front-end processor. The Cisco IOS software and the NCP support two frame formats:

- RFC 1490 routed format for LLC2, specified in the FRF.3 Agreement from the Frame Relay Forum and known in NCP literature as Frame Relay Boundary Network Node (BNN) support. Support for this feature requires NCP 7.1 or higher.

- RFC 1490 802.5 source-route bridged format, known in NCP literature as Frame Relay Boundary Access Node (BAN) support. Support for this feature requires NCP 7.3 or higher.

Management service-point support in FRAS allows the SNA network management application, NetView, to manage Cisco routers over the Frame Relay network as if it were an SNA downstream PU.

FRAS provides dial backup over RSRB in case the Frame Relay network is down. While the backup Public Switched Telephone Network (PSTN) is being used, the Frame Relay connection is tried periodically. As soon as the Frame Relay network is up, it will be used at once.

RFC 1490 Routed Format for LLC2 (BNN)

RFC 1490 specifies a standard method of encapsulating multiprotocol traffic with data link (Level 2 of the OSI model) framing. The encapsulation for SNA data is specified in the FRF.3 Agreement.

The Frame Relay encapsulation method is based on the RFC 1490 frame format for "user-defined" protocols using Q.933 NLPID, as illustrated in Figure I–19.

Figure I–19
Frame Relay encapsulation based on RFC 149.

DLCI Q.922 Address	Control 0x30	NLPID Q.933 0x08	L2 Protocol ID 0x4c (802.2) 0x08	L3 Protocol ID	DSAP SSAP	Control	F C S

NOTES

The protocol ID for SNA subarea FID4 is 0x81. The protocol ID for SNA subarea FID2 is 0x82. The protocol ID for APPN FID2 is 0x83.

Frame Relay access support allows the router acting as a FRAD to take advantage of the SNA BNN support for Frame Relay provided by ACF/NCP 7.1 and OS/400 V2R3. Downstream PU 2.0 and PU 2.1 devices can be attached to the router through SDLC, Token Ring, or Ethernet links. The router acting as a FRAD is connected to the Network Control Program (NCP) or AS/400 through a public or private Frame Relay network, as illustrated in Figure I–20.

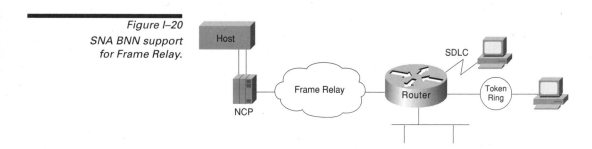

Figure I–20
SNA BNN support
for Frame Relay.

The frame format that communicates across the Frame Relay BNN link is defined in RFC 1490 for routed SNA traffic. From the perspective of the SNA host (for example, an NCP or AS/400), the Frame Relay connection is defined as a switched resource similar to a Token Ring BNN link. Because the frame format does not include link addresses to allow the NCP to distinguish among SNA devices on the same permanent virtual circuit, Cisco supports a feature known as service access point (SAP) multiplexing. SAP multiplexing allows you to configure unique LLC2 SAPs for each downstream SNA device so that they can share a single permanent virtual circuit to the front-end processor.

The Cisco IOS software is responsible for terminating the local data-link control frames (such as SDLC and Token Ring frames) and for modifying the data-link control frames to 802.2 compliant LLC frames. The LLC provides a reliable connection-oriented link-layer transport required by SNA. (For example, 802.2 LLC is used to provide link layer acknowledgment, sequencing, and flow control.)

The Cisco IOS software encapsulates these 802.2 LLC frames according to the RFC 1490 format for SNA traffic. The frames are then forwarded to the SNA host on a Frame Relay permanent virtual circuit (PVC). In the reverse direction, the software is responsible for de-encapsulating the data from the Frame Relay PVC, and for generating and transmitting the appropriate local data-link control frames to the downstream devices.

RFC 1490 Bridged Format for LLC2 (BAN)

BAN provides functionality similar to BNN except that it uses a bridged frame format, as illustrated in Figure I–21.

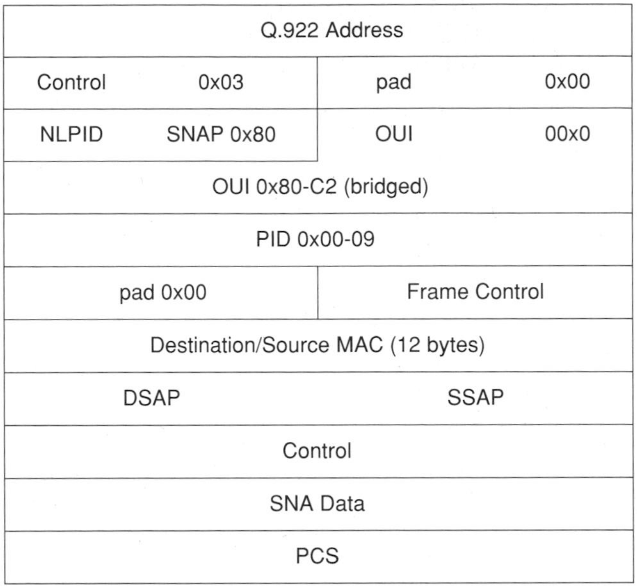

Figure I–21
RFC 1490 bridged
frame format.

Q.922 Address			
Control	0x03	pad	0x00
NLPID	SNAP 0x80	OUI	00x0
OUI 0x80-C2 (bridged)			
PID 0x00-09			
pad 0x00		Frame Control	
Destination/Source MAC (12 bytes)			
DSAP		SSAP	
Control			
SNA Data			
PCS			

Because it includes the MAC header information in every frame, BAN supports multiple SNA devices sharing a single permanent virtual circuit without requiring SAP multiplexing. BAN also supports load balancing across duplicate data-link connection identifiers to the same or different front-end processors at the data center to enhance overall availability. BAN works for devices attached by either Token Ring or Ethernet.

ADVANCED PEER-TO-PEER NETWORKING

Advanced Peer-to-Peer Networking (APPN) is the second generation of SNA. APPN provides support for client/server applications and offers more dynamics than traditional hierarchical SNA, such as dynamic directory and routing services.

Cisco's APPN implementation includes the following features:

- Implements High Performance Routing (HPR), the next step in the evolution of SNA networking. HPR replaced the APPN routing technique called intermediate session routing (ISR) with two elements that provide significant performance improvements:

  ○ Rapid Transport Protocol (RTP) provides functions including error recovery, packet resequencing, segmentation, selective retransmissions, flow control, and congestion control. RTP incorporates a new congestion avoidance algorithm, Adaptive Rate-Based (ARB) congestion control.

  ○ Automatic Network Routing provides a low-level routing mechanism that minimizes cycles and storage requirements for routing packets through intermediate nodes.

- Supports a wide variety of media: Token Ring, Ethernet, FDDI, Frame Relay, QLLC over X.25, and SDLC. APPN also enables interoperability with local and remote source-route bridging via APPN ports that can connect directly to source-route bridge ring groups.

- Supports APPN connection networks over RSRB and DLSw+.

- Enables existing APPN products, such as IBM's Communications Manager/2 (CM/2), Application System/400 (AS/400), System/36 (S/36), and Advanced Communication Facility/Virtual Telecommunications Access Method (ACF/VTAM), to connect as network nodes (NNs) or end nodes (ENs) over a network of Cisco routers.

- Implements APPN across the channel. Cisco routers with Channel Interface Processors (CIPs) can replace FEPs and other channel-attached controllers, enabling ACF/VTAM definition either as an EN or NN that uses the Cisco network for session routing. Both APPN and the CIP offer the ability to communicate through the source-route bridging mechanism in the Cisco router.

- Implements the Dependent Logical Unit Requester (DLUR) feature. Enables Dependent Logical Units (DLUs) that support only legacy applications (such as those using 3270 data streams) to traverse the APPN network to access those applications.

- Allows prioritization of traffic and bandwidth based on user-selected criteria.

- Implements scalability enhancement features, including Locate Throttling and Negative Caching, which allow you to conserve network resources.

- Supports SNMP management via APPN MIB (RFC 1593), an informational RFC provided by IBM.

- Supports a new MIB definition approved by the APPN Implementors Workshop (AIW). The new MIB provides better manageability of APPN network nodes across implementations and adds objects for supporting connection networks. Cisco supports both the current and new MIBs to allow for migration of application customers from the current version, which supports RFC 1593 to a new version for this new MIB.

The following section describes some of the components of an APPN network and reviews basic SNA terminology. The section identifies and compares node types and compares APPN with subarea SNA.

SNA Terminology

The basic component of an SNA network, subarea or APPN, is the network addressable unit (NAU). A NAU is assigned a unique eight-character name and an eight-character network identifier. Examples of NAUs are LUs, PUs, control points (CPs), and system services control points (SSCPs).

Logical Unit

A logical unit (LU) is an interface that enables end users to gain access to network resources and communicate with each other. Examples of LUs are printers, terminals, and applications. LUs communicate with each other via LU-LU sessions. The LU-LU session is the basis of communication in SNA; all end-user data traffic communicates through this session type.

To participate in an SNA network, a DLU requires the services of a VTAM host acting as an SSCP. The SSCP must establish connections with each DLU before the DLU is able to participate in the network. Dependent LUs, such as 3270 terminals, are only capable of maintaining a single LU-LU session at any one time.

An Independent LU (ILU) does not require the services of an SSCP to participate in an SNA network. In addition, an ILU can establish sessions to more than one partner in the network, and can have multiple parallel sessions with the same partner LU. Applications implementing Advanced Program-to-Program Communications (APPC) are examples of independent LUs.

Physical Unit

SNA defines a physical unit (PU) as the representation of the physical device. The PU manages and monitors the resources (such as attached links and adjacent link stations) associated with an SNA node.

Physical Unit Type 2 (PU2), the legacy physical unit, only supports dependent LUs, and requires the services from a VTAM host to perform network functions.

Physical Unit Type 2.1 (PU2.1), also known as a type 2.1 node, offers peer node capabilities in an SNA environment. A PU2.1 can support both dependent and independent LUs. In addition, a PU2.1 can support a control point, which is central to APPN networking.

APPN extends the PU T2.1 architecture to provide dynamic discovery and definition of resources and routing capabilities for large, complex networks.

Control Point

A control point (CP) identifies the networking components of a PU Type 2.1 node. In APPN, CPs are able to communicate with logically adjacent CPs by way of CP-CP sessions. Almost all APPN functions, including searches for network resources and discovery of network topology, use CP-CP sessions as the means of communication between nodes.

APPN Node Types

In an APPN network, different node types distinguish different levels of networking capabilities. This section describes APPN node types.

Low-Entry Networking Node

A Low-Entry Networking (LEN) node, sometimes called a LEN end node, is a PU 2.1 without APPN enhancements. The following are some of the characteristics of a LEN node:

- A LEN node does not support CP-CP sessions. The CP does not communicate with other nodes.

- The LEN node participates in the APPN network by using the services of an adjacent Network Node (NN).

- Destination LUs in an attached APPN network must be defined to the LEN node, and destination LUs on the LEN must be defined on the attached NN.

LEN nodes predate APPN, but are able to interoperate with an APPN network. Because there is no CP-CP session between a LEN node and its NN, resources at the LEN node must be defined at the NN, reducing dynamic resource discovery capabilities.

End Node

An EN is a PU 2.1 that includes the APPN support necessary to gain full access to an APPN network, but is not capable of performing in an intermediate role when routing APPN sessions. The following are the characteristics of an EN:

- Contains a CP to manage its resources.
- Uses the services of an adjacent NN to access the network.
- Provides partial network services.
- May connect to multiple NNs.
- Is always a session end point.

Because an EN lacks full APPN routing capability, it might be thought of as an application host or point-of-user access. The EN establishes CP-CP sessions with its NN server, so topology and directory information can be exchanged dynamically, eliminating the need to define resources on the NN. The EN may connect to multiple network nodes and LU-LU sessions can be established through any of the connected network nodes, although only one network node can be its network node server at any one time.

Network Node

An NN implements the APPN extensions to the PU 2.1 architecture that allow it to provide intermediate routing services to LEN nodes and ENs. An NN contains a CP to manage its own resources and the ENs and LEN nodes in its domain.

An NN provides the following network services:

- Connectivity
- Location of resources in the network
- Route selection
- Intermediate session routing
- Data transport
- Network management

An NN may be a session end point or an intermediate system.

An NN Server is a network node that provides resource location and route-selection services for the LEN nodes, ENs, and LUs it serves. The nodes served, ENs or LEN nodes, are defined as being in the network node server's domain.

APPN Components

This section describes the basic components of APPN and how they interact to provide APPN networking functions.

APPN Connections

The configuration services (CS) component of an APPN node manages local interfaces and connections to the APPN network. CS controls the ports and link stations on the node. A port defines a connection to a transport media accessible to APPN, while a link station identifies the addressing information and characteristics of a connection with another node.

APPN Network: Connection Phase

When two APPN nodes connect, the following activities occur:

- An APPN port is activated, allowing the node to access an interface and its corresponding transport media.
- A link station is activated, initiating a connection-oriented link with the partner node.
- If the CP is APPN capable, and there is no CP-CP session already between these two nodes over a different link, a pair of CP-CP sessions may be established between adjacent CPs. EN-NN and NN-NN CP-CP sessions can be established. Although EN-EN APPN connections can be defined, an EN will not establish CP-CP sessions with another EN. LEN nodes are not capable of establishing CP-CP sessions.

The entire connection phase may be configured to occur automatically, or the connection can be initiated manually via EXEC commands.

A link is defined as both the link stations within the two nodes it connects and the link connection between the nodes. A link station is the hardware or software within a node that enables the node to attach to, and provide control over, a link connection. A link connection is the physical medium over which data is transmitted. In legacy SNA, a transmission group may consist of one or more links between two nodes, but in the APPN architecture, transmission groups are limited to a single link. It is therefore common in APPN to use the terms link and transmission groups interchangeably.

Details of Link Activation

The connection phase in APPN begins with link activation, which initiates communication between nodes. It is independent of the DLC chosen, and may not be required for some DLC types. For switched connections, the connection phase is similar to "dial" and "answer" procedures. In an X.25 network, the connection phase would be the establishment of a virtual circuit. When the connect phase is complete, the two nodes can exchange and establish node characteristics through exchange identification (XID).

The exchange of XIDs allows a node to determine whether the adjacent station is active and to verify the identity of the adjacent node. Node identification fields, including the CP name, will be exchanged. This information exchange allows, for example, a node to correlate an incoming connection with a link station definition on the node.

During XID exchange, primary and secondary link stations are determined. The two link stations compare the XID node identifier values (block number plus ID number). If the link stations are defined as negotiable, then the higher node ID becomes primary. If the nodes have the same node ID, each generates a random number and the node with the higher random number becomes primary. The result of the primary-secondary role negotiation determines which node will send the mode-setting command—Set Normal Response Mode (SNRM) for SDLC, Set Asynchronous Balanced Mode (SABM) for X.25, and so on.

After the link activation XID exchange is complete, CS creates a new path control and instructs the Address Space Manager (ASM) to activate a new address space. Then CS notifies Topology and Routing Services (TRS) that a transmission group (TG) has become active so the APPN topology can be updated. Finally, if a CP-CP session is to be activated, CS notifies SS. SS then activates the CP-CP session.

CP-CP Session Activation

After a link is established, the nodes determine whether CP-CP sessions should be established. Between network nodes, CP-CP sessions are normally activated on the first link to become active between the nodes. An EN determines which of the NNs will be used for a CP-CP session. The EN indicates which NN is the server by sending a request to activate a session, known as a BIND, to the CP on the adjacent NN. The NN accepts by sending BIND for a second LU 6.2 session, completing the CP-CP session pair. Each node uses one session to send CP-CP communication data, while the other is reserved for receiving data from the partner node.

CPSVCMG is the class of service (COS) used for CP-CP sessions. It indicates a transmission priority of network, which is the highest of the four transmission priorities in APPN.

When the CP-CP session is established, the CPs exchange capabilities, and, in the case of EN to NN CP-CP sessions, register the local LUs.

APPN Topology

APPN maintains a map of the APPN network as known to a particular node. TRS is the APPN component responsible for maintaining the topology database.

There are two types of information in a topology database: local topology and network topology.

- Local topology, found in both ENs and NNs, describes the local links attached to a particular node, and the partner control points to which it is connected.

- Network topology, found only in NNs, describes all the NNs in the network and the links that interconnect them.

An EN uses the information in its local topology database to send local TG information to the NN server on APPN search requests and replies. The TG information is passed to the NN server when a route is requested, so the NN can select the best TG from the EN to one of its adjacent NNs. In a NN, the local topology database includes information about the attached ENs and TGs.

Figure I–22 shows the local topology as it is known to EN A, NN2, and EN B.

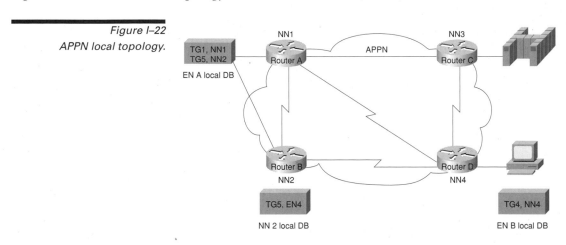

Figure I–22
APPN local topology.

Network topology contains information on all network nodes in the APPN network as well as the TGs interconnecting them. Every NN maintains a fully replicated copy of the network topology database. Figure I–23 illustrates an APPN network topology.

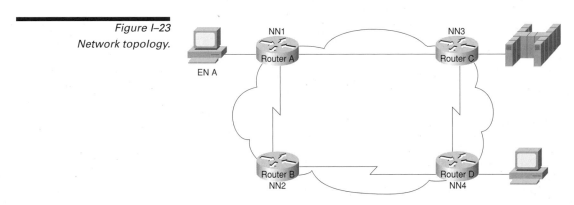

Figure I–23
Network topology.

The network topology database is built from information about the local NN and its TGs to other NNs, and from Topology Database Updates (TDUs) received from adjacent NNs. TDUs are exchanged whenever NNs establish CP-CP sessions with each other. As updates occur in NNs or TGs between NNs, the owning NN sends a TDU to its adjacent NNs, which propagates the TDU to its adjacent NNs until the network topology database is again replicated.

For each NN, certain properties are specified in the topology database. Each node and TG in a network topology database is assigned a unique resource sequence number. These numbers are incremented to the next even value whenever the owning network node creates a TDU for that resource. TG database entries include whether CP-CP sessions are supported, and include the TG weight, TG status (operative or inoperative), TG number, partner node information, and TG characteristics such as cost per byte, cost per connect time, and security level.

TDUs provide updated information to NNs about the node itself and information about all locally owned TGs to other network nodes. TDUs can be triggered by changes in node or TG characteristics.

TRS broadcasts TDUs containing local node information every five days to prevent other network nodes from discarding valid information, which occurs after 15 days with no update. This 15-day cleanup of the database is called garbage collection.

In Figure I–24, NN3 adds itself to the network. NN3 forwards information about itself to NN1. NN1 forwards the information to NN2 and NN4. NN2 and NN4 then forward a second TDU to each other. Because they will have the same RSN and information, the second TDUs will be discarded.

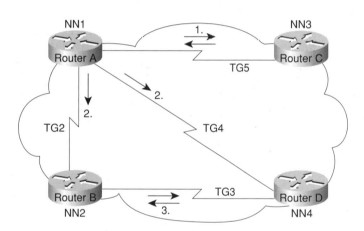

Figure I–24
Topology database update: adding a node.

In Figure I–25, TG6 is activated between NN4 and NN3. TDUs are exchanged between the two nodes, so each node can build a new topology database. New information is propagated to adjacent nodes once NN4 and NN3 have updated topology databases. TG6 could be active, but with no CP-CP session established. The TG still will be included in the network topology and forwarded, so that path can be used for sessions.

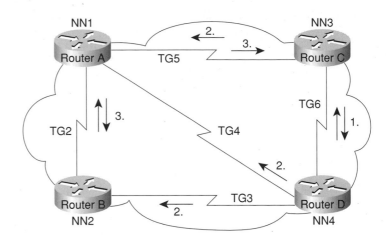

Figure I–25
Topology database update:
adding a transmission group.

APPN Directory and APPN Searches

Directory services is the APPN component responsible for managing the directory database and searching for network resources throughout the APPN network. The directory database should not be confused with the topology database. The directory database maintains information about resource names and their owners, while the topology database maintains a network map of NNs and TGs. Directory services locates a session partner. Topology services computes an optimal route to the session partner when it has been located.

At a minimum, each APPN network resource must be defined on the node where the resource exists. When the resource is defined, it can be found through network searches. Optionally, the resource location may be defined in other nodes to optimize directory services search logic.

Registered directory entries are created dynamically in the local directory of the NN. These entries represent local LUs of an adjacent EN for which the NN is providing network node server function.

Cached directory entries are added dynamically and are based on the results of previous searches. A cache entry allows the node to attempt a directed search straight to the destination resource. If a cache entry does not exist, or the entry is incorrect, a broadcast search is issued to query each NN in the network for the destination resource. Each cache entry is verified before use to make sure the resource is still available. If the resource is not found, a broadcast search is attempted.

Some implementations, including Cisco's, support safe store of the directory cache. The cache entries in a network node's directory database are periodically written to a permanent storage medium. Safe store permits faster access (after a network node failure or initial power-on) by eliminating network broadcast searches for safe-stored resources.

The central resource registration feature implements the registration requester function of the APPN options set 1107, Central Resource Registration of LUs.

An EN registers its local resources at its NN server. The NN server, in turn, registers those resources at a central directory server. This feature significantly reduces the number of network broadcast searches in an APPN network. If every resource is registered, then all network nodes can query the central directory server, which eliminates the need for broadcast searches.

APPN Route Selection

Each APPN session is assigned a route on which the data path for this session will travel. APPN TRS is responsible for computing a route for an LU-LU session. A route is an ordered sequence of nodes and TGs that represents a path from an origin node to a destination node. TRS uses the topology database and its COS definitions to obtain the information necessary to perform a route computation.

While multiple routes may be available between an origin node and a destination node, the best route is selected (see Figure I–26). The lowest-cost path that provides the desired level of service is selected.

When a session is requested, the directory services function locates the target resource, and TRS selects a route.

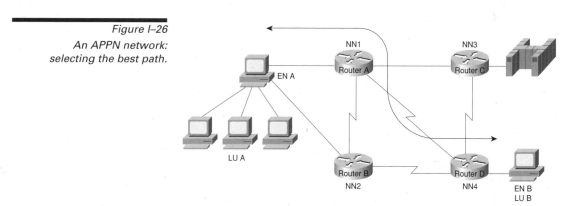

Figure I–26
An APPN network:
selecting the best path.

When the origin LU requests a session, it either specifies a mode or uses a default mode for the session. The mode determines a COS for this session request. Acceptable COS characteristics are compared to node and TG characteristics to select the best route.

A COS table entry specifies transmission priority, COS name and one or multiple rows of COS characteristics that are acceptable for that COS. Note that traffic on sessions with the same COS can only flow at the same transmission priority. You need a separately named entry to achieve a different priority on the same route.

TG characteristics include link speed, cost per connect time, cost per byte, security class (7 levels), propagation delay, and three user-defined fields.

Node properties include route additional resistance (RAR) and a congestion indicator.

The COS table can contain multiple entries meeting the criteria. Some entries are more acceptable than others. The COS table lets you assign weight to each entry to differentiate the value of each entry. For each possible route, compare the characteristics of the component nodes and transmission groups to the ranges of acceptable characteristics as defined in the COS table for that COS. For each NN or TG the characteristics are compared to see if they are within the range of tolerance. If so, a weight is assigned to each node and each TG and is added to the total weight for that particular route.

When all routes are weighed, the one with the lowest weight is selected. Ties are broken by random selection.

Route selection is a complex process and, where multiple routes are available, may involve considerable overhead. To reduce this overhead, TRS uses routing trees to store the best route path to each node in the network for a specific COS. You may configure the number of routing trees the node will maintain at any one time.

Connection Networks

Connection networks provide extensions to the APPN route calculation algorithm to simplify definitions and enhance connectivity on shared transport media. If you specify a node as a member of a connection network, that node can establish a direct connection, when needed, between itself and any other member of the connection network.

For example, on one Token Ring, there may be 50 end nodes with links and a CP-CP session active to the same network node. The end nodes may communicate with each other through the network node, but this data path, which routes data through the network node then back on the same media to the target end node, is an inefficient use of both the network node and the transmission media.

Alternatively, APPN links can be configured between each end node in a mesh fashion, but this would require over 1000 link definitions. Instead, each end node can be configured as a member of the same connection network. This allows APPN route calculation to calculate a route through the connection network between the two end nodes. The resulting data path is a direct connection between end nodes without a corresponding link definition on either node.

APPN Intermediate Session Routing

After a route is selected, a BIND session command flows from the origin LU to the destination LU over the specified route. The BIND includes:

- A route selection control vector (RSCV), the route for this session.
- A fully qualified procedure correlation identifier (FQPCID), which uniquely identifies the session.
- A transmission priority that indicates the relative priority for frames traveling on this session relative to frames on other sessions. There are four priority levels: network, high, medium, and low. The transmission priority is assigned based on the session COS. In SNA, transmission priority provides the mechanism for delivering high priority traffic, such as interactive traffic, ahead of lower priority traffic, such as batch jobs and file transfers.

- A pacing indicator that indicates the maximum window size (the maximum number of messages that can be transmitted prior to receiving a SNA response). It also indicates whether fixed window size or adaptive pacing is supported.

- A segmenting indicator that identifies the capabilities of adjacent nodes to perform segmentation of data frames received on this session.

As the BIND passes through each NN, the NN records the inbound session identifier or local form session identifier (LFSID), and assigns a new session identifier to be used on the outbound port. It also builds a "session connector" that connects the inbound session identifier with the outbound session identifier, so that it knows how to forward subsequent packets on this session. The session connector also stores information carried in the BIND, such as segmentation values and transmission priority, so that other components, such as path control, will be able to use the information on session traffic.

No subsequent data packets contain any routing information—they contain only the local form session identifier. Packets are forwarded based on information in session connectors, including port and outbound LFSID. LFSIDs are swapped at each NN because they have only local significance.

Dependent Logical Unit Requester/Server

A dependent LU (DLU) is an LU that depends on the SSCP in VTAM to provide services for establishing sessions. Common DLU types are DLU 0, 1, 2, and 3.

Dependent LUs originated in subarea SNA. In early APPN environments, only LU 6.2 independent LUs were supported. The PU supporting dependent LUs still required a logical link directly to a subarea network boundary function (VTAM or NCP) in order to operate. Dependent LU Requester (DLUR) provides the extensions to APPN necessary to allow dependent LUs to interoperate in an APPN network and removes the restriction that dependent LUs must have a direct connection to a subarea network boundary function.

DLUR is the client half of Dependent LU Requester/Server (DLUR/DLUS). The Dependent LU Server (DLUS) is currently implemented in IBM's VTAM version 4.2.

There are three main concepts in DLUR/DLUS:

- Control flows to the DLUs from VTAM, such as active logical unit (ACTLU) and active physical unit (ACTPU), and session requests flow on a pair of LU 6.2 session between the DLUR and the DLUS.

- Upon receiving a session request from the LU over control session, the VTAM acting as DLUS notifies the VTAM owning the target application that a session is requested.

- The application initiates the session, and its serving network node selects the best route over the APPN network to the DLUR and destination LU.

The DLUR function resides on an EN or NN that owns the dependent LUs. In addition, the DLUR exists in a network node that offers its DLUR services to PU type 2.0 and PU type 2.1 nodes which connect to the DLUR. This arrangement consolidates the LU6.2 control sessions (only one pair is needed for all downstream PUs that the DLUR serves). In addition, this arrangement provides considerable cost savings over upgrading each device that owns dependent LUs to be APPN and DLUR capable.

The DLUR function does not have to be active in all APPN nodes—only in those nodes with DLUs directly attached. Once encapsulated in the LU 6.2 session, the DLUR control traffic (encapsulated SSCP-PU and SSCP-LU control flows) looks like regular APPN traffic.

By providing DLUS support in VTAM, SSCP support is extended to LUs residing on nodes that are nonadjacent to the VTAM or NCP boundary function. Traditional SSCP-PU and SSCP-LU session flows are multiplexed in LU 6.2 sessions between the DLUR and DLUS.

The benefits of using the DLUS/DLUR function include:

- The ability to use dynamic definition of the dependent LUs in VTAM, providing the served PU supports it, to reduce system definition and allow nodes to be moved in the network. All DLUR-attached resources appear as switched resources that are not associated with a particular communications line or port.

- The SSCP owns resources that are non-adjacent to a VTAM or NCP.

- Dependent LUs are fully visible as VTAM resources for network management purposes.

- APPN routing can be used to select an optimal route for the session path, even though the secondary logical unit (SLU) is not APPN-capable. A key advantage of DLUR over SNA gateway functions is that the LU-LU session path from the application host to the dependent LU can differ from the path between the DLUR to the DLUS. SNA gateway and PU concentration devices are restricted to having their LU-LU session data paths identical to the path over which the SSCP-PU and SSCP-LU traffic flows.

- Because DLUR offers the ability to separate the control functions for dependent LUs from the session traffic, you can interrupt and recover, or even change, DLUS nodes without interrupting currently active LU-LU sessions to the dependent LUs.

- No changes to end-user systems or applications are required.

- Network consolidation—combining the dependent LU traffic with other multiprotocol traffic—provides cost savings.

NATIVE CLIENT INTERFACE ARCHITECTURE (NCIA)

NCIA is a new software architecture introduced by Cisco Systems to make accessing IBM SNA applications over routed internetworks more scalable and flexible. NCIA is a component of the Cisco IOS software. The architecture is intended to combine the benefits of the native SNA interface at end stations and mainframes with those of TCP/IP across the network backbone.

NCIA extends the use of the TCP/IP protocol all the way to the SNA end station. Because of the wide range of media supported by TCP/IP, including dial-up telephone lines for remotely located users, NCIA makes multiprotocol access to corporate backbone networks much more flexible for SNA users.

NCIA allows SNA end stations such as PCs or workstations to encapsulate SNA traffic in TCP/IP, rather than requiring the traffic to travel through routers. The first phase of NCIA (NCIA I) used Cisco remote source-route bridging (RSRB) encapsulation. The current phase (NCIA Server) uses a new client/server model. NCIA Server is not backward compatible to NCIA I.

NCIA I

Using Cisco's RSRB technology, NCIA I encapsulates the Token Ring traffic inside IP datagrams passed over a TCP connection between a router and a client. A virtual ring is created to allow the router to interconnect any client. The virtual ring acts as a logical Token Ring in the router, so that all the Token Rings connected to the router are treated as if they are all on the same Token Ring. The virtual ring is called a ring group. The ring group number is used just like a physical ring number and shows up in any route descriptors contained in packets being bridged. A ring group must be assigned a ring number that is unique throughout the network.

An NCIA I client acts as both an RSRB router and an end station. It must have a "fake" ring number and a "fake" bridge number so that it looks like an end station sitting on a real Token Ring. The fake ring and bridge numbers are visible to both the RSRB router and the NCIA client. The client must also have an LLC2 so that it can handle the LLC2 sessions.

NCIA Server

The NCIA Server feature extends the scalability of NCIA I, enhances its functionality, and provides support for both the installed base of RSRB routers and the growing number of DLSw+ routers. The NCIA Server feature includes the following enhancements:

- No need to configure a ring number on the client.
- No need to configure each client on the router.
- MAC address can be dynamically assigned by the NCIA server running on the router.
- SNA is directly on top of TCP/IP; LLC2 is no longer required at end station.
- A client is a true end station, not a router peer.
- NCIA Server communicates with other components in router, such as RSRB, APPN, DLSw+, and DSPU.
- Supports both connect-in and connect-out.
- NCIA client/server model is independent of the upstream implementation.
- Efficient protocol between client and server.

NCIA Client/Server Model

The NCIA Server feature uses a client/server model (see Figure I–27), where the NCIA server is a software module on a Cisco router and the NCIA client is a PC or workstation. The NCIA server performs two major functions:

- Establishes TCP to NCIA Data Link Control (NDLC) sessions with clients for the purpose of sending and receiving data.

- Uses the Cisco link services interface (CLSI) to communicate with other software modules in the router, such as APPN, DLSw+, and DSPU, and acts as the data intermediary between them and NCIA clients. The NCIA server's role as an intermediary is transparent to the client.

Figure I–27
NCIA server
client/server model.

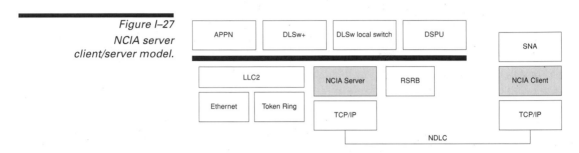

NCIA Data Link Control (NDLC) is the protocol used between clients and servers. NDLC serves two purposes:

- Establishes the peer connection.
- Establishes the circuit between the client and the server.

The peer session must be established before an end-to-end circuit can be set up. During the set up period for the peer session, the MAC address representing a client is defined. The MAC address can be defined by the client or by the server when the client does not have a MAC address.

The NCIA Server feature supports connect-in and connect-out (from the server's perspective), but connect-out is not supported if the client station does not listen for the incoming connection. For a server to connect-out, clients must connect to the server first. After registering itself by providing its own MAC address, the client can then optionally disconnect from the server. When a server receives an explorer, and its destination MAC address is registered, an NCIA server will connect to that client if it is not connected. For NetBIOS explorers (addressed to functional address 0xC00000000080), the TCP session must remain up so that the server can broadcast the explorers to the client. If the TCP session is down, the server will not send the NetBIOS explorers to a client, even when the client is registered.

After the peer session has been established, the NDLC protocol establishes the circuit between the client and server. This circuit is used to transfer end-user data between the client and the server. Because the client and its target station are not on the same transport, they cannot form a direct, end-to-end circuit. Each client must form a circuit between the client and server, and the server must form another circuit between the server and the target station. The server links those two circuits to form an end-to-end circuit. The server acts as a mediator between the client and the target station so that packets can be transferred between them.

In the NCIA server, only peer keepalive is maintained. There is no keepalive at circuit level.

The NCIA server acts as a data-link provider, like Token Ring or Ethernet, in the router. It uses CLSI to communicate with other software modules, just as other data-link providers do. The network administrator configures the router to communicate with specific modules. For data-link users, such as APPN, DLSw+, and DSPU, the NCIA server can interface to them directly. For other data-link providers, the NCIA server must go through a DLSw+ local peer to communicate with them. The DLSw+ local peer passes packets back and forth among different data-link providers.

Advantages of the Client/Server Model

The client/server model used in the NCIA Server feature extends the scalability of NCIA. In addition, it provides support for both the installed base of RSRB routers and the growing number of DLSw+ routers.

Extended Scalability

The client/server model minimizes the number of central site RSRB or DLSw+ peer connections required to support a large network of NCIA clients (see Figure I–28). Rather than each client having a peer connection to a central site router, the clients attach to an IP backbone through an NCIA server that, in turn, has a single peer connection to a central site router. This scheme can greatly reduce the number of central site peer connections required. For example, in a network with 1000 clients and 10 NCIA servers, there would be only 10 central site peer connections. Note that there would still be 1000 LLC2 connections that must be locally acknowledged at the central site router, but this can easily be handled in a single central site router. When the number of LLC2 connections (or the number of clients) is in the tens of thousands, NCIA servers can take advantage of downstream PU concentration to minimize the number of LLC2 connections that must be supported by the central site routers.

Figure I–28
NCIA server provides extended scalability to support large networks.

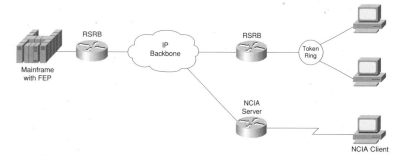

Migration Support

Using a client/server model allows the NCIA Server feature to be independent of the upstream implementation, allowing it to be implemented in a network that is still using RSRB, as well as in a DLSw+ network. It also greatly simplifies migration from RSRB to DLSw+, because it requires no changes at the client. A single NCIA server can support either approach (but not both). As

Figure I–29 illustrates, a central site router can support RSRB and DLSw+ concurrently, allowing a portion of the NCIA servers to communicate using RSRB and another portion to communicate using DLSw+.

Figure I–29

NCIA Server provides independence from the upstream network implementation.

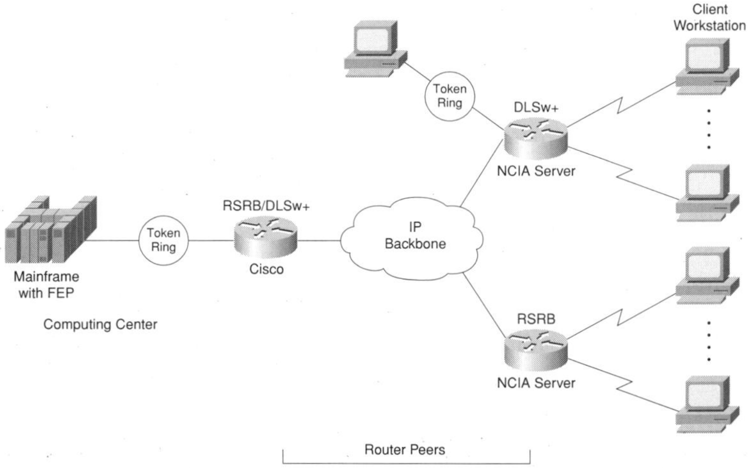

IBM CHANNEL INTERFACE PROCESSOR

The Cisco 7000 series supports the Cisco IOS software mainframe CIP application, which in turn supports the IBM channel attach feature.

IBM (and IBM-compatible) mainframe hosts are connected to each other and to communication controllers through high-performance communication subsystems called mainframe channels. Cisco supports IBM channel attachment technologies, including the fiber-optic Enterprise Systems Connection (ESCON) channel introduced on the ES/9000 mainframe and the parallel bus-and-tag channel supported on System 370 and later mainframes.

The Cisco 7000 series configured with the CIP (and other interface processors) is an ideal connectivity hub for large corporate networks, and provides the following routing services between mainframes and LANs:

- Replaces an IBM 3172 interconnect controller, which enables mainframe and peripheral access from LAN-based workstations.

- Simplifies the network because the number of network devices is reduced, especially in situations where a router can replace an IBM 3172.

- Ensures 100 percent IBM compatibility with the Cisco ESCON Channel Adapter (ECA) which uses the IBM ESCON chipset.

Common Link Access for Workstations (CLAW) Support

Cisco has implemented Common Link Access for Workstations (CLAW) support in the CIP, which is a link-level protocol used by channel-attached RISC System/6000 series systems and by IBM 3172 devices running TCP/IP offload. The CLAW protocol improves channel efficiency and allows the CIP to provide the functionality of an IBM 3172 in TCP/IP environments and support direct channel attachment. The output from TCP/IP mainframe processing is a series of IP datagrams that the router can switch without modifications.

TCP Offload Support

Cisco has implemented offload processing support for TCP/IP. Like the offload feature of the IBM 3172 Model 3, the TCP offload feature on the CIP is designed to remove processing cycles from the mainframe by executing the TCP protocol on the CIP card. But while the IBM 3172-3 executes TCP in an OS/2 environment, the CIP utilizes the MIPS processor and high-speed channel software to deliver vastly improved performance and scalability. The TCP/IP protocol suite runs on the CIP board and delivers routable IP frames to the Cisco 7000 series router.

CIP Systems Network Architecture Support

CIP Systems Network Architecture (CSNA) support in a Cisco 7000 series router provides mainframe connectivity to SNA network nodes. The CIP supports both ECA and Parallel Channel Adapter (PCA) connections to an IBM mainframe using SNA network features. The CSNA feature provides an SNA LAN gateway to VTAM using a high-speed channel connection.

The CSNA feature also allows you to replace currently installed IBM 3172 interconnect controllers with a Cisco 7000 series router and experience no loss of functionality. You will, in fact, gain functionality with minimal or no changes to VTAM or site configuration.

TN3270 Server Support

The Cisco implementation of TN3270 server for CIP and CSNA provides mapping between an SNA 3270 host and a TN3270 client connected to a TCP/IP network as shown in Figure I–30.

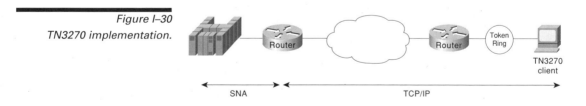

Figure I–30
TN3270 implementation.

Functionally, it is useful to view the TN3270 server from two different perspectives: SNA functions and Telnet Server functions.

- SNA Functions

  From the perspective of an SNA 3270 host connected to the CIP, the TN3270 Server is an SNA device that supports multiple physical units (PUs), with each PU supporting up to 255 Type 1, 2, or 3 logical units (LUs). The SNA host is unaware of the existence of TCP/IP extension on the implementation of these LUs.

  The LUs implemented by the TN3270 server are dependent LUs. To route these dependent LU sessions to multiple VTAM hosts connected to the server in the CIP card, rather than routing in the virtual telecommunications access method (VTAM) hosts, the TN3270 server implements an SNA session switch with end-node Dependent LU Requester (DLUR) function. Using the DLUR is optional, so that the TN3270 server can be used with VTAM versions prior to version 4.2, which provide no APPN support.

  SNA session switch allows you to eliminate SNA subarea routing between hosts of TN3270 traffic by establishing APPN links with the primary LU hosts directly.

- Telnet Server Functions

  From the perspective of a TN3270 client, the TN3270 server is a Telnet server that can support approximately 8000 concurrent Telnet sessions. The server on the CIP card supports Telnet connection negotiation and data format as specified in RFC 1576 (referred to as "traditional TN3270") and RFC 1647 (referred to as "TN3270E").

For more information on TN3270 on the CIP, see Chapter 23, "Configuring IBM Channel Attach."

IBM Channel Attach Hardware Requirements

Support for IBM channel attach requires the following hardware:

- A Cisco 7000 series router with one available card slot.
- A CIP with one or two adapter cards (ECA, PCA, or a combination).
- Cables for interconnecting the adapter cards to the mainframe or ESCON director switch.

IBM Channel Attach Host Software Requirements

Your mainframe host software must meet the following minimum requirements:

- IBM TCP/IP for VM Version 2 Release 2, with program temporary fix (PTF) enhancements for RISC System/6000 series ESCON support.
- IBM TCP/IP for MVS Version 2 Release 2.1, with program temporary fix (PTF) enhancements for RISC System/6000 series ESCON support.

PART 1

BRIDGING

Chapter 1—Configuring Transparent Bridging

Chapter 2—Transparent Bridging Commands

Chapter 3—Configuring Source-Route Bridging

Chapter 4—Source-Route Bridging Commands

Configuring Transparent Bridging

Cisco IOS software bridging functionality combines the advantages of a spanning-tree bridge and a full multiprotocol router. This combination provides the speed and protocol transparency of an adaptive spanning-tree bridge, along with the functionality, reliability, and security of a router.

This chapter describes how to configure transparent bridging and source-route transparent (SRT) bridging. This chapter also describes the concepts of virtual networking, transparent bridging of virtual LANs (VLANs), and routing between VLANs. For a complete description of the commands mentioned in this chapter, see Chapter 2, "Transparent Bridging Commands."

TRANSPARENT AND SRT BRIDGING CONFIGURATION TASK LIST

Perform one or more of the tasks in the following sections to configure transparent bridging or SRT bridging on your router:

- Configuring Transparent Bridging and SRT Bridging
- Configuring Transparently Bridged Virtual LANs (VLANs)
- Configuring Routing Between VLANs
- Configuring Transparent Bridging over WANs
- Configuring Concurrent Routing and Bridging
- Configuring Integrated Routing and Bridging
- Configuring Transparent Bridging Options
- Filtering Transparently Bridged Packets
- Adjusting Spanning-Tree Parameters
- Tuning the Transparently Bridged Network
- Monitoring and Maintaining the Transparent Bridge Network

See the "Transparent and SRT Bridging Configuration Examples" section later in this chapter for configuration examples.

CONFIGURING TRANSPARENT BRIDGING AND SRT BRIDGING

To configure transparent and SRT bridging, you must perform the tasks in the following sections:

- Assigning a Bridge Group Number and Defining the Spanning-Tree Protocol.
- Assigning Each Network Interface to a Bridge Group.
- Choosing the OUI for Ethernet Type II Frames.

Assigning a Bridge Group Number and Defining the Spanning-Tree Protocol

The first step in setting up your transparent bridging network is to define a Spanning-Tree Protocol and assign a bridge group number. You can choose either the IEEE 802.1D Spanning-Tree Protocol or the earlier Digital protocol upon which this IEEE standard is based.

To assign a bridge group number and define a Spanning-Tree Protocol, perform the following task in global configuration mode:

Task	Command
Assign a bridge group number and define a Spanning-Tree Protocol as either IEEE 802.1D standard or Digital.	**bridge** *bridge-group* **protocol** {ieee | dec}

The IEEE 802.1D Spanning-Tree Protocol is the preferred way of running the bridge. Use the Digital Spanning-Tree Protocol only for backward compatibility.

Assigning Each Network Interface to a Bridge Group

A bridge group is an internal organization of network interfaces on a router. Bridge groups cannot be used outside the router on which it is defined to identify traffic switched within the bridge group. Bridge groups within the same router function as distinct bridges; that is, bridged traffic and BPDUs cannot be exchanged between different bridge groups on a router. Furthermore, bridge groups cannot be used to multiplex or demultiplex different streams of bridged traffic on a LAN. An interface can be a member of only one bridge group. Use a bridge group for each separately bridged (topologically distinct) network connected to the router. Typically, only one such network exists in a configuration.

The purpose of placing network interfaces into a bridge group is twofold:

- To bridge all nonrouted traffic among the network interfaces comprising the bridge group. If the packet's destination address is known in the bridge table, it is forwarded on a single interface in the bridge group. If the packet's destination is unknown in the bridge table, it is flooded on all forwarding interfaces in the bridge group. The bridge places source addresses in the bridge table as it learns them during the process of bridging.

- To participate in the spanning-tree algorithm by receiving, and in some cases transmitting, BPDUs on the LANs to which they are attached. A separate spanning process runs for each configured bridge group. Each bridge group participates in a separate spanning tree. A bridge group establishes a spanning tree based on the BPDUs it receives on only its member interfaces.

For SRT bridging, if the Token Ring and serial interfaces are in the same bridge group, changing the serial encapsulation method causes the state of the corresponding Token Ring interface to be reinitialized. Its state will change from "up" to "initializing" to "up" again within a few seconds.

After you assign a bridge group number and define a Spanning-Tree Protocol, assign each network interface to a bridge group by performing the following task in interface configuration mode:

Task	Command
Assign a network interface to a bridge group.	**bridge-group** *bridge-group*

Choosing the OUI for Ethernet Type II Frames

For SRT bridging networks, you must choose the OUI code that will be used in the encapsulation of Ethernet Type II frames across Token Ring backbone networks. To choose the OUI, perform the following task in interface configuration mode:

Task	Command
Select the Ethernet Type II OUI encapsulation code.	**ethernet-transit-oui** [90-compatible | standard | cisco]

CONFIGURING TRANSPARENTLY BRIDGED VIRTUAL LANS (VLANS)

Traditionally, a bridge group is an independently bridged subnetwork. In this definition, bridge groups cannot exchange traffic with other bridge groups, nor can they multiplex or demultiplex different streams of bridged traffic. Cisco's transparently bridged VLAN feature permits a bridge group to extend outside the router to identify traffic switched within the bridge group.

While bridge groups remain internal organizations of network interfaces functioning as distinct bridges within a router, transparent bridging on subinterfaces permits bridge groups to be used to multiplex different streams of bridged traffic on a LAN or HDLC serial interface. In this way, bridged traffic may be switched out of one bridge group on one router, multiplexed across a subinterface, and demultiplexed into a second bridge group on a second router. Together, the first bridge group and the second bridge group form a transparently bridged VLAN. This approach can be extended to impose logical topologies upon transparently bridged networks.

The primary application of transparently bridged VLANs constructed in this way is to separate traffic between bridge groups of local network interfaces, to multiplex bridged traffic from several bridge groups on a shared interface (LAN or HDLC serial), and to form VLANs composed of collections of bridge groups on several routers. These VLANs improve performance because they reduce the propagation of locally bridged traffic, and they improve security benefits because they completely separate traffic.

In Figure 1–1, different bridge groups on different routers are configured into three VLANs that span the bridged network. Each bridge group consists of conventionally bridged local interfaces and a subinterface on the backbone FDDI LAN. Bridged traffic on the subinterface is encapsulated and "colored" with a VLAN identifier known as a *security association identifier* common to all bridge groups participating in the VLAN. In addition, bridges only accept packets bearing security association identifiers for which they have a configured subinterface. Thus, a bridge group is configured to participate in a VLAN if it contains a subinterface configured with the VLAN's characteristic security association identifier. See the section "Transparently Bridged VLANs Configuration Example" later in this chapter for an example configuration of the topology shown in Figure 1–1.

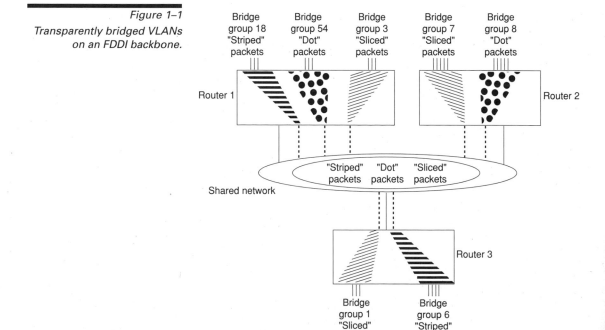

Figure 1–1

Transparently bridged VLANs on an FDDI backbone.

─ **NOTES** ───

The 802.10 encapsulation used to "color" transparently bridged packets on subinterfaces might increase the size of a packet so that it exceeds the MTU size of the LAN from which the packet originated. To avoid MTU violations on the shared network, the originating LANs must either have a smaller native MTU than the shared network (as is the case from Ethernet to FDDI), or the MTU on all packet sources on the originating LAN must be configured to be at least 16 bytes less than the MTU of the shared network.

To configure a VLAN on a transparently bridged network, perform the following tasks, beginning in interface configuration mode:

Task	Command
Step 1 Specify a subinterface.	**interface** *type slot/port.subinterface-number*
Step 2 Specify the IEEE 802.10 Security data exchange security association identifier. (In other words, specify the "color.")	**encapsulation sde** *said*
Step 3 Associate the subinterface with an existing bridge group.	**bridge-group** *bridge-group*

─ **NOTES** ───

Transparently bridged VLANs are supported in conjunction with only the IEEE Spanning-Tree Protocol. When you logically segment a transparently bridged network into VLANs, each VLAN computes its own spanning-tree topology. Configuring each VLAN to compute its own spanning-tree topology provides much greater stability than running a single spanning tree throughout. Traffic bridged within one VLAN is unaffected by physical topology changes occurring within another VLAN.

─ **NOTES** ───

The current implementation of SDE encapsulation is not recommended for serial or Ethernet media.

CONFIGURING ROUTING BETWEEN VLANS

Virtual networking provides a mechanism whereby you can define logical topologies to overlay a physical switched infrastructure, and so establish autonomous VLAN domains. By definition, VLANs provide traffic separation and logical network partitioning. To communicate between VLANs, a routing function is required.

Cisco's VLAN Routing implementation is designed to operate across all router platforms. However, the Inter-Switch Link (ISL) VLAN trunking protocol currently is defined on 100 BaseTX/FX Fast Ethernet interfaces only and therefore is appropriate to the Cisco 7000 and higher-end platforms only. The IEEE 802.10 protocol can run over any LAN or HDLC serial interface. VLAN traffic is fast switched.

The VLAN Routing implementation treats the ISL and 802.10 protocols as encapsulation types. On a physical router interface that receives and transmits VLAN packets, you can select an arbitrary subinterface and map it to the particular VLAN "color" embedded within the VLAN header. This mapping allows you to selectively control how LAN traffic is routed or switched outside of its own VLAN domain. In the VLAN routing paradigm, a switched VLAN corresponds to a single routed subnet, and the network address is assigned to the subinterface.

To route a received VLAN packet, the Cisco IOS software VLAN switching code first extracts the VLAN ID from the packet header (this is a 10-bit field in the case of ISL and a 4-byte entity known as the security association identifier in the case of IEEE 802.10), then demultiplexes the VLAN ID value into a subinterface of the receiving port. If the VLAN color does not resolve to a subinterface, the Cisco IOS software can transparently bridge the foreign packet natively (without modifying the VLAN header) on the condition that the Cisco IOS software is configured to bridge on the subinterface itself. For VLAN packets that bear an ID corresponding to a configured subinterface, received packets are then classified by protocol type before running the appropriate protocol specific fast switching engine. If the subinterface is assigned to a bridge group then non-routed packets are de-encapsulated before they are bridged. This is termed "fall-back bridging" and is most appropriate for non-routable traffic types.

In Figure 1–2, Router A provides inter-VLAN connectivity between multiple Cisco switching platforms where there are three distinct virtual topologies present. For example, for VLAN 300 across the two Catalyst 1200A segments, traffic originating on LAN interface 1 is "tagged" with a VLAN ID of 300 as it is switched onto the FDDI ring. This ID allows the remote Catalyst 1200A to make an intelligent forwarding decision and only switch the traffic to local interfaces configured as belonging to the same VLAN broadcast domain. Router A provides an inter-VLAN mechanism that lets Router A function as a gateway for stations on a given LAN segment by transmitting VLAN encapsulated traffic to and from other switched VLAN domains or simply transmitting traffic in native (non-VLAN) format.

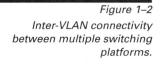

Figure 1–2

Inter-VLAN connectivity between multiple switching platforms.

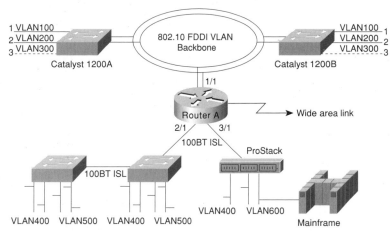

Figure 1–2 illustrates the following scenarios:

- Clients on VLAN 300 want to establish sessions with a server attached to a port in a different VLAN (600). In this scenario, packets originating on LAN interface 3 of the Catalyst 1200B switch are tagged with an 802.10 header with a security association identifier of 300 as they are forwarded onto the FDDI ring. Router A can accept these packets because it is configured to route VLAN 300, classify and make a layer 3 forwarding decision based on the destination network address and the route out (in this case Fast Ethernet 3/1), and adding the ISL VLAN header (color 200) appropriate to the destination subnet as the traffic is switched.

- There is a network requirement to bridge two VLANs together through the system rather than selectively route certain protocols. In this scenario, the two VLAN IDs are placed in the same bridge group. Note that they form a single broadcast domain and spanning tree, effectively forming a single VLAN.

See the section "Routing Between VLANs Configuration Example" later in this chapter for an example configuration of the topology shown in Figure 1–2.

To configure routing between VLANs, perform the following tasks, beginning in interface configuration mode:

Task		Command
Step 1	Specify a subinterface.	**interface** *type slot/port.subinterface-number*
Step 2	Specify the encapsulation type (either ISL or SDE) and the VLAN domain.	**encapsulation** {**sde** | **isl**} *domain*

Task	Command
Step 3 Associate the subinterface with the VLAN.	**bridge-group** *bridge-group*

CONFIGURING TRANSPARENT BRIDGING OVER WANS

You can configure transparent bridging over a variety of networks, as described in the following sections:

- Configuring Fast-Switched Transparent Bridging over ATM
- Configuring Transparent Bridging over DDR
- Configuring Transparent Bridging over Frame Relay
- Configuring Transparent Bridging over Multiprotocol LAPB
- Configuring Transparent Bridging over SMDS
- Configuring Transparent Bridging over X.25

Configuring Fast-Switched Transparent Bridging over ATM

Fast-switched transparent bridging over ATM supports AAL5-SNAP encapsulated packets only. All bridged AAL5-SNAP encapsulated packets are fast switched. Fast-switched transparent bridging supports Ethernet, FDDI, and Token Ring packets sent in AAL5-SNAP encapsulation over ATM. See the section "Fast-Switched Transparent Bridging over ATM Example (Cisco 7000)" for an example configuration of fast-switched transparent bridging over ATM.

Configuring Transparent Bridging over DDR

The Cisco IOS software supports transparent bridging over DDR and provides you some flexibility in controlling access and configuring the interface.

To configure DDR for bridging, complete the tasks in the following sections:

- Defining the Protocols to Bridge
- Specifying the Bridging Protocol
- Determining Access for Bridging
- Configuring an Interface for Bridging

For an example of configuring transparent bridging over DDR, see the "Transparent Bridging over DDR Examples" section near the end of this chapter.

Defining the Protocols to Bridge

IP packets are routed by default unless they are explicitly bridged; all others are bridged by default unless they are explicitly routed.

To bridge IP packets, complete the following task in global configuration mode:

Task	Command
Disable IP routing.	no ip routing

If you choose *not* to bridge another protocol, use the relevant command to enable routing of that protocol.

Specifying the Bridging Protocol

You must specify the type of spanning-tree bridging protocol to use and also identify a bridge group. To specify the Spanning-Tree Protocol and a bridge group number, complete the following task in global configuration mode:

Task	Command
Define the type of Spanning-Tree Protocol and identify a bridge group.	bridge *bridge-group* protocol {ieee	dec}

The bridge group number is used when you configure the interface and assign it to a bridge group. Packets are bridged only among members of the same bridge group.

Determining Access for Bridging

You can determine access by either permitting all bridge packets or by controlling access according to Ethernet type codes.

To permit all transparent bridge packets, complete the following task in global configuration mode:

Task	Command
Define a dialer list that permits all transparent bridge packets.	dialer-list *dialer-group* protocol bridge permit

To control access by Ethernet type codes, complete the following tasks in global configuration mode:

Task	Command
Step 1 Permit packets according to Ethernet type codes (access list numbers must be in the range 200–299).	access-list *access-list-number* {permit	deny} *type-code* [*mask*]

Task	Command
Step 2 Define a dialer list for the specified access list.	**dialer-list** *dialer-group* **protocol bridge list** *access-list-number*

For a table of some common Ethernet type codes, see Appendix A, "Ethernet Type Codes."

Configuring an Interface for Bridging

You can configure serial interfaces or ISDN interfaces for DDR bridging. To configure an interface for DDR bridging, complete the following tasks, starting in global configuration mode:

Task	Command
Step 1 Specify the serial or ISDN interface and enter interface configuration mode.	**interface** *type number*
Step 2 Configure the dial string to call. or Configure a dialer bridge map.	**dialer string** *dial-string* **dialer map bridge** [**name** *hostname*] [**broadcast**] *dial-string*[:*isdn-subaddress*]
Step 3 Assign the specified interface to a bridge group.	**bridge-group** *bridge-group*

Configuring Transparent Bridging over Frame Relay

The transparent bridging software supports bridging of packets over Frame Relay networks. This capability is useful for such tasks as transmitting packets from proprietary protocols across a Frame Relay network. Bridging over a Frame Relay network is supported both on networks that support a multicast facility and those that do not. Both cases are described in this section.

Fast-Switched Transparent Bridging

The transparent bridging software provides fast-switched transparent bridging for Frame Relay encapsulated serial and High-Speed Serial Interface (HSSI) networks.

SVCs are not supported for transparent bridging in this release. All the PVCs configured on a sub-interface must belong to the same bridge group.

Bridging in a Frame Relay Network with No Multicasts

The Frame Relay bridging software uses the same spanning-tree algorithm as the other bridging functions, but allows packets to be encapsulated for transmission across a Frame Relay network. You specify IP-to-DLCI (data-link connection identifier) address mapping, and the system maintains a table of both the Ethernet address and the DLCIs.

To configure bridging in a network not supporting a multicast facility, define the mapping between an address and the DLCI used to connect to the address. To bridge with no multicasts, perform the following task in interface configuration mode:

Task	Command
Define the mapping between an address and the DLCI used to connect to the address.	frame-relay map bridge *dlci* broadcast

An example configuration is provided in the section "Frame Relay Transparent Bridging Examples" at the end of this chapter.

Bridging in a Frame Relay Network with Multicasts

The multicast facility is used to learn about the other bridges on the network, eliminating the need for you to specify any mappings with the **frame-relay map bridge broadcast** command. An example configuration is provided in the section "Frame Relay Transparent Bridging Examples" at the end of the chapter for use as a configuration guide.

Configuring Transparent Bridging over Multiprotocol LAPB

Cisco's software implements transparent bridging over multiprotocol LAPB encapsulation on serial interfaces. To configure transparent bridging over multiprotocol LAPB, perform the following tasks, beginning in global configuration mode:

Task		Command
Step 1	Specify the serial interface.	interface serial *number*
Step 2	Specify no IP address to the interface.	no ip address
Step 3	Configure multiprotocol LAPB encapsulation.	encapsulation lapb multi
Step 4	Assign the interface to a bridge group.	bridge-group *bridge-group*
Step 5	Specify the type of Spanning-Tree Protocol.	bridge *bridge-group* protocol {ieee	dec}

— **NOTES** ——————————————————————————————

Transparent bridging over multiprotocol LAPB requires use of the **encapsulation lapb multi** command. You cannot use the **encapsulation lapb protocol** command with a **bridge** keyword to configure this feature.

For an example of configuring transparent bridging over multiprotocol LAPB, see the section "Transparent Bridging over Multiprotocol LAPB Example" later in this chapter.

Configuring Transparent Bridging over SMDS

Cisco supports fast-switched transparent bridging for Switched Multimegabit Data Service (SMDS) encapsulated serial and HSSI networks. Standard bridging commands are used to enable bridging on an SMDS interface.

To enable transparent bridging over SMDS, perform the following tasks, beginning in interface configuration mode:

Task	Command
Step 1 Specify the serial interface.	**interface serial** *number*
Step 2 Configure SMDS encapsulation on the serial interface.	**encapsulation smds**
Step 3 Associate the interface with a bridge group.	**bridge-group** *bridge-group*
Step 4 Enable transparent bridging of packets across an SMDS network.	**smds multicast bridge** *smds-address*

Broadcast Address Resolution Protocol (ARP) packets are treated differently in transparent bridging over an SMDS network than in other encapsulation methods. For SMDS, two packets are sent to the multicast address. One is sent using a standard (SMDS) ARP encapsulation; the other is sent with the ARP packet encapsulated in an 802.3 MAC header. The native ARP is sent as a regular ARP broadcast.

Cisco's implementation of IEEE 802.6i transparent bridging for SMDS supports 802.3, 802.5, and FDDI frame formats. The router can accept frames with or without frame check sequence (FCS). Fast-switched transparent bridging is the default and is not configurable. If a packet cannot be fast switched, it is process switched.

An example configuration is provided in the section "Fast-Switched Transparent Bridging over SMDS Example" later in this chapter.

Configuring Transparent Bridging over X.25

The transparent bridging software supports bridging of packets in X.25 frames. This capability is useful for such tasks as transmitting packets from proprietary protocols across an X.25 network.

The X.25 bridging software uses the same spanning-tree algorithm as the other bridging functions, but allows packets to be encapsulated in X.25 frames and transmitted across X.25 media. You specify the IP-to-X.121 address mapping, and the system maintains a table of both the Ethernet and

X.121 addresses. To configure X.25 transparent bridging, perform the following task in interface configuration mode:

Task	Command
Specify IP-to-X.121 mapping.	x25 map bridge *x.121-address* broadcast [*options-keywords*]

CONFIGURING CONCURRENT ROUTING AND BRIDGING

You can configure the Cisco IOS software to route a given protocol among one group of interfaces and concurrently bridge that protocol among a separate group of interfaces, all within one router. The given protocol is not switched between the two groups. Rather, routed traffic is confined to the routed interfaces and bridged traffic is confined to the bridged interfaces. A protocol may either be routed or bridged on a given interface, but not both.

The concurrent routing and bridging capability is, by default, disabled. While concurrent routing and bridging is disabled, the Cisco IOS software absorbs and discards bridgeable packets in protocols that are configured for routing on any interface in the router.

When concurrent routing and bridging is first enabled in the presence of existing bridge groups, it will generate a bridge-route configuration command for any protocol for which any interface in the bridge group is configured for routing. This is a precaution that applies only when concurrent routing and bridging is not already enabled, bridge groups exist, and the **bridge crb** command is encountered.

To enable concurrent routing and bridging in the Cisco IOS software, perform the following task in global configuration mode:

Task	Command
Enable concurrent routing and bridging.	bridge crb

Information about which protocols are routed and which are bridged is stored in a table, which can be displayed with the **show interfaces crb** privileged EXEC command.

When concurrent routing and bridging has been enabled, you must configure an explicit bridge route command for any protocol that is to be routed on the interfaces in a bridge group in addition to any required protocol-specific interface configuration.

To configure specific protocols to be routed in a bridge group, perform the following task in interface configuration mode:

Task	Command
Specify a protocol to be routed on a bridge group.	**bridge** *bridge-group* **route** *protocol*

CONFIGURING INTEGRATED ROUTING AND BRIDGING

Perform one or more of the following tasks to configure integrated routing and bridging on your router:

- Assigning a Bridge Group Number and Defining the Spanning-Tree Protocol
- Configuring Interfaces
- Enabling Integrated Routing and Bridging
- Configuring the Bridge-Group Virtual Interface
- Configuring Protocols for Routing or Bridging

Assigning a Bridge Group Number and Defining the Spanning-Tree Protocol

Prior to configuring the router for integrated routing and bridging, you must enable bridging by setting up a bridge group number and specifying a Spanning-Tree Protocol. You can choose either the IEEE 802.1D Spanning-Tree Protocol or the earlier Digital protocol upon which this IEEE standard is based.

To assign a bridge group number and define a Spanning-Tree Protocol, perform the following task in global configuration mode:

Task	Command
Assign a bridge group number and define a Spanning-Tree Protocol as either IEEE 802.1D standard or Digital.	**bridge** *bridge-group* **protocol** {**ieee** | **dec**}

The IEEE 802.1D Spanning-Tree Protocol is the preferred way of running the bridge. Use the Digital Spanning-Tree Protocol only for backward compatibility.

Configuring Interfaces

To configure a router interface in the Cisco IOS software, perform the following tasks, starting in global configuration mode:

Task	Command
Step 1 Specify the interface and enter interface configuration mode.	**interface** *type number*
Step 2 Assign bridge groups to appropriate interfaces.	**bridge-group** *bridge-group*

Enabling Integrated Routing and Bridging

After you have set up the interfaces in the router, you can enable integrated routing and bridging.

To enable integrated routing and bridging in the Cisco IOS software, perform the following task in global configuration mode:

Task	Command
Enable integrated routing and bridging.	**bridge irb**

Use the **show interfaces irb** privileged EXEC command to display the protocols that a given bridged interface can route to the other routed interface when the packet is routable, and to display the protocols that a given bridged interface bridges.

Configuring the Bridge-Group Virtual Interface

The bridge-group virtual interface resides in the router. It acts like a normal routed interface that does not support bridging, but represents the entire corresponding bridge group to routed interfaces within the router. The bridge-group virtual interface is assigned the number of the bridge group that it represents. The bridge-group virtual interface number is the link between the bridge-group virtual interface and its bridge group. Because the bridge-group virtual interface is a virtual routed interface, it has all the network layer attributes, such as a network address and the ability to perform filtering. Only one bridge-group virtual interface is supported for each bridge group.

When you enable routing for a given protocol on the bridge-group virtual interface, packets coming from a routed interface but destined for a host in a bridged domain are routed to the bridge-group virtual interface, and are forwarded to the corresponding bridged interface. All traffic routed to the bridge-group virtual interface is forwarded to the corresponding bridge group as bridged traffic. All routable traffic received on a bridged interface is routed to other routed interfaces as if it is coming directly from the bridge-group virtual interface.

To create a bridge-group virtual interface, perform the following task in interface configuration mode:

Task	Command
Enable a bridge-group virtual interface.	**interface bvi** *bridge-group*

When you intend to bridge and route a given protocol in the same bridge group, you must configure the network-layer attributes of the protocol on the bridge-group virtual interface. Do not configure protocol attributes on the bridged interfaces. No bridging attributes can be configured on the bridge-group virtual interface.

Although it is generally the case that all bridged segments belonging to a bridge group are represented as a single segment or network to the routing protocol, there are situations where several individual networks coexist within the same bridged segment. To make it possible for the routed domain to learn about the other networks behind the bridge-group virtual interface, configure a secondary address on the bridge-group virtual interface to add the corresponding network to the routing process.

Configuring Protocols for Routing or Bridging

When integrated routing and bridging is enabled, the default route/bridge behavior in a bridge group is to bridge all packets.

You then could explicitly configure the bridge group to route a particular protocol, so that routable packets of this protocol are routed, while non-routable packets of this protocol or packets for protocols for which the bridge group is not explicitly configured to route will be bridged.

You also could explicitly configure the bridge group so that it does not bridge a particular protocol, so that routable packets of this protocol are routed when the bridge is explicitly configured to route this protocol, and non-routable packets are dropped because bridging is disabled for this protocol.

— ◀ **NOTES** ▶ ————————————————————————————————————

Packets of non-routable protocols such as LAT are only bridged. You cannot disable bridging for the non-routable traffic.

To configure specific protocols to be routed or bridged in a bridge group, perform one or more of the following tasks in global configuration mode:

Task	Command
Specify a protocol to be routed in a bridge group.	**bridge** *bridge-group* **route** *protocol*

Task	Command
Specify that a protocol is not to be routed in a bridge group.	**no bridge** *bridge-group* **route** *protocol*
Specify that a protocol is to be bridged in the bridge group.	**bridge** *bridge-group* **bridge** *protocol*
Specify that a protocol is not to be bridged in the bridge group.	**no bridge** *bridge-group* **bridge** *protocol*

For example, to bridge AppleTalk, bridge and route IPX, and route IP in the same bridge group, you would do the following:

- Bridge AppleTalk: Because integrated routing and bridging bridges everything by default, no configuration is required to bridge AppleTalk.

- Bridge and route IPX: After using the **bridge irb** command to enable integrated routing and bridging, and the **interface bvi** command to create the bridge-group virtual interface for the bridge group, you would use the **bridge route** command to both bridge and route IPX (bridging is already enabled by default; the **bridge route** command enables routing).

- Route IP: Use the **bridge route** command to enable routing, and then use the **no bridge bridge** command to disable bridging.

— **NOTES** ————————————————————————————————

When integrated routing and bridging is not enabled, routing a given protocol means that protocol is not bridged, and bridging a protocol means that protocol is not routed. When integrated routing and bridging is enabled, the disjunct relationship between routing and bridging is broken down, and a given protocol can be switched between routed and bridged interfaces on a selective, independent basis.

CONFIGURING TRANSPARENT BRIDGING OPTIONS

You can configure one or more transparent bridging options. To configure transparent bridging options, perform one or more of the tasks in the following sections:

- Disabling IP Routing
- Enabling Autonomous Bridging
- Configuring LAT Compression
- Establishing Multiple Spanning-Tree Domains
- Preventing the Forwarding of Dynamically Determined Stations
- Forwarding Multicast Addresses
- Configuring Bridge Table Aging Time

Disabling IP Routing

If you want to bridge IP, you must disable IP routing because IP routing is enabled by default on the Cisco IOS software. You can enable IP routing when you decide to route IP packets. To disable or enable IP routing, perform one of the following tasks in global configuration mode:

Task	Command
Disable IP routing.	no ip routing
Enable IP routing.	ip routing

All interfaces in the bridge group that are bridging IP should have the same IP address. However, if you have more than one bridge group, each bridge group should have its own IP address.

Enabling Autonomous Bridging

Normally, bridging takes place on the processor card at the interrupt level. When autonomous bridging is enabled, bridging takes place entirely on the ciscoBus2 controller, significantly improving performance. Autonomous bridging is a high-speed switching feature that allows bridged traffic to be forwarded and flooded on the ciscoBus2 controller between resident interfaces. If you are using the ciscoBus2 controller, you can maximize performance by enabling autonomous bridging on the following ciscoBus2 interfaces:

- MEC
- FCIT transparent
- HSSI HDLC

Although performance improvements will be seen most in the resident interfaces, the autonomous bridging feature can also be used in bridge groups that include interfaces that are not on the ciscoBus2 controller. These interfaces include the CTR, FCI with encapsulation bridging, and HSSI with encapsulation other than HDLC, such as X.25, Frame Relay, or SMDS, MCI, STR, or SBE16.

If you enable autonomous bridging for a bridge group that includes a combination of interfaces that are resident on the ciscoBus2 controller and some that are not, the ciscoBus2 controller forwards only packets between resident interfaces. Forwarding between nonresident and resident interfaces is done in either the fast or process paths. Flooding between resident interfaces is done by the ciscoBus2 controller. Flooding between nonresident interfaces is done conventionally. If a packet is forwarded from a nonresident to a resident interface, the packet is conventionally forwarded. If packets are flooded from a nonresident interface to a resident interface, the packet is autonomously flooded.

To enable autonomous bridging on a per-interface basis, perform the following task in interface configuration mode:

Task	Command
Enable autonomous bridging (if using the ciscoBus2 controller).	. **bridge-group** *bridge-group* **cbus-bridging**

NOTES

You can filter by MAC-level address on an interface only when autonomous bridging is enabled on that interface. If any filters or priority queuing is configured, autonomous bridging is automatically disabled.

Configuring LAT Compression

The LAT protocol used by Digital and Digital-compatible terminal servers is one of the common protocols that lacks a well-defined network layer (Layer 3) and so always must be bridged.

To reduce the amount of bandwidth that LAT traffic consumes on serial interfaces, you can specify a LAT-specific form of compression. Doing so applies compression to LAT frames being sent out by the Cisco IOS software through the interface in question. To configure LAT compression, perform the following task in interface configuration mode:

Task	Command
Reduce the amount of bandwidth that LAT traffic consumes on a serial interface.	**bridge-group** *bridge-group* **lat-compression**

LAT compression can be specified only for serial interfaces. For the most common LAT operations (user keystrokes and acknowledgment packets), LAT compression reduces LAT's bandwidth requirements by nearly a factor of two.

Establishing Multiple Spanning-Tree Domains

The Cisco IEEE 802.1D bridging software supports spanning-tree domains of bridge groups. Domains are a feature specific to Cisco. This feature is only available if you have specified IEEE as the Spanning-Tree Protocol. A domain establishes an external identification of the BPDUs sent from a bridge group. The purpose of this identification is as follows:

- Bridge groups defined within the domain can recognize that BPDU as belonging to them.
- Two bridged subnetworks in different domains that are sharing a common connection can use the domain identifier to identify and then ignore the BPDUs that belong to another domain. Each bridged subnetwork establishes its own spanning tree based on the BPDUs

that it receives. The BPDUs it receives must contain the domain number to which the bridged subnetwork belongs. Bridged traffic is not domain identified.

> **NOTES**
>
> Domains do not constrain the propagation of bridged traffic. A bridge bridges nonrouted traffic received on its interfaces regardless of domain.

You can place any number of routers or bridges within the domain. The devices in the domain, and only those devices, then share spanning-tree information.

When multiple routers share the same cable and you want to use only certain discrete subsets of those routers to share spanning-tree information with each other, establish spanning-tree domains. This function is most useful when running other applications, such as IP User Datagram Protocol (UDP) flooding, that use the IEEE spanning tree. You also can use this feature to reduce the number of global reconfigurations in large bridged networks.

To establish multiple spanning-tree domains, perform the following task in global configuration mode:

Task	Command
Establish a multiple spanning-tree domain.	**bridge** *bridge-group* **domain** *domain-number*

For an example of how to configure domains, see the "Complex Transparent Bridging Network Topology Example" section later in this chapter.

Preventing the Forwarding of Dynamically Determined Stations

Normally, the system forwards any frames for stations that it has learned about dynamically. By disabling this activity, the bridge will forward only frames whose address have been statically configured into the forwarding cache. To prevent or allow forwarding of dynamically determined stations, perform one of the following tasks in global configuration mode:

Task	Command
Filter out all frames except those whose addresses have been statically configured into the forwarding cache.	**no bridge** *bridge-group* **acquire**
Remove the capability to filter out all frames except those whose addresses have been statically configured into the forwarding cache.	**bridge** *bridge-group* **acquire**

Forwarding Multicast Addresses

A packet with a RIF, indicated by a source address with the multicast bit turned on, is not usually forwarded. However, you can configure bridging support to allow the forwarding of frames that would otherwise be discarded because they have a RIF. Although you can forward these frames, the bridge table will not be updated to include the source addresses of these frames.

To forward frames with multicast addresses, perform the following task in global configuration mode:

Task	Command
Allow the forwarding of frames with multicast source addresses.	**bridge** *bridge-group* **multicast-source**

Configuring Bridge Table Aging Time

A bridge forwards, floods, or drops packets based on the bridge table. The bridge table maintains both static entries and dynamic entries. Static entries are entered by the network manager or by the bridge itself. Dynamic entries are entered by the bridge learning process. A dynamic entry is automatically removed after a specified length of time, known as *aging time*, from the time the entry was created or last updated.

If hosts on a bridged network are likely to move, decrease the aging-time to enable the bridge to adapt to the change quickly. If hosts do not transmit continuously, increase the aging time to record the dynamic entries for a longer time and thus reduce the possibility of flooding when the hosts transmit again.

To set the aging time, perform the following task in global configuration mode:

Task	Command
Set the bridge table aging time.	**bridge-group** *bridge-group* **aging-time** *seconds*

FILTERING TRANSPARENTLY BRIDGED PACKETS

A bridge examines frames and transmits them through the internetwork according to the destination address; a bridge will not forward a frame back to its originating network segment. The bridge software allows you to configure specific administrative filters that filter frames based upon information other than paths to their destinations. You can perform administrative filtering by performing one of the tasks in the following sections:

- Setting Filters at the MAC layer
- Filtering LAT Service Announcements

NOTES

When setting up administrative filtering, remember that there is virtually no performance penalty in filtering by MAC address or vendor code, but there can be a significant performance penalty when filtering by protocol type.

When configuring transparent bridging access control, keep the following points in mind:

- You can assign only one access list to an interface.
- The conditions in the access list are applied to all outgoing packets not sourced by the Cisco IOS software.
- Access lists are scanned in the order you enter them; the first match is used.
- An implicit deny-everything entry is automatically defined at the end of an access list unless you include an explicit permit-everything entry at the end of the list.
- All new entries to an existing list are placed at the end of the list. You cannot add an entry to the middle of a list. This means that if you have previously included an explicit permit-everything entry, new entries will never be scanned. The solution is to delete the access list and retype it with the new entries.
- You can create extended access lists to specify more detailed filters, such as address match only.
- You should not use extended access lists on FDDI interfaces doing transit bridging as opposed to translational bridging.
- Configuring bridging access lists of type 700 may cause a momentary interruption of traffic flow.

Setting Filters at the MAC layer

You can filter transmission of frames at the MAC layer by performing tasks in one of the following sections:

- Filtering by Specific MAC Address
- Filtering by Vendor Code
- Filtering by Protocol Type

When filtering by a MAC-level address, you can use two kinds of access lists: standard access lists that specify a simple address, and extended access lists that specify two addresses. You can also further restrict access by creating filters for these lists. After you have completed one of the preceding tasks, perform the task in the following section:

- Defining and Applying Extended Access Lists

NOTES

MAC addresses on Ethernets are "bit swapped" when compared with MAC addresses on Token Ring and FDDI. For example, address 0110.2222.3333 on Ethernet is 8008.4444.CCCC on Token Ring and FDDI. Access lists always use the canonical Ethernet representation. When using different media and building access lists to filter on MAC addresses, keep this point in mind. Note that when a bridged packet traverses a serial link, it has an Ethernet-style address.

Filtering by Specific MAC Address

You can filter frames with a particular MAC-level station source or destination address. Any number of addresses can be configured into the system without a performance penalty. To filter by the MAC-level address, perform the following task in global configuration mode:

Task	Command
Filter particular MAC-level station addresses.	**bridge** *bridge-group* **address** *mac-address* {**forward**	**discard**} [*interface*]

When filtering specific MAC destination addresses, allow for multicast or broadcast packets that are required by the bridged network protocols. Refer to the example in the section "Multicast or Broadcast Packets Bridging Example" later in this chapter to guide you in building your configuration to allow for multicast or broadcast packets.

Filtering by Vendor Code

The bridging software allows you to create access lists to administratively filter MAC addresses. These access lists can filter groups of MAC addresses, including those with particular vendor codes. There is no noticeable performance loss in using these access lists, and the lists can be of indefinite length. You can filter groups of MAC addresses with particular vendor codes by performing the first task and one or both of the other tasks that follow:

- Establish a vendor code access list.
- Filter source addresses.
- Filter destination addresses.

To establish a vendor code access list, perform the following task in global configuration mode:

Task	Command
Prepare access control information for filtering of frames by canonical (Ethernet-ordered) MAC address.	**access-list** *access-list-number* {**permit**	**deny**} *address mask*

The vendor code is the first three bytes of the MAC address (left to right). For an example of how to filter by vendor code, see "Multicast or Broadcast Packets Bridging Example" later in this chapter.

NOTES ───

Remember that, as with any access list using MAC addresses, Ethernets swap their MAC address bit ordering, and Token Rings and FDDI do not. Therefore, an access list that works for one medium might not work for others.

After you have defined an access list to filter by a particular vendor code, you can assign an access list to a particular interface for filtering on the MAC *source* addresses of packets *received* on that interface or the MAC *destination* addresses of packets that would ordinarily be *forwarded* out that interface. To filter by source or destination addresses, perform one of the following tasks in interface configuration mode:

Task	Command
Assign an access list to an interface for filtering by MAC source addresses.	**bridge-group** *bridge-group* **input-address-list** *access-list-number*
Assign an access list to an interface for filtering by the MAC destination addresses.	**bridge-group** *bridge-group* **output-address-list** *access-list-number*

Filtering by Protocol Type

You can filter by protocol type by using the access-list mechanism and specifying a protocol type code. To filter by protocol type, perform the first task and one or more of the other tasks that follow:

- Establish a protocol-type access list.
- Filter Ethernet- and SNAP-encapsulated packets on input.
- Filter Ethernet- and SNAP-encapsulated packets on output.
- Filter IEEE 802.2-encapsulated packets on input.
- Filter IEEE 802.2-encapsulated packets on output.

NOTES ───

It is not a good idea to have both input- and output-type code filtering on the same interface.

The order in which you enter **access-list** commands affects the order in which the access conditions are checked. Each condition is tested in succession. A matching condition is then used to execute a permit or deny decision. If no conditions match, a "deny" decision is reached.

NOTES

Protocol-type access lists can have an impact on system performance; therefore, keep the lists as short as possible and use wildcard bit masks whenever possible.

Access lists for Ethernet- and IEEE 802.2-encapsulated packets affect only bridging functions. It is not possible to use such access lists to block frames with protocols that are being routed.

You can establish protocol-type access lists. Specify either an Ethernet type code for Ethernet-encapsulated packets or a DSAP/SSAP pair for 802.3 or 802.5-encapsulated packets. Ethernet type codes are listed in Appendix A, "Ethernet Type Codes."

To establish protocol-type access lists, perform the following task in global configuration mode:

Task	Command
Prepare access control information for filtering frames by protocol type.	**access-list** *access-list-number* {**permit** I **deny**} *type-code wild-mask*

You can filter Ethernet- and SNAP-encapsulated packets on input. For SNAP-encapsulated frames, the access list you create is applied against the two-byte TYPE field given after the DSAP/SSAP/OUI fields in the frame. The access list is applied to all Ethernet and SNAP frames received on that interface prior to the bridge learning process. SNAP frames also must pass any applicable IEEE 802.2 DSAP/SSAP access lists.

You also can filter Ethernet- and SNAP-encapsulated packets on output. The access list you create is applied just before sending out a frame to an interface.

To filter these packets on input or output, perform either or both of the following tasks in interface configuration mode:

Task	Command
Add a filter for Ethernet- and SNAP-encapsulated packets on input.	**bridge-group** *bridge-group* **input-type-list** *access-list-number*
Add a filter for Ethernet- and SNAP-encapsulated packets on output.	**bridge-group** *bridge-group* **output-type-list** *access-list-number*

You can filter IEEE 802-encapsulated packets on input. The access list you create is applied to all IEEE 802 frames received on that interface prior to the bridge-learning process. SNAP frames also must pass any applicable Ethernet type-code access list.

You also can filter IEEE 802-encapsulated packets on output. SNAP frames also must pass any applicable Ethernet type-code access list. The access list you create is applied just before sending out a frame to an interface.

To filter these packets on input or output, perform one or both of the following tasks in interface configuration mode:

Task	Command
Add a filter for IEEE 802-encapsulated packets on input.	**bridge-group** *bridge-group* **input-lsap-list** *access-list-number*
Add a filter for IEEE 802-encapsulated packets on output.	**bridge-group** *bridge-group* **output-lsap-list** *access-list-number*

Access lists for Ethernet- and IEEE 802-encapsulated packets affect only bridging functions. You cannot use such access lists to block frames with protocols that are being routed.

Defining and Applying Extended Access Lists

If you are filtering by the MAC-level address, whether it is by a specific MAC address, vendor code, or protocol type, you can define and apply extended access lists. Extended access lists allow finer granularity of control. They allow you to specify both source and destination addresses and arbitrary bytes in the packet.

To define an extended access list, perform the following task in global configuration mode:

Task	Command
Define an extended access list for finer control of bridged traffic.	**access-list** *access-list-number* {**permit** | **deny**} *source source-mask destination destination-mask offset size operator operand*

To apply an extended access list to an interface, perform one or both of the following tasks in interface configuration mode:

Task	Command
Apply an extended access list to the packets being received by an interface.	**bridge-group** *bridge-group* **input-pattern-list** *access-list-number*
Apply an extended access list to the packet being sent by an interface.	**bridge-group** *bridge-group* **output-pattern-list** *access-list-number*

After an access list is created initially, any subsequent additions (possibly entered from the terminal) are placed at the *end* of the list. In other words, you cannot selectively add or remove access list command lines from a specific access list.

— **CAUTION** ————————————————————————————————————

Because of their complexity, only use extended access lists if you are very familiar with the Cisco IOS software. Further, do not specify an offset value that is greater than the size of the packet.

Filtering LAT Service Announcements

The bridging software allows you to filter LAT frames. LAT bridge filtering allows the selective inclusion or exclusion of LAT multicast service announcements on a per-interface basis.

— **NOTES** ————————————————————————————————————

The LAT filtering commands are not implemented for Token Ring interfaces.

In the LAT protocol, a *group code* is defined as a decimal number in the range 0 to 255. Some of the LAT configuration commands take a list of group codes; this is referred to as a *group code list*. The rules for entering numbers in a group code list follow:

- Entries can be individual group code numbers separated with a space. (The Digital LAT implementation specifies that a list of numbers be separated by commas; however, Cisco's implementation expects the numbers to be separated by spaces.)

- Entries also can specify a range of numbers. This is done by separating an ascending order range of group numbers with hyphens.

- Any number of group codes or group code ranges can be listed in one command; just separate each with a space.

In LAT, each node transmits a periodic service advertisement message that announces its existence and availability for connections. Within the message is a group code list; this is a mask of up to 256 bits. Each bit represents a group number. In the traditional use of LAT group codes, a terminal server will connect to a host system only when there is an overlap between the group code list of the user on the terminal server and the group code list in the service advertisement message. In an environment with many bridges and many LAT hosts, the number of multicast messages that each system has to deal with becomes unreasonable. The 256 group codes might not be enough to allocate local assignment policies, such as giving each DECserver 200 device its own group code in large bridged networks. LAT group code filtering allows you to have very fine control over which multicast messages actually get bridged. Through a combination of input and output permit and deny lists, you can implement many different LAT control policies.

You can filter LAT service advertisements by performing any of the tasks in the following sections:

- Enabling LAT Group Code Service Filtering
- Specifying Deny or Permit Conditions for LAT Group Codes on Input
- Specifying Deny or Permit Conditions for LAT Group Codes on Output

Enabling LAT Group Code Service Filtering

You can specify LAT group-code filtering to inform the system that LAT service advertisements require special processing. To enable LAT group-code filtering, perform the following task in global configuration mode:

Task	Command
Enable LAT service filtering.	bridge *bridge-group* lat-service-filtering

Specifying Deny or Permit Conditions for LAT Group Codes on Input

You can specify the group codes by which to deny or permit access upon input. Specifying deny conditions causes the system to not bridge any LAT service advertisements that contain any of the specified groups. Specifying permit conditions causes the system to bridge only those service advertisements that match at least one group in the specified group list.

To specify deny or permit conditions for LAT groups on input, perform one of the following tasks in interface configuration mode:

Task	Command
Specify the group codes with which to deny access upon input.	bridge-group *bridge-group* input-lat-service-deny *group-list*
Specify the group codes with which to permit access upon input.	bridge-group *bridge-group* input-lat-service-permit *group-list*

If a message specifies group codes in both the deny and permit list, the message is not bridged.

Specifying Deny or Permit Conditions for LAT Group Codes on Output

You can specify the group codes by which to deny or permit access upon output. Specifying deny conditions causes the system to not bridge onto the output interface any LAT service advertisements that contain any of the specified groups. Specifying permit conditions causes the system to bridge onto the output interface only those service advertisements that match at least one group in the specified group list.

To specify deny or permit conditions for LAT groups on output, perform one of the following tasks in interface configuration mode:

Task	Command
Specify the group codes with which to deny access upon output.	**bridge-group** *bridge-group* **output-lat-service-deny** *group-list*
Specify the group codes with which to permit access upon output.	**bridge-group** *bridge-group* **output-lat-service-permit** *group-list*

If a message matches both a deny and a permit condition, it will not be bridged.

ADJUSTING SPANNING-TREE PARAMETERS

You might need to adjust certain spanning-tree parameters if the default values are not suitable for your bridge configuration. Parameters affecting the entire spanning tree are configured with variations of the **bridge** global configuration command. Interface-specific parameters are configured with variations of the **bridge-group** interface configuration command.

You can adjust spanning-tree parameters by performing any of the tasks in the following sections:

- Setting the Bridge Priority
- Setting an Interface Priority
- Assigning Path Costs
- Adjusting Bridge Protocol Data Unit (BPDU) Intervals
- Disabling the Spanning Tree on an Interface

NOTES

Only network administrators with a good understanding of how bridges and the Spanning-Tree Protocol work should make adjustments to spanning-tree parameters. Poorly planned adjustments to these parameters can have a negative impact on performance.

Setting the Bridge Priority

You can globally configure the priority of an individual bridge when two bridges tie for position as the root bridge, or you can configure the likelihood that a bridge will be selected as the root bridge. This priority is determined by default; however, you can change it. To set the bridge priority, perform the following task in global configuration mode:

Task	Command
Set the bridge priority.	**bridge** *bridge-group* **priority** *number*

Setting an Interface Priority

You can set a priority for an interface. When two bridges tie for position as the root bridge, you configure an interface priority to break the tie. The bridge with the lowest interface value is elected. To set an interface priority, perform the following task in interface configuration mode:

Task	Command
Establish a priority for a specified interface.	**bridge-group** *bridge-group* **priority** *number*

Assigning Path Costs

Each interface has a path cost associated with it. By convention, the path cost is 1000/data rate of the attached LAN, in Mbps. You can set different path costs.

Task	Command
Set a different path cost other than the defaults.	**bridge-group** *bridge-group* **path-cost** *cost*

Adjusting Bridge Protocol Data Unit (BPDU) Intervals

You can adjust BPDU intervals as described in the following sections:

- Adjusting the Interval between Hello BPDUs
- Defining the Forward Delay Interval
- Defining the Maximum Idle Interval

Each bridge in a spanning tree adopts the interval between hello BPDUs, the forward delay interval, and the maximum idle interval parameters of the root bridge, regardless of what its individual configuration might be.

Adjusting the Interval between Hello BPDUs

You can specify the interval between hello BPDUs. To adjust this interval, perform the following task in global configuration mode:

Task	Command
Specify the interval between hello BPDUs.	**bridge** *bridge-group* **hello-time** *seconds*

Defining the Forward Delay Interval

The forward delay interval is the amount of time spent listening for topology change information after an interface has been activated for bridging and before forwarding actually begins. To change the default interval setting, perform the following task in global configuration mode:

Task	Command
Set the default of the forward delay interval.	**bridge** *bridge-group* **forward-time** *seconds*

Defining the Maximum Idle Interval

If a bridge does not hear BPDUs from the root bridge within a specified interval, it assumes that the network has changed and recomputes the spanning-tree topology. To change the default interval setting, perform the following task in global configuration mode:

Task	Command
Change the amount of time a bridge will wait to hear BPDUs from the root bridge.	**bridge** *bridge-group* **max-age** *seconds*

Disabling the Spanning Tree on an Interface

When a *loop-free* path exists between any two bridged subnetworks, you can prevent BPDUs generated in one transparent bridging subnetwork from impacting nodes in the other transparent bridging subnetwork, yet still permit bridging throughout the bridged network as a whole. For example, when transparently bridged LAN subnetworks are separated by a WAN, BPDUs can be prevented from traveling across the WAN link.

To disable the spanning tree on an interface, perform the following task in interface configuration mode:

Task	Command
Disable the spanning tree on an interface.	**bridge-group** *bridge-group* **spanning-disabled**

TUNING THE TRANSPARENTLY BRIDGED NETWORK

The following sections describe how to configure features that enhance network performance by reducing the number of packets that traverse the backbone network:

- Configuring Circuit Groups
- Configuring Constrained Multicast Flooding

Configuring Circuit Groups

In the process of loop elimination, the spanning-tree algorithm always blocks all but one of a group of parallel network segments between two bridges. When those segments are of limited bandwidth, it might be preferable to augment the aggregate bandwidth between two bridges by forwarding across multiple parallel network segments. Circuit groups can be used to group multiple parallel network segments between two bridges to distribute the load while still maintaining a loop-free spanning tree.

Deterministic load distribution distributes traffic between two bridges across multiple parallel network segments grouped together into a single circuit group. As long as one port of the circuit group is in the forwarding state, all ports in that circuit group will participate in load distribution regardless of their spanning-tree port states. This process guarantees that the computed spanning tree is still adaptive to any topology change and the load is distributed among the multiple segments. Deterministic load distribution guarantees packet ordering between source-destination pairs, and always forwards traffic for a source-destination pair on the same segment in a circuit group for a given circuit-group configuration.

NOTES

You should configure all parallel network segments between two bridges into a single circuit group. Deterministic load distribution across a circuit group adjusts dynamically to the addition or deletion of network segments, and to interface state changes.

If a circuit-group port goes down and up as a result of configuration or a line protocol change, the spanning-tree algorithm will bypass port transition and will time out necessary timers to force the eligible circuit-group ports to enter the forwarding state. This avoids the long disruption time caused by spanning-tree topology recomputation and therefore resumes the load distribution as quickly as possible.

To tune the transparently bridged network, perform the following steps:

Step 1   Define a circuit group.

Step 2   Optionally, configure a transmission pause interval.

Step 3   Modify the load distribution strategy.

To define a circuit group, perform the following task in interface configuration mode:

Task	Command
Add a serial interface to a circuit group.	**bridge-group** *bridge-group* **circuit-group** *circuit-group*

For circuit groups of mixed-bandwidth serial interfaces, it might be necessary to configure a pause interval during which transmission is suspended to avoid misordering packets following changes in the composition of a circuit group. Changes in the composition of a circuit group include the addition or deletion of an interface and interface state changes. To configure a transmission pause interval, perform the following task in global configuration mode:

Task	Command
Configure a transmission pause interval.	**bridge** *bridge-group* **circuit-group** *circuit-group* **pause** *milliseconds*

For applications that depend on the ordering of mixed unicast and multicast traffic from a given source, load distribution must be based upon the source MAC address only. To modify the load distribution strategy to accommodate such applications, perform the following task in global configuration mode:

Task	Command
Base load distribution on the source MAC address only.	**bridge** *bridge-group* **circuit-group** *circuit-group* **source-based**

For an example of how to configure a circuit group, see the "Complex Transparent Bridging Network Topology Example" section later in this chapter.

Configuring Constrained Multicast Flooding

In a transparent bridge, multicast packets are flooded on all forwarding ports on the bridge. For some protocols, it is possible for a bridge to determine the membership of multicast groups, and constrain the flooding of multicasts to a subset of the forwarding ports. Constrained multicast flooding enables a bridge to determine group membership of IP multicast groups dynamically and flood multicast packets only on those ports that reach group members.

To enable constrained multicast flooding, perform the following task in global configuration mode:

Task	Command
Enable constrained multicast flooding for all configured bridge groups.	bridge cmf

MONITORING AND MAINTAINING THE TRANSPARENT BRIDGE NETWORK

This section describes how to monitor and maintain activity on the bridged network. You can perform one or more of the following tasks in privileged EXEC mode:

Task	Command
Remove any learned entries from the forwarding database and clear the transmit and receive counts for any statically configured forwarding entries.	clear bridge *bridge-group*
Remove multicast-group state information and clear the transmit and receive counts.	clear bridge [*bridge-group*] multicast [router-ports I groups I counts] [*group-address*] [*interface-unit*] [counts]
Reinitialize the Silicon Switch Processor (SSP) on the Cisco 7000 series.	clear sse
Remove VLAN statistics from any statically or system configured entries.	clear vlan statistics
Display classes of entries in the bridge forwarding database.	show bridge [*bridge-group*] [*interface*] [*address* [*mask*]] [verbose]
Display the interfaces configured in each circuit group and show whether they are participating in load distribution.	show bridge [*bridge-group*] circuit-group [*circuit-group*] [*src-mac-address*] [*dst-mac-address*]
Display transparent bridging multicast state information.	show bridge [*bridge-group*] multicast [router-ports I groups] [*group-address*]
Display information about configured bridge groups.	show bridge group [verbose]
Display IEEE 802.10 transparently bridged VLAN configuration.	show bridge vlan
Display the configuration for each interface that has been configured for routing or bridging.	show interfaces crb

Task	Command
Display the protocols that can be routed or bridged for the specified interface.	**show interfaces** [*interface*] **irb**
Display the spanning-tree topology known to the router, including whether or not filtering is in effect.	**show span**
Display a summary of SSP statistics.	**show sse summary**
Display a summary of VLAN subinterfaces.	**show vlans**

TRANSPARENT AND SRT BRIDGING CONFIGURATION EXAMPLES

The following sections provide example configurations that you can use as a guide to configuring your bridging environment:

- Basic Bridging Example
- Concurrent Routing and Bridging Example
- Basic Integrated Routing and Bridging Example
- Complex Integrated Routing and Bridging Example
- Integrated Routing and Bridging with Multiple Bridge Groups Example
- Transparently Bridged VLANs Configuration Example
- Routing Between VLANs Configuration Example
- Ethernet to FDDI Transparent Bridging Example
- Ethernet Bridging Example
- SRT Bridging Example
- Multicast or Broadcast Packets Bridging Example
- X.25 Transparent Bridging Example
- Frame Relay Transparent Bridging Examples
- Transparent Bridging over Multiprotocol LAPB Example
- Fast-Switched Transparent Bridging over ATM Example (Cisco 7000)
- Complex Transparent Bridging Network Topology Example

Basic Bridging Example

Figure 1–3 is an example of a basic bridging configuration. The system has two Ethernets, one Token Ring, one FDDI port, and one serial line. The IP is being routed, and everything else is being bridged. The Digital-compatible bridging algorithm with default parameters is being used.

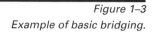

Figure 1–3
Example of basic bridging.

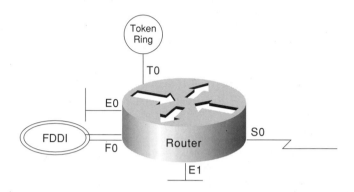

The configuration file for the router depicted in Figure 1–3 would be as follows:

```
interface tokenring 0
 ip address 131.108.1.1 255.255.255.0
 bridge-group 1
!
interface fddi 0
 ip address 131.108.2.1 255.255.255.0
 bridge-group 1
!
interface ethernet 0
 ip address 192.31.7.26 255.255.255.240
 bridge-group 1
!
interface serial 0
 ip address 192.31.7.34 255.255.255.240
 bridge-group 1
!
interface ethernet 1
 ip address 192.31.7.65 255.255.255.240
 bridge-group 1
!
bridge 1 protocol dec
```

Concurrent Routing and Bridging Example

In the following example, DecNet and IPX are concurrently routed and bridged. IP and AppleTalk are routed on all interfaces, DecNet and IP are routed on all interfaces not in the bridge group, and all protocols other than IP and AppleTalk are bridged on all interfaces in the bridge group:

```
!
ipx routing 0000.0c36.7a43
appletalk routing
!
decnet routing 9.65
decnet node-type routing-iv
!
!
interface Ethernet0/0
 ip address 172.19.160.65 255.255.255.0
 ipx network 160
 appletalk address 160.65
 decnet cost 7
!
interface Ethernet0/1
 ip address 172.19.161.65 255.255.255.0
 ipx network 161
 appletalk address 161.65
 decnet cost 7
!
interface Ethernet0/2
 ip address 172.19.162.65 255.255.255.0
 appletalk address 162.65
 bridge-group 1
!
interface Ethernet0/3
 ip address 172.19.14.65 255.255.255.0
 appletalk address 14.65
 appletalk zone california
 bridge-group 1
!
router igrp 666
network 172.19.0.0
!
bridge crb
bridge 1 protocol ieee
bridge 1 route appletalk
bridge 1 route ip
!
```

Basic Integrated Routing and Bridging Example

Figure 1–4 is an example of integrated routing and bridging that uses bridge group 1 to bridge and route IP. The router has three bridged Ethernet interfaces and one routed Ethernet interface.

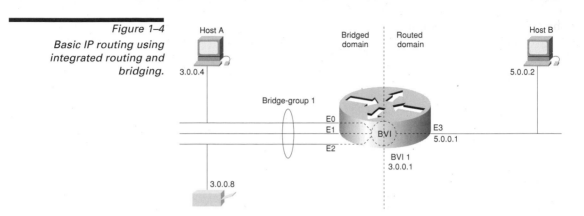

Figure 1–4

Basic IP routing using integrated routing and bridging.

The relevant portions of the configuration for the router are listed below.

```
interface Ethernet 0
 bridge-group 1
!
interface Ethernet 1
 bridge-group 1
!
interface Ethernet 2
 bridge-group 1
!
interface Ethernet 3
 ip address 5.0.0.1 255.0.0.0
!
interface BVI 1
 ip address 3.0.0.1 255.0.0.0
!
bridge irb
bridge 1 protocol ieee
 bridge 1 route ip
```

Complex Integrated Routing and Bridging Example

Figure 1–5 is a more complex example of integrated routing and bridging, where bridge group 1 is used to route IP traffic, bridge IPX traffic, and bridge and route AppleTalk traffic.

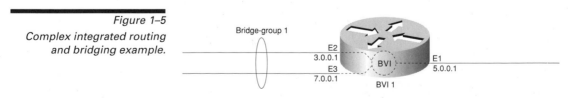

Figure 1–5

Complex integrated routing and bridging example.

The relevant portions of the configuration for the router are listed below.

```
appletalk routing
!
interface Ethernet 1
  ip address 5.0.0.1 255.0.0.0
  appletalk cable-range 35-35 35.1
  appletalk zone Engineering
!
interface Ethernet 2
  ip address 3.0.0.1 255.0.0.0
  bridge-group 1
!
interface Ethernet 3
  ip address 7.0.0.1 255.0.0.0
  bridge-group 1
!
interface BVI 1
  no ip address
  appletalk cable-range 33-33 33.1
  appletalk zone Accounting
!
bridge irb
bridge 1 protocol ieee
  bridge 1 route appletalk
  bridge 1 route ip
  no bridge 1 bridge ip
```

Integrated Routing and Bridging with Multiple Bridge Groups Example

In the example illustrated in Figure 1–6, integrated routing and bridging is used to route and bridge IP between two bridge groups.

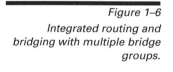

Figure 1–6
Integrated routing and bridging with multiple bridge groups.

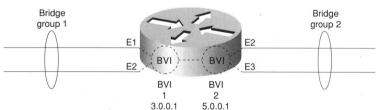

The relevant portions of the configuration for the router are listed as follows.

```
interface Ethernet 1
  bridge-group 1
!
interface Ethernet 2
  bridge-group 1
```

```
!
interface Ethernet 3
 bridge-group 2
!
interface Ethernet 4
 bridge-group 2
!
interface BVI 1
 ip address 3.0.0.1 255.0.0.0
!
interface BVI 2
 ip address 5.0.0.1 255.0.0.0
!
bridge irb
bridge 1 protocol ieee
 bridge 1 route ip
bridge 2 protocol ieee
 bridge 2 route ip
```

Transparently Bridged VLANs Configuration Example

The following example shows the configuration for the topology in Figure 1–1. The "striped" VLAN is identified as security association identifier 45; the "dot" VLAN is identified as security association identifier 1008; the "sliced" VLAN is identified as security association identifier 4321. Note that the assignment of bridge group, interface, and subinterface numbers is of local significance only. You must coordinate only the configuration of a common Security Association Identifier across bridges.

Router One

```
bridge 18 protocol ieee
interface ethernet 0/1
 bridge-group 18
!
interface ethernet 0/2
 bridge group 18
!
interface ethernet 0/3
 bridge-group 18
!
interface fddi 4/0.8
 encapsulation sde 45
 bridge-group 18
!
 bridge 54 protocol ieee

interface ethernet 1/1
 bridge group 54

interface ethernet 1/2
 bridge group 54
```

```
interface ethernet 1/3
 bridge group 54

interface fddi 4/0.13
 encapsulation sde 1008
 bridge group 54
!
bridge 3 protocol ieee

interface ethernet 2/1
 bridge-group 3

interface ethernet 2/2
 bridge-group 3

interface ethernet 2/3
 bridge-group 3

interface fddi 4/0.30
 encapsulation sde 4321
 bridge-group 3
```

Router Two

```
bridge 7 protocol ieee
interface ethernet 0/1
 bridge-group 7

interface ethernet 0/2
 bridge-group 7

interface ethernet 0/3
 bridge-group 7

interface ethernet 0/4
 bridge-group 7

interface fddi 2/0.11
 encapsulation sde 4321
 bridge-group 7
!
bridge 8 protocol ieee
interface ethernet 1/1
 bridge-group 8

interface ethernet 1/2
 bridge-group 8

interface ethernet 1/3
 bridge-group 8
```

```
interface ethernet 1/4
 bridge-group 8

interface fddi 2/0.14
 encapsulation sde 1008
 bridge-group 8
```

Router Three

```
bridge 1 protocol ieee
interface ethernet 0/1
 bridge-group 1
!
interface ethernet 0/2
 bridge-group 1
!
interface ethernet 0/3
 bridge-group 1
!
interface fddi 2/0.5
 encapsulation sde 4321
 bridge-group 1
!
bridge 6 protocol ieee
interface ethernet 1/1
 bridge-group 6
!
interface ethernet 1/2
 bridge-group 6
!
interface ethernet 1/3
 bridge-group 6
!
interface fddi 2/0.3
 encapsulation sde 45
 bridge-group 6
```

Routing Between VLANs Configuration Example

The following example shows the configuration for the topology shown in Figure 1–2. IP traffic is routed to and from switched VLAN domains 300, 400, and 600 to any other IP routing interface, as is IPX for VLANs 500 and 600. Because Fast Ethernet interfaces 2/1.20 and 3/1.40 are combined in bridge group 50, all other nonrouted traffic is bridged between these two subinterfaces.

```
interface FDDI 1/0.10
 ip address 131.108.1.1 255.255.255.0
 encap sde 300
!
interface FastEthernet 2/1.20.
 ip address 171.69.2.2 255.255.255.0
 encap isl 400
 bridge-group 50
```

```
!
interface FastEthernet 2/1.30
 ipx network 1000
 encap isl 500
!
interface FastEthernet 3/1.40
 ip address 198.92.3.3 255.255.255.0
 ipx network 1001
 encap isl 600
 bridge-group 50
!
bridge 50 protocol ieee
!
```

Ethernet to FDDI Transparent Bridging Example

The following configuration example shows the configuration commands that enable transparent bridging between Ethernet and FDDI interfaces. Transparent bridging on an FDDI interface is allowed only on the CSC-C2FCIT interface card.

```
hostname tester
!
buffers small min-free 20
buffers middle min-free 10
buffers big min-free 5
!
no ip routing
!
interface ethernet 0
 ip address 131.108.7.207 255.255.255.0
 no ip route-cache
 bridge-group 1
!
interface ethernet 2
 ip address 131.108.7.208 255.255.255.0
 no ip route-cache
 bridge-group 1
!
interface Fddi 0
 ip address 131.108.7.209 255.255.255.0
 no ip route-cache
 no keepalive
 bridge-group 1
!
bridge 1 protocol ieee
```

If the other side of the FDDI ring were an FDDI interface running in encapsulation mode rather than in transparent mode, the following additional configuration commands would be needed:

```
interface fddi 0
 fddi encapsulate
```

Ethernet Bridging Example

In the following example, two buildings have networks that must be connected via a T1 link. For the most part, the systems in each building use either IP or DECnet, and, therefore, should be routed. There are some systems in each building that must communicate, but they can use only a proprietary protocol.

The example places two Ethernets in each building. One of the Ethernets is attached to the hosts that use a proprietary protocol, and the other is used to attach to the rest of the building network running IP and DECnet. The Ethernet attached to the hosts using a proprietary protocol is enabled for bridging to the serial line and to the other building.

Figure 1–7 shows an example configuration. The interfaces marked with an asterisk (*) are configured as part of Spanning Tree 1. The routers are configured to route IP and DECnet. This configuration permits hosts on any Ethernet to communicate with hosts on any other Ethernet using IP or DECnet. In addition, hosts on Ethernet 1 in either building can communicate using protocols not supported for routing.

Figure 1–7

*Ethernet bridging
configuration example.*

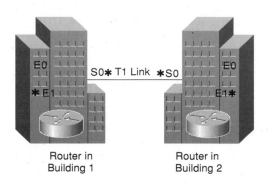

Router in
Building 1

Router in
Building 2

Router/Bridge in Building 1

The configuration file for the router in Building 1 would be as follows. Note that no bridging takes place over Ethernet 0. Both IP and DECnet routing are enabled on all interfaces.

```
decnet address 3.34
interface ethernet 0
 ip address 128.88.1.6 255.255.255.0
 decnet cost 10
!
interface serial 0
 ip address 128.88.2.1 255.255.255.0
 bridge-group 1
 decnet cost 10
!
interface ethernet 1
 ip address 128.88.3.1 255.255.255.0
 bridge-group 1
```

```
   decnet cost 10
 !
 bridge 1 protocol dec
```

Router/Bridge in Building 2

The configuration file for the router in Building 2 is similar:

```
 decnet address 3.56
 !
 interface ethernet 0
  ip address 128.88.11.9 255.255.255.0
  decnet cost 10
 !
 interface serial 0
  ip address 128.88.2.2 255.255.255.0
  bridge-group 1
  decnet cost 10
 !
 interface ethernet 1
  ip address 128.88.16.8 255.255.255.0
  bridge-group 1
  decnet cost 10
 !
 bridge 1 protocol dec
```

SRT Bridging Example

In Figure 1–8, a Token Ring and an Ethernet at a remote sales site in New York City must be configured to pass unroutable bridged traffic across a satellite link to the backbone Token Ring at the corporate headquarters in Thule, Greenland. IP is the only routed protocol. They are running the IEEE Spanning-Tree Protocol to comply with the SRT bridging standard.

If there were source-routed traffic to bridge, the **source-bridge** command also would be used to configure source routing.

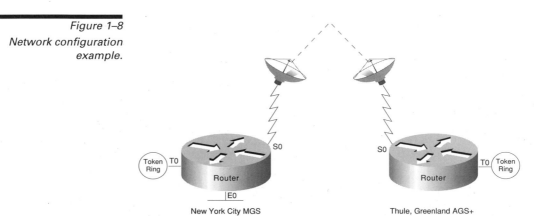

Figure 1–8
Network configuration example.

New York City MGS

Thule, Greenland AGS+

Configuration for the New York City Router

```
interface tokenring 0
 ip address 150.136.1.1 255.255.255.128
 bridge-group 1
!
interface ethernet 0
 ip address 150.136.2.1 255.255.255.128
 bridge-group 1
!
interface serial 0
 ip address 150.136.3.1 255.255.255.128
 bridge-group 1
!
bridge 1 protocol ieee
```

Configuration for the Thule, Greenland Router

```
interface tokenring 0
 ip address 150.136.10.1 255.255.255.128
 bridge-group 1
!
interface serial 0
 ip address 150.136.11.1 255.255.255.128
 bridge-group 1
!
bridge 1 protocol ieee
```

Multicast or Broadcast Packets Bridging Example

When filtering specific MAC destination addresses, allow for multicast or broadcast packets that are required by the bridged network protocols.

Assume you are bridging IP in your network as illustrated in Figure 1–9.

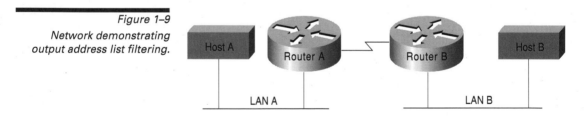

Figure 1–9
Network demonstrating
output address list filtering.

Host A   Router A   Router B   Host B

LAN A   LAN B

The MAC address of Host A is 0800.0907.0207, and the MAC address of Host B is 0260.8c34.0864. The following configuration would work as expected, because input addresses work on the source address on the incoming interface:

```
access-list 700 permit 0260.8c34.0864 0000.0000.0000
access-list 700 deny 0000.0000.0000 FFFF.FFFF.FFFF
interface ethernet 0
 bridge-group 1 input-address-list 700
```

However, the following configuration might work initially, but will eventually fail. The failure occurs because the configuration does not allow for an ARP broadcast with a destination address of FFFF.FFFF.FFFF, even though the destination address on the output interface is correct:

```
access-list 700 permit 0260.8c34.0864 0000.0000.0000
access-list 700 deny 0000.0000.0000 FFFF.FFFF.FFFF
interface ethernet 0
 bridge-group 1 output-address-list 700
```

The correct access list would be as follows:

```
access-list 700 permit 0260.8c34.0864 0000.0000.0000
access-list 700 permit FFFF.FFFF.FFFF 0000.0000.0000
access-list 700 deny 0000.0000.0000 FFFF.FFFF.FFFF
interface ethernet 0
 bridge-group 1 output-address-list 700
```

X.25 Transparent Bridging Example

Figure 1–10 is an example configuration illustrating three bridges connected to each other through an X.25 network.

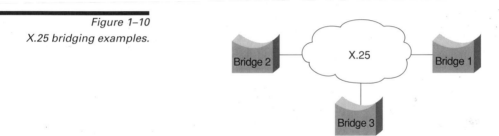

Figure 1–10
X.25 bridging examples.

Following are the configuration commands for each of the bridges depicted in Figure 1–10.

Configuration for Bridge 1

```
interface ethernet 2
 bridge-group 5
 ip address 128.88.11.9 255.255.255.0
!
interface serial 0
 encapsulation x25
 x25 address 31370019027
 bridge-group 5
 x25 map bridge 31370019134 broadcast
 x25 map bridge 31370019565 broadcast
!
bridge 5 protocol ieee
```

Configuration for Bridge 2

```
interface serial 1
 encapsulation x25
 x25 address 31370019134
 bridge-group 5
 x25 map bridge 31370019027 broadcast
 x25 map bridge 31370019565 broadcast
 !
bridge 5 protocol ieee
```

Configuration for Bridge 3

```
interface serial 0
 encapsulation x25
 x25 address 31370019565
 bridge-group 5
 x25 map bridge 31370019027 broadcast
 x25 map bridge 31370019134 broadcast
 !
bridge 5 protocol ieee
```

Frame Relay Transparent Bridging Examples

Figure 1–11 illustrates three bridges connected to each other through a Frame Relay network.

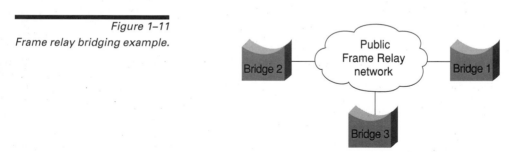

Figure 1–11
Frame relay bridging example.

Bridging in a Frame Relay Network with No Multicasts

The Frame Relay bridging software uses the same spanning-tree algorithm as the other bridging functions, but allows packets to be encapsulated for transmission across a Frame Relay network. The command specifies IP-to-DLCI address mapping and maintains a table of both the Ethernet and DLCIs. Following are the configuration commands for each of the bridges in a network that does not support a multicast facility.

Configuration for Bridge 1

```
interface ethernet 2
 bridge-group 5
 ip address 128.88.11.9 255.255.255.0
```

```
!
interface serial 0
 encapsulation frame-relay
 bridge-group 5
 frame-relay map bridge 134 broadcast
 frame-relay map bridge 565 broadcast
 !
bridge 5 protocol ieee
```

Configuration for Bridge 2

```
interface serial 1
 encapsulation frame-relay
 bridge-group 5
 frame-relay map bridge 27 broadcast
 frame-relay map bridge 565 broadcast
 !
bridge 5 protocol ieee
```

Configuration for Bridge 3

```
interface serial 0
 encapsulation frame-relay
 bridge-group 5
 frame-relay map bridge 27 broadcast
 frame-relay map bridge 134 broadcast
 !
bridge 5 protocol ieee
```

Bridging in a Frame Relay Network with Multicasts

The multicast facility is used to learn about the other bridges on the network, eliminating the need for the **frame-relay map** commands.

Following are the configuration commands for each of the bridges in a network that supports a multicast facility.

Configuration for Bridge 1

```
interface ethernet 2
 bridge-group 5
 ip address 128.88.11.9 255.255.255.0
 !
interface serial 0
 encapsulation frame-relay
 bridge-group 5
 !
bridge 5 protocol ieee
```

Configuration for Bridge 2

```
interface serial 1
 encapsulation frame-relay
 bridge-group 5
!
bridge 5 protocol ieee
```

Configuration for Bridge 3

```
interface serial 0
 encapsulation frame-relay
 bridge-group 5
!
bridge 5 protocol ieee
```

Transparent Bridging over Multiprotocol LAPB Example

The following example illustrates a router configured for transparent bridging over multiprotocol LAPB encapsulation:

```
!
no ip routing
!
interface ethernet 1
 no ip address
 no mop enabled
 bridge-group 1
!
interface serial 0
 no ip address
 encapsulation lapb multi
 bridge-group 1
!
 bridge 1 protocol ieee
```

Fast-Switched Transparent Bridging over ATM Example (Cisco 7000)

The following configuration example enables fast-switched transparent bridging over ATM:

```
interface atm 4/0
 ip address 1.1.1.1 255.0.0.0
 atm pvc 1 1 1 aal5snap
 atm pvc 2 2 2 aal5snap
 atm pvc 3 3 3 aal5snap
 bridge-group 1
!
bridge 1 protocol dec
```

Transparent Bridging over DDR Examples

The following two examples differ only in the packets that cause calls to be placed. The first example specifies by protocol (any bridge packet is permitted to cause a call to be made); the second example allows a finer granularity by specifying the Ethernet type codes of bridge packets.

The first example configures the serial 1 interface for DDR bridging. Any bridge packet is permitted to cause a call to be placed.

```
no ip routing
!
interface Serial1
 no ip address
 encapsulation ppp
 dialer in-band
 dialer enable-timeout 3
 dialer map bridge name urk broadcast 8985
 dialer hold-queue 10
 dialer-group 1
 ppp authentication chap
 bridge-group 1
 pulse-time 1
!
dialer-list 1 protocol bridge permit
bridge 1 protocol ieee
bridge 1 hello 10
```

The second example also configures the serial 1 interface for DDR bridging. However, this example includes an **access-list** command that specifies the Ethernet type codes that can cause calls to be placed and a **dialer list protocol list** command that refers to the specified access list.

```
no ip routing
!
interface Serial1
 no ip address
 encapsulation ppp
 dialer in-band
 dialer enable-timeout 3
 dialer map bridge name urk broadcast 8985
 dialer hold-queue 10
 dialer-group 1
 ppp authentication chap
 bridge-group 1
 pulse-time 1
!
access-list 200 permit 0x0800 0xFFF8
!
dialer-list 1 protocol bridge list 200
bridge 1 protocol ieee
bridge 1 hello 10
```

Fast-Switched Transparent Bridging over SMDS Example

The following configuration example enables fast-switched transparent bridging over SMDS:

```
interface serial 0
 encapsulation smds
 bridge group 1
 smds multicast bridge c141.5797.1313.ffff
```

Complex Transparent Bridging Network Topology Example

Figure 1–12 shows a network topology comprised of four bridged subnetworks. Each bridged subnetwork is defined by the scope of a spanning tree. However, the scope of each spanning tree is not shown in detail because it is unnecessary for purposes of this discussion. Instead, it is shown by a half cloud labeled "To other parts of BSN."

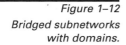

Figure 1–12
Bridged subnetworks
with domains.

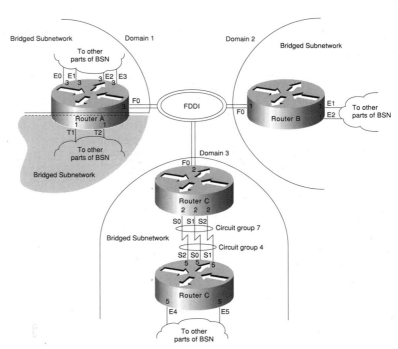

For proper bridging operation, the bridged subnetworks cannot have connections between them, but they can be connected to the same backbone. In this example, three of the four bridged subnetworks are connected to the FDDI backbone and each belongs to a separate domain.

Domains used in this topology allow the bridged subnetworks to be independent of one another while still bridging traffic onto the backbone destined for other connected bridged subnetworks.

Domains can be used in this manner only if the bridged subnetworks have a single point of attachment to one another. In this case, the connection to the FDDI backbone is that single point of attachment.

Each router on which a domain is configured and that has a single point of attachment to the other bridged subnetworks checks whether a BPDU on the backbone is its own. If the BPDU does not belong to the bridged subnetwork, the Cisco IOS software ignores the BPDU.

Separate bridged subnetworks, as in this example, allow spanning-tree reconfiguration of individual bridged subnetworks without disrupting bridging among the other bridged subnetworks.

NOTES

To get spanning-tree information by bridge group, use the **show span** command. Included in this information is the root bridge of the spanning tree. The root bridge for each spanning tree can be any router in the spanning tree.

The routers in this network are configured for bridging and demonstrate some of the bridging features available.

Configuration for Router A

Router A demonstrates multiple bridge groups in one router for bridged traffic separation.

In Router A, the Token Ring interfaces are bridged together entirely independently of the other bridged interfaces in the router and belong to bridge group 1. Bridge group 1 does not use a bridge domain because the interfaces are bridged independently of other bridged subnetworks in the network topology and it has no connection to the FDDI backbone.

Also in Router A, the Ethernet interfaces belong to bridge group 3. Bridge group 3 has a connection to the FDDI backbone and has a domain defined for it so that it can ignore BPDUs for other bridged subnetworks.

```
interface ethernet 0
 bridge-group 3
!
interface ethernet 1
 bridge-group 3
!
interface ethernet 2
 bridge-group 3
!
interface ethernet 3
 bridge-group 3
!
interface fddi 0
 bridge-group 3
!
interface tokenring 1
 bridge-group 1
```

```
!
interface tokenring 2
 bridge-group 1
!
bridge 1 protocol ieee
bridge 3 domain 1
bridge 3 protocol ieee
```

Configuration for Router B

Router B demonstrates a simple bridge configuration. It is connected to the FDDI backbone and has domain 2 defined. As such, it can bridge traffic with the other FDDI-connected BSNs. Note that bridge group 1 has no relationship to bridge group 1 in Router A; bridge groups are an organization internal to each router.

```
interface ethernet 1
 bridge-group 1
!
interface ethernet 2
 bridge-group 1
!
interface fddi 0
 bridge-group 1
!
bridge 1 domain 2
bridge 1 protocol ieee
```

Configuration for Router C

Router C and Router D combine to demonstrate load balancing by means of circuit groups. Circuit groups are used to load balance across multiple parallel serial lines between a pair of routers. The router on each end of the serial lines must have a circuit group defined. The circuit group number can be the same or can be different. In this example, they are different.

Router C and Router D are configured with the same domain, because they must understand one another's BPDUs. If they were configured with separate domains, Router D would ignore Router C's BPDUs and vice versa.

```
interface fddi 0
 bridge-group 2
!
interface serial 0
 bridge-group 2
 bridge-group 2 circuit-group 7
!
interface serial 1
 bridge-group 2
 bridge-group 2 circuit-group 7
!
interface serial 2
 bridge-group 2
 bridge-group 2 circuit-group 7
```

```
!
bridge 2 domain 3
bridge 2 protocol ieee
```

Configuration for Router D

```
interface ethernet 4
 bridge-group 5
!
interface ethernet 5
 bridge-group 5
!
interface serial 0
 bridge-group 5
 bridge-group 5 circuit-group 4
!
interface serial 1
 bridge-group 5
 bridge-group 5 circuit-group 4
!
interface serial 2
 bridge-group 5
 bridge-group 5 circuit-group 4
!
bridge 5 domain 3
bridge 5 protocol ieee
```

CHAPTER 2

Transparent Bridging Commands

Use the commands in this chapter to configure and monitor transparent bridging networks. For transparent bridging configuration information and examples, see Chapter 1, "Configuring Transparent Bridging."

ACCESS-LIST (EXTENDED)

Use the **access-list** global configuration command to provide extended access lists that allow more detailed access lists. These lists allow you to specify both source and destination addresses and arbitrary bytes in the packet.

> **access-list** *access-list-number* {**permit** | **deny**} *source source-mask destination destination-mask offset size operator operand*

Syntax	Description
access-list-number	Integer from 1100 to 1199 that you assign to identify one or more **permit/deny** conditions as an extended access list. Note that a list number in the range 1100 to 1199 distinguishes an extended access list from other access lists.
permit	Allows a connection when a packet matches an access condition. The Cisco IOS software stops checking the extended access list after a match occurs. All conditions must be met to make a match.
deny	Disallows a connection when a packet matches an access condition. The software stops checking the extended access list after a match occurs. All conditions must be met to make a match.
source	Media Access Control (MAC) Ethernet address in the form *xxxx.xxxx.xxxx*.

Syntax	Description
source-mask	Mask of MAC Ethernet source address bits to be ignored. The software uses the *source* and *source-mask* arguments to match the source address of a packet.
destination	MAC Ethernet value used for matching the destination address of a packet.
destination-mask	Mask of MAC Ethernet destination address bits to be ignored. The software uses the *destination* and *destination mask* arguments to match the destination address of a packet.
offset	Range of values that must be satisfied in the access list. Specified in decimal or in hexadecimal format in the form 0x*nn*. The offset is the number of bytes from the destination address field; it is not an offset from the start of the packet. The number of bytes you need to offset from the destination address varies depending on the media encapsulation type you are using.
size	Range of values that must be satisfied in the access list. Must be an integer 1 to 4.
operator	Compares arbitrary bytes within the packet. Can be one of the following keywords:
	lt—less than
	gt—greater than
	eq—equal
	neq—not equal
	and—bitwise and
	xor—bitwise exclusive or
	nop—address match only
operand	Compares arbitrary bytes within the packet. The value to be compared to or masked against.

Default

No extended access lists are established.

Command Mode

Global configuration

Usage Guidelines

This command first appeared in Cisco IOS Release 10.0.

After an access list is initially created, any subsequent additions (possibly entered from the terminal) are placed at the *end* of the list. In other words, you cannot selectively add or remove access list command lines from a specific access list.

An extended access list should not be used on FDDI interfaces that provide transit bridging.

─── **NOTES** ──

Due to their complexity, extended access lists should only be used by those who are very familiar with the Cisco IOS software. For example, to use extended access lists, it is important to understand how different encapsulations on different media would generally require different offset values to access particular fields.

─── **CAUTION** ──

Do not specify offsets into a packet that are greater than the size of the packet.

Examples

The following example permits packets from MAC addresses 000c.1b*xx.xxxx* to any MAC address if the packet contains a value less than 0x55AA in the 2 bytes that begin 0x1e bytes into the packet:

```
interface ethernet 0
 bridge-group 3 output-pattern 1102
access-list 1102 permit 000c.1b00.0000 0000.00ff.ffff
0000.0000.0000 ffff.ffff.ffff 0x1e 2 lt 0x55aa
```

The following example permits an NOP operation:

```
interface ethernet 0
 bridge-group 3 output-pattern 1102
access-list 1101 permit 0000.0000.0000 ffff.ffff.ffff 0000.0000.0000 ffff.ffff.ffff
```

Related Commands

access-list (standard)
access-list (type-code)
bridge-group output-pattern-list

ACCESS-LIST (STANDARD)

Use the **access-list** global configuration command to establish MAC address access lists. Use the **no** form of this command to remove a single access-list entry.

> **access-list** *access-list-number* {**permit** | **deny**} *address mask*
> **no access-list** *access-list-number*

Syntax	Description
access-list-number	Integer from 700 to 799 that you select for the list.
permit	Permits the frame.
deny	Denies the frame.
address mask	48-bit MAC addresses written in dotted triplet form. The ones bits in the *mask* argument are the bits to be ignored in *address*.

Default
No MAC address access lists are established.

Command Mode
Global configuration

Usage Guidelines
This command first appeared in Cisco IOS Release 10.0.

Usage Guidelines
Configuring bridging access lists of type 700 may cause a momentary interruption of traffic flow.

Example
The following example assumes that you want to disallow the bridging of Ethernet packets of all Sun workstations on Ethernet interface 1. Software assumes that all such hosts have Ethernet addresses with the vendor code 0800.2000.0000. The first line of the access list denies access to all Sun workstations, while the second line permits everything else. You then assign the access list to the input side of Ethernet interface 1.

```
access-list 700 deny 0800.2000.0000 0000.00FF.FFFF
access-list 700 permit 0000.0000.0000 FFFF.FFFF.FFFF
interface ethernet 1
 bridge-group 1 input-address-list 700
```

Related Commands
access-list (extended)
access-list (type-code)

ACCESS-LIST (TYPE-CODE)
Use the **access-list** global configuration command to build type-code access lists. Use the **no** form of this command to remove a single access list entry.

> access-list *access-list-number* {**permit** | **deny**} *type-code wild-mask*
> **no** access-list *access-list-number*

Syntax	Description
access-list-number	User-selectable number between 200 and 299 that identifies the list.
permit	Permits the frame.
deny	Denies the frame.
type-code	16-bit hexadecimal number written with a leading "0x"; for example, 0x6000. You can specify either an Ethernet type code for Ethernet-encapsulated packets, or a DSAP/SSAP pair for 802.3 or 802.5-encapsulated packets. Ethernet type codes are listed in Appendix A, "Ethernet Type Codes."
wild-mask	16-bit hexadecimal number whose one bits correspond to bits in the *type-code* argument that should be ignored when making a comparison. (A mask for a DSAP/SSAP pair should always be at least 0x0101. This is because these two bits are used for purposes other than identifying the SAP codes.)

Default

No type-code access lists are built.

Command Mode

Global configuration

Usage Guidelines

This command first appeared in Cisco IOS Release 10.0.

Type-code access lists can have an impact on system performance; therefore, keep the lists as short as possible and use wildcard bit masks whenever possible.

Access lists are evaluated according to the following algorithm:

- If the packet is Ethernet Type II or SNAP, the type-code field is used.
- Other packet type, then the LSAP is used.

If the length/type field is greater than 1500, the packet is treated as an LSAP packet unless the DSAP and SSAP fields are AAAA. If the latter is true, the packet is treated using type-code filtering.

If the LSAP-code filtering is used, all SNAP and Ethernet Type II packets are bridged without obstruction. If type-code filtering is used, all LSAP packets are bridged without obstruction.

If you have both Ethernet Type II and LSAP packets on your network, you should set up access lists for both.

Examples

The following example permits only LAT frames (type 0x6004) and filters out all other frame types:

```
access-list 201 permit 0x6004 0x0000
```

The following example filters out only type codes assigned to Digital (0x6000 to 0x600F) and lets all other types pass:

```
access-list 202 deny 0x6000 0x600F
access-list 202 permit 0x0000 0xFFFF
```

Use the last item of an access list to specify a default action; for example, permit everything else or deny everything else. If nothing else in the access list matches, the default action is normally to deny access; that is, filter out all other type codes.

Related Commands

access-list (extended)
access-list (standard)

BRIDGE ACQUIRE

Use the **bridge acquire** global configuration command to forward any frames for stations that the system has learned about dynamically. Use the **no** form of this command to disable the behavior.

> **bridge** *bridge-group* **acquire**
> **no bridge** *bridge-group* **acquire**

Syntax	Description
bridge-group	Bridge group number specified in the **bridge protocol** command.

Default

Enabled

Command Mode

Global configuration

Usage Guidelines

This command first appeared in Cisco IOS Release 10.0.

When using the command default, the Cisco IOS software forwards any frames from stations that it has learned about dynamically. If you use the **no** form of this command, the bridge stops forwarding frames to stations it has dynamically learned about through the discovery process and limits frame forwarding to statically configured stations. That is, the bridge filters out all frames except those whose sourced-by or destined-to addresses have been statically configured into the forwarding cache. The **no** form of this command prevents the forwarding of a dynamically learned address.

Example

The following example prevents the forwarding of dynamically determined source and destination addresses:

```
no bridge 1 acquire
```

Related Commands

bridge address
bridge protocol

BRIDGE ADDRESS

Use the **bridge address** global configuration command to filter frames with a particular MAC-layer station source or destination address. Use the **no** form of this command to disable the forwarding ability.

bridge *bridge-group* **address** *mac-address* {**forward** | **discard**} [*interface*]
no bridge *bridge-group* **address** *mac-address*

Syntax	Description
bridge-group	Bridge group number. It must be the same number specified in the **bridge protocol** command.
mac-address	48-bit dotted-triplet hardware address such as that displayed by the EXEC **show arp** command, for example, 0800.cb00.45e9. It is either a station address, the broadcast address, or a multicast destination address.
forward	Frame sent from or destined to the specified address is forwarded as appropriate.
discard	Frame sent from or destined to the specified address is discarded without further processing.
interface	(Optional) Interface specification, such as Ethernet 0. It is added after the **forward** or **discard** keyword to indicate the interface on which that address can be reached.

Default

Disabled

Command Mode

Global configuration

Usage Guidelines

This command first appeared in Cisco IOS Release 10.0.

Any number of addresses can be configured into the system without a performance penalty.

> **NOTES**
>
> MAC addresses on Ethernets are "bit swapped" when compared with MAC addresses on Token Ring and FDDI. For example, address 0110.2222.3333 on Ethernet is 8008.4444.CCCC on Token Ring and FDDI. Access lists always use the canonical Ethernet representation. When using different media and building access lists to filter on MAC addresses, keep this point in mind. Note that when a bridged packet traverses a serial link, it has an Ethernet-style address.

Examples

The following example enables frame filtering with MAC address 0800.cb00.45e9. The frame is forwarded through Ethernet interface 1:

```
bridge 1 address 0800.cb00.45e9 forward ethernet 1
```

The following example disables the ability to forward frames with MAC address 0800.cb00.45e9:

```
no bridge 1 address 0800.cb00.45e9
```

Related Commands

bridge acquire
bridge-group input-address-list
bridge-group output-address-list
bridge protocol

BRIDGE BRIDGE

Use the **bridge bridge** global configuration command to enable the bridging of a specified protocol in a specified bridge group. Use the **no** form of this command to disable the bridging of a specified protocol in a specified bridge group.

> **bridge** *bridge-group* **bridge** *protocol*
> **no bridge** *bridge-group* **bridge** *protocol*

Syntax	Description
bridge-group	Bridge-group number. It must be the same number specified in the **bridge protocol** command.
protocol	Any of the supported routing protocols. The default is to bridge all of these protocols.

Default

Bridge every protocol.

Command Mode

Global configuration

Usage Guidelines

This command first appeared in Cisco IOS Release 11.2.

When IRB is enabled, the default route/bridge behavior in a bridge group is to bridge all protocols. You do not have to use the **bridge bridge** command to enable bridging.

You can use the **no bridge bridge** command to disable bridging in a bridge group so that it does not bridge a particular protocol. When you disable bridging for a protocol in a bridge group, routable packets of this protocol are routed when the bridge is explicitly configured to route this protocol, and nonroutable packets are dropped because bridging is disabled for this protocol.

NOTES

Packets of nonroutable protocols such as LAT are only bridged. You cannot disable bridging for the nonroutable traffic.

Example

The following example disables bridging of IP in bridge group 1:

```
no bridge 1 bridge ip
```

Related Commands

bridge irb
bridge protocol
bridge route

BRIDGE CIRCUIT-GROUP PAUSE

Use the **bridge circuit-group pause** global configuration command to configure the interval during which transmission is suspended in a circuit group after circuit group changes take place.

> **bridge** *bridge-group* **circuit-group** *circuit-group* **pause** *milliseconds*

Syntax	Description
bridge-group	Bridge group number specified in the **bridge protocol** command.
circuit-group	Number of the circuit group to which the interface belongs.
milliseconds	Forward delay interval. It must be a value in the range 0 to 10000 ms.

Default

0 ms pause

Command Mode

Global configuration

Usage Guidelines

This command first appeared in Cisco IOS Release 10.3.

Circuit-group changes include the addition or deletion of an interface and interface state changes.

Example

The following example sets the circuit group pause to 5000 ms:

```
bridge 1 circuit-group 1 pause 5000
```

Related Commands

bridge circuit-group source-based
bridge-group circuit-group
bridge protocol
show bridge circuit-group

BRIDGE CIRCUIT-GROUP SOURCE-BASED

Use the **bridge circuit-group source-based** global configuration command to use just the source MAC address for selecting the output interface. Use the **no** form of this command to remove the interface from the bridge group.

> **bridge** *bridge-group* **circuit-group** *circuit-group* **source-based**
> **no bridge** *bridge-group* **circuit-group** *circuit-group* **source-based**

Syntax	Description
bridge-group	Bridge group number specified in the **bridge protocol** command.
circuit-group	Number of the circuit group to which the interface belongs.

Default

No bridge-group interface is assigned.

Command Mode

Global configuration

Usage Guidelines

This command first appeared in Cisco IOS Release 10.3.

For applications that depend on the ordering of mixed unicast and multicast traffic from a given source, load distribution must be based on the source MAC address only. The **bridge circuit-group source-based** command modifies the load distribution strategy to accommodate such applications.

Part
I

Command Reference

Example

The following example uses the source MAC address for selecting the output interface to a bridge group:

```
bridge 1 circuit-group 1 source-based
```

Related Commands

bridge circuit-group pause
bridge-group circuit-group
bridge protocol
show bridge circuit-group

BRIDGE CMF

Use the **bridge cmf** global configuration command to enable constrained multicast flooding (CMF) for all configured bridge groups. Use the **no** form of this command to disable constrained multicast flooding.

bridge cmf
no bridge cmf

Syntax   Description

This command has no arguments or keywords.

Default

Constrained multicast flooding is disabled.

Command Mode

Global configuration

Usage Guidelines

This command first appeared in Cisco IOS Release 11.2.

Example

The following example enables constrained multicast flooding for all configured bridge groups:

```
bridge cmf
```

Related Commands

clear bridge multicast
show bridge multicast

BRIDGE CRB

Use the **bridge crb** global configuration command to enable the Cisco IOS software to both route and bridge a given protocol on separate interfaces within a single router. Use the **no** form of this command to disable the feature.

> **bridge crb**
> **no bridge crb**

Syntax   Description

This command has no arguments or keywords.

Defaults

Concurrent routing and bridging is disabled.

When concurrent routing and bridging has been enabled, the default behavior is to bridge all protocols that are not explicitly routed in a bridge group.

Command Mode

Global configuration

Usage Guidelines

This command first appeared in Cisco IOS Release 11.0.

When concurrent routing and bridging is first enabled in the presence of existing bridge groups, it generates a **bridge route** configuration command for any protocol for which any interface in the bridge group is configured for routing. This is a precaution that applies only when concurrent routing and bridging is not already enabled, bridge groups exist, and the **bridge crb** command is encountered.

Once concurrent routing and bridging has been enabled, you must configure an explicit **bridge route** command for any protocol that is to be routed on interfaces in a bridge group (in addition to any required protocol-specific interface configuration).

Example

The following command enables concurrent routing and bridging:

    bridge crb

Related Commands

bridge route

BRIDGE DOMAIN

Use the **bridge domain** global configuration command to establish a domain by assigning it a decimal value between 1 and 10. Use the **no** form of this command to return it to a single bridge domain by choosing domain zero (0).

> **bridge** *bridge-group* **domain** *domain-number*
> **no bridge** *bridge-group* **domain**

Syntax	Description
bridge-group	Bridge group number specified in the **bridge protocol ieee** command. The **dec** keyword is not valid for this command.
domain-number	Domain ID number you choose. The default domain number is zero; this is the domain number required when communicating to IEEE bridges that do not support this domain extension.

Default

Single bridge domain

Command Mode

Global configuration

Usage Guidelines

This command first appeared in Cisco IOS Release 10.0.

Cisco has implemented a proprietary extension to the IEEE spanning-tree software in order to support multiple spanning-tree domains. You can place any number of routers within the domain. The routers in the domain, and only those routers, will then share spanning-tree information.

Use this feature when multiple routers share the same cable, and you wish to use only certain discrete subsets of these routers to share spanning-tree information with each other. This function is most useful when running other applications, such as IP UDP flooding, that use the IEEE Spanning-Tree Protocol. It also can be used to reduce the number of global reconfigurations in large bridged networks.

CAUTION

Use multiple spanning-tree domains with care. Because bridges in different domains do not share spanning-tree information, bridge loops can be created if the domains are not carefully planned.

NOTES

This command works only when the bridge group is running the IEEE Spanning-Tree Protocol.

Example

The following example places bridge group 1 in bridging domain 3. Only other routers that are in domain 3 will accept spanning-tree information from this router.

```
bridge 1 domain 3
```

Related Commands

bridge protocol

BRIDGE FORWARD-TIME

Use the **bridge forward-time** global configuration command to specify the forward delay interval for the Cisco IOS software. Use the **no** form of this command to return the default interval.

> **bridge** *bridge-group* **forward-time** *seconds*
> **no bridge** *bridge-group* **forward-time** *seconds*

Syntax	Description
bridge-group	Bridge group number specified in the **bridge protocol** command.
seconds	Forward delay interval. It must be a value in the range 10 to 200 seconds.

Default

30-second delay

Command Mode

Global configuration

Usage Guidelines

This command first appeared in Cisco IOS Release 10.0.

The forward delay interval is the amount of time the software spends listening for topology change information after an interface has been activated for bridging and before forwarding actually begins.

Each bridge in a spanning tree adopts the **hello-time, forward-time**, and **max-age** parameters of the root bridge, regardless of what its individual configuration might be.

Example

The following example sets the forward delay interval to 60 seconds:

```
bridge 1 forward-time 60
```

Related Commands

bridge hello-time
bridge max-age
bridge protocol

BRIDGE-GROUP

Use the **bridge-group** interface configuration command to assign each network interface to a bridge group. Use the **no** form of this command to remove the interface from the bridge group.

> **bridge-group** *bridge-group*
> **no bridge-group** *bridge-group*

Syntax	*Description*
bridge-group	Number of the bridge group to which the interface belongs. It must be a number in the range 1 to 63.

Default

No bridge group interface is assigned.

Command Mode

Interface configuration

Usage Guidelines

This command first appeared in Cisco IOS Release 10.0.

You can bridge on any interface, including any serial interface, regardless of encapsulation. Bridging can be configured between interfaces on different cards, although the performance is lower compared with interfaces on the same card. Also note that serial interfaces must be running with HDLC, X.25, or Frame Relay encapsulation.

--- **NOTES** ---

Several modifications to interfaces in bridge groups, including adding interfaces to bridge groups, will result in any Token Ring or FDDI interfaces in that bridge group being reinitialized.

Example

In the following example, Ethernet interface 0 is assigned to bridge-group 1, and bridging is enabled on this interface:

```
interface ethernet 0
 bridge-group 1
```

Related Commands

bridge-group cbus-bridging
bridge-group circuit-group
bridge-group input-pattern-list
bridge-group output-pattern-list
bridge-group spanning-disabled

BRIDGE-GROUP AGING-TIME

Use the **bridge-group aging-time** global configuration command to set the length of time that a dynamic entry can remain in the bridge table from the time the entry was created or last updated. Use the **no** form of this command to return to the default aging-time interval.

> **bridge-group** *bridge-group* **aging-time** *seconds*
> **no bridge-group** *bridge-group* **aging-time**

Syntax	Description
bridge-group	Number of the bridge group to which the interface belongs. It must be a number in the range 1 to 63.
seconds	Aging time, in the range 0 to 1000000 seconds. The default is 300 seconds.

Default

300 seconds

Command Mode

Global configuration

Usage Guidelines

This command first appeared in Cisco IOS Release 10.3.

If hosts on a bridged network are likely to move, decrease the aging time to enable the bridge to adapt quickly to the change. If hosts do not transmit continuously, increase the aging time to record the dynamic entries for a longer time and thus reduce the possibility of flooding when the hosts transmit again.

Example

The following example sets the aging time to 200 seconds:

```
bridge-group 1 aging-time 200
```

Related Commands

bridge-group

BRIDGE-GROUP CBUS-BRIDGING

Use the **bridge-group cbus-bridging** interface configuration command to enable autonomous bridging on a ciscoBus2 controller. Use the **no** form of this command to disable autonomous bridging.

bridge-group *bridge-group* **cbus-bridging**
no bridge-group *bridge-group* **cbus-bridging**

Syntax	Description
bridge-group	Number of the bridge group to which the interface belongs. It must be a number in the range 1 to 63.

Default

Autonomous bridging is disabled.

Command Mode

Interface configuration

Usage Guidelines

This command first appeared in Cisco IOS Release 10.0.

Normally, bridging takes place on the processor card at interrupt level. When autonomous bridging is enabled, bridging takes place entirely on the ciscoBus2 controller, significantly improving performance.

You can enable autonomous bridging on Ethernet, FDDI (FCIT) and HSSI interfaces that reside on a ciscoBus2 controller. Autonomous bridging is not supported on Token Ring interfaces, regardless of the type of bus in use.

To enable autonomous bridging on an interface, that interface must first be defined as part of a bridge group. When a bridge group includes both autonomously and normally bridged interfaces, packets are autonomously bridged in some cases, but bridged normally in others. For example, when packets are forwarded between two autonomously bridged interfaces, those packets are autonomously bridged. But when packets are forwarded between an autonomously bridged interface and one that is not, the packet must be normally bridged. When a packet is flooded, the packet is autonomously bridged on autonomously bridged interfaces, but must be normally bridged on any others.

NOTES

In order to maximize performance when using a ciscoBus2 controller, use the **bridge-group cbus-bridging** command to enable autonomous bridging on any Ethernet, FDDI, or HSSI interface.

> **NOTES**
>
> You can only filter by MAC-level address on an interface when autonomous bridging is enabled on that interface; autonomous bridging disables all other filtering, as well as priority queuing.

Example

In the following example, autonomous bridging is enabled on Ethernet interface 0:

```
interface ethernet 0
 bridge-group 1
 bridge-group 1 cbus-bridging
```

Related Commands

bridge-group

BRIDGE-GROUP CIRCUIT-GROUP

Use the **bridge-group circuit-group** interface configuration command to assign each network interface to a bridge group. Use the **no** form of this command to remove the interface from the bridge group.

> **bridge-group** *bridge-group* **circuit-group** *circuit-group*
> **no bridge-group** *bridge-group* **circuit-group** *circuit-group*

Syntax	Description
bridge-group	Number of the bridge group to which the interface belongs. It must be a number in the range 1 to 63.
circuit-group	Circuit group number. The range is 1 to 9.

Default

No bridge group interface is assigned.

Command Mode

Interface configuration

Usage Guidelines

This command first appeared in Cisco IOS Release 10.3.

Circuit groups are primarily intended for use with HDLC-encapsulated serial interfaces. They are not supported for packet-switched networks such as X.25 or Frame Relay. Circuit groups are best applied to groups of serial lines of equal bandwidth, but can accommodate mixed bandwidths as well.

NOTES ————————————————————————————————————

You must configure bridging before you configure a circuit group on an interface.

Example

In the following example, Ethernet interface 0 is assigned to circuit group 1 of bridge group 1:

```
interface ethernet 0
 bridge-group 1 circuit-group 1
```

Related Commands

bridge circuit-group pause
bridge circuit-group source-based
show bridge circuit-group

BRIDGE-GROUP INPUT-ADDRESS-LIST

Use the **bridge-group input-address-list** interface configuration command to assign an access list to a particular interface. This access list is used to filter packets received on that interface based on their MAC source addresses. Use the **no** form of this command to remove an access list from an interface.

> **bridge-group** *bridge-group* **input-address-list** *access-list-number*
> **no bridge-group** *bridge-group* **input-address-list** *access-list-number*

Syntax	Description
bridge-group	Number of the bridge group to which the interface belongs. It must be a number in the range 1 to 63.
access-list-number	Access list number you assigned with the **access-list** command. It must be in the range 700 to 799.

Default

No access list is assigned.

Command Mode

Interface configuration

Usage Guidelines

This command first appeared in Cisco IOS Release 10.0.

Example

The following example assumes you want to disallow the bridging of Ethernet packets of all Sun workstations on Ethernet interface 1. Software assumes that all such hosts have Ethernet addresses with the vendor code 0800.2000.0000. The first line of the access list denies access to all Sun workstations, while the second line permits everything else. You then assign the access list to the input side of Ethernet interface 1.

```
access-list 700 deny 0800.2000.0000 0000.00FF.FFFF
access-list 700 permit 0000.0000.0000 FFFF.FFFF.FFFF
interface ethernet 1
 bridge-group 1 input-address-list 700
```

Related Commands

access-list (extended)
access-list (standard)
bridge address
bridge-group output-address-list

BRIDGE-GROUP INPUT-LAT-SERVICE-DENY

Use the **bridge-group input-lat-service-deny** interface configuration command to specify the group codes by which to deny access upon input. Use the **no** form of this command to remove this access condition.

> **bridge-group** *bridge-group* **input-lat-service-deny** *group-list*
> **no bridge-group** *bridge-group* **input-lat-service-deny** *group-list*

Syntax	Description
bridge-group	Number of the bridge group to which the interface belongs. It must be a number in the range 1 to 63.
group-list	List of LAT service groups. Single numbers and ranges are permitted. Specify a zero (0) to disable the LAT group code for the bridge group.

Default

No group codes are specified.

Command Mode

Interface configuration

Usage Guidelines

This command first appeared in Cisco IOS Release 10.0.

Autonomous bridging must be disabled to use this command.

This command prevents the system from bridging any LAT service advertisement that has any of the specified groups set.

Example

The following example causes any advertisements with groups 6, 8, and 14 through 20 to be dropped:

```
interface ethernet 0
 bridge-group 1 input-lat-service-deny 6 8 14-20
```

Related Commands

bridge-group
bridge-group input-lat-service-permit
bridge-group output-lat-service-deny

BRIDGE-GROUP INPUT-LAT-SERVICE-PERMIT

Use the **bridge-group input-lat-service-permit** interface configuration command to specify the group codes by which to permit access upon input. Use the **no** form of this command to remove this access condition.

> bridge-group *bridge-group* input-lat-service-permit *group-list*
> no bridge-group *bridge-group* input-lat-service-permit *group-list*

Syntax	Description
bridge-group	Number of the bridge group to which the interface belongs. It must be a number in the range 1 to 63.
group-list	LAT service groups. Single numbers and ranges are permitted. Specify a zero (0) to disable the LAT group code for the bridge group.

Default

No group codes are specified.

Command Mode

Interface configuration

Usage Guidelines

This command first appeared in Cisco IOS Release 10.0.

Autonomous bridging must be disabled to use this command.

This command causes the system to bridge only those service advertisements that match at least one group in the group list specified by the *group-list* argument.

If a message specifies group codes in both the deny and permit list, the message is not bridged.

Example

The following example bridges any advertisements from groups 1, 5, and 12 through 14:

```
interface ethernet 1
  bridge-group 1 input-lat-service-permit 1 5 12-14
```

Related Commands

bridge-group input-lat-service-deny
bridge-group output-lat-service-permit

BRIDGE-GROUP INPUT-LSAP-LIST

Use the **bridge-group input-lsap-list** interface configuration command to filter IEEE 802.2-encapsulated packets on input. Use the **no** form of this command to disable this capability.

> **bridge-group** *bridge-group* **input-lsap-list** *access-list-number*
> **no bridge-group** *bridge-group* **input-lsap-list** *access-list-number*

Syntax	Description
bridge-group	Number of the bridge group to which the interface belongs. It must be a number in the range 1 to 63.
access-list-number	Access list number you assigned with the standard **access-list** command. Specify a zero (0) to disable the application of the access list on the bridge group.

Default

Disabled

Command Mode

Interface configuration

Usage Guidelines

This command first appeared in Cisco IOS Release 10.0.

Autonomous bridging must be disabled to use this command.

This access list is applied to all IEEE 802.2 frames received on that interface prior to the bridge-learning process. SNAP frames must also pass any applicable Ethernet type-code access list.

Example

The following example specifies access list 203 on Ethernet interface 1:

```
interface ethernet 1
  bridge-group 3 input-lsap-list 203
```

Related Commands

access-list (extended)
access-list (standard)
bridge-group
bridge-group output-lsap-list

BRIDGE-GROUP INPUT-PATTERN-LIST

Use the **bridge-group input-pattern-list** interface configuration command to associate an extended access list with a particular interface in a particular bridge group. Use the **no** form of this command to disable this capability.

> **bridge-group** *bridge-group* **input-pattern-list** *access-list-number*
> **no bridge-group** *bridge-group* **input-pattern-list** *access-list-number*

Syntax	*Description*
bridge-group	Number of the bridge group to which the interface belongs. It must be a number in the range 1 to 63.
access-list-number	Access list number you assigned using the standard **access-list** command. Specify a zero (0) to disable the application of the access list on the interface.

Default

Disabled

Command Mode

Interface configuration

Usage Guidelines

This command first appeared in Cisco IOS Release 10.0.

Autonomous bridging must be disabled to use this command.

Example

The following command applies access list 1 to bridge group 3 using the filter defined in group 1:

```
interface ethernet 0
  bridge-group 3 input-pattern-list 1
```

Related Commands

access-list (extended)
access-list (standard)
bridge-group
bridge-group output-pattern-list

BRIDGE-GROUP INPUT-TYPE-LIST

Use the **bridge-group input-type-list** interface configuration command to filter Ethernet- and SNAP-encapsulated packets on input. Use the **no** form of this command to disable this capability.

> **bridge-group** *bridge-group* **input-type-list** *access-list-number*
> **no bridge-group** *bridge-group* **input-type-list** *access-list-number*

Syntax	Description
bridge-group	Number of the bridge group to which the interface belongs. It must be a number in the range 1 to 63.
access-list-number	Access list number you assigned with the standard **access-list** command. Specify a zero (0) to disable the application of the access list on the bridge group.

Default

Disabled

Command Mode

Interface configuration

Usage Guidelines

This command first appeared in Cisco IOS Release 10.0.

Autonomous bridging must be disabled to use this command.

For SNAP-encapsulated frames, the access list is applied against the 2-byte TYPE field given after the DSAP/SSAP/OUI fields in the frame.

This access list is applied to all Ethernet and SNAP frames received on that interface prior to the bridge learning process. SNAP frames must also pass any applicable IEEE 802 DSAP/SSAP access lists.

Example

The following example shows how to configure a Token Ring interface with an access list that allows only the LAT protocol to be bridged:

```
interface tokenring 0
 ip address 131.108.1.1 255.255.255.0
 bridge-group 1
 bridge-group 1 input-type-list 201
```

Related Commands

access-list (extended)
access-list (standard)

bridge-group
bridge-group output-type-list

BRIDGE-GROUP LAT-COMPRESSION

Use the **bridge-group lat-compression** interface configuration command to reduce the amount of bandwidth that LAT traffic consumes on the serial interface by specifying a LAT-specific form of compression. Use the **no** form of this command to disable LAT compression on the bridge group.

> **bridge-group** *bridge-group* **lat-compression**
> **no bridge-group** *bridge-group* **lat-compression**

Syntax	Description
bridge-group	Number of the bridge group to which the interface belongs. It must be a number in the range 1 to 63.

Default
Disabled

Command Mode
Interface configuration

Usage Guidelines
This command first appeared in Cisco IOS Release 10.0.

Autonomous bridging must be disabled to use this command.

Compression is applied to LAT frames being sent out the router through the interface in question.

LAT compression can be specified only for serial interfaces. For the most common LAT operations (user keystrokes and acknowledgment packets), LAT compression reduces LAT's bandwidth requirements by nearly a factor of two.

Example
The following example compresses LAT frames on the bridge assigned to group 1:

```
bridge-group 1 lat-compression
```

Related Commands
bridge-group

BRIDGE-GROUP OUTPUT-ADDRESS-LIST

Use the **bridge-group output-address-list** interface configuration command to assign an access list to a particular interface for filtering the MAC destination addresses of packets that would ordinarily be forwarded out that interface. Use the **no** form of this command to remove an access list from an interface.

> **bridge-group** *bridge-group* **output-address-list** *access-list-number*
> **no bridge-group** *bridge-group* **output-address-list** *access-list-number*

Syntax	*Description*
bridge-group	Number of the bridge group to which the interface belongs. It must be a number in the range 1 to 63.
access-list-number	Access list number you assigned with the standard **access-list** command.

Default

No access list is assigned.

Command Mode

Interface configuration

Usage Guidelines

This command first appeared in Cisco IOS Release 10.0.

Example

The following example assigns access list 703 to Ethernet interface 3:

```
interface ethernet 3
 bridge-group 5 output-address-list 703
```

Related Commands

access-list (extended)
access-list (standard)
bridge address
bridge-group
bridge-group input-address-list

BRIDGE-GROUP OUTPUT-LAT-SERVICE-DENY

Use the **bridge-group output-lat-service-deny** interface configuration command to specify the group codes by which to deny access upon output. Use the **no** form of this command to cancel the specified group codes.

> **bridge-group** *bridge-group* **output-lat-service-deny** *group-list*
> **no bridge-group** *bridge-group* **output-lat-service-deny** *group-list*

Syntax	Description
bridge-group	Number of the bridge group to which the interface belongs. It must be a number in the range 1 to 63.
group-list	List of LAT groups. Single numbers and ranges are permitted.

Default

No group codes are assigned.

Command Mode

Interface configuration

Usage Guidelines

This command first appeared in Cisco IOS Release 10.0.

Autonomous bridging must be disabled to use this command.

This command causes the system to not bridge onto this output interface any service advertisements that contain groups matching any of those in the group list.

Example

The following example prevents bridging of LAT service announcements from groups 12 through 20:

```
interface ethernet 0
 bridge-group 1
 bridge-group 1 output-lat-service-deny 12-20
```

Related Commands

access-list (extended)
access-list (standard)
bridge-group
bridge-group input-lat-service-deny
bridge-group output-lat-service-permit

BRIDGE-GROUP OUTPUT-LAT-SERVICE-PERMIT

Use the **bridge-group output-lat-service-permit** interface configuration command to specify the group codes by which to permit access upon output. Use the **no** form of this command to cancel specified group codes.

bridge-group *bridge-group* output-lat-service-permit *group-list*
no bridge-group *bridge-group* output-lat-service-permit *group-list*

Syntax	Description
bridge-group	Number of the bridge group to which the interface belongs. It must be a number in the range 1 to 63.
group-list	LAT service advertisements.

Default

No group codes are specified.

Command Mode

Interface configuration

Usage Guidelines

This command first appeared in Cisco IOS Release 10.0.

Autonomous bridging must be disabled to use this command.

This command causes the system to bridge onto this output interface only those service advertisements that match at least one group in the specified group code list.

NOTES

If a message matches both a deny and a permit condition, it will not be bridged.

Example

The following example allows only LAT service announcements from groups 5, 12, and 20 on this bridge:

```
interface ethernet 0
 bridge-group 1 output-lat-service-permit 5 12 20
```

Related Commands

bridge-group input-lat-service-permit
bridge-group output-lat-service-deny

BRIDGE-GROUP OUTPUT-LSAP-LIST

Use the **bridge-group output-lsap-list** interface configuration command to filter IEEE 802-encapsulated packets on output. Use the **no** form of this command to disable this capability.

> **bridge-group** *bridge-group* **output-lsap-list** *access-list-number*
> **no bridge-group** *bridge-group* **output-lsap-list** *access-list-number*

Syntax	Description
bridge-group	Number of the bridge group to which the interface belongs. It must be a number in the range 1 to 63.
access-list-number	Access list number you assigned with the standard **access-list** command. Specify a zero (0) to disable the application of the access list on the bridge group.

Default

Disabled

Command Mode

Interface configuration

Usage Guidelines

This command first appeared in Cisco IOS Release 10.0.

Autonomous bridging must be disabled to use this command.

SNAP frames must also pass any applicable Ethernet type-code access list. This access list is applied just before sending out a frame to an interface.

For performance reasons, specify both input and output type code filtering on the same interface.

Access lists for Ethernet- and IEEE 802-encapsulated packets affect only bridging functions. It is not possible to use such access lists to block frames with protocols that are being routed.

Packets bearing an 802.2 LSAP of 0xAAAA qualify for LSAP filtering since they are inherently in 802.3 format. However, because they also carry a Type field, they are matched against any Type filters. Therefore, if you use LSAP filters on an interface that may bear SNAP encapsulated packets, you must explicitly permit 0xAAAA.

Example

The following example specifies access list 204 on Ethernet interface 0:

```
interface ethernet 0
  bridge-group 4 output-lsap-list 204
```

Related Commands

access-list (extended)
access-list (standard)
bridge-group
bridge-group input-lsap-list

BRIDGE-GROUP OUTPUT-PATTERN-LIST

Use the **bridge-group output-pattern-list** interface configuration command to associate an extended access list with a particular interface. Use the **no** form of this command to disable this capability.

> **bridge-group** *bridge-group* **output-pattern-list** *access-list-number*
> **no bridge-group** *bridge-group* **output-pattern-list** *access-list-number*

Syntax	Description
bridge-group	Number of the bridge group to which the interface belongs. It must be a number in the range 1 to 63.
access-list-number	Extended access list number you assigned using the extended **access-list** command. Specify a zero (0) to disable the application of the access list on the interface.

Default

Disabled

Command Mode

Interface configuration

Usage Guidelines

This command first appeared in Cisco IOS Release 10.0.

Autonomous bridging must be disabled to use this command.

Example

The following example filters all packets sent by bridge group 3 using the filter defined in access-list 1102:

```
interface ethernet 0
  bridge-group 3 output-pattern-list 1102
```

Related Commands

access-list (extended)
bridge-group
bridge-group input-pattern-list

BRIDGE-GROUP OUTPUT-TYPE-LIST

Use the **bridge-group output-type-list** interface configuration command to filter Ethernet- and SNAP-encapsulated packets on output. Use the **no** form of this command to disable this capability.

bridge-group *bridge-group* **output-type-list** *access-list-number*
no bridge-group *bridge-group* **output-type-list** *access-list-number*

Syntax	Description
bridge-group	Number of the bridge group to which the interface belongs. It must be a number in the range 1 to 63.
access-list-number	Access list number you assigned with the standard **access-list** command. Specify a zero (0) to disable the application of the access list on the bridge group. This access list is applied just before sending out a frame to an interface.

Default

Disabled

Command Mode

Interface configuration

Usage Guidelines

This command first appeared in Cisco IOS Release 10.0.

Autonomous bridging must be disabled to use this command.

Example

The following example specifies access-list 202 on Ethernet interface 0:

```
interface ethernet 0
 bridge-group 2 output-type-list 202
```

Related Commands

access-list (extended)
access-list (standard)
bridge-group
bridge-group input-type-list

BRIDGE-GROUP PATH-COST

Use the **bridge-group path-cost** interface configuration command to set a different path cost. Use the **no** form of this command to choose the default path cost for the interface.

bridge-group *bridge-group* **path-cost** *cost*
no bridge-group *bridge-group* **path-cost** *cost*

Syntax	Description
bridge-group	Number of the bridge group to which the interface belongs. It must be a number in the range 1 to 63.
cost	Path cost can range from 1 to 65535, with higher values indicating higher costs. This range applies regardless of whether the IEEE or Digital Spanning-Tree Protocol has been specified.

Defaults

The default path cost is computed from the interface's bandwidth setting. The following are IEEE default path cost values. The Digital path cost default values are different.

Ethernet—100
16-Mb Token Ring—62
FDDI—10
HSSI—647
MCI/SCI Serial—647

Command Mode

Interface configuration

Usage Guidelines

This command first appeared in Cisco IOS Release 10.0.

By convention, the path cost is 10000/data rate of the attached LAN (IEEE), or 100000/data rate of the attached LAN (Digital), in megabits per second.

Example

The following example changes the default path cost for Ethernet interface 0:

```
interface ethernet 0
  bridge-group 1 path-cost 250
```

Related Commands

bridge-group

BRIDGE-GROUP PRIORITY

Use the **bridge-group priority** interface configuration command to set an interface priority when two bridges tie for position as the root bridge. The priority you set breaks the tie.

bridge-group *bridge-group* **priority** *number*

Syntax	Description
bridge-group	Number of the bridge group to which the interface belongs. It must be a number in the range 1 to 63.
number	Priority number ranging from 0 to 255 (Digital), or 0 to 64000 (IEEE).

Defaults

When the IEEE Spanning-Tree Protocol is enabled on the router: 32768

When the Digital Spanning-Tree Protocol is enabled on the router: 128

Command Mode

Interface configuration

Usage Guidelines

This command first appeared in Cisco IOS Release 10.0.

The lower the number, the more likely it is that the bridge on the interface will be chosen as the root.

Example

The following example increases the likelihood that the root bridge will be the one on Ethernet interface 0 in bridge group 1:

```
interface ethernet 0
  bridge-group 1 priority 0
```

Related Commands

bridge-group
bridge priority

BRIDGE-GROUP SPANNING-DISABLED

Use the **bridge-group spanning-disabled** interface configuration command to disable the spanning tree on a given interface.

> **bridge-group** *bridge-group* **spanning-disabled**
> **no bridge-group** *bridge-group* **spanning-disabled**

Syntax	Description
bridge-group	Number of the bridge group to which the interface belongs. It must be a number in the range 1 to 63.

Default

Spanning tree enabled

Command Mode

Interface configuration

Usage Guidelines

This command first appeared in Cisco IOS Release 10.0.

To enable transparent bridging on an interface, use the **bridge protocol** command to specify the type of Spanning-Tree Protocol to be used. The **bridge-group spanning-disabled** command can be used to disable that spanning tree on that interface.

When a *loop-free* path exists between any two bridged subnetworks, you can prevent BPDUs generated in one transparent bridging subnetwork from impacting nodes in the other transparent bridging subnetwork, yet still permit bridging throughout the bridged network as a whole.

For example, when transparently bridged LAN subnetworks are separated by a WAN, you can use this command to prevent BPDUs from traveling across the WAN link. You would apply this command to the serial interfaces connecting to the WAN in order to prevent BPDUs generated in one domain from impacting nodes in the remote domain. Because these BPDUs are prevented from traveling across the WAN link, using this command also has the secondary advantage of reducing traffic across the WAN link.

NOTES

In order to disable the spanning tree, you must make sure that no parallel paths exist between transparently bridged interfaces in the network.

Example

In the following example, the spanning tree for the serial interface 0 is disabled:

```
interface serial 0
 bridge-group 1 spanning-disabled
```

Related Commands

bridge-group
bridge protocol

BRIDGE-GROUP SSE

Use the **bridge-group sse** interface configuration command to enable Cisco's silicon switching engine (SSE) switching function. Use the **no** form of this command to disable SSE switching.

> **bridge-group** *bridge-group* **sse**
> **no bridge-group** *bridge-group* **sse**

Syntax	Description
bridge-group	Number of the bridge group to which the interface belongs. It must be a number in the range 1 to 63.

Default
Disabled

Command Mode
Interface configuration

Usage Guidelines
This command first appeared in Cisco IOS Release 10.3.

Example
The following example enables SSE switching:

```
bridge-group 1 sse
```

Related Commands
source-bridge

BRIDGE HELLO-TIME

Use the **bridge hello-time** global configuration command to specify the interval between hello bridge protocol data units (BPDUs). Use the **no** form of this command to return the default interval.

    bridge *bridge-group* **hello-time** *seconds*
    no bridge *bridge-group* **hello-time**

Syntax	Description
bridge-group	Bridge group number. It must be the same number specified in the **bridge protocol** command.
seconds	Interval between 1 and 10 seconds.

Default
1 second

Command Mode
Global configuration

Usage Guidelines

This command first appeared in Cisco IOS Release 10.0.

Each bridge in a spanning tree adopts the **hello-time, forward-time,** and **max-age** parameters of the root bridge, regardless of what its individual configuration might be.

Example

The following example sets the interval to 5 seconds:

```
bridge 1 hello-time 5
```

Related Commands

bridge forward-time
bridge max-age
bridge protocol

BRIDGE IRB

Use the **bridge irb** global configuration command to enable the Cisco IOS software to route a given protocol between routed interfaces and bridge groups or to route a given protocol between bridge groups. Use the **no** form of this command to disable the feature.

> **bridge irb**
> **no bridge irb**

Syntax   Description

This command has no arguments or keywords.

Default

Integrated routing and bridging (IRB) is disabled.

Command Mode

Global configuration

Usage Guidelines

This command first appeared in Cisco IOS Release 10.0.

IRB is supported for transparent bridging, but not for source-route bridging. IRB is supported on all interface media types except X.25 and ISDN bridged interfaces.

Example

The following example command enables integrated routing and bridging:

```
bridge irb
```

Related Commands

bridge bridge
bridge route
interface bvi
show interfaces irb

BRIDGE LAT-SERVICE-FILTERING

Use the **bridge lat-service-filtering** global configuration command to specify LAT group-code filtering. Use the **no** form of this command to disable the use of LAT service filtering on the bridge group.

> **bridge** *bridge-group* **lat-service-filtering**
> **no bridge** *bridge-group* **lat-service-filtering**

Syntax	*Description*
bridge-group	Bridge group number specified in the **bridge protocol** command.

Default

LAT service filtering is disabled.

Command Mode

Global configuration

Usage Guidelines

This command first appeared in Cisco IOS Release 10.0.

This command informs the system that LAT service advertisements require special processing.

Example

The following example specifies that LAT service announcements traveling across bridge group 1 require some special processing:

```
bridge 1 lat-service-filtering
```

Related Commands

bridge protocol

BRIDGE MAX-AGE

Use the **bridge max-age** global configuration command to change the interval the bridge will wait to hear BPDUs from the root bridge. If a bridge does not hear BPDUs from the root bridge within this specified interval, it assumes that the network has changed and will recompute the spanning-tree topology. Use the **no** form of this command to return the default interval.

bridge *bridge-group* **max-age** *seconds*
no bridge *bridge-group* **max-age**

Syntax	Description
bridge-group	Bridge group number specified in the **bridge protocol** command.
seconds	Interval the bridge will wait to hear BPDUs from the root bridge. It must be a value in the range 10 to 200 seconds.

Default

15 seconds

Command Mode

Global configuration

Usage Guidelines

This command first appeared in Cisco IOS Release 10.0.

Each bridge in a spanning tree adopts the **hello-time, forward-time**, and **max-age** parameters of the root bridge, regardless of what its individual configuration might be.

Example

The following example increases the maximum idle interval to 20 seconds:

```
bridge 1 max-age 20
```

Related Commands

bridge forward-time
bridge hello-time
bridge protocol

BRIDGE MULTICAST-SOURCE

Use the **bridge multicast-source** global configuration command to configure bridging support to allow the forwarding, but not the learning, of frames received with multicast source addresses. Use the **no** form of this command to disable this function on the bridge.

bridge *bridge-group* **multicast-source**
no bridge *bridge-group* **multicast-source**

Syntax	Description
bridge-group	Bridge group number specified in the **bridge protocol** command.

Default

Disabled

Command Mode

Global configuration

Usage Guidelines

This command first appeared in Cisco IOS Release 10.0.

If you need to bridge Token Ring over other medium, RSRB is recommended.

Example

The following example allows the forwarding, but not the learning, of frames received with multi-cast source addresses:

```
bridge 2 multicast-source
```

Related Commands

bridge protocol

BRIDGE PRIORITY

Use the **bridge priority** global configuration command to configure the priority of an individual bridge, or the likelihood that it will be selected as the root bridge.

    bridge *bridge-group* **priority** *number*

Syntax	*Description*
bridge-group	Bridge group number specified in the **bridge protocol** command.
number	The lower the number, the more likely the bridge will be chosen as root. When the IEEE Spanning-Tree Protocol is enabled, *number* ranges from 0 to 65535 (default is 32768). When the Digital Spanning-Tree Protocol is enabled, *number* ranges from 0 to 255 (default is 128).

Defaults

When the IEEE Spanning-Tree Protocol is enabled on the router: 32768

When the Digital Spanning-Tree Protocol is enabled on the router: 128

Command Mode

Global configuration

Usage Guidelines

This command first appeared in Cisco IOS Release 10.0.

When two bridges tie for position as the root bridge, an interface priority determines which bridge will serve as the root bridge. Use the **bridge-group priority** interface configuration command to control an interface priority.

Example

The following example establishes this bridge as a likely candidate to be the root bridge:

```
bridge 1 priority 100
```

Related Commands

bridge-group priority
bridge protocol

BRIDGE PROTOCOL

Use the **bridge protocol** global configuration command to define the type of Spanning-Tree Protocol. Use the **no** form of this command, with the appropriate keywords and arguments, to delete the bridge group.

> **bridge** *bridge-group* **protocol** {ieee | dec}
> **no bridge** *bridge-group* **protocol** {ieee | dec}

Syntax	Description
bridge-group	Number in the range 1 to 63 that you choose to refer to a particular set of bridged interfaces. Frames are bridged only among interfaces in the same group. You will use the group number you assign in subsequent bridge configuration commands.
ieee	IEEE Ethernet Spanning-Tree Protocol.
dec	Digital Spanning-Tree Protocol.

Default

No Spanning-Tree Protocol is defined.

Command Mode

Global configuration

Usage Guidelines

This command first appeared in Cisco IOS Release 10.0.

The routers support two Spanning-Tree Protocols: the IEEE 802.1 standard and the earlier Digital Spanning-Tree Protocol upon which the IEEE standard is based. Multiple domains are supported for the IEEE 802.1 Spanning-Tree Protocol.

NOTES

The IEEE 802.1D Spanning-Tree Protocol is the preferred way of running the bridge. Use the Digital Spanning-Tree Protocol only for backward compatibility.

Example
The following example shows bridge 1 as using the Digital Spanning-Tree Protocol:

```
bridge 1 protocol dec
```

Related Commands
bridge domain
bridge-group

BRIDGE ROUTE

Use the **bridge route** global configuration command to enable the routing of a specified protocol in a specified bridge group. Use the **no** form of this command to disable the routing of a specified protocol in a specified bridge group.

> **bridge** *bridge-group* **route** *protocol*
> **no bridge** *bridge-group* **route** *protocol*

Syntax	Description
bridge-group	Bridge-group number. It must be the same number specified in the **bridge protocol** command.
protocol	One of the following protocols: **apollo, appletalk, clns, decnet, ip, ipx, vines, xns.**

Default
No default bridge group or protocol is specified.

Command Mode
Global configuration

Usage Guidelines
This command first appeared in Cisco IOS Release 10.3.

Example

In the following example, AppleTalk and IP are routed on bridge group 1:

```
bridge crb
bridge 1 protocol ieee
bridge 1 route appletalk
bridge 1 route ip
```

Related Commands

bridge crb
bridge protocol

CLEAR BRIDGE

Use the **clear bridge** privileged EXEC command to remove any learned entries from the forwarding database and to clear the transmit and receive counts for any statically or system-configured entries.

> **clear bridge** *bridge-group*

Syntax	*Description*
bridge-group	Bridge group number specified in the **bridge protocol** command.

Command Mode

Privileged EXEC

Usage Guidelines

This command first appeared in Cisco IOS Release 10.0.

Example

The following example shows the use of the **clear bridge** command:

```
clear bridge 1
```

Related Commands

bridge address
bridge protocol

CLEAR BRIDGE MULTICAST

Use the **clear bridge multicast** EXEC command to clear transparent bridging multicast state information.

> **clear bridge** [*bridge-group*] **multicast** [**router-ports** | **groups** | **counts**] [*group-address*]
> [*interface-unit*] [**counts**]

Syntax	Description
bridge-group	(Optional) Bridge group number specified in the **bridge protocol** command.
router-ports	(Optional) Clear multicast router ports.
groups	(Optional) Clear multicast groups.
counts	(Optional) Clear RX and TX counts.
group-address	(Optional) Multicast IP address associated with a specific multicast group.
interface-unit	(Optional) Specific interface, such as Ethernet 0.

Command Mode

EXEC

Usage Guidelines

This command first appeared in Cisco IOS Release 11.2.

If you do not specify arguments or keywords as part of the command, the command clears router ports, group ports, and counts for all configured bridge groups.

Use the **show bridge multicast** command to list transparent bridging multicast state information, then use specific pieces of state information in the **clear bridge multicast** command.

Examples

The following example command clears router ports, group ports, and counts for bridge group 1:

```
clear bridge 1 multicast
```

The following example command clears the group and count information for the group identified as 235.145.145.223, interface Ethernet 0/3 for bridge group 1:

```
clear bridge 1 multicast groups 235.145.145.223 Ethernet0/3 counts
```

Related Commands

bridge cmf
show bridge multicast

CLEAR SSE

Use the **clear sse** privileged EXEC command to reinitialize the Silicon Switch Processor (SSP) on the Cisco 7000 series routers with RSP7000.

clear sse

Syntax   Description

This command has no arguments or keywords.

Default

Disabled

Command Mode

Privileged EXEC

Usage Guidelines

This command first appeared in Cisco IOS Release 10.3.

Example

The following example reinitializes the SSP:

```
clear sse
```

CLEAR VLAN STATISTICS

Use the **clear vlan statistics** privileged EXEC command to remove virtual LAN statistics from any statically or system-configured entries.

clear vlan statistics

Syntax   Description

This command has no arguments or keywords.

Command Mode

Privileged EXEC

Usage Guidelines

This command first appeared in Cisco IOS Release 11.2.

Example

The following example clears VLAN statistics:

```
clear vlan statistics
```

ENCAPSULATION ISL

Use the **encapsulation isl** subinterface configuration command to enable the Inter-Switch Link (ISL), a Cisco proprietary protocol for interconnecting multiple switches and maintaining VLAN information as traffic goes between switches.

encapsulation isl *domain*

Syntax	Description
domain	VLAN domain number.

Default

Disabled

Command Mode

Subinterface configuration

Usage Guidelines

This command first appeared in Cisco IOS Release 11.1.

ISL encapsulation adds a 30-byte header to the beginning of the Ethernet frame. The header contains a 2-byte VLAN identifier that maintains VLAN identities between switches.

Example

The following example enables ISL on FDDI subinterface 2/1.20:

```
interface FastEthernet 2/1.20.
 ip address 171.69.2.2 255.255.255.0
 encapsulation isl 400
 bridge-group 50
```

Related Commands

bridge-group
show bridge vlan
show interfaces
show span

ENCAPSULATION SDE

Use the **encapsulation sde** subinterface configuration command to enable IEEE 802.10 Secure Data Exchange (SDE) encapsulation of transparently bridged traffic on a specified interface within an assigned bridge group.

encapsulation sde *said*

Syntax	*Description*
said	Security association identifier. The valid range is 0 through 0xFFF.

Default

Disabled

Command Mode

Subinterface configuration

Usage Guidelines

This command first appeared in Cisco IOS Release 10.3.

SDE encapsulation is only applicable to transparently bridged traffic, and is configurable on the following interface types:

- Ethernet
- Nonencapsulated FDDI
- Token Ring (except MultiBus Token Ring)
- HDLC serial

--- **NOTES** --

The current implementation of SDE encapsulation is not recommended for serial or Ethernet media.

Example

The following example enables SDE on FDDI subinterface 2/0.1 and assigns a security association identifier of 9999:

```
interface fddi 2/0.1
 encapsulation sde 9999
```

Related Commands

bridge-group
show bridge vlan
show interfaces
show span

ETHERNET-TRANSIT-OUI

Use the **ethernet-transit-oui** interface configuration command to choose the Organizational Unique Identifier (OUI) code to be used in the encapsulation of Ethernet Type II frames across Token Ring backbone networks. Various versions of this OUI code are used by Ethernet/Token Ring transla-tional bridges. The default OUI form is **90-compatible**, which can be chosen with the **no** form of this command.

> **ethernet-transit-oui [90-compatible | standard | cisco]**
> **no ethernet-transit-oui**

Syntax	Description
90-compatible	(Optional) Default OUI form.
standard	(Optional) Standard OUI form.
cisco	(Optional) Cisco's OUI form.

Default

90-compatible

Command Mode

Interface configuration

Usage Guidelines

This command first appeared in Cisco IOS Release 10.0.

This command replaces and extends the **bridge old-oui** command in Software Release 9.0.

The actual OUI codes that are used, when they are used, and how they compare to Software Release 9.0-equivalent commands is shown in Table 2–1.

Table 2–1 *Bridge OUI Codes*

Keyword	OUI Used	When Used/Benefits	9.0 Command Equivalent
90-compatible	0000F8	By default, when talking to other Cisco routers. Provides the most flexibility.	no bridge old-oui
cisco	00000C	Provided for compatibility with future equipment.	None
standard	000000	When talking to IBM 8209 bridges and other vendor equipment. Does not provide for as much flexibility as the other two choices.	bridge old-oui

Do not use the keyword **standard** unless you are forced to interoperate with other vendor equip-ment, such as the IBM 8209, in providing Ethernet and Token Ring mixed media bridged connec-tivity. The use of the **standard** OUI of 000000 in the encapsulation of Ethernet Type II frames creates encapsulated frames on Token Rings that have formats identical to SNAP-encapsulated frames. The router receiving such a frame on a Token Ring for delivery on the Ethernet cannot distinguish between the two, and therefore must make an arbitrary choice between presenting the frame on the Ethernet as a SNAP-encapsulated frame or as an Ethernet Type II frame. The choice has been made to present all such frames as Ethernet Type II. Therefore, it is impossible to use the **standard** keyword if you wish to bridge SNAP-encapsulated frames between Token Rings and Ethernets. Using either the **cisco** or **90-compatible** keywords does not present such a restriction, because SNAP frames and Ethernet Type II-encapsulated frames have different OUI codes on Token Ring networks.

─◀ **NOTES** ▶──

Prior to IOS Software Release 11.1, the default OUI for SNAP on Token Ring for high-end routers was hexadecimal 000F8. and for low-end routers was hexadecimal 00000. If you combine IOS Software Release 11.1 or later with any earlier high-end release on adjacent routers that are bridging over a Token Ring, you must use the **ethernet-transit-oui standard** command to bring the two software versions into agreement.

Example

The following example specifies Cisco's OUI form:

```
interface tokenring 0
 ethernet-transit-oui cisco
```

Related Commands

bridge-group
bridge protocol

FRAME-RELAY MAP BRIDGE BROADCAST

Use the **frame-relay map bridge broadcast** interface configuration command to bridge over a Frame Relay network. Use the **no** form of this command to delete the mapping entry.

> **frame-relay map bridge** *dlci* **broadcast**
> **no frame-relay map bridge** *dlci*

Syntax	Description
dlci	DLCI number. The valid range is 16 to 1007.

Default

No mapping entry is established.

Command Mode

Interface configuration

Usage Guidelines

This command first appeared in Cisco IOS Release 10.0.

Bridging over a Frame Relay network is supported both on networks that support a multicast facility and those that do not.

Example

The following example allows bridging over a Frame Relay network:

```
frame-relay map bridge 144 broadcast
```

Related Commands

encapsulation frame-relay

INTERFACE BVI

Use the **interface bvi** interface configuration command to create the bridge-group virtual interface (BVI) that represents the specified bridge group to the routed world and links the corresponding bridge group to the other routed interfaces. Use the **no** form of this command to delete the BVI.

> **interface bvi** *bridge-group*
> **no interface bvi** *bridge-group*

Syntax	Description
bridge-group	Bridge-group number. It must be the same number specified in the **bridge protocol** command.

Default

No BVI is created.

Command Mode

Interface configuration

Usage Guidelines

This command first appeared in Cisco IOS Release 11.2.

You must enable IRB before attempting to create a BVI.

When you intend to bridge and route a given protocol in the same bridge group, you must configure the network-layer attributes of the protocol on the BVI. Do not configure protocol attributes on the bridged interfaces. No bridging attributes can be configured on the BVI.

Example

The following example creates a bridge-group virtual interface and associates it with bridge group 1:

```
interface bvi 1
```

Related Commands

bridge irb

IP ROUTING

Use the **ip routing** command to enable IP routing. Use the **no** form of this command to disable IP routing so that you can then bridge IP.

> **ip routing**
> **no ip routing**

Syntax   Description

This command has no arguments or keywords.

Default

IP routing is enabled.

Command Mode

Global configuration

Usage Guidelines

This command first appeared in Cisco IOS Release 10.0.

All protocols except IP are bridged by a router unless their routing is explicitly enabled.

Also note that bridging and routing are done on a per-system basis. If a protocol is being routed, it must be routed on all interfaces that are handling that protocol. This is similar for bridging. You cannot route IP on one interface and bridge it on another interface.

Assign the *same* IP address to all network interfaces to manage the system with Telnet, TFTP, SNMP, ICMP (ping), and so forth. Once bridging is enabled, all IP and ARP frames are forwarded or flooded by the router according to standard bridging and spanning-tree rules. IP routing processes such as IGRP or RIP must not be running.

Example

The following example disables IP routing:

```
no ip routing
```

SHOW BRIDGE

Use the **show bridge** privileged EXEC command to view classes of entries in the bridge forwarding database.

> **show bridge** [*bridge-group*] [*interface*] [*address* [*mask*]] [**verbose**]

Syntax	Description
bridge-group	(Optional) Number that specifies a particular spanning tree.
interface	(Optional) Specific interface, such as Ethernet 0.
address	(Optional) 48-bit canonical (Ethernet ordered) MAC address. This may be entered with an optional mask of bits to be ignored in the address, which is specified with the *mask* argument.
mask	(Optional) Bits to be ignored in the address. You must specify the *address* argument if you want to specify a mask.
verbose	(Optional) Shows additional detail, including any Frame Relay DLCI associated with a station address.

Command Mode

Privileged EXEC

Usage Guidelines

This command first appeared in Cisco IOS Release 10.0. The **verbose** keyword first appeared in Cisco IOS Release 11.0.

The following are possible variations of the **show bridge** command:

```
show bridge ethernet 0
show bridge 0000.0c00.0000   0000.00FF.FFFF
show bridge 0000.0c00.0e1a
show bridge
show bridge verbose
```

In the sample output, the first command would display all entries for hosts reachable via Ethernet interface 0, the second command would display all entries with the vendor code of 0000.0c00.0000, and the third command would display the entry for address 0000.0c00.0e1a. In the fourth command, all entries in the forwarding database would be displayed. The fifth command provides additional detail. In all five lines, the bridge-group number has been omitted.

Sample Displays

The following is sample output of the **show bridge** command. The second display is output from the **show bridge** command with the **verbose** argument.

```
Router# show bridge

Total of 300 station blocks, 280 free
Codes: P - permanent, S - self

Bridge Group 32:Bridge Group 32:

    Address       Action   Interface    Age  RX count  TX count
  0180.c200.0000  receive      -          S      0         0
  ffff.ffff.ffff  receive      -          S      0         0
  0900.2b01.0001  receive      -          S      0         0
  0300.0c00.0001  receive      -          S      0         0
  0000.0c05.1000  forward  Ethernet0/1    4      1         0
  0000.0c04.4b5b  receive      -          S      0         0
  0000.0c04.4b5e  receive      -          S      0         0
  0000.0c04.4b5d  receive      -          S      0         0
  0000.0c04.4b5c  receive      -          S      0         0
  0000.0c05.4a62  forward  Ethernet0/1    4      1         0
  aa00.0400.2108  forward  Ethernet0/1    0     42         0
  0000.0c12.b888  forward  Ethernet0/2    4      1         0
  0000.0c12.b886  forward  Ethernet0/1    4      1         0
  aa00.0400.4d09  forward  Ethernet0/1    4      1         0
  0000.0c06.fb9a  forward  Ethernet0/1    4      1         0
  0000.0c04.b039  forward  Ethernet0/1    4      1         0

router# show bridge verbose

Total of 300 station blocks, 287 free
Codes: P - permanent, S - self

BG Hash     Address    Action  Interface    DLCI  Age RX count   TX count
32 00/0  0180.c200.0000 receive     -         -    S      0          0
32 00/1  ffff.ffff.ffff receive     -         -    S      0          0
32 01/0  0900.2b01.0001 receive     -         -    S      0          0
32 01/1  0300.0c00.0001 receive     -         -    S      0          0
32 10/0  0000.0c04.4b5b receive     -         -    S      0          0
32 15/0  0000.0c04.4b5e receive     -         -    S      0          0
32 16/0  0000.0c04.4b5d receive     -         -    S      0          0
32 17/0  0000.0c04.4b5c receive     -         -    S      0          0
32 29/0  aa00.0400.2108 forward Ethernet0/1   -    0     48          0
32 30/0  0000.0c12.b888 forward Ethernet0/2   -    0      1          0
32 A4/0  0800.2002.ff5b forward Ethernet0/1   -    0      6          0
32 E2/0  aa00.0400.e90b forward Ethernet0/1   -    0     65          0
32 F2/0  0000.0c04.b042 forward Ethernet0/2   -    3      2          0
```

Table 2–2 describes significant fields shown in the display.

Table 2–2 *Show Bridge Field Descriptions*

Field	Description
Total of 300 station blocks	Total number of forwarding database elements in the system. The memory to hold bridge entries is allocated in blocks of memory sufficient to hold 300 individual entries. When the number of free entries falls below 25, another block of memory sufficient to hold another 300 entries is allocated. Therefore, the size of the bridge forwarding database is limited to the amount of free memory in the router.
295 free	Number in the free list of forwarding database elements in the system. The total number of forwarding elements is expanded dynamically, as needed.
BG	Bridging group to which the address belongs.
Hash	Hash key/relative position in the keyed list.
Address	Canonical (Ethernet ordered) MAC address.
Action	Action to be taken when that address is looked up; choices are to discard or forward the datagram.
Interface	Interface, if any, on which that address was seen.
Age	Number of minutes since a frame was received from or sent to that address. The letter "P" indicates a permanent entry. The letter "S" indicates the system as recorded by the router. On the modular systems, this is typically the broadcast address and the router's own hardware address; on the IGS, this field will also include certain multicast addresses.
RX count	Number of frames received from that address.
TX count	Number of frames forwarded to that address.

SHOW BRIDGE CIRCUIT-GROUP

Use the **show bridge circuit-group** EXEC command to display the interfaces configured in each circuit group and show whether they are currently participating in load distribution.

> **show bridge** [*bridge-group*] **circuit-group** [*circuit-group*] [*src-mac-address*]
> [*dst-mac-address*]

Syntax	Description
bridge-group	(Optional) Number that specifies a particular bridge group.
circuit-group	(Optional) Number that specifies a particular circuit group.
src-mac-address	(Optional) 48-bit canonical (Ethernet ordered) source MAC address.
dst-mac-address	(Optional) 48-bit canonical (Ethernet ordered) destination MAC address.

Command Mode

EXEC

Usage Guidelines

This command first appeared in Cisco IOS Release 10.3.

Sample Display

The following is sample output of various **show bridge circuit-group** command strings:

```
RouterA> show bridge circuit-group

Bridge group 1 Circuit group 1:
    Interface Serial0 : inserted, learning, forwarding
    Interface Serial3 : inserted, learning, forwarding
Bridge group 1 Circuit group 2:
    Interface Serial2 : inserted, learning, forwarding

RouterA> show bridge 1 circuit-group 1

Bridge group 1 Circuit group 1:
    Interface Serial0 : inserted, learning, forwarding
    Interface Serial3 : inserted, learning, forwarding

RouterA> show bridge 1 circuit-group 2

Bridge group 1 Circuit group 2:
    Interface Serial2 : inserted, learning, forwarding

RouterA> show bridge 1 circuit-group 1 0000.6502.23EA 0000.1234.4567

Output circuit group interface is Serial3
```

```
RouterA> show bridge 1 circuit-group 1 0000.6502.23EA

%Destination MAC address required

RouterB> show bridge 1 circuit-group 1

Bridge group 1 Circuit group 1:
    Transmission pause interval is 250ms
    Output interface selection is source-based
    Interface Serial0 : inserted, learning, forwarding
    Interface Serial3 : inserted, learning, forwarding
    Interface Serial2 is unavailable

RouterB> show bridge 1 circuit-group 1 0000.6502.23EA 0000.1234.4567

%Please enter source MAC address only
```

Table 2–3 describes significant fields shown in the display.

Table 2–3 *Show Bridge Circuit-Group Field Descriptions*

Field	Description
inserted/not inserted	Indicates whether interface is included or not included in circuit-group operation. If the interface is administratively down, or if line protocol is not up, the interface is not included in the circuit-group operation.
learning/not learning	Indicates whether this interface is in Spanning-Tree Protocol (IEEE or Digital) learning or not learning state.
forwarding/not forwarding	Indicates whether this port is in Spanning-Tree Protocol (IEEE or Digital) forwarding or not forwarding state.

SHOW BRIDGE GROUP

Use the **show bridge group** privileged EXEC command to display the status of each bridge group.

show bridge group [verbose]

Syntax	*Description*
verbose	(Optional) Displays detailed information.

Command Mode

Privileged EXEC

Usage Guidelines

This command first appeared in Cisco IOS Release 10.3.

Sample Display

```
Router# show bridge group

Bridge Group 32 is running the IEEE compatible Spanning-Tree Protocol

    Port 43 (Ethernet0/1) of bridge group 32 is forwarding
    Port 44 (Ethernet0/2) of bridge group 32 is forwarding
    Port 45 (Ethernet0/3) of bridge group 32 is forwarding
    Port 62 (Fddi2/0.1) of bridge group 32 is forwarding
    Port 57 (Serial3/4) of bridge group 32 is down
```

"Forwarding" and "down" indicate the port state as determined by the spanning-tree algorithm or via configuration.

SHOW BRIDGE MULTICAST

Use the **show bridge multicast** EXEC command to display transparent bridging multicast state information.

show **bridge** [*bridge-group*] **multicast** [**router-ports** | **groups**] [*group-address*]

Syntax	Description
bridge-group	(Optional) Bridge group number specified in the **bridge protocol** command.
router-ports	(Optional) Display information for multicast router ports.
groups	(Optional) Display information for multicast groups.
group-address	(Optional) Multicast IP address associated with a specific multicast group.

Command Mode

EXEC

Usage Guidelines

This command first appeared in Cisco IOS Release 11.2.

Sample Display

The following is sample output for the **show bridge multicast** command:

```
Router# show bridge multicast

 Multicast router ports for bridge group 1:

  2 multicast router ports
   Fddi2/0          R
   Ethernet0/4      R
```

```
Multicast groups for bridge group 1:

235.145.145.223            RX count    TX count
  Fddi2/0          R              0           2
  Ethernet0/4      R              0           3
  Ethernet0/3      G              1           0

235.5.5.5                  RX count    TX count
  Fddi2/0          R              0           2
  Ethernet0/4      R              0           3
  Ethernet0/3      G              1           0

235.4.4.4                  RX count    TX count
  Fddi2/0          R              0           2
  Ethernet0/4      R              0           3
  Ethernet0/3      G              1           0

Router#
```

Table 2–4 describes significant fields shown in the display.

Table 2–4 *Show Bridge Multicast Field Descriptions*

Field	Description
Multicast router ports for…	List of the multicast router ports by bridge group. Within the bridge group cluster, the display lists the number of multicast router ports and then lists the ports by interface.
Multicast groups for…	List of the multicast groups by bridge group. Within each multicast group, identified by a unique address, the display lists each port by interface name and indicates whether that port is a group member ("G"), a multicast router port ("R"), or both. The RX and TX counts show the number of multicast packets that have constrained to the multicast group by the bridge.

SHOW BRIDGE VLAN

Use the **show bridge vlan** privileged EXEC command to view virtual LAN subinterfaces.

show bridge vlan

Syntax   Description

This command has no arguments or keywords.

Command Mode

Privileged EXEC

Usage Guidelines

This command first appeared in Cisco IOS Release 10.3.

Sample Display

The following is sample output from the **show bridge vlan** command:

```
Router# show bridge vlan

Bridge Group: 50

Virtual LAN Trunking Interface(s):  vLAN Protocol:     vLAN ID:  State

Fddi2/0.1000                        IEEE 802.10        1000      forwarding
FastEthernet4/0.500                 Inter Switch Link  500       listening

Virtual LAN Native Interface(s):    State

Ethernet0/1                         forwarding
Serial1/1                           down
```

Table 2–5 describes the fields shown in the display.

Table 2–5   *Show Bridge VLAN Field Description*

Field	Description
Bridge Group	Bridge group to which these interfaces belong.
Virtual LAN Trunking Interface(s)	VLAN interface.
vLAN Protocol)	IEEE 802.10 or Cisco ISL encapsulation.
vLAN ID	VLAN identifier that maintains VLAN identities between switches.
State	Spanning-tree port state of the interface.
Virtual LAN Native Interface(s):	Interfaces whose transparently bridged traffic will be propagated only to other LAN segments within the same virtual LAN.

SHOW INTERFACES CRB

Use the **show interfaces crb** privileged EXEC command to display the configuration for each interface that has been configured for routing or bridging.

show interfaces crb

Syntax   Description

This command has no arguments or keywords.

Command Mode

Privileged EXEC

Usage Guidelines

This command first appeared in Cisco IOS Release 11.0.

Sample Display

The following is sample output for the **show interfaces crb** command:

```
Router# show interfaces crb

Ethernet0/0

Routed protocols on Ethernet0/0:
appletalk decnet ip novell

Ethernet0/1

Routed protocols on Ethernet0/1:
appletalk  decnet  ip  novell

Ethernet0/2

Routed protocols on Ethernet0/2:
appletalk  ip

Bridged protocols on Ethernet0/2:
clns  decnet  vines  apollo
novell  xns

Software MAC address filter on Ethernet0/2
Hash Len   Address          Matches  Act   Type
0x00: 0    ffff.ffff.ffff   0        RCV   Physical broadcast
0x00: 1    ffff.ffff.ffff   0        RCV   Appletalk zone
0x2A: 0    0900.2b01.0001   0        RCV   DEC spanning tree
0x49: 0    0000.0c36.7a45   0        RCV   Interface MAC address
0xc0: 0    0100.0ccc.cccc   20       RCV   CDP
0xc2: 0    0180.c200.0000   0        RCV   IEEE spanning tree
0xF8: 0    0900.07ff.ffff   0        RCV   Appletalk broadcast

Ethernet0/3

Routed protocols on Ethernet0/3:
appletalk  ip
```

```
Bridged protocols on Ethernet0/3:
clns  decnet  vines  apollo
novell  xns

Software MAC address filter on Ethernet0/3
Hash Len  Address          Matches  Act  Type
0x00: 0   ffff.ffff.ffff   0        RCV  Physical broadcast
0x00: 1   ffff.ffff.ffff   0        RCV  Appletalk zone
0x2A: 0   0900.2b01.0001   0        RCV  DEC spanning tree
0x49: 0   0000.0c36.7a45   0        RCV  Interface MAC address
0xc0: 0   0100.0ccc.cccc   48       RCV  CDP
0xc2: 0   0180.c200.0000   0        RCV  IEEE spanning tree
0xF8: 0   0900.07ff.ffff   0        RCV  Appletalk broadcast

Router#
```

Table 2–6 describes significant fields shown in the display.

Table 2–6   *Show Interfaces CRB Field Descriptions*

Field	Description
Routed protocols on…	List of the routed protocols configured for the specified interface.
Bridged protocols on…	List of the bridged protocols configured for the specified interface.
Software MAC address filter on…	Table of software MAC address filter information for the specified interface.
Hash	Hash key/relative position in the keyed list for this MAC-address entry.
Len	Length of this entry to the beginning element of this hash chain.
Address	Canonical (Ethernet ordered) MAC address.
Matches	Number of received packets matched to this MAC address.
Act	Action to be taken when that address is looked up; choices are to receive or discard the packet.
Type	MAC address type.

SHOW INTERFACES IRB

Use the **show interfaces irb** privileged EXEC command to display the configuration for each interface that has been configured for integrated routing or bridging.

 show interfaces [*interface*] **irb**

Syntax	Description
interface	(Optional) Specific interface, such as Ethernet 0.

Command Mode

Privileged EXEC

Usage Guidelines

This command first appeared in Cisco IOS Release 11.2.

Sample Display

The following is sample output for the **show interfaces irb** command:

```
Router# show interfaces ethernet 2 irb

Ethernet 2

Routed protocols on Ethernet 2:
appletalk ip

Bridged protocols on Ethernet 2:
appletalk   clns    decnet    vines
apollo      ipx     xns

Software MAC address filter on Ethernet 2
Hash Len  Address         Matches  Act   Type
0x00: 0   ffff.ffff.ffff  4886     RCV   Physical broadcast
0x1F: 0   0060.3e2b.a221  7521     RCV   Appletalk zone
0x1F: 1   0060.3e2b.a221  0        RCV   Bridge-group Virtual Interface
0x2A: 0   0900.2b01.0001  0        RCV   DEC spanning tree
0x05: 0   0900.0700.00a2  0        RCV   Appletalk zone
0xC2: 0   0180.c200.0000  0        RCV   IEEE spanning tree
0xF8: 0   0900.07ff.ffff  2110     RCV   Appletalk broadcast
```

Table 2–7 describes significant fields shown in the display.

Table 2–7   *Show Interfaces IRB Field Descriptions*

Field	Description
Routed protocols on...	List of the routed protocols configured for the specified interface.

Table 2-7   *Show Interfaces IRB Field Descriptions, Continued*

Field	Description
Bridged protocols on...	List of the bridged protocols configured for the specified interface.
Software MAC address filter on...	Table of software MAC address filter information for the specified interface.
Hash	Hash key/relative position in the keyed list for this MAC-address entry.
Len	Length of this entry to the beginning element of this hash chain.
Address	Canonical (Ethernet ordered) MAC address.
Matches	Number of received packets matched to this MAC address.
Act	Action to be taken when that address is looked up; choices are to receive or discard the packet.
Type	MAC address type.

SHOW SPAN

Use the **show span** privileged EXEC command to display the spanning-tree topology known to the router. The display indicates whether LAT group code filtering is in effect.

>   **show span**

Syntax   Description

This command has no arguments or keywords.

Command Mode

Privileged EXEC

Usage Guidelines

This command first appeared in Cisco IOS Release 10.0.

Sample Display

The following is sample output for the **show span** command:

```
RouterA# show span

Bridge Group 1 is executing the IEEE compatible Spanning-Tree Protocol
  Bridge Identifier has priority 32768, address 0000.0c15.dba2
  Configured hello time 2, max age 20, forward delay 15
```

```
We are the root of the spanning tree
Topology change flag set, detected flag set
Times:  hold 1, topology change 30, notification 30
        hello 2, max age 20, forward delay 15, aging 300
Timers: hello 1, topology change 14, notification 0

Port 60 (Ethernet0/1.45) of bridge group 1 is forwarding
  Path cost 100, priority 128
  Designated root has priority 32768, address 0000.0c15.dba2
  Designated bridge has priority 32768, address 0000.0c15.dba2
  Designated port is 60, path cost 0
  Timers: message age 0, forward delay 0, hold 0

Port 62 (Ethernet0/2.82) of bridge group 1 is forwarding
  Path cost 100, priority 128
  Designated root has priority 32768, address 0000.0c15.dba2
  Designated bridge has priority 32768, address 0000.0c15.dba2
  Designated port is 62, path cost 0
  Timers: message age 0, forward delay 0, hold 0

Port 65 (Fddi2/0.15) of bridge group 1 is forwarding
  Path cost 10, priority 128
  Designated root has priority 32768, address 0000.0c15.dba2
  Designated bridge has priority 32768, address 0000.0c15.dba2
  Designated port is 65, path cost 0
  Timers: message age 0, forward delay 0, hold 0

Bridge Group 2 is executing the IEEE compatible Spanning-Tree Protocol
  Bridge Identifier has priority 32768, address 0000.0c15.dba4
  Configured hello time 2, max age 20, forward delay 15
  We are the root of the spanning tree
  Topology change flag not set, detected flag not set
  Times:  hold 1, topology change 30, notification 30
          hello 2, max age 20, forward delay 15, aging 300
  Timers: hello 1, topology change 0, notification 0

Port 63 (Ethernet0/3.13) of bridge group 2 is forwarding
  Path cost 100, priority 128
  Designated root has priority 32768, address 0000.0c15.dba4
  Designated bridge has priority 32768, address 0000.0c15.dba4
  Designated port is 63, path cost 0
  Timers: message age 0, forward delay 0, hold 0

Port 64 (Ethernet0/4.19) of bridge group 2 is forwarding
  Path cost 100, priority 128
  Designated root has priority 32768, address 0000.0c15.dba4
  Designated bridge has priority 32768, address 0000.0c15.dba4
  Designated port is 64, path cost 0
  Timers: message age 0, forward delay 0, hold 0
```

```
Port 66 (Fddi2/0.18) of bridge group 2 is forwarding
    Path cost 10, priority 128
    Designated root has priority 32768, address 0000.0c15.dba4
    Designated bridge has priority 32768, address 0000.0c15.dba4
    Designated port is 66, path cost 0
    Timers: message age 0, forward delay 0, hold 0
```

SHOW SSE SUMMARY

Use the **show sse summary** EXEC command to display a summary of Silicon Switch Processor (SSP) statistics:

> **show sse summary**

Syntax   Description

This command has no arguments or keywords.

Command Mode

EXEC

Usage Guidelines

This command first appeared in Cisco IOS Release 10.3.

Sample Display

The following is sample output from the **show sse summary** command:

```
Router# show sse summary

SSE utilization statistics

                 Program words  Rewrite bytes  Internal nodes  Depth
Overhead             499             1               8
IP                     0             0               0          0
IPX                    0             0               0          0
SRB                    0             0               0          0
CLNP                   0             0               0          0
IP access lists        0             0               0
Total used           499             1               8
Total free         65037        262143
Total available    65536        262144

Free program memory
 [499..65535]
Free rewrite memory
 [1..262143]
```

```
Internals
 75032 internal nodes allocated, 75024 freed
 SSE manager process enabled, microcode enabled, 0 hangs
 Longest cache computation 4ms, longest quantum 160ms at 0x53AC8
```

SHOW VLANS

Use the **show vlans** privileged EXEC command to view virtual LAN subinterfaces.

show vlans

Syntax   Description

This command has no arguments or keywords.

Command Mode

Privileged EXEC

Usage Guidelines

This command first appeared in Cisco IOS Release 11.0.

Sample Display

The following is sample output from the **show vlans** command:

```
RouterC7xxx# show vlans

Virtual LAN ID:300 (IEEE 802.10 Encapsulation)

   vLAN Trunk Interface: FDDI 1/1.10

   Protocols Configured:   Address:          Received:       Transmitted:
         IP                31.108.1.1        642             645

Virtual LAN ID:400 (ISL Encapsulation)

   vLAN Trunk Interface: FastEthernet 2/1.20

   Protocols Configured:   Address:          Received:       Transmitted:
         IP                171.69.2.2        123456          654321
         Bridge Group      50                5190            8234

Virtual LAN ID:500 (ISL Encapsulation)

   vLAN Trunk Interface: FastEthernet 2/1.30

   Protocols Configured:   Address:          Received:       Transmitted:
         IPX               1000              987654          456789

Virtual LAN ID:600 (ISL Encapsulation)
```

```
vLAN Trunk Interface: FastEthernet 2/1.30

Protocols Configured:    Address:        Received:       Transmitted:
       IP              198.92.3.3        8114            4508
       IPX             1001              2               3
       Bridge Group    50                8234            5190
```

Table 2–8 describes the fields shown in the display.

Table 2–8 *Show VLAN Field Description*

Field	Description
Virtual LAN ID	The domain number of the virtual LAN.
VLAN Trunk Interface	The subinterface that carries the VLAN traffic.
Protocols Configured	The protocols configured on the VLAN.
Address	The network address.
Received	Packets received.
Transmitted	Packets transmitted.

X25 MAP BRIDGE

Use the **x25 map bridge** interface configuration command to configure the bridging of packets in X.25 frames. Use the **no** form of this command to disable the Internet-to-X.121 mapping.

> **x25 map bridge** *x.121-address* **broadcast** [*options-keywords*]
> **no x25 map bridge**

Syntax

x.121-address

broadcast

options-keywords

Description

The X.121 address.

Required keyword for bridging over X.25.

(Optional) Additional functionality that can be specified for originated calls. Can be any of the options listed in Table 2–9.

Default

Disabled

Command Mode

Interface configuration

Usage Guidelines

This command first appeared in Cisco IOS Release 10.0.

The X.25 bridging software uses the same spanning-tree algorithm as the other bridging functions, but allows packets to be encapsulated in X.25 frames and transmitted across X.25 media. This command specifies IP-to-X.121 address mapping and maintains a table of both the Ethernet and X.121 addresses.

The X.25 bridging implementation supports the map options listed in Table 2–9.

Table 2–9 *X.25 Map Options*

Option	Description
compress	Specifies that X.25 payload compression be used for mapping the traffic to this host. Each virtual circuit established for compressed traffic uses a significant amount of memory (for a table of learned data patterns) and for computation (for compression and decompression of all data). Cisco recommends that compression be used with careful consideration to its impact on overall performance.
method {cisco | ietf | snap | multi}	Specifies the encapsulation method. The choices are as follows: • **cisco**—Cisco's proprietary encapsulation; not available if more than one protocol is to be carried. • **ietf**—Default RFC 1356 operation: protocol identification of single-protocol virtual circuits and protocol identification within multiprotocol virtual circuits uses the standard encoding, which is compatible with RFC 877. Multiprotocol virtual circuits are used only if needed. • **snap**—RFC 1356 operation where IP is identified with SNAP rather than the standard IETF method (the standard method is compatible with RFC 877). • **multi**—Forces a map that specifies a single protocol to set up a multiprotocol virtual circuit when a call is originated; also forces a single-protocol PVC to use multiprotocol data identification methods for all datagrams sent and received.
no-incoming	Use the map only to originate calls.
no-outgoing	Do not originate calls when using the map.
idle *minutes*	Specifies an idle timeout for calls other than the interface default; 0 minutes disables the idle timeout.

Table 2–9 *X.25 Map Options, Continued*

Option	Description
reverse	Specifies reverse charging for outgoing calls.
accept-reverse	Causes the Cisco IOS software to accept incoming reverse-charged calls. If this option is not present, the Cisco IOS software clears reverse-charged calls unless the interface accepts all reverse-charged calls.
broadcast	Causes the Cisco IOS software to direct any broadcasts sent through this interface to the specified X.121 address. This option also simplifies the configuration of OSPF; see "Usage Guidelines" for more detail.
cug *group-number*	Specifies a closed user group number (from 1 to 99) for the mapping in an outgoing call.
nvc *count*	Sets the maximum number of virtual circuits for this map or host. The default *count* is the **x25 nvc** setting of the interface. A maximum number of eight virtual circuits can be configured for each map. Compressed TCP may use only 1 virtual circuit.
packetsize *in-size out-size*	Proposes maximum input packet size (*in-size*) and maximum output packet size (*out-size*) for an outgoing call. Both values typically are the same and must be one of the following values: 16, 32, 64, 128, 256, 512, 1024, 2048, or 4096.
windowsize *in-size out-size*	Proposes the packet count for input window (*in-size*) and output window (*out-size*) for an outgoing call. Both values typically are the same, must be in the range 1 to 127, and must be less than the value set by the **x25 modulo** command.
throughput *in out*	Sets the requested throughput class values for input (*in*) and output (*out*) throughput across the network for an outgoing call. Values for *in* and *out* are in bits per second (bps) and range from 75 to 48000 bps.
transit-delay *milliseconds*	Specifies the transit delay value in milliseconds (0 to 65534) for an outgoing call, for networks that support transit delay.

Table 2–9 *X.25 Map Options, Continued*

Option	Description
nuid *username password*	Specifies that a network user ID (NUID) facility be sent in the outgoing call with the specified Terminal Access Controller Access Control System (TACACS) username and password (in a format defined by Cisco). This option should be used only when connecting to another Cisco router. The combined length of the username and password should not exceed 127 characters.
nudata *string*	Specifies the network user identification in a format determined by the network administrator (as allowed by the standards). This option is provided for connecting to non-Cisco equipment that requires an NUID facility. The string should not exceed 130 characters and must be enclosed in quotation marks (" ") if there are any spaces present.
rpoa *name*	Specifies the name defined by the **x25 roa** command for a list of transit Recognized Operating Agencies (ROAs) to use in outgoing Call Request packets.
passive	Specifies that the X.25 interface should send compressed outgoing TCP datagrams only if they were already compressed when they were received. This option is available only for compressed TCP maps.

Example

The following example allows bridging over an X.25 network:

```
x25 map bridge 31370054065 broadcast
```

Related Commands

x25 address
x25 map

CHAPTER 3

Configuring Source-Route Bridging

This chapter describes source-route bridging (SRB) configuration tasks. For a discussion of remote source-route bridging (RSRB) configuration tasks, see Chapter 5, "Configuring Remote Source-Route Bridging."

For a complete description of the commands mentioned in this chapter, see Chapter 4, "Source-Route Bridging Commands."

SRB CONFIGURATION TASK LIST

Perform the tasks in the following sections to configure SRB:

- Configuring Source-Route Bridging
- Configuring Bridging of Routed Protocols
- Configuring Translation between SRB and Transparent Bridging Environments
- Configuring NetBIOS Support
- Configuring LAN Network Manager (LNM) Support
- Securing the SRB Network
- Tuning the SRB Network
- Establishing SRB Interoperability with Specific Token Ring Implementations
- Monitoring and Maintaining the SRB Network

For SRB Configuration Examples, see "SRB Configuration Examples" at the end of this chapter.

CAUTION

The Cisco IOS software issues a warning if a duplicate bridge definition exists in a router. You must remove an old bridge definition before adding a new bridge definition to a router configuration.

CONFIGURING SOURCE-ROUTE BRIDGING

Cisco's implementation of source-route bridging enables you to connect two or more Token Ring networks using either Token Ring or Fiber Distributed Data Interface (FDDI) media.

The Cisco IOS software offers the ability to encapsulate source-route bridging traffic using RFC 1490 Bridged 802.5 encapsulation. This encapsulation provides SRB over Frame Relay functionality.

You can configure the Cisco IOS software for source-route bridging by performing the tasks in one of the first three sections and, optionally, the tasks in the last section:

- Configuring a Dual-Port Bridge
- Configuring a Multiport Bridge Using a Virtual Ring
- Configuring SRB over FDDI
- Configuring SRB over Frame Relay
- Configuring Fast-Switching SRB over FDDI
- Enabling the Forwarding and Blocking of Spanning-Tree Explorers
- Enabling the Automatic Spanning-Tree Function
- Limiting the Maximum SRB Hops

Configuring a Dual-Port Bridge

A dual-port bridge is the simplest source-route bridging configuration. When configured as a dual-port bridge, the access server or router serves to connect two Token Ring LANs. One LAN is connected through one port (Token Ring interface), and the other LAN is connected through the other port (also a Token Ring interface). Figure 3–1 shows a dual-port bridge.

Figure 3–1
Dual-port bridge.

To configure a dual-port bridge that connects two Token Rings, you must enable source-route bridging on each of the Token Ring interfaces that connect to the two Token Rings. To enable source-route bridging, perform the following task in interface configuration mode for each of the Token Ring interfaces:

Task	Command
Enable local source-route bridging on a Token Ring interface.	**source-bridge** *local-ring bridge-number target-ring*

NOTES

Ring numbers need to be unique across interfaces and networks, so that when you enable source-route bridging over an interface, the local and target rings are defined. Each node on the network will know if it is the target of explorer packets sent on the network.

A dual-port bridge is a limitation imposed by IBM Token Ring chips; the chips can process only two ring numbers. If you have a router with two or more Token Ring interfaces, you can work around the two-ring number limitation. You can configure your router as multiple dual-port bridges or as a multiport bridge using a virtual ring.

You can define several separate dual-port bridges in the same router. However, the routers on the LANs cannot have any-to-any connectivity; that is, they cannot connect to every other router on the bridged LANs. Only the routers connected to the dual-port bridge can communicate with one another. Figure 3–2 shows two separate dual-port bridges (T0-T2 and T1-T3) configured on the same router.

Figure 3–2
Multiple dual-port bridges.

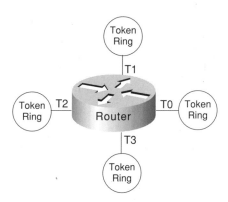

To configure multiple dual-port source-route bridges, repeat the following task in interface configuration mode for each Token Ring interface that is part of a dual-port bridge:

Task	Command
Enable local source-route bridging on a Token Ring interface.	**source-bridge** *local-ring bridge-number target-ring*

If you want your network to use only SRB, you can connect as many routers as you need via Token Rings. Remember, source-route bridging requires you to bridge only Token Ring media.

Configuring a Multiport Bridge Using a Virtual Ring

A better solution for overcoming the two-ring number limitation of IBM Token Ring chips is to configure a multiport bridge using a virtual ring. A virtual ring on a multiport bridge allows the router to interconnect three or more LANs with any-to-any connectivity; that is, connectivity between any of the routers on each of the three LANs is allowed. A virtual ring creates a logical Token Ring internal to the Cisco IOS software, which causes all the Token Rings connected to the router to be treated as if they are all on the same Token Ring. The virtual ring is called a *ring group*. Figure 3–3 shows a multiport bridge using a virtual ring.

Figure 3–3
Multiport bridge using a virtual ring.

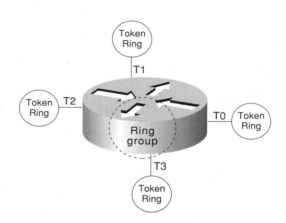

To take advantage of this virtual ring feature, each Token Ring interface on the router must be configured to belong to the same ring group. For information about configuring a multiport bridge using a virtual ring, see the "Configuring a Multiport Bridge Using a Virtual Ring" section later in this chapter.

To configure a source-route bridge to have more than two network interfaces, you must perform the following tasks:

Step 1   Define a *ring group*.

Step 2   Enable source-route bridging and assign a ring group to a Token Ring interface.

Once you have completed these tasks, the router acts as a multiport bridge, not as a dual-port bridge.

NOTES

Ring numbers need to be unique across interfaces and networks.

Defining a Ring Group in SRB Context

Because all IBM Token Ring chips can process only two ring numbers, Cisco has implemented the concept of a ring group or virtual ring. A ring group is a collection of Token Ring interfaces in one or more routers that share the same ring number. This ring number is used just like a physical ring number, showing up in any route descriptors contained in packets being bridged. Within the context of a multiport bridge that uses SRB rather than RSRB, the ring group resides in the same router. See Chapter 5, "Configuring Remote Source-Route Bridging" to compare ring groups in the SRB and RSRB context.

A ring group must be assigned a ring number that is unique throughout the network. It is possible to assign different Token Ring interfaces on the same router to different ring groups, if, for example, you plan to administer them as interfaces in separate domains.

To define or remove a ring group, perform one of the following tasks in global configuration mode:

Task	Command
Define a ring group.	**source-bridge ring-group** *ring-group* [*virtual-mac-address*]
Remove a ring group.	**no source-bridge ring-group** *ring-group* [*virtual-mac-address*]

Enabling SRB and Assigning a Ring Group to an Interface

After you have defined a ring group, you must assign that ring group to those interfaces you plan to include in that ring group. An interface can be assigned to only one ring group. To enable any-to-any connectivity among the end stations connected through this multiport bridge, you must assign the same target ring number to all Token Ring interfaces on the router.

To enable SRB and assign a ring group to an interface, perform the following task in interface configuration mode:

Task	Command
Enable source-route bridging and assign a ring group to a Token Ring interface.	**source-bridge** *local-ring bridge-number target-ring*

Configuring SRB over FDDI

Cisco's implementation of SRB expands the basic functionality to allow autonomous switching of SRB network traffic for FDDI interfaces, adding counters to SRB accounting statistics, and implementing process-level switching of SRB over FDDI. This functionality provides a significant increase in performance for Token Rings interconnected across an FDDI backbone.

SRB over FDDI is supported on the Cisco 4000-M, Cisco 4500-M, Cisco 4700-M, Cisco 7000 series, Cisco 7200 series, and Cisco 7500 routers.

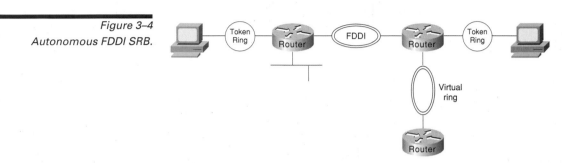

Figure 3–4
Autonomous FDDI SRB.

To configure autonomous FDDI SRB, perform the following tasks, beginning in global configuration mode:

Task	Command
Step 1 Configure an FDDI interface.	**interface fddi** *slot/port*
Step 2 Enable source-route bridging.	**source-bridge** *local-ring bridge-number target-ring*
Step 3 Enable autonomous switching.	**source-bridge route-cache cbus**

Configuring Fast-Switching SRB over FDDI

Fast-Switching SRB over FDDI enhances performance. For example, if you want to use access lists, fast-switching SRB over FDDI provides fast performance and access-list filters capability.

To configure fast-switching SRB over FDDI, perform the following tasks, beginning in global configuration mode:

Task	Command
Step 1 Configure an FDDI interface.	**interface fddi** *slot/port*
Step 2 Enable source-route bridging.	**source-bridge** *local-ring bridge-number target-ring*
Step 3 Enable source-bridge spanning.	**source-bridge spanning**
Step 4 Enable fast-switching.	**source-bridge route-cache**
Step 5 Enable the collection and use of RIF information.	**multiring** *protocol-keyword*

Configuring SRB over Frame Relay

Cisco IOS software offers the ability to encapsulate source-route bridging traffic using RFC 1490 Bridged 802.5 encapsulation. This provides SRB over Frame Relay functionality that is interoperable with other vendors' implementations of SRB over Frame Relay and with some vendors' implementations of FRAS BAN.

NOTES

In the initial release, SRB over Frame Relay does not support the Cisco IOS software proxy explorer, automatic spanning-tree, or LAN Network Manager functions.

To configure SRB over Frame Relay, perform the following tasks in interface configuration mode:

Task	Command
Step 1 Specify the serial port.	**interface serial** *number*
Step 2 Enable Frame Relay encapsulation.	**encapsulation frame-relay**
Step 3 Configure a Frame Relay point-to-point subinterface.	**interface serial** *slot/port.subinterface-number* **point-to-point**
Step 4 Configure a DLCI number for the point-to-point subinterface.	**frame-relay interface-dlci** *dlci* **ietf**
Step 5 Assign a ring number to the Frame Relay permanent virtual circuit.	**source-bridge** *source-ring-number bridge-number target-ring-number* **conserve-ring**

Enabling the Forwarding and Blocking of Spanning-Tree Explorers

When trying to determine the location of remote destinations on a source-route bridge, the source device will need to send explorer packets. Explorer packets are used to collect RIF information. The source device can send spanning-tree explorers or all-routes explorers. Note that some older IBM devices generate only all-routes explorer packets, but many newer IBM devices are capable of generating spanning-tree explorer packets.

A spanning-tree explorer packet is an explorer packet that is sent to a defined group of nodes that comprise a statically configured spanning tree in the network. In contrast, an all-routes explorer packet is an explorer packet that is sent to every node in the network on every path.

Forwarding all-routes explorer packets is the default. However, in complicated source-route bridging topologies, using this default can generate an exponentially large number of explorers that are traversing the network. The number of explorer packets becomes quite large because duplicate explorer packets are sent across the network to every node on every path. Eventually, each explorer packet will reach the destination device. The destination device will respond to each of these explorer packets. It is from these responses that the source device will collect the RIF and determine which route it will use to communicate with the destination device. Usually, the route contained in the first returned response will be used.

The number of explorer packets traversing the network can be reduced by sending spanning-tree explorer packets. Spanning-tree explorer packets are sent to specific nodes; that is, to only the nodes on the spanning tree, not to all nodes in the network. You must manually configure the spanning-tree topology over which the spanning-tree explorers are sent. You do this by configuring which interfaces on the routers will forward spanning-tree explorers and which interfaces will block them.

To enable forwarding of spanning-tree explorers on an outgoing interface, perform the following task in interface configuration mode:

Task	Command
Enable the forwarding of spanning-tree explorer packets on an interface.	**source-bridge spanning**

NOTES

While enabling the forwarding of spanning-tree explorer packets is not an absolute requirement, it is strongly recommended in complex topologies. Configuring an interface to block or forward spanning-tree explorers has no effect on how that interface handles all-routes explorer packets. All-routes explorers can always traverse the network.

To block forwarding of spanning-tree explorers on an outgoing interface, perform the following task in interface configuration mode:

Task	Command
Block spanning-tree explorer packets on an interface.	**no source-bridge spanning**

Enabling the Automatic Spanning-Tree Function

The automatic spanning-tree function supports automatic resolution of spanning trees in SRB networks, which provides a single path for spanning explorer frames to traverse from a given node in the network to another. Spanning explorer frames have a single-route broadcast indicator set in the routing information field. Port identifiers consist of ring numbers and bridge numbers associated with the ports. The spanning-tree algorithm for SRB does not support Topology Change Notification BDPU.

NOTES

Although the automatic spanning-tree function can be configured with SR/TLB, the SRB domain and transparent bridging domain have separate spanning trees. Each Token Ring interface can belong to only one spanning tree. Only one bridge group can run the automatic spanning-tree function at a time.

To create a bridge group that runs an automatic spanning-tree function compatible with the IBM SRB spanning-tree implementation, perform the following task in global configuration mode:

Task	Command
Create a bridge group that runs the automatic spanning-tree function.	**bridge** *bridge-group* **protocol ibm**

To enable the automatic spanning-tree function for a specified group of bridged interfaces, perform the following task in interface configuration mode:

Task	Command
Enable the automatic spanning-tree function on a group of bridged interfaces.	**source-bridge spanning** *bridge-group*

To assign a path cost for a specified interface, perform the following task in interface configuration mode:

Task	Command
Assign a path cost for a specified group of bridged interfaces.	**source-bridge spanning** *bridge-group* **path-cost** *path-cost*

NOTES

Ports running IEEE and IBM protocols form a spanning tree together on the LAN, but they do not mix in the router itself. Make sure the configurations are correct and that each LAN runs only one protocol.

See the end of this chapter for an example of source-route bridging with the automatic spanning-tree function enabled.

Limiting the Maximum SRB Hops

You can minimize explorer storms if you limit the maximum number of source-route bridge hops. For example, if the largest number of hops in the best route between two end stations is six, it might be appropriate to limit the maximum source-route bridging hops to six to eliminate unnecessary traffic. This setting affects spanning-tree explorers and all-routes explorers sent from source devices.

To limit the number of SRB hops, perform one of the following tasks in interface configuration mode:

Task	Command
Control the forwarding or blocking of all-routes explorer frames received on this interface.	**source-bridge max-hops** *count*
Control the forwarding or blocking of spanning-tree explorer frames received on this interface.	**source-bridge max-in-hops** *count*
Control the forwarding or blocking of spanning-tree explorer frames sent from this interface.	**source-bridge max-out-hops** *count*

CONFIGURING BRIDGING OF ROUTED PROTOCOLS

Source-route bridges use MAC information, specifically the information contained in the routing information field (RIF), to bridge packets. A RIF contains a series of ring and bridge numbers that represent the possible paths the source node might use to send packets to the destination. Each ring number in the RIF represents a single Token Ring in the source-route bridged network and is designated by a unique 12-bit ring number. Each bridge number represents a bridge that is between two Token Rings in the SRB network and is designated by a unique 4-bit bridge number. The information in a RIF is derived from explorer packets traversing the source-route bridged network. Without the RIF information, a packet could not be bridged across a source-route bridged network.

Unlike source-route bridges, Level 3 routers use protocol-specific information (for example, Novell IPX or XNS headers) rather than MAC information to route datagrams. As a result, the Cisco IOS software default for routed protocols is to not collect RIF information and to not be able to bridge routed protocols. However, if you want the software to bridge routed protocols across a source-route bridged network, the software must be able to collect and use RIF information to bridge packets across a source-route bridged network. You can configure the software to append

RIF information to routed protocols so that routed protocols can be bridged. Figure 3–5 shows a network topology in which you would want to use this feature.

Figure 3–5
Topology for bridging routed
protocols across a
source-route bridged network.

To configure the Cisco IOS software to bridge routed protocols, you must perform the task in the first section, and optionally, one or both of the tasks in the other sections as follows:

- Enabling use of the RIF
- Configuring a Static RIF Entry
- Configuring the RIF Timeout Interval

Enabling Use of the RIF

You can configure the Cisco IOS software so that it will append RIF information to the routed protocols. This allows routed protocols to be bridged across a source-route bridged network. The routed protocols that you can bridge are as follows:

- Apollo Domain
- AppleTalk
- ISO CLNS
- DECnet
- IP
- IPX
- VINES
- XNS

Enable use of the RIF only on Token Ring interfaces on the router.

To configure the Cisco IOS software to append RIF information, perform the following task in interface configuration mode:

Task	Command
Enable collection and use of RIF information.	**multiring** {*protocol-keyword* [**all-routes**	**spanning**]	**all**	**other**}

For an example of how to configure the software to bridge routed protocols, see the "SRB and Routing Certain Protocols Example" section later in this chapter.

Configuring a Static RIF Entry

If a Token Ring host does not support the use of IEEE 802.2 TEST or XID datagrams as explorer packets, you might need to add static information to the RIF cache of the router.

To configure a static RIF entry, perform the following task in global configuration mode:

Task	Command
Enter static source-route information into the RIF cache.	rif *mac-address rif-string* {*interface-name* | **ring-group** *ring*}

Configuring the RIF Timeout Interval

RIF information that can be used to bridge routed protocols is maintained in a cache whose entries are aged.

NOTES

The **rif validate-enable** commands have no effect on remote entries learned over RSRB.

To configure the number of minutes an inactive RIF entry is kept in the cache, perform the following tasks in global configuration mode:

Task		Command
Step 1	Specify the number of minutes an inactive RIF entry is kept.	rif timeout *minutes*
Step 2	Enable RIF validation for entries learned on an interface (Token Ring or FDDI).	rif validate-enable
Step 3	Enable RIF validation on an SRB that is malfunctioning.	rif validate-enable-age
Step 4	Enable synchronization of the RIF cache with the protocol route cache.	rif validate-enable-route-cache

CONFIGURING TRANSLATION BETWEEN SRB AND TRANSPARENT BRIDGING ENVIRONMENTS

Source-route translational bridging (SR/TLB) is a Cisco IOS software feature that allows you to combine SRB and transparent bridging networks without the need to convert all of your existing source-route bridges to source-route transparent (SRT) nodes. As such, it provides a cost-effective connectivity path between Ethernets and Token Rings.

When a router is configured for SR/TLB, the router operates in fast-switching mode by default, causing packets to be processed in the interrupt handler when the packets first arrive, rather than queuing them for scheduled processing. The **no source-bridge transparent fastswitch** command is provided to disable fast-switched SR/TLB, causing the router to handle packets by process switching. For more information on disabling fast-switched SR/TLB, refer to the "Disabling Fast-Switched SR/TLB" section later in this chapter.

NOTES

When you are translationally bridging, you will have to route routed protocols and translationally bridge all others, such as LAT.

Overview of SR/TLB

You can bridge packets between an SRB domain and a transparent bridging domain. Using this feature, a software "bridge" is created between a specified virtual ring group and a transparent bridge group. To the source-route station, this bridge looks like a standard source-route bridge. There is a ring number and a bridge number associated with a ring that actually represents the entire transparent bridging domain. To the transparent bridging station, the bridge represents just another port in the bridge group.

When bridging from the SRB (typically, Token Ring) domain to the transparent bridging (typically, Ethernet) domain, the source-route fields of the frames are removed. The RIFs are cached for use by subsequent return traffic.

When bridging from the transparent bridging domain to the SRB domain, the router checks the packet to see if it has a multicast or broadcast destination or a unicast (single host) destination. If it is multicast, the packet is sent as a spanning-tree explorer. If it is a unicast destination, the router looks up the path to the destination in the RIF cache. If a path is found, it will be used; otherwise, the router will send the packet as a spanning-tree explorer.

An example of a simple SR/TLB topology is shown in Figure 3–6.

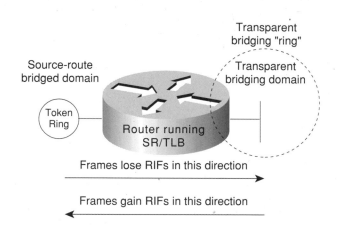

Figure 3–6
Example of a simple
SR/TLB topology.

NOTES

The Spanning-Tree Protocol messages used to prevent loops in the transparent bridging domain are *not* passed between the SRB domain and the transparent bridging domain. Therefore, you must not set up multiple paths between the SRB and transparent bridging domains.

The following notes and caveats apply to all uses of SR/TLB:

- Multiple paths cannot exist between the source-route bridged domain and the transparent bridged domain. Such paths can lead to data loops in the network, because the spanning-tree packets used to avoid these loops in transparent bridging networks do not traverse the SRB network.

- Some devices, notably PS/2s under certain configurations running OS/2 Extended Edition Version 1.3, do not correctly implement the "largest frame" processing on RIFs received from remote source-route bridged hosts. The maximum Ethernet frame size is smaller than that allowed for Token Ring. As such, bridges allowing for communication between Ethernet and Token Ring will tell the Token Ring hosts, through the RIF on frames destined to the Token Ring, that hosts on the Ethernet cannot receive frames larger than a specified maximum, typically 1472 bytes. Some machines ignore this run-time limit specification and send frames larger than the Ethernet can accept. The router and any other Token Ring/Ethernet bridge have no choice but to drop these frames. To allow such hosts to successfully communicate across or to an Ethernet, you must configure their maximum frame sizes manually. For the PS/2, this can be done through Communications Manager.

- Any access filters applied on any frames apply to the frames as they appear on the media to which the interface with the access filter applies. This is important because in the most common use of SR/TLB (Ethernet and Token Ring connectivity), the bit ordering of the MAC addresses in the frame is swapped. Refer to the SR/TLB examples in the "SRB Configuration Examples" section of this chapter.

> **CAUTION**
>
> Bridging between dissimilar media presents several problems that can prevent communication from occurring. These problems include bit-order translation (or usage of MAC addresses as data), maximum transmission unit (MTU) differences, frame status differences, and multicast address usage. Some or all of these problems might be present in a multimedia bridged LAN and prevent communication from taking place. Because of differences in the way end nodes implement Token Ring, these problems are most prevalent when bridging between Token Rings and Ethernets or between Token Ring and FDDI LANs.
>
> We currently know that problems occur with the following protocols when bridged between Token Ring and other media: Novell IPX, DECnet Phase IV, AppleTalk, VINES, XNS, and IP. Further, problems can occur with the Novell IPX and XNS protocols when bridged between FDDI and other media. We recommend that these protocols be routed whenever possible.

To enable SR/TLB, you must perform the task in the following section:

- Enabling Bridging between Transparent Bridging and SRB

In addition, you also can perform the tasks in the following sections:

- Disabling Fast-Switched SR/TLB
- Enabling Translation Compatibility with IBM 8209 Bridges
- Enabling Token Ring LLC2-to-Ethernet Conversion

Enabling Bridging between Transparent Bridging and SRB

Before enabling bridging, you must have completely configured your router using multiport SRB and transparent bridging. Once you have done this, establish bridging between transparent bridging and source-route bridging by performing the following task in global configuration mode:

Task	Command
Enable bridging between transparent bridging and SRB.	**source-bridge transparent** *ring-group pseudo-ring bridge-number tb-group* [*oui*]

Disabling Fast-Switched SR/TLB

To disable fast-switched SR/TLB and cause the router to handle packets by process switching, perform the following task in global configuration mode:

Task	Command
Disable fast-switched SR/TLB.	**no source-bridge transparent** *ring-group* **fastswitch**

Enabling Translation Compatibility with IBM 8209 Bridges

To transfer data between IBM 8209 Ethernet/Token Ring bridges and routers running the SR/TLB software (to create a Token Ring backbone to connect Ethernets), perform the following task on each Token Ring interface in interface configuration mode:

Task	Command
Move data between IBM 8209 Ethernet/Token Ring bridges and routers running translational bridging software.	ethernet-transit-oui [90-compatible | standard | cisco]

Enabling Token Ring LLC2-to-Ethernet Conversion

The Cisco IOS software supports the following types of Token Ring-to-Ethernet frame conversions:

- Token Ring LLC2-to-Ethernet Type II (0x80d5 processing)
- Token Ring LLC2-to-Ethernet 802.3 LLC2 (standard)

For most non-IBM hosts, Token Ring LLC2 frames can be translated in a straightforward manner into Ethernet 802.3 LLC2 frames. This is the default conversion in the Cisco IOS software.

However, many Ethernet-attached IBM devices use nonstandard encapsulation of LLC2 on Ethernet. Such IBM devices, including PS/2s running OS/2 Extended Edition and RT-PCs, do not place their LLC2 data inside an 802.3 format frame, but rather place it into an Ethernet Type 2 frame whose type is specified as *0x80d5*. This nonstandard format is called 0x80d5, named after the type of frame. This format is also sometimes called *RT-PC Ethernet format* because these frames were first widely seen on the RT-PC. Hosts using this nonstandard 0x80d5 format cannot read the standard Token Ring LLC2-to-Ethernet 802.2 LLC frames.

To enable Token Ring LLC2-to-Ethernet LLC2 conversion, you can perform one or both of the following tasks:

- Enabling 0x80d5 Processing
- Enabling Standard Token Ring LLC2-to-Ethernet LLC2 Conversion

Enabling 0x80d5 Processing

You can change the Cisco IOS software's default translation behavior of translating Token Ring LLC-to-Ethernet 802.3 LLC to translate Token Ring LLC2 frames into Ethernet 0x80d5 format frames. To enable this nonstandard conversion, perform the following task in global configuration mode:

Task	Command
Change the Ethernet/Token Ring translation behavior to translate Token Ring LLC2 frames into Ethernet 0x80d5 format frames.	source-bridge enable-80d5

Enabling Standard Token Ring LLC2-to-Ethernet LLC2 Conversion

After you change the translation behavior to perform Token Ring LLC2 frames into Ethernet 0x80d5 format frames, some of the non-IBM hosts in your network topology might use the standard Token Ring conversion of Token Ring LLC2-to-Ethernet 802.3 LLC2 frames. If this is the case, you can change the translation method of those hosts to use the standard translation method on a per-DSAP basis. The translation method for all the IBM hosts still would remain as Token Ring LLC2-to-Ethernet 0x80d5 translation.

To define non-IBM hosts in your network topology to use the standard translation method while the IBM hosts use the nonstandard method, perform the following task in global configuration mode:

Task	Command
Allow some other devices to use normal LLC2/IEEE 802.3 translation on a per-DSAP basis.	source-bridge sap-80d5 *dsap*

CONFIGURING NETBIOS SUPPORT

NetBIOS is a nonroutable protocol that was originally designed to transmit messages between stations, typically IBM PCs, on a Token Ring network. NetBIOS allows messages to be exchanged between the stations using a name rather than a station address. Each station knows its name and is responsible for knowing the names of other stations on the network.

> **NOTES**
>
> In addition to this type of NetBIOS, which runs over LLC2, Cisco has implemented another type of NetBIOS that runs over IPX.

NetBIOS name caching allows the Cisco IOS software to maintain a cache of NetBIOS names, which avoids the high overhead of transmitting many of the broadcasts used between client and server NetBIOS PCs (IBM PCs or PS/2s) in an SRB environment.

When NetBIOS name caching is enabled, the software performs the following actions:

- Notices when any hosts send a series of duplicated "query" frames and reduces them to one frame per period. The time period is configurable.
- Keeps a cache of mappings between NetBIOS server and client names and their MAC addresses. By watching NAME_QUERY and NAME_RECOGNIZED request and response traffic between clients and servers, the Cisco IOS software can forward broadcast requests sent by clients to find servers (and by servers in reply to their clients) directly to their needed destinations, rather than forwarding them for broadcast across the entire bridged network.

The software will time out the entries in the NetBIOS name cache after a specific interval of their initial storage. The timeout value is a user-configurable value. You can configure the timeout value for a particular Token Ring if the NetBIOS name cache is enabled on the interface connecting to that Token Ring. In addition, you can configure static name cache entries that never time out for frequently accessed servers whose locations or paths typically do not change. Static RIF entries are also specified for such hosts.

Generally, NetBIOS name caching is most useful when a large amount of NetBIOS broadcast traffic creates bottlenecks on WAN media connecting distant locations, and the WAN media is overwhelmed with this traffic. However, when two high-speed LAN segments are directly interconnected, the packet savings of NetBIOS name caching is probably not worth the processor overhead associated with it.

NOTES

NetBIOS name caching is not recommended to be turned on in backbone routers, particularly if you have it enabled in all the routers connected to the backbone. NetBIOS caching should be distributed among multiple routers. NetBIOS name caching can be used only between Cisco routers that are running Software Release 9.1 or later.

To enable NetBIOS name caching, you must perform the tasks in the following sections:

- Enabling the Proxy Explorers Feature on the Appropriate Interface
- Specifying Timeout and Enabling NetBIOS Name Caching

In addition, you can configure NetBIOS name caching as described in the following sections:

- Configuring the NetBIOS Cache Name Length
- Enabling NetBIOS Proxying
- Creating Static Entries in the NetBIOS Name Cache
- Specifying Dead-Time Intervals for NetBIOS Packets

Enabling the Proxy Explorers Feature on the Appropriate Interface

In order to enable NetBIOS name caching on an interface, the proxy explorers feature must first be enabled on that interface. This feature must either be enabled for response to all explorer packets or for response to NetBIOS packets only.

To determine whether the proxy explorers feature has been enabled, perform the following task in EXEC mode:

Task	Command
Determine whether the proxy explorers feature has been enabled.	**show startup-config**

To determine whether proxy explorers has been configured for response to all explorer packets, look in the configuration file for the **source-bridge proxy-explorer** entry for the appropriate interface. For example, if the appropriate interface is Token Ring 0, look for an entry similar to the following:

```
interface tokenring 0
source-bridge proxy-explorer
```

If that entry does not exist, look for the **source-bridge proxy-netbios-only** entry for the appropriate interface.

If neither entry exists, proxy explorers has not yet been enabled for the appropriate interface. To enable proxy explorers for response to all explorer packets, refer to the section "Configuring Proxy Explorers" later in this chapter.

Otherwise, enable proxy explorers only for the NetBIOS name-caching function by performing the following task in global configuration mode:

Task	Command
Enable use of proxy explorers only for the NetBIOS name-caching function and not for their general local response to explorers.	**source-bridge proxy-netbios-only**

Specifying Timeout and Enabling NetBIOS Name Caching

After you have ensured that the proxy explorers feature has been enabled for the appropriate interface, you can specify a cache timeout and enable NetBIOS name caching. To do this, perform the following tasks:

Task	Command
Step 1 Specify the timeout for entries in the NetBIOS name cache.	**netbios name-cache timeout** *minutes*
Step 2 Enable NetBIOS name caching for the appropriate interfaces.	**netbios enable-name-cache**

Configuring the NetBIOS Cache Name Length

To specify how many characters of the NetBIOS type name that the name cache will validate, perform the following global configuration task:

Task	Command
Specify the number of characters of the NetBIOS type name to cache.	**netbios name-cache name-len** *length*

Enabling NetBIOS Proxying

The Cisco IOS software can act as a proxy and send NetBIOS datagram type frames. To enable this capability, perform the following global configuration task:

Task	Command
Enable NetBIOS proxying.	**netbios name-cache proxy-datagram** *seconds*

To define the validation time when the software is acting as a proxy for NetBIOS **NAME_QUERY** command or for explorer frames, perform the following global configuration task:

Task	Command
Define validation time.	**rif validate-age** *seconds*

Creating Static Entries in the NetBIOS Name Cache

If the router communicates with one or more NetBIOS stations on a regular basis, adding static entries to the NetBIOS name cache for these stations can reduce network traffic and overhead. You can define a static NetBIOS name cache entry that associates the server with the NetBIOS name and the MAC address. If the router acts as a NetBIOS server, you can specify that the static NetBIOS name cache is available locally through a particular interface. If a remote router acts as the NetBIOS server, you can specify that the NetBIOS name cache is available remotely. To do this, perform one of the following tasks in global configuration mode:

Task	Command
Define a static NetBIOS name cache entry and specify that it is available locally through a particular interface.	**netbios name-cache** *mac-address netbios-name interface-name*
Define a static NetBIOS name cache entry and specify that it is available remotely.	**netbios name-cache** *mac-address netbios-name* **ring-group** *group-number*

If you have defined a NetBIOS name cache entry, you must also define a RIF entry. For an example of how to configure a static NetBIOS entry, see the "NetBIOS Support with a Static NetBIOS Cache Entry Example" section later in this chapter.

Specifying Dead-Time Intervals for NetBIOS Packets

When NetBIOS name caching is enabled and default parameters are set on the router (as well as the NetBIOS name server and the NetBIOS name client), approximately 20 broadcast packets per logon are kept on the local ring where they are generated. The broadcast packets are of the type ADD_NAME_QUERY, ADD_GROUP_NAME, and STATUS_QUERY.

The Cisco IOS software also converts pairs of FIND_NAME and NAME_RECOGNIZED packets received from explorers, which traverse all rings, to specific route frames that are sent only between the two machines that need to see these packets.

You can specify a query-timeout, or "dead-time" interval to prevent repeat or duplicate broadcast of these types of packets for the duration of the interval.

To specify dead-time intervals, perform one or both of the following tasks in global configuration mode:

Task	Command
Specify a dead-time interval during which the Cisco IOS software drops any broadcast (NetBIOS ADD_NAME_QUERY, ADD_GROUP_NAME, or STATUS_QUERY) frames if they are duplicate frames sent by the same host.	**netbios name-cache query-timeout** *seconds*
Specify a dead-time interval during which the software drops FIND_NAME and NAME_RECOGNIZED frames if they are duplicate frames sent by the same host.	**netbios name-cache recognized-timeout** *seconds*

CONFIGURING LAN NETWORK MANAGER (LNM) SUPPORT

LAN Network Manager (LNM), formerly called LAN Manager, is an IBM product for managing a collection of source-route bridges. Using either a proprietary protocol or the Simple Network Management Protocol (SNMP), LNM allows you to monitor the entire collection of Token Rings that comprise your source-route bridged network. You can use LNM to manage the configuration of source-route bridges, monitor Token Ring errors, and gather information from Token Ring parameter servers.

NOTES

LNM is supported on the 4/16-MB Token Ring cards that can be configured for either 4- or 16-MB transmission speeds. LNM support is not provided on CSC-R16M cards with SBEMON 2.0.

LNM is not limited to managing locally attached Token Ring networks; it also can manage any other Token Rings in your source-route bridged network that are connected through non-Token Ring media. To accomplish this task, LNM works in conjunction with the IBM Bridge Program. The IBM Bridge Program gathers data about the local Token Ring network and relays it back to LNM. In this manner, the bridge program becomes a proxy for information about its local Token Ring. Without this ability, you would require direct access to a device on every Token Ring in the network. This process would make managing an SRB environment awkward and cumbersome.

Figure 3–7 shows some Token Rings attached through a cloud and one LNM linking to a source-route bridge on each local ring.

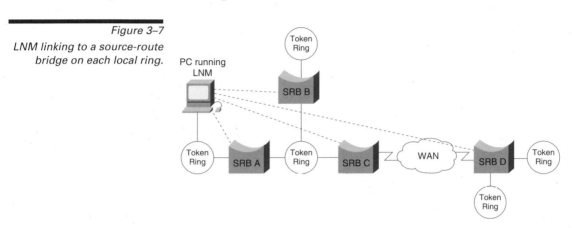

Figure 3–7
LNM linking to a source-route bridge on each local ring.

If LNM requires information about a station somewhere on a Token Ring, it uses a proprietary IBM protocol to query to one of the source-route bridges connected to that ring. If the bridge can provide the requested information, it simply responds directly to LNM. If the bridge does not have the necessary information, it queries the station using a protocol published in the IEEE 802.5 specification. In either case, the bridge uses the proprietary protocol to send a valid response back to LNM, using the proprietary protocol.

As an analogy, consider a language translator who sits between a French-speaking diplomat and a German-speaking diplomat. If the French diplomat asks the translator a question in French for the German diplomat and the translator knows the answer, he or she simply responds without translating the original question into German. If the French diplomat asks a question the translator does not know how to answer, the translator must first translate the question to German, wait for the German diplomat to answer, and then translate the answer back to French.

Similarly, if LNM queries a source-route bridge in the proprietary protocol and the bridge knows the answer, it responds directly using the same protocol. If the bridge does not know the answer, it must first translate the question to the IEEE 802.5 protocol, query the station on the ring, and then translate the response back to the proprietary protocol to send to LNM.

Figure 3–8 illustrates requests from the LNM originating in an IBM proprietary protocol and then translated into IEEE 802.5 MAC-level frames.

Notice that the proprietary protocol LNM uses to communicate with the source-route bridge is an LLC2 connection. Although its protocol cannot be routed, LNM can monitor or manage anything within the SRB network.

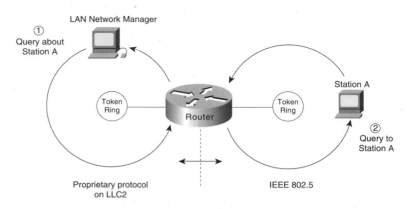

Figure 3–8
LAN Network Manager
monitoring and translating.

How a Router Works with LNM

As of Software Release 9.0, Cisco routers using 4/16-Mbps Token Ring interfaces configured for SRB support the proprietary protocol that LNM uses. These routers provide all functions the IBM Bridge Program currently provides. Thus, LNM can communicate with a router as if it were an IBM source-route bridge, such as the IBM 8209, and can manage or monitor any Token Ring connected to the router.

Through IBM Bridge support, LNM provides three basic services for the SRB network:

- The Configuration Report Server (CRS) monitors the current logical configuration of a Token Ring and reports any changes to LNM. CRS also reports various other events, such as the change of an active monitor on a Token Ring.

- The Ring Error Monitor (REM) monitors errors reported by any station on the ring. In addition, REM monitors whether the ring is in a functional or a failure state.

- The Ring Parameter Server (RPS) reports to LNM when any new station joins a Token Ring and ensures that all stations on a ring are using a consistent set of reporting parameters.

IBM Bridge support for LNM also allows asynchronous notification of some events that can occur on a Token Ring. Examples of these events include notification of a new station joining the Token Ring or of the ring entering failure mode, known as *beaconing*. Support is also provided for LNM to change the operating parameters in the bridge. For a complete description of LNM, refer to the IBM product manual supplied with the LNM program.

LNM support in Cisco's source-route bridges is a powerful tool for managing SRB networks. Through the ability to communicate with LNM and to provide the functionality of the IBM Bridge Program, the Cisco device appears as part of the IBM network. You therefore gain from the interconnectivity of Cisco products without having to learn a new management product or interface.

When SRB is enabled on the router, configuring the Cisco IOS software to perform the functions of an IBM Bridge for communication with LNM occurs automatically. Therefore, if SRB has been enabled, you do not need to perform any tasks to enable LNM support. However, the LNM software residing on a management station on a Token Ring on the network should be configured to properly communicate with the router.

There are several options for modifying LNM parameters in the Cisco IOS software, but none are required for basic functionality. For example, because users can now modify the operation of the Cisco IOS software through SNMP as well as through LNM, there is an option to exclude a user from modifying the Cisco IOS software configuration through LNM. You also can specify which of the three LNM services (CRS, REM, RPS) the source-route bridge will perform.

To configure LNM support, perform the tasks in the following sections:

- Configuring LNM Software on the Management Stations to Communicate with the Router
- Disabling LNM Functionality
- Disabling Automatic Report Path Trace Function
- Preventing LNM Stations from Modifying Cisco IOS Software Parameters
- Enabling Other LRMs to Change Router Parameters
- Applying a Password to an LNM Reporting Link
- Enabling LNM Servers
- Changing Reporting Thresholds
- Changing an LNM Reporting Interval
- Monitoring LNM Operation

Configuring LNM Software on the Management Stations to Communicate with the Router

Because configuring an LNM station is a fairly simple task and is well covered in the LNM documentation, it is not covered in depth here. However, it is important to mention that you must enter the MAC addresses of the interfaces comprising the ports of the bridges as adapter addresses. When you configure the router as a multiport bridge, configuring an LNM station is complicated by the virtual ring that is involved. The basic problem extends from the fact that LNM is designed to understand the concept of only a two-port bridge, and the router with a virtual ring is a *multiport* bridge. The solution is to configure a virtual ring into the LNM Manager station as a series of dual-port bridges.

Disabling LNM Functionality

Under some circumstances, you can disable all LNM server functions on the router without having to determine whether to disable a specific server, such as the ring parameter server or the ring error monitor on a given interface.

To disable LNM functionality, perform the following task in global configuration mode:

Task	Command
Disable LNM functionality.	lnm disabled

The command can be used to terminate all LNM server input and reporting links. In normal circumstances, this command should not be necessary because it is a superset of the functions normally performed on individual interfaces by the **no lnm rem** and **no lnm rps** commands.

Disabling Automatic Report Path Trace Function

Under some circumstances, such as when new hardware has been introduced into the network and is causing problems, the automatic report path trace function can be disabled. The new hardware may be setting bit-fields B1 or B2 (or both) of the routing control field in the routing information field embedded in a source-route bridged frame. This condition may cause the network to be flooded by report path trace frames if the condition is persistent. The **lnm pathtrace-disabled** command, along with its options, allows you to alleviate network congestion that may be occurring by disabling all or part of the automatic report path trace function within LNM.

To disable the automatic report path trace function, perform the following task in global configuration mode:

Task	Command
Disable LNM automatic report path trace function.	lnm pathtrace-disabled [all | origin]

Preventing LNM Stations from Modifying Cisco IOS Software Parameters

Because there is now more than one way to remotely change parameters in a router (either using SNMP or the proprietary IBM protocol), some method is needed to prevent such changes from detrimentally interacting with each other. You can prevent any LNM station from modifying parameters in the Cisco IOS software. It does not affect the ability of LNM to monitor events, only to change parameters on the router.

To prevent the modification of Cisco IOS software parameters by an LNM station, perform the following task in global configuration mode:

Task	Command
Prevent LNM stations from modifying LNM parameters in the Cisco IOS software.	lnm snmp-only

Enabling Other LRMs to Change Router Parameters

LNM has a concept of reporting links and reporting link numbers. A reporting link is simply a connection (or potential connection) between a LAN Reporting Manager (LRM) and a bridge. A reporting link number is a unique number used to identify a reporting link. An IBM bridge allows four simultaneous reporting links numbered 0 through 3. Only the LRM attached on the lowest-numbered connection is allowed to change LNM parameters in the router, and then only when that connection number falls below a certain configurable number. In the default configuration, the LRM connected through link 0 is the only LRM that can change LNM parameters.

To enable other LRMs to change router parameters, perform the following task in interface configuration mode:

Task	Command
Enable a LRM other than that connected through link 0 to change router parameters.	lnm alternate *number*

Applying a Password to an LNM Reporting Link

Each reporting link has its own password that is used not only to prevent unauthorized access from an LRM to a bridge but also to control access to the different reporting links. This is important because it is possible to change parameters through some reporting links.

To apply a password to an LNM reporting link, perform the following task in interface configuration mode:

Task	Command
Apply a password to an LNM reporting link.	lnm password *number string*

Enabling LNM Servers

As in an IBM bridge, the router provides several functions that gather information from a local Token Ring. All of these functions are enabled by default, but also can be disabled. The LNM servers are explained in the section "How a Router Works with LNM" earlier in this chapter.

To enable LNM servers, perform one or more of the following tasks in interface configuration mode:

Task	Command
Enable the LNM Configuration Report Server (CRS).	lnm crs
Enable the LNM Ring Error Monitor (REM).	lnm rem
Enable the LNM Ring Parameter Server (RPS).	lnm rps

Changing Reporting Thresholds

The Cisco IOS software sends a message to all attached LNMs whenever it begins to drop frames. The threshold at which this report is generated is based on a percentage of frames dropped compared with those forwarded. This threshold is configurable, and defaults to a value of 0.10 percent. You can configure the threshold by entering a single number, expressing the percentage loss rate in hundredths of a percent. The valid range is 0 to 9999.

To change reporting thresholds, perform the following task in interface configuration mode:

Task	Command
Change the threshold at which the Cisco IOS software reports the frames-lost percentage to LNM.	**lnm loss-threshold** *number*

Changing an LNM Reporting Interval

All stations on a Token Ring notify the Ring Error Monitor (REM) when they detect errors on the ring. In order to prevent excessive messages, error reports are not sent immediately, but are accumulated for a short interval and then reported. A station learns the duration of this interval from a router (configured as a source-route bridge) when it first enters the ring. This value is expressed in tens of milliseconds between error messages. The default is 200, or 2 seconds. The valid range is 0 to 65,535.

To change an LNM reporting interval, perform the following task in interface configuration mode:

Task	Command
Set the time interval during which stations report ring errors to the Ring Error Monitor (REM).	**lnm softerr** *milliseconds*

Monitoring LNM Operation

Once LNM support is enabled, you can monitor LNM operation. To observe the configuration of the LNM bridge and its operating parameters, perform the following tasks in the EXEC mode:

Task		Command
Step 1	Display all configured bridges and their global parameters.	**show lnm bridge**
Step 2	Display the logical configuration of all bridges configured in the router.	**show lnm config**
Step 3	Display LNM information for an interface or all interfaces of the router.	**show lnm interface** [*type number*]

Task	Command
Step 4 Display LNM information about a Token Ring or all Token Rings on the network.	**show lnm ring** [*ring-number*]
Step 5 Display LNM information about a station or all stations on the network.	**show lnm station** [*address*]

SECURING THE SRB NETWORK

This section describes how to configure three features that are used primarily to provide network security: NetBIOS access filters, administrative filters, and access expressions that can be combined with administrative filters. In addition, these features can be used to increase network performance because they reduce the number of packets that traverse the backbone network.

Configuring NetBIOS Access Filters

NetBIOS packets can be filtered when transmitted across a Token Ring bridge. Two types of filters can be configured: one for source and destination station names and one for arbitrary byte patterns in the packet itself.

As you configure NetBIOS access filters, keep the following issues in mind:

- The access lists that apply filters to an interface are scanned in the order they are entered.

- There is no way to put a new access-list entry in the middle of an access list. All new additions to existing NetBIOS access lists are placed at the end of the existing list.

- Access-list arguments are case sensitive. The software makes a literal translation, so that a lowercase "a" is different from an uppercase "A." (Most nodes are named in uppercase letters.)

- A host NetBIOS access list and byte NetBIOS access list can each use the same name. The two lists are identified as unique and bear no relationship to each other.

- The station names included in the access lists are compared with the source name field for NetBIOS commands 00 and 01 (**ADD_GROUP_NAME_QUERY** and **ADD_NAME_QUERY**), as well as the destination name field for NetBIOS commands 08, 0A, and 0E (**DATAGRAM, NAME_QUERY,** and **NAME_RECOGNIZED**).

- If an access list does not contain a particular station name, the default action is to deny the access to that station.

To minimize any performance degradation, NetBIOS access filters do not examine all packets. Rather, they examine certain packets that are used to establish and maintain NetBIOS client/server connections, thereby effectively stopping new access and load across the router. However, applying a new access filter does not terminate existing sessions immediately. All new sessions will be filtered, but existing sessions could continue for some time.

There are two ways you can configure NetBIOS access filters:

- Configuring NetBIOS Access Filters Using Station Names
- Configuring NetBIOS Access Filters Using a Byte Offset

Configuring NetBIOS Access Filters Using Station Names

To configure access filters using station names, you must do the following:

Step 1   Assign the station access list name.

Step 2   Specify the direction of the message to be filtered on the interface.

The NetBIOS station access list contains the station name to match, along with a permit or deny condition. You must assign the name of the access list to a station or set of stations on the network.

To assign a station access list name, perform the following task in global configuration mode:

Task	Command
Assign the name of an access list to a station or set of stations on the network.	**netbios access-list host** *name* {**permit** | **deny**} *pattern*

When filtering by station name, you can choose to filter either incoming or outgoing messages on the interface. To specify the direction, perform one of the following tasks in interface configuration mode:

Task	Command
Define an access list filter for incoming messages.	**netbios input-access-filter host** *name*
Define an access list filter for outgoing messages.	**netbios output-access-filter host** *name*

Configuring NetBIOS Access Filters Using a Byte Offset

To configure access filters you must do the following:

Step 1   Assign a byte offset access list name.

Step 2   Specify the direction of the message to be filtered on the interface.

Keep the following notes in mind while configuring access filters using a byte offset:

- When an access list entry has an offset plus the length of the pattern that is larger than the packet's length, the entry will not make a match for that packet.

- Because these access lists allow arbitrary byte offsets into packets, these access filters can have a significant impact on the amount of packets per second transiting across the bridge. They should be used only when situations absolutely dictate their use.

The NetBIOS byte offset access list contains a series of offsets and hexadecimal patterns with which to match byte offsets in NetBIOS packets. To assign a byte offset access list name, perform the following task in global configuration mode:

Task	Command
Define the byte offsets and patterns within NetBIOS messages to match with access list parameters.	**netbios access-list bytes** *name* {**permit** | **deny**} *offset pattern*

NOTES

Using NetBIOS Byte Offset access filters disables the autonomous or fast switching of source-route bridging frames.

When filtering by byte offset, you can filter either incoming or outgoing messages on the interface. To specify the direction, perform one of the following tasks in interface configuration mode:

Task	Command
Specify a byte-based access filter on incoming messages.	**netbios input-access-filter bytes** *name*
Specify a byte-based access filter on outgoing messages.	**netbios output-access-filter bytes** *name*

Configuring Administrative Filters for Token Ring Traffic

Source-route bridges normally filter frames according to the routing information contained in the frame. That is, a bridge will not forward a frame back to its originating network segment or any other network segment that the frame has already traversed. This section describes how to configure another type of filter—the administrative filter.

Administrative filters can filter frames based on the following methods:

- Protocol type—IEEE 802 or Subnetwork Access Protocol (SNAP)
- Token Ring vendor code

- Source address
- Destination address

Whereas filtering by Token Ring address or vendor code causes no significant performance penalty, filtering by protocol type significantly affects performance. A list of SNAP (Ethernet) type codes is provided in Appendix A, "Ethernet Type Codes."

Filtering Frames by Protocol Type

You can configure administrative filters by protocol type by specifying protocol type codes in an access list. You then apply that access list to either IEEE 802.2 encapsulated packets or to SNAP-encapsulated packets on the appropriate interface.

The order in which you specify these elements affects the order in which the access conditions are checked. Each condition is tested in succession. A matching condition is then used to execute a permit or deny decision. If no conditions match, a deny decision is reached.

NOTES

If a single condition is to be denied, there must be an **access-list** command that permits everything as well, or all access is denied.

To filter frames by protocol type, perform the following task in global configuration mode:

Task	Command
Create an access list for filtering frames by protocol type.	**access-list** *access-list-number* {**permit** | **deny**} {*type-code wild-mask* | *address mask*}

You can filter IEEE 802-encapsulated packets on either input or output. The access list you specify is the one you created that includes the protocol type codes.

To enable filtering on input or output, perform one of the following tasks in interface configuration mode:

Task	Command
Enable filtering of IEEE 802-encapsulated packets on input by type code.	**source-bridge input-lsap-list** *access-list-number*
Enable filtering of IEEE 802-encapsulated packets on output by type code.	**source-bridge output-lsap-list** *access-list-number*

You can filter SNAP-encapsulated packets on either input or output. The access list you specify is the one you created that includes the protocol type codes.

To enable filtering on input or output, perform one of the following tasks in interface configuration mode:

Task	Command
Filter SNAP-encapsulated packets on input by type code.	**source-bridge input-type-list** *access-list-number*
Filter SNAP-encapsulated frames on output by type code.	**source-bridge output-type-list** *access-list-number*

Filtering Frames by Vendor Code

To configure administrative filters by vendor code or address, define access lists that look for Token Ring addresses or for particular vendor codes for administrative filtering. To do so, perform the following task in global configuration mode:

Task	Command
Configure vendor code access lists.	**access-list** *access-list-number* {**permit** | **deny**} *address mask*

Filtering Source Addresses

To configure filtering on IEEE 802 source addresses, assign an access list to a particular input interface for filtering the Token Ring or IEEE 802 source addresses. To do so, perform the following task in interface configuration mode:

Task	Command
Enable filtering on IEEE 802 source addresses.	**source-bridge input-address-list** *access-list-number*

Filtering Destination Addresses

To configure filtering on IEEE 802 destination addresses, assign an access list to a particular output interface. To do so, perform the following task in interface configuration mode:

Task	Command
Enable filtering on IEEE 802 destination addresses.	**source-bridge output-address-list** *access-list-number*

Configuring Access Expressions that Combine Administrative Filters

You can use access expressions to combine access filters to establish complex conditions under which bridged frames can enter or leave an interface. Using access expressions, you can achieve levels of control on the forwarding of frames that otherwise would be impossible when using only simple access filters. Access expressions are constructed from individual access lists that define administrative filters for the following fields in packets:

- LSAP and SNAP type codes

- MAC addresses

- NetBIOS station names

- NetBIOS arbitrary byte values

--- **NOTES** ---

For any given interface, an access expression cannot be used if an access list has been defined for a given direction. For example, if an input access list is defined for MAC addresses on an interface, no access expression can be specified for the input side of that interface.

In Figure 3–9, two routers each connect a Token Ring to an FDDI backbone. On both Token Rings, SNA and NetBIOS bridging support is required. On Token Ring A, NetBIOS clients must communicate with any NetBIOS server off Token Ring B or any other unpictured router. However, the two 3174 cluster controllers off Token Ring A must communicate with only the one FEP off of Token Ring B, located at MAC address 0110.2222.3333.

Without access expressions, this scenario cannot be achieved. A filter on Router A that restricted access to only the FEP would also restrict access of the NetBIOS clients to the FEP. What is needed is an access *expression* that would state "If it is a NetBIOS frame, pass through, but if it is an SNA frame, only allow access to address 0110.2222.3333."

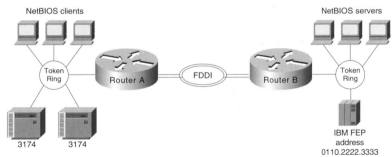

Figure 3–9
Access expression example.

NOTES

Using access expressions that combine access filters disables the autonomous or fast switching of source-route bridging frames.

Configuring Access Expressions

To configure an access expression, perform the following tasks:

- Design the access expression.
- Configure the access lists used by the expression.
- Configure the access expression into the router.

When designing an access expression, you must create some phrase that indicates, in its entirety, all the frames that will *pass* the access expression. This access expression is designed to apply on frames coming from the Token Ring interface on Router A in Figure 3–9:

"Pass the frame if it is a NetBIOS frame or if it is an SNA frame destined to address 0110.2222.3333."

In Boolean form, this phrase can be written as follows:

"Pass if 'NetBIOS or (SNA and destined to 0110.2222.3333).'"

The preceding statement requires three access lists to be configured:

- An access list that passes a frame if it is a NetBIOS frame (SAP = 0xF0F0)
- An access list that passes a frame if it is an SNA frame (SAP = 0x0404)
- An access list that passes a MAC address of 0110.2222.3333

The following configuration allows for all these conditions:

```
! Access list 201 passes NetBIOS frames (command or response)
access-list 201 permit 0xF0F0 0x0001
!
access-list 202 permit 0x0404 0x0001 ! Permits SNA frames (command or response)
access-list 202 permit 0x0004 0x0001 ! Permits SNA Explorers with NULL DSAP
```

```
!
! Access list 701 will permit the FEP MAC address
! of 0110.2222.3333
access-list 701 permit 0110.2222.3333
```

The 0x0001 mask allows command and response frames to pass equally.

Apply the access expression to the appropriate interface by performing the following task in interface configuration mode:

Task	Command
Define a per-interface access expression.	**access-expression** {**in** | **out**} *expression*

Optimizing Access Expressions

It is possible to combine access expressions. Suppose you wanted to transmit SNA traffic through to a single address, but allow other traffic through the router without restriction. The phrase could be written as follows:

"Allow access if the frame is not an SNA frame, or if it is going to host 0110.2222.3333."

More tersely this would be:

"Not SNA or destined to 0110.2222.3333."

The access lists defined in the previous section create the following configuration:

```
interface tokenring 0
 access-expression in ~lsap(202) ¦ dmac(701)
 !
access-list 202 permit 0x0404 0x0001 ! Permits SNA frames (command or response)
access-list 202 permit 0x0004 0x0001 ! Permits SNA Explorers with NULL DSAP
 !
! Access list 701 will permit the FEP MAC address
! of 0110.2222.3333
 access-list 701 permit 0110.2222.3333
```

This is a better and simpler access list than the one originally introduced and probably will result in better run-time execution as a result. Therefore, it is best to simplify your access expressions as much as possible before configuring them into the Cisco IOS software.

Altering Access Lists Used in Access Expressions

Because access expressions are composed of access lists, special care must be taken when deleting and adding access lists that are referenced in these access expressions.

If an access list that is referenced in an access expression is deleted, the access expression merely ignores the deleted access list. However, if you want to redefine an access list, you can create a new access list with the appropriate definition and use the same name as the old access list. The newly defined access list replaces the old one of the same name.

For example, if you want to redefine the NetBIOS access list named MIS that was used in the preceding example, you would enter the following sequence of configuration commands:

```
!  Replace the NetBIOS access list
interface tokenring 0
 access-expression in (smac(701) & netbios-host(accept))
 no netbios access-list host accept permit CISCO*
```

TUNING THE SRB NETWORK

The following sections describe how to configure features that enhance network performance by reducing the number of packets that traverse the backbone network:

- Enabling or Disabling the Source-Route Fast-Switching Cache
- Enabling or Disabling the Source-Route Autonomous-Switching Cache
- Enabling or Disabling the SSE
- Establishing Connection Timeout Interval
- Optimizing Explorer Processing
- Configuring Proxy Explorers

NOTES

In some situations, you might discover that default settings for LLC2 configurations are not acceptable. In such a case, you can configure LLC2 for optimal use. Chapter 11,"Configuring LLC2 and SDLC Parameters," describes how you can use them to optimize your network performance.

Enabling or Disabling the Source-Route Fast-Switching Cache

Rather than processing packets at the process level, the fast-switching feature enables the Cisco IOS software to process packets at the interrupt level. Each packet is transferred from the input interface to the output interface without copying the entire packet to main system memory. Fast switching allows for faster implementations of local SRB between 4/16-Mb Token Ring cards in the same router, or between two routers using the 4/16-Mb Token Ring cards and direct encapsulation.

By default, fast-switching software is enabled when SRB is enabled. To enable or disable source-route fast-switching, perform one of the following tasks in interface configuration mode:

Task	Command
Enable fast-switching.	**source-bridge route-cache**
Disable fast-switching.	**no source-bridge route-cache**

NOTES

Using either NetBIOS Byte Offset access filters or access expressions that combine access filters disables the fast switching of source-route bridging frames.

Enabling or Disabling the Source-Route Autonomous-Switching Cache

Autonomous switching is a feature that enables the Cisco IOS software to transmit packets from the input ciscoBus card to the output ciscoBus card without any involvement on the part of the router processor.

Autonomous switching is available for local SRB between ciscoBus Token Ring (CTR) cards in the same router. Autonomous switching provides higher switching rates than does fast switching between 4/16-Mb Token Ring cards. Autonomous switching works for both two-port bridges and multiport bridges that use ciscoBus Token Ring cards.

In a virtual ring that includes both ciscoBus Token Ring and 4/16-Mb Token Ring interfaces, frames that flow from one CTR interface to another are autonomously switched, and the remainder of the frames are fast switched. The switching that occurs on the CTR interface takes advantage of the high-speed ciscoBus controller processor.

To enable or disable source-route autonomous switching, perform one of the following tasks in interface configuration mode:

Task	Command
Enable autonomous switching.	**source-bridge route-cache cbus**
Disable autonomous switching.	**no source-bridge route-cache cbus**

NOTES

Using either NetBIOS Byte Offset access filters or access expressions that combine access filters disables the autonomous switching of SRB frames.

Enabling or Disabling the SSE

The Silicon Switch Engine (SSE) acts as a programmable cache to speed the switching of packets. To enable or disable the SSE, perform one of the following tasks in interface configuration mode:

Task	Command
Enable the SSE function.	**source-bridge route-cache sse**
Disable the SSE function.	**no source-bridge route-cache sse**

Establishing Connection Timeout Interval

It may be necessary to adjust timeout intervals in a complex topology such as a large multihop WAN with virtual rings or satellite links. The timeout interval is used when a connection to a remote peer is attempted. If the timeout interval expires before a response is received, the connection attempt is aborted.

To set the connection timeout interval, perform the following task in global configuration mode:

Task	Command
Set the connection timeout interval	**source-bridge connection-timeout** *seconds*

Optimizing Explorer Processing

Efficient explorer processing is vital to the operation of SRB. The default configuration is satisfactory for most situations. However, there might be circumstances that create unexpected broadcast storms. You can optimize the handling of explorer frames, thus reducing processor overhead and increasing explorer packet throughput. Optimizing explorer processing enables the router to perform substantially better during explorer broadcast storms.

In networks with redundant topologies—two or more routers connected to the same set of Token Rings and doing source-route bridging—a station on one Token Ring trying to get to a station on another Token Ring may choose a less than optimal route through unnecessary routers, causing explorer storms due to excessive forwarding of explorer frames. For example, in the redundant topology example shown in Figure 3–10, if Station X on Token Ring 1 attempts to get to Station Z on Token Ring 4 by going through Router A, Token Ring 2, and Router B—a less than optimal route—excessive forwarding of explorer frames might cause explorer storms.

The **source-bridge explorer-dup-ARE-filter** command can be used to reduce explorer traffic by filtering explorer frames.

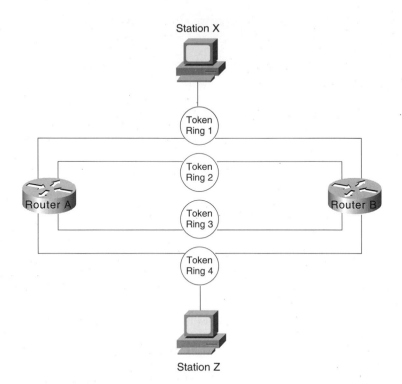

Figure 3–10
Controlling explorer
storms in redundant
network topologies.

To optimize explorer processing, perform one or more of the following tasks in global configuration mode:

Task	Command
Set the maximum explorer queue depth.	**source-bridge explorerq-depth** *depth*
Prevent explorer storms in redundant network topologies by filtering explorers that have already been forwarded once.	**source-bridge explorer-dup-ARE-filter**
Set the maximum byte rate of explorers per ring.	**source-bridge explorer-maxrate** *maxrate*

You must also disable explorer fast switching,which is, by default, enabled. To disable explorer fast switching, perform the following task in global configuration mode:

Task	Command
Disable explorer fast switching.	**no source-bridge explorer-fastswitch**

To enable explorer fast switching after it has been disabled, perform the following task in global configuration mode:

Task	Command
Enable explorer fast switching.	**source-bridge explorer-fastswitch**

Configuring Proxy Explorers

You can use the proxy explorers feature to limit the amount of explorer traffic propagating through the source-bridge network.

To configure proxy explorers, perform the following task in interface configuration mode:

Task	Command
Enable the interface to respond to any explorer packets that meet certain conditions necessary for a proxy response to occur.	**source-bridge proxy-explorer**

The Cisco IOS software does not propagate proxy responses for a station. Instead, the software obtains the RIF path from the RIF cache, changes the explorer to a specific frame, and forwards this frame to the destination. If the Cisco IOS software does not receive a response before the validation timer expires, the RIF entry is marked as invalid. The invalid RIF entry is flushed from the cache table when another explorer for this station is received, and an explorer is forwarded to discover a path to this station.

ESTABLISHING SRB INTEROPERABILITY WITH SPECIFIC TOKEN RING IMPLEMENTATIONS

This section describes how you can establish interoperability between routers and specific Token Ring implementations. It includes the following sections:

- Establishing SRB Interoperability with IBM PC/3270 Emulation Software
- Establishing SRB Interoperability with TI MAC Firmware
- Reporting Spurious Frame-Copied Errors

Establishing SRB Interoperability with IBM PC/3270 Emulation Software

You can establish interoperability with the IBM PC/3270 emulation program Version 3.0, even though it does not properly send packets over a source-route bridge.

Our implementation rewrites the RIF headers of the explorer packets that the PC/3270 emulation program sends to go beyond the local ring, thus confusing the IBM implementation into not looking beyond the local ring for the remote host.

To rewrite RIF headers, perform the following task in interface configuration mode:

Task	Command
Rewrite the RIF headers of explorer packets sent by the PC/3270 emulation program to go beyond the local ring.	source-bridge old-sna

Establishing SRB Interoperability with TI MAC Firmware

You can use a workaround to establish interoperability with Texas Instruments MAC firmware.

There is a known defect in earlier versions of the Texas Instruments Token Ring MAC firmware. This implementation is used by Proteon, Apollo, and IBM RTs. A host using a MAC address whose first two bytes are zeros (such as a Cisco router) will not properly communicate with hosts using that version of Texas Instruments firmware.

There are two solutions. The first involves installing a static RIF entry for every faulty node with which the router communicates. If there are many such nodes on the ring, this might not be practical.

You also can set the MAC address of the Cisco software Token Ring to a value that works around the problem. Resetting the MAC address forces the use of a different MAC address on the specified interface, thereby avoiding the TI MAC firmware problem. However, you must ensure that no other host on the network is using that MAC address.

To reset the MAC address, perform the following task in interface configuration mode:

Task	Command
Reset the MAC address of the Token Ring interface to a value that provides a workaround to a problem in Texas Instruments Token Ring MAC firmware.	mac-address *ieee-address*

Reporting Spurious Frame-Copied Errors

An IBM 3174 cluster controller can be configured to report frame-copied errors to IBM LAN Network Manager software. These errors indicate that another host is responding to the MAC address of the 3174 cluster controller. Both the 3174 cluster controller and the IBM LAN Network Manager software can be configured to ignore frame-copied errors.

MONITORING AND MAINTAINING THE SRB NETWORK

You can display a variety of information about the SRB network. To display the information you require, perform one or more of the following tasks in EXEC mode.

Task	Command
Display internal state information about the Token Ring interfaces in the system.	**show controllers token**
Provide high-level statistics about the state of source bridging for a particular interface.	**show interfaces**
Display all currently configured bridges and all parameters that are related to the bridge as a whole and not to one of its interfaces.	**show lnm bridge**
Display the logical (multiport bridge) configuration of the Cisco IOS software.	**show lnm config**
Display all LNM-relevant information about a specific interface.	**show lnm interface** [*type number*]
Display all LNM-relevant information about a specific ring number.	**show lnm ring** [*ring-number*]
Display all LNM-relevant information about a specific station or about all known stations on the ring.	**show lnm station** [*address*]
Show the current state of any current local acknowledgment for both LLC2 and SDLLC connections.	**show local-ack**
Display the contents of the NetBIOS cache.	**show netbios-cache**
Display the contents of the RIF cache.	**show rif**
Display the current source bridge configuration and miscellaneous statistics.	**show source-bridge**

Task	Command
Display the spanning-tree topology for the router.	**show span**
Display a summary of Silicon Switch Processor (SSP) statistics.	**show sse summary**

To maintain the SRB network, perform any of the following tasks in privileged EXEC mode:

Task	Command
Clear the entries of all dynamically learned NetBIOS names.	**clear netbios-cache**
Clear the entire RIF cache.	**clear rif-cache**
Clear the SRB statistical counters.	**clear source-bridge**
Reinitialize the SSP on the Cisco 7000 series.	**clear sse**

In addition to the EXEC-mode tasks to maintain the SRB network, you can perform the following task in global configuration mode:

Task	Command
Limit the size of the backup queue for RSRB to control the number of packets that can wait for transmission to a remote ring before they start being thrown away.	**source-bridge tcp-queue-max** *number*

SRB CONFIGURATION EXAMPLES

The following sections provide SRB configuration examples:

- Basic SRB with Spanning-Tree Explorers Example
- SRB with Automatic Spanning-Tree Function Configuration Example
- Optimized Explorer Processing Configuration Example
- SRB-Only Example
- SRB and Routing Certain Protocols Example

- Multiport SRB Example
- SRB with Multiple Virtual Ring Groups Example
- SRB over FDDI Configuration Examples
- SRB over FDDI Fast-Switching Example
- SRB over Frame Relay Configuration Example
- Adding a Static RIF Cache Entry Example
- Adding a Static RIF Cache Entry for a Two-Hop Path Example
- SR/TLB for a Simple Network Example
- SR/TLB with Access Filtering Example
- NetBIOS Support with a Static NetBIOS Cache Entry Example
- LNM for a Simple Network Example
- LNM for a More Complex Network Example
- NetBIOS Access Filters Example
- Filtering Bridged Token Ring Packets to IBM Machines Example
- Administrative Access Filters—Filtering SNAP Frames on Output Example
- Creating Access Expressions Example
- Access Expressions Example
- Fast-Switching Example
- Autonomous Switching Example

Basic SRB with Spanning-Tree Explorers Example

Figure 3–11 illustrates a simple two-port bridge configuration. Token Rings 129 and 130 are connected through the router.

Figure 3–11

Dual port source-route bridge configuration.

The example that follows routes IP, but source-route bridges all other protocols using spanning-tree explorers:

```
interface tokenring 0
 ip address 131.108.129.2 255.255.255.0
 source-bridge 129 1 130
 source-bridge spanning
 multiring all
```

```
!
interface tokenring 1
 ip address 131.108.130.2 255.255.255.0
 source-bridge 130 1 129
 source-bridge spanning
! use RIFs, as necessary, with IP routing software
 multiring all
```

SRB with Automatic Spanning-Tree Function Configuration Example

The following example of a Cisco series 7000 router configuration illustrates how to enable the automatic spanning-tree function on an SRB network.

```
source-bridge ring-group 100

interface tokenring 0/0
 no ip address
 ring-speed 16
 multiring all
 source-bridge active 1 10 100
 source-bridge spanning 1
!
interface tokenring 0/1
 no ip address
 ring-speed 16
 multiring all
 source-bridge active 2 10 100
 source-bridge spanning 1
!
bridge 1 protocol ibm
```

Optimized Explorer Processing Configuration Example

The following configuration example improves the handling of explorer frames, enabling the Cisco IOS software to perform substantially better during explorer broadcast storms. In this configuration, the maximum byte rate of explorers is set to 100000.

```
source-bridge explorer-maxrate 100000
source-bridge explorerQ-depth 100
no source-bridge explorer-fastswitch
```

SRB-Only Example

The following example shows that all protocols are bridged, including IP. Because IP is being bridged, the system has only one IP address.

```
no ip routing
!
interface tokenring 0
 ip address 131.108.129.2 255.255.255.0
 source-bridge 129 1 130
 source-bridge spanning
```

```
!
interface tokenring 1
 ip address 131.108.129.2 255.255.255.0
 source-bridge 130 1 129
 source-bridge spanning
!
interface ethernet 0
 ip address 131.108.129.2 255.255.255.0
```

SRB and Routing Certain Protocols Example

In the following configuration, IP, XNS, and IPX are routed, while all other protocols are bridged between rings. While not strictly necessary, the Novell IPX and XNS network numbers are set consistently with the IP subnetwork numbers. This makes the network easier to maintain.

```
xns routing 0000.0C00.02C3
!
novell routing 0000.0C00.02C3
!
interface tokenring 0
 ip address 131.108.129.2 255.255.255.0
 xns network 129
 novell network 129
 source-bridge 129 1 130
 source-bridge spanning
 multiring all
!
interface tokenring 1
 ip address 131.108.130.2 255.255.255.0
 xns network 130
 novell network 130
 source-bridge 130 1 129
 source-bridge spanning
 multiring all
!
interface ethernet 0
 ip address 131.108.2.68 255.255.255.0
 xns network 2
 novell network 2
```

Multiport SRB Example

Figure 3–12 shows an example configuration of a four-port Token Ring source-route bridge. Rings 1000, 1001, 1002, and 1003 are all source-route bridged to each other across ring group 7.

The following is a sample configuration file:

```
source-bridge ring-group 7
!
interface tokenring 0
 source-bridge 1000 1 7
 source-bridge spanning
```

```
!
interface tokenring 1
 source-bridge 1001 1 7
 source-bridge spanning
!
interface tokenring 2
 source-bridge 1002 1 7
 source-bridge spanning
!
interface tokenring 3
 source-bridge 1003 1 7
 source-bridge spanning
```

Figure 3–12
Four-port source-route bridge.

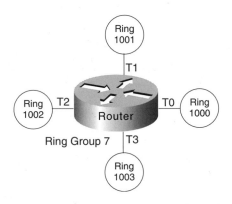

SRB with Multiple Virtual Ring Groups Example

Two virtual ring groups can only be connected through an actual Token Ring. Figure 3–13 shows Virtual Rings 100 and 200 connected through Token Ring 3.

Figure 3–13
Two virtual rings connected by an actual token ring.

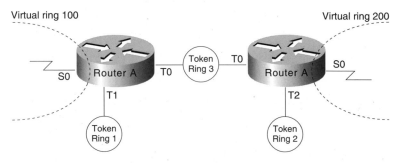

Configuration for Router A

```
source-bridge ring-group 100
!
interface tokenring 0
 source-bridge 3 4 100
 source-bridge spanning
!
interface tokenring 1
 source-bridge 1 4 100
 source-bridge spanning
```

Configuration for Router B

```
source-bridge ring-group 200
!
interface tokenring 0
 source-bridge 3 1 200
 source-bridge spanning
!
interface tokenring 2
 source-bridge 2 1 200
 source-bridge spanning
```

SRB over FDDI Configuration Examples

The following examples show the configuration for SRB over FDDI as illustrated in Figure 3–14.

Router A

```
dlsw local-peer peer-id 132.11.11.2
dlsw remote-peer 0 tcp 132.11.11.3
interface Fddi0
 no ip address
 multiring all
 source-bridge 26 1 10
 source-bridge spanning
```

Router B

```
dlsw local-peer peer-id 132.11.11.2
dlsw remote-peer 0 tcp 132.11.11.3
interface TokenRing0
 no ip address
 ring-speed 16
 multiring all
 source-bridge 25 1 10
 source-bridge spanning
```

Figure 3–14
SRB over FDDI configuration.

SRB over FDDI Fast-Switching Example

The following example enables SRB over FDDI fast-switching:

```
int fddi 2/0
 source-bridge 1 10 2
 source-bridge spanning
 source-bridge route-cache
 multiring ip
```

SRB over Frame Relay Configuration Example

Figure 3–15 illustrates a network with the following characteristics:

- Virtual Ring Number of Router A = 100
- Virtual Ring Number of FRAD B = 200
- Virtual Ring Number of FRAD C = 300
- DLCI number for PVC between Router A and FRAD B = 30
- DLCI number for PVC between Router A and FRAD C = 31

Figure 3–15

FRAD using SRB over frame relay to connect to a Cisco router.

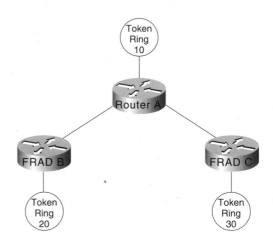

In this example, a new option, **conserve-ring**, is configured on the **source-bridge** interface configuration command. When this option is configured, the SRB software does not add the ring number associated with the Frame Relay PVC (the partner's virtual ring) to outbound explorer frames. This option is permitted for Frame Relay subinterfaces only.

The router configures the partner FRAD's virtual ring number as the ring number for the PVC.

This approach does not require a separate ring number per DLCI. The router configures the partner FRAD's virtual ring number as the ring number for the PVC.

FRAD B would configure its virtual ring as 200 and the ring for the PVC as 100. FRAD C would configure its virtual ring as 300 and the ring for the PVC as 100.

Configuration of Router A

```
source-bridge ring-group 100
!
interface Serial1
 encapsulation frame-relay
!
interface Serial1.1 point-to-point
 frame-relay interface-dlci 30 ietf
 source-bridge 200 1 100 conserve-ring
 source-bridge spanning
!
interface Serial1.2 point-to-point
 frame-relay interface-dlci 31 ietf
 source-bridge 300 1 100 conserve-ring
 source-bridge spanning
!
interface TokenRing0
source-bridge 500 1 100
```

Configuration on Router B

```
source-bridge ring-group 200
!
interface Serial0
 encapsulation frame-relay
!
interface Serial0.30 point-to-point
 frame-relay interface-dlci 30 ietf
 source-bridge 100 1 200 conserve-ring
 source-bridge spanning
!
interface TokenRing0
source-bridge 600 1 200
```

Configuration on Router C

```
source-bridge ring-group 300
!
interface Serial0
 encapsulation frame-relay
!
interface Serial0.31 point-to-point
 frame-relay interface-dlci 31 ietf
 source-bridge 100 1 300 conserve-ring
 source-bridge spanning
!
interface TokenRing0
source-bridge 900 1 300
```

Adding a Static RIF Cache Entry Example

In the example configuration in Figure 3–16, the path between rings 8 and 9 connected via Bridge 1 is described by the route descriptor 0081.0090. A full RIF, including the route control field, would be 0630.0081.0090.

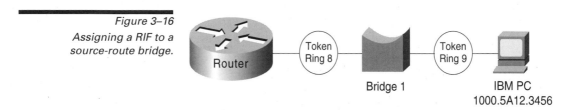

Figure 3–16
Assigning a RIF to a
source-route bridge.

The static RIF entry would be submitted to the router on the left as follows:

```
rif 1000.5A12.3456 0630.0081.0090
```

Adding a Static RIF Cache Entry for a Two-Hop Path Example

In Figure 3–17, assume that a datagram was sent from a router on ring 21 (15 hexadecimal), across Bridge 5 to ring 256 (100 hexadecimal), and then across Bridge 10 (A hexadecimal) to ring 1365 (555 hexadecimal) for delivery to a destination host on that ring.

Figure 3–17
Assigning a RIF
to a two-hop path.

The RIF in the router on the left describing this two-hop path is 0830.0155.100a.5550 and is entered as follows:

```
rif 1000.5A01.0203 0830.0155.100a.5550
```

SR/TLB for a Simple Network Example

In the simple example illustrated in Figure 3–18, a four-port router with two Ethernets and two Token Rings is used to connect transparent bridging on the Ethernets to SRB on the Token Rings.

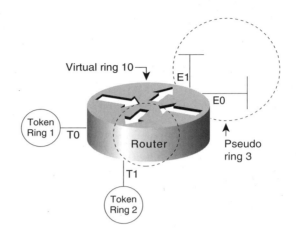

Figure 3–18

Example of a simple SR/TLB configuration.

Assume that the following configuration for SRB and transparent bridging existed before you wanted to enable SR/TLB:

```
interface tokenring 0
 source-bridge 1 1 2
!
interface tokenring 1
 source-bridge 2 1 1
!
interface ethernet 0
 bridge-group 1
!
interface ethernet 0
 bridge-group 1
!
bridge 1 protocol dec
```

To enable SR/TLB, one aspect of this configuration must change immediately—a third ring must be configured. Before SR/TLB, the two Token Ring interfaces were communicating with two-port local source-route bridging; after SR/TLB, these two interfaces must be reconfigured to communicate through a virtual ring, as follows:

```
source-bridge ring-group 10
!
interface tokenring 0
 source-bridge 1 1 10
!
interface tokenring 1
 source-bridge 2 1 10
!
interface ethernet 0
 bridge-group 1
```

```
!
interface ethernet 1
 bridge-group 1
!
bridge 1 protocol dec
```

Now you are ready to determine two things:

- A ring number for the pseudo-ring that is unique throughout the source-route bridged network. For the preceding example configuration, use the number 3.

- A bridge number for the path to the pseudo-ring. For the preceding example configuration, use the number 1.

Once you have determined the ring number and the bridge number, you can add the **source-bridge transparent** command to the file, including these two values as parameters for the command. The following partial configuration includes this **source-bridge transparent** entry:

```
!
source-bridge ring-group 10
source-bridge transparent 10 3 1 1
!
interface tokenring 0
 source-bridge 1 1 10
!
interface tokenring 1
 source-bridge 2 1 10
!
interface ethernet 0
 bridge-group 1
!
interface ethernet 1
 bridge-group 1
!
bridge 1 protocol dec
```

SR/TLB with Access Filtering Example

In the example shown in Figure 3–19, you want to connect only a single machine, Host E, on an Ethernet to a single machine, Host R, on the Token Ring.

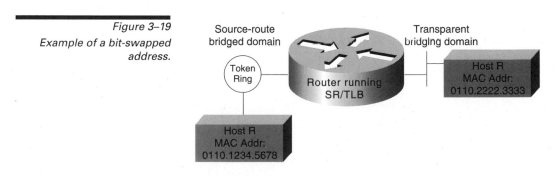

Figure 3–19

Example of a bit-swapped address.

You want to allow only these two machines to communicate across the router. Therefore, you might create the following configuration to restrict the access. However, this configuration will not work, as explained in the paragraph following the sample configuration file.

```
interface tokenring 0
 access-expression output smac(701)
!
interface ethernet 0
 bridge-group 1 input-address-list 701
!
 access-list 701 permit 0110.2222.3333
```

The command for the Token Ring interface specifies that the access list 701 be applied on the source address of frames going out to the Token Ring, and the command for the Ethernet interface specifies that this access list be applied on the source address frames entering the interface from Ethernet. This would work if both interfaces used the same bit ordering, but Token Rings and Ethernets use opposite (swapped) bit orderings in their addresses in relationship to each other. Therefore, the address of Host E on the Token Ring is not 0110.2222.3333, but rather 8008.4444.cccc, resulting in the following configuration. The following configuration is better. This example shows that access lists for Token Ring and Ethernet should be kept completely separate from each other.

```
interface tokenring 0
 source-bridge input-address-list 702
!
interface ethernet 0
 bridge-group 1 input-address-list 701
!
 access-list 701 permit 0110.2222.3333
!!
 access-list 702 permit 0110.1234.5678
```

NetBIOS Support with a Static NetBIOS Cache Entry Example

Figure 3–20 shows a NetBIOS client on a Token Ring connected through a cloud to a NetBIOS server on another Token Ring.

In Figure 3–20, a static entry is created in the router attached to ring 1 on the client side of the ring group. The static entry is to the server DEF, which is reached through the router attached to ring 3.

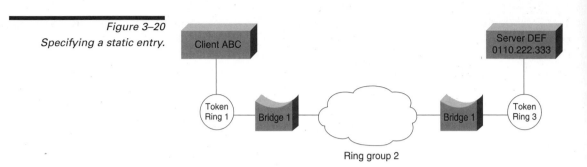

Figure 3–20
Specifying a static entry.

If server DEF has the MAC address 0110.2222.3333, the configuration for the static entry on the client side is as follows:

```
rif 0110.2222.3333 0630.0021.0030 ring-group 2
netbios name-cache 0110.2222.3333 DEF ring-group 2
```

LNM for a Simple Network Example

Figure 3–21 shows a router with two Token Rings configured as a local source-route bridge.

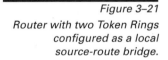

Figure 3–21

Router with two Token Rings configured as a local source-route bridge.

Physical configuration

Logical configuration

The associated configuration file follows:

```
interface tokenring 0
 source-bridge 1 2 3
!
interface tokenring 1
 source-bridge 3 2 1
```

The **show lnm config** command displays the logical configuration of this bridge, including the LNM configuration information that needs to be entered at the LNM Station. A sample **show lnm config** display follows:

```
Wayfarer# show lnm config

Bridge(s) currently configured:
From     ring 001, address 0000.3000.abc4
Across bridge 002
To       ring 003, address 0000.3000.5735
```

In this example, the MAC addresses 0000.3000.abc4 and 000.3000.5735 must be configured as Adapter Addresses at the LNM Station.

LNM for a More Complex Network Example

Figure 3–22 shows a router with three Token Rings configured as a multiport bridge, thus employing the concept of the virtual ring.

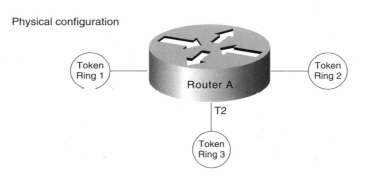

Figure 3–22

Router with three Token Rings configured as a multiport bridge.

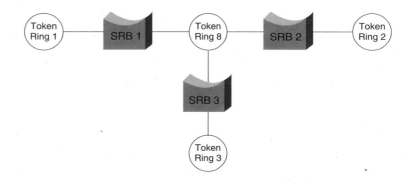

The associated configuration file follows.

```
source-bridge ring-group 8
!
interface tokenring 0
 source-bridge 1 1 8
!
interface tokenring 1
 source-bridge 2 2 8
!
interface tokenring 2
 source-bridge 3 3 8
```

The **show lnm config** command displays the logical configuration of this bridge, including all the pertinent information for configuring this router into LNM:

```
Wayfarer# show lnm config
Bridge(s) currently configured:

        From      ring 001, address 0000.0028.abcd
        Across bridge 001
        To        ring 008, address 4000.0028.abcd

        From      ring 002, address 0000.3000.abc4
        Across bridge 002
        To        ring 008, address 4000.3000.abc4

        From      ring 003, address 0000.3000.5735
        Across bridge 003
        To        ring 008, address 4000.3000.5735
```

In this example, six station definitions must be entered at the LNM Station, one for each of the MAC addresses listed in this sample **show lnm config** display.

NetBIOS Access Filters Example

The following command permits packets that include the station name ABCD to pass through the router, but denies passage to packets that do not include the station name ABCD:

```
netbios access-list host marketing permit ABCD
```

The following command specifies a prefix where the pattern matches any name beginning with the characters DEFG. Note that the string DEFG itself is included in this condition.

```
netbios access-list host marketing deny DEFG*
```

The following command permits any station name with the letter W as the first character and the letter Y as the third character in the name. The second and fourth letters in the name can be any character. This example would allow stations named WXYZ and WAYB; however, stations named WY and WXY would not be included in this statement, because the question mark must match some specific character in the name.

```
netbios access-list host marketing permit W?Y?
```

The following command illustrates how to combine wildcard characters:

```
netbios access-list host marketing deny AC?*
```

The command specifies that the marketing list deny any name beginning with AC that is at least three characters in length (the question mark would match any third character). The string ACBD and ACB would match, but the string AC would not.

The following command removes the entire marketing NetBIOS access list.

```
no netbios access-list host marketing
```

To remove single entries from the list, use a command such as the following:

```
no netbios access-list host marketing deny AC?*
```

This example removes only the list that filters station names with the letters AC at the beginning of the name.

Keep in mind that the access lists are scanned in order. In the following example, the first list denies all entries beginning with the letters ABC, including one named ABCD. This voids the second command, because the entry permitting a name with ABCD comes after the entry denying it.

```
netbios access-list host marketing deny ABC*
netbios access-list host marketing permit ABCD
```

Filtering Bridged Token Ring Packets to IBM Machines Example

The example in Figure 3–23 disallows the bridging of Token Ring packets to all IBM workstations on Token Ring 1.

Figure 3–23

Router filtering bridged Token Ring packets to IBM machines.

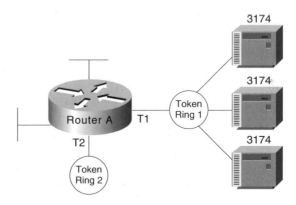

This example assumes that all hosts on Token Ring 1 have Token Ring addresses with the vendor code 1000.5A00.0000. The first line of the access list denies access to all IBM workstations, while the second line permits everything else. The access list is assigned to the input side of Token Ring 1.

```
! deny access to all IBM workstations
access-list 700 deny 1000.5A00.0000    8000.00FF.FFFF
! permit all other traffic
access-list 700 permit 0000.0000.0000    FFFF.FFFF.FFFF
!
interface token ring 1
! apply access list 700 to the input side of Token Ring 1
source-bridge input-address-list 700
```

Administrative Access Filters—Filtering SNAP Frames on Output Example

Figure 3–24 shows a router connecting four Token Rings.

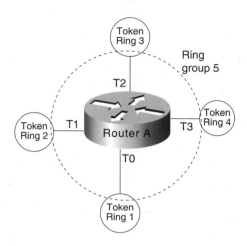

Figure 3–24
Router filtering
SNAP frames on output.

The following example allows only AppleTalk Phase 2 packets to be source-route bridged between Token Rings 0 and 1, and allows Novell packets only to be source-route bridged between Token Rings 2 and 3.

```
source-bridge ring-group 5
!
interface tokenring 0
 ip address 131.108.1.1 255.255.255.0
 source-bridge 1000 1 5
 source-bridge spanning
 source-bridge input-type-list 202
!
interface tokenring 1
 ip address 131.108.11.1 255.255.255.0
 source-bridge 1001 1 5
 source-bridge spanning
 source-bridge input-type-list 202
!
interface tokenring 2
 ip address 131.108.101.1 255.255.255.0
 source-bridge 1002 1 5
 source-bridge spanning
 source-bridge input-lsap-list 203
!
interface tokenring 3
 ip address 131.108.111.1 255.255.255.0
 source-bridge 1003 1 5
 source-bridge spanning
 source-bridge input-lsap-list 203
```

```
!
! SNAP type code filtering
! permit ATp2 data (0x809B)
! permit ATp2 AARP (0x80F3)
access-list 202 permit 0x809B 0x0000
access-list 202 permit 0x80F3 0x0000
access-list 202 deny 0x0000 0xFFFF
!
! LSAP filtering
! permit IPX (0xE0E0)
access-list 203 permit 0xE0E0 0x0101
access-list 203 deny 0x0000 0xFFFF
```

Note that it is not necessary to check for an LSAP of 0xAAAA when filtering SNAP-encapsulated AppleTalk packets, because for source-route bridging, the use of type filters implies SNAP encapsulation.

Creating Access Expressions Example

In math, you have the following:

> $3 \times 4 + 2 = 14$ but $3 \times (4 + 2) = 18$

Similarly, the following access expressions would return TRUE if lsap(201) and dmac(701) returned TRUE or if smac(702) returned TRUE:

> lsap(201) & dmac(701) | smac(702)

However, the following access expression would return TRUE only if lsap(201) returned TRUE and either of dmac(701) or smac(702) returned TRUE:

> lsap(201) & (dmac(701) | smac(702))

Referring to the earlier example, "An Example Using NetBIOS Access Filters," we had the phrase:

> "Pass the frame if it is NetBIOS, or if it is an SNA frame destined to address 0110.2222.3333."

This phrase was converted to the simpler form of:

> Pass if "NetBIOS or (SNA and destined to 0110.2222.3333)."

So, for the following configuration:

```
! Access list 201 passes NetBIOS frames (command or response)
access-list 201 permit 0xF0F0 0x0001
!
access-list 202 permit 0x0404 0x0001 ! Permits SNA frames (command or response)
access-list 202 permit 0x0004 0x0001 ! Permits SNA Explorers with NULL DSAP
!
! Access list 701 will permit the FEP MAC address
! of 0110.2222.3333
access-list 701 permit 0110.2222.3333
```

The following access expression would result:

```
access-expression in lsap(201) ¦ (lsap(202) & dmac(701))
```

Therefore, the full configuration example is as follows:

```
interface tokenring 0
access-expression in lsap(201 ¦ (lsap(202) & dmac(701))
!
! Access list 201 passes NetBIOS frames (command or response
access-list 201 permit 0xF0F0 0x0001
!
access-list 202 permit 0x0404 0x0001 ! Permits SNA frames (command or response)
access-list 202 permit 0x0004 0x0001 ! Permits NSA Explorers with NULL DSAP
!
! Access list 701 will permit the FEP MAC address
! of 0110.2222.3333
access-list 701 permit 0110.2222.3333
```

Access Expressions Example

Figure 3–25 shows two routers connecting two Token Rings to an FDDI backbone.

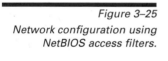

Figure 3–25

Network configuration using NetBIOS access filters.

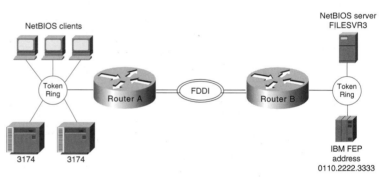

Suppose you want to permit the IBM 3174 cluster controllers to access the FEP at address 0110.2222.3333, and also want the NetBIOS clients to access the NetBIOS server named FILESVR3. The following set of router configuration commands would meet this need:

```
netbios access-list host MIS permit FILESVR3
netbios access-list host MIS deny *
!
access-list 202 permit 0x0404 0x0001 ! Permits SNA frames (command or response)
access-list 202 permit 0x0004 0x0001 ! Permits SNA Explorers with NULL DSAP
!
access-list 701 permit 0110.2222.3333
!
interface tokenring 0
access-expression in (lsap(202) & dmac(701)) ¦ netbios-host(MIS)
```

Fast-Switching Example

The following example disables fast switching between two Token Ring interfaces in the same router:

```
! global command establishing the ring group for the interface configuration commands
source-bridge ring-group 2
!
! commands that follow apply to interface token 0
interface tokenring 0
! enable srb between local ring 1, bridge 1, and target ring 2
source-bridge 1 1 2
!disable source-route fast-switching cache on interface token 0
no source-bridge route-cache
!
interface token 1
! enable srb between local ring 2, bridge 1, and target ring 1
source-bridge 2 1 1
no source-bridge route-cache
```

Frames entering Token Ring interfaces 0 or 1 will not be fast switched to the other interface.

Autonomous Switching Example

The following example enables use of autonomous switching between two ciscoBus Token Ring interfaces in the same router:

```
! global command to apply interface configuration commands to the ring group
source-bridge ring-group 2
!
! commands that follow apply to interface token 0
interface tokenring 0
! enable srb between local ring 1, bridge 1, and target ring 2
source-bridge 1 1 2
! enable autonomous switching for interface token 0
source-bridge route-cache cbus
!
interface tokenring 1
! enable srb between local ring 2, bridge 1, and target ring 1
source-bridge 2 1 1
source-bridge route-cache cbus
```

Frames entering Token Ring interfaces 0 or 1 will be autonomously switched to the other interface.

CHAPTER 4

Source-Route Bridging Commands

Use the commands in this chapter to configure and monitor source-route bridging (SRB) networks. For SRB configuration information and examples, see Chapter 3, "Configuring Source-Route Bridging."

ACCESS-EXPRESSION

Use the **access-expression** interface configuration command to define an access expression. Use the **no** form of this command to remove the access expression from the given interface. You use this command in conjunction with the **access-list** interface configuration command.

> **access-expression** {**in** | **out**} *expression*
> **no access-expression** {**in** | **out**} *expression*

Syntax	Description
in	**out**	Either **in** or **out** is specified to indicate whether the access expression is applied to packets entering or leaving this interface.
	You can specify both an input and an output access expression for an interface, but only one of each.
expression	Boolean access list expression, built as explained in the "Usage Guidelines" section.

Default

No access expression is defined.

Command Mode

Interface configuration

Usage Guidelines

This command first appeared in Cisco IOS Release 10.0.

An access expression consists of a list of terms, separated by Boolean operators, and optionally grouped in parentheses.

An access expression term specifies a type of access list, followed by its name or number. The result of the term is either true or false, depending on whether the access list specified in the term permits or denies the frame. Table 4–1 describes the terms that can be used.

Table 4–1 *Access Expression Terms*

Access Expression Term	Definition
lsap(2nn)	The LSAP access list to be evaluated for this frame (200 series).
type(2nn)	The SNAP type access list to be evaluated for this frame (200 series).
smac(7nn)	The access list to match the source MAC address of the frame (700 series).
dmac(7nn)	The access list to match the destination MAC address of the frame (700 series).
netbios-host(name)	The netbios-host access list to be applied on NetBIOS frames traversing the interface.
netbios-bytes(name)	The netbios-bytes access list to be applied on NetBIOS frames traversing the interface.

NOTES

The *netbios-host* and *netbios-bytes* access expression terms always will return FALSE for frames that are not NetBIOS frames.

Access expression terms are separated by Boolean operators as listed in Table 4–2.

Table 4–2 *Boolean Operators for Access Expression Terms*

Boolean Operators	Definitions
~ (called "not")	Negates, or reverses, the result of the term or group of terms immediately to the right of the ~. Example: "~lsap (201)" returns FALSE if "lsap (201)" itself were TRUE.
& (called "and")	Returns TRUE if the terms or parenthetical expressions to the left and right of the & both return TRUE. Example: "lsap (201) & dmac (701)" returns TRUE if both the lsap (201) and dmac (701) terms return TRUE.
I (called "or")	Returns TRUE if the terms or parenthetical expressions to the left or right of the I either or both of return TRUE. Example: "lsap (201) I dmac (701)" returns TRUE if either the lsap (201) or dmac (701) terms return TRUE, as well as if both return TRUE.

Terms can be grouped in parenthetical expressions. Any of the terms and operators can be placed in parentheses, similar to what is done in arithmetic expressions, to affect order of evaluation.

NOTES

The incorrect use of parentheses can drastically affect the result of an operation, because the expression is read left to right.

Related Commands

access-list

ACCESS-LIST

Use the **access-list** global configuration command to configure the access list mechanism for filtering frames by protocol type or vendor code. Use the **no** form of this command to remove the single specified entry from the access list.

> **access-list** *access-list-number* {**permit** I **deny**} {*type-code wild-mask* I *address mask*}
> **no access-list** *access-list-number* {**permit** I **deny**} {*type-code wild-mask* I *address mask*}

Syntax	Description
access-list-number	Integer that identifies the access list. If the *type-code wild-mask* arguments are included, this integer ranges from 200 to 299, indicating that filtering is by protocol type. If the *address* and *mask* arguments are included, this integer ranges from 700 to 799, indicating that filtering is by vendor code.
permit	Permits the frame.
deny	Denies the frame.
type-code	16-bit hexadecimal number written with a leading 0x; for example, 0x6000. Specify either a Link Service Access Point (LSAP) type code for 802-encapsulated packets or a SNAP type code for SNAP-encapsulated packets. (LSAP, sometimes called SAP, refers to the type codes found in the DSAP and SSAP fields of the 802 header.)
wild-mask	16-bit hexadecimal number whose ones bits correspond to bits in the *type-code* argument. The *wild-mask* indicates which bits in the *type-code* argument should be ignored when making a comparison. (A mask for a DSAP/SSAP pair should always be 0x0101 because these two bits are used for purposes other than identifying the SAP code.)
address	48-bit Token Ring address written in dotted triplet form. This field is used for filtering by vendor code.
mask	48-bit Token Ring address written in dotted triplet form. The ones bits in *mask* are the bits to be ignored in *address*. This field is used for filtering by vendor code.

NOTES

For source address filtering, the mask always should have the high-order bit set. This is because the IEEE 802 standard uses this bit to indicate whether a RIF is present, not as part of the source address.

Default
No access list is configured.

Command Mode
Global configuration

Usage Guidelines
This command first appeared in Cisco IOS Release 10.0.

For a list of type codes, refer to Appendix A, "Ethernet Type Codes."

Examples

In the following example, the access list permits only Novell frames (LSAP 0xE0E0) and filters out all other frame types. This set of access lists would be applied to an interface via the **source-bridge input-lsap list** or **source-bridge input-lsap list** commands (described later in this chapter).

```
access-list 201 permit 0xE0E0 0x0101
access-list 201 deny  0x0000 0xFFFF
```

Combine the DSAP/LSAP fields into one number to do LSAP filtering; for example, 0xE0E0—not 0xE0. Note that the deny condition specified in the preceding example is not required; access lists have an implicit deny as the last statement. Adding this statement can serve as a useful reminder, however.

The following access list filters out only SNAP type codes assigned to DEC (0x6000 to 0x6007) and lets all other types pass. This set of access lists would be applied to an interface using the **source-bridge input-type-list** or **source-bridge output-type-list** commands (described later in this chapter).

```
access-list 202 deny    0x6000 0x0007
access-list 202 permit  0x0000 0xFFFF
```

NOTES

Use the last item of an access list to specify a default action; for example, to permit everything else or to deny everything else. If nothing else in the access list matches, the default action is to deny access; that is, filter out all other type codes.

Type code access lists will negatively affect system performance by greater than 30 percent. Therefore, it is recommended that you keep the lists as short as possible and use wildcard bit masks whenever possible.

Related Commands

access-expression
source-bridge input-address-list
source-bridge input-lsap-list
source-bridge input-type-list
source-bridge output-address-list
source-bridge output-lsap-list
source-bridge output-type-list

BRIDGE PROTOCOL IBM

Use the **bridge protocol ibm** global configuration command to create a bridge group that runs the automatic spanning-tree function. Use the **no** form of this command to cancel the previous assignment.

bridge *bridge-group* **protocol ibm**
no bridge *bridge-group* **protocol ibm**

Syntax   *Description*

bridge-group   Number in the range 1 to 9 that you choose to refer to a particular set
                          of bridged interfaces.

Default

No bridge group is defined.

Command Mode

Global configuration

Usage Guidelines

This command first appeared in Cisco IOS Release 10.3.

Example

The following example specifies bridge 1 to use the automatic spanning-tree function:

```
bridge 1 protocol ibm
```

Related Commands

show source-bridge
source-bridge spanning (automatic)
source-bridge spanning (manual)

CLEAR NETBIOS-CACHE

Use the **clear netbios-cache** privileged EXEC command to clear the entries of all dynamically
learned NetBIOS names. This command will not remove statically defined name cache entries.

clear netbios-cache

Syntax   *Description*

This command has no arguments or keywords.

Command Mode

Privileged EXEC

Usage Guidelines

This command first appeared in Cisco IOS Release 10.0.

The Cisco IOS software automatically learns NetBIOS names. This command clears those entries.

Example

The following example clears all dynamically learned NetBIOS names:

```
clear netbios-cache
```

Related Commands

netbios enable-name-cache
netbios name-cache timeout
show netbios-cache

CLEAR RIF-CACHE

Use the **clear rif-cache** privileged EXEC command to clear the entire RIF cache.

clear rif-cache

Syntax   Description

This command has no arguments or keywords.

Command Mode

Privileged EXEC

Usage Guidelines

This command first appeared in Cisco IOS Release 10.0.

Some entries in the RIF cache are dynamically added and others are static.

Example

The following example clears the entire RIF cache:

```
clear rif-cache
```

Related Commands

rif
rif timeout
show rif

CLEAR SOURCE-BRIDGE

Use the **clear source-bridge** privileged EXEC command to clear the source-bridge statistical counters.

clear source-bridge

Syntax   Description

This command has no arguments or keywords.

Command Mode

Privileged EXEC

Usage Guidelines

This command first appeared in Cisco IOS Release 10.0.

Example

The following example clears the source-bridge statistical counters:

```
clear source-bridge
```

Related Commands

clear bridge

CLEAR SSE

Use the **clear sse** privileged EXEC command to reinitialize the Silicon Switch Processor (SSP) on the Cisco 7000 series routers with RSP7000.

     clear sse

Syntax   Description

This command has no arguments or keywords.

Default

Disabled

Command Mode

Privileged EXEC

Usage Guidelines

This command first appeared in Cisco IOS Release 10.3.

The silicon switching engine (SSE) is on the SSP board in the Cisco 7000 series routers with RSP7000.

Example

The following example reinitializes the SSP:

```
clear sse
```

ETHERNET-TRANSIT-OUI

Use the **ethernet-transit-oui** interface configuration command to choose the Organizational Unique Identifier (OUI) code to be used in the encapsulation of Ethernet Type II frames across Token Ring backbone networks. Various versions of this OUI code are used by Ethernet/Token Ring translational bridges. Use the **no** form of this command to return the default OUI code.

    ethernet-transit-oui [90-compatible | standard | cisco]
    no ethernet-transit-oui

Syntax	*Description*
90-compatible	(Optional) Default OUI form.
standard	(Optional) Standard OUI form.
cisco	(Optional) Cisco's OUI form.

Default

90-compatible

Command Mode

Interface configuration

Usage Guidelines

This command first appeared in Cisco IOS Release 10.0.

This command replaces and extends the **bridge old-oui** command in Software Release 9.0.

Before using this command, you must have completely configured your router using multiport source-bridging and transparent bridging.

The **standard** keyword is used when you are forced to interoperate with other vendor equipment, such as the IBM 8209, in providing Ethernet and Token Ring mixed media bridged connectivity.

The actual OUI codes that are used, when they are used, and how they compare to Software Release 9.0-equivalent commands are shown in Table 4–3.

Table 4–3 *Bridge OUI Codes*

Keyword	OUI Used	When Used/Benefits	Software Release 9.0 Command Equivalent
90-compatible	0000F8	By default, when talking to other Cisco routers. Provides the most flexibility.	no bridge old-oui
cisco	00000C	Provided for compatibility with future equipment.	None
standard	000000	When talking to IBM 8209 bridges and other vendor equipment. Does not provide for as much flexibility as the other two choices.	bridge old-oui

Specify the **90-compatible** keyword when talking to Cisco routers. This keyword provides the most flexibility. When **90-compatible** is specified or the default is used, Token Ring frames with an OUI of 0x0000F8 are translated into Ethernet Type II frames while Token Ring frames with the OUI of 0x000000 are translated into SNAP-encapsulated frames. Specify the **standard** keyword when talking to IBM 8209 bridges and other vendor equipment. This OUI does not provide for as much flexibility as the other two choices. The **cisco** OUI is provided for compatibility with future equipment.

Do not use the **standard** keyword unless you are forced to interoperate with other vendor equipment, such as the IBM 8209, in providing Ethernet and Token Ring mixed media bridged connectivity. Only use the **standard** keyword when you are transferring data between IBM 8209 Ethernet/Token Ring bridges and routers running the SR/TLB software (to create a Token Ring backbone to connect Ethernets).

Use of the **standard** keyword causes the OUI code in Token Ring frames to always be 0x000000. In the context of the **standard** keyword, an OUI of 0x000000 identifies the frame as an Ethernet Type II frame. (Compare with 90-compatible, where 0x000000 OUI means SNAP-encapsulated frames.)

If you use the **90-compatible** keyword, the router, acting as an SR/TLB, can distinguish immediately on Token Ring interfaces between frames that started on an Ethernet Type II frame and those that started on an Ethernet as a SNAP-encapsulated frame. The distinction is possible because the router uses the 0x0000F8 OUI when converting Ethernet Type II frames into Token Ring SNAP frames, and leaves the OUI as 0x000000 for Ethernet SNAP frames going to a Token Ring. This distinction in OUIs leads to efficiencies in the design and execution of the SR/TLB product; no tables need to be kept to know which Ethernet hosts use SNAP encapsulation and which hosts use Ethernet Type II.

The IBM 8209 bridges, however, by using the 0x000000 OUI for all the frames entering the Token Ring, must take extra measures to perform the translation. For every station on each Ethernet, the

8209 bridges attempt to remember the frame format used by each station, and assume that once a station sends out a frame using Ethernet Type II or 802.3, it will always continue to do so. It must do this because in using 0x000000 as an OUI, there is no way to distinguish between SNAP and Type II frame types. Because the SR/TLB router does not need to keep this database, when 8209 compatibility is enabled with the **standard** keyword, the SR/TLB chooses to translate all Token Ring SNAP frames into Ethernet Type II frames as described earlier in this discussion. Because every nonroutable protocol on Ethernet uses either non-SNAP 802.3 (which traverses fully across a mixed IBM 8209/ router Token Ring backbone) or Ethernet Type II, this results in correct interconnectivity for virtually all applications.

Do not use the **standard** OUI if you want SR/TLB to output Ethernet SNAP frames. Using either the **90-compatible** or **cisco** OUI does not present such a restriction, because SNAP frames and Ethernet Type II-encapsulated frames have different OUI codes on Token Ring networks.

Example

The following example specifies standard OUI form:

```
interface tokenring 0
  ethernet-transit-oui standard
```

Related Commands

ethernet-transit-oui
source-bridge transparent

LNM ALTERNATE

Use the **lnm alternate** interface configuration command to specify the threshold reporting link number. In order for a LAN Reporting Manager (LRM) to change parameters, it must be attached to the reporting link with the lowest reporting link number, and that reporting link number must be lower than this threshold reporting link number. Use the **no** form of this command to restore the default of 0.

lnm alternate *number*
no lnm alternate

Syntax	Description
number	Threshold reporting link number. It must be in the range 0 to 3.

Default

0

Command Mode

Interface configuration

Usage Guidelines

This command first appeared in Cisco IOS Release 10.0.

LAN Network Manager (LNM) employs the concepts of reporting links and reporting link numbers. A reporting link is simply a connection (or potential connection) between an LRM and a bridge. A reporting link number is a unique number used to identify a reporting link. An IBM bridge allows four simultaneous reporting links numbered 0 to 3. Only the LRM attached to the lowest number connection is allowed to change any parameters, and then only when that connection number falls below a certain configurable number. In the default configuration, the LRM connected through link 0 is the only LRM allowed to change parameters.

NOTES

Setting the threshold reporting link number on one interface in a source-route bridge will cause it to appear on the other interface of the bridge, because the command applies to the bridge itself and not to either of the interfaces.

Examples

The following example permits LRMs connected through links 0 and 1 to change parameters:

```
! provide appropriate global configuration command if not currently in your config.
!
! permit 0 and 1
lnm alternate 1
```

The following example permits all LRMs to change parameters in the Cisco IOS software:

```
! provide appropriate global configuration command if not currently in your config.
!
! permit 0, 1, 2, and 3
lnm alternate 3
```

Related Commands

lnm password

LNM CRS

Use the **lnm crs** interface configuration command to monitor the current logical configuration of a Token Ring. Use the **no** form of this command to disable this function.

> lnm crs
> no lnm crs

Syntax   Description

This command has no arguments or keywords.

Default

Enabled

Command Mode

Interface configuration

Usage Guidelines

This command first appeared in Cisco IOS Release 10.0.

The Configuration Report Server service keeps track of the current logical configuration of a Token Ring and reports any changes to LNM. It also reports on various other activities such as the change of the Active Monitor on a Token Ring.

Example

The following example disables monitoring of the current logical configuration of a Token Ring:

```
interface tokenring 0
 no lnm crs
```

Related Commands

lnm rem
lnm rps

LNM DISABLED

Use the **lnm disabled** global configuration command to disable LNM functionality. Use the **no** form of this command to restore LNM functionality.

lnm disabled
no lnm disabled

Syntax   Description

This command has no arguments or keywords.

Default

Enabled

Command Mode

Global configuration

Usage Guidelines

This command first appeared in Cisco IOS Release 11.2.

Under some circumstances you can disable all LNM server functions on the router without having to determine whether to disable a specific server, such as the ring parameter server or the ring error monitor on a given interface.

This command can be used to terminate all LNM server input and reporting links. In normal circumstances, this command should not be necessary because it is a superset of the functions normally performed on individual interfaces by the **no lnm rem** and **no lnm rps** commands.

Example

The following example disables LNM functionality:

```
lnm disabled
```

Related Commands

lnm pathtrace-disabled
lnm rem
lnm rps
lnm snmp-only
show lnm bridge

LNM LOSS-THRESHOLD

Use the **lnm loss-threshold** interface configuration command to set the threshold at which the Cisco IOS software sends a message informing all attached LNMs that it is dropping frames. Use the **no** form of this command to return to the default value.

lnm loss-threshold *number*
no lnm loss-threshold

Syntax	Description
number	A single number expressing the percentage loss rate in hundredths of a percent. The valid range is 0 to 9999.

Default

10 (.10 percent)

Command Mode

Interface configuration

Usage Guidelines

This command first appeared in Cisco IOS Release 10.0.

The software sends a message to all attached LNMs whenever it begins to drop frames. The point at which this report is generated (threshold) is a percentage of the number of frames dropped compared with the number of frames forwarded.

When setting this value, remember that 9999 would mean 100 percent of your frames could be dropped before the message is sent. A value of 1000 would mean 10 percent of the frames could be dropped before sending the message. A value of 100 would mean 1 percent of the frames could be dropped before the message is sent.

Example

In the following example, the loss threshold is set to 0.02 percent:

```
interface tokenring 0
  lnm loss-threshold 2
```

LNM PASSWORD

Use the **lnm password** interface configuration command to set the password for the reporting link. Use the **no** form of this command to return the password to its default value of 00000000.

lnm password *number string*
no lnm password *number*

Syntax	Description
number	Number of the reporting link to which to apply the password. This value should be in the range 0 to 3.
string	Password you enter at the keyboard. In order to maintain compatibility with LNM, the parameter *string* should be a six- to eight-character string of the type listed in the "Usage Guidelines" section.

Default

00000000

Command Mode

Interface configuration

Usage Guidelines

This command first appeared in Cisco IOS Release 10.0.

LNM employs the concepts of reporting links and reporting link numbers. A reporting link is simply a connection (or potential connection) between a LAN Reporting Manager (LRM) and a bridge. A reporting link number is a unique number used to identify a reporting link. An IBM bridge allows four simultaneous reporting links numbered 0 to 3. Only the LRM attached to the lowest number connection is allowed to change any parameters, and then only when that connection number falls below a certain configurable number. In the default configuration, the LRM connected through link 0 is the only LRM allowed to change parameters.

Each reporting link has its own password. Passwords are used not only to prevent unauthorized access from an LRM to a bridge, but also to control access to the different reporting links. This is important because of the different abilities associated with the various reporting links.

Characters allowable in the *string* are the following:

- Letters
- Numbers
- Special characters @, #, $, or %

Passwords are displayed only through use of the privileged EXEC **show running-config** command.

NOTES

There are two parameters in an IBM bridge that have no corresponding parameter in the Cisco IOS software. This means that any attempt to modify these parameters from LNM will fail and display an error message. The LNM names of these two parameters are *route active status* and *single route broadcast mode*.

Example

In the following example, the password *Zephyr@* is assigned to reporting link 2:

```
! provide appropriate global configuration command if not currently in your config.
!
lnm password 2 Zephyr@
```

Related Commands

lnm alternate

LNM PATHTRACE-DISABLED

Use the **lnm pathtrace-disabled** global configuration command to disable pathtrace reporting to LNM stations. Use the **no** form of this command to restore pathtrace reporting functionality.

lnm pathtrace-disabled [all | origin]
no lnm pathtrace-disabled

Syntax	Description
all	Disable pathtrace reporting to the LNM and originating stations.
origin	Disable pathtrace reporting to originating stations only.

Default

Enabled

Command Mode

Global configuration

Usage Guidelines

This command first appeared in Cisco IOS Release 11.2.

Under some circumstances, such as when new hardware has been introduced into the network and is causing problems, the automatic report pathtrace function can be disabled. The new hardware might be setting bit-fields B1 or B2 (or both) of the routing control field in the routing information field embedded in a source-route bridged frame. This condition may cause the network to be flooded by report pathtrace frames if the condition is persistent. The **lnm pathtrace-disabled** command, along with its options, allows you to alleviate network congestion that might be occurring by disabling all or part of the automatic report pathtrace function within LNM.

Example

The following example disables all pathtrace reporting:

```
lnm pathtrace-disabled
```

Related Commands

lnm disabled
lnm pathtrace-disabled
show lnm bridge

LNM REM

Use the **lnm rem** interface configuration command to monitor errors reported by any station on the ring. Use the **no** form of this command to disable this function.

> **lnm rem**
> **no lnm rem**

Syntax   Description

This command has no arguments or keywords.

Default

Enabled

Command Mode

Interface configuration

Usage Guidelines

This command first appeared in Cisco IOS Release 10.0.

The Ring Error Monitor (REM) service monitors errors reported by any station on the ring. It also monitors whether the ring is in a functional state or in a failure state.

Example

The following example shows the use of the **lnm rem** command:

```
interface tokenring 0
  lnm rem
```

Related Commands

lnm crs
lnm rps

LNM RPS

Use the **lnm rps** interface configuration command to ensure that all stations on a ring are using a consistent set of reporting parameters. Use the **no** form of this command to disable this function.

> **lnm rps**
> **no lnm rps**

Syntax   Description

This command has no arguments or keywords.

Default

Enabled

Command Mode

Interface configuration

Usage Guidelines

This command first appeared in Cisco IOS Release 10.0.

The Ring Parameter Server (RPS) service ensures that all stations on a ring are using a consistent set of reporting parameters and are reporting to LNM when any new station joins a Token Ring.

Example

The following example shows the use of the **lnm rps** command:

```
interface tokenring 0
  lnm rps
```

Related Commands

lnm crs
lnm rem

LNM SNMP-ONLY

Use the **lnm snmp-only** global configuration command to prevent any LNM stations from modifying parameters in the Cisco IOS software. Use the **no** form of this command to allow modifications.

> lnm snmp-only
> no lnm snmp-only

Syntax   Description

This command has no arguments or keywords.

Default

Enabled

Command Mode

Global configuration

Usage Guidelines

This command first appeared in Cisco IOS Release 10.0.

Configuring a router for LNM support is simple. It happens automatically as a part of configuring the router to act as a source-route bridge. There are several commands available to modify the behavior of the LNM support, but none of them are necessary for it to function.

Because there is now more than one way to remotely change parameters in the Cisco IOS software, this command was developed to prevent them from detrimentally interacting with each other.

This command does not affect the ability of LNM to monitor events, only to modify parameters in the Cisco IOS software.

Example

The following command prevents any LNM stations from modifying parameters in the software:

```
lnm snmp-only
```

LNM SOFTERR

Use the **lnm softerr** interface configuration command to set the time interval in which the Cisco IOS software will accumulate error messages before sending them. Use the **no** form of this command to return to the default value.

lnm softerr *milliseconds*
no lnm softerr

Syntax	Description
milliseconds	Time interval in tens of milliseconds between error messages. The valid range is 0 to 65535.

Default

200 ms (2 seconds)

Command Mode

Interface configuration

Usage Guidelines

This command first appeared in Cisco IOS Release 10.0.

All stations on a Token Ring notify the REM when they detect errors on the ring. To prevent an excessive number of messages, error reports are not sent immediately, but are accumulated for a short period of time and then reported. A station learns this value from a router (configured as a source-route bridge) when it first enters the ring.

Example

The following example changes the error-reporting frequency to once every 5 seconds:

```
lnm softerr 500
```

Related Commands

lnm rem

MAC-ADDRESS

Use the **mac-address** interface configuration command to set the MAC layer address of the Cisco Token Ring.

mac-address *ieee-address*

Syntax	Description
ieee-address	48-bit IEEE MAC address written as a dotted triplet of four-digit hexadecimal numbers

Default

No MAC layer address is set.

Command Mode

Interface configuration

Usage Guidelines

This command first appeared in Cisco IOS Release 10.0.

There is a known defect in earlier forms of this command of the Texas Instruments Token Ring MAC firmware. This implementation is used by Proteon, Apollo, and IBM RTs. A host using a MAC address whose first two bytes are zeros (such as a Cisco router) will not properly communicate with hosts using that form of this command of TI firmware.

There are two solutions. The first involves installing a static RIF entry for every faulty node with which the router communicates. If there are many such nodes on the ring, this might not be practical. The second solution involves setting the MAC address of the Cisco Token Ring to a value that works around the problem.

This command forces the use of a different MAC address on the specified interface, thereby avoiding the Texas Instrument MAC firmware problem. It is up to the network administrator to ensure that no other host on the network is using that MAC address.

Example

The following example sets the MAC layer address, where *xx.xxxx* is an appropriate second half of the MAC address to use:

```
interface tokenring 0
  mac-address 5000.5axx.xxxx
```

MULTIRING

Use the **multiring** interface configuration command to enable collection and use of RIF information. Use the **no** form of this command to disable the use of RIF information for the protocol specified.

> **multiring** {*protocol-keyword* [**all-routes** | **spanning**] | **all** | **other**}
> **no multiring** {*protocol-keyword* [**all-routes** | **spanning**] | **all** | **other**}

Syntax	Description
protocol-keyword	Specifies a protocol; see the keyword list under the "Usage Guidelines" section.
all-routes	Uses all-routes explorers.
spanning	Uses spanning-tree explorers.
all	Enables the multiring for *all* frames.
other	Enables the multiring for *any* routed frame not included in the previous list of supported protocols.

Default

Disabled

Command Mode

Interface configuration

Usage Guidelines

This command first appeared in Cisco IOS Release 10.0. The keywords **all-routes** and **spanning** first appeared in Cisco Release 11.1.

Level 3 routers that use protocol-specific information (for example, Novell IPX or XNS headers) rather than MAC information to route datagrams also must be able to collect and use RIF information to ensure that they can transmit datagrams across a source-route bridge. The software default is to not collect and use RIF information for routed protocols. This allows operation with software that does not understand or properly use RIF information.

The current software allows you to specify a protocol. This is specified by the argument *protocol-keyword*. The protocols supported and the keywords you can enter include the following:

- **apollo**—Apollo Domain
- **appletalk**—AppleTalk Phase 1 and 2
- **clns**—ISO CLNS
- **decnet**—DECnet Phase IV
- **ip**—IP
- **ipx**—Novell IPX
- **vines**—Banyan VINES
- **xns**—XNS

NOTES

When you are configuring DLSw+ over FDDI, the **multiring** command supports only IP and IPX.

The **multiring** command was extended in Software Release 8.3 to allow for per-protocol specification of the interface's ability to append RIFs to routed protocols. When it is enabled for a protocol, the router will source packets that include information used by source-route bridges. This allows a router with Token Ring interfaces, for the protocol or protocols specified, to connect to a source-bridged Token Ring network. If a protocol is not specified for multiring, the router can only route packets to nodes directly connected to its local Token Ring.

Prior to Software Release 8.3, the **multiring** command enabled multiring protocols—in particular, the use of explorers and RIFs—for *all* routable protocols. This sometimes caused problems when multiring-capable devices speaking one particular protocol were attached to the same ring as a nonmultiring-capable device speaking a different network protocol. If the earlier **multiring** command (pre-8.3 release) was not specified, nodes speaking one particular protocol would be able to communicate through the router, but nodes speaking other protocols could not. The reverse was true when the multiring capability was specified on the interface. In 8.3 or later releases of the software, the command **multiring all** is equivalent to the 8.2 and earlier forms of the **multiring** command.

Example

These commands enable IP and Novell IPX bridging on a Token Ring interface. RIFs will be generated for IP frames, but not for the Novell IPX frames.

```
! commands that follow apply to interface token 0
interface tokenring 0
! generate RIFs for IP frames
 multiring ip
! enable the Token Ring interface for IP
 ip address 131.108.183.37 255.255.255.0
! enable the Token Ring interface for Novell IPX
 novell network 33
```

Related Commands

clear rif-cache
rif
rif timeout
show rif
xns encapsulation

NETBIOS ACCESS-LIST BYTES

Use the **netbios access-list bytes** global configuration command to define the offset and hexadecimal patterns with which to match byte offsets in NetBIOS packets. Use the **no** form of this command to remove an entire list or the entry specified with the *pattern* argument.

> netbios access-list bytes *name* {**permit** | **deny**} *offset pattern*
> no netbios access-list bytes *name* {**permit** | **deny**} *offset pattern*

Syntax	Description
name	Name of the access list being defined.
permit	Permits the condition.
deny	Denies the condition.

Syntax	Description
offset	Decimal number indicating the number of bytes into the packet where the byte comparison should begin. An offset of zero points to the very beginning of the NetBIOS header. Therefore, the NetBIOS delimiter string (0xFFEF), for example, begins at offset 2.
pattern	Hexadecimal string of digits representing a byte pattern. The argument *pattern* must conform to certain conventions. These conventions are listed under the "Usage Guidelines" section.

Default

No offset or pattern is defined.

Command Mode

Global configuration

Usage Guidelines

This command first appeared in Cisco IOS Release 10.0.

For offset pattern matching, the byte pattern must be an even number of hexadecimal digits in length.

The byte pattern must be no more than 16 bytes (32 hexadecimal digits) in length.

As with all access lists, the NetBIOS access lists are scanned in order.

You can specify a wildcard character in the byte string indicating that the value of that byte does not matter in the comparison. This is done by specifying two asterisks (**) in place of digits for that byte. For example, the following command would match 0xabaacd, 0xab00cd, and so on:

```
netbios access-list bytes marketing permit 3 0xab**cd
```

Examples

The following example shows how to configure for offset pattern matching:

```
netbios access-list bytes marketing permit 3 0xabcd
```

In the following example, the byte pattern would not be accepted because it must be an even number of hexadecimal digits:

```
netbios access-list bytes marketing permit 3 0xabc
```

In the following example, the byte pattern would not be permitted because the byte pattern is longer than 16 bytes in length:

```
netbios access-list bytes marketing permit 3 00112233445566778899aabbccddeeff00
```

The following example would match 0xabaacd, 0xab00cd, and so on:

```
netbios access-list bytes marketing permit 3 0xab**cd
```

The following example deletes the entire marketing NetBIOS access list named *marketing*:

```
no netbios access-list bytes marketing
```

The following example removes a single entry from the list:

```
no netbios access-list bytes marketing deny 3 0xab**cd
```

In the following example, the first line serves to deny all packets with a byte pattern starting in offset 3 of 0xab. However, this denial would also include the pattern 0xabcd because the entry permitting the pattern 0xabcd comes *after* the first entry:

```
netbios access-list bytes marketing deny 3 0xab
netbios access-list bytes marketing permit 3 0xabcd
```

Related Commands

netbios input-access-filter bytes
netbios output-access-filter bytes

NETBIOS ACCESS-LIST HOST

Use the **netbios access-list host** global configuration command to assign the name of the access list to a station or set of stations on the network. The NetBIOS station access list contains the station name to match, along with a permit or deny condition. Use the **no** form of this command to remove either an entire list or just a single entry from a list, depending upon the argument given for *pattern*.

netbios access-list host *name* {**permit** | **deny**} *pattern*
no netbios access-list host *name* {**permit** | **deny**} *pattern*

Syntax	Description
name	Name of the access list being defined.
permit	Permits the condition.
deny	Denies the condition.
pattern	A set of characters. The characters can be the name of the station, or a combination of characters and pattern-matching symbols that establish a pattern for a set of NetBIOS station names. This combination can be especially useful when stations have names with the same characters, such as a prefix. The table in the "Usage Guidelines" section explains the pattern-matching symbols that can be used.

Default

No access list is assigned.

Command Mode

Global configuration

Usage Guidelines

This command first appeared in Cisco IOS Release 10.0.

Table 4–4 explains the pattern-matching characters that can be used.

Table 4–4   *Station Name Pattern-Matching Characters*

Character	Description
*	Used at the end of a string to match any character or string of characters.
?	Matches any single character. If this wildcard is used as the first letter of the name, you must precede it with a CNTL-V key sequence. Otherwise it will be interpreted by the router as a request for help.

Examples

The following example specifies a full station name to match:

```
netbios access-list host marketing permit ABCD
```

The following example specifies a prefix where the pattern matches any name beginning with the characters DEFG:

```
!The string DEFG itself is included in this condition.
netbios access-list host marketing deny DEFG*
```

The following example permits any station name with the letter W as the first character and the letter Y as the third character in the name. The second and fourth character in the name can be any character. This example would allow stations named WXYZ and WAYB; however, stations named WY and WXY would not be allowed because the question mark (?) must match specific characters in the name:

```
netbios access-list host marketing permit W?Y?
```

The following example illustrates how to combine wildcard characters. In this example, the marketing list denies any name beginning with AC that is not at least three characters in length (the question mark [?] would match any third character). The string ACBD and ACB would match, but the string AC would not:

```
netbios access-list host marketing deny AC?
```

In the following example, a single entry in the marketing NetBIOS access list is removed:

```
no netbios access-list host marketing deny AC?*
```

In the following example, the entire marketing NetBIOS access list is removed:

```
no netbios access-list host marketing
```

Related Commands

netbios input-access-filter host
netbios output-access-filter host

NETBIOS ENABLE-NAME-CACHE

Use the **netbios enable-name-cache** interface configuration command to enable NetBIOS name caching. Use the **no** form of this command to disable the name-cache behavior.

> **netbios enable-name-cache**
> **no netbios enable-name-cache**

Syntax   Description

This command has no arguments or keywords.

Default

Disabled

Command Mode

Interface configuration

Usage Guidelines

This command first appeared in Cisco IOS Release 10.0.

This command enables the NetBIOS name cache on the specified interface. By default, the name cache is disabled for the interface. Proxy explorers must be enabled on any interface that is using the NetBIOS name cache.

Example

The following example enables NetBIOS name caching for Token Ring interface 0:

```
interface tokenring 0
 source-bridge proxy-explorer
 netbios enable-name-cache
```

Related Commands

clear netbios-cache
netbios name-cache timeout
show netbios-cache

NETBIOS INPUT-ACCESS-FILTER BYTES

Use the **netbios input-access-filter bytes** interface configuration command to define a byte access list filter on incoming messages. The actual access filter byte offsets and patterns used are defined in one or more **netbios-access-list bytes** commands. Use the **no** form of this command with the appropriate name to remove the entire access list.

> **netbios input-access-filter bytes** *name*
> **no netbios input-access-filter bytes** *name*

Syntax	Description
name	Name of a NetBIOS access filter previously defined with one or more of the **netbios access-list bytes** global configuration commands.

Default

No access list is defined.

Command Mode

Interface configuration

Usage Guidelines

This command first appeared in Cisco IOS Release 10.0.

Example

The following example applies a previously-defined filter named marketing to packets coming into Token Ring 1:

```
interface tokenring 1
 netbios input-access-filter bytes marketing
```

Related Commands

netbios access-list bytes
netbios input-access-filter bytes

NETBIOS INPUT-ACCESS-FILTER HOST

Use the **netbios input-access-filter host** interface configuration command to define a station access list filter on incoming messages. The access lists of station names are defined in **netbios access-list host** commands. Use the **no** form of this command with the appropriate argument to remove the entire access list.

> **netbios input-access-filter host** *name*
> **no netbios input-access-filter host** *name*

Syntax	Description
name	Name of a NetBIOS access filter previously defined with one or more of the **netbios access-list host** global configuration commands.

Default

No access list is defined.

Command Mode

Interface configuration

Usage Guidelines

This command first appeared in Cisco IOS Release 10.0.

Example

The following example filters packets coming into Token Ring1 using the NetBIOS access list named *marketing*:

```
interface tokenring 1
  netbios access-list host marketing permit W?Y?
  netbios input-access-filter host marketing
```

Related Commands

netbios access-list host
netbios output-access-filter host

NETBIOS NAME-CACHE

Use the **netbios name-cache** global configuration command to define a static NetBIOS name cache entry, tying the server with the name *netbios-name* to the *mac-address*, and specifying that the server is accessible either locally via the *interface-name* specified, or remotely via the **ring-group** *group-number* specified. Use the **no** form of this command to remove the entry.

> **netbios name-cache** *mac-address netbios-name* {*interface-name* | **ring-group** *group-number*}
> **no netbios name-cache** *mac-address netbios-name*

Syntax	Description
mac-address	The MAC address.
netbios-name	Server name linked to the MAC address.
interface-name	Name of the interface by which the server is accessible locally.
ring-group	Specifies that the link is accessible remotely.
group-number	Number of the ring group by which the server is accessible remotely. This ring group number must match the number you have specified with the **source-bridge ring-group** command. The valid range is 1 to 4095.

Default

No entry is defined.

Command Mode

Global configuration

Usage Guidelines

This command first appeared in Cisco IOS Release 10.0.

To specify an entry in the static name cache, first specify a Routing Information Field (RIF) that leads to the server's MAC address. The Cisco IOS software displays an error message if it cannot find a static RIF entry for the server when the NetBIOS name-cache entry is attempted or if the server's type conflicts with that given for the static RIF entry.

NOTES

The names are case sensitive. Therefore "Cc" is not the same as "cC".

Examples

The following example indicates the syntax usage of this command if the NetBIOS server is accessed locally:

```
source-bridge ring-group 2
rif 0220.3333.4444 00c8.042.0060 tokenring 0
netbios name-cache 0220.3333.4444 DEF tokenring 0
```

The following example indicates the syntax usage of this command if the NetBIOS server is accessed remotely:

```
source-bridge ring-group 2
 rif 0110.2222.3333 0630.021.0030 ring group 2
 netbios name-cache 0110.2222.3333 DEF ring-group 2
```

Related Commands

show netbios-cache

NETBIOS NAME-CACHE NAME-LEN

Use the **netbios name-cache name-len** global configuration command to specify how many characters of the NetBIOS type name the name cache will validate.

   netbios name-cache name-len *length*

Syntax	Description
length	Length of the NetBIOS type name. The range is 8 to 16 characters.

Default

15 characters

Command Mode

Global configuration

Usage Guidelines

This command first appeared in Cisco IOS Release 10.0.

Example

The following example specifies that the name cache will validate 16 characters of the NetBIOS type name:

```
netbios name-cache name-len 16
```

Related Commands

netbios enable-name-cache
netbios name-cache
netbios name-cache proxy-datagram
netbios name-cache query-timeout
netbios name-cache recognized-timeout
netbios name-cache timeout

NETBIOS NAME-CACHE PROXY-DATAGRAM

Use the **netbios name-cache proxy-datagram** global configuration command to enable the Cisco IOS software to act as a proxy and send NetBIOS datagram type frames.

netbios name-cache proxy-datagram *seconds*

Syntax	Description
seconds	Time interval, in seconds, that the software forwards a route broadcast datagram type packet. The valid range is any number greater than 0.

Default

There is no default time interval.

Command Mode

Global configuration

Usage Guidelines

This command first appeared in Cisco IOS Release 10.0.

Example

The following example specifies that the software will forward a NetBIOS datagram type frame in 20-second intervals:

```
netbios name-cache proxy-datagram 20
```

Related Commands

netbios enable-name-cache
netbios name-cache
netbios name-cache query-timeout
netbios name-cache recognized-timeout
netbios name-cache timeout

NETBIOS NAME-CACHE QUERY-TIMEOUT

Use the **netbios name-cache query-timeout** global configuration command to specify the "dead" time, in seconds, that starts when a host sends any ADD_NAME_QUERY, ADD_GROUP_NAME, or STATUS_QUERY frame. During this dead time, the Cisco IOS software drops any repeat, duplicate ADD_NAME_QUERY, ADD_GROUP_NAME, or STATUS_QUERY frame sent by the same host. This timeout is only effective at the time of the login negotiation process. Use the **no** form of this command to bring the time back to the default of 6 seconds.

> **netbios name-cache query-timeout** *seconds*
> **no netbios name-cache query-timeout**

Syntax	*Description*
seconds	Dead time period in seconds. Default is 6 seconds.

Default

6 seconds

Command Mode

Global configuration

Usage Guidelines

This command first appeared in Cisco IOS Release 10.0.

Example

The following example sets the timeout to 15 seconds:

```
netbios name-cache query-timeout 15
```

Related Commands

netbios name-cache recognized-timeout

NETBIOS NAME-CACHE RECOGNIZED-TIMEOUT

Use the **netbios name-cache recognized-timeout** global configuration command to specify the "dead" time, in seconds, that starts when a host sends any FIND_NAME or NAME_RECOGNIZED frame. During this "dead" time, the Cisco IOS software drops any repeat, duplicate FIND_NAME or NAME_RECOGNIZED frame sent by the same host. This timeout is only effective at the time of the login negotiation process. Use the **no** form of this command to bring the time back to the default of 6 seconds.

> netbios name-cache recognized-timeout *seconds*
> no netbios name-cache recognized-timeout

Syntax	Description
seconds	Dead time period in seconds. Default is 6 seconds.

Default

6 seconds

Command Mode

Global configuration

Usage Guidelines

This command first appeared in Cisco IOS Release 10.0.

Example

The following example sets the timeout to 15 seconds:

```
netbios name-cache recognized-timeout 15
```

Related Commands

netbios name-cache query-timeout

NETBIOS NAME-CACHE TIMEOUT

Use the **netbios name-cache timeout** global configuration command to enable NetBIOS name caching and to set the time that entries can remain in the NetBIOS name cache. Use the **no** form of this command to bring the time back to the default of 15 minutes.

> netbios name-cache timeout *minutes*
> no netbios name-cache timeout *minutes*

Syntax	Description
minutes	Time, in minutes, that entries can remain in the NetBIOS name cache. Once the time expires, the entry will be deleted from the cache. Default is 15 minutes.

Default

15 minutes

Command Mode

Global configuration

Usage Guidelines

This command first appeared in Cisco IOS Release 10.0.

This command allows you to establish NetBIOS name caching. NetBIOS name caching can be used only between routers that are running Software Release 9.1 or later. NetBIOS name caching does not apply to static entries.

Example

The following example sets the timeout to 10 minutes:

```
interface tokenring 0
  netbios name-cache timeout 10
```

Related Commands

show netbios-cache

NETBIOS OUTPUT-ACCESS-FILTER BYTES

Use the **netbios output-access-filter bytes** interface configuration command to define a byte access list filter on outgoing messages. Use the **no** form of this command to remove the entire access list.

netbios output-access-filter bytes *name*
no netbios output-access-filter bytes *name*

Syntax	Description
name	Name of a NetBIOS access filter previously defined with one or more of the **netbios access-list bytes** global configuration commands.

Default

No access list is defined.

Command Mode

Interface configuration

Usage Guidelines

This command first appeared in Cisco IOS Release 10.0.

Example

The following example filters packets leaving Token Ring 1 using the NetBIOS access list named *engineering*:

```
interface tokenring 1
  netbios access-list bytes engineering permit 3 0xabcd
  netbios output-access-filter bytes engineering
```

Related Commands

netbios access-list bytes
netbios input-access-filter bytes

NETBIOS OUTPUT-ACCESS-FILTER HOST

Use the **netbios output-access-filter host** interface configuration command to define a station access list filter on outgoing messages. Use the **no** form of this command to remove the entire access list.

netbios output-access-filter host *name*
no netbios output-access-filter host *name*

Syntax	Description
name	Name of a NetBIOS access filter previously defined with one or more of the **netbios access-list host** global configuration commands.

Default

No access list filter is defined.

Command Mode

Interface configuration

Usage Guidelines

This command first appeared in Cisco IOS Release 10.0.

Example

The following example filters packets leaving Token Ring 1 using the NetBIOS access list named *engineering*:

```
interface tokenring 1
 netbios access-list host engineering permit W?Y?
 netbios output-access-filter host engineering
```

Related Commands

netbios access-list host
netbios input-access-filter host

RIF

Use the **rif** global configuration command to enter static source-route information into the Routing Information Field (RIF) cache. If a Token Ring host does not support the use of IEEE 802.2 TEST or XID datagrams as explorer packets, you may need to add static information to the RIF cache of the router. Use the **no** form of this command to remove an entry from the cache.

> **rif** *mac-address rif-string* {*interface-name* | **ring-group** *ring*}
> **no rif** *mac-address* {*interface-name* | **ring-group** *ring*}

Syntax	Description
mac-address	12-digit hexadecimal string written as a dotted triplet; for example, 0010.0a00.20a6.
rif-string	Series of 4-digit hexadecimal numbers separated by a period (.). This RIF string is inserted into the packets sent to the specified MAC address.
interface-name	Interface name (for example, tokenring 0) that indicates the origin of the RIF.
ring-group	Specifies the origin of the RIF in a ring group.
ring	Ring-group number that indicates the origin of the RIF. This ring-group number must match the number you have specified with the **source-bridge ring-group** command. The valid range is 1 to 4095.

Default

No static source-route information is entered.

Command Mode

Global configuration

Usage Guidelines

This command first appeared in Cisco IOS Release 10.0.

You must specify either an interface name or a ring-group number to indicate the origin of the RIF. You specify an interface name (for example, tokenring 0) with the *interface-name* argument, and you must specify a ring-group number with the **ring-group** *ring* argument. The ring-group number must match the number you specified with the **source-bridge ring-group** command. Ring groups are explained in Chapter 3, "Configuring Source-Route Bridging."

Using the command **rif** *mac-address* without any other arguments puts an entry into the RIF cache indicating that packets for this MAC address should not have RIF information.

Do not configure a static RIF with any of the *all rings* type codes. Doing so causes traffic for the configured host to appear on more than one ring and leads to unnecessary congestion.

NOTES

Input to the **source-bridge** interface configuration command is in decimal format. RIF displays and input are in hexadecimal format, and IBM source-route bridges use hexadecimal for input. It is essential that bridge and ring numbers are consistent for proper network operation. This means you must explicitly declare the numbers to be hexadecimal by preceding the number with 0x, or you must convert IBM hexadecimal numbers to a decimal equivalent when entering them. For example, IBM hexadecimal bridge number 10 would be entered as hexadecimal number 0x10 or decimal number 16 in the configuration commands. In the displays, these commands always will be in decimal.

Example

The following example configuration sets up a static RIF:

```
! insert entry with MAC address 1000.5A12.3456 and RIF of
! 0630.0081.0090 into RIF cache
rif 1000.5A12.3456 0630.0081.0090 tokenring 0
```

Related Commands

multiring
source-bridge ring-group

RIF TIMEOUT

Use the **rif timeout** global configuration command to determine the number of minutes an inactive RIF entry is kept. RIF information is maintained in a cache whose entries are aged. Use the **no** form of this command to restore the default.

rif timeout *minutes*
no rif timeout

Syntax	Description
minutes	Number of minutes an inactive RIF entry is kept. The value must be greater than 0. Default is 15 minutes.

Default

15 minutes

Command Mode

Global configuration

Usage Guidelines

This command first appeared in Cisco IOS Release 10.0.

A RIF entry is cached based on the MAC address and the interface.

A RIF entry can be aged out even if there is active traffic, but the traffic is fast- or autonomously switched.

A RIF entry is refreshed only if a RIF field of an incoming frame is identical to the RIF information of the RIF entry in the cache.

Until a RIF entry is removed from the cache, no new information is accepted for that RIF entry.

Example

The following example changes the timeout period to 5 minutes:

```
rif timeout 5
```

Related Commands

clear rif-cache
rif validate-enable
show rif

RIF VALIDATE-AGE

Use the **rif validate-age** global configuration command to define the validation time when the Cisco IOS software is acting as a proxy for NetBIOS NAME_QUERY packet or for explorer frames.

> **rif validate-age** *seconds*

Syntax	*Description*
seconds	Interval, in seconds, at which a proxy is sent. The valid range is any number greater than 0. Default is 2 seconds.

Default

2 seconds

Command Mode

Global configuration

Usage Guidelines

This command first appeared in Cisco IOS Release 10.0.

If the timer expires before the response is received, the RIF entry or the NetBIOS cache entry is marked as invalid and is flushed from the cache table when another explorer or NAME_QUERY packet is received.

Example

The following example specifies the interval at which a proxy is sent to be 3 seconds:

```
rif validate-age 3
```

Related Commands

rif
rif timeout

RIF VALIDATE-ENABLE

Use the **rif validate-enable** global configuration command to enable RIF validation for entries learned on an interface (Token Ring or FDDI). Use the **no** form of this command to disable the specification.

rif validate-enable
no rif validate-enable

Syntax   Description

This command has no arguments or keywords.

Default

RIF validation is enabled.

Command Mode

Global configuration

Usage Guidelines

This command first appeared in Cisco IOS Release 11.0.

A RIF validation algorithm is used for the following cases:

- To decrease convergence time to a new source-route path when an intermediate bridge goes down.

- To keep a valid RIF entry in a RIF cache even if a RIF entry is not refreshed either because traffic is fast- or autonomously switched, or because there is no traffic.

A directed IEEE TEST command is sent to the destination MAC address. If a response received in the time specified by **rif validate-age,** the entry is refreshed and is considered valid. Otherwise, the entry is removed from the cache. To prevent sending too many **TEST** commands, any entry that has been refreshed in less than 70 seconds is considered valid.

Validation is triggered as follows:

- When a RIF entry is found in the cache.

- When a RIF field of an incoming frame and the RIF information of the RIF entry is not identical. If, as the result of validation, the entry is removed from the cache, the RIF field of the next incoming frame with the same MAC address is cached.

- When the RIF entry is not refreshed for the time specified in the **rif timeout** command.

NOTES

If the RIF entry has been in the RIF cache for 6 hours, and has not been refreshed for the time specified in the **rif timeout** command, the entry is removed unconditionally from the cache.

NOTES

The **rif validate-enable** commands have no effect on remote entries learned over RSRB.

Example

The following example enables RIF validation:

```
rif validate-enable
```

Related Commands

rif timeout
rif validate-age
rif validate-enable-age
rif validate-enable-route-cache

RIF VALIDATE-ENABLE-AGE

Use the **rif validate-enable-age** global configuration command to enable RIF validation for stations on a source-route bridge network that do not respond to an IEEE TEST command. Use the **no** form of this command to disable the specification.

    rif validate-enable-age
    no rif validate-enable-age

Syntax   Description

This command has no arguments or keywords.

Default

RIF validation is enabled.

Command Mode

Global configuration

Usage Guidelines

This command first appeared in Cisco IOS Release 11.0.

You must first issue the **rif validate-enable** command.

When this command is enabled, a RIF entry is not removed from the cache even if it becomes invalid. If the entry is refreshed, it becomes valid again.

If a RIF field of an incoming frame and the RIF information of the invalid RIF entry are not identical, the old RIF information is replaced by the new information.

NOTES

The **rif validate-enable** commands have no effect on remote entries learned over RSRB.

Example

The following example enables RIF validation:

```
rif validate-enable-age
```

Related Commands

rif validate-enable

RIF VALIDATE-ENABLE-ROUTE-CACHE

Use the **rif validate-enable-route-cache** global configuration command to enable synchronization of the RIF cache with the protocol route cache. Use the **no** form of this command to disable the specification.

> **rif validate-enable-route-cache**
> **no rif validate-enable-route-cache**

Syntax   Description

This command has no arguments or keywords.

Default

This command is disabled by default.

Command Mode

Global configuration

Usage Guidelines

This command first appeared in Cisco IOS Release 11.0.

When a RIF entry is removed from the RIF cache, or the RIF information in the RIF entry is changed, the protocol route caches are synchronized with the RIF cache.

NOTES

The **rif validate-enable** commands have no effect on remote entries learned over RSRB.

Example

The following example synchronizes the RIF cache with the protocol route cache:

```
rif validate-enable-route-cache
```

Related Commands

rif validate-enable

SHOW CONTROLLERS TOKEN

Use the **show controllers token** privileged EXEC command to display information about memory management, error counters, and the board itself. Depending on the board being used, the output can vary. This command also displays proprietary information. Thus, the information that **show controllers token** displays is of primary use to Cisco's technical personnel. Information that is useful to users can be obtained with the **show interfaces tokenring** command, described later.

       show controllers token

Syntax   Description

This command has no arguments or keywords.

Command Mode

Privileged EXEC

Usage Guidelines

This command first appeared in Cisco IOS Release 10.0.

Sample Display

The following is sample output from the **show controllers token** command of a CSC-IR or CSC-2R card:

```
Router# show controllers token

TR Unit 0 is board 0 - ring 0

  state 3, dev blk: 0x1D2EBC, mailbox: 0x2100010, sca: 0x2010000
    current address: 0000.3080.6f40, burned in address: 0000.3080.6f40
    current TX ptr: 0xBA8, current RX ptr: 0x800

  Last Ring Status: none

  Stats: soft:0/0, hard:0/0, sig loss:0/0
         tx beacon: 0/0, wire fault 0/0, recovery: 0/0
         only station: 0/0, remote removal: 0/0
    Bridge: local 3330, bnum 1, target 3583
      max_hops 7, target idb: 0x0, not local
    Interface failures: 0  -- Bkgnd Ints: 0
    TX shorts 0, TX giants 0

    Monitor state: (active)
      flags 0xC0, state 0x0, test 0x0, code 0x0, reason 0x0
  f/w ver: 1.0, chip f/w: '000000.ME31100', [bridge capable]
      SMT form of this command s: 1.0l kernel, 4.02 fastmac
      ring mode: F00, internal enables:  SRB REM RPS CRS/NetMgr
      internal functional: 0000011A (0000011A), group: 00000000 (00000000)
      if_state: 1, ints: 0/0, ghosts: 0/0, bad_states: 0/0
      t2m fifo purges: 0/0
      t2m fifo current: 0, t2m fifo max: 0/0, proto_errs: 0/0
      ring: 3330, bridge num: 1, target: 3583, max hops: 7

Packet counts:
        receive total:  298/6197, small: 298/6197, large 0/0
               runts: 0/0, giants: 0/0
               local: 298/6197, bridged: 0/0, promis: 0/0
            bad rif: 0/0, multiframe: 0/0
        ring num mismatch 0/0, spanning violations 0
        transmit total: 1/25, small: 1/25, large 0/0
               runts: 0/0, giants: 0/0, errors 0/0
bad fs: 0/0, bad ac: 0
congested: 0/0, not present: 0/0
        Unexpected interrupts: 0/0,  last unexp. int: 0

    Internal controller counts:
    line errors:  0/0, internal errors: 0/0
    burst errors: 0/0, ari/fci errors:  0/0
    abort errors: 0/0, lost frame: 0/0
    copy errors:  0/0, rcvr congestion: 0/0
    token errors: 0/0, frequency errors: 0/0
```

```
dma bus errors: -/-, dma parity errors: -/-
 Internal controller smt state:
Adapter MAC:      0000.3080.6f40, Physical drop:     00000000
NAUN Address:     0000.a6e0.11a6, NAUN drop:         00000000
Last source:      0000.a6e0.11a6, Last poll:         0000.3080.6f40
Last MVID:        0006,           Last attn code:    0006
Txmit priority:   0006,           Auth Class:        7FFF
Monitor Error:    0000,           Interface Errors:  FFFF
Correlator:       0000,           Soft Error Timer:  00C8
Local Ring:       0000,           Ring Status:       0000
Beacon rcv type:  0000,           Beacon txmit type: 0000
Beacon type:      0000,           Beacon NAUN:       0000.a6e0.11a6
```

Table 4–5 describes the fields shown in the first line of sample output.

Table 4–5   *Show Controllers Token Field Descriptions—Part 1*

Field	Description
TR Unit 0	Unit number assigned to the Token Ring interface associated with this output.
is board 0	Board number assigned to the Token Ring controller board associated with this interface.
ring 0	Number of the Token Ring associated with this board.

In the following line, state 3 indicates the state of the board. The rest of this output line displays memory mapping that is of primary use to Cisco's engineers.

```
state 3, dev blk: 0x1D2EBC, mailbox: 0x2100010, sca: 0x2010000
```

The following line also appears in **show interface token** output as the address and burned in address (bia), respectively:

```
current address: 0000.3080.6f40, burned in address: 0000.3080.6f40
```

The following line displays buffer management pointers that change by board:

```
current TX ptr: 0xBA8, current RX ptr: 0x800
```

The following line indicates the ring status from the controller chip set. This information is used by LAN Network Manager:

```
Last Ring Status: none
```

The following line displays Token Ring statistics. See the Token Ring specification for more information:

```
Stats: soft:0/0, hard:0/0, sig loss:0/0
       tx beacon: 0/0, wire fault 0/0, recovery: 0/0
       only station: 0/0, remote removal: 0/0
```

The following line indicates that Token Ring communication has been enabled on the interface. If this line of output appears, the message "Source Route Bridge capable" should appear in the **show interfaces tokenring** display.

```
Bridge: local 3330, bnum 1, target 3583
```

Table 4–6 describes the fields shown in the following line of sample output:

```
max_hops 7, target idb: 0x0, not local
```

Table 4–6 *Show Controllers Token Field Descriptions—Part 2*

Field	Description
max_hops 7	Maximum number
target idb: 0x0	Destination interfac
not local	Interface has been de emote bridge.

The following line is specific to the hardware.

```
Interface failures: 0  -- Bkgnd Ints: 0
```

In the following line, TX shorts are the number of packets the interface transmits that are discarded because they are smaller than the medium's minimum packet size. TX giants are the number of packets the interface transmits that are discarded because they exceed the medium's maximum packet size.

```
TX shorts 0, TX giants 0
```

The following line indicates the state of the controller. Possible values include active, failure, inactive, and reset.

```
Monitor state: (active)
```

The following line displays detailed information relating to the monitor state shown in the previous line of output. This information relates to the firmware on the controller. This information is relevant to Cisco's engineers only if the monitor state is something other than active.

```
flags 0xC0, state 0x0, test 0x0, code 0x0, reason 0x0
```

Table 4–7 describes the fields in the following line or output:

```
f/w ver: 1.0 expr 0, chip f/w: '000000.ME31100', [bridge capable]
```

Table 4–7 *Show Controllers Token Field Descriptions—Part 3*

Field	Description
f/w ver: 1.0	Version of Cisco's firmware on the board.
chip f/w: '000000.ME31100'	Firmware on the chip set.
[bridge capable]	Interface has not been configured for bridging, but it has that capability.

The following line displays the version numbers for the kernel and the accelerator microcode of the Madge firmware on the board; this firmware is the LLC interface to the chip set:

```
SMT form of this command s: 1.01 kernel, 4.02 fastmac
```

The following line displays LAN Network Manager information that relates to ring status:

```
ring mode: F00, internal enables:  SRB REM RPS CRS/NetMgr
```

The following line corresponds to the functional address and the group address shown in **show interfaces tokenring** output:

```
internal functional: 0000011A (0000011A), group: 00000000 (00000000)
```

The following line displays interface board state information that is proprietary:

```
if_state: 1, ints: 0/0, ghosts: 0/0, bad_states: 0/0
```

The following lines display information that is proprietary. Cisco's engineers use this information for debugging purposes:

```
t2m fifo purges: 0/0
t2m fifo current: 0, t2m fifo max: 0/0, proto_errs: 0/0
```

Each of the fields in the following line maps to a field in the **show source bridge** display, as follows: ring maps to srn; bridge num maps to bn; target maps to trn; and max hops maps to max:

```
ring: 3330, bridge num: 1, target: 3583, max hops: 7
```

In the following lines of output, the number preceding the slash (/) indicates the count since the value was last displayed; the number following the slash (/) indicates count since the system was last booted:

```
Packet counts:
        receive total:  298/6197, small: 298/6197, large 0/0
```

In the following line, the number preceding the slash (/) indicates the count since the value was last displayed; the number following the slash (/) indicates count since the system was last booted. The runts and giants values that appear here correspond to the runts and giants values that appear in **show interfaces tokenring** output:

```
runts: 0/0, giants: 0/0
```

The following lines are receiver-specific information that Cisco's engineers can use for debugging purposes:

```
local: 298/6197, bridged: 0/0, promis: 0/0
bad rif: 0/0, multiframe: 0/0
ring num mismatch 0/0, spanning violations 0
transmit total: 1/25, small: 1/25, large 0/0
runts: 0/0, giants: 0/0, errors 0/0
```

The following lines include very specific statistics that are not relevant in most cases, but exist for historical purposes. In particular, the internal errors, burst errors, ari/fci, abort errors, copy errors, frequency errors, dma bus errors, and dma parity errors fields are not relevant.

```
Internal controller counts:
 line errors: 0/0,  internal errors: 0/0
 burst errors: 0/0,  ari/fci errors: 0/0
 abort errors: 0/0, lost frame: 0/0
 copy errors: 0/0, rcvr congestion: 0/0
 token errors: 0/0, frequency errors: 0/0
 dma bus errors: -/-, dma parity errors: -/-
```

The following lines are low-level Token Ring interface statistics relating to the state and status of the Token Ring with respect to all other Token Rings on the line:

```
Internal controller smt state:
Adapter MAC:     0000.3080.6f40, Physical drop:      00000000
NAUN Address:    0000.a6e0.11a6, NAUN drop:          00000000
Last source:     0000.a6e0.11a6, Last poll:          0000.3080.6f40
Last MVID:       0006,           Last attn code:     0006
Txmit priority:  0006,           Auth Class:         7FFF
Monitor Error:   0000,           Interface Errors:   FFFF
Correlator:      0000,           Soft Error Timer:   00C8
Local Ring:      0000,           Ring Status:        0000
Beacon rcv type: 0000,           Beacon txmit type:  0000
```

SHOW INTERFACES TOKENRING

Use the **show interfaces tokenring** privileged EXEC command to display information about the Token Ring interface and the state of source-route bridging.

     show interfaces tokenring [*number*]

Syntax	*Description*
number	(Optional) Interface number. If you do not provide a value, the command will display statistics for all Token Ring interfaces.

Command Mode

Privileged EXEC

Usage Guidelines

This command first appeared in Cisco IOS Release 10.0.

Sample Display

The following is sample output from the **show interfaces tokenring** command:

```
Router# show interfaces tokenring

TokenRing 0 is up, line protocol is up
Hardware is 16/4 Token Ring, address is 5500.2000.dc27 (bia 0000.3000.072b)
    Internet address is 150.136.230.203, subnet mask is 255.255.255.0
    MTU 8136 bytes, BW 16000 Kbit, DLY 630 usec, rely 255/255, load 1/255
    Encapsulation SNAP, loopback not set, keepalive set (10 sec)
    ARP type: SNAP, ARP Timeout 4:00:00
    Ring speed: 16 Mbps
    Single ring node, Source Route Bridge capable
    Group Address: 0x00000000, Functional Address: 0x60840000
    Last input 0:00:01, output 0:00:01, output hang never
    Output queue 0/40, 0 drops; input queue 0/75, 0 drops
    Five minute input rate 0 bits/sec, 0 packets/sec
```

```
        Five minute output rate 0 bits/sec, 0 packets/sec
    16339 packets input, 1496515 bytes, 0 no buffer
        Received 9895 broadcasts, 0 runts, 0 giants
          0 input errors, 0 CRC, 0 frame, 0 overrun, 0 ignored, 0 abort
      32648 packets output, 9738303 bytes, 0 underruns
  0 output errors, 0 collisions, 2 interface resets, 0 restarts
        5 transitions
```

Table 4–8 describes significant fields shown in the display.

Table 4–8   *Show Interfaces Tokenring Field Descriptions*

Field	Description
Token Ring is up/down	Interface is currently active and inserted into ring (up) or inactive and not inserted (down).
Token Ring is Reset	Hardware error has occurred. This is not in the sample output; it is informational only.
Token Ring is Initializing	Hardware is up, in the process of inserting the ring. This is not in the sample output; it is informational only.
Token Ring is Administratively Down	Hardware has been taken down by an administrator. This is not in the sample output; it is informational only. "Disabled" indicates the Cisco IOS software has received over 5000 errors in a keepalive interval, which is 10 seconds by default.
line protocol is {up | down | administratively down}	Indicates whether the software processes that handle the line protocol believe the interface is usable (that is, whether keepalives are successful).
Hardware	Specifies the hardware type. "Hardware is ciscoBus Token Ring" indicates that the board is a CSC-C2CTR board. "Hardware is 16/4 Token Ring" indicates that the board is a CSC-1R, CSC-2R, or a CSC-R16M board. Also shows the address of the interface.
Internet address	Lists the Internet address followed by subnet mask.
MTU	Maximum transmission unit of the interface.
BW	Bandwidth of the interface in kilobits per second.
DLY	Delay of the interface in microseconds.
rely	Reliability of the interface as a fraction of 255 (255/255 is 100 percent reliability), calculated as an exponential average over 5 minutes.
load	Load on the interface as a fraction of 255 (255/255 is completely saturated), calculated as an exponential average over 5 minutes.
Encapsulation	Encapsulation method assigned to interface.

Table 4–8 *Show Interfaces Tokenring Field Descriptions, Continued*

Field	Description
loopback	Indicates whether loopback is set.
keepalive	Indicates whether keepalives are set.
ARP type	Type of Address Resolution Protocol assigned.
Ring speed	Speed of Token Ring—4 or 16 Mbps.
{Single ring | multiring node}	Indicates whether a node is enabled to collect and use source RIF for routable Token Ring protocols.
Group Address	Interface's group address, if any. The group address is a multicast address; any number of interfaces on the ring may share the same group address. Each interface may have at most one group address.
Functional Address	Bit-significant group address. Each "on" bit represents a function performed by the station.
Last input	Number of hours, minutes, and seconds since the last packet was successfully received by an interface. Useful for knowing when a dead interface failed.
output hang	Number of hours, minutes, and seconds (or never) since the interface was last reset because of a transmission that took too long. When the number of hours in any of the "last" fields exceeds 24 hours, the number of days and hours is printed. If that field overflows, asterisks are printed.
Output queue, drops Input queue, drops	Number of packets in output and input queues. Each number is followed by a slash, the maximum size of the queue, and the number of packets dropped due to a full queue.
Five minute input rate, Five minute output rate	Average number of bits and packets transmitted per second in the last 5 minutes.
packets input	Total number of error-free packets received by the system.
broadcasts	Total number of broadcast or multicast packets received by the interface.
runts	Number of packets that are discarded because they are smaller than the medium's minimum packet size.
giants	Number of packets that are discarded because they exceed the medium's maximum packet size.

Table 4–8   *Show Interfaces Tokenring Field Descriptions, Continued*

Field	Description
CRC	Cyclic redundancy check generated by the originating LAN station or far-end device does not match the checksum calculated from the data received. On a LAN, this usually indicates noise or transmission problems on the LAN interface or the LAN bus itself. A high number of CRCs is usually the result of a station transmitting bad data.
frame	Number of packets received incorrectly having a CRC error and a noninteger number of octets.
overrun	Number of times the serial receiver hardware was unable to hand received data to a hardware buffer because the input rate exceeded the receiver's ability to handle the data.
ignored	Number of received packets ignored by the interface because the interface hardware ran low on internal buffers. These buffers are different than the system buffers mentioned previously in the buffer description. Broadcast storms and bursts of noise can cause the ignored count to be increased.
packets output	Total number of messages transmitted by the system.
bytes	Total number of bytes, including data and MAC encapsulation, transmitted by the system.
underruns	Number of times that the far-end transmitter has been running faster than the near-end router's receiver can handle. This may never be reported on some interfaces.
output errors	Sum of all errors that prevented the final transmission of datagrams out of the interface being examined. Note that this might not balance with the sum of the enumerated output errors, as some datagrams might have more than one error, and others might have errors that do not fall into any of the specifically tabulated categories.
collisions	Since a Token Ring cannot have collisions, this statistic is nonzero only if an unusual event occurred when frames were being queued or dequeued by the system software.
interface resets	Number of times an interface has been reset. The interface may be reset by the administrator or automatically when an internal error occurs.
Restarts	Should always be zero for Token Ring interfaces.
transitions	Number of times the ring made a transition from up to down, or vice versa. A large number of transitions indicates a problem with the ring or the interface.

SHOW LNM BRIDGE

Use the **show lnm bridge** privileged EXEC command to display all currently configured bridges and all parameters that are related to the bridge as a whole, not to one of its interfaces.

>   **show lnm bridge**

Syntax   Description

This command has no arguments or keywords.

Command Mode

Privileged EXEC

Usage Guidelines

This command first appeared in Cisco IOS Release 10.0.

Sample Display

The following is sample output from the **show lnm bridge** command:

```
Router# show lnm bridge

Bridge 001-2-003, Ports 0000.3000.abc4, 0000.0028.abcd
Active Links:  0000.0000.0000  0000.0000.0000  0000.0000.0000  0000.0000.0000
Notification: 0 min, Threshold 00.10%
```

Table 4–9 describes significant fields shown in the display.

Table 4–9 *Show LNM Bridge Field Descriptions*

Field	Description
Bridge 001-2-003	Ring and bridge numbers of this bridge.
Ports 0000.3000.abc4....	MAC addresses of the two interfaces of this bridge.
Active Links:	Any LNM stations that are currently connected to this bridge. An entry preceded by an asterisk is the controlling LNM.
Notification: 0 min	Current counter notification interval in minutes.
Threshold 00.10%	Current loss threshold that will trigger a message to LNM.

SHOW LNM CONFIG

Use the **show lnm config** privileged EXEC command to display the logical configuration of all bridges configured in a router. This information is needed to configure an LNM Management Station to communicate with a router. This is especially important when the router is configured as a multiport bridge, thus employing the concept of a virtual ring.

>   **show lnm config**

Syntax   Description

This command has no arguments or keywords.

Command Mode

Privileged EXEC

Usage Guidelines

This command first appeared in Cisco IOS Release 10.0.

Sample Displays

The following is sample output from the **show lnm config** command for a simple two-port bridge:

```
Router# show lnm config

Bridge(s) currently configured:

        From     ring 001, address 0000.3000.abc4
        Across bridge 002
        To       ring 003, address 0000.0028.abcd
```

The following is sample output from the **show lnm config** command for a multiport bridge:

```
Router# show lnm config

Bridge(s) currently configured:

        From     ring 001, address 0000.0028.abc4
        Across bridge 001
        To       ring 008, address 4000.0028.abcd

        From     ring 002, address 0000.3000.abc4
        Across bridge 002
        To       ring 008, address 4000.3000.abcd

        From     ring 003, address 0000.3000.5735
        Across bridge 003
        To       ring 008, address 4000.3000.5735
```

Table 4–10 describes significant fields shown in the display.

Table 4–10   *Show I NM Config Field Descriptions*

Field	Description
From ring 001	Ring number of the first interface in the two-port bridge.
address 0000.3000.abc4	MAC address of the first interface in the two-port bridge.
Across bridge 002	Bridge number assigned to this bridge.

Table 4–10 *Show LNM Config Field Descriptions, Continued*

Field	Description
To ring 003	Ring number of the second interface in the two-port bridge.
address 0000.0028.abcd	MAC address of the second interface in the two-port bridge.

SHOW LNM INTERFACE

Use the **show lnm interface** privileged EXEC command to display all LNM-related information about a specific interface or all interfaces.

show lnm interface [*type number*]

Syntax	Description
type	(Optional) Interface type.
number	(Optional) Interface number.

Command Mode

Privileged EXEC

Usage Guidelines

This command first appeared in Cisco IOS Release 10.0.

This command is for all types of interfaces, including Token Ring interfaces. If you want information specific to Token Ring, use the **show lnm ring** command.

Sample Display

The following is sample output from the **show lnm interface** command:

```
router# show lnm interface
 nonisolating error counts
interface ring  Active Monitor  SET  dec  lost  cong.  fc   freq.token
TokenRing1 0001* 1000.5a98.23a0 00200 00001 00000 00000 00000 0000000002

Notification flags: FE00, Ring Intensive: FFFF, Auto Intensive: FFFF
Active Servers: LRM LBS REM RPS CRS
Last NNIN:   never, from 0000.0000.0000.
Last Claim:  never, from 0000.0000.0000.
Last Purge:  never, from 0000.0000.0000.
Last Beacon: never, 'none' from 0000.0000.0000.
Last MonErr: never, 'none' from 0000.0000.0000.

            isolating error counts
 station         int ring   loc.   weight line   inter burst  ac    abort
 1000.5a98.23a0  T1  0001   0000   00 - N00000   00000 00000  00000 00000
```

```
1000.5a98.239e  T1  0001   0000   00 - N00000   00000  00000  00000 00000
1000.5a6f.bc15  T1  0001   0000   00 - N00000   00000  00000  00000 00000
0000.3000.abc4  T1  0001   0000   00 - N00000   00000  00000  00000 00000
1000.5a98.239f  T1  0001   0000   00 - N00000   00000  00000  00000 00000
```

Table 4–11 describes significant fields shown in the display. See the **show lnm station** command for a description of the fields in the bottom half of the sample output.

Table 4–11 *Show LNM Interface Field Descriptions*

Field	Description
interface	Interface about which information was requested.
ring	Number assigned to that Token Ring. An asterisk following the ring number indicates that there are stations with nonzero error counters present on that ring.
Active Monitor	Address of the station that is currently providing "Active Monitor" functions to the ring.
SET	Current soft error reporting time for the ring in units of tens of milliseconds.
dec	Rate at which the various counters of nonisolating errors are being decreased. This number is in errors per 30 seconds.
other nonisolating error counts: lost, cong., fc, and freq.token	Current values of the five nonisolating error counters specified in the 802.5 specification. These are Lost Frame errors, Receiver Congestion errors, FC errors, Frequency errors, and Token errors.
Notification flags:	Representation of which types of ring errors are being reported to LNM.
Ring Intensive:	Representation of which specific ring error messages are being reported to LNM when in the "Ring Intensive" reporting mode.
Auto Intensive:	Representation of which specific ring error messages are being reported to LNM when in the "Auto Intensive" reporting mode.

Table 4–11 *Show LNM Interface Field Descriptions, Continued*

Field	Description
Active Servers:	A list of which servers are currently active on this Token Ring. The possible acronyms and their meanings are as follows: • CRS—Configuration Report Server • LRM—LAN Reporting Manager • LBS—LAN Bridge Server • REM—Ring Error Monitor • RPS—Ring Parameter Server
Last NNIN:	Time since the last "Neighbor Notification Incomplete" frame was received, and the station that sent this message.
Last Claim:	Time since the last "Claim Token" frame was received, and the station that sent this message.
Last Purge:	Time since the last "Purge Ring" frame was received, and the station that sent this message.
Last Beacon:	Time since the last "Beacon" frame was received, the type of the last beacon frame, and the station that sent this message.
Last Mon Err:	Time since the last "Report Active Monitor Error" frame was received, the type of the last monitor error frame, and the station that sent this message.

Related Commands

show lnm ring
show lnm station

SHOW LNM RING

Use the **show lnm ring** privileged EXEC command to display all LNM information about a specific Token Ring or all Token Rings. If a specific interface is requested, it also displays a list of all currently active stations on that interface.

> show lnm ring [*ring-number*]

Syntax	Description
ring-number	(Optional) Number of a specific Token Ring. It can be a value in the range 1 to 4095.

Command Mode

Privileged EXEC

Usage Guidelines

This command first appeared in Cisco IOS Release 10.0.

The output of this command is the same as the output of the **show lnm interface** command. See the **show lnm interface** and **show lnm station** commands for sample output and a description of the fields. The same information can be obtained by using the **show lnm interface** command, but instead of specifying an interface number, you specify a ring number as an argument.

Related Commands

show lnm interface
show lnm station

SHOW LNM STATION

Use the **show lnm station** privileged EXEC command to display LNM-related information about a specific station or all known stations on all rings. If a specific station is requested, it also displays a detailed list of that station's current MAC-level parameters.

   show lnm station [*address*]

Syntax	Description
address	(Optional) Address of a specific LNM station.

Command Mode

Privileged EXEC

Usage Guidelines

This command first appeared in Cisco IOS Release 11.0.

Sample Display

The following is sample output from the **show lnm station** command when a particular address (in this case, 1000.5abc15) has been specified:

```
Router# show lnm station 1000.5a6f.bc15

                                       isolating error counts
      station       int  ring  loc.   weight  line  inter burst   ac   abort
 1000.5a6f.bc15     T1   0001  0000   00 - N  00000 00000 00000 00000 00000

 Unique ID:  0000.0000.0000          NAUN: 0000.3000.abc4
 Functional: C000.0000.0000          Group: C000.0000.0000
```

```
Physical Location:    00000        Enabled Classes:   0000
Allowed Priority:     00000        Address Modifier:  0000
Product ID:       00000000.00000000.00000000.00000000.0000
Ucode Level:      00000000.00000000.0000
Station Status: 00000000.0000
Last transmit status: 00
```

Table 4–12 describes significant fields shown in the display.

Table 4–12 *Show LNM Station Field Descriptions*

Field	Description
station	MAC address of the given station on the Token Ring.
int	Interface used to reach the given station.
ring	Number of the Token Ring where the given station is located.
loc.	Physical location number of the given station.
weight	Weighted accumulation of the errors of the given station, and of its NAUN. The three possible letters and their meanings are as follows: • N—not in a reported error condition. • P—in a "pre-weight" error condition. • W—in a "pre-weight" error condition.
isolating error counts	Current values of the five isolating error counters specified in the 802.5 specification. These are Line errors, Internal errors, Burst errors, AC errors, and Abort errors.
Values below this point will be zero unless LNM has previously requested this information.	
Unique ID:	Uniquely assigned value for this station.
NAUN:	MAC address of this station's "upstream" neighbor.
Functional:	MAC-level functional address currently in use by this station.
Group:	MAC-level group address currently in use by this station.
Physical Location:	Number assigned to this station as its "Physical Location" identifier.
Enabled Classes:	Functional classes that the station is allowed to transmit.
Allowed Priority:	Maximum access priority that the station may use when transmitting onto the Token Ring.
Address Modifier:	Reserved field.
Product ID:	Encoded 18-byte string used to identify what hardware/software combination is running on this station.

Table 4–12 *Show LNM Station Field Descriptions, Continued*

Field	Description
Ucode Level:	10-byte EBCDIC string indicating the microcode level of the station.
Station Status:	Implementation-dependent vector that is not specified anywhere.
Last transmit status:	Contains the strip status of the last "Report Transmit Forward" MAC frame forwarded by this interface.

SHOW NETBIOS-CACHE

Use the **show netbios-cache** privileged EXEC command to display a list of NetBIOS cache entries.

> **show netbios-cache**

Syntax   Description

This command has no arguments or keywords.

Command Mode

Privileged EXEC

Usage Guidelines

This command first appeared in Cisco IOS Release 10.0.

Sample Display

The following is sample output from the **show netbios-cache** command:

```
Router# show netbios-cache

   HW Addr            Name          How      Idle      NetBIOS Packet Savings
  1000.5a89.449a     IC6W06_B      TR1      6         0
  1000.5a8b.14e5     IC_9Q07A      TR1      2         0
  1000.5a25.1b12     IC9Q19_A      TR1      7         0
  1000.5a25.1b12     IC9Q19_A      TR1      10        0
  1000.5a8c.7bb1     BKELSA1       TR1      4         0
  1000.5a8b.6c7c     ICELSB1       TR1      -         0
  1000.5a31.df39     ICASC_01      TR1      -         0
  1000.5ada.47af     BKELSA2       TR1      10        0
  1000.5a8f.018a     ICELSC1       TR1      1         0
```

Table 4–13 describes significant fields shown in the display.

Table 4–13 *Show NetBIOS-Cache Field Descriptions*

Field	Description
HW Addr	MAC address mapped to the NetBIOS name in this entry.
Name	NetBIOS name mapped to the MAC address in this entry.
How	Interface through which this information was learned.
Idle	Period of time (in seconds) since this entry was last accessed. A hyphen in this column indicates it is a static entry in the NetBIOS name cache.
NetBIOS Packet Savings	Number of packets to which local replies were made (thus preventing transmission of these packets over the network).

Related Commands

netbios name-cache
netbios name-cache timeout

SHOW RIF

Use the **show rif** privileged EXEC command to display the current contents of the RIF cache.

   show rif

Syntax   Description

This command has no arguments or keywords.

Command Mode

Privileged EXEC

Usage Guidelines

This command first appeared in Cisco IOS Release 10.0.

Sample Display

The following is sample output from the **show rif** command:

```
Router# show rif

Codes: * interface, - static, + remote
Hardware Addr  How   Idle (min)   Routing Information Field
5C02.0001.4322 rg5        -        0630.0053.00B0
5A00.0000.2333 TR0        3        08B0.0101.2201.0FF0
5B01.0000.4444 -          -        -
0000.1403.4800 TR1        0        -
```

```
0000.2805.4C00 TR0          *    -
0000.2807.4C00 TR1          *    -
0000.28A8.4800 TR0          0    -
0077.2201.0001 rg5          10   0830.0052.2201.0FF0
```

In the display, entries marked with an asterisk (*) are the router's interface addresses. Entries marked with a dash (–) are static entries. Entries with a number denote cached entries. If the RIF timeout is set to something other than the default of 15 minutes, the timeout is displayed at the top of the display.

Table 4–14 describes significant fields shown in the display.

Table 4–14   *Show RIF Field Descriptions*

Field	Description
Hardware Addr	Lists the MAC-level addresses.
How	Describes how the RIF has been learned. Possible values include a ring group (rg), or interface (TR).
Idle (min)	Indicates how long, in minutes, since the last response was received directly from this node.
Routing Information Field	Lists the RIF.

Related Commands

multiring

SHOW SOURCE-BRIDGE

Use the **show source-bridge** privileged EXEC command to display the current source-bridge configuration and miscellaneous statistics.

   show source-bridge

Syntax   Description

This command has no arguments or keywords.

Command Mode

Privileged EXEC

Usage Guidelines

This command first appeared in Cisco IOS Release 10.0.

Sample Display

The following is sample output from the **show source-bridge** command:

```
Router# show source-bridge

Local Interfaces:                          receive     transmit
          srn bn  trn r p s n  max hops      cnt         cnt       drops
TR0         5 1   10 *  *           7       39:1002     23:62923

Ring Group 10:
  This peer: TCP 150.136.92.92
  Maximum output TCP queue length, per peer: 100
  Peers:                   state   lv  pkts_rx  pkts_tx  expl_gn   drops TCP
    TCP 150.136.92.92        -      2      0        0        0      0  0
    TCP 150.136.93.93       open   2*     18       18        3      0  0
Rings:
    bn: 1 rn: 5    local   ma: 4000.3080.844b TokenRing0       fwd: 18
    bn: 1 rn: 2    remote  ma: 4000.3080.8473 TCP 150.136.93.93  fwd: 36

Explorers: ------- input -------       ------- output -------
        spanning  all-rings   total    spanning  all-rings    total
    TR0       0        3         3         3          5          8
Router#
```

The following is sample output from the **show source-bridge** command when Token Ring LANE is configured.

```
Router# show source-bridge

Local Interfaces:                          receive     transmit
          srn bn  trn r p s n  max hops      cnt         cnt       drops
AT2/0.1  2048 5   256 *  f   7 7 7          5073        5072         0
To3/0/0     1 1   256 *  f   7 7 7          4719        4720         0

Global RSRB Parameters:
  TCP Queue Length maximum: 100

Ring Group 256:
  No TCP peername set, TCP transport disabled
  Maximum output TCP queue length, per peer: 100
  Rings:
    bn: 5  rn: 2048 local  ma: 4000.0ca0.5b40 ATM2/0.1        fwd: 5181
    bn: 1  rn: 1    local  ma: 4000.3005.da06 TokenRing3/0/0   fwd: 5180

Explorers: ------- input -------       ------- output -------
        spanning  all-rings   total    spanning  all-rings    total
    AT2/0.1     9        1        10        10         0         10
    To3/0/0    10        0        10         9         1         10

  Local: fastswitched 20       flushed 0        max Bps 38400

          rings     inputs      bursts      throttles    output drops
      To3/0/0        10          0             0              0
```

Table 4–15 describes significant fields shown in the displays.

Table 4–15 *Show Source-Bridge Field Descriptions*

Field	Description
Local Interfaces:	Description of local interfaces.
srn	Ring number of this Token Ring.
bn	Bridge number of this router for this ring.
trn	Group in which the interface is configured. Can be the target ring number or virtual ring group.
r	Ring group is assigned. An asterisk (*) in this field indicates that a ring group has been assigned for this interface.
p	Interface can respond with proxy explorers. An asterisk (*) in this field indicates the interface can respond to proxy explorers.
s	Spanning-tree explorers enabled on the interface. An asterisk (*) indicates that this interface will forward spanning-tree explorers.
n	Interface has NetBIOS name caching enabled. An asterisk (*) in this field indicates the interface has NetBIOS name caching enabled.
max hops	Maximum number of hops.
receive cnt	Bytes received on interface for source bridging.
transmit cnt	Bytes transmitted on interface for source bridging.
drops	Number of dropped packets.
Ring Group *n*:	Describes ring-group *n*, where *n* is the number of the ring group.
This peer:	Address and address type of this peer.
Maximum output TCP queue length, per peer:	Maximum number of packets queued on this peer before the Cisco IOS software starts dropping packets.
Peers:	Addresses and address types of the ring-group peers.
state	Current state of the peer, open or closed. A hyphen indicates this router.
lv	Indicates local acknowledgment.
pkts_rx	Number of packets received.
pkts_tx	Number of packets transmitted.
expl_gn	Explorers generated.

Table 4–15 *Show Source-Bridge Field Descriptions, Continued*

Field	Description
drops	Number of packets dropped.
TCP	Lists the current TCP backup queue length.
Rings:	Describes the ring groups. Information displayed includes the bridge groups, ring groups, whether each group is local or remote, the MAC address, the network address or interface type, and the number of packets forwarded. A type shown as "locvrt" indicates a local virtual ring used by SDLLC or SR/TLB; a type shown as "remvrt" indicates a remote virtual ring used by SDLLC or SR/TLB.
Explorers:	This section describes the explorer packets that the Cisco IOS software has transmitted and received.
input	Explorers received by Cisco IOS software.
output	Explorers generated by Cisco IOS software.
TR0	Interface on which explorers were received.
spanning	Spanning-tree explorers.
all-rings	All-rings explored.
total	Summation of spanning and all-rings.
fastswitched	Number of fast-switched packets.
flushed	Number of flushed packets.
max Bps	Maximum bytes per second.
rings	Interface for the particular ring.
inputs	Number of inputs.
bursts	Number of bursts.
throttles	Number of throttles.
output drops	Number of output drops.

SHOW SPAN

Use the **show span** EXEC command to display the spanning-tree topology known to the router.

> **show span**

Syntax   Description

This command has no arguments or keywords.

Command Mode

EXEC

Usage Guidelines

This command first appeared in Cisco IOS Release 10.3.

Sample Display

The following is sample output from the **show span** command:

```
RouterA> show span

Bridge Group 1 is executing the IBM compatible spanning tree protocol
  Bridge Identifier has priority 32768, address 0000.0c0c.f68b
  Configured hello time 2, max age 6, forward delay 4
  Current root has priority 32768, address 0000.0c0c.f573
  Root port is 001A (TokenRing0/0), cost of root path is 16
  Topology change flag not set, detected flag not set
  Times:  hold 1, topology change 30, notification 30
          hello 2, max age 6, forward delay 4, aging 300
  Timers: hello 0, topology change 0, notification 0
Port 001A (TokenRing0/0) of bridge group 1 is forwarding. Path cost 16
  Designated root has priority 32768, address 0000.0c0c.f573
  Designated bridge has priority 32768, address 0000.0c0c.f573
  Designated port is 001B, path cost 0, peer 0
  Timers: message age 1, forward delay 0, hold 0
Port 002A (TokenRing0/1) of bridge group 1 is blocking. Path cost 16
  Designated root has priority 32768, address 0000.0c0c.f573
  Designated bridge has priority 32768, address 0000.0c0c.f573
  Designated port is 002B, path cost 0, peer 0
  Timers: message age 0, forward delay 0, hold 0
Port 064A (spanRSRB) of bridge group 1 is disabled. Path cost 250
  Designated root has priority 32768, address 0000.0c0c.f573
  Designated bridge has priority 32768, address 0000.0c0c.f68b
  Designated port is 064A, path cost 16, peer 0
  Timers: message age 0, forward delay 0, hold 0
```

A port (spanRSRB) is created with each virtual ring group. The port will be disabled until one or
more peers go into open state in the ring group.

SHOW SSE SUMMARY

Use the **show sse summary** EXEC command to display a summary of Silicon Switch Processor (SSP)
statistics:

show sse summary

Syntax   Description

This command has no arguments or keywords.

Command Mode

EXEC

Usage Guidelines

This command first appeared in Cisco IOS Release 11.0.

Sample Display

The following is sample output from the **show sse summary** command:

```
Router# show sse summary

SSE utilization statistics

                 Program words  Rewrite bytes  Internal nodes  Depth
Overhead              499             1               8
IP                      0             0               0           0
IPX                     0             0               0           0
SRB                     0             0               0           0
CLNP                    0             0               0           0
IP access lists         0             0               0
Total used            499             1               8
Total free          65037        262143
Total available     65536        262144

Free program memory
  [499..65535]
Free rewrite memory
  [1..262143]

Internals
  75032 internal nodes allocated, 75024 freed
  SSE manager process enabled, microcode enabled, 0 hangs
  Longest cache computation 4ms, longest quantum 160ms at 0x53AC8
```

SOURCE-BRIDGE

Use the **source-bridge** interface configuration command to configure an interface for source-route bridging. Use the **no** form of this command to disable source-route bridging on an interface.

> **source-bridge** *source-ring-number bridge-number target-ring-number* [**conserve-ring**]
> **no source-bridge** *source-ring-number bridge-number target-ring-number* [**conserve-ring**]

Syntax	Description
source-ring-number	Ring number for the interface's Token Ring or FDDI ring. It must be a decimal number in the range 1 to 4095 that uniquely identifies a network segment or ring within the bridged Token Ring or FDDI network.
bridge-number	Number that uniquely identifies the bridge connecting the source and target rings. It must be a decimal number in the range 1 to 15.
target-ring-number	Ring number of the destination ring on this router. It must be unique within the bridged Token Ring or FDDI network. The target ring can also be a ring group. Must be a decimal number.
conserve-ring	(Optional) Keyword to enable SRB over Frame Relay. When this option is configured, the SRB software does not add the ring number associated with the Frame Relay PVC (the partner's virtual ring) to outbound explorer frames. This option is permitted for Frame Relay subinterfaces only.

Default

SRB is disabled.

Command Mode

Interface configuration

Usage Guidelines

This command first appeared in Cisco IOS Release 10.0. The revised version of the **source-bridge** command to enable SRB over Frame Relay first appeared in Cisco IOS Release 11.3.

The parser automatically displays the word "active" in the **source-bridge** command in configurations that have SRB enabled. You do not need to enter the **source-bridge** command with the **active** keyword.

Examples

In the following example, Token Rings 129 and 130 are connected via a router:

```
interface tokenring 0
 source-bridge 129 1 130
 !
interface tokenring 1
 source-bridge active 130 1 129
```

In the following example, an FDDI ring on one router is connected to a Token Ring on a second router across a DLSw+ link:

```
dlsw local-peer peer-id 132.11.11.2
dlsw remote-peer 0 tcp 132.11.11.3
```

```
interface fddi 0
 no ip address
 multiring all
 source-bridge active 26 1 10
!
dlsw local-peer peer-id 132.11.11.3
dlsw remote-peer 0 tcp 132.11.11.2
interface tokenring 0
 no ip address
 multiring all
 source-bridge active 25 1 10
```

In the following example, a router forwards frames from a locally attached Token Ring over the Frame Relay using SRB:

```
source-bridge ring-group 200
!
interface Serial0
 encapsulation frame-relay
!
interface Serial0.30 point-to-point
 frame-relay interface-dlci 30 ietf
 source-bridge 100 1 200 conserve-ring
 source-bridge spanning
!
interface TokenRing0
 source-bridge 600 1 200
```

Related Commands

debug frame-relay packet
debug source bridge
debug source error
debug source event
encapsulation frame-relay
frame-relay interface-dlci
source-bridge ring-group
source-bridge transparent

SOURCE-BRIDGE CONNECTION-TIMEOUT

Use the **source-bridge connection-timeout** global configuration command to establish the interval of time between first attempt to open a connection until a timeout is declared. Use the **no** form of this command to disable this feature.

source-bridge connection-timeout *seconds*
no source-bridge connection-timeout *seconds*

Syntax	*Description*
seconds	Interval of time, in seconds, before a connection attempt to a remote peer is aborted.

Default

The default connection-timeout interval is 10 seconds.

Command Mode

Global configuration

Usage Guidelines

This command first appeared in Cisco IOS Release 10.3.

The **source-bridge connection-timeout** command is used for setting timeout intervals in a complex topology such as a large multihop WAN with virtual rings or satellite links. The timeout interval is used when a connection to a remote peer is attempted. If the timeout interval expires before a response is received, the connection attempt is aborted.

Example

The following example sets the connection timeout interval to 60 seconds:

```
source-bridge connection-timeout 60
```

Related Commands

source-bridge ring-group

SOURCE-BRIDGE ENABLE-80D5

Use the **source-bridge enable-80d5** global configuration command to change the router's Token Ring to Ethernet translation behavior. Use the **no** form of this command to disable this function.

> **source-bridge enable-80d5**
> **no source-bridge enable-80d5**

Syntax   Description

This command has no arguments or keywords.

Default

Disabled

Command Mode

Global configuration

Usage Guidelines

This command first appeared in Cisco IOS Release 10.0.

The Cisco IOS software supports two types of Token Ring LLC2-to-Ethernet conversions. They are as follows:

- Token Ring LLC2-to-Ethernet 802.3 LLC2
- Token Ring LLC2-to-Ethernet 0x80d5

Use this global configuration command to change the translation behavior. By default, the Cisco IOS software translates Token Ring LLC2-to-Ethernet 802.3 LLC2. This command allows you to configure the software to translate Token Ring LLC2 frames into Ethernet 0x80d5 format frames.

This command is useful when you have a non-IBM device attached to an IBM network with devices that are using the nonstandard Token Ring LLC2-to-Ethernet 80d5 translation. If you do not configure your router to enable 80d5 processing, the non-IBM and IBM devices will not be able to communicate.

The parameters specifying the current parameters for the processing of 0x80d5 frames are given at the end of the output of the **show span** command.

NOTES

The 80d5 frame processing option is available only with SR/TLB. It is not available when source-route transparent bridging (SRT) is used.

Use the **show span** to check whether 80d5 processing is enabled. If it is, the following line displays in the output:

```
Translation between LLC2 and Ethernet Type II 80d5 is enabled
```

Example

The following example enables 0x80d5 processing, removes the translation for SAP 08, and adds the translation for SAP 1c:

```
source-bridge enable-80d5
 no source-bridge sap-80d5 08
 source-bridge sap-80d5 1c
```

Related Commands

show span
source-bridge sap-80d5

SOURCE-BRIDGE EXPLORER-DUP-**ARE**-FILTER

Use the **source-bridge explorer-dup-ARE-filter** global configuration command to prevent excessive forwarding of explorers in networks with redundant topologies. Use the **no** form of this command to disable this feature.

> **source-bridge explorer-dup-ARE-filter**
> **no source-bridge explorer-dup-ARE-filter**

Syntax   Description

This command has no arguments or keywords.

Default

Duplicate explorer filtering is disabled.

Command Mode

Global configuration

Usage Guidelines

This command first appeared in Cisco IOS Release 11.2.

Example

The following example enables duplicate explorer filtering:

```
source-bridge explorer-dup-ARE-filter
```

SOURCE-BRIDGE EXPLORER-FASTSWITCH

Use the **source-bridge explorer-fastswitch** global configuration command to enable explorer fast switching. To disable explorer fast switching, use the **no** form of this command.

> **source-bridge explorer-fastswitch**
> **no source-bridge explorer-fastswitch**

Syntax   Description

This command has no arguments or keywords.

Default

Fast switching is enabled.

Command Mode

Global configuration

Usage Guidelines

This command first appeared in Cisco IOS Release 10.3.

Use the **no** form of this command in conjunction with the **source-bridge explorerq-depth** and the **source-bridge explorer-maxrate** command to optimize explorer processing.

Example

The following example enables explorer fast switching after it has been previously disabled:

```
source-bridge explorer-fastswitch
```

Related Commands

source-bridge explorer-maxrate
source-bridge explorerq-depth

SOURCE-BRIDGE EXPLORER-MAXRATE

Use the **source-bridge explorer-maxrate** global configuration command to set the maximum byte rate of explorers per ring. To reset the default rate, use the **no** form of this command.

source-bridge explorer-maxrate *maxrate*
no source-bridge explorer-maxrate *maxrate*

Syntax	Description
maxrate	Number in the range 100 to 1000000000 (in bytes per second). The default maximum byte rate is 38400 bytes per second.

Default

The default maximum byte rate is 38400 bytes per second.

Command Mode

Global configuration

Usage Guidelines

This command first appeared in Cisco IOS Release 10.3.

Given the number of different explorer packet types and sizes and the bandwidth limits of the various interfaces, the bus data rate (as opposed to the packet rate) is the common denominator used to decide when to flush incoming explorers. The packets are dropped by the interface before any other processing.

Example

The following command sets the maximum byte rate of explorers on a ring:

```
source-bridge explorer-maxrate 100000
```

SOURCE-BRIDGE EXPLORERQ-DEPTH

Use the **source-bridge explorerq-depth** global configuration command to set the maximum explorer queue depth. To reset the default value, use the **no** form of this command.

> **source-bridge explorerq-depth** *depth*
> **no source-bridge explorerq-depth** *depth*

Syntax	Description
depth	The maximum number of incoming packets. The valid range is 1 to 500.

Default

The default maximum depth is 30.

Command Mode

Global configuration

Usage Guidelines

This command first appeared in Cisco IOS Release 10.0.

In this implementation, the limit is on a per-interface basis such that each interface can have up to the maximum (default 30) outstanding packets on the queue before explorers from that particular interface are dropped.

Example

The following example sets the maximum explorer queue depth:

```
source-bridge explorerq-depth 100
```

SOURCE-BRIDGE INPUT-ADDRESS-LIST

Use the **source-bridge input-address-list** interface configuration command to assign an access list to a particular input interface. This command filters packets coming into the router. Use the **no** form of this command to remove the application of the access list.

> **source-bridge input-address-list** *access-list-number*
> **no source-bridge input-address-list** *access-list-number*

Syntax	Description
access-list-number	Number of the access list. The value must be in the range 700 to 799.

Default

No access list is assigned.

Command Mode

Interface configuration

Usage Guidelines

This command first appeared in Cisco IOS Release 10.3.

Example

The following example assigns access list 700 to Token Ring 0:

```
interface tokenring 0
 source-bridge input-address-list 700
 !
access-list 700 deny 1000.5A00.0000  8000.00FF.FFFF
access-list 700 permit 0000.0000.0000  FFFF.FFFF.FFFF
```

Related Commands

access-list
source-bridge output-address-list

SOURCE-BRIDGE INPUT-LSAP-LIST

Use the **source-bridge input-lsap-list** interface configuration command to filter, on input, FDDI and IEEE 802-encapsulated packets that include the destination service access point (DSAP) and source service access point (SSAP) fields in their frame formats. The access list specifying the type codes to be filtered is given by this variation of the **source-bridge** interface configuration command.

> **source-bridge input-lsap-list** *access-list-number*

Syntax	Description
access-list-number	Number of the access list. This access list is applied to all IEEE 802 or FDDI frames received on that interface prior to the source-routing process. Specify zero (0) to disable the filter. The value must be in the range 200 to 299.

Default

Disabled

Command Mode

Interface configuration

Usage Guidelines

This command first appeared in Cisco IOS Release 10.0.

Example

The following example specifies access list 203:

```
interface tokenring 0
 source-bridge input-lsap-list 203
```

Related Commands

access-list
source-bridge output-lsap-list

SOURCE-BRIDGE INPUT-TYPE-LIST

Use the **source-bridge input-type-list** interface configuration command to filter SNAP-encapsulated packets on input.

  source-bridge input-type-list *access-list-number*

Syntax	*Description*
access-list-number	Number of the access list. This access list is applied to all SNAP frames received on that interface prior to the source-routing process. Specify zero (0) to disable the application of the access list on the bridge group. The value must be in the range 200 to 299.

Default

Disabled

Command Mode

Interface configuration

Usage Guidelines

This command first appeared in Cisco IOS Release 10.0.

Use the **access list** command to specify type code when using the **source-bridge input-type-list** command.

Example

The following example specifies access list 202:

```
interface tokenring 0
 source-bridge input-type-list 202
 !
access-list 202 deny 0x6000 0x0007
access-list 202 permit 0x0000 0xFFFF
```

Related Commands

access-list
source-bridge output-type-list

SOURCE-BRIDGE MAX-HOPS

Use the **source-bridge max-hops** interface configuration command to control the forwarding or blocking of all-routes explorer frames received on an interface. Use the **no** form of this command to reset the count to the maximum value.

> **source-bridge max-hops** *count*
> **no source-bridge max-hops**

Syntax	*Description*
count	Determines the number of bridges an explorer packet can traverse. Typically, the maximum number of bridges for interoperability with IBM equipment is seven.

Default

The maximum number of bridge hops is seven.

Command Mode

Interface configuration

Usage Guidelines

This command first appeared in Cisco IOS Release 11.2.

Frames are forwarded only if the number of hops in the routing information field of the input frame plus hops appended by the router is less than or equal to the specified count. If the interface is connected to a destination interface, the router appends one hop. If the interface is tied to a virtual ring, the router appends two hops. This applies only to all-routes explorer frames on input to this interface.

Example

The following example limits the maximum number of source-route bridge hops to five.

```
source-bridge max-hops 5
```

Related Commands

source-bridge
source-bridge max-in-hops
source-bridge max-out-hops

SOURCE-BRIDGE MAX-IN-HOPS

Use the **source-bridge max-in-hops** interface configuration command to control the forwarding or blocking of spanning-tree explorer frames received on an interface. Use the **no** form of this command to reset the count to the maximum value.

> **source-bridge max-in-hops** *count*
> **no source-bridge max-in-hops**

Syntax	Description
count	Determines the number of bridges an explorer packet can traverse. Typically, the maximum number of bridges for interoperability with IBM equipment is seven.

Default

The maximum number of bridge hops is seven.

Command Mode

Interface configuration

Usage Guidelines

This command first appeared in Cisco IOS Release 11.2.

Frames are forwarded only if the number of hops in the routing information field of the input frame is less than or equal to the specified count. This applies only to spanning-tree explorer frames input to the specified interface.

Example

The following example limits the maximum number of source-route bridge hops to three.

```
source-bridge max-in-hops 3
```

Related Commands

source-bridge
source-bridge max-hops
source-bridge max-out-hops

SOURCE-BRIDGE MAX-OUT-HOPS

Use the **source-bridge max-out-hops** interface configuration command to control the forwarding or blocking of spanning-tree explorer frames sent from this interface. Use the **no** form of this command to reset the count to the maximum value.

> **source-bridge max-out-hops** *count*
> **no source-bridge max-out-hops**

Syntax	Description
count	Determines the number of bridges an explorer packet can traverse. Typically, the maximum number of bridges for interoperability with IBM equipment is seven.

Default

The maximum number of bridge hops is seven.

Command Mode

Interface configuration

Usage Guidelines

This command first appeared in Cisco IOS Release 11.2.

Frames are forwarded only if the number of hops in the routing information field of the frame (including the hops appended by the router) is less than or equal to the specified count. This applies only to spanning-tree explorer frames output from the specified interface.

Example

The following example limits the maximum number of source-route bridge hops to five.

```
source-bridge max-out-hops 5
```

Related Commands

source-bridge
source-bridge max-hops
source-bridge max-in-hops

SOURCE-BRIDGE OUTPUT-ADDRESS-LIST

Use the **source-bridge output-address-list** interface configuration command to assign an access list to a particular output interface. This command filters packets sent out from the router. Use the **no** form of this command to remove the application of the access list.

> **source-bridge output-address-list** *access-list-number*
> **no source-bridge output-address-list** *access-list-number*

Syntax	Description
access-list-number	Number of the access list. The value must be in the range 700 to 799.

Default

No access list is assigned.

Command Mode

Interface configuration

Usage Guidelines

This command first appeared in Cisco IOS Release 10.0.

Example

To disallow the bridging of Token Ring packets of all IBM workstations on Token Ring 1, use this sample configuration. The software assumes that all such hosts have Token Ring addresses with the vendor code 1000.5A00.0000. The vendor portion of the MAC address is the first three bytes (left to right) of the address. The first line of the access list denies access to all IBM workstations, while the second line permits access to all other devices on the network. Then, the access list can be assigned to the input side of Token Ring 1.

```
access-list 700 deny 1000.5A00.0000   8000.00FF.FFFF
access-list 700 permit 0000.0000.0000   FFFF.FFFF.FFFF
interface tokenring 1
 source-bridge output-address-list 700
```

Related Commands

access-list
source-bridge input-address-list

SOURCE-BRIDGE OUTPUT-LSAP-LIST

Use the **source-bridge output-lsap-list** interface configuration command to filter, on output, FDDI and IEEE 802-encapsulated packets that have destination service access point (DSAP) and source service access point (SSAP) fields in their frame formats.

> **source-bridge output-lsap-list** *access-list-number*

Syntax	*Description*
access-list-number	Number of the access list. This access list is applied just before sending out a frame to an interface. Specify zero (0) to disable the filter. The value must be in the range 200 to 299.

Default

No filters are applied.

Command Mode

Interface configuration

Usage Guidelines

This command first appeared in Cisco IOS Release 10.0.

The access list specifying the type codes to be filtered is given by this command.

Example

The following example specifies access list 251:

```
interface tokenring 0
 source-bridge output-lsap-list 251
access-list 251 permit 0xE0E0 0x0101
access-list 251 deny 0x0000 0xFFFF
```

Related Commands

access-list
source-bridge input-lsap-list

SOURCE-BRIDGE OUTPUT-TYPE-LIST

Use the **source-bridge output-type-list** interface configuration command to filter SNAP-encapsulated frames by type code on output.

> **source-bridge output-type-list** *access-list-number*

Syntax	Description
access-list-number	Number of the access list. This access list is applied just before sending out a frame to an interface. Specify zero (0) to disable the application of the access list on the bridge group. The value must be in the range 200 to 299.

Default

No filters are applied.

Command Mode

Interface configuration

Usage Guidelines

This command first appeared in Cisco IOS Release 10.0.

Input and output type code filtering on the same interface reduces performance and is not recommended.

Access lists for Token Ring- and IEEE 802-encapsulated packets affect only source-route bridging functions. Such access lists do not interfere with protocols that are being routed.

Use the access list specifying the types codes in this command.

Example

The following example filters SNAP-encapsulated frames on output:

```
! apply interface configuration commands to interface tokenring 0
interface tokenring 0
! filter SNAP-encapsulated frames on output using access list 202
 source-bridge output-type-list 202
 !
access-list 202 deny 0x6000 0x0007
access-list 202 permit 0x0000 0xFFFF
```

Related Commands

access-list
source-bridge input-type-list

SOURCE-BRIDGE PROXY-EXPLORER

Use the **source-bridge proxy-explorer** interface configuration command to configure the interface to respond to any explorer packets from a source node that meet the conditions described below. Use the **no** form of this command to cancel responding to explorer packets with proxy explorers.

> source-bridge proxy-explorer
> no source-bridge proxy-explorer

Syntax   Description

This command has no arguments or keywords.

Default

Disabled

Command Mode

Interface configuration

Usage Guidelines

This command first appeared in Cisco IOS Release 10.0.

The *proxy explorer* function allows the source-route bridge interface to respond to a source node on behalf of a particular destination node. The interface responds with proxy explorers. The following conditions must be met in order for the interface to respond to a source node with proxy explorers on behalf of a destination node:

- The destination node must be in the RIF cache.
- The destination node must not be on the same ring as the source node.

- The explorer packet must be an IEEE 802.2 XID or TEST packet.
- The packet cannot be from the IBM Token Ring LAN Network Manager source SAP.

If all of the above conditions are met, the source-route bridge interface will turn the packet around, append the appropriate RIF, and reply to the source node.

Use proxy explorers to limit the amount of explorer traffic propagating through the source-bridge network, especially across low-bandwidth serial lines. The proxy explorer is most useful for multiple connections to a single node.

Example

The following example configures the router to use proxy explorers on Token Ring 0:

```
interface tokenring 0
  source-bridge proxy-explorer
```

SOURCE-BRIDGE PROXY-NETBIOS-ONLY

Use the **source-bridge proxy-netbios-only** global configuration command to enable proxy explorers for the NetBIOS name-caching function. Use the **no** form of this command to disable the NetBIOS name-caching function.

source-bridge proxy-netbios-only
no source-bridge proxy-netbios-only

Syntax   Description

This command has no arguments or keywords.

Default

Disabled

Command Mode

Global configuration

Usage Guidelines

This command first appeared in Cisco IOS Release 10.0.

Example

The following example configures the router to use proxy explorers:

```
source-bridge proxy-netbios-only
```

SOURCE-BRIDGE RING-GROUP

Use the **source-bridge ring-group** global configuration command to define or remove a ring group from the configuration. Use the **no** form of this command to cancel previous assignments.

> **source-bridge ring-group** *ring-group* [*virtual-mac-address*]
> **no source-bridge ring-group** *ring-group* [*virtual-mac-address*]

Syntax	Description
ring-group	Ring-group number. The valid range is 1 to 4095.
virtual-mac-address	(Optional) 12-digit hexadecimal string written as a dotted triplet (for example, 0010.0a00.20a6).

Default

No ring group is defined.

Command Mode

Global configuration

Usage Guidelines

This command first appeared in Cisco IOS Release 10.0.

To configure a source-route bridge with more than two network interfaces, the *ring group* concept is used. A ring group is a collection of Token Ring interfaces in one or more routers that are collectively treated as a virtual ring. The ring group is denoted by a ring number that must be unique for the network. The ring group's number is used just like a physical ring number, showing up in any route descriptors contained in packets being bridged.

To configure a specific interface as part of a ring group, its target ring number parameter is set to the ring-group number specified in this command. Do not use the number 0; it is reserved to represent the local ring.

To avoid an address conflict on the virtual MAC address, use a locally administered address in the form 4000.*xxxx.xxxx*.

Example

In the following example, multiple Token Rings are source-route bridged to one another through a single router. These Token Rings are all part of ring group 7.

```
! all token rings attached to this bridge/router are part of ring group 7
source-bridge ring-group 7
!
interface tokenring 0
 source-bridge 1001 1 7
!
interface tokenring 1
 source-bridge 1001 1 7
```

```
!
interface tokenring 2
 source-bridge 1002 1 7
!
interface tokenring 3
 source-bridge 1003 1 7
```

Related Commands

source-bridge

SOURCE-BRIDGE ROUTE-CACHE

Use the **source-bridge route-cache** interface configuration command to enable fast switching. Use the **no** form of this command to disable fast switching.

> **source-bridge route-cache**
> **no source-bridge route-cache**

Syntax   Description

This command has no arguments or keywords.

Default

Enabled

Command Mode

Interface configuration

Usage Guidelines

This command first appeared in Cisco IOS Release 10.0.

By default, fast-switching software is enabled in the source-route bridging software. Fast switching allows for faster implementations of local source-route bridging between 4/16-Mb Token Ring cards in the same router. This feature also allows for faster implementations of local source-route bridging between two routers using the 4/16-Mb Token Ring cards and the direct interface encapsulation.

Example

The following example disables use of fast switching between two 4/16-Mb Token Ring interfaces:

```
interface token 0
 source-bridge 1 1 2
 no source-bridge route-cache
!
interface token 1
 source-bridge 2 1 1
 no source-bridge route-cache
```

Related Commands

source-bridge

SOURCE-BRIDGE ROUTE-CACHE CBUS

Use the **source-bridge route-cache cbus** interface configuration command to enable autonomous switching. Use the **no** form of this command to disable autonomous switching.

> **source-bridge route-cache cbus**
> **no source-bridge route-cache cbus**

Syntax   Description

This command has no arguments or keywords.

Default

Disabled

Command Mode

Interface configuration

Usage Guidelines

This command first appeared in Cisco IOS Release 10.0.

Autonomous switching in source-route bridging software is available for local source-route bridging between ciscoBus Token Ring cards in the same router. Autonomous switching provides higher switching rates than does fast switching between 4/16-Mb Token Ring cards. Autonomous switching works for both two-port bridges and multiport bridges that use ciscoBus Token Ring cards.

In a virtual ring that includes both ciscoBus Token Ring and 4/16-Mb Token Ring interfaces, frames that flow from one ciscoBus Token Ring interface to another are autonomously switched, and the remainder of the frames are fast switched. The switching that occurs on the ciscoBus Token Ring interface takes advantage of the high-speed ciscoBus controller processor.

─◁ **NOTES** ▷──

Using either NetBIOS byte offset access lists or the access expression capability to logically combine the access filters disables the autonomous or fast switching of SRB frames.

Example

The following example enables use of autonomous switching between two ciscoBus Token Ring interfaces:

```
interface token 0
 source-bridge 1 1 2
 source-bridge route-cache cbus
 !
interface token 1
 source-bridge 2 1 1
 source-bridge route-cache cbus
```

Related Commands

source-bridge

SOURCE-BRIDGE ROUTE-CACHE SSE

Use the **source-bridge route-cache sse** interface configuration command to enable Cisco's silicon switching engine (SSE) switching function. Use the **no** form of this command to disable SSE switching.

> source-bridge route-cache sse
> no source-bridge route-cache sse

Syntax   Description

This command has no arguments or keywords.

Default

Disabled

Command Mode

Interface configuration

Usage Guidelines

This command first appeared in Cisco IOS Release 10.0.

Example

The following example enables use of SSE switching between two 4/16-MB Token Ring interfaces:

```
interface token 0
 source-bridge 1 1 2
 source-bridge route-cache sse
 !
interface token 1
 source-bridge 2 1 1
 source-bridge route-cache sse
```

Related Commands

source-bridge

SOURCE-BRIDGE SAP-80D5

Use the **source-bridge sap-80d5** global configuration command to allow non-IBM hosts (attached to a router with 80d5 processing enabled) to use the standard Token Ring-to-Ethernet LLC2 translation instead of the nonstandard Token Ring-to-Ethernet 80d5 translation. This command allows you to set the translation on a per-DSAP basis. Use the **no** form of this command to disable this feature.

> **source-bridge sap-80d5** *dsap*
> **no source-bridge sap-80d5** *dsap*

Syntax	*Description*
dsap	Destination service access point (DSAP).

Default

Enabled

Command Mode

Global configuration

Usage Guidelines

This command first appeared in Cisco IOS Release 10.0.

By default, the following DSAPs are enabled for 0x80d5 translation simply by specifying the **source-bridge enable-80d5** command:

- For SNA—04, 08, 0C, 00
- For NetBIOS—F0

Any of these DSAPs can be disabled with the **no** form of this command.

The parameters specifying the current parameters for the processing of 0x80d5 frames are given at the end of the output of the **show span** command.

— **NOTES** ──

The 80d5 frame processing option is available only with SR/TLB. It is not available when source-route transparent bridging (SRT) is used.

Use the **show span** to check whether 80d5 processing is enabled for a particular DSAP. The following line displays in the output if 80d5 processing is enabled, listing each DSAP for which it is enabled:

```
Translation is enabled for the following DSAPs:
04 0C 1C F0
```

Example

The following example enables 0x80d5 processing, removes the translation for SAP 08, and adds the translation for SAP 1c:

```
source-bridge enable-80d5
no source-bridge sap-80d5 08
source-bridge sap-80d5 1c
```

Related Commands

show span
source-bridge enable-80d5

SOURCE-BRIDGE SPANNING (AUTOMATIC)

Use the automatic version of the **source-bridge spanning** interface configuration command to enable the automatic spanning-tree function for a specified group of bridged interfaces. Use the **no source-bridge spanning** command to return to the default disabled state. Use the **no source-bridge spanning path-cost** command to return an assigned path cost to the default path cost of 16.

> **source-bridge spanning** *bridge-group* [**path-cost** *path-cost*]
> **no source-bridge spanning** *bridge-group* [**path-cost** *path-cost*]

Syntax	Description
bridge-group	Number in the range 1 to 9 that you choose to refer to a particular group of bridged interfaces. This must be the same number as assigned in the **bridge protocol ibm** command.
path-cost	(Optional) Assign a path cost for a specified interface.
path-cost	(Optional) Path cost for the interface. The valid range is 0 to 65535.

Defaults

The automatic spanning-tree function is disabled. The default path cost is 16.

Command Mode

Interface configuration

Usage Guidelines

This command first appeared in Cisco IOS Release 10.3.

Example

The following example adds Token Ring 0 to bridge group 1 and assigns a path cost of 12 to Token Ring 0:

```
interface tokenring 0
 source-bridge spanning 1 path-cost 12
```

Related Commands

bridge protocol ibm
show source-bridge

SOURCE-BRIDGE SPANNING (MANUAL)

Use the **source-bridge spanning** interface configuration command to enable use of spanning explorers. The **no** form of this command disables their use. Only spanning explorers will be blocked; everything else will be forwarded.

> **source-bridge spanning**
> **no source-bridge spanning**

Syntax   Description

This command has no arguments or keywords.

Default

Disabled

Command Mode

Interface configuration

Usage Guidelines

This command first appeared in Cisco IOS Release 10.0.

Use of the **source-bridge spanning** command is recommended. This command puts the interface into a forwarding or active state with respect to the spanning tree. There are two types of explorer packets used to collect RIF information:

- All-rings, all-routes explorer packets follow all possible paths to a destination ring. In a worst-case scenario, the number of all-rings explorers generated may be exponentially large.

- Spanning or limited-route explorer packets follow a spanning tree when looking for paths, greatly reducing the number of explorer packets required. There is currently no dynamic spanning-tree algorithm to establish that spanning tree; it must be manually configured.

Example

The following example enables use of spanning explorers:

```
! Global configuration command establishing the ring group for the interface configuration
commands
 source-bridge ring-group 48
!
! commands that follow apply to interface token 0
interface tokenring 0
! configure interface tokenring 0 to use spanning explorers
 source-bridge spanning
```

Related Commands

source-bridge

SOURCE-BRIDGE TRANSPARENT

Use the **source-bridge transparent** global configuration command to establish bridging between transparent bridging and source-route bridging. Use the **no** form of this command to disable a previously established link between a source-bridge ring group and a transparent bridge group.

source-bridge transparent *ring-group pseudo-ring bridge-number tb-group* [*oui*]
no source-bridge transparent *ring-group pseudo-ring bridge-number tb-group*

Syntax	Description
ring-group	Virtual ring group created by the **source-bridge ring-group** command. This is the source-bridge virtual ring to associate with the transparent bridge group. This ring-group number must match the number you have specified with the **source-bridge ring-group** command. The valid range is 1 to 4095.
pseudo-ring	Ring number used to represent the transparent bridging domain to the source-route bridged domain. This number must be a unique number, not used by any other ring in your source-route bridged network.
bridge-number	Bridge number of the bridge that leads to the transparent bridging domain.
tb-group	Number of the transparent bridge group that you want to tie into your source-route bridged domain. The **no** form of this command disables this feature.
oui	(Optional) Organizational unique identifier. Possible values include the following: • **90-compatible** • **standard** • **cisco**

Default
Not established

Command Mode
Global configuration

Usage Guidelines
This command first appeared in Cisco IOS Release 10.0.

Before using this command, you must have completely configured your router using multiport source-bridging and transparent bridging.

Specify the **90-compatible** OUI when talking to Cisco software routers. This OUI provides the most flexibility. Specify the **standard** OUI when talking to IBM 8209 bridges and other vendor equipment. This OUI does not provide for as much flexibility as the other two choices. The **cisco** OUI is provided for compatibility with future equipment.

Do not use the **standard** OUI unless you are forced to interoperate with other vendor equipment, such as the IBM 8209, in providing Ethernet and Token Ring mixed media bridged connectivity. Only use the **standard** keyword when you are transferring data between IBM 8209 Ethernet/Token Ring bridges and routers running the SR/TLB software (to create a Token Ring backbone to connect Ethernets). Use of the **standard** keyword causes the OUI code in Token Ring frames to always be 0x000000. In the context of the **standard** keyword, an OUI of 0x000000 identifies the frame as an Ethernet Type II frame. If the OUI in Token Ring frame is 0x000000 SR/TLB will output an Ethernet Type II frame.

When 8209 compatibility is enabled with the **ethernet transit-oui standard** command, the SR/TLB chooses to translate all Token Ring SNAP frames into Ethernet Type II frames as described earlier in this chapter.

Example
The following example establishes bridging between a transparent-bridge network and a source-route network:

```
source-bridge ring-group 9
source-bridge transparent 9 6 2 2
!
interface tokenring 0
 source-bridge 5 2 9
!
interface token ring 1
source bridge 4 2 9
!
interface ethernet 0
bridge-group 2
```

```
!
interface ethernet 1
bridge-group 2

bridge 2 protocol ieee
```

Related Commands

bridge-group
source-bridge
source-bridge ring-group

SOURCE-BRIDGE TRANSPARENT FASTSWITCH

Use the **source-bridge transparent fastswitch** global configuration command to enable fast switching of packets between the SRB and transparent domains. Use the **no** form of this command to disable fast switching of packets.

> **source-bridge transparent** *ring-group* **fastswitch**
> **no source-bridge transparent** *ring-group* **fastswitch**

Syntax	Description
ring-group	Virtual ring group created by the **source-bridge ring-group** command. This is the source-bridge virtual ring to associate with the transparent bridge group. This ring-group number must match the number you have specified with the **source-bridge ring-group** command. The valid range is 1 to 4095.
fastswitch	Fast-switched SR/TLB enables the Cisco IOS software to process packets at the interrupt level.

Default

Fast-switched SR/TLB is enabled.

Command Mode

Global configuration

Usage Guidelines

This command first appeared in Cisco IOS Release 11.2.

Because fast-switched SR/TLB is enabled by default when the router is configured for SR/TLB, there are no user-specified changes to the operation of the router, and the enabling command does not appear in the configuration.

The **no source-bridge transparent** *ring-group* **fastswitch** command is provided to disable fast-switched SR/TLB, causing the router to handle packets by process switching. When fast-switched SR/TLB is disabled, the **no** form of the command appears on a separate line of the configuration, immediately below the parent **source-bridge transparent** command.

If fast-switch SR/TLB has been disabled, it can be enabled using the **source-bridge transparent** *ring-group* **fastswitch** command, but the enabling form of the command will not appear in the configuration.

Example

The following example disables fast-switched SR/TLB between a transparent-bridge network and a source-route network:

```
source-bridge ring-group 9
source-bridge transparent 9 6 2 2
no source-bridge transparent 9 fastswitch
!
interface tokenring 0
 source-bridge 5 2 9
interface token ring 1
 source bridge 4 2 9
!
interface ethernet 0
 bridge-group 2
!
interface ethernet 1
 bridge-group 2

bridge 2 protocol ieee
```

Related Commands

bridge-group
source-bridge
source-bridge ring-group

PART 2

IBM NETWORKING

Chapter 5—Configuring Remote Source-Route Bridging

Chapter 6—Remote Source-Route Bridging Commands

Chapter 7—Configuring Data-Link Switching Plus

Chapter 8—DLSw+ Configuration Commands

Chapter 9—Configuring Serial Tunnel and Block Serial Tunnel

Chapter 10 — Serial Tunnel and Block Serial Tunnel Commands

Chapter 11 — Configuring LLC2 and SDLC Parameters

Chapter 12—LLC2 and SDLC Commands

Chapter 13 — Configuring IBM Network Media Translation

Chapter 14 — IBM Network Media Translation Commands

Chapter 15 — Configuring DSPU and SNA Service Point Support

Chapter 16 — DSPU and SNA Service Point Configuration Commands

Chapter 17 — Configuring SNA Frame Relay Access Support

Chapter 18 — SNA Frame Relay Access Support Commands

Chapter 19 — Configuring Advanced Peer-to-Peer Networking

Chapter 20 — APPN Configuration Commands

Chapter 21 — Configuring NCIA Client/Server Topologies

Chapter 22 — NCIA Server Configuration Commands

Chapter 23 — Configuring IBM Channel Attach

Chapter 24 — IBM Channel Attach Commands

CHAPTER 5

Configuring Remote Source-Route Bridging

This chapter describes how to configure remote source-route bridging (RSRB). For a complete description of the commands in this chapter, see Chapter 6, "Remote Source-Route Bridging Commands."

RSRB CONFIGURATION TASK LIST

To configure RSRB, perform the tasks in one of the following sections:

- Configuring RSRB Using Direct Encapsulation
- Configuring RSRB Using IP Encapsulation over an FST Connection
- Configuring RSRB Using IP Encapsulation over a TCP Connection
- Configuring RSRB Using IP Encapsulation over a Fast-Switched TCP Connection
- Configuring RSRB Using TCP and LLC2 Local Acknowledgment
- Configuring Direct Frame Relay Encapsulation Between RSRB Peers

After you configure RSRB, you can establish SAP prioritization by performing the tasks described in the "Establishing SAP Prioritization" section later in this chapter.

To tune and maintain the RSRB network, perform the tasks in the following sections:

- Tuning the RSRB Network
- Monitoring and Maintaining the RSRB Network

See the "RSRB Configuration Examples" section at the end of this chapter for specific configuration samples.

NOTES

Use IP encapsulation over a TCP connection within only complex meshed networks to support connections between peers that are separated by multiple hops and potentially can use multiple paths, and where performance is not an issue. Use direct encapsulation in point-to-point connections. In a point-to-point configuration, using TCP adds unnecessary processing overhead.

CONFIGURING RSRB USING DIRECT ENCAPSULATION

Configuring RSRB via the direct encapsulation method uses an HDLC-like encapsulation to pass frames over a single physical network connection between two routers attached to Token Rings. Use this method when you run source-route bridge traffic over point-to-point, single-hop, serial, or LAN media. Although this method does not have the flexibility of the TCP method, it provides better performance because it involves less overhead. To configure a remote source-route bridge to use a point-to-point serial line or a single Ethernet, or a single FDDI hop, perform the tasks in the following sections:

- Defining a Ring Group in RSRB Context
- Identifying the Remote Peers (Direct Encapsulation)
- Enabling SRB on the Appropriate Interfaces

Defining a Ring Group in RSRB Context

In Cisco's implementation of RSRB, whenever you connect Token Rings using non-Token Ring media, you must treat that non-Token Ring media as a virtual ring by assigning it to a ring group. Every router with which you want to exchange Token Ring traffic must be a member of this same ring group. These routers are referred to as remote-peer bridges. The ring group is therefore made up of interfaces that reside on separate routers.

A ring group must be assigned a ring number that is unique throughout the network. It is possible to assign different interfaces on the same router to different ring groups, if, for example, you plan to administer them as interfaces in separate domains.

To define or remove a ring group, perform one of the following tasks in global configuration mode:

Task	Command
Define a ring group.	**source-bridge ring-group** *ring-group* [*virtual-mac-address*]
Remove a ring group.	**no source-bridge ring-group** *ring-group* [*virtual-mac-address*]

Identifying the Remote Peers (Direct Encapsulation)

The interfaces that you identify as remote-peer bridges must be serial, Ethernet, FDDI, or Token Ring interfaces. On a serial interface, you must use HDLC encapsulation. To identify remote-peer bridges, perform the following task in global configuration mode:

Task	Command
Define the ring group and identify the interface over which to send SRB traffic to another router in the ring group.	**source-bridge remote-peer** *ring-group* **interface** *interface-name* [*mac-address*] [**lf** *size*]

Specify one **source-bridge remote peer** command for each peer router that is part of the virtual ring. Also specify one **source-bridge remote peer** command to identify the IP address of the local router. If you specify a MAC address, make sure it is the MAC address on the remote interface that is directly connected to the system that is being configured. It should not be the MAC address of the Token Ring interface on the remote peer.

You can assign a keepalive interval to the remote source-bridging peer. Perform the following task in interface configuration mode:

Task	Command
Define the keepalive interval of the remote source-bridging peer.	**source-bridge keepalive** *seconds*

Enabling SRB on the Appropriate Interfaces

Enable SRB on each interface through which source-route bridging traffic will pass. The value you specify in the target ring parameter should be the ring-group number you have assigned to the interface. To enable SRB on an interface, perform the following task in interface configuration mode:

Task	Command
Enable source-route bridging on an interface.	**source-bridge** *local-ring bridge-number target-ring*

CONFIGURING RSRB USING IP ENCAPSULATION OVER AN FST CONNECTION

Encapsulating the source-route bridged traffic inside IP datagrams passed over a Fast-Sequenced Transport (FST) connection between two routers is not as fast as direct encapsulation, but it outperforms IP encapsulation over a TCP connection because it has lower overhead. However, this method does not allow for local acknowledgment, nor is it suitable for use in networks that tend to reorder frame sequences. To configure a remote source-route bridge to use IP encapsulation over an FST connection, you must perform the tasks in the following sections:

- Setting Up an FST Peer Name and Assigning an IP Address
- Identifying the Remote Peers (FST Connection)
- Enabling SRB on the Appropriate Interfaces

NOTES

FST encapsulation preserves the dynamic media-independent nature of IP routing to support SNA and NetBIOS applications.

For an example of how to configure RSRB over an FST connection, see the "RSRB Using IP Encapsulation over an FST Connection Example" section later in this chapter.

Setting Up an FST Peer Name and Assigning an IP Address

To set up an FST peer name and provide an IP address to the local router, perform the following task in global configuration mode:

Task	Command
Set up an FST peer name and provide the local router with an IP address.	**source-bridge fst-peername** *local-interface-address*

In Cisco's implementation of RSRB, whenever you connect Token Rings using non-Token Ring media, you must treat that non-Token Ring media as a virtual ring by assigning it to a ring group. Every router with which you want to exchange Token Ring traffic must be a member of this same ring group. Therefore, after you set up an FST peer name, define a ring group. For more information about defining a ring group, see the "Defining a Ring Group in SRB Context" section of Chapter 3, "Configuring Source-Route Bridging."

Identifying the Remote Peers (FST Connection)

All the routers with which you want to exchange Token Ring traffic are referred to as remote-peer bridges. The remote peers can be at the other end of an FST connection. To identify the remote peers, perform the following task in global configuration mode:

Task	Command
Identify your peers and specify an FST connection.	**source-bridge remote-peer** *ring-group* **fst** *ip-address* [**lf** *size*]

Specify one **source-bridge remote-peer** command for each peer router that is part of the virtual ring. Also specify one **source-bridge remote-peer** command to identify the IP address of the local router. The IP address you specify should be the IP address you want the router to reach.

To assign a keepalive interval to the RSRB peer, perform the following task in interface configuration mode:

Task	Command
Define the keepalive interval of the RSRB peer.	**source-bridge keepalive** *seconds*

Enabling SRB on the Appropriate Interfaces

Enable SRB on each interface through which SRB traffic passes. Make the value of the target ring parameter you specify the ring-group number you assigned to the interface. To enable SRB on an interface, perform the following task in interface configuration mode:

Task	Command
Enable local SRB on a Token Ring interface.	**source-bridge** *local-ring bridge-number target-ring*

Performance Considerations When Using FST in a Redundant Network Topology

FST is fast-switched when it receives or sends frames from Ethernet, Token Ring, or FDDI interfaces. It is also fast-switched when it sends and receives from serial interfaces configured with the High-Level Data Link Control (HDLC) encapsulation. In all other cases, FST is slow-switched.

In instances where FST is fast-switched, in either the Cisco routers configured for FST or in the routers contained within the IP "cloud" between a pair of FST peers, only one path is used at a given time between the two FST peers. A single path greatly decreases the likelihood that frames arrive out of sequence. In the rare cases where frames do arrive out of sequence, the FST code on the receiving peer discards the out-of-order frame. Thus, the Token Ring end hosts rarely lose a frame over the FST router cloud, and performance levels remain adequate.

The same conditions are true for any slow-switched topology that provides only a single path (for example, a single X.25 network cloud) between the peers. Similarly, if two slow-switched paths are of different costs such that one always will be chosen over the other, the chances of having frames received out of sequence are also rare.

However, if two or more slow-switched paths of equal cost exist between the two routers (such as two parallel X.25 networks), the routers alternate in sending packets between the two or more equal-cost paths. This results in a high probability of frames arriving out of sequence at the receiver. In such cases, the FST code disposes of every out-of-sequence packet, leading to a large number of drops. This requires that the end hosts retransmit frames, greatly reducing overall throughput.

When parallel paths exist, Cisco strongly recommends choosing one as the preferred path. Choose a preferred path by specifying a higher bandwidth for the path that contains the direct connections to the two or more parallel paths on the router.

Do not use FST when the probability routinely exists for frames to lose their order in your network. If you have a network where frames are routinely reordered, it is far better to use the TCP protocol for remote source-route bridging, because TCP provides the overhead necessary to bring frames back in order on the receiving router. FST, to remain fast, does not provide for such a mechanism, and will discard out-of-order frames.

CONFIGURING RSRB USING IP ENCAPSULATION OVER A TCP CONNECTION

Encapsulating the suorce-route bridged traffic inside IP datagrams passed over a TCP connection between two routers offers lower performance, but is the appropriate method to use under the following conditions:

- You plan to connect Token Ring networks across arbitrary media including Ethernet, FDDI, serial interfaces, X.25 networks, and so forth.
- You plan to connect Token Ring networks across a multiprotocol backbone network.
- You plan to load balance over multiple, redundant paths. Using this topology, when a path fails there is no need for hosts to retransmit explorer packets. IP routing handles the network reconfiguration transparently to the Token Ring hosts.

To configure a remote source-route bridge to use IP encapsulation over a TCP connection, you must perform the tasks in the following sections:

- Identifying the Remote Peer (TCP Connection)
- Enabling SRB on the Appropriate Interfaces

Identifying the Remote Peer (TCP Connection)

In Cisco's implementation, whenever you connect Token Rings using non-Token Ring media, you must treat that non-Token Ring media as a virtual ring by assigning it to a ring group. Every router with which you want to exchange Token Ring traffic must be a member of this same ring group. For more information about defining a ring group, see the "Defining a Ring Group in SRB Context" section of Chapter 3.

To identify the remote peers, perform the following task in global configuration mode:

Task	Command
Identify the IP address of a peer in the ring group with which to exchange source-bridge traffic using TCP.	**source-bridge remote-peer** *ring-group* **tcp** *ip-address* [**lf** *size*] [**tcp-receive-window** *wsize*] [**local-ack**] [**priority**]

Specify one **source-bridge remote-peer** command for each peer router that is part of the virtual ring. Also specify one **source-bridge remote-peer** command to identify the IP address of the local router.

You can assign a keepalive interval to the remote source-bridging peer. Perform the following task in interface configuration mode:

Task	Command
Define the keepalive interval of the remote source-bridging peer.	**source-bridge keepalive** *seconds*

Enabling SRB on the Appropriate Interfaces

To enable SRB on an interface, perform the following task in interface configuration mode:

Task	Command
Enable local source-route bridging on a Token Ring interface.	**source-bridge** *local-ring bridge-number target-ring*

The value of the target ring parameter you specify should be the ring-group number.

CONFIGURING RSRB USING IP ENCAPSULATION OVER A FAST-SWITCHED TCP CONNECTION

The fast-switched TCP (FTCP) encapsulation type speeds up Token Ring-to-Token Ring RSRB over TCP by fast switching Token Ring frames to and from the TCP pipe. FTCP encapsulation supports the same options as TCP, with the exception of priority queueing.

In Cisco's implementation, whenever you connect Token Rings using non-Token Ring media, you must treat that non-Token Ring media as a virtual ring by assigning it to a ring group. Every router with which you wish to exchange Token Ring traffic must be a member of this same ring group. For more information about defining a ring group, see the "Defining a Ring Group in SRB Context" section of Chapter 3.

To configure RSRB fast switching, you must perform the tasks in the following sections:

- Identifying the Remote Peer (FTCP Connection)
- Enabling SRB on the Appropriate Interfaces

Identifying the Remote Peer (FTCP Connection)

Identify the remote peer with which the router communicates. To identify the remote peers, perform the following task in global configuration mode:

Task	Command
Identify the IP address of a peer in the ring group with which to exchange source-bridge traffic using TCP.	**source-bridge remote-peer** *ring-group* **ftcp** *ip-address* [**lf** *size*] [**tcp-receive-window** *wsize*] [**local-ack**]

You must identify a remote peer for each interface you configure for remote source-route bridging. The IP address you specify is the IP address the router tries to reach.

To assign a keepalive interval to the remote peer, perform the following task in interface configuration mode:

Task	Command
Define the keepalive interval of the remote peer.	**source-bridge keepalive** *seconds*

Enabling SRB on the Appropriate Interfaces

To enable SRB on an interface, perform the following task in interface configuration mode:

Task	Command
Enable local SRB on a Token Ring interface.	**source-bridge** *local-ring bridge-number target-ring*

The value of the target ring parameter you specify should be the ring-group number.

CONFIGURING RSRB USING TCP AND LLC2 LOCAL ACKNOWLEDGMENT

Encapsulating source-route bridged traffic inside IP datagrams that traverse a TCP connection between two routers with local acknowledgment enabled is appropriate when you have LANs separated by wide geographic distances and you want to avoid time delays, multiple retransmissions, or loss of user sessions.

Logical Link Control–Type 2 (LLC2) is an ISO standard data-link level protocol used in Token Ring networks. LLC2 was designed to provide reliable transmission of data across LAN media and to cause minimal, or at least predictable, time delays. However, RSRB and wide-area network (WAN) backbones created LANs that are separated by wide, geographic distances spanning countries and continents. As a result, LANs have time delays that are longer than LLC2 allows for bidirectional communication between hosts. Local acknowledgment addresses the problem of unpredictable time delays, multiple retransmissions, and loss of user sessions.

In a typical LLC2 session, when one host sends a frame to another host, the sending host expects the receiving host to respond positively or negatively in a predefined period of time commonly called the *T1 time*. If the sending host does not receive an acknowledgment of the frame it sent within the T1 time, it retries a few times (normally 8 to 10). If there is still no response, the sending host drops the session.

Figure 5–1 illustrates an LLC2 session. A 37x5 on a LAN segment can communicate with a 3x74 on a different LAN segment separated via a wide-area backbone network. Frames are transported between Router A and Router B using RSRB. However, the LLC2 session between the 37x5 and the 3x74 is still end to end; that is, every frame generated by the 37x5 traverses the backbone network to the 3x74, and the 3x74, on receipt of the frame, acknowledges it.

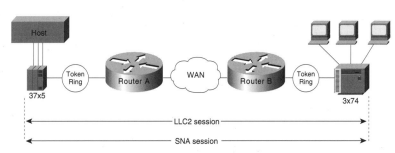

Figure 5–1
LLC2 session without local acknowledgment.

On backbone networks consisting of slow serial links, the T1 timer on end hosts could expire before the frames reach the remote hosts, causing the end host to retransmit. Retransmission results in duplicate frames reaching the remote host at the same time the first frame reaches the remote host. Such frame duplication breaks the LLC2 protocol, resulting in the loss of sessions between the two IBM machines.

One way to solve this time delay is to increase the timeout value on the end nodes to account for the maximum transit time between the two end machines. However, in networks consisting of hundreds or even thousands of nodes, every machine would need to be reconfigured with new values. With local acknowledgment for LLC2 enabled, the LLC2 session between the two end nodes would not be end to end, but instead, would terminate at two local routers. Figure 5–2 shows the LLC2 session with the 37x5 ending at Router A and the LLC2 session with the 3x74 ending at Router B. Both Router A and Router B execute the full LLC2 protocol as part of local acknowledgment for LLC2.

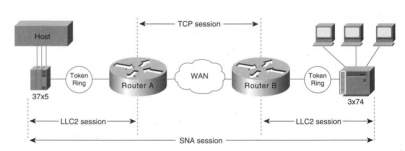

Figure 5–2
LLC2 session with local
acknowledgment.

With local acknowledgment for LLC2 enabled in both routers, Router A acknowledges frames received from the 37x5. The 37x5 still operates as if the acknowledgments it receives are from the 3x74. Router A looks like the 3x74 to the 37x5. Similarly, Router B acknowledges frames received from the 3x74. The 3x74 operates as if the acknowledgments it receives are from the 37x5. Router B looks like the 3x74 to 37x5. Because the frames no longer have to travel the WAN backbone networks to be acknowledged, but instead are locally acknowledged by routers, the end machines do not time out, resulting in no loss of sessions.

Enabling local acknowledgment for LLC2 has the following advantages:

- Local acknowledgment for LLC2 solves the T1 timer problem without having to change any configuration on the end nodes. The end nodes are unaware that the sessions are locally acknowledged. In networks consisting of hundreds or even thousands of machines, this is a definite advantage. All the frames acknowledged by the Cisco IOS software appear to the end hosts to be coming from the remote IBM machine. In fact, by looking at a trace from a protocol analyzer, one cannot say whether a frame was acknowledged by the local router or by a remote IBM machine. The MAC addresses and the RIFs generated by the Cisco IOS software are identical to those generated by the remote IBM machine. The only way to find out whether a session is locally acknowledged is to use either a **show local-ack** command or a **show source-bridge** command on the router.

- All the supervisory (RR, RNR, REJ) frames that are locally acknowledged go no farther than the router. Without local acknowledgment for LLC2, *every* frame traverses the backbone. With local acknowledgment, only data (I-frames) traverse the backbone, resulting in less traffic on the backbone network. For installations in which customers pay for the amount of traffic passing through the backbone, this could be a definite cost-saving measure. A simple protocol exists between the two *peers* to bring up or down a TCP session.

To configure a remote source-route bridge to use IP encapsulation over a TCP connection, perform the tasks in the following sections:

- Enabling LLC2 Local Acknowledgment between Two Remote Peer Bridges
- Enabling SRB on the Appropriate Interfaces

Enabling LLC2 Local Acknowledgment Between Two Remote-Peer Bridges

In Cisco's implementation, whenever you connect Token Rings using non-Token Ring media, you must treat that non-Token Ring media as a virtual ring by assigning it to a ring group. Every router with which you wish to exchange Token Ring traffic must be a member of this same ring group. For more information about defining a ring group, see the "Defining a Ring Group in SRB Context" section of Chapter 3.

To enable LLC2 local acknowledgment, perform the following task in global configuration mode:

Task	Command
Enable LLC2 local acknowledgment on a per-remote-peer basis.	**source-bridge remote-peer** *ring-group* **tcp** *ip-address* **local-ack**

You must use one instance of the **source-bridge remote-peer** command for each interface you configure for RSRB.

Enabling SRB on the Appropriate Interfaces

To enable SRB on an interface, perform the following task in interface configuration mode:

Task	Command
Enable local SRB on a Token Ring interface.	**source-bridge** *local-ring bridge-number target-ring*

The value of the target ring parameter you specify should be the ring-group number.

For an example of how to configure RSRB with local acknowledgment, see the "RSRB with Local Acknowledgment Example" section later in this chapter.

Enabling Local Acknowledgment and Passthrough

To configure some sessions on a few rings to be locally acknowledged while the remaining sessions are passed through, perform the following task in global configuration mode:

Task	Command
Configure the Cisco IOS software for passthrough.	**source-bridge passthrough** *ring-group*

Notes on Using LLC2 Local Acknowledgment

LLC2 local acknowledgment can be enabled with only TCP remote peers (as opposed to LAN or direct serial interface remote peers) because the Cisco IOS software needs the reliable transmission of TCP to provide the same reliability that an LLC2 LAN end-to-end connection provides. Therefore, the direct media encapsulation options for the **source-bridge remote-peer** command cannot be used.

If the LLC2 session between the local host and the router terminates on either side of the connection, the other device will be informed to terminate its connection to its local host.

If the TCP queue length of the connection between the two routers reaches 90 percent of its limit, they send Receiver-not-Ready (RNR) messages to the local hosts until the queue limit is reduced to below this limit.

The configuration of the LLC2 parameters for the local Token Ring interfaces can affect overall performance. See Chapter 11, "Configuring LLC2 and SDLC Parameters" for more details about fine-tuning your network through the LLC2 parameters.

NOTES ──

As previously stated, local acknowledgment for LLC2 is meant only for extreme cases in which communication is not possible otherwise. Because the router must maintain a full LLC2 session, the number of simultaneous sessions it can support before performance degrades depends on the mix of other protocols and their loads.

The routers at each end of the LLC2 session execute the full LLC2 protocol, which can result in some overhead. The decision to turn on local acknowledgment for LLC2 should be based on the speed of the backbone network in relation to the Token Ring speed. For LAN segments separated by slow-speed serial links (for example, 56 kbps), the T1 timer problem could occur more frequently. In such cases, it might be wise to turn on local acknowledgment for LLC2. For LAN segments separated by an FDDI backbone, backbone delays will be minimal; in such cases, local acknowledgment for LLC2 should not be turned on. Speed mismatch between the LAN segments and the backbone network is one criterion to be used in the decision to use local acknowledgment for LLC2.

There are some situations (such as host B failing between the time host A sends data and the time host B receives it) in which host A would behave as if, *at the LLC2 layer*, data had been received when it was not, because the device acknowledges that it received data from host A before it confirms that host B actually can receive the data. But because both NetBIOS and SNA have error recovery in situations where an end device goes down, these higher-level protocols will resend any missing or lost data. These transaction request/confirmation protocols exist above LLC2, so they are not affected by tight timers, as is LLC2. They also are transparent to local acknowledgment.

If you are using NetBIOS applications, note that there are two NetBIOS timers—one at the link level and one at the next-higher level. Local acknowledgment for LLC2 is designed to solve session timeouts at the link level only. If you are experiencing NetBIOS session timeouts, you have two options:

- Experiment with increasing your NetBIOS timers.
- Avoid using NetBIOS applications on slow serial lines.

CONFIGURING DIRECT FRAME RELAY ENCAPSULATION BETWEEN RSRB PEERS

You can configure direct Frame Relay encapsulation to allow the RSRB peers to send RSRB protocol packets on a Frame Relay PVC. This configuration eliminates the overhead introduced by Transmission Control Protocol/Internet Protocol (TCP/IP)-encapsulated Frame Relay packets.

Figure 5–3 illustrates direct Frame Relay encapsulation between RSRB peers.

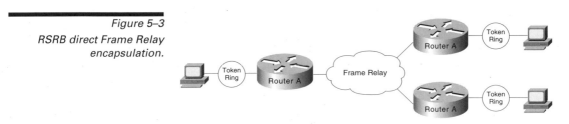

Figure 5–3
RSRB direct Frame Relay
encapsulation.

The RSRB direct encapsulation design can use RFC 1490 format or Cisco Frame Relay encapsulation for routed packets.

To configure RSRB direct Frame Relay encapsulation, perform the following tasks, starting in interface configuration mode:

Task	Command
Step 1 Specify the serial interface on which Frame Relay is configured.	**source-bridge remote-peer** *ring-group* **frame-relay interface** *name* [mac-address] [*dlci-number*] [**lf** *size*]
Step 2 Specify the DLCI number onto which the RSRB traffic is to be mapped.	**frame-relay map rsrb** *dlci-number*

ESTABLISHING SAP PRIORITIZATION

The SAP prioritization feature allows you to use SAP priority lists and filters to specify the priority of one protocol over another across an RSRB or SDLLC WAN.

Defining a SAP Priority List

To establish a SAP priority list, perform the following tasks:

Task	Command
Step 1 Define the priority list.	**sap-priority-list** *number queue-keyword* [**dsap** *ds*] [**ssap** *ss*] [**dmac** *dm*] [**smac** *sm*]
Step 2 Define the priority on an interface.	**sap-priority** *list-number*
Step 3 Apply the priority list to an interface.	**priority-group** *list-number*

Defining SAP Filters

You can define SAP filters and NetBIOS filters on Token Ring and Ethernet interfaces.

To filter by LSAP address on the RSRB WAN interface, perform the following global configuration tasks as appropriate:

Task	Command
Step 1 Filter by LSAP address (TCP encapsulation).	**rsrb remote-peer** *ring-group* **tcp** *ip-address* **lsap-output-list** *access-list-number*
Step 2 Filter by LSAP address (FST encapsulation).	**rsrb remote-peer** *ring-group* **fst** *ip-address* **lsap-output-list** *access-list-number*
Step 3 Filter by LSAP address (direct encapsulation).	**rsrb remote-peer** *ring-group* **interface** *name* **lsap-output-list** *access-list-number*

To filter packets by NetBIOS station name on an RSRB WAN interface, perform one of the following global configuration tasks as appropriate:

Task	Command
Filter by NetBIOS station name (TCP encapsulation).	**rsrb remote-peer** *ring-group* **tcp** *ip-address* **netbios-output-list** *name*
Filter by NetBIOS station name (FST encapsulation).	**rsrb remote-peer** *ring-group* **fst** *ip-address* **netbios-output-list** *name*
Filter by NetBIOS station name (direct encapsulation).	**rsrb remote-peer** *ring-group* **interface** *type* **netbios-output-list** *host*

TUNING THE RSRB NETWORK

The following sections describe how to configure features that enhance network performance by reducing the number of packets that traverse the backbone network:

- Prioritizing Traffic Based on SNA Local LU Addresses
- Enabling Class of Service
- Assigning a Priority Group to an Input Interface
- Configuring the Largest Frame Size

Prioritizing Traffic Based on SNA Local LU Addresses

You can prioritize SNA traffic on an interface configured for either serial tunnel (STUN) or RSRB communication. The SNA local LU address prioritization feature allows SNA traffic to be prioritized according to the address of the logical units (LU) on the FID2 transmission headers. Currently, only dependent LUs are supported. The prioritization takes place on LU-LU traffic between an SNA Node type 5 or Node type 4, and Node type 2.

Figure 5–4 shows how SNA local address prioritization can be used.

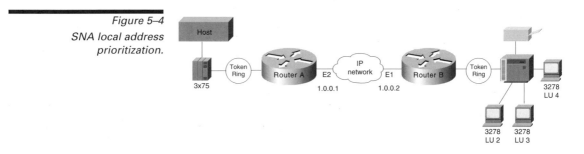

Figure 5–4
SNA local address
prioritization.

In Figure 5–4, the IBM mainframe is channel-attached to a 3x75 FEP, which is connected to a cluster controller via RSRB. Multiple 3270 terminals and printers, each with a unique local LU address, are then attached to the cluster controller. By applying SNA local LU address prioritization, each LU associated with a terminal or printer can be assigned a priority; that is, certain users can have terminals that have better response time than others, and printers can have lowest priority.

NOTES

Both Local Acknowledgment and TCP priority features for STUN or RSRB must be turned on for SNA local address prioritization to take effect.

With the SNA local LU address prioritization feature, you can establish queuing priorities based on the address of the logical unit. To prioritize traffic, perform the following tasks in global configuration mode:

Task	Command
Step 1 Map LUs to TCP port numbers.	**locaddr-priority-list** *list-number address-number queue-keyword* [**dsap** *ds*] [**dmac** *dm*] [**ssap** *ss*] [**smac** *sm*]
Step 2 Set the priority of TCP port numbers.	**priority-list** *list-number* **protocol** *protocol-name queue-keyword*

Enabling Class of Service

To prioritize SNA traffic across the SNA backbone network, you can enable the class of service feature. This feature is useful only between FEP-to-FEP (PU4-to-PU4) communication across the non-SNA backbone. It allows important FEP traffic to flow on high-priority queues.

To enable class of service, IP encapsulation over a TCP connection and LLC2 local acknowledgment must be enabled.

To enable class of service, perform the following task in global configuration mode:

Task	Command
Enable class-of-service.	**source-bridge cos-enable**

Assigning a Priority Group to an Input Interface

To assign a priority group to an input interface, perform the following task in interface configuration mode:

Task	Command
Assign a priority group to an input interface.	**locaddr-priority** *list-number*

Configuring the Largest Frame Size

You can configure the largest frame size that is used to communicate with any peers in the ring group.

Generally, the router and the LLC2 device with which it communicates should support the same maximum SDLC I-frame size. The larger this value, the more efficiently the line is used, thus increasing performance.

Faster screen updates to 3278-style terminals often result from configuring the Token Ring FEP to send as large an I-frame as possible and then allowing the Cisco IOS software to segment the frame into multiple SDLC I-frames.

After you configure the Token Ring FEP to send the largest possible I-frame, configure the software to support the same maximum I-frame size. The default is 516 bytes. The maximum value the software can support is 8144 bytes.

To configure the largest frame size, perform the following task in global configuration mode:

Task	Command
Specify the largest frame size used to communicate with any peers in the ring group.	source-bridge largest-frame *ring-group size*

MONITORING AND MAINTAINING THE RSRB NETWORK

To display a variety of information about the RSRB network, perform one or more of the following tasks in EXEC mode:

Task	Command
Display internal state information about the Token Ring interfaces in the system.	show controllers token
Provide high-level statistics about the state of source bridging for a particular interface.	show interfaces
Show the current state of any current local acknowledgment for both LLC2 and SDLLC connections.	show local-ack

In addition to the EXEC-mode tasks to maintain the RSRB network, you can perform the following task in global configuration mode:

Task	Command
Limit the size of the backup queue for RSRB to control the number of packets that can wait for transmission to a remote ring before they start being discarded.	source-bridge tcp-queue-max *number*

RSRB CONFIGURATION EXAMPLES

The following sections provide RSRB configuration examples:

- RSRB Direct Frame Relay Encapsulation Example
- RSRB Using IP Encapsulation over a TCP Connection Example
- RSRB/TCP Fast-Switching Configuration Example
- RSRB Using IP Encapsulation over an FST Connection Example
- RSRB Using All Types of Transport Methods Example
- RSRB with Local Acknowledgment Example
- RSRB with Local Acknowledgment and Pass-through Example
- Local Acknowledgment for LLC2 Example
- IP for Load Sharing over RSRB Example
- Configuring Priority for Locally Terminated Token Ring Interfaces in RSRB Example
- SNA Traffic Prioritization by LU Address Example

RSRB Direct Frame Relay Encapsulation Example

The following is the configuration file for direct Frame Relay encapsulation between RSRB peers:

```
source-bridge ring-group 200
source-bridge remote-peer 200 frame-relay interface serial0 30
!
interface serial 0
 mtu 3000
 no ip address
 encapsulation frame-relay
 clockrate 56000
 frame-relay lmi-type ansi
 frame-relay map rsrb 30
!
!
interface TokenRing 0
 ip address 10.10.10.1 255.255.255.0
 ring-speed 16
 multiring all
 source-bridge active 102 1 200
 source-bridge spanning
```

RSRB Using IP Encapsulation over a TCP Connection Example

Figure 5–5 illustrates two routers configured for RSRB using TCP as a transport. Each router has two Token Rings. They are connected by an Ethernet segment over which the source-route bridged traffic will pass. The first router configuration is a source-route bridge at address 131.108.2.29.

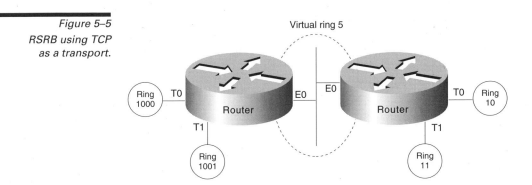

Figure 5–5
RSRB using TCP
as a transport.

Using TCP as the transport, the configuration for the source-route bridge at address 131.108.2.29, as depicted in Figure 5–5, is as follows:

```
source-bridge ring-group 5
source-bridge remote-peer 5 tcp 131.108.2.29
source-bridge remote-peer 5 tcp 131.108.1.27
!
interface ethernet 0
 ip address 131.108.4.4 255.255.255.0
!
interface tokenring 0
 ip address 131.100.2.29 255.255.255.0
 source-bridge 1000 1 5
 source-bridge spanning
!
interface tokenring 1
 ip address 131.108.128.1 255.255.255.0
 source-bridge 1001 1 5
 source-bridge spanning
```

The configuration of the source-route bridge at 131.108.1.27 is as follows:

```
source-bridge ring-group 5
source-bridge remote-peer 5 tcp 131.108.2.29
source-bridge remote-peer 5 tcp 131.108.1.27
!
interface ethernet 0
 ip address 131.108.4.5 255.255.255.0
!
interface tokenring 0
 ip address 131.108.1.27 255.255.255.0
 source-bridge 10 1 5
 source-bridge spanning
!
interface tokenring 1
 ip address 131.108.131.1 255.255.255.0
 source-bridge 11 1 5
 source-bridge spanning
```

RSRB/TCP Fast-Switching Configuration Example

The following configuration enables RSRB/TCP fast switching:

```
source-bridge ring group 100
source-bridge remote-peer 100 ftcp 198.92.88.138
source-bridge remote-peer 100 ftcp 198.92.88.145
```

RSRB Using IP Encapsulation over an FST Connection Example

Figure 5–6 shows two routers connecting IBM hosts on Token Rings through an Ethernet backbone.

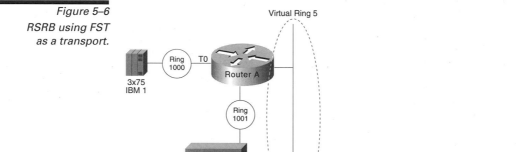

Figure 5–6
RSRB using FST
as a transport.

This sample configuration enables IP encapsulation over an FST connection. In this configuration, the **source-bridge fst-peername** global configuration command is used to provide an IP address for the local router, the **source-bridge ring-group** global configuration command is used to define a ring group, and the **source-bridge remote-peer** command with the **fst** option is used to associate the remote peer's IP address with the router's ring group and specify the remote peer's remote source-route bridging protocol version number. Because all FST peers support version 2 RSRB, the **version** keyword is always specified.

The configuration of the source-route bridge at 131.108.2.29 is as follows:

```
source-bridge fst-peername 131.108.2.29
source-bridge ring-group 5
source-bridge remote-peer 5 fst 131.108.1.27
!
interface ethernet 0
 ip address 131.108.4.4 255.255.255.0
!
interface tokenring 0
 ip address 131.108.2.29 255.255.255.0
 source-bridge 1000 1 5
 source-bridge spanning
```

```
!
interface tokenring 1
 ip address 131.108.128.1 255.255.255.0
 source-bridge 1001 1 5
 source-bridge spanning
```

The configuration of the source-route bridge at 131.108.1.27 is as follows:

```
source-bridge fst-peername 131.108.1.27
source-bridge ring-group 5
source-bridge remote-peer 5 fst 131.108.2.29
!
interface ethernet 0
 ip address 131.108.4.5 255.255.255.0
!
interface tokenring 0
 ip address 131.108.1.27 255.255.255.0
 source-bridge 10 1 5
 source-bridge spanning
!
interface tokenring 1
 ip address 131.108.131.1 255.255.255.0
 source-bridge 11 1 5
 source-bridge spanning
```

RSRB Using All Types of Transport Methods Example

Figure 5–7 shows a router configured for RSRB using all types of transport methods.

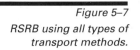

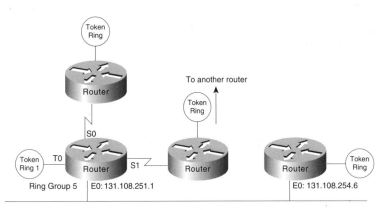

Figure 5–7
RSRB using all types of transport methods.

The configuration for the network in Figure 5–7 is as follows:

```
source-bridge fst-peername 131.108.251.1
source-bridge ring-group 5
source-bridge remote-peer 5 interface serial0
source-bridge remote-peer 5 interface serial1
```

```
source-bridge remote-peer 5 interface Ethernet0 0000.0c00.1234
source-bridge remote-peer 5 tcp 131.108.251.1
source-bridge remote-peer 5 fst 131.108.252.4
source-bridge remote-peer 5 tcp 131.108.253.5
!
interface tokenring 0
 source-bridge 1 1 5
 source-bridge spanning
!
interface ethernet 0
 ip address 131.108.251.1 255.255.255.0
```

The two peers using the serial transport method function correctly only if routers at the other end of the serial line have been configured to use the serial transport. The peers must also belong to the same ring group.

RSRB with Local Acknowledgment Example

In Figure 5–8, a triangular configuration provides the maximum reliability with minimal cost, and one of the links is doubled to gain better bandwidth. In addition to IP and SRB traffic, AppleTalk is also routed between all the sites. In this configuration, all the sessions between Router C and Router D are locally acknowledged. All the sessions between Router C and Router E are not locally acknowledged and are configured for normal remote source-route bridging. This example shows that not every peer must be locally acknowledged but that local acknowledgment can be turned on or off at the customer's discretion.

Figure 5–8

RSRB with local acknowledgment—simple configuration.

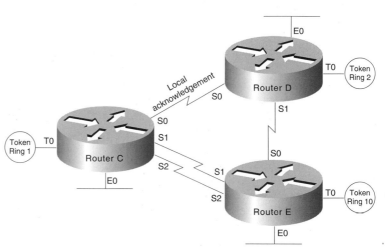

The configuration for the network in Figure 5–8 is as follows:

Configuration for Router C

```
appletalk routing
!
source-bridge ring-group 5
source-bridge remote-peer 5 tcp 132.21.1.1
source-bridge remote-peer 5 tcp 132.21.2.6 local-ack
source-bridge remote-peer 5 tcp 132.21.10.200
!
interface tokenring 0
 ip address 132.21.1.1 255.255.255.0
 source-bridge 1 1 5
 source-bridge spanning
 multiring all
!
interface ethernet 0
 ip address 132.21.4.25 255.255.255.0
 appletalk address 4.25
 appletalk zone Twilight
!
interface serial 0
 ip address 132.21.16.1 255.255.255.0
 appletalk address 16.1
 appletalk zone Twilight
!
interface serial 1
 ip address 132.21.17.1 255.255.255.0
 appletalk address 17.1
 appletalk zone Twilight
!
interface serial 2
 ip address 132.21.18.1 255.255.255.0
 appletalk address 18.1
 appletalk zone Twilight
!
 router igrp 109
 network 132.21.0.0
!
 hostname RouterC
```

Configuration for Router D

```
appletalk routing
!
source-bridge ring-group 5
source-bridge remote-peer 5 tcp 132.21.1.1 local-ack
source-bridge remote-peer 5 tcp 132.21.2.6
source-bridge remote-peer 5 tcp 132.21.10.200
```

```
!
interface tokenring 0
 ip address 132.21.2.6 255.255.255.0
 source-bridge 2 1 5
 source-bridge spanning
 multiring all
!
interface ethernet 0
 ip address 132.21.5.1 255.255.255.0
 appletalk address 5.1
 appletalk zone Twilight
!
interface serial 0
 ip address 132.21.16.2 255.255.255.0
 appletalk address 16.2
 appletalk zone Twilight
!
interface serial 1
 ip address 132.21.19.1 255.255.255.0
 appletalk address 19.1
 appletalk zone Twilight
!
router igrp 109
 network 132.21.0.0
!
hostname RouterD
```

Configuration for Router E

```
appletalk routing
!
source-bridge ring-group 5
source-bridge remote-peer 5 tcp 132.21.1.1
source-bridge remote-peer 5 tcp 132.21.2.6
source-bridge remote-peer 5 tcp 132.21.10.200
!
interface tokenring 0
 ip address 132.21.10.200 255.255.255.0
 source-bridge 10 1 5
 source-bridge spanning
 multiring all
!
interface ethernet 0
 ip address 132.21.7.1 255.255.255.0
 appletalk address 7.1
 appletalk zone Twilight
!
interface serial 0
 ip address 132.21.19.2 255.255.255.0
 appletalk address 19.2
 appletalk zone Twilight
```

```
!
interface serial 1
  ip address 132.21.17.2 255.255.255.0
  appletalk address 17.2
  appletalk zone Twilight
!
interface serial 2
  ip address 132.21.18.2 255.255.255.0
  appletalk address 18.2
  appletalk zone Twilight
!
  router igrp 109
  network 132.21.0.0
!
hostname RouterE
```

RSRB with Local Acknowledgment and Pass-through Example

Figure 5–9 shows two routers configured for remote source-route bridging with local acknowledgment and pass-through over the three serial lines that connect these routers. In turn, five Token Rings connect to each of these routers.

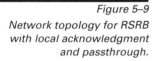

Figure 5–9

Network topology for RSRB with local acknowledgment and passthrough.

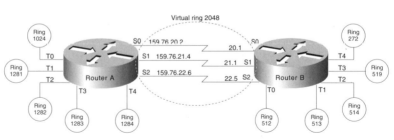

The configuration files for each of these routers follow.

Configuration for Router A

```
source-bridge ring-group 2048
source-bridge remote-peer 2048 tcp 159.76.1.250 local-ack version 2
source-bridge remote-peer 2048 tcp 159.76.7.250 version 2
source-bridge passthrough 1281
source-bridge passthrough 1282
source-bridge passthrough 1283
source-bridge passthrough 1284
!
interface tokenring 0
  ip address 159.76.7.250 255.255.255.0
  llc2 ack-max 1
  llc2 t1-time 1800
  llc2 idle-time 29000
```

```
 llc2 ack-delay-time 5
 source-bridge 1024 1 2048
 source-bridge spanning
 early-token-release
 multiring all
!
interface tokenring 1
 ip address 159.76.8.250 255.255.255.0
 clns-speed 4
 clns mtu 4464
 source-bridge 1281 1 2048
 source-bridge spanning
 multiring all
!
interface tokenring 2
 ip address 159.76.9.250 255.255.255.0
 ring-speed 4
 clns mtu 4464
 source-bridge 1282 1 2048
 source-bridge spanning
 multiring all
!
interface tokenring 3
 ip address 159.76.10.250 255.255.255.0
 ring speed 4
 clns mtu 4464
 source-bridge 1283 1 2048
 source-bridge spanning
 multiring all
!
interface tokenring 4
 ip address 159.78.11.250 255.255.255.0
 ring speed 4
 clns mtu 4464
 source-bridge 1284 1 2048
 source-bridge spanning
 multiring all
!
interface serial 0
 ip address 159.76.20.2 255.255.255.0
!
interface serial 1
 ip address 159.76.21.4 255.255.255.0
!
interface serial 2
 ip address 159.76.22.6 255.255.255.0
 shutdown
!
 interface serial 3
 no ip address
 shutdown
```

Configuration for Router B

```
source-bridge ring-group 2048
source-bridge remote-peer 2048 tcp 159.76.1.250 version 2
source-bridge remote-peer 2048 tcp 159.76.7.250 local-ack version 2
!
interface tokenring 0
 ip address 159.76.1.250 255.255.255.0
 llc2 ack-max 2
 llc2 t1-time 1900
 llc2 idle-time 29000
 llc2 ack-delay-time 5
 source-bridge 512 1 2048
 source-bridge spanning
 early-token-release
 multiring all
!!
interface tokenring 1
 ip address 159.76.2.250 255.255.255.0
 ring-speed 16
 clns mtu 8136
!
 source-bridge 513 1 2048
 source-bridge spanning
 early-token-release
 multiring all
!
interface tokenring 2
 ip address 159.76.3.250 255.255.255.0
 ring speed 16
 clns mtu 8136
 source-bridge 514 1 2048
 source-bridge spanning
 early-token-release
 multiring all
!
interface tokenring 3
 ip address 159.76.4.250 255.255.255.0
 ring-speed 4
 clns mtu 4464
 source-bridge 519 2 2043
 source-bridge spanning
 multiring all
!
interface tokenring 4
 ip address 159.76.5.250 255.255.255.0
 ring-speed 4
 clns mtu 4464
 source-bridge 272 2 2048
 source-bridge spanning
 multiring all
```

```
!
interface serial 0
 ip address 159.76.20.1 255.255.255.0
!
interface serial 1
 ip address 159.76.21.3 255.255.255.0
!
interface serial 2
 ip address 159.76.22.5 255.255.255.0
!
interface serial 3
 no ip address
 shutdown
```

Local Acknowledgment for LLC2 Example

Figure 5–10 shows an IBM FEP located in San Francisco communicating with IBM 3174 cluster controller hosts in Sydney, Paris, and Los Angeles. The session between the FEP and the IBM 3174 system in Los Angeles is not locally terminated, because the distance is great enough to cause time-outs on the line. However, the sessions to Paris and Sydney are locally terminated.

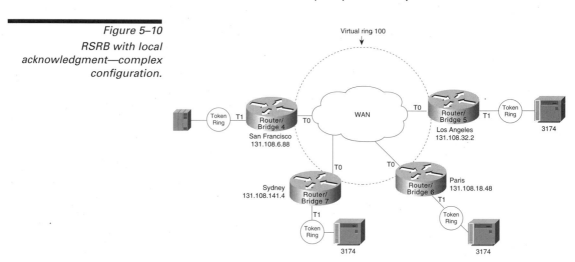

Figure 5–10

RSRB with local acknowledgment—complex configuration.

The configuration described in this example is represented in the following sample configuration files.

Configuration for Router/Bridge 4 in San Francisco

```
source-bridge ring-group 100
! use direct encapsulation across serial link to Los Angeles
source-bridge remote-peer 100 direct 131.108.32.2
 ! use fast sequenced transport with local termination to Paris
source-bridge remote-peer 100 tcp 131.108.18.48 local-ack
```

```
! use tcp encapsulation with local termination to Sydney
source-bridge remote-peer 100 tcp 131.108.141.4 local-ack
!
interface tokenring 0
 ! source ring 1, bridge 4, destination ring 100
source-bridge 1 4 100
! receive up to seven frames before sending an acknowledgment
llc2 ack-max 7
! allow a 30 msec delay before I-frames must be acknowledged
llc2 ack-delay-time 30
!
interface tokenring 1
! source ring 100, bridge 4, destination ring 1
source-bridge 100 4 1
```

Configuration for Router/Bridge 7 in Sydney

```
source-bridge ring-group 100
! use tcp encapsulation with local termination from Sydney
source-bridge remote-peer 100 tcp 131.108.6.88 local-ack
interface tokenring 0
! source ring 1, bridge 7, destination ring 100
source-bridge 1 7 100
! receive up to seven frames before sending an acknowledgment
llc2 ack-max 7
! allow a 30 msec delay before I-frames must be acknowledged
llc2 ack-delay-time 30
!
interface tokenring 1
! source ring 100, bridge 7, destination ring 1
source-bridge 100 7 1
```

Configuration for Router/Bridge 6 in Paris

```
source-bridge ring-group 100
! use fast sequenced transport with local termination from Paris
source-bridge remote-peer 100 tcp 131.108.6.88 local-ack
interface tokenring 0
! source ring 1, bridge 6, destination ring 100
source-bridge 1 6 100
! receive up to seven frames before sending an acknowledgment
llc2 ack-max 7
! allow a 30 msec delay before I-frames must be acknowledged
llc2 ack-delay-time 30
!
interface tokenring 1
! source ring 100, bridge 6, destination ring 1
source-bridge 100 6 1
```

Configuration for Router/Bridge 5 in Los Angeles

```
source-bridge ring-group 100
 ! use direct encapsulation across serial link from Los Angeles
 source-bridge remote-peer 100 direct 131.108.6.88

interface tokenring 0
 ! source ring 1, bridge 5, destination ring 100
 source-bridge 1 5 100
 ! receive up to seven frames before sending an acknowledgment
 llc2 ack-max 7
 ! allow a 30 msec delay before I-frames must be acknowledged
 llc2 ack-delay-time 30
 !
interface tokenring 1
 ! source ring 100, bridge 5, destination ring 1
 source-bridge 100 5 1
```

NOTES

Both peers need to be configured for LLC2 local acknowledgment. If only one is so configured, undesirable results occur.

IP for Load Sharing over RSRB Example

As Figure 5–11 shows, two routers are connected by two serial lines. Each is configured as a basic remote dual-port bridge, but extended to include both reliability and IP load sharing. When both serial lines are up, traffic is split between them, effectively combining the bandwidth of the connections. If either serial line goes down, all traffic is routed to the remaining line with no disruption. This happens transparently with respect to the end connections, unlike other source-route bridges that would abort those connections.

Figure 5–11
RSRB—simple reliability.

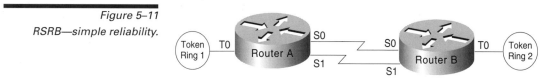

The sample configuration files that enable this configuration follow.

Configuration for Router/Bridge A

```
source-bridge ring-group 5
source-bridge remote-peer 5 tcp 204.31.7.1
source-bridge remote-peer 5 tcp 204.31.8.1
!
interface tokenring 0
 ip address 204.31.7.1 255.255.255.0
```

```
 source-bridge 1 1 5
 source-bridge spanning
 multiring all
 !
interface serial 0
 ip address 204.31.9.1 255.255.255.0
 !
interface serial 1
 ip address 204.31.10.1 255.255.255.0
 !
 router igrp 109
 network 204.31.7.0
 network 204.31.9.0
 network 204.31.10.0
 !
hostname RouterA
```

Configuration for Router/Bridge B

```
 source-bridge ring-group 5
 source-bridge remote-peer 5 tcp 204.31.7.1
 source-bridge remote-peer 5 tcp 204.31.8.1
 !
interface tokenring 0
 ip address 204.31.8.1 255.255.255.0
 source-bridge 2 1 5
 source-bridge spanning
 multiring all
 !
interface serial 0
 ip address 204.31.9.2 255.255.255.0
 !
interface serial 1
 ip address 204.31.10.2 255.255.255.0
 !
 router igrp 109
 network 204.31.8.0
 network 204.31.9.0
 network 204.31.10.0
 !
 hostname RouterB
```

Configuring Priority for Locally Terminated Token Ring Interfaces in RSRB Example

Figure 5–12 shows a network that uses RSRB to bridge Token Ring traffic.

The configuration for the network shown in Figure 5–12 follows.

Figure 5–12
RSRB configuration example.

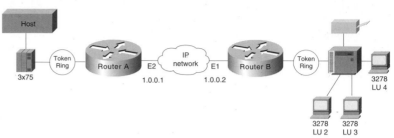

Configuration for Router/Bridge A

```
source-bridge ring-group 2624
source-bridge remote-peer 2624 tcp 1.0.0.1
source-bridge remote-peer 2624 tcp 1.0.0.2 local-ack priority
!
interface tokenring 0
 source-bridge 2576 8 2624
 source-bridge spanning
 multiring all
 locaddr-priority 1
!
interface ethernet 0
 ip address 1.0.0.1 255.255.255.0
 priority-group 1
!
 locaddr-priority-list 1 02 high
 locaddr-priority-list 1 03 high
 locaddr-priority-list 1 04 medium
 locaddr-priority-list 1 05 low
!
 priority-list protocol ip high tcp 1996
 priority-list protocol ip medium tcp 1987
 priority-list protocol ip normal tcp 1988
 priority-list protocol ip low tcp 1989
```

Configuration for Router/Bridge B

```
source-bridge ring-group 2624
source-bridge remote-peer 2624 tcp 1.0.0.2
source-bridge remote-peer 2624 tcp 1.0.0.1 local-ack priority
!
interface tokenring 0
 source-bridge 2626 8 2624
 source-bridge spanning
 multiring all
 locaddr-priority 1
!
interface ethernet 0
 ip address 1.0.0.2 255.255.255.0
 priority-group 1
```

```
!
 locaddr-priority-list 1 02 high
 locaddr-priority-list 1 03 high
 locaddr-priority-list 1 04 medium
 locaddr-priority-list 1 05 low
!
 priority-list protocol ip high tcp 1996
 priority-list protocol ip medium tcp 1987
 priority-list protocol ip normal tcp 1988
 priority-list protocol ip low tcp 1989
```

SNA Traffic Prioritization by LU Address Example

The following example enables SNA traffic prioritization by LU address:

```
locaddr-priority-list 1 01 medium
locaddr-priority-list 1 02 normal
locaddr-priority-list 1 03 low
locaddr-priority-list 1 04 high
!
 priority-list 2 protocol ip low tcp 1996
 priority-list 2 protocol ip high tcp 1987
 priority-list 2 protocol ip medium tcp 1988
 priority-list 2 protocol ip normal tcp 1989
!
interface tokenring 0
 source-bridge 123
 locaddr-priority 1

interface serial 0
 priority-group 2
```

CHAPTER 6

Remote Source-Route Bridging Commands

Use the commands in this chapter to configure remote source-route bridging (RSRB) networks. For RSRB configuration information and examples, see Chapter 5, "Configuring Remote Source-Route Bridging."

LOCADDR-PRIORITY

Use the **locaddr-priority** interface configuration command to assign a remote source-route bridging (RSRB) priority group to an input interface. Use the **no** form of this command to remove the RSRB priority group assignment from the interface.

> **locaddr-priority** *list-number*
> **no locaddr-priority** *list-number*

Syntax	Description
list-number	Priority list number of the input interface

Default

No RSRB priority group is assigned.

Command Mode

Interface configuration

Usage Guidelines

This command first appeared in Cisco IOS Release 10.0.

You must use the **priority-list** command to assign priorities to the ports as shown in Table 6–1.

Table 6–1   *Common RSRB Services and Their Port Numbers*

Service	Port
RSRB high priority	1996
RSRB medium priority	1987
RSRB normal priority	1988
RSRB low priority	1989

Example

In the following example, Token Ring interface 0 is assigned the RSRB priority group 1:

```
source-bridge ring-group 2624
source-bridge remote-peer 2624 tcp 1.0.0.1
source-bridge remote-peer 2624 tcp 1.0.0.2 local-ack priority
!
interface tokenring 0
 source-bridge 2576 8 2624
 locaddr-priority 1
```

Related Commands

locaddr-priority-list
priority-list

LOCADDR-PRIORITY-LIST

Use the **locaddr-priority-list** global configuration command to map logical units (LUs) to queuing priorities as one of the steps to establishing queuing priorities based on LU addresses. Use the **no** form of this command to remove that RSRB priority queuing assignment. You use this command in conjunction with the **priority list** command.

> **locaddr-priority-list** *list-number address-number queue-keyword* [**dsap** *ds*] [**dmac** *dm*]
> [**ssap** *ss*] [**smac** *sm*]
> **no locaddr-priority-list** *list-number address-number queue-keyword* [**dsap** *ds*] [**dmac** *dm*]
> [**ssap** *ss*] [**smac** *sm*]

Syntax	Description
list-number	Arbitrary integer between 1 and 10 that identifies the LU address priority list selected by the user.
address-number	Value of the LOCADDR= parameter on the LU macro, which is a one-byte address of the LU in hexadecimal.
queue-keyword	Priority queue name; one of **high, medium, normal,** or **low**.

Syntax	*Description*
dsap *ds*	(Optional) Indicates that the next argument, *ds*, represents the destination service access point address. The argument *ds* is a hexadecimal value.
dmac *dm*	(Optional) Indicates that the next argument, *dm*, is the destination MAC address. The argument *dm* is a dotted triple of four-digit hexadecimal numbers.
ssap *ss*	(Optional) Indicates that the next argument, *ss*, is the source service access point address. If this is not specified, the default is all source service access point addresses.
smac *sm*	(Optional) Indicates that the next argument, *sm*, is the source MAC address, written as a dotted triple of four-digit hexadecimal numbers. If this is not specified, the default is all source MAC addresses.

Default

The default is no mapping.

Command Mode

Global configuration

Usage Guidelines

This command first appeared in Cisco IOS Release 10.0. The keywords **ssap** and **smac** first appeared in Cisco IOS Release 11.0.

Use this command to map LUs to queuing priorities. Once you establish the priority for each LU, you can assign a priority to a TCP port. Hence you establish a mapping between the LUs and queuing priorities, and queuing priorities and TCP ports.

It is preferable to prioritize NetBIOS traffic below SNA traffic, but by default NetBIOS traffic is assigned the high priority on TCP port 1996.

Example

In the following example, LU 01 is assigned a medium priority and maps to TCP port 1996; LU 02 has been assigned a normal priority and maps to TCP port 1987; LU 03 has been assigned a low priority and maps to TCP port 1988; LU 04 has been assigned high priority and maps to TCP port 1989.

```
locaddr-priority-list 1 01 medium
locaddr-priority-list 1 02 normal
locaddr-priority-list 1 03 low
locaddr-priority-list 1 04 high
```

```
priority-list 1 protocol ip low tcp 1996
priority-list 1 protocol ip high tcp 1987
priority-list 1 protocol ip medium tcp 1988
priority-list 1 protocol ip normal tcp 1989
```

Related Commands
locaddr-priority
priority-list

PRIORITY-GROUP

Use the **priority-group** interface configuration command to assign a specified priority list to an interface.

> **priority-group** *list-number*
> **no priority-group** *list-number*

Syntax	Description
list-number	Priority list number assigned to the interface

Default
No priority list number is established.

Command Mode
Interface configuration

Usage Guidelines
This command first appeared in Cisco IOS Release 10.0.

Example
The following is an example of a priority-group assignment:

```
interface ethernet 0
 ip address 1.0.0.1 255.255.255.0
 priority-group 1
```

Related Commands
locaddr-priority-list
priority-list

PRIORITY-LIST

Use the **priority-list** global configuration command to establish queuing priorities based upon the protocol type as one of the steps to establishing queuing priorities based on logical unit (LU) addresses. Use the **no** form of this command to remove the priority list. Use this command in conjunction with the **locaddr-priority-list** command.

> **priority-list** *list-number* **protocol** *protocol-name queue-keyword*
> **no priority-list** *list-number address-number queue-keyword*

Syntax	Description
list-number	Arbitrary integer between 1 and 10 that identifies the LU address priority list selected by the user.
protocol	Keyword indicating you want the priority list to be based on a protocol type.
protocol-name	Protocol you are using. In most cases, this will be **ip**.
queue-keyword	Priority queue name: **high**, **medium**, **normal**, or **low**.

Default

No queuing priorities are established.

Command Mode

Global configuration

Usage Guidelines

This command first appeared in Cisco IOS Release 10.0.

Use this command to assign the priority level defined to TCP segments originating from or destined to a specified TCP port. Assign priorities to the ports as shown in Table 6–2.

Table 6–2 *Common RSRB Services and Their Port Numbers*

Service	Port
RSRB high priority	1996
RSRB medium priority	1987
RSRB normal priority	1988
RSRB low priority	1989

After you establish the priority for each LU using the **locaddr-priority-list** command, you can assign a priority to a TCP port using the **priority-list** command. By using both commands, you establish a mapping between the LUs and queuing priorities, and between the queuing priorities and TCP ports.

It is preferable to prioritize NetBIOS traffic below SNA traffic, but by default NetBIOS traffic is assigned the high priority on TCP port 1996.

Example

In the following example, LU 01 has been assigned a medium priority and maps to TCP port 1996; LU 02 has been assigned a normal priority and maps to TCP port 1987; LU 03 has been assigned a low priority and maps to TCP port 1988; LU 04 has been assigned high priority and maps to TCP port 1989.

```
locaddr-priority-list 1 01 medium
locaddr-priority-list 1 02 normal
locaddr-priority-list 1 03 low
locaddr-priority-list 1 04 high

priority-list 1 protocol ip low tcp 1996
priority-list 1 protocol ip high tcp 1987
priority-list 1 protocol ip medium tcp 1988
priority-list 1 protocol ip normal tcp 1989
```

Related Commands

locaddr-priority
locaddr-priority-list

RSRB REMOTE-PEER LSAP-OUTPUT-LIST

Use the **rsrb remote-peer lsap-output-list** global configuration command to define service access point (SAP) filters by local SAP (LSAP) address on the remote source-route bridging WAN interface.

> **rsrb remote-peer** *ring-group* **tcp** *ip-address* **lsap-output-list** *access-list-number*
> **rsrb remote-peer** *ring-group* **fst** *ip-address* **lsap-output-list** *access-list-number*
> **rsrb remote-peer** *ring-group* **interface** *name* **lsap-output-list** *access-list-number*

Syntax	Description
ring-group	Virtual ring number of the remote peer
tcp	TCP encapsulation
fst	FST encapsulation
ip-address	IP address
interface	Direct encapsulation
name	Interface name
access-list-number	Number of the access list

Default

No filters are assigned.

Command Mode

Global configuration

Usage Guidelines

This command first appeared in Cisco IOS Release 10.0.

Example

The following example specifies SAP filters by LSAP address:

```
rsrb remote-peer 1000 tcp 131.108.2.30 lsap-output-list 201
```

Related Commands

priority-list
sap-priority
sap-priority-list

RSRB REMOTE-PEER NETBIOS-OUTPUT-LIST

Use the **rsrb remote-peer netbios-output-list** global configuration command to filter packets by NetBIOS station name on a remote source-route bridging WAN interface.

rsrb remote-peer *ring-group* **tcp** *ip-address* **netbios-output-list** *name*
rsrb remote-peer *ring-group* **fst** *ip-address* **netbios-output-list** *name*
rsrb remote-peer *ring-group* **interface** *type* **netbios-output-list** *host*

Syntax	Description
ring-group	Virtual ring number of the remote peer
tcp	TCP encapsulation
fst	FST encapsulation
ip-address	IP address
interface	Direct encapsulation
type	Interface name
name	Name of a NetBIOS access filter previously defined with one or more **netbios access-list host** global configuration commands
host	Host name

Default

No filter is assigned.

Command Mode

Global configuration

Part
II

Command Reference

Usage Guidelines

This command first appeared in Cisco IOS Release 10.0.

Example

The following example filters packets by NetBIOS station name:

```
rsrb remote-peer 1000 tcp 131.108.2.30 netbios-output-list host engineering
```

Related Commands

netbios access-list host
priority-list
sap-priority
sap-priority-list

SAP-PRIORITY

Use the **sap-priority** interface configuration command to define a priority list on an interface.

      sap-priority *list-number*

Syntax	*Description*
list-number	Priority-list number you specified in the **sap-priority-list** command

Default

No priority list is defined.

Command Mode

Interface configuration

Usage Guidelines

This command first appeared in Cisco IOS Release 10.0.

Example

The following example specifies priority list number 1:

```
sap-priority 1
```

Related Commands

sap-priority-list
source-bridge

SAP-PRIORITY-LIST

Use the **sap-priority-list** global configuration command to define a priority list.

    sap-priority-list *list-number queue-keyword* [**dsap** *ds*] [**ssap** *ss*] [**dmac** *dm*] [**smac** *sm*]

Syntax	Description
list-number	Arbitrary integer between 1 and 10 that identifies the priority list.
queue-keyword	Priority queue name or a remote source-route bridge TCP port name.
dsap	(Optional) Indicates that the next argument, *ds*, represents the destination service access point address. The argument *ds* is a hexadecimal number.
ssap	(Optional) Indicates that the next argument, *ss*, represents the source service access point address. The argument *ss* is a hexadecimal number.
dmac	(Optional) Indicates that the next argument, *dm*, represents the destination MAC address. The argument *dm* is written as a dotted triple of four-digit hexadecimal numbers.
smac	(Optional) Indicates that the next argument, *sm*, represents the source MAC address. The argument *sm* is written as a dotted triple of four-digit hexadecimal numbers.

Part II

Command Reference

Default

No priority list is defined.

Command Mode

Global configuration

Usage Guidelines

This command first appeared in Cisco IOS Release 10.0.

To give precedence to traffic on a particular LLC2 session, you must specify all four keywords (**dsap**, **ssap**, **dmac**, and **smac**) to uniquely identify the LLC2 session.

Example

The following example defines priority list 1 and specifies SSAP and DSAP addresses:

```
sap-priority-list 1 high dsap 04 ssap 04
```

SHOW LOCAL-ACK

Use the **show local-ack** privileged EXEC command to display the current state of any current local acknowledgment for both LLC2 and SDLLC connections, as well as for any configured passthrough rings.

      show local-ack

Syntax   Description

This command has no arguments or keywords.

Command Mode

Privileged EXEC

Usage Guidelines

This command first appeared in Cisco IOS Release 10.0.

Sample Display

The following is sample output from the **show local-ack** command:

```
Router# show local-ack

local 1000.5a59.04f9, lsap 04, remote 4000.2222.4444, dsap 04
llc2 = 1798136, local ack state = connected
Passthrough Rings: 4 7
```

Table 6–3 describes significant fields shown in the display.

Table 6–3   *Show Local-Ack Field Descriptions*

Field	Description
local	MAC address of the local Token Ring station with which the route has the LLC2 session.
lsap	Local service access point (LSAP) value of the Token Ring station with which the router has the LLC2 session.
remote	MAC address of the remote Token Ring on whose behalf the router is providing acknowledgments. The remote Token Ring station is separated from the device via the TCP backbone.
dsap	Destination SAP value of the Token Ring station on whose behalf the router is providing acknowledgments.
llc2	Pointer to an internal data structure used by the manufacturer for debugging.

Table 6–3 *Show Local-Ack Field Descriptions, Continued*

Field	Description
local ack state	State of the local acknowledgment for both LLC2 and SDLC connections. The possible states are as follows: • disconnected—No session between the two end nodes. • connected—Full data transfer possible between the two. • awaiting connect—Cisco IOS software is waiting for the other end to confirm a session establishment with the remote host.
Passthrough Rings	Ring numbers of the virtual rings that have been defined as passthroughs using the **source-bridge passthrough** command. If a ring is not a passthrough, it is locally terminated.

SOURCE-BRIDGE COS-ENABLE

Use the **source-bridge cos-enable** global configuration command to force the Cisco IOS software to read the contents of the format identification (FID) frames to prioritize traffic when using TCP. Use the **no** form of this command to disable prioritizing.

> **source-bridge cos-enable**
> **no source-bridge cos-enable**

Syntax   Description

This command has no arguments or keywords.

Default

Enabled

Command Mode

Global configuration

Usage Guidelines

This command first appeared in Cisco IOS Release 10.0.

Use this command to prioritize your SNA traffic across the backbone network. All your important FEP traffic can flow on high-priority queues. This is useful only between FEP-to-FEP (PU4-to-PU4) communications (across the non-SNA backbone.)

NOTES

LLC2 local acknowledgment must be turned on for the class of service (COS) feature to take effect, and the **source-bridge remote-peer tcp** command with the **priority** keyword must be issued.

Example

The following example enables class-of-service for prioritization of SNA traffic across a network:

```
source-bridge cos-enable
```

Related Commands

source-bridge remote-peer tcp

SOURCE-BRIDGE FST-PEERNAME

Use the **source-bridge fst-peername** global configuration command to set up a Fast-Sequenced Transport (FST) peer name. Use the **no** form of this command to disable the IP address assignment.

    source-bridge fst-peername *local-interface-address*
    no source-bridge fst-peername *local-interface-address*

Syntax	Description
local-interface-address	IP address to assign to the local router

Default

Disabled

Command Mode

Global configuration

Usage Guidelines

This command first appeared in Cisco IOS Release 10.0. It is the first step to configuring a remote source-route bridge to use FST.

Example

The following example sets up an FST peer name:

```
source-bridge fst-peername 150.136.64.98
```

Related Commands

source-bridge remote-peer fst

SOURCE-BRIDGE KEEPALIVE

Use the **source-bridge keepalive** interface configuration command to assign the keepalive interval of the remote source-bridging peer. Use the **no** form of this command to cancel previous assignments.

> **source-bridge keepalive** *seconds*
> **no source-bridge keepalive**

Syntax	Description
seconds	Keepalive interval in seconds. The valid range is 10 to 300.

Default

30 seconds

Command Mode

Interface configuration

Usage Guidelines

This command first appeared in Cisco IOS Release 10.0.

Example

The following example sets the keepalive interval to 60 seconds:

```
source-bridge keepalive 60
```

Related Commands

show interface
source-bridge
source-bridge remote-peer fst
source-bridge remote-peer tcp

SOURCE-BRIDGE LARGEST-FRAME

Use the **source-bridge largest-frame** global configuration command to configure the largest frame size that is used to communicate with any peers in the ring group. Use the **no** form of this command to cancel previous assignments.

> **source-bridge largest-frame** *ring-group size*
> **no source-bridge largest-frame** *ring-group*

Syntax	Description
ring-group	Ring-group number. This ring-group number must match the number you have specified with the **source-bridge ring-group** command. The valid range is 1 to 4095.
size	Maximum frame size.

Default

No frame size is assigned.

Command Mode

Global configuration

Usage Guidelines

This command first appeared in Cisco IOS Release 10.0.

The Cisco IOS software negotiates all transit routes down to the specified size or lower. Use the *size* argument with this command to prevent timeouts in end hosts by reducing the amount of data they have to transmit in a fixed interval. For example, in some networks containing slow links, it would be impossible to transmit an 8K frame and receive a response within a few seconds. These are fairly standard defaults for an application on a 16-Mb Token Ring. If the frame size is lowered to 516 bytes, then only 516 bytes must be transmitted and a response received in 2 seconds. This feature is most effective in a network with slow links. The legal values for this argument are 516, 1500, 2052, 4472, 8144, 11407, and 17800 bytes.

Example

The following example sets the largest frame that can be transmitted through a ring group to 1500 bytes:

```
source-bridge largest-frame 8 1500
```

Related Commands

source-bridge ring-group

SOURCE-BRIDGE PASSTHROUGH

Use the **source-bridge passthrough** global configuration command to configure some sessions on a few rings to be locally acknowledged and the remaining to passthrough. Use the **no** form of this command to disable passthrough on all the rings and allow the session to be locally acknowledged.

> **source-bridge passthrough** *ring-group*
> **no source-bridge passthrough** *ring-group*

Syntax	Description
ring-group	Ring-group number. This ring is either the start ring or destination ring of the two IBM end machines for which the passthrough feature is to be configured. This ring-group number must match the number you specified with the **source-bridge ring-group** command. The valid range is 1 to 4095.

Default

Disabled

Command Mode

Global configuration

Usage Guidelines

This command first appeared in Cisco IOS Release 10.0.

Use this command in conjunction with the **source-bridge remote-peer tcp** command that has the **local-ack** keyword specified, which causes every new LLC2 session to be locally terminated. If a machine on the Token Ring attempts to start an LLC2 session to an end host that exists on the *ring number* specified in the **source-bridge passthrough** command, the session will "pass through" and not use local acknowledgment for LLC2.

If you specify passthrough for a ring, LLC2 sessions will never be locally acknowledged on that ring. This is true even if a remote peer accessing the ring has set the **local-ack** keyword in the **source-bridge remote-peer tcp** command. The **source-bridge passthrough** command overrides any setting in the **source-bridge remote-peer tcp** command.

You can define more than one **source-bridge passthrough** command in a configuration.

Example

The following example configures the router to use local acknowledgment on remote peer at 1.1.1.2 but passthrough on rings 9 and 4:

```
source-bridge ring-group 100
source-bridge remote-peer 100 tcp 1.1.1.1
source-bridge remote-peer 100 tcp 1.1.1.2 local-ack
source-bridge passthrough 9
source-bridge passthrough 4
```

Related Commands

source-bridge remote-peer tcp
source-bridge ring-group

SOURCE-BRIDGE REMOTE-PEER FRAME-RELAY (DIRECT ENCAPSULATION)

Use the **source-bridge remote-peer frame-relay** global configuration command when specifying a point-to-point direct encapsulation connection. Use the **no** form of this command to disable previous interface assignments.

> **source-bridge remote-peer** *ring-group* **frame-relay interface** *name* [*mac-address*] [*dlci-number*] [**lf** *size*]
> **no source-bridge remote-peer** *ring-group* **frame-relay interface** *name*

Syntax	Description
ring-group	Ring group number. This ring group number must match the number you specified with the **source-bridge ring-group** command. The valid range is 1 to 4095.
name	Name of the interface over which to send source-route bridged traffic.
mac-address	(Optional) MAC address for the interface on the other side of the virtual ring. This argument is required for nonserial interfaces. You can obtain the value of this MAC address by using the **show interface** command, and then scanning the display for the interface specified by *name*.
dlci-number	(Optional) Data-link connection identifier (DLCI) number for Frame Relay encapsulation.
lf *size*	(Optional) Maximum-sized frame to be sent to this remote peer. The Cisco IOS software negotiates all transit routes down to this size or lower. This argument is useful in preventing timeouts in end hosts by reducing the amount of data they have to transmit in a fixed interval. The legal values for this argument are 516, 1500, 2052, 4472, 8144, 11407 and 17800 bytes.

Default

No point-to-point direct encapsulation connection is specified.

Command Mode

Global configuration

Usage Guidelines

This command first appeared in Cisco IOS Release 11.2.

Use this command to identify the interface over which to send source-route bridged traffic to another router in the ring group. A serial interface does not require that you include a MAC-level address; all other types of interfaces do require MAC addresses.

You must specify one **source-bridge remote-peer** command for each peer router that is part of the virtual ring. You must also specify one **source-bridge remote-peer** command to identify the IP address of the local router.

It is possible to mix all types of transport methods within the same ring group.

NOTES

The two peers using the serial-transport method will function correctly only if there are routers at the end of the serial line that have been configured to use the serial transport. The peers must also belong to the same ring group.

Example

The following example sends source-route bridged traffic over serial interface 0 and Ethernet interface 0:

```
! send source-route bridged traffic over serial 0
source-bridge remote-peer 5 frame-relay interface serial 0
! specify MAC address for source-route bridged traffic on Ethernet 0
source-bridge remote-peer 5 interface Ethernet 0 0000.0c00.1234
```

Related Commands

show interface
source-bridge
source-bridge remote-peer fst
source-bridge remote-peer tcp

SOURCE-BRIDGE REMOTE-PEER FST

Use the **source-bridge remote-peer fst** global configuration command to specify a Fast-Sequenced Transport (FST) encapsulation connection. Use the **no** form of this command to disable the previous assignments.

source-bridge remote-peer *ring-group* **fst** *ip-address* [lf *size*]
no source-bridge remote-peer *ring-group* **fst** *ip-address*

Syntax	Description
ring-group	Ring-group number. This ring-group number must match the number you specified with the **source-bridge ring-group** command. The valid range is 1 to 4095.
ip-address	IP address of the remote peer with which the router will communicate.
lf *size*	(Optional) Maximum-sized frame to be sent to this remote peer. The Cisco IOS software negotiates all transit routes down to this size or lower. Use this argument to prevent timeouts in end hosts by reducing the amount of data they have to transmit in a fixed interval. The legal values for this argument are 516, 1500, 2052, 4472, 8144, 11407, and 17800 bytes.

Default

No FST encapsulation connection is specified.

Command Mode

Global configuration

Usage Guidelines

This command first appeared in Cisco IOS Release 10.0.

The two peers using the serial-transport method will function correctly only if there are routers at the end of the serial line that have been configured to use the serial transport. The peers must also belong to the same ring group.

You must specify one **source-bridge remote-peer** command for each peer router that is part of the virtual ring. You must also specify one **source-bridge remote-peer** command to identify the IP address of the local router.

Example

In the following example, the **source-bridge-fst-peername** command specifies an IP address of 150.136.64.98 for the local router. The **source-bridge ring-group** command assigns the device to a ring group. The **source-bridge remote-peer fst** command specifies ring-group number 100 for the remote peer at IP address 150.136.64.97.

```
source-bridge fst-peername 150.136.64.98
source-bridge ring-group 100
source-bridge remote-peer 100 fst 150.136.64.97
```

Related Commands

source-bridge
source-bridge fst-peername

source-bridge remote-peer frame-relay (direct encapsulation)
source-bridge remote-peer tcp

SOURCE-BRIDGE REMOTE-PEER FTCP

Use the **source-bridge remote-peer ftcp** global configuration command to enable fast switching of Token Ring frames over TCP/IP. Use the **no** form of this command to remove a remote peer from the specified ring group.

> source-bridge remote-peer *ring-group* ftcp *ip-address* [lf *size*] [tcp-receive-window *wsize*]
>   [local-ack]
> no source-bridge remote-peer *ring-group* ftcp *ip-address*

Part
II

Command Reference

Syntax	Description
ring-group	Ring-group number. This ring-group number must match the number you have specified with the **source-bridge ring-group** command. The valid range is 1 to 4095.
ip-address	IP address of the remote peer with which the router will communicate.
lf *size*	(Optional) Maximum-sized frame to be sent to this remote peer. The Cisco IOS software negotiates all transit routes down to this size or lower.
tcp-receive-window *wsize*	(Optional) The TCP receive window size in bytes. The range is 10240 to 65535 bytes. The default window size is 10240 bytes.
local-ack	(Optional) LLC2 sessions destined for a specific remote peer are locally terminated and acknowledged. Use local acknowledgment for LLC2 sessions going to this remote peer.

Default

No IP address is identified. The default window size is 10240 bytes.

Command Mode

Global configuration

Usage Guidelines

This command first appeared in Cisco IOS Release 10.3.

Use this argument to prevent timeouts in end hosts by reducing the amount of data they have to transmit in a fixed interval. The default value for this argument is 516 bytes.

If you change the default TCP receive window size on one peer, you must also change the receive window size on the other peer. Both sides of the connection should have the same window size.

If you configure one peer for LLC2 local acknowledgment, you need to configure both peers for LLC2 local acknowledgment. If only one peer is so configured, unpredictable (and undesirable) results will occur.

Two peers using the serial-transport method will function correctly only if there are routers at the end of the serial line that have been configured to use the serial transport. The peers must also belong to the same ring group.

Examples

In the following example, the remote peer with IP address 131.108.2.291 belongs to ring group 5. It also uses LLC2 local acknowledgment and enables prioritization over a TCP network:

```
source-bridge ring-group 5
source-bridge remote-peer 5 ftcp 131.108.2.291 local-ack priority
```

The following example shows how to locally administer and acknowledge LLC2 sessions destined for a specific remote peer:

```
! identify the ring group as 100
source-bridge ring-group 100
! remote peer at IP address 1.1.1.1 does not use local acknowledgment
source-bridge remote-peer 100 ftcp 1.1.1.1
! remote peer at IP address 1.1.1.2 uses local acknowledgment
source-bridge remote-peer 100 ftcp 1.1.1.2 local-ack
!
interface tokenring 0
source-bridge 1 1 100
```

Sessions between a device on Token Ring 0 that must go through remote peer 1.1.1.2 use local acknowledgment for LLC2, but sessions that go through remote peer 1.1.1.1 do *not* use local acknowledgment (that is, they "pass through").

Related Commands

source-bridge
source-bridge remote-peer fst
source-bridge remote-peer frame-relay (direct encapsulation)

SOURCE-BRIDGE REMOTE-PEER TCP

Use the **source-bridge remote-peer tcp** global configuration command to identify the IP address of a peer in the ring group with which to exchange source-bridge traffic using TCP. Use the **no** form of this command to remove a remote peer for the specified ring group.

> **source-bridge remote-peer** *ring-group* **tcp** *ip-address* [**lf** *size*] [**tcp-receive-window** *wsize*] [**local-ack**] [**priority**]
> **no source-bridge remote-peer** *ring-group* **tcp** *ip-address*

Syntax	Description
ring-group	Ring-group number. This ring-group number must match the number you specified with the **source-bridge ring-group** command. The valid range is 1 to 4095.
ip-address	IP address of the remote peer with which the router will communicate.
If *size*	(Optional) Maximum-sized frame to be sent to this remote peer. The Cisco IOS software negotiates all transit routes down to this size or lower. Use this argument to prevent timeouts in end hosts by reducing the amount of data they have to transmit in a fixed interval. The valid values for this argument are 516, 1500, 2052, 4472, 8144, 11407, and 17800 bytes.
tcp-receive-window *wsize*	(Optional) The TCP receive window size in bytes. The range is 10240 to 65535 bytes. The default window size is 10240 bytes.
local-ack	(Optional) LLC2 sessions destined for a specific remote peer are locally terminated and acknowledged. Use local acknowledgment for LLC2 sessions going to this remote peer.
priority	(Optional) Enables prioritization over a TCP network. You must specify the keyword **local-ack** earlier in the same **source-bridge remote-peer** command. The keyword **priority** is a prerequisite for features such as System Network Architecture (SNA) class of service and SNA LU address prioritization over a TCP network.

Default

No IP address is identified. The default window size is 10240 bytes.

Command Mode

Global configuration

Usage Guidelines

This command first appeared in Cisco IOS Release 10.0. The **tcp-receive-window** keyword and *wsize* argument first appeared in Cisco IOS Release 11.1.

If you change the default TCP receive window size on one peer, you must also change the receive window size on the other peer. Both sides of the connection should have the same window size.

If you configure one peer for LLC2 local acknowledgment, you need to configure both peers for LLC2 local acknowledgment. If only one peer is so configured, unpredictable results occur.

You must specify one **source-bridge remote-peer** command for each peer router that is part of the virtual ring. You must also specify one **source-bridge remote-peer** command to identify the IP address of the local router.

The two peers using the serial-transport method will function correctly only if there are routers at the end of the serial line that have been configured to use the serial transport. The peers must also belong to the same ring group.

Examples

In the following example, the remote peer with IP address 131.108.2.291 belongs to ring group 5. It also uses LLC2 local acknowledgment, priority, and RSRB protocol version 2:

```
! identify the ring group as 5
source-bridge ring-group 5
! remote peer at IP address 131.108.2.291 belongs to ring group 5, uses
! tcp as the transport, is set up for local acknowledgment, and uses priority
source-bridge remote-peer 5 tcp 131.108.2.291 local-ack priority
```

The following example shows how to locally administer and acknowledge LLC2 sessions destined for a specific remote peer:

```
! identify the ring group as 100
source-bridge ring-group 100
! remote peer at IP address 1.1.1.1 does not use local acknowledgment
source-bridge remote-peer 100 tcp 1.1.1.1
! remote peer at IP address 1.1.1.2 uses local acknowledgment
source-bridge remote-peer 100 tcp 1.1.1.2 local-ack
!
interface tokenring 0
 source-bridge 1 1 100
```

Sessions between a device on Token Ring 0 that must go through remote peer 1.1.1.2 use local acknowledgment for LLC2, but sessions that go through remote peer 1.1.1.1 do *not* use local acknowledgment (that is, they "pass through").

Related Commands

source-bridge
source-bridge remote-peer fst
source-bridge remote-peer frame-relay (direct encapsulation)

SOURCE-BRIDGE TCP-QUEUE-MAX

Use the **source-bridge tcp-queue-max** global configuration command to modify the size of the backup queue for remote source-route bridging. This backup queue determines the number of packets that can wait for transmission to a remote ring before packets start being thrown away. Use the **no** form of this command to return to the default value.

> source-bridge tcp-queue-max *number*
> no source-bridge tcp-queue-max

Syntax	Description
number	Number of packets to hold in any single outgoing TCP queue to a remote router. The default is 100 packets.

Default

The default number of packets is 100.

Command Mode

Global configuration

Usage Guidelines

This command first appeared in Cisco IOS Release 10.3.

Example

If, for example, your network experiences temporary bursts of traffic using the default packet queue length, the following command raises the limit from 100 to 150 packets:

```
source-bridge tcp-queue-max 150
```

CHAPTER 7

Configuring Data-Link Switching Plus

This chapter describes how to configure data-link switching plus (DLSw+), Cisco's implementation of the DLSw standard for Systems Network Architecture (SNA) and NetBIOS devices. For a complete description of the commands in this chapter, see Chapter 8, "DLSw+ Configuration Commands."

DLSw+ CONFIGURATION TASK LIST

DLSw+ supports local or remote media conversion between LANs and SDLC or QLLC. For clarity, the configuration task list below describes configuration in a Token Ring environment. The only differences for SDLC and Ethernet are the specific commands needed to configure those media, plus a media-specific command to associate the interface with DLSw+.

─── NOTES ───

By default, the Cisco IOS software translates Token Ring LLC2 to Ethernet 802.3 LLC2. To configure the router to translate Token Ring LLC2 frames into Ethernet 0x80d5 format frames, refer to the section "Enabling Token Ring LLC2-to-Ethernet Conversion" in Chapter 3, "Configuring Source-Route Bridging."

───

To configure DLSw+, complete the tasks in the following sections:

- Defining a Source-Bridge Ring Group for DLSw+
- Defining a DLSw+ Local Peer for the Router
- Defining a DLSw+ Ring List or Port List
- Defining a DLSw+ Bridge Group List
- Defining DLSw+ Remote Peers

- Enabling DLSw+ over Frame Relay
- Enabling DLSw+ on a Token Ring or FDDI Interface
- Enabling DLSw+ on an Ethernet Interface
- Enabling DLSw+ on an SDLC Interface
- Enabling DLSw+ over QLLC
- Enabling NetBIOS Dial-on-Demand Routing
- Tuning the DLSw+ Configuration

See the end of this chapter for "DLSw+ Configuration Examples." Media-specific configuration examples for Ethernet and SDLC are also provided. For details of SDLC commands in the sample SDLC configuration, see Chapter 12, "LLC2 and SDLC Commands."

DEFINING A SOURCE-BRIDGE RING GROUP FOR DLSW+

The source-bridge ring can be shared between DLSw+ and SRB/RSRB. In DLSw+, the source-bridge ring group specifies the virtual ring that will appear to be the last ring in the RIF. Because RIFs are terminated at the router, there is no correlation between the ring-group number specified in DLSw+ peers. The numbers can be the same for management simplicity, but they do not have to be. To define a source-bridge ring group for DLSw+, perform the following task in global configuration mode:

Task	Command
Define a ring group.	**source-bridge ring-group** *ring-group* [*virtual-mac-address*]

See "DLSw+ Using TCP Encapsulation and LLC2 Local Acknowledgment—Basic Configuration Example" later in this chapter for a sample configuration file.

DEFINING A DLSW+ LOCAL PEER FOR THE ROUTER

Defining a DLSw+ local peer for a router enables DLSw+. You specify all local DLSw+ parameters as part of the local peer definition. To define a local peer, perform the following task in global configuration mode:

Task	Command
Define the DLSw+ local peer.	**dlsw local-peer** [**peer-id** *ip-address*] [**group** *group*] [**border**] [**cost** *cost*] [**lf** *size*] [**keepalive** *seconds*] [**passive**] [**promiscuous**] [**init-pacing-window** *size*] [**max-pacing-window** *size*][**biu-segment**]

See "DLSw+ Using TCP Encapsulation and LLC2 Local Acknowledgment—Basic Configuration Example" for a sample configuration.

DEFINING A DLSW+ RING LIST OR PORT LIST

DLSw+ ring lists map traffic on a local interface to remote peers. You can create a ring list of local ring numbers and apply the list to remote peer definitions. Traffic received from a remote peer is forwarded to only the rings specified in the ring list. Traffic received from a local interface is forwarded to peers only if the input ring number appears in the ring list applied to the remote peer definition. The definition of a ring list is optional. If you want all peers and all rings to receive all traffic, you do not have to define a ring list. Specify 0 for the list number in the remote peer statement.

To define a ring list, perform the following task in global configuration mode:

Task	Command
Define a ring list.	**dlsw ring-list** *list-number* **rings** *ring-number*

DLSw+ port lists map traffic on a local interface (either Token Ring or serial) to remote peers. You can create a port list of local ports and apply the list to remote peer definitions. Traffic received from a remote peer is forwarded to peers only if the input port number appears in the port list applied to the remote peer definition. The **port list** command provides a single command to specify both serial and Token Ring interfaces. Figure 7–1 shows how port lists are used to map traffic.

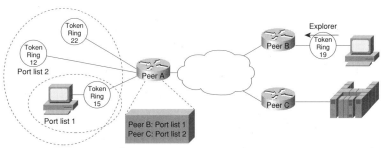

Figure 7–1
Mapping traffic using port lists.

The definition of a port list is optional. If you want all peers and all interfaces to receive all traffic, you do not have to define a port list. Simply specify 0 for the list number in the remote peer statement.

To define a port list, perform the following task in global configuration mode:

Task	Command
Define a port list.	**dlsw port-list** *list-number type number*

Either the **ring list** or the **port list** command can be used to associate rings with a given ring list. The **ring list** command is easier to type in if you have a large number of rings to define.

DEFINING A DLSW+ BRIDGE GROUP LIST

DLSw+ bridge group lists map traffic on the local Ethernet bridge group interface to remote peers. You can create a bridge group list and apply the list to remote peer definitions. Traffic received from a remote peer is forwarded to only the bridge group specified in the bridge group list. Traffic received from a local interface is forwarded to peers only if the input bridge-group number appears in the bridge group list applied to the remote peer definition. The definition of a bridge group list is optional. Because each remote peer has a single list number associated with it, if you want traffic to go to a bridge group and to either a ring list or port list, you should specify the same list number in each definition.

Task	Command
Define a ring list.	**dlsw bgroup-list** *list-number* **bgroups** *number*

DEFINING DLSW+ REMOTE PEERS

You can define three types of encapsulation on a remote peer by performing the following tasks:

- Configuring Direct Encapsulation
- Configuring FST Encapsulation
- Configuring TCP Encapsulation

The configuration commands for each of the encapsulation methods share some optional parameters that permit support for specific features, such as backup peers. There are some command options for TCP encapsulation support features that are not available with other encapsulation types: SNA dial-on-demand routing (DDR) and configured dynamic peers. The configuration combinations for each of the encapsulation methods and features are described in greater detail following the task tables.

Configuring Direct Encapsulation

Direct encapsulation is supported over HDLC and Frame Relay. Direct encapsulation over Frame Relay comes in two forms: DLSw Lite (LLC2 encapsulation) and Passthru. To configure direct encapsulation, perform the following tasks in global configuration mode:

To distinguish between DLSw Lite and Passthru, use the **pass-thru** option in the **dlsw remote-peer** command.

Task	Command
Step 1 Define a direct encapsulation in Frame Relay for the remote peer.	**dlsw remote-peer** *list-number* **frame-relay interface serial** *number dlci-number* [**backup-peer** [*ip-address* | **frame-relay interface serial** *number dlci-number* | **interface** *name*]] [**bytes-netbios-out** *bytes-list-name*] [**cost** *cost*] [**dest-mac** *mac-address*] [**dmac-output-list** *access-list-number*] [**host-netbios-out** *host-list-name*] [**keepalive** *seconds*] [**lf** *size*] [**linger** *minutes*] [**lsap-output-list** *list*] [**pass-thru**]
Step 2 Define a direct encapsulation in HDLC for the remote peer.	**dlsw remote-peer** *list-number* **interface serial** *number* [**backup-peer** [*ip-address* | **frame-relay interface serial** *number dlci-number* | **interface** *name*]] [**bytes-netbios-out** *bytes-list-name*] [**cost** *cost*] [**dest-mac** *mac-address*] [**dmac-output-list** *access-list-number*] [**host-netbios-out** *host-list-name*] [**keepalive** *seconds*] [**lf** *size*] [**linger** *minutes*] [**lsap-output-list** *list*] [**pass-thru**]

Configuring FST Encapsulation

To configure FST encapsulation on a remote peer, perform the following task in global configuration mode:

Task	Command
Define an FST encapsulation remote peer.	**dlsw remote-peer** *list-number* **fst** *ip-address* [**backup-peer** [*ip-address* | **frame-relay interface serial** *number dlci-number* | **interface** *name*]] [**bytes-netbios-out** *bytes-list-name*] [**cost** *cost*] [**dest-mac** *mac-address*] [**dmac-output-list** *access-list-number*] [**host-netbios-out** *host-list-name*] [**keepalive** *seconds*] [**lf** *size*] [**linger** *minutes*] [**lsap-output-list** *list*]

Configuring TCP Encapsulation

To configure TCP encapsulation on a remote peer, perform the following task in global configuration mode:

Task	Command
Define a TCP encapsulation remote peer.	**dlsw remote-peer** *list-number* **tcp** *ip-addres*s [**backup-peer** [*ip-address* | **frame-relay interface serial** *number dlci-number* | **interface** *name*]] [**bytes-netbios-out** *bytes-list-name*] [**cost** *cost*] [**dest-mac** *mac-address*] [**dmac-output-list** *access-list-number*] [**dynamic**] [**host-netbios-out** *host-list-name*] [**keepalive** *seconds*] [**lf** *size*] [**linger** *minutes*] [**lsap-output-list** *list*] [**no-llc** *minutes*] [**priority**] [**tcp-queue-max** *size*] [**timeout** *seconds*]

Table 7–1 is a list of valid port numbers used for TCP connections when the **priority** keyword is used with the **dlsw remote-peer** command:

Table 7–1   *Valid port Numbers for TCP Connections*

Priority	Port
High	2065
Medium	1981
Normal	1982
Low	1983

Backup Peers

The **backup-peer** option is common to all encapsulation types (direct, FST, and TCP) on a remote peer and specifies that this remote peer is a backup peer for the router with the specified IP-address, Frame Relay DLCI number, or interface name. When the primary peer fails, all circuits over this peer are disconnected and the user can start a new session via their backup peer. Prior to Cisco IOS Release 11.2(6)F, you could configure backup peers only for primary FST and TCP.

Also, when you specify the **backup-peer** option in a **dlsw remote-peer tcp** command, the backup peer is activated only when the primary peer becomes unreachable. Once the primary peer is reactivated, all new sessions use the primary peer and the backup peer remains active only as long as there are LLC2 connections using it. You can use the **linger** option to specify a period (in minutes) that the backup peer remains connected after the connection to the primary peer is reestablished. When the linger period expires, the backup peer connection is taken down.

NOTES

Because the expiration of the linger period may cause active SNA sessions to be terminated, you should not use the **linger** option unless you want active SNA sessions over the backup peer to be terminated.

SNA Dial-on-Demand Routing

In TCP encapsulation, you can use the **keepalive** and **timeout** options to run DLSw+ over a switched line and have the Cisco IOS software take the switched line down dynamically when it is not in use. Utilizing these options gives the IP Routing table more time to converge when a network problem hinders a remote peer connection. In small networks with good IP convergence time and ISDN lines that start quickly, it is not as neccesary to use the **keepalive** option. To use this feature, you must set the **keepalive** value to zero, and you might need to use a lower value for the **timeout** option than the default, which is 90 seconds.

Configured Dynamic Peers

In TCP encapsulation, the **dynamic** option and its suboptions **no-llc** and **inactivity** allow you to specify and control the activation of dynamic peers, which are configured peers that are activated only when required. Dynamic peer connections are established only when there is DLSw+ data to send. The dynamic peer connections are taken down when the last LLC2 connection using them terminates and the time period specified in the **no-llc** option expires. You also can use the **inactivity** option to take down dynamic peers when the circuits using them are inactive for a specified number of minutes.

NOTES

Because the **inactivity** option might cause active SNA sessions to be terminated, you should not use this option unless you want active SNA sessions to be terminated.

The **dest-mac** and **dmac-output-list** options allow you to specify filter lists as part of the **dlsw remote-peer** command to control access to remote peers. For static peers in direct, FST, or TCP encapsulation, these filters control which explorers are sent to remote peers. For dynamic peers in TCP encapsulation, these filters also control the activation of the dynamic peer. For example, you can specify at a branch office that a remote peer is only activated when there is an explorer frame destined for the MAC address of an FEP.

The **dest-mac** option permits the connection to be established only when there is an explorer frame destined for the specified MAC address. The **dmac-output-list** option permits the connection to be established only when the explorer frame passes the specified access list. To permit access to a single MAC address, use the **dest-mac** option, because it is a configuration shortcut compared to the **dmac-output-list** option.

See "DLSw+ Using TCP Encapsulation and LLC2 Local Acknowledgment—Basic Configuration Example" later in this chapter for a sample configuration.

ENABLING DLSw+ OVER FRAME RELAY

You can configure the Cisco IOS software for direct encapsulation of DLSw+ in Frame Relay according to RFC 1490. DLSw+ direct encapsulation over RFC 1490 supports either pass-through or local acknowledgment (data link control termination). DLSw+ supports transport for both SNA and NetBIOS data. SNA PU 2.0 and PU 2.1 are supported.

The configuration requires a minimum number of PVCs (since multiple protocols can share a single PVC). A minimum number of PVCs simplifies configuration because multiple PUs can share a PVC without requiring configuration of multiple SAPs.

The **pass-thru** option adds the smallest amount of link overhead and requires minimal processing cycles in the attaching routers when compared to TCP/IP encapsulation.

The local acknowledgment option prevents data link control timeouts during periods of WAN congestion. It also minimizes WAN traffic by keeping data link control acknowledgments and keep-alives off the WAN.

No controller or FEP upgrades are required to take advantage of this feature (if already Token Ring attached), reducing costs and simplifying migration to Frame Relay.

To enable DLSw+ over Frame Relay with passthrough, perform the following tasks, beginning in global configuration mode:

Task	Command
Step 1 Specify the serial port.	**interface serial** *number*
Step 2 Enable Frame Relay encapsulation.	**encapsulation frame-relay**
Step 3 Define the mapping between DLSw+ and the DLCI.	**frame-relay map dlsw** *dlci-number*
Step 4 Define direct encapsulation in Frame Relay.	**dlsw remote-peer** *list-number* **frame-relay interface serial** *number dlci-number* **pass-thru**

NOTES

The DLSw+ remote peer statement should specify **pass-thru**.

To enable DLSw+ over Frame Relay with local acknowledgment (also known as DLSw Lite), perform the following tasks, beginning in global configuration mode:

Task		Command
Step 1	Specify the serial port.	**interface serial** *number*
Step 2	Enable Frame Relay encapsulation.	**encapsulation frame-relay**
Step 3	Define the mapping between DLSw+ and the DLCI.	**frame-relay map llc2** *dlci-number*
Step 4	Define direct encapsulation in Frame Relay.	**fdlsw remote-peer** *list-number* **frame-relay interface serial** *number dlci-number*

ENABLING DLSW+ ON A TOKEN RING OR FDDI INTERFACE

To enable DLSw+ on a Token Ring or FDDI interface, perform the following task in interface configuration mode:

Task	Command
Enable DLSw+ on a Token Ring or FDDI interface.	**source-bridge** *local-ring bridge-number ring-group*

ENABLING DLSW+ ON AN ETHERNET INTERFACE

To enable DLSw+ on certain Ethernet interfaces, perform the following task in global configuration mode:

Task	Command
Enable DLSw+ on an Ethernet interface.	**dlsw bridge-group** *group-number*

In interface mode, the interfaces must also be put into the bridge group.

ENABLING DLSw+ ON AN SDLC INTERFACE

To establish devices as SDLC stations, complete the following tasks in interface configuration mode:

Task	Command
Step 1 Set the encapsulation type of the serial interface to SDLC.	**encapsulation sdlc**
Step 2 Establish the role of the interface.	**sdlc role** {**none** | **primary** | **secondary** | **prim-xid-poll**}
Step 3 Configure a MAC address for the serial interface.	**sdlc vmac** *mac-address**
Step 4 Assign a set of secondary stations attached to the serial link.	**sdlc address** *hexbyte* [**echo**]
Step 5 Specify the destination address with which an LLC session is established for the SDLC station.	**sdlc partner** *mac-address sdlc-address*

* The last byte of the MAC address must be 00.

To enable DLSw+ on an SDLC interface, perform the following task in interface configuration mode:

Task	Command
Enable DLSw+ on an SDLC interface.	**sdlc dlsw** {*sdlc-address* | **default** | **partner** *mac address* [**inbound** | **outbound**]}

Use the **default** option if you have more than 10 SDLC devices to attach to the DLSw+ network. To configure an SDLC multidrop line downstream, you configure the SDLC role as either **primary** or **prim-xid-poll**. SDLC role **primary** specifies that any PU without the **xid-poll** parameter in the **sdlc address** command is a PU 2.0 device. SDLC role **prim-xid-poll** specifies that every PU is type 2.1. Cisco recommends that you specify **sdlc role primary** if all SDLC devices are type PU 2.0 or a mix of PU 2.0 and PU 2.1. Specify **sdlc role prim-xid-poll** if all devices are type PU 2.1

To configure DLSw+ to support LLC2-to-SDLC conversion for PU 4 or PU 5 devices, specify the **echo** option in the **sdlc address** command. A PU 4-to-PU 4 configuration requires that none be specified in the **sdlc role** command.

See "DLSw+ with SDLC Multidrop Support Configuration Example" and "DLSw+ with LLC2-to-SDLC Conversion Between PU 4-to-PU 4 Communication" later in this chapter for sample configurations.

ENABLING DLSW+ OVER QLLC

You can configure DLSw+ for QLLC connectivity, which enables both of the following two scenarios:

- Remote LAN-attached devices (physical units) or SDLC-attached devices can access a front-end processor (FEP) or an AS/400 over an X.25 network.

  Cisco's QLLC support allows remote X.25-attached SNA devices to access a FEP without requiring NPSI in the FEP. This might eliminate the requirement for NPSI (if GATE and DATE are not required), thereby eliminating the recurring license cost. In addition, because the QLLC-attached devices appear to be Token Ring-attached to the NCP, they require no preconfiguration in the FEP. Remote X.25-attached SNA devices also can connect to an AS/400 over Token Ring using this support.

- Remote X.25-attached SNA devices can access a FEP or an AS/400 over a Token Ring or over SDLC.

  For environments just beginning to migrate to LANs, Cisco's QLLC support allows deployment of LANs in remote sites while maintaining access to the FEP over existing NPSI links. Remote LAN-attached devices (physical units) or SDLC- attached devices can access a FEP over an X.25 network without requiring X.25 hardware or software in the LAN-attached devices. The Cisco IOS software supports direct attachment to the FEP over X.25 without the need for routers at the data center for SNA traffic.

To enable QLLC connectivity for DLSw+, perform the following tasks in interface configuration mode:

Task	Command
Step 1 Specify an interface as an X.25 device.	**encapsulation x.25**
Step 2 Activate X.25 subaddresses.	**x25 address** *subaddress*
Step 3 Associate a virtual MAC address with the X.121 address of the remote X.25 device.	**x25 map qllc** *x121-addr* [*x25-map-options*]
Step 4 Enable DLSw+ over QLLC.	**qllc dlsw** {**subaddress** *subaddress* | **pvc** *pvc-low* [*pvc-high*]} [**vmac** *vmacaddr* [*poolsize*]] [**partner** *partner-macaddr*] [**sap** *ssap dsap*] [**xid** *xidstring*] [**npsi-poll**]

ENABLING NETBIOS DIAL-ON-DEMAND ROUTING

DLSw+ can filter NetBIOS Session Alive packets from the WAN. NetBIOS periodically sends Session Alive packets as LLC2 I-frames. These packets do not require a response and are superfluous to the function of proper data flow. Furthermore, these packets keep dial-on-demand interfaces up and this up time causes unwanted per-packet charges in DDR networks. By filtering these NetBIOS Session Alive packets, you reduce traffic on the WAN as well as some costs that are associated with DDR.

To enable NetBIOS Dial-on-Demand Routing, perform the following task in global configuration mode:

Task	Command
Enable NetBIOS DDR.	dlsw netbios keepalive-filter

TUNING THE DLSW+ CONFIGURATION

To modify an existing configuration parameter, perform one or more of the tasks in the following sections:

- Configuring DLSw+ Timers
- Configuring Maximum Entries in Group Cache
- Configuring Peer-on-Demand Defaults
- Configuring Promiscuous Peer Defaults
- Configuring Static Resources Capabilities Exchange
- Configuring Static Paths
- Configuring Duplicate Path Handling
- Disabling Border Peer Caching
- Disabling UDP Unicast

Configuring DLSw+ Timers

To configure DLSw+ timers (including group cache entries), perform the following task in global configuration mode:

Task	Command
Configure DLSw+ timers.	dlsw timer {icannotreach-block-time | netbios-cache-timeout | netbios-explorer-timeout |netbios-group-cache | netbios-retry-interval | netbios-verify-interval | sna-cache-timeout | sna-explorer-timeout | sna-group-cache | sna-retry-interval | sna-verify-interval} *time*

Configuring Maximum Entries in Group Cache

To define the maximum entries in a group cache, perform the following task in global configuration mode:

Task	Command
Define the maximum entries in a group cache.	dlsw group-cache max-entries *number*

Configuring Peer-on-Demand Defaults

To configure peer-on-demand defaults, perform the following task in global configuration mode:

Task	Command
Configure peer-on-demand defaults.	dlsw peer-on-demand-defaults [fst] [bytes-netbios-out *bytes-list-name*] [cost *cost*] [dest-mac *destination mac address*] [dmac-output-list *access list number*] [host-netbios-out *host-list-name*] [inactivity *minutes*] [keepalive *seconds*] [lf *size*] [lsap-output-list *list*] [port-list *port-list-number*] [priority] [tcp-queue-max]

Configuring Promiscuous Peer Defaults

To configure promiscuous peer defaults, perform the following task in global configuration mode:

Task	Command
Configure promiscuous peer defaults.	dlsw prom-peer-defaults [bytes-netbios-out *bytes-list-name*] [cost *cost*] [dest-mac *destination mac address*] [dmac-output-list *access list number*] [host-netbios-out *host-list-name*] [keepalive *seconds*] [lf *size*] [lsap-output-list *list*] [tcp-queue-max *size*]

Configuring Static Resources Capabilities Exchange

To reduce explorer traffic destined for this peer, the peer can send other peers a list of resources for which it has information (**icanreach**) or does not have information (**icannotreach**). This information is exchanged as part of a capabilities exchange. To configure static resources that will be exchanged as part of a capabilities exchange, perform one of the following tasks in global configuration mode:

Task	Command
Configure a resource not locally reachable by the router.	**dlsw icannotreach saps** *sap* [*sap...*]
Configure a resource locally reachable by the router.	**dlsw icanreach {mac-exclusive	netbios-exclusive	mac-address** *mac-addr* [**mask** *mask*] **| netbios-name** *name* **| saps}**

Configuring Static Paths

To configure static paths to minimize explorer traffic originating in this peer, perform one of the following tasks in global configuration mode:

Task	Command
Configure the location or path of a static MAC address.	**dlsw mac-addr** *mac-addr* **{ring** *ring number* **| remote-peer {interface serial** *number* **| ip-address** *ip-address***}	rif** *rif string* **| group** *group***}**
Configure a static NetBIOS name.	**dlsw netbios-name** *netbios-name* **{ring** *ring number*\ **remote-peer {interface serial** *number* **| ip-address** *ip-address***}	rif** *rif string* **| group** *group***}**

Configuring Duplicate Path Handling

To configure duplicate path handling, perform the following task in global configuration mode:

Task	Command
Configure duplicate path handling.	**dlsw duplicate-path-bias [load-balance]**

Disabling Border Peer Caching

To disable the border peer caching feature, perform the following task in global configuration mode:

Task	Command
Disable the border peer caching feature.	dlsw group-cache disable

Disabling UDP Unicast

To disable UDP Unicast, perform the following task in global configuration mode:

Task	Command
Disable UDP Unicast.	dlsw udp-disable

MONITORING AND MAINTAINING THE DLSW+ NETWORK

To monitor and maintain activity on the DLSw+ network, perform one or more of the following tasks in privileged EXEC mode:

Task	Command
Close all the DLSw+ circuits.	clear dlsw circuit
Remove all entries from the DLSw+ reachability cache.	clear dlsw reachability
Reset to zero the number of frames that have been processed in the local, remote, and group caches.	clear dlsw statistics
Display capabilities of a direct-encapsulated remote peer.	show dlsw capabilities interface *type number*
Display capabilities of a TCP/FST remote peer.	show dlsw capabilities ip-address *ip-address*
Display capabilities of the local peer.	show dlsw capabilities local
Display DLSw+ circuit information.	show dlsw circuits
Display the fast cache for FST and direct-encapsulated peers.	show dlsw fastcache

Task	Command
Display DLSw+ peer information.	**show dlsw peers**
Display DLSw+ reachability information.	**show dlsw reachability**
Disable and re-enable DLSw+ without altering the configuration.	**dlsw disable**
Display the number of frames that have been processed in the local, remote, and group caches.	**show dlsw statistics [border-peers]**

DLSw+ Configuration Examples

The following sections provide DLSw+ configuration examples:

- DLSw+ Using TCP Encapsulation and LLC2 Local Acknowledgment—Basic Configuration Example.
- DLSw+ Using TCP Encapsulation with Local Acknowledgment—Peer Groups Configuration Example 1
- DLSw+ Using TCP Encapsulation with Local Acknowledgment—Peer Group Configuration Example 2
- DLSw+ with SDLC Multidrop Support Configuration Example
- DLSw+ with LLC2-to-SDLC Conversion Between PU 4-to-PU 4 Communication
- DLSw+ Translation Between Ethernet and Token Ring Configuration Example
- DLSw+ Translation Between FDDI and Token Ring Configuration Example
- DLSw+ Translation Between SDLC and Token Ring Media Example
- DLSw+ over Frame Relay Configuration Example
- DLSw+ over QLLC Configuration Examples

DLSw+ Using TCP Encapsulation and LLC2 Local Acknowledgment—Basic Configuration Example

This sample configuration requires the following tasks, which are described in earlier sections of this document:

- Defining a Source-Bridge Ring Group for DLSw+
- Defining a DLSw+ Local Peer for the Router

- Defining DLSw+ Remote Peers
- Enabling DLSw+ on the Appropriate LAN Interface

Encapsulate the source-route bridged traffic inside IP datagrams passed over a TCP connection between two routers with local acknowledgment enabled when you have LANs separated by wide geographic distances, and you want to avoid multiple retransmissions or loss of user sessions that can occur with time delays.

Logical Link Control, type 2 (LLC2) is an ISO standard data-link level protocol used in Token Ring networks. LLC2 was designed to provide reliable transmission of data across LAN media and to cause minimal, or at least predictable, time delays. However, RSRB and WAN backbones created LANs that are separated by wide, geographic distances spanning countries and continents. As a result, LANs have time delays that are longer than LLC2 allows for bidirectional communication between hosts. Local acknowledgment addresses the problem of unpredictable time delays, multiple retransmissions, and loss of user sessions.

In a typical LLC2 session, when one host sends a frame to another host, the sending host expects the receiving host to respond positively or negatively in a predefined period of time commonly called the *T1 time*. If the sending host does not receive an acknowledgment of the frame it sent within the T1 time, it retries a few times (normally 8 to 10). If there is still no response, the sending host drops the session.

Figure 7–2 illustrates an LLC2 session. A 37x5 on a LAN segment can communicate with a 3x74 on a different LAN segment separated via a wide-area backbone network. Frames are transported between Router A and Router B by means of DLSw+. However, the LLC2 session between the 37x5 and the 3x74 is still end to end; that is, every frame generated by the 37x5 traverses the backbone network to the 3x74, and the 3x74, on receipt of the frame, acknowledges it.

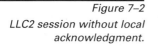

Figure 7–2

LLC2 session without local acknowledgment.

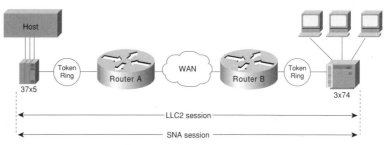

On backbone networks consisting of slow serial links, the T1 timer on end hosts could expire before the frames reach the remote hosts, causing the end host to retransmit. Retransmission results in duplicate frames reaching the remote host at the same time as the first frame reaches the remote host. Such frame duplication breaks the LLC2 protocol, resulting in the loss of sessions between the two IBM machines.

One way to solve this time delay is to increase the timeout value on the end nodes to account for the maximum transit time between the two end machines. However, in networks consisting of hundreds or even thousands of nodes, every machine would need to be reconfigured with new values. With local acknowledgment for LLC2 enabled, the LLC2 session between the two end nodes would not be not end-to-end, but instead, would terminate at two local routers. Figure 7–3 shows the LLC2 session with the 37x5 ending at Router A and the LLC2 session with the 3x74 ending at Router B. Both Router A and Router B execute the full LLC2 protocol as part of local acknowledgment for LLC2.

Figure 7–3

LLC2 session with local acknowledgment.

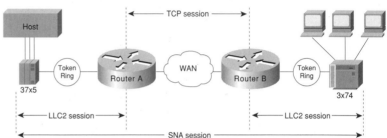

With local acknowledgment for LLC2 enabled in both routers, Router A acknowledges frames received from the 37x5. The 37x5 still operates as if the acknowledgments it receives are from the 3x74. Router A looks like the 3x74 to the 37x5. Similarly, Router B acknowledges frames received from the 3x74. The 3x74 operates as if the acknowledgments it receives are from the 37x5. Router B looks like the 3x74 to 37x5. Because the frames no longer have to travel the WAN backbone networks to be acknowledged, but instead are locally acknowledged by routers, the end machines do not time out, resulting in no loss of sessions.

Enabling local acknowledgment for LLC2 has the following advantages:

- Local acknowledgment for LLC2 solves the T1 timer problem without having to change any configuration on the end nodes. The end nodes are unaware that the sessions are locally acknowledged. In networks consisting of hundreds or even thousands of machines, this is a definite advantage. All the frames acknowledged by the Cisco IOS software appear to the end hosts to be coming from the remote IBM machine. In fact, by looking at a trace from a protocol analyzer, one cannot say whether a frame was acknowledged by the local router or by a remote IBM machine. The MAC addresses and the RIFs generated by the Cisco IOS software are identical to those generated by the remote IBM machine. The only way to find out whether a session is locally acknowledged is to use either a **show local-ack** command or a **show source-bridge** command on the router.

- All the supervisory (RR, RNR, REJ) frames that are locally acknowledged go no farther than the router. Without local acknowledgment for LLC2, *every* frame traverses the backbone. With local acknowledgment, only data (I-frames) traverse the backbone, resulting in less traffic on the backbone network. For installations in which customers pay for the amount of traffic passing through the backbone, this could be a definite cost-saving measure. A simple protocol exists between the two *peers* to bring up or down a TCP session.

Notes on Using LLC2 Local Acknowledgment

LLC2 local acknowledgment is enabled with TCP and DLSw+ lite remote peers.

If the LLC2 session between the local host and the router terminates in either router, the other will be informed to terminate its connection to its local host.

If the TCP queue length of the connection between the two routers reaches the high-water mark, the routers send Receiver-Not-Ready (RNR) messages to the local hosts until the queue limit is reduced to below this limit. It is possible, however, to prevent the RNR messages from being sent by using the **dlsw llc2 nornr** command.

The configuration of the LLC2 parameters for the local Token Ring interfaces can affect overall performance. See Chapter 11, "Configuring LLC2 and SDLC Parameters" for more details about fine-tuning your network through the LLC2 parameters.

The routers at each end of the LLC2 session execute the full LLC2 protocol, which could result in some overhead. The decision to use local acknowledgment for LLC2 should be based on the speed of the backbone network in relation to the Token Ring speed. For LAN segments separated by slow-speed serial links (for example, 56 kbps), the T1 timer problem could occur more frequently. In such cases, it might be wise to turn on local acknowledgment for LLC2. For LAN segments separated by a T1, backbone delays will be minimal. In such cases, FST or direct should be considered. Speed mismatch between the LAN segments and the backbone network is one criterion to help you decide to use local acknowledgment for LLC2.

There are some situations (such as the receiving host failing between the time the sending host sends data and the time the receiving host receives it), in which the sending host would determine, *at the LLC2 layer*, that data was received when it actually was not. This error occurs because the router acknowledges that it received data from the sending host before it determines that the receiving host actually can receive the data. But because both NetBIOS and SNA have error recovery in situations where an end device goes down, these higher-level protocols will resend any missing or lost data. Because these transaction request/confirmation protocols exist above LLC2, they are not affected by tight timers, as is LLC2. They also are transparent to local acknowledgment.

If you are using NetBIOS applications, note that there are two NetBIOS timers—one at the link level and one at the next higher level. Local acknowledgment for LLC2 is designed to solve link timeouts only. If you are experiencing NetBIOS session timeouts, you have two options:

- Experiment with increasing your NetBIOS timers and decreasing your maximum NetBIOS frame size.
- Avoid using NetBIOS applications on slow serial lines.

Figure 7–4 illustrates a DLSw+ configuration with local acknowledgment.

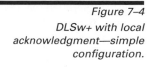
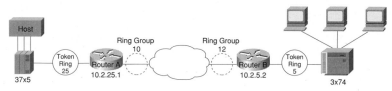

Figure 7–4
DLSw+ with local
acknowledgment—simple
configuration.

Configuration for Router A

```
source-bridge ring-group 10
!
dlsw local-peer peer-id 10.2.25.1
dlsw remote-peer 0 tcp 10.2.5.2
 interface loopback 0
 ip address 10.2.25.1 255.255.255.0
 .

 .

interface tokenring 0
 no ip address
 ring-speed 16
 source-bridge active 25 1 10
 source-bridge spanning
```

Configuration for Router B

```
source-bridge ring-group 12
dlsw local-peer peer-id 10.2.5.2
dlsw remote-peer 0 tcp 10.2.25.1
 interface loopback 0
 ip address 10.2.5.2 255.255.255.0
 .

 .

interface tokenring 0
 no ip address
 ring-speed 16
 source-bridge active 5 1 12
 source-bridge spanning
```

DLSw+ Using TCP Encapsulation with Local Acknowledgment—Peer Groups Configuration Example 1

Figure 7–5 illustrates DLSw+ configured using acknowledgment border peers, showing circuits to each other. Router A is configured to operate in promiscuous mode, and border peers Routers B and C forward broadcasts. This configuration reduces processing requirements in Router A (the access router) and still supports any-to-any networks.

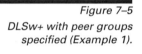

Figure 7–5
DLSw+ with peer groups
specified (Example 1).

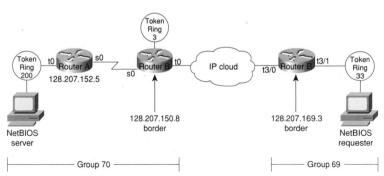

The following are configuration files for the routers in Figure 7–5.

Configuration for Router A

```
hostname RouterA
!
source-bridge ring group 31
dlsw local-peer peer-id 128.207.152.5 group 70 promiscuous
dlsw remote peer 0 tcp 128.207.150.8
!
interface serial 0
 ip unnumbered tokenring
 clockrate 56000
!
interface tokenring 0
 ip address 128.207.152.5 255.255.255.0
 ring-speed 16
 source-bridge 200 13 31
 source-bridge spanning
!
 .
 .
 .
router igrp 777
network 128.207.0.0
```

Configuration for Router B

```
hostname RouterB
!
 .
 .
 .
source-bridge ring-group 31
dlsw local-peer peer-id 128.207.150.8 group 70 border promiscuous
dlsw remote-peer 0 tcp 128.207.169.3
dlsw remote-peer 0 tcp 128.207.152.5
```

```
!
.
.

.
interface serial 0
 ip unnumbered tokenring 0
 bandwidth 56
!
.

.

.
interface tokenring 0
 ip address 128.207.150.8 255.255.255.0
 ring-speed 16
source-bridge 3 14 31
 source-bridge spanning
!
router igrp 777
network 128.207.0.0
```

Configuration for Router C

```
hostname RouterC
!
.

.

.
source-bridge ring-group 69
dlsw local-peer peer-id 128.207.169.3 group 69 border promiscuous
dlsw remote-peer 0 tcp 128.207.150.8
!
.

.

.
interface tokenring 3/0
description fixed to flashnet
 ip address 128.207.2.152 255.255.255.0
 ring-speed 16
 multiring all
!
interface tokenring 3/1
 ip address 128.207.169.3 255.255.255.0
 ring-speed 16
source-bridge 33 2 69
 source-bridge spanning
!
.

.

.
router igrp 777
network 128.207.0.0
```

DLSw+ Using TCP Encapsulation with Local Acknowledgment—Peer Group Configuration Example 2

Figure 7–6 illustrates a peer group configuration that allows any-to-any connection except for Router B. Router B has no connectivity to anything except router C because the **promiscuous** keyword is omitted

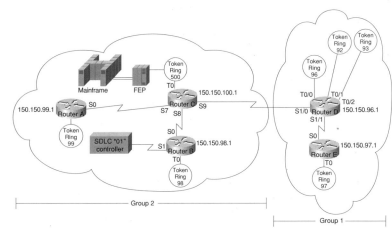

Figure 7–6

DLSw+ with peer groups specified (Example 2).

The following are configuration files for the routers in Figure 7–6.

Configuration for Router A

```
hostname Router A
!
.
.
.
source-bridge ring-group 2000
dlsw local-peer peer-id 150.150.99.1 group 2 promiscuous
dlsw remote-peer 0 tcp 150.150.100.1
!
interface loopback 0
 ip address 150.150.99.1 255.255.255.192
!
interface serial 0
 ip address 150.150.9.1 255.255.255.192
!
.
.
.
interface tokenring 0
 no ip address
 ring-speed 16
```

```
 source-bridge 99 1 2000
  source-bridge spanning
 !
 .
 .
 .
 router eigrp 202
 network 150.150.0.0
```

Configuration for Router B

```
 hostname RouterB
 !
 .
 .
 .
 source-bridge ring-group 2000
 dlsw local-peer peer-id 150.150.98.1 group 2
 dlsw remote-peer 0 tcp 150.150.100.1
 !
 interface loopback 0
  ip address 150.150.98.1 255.255.255.192
 !
 .
 .
 .
 interface serial 1
  no ip address
  encapsulation sdlc
  no keepalive
  priority-group 1
  clockrate 9600
  sdlc role primary
  sdlc vmac 4000.8888.0100
  sdlc address 01
  sdlc xid 01 05d20006
  sdlc partner 4000.1020.1000 01
  sdlc dlsw 1
 !
 interface tokenring 0
  no ip address
  ring-speed 16
  multiring all
 source-bridge 98 1 2000
  source-bridge spanning
 !
 .
 .
 .
 router eigrp 202
 network 150.150.0.0
```

Configuration for Router C

```
hostname RouterC
!
.
.
.
source-bridge ring-group 2000
dlsw local-peer peer-id 150.150.100.1 group 2 border promiscuous
dlsw remote-peer 0 tcp 150.150.96.1
dlsw remote-peer 0 tcp 150.150.98.1
dlsw remote-peer 0 tcp 150.150.99.1
!
interface loopback 0
 ip address 150.150.100.1 255.255.255.192
!
.
.
.
interface serial 7
 ip address 150.150.9.2 255.255.255.192
 clockrate 56000
!
interface serial 8
 ip address 150.150.10.2 255.255.255.192
!
interface serial 9
 ip address 150.150.8.2 255.255.255.192
!
interface tokenring 0
 no ip address
 ring-speed 16
 multiring all
source-bridge 500 1 2000
!
router eigrp 202
network 150.150.0.0
```

Configuration for Router D

```
hostname RouterD
!
.
.
.
source-bridge ring-group 2000
dlsw local-peer peer-id 150.150.96.1 group 1 border promiscuous
dlsw remote-peer 0 tcp 150.150.97.1
dlsw remote-peer 0 tcp 150.150.100.1
!
interface loopback 0
 ip address 150.150.96.1 255.255.255.192
```

```
!
.
.
.
interface serial 1/0
 ip address 150.150.8.1 255.255.255.192
 clockrate 56000
!
interface serial 1/1
 ip address 150.150.16.1 255.255.255.192
!
.
.
.
interface tokenring g0/0
 ip address 150.150.2.1 255.255.255.192
 ring-speed 16
source-bridge 96 1 2000
 source-bridge spanning
!
interface tokenring 0/1
 ip address 150.150.13.1 255.255.255.192
 no ip address
 ring-speed 16
source-bridge 92 1 2000
 source-bridge spanning
!
.
.
.
router eigrp 202
network 150.150.0.0
```

Configuration for Router E

```
hostname RouterE
!
.
.
.
source-bridge ring-group 2000
dlsw local-peer peer-id 150.150.97.1 group 1 promiscuous
dlsw remote-peer 0 tcp 150.150.96.1
!
interface loopback 0
 ip address 150.150.97.1 255.255.255.192
!
interface serial 0
 mtu 1400
 ip address 150.150.16.2 255.255.255.192
```

```
!
.
.
.
interface tokenring 0
 no ip address
 no ip route-cache
 ring-speed 16
source-bridge 97 1 2000
 source-bridge spanning
!
.
.
.
router eigrp 202
network 150.150.0.0
```

DLSw+ with SDLC Multidrop Support Configuration Example

In the following example all devices are type PU 2.0:

```
interface serial 2
 mtu 4400
 no ip address
 encapsulation sdlc
 no keepalive
 clockrate 19200
 sdlc role primary
 sdlc vmac 4000.1234.5600
 sdlc N1 27200
 sdlc address C1
 sdlc xid C1 05DCCCC1
 sdlc partner 4001.3745.1088 C1
 sdlc address C2
 sdlc xid C2 05DCCCC2
 sdlc partner 4001.3745.1088 C2
 sdlc dlsw C1 C2
```

The following example shows mixed PU 2.0 (device using address C1) and PU 2.1 (device using address C2) devices:

```
interface serial 2
 mtu 4400
 no ip address
 encapsulation sdlc
 no keepalive
 clockrate 19200
 sdlc role primary
 sdlc vmac 4000.1234.5600
 sdlc N1 27200
 sdlc address C1
 sdlc xid C1 05DCCCC1
 sdlc partner 4001.3745.1088 C1
```

```
sdlc address C2 xid-poll
sdlc partner 4001.3745.1088 C2
sdlc dlsw C1 C2
```

In the following example, all devices are type PU 2.1 (Method 1):

```
interface serial 2
mtu 4400
no ip address
encapsulation sdlc
no keepalive
clockrate 19200
sdlc role primary
sdlc vmac 4000.1234.5600
sdlc N1 27200
sdlc address C1 xid-poll
sdlc partner 4001.3745.1088 C1
sdlc address C2 xid-poll
sdlc partner 4001.3745.1088 C2
sdlc dlsw C1 C2
```

In the following example, all devices are type PU 2.1 (Method 2):

```
interface serial 2
mtu 4400
no ip address
encapsulation sdlc
no keepalive
clockrate 19200
sdlc role prim-xid-poll
sdlc vmac 4000.1234.5600
sdlc N1 27200
sdlc address C1 xid-poll
sdlc partner 4001.3745.1088 C1
sdlc address C2
sdlc xid C2 05DCCCC2
sdlc partner 4001.3745.1088 C2
sdlc dlsw C1 C2
```

DLSw+ with LLC2-to-SDLC Conversion Between PU 4-to-PU 4 Communication

The following example is a sample configuration for LLC2-to-SDLC conversion for PU 4-to-PU 4 communication as shown in Figure 7–7:

Figure 7–7

LLC2-to-SDLC conversion for PU 4-to-PU 4 communication.

Router A

```
interface serial 0
 mtu 4096
 ip address 10.4.21.2 255.255.255.0
 encapsulation frame-relay IETF
 keepalive 12
 frame-relay map llc2  46
 frame-relay map llc2  45
 frame-relay map ip 10.4.21.1 43 broadcast
 frame-relay map ip 10.4.21.3 45 broadcast
 frame-relay map ip 10.4.21.4 46 broadcast
 frame-relay lmi-type ansi

interface TokenRing 0
 mac-address 4000.1250.1001
 no ip address
 ring-speed 16
 fras map llc 4000.1060.1000 4 4 Serial0 frame-relay 45 4 4
```

Router B

```
interface serial 0
 mtu 4096
 ip address 10.4.21.3 255.255.255.0
 encapsulation frame-relay IETF
 keepalive 12
 no fair-queue
 frame-relay map llc2  53
 frame-relay map llc2  54
 frame-relay map llc2  56
 frame-relay map ip 10.4.21.1 53 broadcast
 frame-relay map ip 10.4.21.2 54 broadcast
 frame-relay map ip 10.4.21.4 56 broadcast
 frame-relay lmi-type ansi

interface serial 1
 no ip address
 encapsulation sdlc
 no keepalive
 clockrate 9600
 sdlc address 01 echo
 fras map sdlc 1 Serial0 frame-relay 54 4 4 fid4
```

DLSw+ Translation Between Ethernet and Token Ring Configuration Example

DLSw+ also supports Ethernet media. Except for configuring for a specific media, in this case Ethernet, the configuration is similar to other DLSw+ configuration (see Figure 7–8).

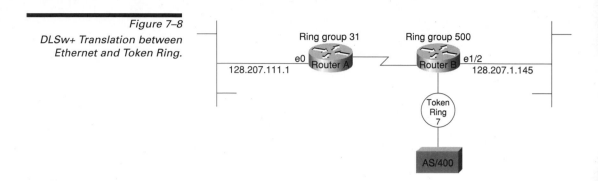

Figure 7–8
DLSw+ Translation between
Ethernet and Token Ring.

The following are the configuration files for the routers in Figure 7–8.

Configuration for Router A

```
hostname RouterA
!
.
.
.
source-bridge ring-group 31
dlsw local-peer peer-id 128.207.111.1
dlsw remote-peer 0 tcp 128.207.1.145 lf 1500
dlsw bridge-group 5
!
interface Ethernet 0
 ip address 128.207.111.1 255.255.255.0
 bridge-group 5
!
.
.
bridge 5 protocol ieee
!
.
```

Configuration for Router B

```
hostname RouterB
!
.
.
.
source-bridge ring-group 500
dlsw local-peer peer-id 128.207.1.145
dlsw remote-peer 0 tcp 128.207.111.1 lf 1500
 dlsw bridge-group 5
 .
 .
 .
```

```
interface ethernet 1/2
 ip address 128.207.1.145 255.255.255.0
 bridge-group 5
 .
 .
 .
interface tokenring 2/0
 no ip address
 ring-speed 16
 source-bridge 7 1 500
 source-bridge spanning
!
 .
 .
 .
bridge 5 protocol ieee
```

DLSw+ Translation Between FDDI and Token Ring Configuration Example

DLSw+ also supports FDDI media. Except for configuring for a specific media type, in this case FDDI (see Figure 7–9), the configuration is similar to other DLSw+ configurations.

Figure 7–9
DLSw+ Translation between
FDDI and Token Ring.

In the following example, an FDDI ring on Router A is connected to a Token Ring on Router B across a DLSw+ link.

Configuration for Router A

```
source-bridge ring-group 10
dlsw local-peer peer-id 132.11.11.2
dlsw remote-peer 0 tcp 132.11.11.3
interface fddi 0
 no ip address
source-bridge active 26 1 10
 source-bridge spanning
```

Configuration for Router B

```
source-bridge ring-group 10
dlsw local peer peer-id 132.11.
dlsw remote-peer 0 tcp 132.11.11.2
interface tokenring 0
no ip address
source-bridge active 25 1 10
 source-bridge spanning
```

DLSw+ Translation Between SDLC and Token Ring Media Example

DLSw+ provides media conversion between local or remote LANs and SDLC. For additional information about configuring SDLC parameters, see Chapter 11, "Configuring LLC2 and SDLC Parameters."

Figure 7–10 illustrates DLSw+ with SDLC encapsulation. For this example, 4000.1020.1000 is the MAC address of the FEP host (PU 4.0). The MAC address of the AS/400 host is 1000.5aed.1f53, which is defined as Node Type 2.1. Router B serves as the primary station for the remote secondary station 01. Router B can serve as either primary station or secondary station to remote station D2.

Figure 7–10

DLSw+ Translation between SDLC and Token Ring media.

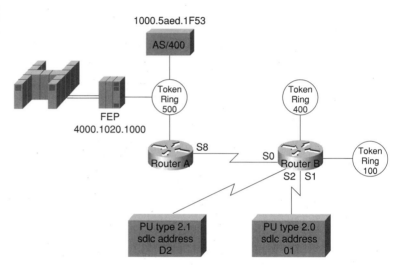

The following is the configuration file for Router A.

Configuration for Router A

```
hostname RouterA
!
.
.
.
source-bridge ring-group 2000
dlsw local-peer peer-id 150.150.10.2
dlsw remote-peer 0 tcp 150.150.10.1
!
.
.
.
interface serial 8
 ip address 150.150.10.2 255.255.255.192
 clockrate 56000
```

```
!
.
.
.
interface tokenring 0
 no ip address
 ring-speed 16
 source-bridge 500 1 2000
 source-bridge spanning
!
.
.
.
router eigrp 202
 network 150.150.0.0
```

Configuration for Router B

```
hostname RouterB
!
.
.
.
source-bridge ring-group 2000
dlsw local-peer peer-id 150.150.10.1
dlsw remote-peer 0 tcp 150.150.10.2
!
.
.
.
interface serial 0
 ip address 150.150.10.1 255.255.255.192
!
interface serial 1
 description PU2 with SDLC station role set to secondary
 no ip address
 encapsulation sdlc
 no keepalive
 clockrate 9600
 sdlc role primary
 sdlc vmac 4000.9999.0100
 sdlc address 01
 sdlc xid 01 05d20006
 sdlc partner 4000.1020.1000 01
 sdlc dlsw 1
!
interface serial 2
 description Node Type 2.1 with SDLC station role set to negotiable or primary
 encapsulation sdlc
 sdlc role none
 sdlc vmac 1234.3174.0000
 sdlc address d2
 sdlc partner 1000.5aed.1f53 d2
 sdlc dlsw d2
```

```
!
interface tokenring 0
 no ip address
 early-token-release
 ring-speed 16
 multiring all
 source-bridge 100 1 2000
 source-bridge spanning
!
interface tokenring 1
 no ip address
 ring-speed 16
 multiring all
 source-bridge 400 1 2000
 source-bridge spanning
!
router eigrp 202
 network 150.150.0.0
```

DLSw+ over Frame Relay Configuration Example

Frame Relay support extends the DLSw+ capabilities to include Frame Relay in direct mode. Frame Relay support includes permanent virtual circuit capability. DLSw+ runs over Frame Relay with or without local acknowledgment. It supports the Token Ring-to-Token Ring connections similar to Fast-Sequenced Transport and other direct data link controls. Figure 7–11 illustrates a DLSw+ configuration over Frame Relay with local acknowledgment.

Figure 7–11
DLSw+ over Frame Relay.

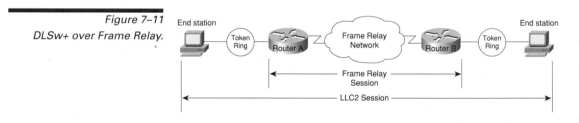

The following configuration examples are based on Figure 7–11. The Token Rings in the illustration are in Ring 2.

Configuration for Router A

```
source-bridge ring-group 100
dlsw local-peer peer-id 1.1.1.1
dlsw remote-peer 0 frame-relay interface serial 0 30
!
interface tokenring 0
 ring-speed 16
source-bridge active 1 1 100
```

```
!
interface serial 0
 mtu 3000
 no ip address
 encapsulation frame-relay
 frame-relay lmi-type ansi
 frame-relay map llc2 30
```

Configuration for Router B

```
source-bridge ring-group 100
dlsw local-peer peer-id 1.1.1.2
dlsw remote-peer 0 frame-relay interface serial 0 30
 !
interface tokenring 0
 ring-speed 16
 source-bridge active 2 1 100
 !
interface serial 0
 mtu 3000
 no ip address
 encapsulation frame-relay
 frame-relay lmi-type ansi
 frame-relay map llc2 30
```

DLSw+ over QLLC Configuration Examples

The following three examples describe QLLC support for DLSw+.

Example 1

In this configuration, DLSw+ is used to allow remote devices to connect to a DLSw+ network over an X.25 public packet-switched network.

In this example, all QLLC traffic is addressed to destination address 4000.1161.1234, which is the MAC address of the FEP.

The remote X.25-attached IBM 3174 cluster controller is given a virtual MAC address of 1000.0000.0001. This virtual MAC address is mapped to the X.121 address of the 3174 (31104150101) in the X.25 attached router.

```
interface serial 0
 encapsulation x25
 x25 address 3110212011
 x25 map qllc 1000.0000.0001 31104150101
 qllc dlsw partner 4000.1611.1234
```

Example 2

In this configuration, a single IBM 3174 cluster controller needs to communicate with both an AS/400 and a FEP. The FEP is associated with subaddress 150101 and the AS/400 is associated with subaddress 151102.

If an X.25 call comes in for 33204150101, the call is mapped to the FEP and forwarded to MAC address 4000.1161.1234. The IBM 3174 appears to the FEP as a Token Ring-attached resource with MAC address 1000.0000.0001. The IBM 3174 uses a source SAP of 04 when communicating with the FEP, and a source SAP of 08 when communicating with the AS/400.

```
interface serial 0
 encapsulation x25
 x25 address 31102
 x25 map qllc 1000.0000.0001 33204
 qllc dlsw subaddress 150101 partner 4000.1161.1234
 qllc dlsw subaddress 150102 partner 4000.2034.5678 sap 04 08
```

Example 3

In this example, two different X.25 resources want to communicate over X.25 to the same FEP.

In the router attached to the X.25 network, every X.25 connection request for X.121 address 31102150101 is directed to DLSw+. The first SVC to be established will be mapped to virtual MAC address 1000.0000.0001. The second SVC to be established will be mapped to virtual MAC address 1000.0000.0002.

```
interface serial 0
 encapsulation x25
 x25 address 31102
 x25 map qllc 33204
 x25 map qllc 35765
 qllc dlsw subaddress 150101 vmacaddr 1000.0000.0001 2 partner 4000.1611.1234
```

CHAPTER 8

DLSw+ Configuration Commands

This chapter describes the commands to configure data-link switching plus (DLSw+), Cisco's implementation of the DLSw standard. For DLSw+ configuration tasks and examples, see Chapter 7, "Configuring Data-Link Switching Plus." For specific SDLC commands to configure DLSw+ for SDLC, see Chapter 12, "LLC2 and SDLC Commands."

CLEAR DLSW CIRCUIT

Use the **clear dlsw circuit** privileged EXEC command to cause all DLSw+ circuits to be closed.

   clear dlsw circuit

Syntax   Description

This command has no arguments or keywords.

Command Mode

Privileged EXEC

Usage Guidelines

This command first appeared in Cisco IOS Release 11.2 F.

CAUTION

This command also drops the associated LLC2 session. The command usage should be used with caution and under the advice of a Cisco engineer.

Example

The following example closes all DLSw+ circuits:

```
clear dlsw circuit
```

CLEAR DLSW REACHABILITY

Use the **clear dlsw reachability** privileged EXEC command to remove all entries from the dlsw reachability cache.

clear dlsw reachability

Syntax   Description

This command has no arguments or keywords.

Command Mode

Privileged EXEC

Usage Guidelines

This command first appeared in Cisco IOS Release 11.2 F.

This command does not affect existing sessions.

Example

The following example removes all entries from the dlsw reachability cache:

```
clear dlsw reachability
```

CLEAR DLSW STATISTICS

Use the **clear dlsw statistics** privileged EXEC command to reset to zero the number of frames that have been processed in the local, remote, and group cache.

clear dlsw statistics

Syntax   Description

This command has no arguments or keywords.

Command Mode

Privileged EXEC

Usage Guidelines

This command first appeared in Cisco IOS Release 11.2 F.

Example

The following example resets to zero the number of frames in the local, remote, and group cache:

```
clear dlsw statistics
```

DLSW ALLROUTE-NETBIOS

Use the **dlsw allroute-netbios** global configuration command to change the single-route explorer to an all-route broadcast for NetBIOS. Use the **no** form of this command to return to the default single-route explorer.

    dlsw allroute-netbios
    no dlsw allroute-netbios

Syntax   Description

This command has no arguments or keywords.

Default

Single-route explorer.

Command Mode

Global configuration

Usage Guidelines

This command first appeared in Cisco IOS Release 11.1.

Example

The following example specifies all-route broadcasts:

```
dlsw allroute-netbios
```

DLSW ALLROUTE-SNA

Use the **dlsw allroute-sna** global configuration command to change the single-route explorer to an all-route broadcast for SNA. Use the **no** form of this command to return to the default single-route explorer.

    dlsw allroute-sna
    no dlsw allroute-sna

Syntax   Description

This command has no arguments or keywords.

Default

Single-route explorer.

Command Mode

Global configuration

Usage Guidelines

This command first appeared in Cisco IOS Release 11.1.

Example

The following example specifies all-route broadcasts:

```
dlsw allroute-sna
```

DLSW BGROUP-LIST

Use the **dlsw bgroup-list** global configuration command to map traffic on the local Ethernet bridge group interface to remote peers. Use the **no** form of this command to cancel the map.

> **dlsw bgroup-list** *list-number* **bgroups** *number*
> **no dlsw bgroup-list**

Syntax	Description
list-number	The ring-list number. This number is subsequently used in the **dlsw remote-peer** command to define the segment to which the bridge group should be applied. The valid range is 1 to 255.
bgroups	The transparent bridge group to which DLSw+ will be attached. The valid range is 1 to 63.
number	The transparent bridge group list number. The valid range is 1 to 63.

Default

There is no default setting.

Command Mode

Global configuration

Usage Guidelines

This command first appeared in Cisco IOS Release 11.0.

Traffic received from a remote peer is forwarded only to the bridge group specified in the bridge group list. Traffic received from a local interface is forwarded to peers if the input bridge group number appears in the bridge group list applied to the remote peer definition. The definition of a bridge group list is optional. Each remote peer has a single list number associated with it; therefore, if you want traffic to go to a bridge group and to either a ring list or port list, you should specify the same list number in each definition.

Example

The following example configures bgroup list 1:

```
dlsw bgroup-list 1 bgroups 33
```

Related Commands

dlsw bridge-group
dlsw ring-list

DLSW BRIDGE-GROUP

Use the **dlsw bridge-group** global configuration command to link DLSw+ to the bridge group of the Ethernet LANs. Use the **no** form of this command to disable the link.

dlsw bridge-group *group-number* [llc2 [N2 *number*] [ack-delay-time *milliseconds*]
    [ack-max *number*] [idle-time *milliseconds*] [local-window *number*] [t1-time *milliseconds*]
    [tbusy-time *milliseconds*] [tpf-time *milliseconds*] [trej-time *milliseconds*]
    [txq-max *number*] [xid-neg-val-time *milliseconds*] [xid-retry-time *milliseconds*]]
    [locaddr-priority] [sap-priority]

no dlsw bridge-group *group-number* [llc2 [N2 *number*] [ack-delay-time *milliseconds*]
    [ack-max *number*] [idle-time *milliseconds*] [local-window *number*] [t1-time *milliseconds*]
    [tbusy-time *milliseconds*] [tpf-time *milliseconds*] [trej-time *milliseconds*]
    [txq-max *number*] [xid-neg-val-time *milliseconds*] [xid-retry-time *milliseconds*]]
    [locaddr-priority] [sap-priority]

Syntax	Description
group-number	The transparent bridge group to which DLSw+ will be attached. The valid range is 1 to 63.
llc2	LLC2 interface subcommands.
N2 *number*	Number of times router should retry various operations. The valid range is 1 to 255.
ack-delay-time *milliseconds*	Max time the router allows incoming I-frames to stay unacknowledged. The valid range is 1 to 60000.
ack-max *number*	Max number of I-frames received before an acknowledgment must be sent. The valid range is 1 to 255.
idle-time *milliseconds*	Frequency of polls during periods of idle traffic. The valid range is 1 to 60000.
local-window *number*	Max number of I-frames to send before waiting for an acknowledgment. The valid range is 1 to 127.

Syntax	Description
t1-time *milliseconds*	How long router waits for an acknowledgment to transmitted I-frames. The valid range is 1 to 60000.
tbusy-time *milliseconds*	Amount of time router waits while the other LLC2 station is in a busy state before attempting to poll the remote station. The valid range is 1 to 60000.
tpf-time *milliseconds*	Amount of time router waits for a final response to a poll frame before resending the original poll frame. The valid range is 1 to 60000.
trej-time *milliseconds*	Amount of time router waits for a resend of a rejected frame before sending the reject command. The valid range is 1 to 60000.
txq-max *number*	Queue for holding llc2 information frames. The valid range is 20 to 200.
xid-neg-val-time *milliseconds*]	Frequency of exchange of identification (XID). The valid range is 1 to 60000.
xid-retry-time *milliseconds*	How long router waits for reply to XID The valid range is 1 to 60000.
locaddr-priority	Assign an input SNA LU Addr priority list to this bridge group.
sap-priority	Assign an input sap priority list to this bridge group.

Syntax Description

Default

There is no default setting.

Command Mode

Global configuration

Usage Guidelines

This command first appeared in Cisco IOS Release 11.0.

More than one bridge group can be attached to DLSw+ by using this command multiple times. Multiple bridge group support is available in Cisco IOS Release 11.3.

Example

The following example links DLSw+ to bridge group 1, 2 and 3:

```
dlsw local-peer peer-id 1.1.1.1
dlsw remote-peer 0 tcp 2.2.2.2
dlsw bridge-group 1
```

```
dlsw bridge-group 2
dlsw bridge-group 3

interface Ethernet0
 bridge-group 1

interface Ethernet1
 bridge-group 2

interface Ethernet2
 bridge-group 3

bridge 1 protocol ieee
bridge 2 protocol ieee
bridge 3 protocol ieee
```

Related Commands

dlsw bgroup-list

DLSW DISABLE

Use the **dlsw disable** global configuration command to disable and re-enable DLSw+ without altering the configuration.

> **dlsw disable**
> **no dlsw disable**

Syntax　　　Description

This command has no arguments or keywords.

Default

There is no default setting.

Command Mode

Global configuration

Usage Guidelines

This command first appeared in Cisco IOS Release 11.0.

Example

The following example re-enables DLSw+:

```
no dlsw disable
```

DLSW DUPLICATE-PATH-BIAS

Use the **dlsw duplicate-path-bias** global configuration command to specify how DLSw+ handles duplicate paths to the same Media Access Control (MAC) address or NetBIOS name. Use the **no** form of the command to return to the default (fault-tolerance).

> **dlsw duplicate-path-bias** [**load-balance**]
> **no dlsw duplicate-path-bias** [**load-balance**]

Syntax	*Description*
load-balance	(Optional) Specifies that sessions are load-balanced across duplicate paths.

Default

Fault-tolerance is the default logic used to handle duplicate paths.

Command Mode

Global configuration

Usage Guidelines

This command first appeared in Cisco IOS Release 11.0.

A path is either a remote peer or a local port.

In full-tolerance mode, the preferred path is always used unless it is unavailable. The preferred path is either the path over which the first response to an explorer was received or, in the case of remote peers, the peer with the least cost.

Example

The following example specifies load balancing to resolve duplicate paths:

```
dlsw duplicate-path-bias load-balance
```

DLSW GROUP-CACHE DISABLE

Use the **dlsw group cache disable** global configuration command to disable the border peer caching feature. Use the **no** form of this command to return to the default peer caching feature.

> **dlsw group-cache disable**
> **no dlsw group-cache disable**

Syntax	*Description*

This command has no arguments or keywords.

Default

This command is enabled by default.

Command Mode

Global configuration

Usage Guidelines

This command first appeared in Cisco IOS Release 11.2 F.

If a border peer becomes a non-border peer, then the group cache is automatically deleted.

This command prevents a border peer from learning reachability information from relay responses. This command also prevents a border peer from using local or remote caches to make forwarding decisions.

Example

The following example disables the group cache:

```
dlsw group-cache disable
```

Related Commands

dlsw group-cache max-entries

DLSW GROUP-CACHE MAX-ENTRIES

Use the **dlsw group-cache max entries** global configuration command to limit the number of entries in the group cache. Use the **no** form of this command to return to the default.

> **dlsw group-cache max-entries** *number*
> **no dlsw group-cache max entries**

Syntax	Description
number	Maximum number of entries allowed in the group cache. The valid range is 0 through 12000. If the value is set to 0, then there is no limit to the number of entries. The default is 2000.

Default

The default setting is 2000.

Command Mode

Global configuration

Usage Guidelines

This command first appeared in Cisco IOS Release 11.2 F.

Once the number of entries has reached the maximum number specified, if a new entry needs to be added, an entry will be removed to make room.

The value set for *cache max* applies to both the NetBIOS and SNA group cache.

Example

The following configuration defines the maximum number of entries allowed in the NetBIOS or SNA group cache as 1800:

```
dlsw group-cache max-entries 1800
```

Releated Commands

dlsw group-cache disable

DLSW ICANNOTREACH SAPS

Use the **dlsw icannotreach saps** global configuration command to configure a list of service access points (SAPs) not locally reachable by the router. Use the **no** form of this command to remove the list.

> **dlsw icannotreach saps** *sap* [*sap...*]
> **no dlsw icannotreach saps** *sap* [*sap...*]

Syntax	Description
sap sap...	Array of SAPs.

Default

No lists are configured.

Command Mode

Global configuration

Usage Guidelines

This command first appeared in Cisco IOS Release 10.3

The **dlsw icannot reach saps** command causes the local router to send a control vector to its peers during the capabilities exchange, which tells the peers not to send canureach messages to the local router for sessions using those DSAPs. (They are DSAPs from the peer's perspective, and SSAPs from the perspective of the devices attached to the local router.) The effect is that devices attached to the peer will not be able to initiate sessions to devices attached to the local router using the listed DSAPs. Devices attached to the local router, however, still will be able to start sessions with devices on its peers using the listed saps as SSAPs. The reason is that the local router still can send canureach requests to its peers, since no filtering is actually done on the local router. The filtering done by the peers does not prohibit the peers from responding to canureach requests from the local router sending the control vector, only sending canureach requests to the local router.

Example

The following example specifies a list of SAPs that are not reachable:

```
dlsw icannotreach saps F0
```

DLSW ICANREACH

Use the **dlsw icanreach** global configuration command to configure a resource that is locally reachable by this router. Use the **no** form of this command to remove the resource.

Part
II

Command Reference

> **dlsw icanreach** {**mac-exclusive** | **netbios-exclusive** | **mac-address** *mac-addr*
>   [**mask** *mask*] | **netbios-name** *name* | **saps**}
> **no dlsw icanreach** {**mac-exclusive** | **netbios-exclusive** | **mac-address** *mac-addr*
>   [**mask** *mask*] | **netbios-name** *name* | **saps**}

Syntax	Description
mac-exclusive	Router can reach only the MAC addresses that are user configured.
netbios-exclusive	Router can reach only the NetBIOS names that are user configured.
mac-address *mac-addr*	Configures a MAC address that this router can reach locally.
mask *mask*	(Optional) MAC address mask in hexadecimal *h.h.h*. The mask indicates which bits in the MAC address are relevant.
netbios-name *name*	Configures a NetBIOS name that this router can locally reach. Wildcards (*) are allowed at the end of the name. Trailing white spaces are ignored when comparing against an actual name in a NetBIOS frame.
saps	(Optional) Array of saps.

Default

No resources are configured.

Command Mode

Global configuration

Usage Guidelines

This command first appeared in Cisco IOS Release 11.0.

This command can be entered at any time. It causes a capabilities exchange to relay the information to all active peers. By specifying resource names or MAC addresses in this command, you can avoid broadcasts from remote peers that are looking for this resource. By specifying "exclusive," you can avoid broadcasts to this router or any resources. For example, you could configure the front-end processor (FEP) MAC address or corporate site LAN servers in central site routers to avoid any broadcasts over the WAN for these resources.

Example

The following example indicates that this peer only has information about a single NetBIOS server, and that no peers should send this peer explorer searching for other NetBIOS names:

```
dlsw icanreach netbios-exclusive
dlsw icanreach netbios-name lanserv
```

Related Commands

show dlsw capabilities

DLSW LLC2 NORNR

Use the **dlsw llc2 nornr** global configuration command to prevent the receiver not ready (RNR) message from being sent while establishing an LLC2 connection. Use the **no** form of this command to return to the default.

> **dlsw llc2 nornr**
> **no dlsw llc2 nornr**

Default

The command is disabled by default.

Command Mode

Global configuration

Usage Guidelines

This command first appeared in Cisco IOS Release 11.0.

This command is used when any device does not handle the LLC2 RNR frames.

Examples

The following configuration keeps the receiver not ready message from being sent when establishing an LLC2 connection.

```
router# dlsw llc2 nornr
```

The following is output from a sniffer trace showing when it would be appropriate to use the **dlsw llc2 nornr** command because the RNR message is being rejected from the FEP when the router is trying to establish an LLC2 connection

```
SUMMARY  Delta T    From 400020401003              From 400023491026
8    0.173                                  LLC C D=00 S=04 TEST P
9    0.003    LLC R D=04 S=00 TEST F
10   0.002                                  SNA XID Fmt 2 T4
11   0.059    SNA XID Fmt 2 T4
12   0.004                                  SNA XID Fmt 2 T4
13   0.065    SNA XID Fmt 2 T4
14   0.005                                  SNA XID Fmt 2 T4
16   0.054    LLC C D=04 S=04 SABME P
17   0.003                                  LLC R D=04 S=04 UA
```

The router sends a receiver not ready message.

```
18   0.001    LLC C D=04 S=04 RNR NR=0
```

From frames 19 to 35, the FEP does not respond.

```
19   0.002    LLC C D=04 S=04 RR NR=0
20   0.048    SNA  C NC  NC-ER-OP
21   0.997    LLC C D=04 S=04 RR NR=0 P
22   1.000    LLC C D=04 S=04 RR NR=0 P
24   1.000    LLC C D=04 S=04 RR NR=0 P
25   1.000    LLC C D=04 S=04 RR NR=0 P
31   1.000    LLC C D=04 S=04 RR NR=0 P
32   1.000    LLC C D=04 S=04 RR NR=0 P
34   1.000    LLC C D=04 S=04 RR NR=0 P
35   1.000    LLC C D=04 S=04 RR NR=0 P
```

The router disconnects the circuit.

```
37   1.000    LLC C D=04 S=04 DISC P
38   0.002                                  LLC R D=04 S=04 UA F
```

The sequence repeats.

```
39   0.179                                  LLC C D=00 S=04 TEST P
41   0.767    SNA XID Fmt 2 T4
42   0.634    SNA XID Fmt 2 T4
43   0.173                                  LLC C D=00 S=04 TEST
44   0.003    LLC R D=04 S=00 TEST F
45   0.002                                  SNA XID Fmt 2 T4
46   0.060    SNA XID Fmt 2 T4
47   0.004                                  SNA XID Fmt 2 T4
48   0.063    SNA XID Fmt 2 T4
49   0.005                                  SNA XID Fmt 2 T4
```

DLSW LOCAL-PEER

Use the **dlsw local-peer** global configuration command to define the parameters of the DLSw+ local peer. Use the **no** form of this command to cancel the definitions.

dlsw local-peer [peer-id *ip-address*] [group *group*] [border] [cost *cost*]
  [lf *size*] [keepalive *seconds*] [passive] [promiscuous] [biu-segment]
  [init-pacing-window *size*] [max-pacing-window *size*]
no dlsw local-peer [peer-id *ip-address*] [group *group*] [border] [cost *cost*]
  [lf *size*] [keepalive *seconds*] [passive] [promiscuous] [biu-segment]
  [init-pacing-window *size*] [max-pacing-window *size*]

Syntax	Description
peer-id *ip-address*	(Optional) Local peer IP address; required for Fast-Sequenced Transport (FST) and TCP.
group *group*	(Optional) Peer-group number for this router. The valid range is 1 to 255.
border	(Optional) Enables as a border peer. Group option must be specified in order to use the border peer option.
cost *cost*	(Optional) Peer cost advertised to remote peers in the capabilities exchange. The valid range is 1 to 5.
lf *size*	(Optional) Largest frame size for this local peer. Valid sizes are the following: 516-516 byte maximum frame size 1470-1470 byte maximum frame size 1500-1500 byte maximum frame size 2052-2052 byte maximum frame size 4472-4472 byte maximum frame size 8144-8144 byte maximum frame size 11407-11407 byte maximum frame size 11454-11454 byte maximum frame size 17800-17800 byte maximum frame size
keepalive *seconds*	(Optional) Default remote-peer keepalive interval in seconds. The valid range is 0 to 1200 seconds. The default is 30 seconds. The value 0 means no keepalives.
passive	(Optional) Specifies that this router will not initiate remote peer connections to configured peers.
promiscuous	(Optional) Accepts connections from nonconfigured remote peers.
biu-segment	(Optional) Causes DLSw+ to spoof the maximum receivable I-frame size in XID so that each end station sends the largest frame it can.
init-pacing-window *size*	(Optional) Size of the initial pacing window, as defined in RFC 1795. The valid range is 1–2000.
max-pacing-window *size*	(Optional) Maximum size of the pacing window, as defined in RFC 1795. The valid range is 1–2000.

Default

No parameters are defined.

Command Mode

Global configuration

Usage Guidelines

This command first appeared in Cisco IOS Release 10.3.

When there are multiple peers to a given destination, use the **cost** keyword to determine which router is preferred and which is capable. The **cost** keyword only applies in fault-tolerance mode.

The **biu-segment** option is a performance/utilization improvement. If a frame that arrives from a remote peer is too large for the destination station to handle, DLSw+ segments the frame. If you choose to implement this option, you must add the option to both DLSw peer partners.

Example

The following command defines the local peer IP address and specifies the peer-group number for this router:

```
dlsw local-peer peer-id 10.2.17.1 group 2
```

Related Commands

dlsw duplicate-path-bias
show dlsw capabilities

DLSW MAC-ADDR

Use the **dlsw mac-addr** global configuration command to configure a static MAC address. Use the **no** form of this command to cancel the configuration.

> **dlsw mac-addr** *mac-addr* {**ring** *ring -number*| **remote-peer** {**interface serial** *number* |
> **ip-address** *ip-address*}| **rif** *rif-string* | }
> **no dlsw mac-addr** *mac-addr* {**ring** *ring -number*| **remote-peer** {**interface serial** *number* |
> **ip-address** *ip-address*}| **rif** *rif-string* | **group** *group*}

Syntax	Description
mac-addr	Specifies the MAC address.
ring *ring-number*	Maps the MAC address to a ring number or ring-group number. The valid range is 1 to 4095.
remote-peer	Maps the MAC address to a specific remote peer.
interface serial *number*	Specifies the remote peer by direct serial interface.

Syntax	Description
ip-address *ip-address*	Specifies the remote peer by IP address.
rif *rif-string*	Maps the MAC address to a local interface using a RIF string. The RIF string describes a source-routed path from the router to the MAC address. It starts at the router's ring group and ends on the ring where the MAC address is located. The direction should be from the router toward the MAC address. See IEEE 802.5 standard for details.
group *group*	Maps the MAC address to a specified peer group. Valid numbers are in the range 1 to 255.

Default

No static MAC address is configured.

Command Mode

Global configuration

Usage Guidelines

This command first appeared in Cisco IOS Release 11.0.

You can statically define resources to prevent the Cisco IOS software from sending explorer frames for the specified resource. For example, you can include the MAC address of a FEP in the configuration for each remote router to eliminate any broadcasts that are searching for a FEP. Alternatively, you can specify a single **dlsw icanreach** statement in the router attached to the FEP indicating the MAC address of the FEP. This information is sent to all remote routers as part of the capabilities exchange.

Example

The following example maps the static MAC address 1000.5A12.3456 to the remote peer at IP address 10.17.3.2:

```
dlsw mac-addr 1000.5A12.3456 remote-peer ip-address 10.17.3.2
```

Related Commands

show dlsw reachability

DLSW NETBIOS-KEEPALIVE-FILTER

Use the **dlsw netbios-keepalive-filter** global configuration command to enable the NetBIOS Dial-on-Demanding Routing (DDR) feature. Use the **no** form of this command to turn off the feature.

> **dlsw netbios-keepalive-filter**
> **no dlsw netbios-keepalive-filter**

Syntax   Description

This command has no arguments or keywords.

Default

Disabled

Command Mode

Global configuration

Usage Guidelines

This command first appeared in 11.2 F.

See the "Bridging and IBM Networking Overview" at the beginning of this book for more details on the NetBIOS DDR feature.

Example

The following example enables NetBIOS DDR:

```
dlsw netbios-keepalive-filter
```

DLSW NETBIOS-NAME

Use the **dlsw netbios-name** global configuration command to configure a static NetBIOS name. Use the **no** form of this command to cancel the configuration.

dlsw netbios-name *netbios-name* {**ring** *ring-number* | **remote-peer** {**interface serial** *number* | **ip-address** *ip-address*}| **rif** *rif-string* | **group** *group*}
no dlsw netbios-name *netbios-name* {**ring** *ring-number* | **remote-peer**
{**interface serial** *number* | **ip-address** *ip-address*}| **rif** *rif-string* | **group** *group*}

Syntax	Description
netbios-name	Specifies the NetBIOS name. Wildcards are allowed.
ring *ring number*	Maps the NetBIOS name to a ring number or ring-group number. Test frames for this name will be sent only to LAN ports in this ring group.
remote-peer	Maps the NetBIOS name to a specific remote peer.
interface serial *number*	Specifies the remote peer by direct interface.
ip-address *ip-address*	Specifies the remote peer by IP address.

Syntax	Description
rif *rif- string*	Maps the MAC address to a local interface using a RIF string. The RIF string describes a source-routed path from the router to the MAC address. It starts at the router's ring group and ends on the ring where the MAC address is located. The direction should be from the router towards the MAC address. See IEEE 802.5 standard for details
group *group*	Maps the NetBIOS name to a specified peer group. Valid numbers are in the range 1 to 255.

Default

No static NetBIOS name is configured.

Command Mode

Global configuration

Usage Guidelines

This command first appeared in Cisco IOS Release 11.0.

Example

The following example configures a static NetBIOS name and links it to group 3:

```
dlsw netbios-name netname group 3
```

Related Commands

show dlsw reachability

DLSW PEER-ON-DEMAND-DEFAULTS

Use the **dlsw peer-on-demand-defaults** global configuration command to configure defaults for peer-on-demand transport. Use the **no** form of this command to disable the previous assignment.

> **dlsw peer-on-demand-defaults** [**fst**] [**bytes-netbios-out** *bytes-list-name*] [**cost** *cost*]
> [**dest-mac** *destination mac address*] [**dmac-output-list** *access list number*]
> [**host-netbios-out** *host-list-name*] [**inactivity** *minutes*] [**keepalive** *seconds*] [**lf** size]
> [**lsap-output-list** *list*] [**port-list** *port-list-number*] [**priority**] [**tcp-queue-max**]
> **no dlsw peer-on-demand-defaults** [**fst**] [**bytes-netbios-out** *bytes-list-name*] [**cost** *cost*]
> [**dest-mac** *destination mac address*] [**dmac-output-list** *access list number*]
> [**host-netbios-out** *host-list-name*] [**inactivity** *minutes*] [**keepalive** *seconds*] [**lf** size]
> [**lsap-output-list** *list*] [**port-list** *port-list-number*] [**priority**] [**tcp-queue-max**]

Syntax	Description
fst	(Optional) Use FST encapsulation for all peer-on-demand peers being established by this router.
bytes-netbios-out *bytes-list-name*	(Optional) Configures NetBIOS bytes output filtering for peer-on-demand peers. The *bytes-list-name* is the name of the previously defined netbios bytes access list filter.
cost *cost*	(Optional) Specifies the cost to reach peer-on-demand peers. The valid range is 1 to 5. The default cost is 3.
dest-mac *destination mac address*	(Optional) Specifies the exclusive destination MAC address for peer-on-demand peers.
dmac-output-list *access list number*	(Optional) Specifies the filter output destination MAC addresses.
host-netbios-out *host-list-name*	(Optional) Configures NetBIOS host output filtering for peer-on-demand peers. The *host-list-name* is the name of the previously defined NetBIOS host access list filter.
inactivity *minutes*	(Optional) Configures the length of time after the peer's circuit count is zero that the peer-on-demand is disconnected. The valid range is 0 to 1440 seconds. The default is 10 minutes.
keepalive *seconds*	(Optional) Configures the peer-on-demand keepalive interval. The valid range is 0 to 1200 seconds. The default is 30 seconds.
lf *size*	(Optional) Largest frame size for this remote peer. Valid sizes are the following: 516-516 byte maximum frame size 1470-1470 byte maximum frame size 1500-1500 byte maximum frame size 2052-2052 byte maximum frame size 4472-4472 byte maximum frame size 8144-8144 byte maximum frame size 11407-11407 byte maximum frame size 11454-11454 byte maximum frame size 17800-17800 byte maximum frame size
lsap-output-list *list*	(Optional) Configures local service access point (LSAP) output filtering for peer-on-demand peers. Valid numbers are in the range 200 to 299.
port-list *port-list-number*	(Optional) Configures a port list for peer-on-demand peers. Valid numbers are in the range 0 to 4095.

Syntax	Description
priority	(Optional) Configures prioritization for peer-on-demand peers. The default state is off.
tcp-queue-max	(Optional) Configures the maximum output TCP queue size for peer-on-demand peers.

Default

The default peer-on-demand transport is TCP.

Command Mode

Global configuration

Usage Guidelines

This command first appeared in Cisco IOS Release 11.0.

Example

The following example configures FST for peer-on-demand transport:

```
dlsw peer-on-demand-defaults fst
```

Related Commands

show dlsw peers

DLSW PORT-LIST

Use the **dlsw port-list** global configuration command to map traffic on a local interface (Ethernet, Token Ring, or serial) to remote peers. Use the **no** form of this command to disable the previous map assignment.

> **dlsw port-list** *list-number type number*
> **no dlsw port-list** *list-number type number*

Syntax	Description
list-number	Port-list number. The valid range is 1 to 255.
type	Interface type.
number	Interface number.

Default

No port list is configured.

Command Mode

Global configuration

Usage Guidelines

This command first appeared in Cisco IOS Release 11.0.

Traffic received from a remote peer is forwarded only to the ports specified in the port list. Traffic received from a local interface is forwarded to peers if the input port number appears in the port list applied to the remote peer definition. The definition of a port list is optional.

Example

The following example configures a DLSw peer port list for token ring interface 1:

```
dlsw port-list 3 token ring 1
```

Related Commands

dlsw bgroup-list
dlsw ring-list

DLSW PROM-PEER-DEFAULTS

Use the **dlsw prom-peer-defaults** global configuration command to configure defaults for promiscuous transport. Use the **no** form of this command to disable the previous assignment.

> **dlsw prom-peer-defaults** [**fst**] [**bytes-netbios-out** *bytes-list-name*] [**cost** *cost*]
> [**dest-mac** *destination mac address*] [**dmac-output-list** *access list number*]
> [**host-netbios-out** *host-list-name*] [**keepalive** *seconds*] [**lf** *size*]
> [**lsap-output-list** *list*] [**tcp-queue-max** *size*]
> **no dlsw prom-peer-defaults** [**fst**] [**bytes-netbios-out** *bytes-list-name*] [**cost** *cost*]
> [**dest-mac** *destination mac address*] [**dmac-output-list** *access list number*]
> [**host-netbios-out** *host-list-name*] [**keepalive** *seconds*] [**lf** *size*]
> [**lsap-output-list** *list*] [**tcp-queue-max** *size*]

Syntax	Description
bytes-netbios-out *bytes-list-name*	(Optional) Configures NetBIOS bytes output filtering for promiscuous peers. The *bytes-list-name* is the name of the previously defined NetBIOS bytes access list filter.
cost *cost*	(Optional) Specifies the cost to reach promiscuous peers. The valid range is 1 to 5. The default cost is 3.
dest-mac *destination mac address*	Specifies the exclusive destination MAC address for promiscuous peers.
dmac-output-list *access list number*	Specifies the filter output destination MAC addresses.

Syntax	Description
fst	(Optional) Use FST encapsulation for all prom peers being established by this router.
host-netbios-out *host-list-name*	(Optional) Configures NetBIOS host output filtering for promiscuous peers. The *host-list-name* is the name of the previously defined NetBIOS host access list filter.
keepalive *seconds*	(Optional) Configures the promiscuous keepalive interval. The valid range is 0 to 1200 seconds. The default is 30 seconds.
lf *size*	(Optional) Largest frame size for this promiscuous peer. Valid sizes are the following: 516-516 byte maximum frame size 1470-1470 byte maximum frame size 1500-1500 byte maximum frame size 2052-2052 byte maximum frame size 4472-4472 byte maximum frame size 8144-8144 byte maximum frame size 11407-11407 byte maximum frame size 11454-11454 byte maximum frame size 17800-17800 byte maximum frame size
lsap-output-list *list*	(Optional) Configures LSAP output filtering for promiscuous peers. Valid numbers are in the range 200 to 299.
tcp-queue-max *size*	(Optional) Configures the maximum output TCP queue size for promiscuous peers.

Default

The default prom-peer transport is TCP.

Command Mode

Global configuration

Usage Guidelines

This command first appeared in Cisco IOS Release 11.0.

Example

The following example configures cost for promiscuous peers:

```
dlsw prom-peer-defaults cost 4
```

Related Commands

show dlsw capabilities

DLSW REMOTE-PEER FRAME RELAY

Use the **dlsw remote-peer frame relay** global configuration command to specify the remote peer with which the router will connect. Use the **no** form of this command to disable the previous assignments.

> dlsw remote-peer *list-number* **frame-relay interface serial** *number dlci-number*
> [**backup-peer** [*ip-address* | **frame-relay interface serial** *number dlci-number* |
> **interface** *name*]] [**bytes-netbios-out** *bytes-list-name*] [**cost** *cost*]
> [**dest-mac** *mac-address*] [**dmac-output-list** *access-list-number*]
> [**host-netbios-out** *host-list-name*] [**keepalive** *seconds*] [**lf** *size*] [**linger** *minutes*]
> [**lsap-output-list** *list*] [**passive**] [pass-**thru**]

> no dlsw remote-peer *list-number* **frame-relay interface serial** *number dlci-number*
> [**backup-peer** [*ip-address* | **frame-relay interface serial** *number dlci-number* |
> **interface** *name*]] [**bytes-netbios-out** *bytes-list-name*] [**cost** *cost*]
> [**dest-mac** *mac-address*] [**dmac-output-list** *access-list-number*]
> [**host-netbios-out** *host-list-name*] [**keepalive** *seconds*] [**lf** *size*] [**linger** *minutes*]
> [**lsap-output-list** *list*] [**passive**] [pass-**thru**]

Syntax	Description
list-number	Ring-list number. The valid range is 1 to 255. The default is 0, which means DLSw+ forwards explorers over all ports or bridge groups on which DLSw+ is enabled.
interface serial *number*	Serial interface number of the remote peer with which the router is to communicate.
dlci-number	DLCI number of the remote peer.
backup-peer *ip-address*	(Optional) IP address of the existing TCP/FST peer for which this peer is the backup peer.
backup-peer frame-relay interface serial *number dlci-number*	(Optional) Serial interface and DLCI number of the existing Direct/LLC2 frame-relay peer for which this peer is the backup peer.
backup-peer interface *name*	(Optional) Interface name of the existing direct peer for which this peer is the backup peer.
bytes-netbios-out *bytes-list-name*	(Optional) Configures NetBIOS bytes output filtering for this peer. The *bytes-list-name* argument is the name of the previously defined NetBIOS bytes access list filter.
cost *cost*	(Optional) Cost to reach this remote peer. The valid range is 1 to 5.
dest-mac *mac-address*	(Optional) Permits the connection to be established only when there is an explorer frame destined for the specified 48-bit MAC address written in dotted triplet form.

Syntax	Description
dmac-output-list *access-list-number*	(Optional) Permits the connection to be established only when the explorer frame passes the specified access list. The *access-list-number* is the list number specified in the **access-list** command.
host-netbios-out *host-list-name*	(Optional) Configures NetBIOS host output filtering for this peer. The *host-list-name* is the name of the previously defined NetBIOS host access list filter.
keepalive *seconds*	(Optional) Sets the keepalive interval for this remote peer. The range is 0 to 1200 seconds.
lf *size*	(Optional) Largest frame size, in bytes, this local peer will use on a circuit to avoid segmented frames. Valid sizes are 516, 1470, 1500, 2052, 4472, 8144, 11407, 11454, and 17800 bytes.
linger *minutes*	(Optional) Configures length of time the backup peer remains connected after the primary peer connection is re-established. The valid range is 1 to 300 minutes. The default is 5 minutes.
lsap-output-list *list*	(Optional) Filters output IEEE 802.5 encapsulated packets. Valid access list numbers are in the range 200 to 299.
passive	(Optional) Designates this remote peer as passive.
pass-thru	(Optional) Selects passthrough mode. The default is local acknowledgment mode.

Default

No remote peers are specified.

Command Mode

Global configuration

Usage Guidelines

This command first appeared in Cisco IOS Release 11.0. The following keywords and arguments first appeared in Cisco IOS Release 11.2: **dest-mac** *mac-address*, **dmacoutput-list** *access-list-number* and **linger** *minutes*.

The **cost** keyword specified in a remote peer statement takes precedence over the cost learned as part of the capabilities exchange with the remote peer. The **cost** keyword is relevant only in fault-tolerance mode.

When you need to permit access to only a single MAC address, the **dest-mac** option is a shortcut over the **dmac-output-list** option.

When **pass-thru** is not specified, traffic will be locally acknowledged and reliably transported in LLC2 across the WAN.

Examples

The following example specifies a DLSw Lite peer as a backup to a primary direct peer:

```
dlsw remote-peer 0 frame-relay interface serial 1 40 pass-thru
dlsw remote-peer 0 frame-relay interface serial 0 30 backup-peer frame-relay interface
serial 1 40
```

The following example specifies Frame Relay encapsulation connection for remote peer transport:

```
dlsw remote-peer 0 frame-relay interface 0 30
```

Related Commands

show dlsw peers

DLSW REMOTE-PEER FST

Use the **dlsw remote-peer fst** global configuration command to specify an FST encapsulation connection for remote peer transport. Use the **no** form of this command to disable the previous FST assignments.

> dlsw remote-peer *list-number* **fst** *ip-address* [**backup-peer** [*ip-address* | **frame-relay**
>   **interface serial** *number dlci-number* | **interface** *name*]]
>   [**bytes-netbios-out** *bytes-list-name*] [*cost cost*] [**dest-mac** *mac-address*]
>   [**dmac-output-list** *access-list-number*] [**host-netbios-out** *host-list-name*]
>   [**keepalive** *seconds*] [**lf** *size*] [**linger** *minutes*] [**lsap-output-list** *list*] [**passive**]
> no dlsw remote-peer *list-number* **fst** *ip-address* [**backup-peer** [*ip-address* | **frame-relay**
>   **interface serial** *number dlci-number* | **interface** *name*]]
>   [**bytes-netbios-out** *bytes-list-name*] [*cost cost*] [**dest-mac** *mac-address*]
>   [**dmac-output-list** *access-list-number*] [**host-netbios-out** *host-list-name*]
>   **keepalive** *seconds*] [**lf** *size*] [**linger** *minutes*] [**lsap-output-list** *list*] [**passive**]

Syntax	Description
list-number	Ring-list number. The valid range is 1 to 255. The default is 0, which means DLSw+ forwards explorers over all ports or bridge groups on which DLSw+ is enabled.
ip-address	IP address of the remote peer with which the router is to communicate.
backup-peer *ip-address*	(Optional) IP address of the existing TCP/FST peer for which this peer is the backup peer.

Syntax	Description
backup-peer frame-relay-interface serial *number dlci number*	(Optional) Serial interface and DLCI number of the existing Direct/LLC2 frame-relay peer for which this peer is the backup peer.
backup-peer interface *name*	(Optional) Interface name of the existing direct peer for which this peer is the backup peer.
bytes-netbios-out *bytes-list-name*	(Optional) Configures NetBIOS bytes output filtering for this peer. The *bytes-list-name* argument is the name of the previously defined NetBIOS bytes access list filter.
cost *cost*	(Optional) Cost to reach this remote peer. The valid range is 1 to 5.
dest-mac *mac-address*	(Optional) Permits the connection to be established only when there is an explorer frame destined for the specified 48-bit MAC address written in dotted triplet form.
dmac-output-list *access-list-number*	(Optional) Permits the connection to be established only when the explorer frame passes the specified access list. The *access-list-number* is the list number specified in the **access-list** command.
host-netbios-out *host-list-name*	(Optional) Configures NetBIOS host output filtering for this peer. The *host-list-name* is the name of the previously defined NetBIOS host access list filter.
keepalive *seconds*	(Optional) Sets the keepalive interval for this remote peer. The range is 0 to 1200 seconds.
lf *size*	(Optional) Largest frame size this local peer will use on a circuit to avoid segmented frames. Valid sizes are 516, 1470, 1500, 2052, 4472, 8144, 11407, 11454, and 17800 bytes.
linger *minutes*	(Optional) Configures length of time the backup peer remains connected after the primary peer connection is reestablished. The valid range is 1 to 300 minutes. The default is 5 minutes.
lsap-output-list *list*	(Optional) Filters output IEEE 802.5 encapsulated packets. Valid access list numbers are in the range 200 to 299.
passive	(Optional) Designates this remote peer as passive.

Default

No FST encapsulation connection is specified.

Command Mode

Global configuration

Usage Guidelines

This command first appeared in Cisco IOS Release 10.3. The following keywords and arguments first appeared in Cisco IOS Release 11.2: **dest-mac** *mac-address*, **dmacoutput-list** *access-list-number*, and **linger** *minutes*.

The **cost** keyword specified in a remote peer statement takes precedence over the cost learned as part of the capabilities exchange with the remote peer. The **cost** keyword is relevant only in fault-tolerance mode.

When you need to permit access to a single MAC address, the **dest-mac** option is a shortcut over the **dmac-output-list** option.

Examples

The following example specifies an FST peer as backup to a primary TCP peer:

```
dlsw remote-peer 0 tcp 10.2.18.1
dlsw remote-peer 1 fst 10.2.17.8 backup-peer 10.2.18.1
```

The following example specifies an FST encapsulation connection for remote peer transport:

```
dlsw remote-peer 1 fst 10.2.17.8
```

Related Commands

show dlsw peers

DLSW REMOTE-PEER INTERFACE

Use the **dlsw remote-peer interface** global configuration command when specifying a point-to-point direct encapsulation. Use the **no** form of this command to disable previous interface assignments.

> **dlsw remote-peer** *list-number* **interface serial** *number* [**backup-peer** [*ip-address* | **frame-relay**
> **interface serial** *number dlci-number* | **interface** *name*]] [**bytes-netbios-out**
> *bytes-list-name*] [**cost** *cost*] [**dest-mac** *mac-address*]
> [**dmac-output-list** *access-list-number*] [**host-netbios-out** *host-list-name*]
> [**keepalive** *seconds*] [**lf** *size*] [**linger** *minutes*] [**lsap-output-list** *list*] [**passive**]
> [**pass-thru**]
>
> **no dlsw remote-peer** *list-number* **interface serial** *number* [**backup-peer** [*ip-address* |
> **frame-relay interface serial** *number dlci-number* | **interface** *name*]]
> [**bytes-netbios-out** *bytes-list-name*] [**cost** *cost*] [**dest-mac** *mac-address*]
> [**dmac-output-list** *access-list-number*] [**host-netbios-out** *host-list-name*]
> [**keepalive** *seconds*] [**lf** *size*] [**linger** *minutes*] [**lsap-output-list** *list*] [**passive**]
> [**pass-thru**]

Syntax	Description
list-number	Ring-list number. The valid range is 1 to 255. The default is 0, which means all.
serial *number*	Specifies the remote peer by direct serial interface.
backup-peer *ip-address*	(Optional) IP address of the existing TCP/FST peer for which this peer is the backup peer.
backup-peer frame-relay interface serial *number dlci number*	(Optional) Serial interface and DLCI number of the existing Direct /LLC2 frame relay peer for which this peer is the backup peer.
backup-peer interface *name*	(Optional) Interface name of the existing direct peer for which this peer is the backup peer.
bytes-netbios-out *bytes-list-name*	(Optional) Configures NetBIOS bytes output filtering for this peer. The *bytes-list-name* argument is the name of the previously defined NetBIOS bytes access list filter.
cost *cost*	(Optional) Cost to reach this remote peer. The valid range is 1 to 5.
dest-mac *mac-address*	(Optional) Permits the connection to be established only when there is an explorer frame destined for the specified 48-bit MAC address written in dotted triplet form.
dmac-output-list *access-list-number*	(Optional) Permits the connection to be established only when the explorer frame passes the specified access list. The *access-list-number* is the list number specified in the **access-list** command.
host-netbios-out *host-list-name*	(Optional) Configures NetBIOS host output filtering for this peer. The *host-list-name* is the name of the previously defined NetBIOS host access list filter.
keepalive *seconds*	(Optional) Sets the keepalive interval for this remote peer. The range is 0 to 1200 seconds.
lf *size*	(Optional) Largest frame size, in bytes, this local peer will use on a circuit to avoid segmented frames. Valid sizes are 516, 1470, 1500, 2052, 4472, 8144, 11407, 11454, and 17800 bytes.
linger *minutes*	(Optional) Configures length of time the backup peer remains connected after the primary peer connection is re-established. The valid range is 1 to 300 minutes. The default is 5 minutes.
lsap-output-list *list*	(Optional) Filters output IEEE 802.5 encapsulated packets. Valid access list numbers are in the range 200 to 299.
passive	(Optional) Designates this remote peer as passive.
pass-thru	(Optional) Selects passthrough mode. The default is local acknowledgment mode.

Default

No point-to-point direct encapsulation connection is specified.

Command Mode

Global configuration

Usage Guidelines

This command first appeared in Cisco IOS Release 10.3. The following keywords and arguments first appeared in Cisco IOS Release 11.2: **dest-mac** *mac-address*, **dmacoutput-list** *access-list-number*, **linger** *minutes*.

The **cost** keyword specified in a remote peer statement takes precedence over the cost learned as part of the capabilities exchange with the remote peer. The **cost** keyword is relevant only in fault-tolerance mode.

When you need to permit access to a single MAC address only, the **dest-mac** option is a shortcut over the **dmac-output-list** option.

Examples

The following example specifies a point-to-point direct peer backup to a primary direct peer:

```
dlsw remote-peer 0 interface serial 1 pass-thru
dlsw remote-peer 1 interface serial 2 pass-thru backup-peer interface serial 1
```

The following example specifies a point-to-point direct encapsulation connection for remote peer transport:

```
dlsw remote-peer 1 interface serial 2 pass-thru
```

Related Commands

show dlsw peers

DLSW REMOTE-PEER TCP

Use the **dlsw remote-peer tcp** global configuration command to identify the IP address of a peer with which to exchange traffic using TCP. Use the **no** form of this command to remove a remote peer.

> **dlsw remote-peer** *list-number* **tcp** *ip-address* [**backup-peer** [*ip-address* | **frame-relay**
> **interface serial** *number dlci-number* | **interface** *name*]] [**bytes-netbios-out**
> *bytes-list-name*] [**cost** *cost*] [**dest-mac** *mac-address*]
> [**dmac-output-list** *access-list-number*] [**dynamic**] [**host-netbios-out** *host-list-name*]
> [**inactivity** *minutes*] [**dynamic**] [**keepalive** *seconds*] [**lf** *size*] [**linger** *minutes*]
> [**lsap-output-list** *list*] [**no-llc** *minutes*] [**passive**] [**priority**] [**tcp-queue-max** *size*]
> [**timeout** *seconds*]

no dlsw remote-peer *list-number* tcp *ip-address* [backup-peer [*ip-address* | frame-relay
interface serial *number dlci-number* | interface *name*]] [bytes-netbios-out
bytes-list-name] [cost *cost*] [dest-mac *mac-address*]
[dmac-output-list *access-list-number*] [dynamic]
[host-netbios-out *host-list-name*] [inactivity *minutes*] [dynamic] [keepalive *seconds*]
[lf *size*] [linger *minutes*] [lsap-output-list *list*] [no-llc *minutes*] [passive]
[priority]
[tcp-queue-max *size*] [timeout *seconds*]

Syntax	Description
list-number	Remote peer ring-group list number. This ring-group list number default is 0. Otherwise, this value must match the number you specify with the **dlsw ring-list, dlsw port-list,** or **dlsw bgroup-list** command.
tcp *ip-address*	IP address of the remote peer with which the router is to communicate.
backup-peer *ip-address*	(Optional) IP address of the existing TCP/FST peer for which this peer is the backup peer.
backup-peer frame-relay interface serial *number dlci number*	(Optional) Serial interface and DLCI number of the existing Direct /LLC2 frame relay peer for which this peer is the backup peer.
backup-peer interface *name*	(Optional) Interface name of the existing direct peer for which this peer is the backup peer.
bytes-netbios-out *bytes-list-name*	(Optional) Configures NetBIOS bytes output filtering for this peer. The *bytes-list-name* argument is the name of the previously defined NetBIOS bytes access list filter.
cost *cost*	(Optional) The cost to reach this remote peer. The valid range is 1 to 5.
dest-mac *mac-address*	(Optional) Permits the TCP connection to be established only when there is an explorer frame destined for the specified 48-bit MAC address written in dotted triplet form.
dmac-output-list *access-list-number*	(Optional) Permits the TCP connection to be established only when the explorer frame passes the specified access list. The *access-list-number* is the list number specified in an **access-list** command.
dynamic	(Optional) Permits the TCP connection to be established only when there is DLSw+ data to send.
host-netbios-out *host-list-name*	(Optional) Configures NetBIOS host output filtering for this peer. The *host-list-name* is the name of the previously defined NetBIOS host access list filter.
inactivity *minutes*	(Optional) Configures the length of time a connection can be idle before closing the dynamic remote peer connection. The valid range is 1 to 300 minutes. The default is 5 minutes.

Syntax	Description
keepalive *seconds*	(Required) Sets the keepalive interval for this remote peer. The range is 0 to 1200 seconds.
lf *size*	(Optional) Largest frame size, in bytes, this local peer will use on a circuit to avoid segmented frames. Valid sizes are 516, 1470, 1500, 2052, 4472, 8144, 11407, 11454, and 17800 bytes.
linger *minutes*	(Optional) Configures length of time the backup peer remains connected after the primary peer connection is reestablished. The valid range is 1 to 300 minutes. The default is 5 minutes.
lsap-output-list *list*	(Optional) Filters output IEEE 802.5 encapsulated packets. Valid access list numbers are in the range 200 to 299.
no-llc *minutes*	(Optional) Configures the length of time a remote peer remains connected after all LLC2 connections are gone. The valid range is 1 to 300 minutes. The default is 5 minutes.
passive	(Optional) Designates this remote peer as passive.

Defaults

No peer IP address is identified.

The **linger** option is inactive. If the linger option is added with no minutes specified, the default is 5 minutes.

The **dynamic** option is not on by default. If the dynamic option is added without either the **inactivity** or **no-llc** argument specified, the default is to terminate the TCP connection to the remote peer after 5 minutes of no active LLC2 connection.

Command Mode

Global configuration

Usage Guidelines

This command first appeared in Cisco IOS Release 10.3. The following keywords and arguments first appeared in Cisco IOS Release 11.1: **dynamic, inactivity** *minutes*, **linger** *minutes*, **no-llc** *minutes* and **timeout** *seconds*. The following keywords and arguments first appeared in Cisco IOS Release 11.2: **dest-mac** *mac-address*, **dmac-output-list** *access-list-number*, **linger** *minutes*.

SNA DDR technology allows switched links to be closed during idle periods. To enable this feature, set the **keepalive** option to 0 and configure the **timeout** option. When the **dynamic** option is configured, the **keepalive** option is automatically set to 0.

To enhance DDR cost-savings, you can configure the TCP connection to a remote peer to be dynamically established (that is, established only when there is DLSw data to send). You can further configure the TCP connection to terminate after a specified period of idle time on the peer or after a specified period of no active LLC sessions on the peer.

You cannot use both **no-llc** and **inactivity** in a command specifying a dynamic peer.

When you need to permit access to a single MAC address, the **dest-mac** option is a shortcut over the **dmac-output-list** option.

Use the **linger** option to specify that a backup peer will remain connected for a specified period of time after the primary connection is gone.

When the **priority** option on the **dlsw remote-peer** command is configured, DLSw+ automatically activates four TCP ports to that remote peer (ports 2065, 1981, 1982, and 1983) and assigns traffic to specific ports. Furthermore, if APPN is running with DLSw+ and you specify the **priority** option on the **dlsw remote-peer** command, then the SNA TOS will map APPN class of service (COS) to TCP TOS and will preserve the APPN COS characteristics throughout the network.

Examples

The following example specifies a TCP peer as backup to a primary FST peer:

```
dlsw remote-peer 0 fst 10.2.18.9
dlsw remote-peer 1 tcp 10.2.17.8 backup-peer 10.2.18.9
```

The following example specifies a TCP encapsulation connection for remote peer transport:

```
dlsw remote-peer 1 tcp 10.2.17.8
```

The following is an example policy routing configuration that shows how to modify the default setting of TCP port 2065. The configuration changes the default setting on IP packets from network control precedence to routine precedence.

```
ip local policy route-map test
access-list 101 permit tcp any eq 2065 any
access-list 101 permit tcp any any eq 2065
route-map test permit 20
match ip address 101
set ip precedence routine
```

Related Commands

show dlsw peers

DLSW RING-LIST

Use the **dlsw ring-list** to configure a ring list, mapping traffic on a local interface to remote peers. Use the **no** form of this command to cancel the definition.

> **dlsw ring-list** *list-number* **rings** *ring-number*
> **no dlsw ring-list** *list-number* **rings** *ring-number*

Default

There is no default setting.

Syntax	Description
list-number	Ring-list number. The valid range is 1 to 255.
rings	Specify one or more physical or virtual rings.

Command Mode

Global configuration

Usage Guidelines

This command first appeared in Cisco IOS Release 11.0.

Traffic received from a remote peer is forwarded only to the rings specified in the ring list. Traffic received from a local interface is forwarded to peers if the input ring number appears in the ring list applied to the remote peer definition. The definition of a ring list is optional.

Example

The following example configures a DLSw ring list, assigning rings 1, 2, and 3 to ring list 3:

```
dlsw ring-list 3 rings 1 2 3
```

Related Commands

dlsw port-list
show dlsw capabilities
dlsw remote-peer frame relay

DLSW TIMER

Use the **dlsw timer** global configuration command to tune an existing configuration parameter. Use the **no** form of this command to restore the default parameters.

dlsw timer {icannotreach-block-time | netbios-cache-timeout | netbios-explorer-timeout |
    netbios-group-cache | netbios-retry-interval | netbios-verify-interval |
    sna-cache-timeout | explorer-delay-time | sna-explorer-timeout | explorer-wait-time |
    sna-group-cache | sna-retry-interval | sna-verify-interval} *time*
no dlsw timer {icannotreach-block-time | netbios-cache-timeout |
    netbios-explorer-timeout | netbios-group-cache | netbios-retry-interval |
    netbios-verify-interval | sna-cache-timeout | explorer-delay-time |
    sna-explorer-timeout | explorer-wait-time | sna-group-cache | sna-retry-interval |
    sna-verify-interval} *time*

Syntax	Description
icannotreach-block-time	Cache life of unreachable resource; during this time searches for the resource are blocked. The valid range is 1 to 86400 seconds. The default is 0 (disabled).
netbios-cache-timeout	Cache life of NetBIOS name location for the local and remote reachability caches. The valid range is 1 to 86400 seconds. The default is 960 seconds (16 minutes).
netbios-explorer-timeout	Length of time that the Cisco IOS software waits for an explorer response before marking a resource unreachable (on both a LAN and a WAN). The valid range is 1 to 86400 seconds. The default is 6 seconds.
netbios-group-cache	Cache life of NetBIOS entries in the group cache. The valid range is 1 to 86000 seconds. The default is 240 seconds (4 minutes).
netbios-retry-interval	NetBIOS explorer retry interval (on a LAN only). The valid range is 1 to 86400 seconds. The default is 1 second.
netbios-verify-interval	Number of seconds between a cache entry's creation and its marking as stale. If a search request comes in for a stale cache entry, a directed verify query is sent to ensure the cache still exists. The valid range is 1 to 86400 seconds. The default is 240 seconds (4 minutes).
sna-cache-timeout	Length of time that an SNA MAC/service access point (SAP) location cache entry exists before it is discarded (for local and remote caches). The valid range is 1 to 86400 seconds. The default is 960 seconds (16 minutes).
explorer-delay-time	Time to wait before sending or accepting explorers. The valid range is 1 to 5 minutes. The default is 0.
sna-group-cache	Cache life of SNA entries in the group cache. The valid range is 1 to 86000 seconds. The default is 240 seconds (4 minutes).
sna-explorer-timeout	Length of time that the Cisco IOS software waits for an explorer response before marking a resource unreachable (on a LAN and WAN). The valid range is 1 to 86400 seconds. The default is 180 seconds (3 minutes).
explorer-wait-time	Time to wait for all stations to respond to explorers. The valid range is 1 to 86400 seconds. The default is 0.
sna-retry-interval	Interval between SNA explorer retries (on a LAN). The valid range is 1 to 86400 seconds. The default is 30 seconds.
sna-verify-interval	Number of seconds between a cache entry's creation and its marking as stale. If a search request comes in for a stale cache entry, a directed verify query is sent to ensure that the cache still exists. The valid range is 1 to 86400 seconds. The default is 240 seconds (4 minutes).

Command Mode

Global configuration

Usage Guidelines

This command first appeared in Cisco IOS Release 10.3.

The **netbios-group-cache** and **sna-group-cache** options were added to this command for the Border Peer Caching feature.

Examples

The following configuration defines the length of time that an entry will stay in the group cache as 120 seconds (2 minutes):

```
dlsw timers sna-group-cache 120
```

The following example configures the length of time that an SNA MAC location cache entry exists before it is discarded:

```
dlsw timer sna-cache-timeout 3
```

DLSW UDP-DISABLE

Use the **dlsw udp-disable** global configuration command to disable the UDP Unicast feature. Use the **no** form of this command to return to the default UDP Unicast feature.

dlsw udp-disable
no dlsw udp-disable

Syntax   Description

This command has no arguments or keywords.

Default

The UDP Unicast feature is enabled.

Command Mode

Global configuration

Usage Guidelines

This command first appeared in Cisco IOS Release 11.2 F.

If the **dlsw udp-disable** command is configured, then a DLSw+ node will not send packets via UDP Unicast and will not advertise UDP Unicast support in its capabilities exchange message.

See "Bridging and IBM Networking Overview" at the beginning of this book for more information on the UDP Unicast feature.

Example

The following example disables the UDP Unicast feature:

```
dlsw udp-disable
```

QLLC DLSW

Use the **qllc dlsw** interface configuration command to enable DLSw+ over Qualified Logical Link Control (QLLC). Use the **no** form of this command to cancel the configuration.

> **qllc dlsw** {**subaddress** *subaddress* | **pvc** *pvc-low* [*pvc-high*]} [**vmac** *vmacaddr*
>   [*poolsize*]] [**partner** *partner-macaddr*] [**sap** *ssap dsap*] [**xid** *xidstring*] [**npsi-poll**]
> **no qllc dlsw** {**subaddress** *subaddress* | **pvc** *pvc-low* [*pvc-high*]} [**vmac** *vmacaddr*
>   [*poolsize*]] [**partner** *partner-macaddr*] [**sap** *ssap dsap*] [**xid** *xidstring*] [**npsi-poll**]

Syntax	Description
subaddress *subaddress*	An X.121 subaddress.
pvc	Map one or more permanent virtual circuits (PVCs) to a particular QLLC service (in this case DLSw+). QLLC will attempt to reach the partner by sending and ID.STN.IND to DLSw+.
pvc-low	Lowest logical channel number (LCN) for a range of X.25 PVCs. Acceptable values for PVCs are decimal numbers between 1 and 4095. There is no default value.
pvc-high	(Optional) Highest LCN. If not specified the range of PVCs consists of just one PVC.
vmac *vmacaddr*	(Optional) Defines either the only virtual MAC address used for DLSw+ or the lowest virtual MAC address in a pool of virtual MAC addresses.
poolsize	(Optional) Specify the number of contiguous virtual MAC addresses that have been reserved for DLSw+. If the parameter is not present, then just one virtual MAC address is available.
partner *partner-macaddr*	Virtual MAC address to which an incoming call wishes to connect. The **qllc dlsw** command must be repeated for each different partner. Each partner is identified by a unique subaddress.
sap *ssap dsap*	Overrides the default SAP values (04) for a Token Ring connection. *dsap* refers to the partner's SAP address; *ssap* applies to the virtual MAC address that corresponds to the X.121 device.
xid *xidstring*	XID format 0 type 2 string.
npsi-poll	Inhibits forwarding a null XID on the X.25 link. Instead the Cisco IOS software will send a null XID response back to the device that sent the null XID command.

Default

No defaults are specified.

Command Mode

Interface configuration

Usage Guidelines

This command first appeared in Cisco IOS Release 11.0.

Any incoming call whose X.121 destination address matches the router's X.121 address and this subaddress will be dispatched to DLSw+ (with an ID.STN IND). If a router is providing several QLLC services, different subaddresses must be used to discriminate between them. Subaddresses can be used even if a remote X.25 device is not explicitly mapped to a specific virtual MAC address. This is most useful when PU 2.1 devices are connecting to a host because the X.25 device's control point name and network name are used to validate the connection, rather than some virtual MAC address. The subaddress is optional. If no subaddress is provided, any incoming call that matches the router's X.121 address will be dispatched to DLSw+. On outgoing calls, the subaddress is concatenated to the interface's X.121 address.

When DLSw+ receives a Can You Reach inquiry about a virtual MAC address in the pool, the QLLC code will attempt to set up a virtual circuit to the X.121 address that maps to the virtual MAC address specified. If an incoming call is received, QLLC sends an ID.STN.IND with a virtual MAC address from the pool to DLSw+. If there is no virtual MAC address, then the **x25 map qllc** or **x25 pvc qllc** command must provide a virtual MAC address.

The **npsi-poll** parameter is needed to support PU 2.0 on the partner side that wishes to connect to a FEP on the X.25 side. In a Token Ring or DLSw+ environment, the PU 2.0 will send a null XID to the FEP. If the software forwards this null XID to an X.25 attached FEP, the FEP will assume that it is connecting to PU2.1, and will break off the connection when the PU 2.0 next send an XID Format 0 Type 2.

Example

The following commands assign virtual MAC address 1000.0000.0001 to a remote X.25-attached 3174, which is then mapped to the X.121 address of the 3174 (31104150101) in an X.25-attached router:

```
interface serial 0
  x25 address 3110212011
  x25 map qllc 1000.000.0001 31104150101
  qllc dlsw partner 4000.1161.1234
```

SDLC DLSW

Use the **sdlc dlsw** interface configuration command to attach SDLC addresses to DLSw+. Use the **no** form of this command to cancel the configuration.

sdlc dlsw {*sdlc-address* | **default** | **partner** *mac address* [**inbound** | **outbound**]}
no sdlc dlsw {sdlc-*address* | **default** | **partner** *mac address* [**inbound** | **outbound**]}

Syntax	Description
sdlc-address	SDLC address in hexadecimal. The valid range is 1 to FE.
default	Allows the user to configure an unlimited number of SDLC addresses to DLSw+.
partner *mac address*	MAC address for default partner.
inbound	Partner will initiate connection.
outbound	Initiate connection to partner.

Default

No correspondence is defined.

Command Mode

Interface configuration

Usage Guidelines

This command first appeared in Cisco IOS Release 11.0.

Examples

The following command attaches SDLC address d2 to DLSw+:

```
sdlc dlsw d2
```

The following command attaches SDLC addresses d2, d5, e3, e4, e6, b1, c3, d4, a1, and a5:

```
sdlc dlsw d2 d5 e3 e4 e6 b1 c3 d4 a1 a5
```

Related Commands

encapsulation sdlc
sdlc address
sdlc role

SHOW DLSW CAPABILITIES

Use the **show dlsw capabilities** privileged EXEC command to display the configuration of a specific peer or all peers.

show dlsw capabilities [**interface** *type number* | **ip-address** *ip-address* | **local**]

Syntax	Description
interface	(Optional) Specifies the interface for which the DLSw+ capabilities are to be displayed.
type	Interface type is indicated by the keyword *serial*.
number	Interface number.
ip-address *ip-address*	(Optional) Specifies a peer by its IP address.
local	(Optional) Specifies the local DLSw+ peer.

Command Mode

Privileged EXEC

Usage Guidelines

This command first appeared in Cisco IOS Release 10.3.

Sample Display

The following is sample output from the **show dlsw capabilities** command:

```
Router# show dlsw capabilities

DLSw: Capabilities for peer 1.1.1.6(2065)
   vendor id (OUI)        : '00C' (cisco)
   version number         : 1
   release number         : 0
   init pacing window     : 20
   unsupported saps       : none
   num of tcp sessions    : 1
   loop prevent support   : no
   icanreach mac-exclusive : no
   icanreach netbios-excl. : no
   reachable mac addresses : none
   reachable netbios names : none
   cisco version number   : 1
   peer group number      : 0
   border peer capable    : no
   peer cost              : 3
   biu-segment configured : no
   UDP Unicast support    : yes
   local-ack configured   : yes
   priority configured    : no
   configured ip address  : 1.1.1.6
   peer type              : conf
   version string         :
```

Table 8–1 describes significant fields shown from the **show dlsw capabilities** command.

Table 8–1 *Show DLSw Capabilities Field Descriptions*

Field	Description
vendor id (OUI)	Vendor ID.
version number	RFC 1795 version of SSP protocol.
release number	RFC 1795 release of SSP protocol
init pacing window	Initial pacing window.
unsupported saps	Unsupported SAPs.
num of tcp sessions	Number of TCP sessions.
loop prevent support	No loop prevent support.
icanreach mac-exclusive	Configured MAC addresses that the router can reach
icanreach netbios-excl.	Configured NetBIOS names that the router can reach
reachable mac addresses	Reachable MAC addresses.
reachable netbios name	Reachable NetBIOS names.
cisco version number	Cisco version number.
peer group number	Peer group member number.
border peer capable	Border peer capability.
peer cost	Peer cost.
biu-segment configured	BIU segment configured.
UDP Unicast support	UDP unicast support.
local-ack configured	Local acknowledgment capable.
priority configured	Priority capability.
configured ip address	Configured IP address.
peer type	Peer type can be peer-on-demand or promiscuous.
version string	Cisco IOS software version information.

SHOW DLSW CIRCUITS

Use the **show dlsw circuits** privileged EXEC command to display the state of all circuits involving this MAC address as a source and destination.

      show dlsw circuits [**detail**] [**mac-address** *address* | **sap-value** *value* | **circuit ID**]

Syntax	Description
detail	(Optional) Display circuit state information in expanded format.
mac-address *address*	(Optional) Specifies the MAC address to be used in the circuit search.
sap-value *value*	(Optional) Specifies the SAP to be used in the circuit search.
circuit id	(Optional) Specifies the circuit ID of the circuit index.

Command Mode

Privileged EXEC

Usage Guidelines

This command first appeared in Cisco IOS Release 10.3.

Sample Displays

The following is sample output from the **show dlsw circuits** command:

```
Router# show dlsw circuits

Index    local addr(lsap)     remote addr(dsap)    state
75    1000.5acc.5acc(F0)   1000.5acc.800d(F0)   CONNECTED
119   1000.5acc.88ea(04)   1000.5acc.800d(08)   CONNECTED
121   4006.315b.568e(F0)   0006.311d.eea1(F0)   CONNECTED
```

The following is sample output from the **show dlsw circuits** command with the **detail** argument:

```
Router# show dlsw circuits detail

Index    local addr(lsap)      remote addr(dsap)     state
194 0800.5a9b.b3b2(F0)   0800.5ac1.302d(F0)   CONNECTED
         PCEP: 995AA4      UCEP: A52274
         Port: To0/0       peer 172.18.15.166(2065)
         Flow-Control-Tx CW:20, Permitted:28; Rx CW:22, Granted:25
         RIF = 0680.0011.0640
```

Table 8–2 describes significant fields shown in the display.

Table 8–2 *Show DLSw Circuits Field Descriptions*

Field	Description
Index	Index = 4D00
local addr (lsap)	Local Address (LSAP) = 4006.313c.a07f (F0)
remote addr (dsap)	Remote Address (DSAP) = 0800.5a8f.8822
state	Connected

SHOW DLSW FASTCACHE

Use the **show dlsw fastcache** privileged EXEC command to display the fast cache for FST and direct-encapsulated peers.

> **show dlsw fastcache**

Syntax   Description

This command has no arguments or keywords.

Command Mode

Privileged EXEC

Usage Guidelines

This command first appeared in Cisco IOS Release 11.0.

Sample Display

The following is sample output from the **show dlsw fastcache** command with an FST peer:

```
Router# show dlsw fastcache

    peer                 local-mac        remote-mac    l/r sap rif
 FST 10.2.32.1         0800.5a8f.881c 0800.5a8f.8822  04/04   0680.02D5.1360
```

The following is sample output from the **show dlsw fastcache** command:

```
Router# show dlsw fastcache

    peer                 local-mac        remote-mac    l/r sap rif
 IF Se1 0800.5a8f.881c  0800.5a8f.8822 F0/F0 0680.02D5.1360
```

Table 8–3 describes significant fields shown in the display.

Table 8–3 *Show DLSw Fastcache Field Descriptions*

Field	Description
peer	The FST peer in which the router is connected. Could represent either an ip address or interface.
local-mac	Local MAC address
remote-mac	Remote MAC address
l/r sap	Local/remote SAP value.
rif	RIF value.

SHOW DLSW PEERS

Use the **show dlsw peers** privileged EXEC command to display DLSw peer information.

   show dlsw peers [**interface** *type number* | ip-address *ip-address* | **udp**]

Syntax	Description
interface	(Optional) Specifies the interface for which the DLSw+ peer information is to be displayed.
type	Interface type, indicated by the keyword *serial*.
number	Interface number.
ip-address *ip-address*	(Optional) Specifies a remote peer by its IP address.
udp	(Optional) Specifies a remote peer by its UDP capabilities.

Command Mode

Privileged EXEC

Usage Guidelines

This command first appeared in Cisco IOS Release 11.0.

Sample Displays

The following is sample output from the **show dlsw peers** command:

```
Router# show dlsw peers udp

Peers:  tot-Q'd  total-rx  total-tx  tot-retx  tot-drop  curr-Q'd TCP
1.1.1.602300000
```

The following is sample output from the **show dlsw peers** command with a TCP connection:

```
Router# show dlsw peers ip-address 10.2.32.1

Peers:              state pkts_rx  pkts_tx  type  drops
  TCP 10.2.32.1     CONNECT 79170   50816  conf    0
```

The following is sample output from the **show dlsw peers** command with a Direct Frame Relay connection:

```
Router # show dlsw peers

Peers:              state pkts_rx pkts_tx  type  drops ckts TCP uptime
  IF SE116connect652597conf0--00:04:09
```

The following is sample output from the **show dlsw peers** command with a Direct Frame Relay with local acknowledgment (LLC2) connection:

```
Router # show dlsw peers

Peers:              state pkts_rx pkts_tx  type  drops ckts TCP uptime
LLC2 SE116connect1179108conf01-00:04:09
```

Table 8–4 describes the significant fields shown in the **show dlsw peers** command display.

Table 8–4 *Show DLSw Peers Field Descriptions*

Field	Description
Peers	Information related to the remote peer, including encapsulation type, IP address (if using FST or TCP), and interface number (if using direct encapsulation).
tot-Q'd	Number of UDP packets that have been queued because of TCP congestion.
total-rx	Number UDP packets received from the peer.
total-tx	Number of UDP packets transmitted to the peer.
tot-retx	Number of reachability retransmits (for example, DLSw+ retries NQ_ex and CUR_ex) when originally sent via UDP.
tot-drop	Number of queued UDP packets that were dropped because of persistent TCP congestion.
curr-Q'd	Number of current UDP packets queued because of TCP congestion.
TCP	Number of packets currently on TCP output queue.
state	State of the peer: CONNECT: normal working peer DISCONN: peer is not connected CAP_EXG: capabilities exchange mode. Waiting for capabilities response. WAIT_RD: TCP write pipe (local port 2065) is open and peer is waiting for remote peer to open the read port (local port 2067). This field applies only to TCP peers. WAN_BUSY: TCP outbound queue is full. This field applies only to TCP peers.
pkts_rx	Number of received packets.
pkts_tx	Number of transmitted packets.
type	Type of remote peer: conf : configured prom : promiscuous pod : peer on demand

Table 8-4 *Show DLSw Peers Field Descriptions, Continued*

Field	Description
drops	The number of drops done by this peer. Reasons for the counter to increment: • WAN interface not up for a direct peer. • DLSW tries to send a packet before the peer is fully connected (waiting for TCP event or capabilities event). • Outbound TCP queue full. • FST sequence number count mismatch. • Cannot get buffer to "slow switch" FST packet. • CiscoBus controller failure on high end (cannot move packet from receive buffer to transmit buffer, or vice versa). • Destination IP address of FST packet does not match local peer-ID. • WAN interface not up for an FST peer. • No SRB route cache command configured. • Madge ring buffer is full on low end systems (WAN feeding LAN too fast).
uptime	How long the connection has been established to this peer.
ckts	Number of active circuits through this peer. This field applies only to TCP and LLC2 transport peer types.

SHOW DLSW REACHABILITY

Use the **show dlsw reachability** privileged EXEC command to display DLSw reachability information.

> **show dlsw reachability** [[**group** [*value*] | **local** | **remote**] | [**mac-address** [*address*] [**netbios-names** [*name*]]

Syntax	Description
group	(Optional) Displays contents of group reachability cache only.
value	(Optional) Specifies the group number for the reachability check. Only displays group cache entries for the specified group. The valid range is 1 to 255.
local	(Optional) Displays contents of local reachability cache only.
remote	(Optional) Displays contents of remote reachability cache only.
mac-address	(Optional) Displays DLSw reachability for MAC addresses only.
address	(Optional) Specifies the MAC address for which to search in the reachability cache.

Part II

Command Reference

Syntax	Description
netbios-names	(Optional) Displays DLSw reachability for NetBIOS names only.
name	(Optional) Specifies the NetBIOS name for which to search in the reachability cache.

Command Mode
Privileged EXEC

Usage Guidelines
This command first appeared in Cisco IOS Release 11.0.

If none of the group, local, or remote options are specified, then the caches will be displayed in the following order: local, remote, and group.

Sample Displays
The following is sample output from the **show dlsw reachability group** command:

```
router# show dlsw reachability group

DLSw Group MAC address reachability cache list
Mac Addr Group
0000.3072.1070      10
DLSW Group NetBIOS Name reachability cache list
NetBIOS Name    Group
```

The following is sample output from the **show dlsw reachability** command:

```
Router# show dlsw reachability

DLSw MAC address reachability cache list
Mac Addr        status     Loc.    peer/port        rif
0000.f641.91e8  SEARCHING  LOCAL
0006.7c9a.7a48  FOUND      LOCAL   TokenRing0/0     0CB0.0011.3E71.A041.0DE5.0640
0800.5a4b.1cbc  SEARCHING  LOCAL
0800.5a54.ee59  SEARCHING  LOCAL
0800.5a8f.9c3f  FOUND      LOCAL   TokenRing0/0     08B0.A041.0DE5.0640
4000.0000.0050  FOUND      LOCAL   TokenRing0/0     0CB0.0011.3E71.A041.0DE5.0640
4000.0000.0306  FOUND      LOCAL   TokenRing0/0     0CB0.0011.3E71.A041.0DE5.0640
4000.0000.0307  SEARCHING  LOCAL
4000.0000.0308  SEARCHING  LOCAL
4000.1234.56c1  FOUND      LOCAL   Serial3/7        --no rif--
4000.1234.56c2  FOUND      LOCAL   Serial3/7        --no rif--
4000.3000.0100  FOUND      LOCAL   TokenRing0/0     08B0.A041.0DE5.0640
4000.4000.ff40  SEARCHING  LOCAL
4000.7470.00e7  SEARCHING  LOCAL
4000.ac0b.0001  FOUND      LOCAL   TokenRing0/0     08B0.A041.0DE5.0640
4001.0000.0064  FOUND      LOCAL   TokenRing0/0     0CB0.0011.3E71.A041.0DE5.0640
4001.3745.1088  FOUND      LOCAL   TokenRing0/0     08B0.A041.0DE5.0640
```

```
4100.0131.1030  FOUND      LOCAL   TokenRing0/0
10B0.FFF1.4041.0041.3E71.A041.0DE5.0640

DLSw NetBIOS Name reachability cache list
NetBIOS Name   status   Loc.   peer/port       rif
APPNCLT2       FOUND    LOCAL  TokenRing0/0   08B0.A041.0DE5.0640
```

The following is sample output from the **show dlsw reachability** command with the **mac-address** argument:

```
Router# show dlsw reachability mac-address 4000.00000306

DLSw MAC address reachability cache list
Mac Addr        status   Loc.   peer/port       rif
4000.0000.0306  FOUND    LOCAL  TokenRing0/0   0CB0.0011.3E71.A041.0DE5.0640
```

The following is sample output from the **show dlsw reachability** command with the **netbios-names** argument:

```
Router# show dlsw reachability netbios-names

DLSw NetBIOS Name reachability cache list
NetBIOS Name   status   Loc.   peer/port       rif
APPNCLT2       FOUND    LOCAL  TokenRing0/0   08B0.A041.0DE5.0640
```

Table 8–5 describes the significant fields shown in the **show dlsw reachability** command.

Table 8–5 *Show DLSw Reachability Field Descriptions*

Field	Description
Mac Addr	MAC address of station being sought (destination MAC address of canureach_ex packet).
NetBIOS Name	NetBIOS name of station being sought (destination MAC address of NQ_ex packet).
status	Result of station search. The status can be one of the following: • FOUND: Station has recently sent a broadcast or responded to a broadcast. • SEARCHING: Router has sent broadcast to this station and is waiting for a response. • NOT_FOUND: Negative caching is on, and the station has not responded to queries. • UNCONFIRMED: Station is configured, but DLSw has not verified it. • VERIFY: Cache information is being verified because cache is going stale, or the user configuration is being verified.
Loc.	Location of station. LOCAL indicates that the station is on the local network. REMOTE indicates that the station is on the remote network.

Table 8–5   *Show DLSw Reachability Field Descriptions, Continued*

Field	Description
peer/port	Peer/port number. If the Loc. field lists a REMOTE station, the peer/port field indicates the peer through which the remote station is reachable. If the Loc. field lists a LOCAL station, the peer/port field indicates the port through which the local station is reachable. For ports, the port number and slot number are given. Pxxx-Syyy denotes port xxx slot yyy. If the station is reachable through a bridge group, that is shown by TBridge-xxx.
rif	Shows the RIF in the cache. This column applies only to LOCAL stations. If the station was reached through a medium that does not support RIFs (such as SDLC or Ethernet) then "--no rif--" is shown.

SHOW DLSW STATISTICS

Use the **show dlsw statistics** privileged EXEC command to display the number of frames that have been processed in the local, remote, and group cache.

> **show dlsw statistics [border-peers]**

Syntax	*Description*
border-peers	(Optional) Displays the number of frames processed in the local, remote, and group caches.

Command Mode

Privileged EXEC

Usage Guidelines

This command first appeared in Cisco IOS Release 11.2 F.

Example

The following sample displays the number of frames processed in the local, remote, and group cache:

```
router# show dlsw statistics border-peers

100 Border Peer Frames processed
10 Border frames found Local
20 Border frames found Remote
17 Border frames found Group Cache
```

CHAPTER 9

Configuring Serial Tunnel and Block Serial Tunnel

Cisco's serial tunnel (STUN) implementation allows Synchronous Data Link Control (SDLC) protocol devices and High-Level Data Link Control (HDLC) devices to connect to one another through a multiprotocol internetwork rather than through a direct serial link. STUN encapsulates SDLC frames in either the Transmission Control Protocol/Internet Protocol (TCP/IP) or the HDLC protocol. STUN provides a straight passthru of all SDLC traffic (including control frames, such as Receiver Ready) end-to-end between Systems Network Architecture (SNA) devices.

Cisco's SDLC local acknowledgment provides local termination of the SDLC session so that control frames no longer travel the WAN backbone networks. This means end nodes do not time out, and a loss of sessions does not occur. You can configure your network with STUN, or with STUN and SDLC local acknowledgment. To enable SDLC local acknowledgment, the Cisco IOS software must first be enabled for STUN and routers configured to appear on the network as primary or secondary SDLC nodes. TCP/IP encapsulation must be enabled. Cisco's SDLC Transport feature also provides priority queuing for TCP encapsulated frames.

Cisco's block serial tunnel (BSTUN) implementation enables Cisco series 2500, 4000, and 4500, 4700, 7200 routers to support devices that use the Binary Synchronous Communications (Bisync) datalink protocol and asynchronous security protocols that include Adplex, ADT Security Systems, Inc., Diebold, and asynchronous generic traffic. BSTUN implementation is also supported on the 4T network interface module (NIM) on the Cisco series 4000 and 4500. Cisco's support of the bisync protocol enables enterprises to transport Bisync traffic and SNA multiprotocol traffic over the same network.

This chapter describes how to configure STUN and BSTUN. For a complete description of the STUN and BSTUN commands in this chapter, see Chapter 10, "Serial Tunnel and Block Serial Tunnel Commands."

STUN CONFIGURATION TASK LIST

To configure and monitor STUN, or STUN local acknowledgment, complete the tasks in the following sections:

- Enabling STUN
- Configuring SDLC Broadcast
- Specifying STUN Protocol Group
- Enabling STUN Interfaces
- Establishing the Frame Encapsulation Method
- Configuring STUN with Multilink Transmission Groups
- Setting Up STUN Traffic Priorities
- Monitoring STUN Network Activity

The "STUN Configuration Examples" section follows these configuration tasks.

ENABLING STUN

To enable STUN, perform the following task in global configuration mode:

Task	Command
Enable STUN for a particular IP address.	**stun peer-name** *ip-address*

When configuring redundant links, ensure that the STUN peer names you choose on each router are the IP addresses of the most stable interfaces on each device, such as a loopback or Ethernet interface. See "STUN Configuration Examples" later in this chapter.

CONFIGURING SDLC BROADCAST

The SDLC broadcast feature allows SDLC broadcast address FF to be replicated for each of the STUN peers, so each of the end stations receives the broadcast frame. For example, in Figure 9–1, the FEP views the end stations 1, 2, and 3 as if they are on an SDLC multidrop link. Any broadcast frame sent from the FEP to Router A is duplicated and sent to each of the downstream routers (B and C).

Figure 9–1
SDLC Broadcast across
virtual multidrop lines.

To enable SDLC broadcast, perform the following task in interface configuration mode:

Task	Command
Enable SDLC broadcast.	**sdlc virtual-multidrop**

Only enable SDLC broadcast on the device that is configured to be the secondary station on the SDLC link (Router A in Figure 9–1).

You must also configure SDLC address FF on Router A for each of the STUN peers. To do so, perform the following task in interface configuration mode:

Task	Command
Configure SDLC address FF on Router A for each STUN peer.	**stun route address** *address-number* **tcp** *ip-address* [**local-ack**] [**priority**] [**tcp-queue-max**]

SPECIFYING STUN PROTOCOL GROUP

Place each STUN interface in a group that defines the ISO 3309-compliant framed protocol running on that link. Packets will travel only between STUN interfaces that are in the same protocol group.

There are three predefined STUN protocols:

- Basic
- SDLC
- SDLC transmission group

You also can specify a custom STUN protocol.

If you want to use the STUN Local Acknowledgment feature, you must specify either the SDLC protocol or the SDLC transmission group protocol.

─ NOTES ───

Before you can specify a custom protocol, you must first define the protocol. See the "Creating and Specifying a Custom STUN Protocol" section later in this chapter for the procedure.

Specifying a Basic STUN Group

The basic STUN protocol does not depend on the details of serial protocol addressing and is used when addressing is unimportant. Use this when your goal is to replace one or more sets of point-to-point (not multidrop) serial links by using a protocol other than SDLC. Perform the following task in global configuration mode:

Task	Command
Specify a basic protocol group and assign a group number.	**stun protocol-group** *group-number* **basic**

Specifying an SDLC Group

You can specify SDLC protocol groups to associate interfaces with the SDLC protocol. Use the SDLC STUN protocol to place the routers in the midst of either point-to-point or multipoint (multidrop) SDLC links. To define an SDLC protocol group, perform the following task in global configuration mode:

Task	Command
Specify an SDLC protocol group and assign a group number.	**stun protocol-group** *group-number* **sdlc**

If you specify an SDLC protocol group, you cannot specify the **stun route all** command on any interface of that group.

For an example of how to configure an SDLC protocol group, see "Configuring Serial Link Address Prioritization Using STUN TCP/IP Encapsulation Example" later in this chapter.

Specifying an SDLC Transmission Group

An SNA transmission group is a set of lines providing parallel links to the same pair of SNA front-end-processor (FEP) devices. This provides redundancy of paths for fault tolerance and load sharing. To define an SDLC transmission group, perform the following task in global configuration mode:

Task	Command
Specify an SDLC protocol group, assign a group number, and create an SNA transmission group.	**stun protocol-group** *group-number* **sdlc sdlc-tg**

All STUN connections in a transmission group must connect to the same IP address and use the SDLC local acknowledgment feature.

Creating and Specifying a Custom STUN Protocol

To define a custom protocol and tie STUN groups to the new protocol, perform the following tasks in global configuration mode:

Task	Command
Step 1 Create a custom protocol.	**stun schema** *name* **offset** *constant-offset* **length** *address-length* **format** *format-keyword*
Step 2 Specify the custom protocol group and assign a group number.	**stun protocol-group** *group-number* **schema**

ENABLING STUN INTERFACES

You must enable STUN on serial interfaces and place these interfaces in the protocol groups you have defined. To enable STUN on an interface and to place the interface in a STUN group, perform the following tasks in interface configuration mode:

Task	Command
Step 1 Enable STUN function on a serial interface.	**encapsulation stun**
Step 2 Place the interface in a previously defined STUN group.	**stun group** *group-number*

When a given serial link is configured for the STUN function, it is no longer a shared multiprotocol link. All traffic that arrives on the link will be transported to the corresponding peer as determined by the current STUN configuration.

ESTABLISHING THE FRAME ENCAPSULATION METHOD

To allow SDLC frames to travel across a multimedia, multiprotocol network, you must encapsulate them using one of the methods in the following sections:

- Configuring HDLC Encapsulation Without Local Acknowledgment
- Configuring TCP Encapsulation Without Local Acknowledgment
- Configuring TCP Encapsulation with SDLC Local Acknowledgment and Priority Queuing
- Configuring Local Acknowledgment for Direct Frame Relay Connectiviity

Configuring HDLC Encapsulation Without Local Acknowledgment

You can encapsulate SDLC or HDLC frames using the HDLC protocol. The outgoing serial link can still be used for other kinds of traffic. The frame is not TCP encapsulated. To configure HDLC encapsulation, perform one of the following tasks in interface configuration mode:

Task	Command
Forward all HDLC or SDLC traffic of the identified interface number.	**stun route all interface serial** *number*
Forward all HDLC or SDLC traffic on a direct STUN link.	**stun route all interface serial** *number* **direct**
Forward HDLC or SDLC traffic of the identified address.	**stun route address** *address-number* **interface serial** *number*
Forward HDLC or SDLC traffic of the identified address across a direct STUN link.	**stun route address** *address-number* **interface serial** *number* **direct**

Use the **no** forms of these commands to disable HDLC encapsulation.

> **NOTES**
>
> You can forward all traffic only when you are using basic STUN protocol groups.

Configuring TCP Encapsulation without Local Acknowledgment

If you do not want to use SDLC local acknowledgment and only need to forward all SDLC frames encapsulated in TCP, complete the following tasks in interface configuration mode:

Task	Command
Step 1 Forward all TCP traffic for this IP address.	**stun route all tcp** *ip-address*
Step 2 Specify TCP encapsulation.	**stun route address** *address-number* **tcp** *ip-address* [**local-ack**] [**priority**] [**tcp-queue-max**]

Use the **no** form of these commands to disable forwarding of all TCP traffic.

This configuration is typically used when two routers can be connected via an IP network as opposed to a point-to-point link.

Configuring TCP Encapsulation with SDLC Local Acknowledgment and Priority Queuing

You configure SDLC local acknowledgment using TCP encapsulation. When you configure SDLC local acknowledgment, you also have the option to enable support for priority queuing.

NOTES

To enable SDLC local acknowledgment, you must specify an SDLC or SDLC transmission group.

SDLC local acknowledgment provides local termination of the SDLC session so that control frames no longer travel the WAN backbone networks. This means that time-outs are less likely to occur.

Figure 9–2 illustrates an SDLC session. IBM 1, using a serial link, can communicate with IBM 2 on a different serial link separated by a wide-area backbone network. Frames are transported between Router A and Router B using STUN, but the SDLC session between IBM 1 and IBM 2 is still end-to-end. Every frame generated by IBM 1 traverses the backbone network to IBM 2, which, upon receipt of the frame, acknowledges it.

Figure 9–2
SDLC session without local
acknowledgment.

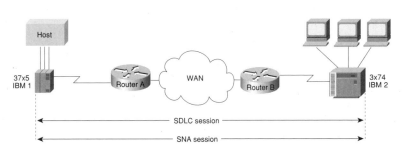

With SDLC local acknowledgment, the SDLC session between the two end nodes is not end-to-end, but instead terminates at the two local routers, as shown in Figure 9–3. The SDLC session with IBM 1 ends at Router A, and the SDLC session with IBM 2 ends at Router B. Both Router A and Router B execute the full SDLC protocol as part of SDLC Local Acknowledgment. Router A acknowledges frames received from IBM 1. The node IBM 1 treats the acknowledgments it receives as if they are from IBM 2. Similarly, Router B acknowledges frames received from IBM 2. The node IBM 2 treats the acknowledgments it receives as if they are from IBM 1.

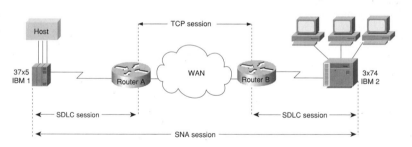

Figure 9–3
SDLC session with local
acknowledgment.

To configure TCP encapsulation with SDLC local acknowledgment and priority queuing, perform the tasks in the following sections:

- Assigning the Router an SDLC Primary or Secondary Role
- Enabling the SDLC Local Acknowledgment Feature
- Establishing Priority Queuing Levels

Assigning the Router an SDLC Primary or Secondary Role

To establish local acknowledgment, the router must play the role of an SDLC primary or secondary node. Primary nodes poll secondary nodes in a predetermined order. Secondaries then transmit if they have outgoing data.

For example, in the IBM environment, an FEP is the primary station and cluster controllers are secondary stations. If the router is connected to a cluster controller, the router should appear as an FEP and must therefore be assigned the role of a primary SDLC node. If the router is connected to an FEP, the router should appear as a cluster controller and must therefore be assigned the role of a secondary SDLC node. Devices connected to SDLC primary end stations must play the role of an SDLC secondary and routers attached to SDLC secondary end stations must play the role of an SDLC primary station.

To assign the router a primary or secondary role, perform one of the following tasks in interface configuration mode:

Task	Command
Assign the STUN-enabled router an SDLC primary role.	**stun sdlc-role primary**
Assign the STUN-enabled router an SDLC secondary role.	**stun sdlc-role secondary**

Enabling the SDLC Local Acknowledgment Feature

To enable SDLC local acknowledgment, complete the following task in interface configuration mode:

Task	Command
Establish SDLC local acknowledgment using TCP encapsulation.	**stun route address** *address-number* **tcp** *ip-address* [**local-ack**] [**priority**] [**tcp-queue-max**]

The **stun route address 1 tcp local-ack priority tcp-queue-max** interface configuration command enables local acknowledgment and TCP encapsulation. Both options are required to use transmission groups. You should specify the SDLC address with the echo bit turned off for transmission group interfaces. The SDLC broadcast address 0xFF is routed automatically for transmission group interfaces. The **priority** keyword creates multiple TCP sessions for this route. The **tcp-queue-max** keyword sets the maximum size of the outbound TCP queue for the SDLC. The default TCP queue size is 100. The value for **hold-queue in** should be greater than the value for **tcp-queue-max**.

You can use the **priority** keyword (to set up the four levels of priorities to be used for TCP encapsulated frames) at the same time you enable local acknowledgment. The **priority** keyword is described in the following section. Use the **no** form of this command to disable SDLC Local Acknowledgment. For an example of how to enable local acknowledgment, see "Configuring Serial Link Address Prioritization Using STUN TCP/IP Encapsulation Example" later in this chapter.

Establishing Priority Queuing Levels

With SDLC local acknowledgment enabled, you can establish priority levels used in priority queuing for serial interfaces. The priority levels are as follows:

- Low
- Medium
- Normal
- High

To set the priority queuing level, perform the following task in interface configuration mode:

Task	Command
Establish the four levels of priorities to be used in priority queuing.	**stun route address** *address-number* **tcp** *ip-address* [**local-ack**] **priority** [**tcp-queue-max**]

Use the **no** form of this command to disable priority settings. For an example of how to establish priority queuing levels, see "Configuring Serial Link Address Prioritization Using STUN TCP/IP Encapsulation Example" later in this chapter.

Configuring Local Acknowledgment for Direct Frame Relay Connectivity

To implement STUN with local acknowledgment using direct Frame Relay encapsulation, perform the following task in interface configuration mode:

Task	Command
Configure Frame Relay encapsulation between STUN peers with local acknowledgment.	**stun route address** *sdlc-addr* **interface** *frame-relay-port* **dlci** *number localsap* **local-ack**

CONFIGURING STUN WITH MULTILINK TRANSMISSION GROUPS

You can configure multilink SDLC transmission groups across STUN connections between IBM communications controllers such as IBM 37x5s. Multilink transmission groups allow you to collapse multiple WAN leased lines into one leased line.

SDLC multilink transmission groups provide the following features:

- Network Control Program (NCP) SDLC address allowances, including echo and broadcast addressing.

- Remote NCP load sequence. After a SIM/RIM exchange but before a SNRM/UA exchange, NCPs send numbered I-frames. During this period, I-frames are not locally acknowledged, but instead are passed through. After the SNRM/UA exchange, local acknowledgment occurs.

- Rerouting of I-frames sent by the Cisco IOS software to the NCP if a link is lost in a multilink transmission group.

- Flow control rate tuning causes a sending NCP to "feel" WAN congestion and hold frames that would otherwise be held by the Cisco IOS software waiting to be transmitted on the WAN. This allows the NCP to perform its class-of-service algorithm more efficiently based on a greater knowledge of network congestion.

STUN connections that are part of a transmission group must have local acknowledgment enabled. Local acknowledgment keeps SDLC poll traffic off the WAN and reduces store-and-forward delays through the router. It also might minimize the number of NCP timers that expire due to network delay. Also, these STUN connections must go to the same IP address. This is because SNA transmission groups are parallel links between the same pair of IBM communications controllers.

Design Recommendations

This section provides some recommendations that are useful in configuring SDLC multilink transmission groups.

The bandwidth of the WAN should be larger than or equal to the aggregate bandwidth of all serial lines to avoid excessive flow control and ensure response time does not degrade. If other protocols are also using the WAN, ensure that the WAN bandwidth is significantly greater than the aggregate SNA serial line bandwidth to ensure that the SNA traffic does not monopolize the WAN.

When you use a combination of routed transmission groups and directly connected NCP transmission groups, you need to plan the configuration carefully to ensure that SNA sessions do not stop unexpectedly. Assuming that hardware reliability is not an issue, single-link routed transmission groups are as reliable as direct NCP-to-NCP single-link transmission groups. This is true because neither the NCP nor the Cisco IOS software can reroute I-frames when a transmission group has only one link. Additionally, a multilink transmission group directed between NCPs and a multilink transmission group through a router are equally reliable. Both can perform rerouting.

However, you might run into problems if you have a configuration in which two NCPs are directly connected (via one or more transmission group links) and one link in the transmission group is routed. The NCPs treat this as a multilink transmission group. However, the Cisco IOS software views the transmission group as a single-link transmission group.

A problem can arise in the following situation: Assume that an I-frame is being transmitted from NCP A (connected to router A) to NCP B (connected to router B) and that all SDLC links are currently active. Router A acknowledges the I-frame sent from NCP A and sends it over the WAN. If, before the I-frame reaches Router B, the SDLC link between router B and NCP B goes down, Router B attempts to reroute the I-frame on another link in the transmission group when it receives the I-frame. However, because this is a single-link transmission group, there are no other routes, and Router B drops the I-frame. NCP B never receives this I-frame because Router A acknowledges its receipt, and NCP A marks it as transmitted and deletes it. NCP B detects a gap in the transmission group sequence numbers and waits to receive the missing I-frame. NCP B waits forever for this I-frame, and does not send or receive any other frames. NCP B is technically not operational and all SNA sessions through NCP B are lost.

Finally, consider a configuration in which one or more lines of an NCP transmission group are connected to a router and one or more lines are directly connected between NCPs. If the network delay associated with one line of an NCP transmission group is different from the delay of another line in the same NCP transmission group, the receiving NCP spends additional time resequencing PIUs.

SETTING UP STUN TRAFFIC PRIORITIES

Use the methods described in the following sections to determine the order in which traffic should be handled on the network:

- Assigning Queuing Priorties
- Prioritizing STUN Traffic over All Other Traffic

Assigning Queuing Priorities

You can assign queuing priorities by one of the following:

- Serial interface address or TCP port
- Logical unit (LU) address

Prioritizing by Serial Interface Address or TCP Port

You can prioritize traffic on a per-serial-interface address or TCP port basis. You might want to do this so that traffic between one source-destination pair is always sent before traffic between another source-destination pair.

NOTES

You must first enable local acknowledgment and priority levels as described earlier in this chapter.

To prioritize traffic, perform one of the following tasks in global configuration mode:

Task	Command
Assign a queuing priority to the address of the STUN serial interface.	**priority-list** *list-number* **stun** *queue* **address** *group-number address-number*
Assign a queuing priority to a TCP port.	**priority-list** *list-number* **protocol ip** *queue* **tcp** *tcp-port-number*

You must also perform the following task in interface configuration mode:

Task	Command
Assign a priority list to a priority group.	**priority-group** *list-number*

Figure 9–4 illustrates serial link address prioritization. Device A communicates with Device C, and Device B communicates with Device D. With the serial link address prioritization, you can choose to give A-C a higher priority over B-D across the serial tunnel.

Figure 9–4
Serial link address
prioritization.

To disable priorities, use the **no** forms of these commands.

For an example of how to prioritize traffic according to serial link address, see "Configuring Serial Link Address Prioritization Using STUN TCP/IP Encapsulation Example" later in this chapter.

Prioritizing by Logical Unit Address

SNA local logical unit (LU) address prioritization is specific to IBM SNA connectivity and is used to prioritize SNA traffic on either STUN or remote source-route bridging (RSRB). To set the queuing priority by LU address, perform the following task in interface configuration mode:

Task	Command
Assign a queuing priority based on the logical unit address.	**locaddr-priority-list** *list-number* *address-number queue-keyword*

In Figure 9–5, LU address prioritization can be set so that particular LUs receive data in preference to others or so that LUs have priority over the printer, for example.

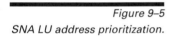

Figure 9–5
SNA LU address prioritization.

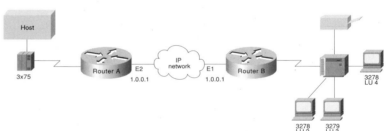

To disable this priority, use the **no** form of this command.

For an example of how to prioritize traffic according to logical unit address, see "Configuring LOCADDR Priority Groups for STUN Example" later in this chapter.

Prioritizing STUN Traffic over All Other Traffic

You can prioritize STUN traffic to be routed first before all other traffic on the network. To give STUN traffic this priority, perform the following task in global configuration mode:

Task	Command
Prioritize STUN traffic in your network over that of other protocols.	**priority-list** *list-number* **stun** *queue* **address** *group-number address-number*

To disable this priority, use the **no** form of this command.

For an example of how to prioritize STUN traffic over all other traffic, see "Configuring Serial Link Address Prioritization Using STUN TCP/IP Encapsulation Example" later in this chapter.

MONITORING STUN NETWORK ACTIVITY

You can list statistics regarding STUN interfaces, protocol groups, number of packets sent and received, local acknowledgment states, and more. To get activity information, perform the following task in EXEC mode:

Task	Command
List the status display fields for STUN interfaces.	**show stun**

STUN CONFIGURATION EXAMPLES

The following sections provide STUN configuration examples:

- Configuring STUN Priorities Using HDLC Encapsulation Example
- Configuring SDLC Broadcast Example
- Configuring Serial Link Address Prioritization Using STUN TCP/IP Encapsulation Example
- Configuring STUN Multipoint Implementation Using a Line-Sharing Device Example
- Configuring STUN Local Acknowledgment for SDLC Example
- Configuring STUN Local Acknowledgment for Frame Relay Example
- Configuring LOCADDR Priority Groups—Simple Example
- Configuring LOCADDR Priority Groups for STUN Example

Configuring STUN Priorities Using HDLC Encapsulation Example

Assume that the link between Router A and Router B in Figure 9–6 is a serial tunnel that uses the simple serial transport mechanism. Device A communicates with Device C (SDLC address C1) with a high priority. Device B communicates with Device D (SDLC address A7) with a normal priority.

Figure 9–6
STUN simple serial transport.

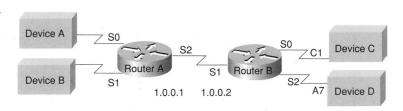

The following configurations set the priority of STUN hosts A, B, C, and D.

Configuration for Router A

```
stun peer-name 1.0.0.1
stun protocol-group 1 sdlc
stun protocol-group 2 sdlc
!
interface serial 0
 no ip address
 encapsulation stun
 stun group 1
 stun route address C1 interface serial 2
!
interface serial 1
 no ip address
 encapsulation stun
 stun group 2
 stun route address A7 interface serial 2
!
interface serial 2
 ip address 1.0.0.1 255.0.0.0
 priority-group 1
!
priority-list 1 stun high address 1 C1
priority-list 1 stun low address 2 A7
```

Configuration for Router B

```
stun peer-name 1.0.0.2
stun protocol-group 1 sdlc
stun protocol-group 2 sdlc
!
interface serial 0
 no ip address
 encapsulation stun
 stun group 1
 stun route address C1 interface serial 1
!
interface serial 1
 ip address 1.0.0.2 255.0.0.0
 priority-group 1
!
interface serial 2
 no ip address
 encapsulation stun
 stun group 2
 stun route address A7 interface serial 1
!
priority-list 1 stun high address 1 C1
priority-list 1 stun low address 2 A7
```

Configuring SDLC Broadcast Example

In the following example, an FEP views end stations 1, 2, and 3 as if they were on an SDLC multi-drop link. Any broadcast frame sent from the FEP to Router A is duplicated and sent to each of the downstream routers (B and C):

```
stun peer-name xxx.xxx.xxx.xxx
stun protocol-group 1 sdlc
interface serial 1
encapsulation stun
 stun group 1
 stun sdlc-role secondary
 sdlc virtual-multidrop
 sdlc address 1
 sdlc address 2
 sdlc address 3
 stun route address 1 tcp yyy.yyy.yyy.yyy local-ack
 stun route address 2 tcp zzz.zzz.zzz.zzz local-ack
 stun route address 3 tcp zzz.zzz.zzz.zzz local-ack
 stun route address FF tcp yyy.yyy.yyy.yyy
 stun route address FF tcp zzz.zzz.zzz.zzz
```

Configuring Serial Link Address Prioritization Using STUN TCP/IP Encapsulation Example

Assume that the link between Router A and Router B is a serial tunnel that uses the TCP/IP encapsulation as shown in Figure 9–7. Device A communicates with Device C (SDLC address C1) with a high priority. Device B communicates with Device D (SDLC address A7) with a normal priority. The configuration file for each router follows the figure.

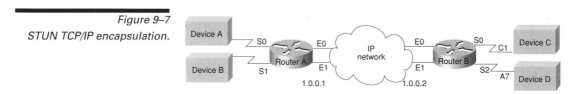

Figure 9–7
STUN TCP/IP encapsulation.

Configuration for Router A

```
stun peer-name 1.0.0.1
stun protocol-group 1 sdlc
stun protocol-group 2 sdlc
!
interface serial 0
 no ip address
 encapsulation stun
 stun group 1
 stun route address C1 tcp 1.0.0.2 local-ack priority
 priority-group 1
```

```
!
interface serial 1
 no ip address
 encapsulation stun
 stun group 2
 stun route address A7 tcp 1.0.0.2 local-ack priority
 priority-group 2
!
interface ethernet 0
 ip address 1.0.0.1 255.0.0.0
 !
interface ethernet 1
 ip address 1.0.0.3 255.0.0.0
 !
priority-list 1 protocol ip high tcp 1994
priority-list 1 protocol ip medium tcp 1990
priority-list 1 protocol ip normal tcp 1991
priority-list 1 protocol ip low tcp 1992
priority-list 1 stun high address 1 C1
 !
priority-list 2 protocol ip high tcp 1994
priority-list 2 protocol ip medium tcp 1990
priority-list 2 protocol ip normal tcp 1991
priority-list 2 protocol ip low tcp 1992
priority-list 2 stun normal address 2 A7
 !
hostname routerA
router igrp
network 1.0.0.0
```

Configuration for Router B

```
stun peer-name 1.0.0.2
stun protocol-group 1 sdlc
stun protocol-group 2 sdlc
!
interface serial 0
 no ip address
 encapsulation stun
 stun group 1
 stun route address C1 tcp 1.0.0.1 local-ack priority
 priority-group 1
 !
interface serial 2
 no ip address
 encapsulation stun
 stun group 2
 stun route address A7 tcp 1.0.0.1 local-ack priority
 priority-group 2
 !
interface ethernet 0
 ip address 1.0.0.2 255.0.0.0
```

```
!
interface ethernet 1
 ip address 1.0.0.4 255.0.0.0
 !
priority-list 1 protocol ip high tcp 1994
priority-list 1 protocol ip medium tcp 1990
priority-list 1 protocol ip normal tcp 1991
priority-list 1 protocol ip low tcp 1992
priority-list 1 stun high address 1 C1
!
priority-list 2 protocol ip high tcp 1994
priority-list 2 protocol ip medium tcp 1990
priority-list 2 protocol ip normal tcp 1991
priority-list 2 protocol ip low tcp 1992
priority-list 2 stun normal address 2 A7
!
hostname routerB
router igrp 109
network 1.0.0.0
```

Configuring STUN Multipoint Implementation Using a Line-Sharing Device Example

In Figure 9–8, four separate PS/2 computers are connected to a line-sharing device off of Router B. Each PS/2 computer has four sessions open on an AS/400 device attached to Router A. Router B functions as the primary station, while Router A functions as the secondary station. Both routers locally acknowledge packets from the IBM PS/2 systems.

Figure 9–8
STUN communication involving a line-sharing device.

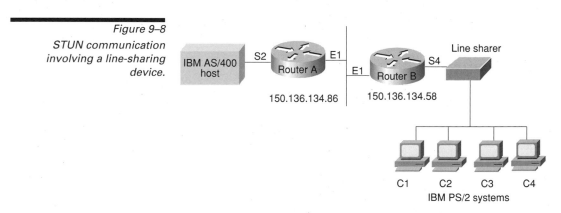

The configuration file for the routers shown in Figure 9–8 follows.

Configuration for Router A

```
! enter the address of the stun peer
stun peer-name 150.136.134.86
! specify that group 4 uses the SDLC protocol
stun protocol-group 4 sdlc
stun remote-peer-keepalive

interface ethernet 1
! enter the IP address for the Ethernet interface
 ip address 150.136.134.86 255.255.255.0
 !
 ! description of IBM AS/400 link
interface serial 2
 ! description of IBM AS/400 link; disable the IP address on a serial interface
 no ip address
 ! enable STUN encapsulation on this interface
 encapsulation stun
 ! apply previously defined stun group 4 to serial interface 2
 stun group 4
 ! establish this router as a secondary station
 stun sdlc-role secondary
 ! wait up to 63000 msec for a poll from the primary before timing out
 sdlc poll-wait-timeout 63000
 ! list addresses of secondary stations (PS/2 systems) attached to link
 sdlc address C1
 sdlc address C2
 sdlc address C3
 sdlc address C4
 ! use tcp encapsulation to send frames to SDLC stations C1, C2, C3, or
 ! C4 and locally terminate sessions with these stations
 stun route address C1 tcp 150.136.134.58 local-ack
 stun route address C2 tcp 150.136.134.58 local-ack
 stun route address C3 tcp 150.136.134.58 local-ack
 stun route address C4 tcp 150.136.134.58 local-ack
```

Configuration for Router B

```
! enter the address of the stun peer
stun peer-name 150.136.134.58
! this router is part of SDLC group 4
stun protocol-group 4 sdlc
stun remote-peer-keepalive
!
interface ethernet 1
! enter the IP address for the Ethernet interface
ip address 150.136.134.58 255.255.255.0
!
! description of PS/2 link
interface serial 4
! disable the IP address on a serial interface
 no ip address
```

```
! enable STUN encapsulation on this interface
 encapsulation stun
! apply previously defined stun group 4 to serial interface 2
stun group 4
! establish this router as a primary station
stun sdlc-role primary
sdlc line-speed 9600
! wait 2000 milliseconds for a reply to a frame before resending it
sdlc t1 2000
! resend a frame up to four times if not acknowledged
sdlc n2 4
! list addresses of secondary stations (PS/2 systems) attached to link
sdlc address C1
sdlc address C2
sdlc address C3
sdlc address C4
! use tcp encapsulation to send frames to SDLC stations C1, C2, C3, or
! C4 and locally terminate sessions with these stations
stun route address C3 tcp 150.136.134.86 local-ack
stun route address C1 tcp 150.136.134.86 local-ack
stun route address C4 tcp 150.136.134.86 local-ack
stun route address C2 tcp 150.136.134.86 local-ack
! set the clockrate on this interface to 9600 bits per second
clockrate 9600
```

Configuring STUN Local Acknowledgment for SDLC Example

The following example shows a sample configuration for a pair of routers performing SDLC local acknowledgment.

Configuration for Router A

```
stun peer-name 150.136.64.92
stun protocol-group 1 sdlc
stun remote-peer-keepalive
!
interface Serial 0
 no ip address
 encapsulation stun
 stun group 1
 stun sdlc-role secondary
 sdlc address C1
 stun route address C1 tcp 150.136.64.93 local-ack
 clockrate 19200
```

Configuration for Router B

```
stun peer-name 150.136.64.93
stun protocol-group 1 sdlc
stun remote-peer-keepalive
```

```
!
interface Serial 0
 no ip address
 encapsulation stun
 stun group 1
 stun sdlc-role primary
 sdlc line-speed 19200
 sdlc address C1
 stun route address C1 tcp 150.136.64.92 local-ack
 clockrate 19200
```

Configuring STUN Local Acknowledgment for Frame Relay Example

The following example describes an interface configuration for Frame Relay STUN with local acknowledgment:

```
stun peer-name 10.1.21.1
stun protocol-group 120 sdlc
!
interface serial 1
 no ip address
 encapsulation frame-relay
 frame-relay lmi-type ansi
 frame-relay map llc2 22
!
interface seria 14
 no ip address
 encapsulation stun
 clockrate 9600
 stun group 120
 stun sdlc-role secondary
 sdlc address C1
 sdlc address C2
 stun route address C1 interface Serial1 dlci 22 04 local-ack
 stun route address C2 interface Serial1 dlci 22 08 local-ack
```

Configuring LOCADDR Priority Groups—Simple Example

The following example shows how to establish queuing priorities on a STUN interface based on an LU address:

```
! sample stun peer-name global command
stun peer-name 131.108.254.6
! sample protocol-group command for reference
stun protocol-group 1 sdlc
!
interface serial 0
! disable the ip address for interface serial 0
 no ip address
! enable the interface for STUN
 encapsulation stun
```

```
! sample stun group command
stun group 2
! sample stun route command
stun route address 10 tcp 131.108.254.8 local-ack priority
!
! assign priority group 1 to the input side of interface serial 0
locaddr-priority 1
priority-group 1
!
interface Ethernet 0
! give locaddr-priority-list 1 a high priority for LU 02
 locaddr-priority-list 1 02 high
! give locaddr-priority-list 1 a low priority for LU 05
 locaddr-priority-list 1 05 low
```

Configuring LOCADDR Priority Groups for STUN Example

The following configuration example shows how to assign a priority group to an input interface:

Configuration for Router A

```
stun peer-name 1.0.0.1
stun protocol-group 1 sdlc
!
interface serial 0
 no ip address
 encapsulation stun
 stun group 1
 stun route address C1 tcp 1.0.0.2 local-ack priority
 clockrate 19200
 locaddr-priority 1
 priority-group 1
!
interface Ethernet 0
 ip address 1.0.0.1 255.255.255.0
!
 locaddr-priority-list 1 02 high
 locaddr-priority-list 1 03 high
 locaddr-priority-list 1 04 medium
 locaddr-priority-list 1 05 low
!
 priority-list 1 protocol ip high tcp 1994
 priority-list 1 protocol ip medium tcp 1990
 priority-list 1 protocol ip normal tcp 1991
 priority-list 1 protocol ip low tcp 1992
```

Configuration for Router B

```
stun peer-name 1.0.0.2
stun protocol-group 1 sdlc
```

```
!
interface serial 0
 no ip address
 encapsulation stun
 stun group 1
 stun route address C1 tcp 1.0.0.1 local-ack priority
 clockrate 19200
 locaddr-priority 1
 priority-group 1
!
interface Ethernet 0
 ip address 1.0.0.2 255.255.255.0
!
 locaddr-priority-list 1 02 high
 locaddr-priority-list 1 03 high
 locaddr-priority-list 1 04 medium
 locaddr-priority-list 1 05 low
!
 priority-list 1 protocol ip high tcp 1994
 priority-list 1 protocol ip medium tcp 1990
 priority-list 1 protocol ip normal tcp 1991
 priority-list 1 protocol ip low tcp 1992
```

BLOCK SERIAL TUNNELING (BSTUN)

Cisco's implementation of BSTUN provides the following features:

- Encapsulates Bisync, Adplex, ADT Security Systems, Inc., Diebold, and asynchronous generic traffic for transfer over router links. The tunneling of asynchronous security protocols (ASP) feature enables your Cisco 2500, 3600, 4000, 4500, or 7200 series router to support devices that use the following asynchronous security protocols:
  - ○ adplex
  - ○ adt-poll-select
  - ○ adt-vari-poll
  - ○ diebold
  - ○ async-generic
  - ○ mdi
- Provides a tunnel mechanism for BSTUN over Frame Relay, without using TCP/IP encapsulation.
- Supports legacy Bisync devices and host applications without modification.
- Uses standard synchronous serial interfaces on Cisco 2500 series and the 4T network interface module (NIM) on the Cisco 4000 series and Cisco 4500 series.
- Supports point-to-point, multidrop, and virtual multidrop configurations.

The async-generic item listed above is not a protocol name. It is a command keyword used to indicate generic support of other asynchronous security protocols that are not explicitly supported.

BISYNC NETWORK OVERVIEW

The Bisync feature enables your Cisco series 2500, 3600, 4000, 4500, 4700, and 7200 series router to support devices that use the Bisync datalink protocol. This protocol enables enterprises to transport Bisync traffic over the same network that supports their SNA and multiprotocol traffic, eliminating the need for separate Bisync facilities.

At the access router, traffic from the attached Bisync device is encapsulated in IP. The Bisync traffic then can be routed across arbitrary media to the host site where another router supporting Bisync will remove the IP encapsulation headers and present the Bisync traffic to the Bisync host or controller over a serial connection. HDLC can be used as an alternative encapsulation method for point-to-point links. Figure 9–9 shows how you can reconfigure an existing Bisync link between two devices and provide the same logical link without any changes to the existing Bisync devices.

Figure 9–9

Routers consolidate bisync traffic by encapsulation in IP or HDLC.

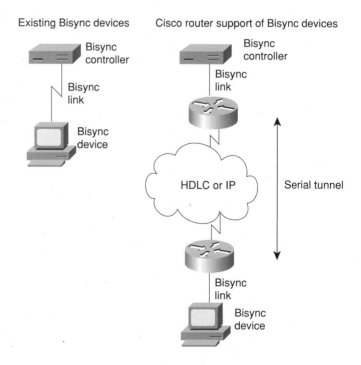

The routers transport all Bisync blocks between the two devices in pass-through mode using BSTUN as encapsulation. BSTUN uses the same encapsulation architecture as STUN, but is implemented on an independent tunnel.

Point-to-Point and Multidrop Support

The Bisync feature supports point-to-point, multidrop, and virtual multidrop Bisync configurations.

Point-to-Point Operation

In point-to-point operation, the Bisync blocks between the two point-to-point devices are received and forwarded transparently by the Cisco IOS software. The contention to acquire the line for transmission is handled by the devices themselves.

Cisco's Bisync multipoint operation is provided as a logical multipoint configuration. Figure 9–10 shows how a multipoint Bisync link is reconfigured using Cisco routers. Router A is configured as Bisync secondary. It monitors the address field of the polling or selection block and uses this address information to put into the BSTUN frame for BSTUN to deliver to the correct destination router. To simulate the Bisync multidrop, an EOT block is sent by the Bisync primary router before a poll or selection block. This ensures that Bisync tributary stations are in control mode before being polled or selected.

Figure 9–10
Multipoint Bisync link reconfigured using routers.

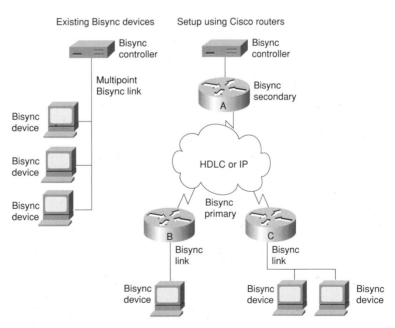

Multidrop Configuration

Multidrop configurations are common in Bisync networks where up to 8 or 10 Bisync devices are frequently connected to a Bisync controller port over a single low-speed link. Cisco's router allows Bisync devices from different physical locations in the network to appear as a single multidrop line to the Bisync host or controller. Figure 9–11 illustrates a multidrop Bisync configuration before and after implementing routers.

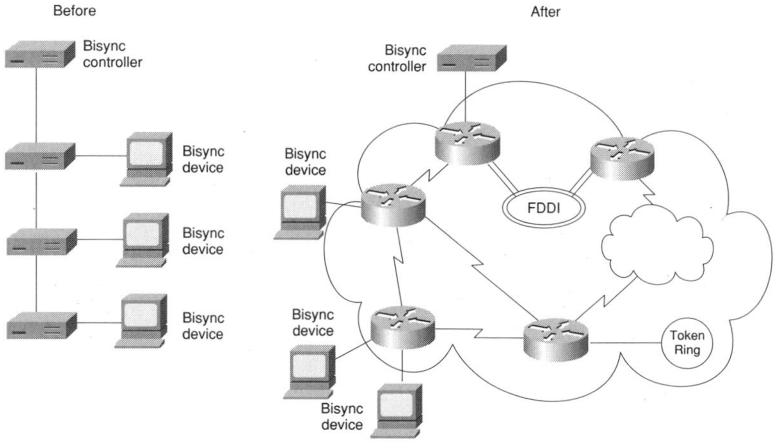

Figure 9–11
Integrating Bisync devices over a multiprotocol network.

ASYNCHRONOUS NETWORK OVERVIEW

These protocols enable enterprises to transport polled asynchronous traffic over the same network that supports their SNA and multiprotocol traffic, eliminating the need for separate facilities. Figure 9–12 shows how you can reconfigure an existing asynchronous link between two security devices and provide the same logical link without any changes to the existing devices.

Router A is configured as the secondary end of the BSTUN asynchronous link and is attached to the security control station. Router B is configured as the primary end of the BSTUN asynchronous link and has one or more alarm panels attached to it.

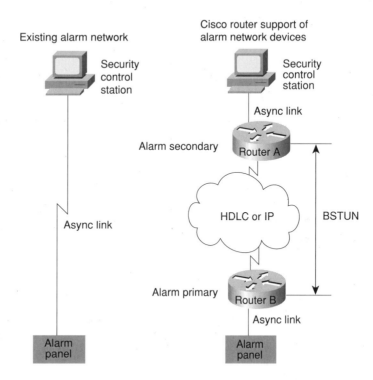

Figure 9–12
Routers consolidate polled asynchronous traffic using encapsulation in IP or HDLC.

At the downstream router, traffic from the attached alarm panels is encapsulated in IP. The asynchronous (alarm) traffic can be routed across arbitrary media to the host site where the upstream router supporting these protocols removes the IP encapsulation headers and presents the original traffic to the security control station over a serial connection. High-Level Data Link Control (HDLC) can be used as an alternative encapsulation method for point-to-point links.

The routers transport all asynchronous (alarm) blocks between the two devices in passthru mode using BSTUN for encapsulation. BSTUN uses the same encapsulation architecture as serial tunnel (STUN), but is implemented on an independent tunnel. As each asynchronous frame is received from the line, a BSTUN header is added to create a BSTUN frame, and then BSTUN is used to deliver the frame to the correct destination router.

The Cisco routers do not perform any local acknowledgment or cyclic redundancy check (CRC) calculations on the asynchronous alarm blocks. The two end devices are responsible for error recovery in the asynchronous alarm protocol.

Virtual Multidrop Support for Multipoint Security Network Configurations

Multipoint configurations are common in security networks where a number of alarm panels are frequently connected to a security control station over a single low-speed link. Cisco's virtual multidrop support allows alarm panels from different physical locations in the network to appear as a single multidrop line to the security control station. Both Adplex and ADT are virtual multidropped protocols.

Multidrop operation is provided as a logical multipoint configuration. Figure 9–13 shows how a multipoint security network is reconfigured using Cisco routers. Router A is configured as an alarm secondary node, routers B and C are configured as alarm primary nodes. Router A monitors the address field of the polling or selection block and puts this address information in the BSTUN frame so BSTUN can deliver the frame to the correct downstream node.

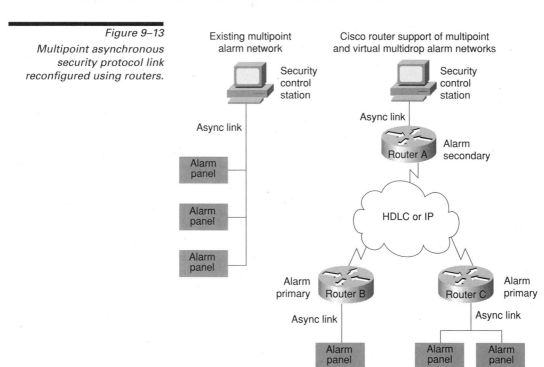

Figure 9–13
Multipoint asynchronous security protocol link reconfigured using routers.

FRAME SEQUENCING

Both Bisync and asynchronous alarm protocols are half-duplex protocols. Transmission can occur in either direction, but only in one direction at a time. Each block of transmission is acknowledged explicitly by the remote end. To avoid the problem associated with simultaneous transmisssion, there is an implicit role of primary and secondary station.

Frame Sequencing in Bisync Networks

In a multidrop setup in Bisync networks, the Bisync control station is primary and the tributary stations are secondary. In a point-to-point configuration, the primary role is assumed by the Bisync device that has successfully acquired the line for transmission through the ENQ bidding sequence. The primary role stays with this station until it sends EOT.

To protect against occasional network latency, which causes the primary station to time out and resend the block before the Bisync block sent by the secondary is received, the control byte of the encapsulating frame is used as a sequence number. This sequence number is controlled and monitored by the primary Bisync router. This allows the primary Bisync router to detect and discard "late" Bisync blocks sent by the secondary router and ensure integrity of the Bisync link.

NOTES

Frame sequencing is implemented in passthru mode only.

Frame Sequencing in Asynchronous Networks

Network delays in asynchronous networks make it possible for a frame to arrive "late," meaning that the poll-cycling mechanism at the security control station already has moved on to poll the next alarm panel in sequence when it receives the poll response from the previous alarm panel.

To protect against this situation, routers configured for adplex or for adt-poll-select protocols use a sequence number built into the encapsulating frame to detect and discard late frames. The "upstream" router (connected to the security control station) inserts a frame-sequence number into the protocol header, which is shipped through the BSTUN tunnel and bounced back by the "downstream" router (connected to the alarm panel). The upstream router maintains a frame-sequence count for the line, and checks the incoming frame sequence number from the downstream router. If the two frame sequence numbers do not agree, the frame is considered late (out of sequence) and is discarded.

Because the adt-vari-poll option allows the transmission of unsolicited messages from the alarm panel, frame sequencing is not supported for this protocol.

NOTES

Polled asynchronous (alarm) protocols are implemented only in passthru mode. There is no support for local acknowledgment.

BSTUN CONFIGURATION TASK LIST

The Bisync feature is configured similar to SDLC STUN, but is configured as a protocol within a BSTUN feature. To configure and monitor Bisync with BSTUN, complete the tasks in the following sections:

- Enabling BSTUN
- Defining the Protocol Group
- Enabling Frame Relay Encapsulation
- Defining Mapping Between BSTUN and DLCI
- Configuring BSTUN on the Serial Interface
- Placing a Serial Interface in a BSTUN Group
- Specifying How Frames are Forwarded
- Setting Up BSTUN Traffic Priorities
- Configuring Protocol Group Options on a Serial Interface
- Configuring Direct Serial Encapsulation for Passthru Peers
- Configuring Local Acknowledgment Peers
- Monitoring the Status of BSTUN

The "BSTUN Configuration Examples" section follows these tasks.

ENABLING BSTUN

To enable BSTUN in IP networks, perform the following task in global configuration mode:

Task	Command
Step 1 Enable BSTUN.	**bstun peer-name** *ip-address*
Step 2 Enable BSTUN for Frame Relay transport.	**bstun lisnsap** *sap-value*

The IP address in the **bstun peer-name** command defines the address by which this BSTUN peer is known to other BSTUN peers that are using the TCP transport. If this command is unconfigured or the **no** form of this command is specified, all BSTUN routing commands with IP addresses are deleted. BSTUN routing commands without IP addresses are not affected by this command.

The **bstun lisnsap** command specifies a SAP on which to detect incoming calls.

DEFINING THE PROTOCOL GROUP

Define a BSTUN group and specify the protocol it uses. To define the protocol group, perform the following task in global configuration mode:

Task	Command
Define the protocol group.	**bstun protocol-group** *group-number* {bsc | bsc-local-ack | adplex | adt-poll | adt-poll-select | adt-vari-poll | diebold | async-generic | mdi}

The **bsc-local-ack** protocol option only works for 3270 Bisync uses.

The block serial protocols include bsc, bsc-local-ack, adplex, adt-poll-select, adt-vari-poll, diebold, async-generic, and mdi.

Traditionally, the adt-poll-select protocol is used over land-based links, while the adt-vari-poll protocol is used over satellite (VSAT) links. The adt-vari-poll protocol typically uses a much slower polling rate when alarm consoles poll alarm panels because adt-vari-poll allows alarm panels to send unsolicited messages to the alarm console. In an adt-vari-poll configuration, alarm panels do not have to wait for the console to poll them before responding with an alarm. They automatically send the alarm.

Interfaces configured to run the adplex protocol have their baud rate set to 4800 bps, use even parity, 8 data bits, 1 start bit, and 1 stop bit.

Interfaces configured to run the adt-poll-select and adt-vari-poll protocols have their baud rate set to 600 bps, use even parity, 8 data bits, 1 start bit, and 1.5 stop bits. If different line configurations are required, use the **rxspeed, txspeed, databits, stopbits,** and **parity** line configuration commands to change the line attributes.

Interfaces configured to run the diebold protocol have their baud rate set to 300 bps, use even parity, 8 data bits, 1 start bit, and 2 stop bits. If different line configurations are required, use the **rxspeed, txspeed, databits,** and **parity** line configuration commands to change the line attributes.

Interfaces configured to run the async-generic protocol have their baud rate set to 9600 bps, use no parity, 8 data bits, 1 start bit, and 1 stop bit. If different line configurations are required, use the **rxspeed, txspeed, databits, stopbits,** and **parity** line configuration commands to change the line attributes.

Interfaces configured to run the mdi protocol have their baud rate set to 600 bps, use even parity, 8 data bits, 1 start bit, and 1.5 stop bits. If different line configurations are required, use the **rxspeed, txspeed, databits, stopbits,** and **parity** line configuration commands to change the line attributes. The mdi protocol allows alarm panels to be sent to the the MDI alarm console.

ENABLING FRAME RELAY ENCAPSULATION

To enable Frame Relay encapsulation, perform the following tasks, beginning in global configuration mode:

Task	Command
Step 1 Specify a serial port.	**interface serial** *number*
Step 2 Enable Frame Relay encapsulation on the serial port.	**encapsulation frame-relay**

DEFINING MAPPING BETWEEN BSTUN AND DLCI

To configure the mapping between BSTUN and the DLCI, perform one of the following tasks in interface configuration mode:

Task	Command
Step 1 Define the mapping between BSTUN and the DLCI when using BSC passthru.	**frame-relay map bstun** *dlci*
Step 2 Define the mapping between BSTUN and the DLCI when using BSC local acknowledgment.	**frame-relay map llc2** *dlci*

CONFIGURING BSTUN ON THE SERIAL INTERFACE

Configure BSTUN on the serial interface before issuing any further BSTUN or protocol configuration commands for the interface. To configure the BSTUN function on a specified interface, perform the following command in interface configuration mode:

Task	Command
Step 1 Specify a serial port.	**interface serial** *number*
Step 2 Configure BSTUN on an interface.	**encapsulation bstun**[*]

[*] This command must be configured on an interface before any other BSTUN commands are configured for this interface.

PLACING A SERIAL INTERFACE IN A BSTUN GROUP

Each BSTUN-enabled interface on a router must be placed in a previously defined BSTUN group. Packets will travel only between BSTUN-enabled interfaces that are in the same group. To assign a serial interface to a BSTUN group, perform the following task in interface configuration mode:

Task	Command
Assign a serial interface to a BSTUN group.	**bstun group** *group-number*

SPECIFYING HOW FRAMES ARE FORWARDED

To specify how frames are forwarded when received on a BSTUN interface, perform one of the following tasks in interface configuration mode:

Task	Command
Propagate the serial frame that contains a specific address. HDLC encapsulation is used to propagate the serial frames.	**bstun route address** *address-number* **interface serial** *number*
Propagate all BSTUN traffic received on the input interface, regardless of the address contained in the serial frame. HDLC encapsulation is used to propagate the serial frames.	**bstun route all interface serial** *number*
Propagate the serial frame that contains a specific address. TCP encapsulation is used to propagate frames that match the entry.	**bstun route address** *address-number* **tcp** *ip-address*
Propagate all BSTUN traffic received on the input interface, regardless of the address contained in the serial frame. TCP encapsulation is used to propagate frames that match the entry.	**bstun route all tcp** *ip-address*[*]
Propagate the serial frame that contains a specific address. Specify the control unit address for the Bisync end station. Frame Relay encapsulation is used to propagate the serial frames.	**bstun route address** *cu-address* **interface serial** *serial-int* **dlci** *dlci*
Propagate all frames regardless of the control unit address for the Bisync end station. Frame Relay encapsulation is used to propagate the serial frames in bisync passthru mode.	**bstun route all interface serial** *serial-int* **dlci** *dlci*

Task	Command
Propagate the serial frame that contains a specific address. Specify the control unit address for the bisync end station. Frame Relay encapsulation is used to propagate the serial frames for bisync local acknowledgment mode.	**bstun route address** *cu-address* **interface serial** *serial-int* **dlci** *dlci rsap* **priority** *priority*
Propagate all BSTUN traffic received on the input interface, regardless of the address contained in the serial frame. Frame Relay encapsulation is used to propagate the serial frames.	**bstun route all interface serial** *serial-int* **dlci** *dlci rsap* **priority** *priority*

* This command functions in either passthru or local acknowledgment mode.

For Bisync local acknowledgment, Cisco recommends that you use the **bstun route all tcp** command. This command reduces the amount of duplicate configuration detail that otherwise would be needed to specify devices at each end of the tunnel.

SETTING UP BSTUN TRAFFIC PRIORITIES

You can assign BSTUN traffic priorities based on either the BSTUN header or the TCP port. To prioritize traffic, perform one of the following tasks in global configuration mode:

Task	Command
Establish BSTUN queuing priorities based on the BSTUN header.	**priority-list** *list-number* **protocol bstun** *queue* [**gt** *packetsize*] [**lt** *packetsize*] **address** *bstun-group bsc-addr*
Assign a queuing priority to TCP port.	**priority-list** *list-number* **protocol ip** *queue* **tcp** *tcp-port-number*

You can customize BSTUN queuing priorities based on either the BSTUN header or TCP port. To customize priorities, perform one of the following tasks in global configuration mode:

Task	Command
Customize BSTUN queuing priorities based on the BSTUN header.	**queue-list** *list-number* **protocol bstun** *queue* [**gt** *packetsize*] [**lt** *packetsize*] **address** *bstun-group bsc-addr*
Customize BSTUN queuing priorities based on the TCP port.	**queue-list** *list-number* **protocol ip** *queue* **tcp** *tcp-port-number*

NOTES

Because the asynchronous security protocols share the same tunnels with Bisync when configured on the same routers, any traffic priorities configured for the tunnel apply to both Bisync and the various asynchronous security protocols.

CONFIGURING PROTOCOL GROUP OPTIONS ON A SERIAL INTERFACE

Depending on the selected block serial protocol group, you must configure one or more options for that protocol group. The options for each of these protocol groups are explained in the following sections:

- Configuring Bisync Options on a Serial Interface
- Configuring Asynchronous Security Protocol Options on a Serial Interface

Configuring Bisync Options on a Serial Interface

To configure Bisync options on a serial interface, perform one of the following tasks in interface configuration mode:

Task	Command
Specify the character set used by the Bisync support feature.	**bsc char-set** {**ascii** | **ebcdic**}
Specify an address on a contention interface.	**bsc contention** *address*
Specify that the router at the central site will behave as a central router with dynamic allocation of serial interfaces. The timeout value is the length of time an interface can be idle before it is returned to the idle interface pool.	**bsc dial-contention** *time-out*
Specify a nonstandard Bisync address.	**bsc extended-address** *poll-address select-address*
Specify that the interface can run Bisync in full-duplex mode.	**full-duplex**
Specify the amount of time between the start of one polling cycle and the next.	**bsc pause** *time*
Specify the timeout for a poll or a select sequence.	**bsc poll-timeout** *time*

Task	Command
Specify the timeout for a nonreception of poll or a select sequence from the host. If the frame is not received within this time the remote connection will be deactivated.	**bsc host-timeout** *time*
Specify that the router is acting as the primary end of the Bisync link.	**bsc primary**
Specify the number of retries before a device is considered to have failed.	**bsc retries** *retry-count*
Specify that the router is acting as the secondary end of the Bisync link.	**bsc secondary**
Specify the number of cycles of the active poll list that are performed between polls to control units in the inactive poll list.	**bsc servlim** *servlim-count*

Configuring Asynchronous Security Protocol Options on a Serial Interface

To configure asynchronous security protocol options on a serial interface, perform one or more of the following tasks in interface configuration mode:

Task	Command
Specify that the router is acting as the primary end of the polled asynchronous link.	**asp role primary**
Specify that the router is acting as the secondary end of the polled asynchronous link.	**asp role secondary**
For asynchronous-generic configurations, specify the location of the address byte within the polled asynchronous frame being received.	**asp addr-offset** *address-offset*
For asynchronous-generic configurations, specify the timeout period between frames to delineate the end of one frame being received from the start of the next frame.	**asp rx-ift** *interframe-timeout*

CONFIGURING DIRECT SERIAL ENCAPSULATION FOR PASSTHRU PEERS

To configure direct serial encapsulation for passthru peers, perform the following task in interface configuration mode:

Task	Command
Configure the Frame Relay interface for passthru.	**frame relay map bstun**

CONFIGURING LOCAL ACKNOWLEDGMENT PEERS

To configure local acknowledgment peers, perform the following task in interface configuration mode:

Task	Command
Configure the Frame Relay interface for local acknowledgment.	**frame-relay map llc2** *dlci*

MONITORING THE STATUS OF BSTUN

To list statistics for BSTUN interfaces, protocol groups, number of packets sent and received, local acknowledgment states, and other activity information, perform the following tasks in EXEC mode:

Task		Command
Step 1	List the status display fields for BSTUN interfaces.	**show bstun [group** *bstun-group-number*] **[address** *address-list*]
Step 2	Display status of the interfaces on which Bisync is configured.	**show bsc [group** *bstun-group-number*] **[address** *address-list*]

BSTUN CONFIGURATION EXAMPLES

The following sections provide BSTUN configuration examples:

- Simple Bisync Configuration Example
- Bisync Addressing on Contention Interfaces
- Nonstandard Bisync Addressing
- Priority Queuing: Prioritization Based on BSTUN Header Example
- Priority Queuing: Prioritization Based on BSTUN Header and Packet Sizes Example
- Priority Queuing: Prioritization Based on BSTUN Header and Bisync Address Example

- Priority Queuing: Prioritization Based on BSTUN TCP Ports Example
- Priority Queuing: Prioritization Based on BSTUN TCP Ports and Bisync Address Example
- Custom Queuing: Prioritization Based on BSTUN Header Example
- Custom Queuing: Prioritization Based on BSTUN Header and Packet Size Example
- Custom Queuing: Prioritization Based on BSTUN Header and Bisync Address Example
- Custom Queuing: Prioritization Based on BSTUN TCP Ports Example
- Custom Queuing: Prioritization Based on BSTUN TCP Ports and Bisync Address Example
- Asynchronous Configuration Example
- BSTUN-over-Frame Relay Configuration Example for Local Acknowledgment
- BSTUN-over-Frame Relay Configuration Example for Passthru

Simple Bisync Configuration Example

Figure 9–14 shows a simple Bisync configuration example.

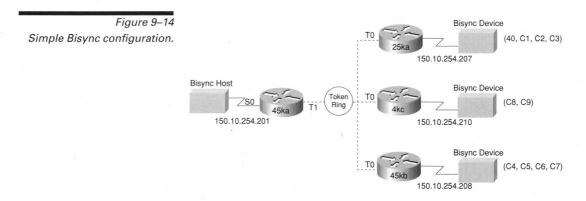

Figure 9–14
Simple Bisync configuration.

The configuration files for the routers shown in Figure 9–14 follow.

Configuration for Router 45ka

```
version 10.2
!
hostname 45ka
!
no ip domain-lookup
!
bstun peer-name 150.10.254.201
bstun protocol-group 1 bsc
!
interface ethernet 0
 ip address 198.92.0.201 255.255.255.0
 media-type 10BaseT
```

```
!
interface ethernet 1
 no ip address
 shutdown
 media-type 10BaseT
!
interface serial 0
 no ip address
 encapsulation bstun
 clockrate 19200
 bstun group 1
 bsc char-set ebcdic
 bsc secondary
 bstun route address C9 tcp 150.10.254.210
bstun route address C8 tcp 150.10.254.210
bstun route address C7 tcp 150.10.254.208
bstun route address C6 tcp 150.10.254.208
bstun route address C5 tcp 150.10.254.208
bstun route address C4 tcp 150.10.254.208
bstun route address C3 tcp 150.10.254.207
bstun route address C2 tcp 150.10.254.207
bstun route address C1 tcp 150.10.254.207
bstun route address 40 tcp 150.10.254.207
!
interface serial 1
no ip address
shutdown
!
interface serial 2
 no ip address
 shutdown
!
interface serial 3
 no ip address
 shutdown
!
interface tokenring 0
 no ip address
 shutdown
!
interface tokenring 1
 ip address 150.10.254.201 255.255.255.0
 ring-speed 16
!
line con 0
line aux 0
line vty 0 4
login
!
end
```

Configuration for Router 25ka

```
version 10.2
!
hostname 25ka
!
no ip domain-lookup
!
bstun peer-name 150.10.254.207
bstun protocol-group 1 bsc
!
interface serial 0
 no ip address
 shutdown
!
interface serial 1
 no ip address
 encapsulation bstun
 clockrate 19200
 bstun group 1
 bsc char-set ebcdic
 bsc primary
 bstun route address C3 tcp 150.10.254.201
 bstun route address C2 tcp 150.10.254.201
 bstun route address C1 tcp 150.10.254.201
 bstun route address 40 tcp 150.10.254.201
!
interface tokenring 0
 ip address 150.10.254.207 255.255.255.0
 ring-speed 16
!
interface bri 0
 no ip address
 shutdown
!
line con 0
line aux 0
line vty 0 4
login
!
end
```

Configuration for Router 4kc

```
version 10.2
!
hostname 4kc
!
no ip domain-lookup
!
bstun peer-name 150.10.254.210
bstun protocol-group 1 bsc
```

```
 !
 interface ethernet 0
  ip address 198.92.0.210 255.255.255.0
  media-type 10BaseT
 !
 interface serial 0
  no ip address
  encapsulation bstun
  clockrate 19200
  bstun group 1
  bsc char-set ebcdic
  bsc primary
  bstun route address C9 tcp 150.10.254.201
  bstun route address C8 tcp 150.10.254.201
 !
 interface serial 1
  no ip address
  shutdown
 !
 interface serial 2
  no ip address
  shutdown
 !
 interface serial 3
  no ip address
  shutdown
 !
 interface tokenring 0
  ip address 150.10.254.210 255.255.255.0
  ring-speed 16
 !
 interface tokenring 1
  no ip address
  shutdown
 !
 line con 0
 line aux 0
 line vty 0 4
 login
 !
 end
```

Configuration for Router 25kb

```
 version 10.2
 !
 hostname 25kb
 !
 no ip domain-lookup
 !
 bstun peer-name 150.10.254.208
 bstun protocol-group 1 bsc
```

```
!
interface serial 0
 no ip address
 encapsulation bstun
 no keepalive
 clockrate 19200
 bstun group 1
 bsc char-set ebcdic
 bsc primary
 bstun route address C7 tcp 150.10.254.201
 bstun route address C6 tcp 150.10.254.201
 bstun route address C5 tcp 150.10.254.201
 bstun route address C4 tcp 150.10.254.201
!
interface serial 1
 no ip address
 shutdown
!
interface tokenring 0
 ip address 150.10.254.208 255.255.255.0
 ring-speed 16
!
!
line con 0
line aux 0
line vty 0 4
login
!
end
```

Bisync Addressing on Contention Interfaces

The following two examples show user-configurable addressing on contention interfaces:

Remote Devices

```
bstun peer-name 1.1.1.20
bstun protocol-group 1 bsc
interface serial 0
 bstun group 1
 bsc contention 20
 bstun route address 20 tcp 1.1.1.1
```

Host Device

```
bstun peer-name 1.1.1.1
bstun protocol-group 1 bsc
interface serial 0
 bstun group 1
 bsc dial-contention 100
 bstun route address 20 tcp 1.1.1.20
 bstun route address 21 tcp 1.1.1.21
```

Nonstandard Bisync Addressing

This example specifies an extended address on serial interface 0:

```
bstun peer-name 1.1.1.1
bstun protocol-group 1 bsc
!
interface serial 0
 bstun group 1
 bsc extended-address 23 83
 bsc extended-address 87 42
 bsc primary
 bstun route address 23 tcp 1.1.1.20
```

Priority Queuing: Prioritization Based on BSTUN Header Example

In this example, the output interface examines header information and places packets with the BSTUN header on specified output queue.

```
priority-list 1 protocol bstun normal
interface serial 0
 priority-group 1
interface serial 1
 encapsulation bstun
 bstun group 1
 bstun route all interface serial 0
              ...or...
bstun route address <bsc-addr> interface serial 0
```

Priority Queuing: Prioritization Based on BSTUN Header and Packet Sizes Example

In this example, the output interface examines header information and packet size and places packets with the BSTUN header that match criteria (gt- or lt-specified packet size) on specified output queue.

```
priority-list 1 protocol bstun low gt 1500
priority-list 1 protocol bstun hi lt 500
interface serial 0
 priority-group 1
interface serial 1
 encapsulation bstun
 bstun group 1
 bstun route all interface serial 0
              ...or...
bstun route address <bsc-addr> interface serial 0
```

Priority Queuing: Prioritization Based on BSTUN Header and Bisync Address Example

In this example, the output interface examines header information and Bisync address and places packets with the BSTUN header that match Bisync address on specified output queue.

```
priority-list 1 protocol bstun normal
address <bstun-group> <bsc-addr>
interface serial 0
 priority-group 1
interface serial 1
 encapsulation bstun
 bstun group 1
 bstun route address <bsc-addr> interface serial 0
```

Priority Queuing: Prioritization Based on BSTUN TCP Ports Example

In this example, the output interface examines TCP port number and places packets with the BSTUN port number (1976) on specified output queue.

```
priority-list 1 protocol ip high tcp 1976
interface serial 0
 priority-group 1
interface serial 1
 encapsulation bstun
 bstun group 1
 bstun route all tcp <bstun-peer-ip-addr>
```

Priority Queuing: Prioritization Based on BSTUN TCP Ports and Bisync Address Example

In this example, four TCP/IP sessions (high, medium, normal, and low) are established with BSTUN peers using BSTUN port numbers. The input interface examines the Bisync address and uses the specified output queue definition to determine which BSTUN TCP session to use for sending the packet to the BSTUN peer.

The output interface examines the TCP port number and places packets with the BSTUN port numbers on the specified output queue.

```
priority-list 1 protocol ip high   tcp 1976
priority-list 1 protocol ip medium tcp 1977
priority-list 1 protocol ip normal tcp 1978
priority-list 1 protocol ip low    tcp 1979
!
priority-list 1 protocol bstun <outputQ>
address <bstun-group> <bsc-addr>
!
interface serial 0
 priority-group 1
!
interface serial 1
 encapsulation bstun
 bstun group 1
 bstun route address <bsc-addr> tcp <bstun-peer-ip-addr> priority
 priority-group 1
```

Custom Queuing: Prioritization Based on BSTUN Header Example

In this example, the output interface examines header information and places packets with the BSTUN header on specified output queue.

```
queue-list 1 protocol bstun normal
!
interface serial 0
 custom-queue-list 1
!
interface serial 1
 encapsulation bstun
 bstun group 1
 bstun route all interface serial 0
```

Custom Queuing: Prioritization Based on BSTUN Header and Packet Size Example

In this example, the output interface examines header information and packet size and places packets with the BSTUN header that match criteria (gt- or lt-specified packet size) on specified output queue.

```
queue-list 1 protocol bstun low gt 1500
queue-list 1 protocol bstun high lt 500
!
interface serial 0
 custom-queue-list 1
!
interface serial 1
 encapsulation bstun
 bstun group 1
 bstun route all interface serial 0
```

Custom Queuing: Prioritization Based on BSTUN Header and Bisync Address Example

In this example, the output interface examines header information and Bisync address and places packets with the BSTUN header that match Bisync address on specified output queue.

```
queue-list 1 protocol bstun normal
address <bstun-group> <bsc-addr>
!
interface serial 0
 custom-queue-list 1
!
interface serial 1
 encapsulation bstun
 bstun group 1
 bstun route address <bsc-addr> interface serial 0
```

Custom Queuing: Prioritization Based on BSTUN TCP Ports Example

In this example, the output interface examines the TCP port number and places packets with the BSTUN port number (1976) on specified output queue.

```
queue-list 1 protocol ip high tcp 1976
!
interface serial 0
 custom-queue-list 1
!
interface serial 1
 encapsulation bstun
 bstun group 1
 bstun route all tcp <bstun-peer-ip-addr>
```

Custom Queuing: Prioritization Based on BSTUN TCP Ports and Bisync Address Example

In this example, four TCP/IP sessions (high, medium, normal, and low) are established with BSTUN peers using BSTUN port numbers. The input interface examines the Bisync address and uses the specified output queue definition to determine which BSTUN TCP session to use.

The output interface examines the TCP port number and places packets with the BSTUN port numbers on the specified output queue.

For Bisync addressing, output queues map as shown in Table 9–1:

Table 9–1 *Bisync Addressing Output Queues*

Output Queue	Session Mapped	BSTUN Port
1	Medium	1977
2	Normal	1978
3	Low	1979
4–10	High	1976

```
queue-list 1 protocol ip high tcp 1976
queue-list 1 protocol ip medium tcp 1977
queue-list 1 protocol ip normal tcp 1978
queue-list 1 protocol ip low tcp 1979
!
priority-list 1 protocol bstun normal
address <bstun-group> <bsc-addr>
!
interface serial 0
 custom-queue-list 1
!
interface serial 1
 encapsulation bstun
```

```
bstun group 1
bstun route address <bsc-addr> tcp <bstun-peer-ip-addr> priority
custom-queue-list 1
```

Asynchronous Configuration Example

In this example, Router A and Router B are configured for both Adplex and Bisync across the same block serial tunnel, as shown in Figure 9–15.

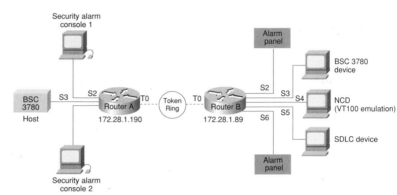

Figure 9–15
Combined Adplex and Bisync configuration example.

Configuration for Router A

```
version 11.0
!
hostname router-a
!
bstun peer-name 172.28.1.190
bstun protocol-group 1 bsc
bstun protocol-group 2 adplex
bstun protocol-group 3 adplex
!
interface serial 0
 no ip address
!
interface serial 1
 no ip address
!
interface serial 2
 physical-layer async
 description Connection to 1st Security Alarm Console.
 no ip address
 encapsulation bstun
 no keepalive
 bstun group 2
 bstun route address 2 tcp 172.28.1.189
 bstun route address 3 tcp 172.28.1.189
 adplex secondary
```

```
!
interface serial 3
 description Connection to BSC 3780 host.
 no ip address
 encapsulation bstun
 no keepalive
 clockrate 9600
 bstun group 1
 bstun route all tcp 172.28.1.189
 bsc char-set ebcdic
 bsc contention
!
interface serial 4
 physical-layer async
 description Connection to 2nd Security Alarm Console.
 no ip address
 encapsulation bstun
 no keepalive
 bstun group 3
 bstun route address 2 tcp 172.28.1.189
 bstun route address 3 tcp 172.28.1.189
 adplex secondary
!
interface serial 5
 no ip address
!
interface serial 6
 no ip address
!
interface serial 7
 no ip address
!
interface serial 8
 no ip address
!
interface serial 9
 no ip address
!
interface tokenring 0
 ip address 172.28.1.190 255.255.255.192
 ring-speed 16
!
interface BRI0
 ip address
 shutdown
!
ip host ss10 172.28.0.40
ip host s2000 172.31.0.2
ip route 0.0.0.0 0.0.0.0 172.28.1.129
!
snmp-server community public RO
```

```
!
line con 0
 exec-timeout 0 0
line 2
 no activation-character
 transport input-all
 parity even
 stopbits 1
 rxspeed 4800
 txspeed 4800
line 4
 transport input all
 parity even
 stopbits 1
 rxspeed 4800
 txspeed 4800
line aux 0
 transport input all
line vty 0 4
 password mango
 login
!
end
```

Configuration for Router B

```
version 11.0
!
hostname router-b
!
bstun peer-name 172.28.1.189
bstun protocol-group 1 bsc
bstun protocol-group 2 adplex
bstun protocol-group 3 adplex
source-bridge ring-group 100
!
interface serial 0
 no ip address
!
interface serial 1
 no ip address
!
interface serial 2
 physical-layer async
 description Connection to Security Alarm Panel.
 no ip address
 encapsulation bstun
 no keepalive
 bstun group 2
 bstun route all tcp 172.28.1.190
 adplex primary
```

```
!
interface serial 3
 description Connection to BSC 3780 device.
 no ip address
 encapsulation bstun
 no keepalive
 clockrate 9600
 bstun group 1
 bstun route all tcp 172.28.1.190
 bsc char-set ebcdic
 bsc contention
!
interface serial 4
 physical-layer async
 description Connection to async port on NCD (VT100 terminal emulation).
 no ip address
!
interface serial 5
 no ip address
 encapsulation sdlc-primary
 no keepalive
 nrzi-encoding
 clockrate 9600
 sdllc traddr 4000.0000.4100 222 2 100
 sdlc address C1
 sdllc xid C1 05D40003
 sdllc partner 4000.0000.0307 C1
!
interface serial 6
 description Connection to alarm panel.
 physical-layer async
 no ip address
 encapsulation bstun
 no keepalive
 bstun group 3
 bstun route all tcp 172.28.1.190
 adplex primary
!interface serial 7
 no ip address
!
interface serial 8
 no ip address
!
interface serial 9
 no ip address
!
interface tokenring 0
 ip address 172.28.1.189 255.255.255.192
 ring-speed 16
 source-bridge 4 1 100
```

```
!
interface BRI0
 ip address
 shutdown
!
ip host ss10 172.28.0.40
ip host s2000 172.31.0.2
ip route 0.0.0.0 0.0.0.0 172.28.1.129
!
snmp-server community public RO
!
line con 0
 exec-timeout 0 0
line 2
 no activation-character
 transport input-all
 parity even
 stopbits 1
 rxspeed 4800
 txspeed 4800
line 4
 transport input all
 stopbits 1
line 6
 transport input all
 parity even
 stopbits 1
 rxspeed 4800
 txspeed 4800
line 7
 transport input all
line aux 0
 transport input all
line vty 0 4
 password mango
 login
!
end
```

BSTUN-over-Frame Relay Configuration Example for Local Acknowledgment

```
bstun protocol-group 1 bsc-local-ack

interface Serial1
encapsulation frame-relay ietf
clockrate 125000
frame-relay map llc2 16
```

```
interface Serial4
 no ip address
encapsulation bstun
bstun group 1
bsc secondary
bstun route address C3 interface Serial1 dlci 16 C
bstun route address C2 interface Serial1 dlci 16 8
bstun route address C1 interface Serial1 dlci 16 4
```

BSTUN-over-Frame Relay Configuration Example for Passthru

```
bstun protocol-group 1 bsc

interface Serial1
encapsulation frame-relay
clockrate 125000
frame-relay map bstun 16

interface Serial4
 no ip address
encapsulation bstun
bstun group 1
bsc secondary
bstun route address C3 interface Serial1 dlci 16
bstun route address C2 interface Serial1 dlci 16
bstun route address C1 interface Serial1 dlci 16
```

10

Serial Tunnel and Block Serial Tunnel Commands

Cisco's serial tunnel (STUN) feature allows Synchronous Data Link Control (SDLC) or High-Level Data Link Control (HDLC) devices to connect to one another through a multiprotocol internetwork rather than through a direct serial link. STUN encapsulates SDLC frames in either the Transmission Control Protocol/Internet Protocol (TCP/IP) or the HDLC protocol. STUN provides a straight passthrough of all SDLC traffic (including control frames, such as Receiver Ready) end-to-end between Systems Network Architecture (SNA) devices.

Cisco's SDLC local acknowledgment provides local termination of the SDLC session so that control frames no longer travel the WAN backbone networks. This means end nodes do not time out, and a loss of sessions does not occur. You can configure your network with STUN, or with STUN and SDLC local acknowledgment. To enable SDLC local acknowledgment, the Cisco IOS software must first be enabled for STUN and routers configured to appear on the network as primary or secondary SDLC nodes. TCP/IP encapsulation must be enabled. Cisco's SDLC transport feature also provides priority queuing for TCP encapsulated frames.

Cisco's block serial tunnel (BSTUN) implementation enables Cisco series 2500, 3600, 4000, 4500, 4700, and 7200 routers to support devices that use the Binary Synchronous Communications (Bisync) datalink protocol and asynchronous security protocols that include Adplex, ADT Security Systems, Inc., Diebold, asynchronous generic, and mdi traffic. Cisco's support of the Bisync protocol enables enterprises to transport Bisync traffic and SNA multiprotocol traffic over the same network.

Use the commands in this chapter to configure BSTUN, Bisync, STUN, and SDLC local acknowledgment networks. For STUN and BSTUN configuration information and examples, see Chapter 9, "Configuring Serial Tunnel and Block Serial Tunnel."

ASP ADDR-OFFSET

Use the **asp addr-offset** interface configuration command to configure an asynchronous port to transmit and receive polled asynchronous traffic through a BSTUN tunnel. Use the **no** form of this command to cancel the specification.

> **asp addr-offset** *address-offset*
> **no asp addr-offset**

Syntax	Description
address-offset	Location of the address byte within the polled asynchronous frame being received.

Default

No default is specified.

Command Mode

Interface configuration

Usage Guidelines

This command first appeared in Cisco IOS Release 11.2 F.

This command is used to specify the offset from the start of the frame where the address byte is located. This command only applies when the asynchronous-generic protocol has been specified on an interface using a combination of the **bstun protocol-group** global configuration command and the **bstun group** interface configuration command.

Interfaces configured to run the asynchronous-generic protocol have their baud rate set to 9600 bps, use 8 data bits, no parity, 1 start bit, and 1 stop bit. If different line configurations are required, use the **rxspeed, txspeed, databits, stopbits,** and **parity** line configuration commands to change the line attributes.

The addresses of the alarm panels should be used in the address field of the **bstun route address** interface configuration command.

Example

The following example specifies that the first byte in the polled asynchronous frame contains the device address:

```
asp addr-offset 0
```

Related Commands

asp role
asp rx-ift
bstun protocol-group
bstun route

ASP ROLE

Use the **asp role** interface configuration command to specify whether the router is acting as the primary end of the polled asynchronous link or as the secondary end of the polled asynchronous link connected to the serial interface and the attached remote device is a security alarm control station. Use the **no** form of this command to cancel the specification.

> **asp role {primary | secondary}**
> **no asp role {primary | secondary}**

Syntax	Description
primary	Router is the primary end of the polled asynchronous link connected to the serial interface, and the attached remote devices are alarm panels.
secondary	Router is the secondary end of the polled asynchronous link connected to the serial interface, and the attached remote device is a security alarm control station.

Part II

Command Reference

Default

No default is specified.

Command Mode

Interface configuration

Usage Guidelines

This command first appeared in Cisco IOS Release 11.2 F.

This command enables the interface on which ASP is configured. Configure the interface connected to the alarm console as a secondary router and the interface connected to the alarm panel as a primary router.

The addresses of the alarm panels should be used in the address field of the **bstun route address** interface configuration command.

Example

The following example specifies the router as the primary end of the link:

```
asp role primary
```

Related Commands

bstun route

ASP RX-IFT

Use the **asp rx-ift** interface configuration command to specify a time period that, by expiring, signals the end of one frame being received and the start of the next. Use the **no** form of this command to cancel the specification.

> **asp rx-ift** *interframe-timeout*
> **no asp rx-ift**

Syntax	Description
interframe-timeout	Number of milliseconds between the end of one frame being received and the start of the next frame.

Default

The default timeout value is 40 ms.

Command Mode

Interface configuration

Usage Guidelines

This command first appeared in Cisco IOS Release 11.2 F.

The interframe timeout is useful when different baud rates are used between the router and the alarm console or alarm panel. For example, you might set an interframe timeout of 6 ms if the polled asynchronous protocol is running at 9600 bps, but set the value to 40 ms if the protocol is running at 300 bps.

This command applies only when the asynchronous-generic protocol has been specified on an interface using a combination of the **bstun protocol-group** global configuration command and the **bstun group** interface configuration command.

Interfaces configured to run the asynchronous-generic protocol have their baud rate set to 9600 bps, use 8 data bits, no parity, 1 start bit, and 1 stop bit. If different line configurations are required, use the **rxspeed, txspeed, databits, stopbits,** and **parity** line configuration commands to change the line attributes.

The addresses of the alarm panels should be used in the address field of the **bstun route address** interface configuration command.

Example

The following example sets the interframe timeout value to 6 ms because the polled asynchronous protocol is running at 9600 bps:

```
asp rx-ift 6
```

Related Commands

asp addr-offset
asp role
bstun protocol-group
bstun route

BSC CHAR-SET

Use the **bsc char-set** interface configuration command to specify the character set used by the Bisync support feature in this serial interface as either EBCDIC or ASCII. Use the **no** form of this command to cancel the character set specification.

> bsc char-set {ascii | ebcdic}
> no bsc char-set {ascii | ebcdic}

Syntax	Description
ascii	ASCII character set.
ebcdic	EBCDIC character set.

Default

EBCDIC

Command Mode

Interface configuration

Usage Guidelines

This command first appeared in Cisco IOS Release 11.0.

Example

The following command specifies that the ASCII character set will be used:

```
bsc char-set ascii
```

BSC CONTENTION

Use the **bsc contention** interface configuration command to specify an address on a contention interface. Use the **no** form of this command to cancel the specification.

bsc contention *address*
no bsc contention

Syntax   *Description*

address   Address assigned to contention interface. The range is 1 to 255. The
                          default is 0x01.

Default

The default address is 0x01 to accommodate backward compatibility to the previous point-to-point
contention implementation.

Command Mode

Interface configuration

Usage Guidelines

This command first appeared in Cisco IOS Release 11.0.

Example

The following command specifies address 20 on the remote device:

```
bsc contention 20
```

Related Commands

bsc dial-contention

BSC DIAL-CONTENTION

Use the **bsc dial-contention** interface configuration command to specify a router at the central site
as a central router with dynamic allocation of serial interfaces. Use the **no** form of this command
to cancel the specification. A timeout value is configurable to ensure that an interface does not get
locked out because of a device outage during transmission.

bsc dial-contention *time-out*
no bsc dial-contention

Syntax   *Description*

time-out   Amount of time interface can sit idle before it is returned to the idle
                          interface pool. The range is 2 to 30 seconds. The default is 5 seconds.

Default

5 seconds

Command Mode

Interface configuration

Usage Guidelines

This command first appeared in Cisco IOS Release 11.2 F.

Example

The following command defines a dial-in interface at the central site with an idle timeout of 10 seconds:

```
bsc dial-contention 10
```

Related Commands

bsc contention

BSC HOST-TIMEOUT

Use the **bsc host-timeout** interface configuration command to detect deactivation of devices at the host. Use the **no** form of this command to cancel the configuration.

bsc host-timeout *interval*
no host-timeout *interval*

Syntax	Description
interval	Timeout interval within which a poll or select for a control unit must be received. If this interval expires, the remote router is sent a teardown peer signal. The range is 30 to 3000 deciseconds. The default is 60 seconds.

Default

The default interval is 60 seconds.

Command Mode

Interface configuration

Usage Guidelines

This command first appeared in Cisco IOS Release 11.2 F.

This command is used to detect deactivation of devices at the host. If the host is told to deactivate or not poll a device, it will take time for the signal to propagate the network and get the remote end from polling. The timeout can be used to fine tune the delay in detecting the host outage. The remote peer will stop polling the control unit that has timed-out in the interval 1 to 2 times the configured timeout value.

Example

The following example configures a timeout of 50 seconds:

```
bsc host-timeout 500
```

Related Commands

bsc secondary
bstun group
bstun protocol-group

BSC PAUSE

Use the **bsc pause** interface configuration command to specify the interval to the tenth of a second, between starts of the polling cycle. Use the **no** form of this command to cancel the specification.

> **bsc pause** *time*
> **no bsc pause** *time*

Syntax   *Description*

time   Interval in tenths of a second. The default value is 10 (1 second). The maximum time is 25.5 seconds.

Default

10 (1 second)

Command Mode

Interface configuration

Usage Guidelines

This command first appeared in Cisco IOS Release 11.0.

Example

The following command sets the interval to 2 seconds:

```
bsc pause 20
```

BSC POLL-TIMEOUT

Use the **bsc poll-timeout** interface configuration command to specify the timeout, in tenths of a second, for a poll or select sequence. Use the **no** form of this command to cancel the specification.

> **bsc poll-timeout** *time*
> **no bsc poll-timeout** *time*

Syntax	Description
time	Time in tenths of a second. The default value is 10 (1 second).

Default

10 (1 second)

Command Mode

Interface configuration

Usage Guidelines

This command first appeared in Cisco IOS Release 11.0.

Example

The following command sets the interval to 2 seconds:

```
bsc poll-timeout 20
```

BSC PRIMARY

Use the **bsc primary** interface configuration command to specify that the router is acting as the primary end of the Bisync link connected to the serial interface, and that the attached remote devices are Bisync tributary stations. Use the **no** form of this command to cancel the specification.

> **bsc primary**
> **no bsc primary**

Syntax   Description

This command has no arguments or keywords.

Default

No default is specified.

Command Mode

Interface configuration

Usage Guidelines

This command first appeared in Cisco IOS Release 11.0.

The Bisync support feature in the serial interface uses the address of the incoming encapsulation for reply.

Example

The following example specifies the router as the primary role:

```
bsc primary
```

Related Commands

bstun route

BSC RETRIES

Use the **bsc retries** interface configuration command to specify the number of retries performed before a device is considered to have failed. Use the **no** form of this command to cancel the specification.

> **bsc retries** *retries*
> **no bsc retries** *retries*

Syntax	*Description*
retries	Number of retries before a device fails. The default is 5.

Default

5 retries

Command Mode

Interface configuration

Usage Guidelines

This command first appeared in Cisco IOS Release 11.0.

Example

The following command sets the retry count to 10:

```
bsc retries 10
```

BSC SECONDARY

Use the **bsc secondary** interface configuration command to specify that the router is acting as the secondary end of the Bisync link connected to the serial interface, and the attached remote device is a Bisync control station. Use the **no** form of this command to cancel the specification.

> **bsc secondary**
> **no bsc secondary**

Syntax Description

This command has no arguments or keywords.

Default

No default is specified.

Command Mode

Interface configuration

Usage Guidelines

This command first appeared in Cisco IOS Release 11.0.

The Bisync support feature in this serial interface uses the address of the poll or selection block in the framing encapsulation. It also generates an end of transmission (EOT) frame preceding each Bisync poll and selection.

Example

The following example specifies the router as the secondary role:

```
bsc secondary
```

Related Commands

bstun route

BSC SERVLIM

Use the **bsc servlim** interface configuration command to specify the number of cycles of the active poll list that are performed between polls to control units in the inactive poll list. Use the **no** form of this command to cancel the specification.

> **bsc servlim** *servlim-count*
> **no bsc servlim** *servlim-count*

Syntax   Description

servlim-count   Number of cycles. The range is 1 to 50. The default is 3.

Default

3 cycles

Command Mode

Interface configuration

Usage Guidelines

This command first appeared in Cisco IOS Release 11.0.

Example

The following command sets the number of cycles to 2:

```
bsc servlim 2
```

BSC SPEC-POLL

Use the **bsc spec-poll** interface configuration command to set specific polls, rather than general polls, used on the host-to-router connection. Use the **no** form of this command to cancel the specification.

> **bsc spec-poll**
> **no spec-poll**

Syntax   Description

This command has no arguments or keywords.

Default

No default is specified.

Command Mode

Interface configuration

Usage Guidelines

This command first appeared in Cisco IOS Release 11.1.

Use the **bsc spec-poll** command when a router is connected to a host, and only when that host issues specific polls rather than general polls. Tandem hosts that poll ATM cash machines typically are configured to use specific polls rather than general polls.

Configuring a downstream (control-unit/device connected) router to support specific polling has no effect.

Example

The following commands configure interface serial 0 to use specific poll:

```
interface serial 0
 description Connection to host.
 encapsulation bstun
 bstun group 1
 bsc secondary
 bsc spec-poll
 bsc char-set ebcdic
 bstun route all tcp <ip-addr-of-remote-peer>
```

BSTUN GROUP

Use the **bstun group** interface configuration command to specify the BSTUN group to which the interface belongs. Use the **no** form of this command to remove the interface from the BSTUN group.

> **bstun group** *group-number*
> **no bstun group** *group-number*

Syntax	Description
group-number	BSTUN group to which the interface belongs.

Default

No default is specified.

Command Mode

Interface configuration

Usage Guidelines

This command first appeared in Cisco IOS Release 11.0.

Each BSTUN-enabled interface must be placed in a BSTUN group previously defined by the **bstun protocol-group** command. Packets only travel between BSTUN-enabled interfaces that are in the same group.

Example

The following example specifies that serial interface 1 belongs to the previously defined protocol group 1:

```
interface serial 1
 encapsulation bstun
 bstun group 1
```

Related Commands

bstun protocol-group
encapsulation bstun

BSTUN KEEPALIVE-COUNT

Use the **bstun keepalive-count** global configuration command to define the number of times to attempt a peer connection before declaring the peer connection to be down. Use the **no** form of this command to cancel the definition.

> **bstun keepalive-count** *count*
> **no bstun keepalive-count**

Syntax	Description
count	Number of connection attempts. The range is between 2 and 10 retries.

Default

No default is specified.

Command Mode

Global configuration

Usage Guidelines

This command first appeared in Cisco IOS Release 11.1.

Example

The following example sets the number of times to retry a connection to a peer to 4:

```
bstun keepalive-count 4
```

Related Commands

bstun remote-peer-keepalive

BSTUN LISNSAP

Use the **bstun lisnsap** global configuration command to configure a SAP on which to listen for incoming calls. Use the **no** form of this command to cancel the lisnsap.

> **bstun lisnsap** *sap-value*
> **no bstun lisnsap**

Syntax	Description
sap-value	SAP on which to listen for incoming calls. The default is 04.

Default

The default SAP value is 04.

Command Mode

Global configuration

Usage Guidelines

This command first appeared in Cisco IOS Release 11.2 F.

Changes to the **bstun lisnsap** command configuration will not take effect until after the router has been reloaded.

Example

The following example configures a SAP for listening:

```
bstun lisnsap
```

Related Commands

bstun route (Frame Relay)
frame-relay map bstun
frame-relay map llc2

BSTUN PEER-NAME

Use the **bstun peer-name** global configuration command to enable the block serial tunneling function. Use the **no** form of this command to disable the function.

> **bstun peer-name** *ip-address*
> **no bstun peer-name** *ip-address*

Syntax	Description
ip-address	Address by which this BSTUN peer is known to other BSTUN peers that are using the TCP transport.

Default

No default is specified.

Command Mode

Global configuration

Usage Guidelines

This command first appeared in Cisco IOS Release 11.0.

The IP address defines the address by which this BSTUN peer is known to other BSTUN peers that are using the TCP transport. If this command is unconfigured or the **no** form of this command is specified, all BSTUN routing commands with IP addresses are deleted. BSTUN routing commands without IP addresses are not affected by this command.

Example

The following example enables the block serial tunneling function:

```
bstun peer-name 150.10.254.201
```

Related Commands

bstun protocol-group

BSTUN PROTOCOL-GROUP

Use the **bstun protocol-group** global configuration command to define a BSTUN group and the protocol it uses. Use the **no** form of this command to delete the BSTUN group.

> **bstun protocol-group** *group-number protocol*
> **no bstun protocol-group** *group-number protocol*

Syntax	*Description*
group-number	BSTUN group number. Valid numbers are decimal integers in the range 1 to 255.
protocol	Block serial protocol, selected from the following:

adplex
adt-poll-select
adt-vari-poll
async-generic
bsc
bsc-local-ack
diebold
mdi

Default

No defaults are specified.

Command Mode

Global configuration

Usage Guidelines

This command first appeared in Cisco IOS Release 11.0.

Interfaces configured to run the Adplex protocol have their baud rate set to 4800 bps, use even parity, 8 data bits, 1 start bit, and 1 stop bit.

Interfaces configured to run the adt-vari-poll and adt-poll-select protocols have their baud rate set to 600 bps, use even parity, 8 data bits, 1 start bit, and 1.5 stop bits. If different line configurations are required, use the **rxspeed, txspeed, databits, stopbits,** and **parity** line configuration commands to change the line attributes.

Interfaces configured to run the asynchronous-generic protocol have their baud rate set to 9600 bps, use no parity, 8 data bits, 1 start bit, and 1 stop bit. If different line configurations are required, use the **rxspeed, txspeed, databits, stopbits,** and **parity** line configuration commands to change the line attributes.

Interfaces configured to run the mdi protocol have their baud rate set to 600 bps, use even parity, 8 data bits, 1 start bit, and 1.5 stop bits. If different line configurations are required, use the **rxspeed, txspeed, databits, stopbits,** and **parity** line configuration commands to change the line attributes. The mdi protocol allows alarm panels to be sent to the the MDI alarm console.

Example

The following example defines BSTUN group 1, specifies that it uses the Bisync protocol, and indicates that frames will be locally acknowledged:

```
bstun protocol-group 1 bsc-local-ack
```

Related Commands

bstun group

BSTUN REMOTE-PEER-KEEPALIVE

Use the **bstun remote-peer-keepalive** global configuration command to enable detection of the loss of a peer. Use the **no** form of this command to disable detection.

bstun remote-peer-keepalive *seconds*
no bstun remote-peer-keepalive

Syntax	*Description*
seconds	Keepalive interval, in seconds. The range is 1 to 300 seconds.

Default

30 seconds

Command Mode

Global configuration

Usage Guidelines

This command first appeared in Cisco IOS Release 11.1.

Example

In the following example, the remote-peer-keepalive interval is set to 60 seconds:

```
bstun remote-peer-keepalive 60
```

Related Commands

bstun keepalive-count

BSTUN ROUTE

Use the **bstun route** interface configuration command to define how frames will be forwarded from a BSTUN interface to a remote BSTUN peer. Use the **no** form of this command to cancel the definition.

> **bstun route** {**all** | **address** *address-number*} {**tcp** *ip-address* | **interface serial** *number*} [**direct**]
>
> **no bstun route** {**all** | **address** *address-number*} {**tcp** *ip-address* | **interface serial** *number*} [**direct**]

Syntax	Description
all	All BSTUN traffic received on the input interface is propagated, regardless of the address contained in the serial frame.
address	Serial frame that contains a specific address is propagated.
address-number	Poll address, a hexadecimal number from 01 to FF (but not all values are valid). The reply address to be used on the return leg is calculated from the configured poll address.
tcp	TCP encapsulation is used to propagate frames that match the entry.
ip-address	IP address of the remote BSTUN peer.
interface serial	HDLC encapsulation is used to propagate the serial frames.
number	Serial line to an appropriately configured router on the other end.
direct	(Optional) Specified interface is also a direct BSTUN link, rather than a serial connection to another peer.

Default

No defaults are specified.

Command Mode

Interface configuration

Usage Guidelines

This command first appeared in Cisco IOS Release 11.0.

When the ADplex protocol is specified in the **bstun protocol-group** command, ADplex device addresses are limited to the range 1 to 127 because ADplex alarm panels invert the device address in the ADplex frame when responding to alarm console commands.

When the adt-poll-select protocol is specified in the **bstun protocol-group** command, routes for specific addresses cannot be specified on the downstream router (connected to the alarm panel), because no address field is provided within frames that are sent back to the alarm console. The only way to route traffic back to the alarm console is to use the **bstun route all** form of the **bstun route** command. This is also true for the diebold protocol and any other protocol supported by the asynchronous-generic protocol group that does not include a device address in the frame.

When the adt-vari-poll protocol is specified in the **bstun protocol-group** command, ADT device addresses are limited to the range 0 to 255, and address 0 is reserved for use as a broadcast address for adt-vari-poll only. If address 0 is specified in the **bstun route address** form of the **bstun route** command, the address is propagated to all configured BSTUN peers.

It is possible to use both the **all** and the **address** keywords on different **bstun route** commands on the same serial interface. When this is done, the **address** specifications take precedence; if none of these match, then the **all** specification is used to propagate the frame.

Example

In the following example, all BSTUN traffic received on serial interface 0 is propagated, regardless of the address contained in the serial frame:

```
bstun route all interface serial 0
```

BSTUN ROUTE (FRAME RELAY)

Use the **bstun route** interface configuration command to define how frames will be forwarded from a BSTUN interface to a remote BSTUN peer over Frame Relay. Use the **no** form of this command to cancel the definition.

> **bstun route** {**all** | **address** *cu-address*} **interface serial** *number* **dlci** *dlci rsap* **priority** *priority*
>
> **no bstun route** {**all** | **address** *cu-address*} **interface serial** *number* **dlci** *dlci rsap* **priority** *priority*]

Syntax	Description
all	All BSTUN traffic received on the input interface is propagated, regardless of the address contained in the serial frame.
address	Serial frames that contain a specific address are propagated.
cu-address	Control unit address for the Bisync end station.
interface serial *number*	Specify a serial interface on which Frame Relay encapsulation is used to propagate serial frames.
dlci *dlci*	Data-link connection identifier to be used on the Frame Relay interface.
rsap	Remote SAP, to be used when initiating an LLC2 session. This argument is configurable only if the interface group number supports local acknowledgment.
priority *priority*	Priority port to be used for this LLC2 session. Configurable only if the interface group number supports local acknowledgment.

Default

No defaults are specified.

Command Mode

Interface configuration

Usage Guidelines

This command first appeared in Cisco IOS Release 11.1.

Example

The following example configures BSTUN over Frame Relay. All BSTUN traffic is propagated to serial interface 0 regardless of the address contained in the serial frame:

```
bstun route all interface serial 0 dlci 16
```

ENCAPSULATION BSTUN

Use the **encapsulation bstun** interface configuration command to configure BSTUN on a particular serial interface. Use the **no** form of this command to disable the BSTUN function on the interface.

> **encapsulation bstun**
> **no encapsulation bstun**

Syntax   Description

This command has no arguments or keywords.

Default

No default is specified.

Command Mode

Interface configuration

Usage Guidelines

This command first appeared in Cisco IOS Release 11.0.

The **encapsulation bstun** command must be configured on an interface before any further BSTUN or Bisync commands are configured for the interface.

You must use this command to enable BSTUN on an interface. Before using this command, complete the following two tasks:

- Enable BSTUN on a global basis by identifying BSTUN on IP addresses. The command is **bstun peer-name**.
- Define a protocol-group number to be applied to the interface. Packets only travel between interfaces that are in the same protocol group. The command is **bstun protocol-group**.

After using the **encapsulation bstun** command, use the **bstun group** command to place the interface in the previously defined protocol group.

Example

The following example configures the BSTUN function on serial interface 0:

```
interface serial 0
  no ip address
  encapsulation bstun
```

Related Commands

bstun group
bstun peer-name
bstun protocol-group

ENCAPSULATION STUN

Use the **encapsulation stun** interface configuration command to enable STUN encapsulation on a specified serial interface.

encapsulation stun

Syntax   Description

This command has no arguments or keywords.

Default

STUN encapsulation is disabled.

Command Mode

Interface configuration

Usage Guidelines

This command first appeared in Cisco IOS Release 10.0.

Use this command to enable STUN on an interface. Before using this command, complete the following two tasks:

- Enable STUN on a global basis by identifying STUN on IP addresses. The command is **stun peer-name**.
- Define a protocol-group number to be applied to the interface. Packets only travel between interfaces that are in the same protocol group. The command is **stun protocol-group**.

After using the **encapsulation stun** command, use the **stun group** command to place the interface in the previously defined protocol group.

Example

This partial configuration example shows how to enable serial interface 5 for STUN traffic:

```
! sample stun peer name and stun protocol-group global commands
stun peer-name 131.108.254.6
stun protocol-group 2 sdlc
!
interface serial 5
! sample ip address command
no ip address
! enable the interface for STUN; must specify encapsulation stun
! command to further configure the interface
encapsulation stun
! place interface serial 5 in previously defined STUN group 2
stun group 2
! enter stun route command
stun route 7 tcp 131.108.254.7
```

Related Commands

stun group
stun peer-name
stun protocol-group

FRAME-RELAY MAP BSTUN

Use the **frame-relay map bstun** interface configuration command to configure BSTUN over Frame Relay for passthru. Use the **no** form of this command to cancel the configuration.

> **frame-relay map bstun** *dlci*
> **no frame-relay map bstun** *dlci*

Syntax	Description
dlci	Frame Relay DLCI number on which to support passthru.

Default

No default is specified.

Command Mode

Interface configuration

Usage Guidelines

This command first appeared in Cisco IOS Release 11.2 F.

Example

The following example maps BSTUN traffic to DLCI number 16:

```
frame-relay map bstun 16
```

Related Commands

bstun lisnsap
bstun protocol-group
encapsulation frame-relay

FRAME-RELAY MAP LLC2

Use the **frame-relay map llc2** interface configuration command to configure BSTUN over Frame Relay when using Bisync local acknowledgment. Use the **no** form of this command to cancel the configuration.

> **frame-relay map llc2** *dlci*
> **no frame-relay map llc2** *dlci*

Syntax	Description
dlci	Frame Relay DLCI number on which to support local acknowledgment.

Default

No default is specified.

Command Mode

Interface configuration

Usage Guidelines

This command first appeared in Cisco IOS Release 11.2 F.

Example

The following example maps BSTUN traffic to DLCI number 16:

```
frame-relay map DLCI 16
```

Related Commands

bstun lisnsap
bstun protocol-group
encapsulation frame-relay

LOCADDR-PRIORITY-LIST

Use the **locaddr-priority-list** interface configuration command to establish queuing priorities based upon the address of the logical unit (LU). Use the **no** form of this command to cancel all previous assignments.

> **locaddr-priority-list** *list-number address-number queue-keyword*
> **no locaddr-priority-list**

Syntax	Description
list-number	Arbitrary integer between 1 and 10 that identifies the LU address priority list.
address-number	Value of the LOCADDR=parameter on the LU macro, which is a 1-byte address of the LU in hexadecimal.
queue-keyword	Priority queue type: **high, medium, normal,** or **low.**

Default

No queuing priorities are established.

Command Mode

Interface configuration

Usage Guidelines

This command first appeared in Cisco IOS Release 10.0.

Example

The following example shows how to establish queuing priorities based on the address of the serial link on a STUN connection. Note that you must use the **priority-group** interface configuration command to assign a priority group to an input interface:

```
stun peer-name 131.108.254.6
stun protocol-group 1 sdlc
!
interface serial 0
 no ip address
 encapsulation stun
 stun group 1
 stun route address 4 interface serial 0 direct
 locaddr priority 1
 priority-group 1
!
 locaddr-priority-list 1 02 high
 locaddr-priority-list 1 03 high
 locaddr-priority-list 1 04 medium
 locaddr-priority-list 1 05 low
```

Related Commands

priority-group

PRIORITY-GROUP

Use the **priority-group** interface configuration command to assign a priority group to an interface. Use the **no** form of this command to remove assignments.

> **priority-group** *list-number*
> **no priority-group** *list-number*

Syntax	*Description*
list-number	Priority list number assigned to the interface.

Default

No priority group is assigned.

Command Mode

Interface configuration

Usage Guidelines

This command first appeared in Cisco IOS Release 10.0.

Example

The following example shows how to establish queuing priorities based on the address of the serial link on a STUN connection. Note that you must use the **priority-group** interface configuration command to assign a priority group to an output interface.

```
! sample stun peer-name global command
stun peer-name 131.108.254.6
! sample protocol-group command for reference
stun protocol-group 1 sdlc
!
interface serial 0
! disable the ip address for interface serial 0
no ip address
! enable the interface for STUN
encapsulation stun
! sample stun group command
stun group 2
! sample stun route command
stun route address 10 tcp 131.108.254.8 local-ack priority
!
! assign priority group 1 to the input side of interface serial 0
priority-group 1
```

```
! assign a low priority to priority list 1 on serial link identified
! by group 2 and address A7
priority-list 1 stun low address 2 A7
```

Related Commands

locaddr-priority-list
priority-list protocol ip tcp
priority-list stun address

PRIORITY-LIST PROTOCOL BSTUN

Use the **priority-list protocol bstun** global configuration command to establish BSTUN queuing priorities based on the BSTUN header. Use the **no** form of this command to revert to normal priorities.

> **priority-list** *list-number* **protocol bstun** *queue* [**gt** | **lt** *packetsize*]
>   [**address** *bstun-group bsc-addr*]
> **no priority-list** *list-number* **protocol bstun** *queue* [**gt** | **lt** *packetsize*]
>   [**address** *bstun-group bsc-addr*]

Syntax	Description
list-number	Arbitrary integer between 1 and 10 that identifies the priority list selected by the user.
queue	Priority queue type: **high, medium, normal,** or **low.**
gt	**lt** *packetsize*	(Optional) Output interface examines header information *and* packet size and places packets with the BSTUN header that match criteria (gt- or lt-specified packet size) on specified output.
address *bstun-group bsc-addr*	(Optional) Output interface examines header information and Bisync address and places packets with the BSTUN header that match Bisync address on the specified output queue.

Default

Prioritize based on BSTUN header.

Command Mode

Global configuration

Usage Guidelines

This command first appeared in Cisco IOS Release 11.0.

Example

In the following example, the output interface examines the header information and places packets with the BSTUN header on the output queue specified as medium.

```
priority-list 1 protocol bstun medium
```

Related Commands

encapsulation bstun

PRIORITY-LIST PROTOCOL IP TCP

Use the **priority-list protocol ip tcp** global configuration command to establish BSTUN or STUN queuing priorities based on the TCP port. Use the **no** form of this command to revert to normal priorities.

priority-list *list-number* **protocol ip** *queue* **tcp** *tcp-port-number*
no priority-list *list-number* **protocol ip** *queue* **tcp** *tcp-port-number*

Syntax	Description
list-number	Arbitrary integer between 1 and 10 that identifies the priority list selected by the user.
queue	Priority queue type: **high, medium, normal,** or **low.**
tcp-port-number	BSTUN port and priority settings are as follows: High—BSTUN port 1976 Medium—BSTUN port 1977 Normal—BSTUN port 1978 Low—BSTUN port 1979
	STUN port and priority settings are as follows: High—STUN port 1994 Medium—STUN port 1990 Normal—STUN port 1991 Low—STUN port 1992

Default

The default is normal queue.

Command Mode

Global configuration

Usage Guidelines

This command first appeared in Cisco IOS Release 10.0.

Use the **priority-list stun address** command first. Priority settings created with this command are assigned to SDLC ports.

NOTES

SDLC local acknowledgment with the priority option must be enabled using the **stun route address tcp** command.

Examples

In the following example, queuing priority for address C1 using priority list 1 is set to high. A priority queue of high is assigned to the SDLC port 1994.

```
priority-list 1 stun high address 1 c1
priority-list 1 protocol ip high tcp 1994
```

In the following example, queuing priority for address C1 using priority list 1 is set to high. A priority queue of high is assigned to BSTUN port 1976.

```
priority-list bstun high address 1 c1
priority-list 1 protocol ip high 1976
```

Related Commands

bstun protocol-group
encapsulation bstun
encapsulation stun
priority-group
priority-list stun address
stun route address tcp

PRIORITY-LIST STUN ADDRESS

Use the **priority-list stun address** global configuration command to establish STUN queuing priorities based on the address of the serial link. Use the **no** form of this command to revert to normal priorities.

> priority-list *list-number* **stun** *queue* **address** *group-number address-number*
> no priority-list *list-number* **stun** *queue-keyword* **address** *group-number address-number*

Syntax	Description
list-number	Arbitrary integer between 1 and 10 that identifies the priority list selected by the user.
queue	Priority queue type: **high, medium, normal,** or **low.**
group-number	Group number that is used in the **stun group** command.
address-number	Address of the serial link. For an SDLC link, the format is a 1-byte hex value (for example, C1). For a non-SDLC link, the address format can be specified by the **stun schema** command.

Default

The default is normal queue.

Command Mode

Global configuration

Usage Guidelines

This command first appeared in Cisco IOS Release 10.0.

NOTES

SDLC local acknowledgment with the priority option must be enabled using the **stun route address interface serial** command.

Example

In the following example, queuing priority for address C1 using priority list 1 is set to high:

```
priority-list 1 stun high address 1 c1
```

Related Commands

priority-list protocol ip tcp
stun group
stun route address interface serial
stun schema offset length format

QUEUE-LIST PROTOCOL BSTUN

Use the **queue-list protocol bstun** global configuration command to customize BSTUN queuing priorities based on the BSTUN header. Use the **no** form of this command to revert to normal priorities.

> **queue-list** *list-number* **protocol bstun** *queue* [**gt** | **lt** *packetsize*]
>   [**address** *bstun-group bsc-addr*]
> **no queue-list** *list-number* **protocol bstun** *queue* [**gt** | **lt** *packetsize*]
>   [**address** *bstun-group bsc-addr*]

Syntax	Description
list-number	Arbitrary integer between 1 and 10 that identifies the priority list selected by the user.
queue	Priority queue type: **high, medium, normal,** or **low.**

Syntax	Description
gt | **lt** *packetsize*	(Optional) Output interface examines header information *and* packet size and places packets with the BSTUN header that match criteria (gt- or lt-specified packet size) on specified output.
address *bstun-group bsc-addr*	(Optional) Output interface examines header information and Bisync address and places packets with the BSTUN header that match Bisync address on the specified output queue.

Default
Prioritize based on BSTUN header.

Command Mode
Global configuration

Usage Guidelines
This command first appeared in Cisco IOS Release 11.0.

Example
In the following example, the output interface examines the header information and places packets with the BSTUN header on the output queue specified as medium.

```
queue-list 1 protocol bstun medium
```

Related Commands
encapsulation bstun

QUEUE-LIST PROTOCOL IP TCP

Use the **queue-list protocol ip tcp** global configuration command to customize BSTUN queuing priorities based on the TCP port. Use the **no** form of this command to revert to normal priorities.

> **queue-list** *list-number* **protocol ip** *queue* **tcp** *tcp-port-number*
> **no queue-list** *list-number* **protocol ip** *queue* **tcp** *tcp-port-number*

Syntax	Description
list-number	Arbitrary integer between 1 and 10 that identifies the priority list selected by the user.
queue	Priority queue type: **high, medium, normal,** or **low.**

Syntax	Description
tcp-port-number	BSTUN port and priority settings are as follows: High—BSTUN port 1976 Medium—BSTUN port 1977 Normal—BSTUN port 1978 Low—BSTUN port 1979
	STUN port and priority settings are as follows: High—STUN port 1994 Medium—STUN port 1990 Normal—STUN port 1991 Low—STUN port 1992

Default

The default is normal queue.

Command Mode

Global configuration

Usage Guidelines

This command first appeared in Cisco IOS Release 11.0.

Example

In the following example, queuing priority for address C1 using priority list 1 is set to high. A priority queue of high is assigned to BSTUN port 1976.

```
queue-list bstun high address 1 c1
queue-list 1 protocol ip high 1976
```

Related Commands

encapsulation bstun

SDLC VIRTUAL-MULTIDROP

Use the **sdlc virtual-multidrop** interface configuration command to allow SDLC broadcast address FF to be replicated for each of the STUN peers so each of the end stations receive the broadcast frame. Use the **no** form of this command to disable the SDLC broadcast feature.

> sdlc virtual-multidrop
> no sdlc virtual-multidrop

Syntax   Description

This command has no arguments or keywords.

Default

SDLC broadcast is disabled.

Command Mode

Interface configuration

Usage Guidelines

This command first appeared in Cisco IOS Release 10.3.

Example

The following example allows each STUN peer to receive a broadcast frame:

```
sdlc virtual-multidrop
```

Related Commands

stun route address tcp

SHOW BSC

Use the **show bsc** privileged EXEC command to display statistics about the interfaces on which Bisync is configured.

> **show bsc** [**group** *bstun-group-number*] [**address** *address-list*]

Syntax	Description
bstun-group-number	BSTUN group number. Valid numbers are decimal integers in the range 1 to 255.
address-list	List of poll addresses.

Command Mode

Privileged EXEC

Usage Guidelines

This command first appeared in Cisco IOS Release 11.0.

Sample Displays

The following is sample output from the **show bsc** command:

```
Router# show bsc

BSC pass-through on Serial4:
HDX enforcement state: IDLE.
Frame sequencing state: IDLE.
```

```
Total Tx Counts: 0 frames(total). 0 frames(data). 0 bytes.
Total Rx Counts: 0 frames(total). 0 frames(data). 0 bytes.

BSC local-ack on serial5:
Secondary state is CU_Idle.
Control units on this interface:

        Poll address: C2. Select address: E2.
        State is Active.
        Tx Counts: 1137 frames(total). 0 frames(data). 1137 bytes.
        Rx Counts: 1142 frames(total). 0 frames(data). 5710 bytes.

        Poll address: C3. Select address: E3 *CURRENT-CU*
        State is Active.
        Tx Counts: 1136 frames(total). 0 frames(data). 1136 bytes.
        Rx Counts: 1142 frames(total). 0 frames(data). 5710 bytes.

Total Tx Counts: 2273 frames(total). 0 frames(data). 2273 bytes.
Total Rx Counts: 2284 frames(total). 0 frames(data). 11420 bytes.
```

Table 10–1 describes significant fields shown in the display.

Table 10–1 *Show BSC Command Field Descriptions*

Field	Description
BSC *x* on *interface y*	Indicates whether the router is configured for passthru or local acknowledgment on the indicated interface.
Output queue depth	Packets queued on this interface. This field is only displayed when the value is not zero.
Frame builder state	Current frame building state. This field is only displayed when the state is not IDLE.
HDX enforcement state	Current half-duplex transmit enforcement state. The possible values are: • IDLE—Waiting for communication activity. • PND_COMP—Waiting for router to transmit. • PND_RCV—Waiting for attached device to respond to transmission.
Frame sequencing state	Frame sequencing state to protect against network latencies. When the router is configured as the primary end of the link, the possible values are: • IDLE—Waiting for a poll. • SEC—In a session with a device.

Table 10–1   *Show BSC Command Field Descriptions, Continued*

Field	Description
Frame sequencing state (*Continued*)	When the router is configured as the secondary end of the link, the possible values are: • IDLE—Waiting for a poll. • PRI—In a session with a device. When the router is configured for point-to-point contention, the possible values are: • IDLE—Waiting for a poll. • PEND—Waiting for the first data frame. • PRI—Connected device is acting as a primary device. • SEC—Connected device is acting as a secondary device.
Total Tx Counts	Total transmit frame count for the indicated interface.
Total Rx Count	Total receive frame count for the indicated interface.
Primary state is …	The current state when the router is configured as the primary end of the link. The possible values are: • TCU_Down—Waiting for the line to become active. • TCU_EOFile—A valid block ending in ETX has been received. • TCU_Idle—Waiting for work or notification of completion of the transmission of EOT. • TCU_InFile—A valid block ending in ETB has been received. • TCU_Polled—A general poll has been issued. • TCU_Selected—A select has been issued. • TCU_SpecPolled—A specific poll has been sent. • TCU_TtdDelay—An ETB block was acknowledged, but the next block to be transmitted has not yet been received. • TCU_TtdSent—A TTD has been transmitted because no data was received by the time the timeout for sending Ttd expired. • TCU_TxEOFile—A block of data ending in ETX has been transmitted. • TCU_TxInFile—A block of data ending in ETB has been transmitted. • TCU_TxRetry—Trying to transmit a frame again.

Table 10–1 *Show BSC Command Field Descriptions, Continued*

Field	Description
Secondary state is ...	The current state when the router is configured as the secondary end of the link. The possible values are: • CU_DevBusy—A select has been refused with WACK or RVI. • CU_Down—Waiting for the line to become active. • CU_EOFile—A valid block ending in ETX has been received. • CU_Idle—Waiting for a poll or select action. • CU_InFile—A valid block ending in ETB has been received. • CU_Selected—A select has been acknowledged. • CU_TtdDelay—An ETB block was acknowledged, but the next block to be transmitted has not yet been received. • CU_TtdSent—A TTD has been transmitted because no data was received by the time the timeout for sending Ttd expired. • CU_TxEOFile—A block of data ending in ETX has been transmitted. • CU_TxInFile—A block of data ending in ETB has been transmitted. • CU_TxRetry—Trying to transmit a frame again. • CU_TxSpecPollData—A data frame (typically S/S) has been used to answer a specific poll. • CU_TxStatus—Host has polled for device-specific status.
Poll address	Address used when the host wants to get device information.
Select address	Address used when the host wants to send data to the device.
State is ...	Current initialization state of this control unit. The possible values are: • Active—The remote device is active. • Inactive—The remote device is dead. • Initializing—No response from remote device yet.
Tx Counts	Transmit frame count for this control unit.
Rx Counts	Receive frame count for this control unit.
Total Tx Counts	Total transmit frame count for the indicated interface.
Total Rx Counts	Total receive frame count for the indicated interface.

Part II

Command Reference

The following is sample output from the **show bsc** command specifying BSTUN group 50:

```
Router# show bsc group 50

BSC local-ack on serial5:
Secondary state is CU_Idle.
Control units on this interface:

        Poll address: C2. Select address: E2.
        State is Active.
        Tx Counts: 1217 frames(total). 0 frames(data). 1217 bytes.
        Rx Counts: 1222 frames(total). 0 frames(data). 6110 bytes.

        Poll address: C3. Select address: E3 *CURRENT-CU*
        State is Active.
        Tx Counts: 1214 frames(total). 0 frames(data). 1214 bytes.
        Rx Counts: 1220 frames(total). 0 frames(data). 6100 bytes.

Total Tx Counts: 2431 frames(total). 0 frames(data). 2431 bytes.
Total Rx Counts: 2442 frames(total). 0 frames(data). 12200 bytes.
```

The following is sample output from the **show bsc** command specifying BSTUN group 50 and poll address C2:

```
Router# show bsc group 50 address C2

BSC local-ack on serial5:
Secondary state is CU_Idle.
Control units on this interface:

        Poll address: C2. Select address: E2.
        State is Active.
        Tx Counts: 1217 frames(total). 0 frames(data). 1217 bytes.
        Rx Counts: 1222 frames(total). 0 frames(data). 6110 bytes.

Total Tx Counts: 1217 frames(total). 0 frames(data). 1217 bytes.
Total Rx Counts: 1222 frames(total). 0 frames(data). 6110 bytes.
```

The following is sample output from the **show bsc** command specifying poll address C2:

```
Router# show bsc address C2

BSC pass-through on Serial4:
HDX enforcement state: IDLE.
Frame sequencing state: IDLE.
Total Tx Counts: 0 frames(total). 0 frames(data). 0 bytes.
Total Rx Counts: 0 frames(total). 0 frames(data). 0 bytes.

BSC local-ack on serial5:
Secondary state is CU_Idle.
Control units on this interface:
```

```
Poll address: C2. Select address: E2.
State is Active.
Tx Counts: 1137 frames(total). 0 frames(data). 1137 bytes.
Rx Counts: 1142 frames(total). 0 frames(data). 5710 bytes.
```

```
Total Tx Counts: 1137 frames(total). 0 frames(data). 1137 bytes.
Total Rx Counts: 1142 frames(total). 0 frames(data). 5710 bytes.
```

SHOW BSTUN

Use the **show bstun** privileged EXEC command to display the current status of STUN connections.

show bstun [**group** *bstun-group-number*] [**address** *address-list*]

Part
II

Command Reference

Syntax	Description
group *bstun-group-number*	BSTUN group number. Valid numbers are decimal integers in the range 1 to 255.
address *address-list*	List of poll addresses.

Command Mode

Privileged EXEC

Usage Guidelines

This command first appeared in Cisco IOS Release 11.0.

Sample Displays

The following is sample output from the **show bstun** command with no options:

```
Router# show bstun

This peer: 22.22.1.107
 *Serial0  (group 1 [bsc])
route  transport  address      state   rx_pkts  tx_pkts  drops
all    TCP        22.22.1.108 closed      0        0        0

  Serial4  (group 3 [bsc])
route  transport  address      state   rx_pkts  tx_pkts  drops
C2     TCP        22.22.2.108 closed      0        0        0
C1     TCP        22.22.2.108 closed      0        0        0
40     TCP        22.22.1.108 closed      0        0        0

  Serial5  (group 50 [bsc])
route  transport  address      state   rx_pkts  tx_pkts  drops
C2     TCP        22.22.2.108 open        4        4        0
C3     TCP        22.22.2.108 open        3        3        0
```

The following is sample output from the **show bstun** command specifying BSTUN group 3:

```
Router# show bstun group 3

This peer: 22.22.1.107
  Serial4 (group 3 [bsc])
  route  transport  address       state   rx_pkts  tx_pkts  drops
  C2     TCP        22.22.2.108 closed       0         0       0
  C1     TCP        22.22.2.108 closed       0         0       0
  40     TCP        22.22.1.108 closed       0         0       0
```

The following is sample output from the **show bstun** command specifying BSTUN group 3 and poll address C1:

```
Router# show bstun group 3 address C1

This peer: 22.22.1.107
  Serial4 (group 3 [bsc])
  route  transport  address       state   rx_pkts  tx_pkts  drops
  C1     TCP        22.22.2.108 closed       0         0       0
```

The following is sample output from the **show bstun** command specifying poll address C2:

```
Router# show bstun address C2

This peer: 22.22.1.107
  Serial4 (group 3 [bsc])
  route  transport  address       state   rx_pkts  tx_pkts  drops
  C2     TCP        22.22.2.108 closed       0         0       0

  Serial5 (group 50 [bsc])
  route  transport  address       state   rx_pkts  tx_pkts  drops
  C2     TCP        22.22.2.108 open         4         4       0
```

Table 10–2 describes significant fields shown in the output.

Table 10–2   *Show BSTUN Command Field Descriptions*

Field	Description
This peer	Lists the peer name or address. The interface name (as defined by the **description** command), its BSTUN group number, and the protocol associated with the group are shown on the next header line.
route	Bisync control unit address.
transport	Description of link, either a serial interface using serial transport (indicated by IF followed by interface name), or a TCP connection to a remote router (TCP followed by IP address).
address	Address or the word *all* if the default forwarding entry is specified, followed by a repeat of the group number given for the interface.

Table 10–2 *Show BSTUN Command Field Descriptions, Continued*

Field	Description
state	State of the link: open is the normal, working state; direct indicates a direct link to another line, as specified with the **direct** keyword on the **bstun route** command.
rx_pkts	Number of received packets.
tx_pkts	Number of transmitted packets.
drops	Number of packets that had to be dropped for whatever reason.

SHOW STUN

Use the **show stun** privileged EXEC command to display the current status of STUN connections.

> **show stun**

Syntax   Description

This command has no arguments or keywords.

Command Mode

Privileged EXEC

Usage Guidelines

This command first appeared in Cisco IOS Release 10.0.

Sample Display

The following is sample output from the **show stun** command:

```
Router# show stun

This peer: 131.108.10.1
Serial0 -- 3174 Controller for test lab (group 1 [sdlc])
                        state   rx-pkts   tx-pkts   drops   poll
   7[ 1] IF Serial1     open     20334     86440       5   8P
  10[ 1] TCP 131.108.8.1 open      6771      7331       0
 all[ 1] TCP 131.108.8.1 open    612301   2338550    1005
```

In the display, the first entry reports proxy polling is enabled for address 7 and serial 0 is running with modulus 8 on the primary side of the link. The link has received 20,334 packets, transmitted 86,440 packets, and dropped 5 packets.

Table 10–3 describes significant fields shown in the output.

Table 10–3 *Show STUN Command Field Descriptions*

Field	Description
This peer	Lists the peer name or address. The interface name (as defined by the **description** command), its STUN group number, and the protocol associated with the group are shown on the header line.
STUN address	Address or the word *all* if the default forwarding entry is specified, followed by a repeat of the group number given for the interface.
Type of link	Description of link, either a serial interface using serial transport (indicated by IF followed by interface name), or a TCP connection to a remote router (TCP followed by IP address).
state	State of the link: open is the normal, working state; direct indicates a direct link to another line, as specified with the **direct** keyword on the **stun route** command.
rx_pkts	Number of received packets.
tx_pkts	Number of transmitted packets.
drops	Number of packets that, for whatever reason, had to be dropped.
poll	Report of the proxy poll parameters, if any. P indicates a primary and S indicates a secondary node. The number before the letter is the modulus of the link.

STUN GROUP

Use the **stun group** interface configuration command to place each STUN-enabled interface on a router in a previously defined STUN group. Use the **no** form of this command to remove an interface from a group.

> **stun group** *group-number*
> **no stun group** *group-number*

Syntax   *Description*

group-number   Integer in the range 1 to 255.

Default

Disabled

Command Mode

Interface configuration

Usage Guidelines

This command first appeared in Cisco IOS Release 10.0.

Before using this command, complete the following steps:

Step 1   Enable STUN on a global basis with the **stun peer-name** command.

Step 2   Define the protocol group in which you want to place this interface with the **stun protocol-group** command.

Step 3   Enable STUN on the interface using the **encapsulation stun** command.

Packets only travel between STUN-enabled interfaces that are in the same group. Once a given serial link is configured for the STUN function, it is no longer a shared multiprotocol link. All traffic that arrives on the link is transported to the corresponding peer as determined by the current STUN configuration.

Example

The following example places serial interface 0 in STUN group 2, which is defined to run the SDLC transport:

```
! sample stun peer-name global command
stun peer-name 131.108.254.6
! sample protocol-group command telling group 2 to use the SDLC protocol
stun protocol-group 2 sdlc
!
interface serial 0
! sample ip address subcommand
 no ip address
! sample encapsulation stun subcommand
 encapsulation stun
! place interface serial0 in previously defined STUN group 2
 stun group 2
! enter stun route command
 stun route 7 tcp 131.108.254.7
```

Related Commands

encapsulation stun
priority-list stun address
stun peer-name
stun protocol-group

STUN KEEPALIVE-COUNT

Use the **stun keepalive-count** global configuration command to define the number of times to attempt a peer connection before declaring the peer connection to be down. Use the **no** form of this command to cancel the definition.

stun keepalive-count *count*
no stun keepalive-count

Syntax	Description
count	Number of connection attempts. The range is between 2 and 10 retries.

Default
No default is specified.

Command Mode
Global configuration

Usage Guidelines
This command first appeared in Cisco IOS Release 10.0.

Example
The following example sets the number of times to retry a connection to a peer to 4:

```
stun keepalive-count 4
```

Related Commands
stun remote-peer-keepalive

STUN PEER-NAME

Use the **stun peer-name** global configuration command to enable STUN for an IP address. Use the **no** form of this command to disable STUN for an IP address.

> **stun peer-name** *ip-address* **cls**
> **no stun peer-name** *ip-address* **cls**

Syntax	Description
ip-address	IP address by which this STUN peer is known to other STUN peers.

Default
STUN is disabled

Command Mode
Global configuration

Usage Guidelines
This command first appeared in Cisco IOS Release 10.0.

Use this command to enable any further STUN features. After using this command, complete the following steps:

Step 1   Define the protocol group in which you want to place this interface with the **stun protocol-group** command.

Step 2   Enable STUN on the interface using the **encapsulation stun** command.

Step 3   Place the interface in a STUN group with the **stun group** command.

Example

The following example assigns IP address 131.108.254.6 as the STUN peer:

```
stun peer-name 131.108.254.6 cls
```

Related Commands

encapsulation stun
stun group
stun protocol-group

STUN PROTOCOL-GROUP

Use the **stun protocol-group** global configuration command to create a protocol group. Use the **no** form of this command to remove an interface from the group.

　　stun protocol-group *group-number* {**basic** | **sdlc** [**sdlc-tg**] | **schema**}
　　no stun protocol-group

Syntax	Description
group-number	Integer in the range 1 to 255.
basic	Indicates a non-SDLC protocol.
sdlc	Indicates an SDLC protocol.
sdlc-tg	(Optional) Identifies the group as part of an SNA transmission group.
schema	Indicates a custom protocol.

Default

No protocol group established.

Command Mode

Global configuration

Usage Guidelines

This command first appeared in Cisco IOS Release 10.0.

Use the **sdlc** keyword to specify an SDLC protocol. You must specify either the **sdlc** or the **sdlc-tg** keyword before you can enable SDLC local acknowledgment. SDLC local acknowledgment is established with the **stun route address tcp** command.

Use the **basic** keyword to specify a non-SDLC protocol, such as HDLC.

Use the **schema** keyword to specify a custom protocol. The custom protocol must have been previously created with the **stun schema** command.

Use the optional **sdlc-tg** keyword, in conjunction with the **sdlc** keyword, to establish an SNA transmission group. A transmission group is a set of protocol groups providing parallel links to the same pair of IBM establishment controllers. This provides redundancy of paths. In case one or more links go down, an alternate path will be used. All STUN connections in a transmission group must connect to the same IP address. SDLC local acknowledgment must be enabled.

NOTES

If you specify the keyword **sdlc** in the **stun protocol group** command string, you cannot specify the **stun route all** command on that interface.

Examples

The following example specifies that group 7 will use the SDLC STUN protocol to route frames within that group:

```
stun protocol-group 7 sdlc
```

The following example specifies that group 5 use the basic protocol, wherein the serial addressing is unimportant and you have a point-to-point link:

```
stun protocol-group 5 basic
```

Related Commands

encapsulation stun
stun route address interface serial
stun route address tcp
stun schema offset length format

STUN REMOTE-PEER-KEEPALIVE

Use the **stun remote-peer-keepalive** global configuration command to enable detection of the loss of a peer. Use the **no** form of this command to disable detection.

stun remote-peer-keepalive *seconds*
no stun remote-peer-keepalive

Syntax

seconds

Description

Keepalive interval, in seconds. The range is 1 to 300 seconds. The default is 30 seconds.

Default

30 seconds

Command Mode

Global configuration

Usage Guidelines

This command first appeared in Cisco IOS Release 10.0.

Example

In the following example, the remote-peer-keepalive interval is set to 60 seconds:

```
stun remote-peer-keepalive 60
```

Related Commands

stun keepalive-count

STUN ROUTE ADDRESS INTERFACE DLCI

Use the **stun route address interface dlci** interface configuration command to configure direct Frame Relay encapsulation between STUN peers with SDLC local acknowledgment. Use the **no** form of this command to disable the configuration.

stun route address *sdlc-addr* **interface** *frame-relay-port* **dlci** *number localsap* **local-ack**
no stun route address *sdlc-addr* **interface** *frame-relay-port* **dlci** *number localsap* **local-ack**

Syntax	*Description*
sdlc-addr	Address of the serial interface.
frame-relay-port	Port number.
number	Data-link connection identifier (DLCI) number.
localsap	Local connecting SAP.
local-ack	Enable local acknowledgment.

Default

The configuration is disabled.

Command Mode

Interface configuration

Usage Guidelines

This command first appeared in Cisco IOS Release 11.0.

Example

The following command enables Frame Relay encapsulation between STUN peers with SDLC local acknowledgment:

```
stun route address c1 interface serial1 dlci 22 04 local-ack
```

Related Commands

stun route all interface serial

STUN ROUTE ADDRESS INTERFACE SERIAL

Use the **stun route address interface serial** interface configuration command to forward all HDLC traffic on a serial interface. Use the **no** form of this command to disable this method of HDLC encapsulation.

> **stun route address** *address-number* **interface serial** *number* [**direct**]
> **no stun route address** *address-number* **interface serial** *number*

Syntax	Description
address-number	Address of the serial interface.
number	Number assigned to the serial interface.
direct	(Optional) Forwards all HDLC traffic on a direct STUN link.

Default

The configuration is disabled

Command Mode

Interface configuration

Usage Guidelines

This command first appeared in Cisco IOS Release 10.0.

Examples

In the following example, serial frames with a STUN route address of 4 are forwarded through serial interface 0 using HDLC encapsulation:

```
stun route address 4 interface serial 0
```

In the following example, serial frames with STUN route address 4 are propagated through serial interface 0 using STUN encapsulation:

```
stun route address 4 interface serial 0 direct
```

Related Commands

stun route all interface serial

STUN ROUTE ADDRESS TCP

Use the **stun route address tcp** interface configuration command to specify TCP encapsulation and optionally establish SDLC local acknowledgment (SDLC transport) for STUN. Use the **no** form of this command to disable this method of TCP encapsulation.

stun route address *address-number* **tcp** *ip-address* [**local-ack**] [**priority**] [**tcp-queue-max**]

no stun route address *address-number* **tcp** *ip-address* [**local-ack**] [**priority**][**tcp-queue-max**]

Syntax	Description
address-number	Number that conforms to TCP addressing conventions.
ip-address	IP address by which this STUN peer is known to other STUN peers that are using the TCP as the STUN encapsulation.
local-ack	(Optional) Enables local acknowledgment for STUN.
priority	(Optional) Establishes the four levels used in priority queuing: low, medium, normal, and high.
tcp-queue-max	(Optional) Sets the maximum size of the outbound TCP queue for the SDLC link.

Defaults

TCP encapsulation is not established; TCP queue size default is 100.

Command Mode

Interface configuration

Usage Guidelines

This command first appeared in Cisco IOS Release 10.0. The **tcp-queue-max** keyword first appeared in Cisco IOS Release 11.1.

SDLC transport participates in SDLC windowing and re-transmission through support of local acknowledgment. SDLC sessions require that end nodes send acknowledgments for a set amount of data frames received before allowing further data to be transmitted. Local acknowledgment provides local termination of the SDLC session so that control frames no longer travel the WAN backbone networks. This means end nodes do not time out, and a loss of sessions does not occur.

Example

In the following example, a frame with a source-route address of 10 is propagated using TCP encapsulation to a device with an IP address of 131.108.8.1:

```
stun route address 10 tcp 131.108.8.1
```

Related Commands

sdlc address ff ack-mode
stun route all tcp

STUN ROUTE ALL INTERFACE SERIAL

Use the **stun route all interface serial** interface configuration command to encapsulate and forward all STUN traffic using HDLC encapsulation on a serial interface.

> **stun route all interface serial** *number* [**direct**]

Syntax	Description
number	Number assigned to the serial interface.
direct	(Optional) Indicates that the specified interface is also a direct STUN link, rather than a serial connection to another peer.

Default

No default is specified.

Command Mode

Interface configuration

Usage Guidelines

This command first appeared in Cisco IOS Release 10.0.

An appropriately configured router must exist on the other end of the designated serial line. The outgoing serial link still can be used for other kinds of traffic (the frame is not TCP encapsulated). This mode is used when TCP/IP encapsulation is not needed or when higher performance is required. Enter the serial line number connected to the router for the *interface-number* argument.

Examples

In the following example, all traffic on serial interface 0 is propagated using STUN encapsulation:

```
stun route all interface serial 0
```

In the following example, serial interface 1 is a direct STUN link, not a serial connection to another peer:

```
stun route all interface serial 1 direct
```

Related Commands

stun route address interface serial

STUN ROUTE ALL TCP

Use the **stun route all tcp** interface configuration command with TCP encapsulation to forward all STUN traffic on an interface regardless of what address is contained in the serial frame.

> **stun route all tcp** *ip-address*

Syntax	Description
ip-address	IP address by which this remote STUN peer is known to other STUN peers. Use the address that identifies the remote STUN peer that is connected to the far serial link.

Default

Disabled

Command Mode

Interface configuration

Usage Guidelines

This command first appeared in Cisco IOS Release 10.0.

TCP/IP encapsulation allows movement of serial frames across arbitrary media types and topologies. This is particularly useful for building shared, multiprotocol enterprise network backbones.

Example

In the following example, all STUN traffic received will be propagated through the bridge:

```
stun route all tcp 131.108.10.1
```

STUN SCHEMA OFFSET LENGTH FORMAT

Use the **stun schema offset length format** global configuration command to define a protocol other than SDLC for use with STUN. Use the **no** form of this command to disable the new protocol.

> **stun schema** *name* **offset** *constant-offset* **length** *address-length* **format** *format-keyword*
> **no stun schema** *name* **offset** *constant-offset* **length** *address-length* **format** *format-keyword*

Syntax	Description
name	Name that defines your protocol. It can be up to 20 characters in length.
constant-offset	Constant offset, in bytes, for the address to be found in the frame.

Syntax	Description
address-length	Length in one of the following formats: decimal (4 bytes), hexadecimal (8 bytes), or octal (4 bytes).
format-keyword	Format to be used to specify and display addresses for routes on interfaces that use this STUN protocol. The allowable format keywords are **decimal** (0 to 9), **hexadecimal** (0 to F), and **octal** (0 to 7).

Default

No protocol is defined.

Command Mode

Global configuration

Usage Guidelines

This command first appeared in Cisco IOS Release 10.0.

Use this command before defining the protocol group (**stun protocol-group** command). The serial protocol you define must meet the following criteria:

- The protocol uses full-duplex conventions (RTS/CTS always high).
- The protocol uses standard HDLC checksum and framing (beginning and end of frames, data between frames).
- Addresses are contained in a constant location (offset) within the frame.
- Addresses are found on a byte boundary.

Example

In the following example, a protocol named *new-sdlc* is created. In the protocol frame structure, the constant offset is 0, the address length is 1 byte, and the address format is hexadecimal:

```
stun schema new-sdlc offset 0 length 1 format hexadecimal
```

Related Commands

priority-list stun
stun protocol-group

STUN SDLC-ROLE PRIMARY

Use the **stun sdlc-role primary** interface configuration command to assign the router the role of SDLC primary node. Primary nodes poll secondary nodes in a predetermined order.

   stun sdlc-role primary

Syntax   Description

This command has no arguments or keywords.

Default

No role is assigned.

Command Mode

Interface configuration

Usage Guidelines

This command first appeared in Cisco IOS Release 10.0.

If the router is connected to a cluster controller, for example a 3x74, it should appear as a front-end processor such as a 37x5, and must be assigned the role of a primary node.

Example

The following example assigns the router the role of SDLC primary node:

```
stun sdlc-role primary
```

Related Commands

encapsulation stun
stun sdlc-role secondary

Part II

Command Reference

STUN SDLC-ROLE SECONDARY

Use the **stun sdlc-role secondary** interface configuration command to assign the router the role of SDLC secondary node. Secondary nodes respond to polls sent by the SDLC primary by transmitting any outgoing data they might have.

stun sdlc-role secondary

Syntax   Description

This command has no arguments or keywords.

Default

No secondary role is assigned.

Command Mode

Interface configuration

Usage Guidelines

This command first appeared in Cisco IOS Release 10.0.

If the router is connected to a front-end processor, for example a 37x5, it should appear as a cluster controller such as a 3x74, and must be assigned the role of a secondary node.

Example

The following example assigns the router the role of SDLC secondary node:

```
stun sdlc-role secondary
```

Related Commands

encapsulation stun
stun sdlc-role primary

CHAPTER 11

Configuring LLC2 and SDLC Parameters

You do not need to configure Logical Link Control, type 2 (LLC2) because it already is enabled on Token Ring interfaces. This chapter describes how to modify the default settings of LLC2 parameters as needed. To support the Synchronous Data Link Control (SDLC) protocol, you must configure the Cisco IOS software to act as a primary or secondary SDLC station. You also can change default settings on any SDLC parameters. Configuration examples for both LLC2 and SDLC are given at the end of the chapter.

For a complete description of the commands mentioned in this chapter, see Chapter 12, "LLC2 and SDLC Commands."

LLC2 CONFIGURATION TASK LIST

Because LLC2 already is enabled on a Token Ring, you do not need to enable it on the router. However, you can complete the tasks in the following sections to enhance LLC2 performance:

- Controlling Transmission of I-Frames
- Establishing Polling Level
- Setting Up XID Transmissions

To determine which LLC2 parameters need adjustment, you can perform the task in the following section:

- Monitoring LLC2 Stations

See the end of this chapter for an LLC2 configuration example.

CONTROLLING TRANSMISSION OF I-FRAMES

Control the number of information frames (I-frames) and acknowledgments sent on the LLC2 network by completing the tasks described in the following sections.

- Setting the Maximum Number of I-Frames Received before Sending an Acknowledgment
- Setting the Maximum Delay for Acknowledgments
- Setting the Maximum Number of I-Frames Sent Before Requiring Acknowledgment
- Setting the Number of Retries Allowed
- Setting the Time for Resending I-Frames
- Setting the Time for Resending Rejected Frames

Setting the Maximum Number of I-Frames Received Before Sending an Acknowledgment

You can reduce overhead on the network by increasing the maximum number of frames the Cisco IOS software can receive at once before it must send the sender an acknowledgment. To do so, perform the following task in interface configuration mode:

Task	Command
Set maximum number of I-frames the Cisco IOS software can receive before it sends an acknowledgment.	**llc2 ack-max** *packet-count*

Setting the Maximum Delay for Acknowledgments

You can ensure timely receipt of acknowledgments so that transmission of data is not delayed. Even if the maximum amount of frames has not been reached, you can set a timer forcing the Cisco IOS software to send an acknowledgment and reset the maximum amount counter to 0.

To set the maximum delay time, perform the following task in interface configuration mode:

Task	Command
Set the I-frame acknowledgment time.	**llc2 ack-delay-time** *milliseconds*

Setting the Maximum Number of I-Frames Sent Before Requiring Acknowledgment

You can set the maximum number of I-frames that the Cisco IOS software sends to an LLC2 station before the software requires an acknowledgment from the receiving end. A higher value reduces overhead on the network. Ensure that the receiving LLC2 station can handle the number of frames set by this value.

To set this value, perform the following task in interface configuration mode:

Task	Command
Set the maximum number of I-frames the Cisco IOS software sends before it requires an acknowledgment.	**llc2 local-window** *packet-count*

Setting the Number of Retries Allowed

You can set the number of times the Cisco IOS software will resend a frame when the receiving station does not acknowledge the frame. Once this value is reached, the session is dropped. This value also is used to determine how often the software will retry polling a busy station. This task should be done in conjunction with the task for setting the time for resending I-frames (described next). Performing them together ensures that frame transmission is monitored at a reasonable level, while limiting the number of unsuccessful repeated tries.

To set the number of retries, perform the following task in interface configuration mode:

Task	Command
Establish number of times the Cisco IOS software will resend unacknowledged frames or try polling a busy station.	**llc2 n2** *retry-count*

Setting the Time for Resending I-Frames

You can set the amount of time the Cisco IOS software waits before resending unacknowledged I-frames. This interval is called the *T1 time*. Perform this task in conjunction with setting the number of retries and setting the transit poll-frame timer. Performing these tasks in conjunction with each other provides a balance of network monitoring and performance.

To set the T1 time, perform the following task in interface configuration mode:

Task	Command
Control how long the Cisco IOS software waits for an acknowledgment of transmitted I-frames.	**llc2 t1-time** *milliseconds*

— **NOTES** —

Ensure that you allow enough time for the round trip between the router and its LLC2-speaking stations. Under heavy network loading conditions, resending I-frames every 3000 ms is appropriate.

Setting the Time for Resending Rejected Frames

You can set the amount of time that the Cisco IOS software will wait for an expected frame before sending a reject command (REJ). Typically, when an LLC2 station sends an I-frame, a sequence number is included in the frame. The LLC2 station that receives these frames will expect to receive them in order. If it does not, it can reject a frame and indicate which frame it is expecting to receive instead. If the correct frame is not sent to the software before the reject timer expires, the software sends a REJ to the remote station and disconnects the LLC2 session.

To set the reject timer, perform the following task in interface configuration mode:

Task	Command
Set the time a Cisco IOS software waits for a resend of a rejected frame before sending a reject command to the remote station.	**llc2 trej-time** *milliseconds*

ESTABLISHING POLLING LEVEL

You can control the amount of polling that occurs on the LLC2 network by completing the tasks described in the following sections:

- Setting the Polling Frequency
- Setting the Polling Interval
- Setting the Transmit-Poll-Frame Timer

Setting the Polling Frequency

You can set the optimum interval of time after which the Cisco IOS software sends Receiver Ready messages or frames that tell other LLC2 stations that the router is available. These polls occur during periods of idle time on the network.

To set polling frequency, perform the following task in interface configuration mode:

Task	Command
Control the polling frequency during idle traffic.	**llc2 idle-time** *milliseconds*

Setting the Polling Interval

The amount of time the Cisco IOS software waits until repolling a busy station also can be set. Perform this task in conjunction with setting the number of retries. Typically, you do not need to perform this task unless an LLC2 station has unusually long busy periods before clearing the busy state. In this case, you should increase the value so that the station does not time out.

To set the polling interval, perform the following task in interface configuration mode:

Task	Command
Set the amount of time the Cisco IOS software will wait before repolling a busy station.	**llc2 tbusy-time** *milliseconds*

Setting the Transmit-Poll-Frame Timer

When the Cisco IOS software sends a command that must receive a response, a poll bit is sent in the frame. When the software sends the poll bit, it cannot send any other frame with the poll bit set until the receiver replies to that poll frame with a frame containing a final bit set. When the timer expires, the software assumes that it can send another frame with a poll bit.

Set the transmit-poll-frame timer to reduce problems with receiving stations that are faulty and cannot send the frame with the final bit set by performing the following task in interface configuration mode:

Task	Command
Set the amount of time the Cisco IOS software waits for a final response to a poll frame before resending it.	**llc2 tpf-time** *milliseconds*

This value should be larger than the T1 time. The T1 time determines how long the software waits for receipt of an acknowledgment before sending the next set of frames. See the section "Setting the Time for Resending I-Frames" earlier in this chapter for more information.

SETTING UP XID TRANSMISSIONS

You can control the number of frames used for identification on the LLC2 network by completing the tasks described in the following sections:

- Setting the Frequency of Exchange Identification (XID) Transmissions
- Setting the Time for XID Retries

Setting the Frequency of Exchange Identification (XID) Transmissions

Exchange identification (XID) frames identify LLC2 stations at a higher level than the MAC address and contain information about the configuration of the stations. You can set how often the Cisco IOS software sends an XID frame by performing the following task in interface configuration mode:

Task	Command
Set the frequency of XID transmissions.	**llc2 xid-neg-val-time** *milliseconds*

CAUTION

Do not change the value unless requested by your technical support representative.

Setting the Time for XID Retries

You can set the amount of time the Cisco IOS software waits for a reply to the XID frames it sends to remote stations. The value should be larger than the T1 time, which indicates how long the software waits for an acknowledgment before dropping the session.

To set the time for XID retries, perform the following task in interface configuration mode:

Task	Command
Set how long the Cisco IOS software waits for a reply to the XID frames it sends to remote stations.	**llc2 xid-retry-time** *milliseconds*

MONITORING LLC2 STATIONS

You can display the configuration of LLC2 stations to determine which LLC2 parameters need adjustment. Perform the following task in EXEC mode:

Task	Command
Display the configuration of LLC2 stations.	**show llc2**

SDLC CONFIGURATION TASK LIST

The SDLC tasks described in this section configure the router as an SDLC station. (This is in contrast to a router configured for SDLC Transport, where the device is not an SDLC station, but passes SDLC frames between two SDLC stations across a mixed-media, multiprotocol environment). The first task is required; you accomplish it with the appropriate set of commands for your network needs. The remaining tasks are optional: You can use them as necessary to enhance SDLC performance.

- Enabling the Router as a Primary or a Secondary SDLC Station
- Enabling SDLC Two-Way Simultaneous Mode
- Determining the Use of Frame Rejects
- Setting SDLC Timer and Retry Counts
- Setting SDLC Timer and Retry Counts
- Setting SDLC Frame and Window Sizes
- Controlling the Buffer Size
- Controlling Polling of Secondary Stations
- Configuring an SDLC Interface for Half-Duplex Mode
- Specifying the XID Value
- Setting the Largest SDLC I-Frame Size

To determine which SDLC parameters need adjustment, you can perform the task in the following section:

- Monitoring SDLC Stations

See the end of this chapter for SDLC configuration examples.

ENABLING THE ROUTER AS A PRIMARY OR A SECONDARY SDLC STATION

SDLC defines two types of network nodes: primary and secondary. Primary nodes poll secondary nodes in a predetermined order. Secondaries then transmit if they have outgoing data. When configured as primary and secondary nodes, Cisco's devices are established as SDLC stations.

Depending on your particular network needs, perform the tasks in one of the following sections to enable the router as an SDLC station:

- Establishing an SDLC Station for Frame Relay Access Support
- Establishing an SDLC Station for DLSw+ Support
- Establishing an SDLC Station for SDLLC Media Translation

Establishing an SDLC Station for Frame Relay Access Support

You can establish the router to be any of the following:

- A primary SDLC station
- A secondary SDLC station
- Either primary or secondary, depending on the role of the end stations or on XID negotiations
- A primary Node Type 2.1 (NT2.1) node

To establish devices as SDLC stations when you plan to configure Frame Relay access support, complete the following tasks in interface configuration mode:

Task	Command
Step 1 Set the encapsulation type of the serial interface to SDLC.	**encapsulation sdlc**
Step 2 Establish the role of the interface.	**sdlc role {none	primary	secondary	prim-xid-poll}**

If the interface does not play a role, the router can be either primary or secondary, depending on the end stations. The SDLC end station must be configured as negotiable or primary NT2.1. When the end stations are configured as physical unit (PU) type 2, you can set the role of the interface to primary or secondary. When the end station is configured as secondary NT2.1, you must set the role of the interface to poll the primary XID.

— **NOTES** —————————————————————————————

Currently, Frame Relay access support does not support the secondary role.

Establishing an SDLC Station for DLSw+ Support

To establish devices as SDLC stations when you plan to configure Cisco's DLSw+ feature, complete the following tasks in interface configuration mode:

Task	Command
Step 1 Set the encapsulation type of the serial interface to SDLC.	**encapsulation sdlc**
Step 2 Establish the role of the interface.	**sdlc role {none	primary	secondary	prim-xid-poll}**
Step 3 Configure a MAC address for the serial interface.	**sdlc vmac** *mac-address*
Step 4 Specify the destination address with which an LLC session is established for the SDLC station.	**sdlc partner** *mac-address sdlc-address*
Step 5 Attach SDLC addresses to DLSw+.	**sdlc dlsw** *sdlc-address sdlc-address...*

To configure an SDLC multidrop line downstream, you configure the SDLC role as either **primary** or **prim-xid-poll**. SDLC role **primary** specifies that any PU without the xid-poll parameter in the **sdlc address** command is a PU 2.0 device. SDLC role **prim-xid-poll** specifies that every PU is type 2.1. Cisco recommends that you specify **sdlc role primary** if all SDLC devices are type PU 2.0 or a mix of PU 2.0 and PU 2.1. Specify **sdlc role prim-xid-poll** if all devices are type PU 2.1

For more DLSw+ configuration tasks, see Chapter 7, "Configuring Data-Link Switching Plus."

Establishing an SDLC Station for SDLLC Media Translation

To establish devices as SDLC stations when you plan to configure Cisco's SDLLC media translation feature, complete tasks in the order listed in the following table. One serial interface can have two or more secondary stations attached to it through a modem-sharing device. Each secondary station address must be assigned to the primary station. You must perform the following tasks in interface configuration mode for the serial interface:

Task	Command
Step 1 Establish a router as the primary SDLC station on the serial line.	**encapsulation sdlc-primary**
Step 2 Establish other routers as secondary SDLC stations.	**encapsulation sdlc-secondary**
Step 3 Assign secondary stations to a primary station.	**sdlc address** *hexbyte* [*echo*]

Use the **show interfaces** command to list the configuration of the SDLC serial lines. Use the **no sdlc address** command to remove a secondary address assignment. Addresses are hexadecimal (base 16).

ENABLING SDLC TWO-WAY SIMULTANEOUS MODE

SDLC two-way simultaneous mode allows a primary SDLC link station to achieve more efficient use of a full-duplex serial line. With two-way simultaneous mode, the primary link station can send data to one secondary link station while there is a poll outstanding. Two-way simultaneous mode works on the SDLC primary side only. On a secondary link station, it responds to a poll from the primary station.

SDLC two-way simultaneous mode operates in either a multidrop link environment or point-to-point link environment.

In a multidrop link environment, a two-way simultaneous primary station is able to poll a secondary station and receive data from the station, and send data (I-frames) to other secondary stations.

In a point-to-point link environment, a two-way simultaneous primary station can send data (I-frames) to the secondary station, although there is a poll outstanding, as long as the window limit is not reached.

To enable two-way simultaneous mode, perform either of the following tasks in interface configuration mode:

Task	Command
Enable the primary station to send data to and receive data from the polled secondary station.	**sdlc simultaneous full-datamode**
Prohibit the primary stations from sending data to the polled secondary station.	**sdlc simultaneous half-datamode**

DETERMINING THE USE OF FRAME REJECTS

You can specify that a secondary station not send frame reject messages, or reject commands indicating frame errors. If you do so, the Cisco IOS software drops an SDLC connection if the system receives an error from the secondary station. To determine handling of frame rejects, perform the following task in interface configuration mode:

Task	Command
Specify that this secondary station does not support frame rejects.	**sdlc frmr-disable**

To specify that the secondary station does support frame rejects, use the **no sdlc frmr-disable** command.

SETTING SDLC TIMER AND RETRY COUNTS

When an SDLC station sends a frame, it waits for an acknowledgment from the receiver indicating that this frame has been received. You can modify the time the Cisco IOS software allows for an acknowledgment before resending the frame. You also can determine the number of times that a software resends a frame before terminating the SDLC session. By controlling these values, you can reduce network overhead while continuing to check transmission of frames.

To set the SDLC timer and retry counts, perform one or both of the following tasks in interface configuration mode:

Task	Command
Control the amount of time the Cisco IOS software waits for a reply.	**sdlc t1** *milliseconds*
Set the number of times a Cisco IOS software will retry an operation that has timed out.	**sdlc n2** *retry-count*

SETTING SDLC FRAME AND WINDOW SIZES

You can set the maximum size of an incoming frame and set the maximum number of I-frames (or window size) the Cisco IOS software will receive before sending an acknowledgment to the sender. By using higher values, you can reduce network overhead.

To set SDLC frame and window sizes, perform any of the following tasks in interface configuration mode:

Task	Command
Set the maximum size of an incoming frame.	**sdlc n1** *bit-count*
Set the local window size of the router.	**sdlc k** *window-size*
Set how many times a primary station will poll a secondary station.	**sdlc poll-limit-value** *count*

CONTROLLING THE BUFFER SIZE

You can control the buffer size of the router. The buffer holds data that is pending transmission to a remote SDLC station. This task is particularly useful in the case of the SDLLC media translator, which allows an LLC2-speaking SNA station on a Token Ring to communicate with an SDLC-speaking SNA station on a serial link. The frame sizes and window sizes on Token Rings are often much larger than those acceptable for serial links, and serial links are often slower than Token Rings.

To control backlogs that can occur during periods of high data transfer from the Token Ring to the serial line, perform the following task in interface configuration mode on a per-address basis:

Task	Command
Set the maximum number of packets held in queue before transmitting.	**sdlc holdq** *address queue-size*

CONTROLLING POLLING OF SECONDARY STATIONS

You can control the intervals at which the Cisco IOS software polls secondary stations, the length of time a primary station can send data to a secondary station, and how often the software polls one secondary station before moving on to the next station.

Keep the following points in mind when performing these tasks:

- Secondary stations cannot transmit data until they are polled by a primary station. Increasing the poll-pause timer increases the response time of the secondary stations. Decreasing the timer can flood the serial link with unneeded polls, requiring secondary stations to spend wasted CPU time processing them.
- Increasing the value of the poll limit allows for smoother transactions between a primary station and a single secondary station, but can delay polling of other secondary stations.

To control polling of secondary stations, perform one or more of the following tasks in interface configuration mode:

Task	Command
Set the length of time the Cisco IOS software pauses between sending each poll frame to secondary stations on a single serial interface.	**sdlc poll-pause-timer** *milliseconds*
Set how many times a primary station will poll a secondary station.	**sdlc poll-limit-value** *count*

To retrieve default polling values for these operations, use the **no** forms of these commands.

Configuring an SDLC Interface for Half-Duplex Mode

By default, SDLC interfaces operate in full-duplex mode. To configure an SDLC interface for half-duplex mode, perform the following task in interface configuration mode:

Task	Command
Configure an SDLC interface for half-duplex mode.	**half-duplex**

On an interface that is in half-duplex mode and that has been configured for DCE, you can adjust the delay between the detection of a Request To Send (RTS) signal and the assertion of the Clear To Send (CTS) signal. To do so, perform the following task in interface configuration mode:

Task	Command
Delay the assertion of a CTS.	**half-duplex timer cts-delay** *value*

On an interface that is in half-duplex mode and that has been configured for DTE, you can adjust the time the interface waits for the DCE to assert CTS before dropping an RTS. To do so, perform the following task in interface configuration mode:

Task	Command
Adjust the amount of time before interface drops an RTS.	**half-duplex timer rts-timeout** *value*

Specifying the XID Value

The exchange of identification (XID) value you define on the router must match that of the IDBLK and IDNUM system generation parameters defined in VTAM on the Token Ring host to which the SDLC device will be communicating. To specify the XID value, perform the following task in interface configuration mode:

Task	Command
Specify the XID value to be associated with the SDLC station.	**sdlc xid** *address xid*

Setting the Largest SDLC I-Frame Size

Generally, the router and the SDLC device with which it communicates should support the same maximum SDLC I-frame size. The larger this value, the more efficient the line use, thus increasing performance.

After the SDLC device has been configured to send the largest possible I-frame, you must configure the Cisco IOS software to support the same maximum I-frame size. The default is 265 bytes. The maximum value the software can support must be less than the value of the LLC2 largest frame value defined when setting the largest LLC2 I-frame size.

To set the largest SDLC I-frame size, perform the following task in interface configuration mode:

Task	Command
Set the largest I-frame size that can be sent or received by the designated SDLC station.	**sdlc sdlc-largest-frame** *address size*

Monitoring SDLC Stations

To monitor the configuration of SDLC stations to determine which SDLC parameters need adjustment, perform the following task in EXEC mode:

Task	Command
Display SDLC station configuration information.	**show interfaces**

You determine the status of end stations by sending an SDLC test frame to a physical unit via its SDLC address and router interface. You can send out either the default information string or a predefined one. You can send a preset number of test frames a continuous stream that can later be halted. The **sdlc test serial** command pre-checks for correct interface and SDLC address of the end station. You can view the results of the test frames after the frames have been sent or a SDLC test frame stop has been executed. To send an SDLC test frame, perform the following task in EXEC mode:

Task	Command
Send an SDLC test frame.	**sdlc test serial** *number address* [*iterations* | **continuous** | **stop** | **string** *string*]

NOTES

Only a device configured as primary is allowed to send test frames.

CONFIGURATION EXAMPLES

The following sections provide LLC2 and SDLC configuration examples:

- LLC2 Configuration Example
- SDLC Two-Way Simultaneous Mode Configuration Example
- SDLC Encapsulation for Frame Relay Access Support Configuration Examples
- SDLC Configuration for DLSw+ Example
- Half-Duplex Configuration Example

LLC2 Configuration Example

You can configure the number of LLC2 frames received before an acknowledgment. For this example, assume that at time 0, two I-frames are received. The maximum amount of three has not been reached, so no acknowledgment for these frames is sent. If a third frame, which would force the Cisco IOS software to send an acknowledgment, is not received within 800 ms, an acknowledgment is sent anyway, because the delay timer alarm is activated.

```
interface tokenring 0
 llc2 ack-max 3
 llc2 ack-delay-time 800
```

At this point, because all frames are acknowledged, the counter for the maximum amount of I-frames will be reset to zero.

SDLC Two-Way Simultaneous Mode Configuration Example

The following configuration defines serial interface 0 as the primary SDLC station with two SDLC secondary stations, C1 and C2, attached to it through a modem-sharing device. Two-way simultaneous mode is enabled.

```
interface serial 0
 encapsulation sdlc-primary
 sdlc address c1
 sdlc address c2
 sdlc simultaneous full-datamode
```

The network for this configuration is shown in Figure 11–1.

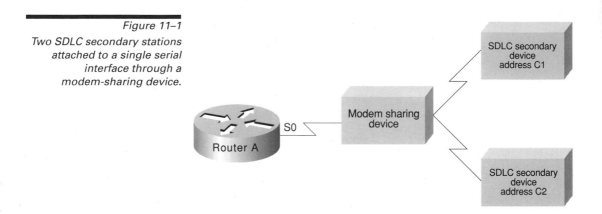

Figure 11–1
Two SDLC secondary stations attached to a single serial interface through a modem-sharing device.

SDLC Encapsulation for Frame Relay Access Support Configuration Examples

The following examples describe possible SDLC encapsulation configurations if you plan to configure Frame Relay access support.

The following configuration is appropriate if the SDLC station is a negotiable or primary Node Type 2.1 station:

```
interface serial 2/6
 no ip address
 encapsulation sdlc
 clockrate 9600
 fras map sdlc C1 serial 2/0 frame-relay 32 4 4
 sdlc address C1
```

The following configuration is appropriate if the SDLC station is a secondary Node Type 2.1 station:

```
interface serial 2/6
 no ip address
 encapsulation sdlc
 clockrate 9600
 fras map sdlc C1 serial 2/0 frame-relay 32 4 4
 sdlc role prim-xid-poll
 sdlc address C1
```

The following configuration is appropriate if the SDLC station is a secondary PU 2 station:

```
interface serial 2/6
 no ip address
 encapsulation sdlc
 clockrate 9600
 fras map sdlc C1 serial 2/0 frame-relay 32 4 4
 sdlc role primary
 sdlc address C1
 sdlc xid C1 01700001
```

SDLC Configuration for DLSw+ Example

The following example describes an SDLC configuration if you plan to implement DLSw+ support. In this example, 4000.3745.001 is the MAC address of the host. The router serves as the primary station for the remote secondary stations, C1 and C2. Both C1 and C2 are reserved for DLSw+ and cannot be used by any other data link user.

```
interface serial 0
 encapsulation sdlc
 sdlc vmac 4000.3174.0000
 sdlc address c1
 sdlc xid c1 01712345
 sdlc partner 4000.3745.0001 c1
 sdlc address c2
 sdlc xid c2 01767890
 sdlc partner 4000.3745.0001 c2
 sdlc dlsw c1 c2
 sdlc role primary
```

Half-Duplex Configuration Example

In the following example, an SDLC interface has been configured for half-duplex mode:

```
encapsulation sdlc-primary
 half-duplex
```

CHAPTER **12**

LLC2 and SDLC Commands

Logical Link Control, type 2 (LLC2) protocol provides connection-oriented service and is widely used in LAN environments, particularly among IBM communication systems connected by Token Ring. The Cisco IOS software supports LLC2 connections over Ethernet, Token Ring, and Fiber Distributed Data Interface (FDDI).

The LLC2 commands provide operations that support the following features:

- Local acknowledgment in remote source-route bridging (RSRB)
- IBM LAN Network Manager (LNM) support used in source-route bridging (SRB)
- Synchronous Data Link Control (SDLC)/LLC2 Media Translation (SDLLC)
- ISO Connection-Mode Network Services (CMNS) running X.25 packets over LLC2

SDLC is used as the primary Systems Network Architecture (SNA) link-layer protocol for WAN links. SDLC defines two types of network nodes: primary and secondary. Primary nodes poll secondary nodes in a predetermined order. Secondaries then transmit if they have outgoing data. When configured as primary and secondary nodes, routers are established as SDLC stations.

The SDLC commands described in this chapter pertain to routers configured as SDLC stations. This is in contrast to a device configured for SDLC Transport where the router is not configured as an SDLC station, but acts as an intermediary, passing SDLC frames between two SDLC stations across a mixed-media, multiprotocol environment.

The SDLC commands support the following features:

- SDLLC SDLC/LLC2 media translation
- SDLC local acknowledgment for serial tunnel (STUN)-enabled interfaces

Use the commands in this chapter to adjust the LLC2 and SDLC parameters. For LLC2 and SDLC parameter configuration information and examples, see Chapter 11, "Configuring LLC2 and SDLC Parameters."

609

ENCAPSULATION SDLC

Use the **encapsulation sdlc** interface configuration command to configure an SDLC interface.

    encapsulation sdlc

Syntax   Description

This command has no arguments or keywords.

Default

Disabled

Command Mode

Interface configuration

Usage Guidelines

This command first appeared in Cisco IOS Release 10.3.

The **encapsulation sdlc** command must be used to configure an SDLC interface if you plan to implement DLSw+ or Frame Relay access support.

SDLC defines two types of network nodes: primary and secondary. Primary nodes poll secondary nodes in a predetermined order. Secondaries then transmit if they have outgoing data. When configured as primary and secondary nodes, Cisco routers are established as SDLC stations. Use the sdlc role interface configuration command to establish the role as primary or secondary.

In the IBM environment, a front-end processor (FEP) is the primary station and establishment controllers (ECs) are secondary stations. In a typical scenario, an EC may be connected to dumb terminals and to a Token Ring network at a local site. At the remote site, an IBM host connects to an IBM FEP, which also can have links to another Token Ring LAN. Typically, the two sites are connected through an SDLC leased line.

If a router is connected to an EC, it takes over the function of the FEP, and must therefore be configured as a primary SDLC station. If the router is connected to a FEP, it takes the place of the EC, and must therefore be configured as a secondary SDLC station.

Example

The following example configures an SDLC interface:

```
interface serial 2/6
 no ip address
 encapsulation sdlc
```

Related Commands

sdlc role

ENCAPSULATION SDLC-PRIMARY

Use the **encapsulation sdlc-primary** interface configuration command to configure the router as the primary SDLC station if you plan to configure the SDLLC media translation feature.

encapsulation sdlc-primary

Syntax   Description

This command has no arguments or keywords.

Default

Disabled

Command Mode

Interface configuration

Usage Guidelines

This command first appeared in Cisco IOS Release 10.0.

The **encapsulation sdlc-primary** or **encapsulation sdlc-secondary** command must be used to configure an SDLC interface. To use the **encapsulation sdlc-primary** command, first select the interface on which you want to enable SDLC. Then establish the router as a primary station. Next, assign secondary station addresses to the primary station using the **sdlc address** command.

SDLC defines two types of network nodes: primary and secondary. Primary nodes poll secondary nodes in a predetermined order. Secondaries then transmit if they have outgoing data. When configured as primary and secondary nodes, Cisco routers are established as SDLC stations.

In the IBM environment, a front-end processor (FEP) is the primary station and establishment controllers (ECs) are secondary stations. In a typical scenario, an EC may be connected to dumb terminals and to a Token Ring network at a local site. At the remote site, an IBM host connects to an IBM FEP, which also can have links to another Token Ring LAN. Typically, the two sites are connected through an SDLC leased line.

If a router is connected to an EC, it takes over the function of the FEP, and must therefore be configured as a primary SDLC station. If the router is connected to an FEP, it takes the place of the EC, and must therefore be configured as a secondary SDLC station.

Example

The following example configures serial interface 0 on your router to allow two SDLC secondary stations to attach through a modem-sharing device (MSD) with addresses C1 and C2:

```
! enter a global command if you have not already
interface serial 0
 encapsulation sdlc-primary
 sdlc address c1
 sdlc address c2
```

Related Commands

encapsulation sdlc-secondary
sdlc address
show interfaces

ENCAPSULATION SDLC-SECONDARY

Use the **encapsulation sdlc-secondary** interface configuration command to configure the router as a secondary SDLC station if you plan to configure the SDLLC media translation feature.

>   **encapsulation sdlc-secondary**

Syntax   Description

This command has no arguments or keywords.

Default

Disabled

Command Mode

Interface configuration

Usage Guidelines

This command first appeared in Cisco IOS Release 10.0.

An **encapsulation sdlc-primary** or **encapsulation sdlc-secondary** command must be used to configure an SDLC interface. To use the **encapsulation sdlc-secondary** command, first select the interface on which you want to enable SDLC. Then establish the router as a secondary station. Next, assign secondary station addresses to the primary station using the **sdlc address** command.

SDLC defines two types of network nodes: primary and secondary. Primary nodes poll secondary nodes in a predetermined order. Secondaries then transmit if they have outgoing data. When configured as primary and secondary nodes, Cisco devices are established as SDLC stations.

In the IBM environment, a front-end processor (FEP) is the primary station and establishment controllers (ECs) are secondary stations. In a typical scenario, an EC may be connected to dumb terminals and to a Token Ring network at a local site. At the remote site, an IBM host connects to an IBM FEP, which also can have links to another Token Ring LAN. Typically, the two sites are connected through an SDLC leased line.

If a router is connected to an EC, it takes over the function of the FEP, and must therefore be configured as a primary SDLC station. If the router is connected to a FEP, it takes the place of the EC, and must therefore be configured as a secondary SDLC station.

Example

The following example establishes the router as a secondary SDLC station:

```
interface serial 0
  encapsulation sdlc-secondary
```

Related Commands

encapsulation sdlc-primary
sdlc address
show interfaces

LLC2 ACK-DELAY-TIME

Use the **llc2 ack-delay-time** interface configuration command to set the amount of time the Cisco IOS software waits for an acknowledgment before sending the next set of information frames.

llc2 ack-delay-time *milliseconds*

Syntax	Description
milliseconds	Number of milliseconds the software allows incoming information frames to stay unacknowledged. The minimum is 1 ms and the maximum is 60000 ms. The default is 100 ms.

Default

100 ms

Command Mode

Interface configuration

Usage Guidelines

This command first appeared in Cisco IOS Release 10.0.

Upon receiving an information frame, each LLC2 station starts a timer. If the timer expires, an acknowledgment will be sent for the frame, even if the **llc2 ack-max** number of received frames has not been reached. Experiment with the value of the **llc2 ack-delay-time** command to determine the configuration that balances acknowledgment network overhead and quick response time (by receipt of timely acknowledgments).

Use this command in conjunction with the **llc2 ack-max** command to determine the maximum number of information frames the Cisco IOS software can receive before sending an acknowledgment.

Example

In the following example, the software allows a 100-ms delay before I-frames must be acknowledged:

```
! enter a global command, if you have not already
interface tokenring 0
! sample ack-max command
 llc2 ack-max 3
! allow a 100 millisecond delay before I-frames must be acknowledged
 llc2 ack-delay-time 100
```

At time 0, two information frames are received. The llc2 ack-max amount of three has not been reached, so no acknowledgment for these frames is sent. If a third frame, which would force the software to send an acknowledgment, is not received in 100 ms, an acknowledgment will be sent anyway, because the llc2 ack-delay timer expires. At this point, because all frames are acknowledged, the counter for the ack-max purposes will be reset to zero.

Related Commands

llc2 ack-max
show llc2

LLC2 ACK-MAX

Use the **llc2 ack-max** interface configuration command to control the maximum amount of information frames the Cisco IOS software can receive before it must send an acknowledgment.

　　　llc2 ack-max *packet-count*

Syntax	*Description*
packet-count	Maximum number of packets the software will receive before sending an acknowledgment. The minimum is 1 packet and the maximum is 127 packets. The default is 3 packets.

Default

3 packets

Command Mode

Interface configuration

Usage Guidelines

This command first appeared in Cisco IOS Release 10.0.

An LLC2-speaking station can send only a predetermined number of frames before it must wait for an acknowledgment from the receiver. If the receiver waits until receiving a large number of frames before acknowledging any of them, and then acknowledges them all at once, it reduces overhead on the network.

For example, an acknowledgment for five frames can specify that all five have been received, as opposed to sending a separate acknowledgment for each frame. To keep network overhead low, make this parameter as large as possible.

However, some LLC2-speaking stations expect this to be a low number. Some NetBIOS-speaking stations expect an acknowledgment to every frame. Therefore, for these stations, this number is best set to 1. Experiment with this parameter to determine the best configuration.

Example

In the following example, the software is configured to receive up to seven frames before it must send an acknowledgment. Seven frames is the maximum allowed by SNA before a reply must be received:

```
! enter a global command, if you have not already
interface tokenring 0
! receive up to seven frames before sending an acknowledgment
 llc2 ack-max 7
! sample delay-time command
 llc2 ack-delay-time 100
```

Related Commands

llc2 ack-delay-time
llc2 local-window
show llc2

LLC2 IDLE-TIME

Use the **llc2 idle-time** interface configuration command to control the frequency of polls during periods of idle time (no traffic).

    llc2 idle-time *milliseconds*

Syntax	Description
milliseconds	Number of milliseconds that can pass with no traffic before the LLC2 station sends a Receiver Ready frame. The minimum is 1 ms and the maximum is 60000 ms. The default is 10000 ms.

Default

10000 ms

Command Mode

Interface configuration

Usage Guidelines

This command first appeared in Cisco IOS Release 10.0.

Periodically, when no information frames are being transmitted during an LLC2 session, LLC2 stations are sent a Receiver Ready frame to indicate they are available. Set the value for this command low enough to ensure a timely discovery of available stations, but not too low, or you will create a network overhead with too many Receiver Ready frames.

Example

In the following example, the Cisco IOS software waits 20000 ms before sending a Receiver Ready ("are you there") frame:

```
! enter a global command, if you have not already
interface tokenring 0
! wait 20000 ms before sending receiver-ready frames
 llc2 idle-time 20000
```

Related Commands

llc2 tbusy-time
llc2 tpf-time
show llc2

LLC2 LOCAL-WINDOW

Use the **llc2 local-window** interface configuration command to control the maximum number of information frames the Cisco IOS software sends before it waits for an acknowledgment.

llc2 local-window *packet-count*

Syntax	*Description*
packet-count	Maximum number of packets that can be sent before the software must wait for an acknowledgment. The minimum is 1 packet and the maximum is 127 packets. The default is 7 packets.

Default

7 packets

Command Mode

Interface configuration

Usage Guidelines

This command first appeared in Cisco IOS Release 10.0.

An LLC2-speaking station can send only a predetermined number of frames before it must wait for an acknowledgment from the receiver. Set this number to the maximum value that can be supported by the stations with which the router communicates. Setting this value too large can cause frames to be lost because the receiving station might not be able to receive all of them.

Example

In the following example, the software will send as many as 30 information frames through Token Ring interface 1 before it must receive an acknowledgment:

```
! enter a global command, if you have not already
interface tokenring 1
 llc2 local-window 30
```

Related Commands

llc2 ack-max
show llc2

LLC2 N2

Use the **llc2 n2** interface configuration command to control the number of times the Cisco IOS software retries sending unacknowledged frames or repolls remote busy stations.

    llc2 n2 *retry-count*

Syntax	Description
retry-count	Number of times the software retries operations. The minimum is 1 retry and the maximum is 255 retries. The default is 8 retries.

Default

8 retries

Command Mode

Interface configuration

Usage Guidelines

This command first appeared in Cisco IOS Release 10.0.

An LLC2 station must have some limit to the number of times it will resend a frame when the receiver of that frame has not acknowledged it. After the software is told that a remote station is busy, it will poll again based on the *retry-count* value. When this retry count is exceeded, the LLC2 station terminates its session with the other station. Set this parameter to a value that balances between frame checking and network performance.

Example

In the following example, the software will resend a frame up to four times through Token Ring interface 1 before it must receive an acknowledgment. Because you generally do not need to change the retry limit, this example shows you how to reset the limit to the default of 8:

```
! enter a global command, if you have not already
interface tokenring 1
! retry value of 8
 llc2 n2 8
```

Related Commands

llc2 t1-time
llc2 tbusy-time
llc2 trej-time
show llc2

LLC2 T1-TIME

Use the **llc2 t1-time** interface configuration command to control the amount of time the Cisco IOS software will wait before resending unacknowledged information frames.

> **llc2 t1-time** *milliseconds*

Syntax	*Description*
milliseconds	Number of milliseconds the software waits before resending unacknowledged information frames. The minimum is 1 ms and the maximum is 60000 ms. The default is 1000 ms.

Default

1000 ms

Command Mode

Interface configuration

Usage Guidelines

This command first appeared in Cisco IOS Release 10.0.

Use this command in conjunction with the **llc2 n2** command to provide a balance of network monitoring and performance. Ensure that enough time is allowed to account for the round trip between the router and its LLC2-speaking stations under heavy network loading conditions.

Example

In the following example, the software will wait 4000 ms before resending an unacknowledged frame through Token Ring interface 2:

```
! enter a global command, if you have not already
interface tokenring 2
! wait 4000 ms before retransmitting a frame through tokenring 2
 llc2 t1-time 4000
```

Related Commands

llc2 n2
llc2 tpf-time
llc2 xid-retry-time
show llc2

LLC2 TBUSY-TIME

Use the **llc2 tbusy-time** interface configuration command to control the amount of time the Cisco IOS software waits until repolling a busy remote station.

    llc2 tbusy-time *milliseconds*

Syntax	Description
milliseconds	Number of milliseconds the software waits before repolling a busy remote station. The minimum is 1 ms and the maximum is 60000 ms. The default is 9600 ms.

Default

9600 ms

Command Mode

Interface configuration

Usage Guidelines

This command first appeared in Cisco IOS Release 10.0.

An LLC2 station has the ability to notify other stations that it is temporarily busy so the other stations will not attempt to send any new information frames. The frames sent to indicate this are called Receiver Not Ready (RNR) frames. Change the value of this parameter only to increase the value for LLC2-speaking stations that have unusually long busy periods before they clear their busy status. Increasing the value will prevent the stations from timing out.

Example

In the following example, the software will wait up to 12000 ms before attempting to poll a remote station through Token Ring interface 0 to learn the station's status:

```
! enter a global command, if you have not already
interface tokenring 0
! wait 12000 ms before polling a station through tokenring 0
 llc2 tbusy-time 12000
```

Related Commands

llc2 n2
llc2 idle-time
show llc2

LLC2 TPF-TIME

Use the **llc2 tpf-time** interface configuration command to set the amount of time the Cisco IOS software waits for a final response to a poll frame before resending the poll frame.

> **llc2 tpf-time** *milliseconds*

Syntax	Description
milliseconds	Number of milliseconds the software waits for a final response to a poll frame before resending the poll frame. The minimum is 1 ms and the maximum is 60000 ms. The default is 1000 ms.

Default

1000 ms

Command Mode

Interface configuration

Usage Guidelines

This command first appeared in Cisco IOS Release 10.0.

When sending a command that must receive a response, a poll bit is sent in the frame. This is the receiving station's clue that the sender is expecting some response from it, be it an acknowledgment of information frames or an acknowledgment of more administrative tasks, such as starting and stopping the session. Once a sender gives out the poll bit, it cannot send any other frame with the poll bit set until the receiver replies with a frame containing a final bit set. If the receiver is faulty, it might never return the final bit to the sender. Therefore, the sender could be waiting for a reply that will never come. To avoid this problem, when a poll-bit-set frame is sent, a transmit-poll-frame (TPF) timer is started. If this timer expires, the software assumes that it can send another frame with a poll bit.

Usually, you will not want to change this value. If you do, the value should be larger than the T1 time, set with the **llc2 t1-time** command. The T1 time determines how long the software waits for receipt of an acknowledgment before sending the next set of frames.

Example

While you generally will not want to change the transmit-poll-frame time, this example sets the TPF time to 3000 ms. Because the TPF time should be larger than the LLC2 T1 time, this example shows the TPF time as double the LLC2 T1 time:

```
! enter a global command, if you have not already
interface tokenring 0
! send a poll bit set through tokenring 0 after a 3000 ms delay
 llc2 tpf-time 3000
! wait 1500 ms for an acknowledgment before resending I-frames
 llc2 t1-time 1500
```

Related Commands

llc2 idle-time
llc2 n2
llc2 t1-time
show llc2

LLC2 TREJ-TIME

Use the **llc2 trej-time** interface configuration command to control the amount of time the Cisco IOS software waits for a correct frame after sending a reject command to the remote LLC2 station.

   llc2 trej-time *milliseconds*

Syntax	Description
milliseconds	Number of milliseconds the software waits for a resend of a rejected frame before sending a reject command to the remote station. The minimum is 1 ms and the maximum is 60000 ms. The default is 3200 ms.

Default

3200 ms

Command Mode

Interface configuration

Usage Guidelines

This command first appeared in Cisco IOS Release 10.0.

When an LLC2 station sends an information frame, a sequence number is included in the frame. The LLC2 station that receives these frames will expect to receive them in order. If it does not, it can reject a frame and indicate which frame it is expecting to receive instead. Upon sending a reject, the LLC2 station starts a reject timer. If the frames are not received before this timer expires, the session is disconnected.

Example

In the following example, the software will wait up to 1000 ms to receive a previously rejected frame before resending its reject message to the station that sent the frame:

```
! enter a global command, if you have not already
interface tokenring 0
! wait 1000 ms before resending a reject message through tokenring 0
 llc2 trej-time 1000
```

Related Commands

llc2 n2
show llc2

LLC2 XID-NEG-VAL-TIME

Use the **llc2 xid-neg-val-time** interface configuration command to control the frequency of exchange of identification (XID) transmissions by the Cisco IOS software.

llc2 xid-neg-val-time *milliseconds*

Syntax	Description
milliseconds	Number of milliseconds after which the software sends XID frames to other LLC2-speaking stations. The minimum is 0 ms and the maximum is 60000 ms. The default is 0 ms.

Default

0 ms

Command Mode

Interface configuration

Usage Guidelines

This command first appeared in Cisco IOS Release 10.0.

Do not change the **llc2 xid-neg-val-time** parameter unless requested by your technical support representative.

LLC2-speaking stations can communicate exchange of identification (XID) frames to each other. These frames identify the stations at a higher level than the MAC address and also can contain information about the configuration of the station. These frames typically are sent only during setup and configuration periods when it is deemed that sending them is useful. The greatest frequency at which this information is transferred is controlled by this timer.

Example

The following example shows how to reset the frequency of XID transmissions to the default of 0 ms:

```
! enter a global command, if you have not already
interface tokenring 0
! set the frequency of XID transmissions to 0
 llc2 xid-neg-val-time 0
```

Related Commands

llc2 xid-retry-time
show llc2

LLC2 XID-RETRY-TIME

Use the **llc2 xid-retry-time** interface configuration command to set the amount of time the Cisco IOS software waits for a reply to exchange of identification (XID) frames before dropping the session.

llc2 xid-retry-time *milliseconds*

Syntax	Description
milliseconds	Number of milliseconds the software waits for a reply to XID frames before dropping a session. The minimum is 1 ms and the maximum is 60000 ms. The default is 60000 ms.

Default

60000 ms

Command Mode

Interface configuration

Usage Guidelines

This command first appeared in Cisco IOS Release 10.0.

Part
II

Command Reference

Set this value greater than the value of the T1 time, or the time the software waits for an acknowledgment before dropping the session. T1 time is set with the **llc2 t1-time** command.

Example

The following example sets the software to wait up to 60000 ms for a reply to XID frames it sent to remote stations (which resets the value to its default):

```
! enter a global command, if you have not already
interface tokenring 0
! wait 60000 ms for a reply to XID frames
 llc2 xid-retry-time 60000
```

Related Commands

llc2 t1-time
llc2 xid-neg-val-time
show llc2

SDLC ADDRESS

Use the **sdlc address** interface configuration command to assign a set of secondary stations attached to the serial link. Use the **no** form of this command to remove an assigned secondary station.

> **sdlc address** *hexbyte* [**echo**]
> **no sdlc address** *hexbyte*

Syntax	Description
hexbyte	Hexadecimal number (base 16) indicating the address of the serial link.
echo	(Optional) Treats nonecho and echo SDLC addresses as the same address.

Default

No secondary stations are assigned.

Command Mode

Interface configuration

Usage Guidelines

This command first appeared in Cisco IOS Release 10.0.

Before using this command, first select the interface on which you want to enable SDLC. Then establish the router as a primary station with the **encapsulation sdlc-primary** command. Next, assign secondary station addresses to the primary station using the **sdlc address** command. The addresses are given in hexadecimal (base 16) and are given one per line.

The optional keyword **echo** is valid only for TG interfaces. When you use the **echo** keyword, *hex-byte* is the nonecho SDLC address.

Example

The following example shows how to configure serial interface 0 to have two SDLC secondary stations attached to it through a modem-sharing device with addresses C1 and C2:

```
interface serial 0
 encapsulation sdlc-primary
 sdlc address c1
 sdlc address c2
```

Related Commands

encapsulation sdlc-primary
encapsulation sdlc-secondary
show interfaces

SDLC ADDRESS FF ACK-MODE

Use the **sdlc address ff ack-mode** interface configuration command to configure the IBM reserved address ff as a valid local address.

sdlc address ff ack-mode

Syntax   Description

This command has no arguments or keywords.

Command Mode

Interface configuration

Usage Guidelines

This command first appeared in Cisco IOS Release 11.0.

The **sdlc address ff ack-mode** command is used to support applications that require local termination of an SDLC connection with address FF. This command should be used only if you use the SDLC address FF as a regular (not a broadcast) address.

Example

The following example enables local acknowledgment of SDLC address FF:

```
stun peer-name xxx.xxx.xxx.xxx
stun protocol-group 1 sdlc
interface serial 1
 encapsulation stun
 stun group 1
 stun sdlc-role secondary
```

```
sdlc address c1
sdlc address ff ack-mode
stun route address c1 tcp yyy.yyy.yyy.yyy local-ack
stun route address ff tcp yyy.yyy.yyy.yyy local-ack
```

Related Commands

stun route address tcp

SDLC DLSW

Use the **sdlc dlsw** interface configuration command to attach SDLC addresses to DLSw+. Use the **no** form of this command to cancel the configuration.

> **sdlc dlsw** *sdlc-address sdlc-address ...*
> **no sdlc dlsw** *sdlc-address sdlc-address ...*

Syntax	*Description*
sdlc-address	SDLC address in hexadecimal. The valid range is 1 to FE.

Default

No correspondence is defined.

Command Mode

Interface configuration

Usage Guidelines

This command first appeared in Cisco IOS Release 11.0.

Example

The following command attaches SDLC address D2 to DLSw+:

```
sdlc dlsw d2
```

Related Commands

encapsulation sdlc
sdlc address
sdlc role

SDLC DTE-TIMEOUT

Use the **sdlc dte-timeout** interface configuration command to adjust the amount of time a data terminal equipment (DTE) interface waits for the data circuit-terminating equipment (DCE) to assert a Clear To Send (CTS) signal before dropping a Request To Send (RTS).

> **sdlc dte-timeout** *unit*

Syntax

Description

unit   Timeout wait interval in microseconds. The valid range is 10 to 64000.
                       Each unit is approximately 5 microseconds. The default is 10 units.

Default

10 units (approximately 50 microseconds)

Command Mode

Interface configuration

Usage Guidelines

This command first appeared in Cisco IOS Release 10.0.

Use this command on an interface that is in half-duplex mode and that has been configured for DTE.

Example

The following example sets the amount of time that the DTE waits for the DCE to assert a CTS to 100 units (approximately 500 microseconds):

```
sdlc dte-timeout 100
```

Related Commands

half-duplex
half-duplex timer

SDLC FRMR-DISABLE

Use the **sdlc frmr-disable** interface configuration command to indicate that secondary stations on a particular serial link do not support Frame Rejects (FRMRs) or error indications. Use the **no** form of this command to specify that the secondary station does support FRMRs.

sdlc frmr-disable
no sdlc framer-disable

Syntax   Description

This command has no arguments or keywords.

Default

Support of FRMRs or error indications

Part
II

Command Reference

Command Mode

Interface configuration

Usage Guidelines

This command first appeared in Cisco IOS Release 10.0.

FRMRs are error indications that can be sent to an SDLC station indicating that a protocol error has occurred. Not all SDLC stations support FRMRs. If this command is enabled, when the Cisco IOS software receives an error it drops the line by sending a disconnect request to the remote station.

Example

In the following example, the software is set to drop the serial line when it receives a protocol error:

```
interface serial 0
  sdlc frmr-disable
```

Related Commands

show interfaces

SDLC HOLDQ

Use the **sdlc holdq** interface configuration command to control the maximum number of packets that can be held in a buffer before being transmitted to a remote SDLC station.

    sdlc holdq *address queue-size*

Syntax	*Description*
address	SDLC address for which you are specifying a queue size.
queue-size	Local send window size. The minimum is 1 packet. No maximum value has been established. The default is 200 packets.

Default

200 packets

Command Mode

Interface configuration

Usage Guidelines

This command first appeared in Cisco IOS Release 10.0.

This command is particularly useful with the SDLLC feature that allows an LLC2-speaking SNA station on a Token Ring to communicate with an SDLC-speaking SNA station on a serial link.

Frame sizes and window sizes on Token Rings are often much larger than those acceptable for serial links. The fact that serial links are often much slower than Token Rings often makes this problem worse. Therefore, temporary backlogs can exist in periods of high data transfer from the Token Ring station to the serial station. A buffer creates a holding place for backlogged frames awaiting transmission on the serial link. This command is specified for each SDLC address and, therefore, for each SDLC secondary station on the serial link.

Example

The following example shows how to change the output hold queue length to 30 frames on an SDLC station of address C1 off serial interface 0:

```
! enter a global command, if you have not already
interface serial 0
! use SDLC encapsulation
 encapsulation sdlc-primary
! establish address of SDLC station off serial 0 as c1
 sdlc address c1
! change the output hold queue length to 30 frames on the SDLC station
 sdlc holdq c1 30
```

Related Commands

show interfaces

SDLC K

Use the **sdlc k** interface configuration command to set the window size in order to control the maximum number of information frames the Cisco IOS software transmits before it must stop transmitting and wait for an acknowledgment from the receiving router.

sdlc k *window-size*

Syntax	Description
window-size	Local send window size. The minimum is 1 frame. The maximum is 7 frames, which is the default.

Default

7 frames

Command Mode

Interface configuration

Usage Guidelines

This command first appeared in Cisco IOS Release 10.0.

Part II

Command Reference

When the Cisco IOS software is communicating with SDLC, it must have a parameter that controls the maximum number of information frames it will send before it must stop sending and wait for an acknowledgment. The **k** parameter controls this window of acceptable frames. Use this command in conjunction with the **sdlc n1** command to create a balance between frame checking and network performance.

Example

In the following example, the software can send up to five frames before it must receive an acknowledgment:

```
! enter a global command, if you have not already
interface tokenring 0
!send up to 5 frames, then wait for acknowledgment
 sdlc k 5
```

Related Commands

sdlc n1
show interfaces

SDLC LINE-SPEED

Use the **sdlc line-speed** interface configuration command to enable adaptive SDLC T1.

> **sdlc line-speed** *rate*
> **no sdlc line-speed** *rate*

Syntax	Description
rate	Clockrate in bits per second.

Default

No default rate

Command Mode

Interface configuration

Usage Guidelines

This command first appeared in Cisco IOS Release 10.0.

This feature is used to calculate the adjusted SDLC T1 value. The adjusted T1 is used to compensate for the delay between the time the system software passes a packet to the microcode and the time the packet is actually sent out on the line. For a DCE device, this should be equal to the clockrate on the interface. For a DTE device, it should be equal to the clockrate on the DCE device to which the DTE is connected.

Example

In the following example, the SDLC line-speed rate is set to *rate:*

```
sdlc line-speed rate
```

Related Commands

sdlc n2
sdlc t1

SDLC N1

Use the **sdlc n1** interface configuration command to control the maximum size of an incoming frame.

Part
II

    sdlc n1 *bit-count*

Syntax	Description
bit-count	Number indicating bit size. Frames that exceed this size are rejected. The minimum is 1 bit. The maximum is 12,000 bits, which is the default.

Default

12,000 bits

Command Mode

Interface configuration

Usage Guidelines

This command first appeared in Cisco IOS Release 10.0.

Use with the **sdlc k** command to reduce network overhead while continuing to check frame transmission.

Example

In the following example, the Cisco IOS software rejects frames larger than 10000 bits:

```
! enter a global command, if you have not already
interface tokenring 0
! reject frames larger than 10000 bits
 sdlc n1 10000
```

Related Commands

sdlc k
show interfaces

SDLC N2

Use the **sdlc n2** interface configuration command to determine the number of times that the Cisco IOS software resends a frame before terminating the SDLC session.

> **sdlc n2** *retry-count*

Syntax	Description
retry-count	Number of retry attempts. When this number is exceeded, the SDLC station terminates its session with the other station. The minimum is 1 and the maximum is 255. The default is 20 retries.

Default

20 retries

Command Mode

Interface configuration

Usage Guidelines

This command first appeared in Cisco IOS Release 10.0.

Use with the **sdlc t1** command to reduce network overhead while continuing to check transmission.

Example

In the following example, the software is set to drop an SDLC station after five unsuccessful attempts to receive an acknowledgment for a frame:

```
interface serial 0
  sdlc n2 5
```

Related Commands

sdlc t1
show interfaces

SDLC PARTNER

Use the **sdlc partner** interface configuration command to specify the destination address with which an LLC session is established for the SDLC station. Use the **no** form of this command to cancel the configuration.

> **sdlc partner** *mac-address sdlc-address*
> **no sdlc partner** *mac-address sdlc-address*

Syntax Description

mac-address   The 48-bit Media Access Control (MAC) address of the Token Ring host.

sdlc-address   SDLC address of the serial device that will communicate with the Token Ring host. The valid range is 1 to FE.

Default

No partner is defined.

Command Mode

Interface configuration

Usage Guidelines

This command first appeared in Cisco IOS Release 11.0.

Example

The following command establishes the correspondence between an SDLC and QLLC connection:

```
sdlc partner 1000.5aed.1f53 d2
```

Related Commands

encapsulation sdlc
sdlc dlsw
sdlc vmac

SDLC POLL-LIMIT-VALUE

Use the **sdlc poll-limit-value** interface configuration command to control how many times a single secondary station can be polled for input before the next station must be polled. Use the **no** form of this command to retrieve the default value.

    sdlc poll-limit-value *count*
    no sdlc poll-limit-value *count*

Syntax	Description
count	Number of times the Cisco IOS software can poll one secondary station before proceeding to the next station. The minimum is 1 time, which is the default. The maximum is 10 times.

Default

1 time

Command Mode

Interface configuration

Usage Guidelines

This command first appeared in Cisco IOS Release 10.0.

As is typical for the primary station of an SDLC connection, if a secondary station sends its full possible window of input to the primary router or access server, the Cisco IOS software immediately will re-poll the same secondary for more data in an attempt to capture the complete transaction at one time. The **sdlc poll-limit-value** command indicates how many times this can happen before the next station in the poll loop must be polled.

Increasing the value allows for smoother transaction processing but can delay polling of other stations or giving output to other stations.

Example

The following example specifies that the router can be polled two times before the next station in the poll list must be polled:

```
! enter a global command, if you have not already
interface serial 4
 no ip address
! use stun encapsulation
encapsulation stun
! establish stun group 4 on interface serial 4
 stun group 4
 stun sdlc-role primary
! poll the router up to two times before polling the next station
 sdlc poll-limit-value 2
```

Related Commands

sdlc poll-pause-timer
show interfaces

SDLC POLL-PAUSE-TIMER

Use the **sdlc poll-pause-timer** interface configuration command to control how long the Cisco IOS software pauses between sending each poll frame to secondary stations on a single serial interface. Use the **no** form of this command to retrieve the default value.

> sdlc poll-pause-timer *milliseconds*
> no sdlc poll-pause-timer *milliseconds*

Syntax	*Description*
milliseconds	Number of milliseconds that the software waits before sending the poll frame to a single serial interface. This is a number in the range 1 to 10000. The default is 10 ms.

Default

10 ms

Command Mode

Interface configuration

Usage Guidelines

This command first appeared in Cisco IOS Release 10.0.

As is typical for the primary station of an SDLC connection, the software generates polls periodically to each of the secondary stations to solicit their input. After polling each station on a single serial interface, the software will pause before beginning to poll the next station.

Because the secondaries cannot transmit data until they are polled, increasing this timer can increase response time to the users. However, making this parameter too small can flood the serial link with unneeded polls and require the secondary stations to spend wasted CPU time processing them.

Example

In the following example, the software pauses 2000 ms before sending a series of poll frames through serial interface 4:

```
! enter a global command, if you have not already
interface serial 4
no ip address
! use STUN encapsulation
 encapsulation stun
! establish stun group 4 on interface serial 4
 stun group 4
 !
 stun sdlc-role primary
! wait 2000 ms before sending each series of poll frames
 sdlc poll-pause-timer 2000
```

Related Commands

sdlc poll-limit-value
show interfaces

SDLC POLL-WAIT-TIMEOUT

Use the **sdlc poll-wait-timeout** interface configuration command when the router has been configured for local acknowledgment and some form of SDLC communication (SDLLC or STUN, for example) to specify the interval the Cisco IOS software will wait for polls from a primary node before timing out that connection.

> **sdlc poll-wait-timeout** *milliseconds*

Syntax	Description
milliseconds	Number of milliseconds the software will wait for a poll from the primary station before timing out the connection to the primary station. The minimum is 10 ms and the maximum is 64000 ms. The default is 10,000 ms.

Default

10,000 ms

Command Mode

Interface configuration

Usage Guidelines

This command first appeared in Cisco IOS Release 10.0.

This command can be used on an interface that has been configured as a secondary node, but is not to be used on an interface that has been configured as a primary node.

In a locally acknowledged multidrop environment, the polls the primary node sends to the router can be delayed because the primary node is busy polling other secondary nodes. In such situations, this command can be used to extend the timeout, thus reducing the likelihood the Cisco IOS software times out the connection to the primary node.

Example

The following example specifies that the local software will wait an interval of 63000 ms for a poll from a primary station before timing out:

```
! sample stun peer-name global command
stun peer-name 150.136.134.86
! sample protocol-group command
stun protocol-group 4 sdlc
!
interface serial 0
! sample ip address command
 no ip address
! sample encapsulation stun command
 encapsulation stun
```

```
! place interface serial0 in previously defined STUN group 4
 stun group 4
! must enter the next command to use the sdlc poll-wait-timeout command
 stun sdlc-role secondary
! set timeout period for polls from primary station to 63000 ms.
 sdlc poll-wait-timeout 63000
! list the addresses of the sdlc stations on the link
 sdlc address C1
 sdlc address C2
! provide stun route command
 stun route address C2 tcp 150.136.134.58
 stun route address C1 tcp 150.136.134.58
```

Related Commands

sdlc poll-limit-value
sdlc poll-pause-timer

SDLC QLLC-PRTNR

To establish correspondence between an SDLC and QLLC connection, use the **sdlc qllc-prtnr** interface configuration command.

> **sdlc qllc-prtnr** *virtual-mac-address sdlc-address*

Syntax	Description
virtual-mac-address	The virtual Media Access Control (MAC) address in the form *h.h.h*.
sdlc-address	SDLC address in hexadecimal. The valid range is 1 to FE.

Default

No correspondence is defined.

Command Mode

Interface configuration

Usage Guidelines

This command first appeared in Cisco IOS Release 10.3.

Example

The following command establishes the correspondence between an SDLC and QLLC connection:

```
sdlc qllc-prtnr 4000.0122.0001 c1
```

Related Commands

show interfaces

SDLC ROLE

Use the **sdlc role** interface configuration command to establish the router to be either a primary or secondary SDLC station. Use the **no** form of this command to cancel the designation.

> **sdlc role** {**none** | **primary** | **secondary** | **prim-xid-poll**}
> **no sdlc role** {**none** | **primary** | **secondary** | **prim-xid-poll**}

Syntax	Description
none	Establishes the router as either a primary or secondary station, depending on the end stations.
primary	Establishes the router as a primary station.
secondary	Establishes the router as a secondary station.
prim-xid-poll	Establishes the router as a primary station when the end station is configured as a secondary NT2.1.

Default

No default role is assigned.

Command Mode

Interface configuration

Usage Guidelines

This command first appeared in Cisco IOS Release 10.3.

If the role is **none,** the router can be either primary or secondary, depending on the end stations. The SDLC end station must be configured as negotiable or primary NT2.1. When the end stations are configured as Physical Unit type 2 (PU 2), you can set the role of the interface to **primary** or **secondary.** When the end station is configured as secondary NT2.1, you must set the role of the interface to **prim-xid-poll.**

To configure an SDLC multidrop line (downstream), configure the SDLC role as follows:

- **primary** if all SDLC devices are type PU 2.0 or mixed PU 2.0 and 2.1
- **prim-xid-poll** if all devices are type PU 2.1

Example

The following example configures the router as a primary SDLC station:

```
interface serial 2/6
 no ip address
 encapsulation sdlc
 fras map sdlc c1 serial 2/0 frame-relay 32 4 4
 sdlc role primary
 sdlc address c1
 sdlc xid c1 01700001
```

Related Commands

encapsulation sdlc

SDLC SDLC-LARGEST-FRAME

Use the **sdlc sdlc-largest-frame** interface configuration command to indicate the largest information frame (I-frame) size that can be sent or received by the designated SDLC station. Use the **no** form of this command to return to the default value.

   sdlc sdlc-largest-frame *address size*
   no sdlc sdlc-largest-frame *address size*

Syntax	Description
address	Address of the SDLC station that will communicate with the router.
size	Largest frame size that can be sent or received. The default is 265 bytes.

Default

The default largest I-frame is 265 bytes.

Command Mode

Interface configuration

Usage Guidelines

This command first appeared in Cisco IOS Release 10.3.

Example

In the following example, the Cisco IOS software can send or receive a frame as large as 265 bytes (the default) from the SDLC station at address C6. Any frames larger will be fragmented by the software.

```
interface serial 4
 sdlc sdlc-largest-frame c6 265
```

SDLC SIMULTANEOUS

To enable an interface configured as a primary SDLC station to operate in two-way simultaneous mode, use the **sdlc simultaneous** interface configuration command.

   sdlc simultaneous [**full-datamode** | **half-datamode**]

Syntax	Description
full-datamode	(Optional) Enables the primary station to send data to and receive data from the polled secondary station.
half-datamode	(Optional) Prohibits the primary station from sending data to the polled secondary station.

Default

Two-way simultaneous mode is disabled.

Command Mode

Interface configuration

Usage Guidelines

This command first appeared in Cisco IOS Release 10.3.

By default, the SDLC driver supports alternative mode. This means that in a multidrop environment, the primary station cannot send data to another secondary station until it receives a response (F bit) from the secondary station with which it is currently communicating.

In contrast, two-way simultaneous mode enables the interface configured as a primary SDLC station to send data to a second secondary station, even when it is receiving data from another secondary station. This capability improves utilization of a full-duplex serial line.

Examples

The following example enables all primary stations to send and receive data at the same time:

```
sdlc simultaneous full-datamode
```

The following example enables all secondary stations to send or receive data at the same time:

```
sdlc simultaneous half-datamode
```

Related Commands

encapsulation sdlc-primary
show interfaces

SDLC SLOW-POLL

Use the **sdlc slow-poll** interface configuration command to enable the slow-poll capability of the router as a primary SDLC station. Use the **no** form of this command to disable slow-poll capability.

sdlc slow-poll *seconds*
no sdlc slow-poll

Syntax

seconds

Description

Amount of time in seconds.

Default

10 seconds

Command Mode

Interface configuration

Usage Guidelines

This command first appeared in Cisco IOS Release 10.0.

You can use this command to improve the performance of a multidropped SDLC configuration when one or more of the secondary stations are inactive.

When slow-poll is enabled, if the router acting as a primary station detects that a secondary SDLC station is not responding, it polls that secondary SDLC station less frequently. The router spends less time waiting for the inactive secondary station to respond, thereby minimizing the performance degradation on the active secondary SDLC stations on the multidropped line.

Example

The following example enables the slow-poll capability:

```
interface serial 0
 sdlc slow-poll
```

Related Commands

sdlc poll-limit-value
sdlc poll-pause-timer
show interfaces

SDLC T1

Use the **sdlc t1** interface configuration command to control the amount of time the Cisco IOS software waits for an acknowledgment to a frame or sequence of frames.

sdlc t1 *milliseconds*

Syntax

milliseconds

Description

Number of milliseconds that the software waits. The minimum is 1 ms and the maximum is 64,000 ms. The default is 3000 ms.

Part II

Command Reference

Default

3000 ms

Command Mode

Interface configuration

Usage Guidelines

This command first appeared in Cisco IOS Release 10.0.

When an SDLC station sends a frame, it waits for an acknowledgment from the receiver that the frame has been received. The sending station cannot wait indefinitely for a response. When the frame is sent, a timer is started. To be consistent with the original specification of SDLC, this timer is called the T1 timer and is controlled by this parameter. If this timer reaches its limit before the acknowledgment is received, the software will try again and resend the frame.

Example

In the following example, the software waits up to 4000 ms for a reply to a frame or sequence of frames:

```
! enter a global command, if you have not already
interface tokenring 0
 sdlc t1 4000
```

Related Commands

sdlc n2
show interfaces

SDLC TEST SERIAL

Use the **sdlc test serial** EXEC command to determine the status of end stations. Use the **sdlc test serial** command with the **stop** keyword to halt the sending of the test frames.

> **sdlc test serial** *number address* [*iterations* | **continuous** | **stop** | **string** *string*]

Syntax	Description
serial *number*	Serial interface on which the test frame is to be sent out.
address	SDLC address (in hexadecimal) of the end station to receive the test frame.
iterations	(Optional) Number of test frames to be sent. The valid range is 1 to 25 frames. The default is 10 frames.
continuous	(Optional) Sends frames continuously until the **sdlc test serial** command is issued with the **stop** keyword.

Syntax	Description
stop	(Optional) Halts the sending of test frames.
string *string*	(Optional) Specifies a string of characters as data within the test frame. If this option is not specified, the default test string is ABCDEFGHIJKLMNOPQRSTUVWXYZ.

Defaults

The **sdlc test serial** command is not active.

The default test string is "ABCDEFGHIJKLMNOPQRSTUVWXYZ."

Command Mode

EXEC

Usage Guidelines

This command first appeared in Cisco IOS Release 11.2.

The command will pre-check for correct interface and SDLC address. The results of the test frames sent can be viewed after the frames have been sent or an **sdlc test serial** command with the **stop** keyword has been issued.

Sample Displays

The following are variations of the **sdlc test serial** command, followed by the response for each:

```
Router# sdlc test serial 0 c1

SDLC Test for address C1 completed
Frames sent=10 Frames received=10

Router# sdlc test serial 0 c1 255

SDLC Test for address C1 completed
Frames sent=255 Frames received=255

Router# sdlc test serial 0 C1 stop

SDLC Test for address C1 completed
Frames sent=44 Frames received=44

Router# sdlc test serial 0 c1 string HeyMrPUareyouthere

SDLC Test for address C1 completed
Frames sent=10 Frames received=10
```

Part
II

Command Reference

Related Commands

show interfaces

SDLC VMAC

Use the **sdlc vmac** interface configuration command to configure a MAC address for the serial interface. Use the **no** form of this command to disable the configuration.

> sdlc vmac *mac-address*
> no sdlc vmac *mac-address*

Syntax	Description
mac-address	48-bit MAC address of the Token Ring host.

Default

Disabled

Command Mode

Interface configuration

Usage Guidelines

This command first appeared in Cisco IOS Release 11.0.

This command must be configured if you plan to configure DLSw+. The last byte of the address must be 00.

Example

The following example specifies a MAC address for the serial interface:

```
sdlc vmac 1234.3174.0000
```

Related Commands

encapsulation sdlc
sdlc dlsw

SDLC XID

Use the **sdlc xid** interface configuration command to specify an exchange ID (XID) value appropriate for the designated SDLC station associated with this serial interface. Use the **no** form of this command to disable XID processing for this address.

> sdlc xid *address xid*
> no sdlc xid *address xid*

Syntax	Description
address	Address of the SDLC station associated with this interface.
xid	XID the Cisco IOS software will use to respond to XID requests the router receives. This value must be 4 bytes (8 digits) in length and is specified with hexadecimal digits.

Default

Disabled

Command Mode

Interface configuration

Part
II

Command Reference

Usage Guidelines

This command first appeared in Cisco IOS Release 10.3.

XID requests and responses are usually exchanged before sessions are started. Be sure that the XID value configured in the Cisco IOS software matches the IDBLK and IDNUM parameters configured on the host. The XID response to an XID request will contain the information you configured in the **sdlc xid** command. The host will check the XID response it receives with the IDBLK and IDNUM parameters (that are configured in the VTAM). If they match, the host will initiate a session with the router. If they do not match, the host will not initiate a session.

Example

The following example specifies an XID value of 01720002 at address C2:

```
interface serial 0
 sdlc xid c2 01720002
```

Related Commands

encapsulation sdlc

SHOW INTERFACES

Use the **show interfaces** privileged EXEC command to display the SDLC information for a given SDLC interface.

   show interfaces

Syntax   Description

This command has no arguments or keywords.

Command Mode

Privileged EXEC

Usage Guidelines

This command first appeared in Cisco IOS Release 10.0.

Sample Display

The following is sample output from the **show interfaces** command for an SDLC primary interface supporting the SDLLC function:

```
Router# show interfaces

Serial 0 is up, line protocol is up
 Hardware is MCI Serial
 MTU 1500 bytes, BW 1544 Kbit, DLY 20000 usec, rely 255/255, load 1/255
 Encapsulation SDLC-PRIMARY, loopback not set
      Timers (msec): poll pause 100 fair poll 500. Poll limit 1
      [T1 3000, N1 12016, N2 20, K 7] timer: 56608 Last polled device: none
      SDLLC [ma: 0000.0C01.14--, ring: 7 bridge: 1, target ring: 10
            largest token ring frame 2052]
SDLC addr C1 state is CONNECT
      VS 6, VR 3, RCNT 0, Remote VR 6, Current retransmit count 0
      Hold queue: 0/12 IFRAMEs 77/22 RNRs 0/0 SNRMs 1/0 DISCs 0/0
      Poll: clear, Poll count: 0, chain: p: C1 n: C1
      SDLLC [largest SDLC frame: 265, XID: disabled]
   Last input 00:00:02, output 00:00:01, output hang never
 Output queue 0/40, 0 drops; input queue 0/75, 0 drops
 Five minute input rate 517 bits/sec, 30 packets/sec
 Five minute output rate 672 bits/sec, 20 packets/sec
      357 packets input, 28382 bytes, 0 no buffer
      Received 0 broadcasts, 0 runts, 0 giants
      0 input errors, 0 CRC, 0 frame, 0 overrun, 0 ignored, 0 abort
      926 packets output, 77274 bytes, 0 underruns
      0 output errors, 0 collisions, 0 interface resets, 0 restarts
      2 carrier transitions
```

Table 12–1 shows the timer fields relevant to all SDLC connections.

Table 12–1   *Timer Fields and Descriptions when SDLC Is Enabled*

Field	Description
Timers (msec):	Lists the timers and their current values.
poll pause, fair poll, Poll limit	Current values of these timers, as described in the individual command sections in this chapter.
T1, N1, N2, K	Current values for these timers, as described in the individual command sections in this chapter.

Table 12–2 shows other data given for each SDLC secondary station configured to be attached to this interface.

Table 12–2 *SDLC Field Descriptions*

Field	Description
addr	Address of this secondary SDLC station.
state is	Current state of this connection. The possible values are: • DISCONNECT—No communication is being attempted to this secondary. • CONNECT—A normal connect state exists between this router and this secondary. • DISCSENT—This router has sent a disconnect request to this secondary and is awaiting its response. • SNRMSENT—This router has sent a connect request (SNRM) to this secondary and is awaiting its response. • THEMBUSY—This secondary has told this router that it is temporarily unable to receive any more information frames. • USBUSY—This router has told this secondary that it is temporarily unable to receive anymore information frames. • BOTHBUSY—Both sides have told each other that they are temporarily unable to receive anymore information frames. • ERROR—This router has detected an error, and is waiting for a response from the secondary acknowledging this.
VS	Sequence number of the next information frame this station sends.
VR	Sequence number of the next information frame from this secondary that this station expects to receive.
Remote VR	Last frame transmitted by this station that has been acknowledged by the other station.
Current retransmit count	Number of times the current I-frame or sequence of I-frames has been retransmitted.
Hold queue:	Number of frames in hold queue/Maximum size of hold queue.
IFRAMEs, RNRs, SNRMs, DISCs	Sent/received count for these frames.
Poll:	"Set" if this router has a poll outstanding to the secondary; "clear" if it does not.

Table 12–2   *SDLC Field Descriptions, Continued*

Field	Description
Poll count:	Number of polls, in a row, given to this secondary station at this time.
chain:	Shows the previous (p) and next (n) secondary address on this interface in the round robin loop of polled devices.

Related Commands

encapsulation sdlc-primary
encapsulation sdlc-secondary
sdlc frmr-disable
sdlc holdq
sdlc n1
sdlc n2
sdlc poll-limit-value
sdlc poll-pause-timer

SHOW LLC2

Use the **show llc2** privileged EXEC command to display the LLC2 connections active in the router.

> show llc2

Syntax   Description

This command has no arguments or keywords.

Command Mode

Privileged EXEC

Usage Guidelines

This command first appeared in Cisco IOS Release 10.0.

Sample Display

The following is sample output from the **show llc2** command:

```
Router# show llc2

TokenRing0 DTE=1000.5A59.04F9,400022224444 SAP=04/04, State=NORMAL
V(S)=5, V(R)=5, Last N(R)=5, Local window=7, Remote Window=127
ack-max=3, n2=8, Next timer in 7768
xid-retry timer 0/60000 ack timer 0/1000
p timer 0/1000 idle timer 7768/10000
```

```
rej timer 0/3200 busy timer 0/9600
ack-delay timer 0/3200
CMNS Connections to:
 Address 1000.5A59.04F9 via Ethernet2
 Protocol is up
 Interface type X25-DCE RESTARTS 0/1
 Timers: T10 1 T11 1 T12 1 T13 1
```

The display includes a CMNS addendum, indicating LLC2 is running with CMNS. When LLC2 is not running with CMNS, the **show llc2** command does not display a CMNS addendum.

Table 12–3 describes significant fields shown in the display.

Table 12–3 *Show LLC2 Field Descriptions*

Field	Description
TokenRing0	Name of interface on which the session is established.
DTE=1000.5A59.04F9, 400022224444	Address of the station to which the router is talking on this session. (The address is the MAC address of the interface on which the connection is established, except when Local Acknowledgment or SDLLC is used, in which case the address used by the Cisco IOS software is shown, as in this example, following the DTE address and separated by a comma.)
SAP=04/04	Other station's and the router's (remote/local) service access point (SAP) for this connection. The SAP is analogous to a "port number" on the router and allows for multiple sessions between the same two stations.
State=NORMAL	Current state of the LLC2 session. The possible values are: • ADM—Asynchronous Disconnect Mode—A connection is not established, and either end can begin one. • SETUP—Request to begin a connection has been sent to the remote station, and this station is waiting for a response to that request. • RESET—A previously open connection has been reset because of some error by this station, and this station is waiting for a response to that reset command. • D_CONN—This station has requested a normal, expected, end of communications with the remote, and is waiting for a response to that disconnect request. • ERROR—This station has detected an error in communications and has told the other station of this. This station is waiting for a reply to its posting of this error.

Table 12–3 *Show LLC2 Field Descriptions, Continued*

Field	Description
	• NORMAL—Connection between the two sides is fully established, and normal communication is occurring. • BUSY—Normal communication state exists, except busy conditions on this station make it such that this station cannot receive information frames from the other station at this time. • REJECT—Out-of-sequence frame has been detected on this station, and this station has requested that the other resend this information. • AWAIT—Normal communication exists, but this station has had a timer expire, and is trying to recover from it (usually by resending the frame that started the timer). • AWAIT_BUSY—A combination of the AWAIT and BUSY states. • AWAIT_REJ—A combination of the AWAIT and REJECT states.
V(S)=5	Sequence number of the next information frame this station will send.
V(R)=5	Sequence number of the next information frame this station expects to receive from the other station.
Last N (R)=5	Last sequence number of this station's transmitted frames acknowledged by the remote station.
Local Window=7	Number of frames this station may send before requiring an acknowledgment from the remote station.
Remote Window=127	Number of frames this station can accept from the remote.
ack-max=3, n2=8	Value of these parameters, as given in the previous configuration section.
Next timer in 7768	Number of milliseconds before the next timer, for any reason, goes off.
xid-retry timer 0/60000....	Series of timer values in the form of next-time/time-between, where "next-time" is the next time, in milliseconds, that the timer will wake, and "time-between" is the time, in milliseconds, between each timer wakeup. A "next-time" of zero indicates that the given timer is not enabled, and will never wake.
CMNS Connections to:	List of values that affect the interface if CMNS is enabled.

Table 12–3 *Show LLC2 Field Descriptions, Continued*

Field	Description
Address 1000.5A59.04F9 via Ethernet2	MAC address of remote station.
Protocol is up	Up indicates the LLC2 and X.25 protocols are in a state where incoming and outgoing Call Requests can be made on this LLC2 connection.
Interface type X25-DCE	One of X25-DCE, X25-DTE, or X25-DXE (both DTE and DCE).
RESTARTS 0/1	Restarts sent/received on this LLC2 connection.
Timers:	T10, T11, T12, T13 (or T20, T21, T22, T23 for DTE); these are Request packet timers. These are similar in function to X.25 parameters of the same name.

Related Commands

llc2 ack-delay-time
llc2 ack-max
llc2 idle-time
llc2 local-window
llc2 n2
llc2 t1-time
llc2 tbusy-time
llc2 tpf-time
llc2 trej-time
llc2 xid-neg-val-time
llc2 xid-retry-time

Part II

Command Reference

CHAPTER 13

Configuring IBM Network Media Translation

This chapter describes how to configure the Cisco IOS software for IBM network media translation with SDLLC or Qualified Logical Link Control (QLLC). For a complete description of the commands in this chapter, see Chapter 14, "IBM Network Media Translation Commands."

SDLLC CONFIGURATION TASK LIST

To configure SDLLC, perform the tasks in the following sections:

- Configuring SDLLC with Direct Connection
- Configuring SDLLC with Remote Source-Route Bridging (RSRB)
- Configuring SDLLC with RSRB and Local Acknowledgment
- Configuring SDLLC with Ethernet and Translational Bridging
- Customizing SDLLC Media Translation
- Monitoring SDLLC Media Translation

NOTES

Because data-link switching plus (DLSw+) contains its own media conversion, SDLLC is not required when using DLSw+.

See the "SDLLC Configuration Examples" section at the end of this chapter for specific configuration samples.

CONFIGURING SDLLC WITH DIRECT CONNECTION

In the SDLLC configuration with direct connection, a 37x5 front-end processor (FEP) on a Token Ring and a 3x74 cluster controller connected to a serial line each are connected to an interface on the same router configured with SDLLC. In this configuration, the Logical Link Control, type 2 (LLC2) session extends from the 37x5 FEP across the Token Ring to the router. The SDLLC session extends from the router across the serial line to the 3x74 cluster controller. The Systems Network Architecture (SNA) session extends across the Token Ring and the serial line to provide an end-to-end connection. The router is configured with source-route bridging (SRB).

To configure SDLLC with direct connection, you must perform the tasks in the following sections:

- Enabling SDLLC Media Translation
- Associating a Service Access Point (SAP) Value
- Specifying the Exchange Identification (XID) Value
- Initiating Connection to Token Ring Host

For an example of how to configure SDLLC with direct connection, see the "SDLLC with Direct Connection Example" later in this chapter.

Enabling SDLLC Media Translation

The interfaces you will configure for SDLLC media translation are the serial interfaces that connect to the serial lines linking the remote Synchronous Data Link Control (SDLC) devices. To configure them, perform the following task in interface configuration mode:

Task	Command
Enable SDLLC media translation on a serial interface.	**sdllc traddr** *xxxx.xxxx.xx00 lr bn tr*

Associating a Service Access Point (SAP) Value

You can associate a SAP value by performing the following task in interface configuration mode:

Task	Command
Associate a SAP value.	**sdllc sap** *sdlc-address ssap dsap*

Specifying the Exchange Identification (XID) Value

The XID value you define in the Cisco IOS software must match that of the IDBLK and IDNUM system generation parameters defined in VTAM of the Token Ring host to which the SDLC device will be communicating. To define XID, perform the following task in interface configuration mode:

Task	Command
Specify the XID value appropriate for the SDLC station to match VTAM values.	**sdllc xid** *address xxxxxxxx*

Initiating Connection to Token Ring Host

The Token Ring host is always kept in a state ready to accept a connection from the remote serial device. The remote serial device is responsible for initiating connections. The advantage of this scheme is that the serial device can communicate with the Token Ring host whenever it chooses without requiring personnel to be on the host site.

The Cisco IOS software actually initiates the connection on behalf of the serial device. To initiate connections, both the media access control (MAC) address of the Token Ring host and the SDLC line address are required. You must configure the Cisco IOS software to define the Token Ring host as the partner of the serial device. To do so, perform the following task in interface configuration mode:

Task	Command
Enable connections for SDLLC.	**sdllc partner** *mac-address sdlc-address*

CONFIGURING SDLLC WITH REMOTE SOURCE-ROUTE BRIDGING (RSRB)

A router need not directly connect the two IBM end nodes: a 37x5 FEP on a Token Ring and a 3x74 cluster controller connected to a serial line can be connected to different routers. However, the router to which the 3x74 is connected must be configured with SDLLC. They communicate via RSRB using direct encapsulation, RSRB over an FST connection, or RSRB over a TCP connection. RSRB transports packets between Router A and Router B, while Router B performs all conversions between the LLC2 and SDLC protocols by means of the SDLLC software.

To configure the router for SDLLC with RSRB, you must perform all the tasks in the "Configuring SDLLC with Direct Connection" section earlier in this chapter. You also must perform one of the sets of tasks in the following sections:

- Configuring RSRB Using Direct Encapsulation
- Configuring RSRB over FST Connection
- Configuring RSRB over TCP Connection

For more information about configuring RSRB, see Chapter 3, "Configuring Source-Route Bridging" and Chapter 4, "Source-Route Bridging Commands."

— **NOTES** —

When you configure RSRB, you must include a **source-bridge remote-peer** command on the router connected to the serial line and another **source-bridge remote-peer** command on the one connected to the Token Ring. If you have more than one serial line connected to the same router, then you will have a **source-bridge remote-peer** command for each interface in its configuration that will be using SDLLC with RSRB.

For an example of how to configure SDLLC with RSRB, see the section "SDLLC with RSRB (Multiple 3x74s) Example" later in this chapter.

Configuring RSRB Using Direct Encapsulation

To configure SDLLC with RSRB using direct encapsulation, perform the following tasks in global configuration mode:

Task	Command
Step 1 Define a ring group.	**source-bridge ring-group** *ring-group* [*virtual-mac-address*]
Step 2 Define a remote peer.	**source-bridge remote-peer** *ring-group* **interface** *interface-name* [*mac-address*]

Configuring RSRB over FST Connection

To configure SDLLC with RSRB over an FST connection, perform the following tasks in global configuration mode:

Task	Command
Step 1 Define a ring group.	**source-bridge ring-group** *ring-group* [*virtual-mac-address*]
Step 2 For FST connection only, set up an FST peer name.	**source-bridge fst-peername** *local-interface-address*
Step 3 Define a remote peer.	**source-bridge remote-peer** *ring-group* **fst** *ip-address*

Configuring RSRB over TCP Connection

To configure SDLLC with RSRB over a TCP connection, perform the following tasks in global configuration mode:

Task	Command
Step 1 Define a ring group.	**source-bridge ring-group** *ring-group* [*virtual-mac-address*]
Step 2 Define a remote peer.	**source-bridge remote-peer** *ring-group* **tcp** *ip-address*

CONFIGURING SDLLC WITH RSRB AND LOCAL ACKNOWLEDGMENT

RSRB can be configured for only local acknowledgment with RSRB using IP encapsulation over a TCP connection. Configuring SDLLC local acknowledgment can reduce time-outs and keepalive traffic on the connection.

If LLC2 local acknowledgment is configured, it must be configured on the serial interface of the router on the 3x74 cluster controller side of the connection and on the Token Ring interface of the router on the 37x5 FEP side of the connection. Whether local acknowledgment is configured, the SNA session extends end-to-end and the SDLC session extends from the router configured with the serial interface to the 3x74 cluster controller. However, the LLC2 session extends from the 37x5 FEP to the router with the Token Ring interface configured. The LLC2 session is locally terminated at that router. A TCP session then is established across the WAN to a router on the 3x74 side of the connection.

To configure the Cisco IOS software for SDLLC with RSRB and local acknowledgment, you must perform all the tasks in the "Configuring SDLLC with Direct Connection" section earlier in this chapter. You also must perform the following tasks in global configuration mode:

Task	Command
Step 1 Define a ring group.	**source-bridge ring-group** *ring-group* [*virtual-mac-address*]
Step 2 Define a remote peer with the local acknowledgment feature.	**source-bridge remote-peer** *ring-group* **tcp** *ip-address* **local-ack**
Step 3 Enable local acknowledgment for connections involving SDLLC media translation.	**source-bridge sdllc-local-ack**

Local acknowledgment is not supported when the LLC2 device is attached to an Ethernet rather than to a Token Ring.

For an example of how to configure SDLLC with RSRB and local acknowledgment, see the section "SDLLC with RSRB and Local Acknowledgment Example" later in this chapter.

For more information about configuring RSRB and local acknowledgment, see Chapter 3 and Chapter 4.

CONFIGURING SDLLC WITH ETHERNET AND TRANSLATIONAL BRIDGING

SDLLC support over Ethernet combines translational bridging with Ethernet support of 37x5 FEP connections. Figure 13–1 shows SDLLC with Ethernet and translational bridging. The 3x75 FEP is attached to Router A through Ethernet. The same router is configured for translational bridging, which translates Ethernet packets into Token Ring packets and passes them across the WAN to Router B connected to the 3x74 cluster controller via a serial line. The LLC2 session terminates at

Router B connected to the 3x74 cluster controller. In addition, Router B maintains an SDLC session from itself to the cluster controller.

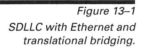
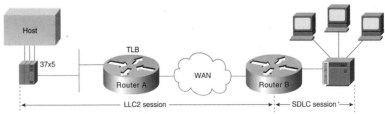

Figure 13–1
SDLLC with Ethernet and translational bridging.

CUSTOMIZING SDLLC MEDIA TRANSLATION

To increase performance on connections involving SDLLC media translation, perform the tasks in the following sections:

- Setting the Largest LLC2 I-Frame Size
- Setting the Largest SDLC I-Frame Size
- Increasing the SDLC Line Speed

See "Other Customizing Considerations" at the end of this section for more information.

Setting the Largest LLC2 I-Frame Size

Generally, the router and the LLC2 device with which it communicates should support the same maximum SDLC I-frame size. The larger this value, the better the line is used, thus increasing performance.

Faster screen updates to 3278-style terminals often result by configuring the Token Ring FEP to send as large an I-frame as possible and then allowing the Cisco IOS software to segment the frame into multiple SDLC I-frames.

After the Token Ring FEP has been configured to send the largest possible I-frame, it is best to configure the software to support the same maximum I-frame size. The default is 516 bytes. The maximum value the software can support is 8144 bytes.

To set the largest LLC2 I-frame size, perform the following task in interface configuration mode:

Task	Command
Specify the largest I-frame size that can be sent or received by the designated LLC2 primary station.	**sdllc ring-largest-frame** *value*

Setting the Largest SDLC I-Frame Size

Generally, the router and the SDLC device with which it communicates should support the same maximum SDLC I-frame size. The larger this value, the better the line is utilized, thus increasing performance.

After the SDLC device has been configured to send the largest possible I-frame, you must configure the Cisco IOS software to support the same maximum I-frame size. The default is 265 bytes. The maximum value the software can support must be less than the value of the LLC2 largest frame value defined when setting the largest LLC2 I-frame size.

To set the largest SDLC I-frame size, perform the following task in interface configuration mode:

Task	Command
Set the largest I-frame size that can be sent or received by the designated SDLC station.	**sdllc sdlc-largest-frame** *address value*

Increasing the SDLC Line Speed

You can increase the data transfer rate by increasing the SDLC line speed on the serial interface. If possible, increase the link speed of the 3x74 to 19.2 kbps on older units, or to 64 kbps on new units.

To increase the SDLC line speed, perform the following task in interface configuration mode:

Task	Command
Adjust the clock rate on the serial interface of the SCI and MCI cards to an acceptable bit rate.	**clock rate** *bps*

Other Customizing Considerations

In addition to adjusting the SDLLC parameters described in this section, you can improve performance on the connection by adjusting the LLC2 and SDLC parameters described in Chapter 11, "Configuring LLC2 and SDLC Parameters."

For IBM host configuration, consider changing the default MAXOUT (window size) value. Widely used installation guides for IBM equipment show a MAXOUT value of 1 in the VTAM-switched major node for the IBM 3174 PU. Changing this value to 7 improves the performance because VTAM can send seven frames before requiring an acknowledgment.

MONITORING SDLLC MEDIA TRANSLATION

To monitor connections using SDLLC media translation, perform the following monitoring tasks in privileged EXEC mode:

Task	Command
Step 1 Display information about SDLC and LLC2 connections involving interfaces on which SDLLC media translation has been enabled.	**show interfaces**
Step 2 Display the current state of any connections using local acknowledgment for LLC2 and SDLLC connections.	**show sdllc local-ack**
Step 3 Display information about LLC2 connections involving interfaces on which SDLLC media translation has been enabled.	**show llc2**

In **show llc2** output, look for the LLC2 connections that correspond to the MAC addresses you assigned to the SDLLC interfaces using the **sdllc traddr** command. For information about these commands, see Chapter 12, "LLC2 and SDLC Commands," and Chapter 14, "IBM Network Media Translation Commands."

QLLC CONVERSION CONFIGURATION TASK LIST

Perform the tasks in the following sections to configure QLLC conversion. The first task is required; all others are optional and depend on your specific needs.

- Enabling QLLC Conversion on a Serial Interface
- Customizing QLLC Conversion
- Monitoring QLLC Conversion

See the end of this chapter for QLLC configuration examples.

ENABLING QLLC CONVERSION ON A SERIAL INTERFACE

The interfaces you configure for QLLC conversion are the serial interfaces that connect to the X.25 network linking the remote devices with which you plan to communicate.

To enable QLLC conversion, you must perform the tasks in the first of the following sections. Perform the tasks in the remaining sections as appropriate.

- Enabling QLLC Conversion on the Appropriate Serial Interfaces
- Defining the XID Value Associated with an X.25 Device
- Enabling to Open a Connection to the Local Token Ring Device

Enabling QLLC Conversion on the Appropriate Serial Interfaces

You can enable QLLC conversion on a serial interface to support either a switched virtual circuit (SVC) or a permanent virtual circuit (PVC). The tasks you perform differ somewhat depending on the type of virtual circuit you plan to support on the interface. In either case, first verify that RSRB is enabled by performing the following task in privileged EXEC mode:

Task	Command
Ensure that RSRB is enabled on the interfaces.	show configuration

In the sections for the appropriate serial interfaces of the **show configuration** display, look for one or more **source-bridge remote-peer** entries and a **source-bridge** *rn* entry. For more information about configuring a serial interface for RSRB, see Chapter 11.

To enable QLLC conversion to support an SVC, perform the following tasks in interface configuration mode:

Task	Command
Step 1 Map a virtual Token Ring MAC address for the interface to its X.121 address.	**x25 map qllc** *x121-addr* [*x25-map-options*]
Step 2 Enable the use of QLLC conversion on the interface.	**qllc srb** *virtual-mac-addr srn trn*

To enable QLLC conversion to support a PVC, perform the following task in interface configuration mode:

Task	Command
Step 1 Set up a PVC for QLLC conversion.	**x25 pvc** *circuit* **qllc** *x121-address* [*x25-map-options*]
Step 2 Enable the use of QLLC conversion on the interface.	**qllc srb** *virtual-mac-addr srn trn*

To configure QLLC to accept a call from any remote X.25 device, perform the following task in interface configuration mode:

Task	Command
Configure QLLC to accept a call from any remote X.25 device.	qllc accept-all-calls

In a Token Ring or RSRB environment, the LAN-attached devices initiate a connection by sending a null XID packet upstream. If the Cisco IOS software forwards this null XID to an X.25-attached FEP, the FEP responds as if it were connecting to a PU2.1 device and breaks the connection when the PU 2.0 next sends an XID Format 0 Type 2. To resolve this situation and to enable the connection, perform the following task in interface configuration mode:

Task	Command
Enable connection between a PU 2.0 on the LAN side and a FEP running NPSI on the X.25 side.	qllc npsi-poll *virtual-mac-addr*

The **qllc npsi-poll** command intercepts any null XID packet that the router receives on the LAN interface and returns a null XID response to the downstream device. It continues to allow XID Format 3 and XID Format 0 packets through the X.25 device.

Defining the XID Value Associated with an X.25 Device

The exchange identification (XID) serves as a password to ensure that only those devices that should communicate with the Token Ring host have that privilege. If the XID is defined in NCP on the host, you must enable the Cisco IOS software to reply (on behalf of the X.25 device) to the Token Ring host's requests for an XID reply. Although the XID value is used to reply to XID requests received on the LLC2 side of the connection, you apply this command on the serial interface defined for X.25. This XID value must match that of IDBLK and IDNUM defined in the NCP.

— **NOTES** —————————————————————————————————————

For most QLLC installations, you do not need to define the XID value. You only need to do so if the remote X.25 device is not configured to send its own XID. This is only possible for a device that is attached through a PVC, although most devices that are connected through X.25 send their own XIDs.

To define the XID value associated with an X.25 device, perform the following task in interface configuration mode:

Task	Command
Specify the XID value appropriate for the X.25 device associated with the Token Ring interface.	**qllc xid** *virtual-mac-addr xid*

Enabling to Open a Connection to the Local Token Ring Device

If you plan to use SVCs rather than PVCs, you must enable the Cisco IOS software to open a connection to the local Token Ring device on behalf of the remote X.25 device when an incoming call is received. When QLLC conversion is used over an SVC, the remote X.25 device typically initiates the X.25/QLLC session, and the software in turn initiates the LLC2 session.

To enable the software to open a connection to the local Token Ring device, perform the following task in interface configuration mode:

Task	Command
Enable the software to open a connection to the local Token Ring device.	**qllc partner** *virtual-mac-addr mac-addr*

CUSTOMIZING QLLC CONVERSION

To customize your configuration of QLLC conversion, you can perform one or more of the following tasks:

- Enable QLLC local acknowledgment for remote source-route-bridged connections.
- Specify a SAP value other than the IBM default SAP value.
- Specify the largest packet that can be sent or received on the X.25 interface.

These tasks are described in the following sections.

Enabling QLLC Local Acknowledgment for Remote Source-Route-Bridged Connections

Enable local acknowledgment when the round-trip time through the TCP/IP network is as large or larger than the LLC2 timeout period.

To enable QLLC local acknowledgment for RSRB connections, perform the following global configuration task on the router connected to the X.25 interface and configure the remote peers for local acknowledgment:

Task	Command
Enable QLLC local acknowledgment for remote source-route-bridged connections.	**source-bridge qllc-local-ack**

If, for example, Router B with X.25 interface has the IP address *ip1*, and the remote peer (Router A) has the address *ip2*, and they use a virtual ring group *vrg*, then both routers use the following configuration commands:

```
source-bridge ring-group vrg
source-bridge remote-peer vrg tcp ip1 local-ack
source-bridge remote-peer vrg tcp ip2
```

The configuration for Router B is as follows:

```
source-bridge ring-group vrg
source-bridge remote-peer vrg tcp ip1
source-bridge remote-peer vrg tcp ip2 local-ack
```

This will not affect Router A.

Specifying SAP Values Other Than the Default IBM SAP Values

To use SAP values other than the default IBM SAP values, perform the following task in interface configuration mode:

Task	Command
Specify a SAP value other than the default IBM SAP value.	**qllc sap** *virtual-mac-addr ssap dsap*

Specifying the Largest Packet That Can Be Sent or Received on the X.25 Interface

There are two ways for a packet to become segmented:

- The X.25 software performs the segmentation and the other X.25 station re-assembles the packet.
- The QLLC conversion performs SNA header segmentation. In this case, QLLC does not re-assemble, but passes smaller SNA segments to the IBM end station.

If the QLLC software does not perform SNA segmentation, then the X.25 software must be capable of performing X.25 segmentation of the largest packet that it can receive from the LLC2 side. This packet can be several thousand bytes long, whereas the typical size for X.25 packets is 1024 bytes or less. (The default is 128, but that can be overridden with larger values.) The X.25 software, especially in the X.25-attached IBM end station, might not be able to re-assemble a very large packet. In this situation, specifying the largest QLLC packet can be useful.

By default, the maximum SNA data unit size established for the virtual circuit is the maximum packet size that can be sent or received on the X.25 interface. If packets received on the LLC2 interface are larger than the largest value allowed on the X.25 connection, they can be segmented by the X.25 software before being sent on the X.25 interface. Moreover, there is no re-assembly on receiving packets on the X.25 interface before sending them on the LLC2 interface. Thus, you might need to reconfigure the maximum packet size for the X.25 interface to match that for the LLC2 interface.

When the remote X.25 device has a limit on the maximum total length of recombined X.25 segments it will support, you must ensure the length is not exceeded. For example, a device whose maximum SNA packet size is limited to 265 bytes might not be able to handle a series of X.25 packets that it has to recombine to make a 4, 8, or 17 KB SNA packet, such as one often encounters in an LLC2 environment.

You cannot configure the X.25 interface with a larger packet size than the LLC2 interface.

To specify the largest packet that can be sent or received on the X.25 interface, perform the following task in interface configuration mode:

Task	Command
Specify the largest packet that can be sent or received on the X.25 interface.	**qllc largest-packet** *virtual-mac-address max-size*

MONITORING QLLC CONVERSION

To monitor connections using QLLC conversion, perform the following tasks in privileged EXEC mode:

Task		Command
Step 1	Display information about X.25 and LLC2 connections involving interfaces on which QLLC conversion has been enabled.	**show interfaces serial** *number*
Step 2	Display the current state of any connections using QLLC local acknowledgment.	**show qllc**

Task		Command
Step 3	Display information about LLC2 connections involving interfaces on which QLLC conversion has been enabled.	**show llc2**

SDLLC CONFIGURATION EXAMPLES

The following sections provide SDLLC configuration examples:

- SDLLC with Direct Connection Example
- SDLLC with Single Router Using RSRB Example
- SDLLC with RSRB (Single 3x74) Example
- SDLLC with RSRB (Multiple 3x74s) Example
- SDLLC with RSRB and Local Acknowledgment Example

Refer to the "NCP and VTAM Sysgen Parameters" section for sample NCP definitions that the 37x5 FEP in these topologies could use and VTAM definitions that the IBM host in these topologies could use to reflect the routers in the communication path.

SDLLC with Direct Connection Example

Figure 13–2 shows a router configuration when the router directly connects the Token Ring and the serial line. The Cisco IOS software is configured with SRB.

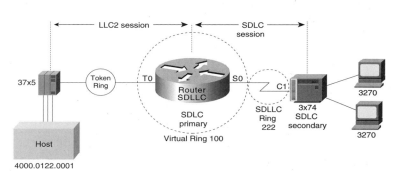

Figure 13–2

SDLLC communication between a 37x5 and a 3x74 connected to the same router (direct connection).

A configuration file that enables direct connection follows:

```
source-bridge ring-group 100
!
interface tokenring 0
 source-bridge 111 1 100
```

```
!
interface serial 0
 encapsulation sdlc-primary
 sdlc address c1
 sdllc traddr 0110.2222.3300 222 2 100
 sdllc partner 4000.0122.0001 c1
 sdllc xid c1 1720001
```

SDLLC with Single Router Using RSRB Example

Figure 13–3 shows a software configuration in which the router directly connects the Token Ring and the serial line, but uses RSRB to create a virtual ring 100. This configuration has the following characteristics:

- The FEP (37x5) sees C1 3x74 at MAC address 0110.2222.3300

- The RIF from the FEP to the devices would appear as:

  ring 111—bridge 1—ring 100—bridge 1—ring 8

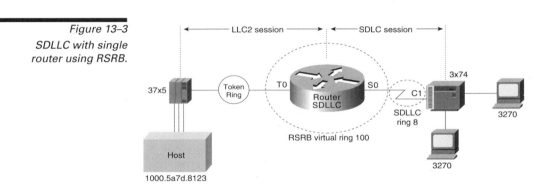

Figure 13–3
SDLLC with single router using RSRB.

The following sample configuration file is for SDLLC with a single router using RSRB:

```
source-bridge ring-group 100
source-bridge remote-peer 100 tcp 131.108.1.1
source-bridge remote-peer 100 tcp 131.108.2.2

interface tokenring 0
 ip address 131.108.2.2 255.255.255.0
 source-bridge 111 1 100

interface serial 0
 encapsulation sdlc-primary
 sdlc address c1
 sdllc traddr 0110.2222.3300 8 1 100
 sdllc partner 1000.5a7d.8123 c1
 sdllc xid c1 17200c1
```

SDLLC with RSRB (Single 3x74) Example

In Figure 13–4, SDLLC with RSRB connects a FEP (37x5) and a single 3x74 cluster controller. The host wants to communicate with a single 3x74 that its FEP sees on a Token Ring. However, the 3x74 seen by the FEP is in fact SDLC device C1 connected by means of a serial link through a remote router.

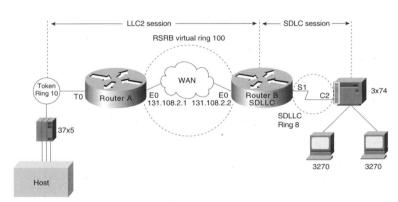

Figure 13–4
SDLLC with RSRB
with a single 3x74.

The configuration files for the network shown in Figure 13–4 follow.

Configuration for Router A

```
source-bridge ring-group 100
source-bridge remote-peer 100 tcp 131.108.1.1
source-bridge remote-peer 100 tcp 131.108.2.2
!
interface tokenring 0
 ip address 131.108.1.1 255.255.255.0
 source-bridge 10 1 100
!
interface ethernet 0
 ip address 131.108.2.1 255.255.255.0
```

Configuration for Router B

```
source-bridge ring-group 100
source-bridge remote-peer 100 tcp 131.108.1.1
source-bridge remote-peer 100 tcp 131.108.2.2
!
interface tokenring 0
 ip address 131.108.2.2 255.255.255.0
 source-bridge 1 1 100
!
interface serial 0
 encapsulation sdlc-primary
 sdlc address c1
```

```
sdllc traddr 0110.2222.3300 8 1 100
sdllc partner 1000.5a7d.8123 c1
sdllc xid c1 17200c1
```

SDLLC with RSRB (Multiple 3x74s) Example

In the setup shown in Figure 13–5, Router A needs no SDLLC configuration; Router B has the SDLLC configuration and supports multipoint on the SDLC link with a modem-sharing device, and Router C also is configured with SDLLC. For information about the NCP and VTAM system generation (sysgen) parameters that are used in this configuration, see the "NCP and VTAM Sysgen Parameters" section later in this chapter.

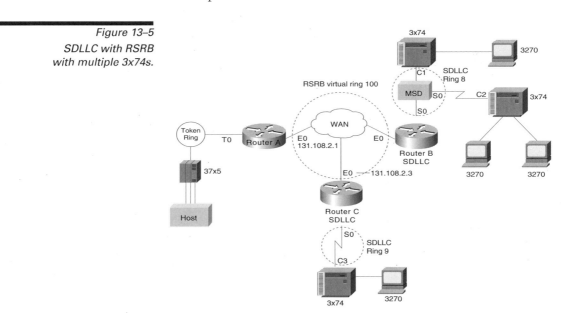

Figure 13–5
SDLLC with RSRB
with multiple 3x74s.

The following configuration files describe the network shown in Figure 13–5. The note references to the right of the configuration files refer to the "Notes" section at the end of this chapter.

Configuration for Router A

```
source-bridge ring-group 100
source-bridge remote-peer 100 tcp 131.108.2.1
source-bridge remote-peer 100 tcp 131.108.2.2
source-bridge remote-peer 100 tcp 131.108.2.3
!
interface tokenring 0
 ip address 131.108.1.1 255.255.255.0
 source-bridge 10 1 100
```

```
!
interface ethernet 0
 ip address 131.108.2.1 255.255.255.0
```

Configuration for Router B

```
source-bridge ring-group 100
source-bridge remote-peer 100 tcp 11.108.2.1
source-bridge remote-peer 100 tcp 11.108.2.2
source-bridge remote-peer 100 tcp 11.108.2.3
!
interface ethernet 0
 ip address 131.108.2.2 255.255.255.0
!
interface serial 0
 encapsulation sdlc-primary
 sdlc address c1
 sdlc address c2
 sdllc traddr 0110.2222.3300 7 1 100
 sdllc partner 1000.5a7d.8123 c1
 sdllc partner 1000.5a7d.8123 c2
 sdllc xid c1 17200c1
 sdllc xid c2 17200c2
```

Configuration for Router C

```
source-bridge ring-group 100
source-bridge remote-peer 100 tcp 131.108.2.1
source-bridge remote-peer 100 tcp 131.108.2.2
source-bridge remote-peer 100 tcp 131.108.2.3
!
interface ethernet 0
 ip address 131.108.2.3 255.255.255.0
!
interface serial 0
 encapsulation sdlc-primary
 sdlc address c3
 sdllc traddr 0110.2222.3300 9 1 100
 sdllc partner 1000.5a7d.8123 c3
 sdllc xid c3 17200c3
```

SDLLC with RSRB and Local Acknowledgment Example

The configuration shown in Figure 13–6 enables local acknowledgment for Router B, which means that the LLC session terminates at Router A. However, the LLC2 session between Router A and Router C is not locally acknowledged and terminates at Router C.

For information about the NCP and VTAM system generation (sysgen) parameters that are used in this configuration, see the "NCP and VTAM Sysgen Parameters" section later in this chapter.

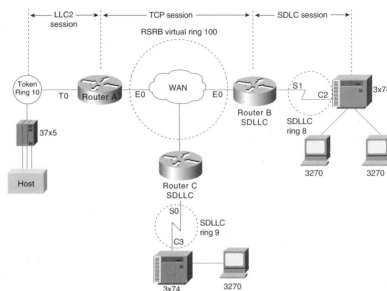

Figure 13–6
SDLLC with RSRB and local
acknowledgment.

The following sample configuration files describe the network shown in Figure 13–6. (The notes in the sample configuration files refer to the "Notes" section at the end of this chapter.)

Configuration for Router A

```
source-bridge ring-group 100
source-bridge remote-peer 100 tcp 131.108.2.1
source-bridge remote-peer 100 tcp 131.108.2.2 local-ack
source-bridge remote-peer 100 tcp 131.108.2.3
!
interface tokenring 0
 ip address 131.108.1.1 255.255.255.0
 source-bridge 1 1 100
!
interface ethernet 0
 ip address 131.108.2.1 255.255.255.0
```

Configuration for Router B

```
source-bridge ring-group 100
source-bridge remote-peer 100 tcp 131.108.2.1 local-ack
source-bridge remote-peer 100 tcp 131.108.2.2
source-bridge remote-peer 100 tcp 131.108.2.3

source-bridge sdllc local-ack
!
interface ethernet 0
 ip address 131.108.2.2 255.255.255.0
```

```
!
interface serial 0
 encapsulation sdlc-primary
 sdlc address c1
 sdllc traddr 4000.3174.0b0d 7 1 100
 sdllc partner 1000.5a7d.8123 c1
 !Must match TIC LOCADD [See NOTE 2.]
 sdllc xid c1 017200c1
 !Must match VTAM IDBLK/IDNUM [See NOTE 4.]
!
interface serial 1
 encapsulation sdlc-primary
 sdlc address c2
 sdllc traddr 0110.2222.3200 8 1 100
 sdllc partner 1000.5a7d.8123 c2
 !Must match TIC LOCADD [See NOTE 2.]
 sdllc xid c2 017200c2
 !Must match VTAM IDBLK/IDNUM [See NOTE 4.]
```

Configuration for Router C

```
source-bridge ring-group 100
source-bridge remote-peer 100 tcp 131.108.2.1
source-bridge remote-peer 100 tcp 131.108.2.2
source-bridge remote-peer 100 tcp 131.108.2.3
!
interface ethernet 0
ip address 131.108.2.3 255.255.255.0
!
interface serial 0
 encapsulation sdlc-primary
 sdlc address c3
 sdllc traddr 4000.3174.0c00 9 1 100
 sdllc partner 1000.5a7d.8123 c3
 Must match TIC LOCADD [See NOTE 2.]
 sdllc xid c3 017200c3
 !Must match VTAM IDBLK/IDNUM [See NOTE 4.]
```

QLLC CONVERSION CONFIGURATION EXAMPLES

The following sections provide QLLC conversion configuration examples:

- QLLC Conversion Between a Single 37x5 and a Single 3x74 Example
- QLLC Conversion Between a Single 37x5 and Multiple 3x74s Example
- QLLC Conversion Between Multiple 37x5s and Multiple 3x74s Example
- QLLC Conversion Between a Single 37x5 and Multiple 3x74s Across an Arbitrary WAN Example
- NCP and VTAM Sysgen Parameters

The examples describe four increasingly complex QLLC conversion topologies and possible software configurations for each. Following the examples are sample NCP definitions that the 37x5 FEP in these topologies could use and VTAM definitions that the IBM host in these topologies could use to reflect the routers in the communication path.

QLLC Conversion Between a Single 37x5 and a Single 3x74 Example

Figure 13–6, shown previously, illustrates the simplest QLLC conversion topology—a single 37x5 FEP on a Token Ring communicating with a single 3x74 cluster controller across an X.25 network. A router connects the Token Ring to the X.25 network. In Figure 13–6, notice that the router's X.25 interface is treated as a virtual ring for configuration purposes.

The following configuration file configures the Cisco IOS software to support the network topology shown in Figure 13–6:

```
source-bridge ring-group 100
!
interface serial 0
 encapsulation x25
 x25 address 31102120100
 x25 map qllc 0100.0000.0001 31104150101
 qllc srb 0100.0000.0001 201 100
!
! Allow the 3x74 to initiate the connection.
!
 qllc partner 0100.0000.0001 4000.0101.0132

interface tokenring 0
 source-bridge 1 1 100
```

In this configuration file, the **source-bridge ring-group** command defines a virtual ring number 100. The serial 0 interface that connects to the X.25 network then is configured for X.25 DTE operation using the **encapsulation x25** command and assigned the X.121 address of 31102120100 using the **x25 address** command. The **x25 map qllc** command associates the X.121 address of the remote X.25 device (31104150101) with a virtual Token Ring MAC address (0100.0000.0001) the Token Ring device will use to communicate with this remote X.25 device. The **qllc srb** command indicates that the virtual MAC address of the X.25 device will be used to communicate with the real MAC address of the Token Ring device.

The **qllc partner** command enables the software to open a connection to the local Token Ring device at MAC address 4000.0101.0132 on behalf of the remote X.25 device at virtual Token Ring MAC address 0100.0000.0001. The **source-bridge** command configures the router's Token Ring 0 interface for local source-route bridging by associating the router's virtual ring number 100 with the ring number (1) of the local Token Ring and the bridge number (1) that uniquely identifies this bridge interface.

QLLC Conversion Between a Single 37x5 and Multiple 3x74s Example

Figure 13–7 shows a slightly more complex QLLC conversion topology. The same 37x5 FEP on a Token Ring connects through a router to an X.25 network, but communicates with multiple 3x74 cluster controllers through X.25.

Figure 13–7
QLLC conversion
between a single 37x5
and multiple 3x74s.

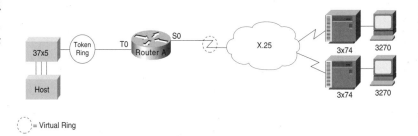

= Virtual Ring

The following configuration file configures the Cisco IOS software to support the network topology shown in Figure 13–7:

```
source-bridge ring-group 100
!
interface serial 0
 encapsulation x25
 x25 address 3137005469
!
 ! configure the first 3174
!
 x25 map qllc 0000.0cff.0001 31370054111
!
 ! 1001 - virtual ring used by all qllc devices
 ! 100 - the virtual ring group
!
 qllc srb 0000.0cff.0001 1001 100
 qllc partner 0000.0cff.0001 4000.1160.0000
 qllc xid 0000.0cff.0001 01710017
!
 ! configure the second 3174
!
 x25 map qllc 0000.0cff.0002 313700543247
!
 ! 1001 - virtual ring used by all qllc devices
 ! 100 - the virtual ring group
!
 qllc srb 0000.0cff.0002 1001 100
 qllc partner 0000.0cff.0002 4000.1160.0000
 qllc xid 0000.0cff.0002 01710017
!
interface tokenring 0
```

```
!
! Since this is a real bridge, we have to define the way it
! bridges to the Qllc virtual ring.
!
source-bridge 1 1 100
source-bridge spanning
```

QLLC Conversion Between Multiple 37x5s and Multiple 3x74s Example

In the following example, two 3x74s on a Token Ring each attach to a different 37x5 on the other side of an X.25 network. Only one Token Ring interface is used. Do not create a bridge from the QLLC virtual ring (1001) to the physical Token Ring (1). Instead, define a virtual-ring group (for example, 100).

```
interface serial 0
 encapsulation x25
 x25 address 3137005469
!
! configure the router for the first 3x74
!
 x25 map qllc 0000.0cff.0001 31370054111
!
! 1001 - virtual ring used by all qllc devices
! 1 - the local Token Ring number
!
 qllc srb 0000.0cff.0001 1001 1
 qllc partner 0000.0cff.0001 4000.1160.0000
!
! configure the router for the second 3x74
!
 x25 map qllc 0000.0cff.0002 31370053247
!
! 1001 - virtual ring used by all qllc devices
! 1 - the local Token Ring number
!
! Note that the partner's MAC address and XID are different from
! those in the first 3x74.
!
 qllc srb 0000.0cff.0001 1001 1
 qllc partner 0000.0cff.0002 4000.1161.1234
!
interface tokenring 0
!
! Since this is a real bridge, we have to define the way it bridges
! to the QLLC virtual ring.
!
 source-bridge 1 1 1001
 source-bridge spanning
```

QLLC Conversion Between a Single 37x5 and Multiple 3x74s Across an Arbitrary WAN Example

Figure 13–7, shown previously, includes an added arbitrary WAN in the communication path between the 37x5 FEP and the multiple 3x74 cluster controllers. The arbitrary WAN can be a multihop network, whereas QLLC conversion treats the X.25 network as a single-hop network.

In Figure 13–7, notice that the arbitrary WAN and the routers on either side of it form a single virtual ring, as configured using the **source-bridge ring-group** global configuration command.

In this configuration file, Router A uses an IP address of 131.108.2.2 and its Token Ring interface is attached to Token Ring 1. Because Router A connects to the Token Ring, it does not need to be configured for QLLC conversion. Router B, configured for QLLC conversion because it connects directly to the X.25 network through its serial interface, uses an X.121 address of 31102120100 and an IP address of 131.108.1.1. The 37x5 device uses a MAC address of 4000.0101.0132. The virtual MAC address of 0100.0000.0001 has been assigned to the 3x74 device.

Sample Configuration for Router A

The following configuration file configures the Router A in Figure 13–7:

```
source-bridge ring-group 100
source-bridge remote-peer 100 tcp 131.108.1.1 local-ack
source-bridge remote-peer 100 tcp 131.108.2.2 local-ack
!
interface ethernet 0
 ip address 131.108.3.3 255.255.255.0
!
interface tokenring 0
 ip address 131.108.2.2 255.255.255.0
 source-bridge 1 1 100
 source-bridge spanning
```

Sample Configuration for Router B

The following configuration file configures the Router B in :

```
source-bridge ring-group 100
source-bridge remote-peer 100 tcp 131.108.1.1 local-ack
source-bridge remote-peer 100 tcp 131.108.2.2 local-ack
source-bridge qllc-local-ack
!
interface serial 0
 encapsulation x25
 x25 address 31102120100
 x25 map qllc 0100.0000.0001 31104150101
 x25 map qllc 0100.0000.0002 31104150102
 qllc srb 0100.0000.0001 201 100
 qllc srb 0100.0000.0002 201 100
!
! Allow the 3174 to initiate the connection.
```

```
!
 qllc partner 0100.0000.0001 4000.0101.0132
 qllc partner 0100.0000.0002 4000.0101.0132
!
interface ethernet 0
 ip address 131.108.1.1 255.255.255.0
```

NCP and VTAM Sysgen Parameters

The sample system generation (sysgen) parameters in this section show typical NCP and VTAM values that correspond with the Router A, Router B, and Router C configurations shown in Figure 13–5 and Figure 13–6 for SDLLC media translation and in Figure 13–7 for QLLC conversion.

IBM's ACF/NCP uses a function called NTRI (NCP/Token Ring Interconnection) to support Token Ring-attached SNA devices. NTRI also provides translation from Token Ring-attached SNA devices (Physical Units) to switched (dial-up) devices. VTAM provides the resolution for these devices in a Switched Major Node. VTAM treats these devices on NTRI logical lines as switched devices.

Using SDLLC, the Cisco IOS software translates SDLC leased line protocol into Token Ring LLC2 protocol, then the NTRI function in ACF/NCP translates Token Ring LLC2 protocol into an SNA switched protocol.

NCP Generation Definitions

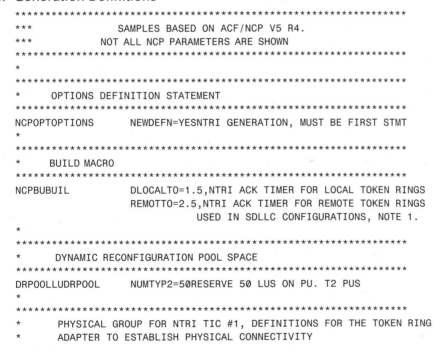

```
*******************************************************************
***              SAMPLES BASED ON ACF/NCP V5 R4.
***           NOT ALL NCP PARAMETERS ARE SHOWN
*******************************************************************
*
*******************************************************************
*     OPTIONS DEFINITION STATEMENT
*******************************************************************
NCPOPT OPTIONS       NEWDEFN=YES NTRI GENERATION, MUST BE FIRST STMT
*
*******************************************************************
*     BUILD MACRO
*******************************************************************
NCPBU BUILD          DLOCALTO=1.5,NTRI ACK TIMER FOR LOCAL TOKEN RINGS
                     REMOTTO=2.5,NTRI ACK TIMER FOR REMOTE TOKEN RINGS
                              USED IN SDLLC CONFIGURATIONS, NOTE 1.
*
*******************************************************************
*     DYNAMIC RECONFIGURATION POOL SPACE
*******************************************************************
DRPOOLL UDRPOOL      NUMTYP2=50 RESERVE 50 LUS ON PU. T2 PUS
*
*******************************************************************
*     PHYSICAL GROUP FOR NTRI TIC #1, DEFINITIONS FOR THE TOKEN RING
*     ADAPTER TO ESTABLISH PHYSICAL CONNECTIVITY
```

```
******************************************************************
EPHYGGROUP          ECLTYPE=PHYSICAL
*
EPHYLLINE           ADAPTER=TIC2,        TYPE OF ADAPTER
                    ADDRESS=(16,FULL),   INTERNAL FEP TIC ADDRESS
                    PORTADD=0,
                    LOCADD=10005a7d8123,TIC ADDRESS, NOTE 2.
                    RCVBUFC=1440,
                    MAXTSL=2012,
                    TRSPEED=16           TOKEN RING SPEED
*
EPHYPUPU
*
EPHYLULU            ISTATUS=INACTIVE
*
******************************************************************
*     NTRI PERIPHERAL LOGICAL LINE GROUP, LINE AND PU PAIRS ARE
*     GENERATED BY THE AUTOGEN PARAMETER.
******************************************************************
ELOGGGROUP          ECLTYPE=LOGICAL,
                    PHYPORT=0,
                    CALL=INOUT,
                    AUTOGEN=3            ONE PER SDLLC CONTROLLER,
                                         NOTE 3.
******************************************************************
```

VTAM Definitions

```
******************************************************************
*         VTAM SWITCHED MAJOR NODE, BASED ON ACF/VTAM V3 R4.
*         THE CODING BELOW SUPPORTS DIAL IN OPERATION ONLY. TYPICALLY,
*         NTRI IMPLEMENTATIONS USE ONLY DIAL IN. IF DIAL OUT FROM AN
*         APPLICATION IS REQUIRED, PATH MACROS MUST BE USED. CONSULT
*         THE APPROPRIATE VTAM INSTALLATION REFERENCE MANUAL.
******************************************************************
VSWITCH   VBUILD     TYPE=SWNET
*
VPU1      PU         ADDR=13,      COULD BE ANYTHING (NOT USED)
                     IDBLK=017,    XID PARM, NOTE 4.
                     IDNUM=200c1,  XID PARM, NOTE 4.
                     MAXOUT=7,
                     MAXDATA=265,
                     MODETAB=AMODETAB,
                     DLOGMOD=US327X,
                     PUTYPE=2,
                     USSTAB=USS327X
*
VLU1A     LU         LOCADDR=2,
VLU1B     LU         LOCADDR=3
*
VPU2PU               ADDR=13,      COULD BE ANYTHING (NOT USED)
                     IDBLK=017,    XID PARM, NOTE 4.
```

```
                         IDNUM=200c2, XID PARM, NOTE 4.
                         MAXOUT=7,
                         MAXDATA=265,
                         MODETAB=AMODETAB,
                         DLOGMOD=US327X,
                         PUTYPE=2,
                         USSTAB=USS327X
*
VLU2A        LU          LOCADDR=2,
VLU2B        LU          LOCADDR=3
*
VPU3         PU          ADDR=13,      COULD BE ANYTHING (NOT USED)
                         IDBLK=017,    XID PARM, NOTE 4.
                         IDNUM=200c3, XID PARM, NOTE 4.
                         MAXOUT=7,
                         MAXDATA=265,
                         MODETAB=AMODETAB,
                         DLOGMOD=US327X,
                         PUTYPE=2,
                         USSTAB=USS327X
*
VLU3A        LU          LOCADDR=2,
VLU3B        LU          LOCADDR=3
*
```

Notes

In these sample definitions:

1. REMOTTO is the NCP's T1 timer for remote Token Rings. All connections use RIF information and therefore look like remote Token Ring devices. The default is 2.5 seconds, which is adequate for most situations; however, when slow-speed links are used, this parameter should be reviewed to ensure enough time for link-level acknowledgments.

2. The LOCADD parameter defines the locally administered address of the TIC in the NCP. The Cisco IOS software, configured for SDLLC, will insert this address as the 802.5 destination address field in TEST and XID frames to establish connectivity and then in data frames during the session. The **sdllc partner** and **qllc partner** commands define this connection in the Cisco IOS software. Each SDLC control unit is defined with an **sdllc partner** or **qllc partner** command.

3. The AUTOGEN parameter specifies the number of LINE and PU pairs that are automatically generated by NDF (Network Definition Facility). Each controller requires a LINE and PU definition in the ELCTYPE LOGICAL group. These represent control block space in the NCP simulating switched line as described earlier.

4. The IDBLK and IDNUM parameters in VTAM are used to identify incoming connection requests. IDBLK is typically unique for each type of IBM device. IDNUM is any five hexadecimal digit combination. The Cisco routers configured for SDLLC or QLLC conversion must associate an IDBLK/IDNUM combination with a controller by using the **sdllc xid** or

qllc xid command. If not using the **qllc xid** command, then IDBLK/IDNUM must agree with the values of the X.25-attached devices. During activation, an XID will be sent to the NCP containing the specific IDBLK/IDNUM. NCP will send these values to VTAM in an SNA command called REQCONT. VTAM will search its switched major nodes to find a match. If found, VTAM will establish sessions with the device by sending activation commands (ACTPU, ACTLUs).

CHAPTER 14

IBM Network Media Translation Commands

Use the commands in this chapter to configure and monitor Qualified Logical Link Control (QLLC) or SDLLC connections. SDLLC is a Cisco IOS software feature that provides translation between Synchronous Data Link Control (SDLC) and Logical Link Control, type 2 (LLC2). For QLLC conversion or SDLLC parameter configuration information and examples, see Chapter 13, "Configuring IBM Network Media Translation."

QLLC ACCEPT-ALL-CALLS

Use the **qllc accept-all-calls** interface configuration command to enable the router to accept a call from any remote X.25 device. Use the **no** form of this command to cancel the request.

> qllc accept-all-calls
> no qllc accept-all-calls

Syntax   Description

This command has no arguments or keywords.

Default

Disabled

Command Mode

Interface configuration

Usage Guidelines

This command first appeared in Cisco IOS Release 11.2 F.

This command allows QLLC to accept all inbound X.25 calls, provided that the QLLC Call User Data (CUD) is in the call packet and the destination X.121 address in the call packet matches the serial interface's configured destination X.121 address or subaddress. When using this command, the source X.121 address does not need to be configured via an **x25 map qllc** command for the call to be accepted.

This command is applicable to QLLC support for DLSw+, APPN, and DSPU. It is not applicable to QLLC support for SRB and RSRB.

Example

The following example enables QLLC connectivity for DLSw+ and allows QLLC to accept all inbound X.25 calls. Every X.25 connection request for X.121 address 0308 with QLLC CUD is directed to DLSw+. The first SVC to be established will be mapped to virtual MAC address 4000.0B0B.0001. If a call comes in with an X.121 address of 0308, the call will be forwarded to MAC address 4001.1161.1234.

```
interface serial 0
 encapsulation x25
 x25 address 0308
 qllc accept-all-calls
 qllc dlsw vmac 4000.0B0B.0001 500 partner 4001.1161.1234
```

Related Commands

x25 map qllc

QLLC LARGEST-PACKET

Use the **qllc largest-packet** interface configuration command to indicate the maximum size of the Systems Network Architecture (SNA) packet that can be sent or received on an X.25 interface configured for QLLC conversion. Use the **no** form of this command to restore the default largest packet size.

> **qllc largest-packet** *virtual-mac-addr max-size*
> **no qllc largest-packet** *virtual-mac-addr max-size*

Syntax	Description
virtual-mac-addr	Virtual Media Access Control (MAC) address associated with the remote X.25 device, as defined using the **x25 map qllc** or **x25 pvc qllc** interface configuration commands. This address is written as a dotted triple of four-digit hexadecimal numbers.
max-size	Maximum size, in bytes, of the SNA packet that can be sent or received on the X.25 interface configured for QLLC conversion. This value agrees with the value configured in the remote SNA device. The valid range is 0 to 1024.

Default

265 bytes

Command Mode

Interface configuration

Usage Guidelines

This command first appeared in Cisco IOS Release 10.3.

SNA packets that are larger than the largest value allowed on the X.25 connection and are received on the LLC2 interface are segmented before being sent on the X.25 interface. When a segmented packet is received on the X.25 interface, it is passed immediately to the LLC2 interface, and no effort is made to wait for the segment to be completed.

When the remote X.25 device has a limit on the maximum total length of recombined X.25 segments it will support, you can use the **qllc largest-packet** command to ensure the length is not exceeded. For example, a device whose maximum SNA packet size is limited to 265 bytes might not be able to handle a series of X.25 packets that it has to recombine to make a 4, 8, or 17 KM SNA packet, such as one often encounters in an LLC2 environment.

You use the **qllc largest-packet** command in conjunction with the **x25 map qllc** and **qllc srb** commands.

─── **NOTES** ──

Do not configure the maximum SNA packet size on an X.25 interface to be larger than the maximum SNA packet size allowed on the LLC2 interface.

──

Consult your IBM documentation to set the maximum packet size on the remote X.25 device.

Example

In the following example, the maximum packet size that has been established for the virtual circuit is used as the maximum packet size that can be sent or received on the X.25 interface:

```
interface serial 0
 encapsulation x25
 x25 address 31102120100
 x25 map qllc 0100.0000.0001 31104150101
 qllc srb 0100.0000.0001 201 100
!
 qllc partner 0100.0000.0001 4000.0101.0132
 qllc xid 0100.0000.0001 01720001
 qllc largest-packet 0100.0000.0001 521
```

Part
II

Command Reference

Related Commands

qllc srb
x25 map qllc
x25 pvc qllc

QLLC NPSI-POLL

Use the **qllc npsi-poll** interface configuration command to enable a connection between a PU 2 on the LAN side and a front-end processor (FEP) running NPSI on the X.25 side. Use the **no** form of this command to disable this capability.

> qllc npsi-poll *virtual-mac-addr*
> no qllc npsi-poll *virtual-mac-addr*

Syntax	Description
virtual-mac-addr	MAC address associated with the remote X.25 device, as defined using the **x25 map qllc** or **x25 pvc qllc** interface configuration commands. This address is written as a dotted triple of four-digit hexadecimal numbers.

Default

Disabled

Command Mode

Interface configuration

Usage Guidelines

This command first appeared in Cisco IOS Release 11.1.

The **qllc npsi-poll** command is necessary only when the upstream device is a FEP running NPSI and the downstream device is a PU 2.

This command is necessary because in a Token Ring or RSRB environment, the LAN-attached devices start up by sending a null exchange ID packet upstream. If the Cisco IOS software forwards this null XID to an X.25-attached FEP, the FEP responds as if it were connecting to an PU2.1 device, and breaks the connection when the PU 2 next sends an XID Format 0 Type 2. The **qllc npsi-poll** command intercepts any null XID packet that the software receives on the LAN interface, and returns a null XID response to the downstream device. It continues to allow XID Format 3 and XID Format 0 packets through the X.25 device.

Example

The following example facilitates a connection between a FEP running NPSI and a downstream PU 2.0.

```
qllc npsi-poll 0100.0000.0001
```

Related Commands

qllc srb
sdlc qllc-prtnr
x25 map qllc
x25 pvc qllc

QLLC PARTNER

Use the **qllc partner** interface configuration command to enable a router configured for QLLC conversion to open a connection to the local Token Ring device on behalf of the remote X.25 device when an incoming call is received. Use the **no** form of this command to disable this capability.

> **qllc partner** *virtual-mac-addr mac-addr*
> **no qllc partner** *virtual-mac-addr mac-addr*

Syntax	*Description*
virtual-mac-addr	MAC address associated with the remote X.25 device, as defined using the **x25 map qllc** or **x25 pvc qllc** interface configuration commands. This address is written as a dotted triple of four-digit hexadecimal numbers.
mac-addr	48-bit MAC address of the Token Ring host that will communicate with the remote X.25 device.

Default

Disabled

Command Mode

Interface configuration

Usage Guidelines

This command first appeared in Cisco IOS Release 10.3.

When the Cisco IOS software receives an incoming call from the designated X.121 address, it opens an LLC2 connection with the device at the given MAC address. Both the MAC address of the Token Ring device and the virtual MAC address for the remote X.25 device with which it is to communicate are required in order for the software to initiate connections with the Token Ring device. This allows the Token Ring host to be permanently ready to accept a connection rather than requiring operator action at the host to initiate the connection with the X.25 device.

You must issue the **qllc partner** command for each remote X.25 device that will communicate with the local Token Ring host through this interface.

You use the **qllc partner** command in conjunction with the **x25 map qllc** and **qllc srb** commands.

Example

In the following example, the **qllc partner** command is used to associate the virtual MAC address 0100.0000.0001, as defined in the previous **x25 map qllc** entry, with the MAC address of the Token Ring host that will communicate with the remote X.25 device:

```
interface serial 0
 encapsulation x25
 x25 address 31102120100
 x25 map qllc 0100.0000.0001 31104150101
 qllc srb 0100.0000.0001 201 100
!
 qllc partner 0100.0000.0001 4000.0101.0132
 qllc xid 0100.0000.0001 01720001
```

Related Commands

qllc srb
sdlc qllc-prtnr
x25 map qllc
x25 pvc qllc

QLLC SAP

Use the **qllc sap** interface configuration command to associate a service access point (SAP) value other than the default SAP value with a serial interface configured for X.25 communication and QLLC conversion. The **no** form of this command returns this SAP value to its default state.

> **qllc sap** *virtual-mac-addr ssap dsap*
> **no qllc sap** *virtual-mac-addr ssap dsap*

Syntax	Description
virtual-mac-addr	MAC address associated with the remote X.25 device, as defined using the **x25 map qllc** or **x25 pvc qllc** interface configuration commands. This address is written as a dotted triple of four-digit hexadecimal numbers.
ssap	Source SAP value. It can be a decimal number in the range 2 to 254. The default is 4.
dsap	Destination SAP value. It can be a decimal number in the range 2 to 254. The default is 4.

Defaults

The default source SAP value is 4.

The default destination SAP value is 4.

Command Mode

Interface configuration

Usage Guidelines

This command first appeared in Cisco IOS Release 10.3.

A SAP can be viewed as a port through which a higher-layer application can communicate with its counterpart (peer) operating on another system. While the standard SAP value for IBM devices is 4, other values are allowed.

You use the **qllc sap** command in conjunction with the **x25 map qllc** and **qllc srb** interface configuration commands.

Example

In the following example, source SAP and destination SAP values of 2 are specified for the remote X.25 device at the X.121 address 31370054065:

```
interface serial 0
  x25 map qllc 31370054065 4000.0122.0001
  qllc srb 9 100
  qllc sap 4000.0122.0001 02 02
```

Related Commands

qllc srb
x25 map qllc
x25 pvc qllc

QLLC SRB

Use the **qllc srb** interface configuration command to enable QLLC conversion on a serial interface configured for X.25 communication. The **no** form of this command disables QLLC conversion on the interface.

qllc srb *virtual-mac-addr srn trn*
no qllc srb *srn trn*

Syntax	Description
virtual-mac-addr	MAC address associated with the remote X.25 device, as defined using the **x25 map qllc** or **x25 pvc qllc** interface configuration commands. It can be 1 to 15 digits long.
srn	Source ring number. This value defines a virtual ring for all of the remote X.25 devices attached to the QLLC interface.
trn	Target ring number. It must be a virtual ring group that has been defined with the **source-bridge ring-group** global configuration command.

Default

QLLC conversion is not enabled.

Usage Guidelines

Any number of QLLC conversion connections using the same X.25 serial interface can share a common source ring. However, this source ring must be a unique hexadecimal ring number within the source-bridged network.

If the router has only one Token Ring interface and is bridging from the remote X.25 devices to this interface, then *trn* is the number of the ring on that Token Ring interface. If the router has several Token Ring interfaces and interconnects them by means of the **source-bridge ring-group** command, then *trn* is the number of that virtual ring group, as assigned using the **source-bridge ring-group** global configuration command.

Command Mode

Interface configuration

Usage Guidelines

This command first appeared in Cisco IOS Release 10.3.

Use the **qllc srb** command to associate the ring number and bridge number that have been assigned to the interface with a virtual ring group of which the interface will be a part. The serial interface appears to be a ring, or source-ring number, on a source-route bridge network, and ties in to the virtual ring group, or target ring number. The target ring number provides access to other real rings that have been designated using the **source-bridge** global configuration command. Note that you can configure QLLC conversion on a router containing no Token Ring interface cards, such as a router connecting a serial-attached device to an X.25 public data network (PDN).

The **qllc srb** command automatically turns on the LLC2 process with default values. To change any of the LLC2 parameters (described in Chapter 12, "LLC2 and SDLC Commands"), apply their values to the serial interface that has been configured for QLLC conversion. This is done on the serial interface, even though LLC2 does not technically run on the serial interface, but on the virtual ring associated with the serial interface.

You use the **qllc srb** command in conjunction with the **x25 map qllc** command.

Example

In the following example, the **qllc srb** command is used to define a virtual ring number of 201 for the remote X.25 device, and an actual or virtual ring number of 100 for the Token Ring interface:

```
interface serial 0
 encapsulation x25
 x25 address 31102120100
 x25 map qllc 0100.0000.0001 31104150101
 qllc srb 0100.0000.0001 201 100
```

Related Commands

source-bridge
source-bridge ring-group
x25 map qllc
x25 pvc qllc

QLLC XID

Use the **qllc xid** interface configuration command to associate an exchange ID (XID) value with the remote X.25 device that communicates through the Cisco IOS software using QLLC conversion. The **no** form of this command disables XID processing for this address.

qllc xid *virtual-mac-addr xid*
no qllc xid *virtual-mac-addr xid*

Syntax	Description
virtual-mac-addr	MAC address associated with the remote X.25 device, as defined using the **x25 map qllc** or **x25 pvc qllc** interface configuration command. This address is written as a dotted triple of four-digit hexadecimal numbers.
xid	Combined XID IDBLK and XID IDNUM you are associating with the X.25 device at this X.121 address. This hexadecimal value must be four bytes (eight digits) in length.

Default

XID processing is not enabled.

Command Mode

Interface configuration

Usage Guidelines

This command first appeared in Cisco IOS Release 10.3.

Most QLLC installations do not need the **qllc xid** configuration command. It is only needed if the remote X.25 device is not configured to send its own XID. This is only possible for a device that is attached via a permanent virtual circuit (PVC). Even so, most devices that are connected via X.25 will send their own XIDs. Use the **qllc xid** command when the Token Ring host requires login validation for security purposes and the remote X.25 device does not send an XID. The XID value is used to reply to XID requests received on the Token Ring (LLC2) side of the connection. XID requests and responses usually are exchanged before sessions are started. The XID response to the XID request from the Token Ring host will contain the information you configure using the **qllc xid** command. The host will check the XID response it receives with the IDBLK and IDNUM parameters (configured in VTAM). If they match, the Token Ring host will initiate a session with the router. If they do not match, the host will not initiate a session with the router.

You use the **qllc xid** command in conjunction with the **x25 map qllc** and the **qllc srb** commands.

Example

In the following example, the X.25 device at X.121 address 31104150101 must use an XID IDBLK of 017 and XID IDNUM of 20001 to access the Token Ring host whose MAC address is associated with the remote X.25 device, as applied using the **sdllc partner** command:

```
interface serial 0
 encapsulation x25
 x25 address 31102120100
 x25 map qllc 0100.0000.0001 31104150101
 qllc srb 0100.0000.0001 201 100
!
 qllc partner 0100.0000.0001 4000.0101.0132
 qllc xid 0100.0000.0001 01720001
```

Related Commands

qllc srb
sdllc partner
x25 map qllc
x25 pvc qllc

SDLLC PARTNER

Use the **sdllc partner** interface configuration command to enable device-initiated connections for SDLLC. This command must be specified for the serial interface that links to the serial line device. Use the **no** form of this command to cancel the original instruction.

> **sdllc partner** *mac-address sdlc-address*
> **no sdllc partner** *mac-address sdlc-address*

Syntax	Description
mac-address	MAC address of the Token Ring host.
sdlc-address	SDLC address of the serial device that will communicate with the Token Ring host.

Default

Disabled

Command Mode

Interface configuration

Usage Guidelines

This command first appeared in Cisco IOS Release 10.0.

Both the MAC address of the Token Ring host and the SDLC serial line address are required to initiate connections with the Token Ring host.

The Token Ring host and the serial device communicate with each other through the Cisco IOS software. Although the device is said to initiate connections, the software actually initiates connections with the Token Ring host on behalf of the serial device. As part of Cisco's SDLLC implementation, the serial device "thinks" that it is communicating with a host also on a serial line. It is actually the software that does all the frame and protocol conversions between serial and Token Ring devices.

There are two conditions under which the Cisco IOS software will attempt to initiate a connection to a host on behalf of a serial device:

- When the serial device attached to the router is powered on. In this case, the router attached to the serial line detects a change in interface signals and initiates a connection with the Token Ring hosts by exchanging explorer and XID packets.

- When a previously shut-down serial interface is brought back on-line. When the **no shutdown** command is issued, the software will detect a change in the serial line state from down to up and initiate a session with the Token Ring host by exchanging explorer and XID packets.

The Cisco IOS software will continue trying once a minute to initiate a connection whenever one of these two conditions is met, until the host responds to its requests. When you no longer want the software to initiate connections with a host, use the **no sdllc partner** command.

Part II

Command Reference

NOTES

For device-initiated sessions, the host will check the IDBLK and IDNUM parameters of the serial device it receives in the XID packet against the information configured on the host. If the information in the XID packet does not match with what is configured on the host, the host will drop the session. Therefore, for device-initiated connections, always specify the correct IDBLK and IDNUM parameters on the router serial interfaces with the **sdllc xid** command.

Example

In the following example, a serial device at SDLC address C2 wants to initiate a connection with a Token Ring host at MAC address 4000.0122.0001. The router initiates the connection on behalf of a serial device:

```
! sample global command
source-bridge ring-group 100
!
interface serial 0
! router initiates connections with Token Ring host at MAC address
! 4000.0122.0001 on behalf of serial device c2
sdllc partner 4000.0122.0001 c2
```

Related Commands

sdllc xid

SDLLC RING-LARGEST-FRAME

Use the **sdllc ring-largest-frame** interface configuration command to indicate the largest I-frame size that can be sent to or received from the LLC2 primary station. Use the **no** form of this command to return to the default.

> sdllc ring-largest-frame *value*
> no sdllc ring-largest-frame *value*

Syntax	*Description*
value	Frame size in bytes. Possible values include 516, 1500, 2052, 4472, 8144, 11407, and 17800.

Default

516 bytes

Command Mode

Interface configuration

Usage Guidelines

This command first appeared in Cisco IOS Release 10.0.

Possible values for the *value* argument match those that are possible for the **lf** *size* of the various **source-bridge remote-peer** commands. You must ensure that your remote peer connection can support this largest frame size. Possible values for the *value* argument include 516, 1500, 2052, 4472, 8144, 11407, and 17800.

Faster screen updates to 3278-style terminals often can be obtained by allowing the Token Ring FEP to send as large a frame as possible and by allowing the Cisco IOS software to segment the frame into multiple SDLC I-frames.

Example

In the following example, the software can send or receive a frame as large as 11407 bytes from the LLC2 primary station. Any frames larger will be fragmented by the software.

```
! sample global command
source-bridge ring-group 100
!
interface serial 3
! largest frame sent or received on serial 3 is 11407 bytes
sdllc ring-largest-frame 11407
```

Related Commands

source-bridge remote-peer fst
source-bridge remote-peer interface
source-bridge remote-peer tcp

SDLLC SAP

Use the **sdllc sap** interface configuration command to associate a SAP value other than the default SAP value with a serial interface configured for SDLLC. Use the **no** form of this command to return this SAP value to its default state.

> sdllc sap *sdlc-address ssap dsap*
> no sdllc sap *sdlc-address ssap dsap*

Syntax	Description
sdlc-address	MAC address associated with the remote SDLC device.
ssap	Source SAP value. It must be in the range 1 to 254. The default is 4.
dsap	Destination SAP value. It must be in the range 1 to 254. The default is 4.

Default

The default SAP value for IBM SNA devices is 4.

Command Mode

Interface configuration

Usage Guidelines

This command first appeared in Cisco IOS Release 10.0.

You use the **sdllc sap** command in conjunction with the **sdllc traddr** interface configuration commands. A SAP can be viewed as a port through which a higher-layer application can communicate with its counterpart (peer) operating on another system. While the standard SAP value for IBM SNA devices is 4, and NetBIOS devices is xF0, other values are allowed.

Example

In the following example, source SAP and destination SAP values of 2 are specified for the remote SDLC device at the SDLC address C1 02 02:

```
interface serial 0
 sdllc sap c1 02 02
```

Related Commands

sdllc traddr

SDLLC SDLC-LARGEST-FRAME

Use the **sdllc sdlc-largest-frame** interface configuration command to indicate the largest information frame (I-frame) size that can be sent or received by the designated SDLC station. Use the **no** form of this command to return to the default value.

> sdllc sdlc-largest-frame *address value*
> **no** sdllc sdlc-largest-frame *address value*

Syntax	*Description*
address	Address of the SDLC station that will communicate with the Token Ring host.
value	Largest frame size that can be sent or received by this SDLC station. The default is 265 bytes.

Default

265 bytes

Command Mode

Interface configuration

Usage Guidelines

This command first appeared in Cisco IOS Release 10.0.

Most SDLC devices are limited to frames of 265 bytes. I-frames received from the Token Ring station that are larger than this size will be properly fragmented.

Example

In the following example, the Cisco IOS software can send or receive a frame as large as 265 bytes (the default) from the SDLC station at address C6. Any frames larger will be fragmented by the software.

```
! sample global command
source-bridge ring-group 100
!
interface serial 4
! largest frame sent or received on serial 4 is 265 bytes
 sdllc sdlc-largest-frame c6 265
```

SDLLC TRADDR

Use the **sdllc traddr** interface configuration command to enable SDLLC media translation on a serial interface. The address specified is a MAC address to be assigned to the serial station. Use the **no** form of this command to disable SDLLC media translation on the interface.

> **sdllc traddr** *xxxx.xxxx.xx00 lr bn tr*
> **no sdllc traddr** *xxxx.xxxx.xx00 lr bn tr*

Syntax	Description
xxxx.xxxx.xx00	MAC address to be assigned to the serial interface.
lr	SDLLC virtual ring number.
bn	SDLLC bridge number.
tr	SDLLC target ring number.

Default

Disabled

Command Mode

Interface configuration

Usage Guidelines

This command first appeared in Cisco IOS Release 10.0.

Every control unit hooked off the serial line requires a virtual Token Ring address (VTRA).This usually is assigned by the system administrator as a locally administered MAC address (unique across the network).

When you enable SDLLC Media Translation by specifying the **sdllc traddr** command on a serial interface, you must specify a VTRA for each serial station attached to the serial line. The last two hexadecimal digits (that is, the last byte) of the VTRA *must* be 00. The Cisco IOS software uses this byte to represent the SDLC address of a station on the serial link.

NOTES

Addresses in the range *xxxx.xxxx.xx*00 to *xxxx.xxxx.xx*FF are reserved for use by the Cisco IOS software. You must adhere to this addressing requirement. If you do not follow this addressing requirement, there might be a conflict between the VTRA and the addresses reserved by the software for the SDLC link.

The variables *lr*, *bn*, and *tr* represent the SDLLC virtual ring number, bridge number, and target ring number, respectively, that you assign to the interface. In design, the serial interface appears to be a ring, *lr*, on a source-route bridged network, and ties in through the bridge, *bn*, to the virtual-ring group, *tr*. This provides access to other, real rings through remote source-route bridging **source-bridge remote-peer** commands. Note that SDLLC can be configured on a router containing no Token Ring interface cards.

The **sdllc traddr** command automatically turns on the LLC2 process with default values. To change any of the LLC2 parameters, specify their values on the serial interface that is being enabled for SDLLC. This is done on the serial interface, even though LLC2 does not technically run on the serial interface, but on the SDLLC virtual ring associated with the serial interface. LLC2 commands can be configured after specifying the **sdllc traddr** command.

Example

In the following example, SDLLC media translation is enabled off the serial 0 interface to a serial station at MAC address 0110.2222.3300. The SDLLC virtual ring number is 8, the bridge number is 1, and the target ring number is 100:

```
! global command to apply commands to the ring group
source-bridge ring-group 100
! remote peer at IP address 131.108.1.1 belongs to ring group 100 and uses
! tcp as the transport
source-bridge remote-peer 100 tcp 131.108.1.1
source-bridge remote-peer 100 tcp 131.108.2.2
!
interface serial 0
 encapsulation sdlc-primary
! establish address of SDLC station off serial-0 as c1
 sdlc address c1
! enable SDLLC media translation to serial station 0110.2222.3300
! on virtual ring 8, bridge 1, to target ring 100
 sdllc traddr 0110.2222.3300 8 1 100
```

Related Commands

sdllc sap
source-bridge remote-peer fst
source-bridge remote-peer interface
source-bridge remote-peer tcp

SDLLC XID

Use the **sdllc xid** interface configuration command to specify an XID value appropriate for the designated SDLC station associated with this serial interface. Use the **no** form of this command to disable XID processing for this address.

> sdllc xid *address xxxxxxxx*
> no sdllc xid *address xxxxxxxx*

Syntax	Description
address	Address of the SDLC station associated with this interface.
xxxxxxxx	XID the Cisco IOS software will use to respond to XID requests received on the Token Ring (LLC2) side of the connection. This value must be 4 bytes (8 digits) in length and is specified with hexadecimal digits.

Default

Disabled

Command Mode

Interface configuration

Part
II

Command Reference

Usage Guidelines

This command first appeared in Cisco IOS Release 10.0.

XID requests and responses usually are exchanged before sessions are started. Be sure that the XID value configured on the router matches the IDBLK and IDNUM parameters configured on the host. The XID response to an XID request from the Token Ring host will contain the information you configured in the **sdllc xid** command. The host will check the XID response it receives with the IDBLK and IDNUM parameters (that are configured in virtual telecommunications access method (VTAM)). If they match, the Token Ring host will initiate a session with the router. If they do not match, the host will not initiate a session.

Example

The following example specifies an XID value of 01720002 at address C2:

```
! sample global command
source-bridge ring-group 100
!
interface serial 0
! sdllc exchange identification value of 01720002 at address c2
 sdllc xid c2 01720002
```

Related Commands

sdllc partner

SHOW INTERFACES

Use the **show interfaces** privileged EXEC command to display the SDLC information for a given SDLC interface.

> show interfaces

Syntax   Description

This command has no arguments or keywords.

Command Mode

Privileged EXEC

Usage Guidelines

This command first appeared in Cisco IOS Release 10.0.

Sample Display

The following is sample output from the **show interfaces** command for an SDLC primary interface supporting the SDLLC function:

```
Router# show interfaces

Serial 0 is up, line protocol is up
    Hardware is MCI Serial
    MTU 1500 bytes, BW 1544 Kbit, DLY 20000 usec, rely 255/255, load 1/255
    Encapsulation SDLC-PRIMARY, loopback not set
    Timers (msec): poll pause 100 fair poll 500. Poll limit 1
    [T1 3000, N1 12016, N2 20, K 7] timer: 56608 Last polled device: none
    SDLLC [ma: 0000.0C01.14--, ring: 7 bridge: 1, target ring: 10
            largest token ring frame 2052]
SDLC addr C1 state is CONNECT
    VS 6, VR 3, RCNT 0, Remote VR 6, Current retransmit count 0
    Hold queue: 0/12 IFRAMEs 77/22 RNRs 0/0 SNRMs 1/0 DISCs 0/0
    Poll: clear, Poll count: 0, chain: p: C1 n: C1
    SDLLC [largest SDLC frame: 265, XID: disabled]
 Last input 00:00:02, output 00:00:01, output hang never
 Output queue 0/40, 0 drops; input queue 0/75, 0 drops
 Five minute input rate 517 bits/sec, 30 packets/sec
 Five minute output rate 672 bits/sec, 20 packets/sec
    357 packets input, 28382 bytes, 0 no buffer
    Received 0 broadcasts, 0 runts, 0 giants
    0 input errors, 0 CRC, 0 frame, 0 overrun, 0 ignored, 0 abort
    926 packets output, 77274 bytes, 0 underruns
    0 output errors, 0 collisions, 0 interface resets, 0 restarts
    2 carrier transitions
```

Table 14–1 shows the fields relevant to all SDLC connections.

Table 14–1 *Show Interfaces Field Descriptions when SDLC Is Enabled*

Field	Description
Timers (msec)	List of timers in milliseconds.
poll pause, fair poll, Poll limit	Current values of these timers, as described in the individual commands in this chapter.
T1, N1, N2, K	Current values for these variables, as described in the individual commands in this chapter.

Table 14–2 shows other data given for each SDLC secondary configured to be attached to this interface.

Table 14–2 *SDLC Field Descriptions*

Field	Description
addr	Address of this secondary.
State	Current state of this connection. The possible values are: • DISCONNECT—No communication is being attempted to this secondary. • CONNECT—A normal connect state exists between this router and this secondary. • DISCSENT—This router has sent a disconnect request to this secondary and is awaiting its response. • SNRMSENT—This router has sent a connect request (SNRM) to this secondary and is awaiting its response. • THEMBUSY—This secondary has told this router that it is temporarily unable to receive any more information frames. • USBUSY—This router has told this secondary that it is temporarily unable to receive any more information frames. • BOTHBUSY—Both sides have told each other that they are temporarily unable to receive any more information frames. • ERROR—This router has detected an error, and is waiting for a response from the secondary acknowledging this.
VS	Sequence number of the next information frame this station sends.
VR	Sequence number of the next information frame from this secondary that this station expects to receive.

Table 14–2 *SDLC Field Descriptions, Continued*

Field	Description
RCNT	Number of correctly sequenced I-frames received when the Cisco IOS software was in a state in which it is acceptable to receive I-frames.
Remote VR	Last frame transmitted by this station that has been acknowledged by the other station.
Current retransmit count	Number of times the current I-frame or sequence of I-frames has been retransmitted.
Hold queue	Number of frames in hold queue/Maximum size of hold queue.
IFRAMEs, RNRs, SNRMs, DISCs	Sent/received count for these frames.
Poll	"Set" if this router has a poll outstanding to the secondary; "clear" if it does not.
Poll count	Number of polls, in a row, given to this secondary at this time.
chain	Shows the previous (p) and next (n) secondary address on this interface in the round robin loop of polled devices.

SHOW QLLC

Use the **show qllc** EXEC command to display the current state of any QLLC connections.

> **show qllc**

Syntax   Description

This command has no arguments or keywords.

Command Mode

Privileged EXEC.

Usage Guidelines

This command first appeared in Cisco IOS Release 10.3.

Sample Display

The following is sample output from the **show qllc** command.

```
Router# show qllc

QLLC Connections:
Serial2: 1000.5a35.3a4f->1000.5a59.04f9. SAPs 4 4. Rings Src 200, Tgt 100.
State Connect
Remote DTE 1002. QLLC Protocol State NORMAL lci 1 (PVC)
```

In the display, the first two lines of the **show qllc** command show that there is a QLLC session between a Token Ring device and an X.25 remote device. The X.25 device has a virtual MAC address of 100.5a35.3a4f with a SAP of 04. It is using a PVC with logical channel number 1. The Token Ring device has a MAC address of 1000.5a59.04f9 with a SAP of 04. The state of the QLLC session is CONNECTED.

Table 14–3 describes the fields shown in the display.

Table 14–3   *Show QLLC Field Descriptions*

Field	Description
Serial2	Serial interface for the X.25 link.
1000.5a35.3a4f	Virtual MAC address for the X.25 attached device.
1000.5a59.04f9	MAC address of the Token Ring-attached device with which the X.25 attached device is communicating. This device might be on a local Token Ring or attached via source-route bridging (SRB) or remote source-route bridging (RSRB).
SAPs 4 4	Source SAP value at the virtual MAC address and destination SAP value at the Token Ring station.
Rings Src 200	Ring number for the source virtual ring defined by the **qllc srb** command.
Tgt 100	Ring number for the target virtual ring defined by the **source-bridge ring-group** command.

Table 14–3 *Show QLLC Field Descriptions, Continued*

Field	Description
State	State of the QLLC-LLC2 conversion. This can be any of the following: • DISCONNECT—No connection exists. • NET DISC WAIT—X.25 device is disconnecting. The QLLC conversion is waiting for the Token Ring device to disconnect. • QLLC DISC WAIT—The Token Ring device is disconnecting. The QLLC conversion is waiting for the X.25 device to disconnect. • QLLC PRI WAIT—Connection is being established. The Token Ring device is ready to complete the connection, and the Cisco IOS software is establishing the QLLC connection with the X.25 device. • NET CONTACT REPLY WAIT—Remote X.25 device is a FEP, and has made contact with the Cisco IOS software. The software is attempting to reach Token Ring device. • QLLC SEC WAIT—Connection is being established. • NET UP WAIT—Connection is being established. QLLC connection to X.25 device has been established; awaiting completion on the connection to the Token Ring-attached device. • CONNECT—Connections from the software to X.25 and Token Ring devices are established. Data can flow end to end.
Remote DTE 1002	X.121 address of X.25 connected device.
QLLC Protocol State	State of the QLLC protocol between the software and the X.25-attached device. These states are different from the state of the underlying X.25 virtual circuit. The following are possible values: • ADM—Asynchronous Disconnected Mode. • SETUP—Cisco IOS software has initiated QLLC connection, awaiting confirmation from the X.25 device. • RESET—Cisco IOS software has initiated QLLC Reset, awaiting confirmation from the X.25 device. • DISCONNECTING—Cisco IOS software has initiated QLLC Disconnect, awaiting confirmation from the X.25 device. • NORMAL—QLLC connection has been completed. SNA data can be transmitted and received.
lci 1 (PVC)	Logical channel number used on the X.25 interface.

SHOW SDLLC LOCAL-ACK

Use the **show sdllc local-ack** privileged EXEC command to display the current state of any current local acknowledgment connections, as well as any configured passthrough rings.

> **show sdllc local-ack**

Syntax   Description

This command has no arguments or keywords.

Command Mode

Privileged EXEC

Usage Guidelines

This command first appeared in Cisco IOS Release 10.0.

Sample Display

The following is sample output from the **show sdllc local-ack** command:

```
Router# show sdllc local-ack

local 1000.5a59.04f9, lsap 04, remote 4000.2222.4444, dsap 04
llc2 = 1798136, local act state = connected
Passthrough Rings: 4 7
```

In the display, the first two lines of the **show sdllc local-ack** command show that there is a local acknowledgment session between two Token Ring devices. The device on the local ring has a MAC address of 1000.5a59.04f9 with a SAP of 04. The remote device has a MAC address of 4000.2222.4444 with a SAP of 04. The state of the local acknowledgment session is connected.

The passthrough rings display is independent of the rest of the **show sdllc local-ack** command. The passthrough rings display indicates that there are two rings, 4 and 7, configured for passthrough. This means that stations on these rings will not have their sessions locally acknowledged but will instead have their acknowledgments end-to-end.

Table 14–4 describes significant fields shown in the display.

Table 14–4   *Show SDLLC Local-Ack Field Descriptions*

Field	Description
local	MAC address of the local Token Ring station with which the router has the LLC2 session.
lsap	Local SAP value of the Token Ring station with which the router has the LLC2 session.

Table 14–4   *Show SDLLC Local-Ack Field Descriptions, Continued*

Field	Description
remote	MAC address of the remote Token Ring station on whose behalf the router is providing acknowledgments. The remote Token Ring station is separated from the router via the TCP backbone.
dsap	Destination SAP value of the remote Token Ring station on whose behalf the router is providing acknowledgments.
llc2	Pointer to an internal data structure used by technical support staff for debugging.
local-ack state:	Current state. Possible values are as follows: • disconnected—No session between the two end hosts. • connected—Full data transfer possible between the two end hosts. • awaiting connect—This router is waiting for the other end to confirm a session establishment with the remote host.
Passthrough Rings	Ring number of the start ring and destination ring for the two IBM machines when you do not have local acknowledgment for LLC2 configured for your routers using RSRB.

SOURCE-BRIDGE FST-PEERNAME

Use the **source-bridge fst-peername** global configuration command to set up a Fast-Sequenced Transport (FST) peer name. Use the **no** form of this command to disable the IP address assignment.

>   **source-bridge fst-peername** *local-interface-address*
>   **no source-bridge fst-peername** *local-interface-address*

Syntax   *Description*

local-interface-address   IP address to assign to the local router.

Default

Disabled

Command Mode

Global configuration

Usage Guidelines

This command first appeared in Cisco IOS Release 10.0.

Using this command is the first step to configuring a remote source-route bridge to use FST.

Example

The following example configures FST peer for IP address 150.136.64.98:

```
source-bridge fst-peername 150.136.64.98
```

Related Commands

source-bridge remote-peer fst

SOURCE-BRIDGE QLLC-LOCAL-ACK

Use the **source-bridge qllc-local-ack** global configuration command to enable or disable QLLC local acknowledgment for all QLLC conversion connections. The **no** form of this command disables this capability.

> **source-bridge qllc-local-ack**
> **no source-bridge qllc-local-ack**

Syntax   Description

This command has no arguments or keywords.

Default

QLLC local acknowledgment is disabled.

Command Mode

Global configuration

Usage Guidelines

This command first appeared in Cisco IOS Release 10.3.

In a remote source-route bridged topology, QLLC local acknowledgment is used to configure the QLLC conversion router (connecting the remote X.25 devices) to exchange local acknowledgment information with the Token Ring router (on the Token Ring side of the cloud). This Token Ring device has been configured for LLC2 local acknowledgment using the **source-bridge remote peer tcp local-ack** command.

You only have to issue the **source-bridge qllc-local-ack** command on the QLLC conversion router. When this command is issued, all of the QLLC conversion sessions are locally acknowledged at the Token Ring interface of the Token Ring router with which it is communicating using QLLC conversion.

Example

The following configuration indicates that the local router (131.108.2.2) QLLC conversion sessions will be locally acknowledged at the remote router:

```
source-bridge ring-group 100
source-bridge remote-peer 100 tcp 131.108.1.1 local-ack
source-bridge remote-peer 100 tcp 131.108.2.2
source-bridge qllc-local-ack
```

Related Commands

source-bridge remote-peer tcp
source-bridge ring-group

SOURCE-BRIDGE REMOTE-PEER FST

Use the **source-bridge remote-peer fst** global configuration command to specify a Fast-Sequenced Transport (FST) encapsulation connection. Use the **no** form of this command to disable the previous assignments.

source-bridge remote-peer *ring-group* **fst** *ip-address* [**lf** *size*] [**version** *number*]
no source-bridge remote-peer *ring-group* **fst** *ip-address*

Syntax	*Description*
ring-group	Ring-group number. This ring-group number must match the number you have specified with the **source-bridge ring-group** command. The valid range is 1 to 4095.
ip-address	IP address of the remote peer with which the router will communicate.
lf *size*	(Optional) Maximum size frame to be sent to this remote peer. The Cisco IOS software negotiates all transit routes down to this size or lower. Use this argument to prevent timeouts in end hosts by reducing the amount of data they have to transmit in a fixed interval. The legal values for this argument are 516, 1500, 2052, 4472, 8144, 11407, and 17800 bytes.
version *number*	(Optional) Forces RSRB protocol version number for the remote peer. Because all FST peers support version 2 RSRB, the **version** keyword is always specified.

Default

No FST encapsulation connection is specified.

Command Mode

Global configuration

Usage Guidelines

This command first appeared in Cisco IOS Release 10.0. The **version** *number* option first appeared in Cisco IOS Release 10.3.

The two peers using the serial-transport method will function correctly only if there are routers at the end of the serial line that have been configured to use the serial transport. The peers also must belong to the same ring group.

Example

In the following example the **source-bridge fst-peername** command specifies an IP address of 150.136.64.98 for the local router. The **source-bridge ring-group** command assigns the router to a ring group. The **source-bridge remote-peer fst** command specifies ring-group number 100 for the remote peer at IP address 150.136.64.97.

```
source-bridge fst-peername 150.136.64.98
source-bridge ring-group 100
source-bridge remote-peer 100 fst 150.136.64.97 version 2 RSRB
```

Part II

Command Reference

Related Commands

source-bridge
source-bridge fst-peername
source-bridge remote-peer interface
source-bridge remote-peer tcp

SOURCE-BRIDGE REMOTE-PEER INTERFACE

Use the **source-bridge remote-peer interface** global configuration command when specifying a point-to-point direct encapsulation connection. Use the **no** form of this command to disable previous interface assignments.

> **source-bridge remote-peer** *ring-group* **interface** *interface-name* [*mac-address*] [**lf** *size*]
> **no source-bridge remote-peer** *ring-group* **interface** *interface-name*

Syntax	Description
ring-group	Ring-group number. This ring-group number must match the number you have specified with the **source-bridge ring-group** command. The valid range is 1 to 4095.
interface-name	Name of the serial interface over which to send source-route bridged traffic.

Syntax	Description
mac-address	(Optional) MAC address for the interface you specify using the *interface-name* argument. This argument is required for nonserial interfaces. You can obtain the value of this MAC address by using the **show interfaces** command, and then scanning the display for the interface specified by *interface-name*.
lf *size*	(Optional) Maximum size frame to be sent to this remote peer. The Cisco IOS software negotiates all transit routes down to this size or lower. This argument is useful in preventing timeouts in end hosts by reducing the amount of data they have to transmit in a fixed interval. The legal values for this argument are 516, 1500, 2052, 4472, 8144, 11407, and 17800 bytes.

Default

No point-to-point direct encapsulation connection is specified.

Command Mode

Global configuration

Usage Guidelines

This command first appeared in Cisco IOS Release 10.0.

Use this command to identify the interface over which to send source-route bridged traffic to another router/bridge in the ring group. A serial interface does not require that you include a MAC-level address; all other types of interfaces do require MAC addresses.

It is possible to mix all types of transport methods within the same ring group.

NOTES ———————————————————————————————————

The two peers using the serial-transport method will function correctly only if there are routers at the end of the serial line that have been configured to use the serial transport. The peers also must belong to the same ring group.

Example

The following example shows how to send source-route bridged traffic over interfaces serial 0 and Ethernet 0:

```
! send source-route bridged traffic over serial 0
source-bridge remote-peer 5 interface serial 0
! specify MAC address for source-route bridged traffic on Ethernet 0
source-bridge remote-peer 5 interface ethernet 0 0000.0c00.1234
```

Related Commands

show interfaces
source-bridge remote-peer tcp

SOURCE-BRIDGE REMOTE-PEER TCP

Use the **source-bridge remote-peer tcp** global configuration command to identify the IP address of a peer in the ring group with which to exchange source-bridge traffic using TCP. Use the **no** form of this command to remove a remote peer for the specified ring group.

> **source-bridge remote-peer** *ring-group* **tcp** *ip-address* [**lf** *size*] [**local-ack**] [**priority**]
> **no source-bridge remote-peer** *ring-group* **tcp** *ip-address*

Part II

Command Reference

Syntax	Description
ring-group	Ring-group number. This ring-group number must match the number you have specified with the **source-bridge ring-group** command. The valid range is 1 to 4095.
ip-address	IP address of the remote peer with which the router will communicate.
lf *size*	(Optional) Maximum size frame to be sent to this remote peer. The Cisco IOS software negotiates all transit routes down to this size or lower. Use this argument to prevent timeouts in end hosts by reducing the amount of data they have to transmit in a fixed interval. The valid values for this argument are 516, 1500, 2052, 4472, 8144, 11407, and 17800 bytes.
local-ack	(Optional) LLC2 sessions destined for a specific remote peer are to be locally terminated and acknowledged. Local acknowledgment should be used for LLC2 sessions going to this remote peer.
priority	(Optional) Enables prioritization over a TCP network. You must specify the keyword **local-ack** earlier in the same **source-bridge remote-peer** command. The keyword **priority** is a prerequisite for features such as SNA class of service and SNA logical unit (LU) address prioritization over a TCP network.

Default

No IP address is identified.

Command Mode

Global configuration

Usage Guidelines

This command first appeared in Cisco IOS Release 10.0.

If you configure one peer for LLC2 local acknowledgment, you need to configure both peers for LLC2 local acknowledgment. If only one peer is so configured, unpredictable (and undesirable) results will occur.

The two peers using the serial-transport method will function correctly only if there are routers at the end of the serial line that have been configured to use the serial transport. The peers also must belong to the same ring group.

Examples

In the following example, the remote peer with IP address 131.108.2.291 belongs to ring group 5. It also uses LLC2 local acknowledgment, priority, and RSRB protocol version 2:

```
! identify the ring group as 5
source-bridge ring-group 5
! remote peer at IP address 131.108.2.291 belongs to ring group 5, uses
! tcp as the transport, is set up for local acknowledgment, uses
! priority, and uses RSRB protocol form of this command
source-bridge remote-peer 5 tcp 131.108.2.291 local-ack priority
```

The following example shows how to administer locally and acknowledge LLC2 sessions destined for a specific remote peer:

```
! identify the ring group as 100
source-bridge ring-group 100
! remote peer at IP address 1.1.1.1 does not use local acknowledgment
source-bridge remote-peer 100 tcp 1.1.1.1
! remote peer at IP address 1.1.1.2 uses local acknowledgment
source-bridge remote-peer 100 tcp 1.1.1.2 local-ack
!
interface tokenring 0
 source-bridge 1 1 100
```

Sessions between a device on Token Ring 0 that must go through remote peer 1.1.1.2 use local acknowledgment for LLC2, but sessions that go through remote peer 1.1.1.1 do *not* use local acknowledgment (that is, they "pass through").

Related Commands

source-bridge remote-peer fst
source-bridge remote-peer interface

SOURCE-BRIDGE RING-GROUP

Use the **source-bridge ring-group** global configuration command to define or remove a ring group from the configuration. Use the **no** form of this command to cancel previous assignments.

> **source-bridge ring-group** *ring-group* [*virtual-mac-address*]
> **no source-bridge ring-group** *ring-group* [*virtual-mac-address*]

Syntax	*Description*
ring-group	Ring-group number. The valid range is 1 to 4095.
virtual-mac-address	(Optional) 12-digit hexadecimal string written as a dotted triplet (for example, 0010.0a00.20a6).

Default

No ring group is defined.

Command Mode

Global configuration

Usage Guidelines

This command first appeared in Cisco IOS Release 10.0.

To configure a source-route bridge with more than two network interfaces, the *ring-group* concept is used. A ring group is a collection of Token Ring interfaces in one or more routers that are collectively treated as a virtual ring. The ring group is denoted by a ring number that must be unique for the network. The ring group's number is used just like a physical ring number, showing up in any route descriptors contained in packets being bridged.

To configure a specific interface as part of a ring group, its target ring number parameter is set to the ring-group number specified in this command. Do not use the number 0. It is reserved to represent the local ring.

To avoid an address conflict on the virtual MAC address, use a locally administered address in the form 4000.*xxxx.xxxx*.

Example

In the following example, multiple Token Rings are source-route bridged to one another through a single router/bridge. These Token Rings are all part of ring group 7.

```
! all token rings attached to this bridge/router are part of ring group 7
source-bridge ring-group 7
!
interface tokenring 0
 source-bridge 1000 1 7
!
interface tokenring 1
 source-bridge 1001 1 7
!
interface tokenring 2
 source-bridge 1002 1 7
!
interface tokenring 3
 source-bridge 1003 1 7
```

Related Commands

source-bridge

SOURCE-BRIDGE SDLLC-LOCAL-ACK

Use the **source-bridge sdllc-local-ack** global configuration command to activate local acknowledgment for SDLLC sessions on a particular interface. Use the **no** form of this command to deactivate local acknowledgment for SDLLC sessions.

source-bridge sdllc-local-ack
no source-bridge sdllc-local-ack

Syntax   Description

This command has no arguments or keywords.

Default

Disabled

Command Mode

Global configuration

Usage Guidelines

This command first appeared in Cisco IOS Release 10.0.

This command must be issued only on a router with a serial interface. Once the command is issued, *all* SDLLC sessions between the two devices will be locally acknowledged. You cannot selectively choose which SDLLC sessions are to be locally acknowledged and which are not. Also, local acknowledgment is not supported when the LLC2 station is attached to Ethernet rather than to Token Ring.

NOTES

You must use the TCP encapsulation option if you use local acknowledgment for SDLLC.

Example

The following example activates local acknowledgment for SDLLC sessions:

```
source-bridge ring-group 100
source-bridge remote-peer 100 tcp 131.108.1.1 local-ack
source-bridge remote-peer 100 tcp 131.108.2.2
source-bridge sdllc-local-ack
```

X25 MAP QLLC

Use the **x25 map qllc** interface configuration command to specify the X.121 address of the remote X.25 device with which you plan to communicate using QLLC conversion. The **no** form of this command disables QLLC conversion to this X.121 address.

x25 map qllc *x121-addr* [*x25-map-options*]
no x25 map qllc *x121-addr* [*x25-map-options*]

Syntax	Description
x121-addr	X.121 address of the remote X.25 device you are associating with this virtual MAC address. It can be from 1 to 15 digits long.
x25-map-options	(Optional) Additional functionality that can be specified for originated calls. Can be any of the options listed in Table 14–5.

Default

No association is made.

Command Mode

Interface configuration

Usage Guidelines

This command first appeared in Cisco IOS Release 10.3.

The central notion that binds the QLLC conversion interface to the X.25 and SRB facilities is the X.25 address map. For each remote client an X.121 address is associated with a virtual MAC address. The rest of the configuration is specified by using the virtual Token Ring address to refer to the connection.

When a Token Ring device wishes to open communications with another device, it will send the request to the address it knows, which is the MAC address. The Cisco IOS software accepts this connection request and must transform it into a known X.121 address. The **x25 map qllc** command matches the MAC address with the X.121 address.

You must enter a mapping for each X.25 device with which the router will exchange traffic.

All QLLC conversion commands use the *virtual-mac-addr* parameter that you define with the **x25 map qllc** command to refer to the connection.

You use the **x25 map qllc** command in conjunction with the **qllc srb** command.

Table 14–5   *X.25 Map Options*

Option	Description
compress	Specifies that X.25 payload compression be used for mapping the traffic to this host. Each virtual circuit established for compressed traffic uses a significant amount of memory (for a table of learned data patterns) and for computation (for compression and decompression of all data). Cisco recommends that compression be used with careful consideration to its impact on overall performance.
method {cisco | ietf | snap | multi}	Specifies the encapsulation method. The choices are as follows: • **cisco**—Cisco's proprietary encapsulation; not available if more than one protocol is to be carried. • **ietf**—Default RFC 1356 operation: protocol identification of single-protocol virtual circuits and protocol identification within multiprotocol virtual circuits uses the standard encoding, which is compatible with RFC 877. Multiprotocol virtual circuits are used only if needed. • **snap**—RFC 1356 operation where IP is identified with SNAP rather than the standard IETF method (the standard method is compatible with RFC 877). • **multi**—Forces a map that specifies a single protocol to set up a multiprotocol virtual circuit when a call is originated; also forces a single-protocol PVC to use multiprotocol data identification methods for all datagrams sent and received.
no-incoming	Use the map only to originate calls.
no-outgoing	Do not originate calls when using the map.
idle *minutes*	Specifies an idle timeout for calls other than the interface default; 0 minutes disables the idle timeout.
reverse	Specifies reverse charging for outgoing calls.
accept-reverse	Causes the Cisco IOS software to accept incoming reverse-charged calls. If this option is not present, the Cisco IOS software clears reverse-charged calls unless the interface accepts all reverse-charged calls.

Table 14–5 *X.25 Map Options, Continued*

Option	Description
broadcast	Causes the Cisco IOS software to direct any broadcasts sent through this interface to the specified X.121 address. This option also simplifies the configuration of OSPF; see "Usage Guidelines" for more detail.
cug *group-number*	Specifies a closed user group number (from 1 to 99) for the mapping in an outgoing call.
nvc *count*	Sets the maximum number of virtual circuits for this map or host. The default *count* is the **x25 nvc** setting of the interface. A maximum number of eight virtual circuits can be configured for each map. Compressed TCP may use only 1 virtual circuit.
packetsize *in-size out-size*	Proposes maximum input packet size (*in-size*) and maximum output packet size (*out-size*) for an outgoing call. Both values typically are the same and must be one of the following values: 16, 32, 64, 128, 256, 512, 1024, 2048, or 4096.
windowsize *in-size out-size*	Proposes the packet count for input window (*in-size*) and output window (*out-size*) for an outgoing call. Both values typically are the same, must be in the range 1 to 127, and must be less than the value set by the **x25 modulo** command.
throughput *in out*	Sets the requested throughput class values for input (*in*) and output (*out*) throughput across the network for an outgoing call. Values for *in* and *out* are in bits per second (bps) and range from 75 to 48000 bps.
transit-delay *milliseconds*	Specifies the transit delay value in milliseconds (0 to 65534) for an outgoing call, for networks that support transit delay.
nuid *username password*	Specifies that a network user ID (NUID) facility be sent in the outgoing call with the specified Terminal Access Controller Access Control System (TACACS) username and password (in a format defined by Cisco). This option should be used only when connecting to another Cisco router. The combined length of the username and password should not exceed 127 characters.

Part
II

Command Reference

Table 14–5   *X.25 Map Options, Continued*

Option	Description
nudata *string*	Specifies the network user identification in a format determined by the network administrator (as allowed by the standards). This option is provided for connecting to non-Cisco equipment that requires an NUID facility. The string should not exceed 130 characters and must be enclosed in quotation marks (" ") if there are any spaces present.
roa *name*	Specifies the name defined by the **x25 roa** command for a list of transit Recognized Operating Agencies (ROAs) to use in outgoing Call Request packets.
passive	Specifies that the X.25 interface should send compressed outgoing TCP datagrams only if they were already compressed when they were received. This option is available only for compressed TCP maps.

Example

In the following example, the **x25 map qllc** command is used to associate the remote X.25 device at X.121 address 31104150101 with the virtual MAC address 0100.000.0001:

```
interface serial 0
 encapsulation x25
 x25 address 31102120100
 x25 map qllc 31104150101
 qllc srb 0100.0000.0001 201 100
```

Related Commands

qllc srb
qllc accept-all-calls

X25 PVC QLLC

Use the **x25 pvc qllc** interface configuration command to associate a virtual MAC address with a PVC for communication using QLLC conversion. The **no** form of this command removes the association.

> **x25 pvc** *circuit* **qllc** *x121-address* [*x25-map-options*]
> **no x25 pvc** *circuit* **qllc** *x121-address* [*x25-map-options*]

Syntax	Description
circuit	PVC you are associating with the virtual MAC address. This must be lower than any number assigned to switched virtual circuits.
x121-address	X.121 address.
x25-map-options	(Optional) Additional functionality that can be specified for originated calls. Can be any of the options listed in Table 14–5 shown earlier in this publication.

Default

No association is made.

Command Mode

Interface configuration

Usage Guidelines

This command first appeared in Cisco IOS Release 11.0.

When a Token Ring device wishes to communicate with another device, it will send the request to the address it knows, which is the MAC address. The Cisco IOS software accepts this connection request and transforms it into the known X.121 address and virtual circuit. You must use the **x25 map qllc** command to specify the required protocol-to-X.121 address mapping before you use the **x25 pvc qllc** command. The **x25 map qllc** command associates the MAC address with the X.121 address, and the **x25 pvc qllc** command further associates that address with a known PVC.

You use the **x25 pvc** command in conjunction with the **x25 map qllc** and **qllc srb** commands.

Example

In the following example, the **x25 pvc qllc** command associates the virtual MAC address 0100.0000.0001, as defined in the previous **x25 map qllc** command entry, with PVC 3:

```
interface serial 0
 encapsulation x25
 x25 address 31102120100
 x25 map qllc 0100.0000.0001 31104150101
 x25 pvc 3 qllc 0100.0000.0001
```

Related Commands

qllc srb
x25 map qllc

15

Configuring DSPU and SNA Service Point Support

This chapter describes Cisco's support for Systems Network Architecture (SNA) downstream physical unit (DSPU) devices and SNA Service Point. For a complete description of the commands mentioned in this chapter, see Chapter 16, "DSPU and SNA Service Point Configuration Commands."

DSPU CONFIGURATION TASK LIST

To configure DSPU, perform the tasks in the following sections. The last two tasks are optional.

- Defining DSPU Upstream Hosts
- Defining Downstream PUs
- Defining DSPU LUs
- Configuring DSPU to Use a Data-Link Control
- Defining the Number of Outstanding, Unacknowledged Activation RUs
- Configuring SNA Service Point Support
- Monitoring DSPU and SNA Service Point Feature Status

See the end of this chapter for "DSPU and SNA Service Point Configuration Examples."

DEFINING DSPU UPSTREAM HOSTS

The upstream host provides logical units (LUs) that the Cisco IOS software assigns for use by its downstream PUs. Because one upstream host can provide only a maximum of 255 LUs, the DSPU feature supports multiple hosts. Multiple upstream host support allows the DSPU router to provide more than 255 LUs for use by its downstream PUs.

To define a DSPU host over Token Ring, Ethernet, FDDI, remote source-route bridging (RSRB), or virtual data-link control connections, perform the following task in global configuration mode:

Task	Command
Define a DSPU host over Token Ring, Ethernet, FDDI, RSRB, or virtual data-link control connections.	dspu host *host-name* xid-snd *xid* rmac *remote-mac* [rsap *remote-sap*] [lsap *local-sap*] [interface *slot/port*] [window *window-size*] [maxiframe *max-iframe*] [retries *retry-count*] [retry-timeout *retry-timeout*] [focalpoint]

To define a DSPU host over an SDLC connection, perform the following task in global configuration mode:

Task	Command
Define a DSPU host over an SDLC connection	dspu host *host-name* xid-snd *xid* sdlc *sdlc-addr* [interface *slot/port*] [window *window-size*] [maxiframe *max-iframe*] [retries *retry-count*] [retry-timeout *retry-timeout*] [focalpoint]

To define a DSPU host over an X.25/QLLC connection, perform the following task in global configuration mode:

Task	Command
Define a DSPU host over an X.25/QLLC connection.	dspu host *host-name* xid-snd *xid* x25 *remote-x121-addr* [qllc *local-x121-subaddr*] [interface *slot/port*] [window *window-size*] [maxiframe *max-iframe*] [retries *retry-count*] [retry-timeout *retry-timeout*] [focalpoint]

To define a DSPU host over a Frame Relay connection, perform the following task in global configuration mode:

Task	Command
Define a DSPU host over a Frame Relay connection.	dspu host *host-name* xid-snd *xid* dlci *dlci-number* [rsap *remote-sap*] [lsap *local-sap*] [interface *slot/port*] [window *window-size*] [maxiframe *max-iframe*] [retries *retry-count*] [retry-timeout *retry-timeout*] [focalpoint]

DEFINING DOWNSTREAM PUs

To define the downstream PUs, perform either of the tasks in the following sections, depending on your circumstances:

- Explicitly Defining a Downstream PU
- Enabling the Default PU Option

Explicitly Defining a Downstream PU

Explicitly define a downstream PU if you require the Cisco IOS software to perform verification checking on incoming downstream connections or to initiate an outgoing downstream connection.

To explicitly define a downstream PU over Token Ring, Ethernet, FDDI, RSRB, virtual data-link control, or NCIA connections, perform the following task in global configuration mode:

Task	Command
Explicitly define a downstream PU over Token Ring, Ethernet, FDDI, RSRB, virtual data-link control, or NCIA connections.	**dspu pu** *pu-name* [**rmac** *remote-mac*] [**rsap** *remote-sap*] [**lsap** *local-sap*] [**xid-rcv** *xid*] [**interface** *slot/port*] [**window** *window-size*] [**maxiframe** *max-iframe*] [**retries** *retry-count*] [**retry-timeout** *retry-timeout*]

To explicitly define a downstream PU over an SDLC connection, perform the following task in global configuration mode:

Task	Command
Explicitly define a downstream PU over an SDLC connection.	**dspu pu** *pu-name* **sdlc** *sdlc-addr* [**xid-rcv** *xid*] [**interface** *slot/port*] [**window** *window-size*] [**maxiframe** *max-iframe*] [**retries** *retry-count*] [**retry-timeout** *retry-timeout*]

To explicitly define a downstream PU over an X.25/QLLC connection, perform the following task in global configuration mode:

Task	Command
Explicitly define a downstream PU over an X.25/QLLC connection.	**dspu pu** *pu-name* **x25** *remote-x121-addr* [**qllc** *local-x121-subaddr*] [**xid-rcv** *xid*] [**interface** *slot/port*] [**window** *window-size*] [**maxiframe** *max-iframe*] [**retries** *retry-count*] [**retry-timeout** *retry-timeout*]

To explicitly define a downstream PU over a Frame Relay connection, perform the following task in global configuration mode:

Task	Command
Explicitly define a downstream PU over a Frame Relay connection.	**dspu pu** *pu-name* **dlci** *dlci-number* [**rsap** *remote-sap*] [**lsap** *local-sap*] [**xid-rcv** *xid*] [**interface** *type slot/port*] [**window** *window-size*] [**maxiframe** *max-iframe*] [**retries** *retry-count*] [**retry-timeout** *retry-timeout*]

If the Cisco IOS software will perform verification checking on incoming downstream connections, there are several combinations of parameters that you can configure for verification matching:

- Match on xid-rcv value only.

    User may define a downstream PU using only the xid-rcv value so that any connecting PU that specifies the value of the configured XID will match that PU definition.

- Match on xid-rcv and interface values.

    User may define a downstream PU using the xid-rcv and interface values so that any PU connecting into the configured interface that specifies the value of the configured XID will match the PU definition.

- Match on addressing values only.

    User may define a downstream PU using only the addressing values (RMAC/RSAP/LSAP, SDLC, DLCI/RSAP/LSAP, or X25/QLLC) so that any connecting PU with addressing that matches the configured addressing will match that PU definition.

- Match on xid-rcv and addressing values.

    User may define a downstream PU using the xid-rcv and addressing values (RMAC/RSAP/LSAP, SDLC, DLCI/RSAP/LSAP, or X25/QLLC) so that any connecting PU with addressing that matches the configured addressing and specifies the value of the configured xid will match the PU definition.

- Match on addressing and interface values.

    User may define a downstream PU using the interface and addressing values (RMAC/RSAP/LSAP, SDLC, DLCI/RSAP/LSAP, or X25/QLLC) so that any PU connecting into the configured interface with addressing that matches the configured addressing will match the PU definition.

- Match on xid, addressing, and interface values.

    User may define a downstream PU using the xid, interface, and addressing parameters (RMAC/RSAP/LSAP, SDLC, DLCI/RSAP/LSAP, or X25/QLLC) so that any PU connecting into the configured interface with addressing that matches the configured addressing and specifies the value of the configured xid will match the PU definition.

The Cisco IOS software rejects any incoming downstream connections that do not match the parameters of a defined downstream PU unless the default PU option is also enabled.

Enabling the Default PU Option

Configure the DSPU default PU option if you do not require the Cisco IOS software to verify incoming downstream connections. The default PU option allows the software to accept incoming downstream connections without an explicit definition for the downstream PU.

To enable the default PU option, perform the following task in global configuration mode:

Task	Command
Enable the default PU option.	dspu default-pu [window *window-size*] [maxiframe *max-iframe*]

DEFINING DSPU LUs

Specify the LU routing algorithm used to map the upstream LUs to the downstream LUs and to define all LUs for each upstream and downstream PU.

The DSPU feature assigns upstream LUs to downstream LUs based on the selected LU routing algorithm and performs the mapping necessary for SNA data transfer.

The DSPU feature supports two alternative mapping algorithms that are described in the following sections:

- Defining Dedicated LU Routing
- Defining Pooled LU Routing

An upstream host PU or downstream PU can support up to 255 LU sessions. The DSPU feature allows each LU to be configured individually for either dedicated LU routing or pooled LU routing.

Defining Dedicated LU Routing

You can configure an upstream LU so that it is reserved, or dedicated, for use by a specific downstream LU.

To define a dedicated LU or a range of dedicated LUs for an upstream host and downstream PU, perform the following task in global configuration mode:

Task	Command
Define a dedicated LU or a range of dedicated LUs for a downstream PU.	dspu lu *lu-start* [*lu-end*] {host *host-name host-lu-start* | pool *pool-name*} [pu *pu-name*]

See the "Dedicated LU Routing Example" section later in this chapter for an example of dedicated LU routing.

Defining Pooled LU Routing

You can configure an upstream host LU so that it is a member of a pool of LUs. When a downstream connection is established and the downstream LU is configured as a pooled LU, the Cisco IOS software selects an upstream LU from the pool for assignment to the downstream LU.

Pooled LU routing allows a limited number of upstream host LUs to be shared (at different times) among many downstream LUs.

To define a host LU or a range of host LUs in an LU pool, perform the following task in global configuration mode:

Task	Command
Define a host LU or a range of host LUs in an LU pool.	**dspu pool** *pool-name* **host** *host-name* **lu** *lu-start* [*lu-end*] [**inactivity-timeout** *inactivity-minutes*]

You can configure a downstream LU as a pooled LU. When a downstream connection is established and the downstream LU is configured as a pooled LU, the software selects an upstream LU from the specified pool for assignment to the downstream LU.

To define a pooled LU or a range of pooled LUs for a downstream PU, perform the following task in global configuration mode:

Task	Command
Define a pooled LU or a range of pooled LUs for a downstream PU.	**dspu lu** *lu-start* [*lu-end*] **pool** *pool-name* **pu** *pu-name*

See the "Pooled LU Routing Example" section later in this chapter for an example of pooled LU routing.

CONFIGURING DSPU TO USE A DATA-LINK CONTROL

The final step in configuring DSPU is to define the data-link controls that will be used for upstream host and downstream PU connections.

The DSPU feature supports the data-link controls described in the following sections:

- Configuring DSPU to Use Token Ring, Ethernet, or FDDI
- Configuring DSPU to Use RSRB

- Configuring DSPU to Use RSRB with Local Acknowledgment
- Configuring DSPU to Use Virtual Data-link Control
- Configuring DSPU to Use SDLC
- Configuring DSPU to Use QLLC
- Configuring DSPU to Use Frame Relay
- Configuring DSPU to Use NCIA

Configuring DSPU to Use Token Ring, Ethernet, or FDDI

You can configure DSPU to use the Token Ring, Ethernet, or FDDI data-link controls or both by enabling a service access point (SAP) address on the interface. Each interface can support up to 254 local SAPs enabled for either upstream or downstream connections; a local SAP cannot be enabled for both upstream and downstream connections on the same interface.

To enable a local SAP on the Token Ring, Ethernet, or FDDI interfaces for use by upstream hosts, perform the following task in interface configuration mode:

Task	Command
Enable local SAP for upstream hosts.	**dspu enable-host** [lsap *local-sap*]

To enable a local SAP on the Token Ring, Ethernet, or FDDI interfaces for use by downstream PUs, perform the following task in interface configuration mode:

Task	Command
Enable local SAP for downstream PUs.	**dspu enable-pu** [lsap *local-sap*]

Once a local SAP is enabled, it is ready to accept incoming connection attempts from the remote device (upstream host or downstream PU). Alternatively, initiate an outgoing connection to the remote device by performing the following task in interface configuration mode:

Task	Command
Initiate connection with upstream host or downstream PU via Token Ring or Ethernet.	**dspu start** {*host-name* | *pu-name*}

Configuring DSPU to Use RSRB

To configure DSPU to use RSRB, you must create a DSPU/RSRB data-link control.

Similar to Cisco's implementation of SDLLC, the DSPU/RSRB data-link control uses the concept of a virtual Token Ring device residing on a virtual Token Ring to represent the Cisco IOS software to upstream hosts and downstream PUs across an RSRB network.

Because the upstream host and downstream PU expects its peer also to be on a Token Ring, you must assign a virtual Token Ring address (the DSPU virtual MAC address) to the DSPU/RSRB data-link control. Like real Token Ring addresses, the DSPU virtual MAC address must be unique across the network.

In addition to assigning the DSPU virtual MAC address, you also must assign a DSPU virtual ring number to the DSPU/RSRB data-link control. The DSPU virtual ring number must be unique across the network.

NOTES

The DSPU virtual ring number is a different number from the virtual ring-group numbers that you use to configure RSRB and multiport bridging.

The combination of the DSPU virtual MAC address and the DSPU virtual ring number identifies the DSPU/RSRB data-link control interface to the rest of an RSRB network.

When an end station (either an upstream host or a downstream PU) attempts to connect with the DSPU software, the following events occur:

1. The end station sends explorer packets with the locally administered MAC address on the router interface to which the end station is connected.

2. The router configured with that locally administered MAC address or with the hardware MAC address intercepts the frame, fills in the DSPU virtual ring number and the DSPU bridge number in the routing information field (RIF), and sends a response to the end station.

3. The end station establishes a session with the DSPU router.

To define the DSPU/RSRB data-link control interface, perform the following tasks in global configuration mode:

Task	Command
Step 1 Define an RSRB ring group.	**source-bridge ring-group** *ring-group* [*virtual-mac-address*]
Step 2 Define a remote peer with the local acknowledgment feature.	**source-bridge remote-peer** *ring-group* **tcp** *ip-address* **local-ack**
Step 3 Define the DSPU/RSRB interface.	**dspu rsrb** *local-virtual-ring bridge-number target-virtual-ring virtual-macaddr*

After you define the DSPU RSRB data-link control, configure DSPU to use the RSRB data-link control by enabling a local SAP for either upstream or downstream connections.

To enable a local SAP on RSRB for use by upstream hosts, perform the following task in global configuration mode:

Task	Command
Enable local SAP for upstream hosts.	**dspu rsrb enable-host** [**lsap** *local-sap*]

To enable a local SAP on RSRB for use by downstream PUs, perform the following task in global configuration mode:

Task	Command
Enable local SAP for downstream PUs.	**dspu rsrb enable-pu** [**lsap** *local-sap*]

Once a local SAP is enabled, it is ready to accept incoming connection attempts from the remote device (upstream host or downstream PU) over RSRB. Alternatively, initiate an outgoing connection to the remote device by performing the following task in global configuration mode:

Task	Command
Initiate connection with upstream host or downstream PU via RSRB.	**dspu rsrb start** {*host-name* | *pu-name*}

Configuring DSPU to Use RSRB with Local Acknowledgment

Configuring DSPU to use RSRB with local acknowledgment is identical to configuring RSRB with local acknowledgment. If you add the **local-ack** keyword to the **source-bridge remote-peer** configuration command, DSPU will use local acknowledgment for any end stations that connect to DSPU from that peer.

To configure DSPU to use RSRB with local acknowledgment, perform the following tasks in global configuration mode:

Task	Command
Step 1 Define an RSRB ring group.	**source-bridge ring-group** *ring-group* [*virtual-mac-address*]
Step 2 Define a remote peer with the local acknowledgment feature.	**source-bridge remote-peer** *ring-group* **tcp** *ip-address* **local-ack**

Task	Command
Step 3 Define the DSPU/RSRB interface.	**dspu rsrb** *local-virtual-ring bridge-number target-virtual-ring virtual-macaddr*

Configuring DSPU to Use Virtual Data-link Control

To configure DSPU to use virtual data-link control, you must create a DSPU virtual data-link control interface.

Similar to Cisco's implementation of SDLLC, the DSPU virtual data-link control interface uses the concept of a virtual Token Ring device residing on a virtual Token Ring to represent the Cisco IOS software to upstream hosts and downstream PUs across a network.

Because the upstream host and downstream PU expects its peer also to be on a Token Ring, you must assign a virtual Token Ring address (the DSPU virtual MAC address) to the DSPU virtual data-link control interface. Like real Token Ring addresses, the DSPU virtual MAC address must be unique across the network.

In addition to assigning the DSPU virtual MAC address, you also must identify the source-route bridging virtual ring number with which the DSPU virtual MAC address will be associated. The source-route bridging virtual ring number is set using the **source-bridge ring-group** command, which is documented in Chapter 4, "Source-Route Bridging Commands."

The combination of the DSPU virtual MAC address and the source-route bridging virtual ring number identifies the DSPU virtual data-link control interface to the rest of the DLSw+ network.

When an end station (either an upstream host or a downstream PU) attempts to connect with the DSPU software, the following events occur:

1. The end station sends explorer packets with the locally administered MAC address on the router interface to which the end station is connected.

2. The router configured with that locally administered MAC address intercepts the frame and DLSw+ adjusts the routing information field (RIF) and sends a response to the end station.

3. The end station establishes a session with the DSPU router.

Prior to creating the DSPU virtual data-link control interface, you also must configure DLSw+ peers so that DLSw+ can provide the communication path. Commands for defining DLSw+ local and remote peers can be found in Chapter 8, "DLSw+ Configuration Commands."

To define the DSPU virtual data-link control interface, perform the following task in global configuration mode:

Task	Command
Define the DSPU virtual data-link control interface.	**dspu vdlc** *ring-group virtual-mac-address*

After you define the DSPU virtual data-link control interface, configure DSPU to use virtual data-link control by enabling a local SAP for either upstream or downstream connections.

To enable a local SAP on the virtual data-link control for use by upstream hosts, perform the following task in global configuration mode:

Task	Command
Enable local SAP for upstream hosts.	**dspu vdlc enable-host** [**lsap** *local-sap*]

To enable a local SAP on the virtual data-link control for use by downstream PUs, perform the following task in global configuration mode:

Task	Command
Enable local SAP for downstream PUs.	**dspu vdlc enable-pu** [**lsap** *local-sap*]

Once a local SAP is enabled, it is ready to accept incoming connection attempts from the remote device (upstream host or downstream PU) using virtual data-link control. Alternatively, initiate an outgoing connection to the remote device by performing the following task in global configuration mode:

Task	Command
Initiate connection with upstream host or downstream PU via virtual data-link control.	**dspu vdlc start** {*host-name* | *pu-name*}

Configuring DSPU to Use SDLC

Before DSPU may be configured to use the SDLC data-link control, the serial interface must be defined for SDLC encapsulation and assigned an SDLC role.

To define the serial interface to use SDLC and specify the SDLC role, perform the following tasks in interface configuration mode:

Task	Command
Step 1 Enable SDLC encapsulation on the serial interface.	**encapsulation sdlc**
Step 2 Specify the SDLC role of the router.	**sdlc role** {**none** | **primary** | **secondary** | **prim-xid-poll**}

For the connection to be established without XID exchange, the SDLC role must be **primary** if DSPU will be initiating connections to the SDLC partner. The SDLC role must be **secondary** or **none** if the SDLC partner will be initiating connections with DSPU.

When an XID exchange is required, the SDLC role must be **prim-xid-poll** or **none** if DSPU will be initiating connections to the SDLC partner. The role must be **none** if the SDLC partner will be initiating connections with DSPU.

The SDLC address(es) used on the SDLC link also must be defined. If DSPU is configured to initiate the connection, then the SDLC address identifies the SDLC partner. If the remote SDLC device initiates the connection, then the SDLC address identifies the address for which a connection will be accepted.

To configure the SDLC address, perform the following task in interface configuration mode:

Task	Command
Define the SDLC address.	**sdlc address** *hexbyte*

Finally, the SDLC address must be enabled for use by DSPU. Each interface can support up to 255 SDLC addresses enabled for either upstream or downstream connections; an SDLC address cannot be enabled for both upstream and downstream connections on the same interface. If the SDLC role is **none**, there can be only one SDLC address on that interface.

To enable an SDLC address for use by upstream host connections, perform the following task in interface configuration mode:

Task	Command
Enable SDLC address for upstream host.	**dspu enable-host sdlc** *sdlc-address*

To enable an SDLC address for use by downstream PU connections, perform the following task in interface configuration mode:

Task	Command
Enable SDLC address for downstream PU.	**dspu enable-pu sdlc** *sdlc-address*

When the SDLC role is configured as **primary**, DSPU initiates a connection with the remote device by sending set normal response mode (SNRM) when the SDLC address is enabled for DSPU.

When the SDLC role is configured as **prim-xid-poll**, DSPU initiates a connection with the remote device by sending a NULL XID when the SDLC address is enabled for DSPU.

When the SDLC role is configured as **secondary**, DSPU will not be ready to respond to SNRM until a **dspu start** *pu-name* command is issued.

When the SDLC role is configured as **none**, DSPU is ready to respond to a received XID or SNRM when the SDLC address is enabled for DSPU; otherwise, the connection may be initiated by issuing the **dspu start** *pu-name* command.

To configure DSPU to respond to SNRM when the SDLC role is configured as **secondary**, or to initiate a connection when the SDLC role is configured as **none**, perform the following task in interface configuration mode:

Task	Command
Initiate a connection with a remote device when the SDLC role is configured as **secondary** or **none**.	**dspu start** {*host-name* | *pu-name*}

Configuring DSPU to Use QLLC

Before DSPU may be configured to use the QLLC data-link control, the serial interface must be defined for X.25 encapsulation and assigned an X.121 address.

To define the serial interface to use X.25, perform the following tasks in interface configuration mode:

Task	Command
Step 1	Enable X.25 encapsulation on serial interface.	**encapsulation x25** [dce]
Step 2	Define an X.121 address.	**x25 address** *x121-addr*

X.25 routing also must be configured so that incoming calls to the local X.121 address can be appropriately routed to the serial interface and mapped into the QLLC data-link control.

To define X.25 routing, perform the following tasks in global configuration mode:

Task	Command
Step 1	Enable X.25 routing.	**x25 routing**
Step 2	Enable routing of X.25 packets to serial interface.	**x25 route** ^*local-x121-addr*.* **alias serial** **slot/port**

To define which calls get mapped into QLLC, perform the following task in interface configuration mode:

Task	Command
Define remote X.121 address for mapping into QLLC.	**x25 map qllc** *x121-addr*

Finally, the local X.121 subaddress must be enabled for use by DSPU. An X.121 subaddress can be enabled for either upstream or downstream connections; an X.121 subaddress cannot be enabled for both upstream and downstream connections on the same interface.

To enable an X.121 subaddress for use by upstream host connections via QLLC, perform the following task in interface configuration mode:

Task	Command
Enable X.121 subaddress for upstream host.	**dspu enable-host qllc** *x121-subaddress*

To enable an X.121 subaddress for use by downstream PU connections via QLLC, perform the following task in interface configuration mode:

Task	Command
Enable X.121 subaddress for downstream PU.	**dspu enable-pu qllc** *x121-subaddress*

Once an X.121 subaddress is enabled, it is ready to accept incoming connection attempts from the remote device (upstream host or downstream PU) over QLLC. Alternatively, initiate an outgoing connection to the remote device by performing the following task in interface configuration mode:

Task	Command
Initiate connection with upstream host or downstream PU via QLLC.	**dspu start** {*host-name* | *pu-name*}

Configuring DSPU to Use Frame Relay

Before DSPU may be configured to use the LLC2/Frame Relay data-link control, the serial interface must be defined for Frame Relay encapsulation.

To define the serial interface for Frame Relay encapsulation, perform the following task in interface configuration mode:

Task	Command
Enable Frame Relay encapsulation on a serial interface.	**encapsulation frame-relay ietf**

The DLCI used on the Frame Relay link must be mapped into LLC2.

To configure the mapping of a DLCI into LLC2, perform the following task in interface configuration mode:

Task	Command
Configure DLCI mapping into LLC2.	**frame-relay map llc2** *dlci-number*

Finally, the local SAP address must be enabled for use by DSPU. A SAP address can be enabled for either upstream or downstream connections; a SAP address cannot be enabled for both upstream and downstream connections on the same interface.

To enable a local SAP on the LLC2/Frame Relay interface for use by upstream hosts, perform the following task in interface configuration mode:

Task	Command
Enable local SAP for upstream hosts.	**dspu enable-host** [**lsap** *local-sap*]

To enable a local SAP for the LLC2/Frame Relay interface for use by downstream PUs, perform the following task in interface configuration mode:

Task	Command
Enable local SAP for downstream PUs.	**dspu enable-pu** [**lsap** *local-sap*]

Once a local SAP is enabled, it is ready to accept incoming connection attempts from the remote device (upstream host or downstream PU) over Frame Relay. Alternatively, initiate an outgoing connection to the remote device by performing the following task in interface configuration mode:

Task	Command
Initiate connection with upstream host or downstream PU via LLC2/Frame Relay.	**dspu start** {*host-name*	*pu-name*}

Configuring DSPU to Use NCIA

To configure DSPU to use NCIA, you must perform the following tasks:

- Configure the NCIA server as the underlying transport mechanism.
- Enable a local SAP on the NCIA server for use by downstream PUs.

To configure the NCIA server as the underlying transport mechanism, perform the following task in global configuration mode:

Task	Command
Configure the NCIA server as the underlying transport mechanism.	**dspu ncia** *server-number*

To enable a local SAP on the NCIA server for use by downstream PUs, perform the following task in global configuration mode:

Task	Command
Enable local SAP for downstream PUs.	**dspu ncia enable-pu** [lsap *local-sap*]

DEFINING THE NUMBER OF OUTSTANDING, UNACKNOWLEDGED ACTIVATION RUS

The DSPU feature allows you to define the number of activation request/response units (RUs) such as ACTLUs or DDDLU NMVTs that can be sent by the Cisco IOS software before waiting for responses from the remote PU.

The DSPU activation window provides pacing to avoid depleting the router buffer pool during PU activation. Increasing the window size allows more LUs to become active in a shorter amount of time (assuming the required buffers for activation RUs are available). Decreasing the window size limits the amount of buffers the DSPU may use during PU activation. Typically, you do not need to change the default window size.

To define the number of unacknowledged activation RUs that can be outstanding, perform the following task in global configuration mode:

Task	Command
Define the number of unacknowledged activation RUs.	**dspu activation-window** *window-size*

CONFIGURING SNA SERVICE POINT SUPPORT

Cisco's implementation of SNA Service Point support includes support for three commands: Alerts, RUNCMD, and Vital Product Data support.

Alert support is provided as the Cisco IOS software sends unsolicited Alerts to NetView (or an equivalent network management application) at the host. This function occurs at the various router interfaces and protocol layers within the device.

RUNCMD support enables you to send commands to the router from the NetView console using the NetView RUNCMD facility, and the router sends the relevant replies back to the RUNCMD screen.

Vital Product Data support allows you to request Vital Product Data from the NetView console. The router replies to NetView with the relevant information.

To configure SNA Service Point support, perform the tasks in the following sections:

- Defining a Link to an SNA Host
- Configuring Service Point Support to Use a Data-Link Control
- Specifying Names for All Attached LANs
- Specifying the Physical Location of the Router

NOTES ────────────────────────────────

You do not need to perform the tasks in the next section if you have configured a DSPU host with the **focalpoint** parameter.

Defining a Link to an SNA Host

To define a link to an SNA host over Token Ring, Ethernet, FDDI, RSRB, or virtual data-link control connections, perform the following task in global configuration mode:

Task	Command
Define a link to an SNA host over Token Ring, Ethernet, FDDI, RSRB, or virtual data-link control connections.	**sna host** *host-name* **xid-snd** *xid* **rmac** *remote-mac* [**rsap** *remote-sap*] [**lsap** *local-sap*] [**interface** *slot/port*] [**window** *window-size*] [**maxiframe** *max-iframe*] [**retries** *retry-count*] [**retry-timeout** *retry-timeout*] [**focalpoint**]

To define a link to an SNA host over an SDLC connection, perform the following task in global configuration mode:

Task	Command
Define a link to an SNA host over an SDLC connection.	**sna host** *host-name* **xid-snd** *xid* **sdlc** *sdlc-addr* [**interface** *slot/port*] [**window** *window-size*] [**maxiframe** *max-iframe*] [**retries** *retry-count*] [**retry-timeout** *retry-timeout*] [**focalpoint**]

To define a link to an SNA host over an X.25/QLLC connection, perform the following task in global configuration mode:

Task	Command
Define a link to an SNA host over an X.25/QLLC connection.	**sna host** *host-name* **xid-snd** *xid* **x25** *remote-x121-addr* [**qllc** *local-x121-subaddr*] [**interface** *slot/port*] [**window** *window-size*] [**maxiframe** *max-iframe*] [**retries** *retry-count*] [**retry-timeout** *retry-timeout*] [**focalpoint**]

To define a link to an SNA host over a Frame Relay connection, perform the following task in global configuration mode:

Task	Command
Define a link to an SNA host over a Frame Relay connection.	**sna host** *host-name* **xid-snd** *xid* **dlci** *dlci-number* [**rsap** *remote-sap*] [**lsap** *local-sap*] [**interface** *slot/port*] [**window** *window-size*] [**maxiframe** *max-iframe*] [**retries** *retry-count*] [**retry-timeout** *retry-timeout*] [**focalpoint**]

Configuring Service Point Support to Use a Data-Link Control

To configure Service Point to use a data-link control, perform the tasks in one of the following sections:

- Configuring Service Point to Use Token Ring, Ethernet, or FDDI
- Configuring Service Point to Use RSRB
- Configuring Service Point to Use RSRB with Local Acknowledgment
- Configuring Service Point to Use Virtual Data-Link Control
- Configuring Service Point Support for Frame Relay
- Configuring Service Point Support for SDLC
- Configuring Service Point Support for X.25

NOTES

You do not need to perform this task if you have configured a DSPU host with the **focalpoint** parameter and have configured the DSPU host to use a data-link control.

Configuring Service Point to Use Token Ring, Ethernet, or FDDI

To enable a local SAP on the Token Ring, Ethernet, or FDDI interfaces for use by SNA Service Point, perform the following task in interface configuration mode:

Task	Command
Enable local SAP for Service Point.	**sna enable-host** [**lsap** *lsap-address*]

Once a local SAP is enabled, it is ready to accept incoming connection attempts from the remote host. Alternatively, initiate an outgoing connection to the remote host by performing the following task in interface configuration mode:

Task	Command
Initiate connection with host via Token Ring, Ethernet, or FDDI.	**sna start** *host-name*

Configuring Service Point to Use RSRB

To define the Service Point/RSRB data-link control interface, perform the following tasks in global configuration mode:

Task	Command
Step 1 Define an RSRB ring group.	source-bridge ring-group *ring-group* [*virtual-mac-address*]
Step 2 Define the Service Point/RSRB interface.	sna rsrb *local-virtual-ring bridge-number target-virtual-ring virtual-macaddr*

To enable a local SAP on RSRB for use by hosts, perform the following task in global configuration mode:

Task	Command
Enable local SAP for hosts.	sna rsrb enable-host [lsap *local-sap*]

Once a local SAP is enabled, it is ready to accept incoming connection attempts from the remote host over RSRB. Alternatively, initiate an outgoing connection to the remote host by performing the following task in global configuration mode:

Task	Command
Initiate connection with host via RSRB.	sna rsrb start *host-name*

Configuring Service Point to Use RSRB with Local Acknowledgment

To configure Service Point to use RSRB with local acknowledgment, perform the following tasks in global configuration mode:

Task	Command
Step 1 Define an RSRB ring group.	source-bridge ring-group *ring-group* [*virtual-mac-address*]
Step 2 Define a remote peer with the local acknowledgment feature.	source-bridge remote-peer *ring-group* tcp *ip-address* local-ack

Task	Command
Step 3 Define the Service Point/RSRB interface.	**sna rsrb** *local-virtual-ring bridge-number target-virtual-ring virtual-macaddr*

Configuring Service Point to Use Virtual Data-Link Control

To configure SNA Service Point to use virtual data-link control, you must create an SNA virtual data-link control interface.

Similar to Cisco's implementation of SDLLC, the SNA virtual data-link control interface uses the concept of a virtual Token Ring device residing on a virtual Token Ring to represent the Cisco IOS software to upstream hosts and downstream PUs across a network.

Because the upstream host and downstream PU expect their peer also to be on a Token Ring, you must assign a virtual Token Ring address (the SNA virtual data-link control virtual MAC address) to the SNA virtual data-link control interface. Like real Token Ring addresses, the SNA virtual MAC address must be unique across the network.

In addition to assigning the SNA virtual data-link control virtual MAC address, you also must identify the source-route bridging virtual ring number with which the SNA virtual MAC address will be associated. The source-route bridging virtual ring number is set using the **source-bridge ring-group** command, which is documented in Chapter 4, "Source-Route Bridging Commands."

The combination of the SNA virtual MAC address and the source-route bridging virtual ring number identifies the SNA virtual data-link control interface to the rest of the DLSw+ network.

When an end station (either an upstream host or a downstream PU) attempts to connect with the SNA Service Point software, the following events occur:

1. The end station sends explorer packets with the locally administered MAC address on the router interface to which the end station is connected.

2. The router configured with that locally administered MAC address intercepts the frame, and DLSw+ adjusts the routing information field (RIF) and sends a response to the end station.

3. The end station establishes a session with the SNA Service Point router.

Prior to creating the SNA virtual data-link control interface, you also must configure DLSw+ peers so that DLSw+ can provide the communication path. The commands for defining DLSw+ local and remote peers are documented in Chapter 8.

To define the Service Point virtual data-link control interface, perform the following task in global configuration mode:

Task	Command
Define the Service Point virtual data-link control interface.	**sna vdlc** *ring-group virtual-mac-address*

After you create the SNA virtual data-link control interface, configure SNA Service Point to use virtual data-link control by enabling a local SAP for upstream connections. To enable a local SAP on virtual data-link control for use by hosts, perform the following task in global configuration mode:

Task	Command
Enable local SAP for hosts.	**sna vdlc enable-host** [**lsap** *local-sap*]

Once a local SAP is enabled, it is ready to accept incoming connection attempts from the remote host using virtual data-link control. Alternatively, initiate an outgoing connection to the remote host by performing the following task in global configuration mode:

Task	Command
Initiate connection with host via virtual data-link control.	**sna vdlc start** *host-name*

Configuring Service Point Support for Frame Relay

To configure Service Point support for Frame Relay, perform the following tasks in interface configuration mode:

Task		Command
Step 1	Define DLCI mapping into LLC2.	**frame-relay map llc2** *dlci-number*
Step 2	Enable a local SAP for hosts.	**sna enable-host lsap** *lsap-address*

Configuring Service Point Support for SDLC

To configure Service Point support for SDLC, perform the following tasks in interface configuration mode:

Task		Command
Step 1	Specify the SDLC role of the router.	**sdlc role** {**none** | **primary** | **secondary** | **prim-xid-poll**}
Step 2	Define the SDLC address.	**sdlc address** *hexbyte*
Step 3	Enable the SDLC address for the host.	**sna enable-host sdlc** *sdlc-address*

Configuring Service Point Support for X.25

To configure Service Point support for X.25, perform the following tasks in interface configuration mode:

Task	Command
Step 1 Define an X.121 address.	**x25 address** *x121-address*
Step 2 Define remote X.121 address for mapping to QLLC.	**x25 map qllc** *x121-addr*
Step 3 Enable QLLC subaddress for host.	**sna enable-host qllc** *x121-subaddress*
Step 4 Enable routing of X.25 packets to serial interface.	**x25 route** ^*x121-addr.** **alias** *serial interface*

Specifying Names for All Attached LANs

You can specify names for all Token Ring or Ethernet LANs attached to the router. These names are used to identify the LAN when the Cisco IOS software sends an Alert to the host. To specify names for all attached LANs, perform the following tasks in interface configuration mode:

Task	Command
Define the name of an attached LAN.	**lan-name** *lan-name*

Specifying the Physical Location of the Router

You can specify the physical location of the router if you intend requesting vital product information from the router. To specify the physical location, perform the following tasks in interface configuration mode:

Task	Command
Define the physical location of the router.	**location** *location-description*

MONITORING DSPU AND SNA SERVICE POINT FEATURE STATUS

You can monitor the status of the DSPU and SNA Service Point features. To display information about the state of the DSPU and SNA Service Point features, perform the following tasks in EXEC mode:

Task	Command
Step 1 Show the status of all DSPU resources.	**show dspu**
Step 2 Show the status of DSPU hosts or downstream PUs.	**show dspu pu** {*host-name* | *pu-name*} [**all**]
Step 3 Show the status of a DSPU pool.	**show dspu pool** *pool-name* [**all**]
Step 4 Show the status of all SNA hosts.	**show sna**
Step 5 Show the status of an SNA host.	**show sna pu** *host-name* [**all**]

To control the reporting of DSPU notification events (DSPU-specific SNMP Traps and Unsolicited SNA Messages to Operator), perform the following command in global configuration mode:

Task	Command
Specify the level of notification event reporting.	**dspu notification-level** {**off** | **low** | **medium** | **high**}

DSPU AND SNA SERVICE POINT CONFIGURATION EXAMPLES

The following sections provide DSPU and SNA Service Point configuration examples:

- Dedicated LU Routing Example
- Pooled LU Routing Example
- Upstream Host via RSRB DSPU Configuration Example
- DSPU over DLSw+ Using Virtual Data-Link Control Configuration Example
- Downstream PU via SDLC DSPU Configuration Example
- Upstream Host via SDLC DSPU Configuration Example
- Downstream PU via QLLC/X.25 DSPU Configuration Example
- Upstream Host via Frame Relay DSPU Configuration Example
- DSPU NCIA Configuration Example
- SNA Service Point Support Configuration Example
- SNA Service Point over DLSw+ Using Virtual Data-Link Control Configuration Example

Dedicated LU Routing Example

Figure 15–1 illustrates the use of dedicated LU routing. Each upstream host LU is dedicated for use by a specific downstream LU.

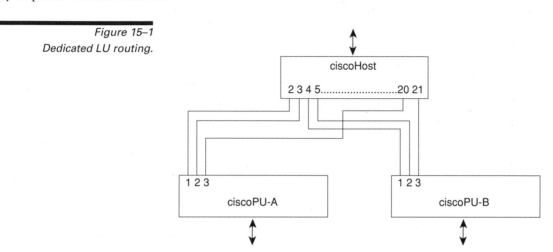

Figure 15–1
Dedicated LU routing.

The following is a configuration file for the dedicated LU routing shown in Figure 15–1:

```
dspu host ciscohost xid-snd 06500001 rmac 4000.3745.0001
dspu pu ciscopu-a xid-rcv 05D00001 rmac 1000.5AED.0001
dspu lu 1 2 host ciscohost 2
dspu lu 3 3 host ciscohost 20
dspu pu ciscopu-b xid-rcv 05D00002 rmac 1000.5AED.0002
dspu lu 1 2 host ciscohost 4
dspu lu 3 3 host ciscohost 21
```

Pooled LU Routing Example

Figure 15–2 illustrates the use of pooled LU routing. Each upstream LU is configured in the LU pool and each downstream LU is configured as a pooled LU.

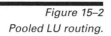

Figure 15–2
Pooled LU routing.

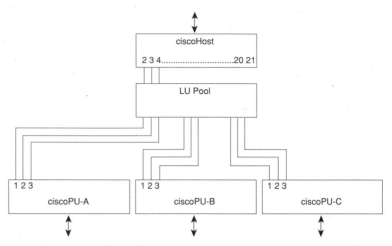

The following is a configuration file for the pooled LU routing shown in Figure 15–2:

```
dspu host ciscohost xid-snd 06500001 rmac 4000.3745.0001
dspu pool lupool host ciscohost lu 2 21
dspu pu ciscopu-a xid-rcv 05D00001 rmac 1000.5AED.0001
dspu lu 1 3 pool lupool
dspu pu ciscopu-b xid-rcv 05D00002 rmac 1000.5AED.0002
dspu lu 1 3 pool lupool
dspu pu ciscopu-c xid-rcv 05D00003 rmac 1000.5AED.0003
dspu lu 1 3 pool lupool
```

Upstream Host via RSRB DSPU Configuration Example

The following configuration example represents one possible definition for the network topology shown earlier in Figure 15–1. This example demonstrates the configuration of an upstream host via RSRB (with local acknowledgment) and downstream PUs via Token Ring.

```
source-bridge ring-group 99
source-bridge remote-peer 99 tcp 150.10.13.1
source-bridge remote-peer 99 tcp 150.10.13.2 local-ack

dspu rsrb 88 1 99 4000.ffff.0001
dspu rsrb enable-host lsap 4

dspu host ciscohost xid-snd 06500001 rmac 4000.3172.0001 rsap 4 lsap 4
dspu pool ciscopool host ciscohost lu 2 8
dspu rsrb start ciscohost

dspu pu ciscopu1 xid-rcv 05d00001
dspu lu 2 3 pool ciscopool

dspu pu ciscopu2 xid-rcv 05d00002
dspu lu 2 4 pool ciscopool
```

```
dspu pu ciscopu3 xid-rcv 05d00003
dspu lu 2 2 pool ciscopool

dspu pu ciscopu4 xid-rcv 05d00004
dspu lu 2 2 pool ciscopool
dspu lu 3 3 host ciscohost 9

interface tokenring 0
 description tokenring connection for downstream PUs
 ring-speed 16
 dspu enable-pu lsap 8
```

DSPU over DLSw+ Using Virtual Data-Link Control Configuration Example

This configuration example illustrates pooled LU routing over DLSw+ using virtual data-link control.

```
source-bridge ring-group 99
dlsw local-peer peer-id 150.10.16.2
dlsw remote-peer 0 tcp 150.10.16.1
!
dspu vdlc 99 4000.4500.01f0
dspu vdlc enable-pu lsap 8
dspu vdlc enable-host lsap 12
!
dspu host HOST-B xid-snd 065bbbb0 rmac 4000.7000.01f1 rsap 4 lsap 12 focalpoint
dspu pool pool-b host HOST-B lu 2 254
!
dspu pu PU3K-A xid-rcv 05d0000a rmac 4000.3000.0100 rsap 10 lsap 8
dspu lu 2 254 pool pool-b
!
dspu default-pu
dspu lu 2 5 pool pool3k-a
!
dspu vdlc start HOST-B
dspu vdlc start PU3K-A
!
interface serial 3
 description IP connection to dspu7k
 ip address 150.10.16.2 255.255.255.0
 clockrate 4000000
```

Downstream PU via SDLC DSPU Configuration Example

This example demonstrates the configuration of downstream PUs via SDLC and an upstream host via Token Ring.

```
dspu host ciscohost xid-snd 06500001 rmac 4000.3172.0001 rsap 4 lsap 12
dspu pool ciscopool host ciscohost lu 2 11
!
dspu pu pu-sdlc0 sdlc C1 interface serial 0
dspu lu 2 6 pool ciscopool
```

```
!
dspu pu pu-sdlc1 sdlc C1 interface serial 1
dspu lu 2 6 pool ciscopool
!
interface serial 0
 description SDLC connection for pu-sdlc0
 encapsulation sdlc
 sdlc role primary
 sdlc address C1
 dspu enable-pu sdlc C1
 clockrate 56000
!
interface serial 1
 description SDLC connection for pu-sdlc1
 encapsulation sdlc
 sdlc role primary
 sdlc address C1
 dspu enable-pu sdlc C1
 clockrate 56000
!
interface tokenring 0
 description tokenring connection for ciscohost
 ring-speed 16
 dspu enable-host lsap 12
 dspu start ciscohost
```

Upstream Host via SDLC DSPU Configuration Example

This example demonstrates the configuration of an upstream host via SDLC and downstream PUs via Token Ring and Ethernet.

```
dspu host ciscohost xid-snd 06500001 sdlc C1 interface serial 0
dspu pool ciscopool host ciscohost lu 2 11
!
dspu pu pu-token rmac 4000.4444.0001 rsap 4 lsap 8
dspu lu 2 6 pool ciscopool
!
dspu pu pu-ether rmac 0200.2222.0001 rsap 4 lsap 8
dspu lu 2 6 pool ciscopool
!
interface serial 0
 description SDLC connection for ciscohost
 encapsulation sdlc
 sdlc role secondary
 sdlc address C1
 dspu enable-host sdlc C1
 clockrate 56000
!
interface tokenring 0
 description tokenring connection for pu-token
 ring-speed 16
 dspu enable-pu lsap 8
```

```
!
interface ethernet 0
 description Ethernet connection for pu-ether
 dspu enable-pu lsap 8
```

Downstream PU via QLLC/X.25 DSPU Configuration Example

This example demonstrates the configuration of a downstream PU via QLLC/X.25 and upstream host via Ethernet.

```
x25 routing
!
dspu host ciscohost xid-snd 06500001 rmac 0200.2222.0001 rsap 4 lsap 12
dspu pool ciscopool host ciscohost lu 2 11
!
dspu pu pu-qllc x25 320108 qllc 08
dspu lu 2 11 pool ciscopool
!
interface serial 0
 description QLLC connection for pu-qllc
 encapsulation x25
 x25 address 3202
 x25 map qllc 320108
 dspu enable-pu qllc 8
!
interface ethernet 0
 description Ethernet connection for pu-ether
 dspu enable-host lsap 12
 dspu start ciscohost
!
 x25 route ^3202.* alias serial 0
```

Upstream Host via Frame Relay DSPU Configuration Example

This example demonstrates the configuration of an upstream host via Frame Relay and downstream PUs via Token Ring and Ethernet.

```
dspu host ciscohost xid-snd 06500001 dlci 200 rsap 4 lsap 12
dspu pool ciscopool host ciscohost lu 2 11
!
dspu pu pu-token rmac 4000.4444.0001 rsap 4 lsap 8
dspu lu 2 6 pool ciscopool
!
dspu pu pu-ether rmac 0200.2222.0001 rsap 4 lsap 8
dspu lu 2 6 pool ciscopool
!
interface serial 0
 description Frame Relay connection for ciscohost
 encapsulation frame-relay ietf
 frame-relay map llc2 200
 dspu enable-host lsap 12
 dspu start ciscohost
```

```
!
interface tokenring 0
 description tokenring connection for pu-token
 ring-speed 16
 dspu enable-pu lsap 8
!
interface ethernet 0
 description Ethernet connection for pu-ether
 dspu enable-pu lsap 8
```

DSPU NCIA Configuration Example

This configuration example illustrates an NCIA client-server session using DSPU.

```
ncia server 1 10.2.20.4 4000.3745.0001 1000.0000.0001 128
!
dspu ncia 1
dspu ncia enable-pu lsap 8
!
dspu host HOST-9370 xid-snd 11100001 rmac 4000.1060.1000 rsap 4 lsap 4
!
dspu pu CISCOPU-A xid-rcv 01700001
dspu lu 2 6 host HOST-9370 2
!
interface TokenRing 0
 ring-speed 16
 llc2 xid-retry-time 0
 dspu enable-host lsap 4
 dspu start HOST-9370
!
```

SNA Service Point Support Configuration Example

The following is an example of an RSRB configuration that implements SNA Service Point:

```
source-bridge ring-group 99
source-bridge remote-peer 99 tcp 150.10.13.2 local-ack
!
sna rsrb 88 1 99 4000.ffff.0001
!
sna host CNM02 xid-snd 05dbc000 rmac 4001.3745.1088 rsap 4 lsap 4 focalpoint
sna rsrb enable-host lsap 4
sna rsrb start CNM02
!
```

SNA Service Point over DLSw+ Using Virtual Data-Link Control Configuration Example

The following is an example of an SNA Service Point configuration that uses virtual data-link control over DLSw+:

```
source-bridge ring-group 99
dlsw local-peer peer-id 150.10.16.2
dlsw remote-peer 0 tcp 150.10.16.1
```

```
!
sna vdlc 99 4000.4500.01f0
sna vdlc enable-host lsap 12
!
sna host HOST-B xid-snd 065bbbb0 rmac 4000.7000.01f1 rsap 4 lsap 12 focalpoint
!
sna vdlc start HOST-B
!
interface serial 3
 description IP connection to dspu7k
 ip address 150.10.16.2 255.255.255.0
 clockrate 4000000
```

CHAPTER 16

DSPU and SNA Service Point Configuration Commands

This chapter describes the commands you use to configure the downstream physical unit (DSPU) feature, which provides a gateway facility for downstream Systems Network Architecture (SNA) physical units (PUs) and SNA Service Point support. For DSPU and SNA Service Point configuration tasks and examples, see Chapter 15, "Configuring DSPU and SNA Service Point Support."

DSPU ACTIVATION-WINDOW

Use the **dspu activation-window** global configuration command to define the number of activation request units (RUs) and response messages (such as ACTLUs or DDDLU NMVTs) that can be sent without waiting for responses from the remote PU. Use the **no** form of this command to return to the default window size.

    dspu activation-window *window-size*
    no dspu activation-window

Syntax	Description
window-size	Number of outstanding unacknowledged activation RUs. The default is 5.

Default

The default window size is 5 outstanding unacknowledged activation RUs.

Command Mode

Global configuration

Usage Guidelines

This command first appeared in Cisco IOS Release 10.3.

You do not typically need to define the number of activation RUs, but doing so can enhance activation performance in some situations. Increasing the DSPU activation window allows more LUs to become active in a shorter amount of time (assuming the required buffers for activation RUs are available). Conversely, decreasing the DSPU activation window limits the amount of buffers the DSPU can use during PU/LU activation. This command provides pacing to avoid depleting the buffer pool during PU activation.

Example

In the following example, the DSPU activation window is configured to 10. The DSPU can send up to 10 activation RUs without a response from the remote PU. However, the DSPU cannot send any additional activation RUs until a response is received. The DSPU can have only 10 activation RUs awaiting response at any given time.

```
dspu activation-window 10
```

DSPU DEFAULT-PU

Use the **dspu default-pu** global configuration command to enable the default PU feature to be used when a downstream PU attempts to connect, but does not match any of the explicit PU definitions. Use the **no** form of this command to disable the default PU feature.

> **dspu default-pu** [**window** *window-size*] [**maxiframe** *max-iframe*]
> **no dspu default-pu** [**window** *window-size*] [**maxiframe** *max-iframe*]

Syntax	Description
window *window-size*	(Optional) Send and receive window sizes used across the link. The range is 1 to 127. The default is 7.
maxiframe *max-iframe*	(Optional) Maximum size (in bytes) of an I-frame that can be transmitted or received across the link. The range is 64 bytes to 18,432 bytes. The default is 1472.

Defaults

The default window size is 7.
The default maximum I-frame size is 1472.

Command Mode

Global configuration

Usage Guidelines

This command first appeared in Cisco IOS Release 10.3.

If the DSPU default PU is not defined, a connection attempt by a downstream PU that does not match any explicit PU definition is rejected.

The **dspu default-pu** command must be followed by at least one **dspu lu** command to define from which pool the default LUs will be assigned. Note that default LUs cannot be defined as dedicated LUs from a host.

The maximum I-frame size includes the SNA transmission header (TH), request header (RH), and request unit (RU), but does not include the DLC header. The DSPU feature segments frames being transmitted to fit within this frame size. If an XID is received from a remote PU which indicates that it supports a different maximum I-frame size, then the smaller of the two values is used.

Example

In the following example, the default PU feature is enabled with a window size of 5 and a maximum I-frame size of 128. Each default PU can have up to 3 LUs assigned from the *hostpool* pool of LUs.

```
dspu pool hostpool host ibm3745 lu 2 254
dspu default-pu window 5 maxiframe 128
dspu lu 2 4 pool hostpool
```

Related Commands

dspu lu
dspu pool

DSPU ENABLE-HOST (ETHERNET, FRAME RELAY, TOKEN RING, FDDI)

Use the **dspu enable-host** interface configuration command to enable a local SAP on Token Ring, Ethernet, FDDI, or Frame Relay interfaces for use by upstream hosts. Use the **no** form of this command to cancel the definition.

dspu enable-host [**lsap** *local-sap*]
no dspu enable-host [**lsap** *local-sap*]

Syntax	Description
lsap	(Optional) Specifies that the local SAP will be activated as an upstream SAP for both receiving incoming connection attempts and for starting outgoing connection attempts.
local-sap	(Optional) Local SAP address. The default is 12.

Default

The default local SAP address is 12.

Command Mode

Interface configuration

Usage Guidelines

This command first appeared in Cisco IOS Release 10.3.

Example

In the following example, the local SAP address 10 on Token Ring interface 0 is enabled for use by upstream host connections:

```
interface tokenring 0
 dspu enable-host lsap 10
```

Related Commands

dspu host (Frame Relay)
dspu host (Token Ring, Ethernet, FDDI, RSRB, VDLC)

DSPU ENABLE-HOST (QLLC)

Use the **dspu enable-host** interface configuration command to enable an X.121 subaddress for use by upstream host connections via QLLC. Use the **no** form of this command to disable the X.121 subaddress.

> **dspu enable-host** qllc *x121-subaddress*
> **no dspu enable-host** qllc *x121-subaddress*

Syntax	Description
qllc	Required keyword for QLLC data-link control.
x121-subaddress	X.121 subaddress.

Default

No default X.121 subaddress is specified.

Command Mode

Interface configuration

Usage Guidelines

This command first appeared in Cisco IOS Release 11.0.

Example

In the following example, X.121 subaddress 320108 is enabled for use by upstream host connections:

```
interface serial 0
 encapsulation x35
 x25 address 3202
 x25 map qllc 320112
 dspu enable-host qllc 320108
```

Related Commands

dspu host (QLLC)
x25 map qllc

DSPU ENABLE-HOST (**SDLC**)

Use the **dspu enable-host** interface configuration command to enable an SDLC address for use by upstream host connections. Use the **no** form of this command to cancel the definition.

> **dspu enable-host sdlc** *sdlc-address*
> **no dspu enable-host sdlc** *sdlc-address*

Syntax	Description
sdlc	Required keyword for SDLC data-link control.
sdlc-address	SDLC address.

Default

No default SDLC address is specified.

Command Mode

Interface configuration

Usage Guidelines

This command first appeared in Cisco IOS Release 11.0.

Example

In the following example, SDLC address C1 is enabled for use by upstream host connections:

```
interface serial 0
 encapsulation sdlc
 sdlc role secondary
 sdlc address c1
 dspu enable-host sdlc c1
```

Related Commands

dspu host (SDLC)
sdlc address
sdlc role

DSPU ENABLE-PU (ETHERNET, FRAME RELAY, TOKEN RING, FDDI)

Use the **dspu enable-pu** interface configuration command to enable an Ethernet, Frame Relay, Token Ring, or FDDI address for use by downstream PU connections. Use the **no** form of this command to disable the connection.

> **dspu enable-pu** [**lsap** *local-sap*]
> **no dspu enable-pu** [**lsap** *local-sap*]

Syntax	Description
lsap *local-sap*	(Optional) Local SAP address used by the DSPU to establish connection with the remote host. The default local SAP address is 8.

Default

The default local SAP address is 8.

Command Mode

Interface configuration

Usage Guidelines

This command first appeared in Cisco IOS Release 10.3.

Example

The following example demonstrates the configuration of a downstream PU via Token Ring and Ethernet:

```
interface tokenring 0
 ring-speed 16
 dspu enable-pu lsap 8

interface ethernet 0
 dspu enable-pu lsap 8
```

Related Commands

dspu pu (Frame Relay)
dspu pu (Token Ring, Ethernet, FDDI, RSRB, VDLC, NCIA)

DSPU ENABLE-PU (QLLC)

Use the **dspu enable-pu** interface configuration command to enable an X.121 subaddress for use by downstream PU connections via QLLC. Use the **no** form of this command to cancel the definition.

> **dspu enable-pu qllc** *x121-subaddress*
> **no dspu enable-pu qllc** *x121-subaddress*

Syntax	Description
qllc	Required keyword for QLLC data-link control.
x121-subaddress	Variable-length X.121 address. It is assigned by the X.25 network service provider.

Default

No default address is assigned.

Command Mode

Interface configuration

Usage Guidelines

This command first appeared in Cisco IOS Release 11.0.

Example

The following command enables an X.121 subaddress for use by downstream PU connections:

```
interface serial 0
  encapsulation x25
  x25 address 3201
  x25 map qllc 320208
  dspu enable-pu qllc 08
```

Related Commands

dspu pu (QLLC)
x25 map qllc

DSPU ENABLE-PU (SDLC)

Use the **dspu enable-pu** interface configuration command to enable an SDLC address for use by downstream PU connections. Use the **no** form of this command to disable the connection.

dspu enable-pu sdlc *sdlc-address*
no dspu enable-pu sdlc *sdlc-address*

Syntax	Description
sdlc	Required keyword for SDLC data-link control.
sdlc-address	SDLC address.

Default

No default address is specified.

Command Mode

Interface configuration

Usage Guidelines

This command first appeared in Cisco IOS Release 11.0.

Example

The following command enables a DSPU downstream connection:

```
interface serial 0
 encapsulation x25
 sdlc role primary
 sdlc address c1
 dspu enable-pu sdlc c1
```

Related Commands

dspu pu (SDLC)
sdlc address
sdlc role

DSPU HOST (FRAME RELAY)

Use the **dspu host** global configuration command to define a DSPU host over a Frame Relay connection. Use the **no** form of this command to cancel the definition.

> **dspu host** *host-name* **xid-snd** *xid* **dlci** *dlci-number* [**rsap** *remote-sap*] [**lsap** *local-sap*]
>   [**interface** *slot/port*] [**window** *window-size*] [**maxiframe** *max-iframe*] [**retries**
>   *retry-count*] [**retry-timeout** *retry-timeout*] [**focalpoint**]
> **no dspu host** *host-name* **xid-snd** *xid* **dlci** *dlci-number* [**rsap** *remote-sap*] [**lsap** *local-sap*]
>   [**interface** *slot/port*] [**window** *window-size*] [**maxiframe** *max-iframe*] [**retries**
>   *retry-count*] [**retry-timeout** *retry-timeout*] [**focalpoint**]

Syntax	Description
host-name	The specified DSPU host.
xid-snd *xid*	XID that will be sent to the host during connection establishment. The XID value is 8 hexadecimal digits that include both block and ID numbers. For example, if the XID value is 05D00001, the block number is 05D and the ID number is 00001.
dlci *dlci-number*	Frame Relay data-link connection identifier (DLCI) number; a decimal number.
rsap *rsap-addr*	(Optional) Remote service access point (SAP) address.
lsap *lsap-addr*	(Optional) Local SAP address.

Syntax	Description
interface *slot/port*	(Optional) Slot and port number of the interface.
window *window-size*	(Optional) Send and receive window sizes used for the host link. The range is 1 to 127.
maxiframe *max-iframe*	(Optional) Send and receive maximum I-frame sizes used for the host link. The range is 64 to 18432. The default is 1472.
retries *retry-count*	(Optional) Number of times the DSPU attempts to retry establishing connection with remote host PU. The range is 0 to 255 (0 = no retry attempts, 255 = infinite retry attempts). The default is 255.
retry-timeout *retry-timeout*	(Optional) Delay (in seconds) between DSPU attempts to retry establishing connection with remote host PU. The range is 1 to 600 seconds. The default is 30 seconds.
focalpoint	(Optional) Specifies that the host link will be used for the focal point support.

Default

The default remote SAP is 4.
The default local SAP is 12.
The default window size is 7.
The default maximum I-frame is 1472.
The default retry count is 255.
The default retry timeout is 30 seconds.

Command Mode

Global configuration

Usage Guidelines

This command first appeared in Cisco IOS Release 10.3.

The local SAP address must be enabled by a **dspu enable-host (Ethernet, Frame Relay, Token Ring, FDDI)** command.

If an XID is received from a remote PU that indicates it supports a different maximum I-frame size, then the smaller of the two values is used.

Alerts from downstream PUs will be forwarded to the focalpoint host. The **focalpoint** parameter must be included in no more than one **dspu host** command.

Example

The following command defines a DSPU host for Frame Relay support:

```
dspu host rosebud xid-snd 06500001 dlci 200 rsap 4 lsap 12
```

Related Commands

dspu enable-host (Ethernet, Frame Relay, Token Ring, FDDI)
dspu pool

DSPU HOST (QLLC)

Use the **dspu host** global configuration command to define a DSPU host over an X.25/QLLC connection. Use the **no** form of this command to delete the DSPU host definition.

> **dspu host** *host-name* **xid-snd** *xid* **x25** *remote-x121-addr* [**qllc** *local-x121-subaddr*]
> [**interface** *slot/port*] [**window** *window-size*] [**maxiframe** *max-iframe*] [**retries**
> *retry-count*] [**retry-timeout** *retry-timeout*] [**focalpoint**]
> **no dspu host** *host-name* **xid-snd** *xid* **x25** *remote-x121-addr* [**qllc** *local-x121-subaddr*]
> [**interface** *slot/port*] [**window** *window-size*] [**maxiframe** *max-iframe*] [**retries**
> *retry-count*] [**retry-timeout** *retry-timeout*] [**focalpoint**]

Syntax	Description
host-name	The specified DSPU host.
xid-snd *xid*	XID that will be sent to the host during connection establishment. The *xid* value is 8 hexadecimal digits that include both block and ID numbers. For example, if the *xid* value is 05D00001, the Block number is 05D and the ID number is 00001.
x25 *remote-x121-addr*	Remote X.121 address.
qllc *local-x121-subaddr*	(Optional) Local X.121 subaddress.
interface *slot/port*	(Optional) Slot and port number of the interface.
window *window-size*	(Optional) Send and receive window sizes used for the host link. The range is 1 to 127. The default is 7.
maxiframe *max-iframe*	(Optional) Send and receive maximum I-frame sizes used for the host link. The range is 64 to 18432. The default is 1472.
retries *retry-count*	(Optional) Number of times the DSPU attempts to retry establishing connection with remote host PU. The range is 0 to 255 (0 = no retry attempts, 255 = infinite retry attempts). The default is 255.
retry-timeout *retry-timeout*	(Optional) Delay (in seconds) between DSPU attempts to retry establishing connection with remote host PU. The range is 1 to 600 seconds. The default is 30 seconds.
focalpoint	(Optional) Specifies that the host link will be used for the focal point support.

Default

The default window size is 7.
The default maximum I-frame is 1472.
The default retry count is 255.
The default retry timeout is 30 seconds.

Command Mode

Global configuration

Usage Guidelines

This command first appeared in Cisco IOS Release 11.0.

The X.121 subaddress must be enabled by a **dspu enable-host (QLLC)** command.

If an XID is received from a remote PU that indicates it supports a different maximum I-frame size, then the smaller of the two values is used.

Alerts from downstream PUs will be forwarded to the focalpoint host. The **focalpoint** parameter must be included in no more than one **dspu host** command.

Example

The following command defines a DSPU host:

```
dspu host hosta xid-snd 065ffff0 x25 00000123005 qllc 12
```

Related Commands

dspu enable-host (QLLC)
dspu pool
dspu start

DSPU HOST (SDLC)

Use the **dspu host** global configuration command to define a DSPU host over an SDLC connection. Use the **no** form of this command to cancel the definition.

> **dspu host** *host-name* **xid-snd** *xid* **sdlc** *sdlc-addr* [**interface** *slot/port*] [**window** *window-size*] [**maxiframe** *max-iframe*] [**retries** *retry-count*] [**retry-timeout** *retry-timeout*] [**focalpoint**]
>
> **no dspu host** *host-name* **xid-snd** *xid* **sdlc** *sdlc-addr* [**interface** *slot/port*] [**window** *window-size*] [**maxiframe** *max-iframe*] [**retries** *retry-count*] [**retry-timeout** *retry-timeout*] [**focalpoint**]

Syntax	Description
host-name	The specified DSPU host.
xid-snd *xid*	XID that will be sent to the host during connection establishment. The XID value is 8 hexadecimal digits that include both Block and ID numbers. For example, if the XID value is 05D00001, the Block number is 05D and the ID number is 00001.
sdlc *sdlc-addr*	SDLC hexadecimal address.
interface *slot/port*	(Optional) Slot and port number of the interface.
window *window-size*	(Optional) Send and receive window sizes used for the host link. The range is 1 to 127. The default window size is 7.
maxiframe *max-iframe*	(Optional) Send and receive maximum I-frame sizes used for the host link. The range is 64 to 18432. The default is 1472.
retries *retry-count*	(Optional) Number of times the DSPU attempts to retry establishing connection with remote host PU. The range is 0 to 255 (0 = no retry attempts, 255 = infinite retry attempts). The default is 255.
retry-timeout *retry-timeout*	(Optional) Delay (in seconds) between DSPU attempts to retry establishing connection with remote host PU. The range is 1 to 600 seconds. The default is 30 seconds.
focalpoint	(Optional) Specifies that the host link will be used for the focal point support.

Defaults

The default window size is 7.
The default maximum I-frame is 1472.
The default number of retries is 255.
The default retry timeout is 30 seconds.

Command Mode

Global configuration

Usage Guidelines

This command first appeared in Cisco IOS Release 11.0.

The SDLC address must be enabled by a **dspu enable-host (SDLC)** command.

If an XID is received from a remote PU that indicates it supports a different maximum I-frame size, then the smaller of the two values is used.

Alerts from downstream PUs will be forwarded to the focalpoint host. The **focalpoint** parameter must be included in no more than one **dspu host** command.

Example

The following command defines a DSPU host for SDLC:

```
dspu host hosta xid-snd 065ffff0 sdlc c1
```

Related Commands

dspu enable-host (SDLC)
dspu pool

DSPU HOST (TOKEN RING, ETHERNET, FDDI, RSRB, VDLC)

Use the **dspu host** global configuration command to define a DSPU host over Token Ring, Ethernet, FDDI, RSRB, or virtual data-link control (VDLC) connections. Use the **no** form of this command to cancel the definition.

dspu host *host-name* **xid-snd** *xid* **rmac** *remote-mac* [**rsap** *remote-sap*] [**lsap** *local-sap*]
  [**interface** *slot/port*] [**window** *window-size*] [**maxiframe** *max-iframe*] [**retries**
  retry-count] [**retry-timeout** *retry-timeout*] [**focalpoint**]
no dspu host *host-name* **xid-snd** *xid* **rmac** *remote-mac* [**rsap** *remote-sap*] [**lsap** *local-sap*]
  [**interface** *slot/port*] [**window** *window-size*] [**maxiframe** *max-iframe*] [**retries**
  retry-count] [**retry-timeout** *retry-timeout*] [**focalpoint**]

Syntax	Description
host-name	The specified DSPU host.
xid-snd *xid*	XID that will be sent to the host during connection establishment. The XID value is 8 hexadecimal digits that include both Block and ID numbers. For example, if the XID value is 05D00001, the Block number is 05D and the ID number is 00001.
rmac *remote-mac*	MAC address of the remote host PU.
rsap *remote-sap*	(Optional) SAP address of the remote host PU. The default is 4.
lsap *local-sap*	(Optional) Local SAP address used by the DSPU to establish connection with the remote host. The default is 12.
interface *slot/port*	(Optional) Slot and port number of the interface.
window *window-size*	(Optional) Send and receive window sizes used for the host link. The range is 1 to 127. The default is 7.
maxiframe *max-iframe*	(Optional) Send and receive maximum I-frame sizes used for the host link. The range is 64 to 18432. The default is 1472.
retries *retry-count*	(Optional) Number of times the DSPU attempts to retry establishing connection with remote host PU. The range is 0 to 255 (0 = no retry attempts, 255 = infinite retry attempts). The default is 255.

Syntax	Description
retry-timeout *retry-timeout*	(Optional) Delay (in seconds) between DSPU attempts to retry establishing connection with remote host PU. The range is 1 to 600 seconds. The default is 30 seconds.
focalpoint	(Optional) Specifies that the host link will be used for the focalpoint support.

Defaults

The default remote SAP address is 4.
The default local SAP address is 12.
The default window size is 7.
The default maximum I-frame is 1472.
The default number of retries is 255.
The default retry timeout is 30 seconds.

Command Mode

Global configuration

Usage Guidelines

This command first appeared in Cisco IOS Release 11.0.

The local SAP address must be enabled by one of the following commands: **dspu enable-host** (**Ethernet, Frame Relay, Token Ring, FDDI**), **dspu rsrb enable-host**, or **dspu vdlc enable-host**.

If an XID is received from a remote PU that indicates it supports a different maximum I-frame size, then the smaller of the two values is used.

Alerts from downstream PUs will be forwarded to the focalpoint host. The **focalpoint** parameter must be included in no more than one **dspu host** command.

Example

The following example shows the definition for a DSPU host with 252 LUs and a connection to be established across an RSRB link:

```
dspu rsrb 88 1 99 4000.ffff.0001
dspu rsrb enable-host lsap 10
dspu host ibm3745 xid 06500001 rmac 4000.3745.0001 lsap 10
dspu pool hostpool lu 2 253 host ibm3745
```

Related Commands

dspu enable-host (Ethernet, Frame Relay, Token Ring, FDDI)
dspu pool
dspu rsrb enable-host

dspu rsrb start
dspu start
dspu vdlc enable-host

DSPU LU

Use the **dspu lu** global configuration command to define a dedicated LU or a range of LUs for an upstream host and a downstream PU. Use the **no** form of this command to cancel the definition.

> **dspu lu** *lu-start* [*lu-end*] {**host** *host-name host-lu-start* | **pool** *pool-name*} [**pu** *pu-name*]
>
> **no dspu lu** *lu-start* [*lu-end*] {**host** *host-name host-lu-start* | **pool** *pool-name*} [**pu** *pu-name*]

Syntax	Description
lu-start	Starting LU address in the range of LUs to be assigned from a pool or dedicated to a host.
lu-end	(Optional) Ending LU address in the range of LUs to be assigned from a pool or dedicated to a host.
host *host-name host-lu-start*	Specifies that each LU in the range of LUs will be dedicated to a host LU *host-name*. The range of host LUs starts with the address *host-lu-start*.
pool *pool-name*	Specifies that each LU in the range of LUs will be assigned from the specified pool.
pu *pu-name*	(Optional) Downstream PU for which this range of LUs is being defined.

Default

There are no default specifications.

Command Mode

Global configuration

Usage Guidelines

This command first appeared in Cisco IOS Release 10.3.

If the **dspu lu** command immediately follows one of these commands:

dspu default-pu
dspu pu (Frame Relay)
dspu pu (QLLC)
dspu pu (SDLC)
dspu pu (Token Ring, Ethernet, FDDI, RSRB, VDLC, NCIA)

The **dspu lu** command is applied to that PU, and the **pu** keyword and *pu-name* are not required. If the keyword and argument are included, the LU defined by the **dspu lu** command will be applied to the named PU.

The pool and host parameters are mutually exclusive. You can define a range of LUs to be either assigned from a pool or dedicated to a host.

Example

The following example defines downstream LUs as dedicated LUs. The downstream PU, ciscopu, has three downstream LUs with addresses 2, 3, and 4. When ciscopu establishes a connection with the DSPU, the three downstream LUs (2, 3, and 4) are dedicated to LUs 22, 23, and 24, respectively, from the IBM 3745 host.

```
dspu host ibm3745 xid-snd 065000001 rmac 4000.3745.0001
dspu pu ciscopu xid-rcv 05D00001 rmac 1000.5AED.1F53
dspu lu 2 4 host ibm3745 22
```

Related Commands

dspu default-pu
dspu host (Frame Relay)
dspu host (QLLC)
dspu host (SDLC)
dspu host (Token Ring, Ethernet, FDDI, RSRB, VDLC)
dspu pool
dspu pu (Frame Relay)
dspu pu (QLLC)
dspu pu (SDLC)
dspu pu (Token Ring, Ethernet, FDDI, RSRB, VDLC, NCIA)

DSPU NCIA

Use the **dspu ncia** global configuration command to configure the NCIA server as the underlying transport. Use the **no** form of this command to cancel the definition.

> **dspu ncia** [*server-number*]
> **no dspu ncia** [*server-number*]

Syntax	Description
server-number	(Optional) Server number configured in the **ncia server** command. Currently, only one NCIA server is supported.

Default

There are no default settings.

Command Mode

Global configuration

Usage Guidelines

This command first appeared in Cisco IOS Release 11.2.

You must use the **ncia server** command to configure an NCIA server on the router before using the **dspu ncia** command to configure the NCIA server as the underlying transport.

Example

The following example configures the NCIA server as the underlying transport mechanism communicating directly with DSPU.

```
dspu ncia 1
```

Related Commands

dspu ncia enable-pu
ncia server

DSPU NCIA ENABLE-PU

Use the **dspu ncia enable-pu** global configuration command to enable a SAP on the NCIA server for use by downstream connections. Use the **no** form of this command to disable the SAP.

dspu ncia enable-pu [lsap *local-sap*]
no dspu ncia enable-pu [lsap *local-sap*]

Syntax	Description
lsap *local-sap*	(Optional) Specifies that the local SAP address will be activated as an upstream SAP for receiving incoming connection attempts. The default is 8.

Default

The default local SAP is 8.

Command Mode

Global configuration

Usage Guidelines

This command first appeared in Cisco IOS Release 11.2.

Example

In the following example, the local SAP address 8 is enabled for use by the downstream PU CISCOPU-A:

```
dspu ncia 1
dspu ncia enable-pu lsap 8
!
dspu host HOST-9370 xid-snd 11100001 rmac 4000.1060.1000 rsap 4 lsap 4
!
dspu pu CISCOPU-A xid-rcv 01700001
dspu lu 2 6 host HOST-9370 2
!
interface TokenRing 0
 ring-speed 16
 llc2 xid-retry-time 0
 dspu enable-host lsap 4
 dspu start HOST-9370
```

Related Commands

dspu ncia
dspu pu (Token Ring, Ethernet, FDDI, RSRB, VDLC, NCIA)

DSPU NOTIFICATION-LEVEL

Use the **dspu notification-level** global configuration command to specify the DSPU notifications to send to SNMP and SNA network management. Use the **no** form of this command to specify the default notification level, **low**.

> **dspu notification-level** {**off** | **low** | **medium** | **high**}
> **no dspu notification-level**

Syntax	Description
off	Sends neither SNMP traps nor unsolicited SNA messages for DSPU.
low	Sends PU and LU activation failures only.
medium	Sends PU state changes and PU and LU activation failures.
high	Sends both PU and LU state changes and activation failures.

Default

The default notification level is **low**.

Command Mode

Global configuration

Usage Guidelines

This command first appeared in Cisco IOS Release 11.1.

This command applies to both SNMP traps and unsolicited SNA messages to operator. Note that the upstream PU and LU notification events and the LU state change notification events are not sent as unsolicited SNA messages to operator. These events are sent as SNMP traps only.

Example

The following command sets the notification level to enable DSPU to send notifications to network management for both PU and LU state changes and activation failures:

```
dspu notification-level high
```

Related Commands

snmp-server host

DSPU POOL

Use the **dspu pool** global configuration command to define a range of host LUs in an LU pool. Use the **no** form of this command to remove the definition.

> **dspu pool** *pool-name* **host** *host-name* **lu** *lu-start* [*lu-end*] [**inactivity-timeout** *minutes*]
> **no dspu pool** *pool-name* **host** *host-name* **lu** *lu-start* [*lu-end*] [**inactivity-timeout** *minutes*]

Syntax	Description
pool-name	Name identifier of the pool.
host *host-name*	Name of the host that owns the range of host LUs in the pool.
lu *lu-start*	Starting LU address in the range of host LUs in the pool.
lu-end	(Optional) Ending address (inclusive) of the range of host LUs in the pool. If no ending address is specified, only one LU (identified by *lu-start*) will be defined in the pool.
inactivity-timeout *minutes*	(Optional) Interval of inactivity (in minutes) on either the SSCP-LU or LU-LU sessions, which will cause the downstream LU to be disconnected from the upstream LU. The default is disabled.

Default

The **inactivity-timeout** is disabled.

Command Mode

Global configuration

Usage Guidelines

This command first appeared in Cisco IOS Release 10.3.

You can include multiple **dspu pool** commands that specify the same pool name. In this way, an LU pool can include several LU ranges from the one host PU, or it can include LUs from different host PUs. The LUs from host *host-name* starting at *lu-start* and ending with *lu-end*, inclusive, will be included in the pool *pool-name*. For the LUs in this pool, if there is no traffic on either the SSCP-LU or LU-LU sessions for the inactivity-timeout number of minutes, the downstream LU will be disconnected from the upstream LU, and the upstream LU will be allocated to any downstream LU waiting for a session. A value of zero for inactivity minutes means no timeouts. (Note that the nactivity-timeout applies to all LUs in this pool, not just the LUs defined by this **dspu pool** command. The last value configured will be used.)

Examples

The following example defines a pool of host LUs. A pool of 253 host LUs is defined with all LUs supplied from the *ibm3745* host PU:

```
dspu host ibm3745 xid-snd 065000001 rmac 4000.3745.0001
dspu pool hostpool host ibm3745 lu 2 254
```

The following example defines multiple pools and defines a disjoint pool of host LUs. One pool with a total of 205 host LUs and second pool with a total of 48 host LUs are defined with all LUs supplied from the same *ibm3745* host PU. Host LUs with addresses 2 to 201 and 250 to 254 are defined in *hostpool1*. Host LUs with addresses 202 to 249 are defined in *hostpool2*.

```
dspu host ibm3745 xid-snd 065000001 rmac 4000.3745.0001
dspu pool hostpool1 host ibm3745 lu 2 201
dspu pool hostpool2 host ibm3745 lu 202 249
dspu pool hostpool1 host ibm3745 lu 250 254
```

The following example defines a pool of LUs from multiple hosts. A pool of 506 host LUs is defined with 253 LUs supplied by the *ibm3745* host PU and 253 supplied by the *ibm3172* hostPU.

```
dspu host ibm3745 xid-snd 065000001 rmac 4000.3745.0001
dspu host ibm3172 xid 06500002 rmac 4000.3172.0001
dspu pool hostpool host ibm3745 lu 2 254
dspu pool hostpool host ibm3172 lu 2 254
```

Related Commands

dspu host (Frame Relay)
dspu host (QLLC)
dspu host (Token Ring, Ethernet, FDDI, RSRB, VDLC)
dspu lu

DSPU PU (FRAME RELAY)

Use the **dspu pu** global configuration command to define a DSPU host over a Frame Relay connection. Use the **no** form of this command to cancel the definition.

dspu pu *pu-name* dlci *dlci-number* [rsap *remote-sap*] [lsap *local-sap*] [xid-rcv *xid*]
[interface *slot/port*] [window *window-size*] [maxiframe *max-iframe*] [retries
retry-count] [retry-timeout *retry-timeout*]
no dspu pu *pu-name* dlci *dlci-number* [rsap *remote-sap*] [lsap *local-sap*] [xid-rcv *xid*]
[interface *slot/port*] [window *window-size*] [maxiframe *max-iframe*] [retries
retry-count] [retry-timeout *retry-timeout*]

Syntax	Description
pu-name	Name of the downstream PU.
dlci *dlci-number*	Frame Relay data-link connection identifier (DLCI) number; a decimal number.
rsap *remote-sap*	(Optional) SAP address of the downstream PU. The default is 4.
lsap *local-sap*	(Optional) Local SAP address used by the DSPU to establish connection with the downstream PU. The default is 8.
xid-rcv *xid*	(Optional) Specifies a match on XID.
interface *slot/port*	(Optional) Slot and port number of the interface.
window *window-size*	(Optional) Send and receive sizes used for the downstream PU link. The range is 1 to 127. The default is 7.
maxiframe *max-iframe*	(Optional) Maximum I-frame that can be transmitted or received across the link. The range is 64 to 18432. The default is 1472.
retries *retry-count*	Number of times the DSPU attempts to retry establishing connection with downstream PU. The range is 0 to 255 (0 = no retry attempts, 255 = infinite retry attempts). The default is 4.
retry-timeout *retry-timeout*	(Optional) Delay (in seconds) between DSPU attempts to retry establishing connection with downstream PU. The range is 1 to 600 seconds. The default is 30 seconds.

Defaults

The default remote SAP is 4.
The default local SAP is 8.
The default window size is 7.
The default maximum I-frame is 1472.
The default retry count is 4.
The default retry timeout is 30 seconds.

Command Mode

Global configuration

Usage Guidelines

This command first appeared in Cisco IOS Release 11.0.

Example

The following example defines a downstream PU:

```
dspu pu pub dlci 8
```

Related Commands

dspu enable-pu (Ethernet, Frame Relay, Token Ring, FDDI)
dspu lu

DSPU PU (QLLC)

Use the **dspu pu** global configuration command to explicitly define a downstream PU over an X.25 connection. Use the **no** form of this command to cancel the definition.

> **dspu pu** *pu-name* **x25** *remote-x121-addr* [**qllc** *local-x121-subaddr*] [**xid-rcv** *xid*]
> [**interface** *slot/port*] [**window** *window-size*] [**maxiframe** *max-iframe*] [**retries**
> *retry-count*] [**retry-timeout** *retry-timeout*]
> **no dspu pu** *pu-name* **x25** *remote-x121-addr* [**qllc** *local-x121-subaddr*] [**xid-rcv** *xid*]
> [**interface** *slot/port*] [**window** *window-size*] [**maxiframe** *max-iframe*] [**retries**
> *retry-count*] [**retry-timeout** *retry-timeout*]

Syntax	Description
pu-name	Name of the downstream PU.
x25 *remote-x121-addr*	Variable-length X.121 address. It is assigned by the X.25 network service provider.
qllc *local-x121-subaddr*	(Optional) Local X.121 subaddress.
xid-rcv *xid*	(Optional) Specifies a match on XID.
interface *slot/port*	(Optional) Slot and port number of the interface.
window *window-size*	(Optional) Send and receive sizes used for the downstream PU link. The range is 1 to 127. The default is 7.
maxiframe *max-iframe*	(Optional) Maximum I-frame that can be transmitted or received across the link. The range is 64 to 18432. The default is 1472.
retries *retry-count*	Number of times the DSPU attempts to retry establishing connection with downstream PU. The range is 0 to 255 (0 = no retry attempts, 255 = infinite retry attempts). The default is 4.
retry-timeout *retry-timeout*	(Optional) Delay (in seconds) between DSPU attempts to retry establishing connection with downstream PU. The range is 1 to 600 seconds. The default is 30 seconds.

Defaults

The default window size is 7.
The default maximum I-frame is 1472.
The default retry count is 4.
The default retry timeout is 30 seconds.

Command Mode

Global configuration

Usage Guidelines

This command first appeared in Cisco IOS Release 11.0.

Part II

Example

The following command defines a downstream PU:

```
dspu pu testpu xid-rcv 05d00001 x25 32012 qllc 12
```

Related Commands

dspu enable-pu (QLLC)
dspu lu

DSPU PU (SDLC)

Use the **dspu pu** global configuration command to define a DSPU host over an SDLC connection.
Use the **no** form of this command to cancel the definition.

> **dspu pu** *pu-name* **sdlc** *sdlc-addr* [**xid-rcv** *xid*] [**interface** *slot/port*] [**window** *window-size*]
> [**maxiframe** *max-iframe*] [**retries** *retry-count*] [**retry-timeout** *retry-timeout*]
> **no dspu pu** *pu-name* **sdlc** *sdlc-addr* [**xid-rcv** *xid*] [**interface** *slot/port*] [**window** *window-size*]
> [**maxiframe** *max-iframe*] [**retries** *retry-count*] [**retry-timeout** *retry-timeout*]

Syntax	Description
pu-name	Name of the downstream PU.
sdlc *sdlc-addr*	SDLC address.
xid-rcv *xid*	(Optional) Specifies a match on XID.
interface *slot/port*	(Optional) Slot and port number of the interface.
window *window-size*	(Optional) Send and receive sizes used for the downstream PU link. The range is 1 to 127. The default is 7.
maxiframe *max-iframe*	(Optional) Maximum I-frame that can be transmitted or received across the link. The range is 64 to 18432. The default is 1472.

Syntax	Description
retries *retry-count*	(Optional) Number of times the DSPU attempts to retry establishing connection with downstream PU. The range is 0 to 255 (0 = no retry attempts, 255 = infinite retry attempts). The default is 4.
retry-timeout *retry-timeout*	(Optional) Delay (in seconds) between DSPU attempts to retry establishing connection with downstream PU. The range is 1 to 600 seconds. The default is 30 seconds.

Defaults

The default window size is 7.
The default maximum I-frame is 1472.
The default retry count is 4.
The default retry timeout is 30 seconds.

Command Mode

Global configuration

Usage Guidelines

This command first appeared in Cisco IOS Release 11.0.

Example

The following command defines a downstream PU:

```
dspu pu testpu sdlc c1 interface serial 0
```

Related Commands

dspu enable-pu (SDLC)
dspu lu

DSPU PU (TOKEN RING, ETHERNET, FDDI, RSRB, VDLC, NCIA)

Use the **dspu pu** global configuration command to define an explicit downstream PU over Token Ring, Ethernet, FDDI, RSRB, virtual data-link control, or NCIA connections. Use the **no** form of this command to cancel the definition.

> **dspu pu** *pu-name* [**rmac** *remote-mac*] [**rsap** *remote-sap*] [**lsap** *local-sap*] [**xid-rcv** *xid*]
> [**interface** *slot/port*] [**window** *window-size*] [**maxiframe** *max-iframe*] [**retries**
> *retry-count*] [**retry-timeout** *retry-timeout*]
> **no dspu pu** *pu-name* [**rmac** *remote-mac*] [**rsap** *remote-sap*] [**lsap** *local-sap*] [**xid-rcv** *xid*]
> [**interface** *slot/port*] [**window** *window-size*] [**maxiframe** *max-iframe*] [**retries**
> *retry-count*] [**retry-timeout** *retry-timeout*]

Syntax	Description
pu-name	Name of the downstream PU.
rmac *remote-mac*	(Optional) MAC address of the downstream PU.
rsap *remote-sap*	(Optional) SAP address of the downstream PU. The default is 4.
lsap *local-sap*	(Optional) Local SAP address used by the DSPU to establish connection with the downstream PU. The default is 8.
xid-rcv *xid*	(Optional) Specifies a match on XID.
interface *slot/port*	(Optional) Slot and port number of the interface.
window *window-size*	(Optional) Send and receive sizes used for the downstream PU link. The range is 1 to 127. The default is 7.
maxiframe *max-iframe*	(Optional) Maximum I-frame that can be transmitted or received across the link. The range is 64 to 18432. The default is 1472.
retries *retry-count*	Number of times the DSPU attempts to retry establishing connection with downstream PU. The range is 0 to 255 (0 = no retry attempts, 255 = infinite retry attempts). The default is 4.
retry-timeout *retry-timeout*	(Optional) Delay (in seconds) between DSPU attempts to retry establishing connection with downstream PU. The range is 1 to 600 seconds. The default is 30 seconds.

Part II

Command Reference

Defaults

The default remote SAP is 4.
The default local SAP is 8.
The default window size is 7.
The default maximum I-frame is 1472.
The default retry count is 4.
The default retry timeout is 30 seconds.

Command Mode

Global configuration

Usage Guidelines

This command first appeared in Cisco IOS Release 10.3.

The local SAP address must be enabled by one of the following commands:

- **dspu enable-pu (Ethernet, Frame Relay, Token Ring, FDDI) lsap**
- **dspu ncia enable-pu lsap**
- **dspu rsrb enable-pu lsap**
- **dspu vdlc enable-pu lsap**

The send and receive maximum I-frame size includes the SNA TH and RH, but does not include the data-link control header. The DSPU feature will segment frames being transmitted to fit within this frame size. If an XID is received from a remote PU that indicates that it supports a different maximum I-frame size, then the smaller of the two values is used.

If you want the DSPU to attempt a ConnectOut to the remote node using the **dspu start** command, you must configure the **rmac** keyword and argument. If you want this PU to match against a ConnectIn attempt, then several combinations of **rmac**, **rsap**, **xid-rcv** are possible. The matching algorithms are as follows:

- **rmac**—Match on remote MAC/SAP address of downstream PU

- **xid-rcv**—Match on XID value received from downstream PU.

- **rmac/rsap, xid-rcv**—Match on remote MAC/SAP address of downstream PU and XID value received from downstream PU.

If an XID is received from a remote PU that indicates that it supports a different maximum I-frame size, then the smaller of the two values is used.

Examples

In the following example, a downstream PU is defined with only the MAC address and SAP address specified. A downstream PU that attempts an incoming connection to the DSPU will only be accepted if the remote MAC/SAP address matches the configured values for this downstream PU (and the proper local SAP address is enabled).

```
dspu pu ciscopu rmac 1000.5AED.1F53 rsap 20
dspu lu 2 5 pool hostpool
interface tokenring 0
dspu enable-pu lsap 8
```

In the following example, a downstream PU is defined with only an **xid-rcv** value. Any downstream PU that attempts an incoming connection specifying the **xid-rcv** value, 05D00001, will be accepted without regard to remote MAC or SAP address (although the proper local SAP address must be enabled).

```
dspu pu ciscopu xid-rcv 05d00001
dspu lu 2 5 pool hostpool
interface tokenring 0
 dspu enable-pu lsap 8
```

In the following example, a downstream PU is defined with **xid-rcv**, **rmac**, and **rsap** keywords. Any downstream PU that attempts to ConnectIn to the DSPU must match all three configured values for the connection to be accepted (the proper local SAP address must also be enabled).

```
dspu pu ciscopu xid-rcv 05d00001 rmac 1000.5AED.1F53 rsap 20
dspu lu 2 5 pool hostpool
interface tokenring 0
 dspu enable-pu lsap 8
```

Related Commands

dspu enable-pu (Ethernet, Frame Relay, Token Ring, FDDI)
dspu lu
dspu ncia enable-pu
dspu rsrb enable-pu
dspu rsrb start
dspu start
dspu vdlc enable-pu

DSPU RSRB

Use the **dspu rsrb** global configuration command to define the local virtual ring, virtual bridge, target virtual ring, and virtual MAC address that the DSPU feature will simulate at the RSRB. Use the **no** form of this command to cancel the definition.

> **dspu rsrb** *local-virtual-ring bridge-number target-virtual-ring virtual-macaddr*
> **no dspu rsrb** *local-virtual-ring bridge-number target-virtual-ring virtual-macaddr*

Syntax	Description
local-virtual-ring	DSPU local virtual ring number.
bridge-number	Bridge number connecting the DSPU local virtual ring and the RSRB target virtual ring. The valid range is 1 to 15.
target-virtual-ring	RSRB target virtual ring number. The RSRB target virtual ring corresponds to the ring-number parameter defined by a **source-bridge ring-group** command.
virtual-macaddr	DSPU virtual MAC address.

Default

There are no default settings.

Command Mode

Global configuration

Usage Guidelines

This command first appeared in Cisco IOS Release 10.3.

The bridge number parameter can be specified only once in a configuration.

Use the **dspu rsrb** command to enable DSPU host and downstream connections to be established across an RSRB link.

If the **local-ack** parameter is specified on the **source-bridge remote-peer** statement, DSPU will establish host connections across RSRB using local acknowledgment. DSPU cannot support local acknowledgment for downstream PU connections across RSRB.

Examples

The following example defines DSPU to start a connection to the host across an RSRB link (without local acknowledgment). The DSPU is identified by its local ring number 88 and its virtual MAC address 4000.FFFF.0001. When the DSPU attempts an outgoing connection to the *ibm3745* host, the connection will be established across the RSRB virtual ring 99.

```
source-bridge ring-group 99
source-bridge remote-peer 99 tcp 150.10.13.1
source-bridge remote-peer 99 tcp 150.10.13.2

dspu rsrb 88 1 99 4000.FFFF.0001
dspu rsrb enable-host lsap 10

dspu host ibm3745 xid-snd 06500001 rmac 4000.3745.0001 lsap 10
dspu rsrb start ibm3745
interface serial 0
 ip address 150.10.13.1 255.255.255.0
```

The following example defines DSPU to start a connection to the host across an RSRB link (with local acknowledgment). The DSPU is identified by its local ring number 88 and its virtual MAC address 4000.FFFF.0001. When the DSPU attempts an outward connection to the *ibm3745* host, the connection will be established across the RSRB virtual ring 99 using RSRB local acknowledgment.

```
source-bridge ring-group 99
source-bridge remote-peer 99 tcp 150.10.13.1
source-bridge remote-peer 99 tcp 150.10.13.2 local-ack

dspu rsrb 88 1 99 4000.FFFF.0001
dspu rsrb enable-host lsap 10

dspu host ibm3745 xid-snd 06500001 rmac 4000.3745.0001 lsap 10
dspu rsrb start ibm3745

interface serial 0
 ip address 150.10.13.1 255.255.255.0
```

The following example defines DSPU to allow a connection from the downstream PU across an RSRB link.The DSPU is identified by its local ring number 88 and its virtual MAC address 4000.FFFF.0001. The downstream PU will specify the DSPU virtual MAC address 4000.FFFF.0001 and SAP address 20 in its host definitions. The DSPU will accept incoming connections from the downstream PU across the RSRB virtual ring 99.

```
source-bridge ring-group 99
source-bridge remote-peer 99 tcp 150.10.13.1
source-bridge remote-peer 99 tcp 150.10.13.2
```

```
dspu rsrb 88 1 99 4000.FFFF.0001
dspu rsrb enable-pu lsap 20

dspu pu ciscopu xid-rcv 05D00001 lsap 20

interface serial 0
 ip address 150.10.13.1 255.255.255.0
```

Related Commands

dspu rsrb enable-host
dspu rsrb enable-pu
dspu rsrb start
source-bridge ring-group
source-bridge remote-peer

DSPU RSRB ENABLE-HOST

Use the **dspu rsrb enable-host** global configuration command to enable an RSRB SAP for use by DSPU host connections. Use the **no** form of this command to disable the RSRB SAP.

> **dspu rsrb enable-host** [**lsap** *local-sap*]
> **no dspu rsrb enable-host** [**lsap** *local-sap*]

Syntax	*Description*
lsap *local-sap*	(Optional) Specifies that the local SAP address will be activated as an upstream SAP for both receiving incoming connection attempts and for starting outgoing connection attempts. The default is 12.

Default

The default local SAP is 12.

Command Mode

Global configuration

Usage Guidelines

This command first appeared in Cisco IOS Release 10.3.

Example

In the following example, the local SAP address 10 of the RSRB is enabled for use by the *ibm3745* host PU:

```
source-bridge ring-group 99
source-bridge remote-peer 99 tcp 150.10.13.1
source-bridge remote-peer 99 tcp 150.10.13.2
```

```
dspu rsrb 88 1 99 4000.FFFF.0001
dspu rsrb enable-host lsap 10

dspu host ibm3745 xid-snd 06500001 rmac 4000.3745.0001 lsap 10

interface serial 0
 ip address 150.10.13.1 255.255.255.0
```

Related Commands

dspu host (Token Ring, Ethernet, FDDI, RSRB, VDLC)
dspu rsrb

DSPU RSRB ENABLE-PU

Use the **dspu rsrb enable-pu** global configuration command to enable an RSRB SAP for use by DSPU downstream connections. Use the **no** form of this command to disable the SAP.

> **dspu rsrb enable-pu** [**lsap** *local-sap*]
> **no dspu rsrb enable-pu** [**lsap** *local-sap*]

Syntax	Description
lsap *local-sap*	(Optional) Specifies that the local SAP address will be activated as an upstream SAP for both receiving incoming connection attempts and for starting outgoing connection attempts.

Default

The default local SAP is 8.

Command Mode

Global configuration

Usage Guidelines

This command first appeared in Cisco IOS Release 10.3.

Example

In the following example, the local SAP address 20 of the RSRB is enabled for use by the *ciscopu* DSPU downstream PU:

```
source-bridge ring-group 99
source-bridge remote-peer 99 tcp 150.10.13.1
source-bridge remote-peer 99 tcp 150.10.13.2

dspu rsrb 88 1 99 4000.FFFF.0001
dspu rsrb enable-pu lsap 20

dspu pu ciscopu xid-rcv 05D00001 lsap 20
```

Related Commands

dspu pu (Token Ring, Ethernet, FDDI, RSRB, VDLC, NCIA)
dspu rsrb

DSPU RSRB START

Use the **dspu rsrb start** global configuration command to specify that an attempt will be made to connect to the remote resource defined by host name or PU name through the RSRB. Use the **no** form of this command to cancel the definition.

> **dspu rsrb start** {*host-name* | *pu-name*}
> **no dspu rsrb start** {*host-name* | *pu-name*}

Syntax	Description
host-name	Name of a host defined in a **dspu host** (Token Ring, Ethernet, FDDI, RSRB, VDLC) command.
pu-name	Name of a PU defined in a **dspu pu** (Token Ring, Ethernet, FDDI, RSRB, VDLC, NCIA) command.

Default

There are no default settings.

Command Mode

Global configuration

Usage Guidelines

This command first appeared in Cisco IOS Release 10.3.

Before issuing this command, you must enable the correct local SAP with the appropriate enable command (**dspu rsrb enable-host** for a host resource, and **dspu rsrb enable-pu** for a PU resource).

This command is only valid if the target MAC address has been defined in the resource. For a host resource, this is not a problem because the MAC address is mandatory. However, for a PU resource, the MAC address is optional. The command will fail if the MAC address is missing.

Example

In the following example, the DSPU will initiate a connection with the *ibm3745* host PU across the RSRB link:

```
source-bridge ring-group 99
source-bridge remote-peer 99 tcp 150.10.13.1
source-bridge remote-peer 99 tcp 150.10.13.2

dspu rsrb 88 1 99 4000.FFFF.0001
dspu rsrb enable-host lsap 10
```

```
dspu host ibm3745 xid-snd 06500001 rmac 4000.3745.0001 lsap 10
dspu rsrb start ibm3745

interface serial 0
 ip address 150.10.13.1 255.255.255.0
```

Related Commands

dspu host (Token Ring, Ethernet, FDDI, RSRB, VDLC)
dspu pu (Token Ring, Ethernet, FDDI, RSRB, VDLC, NCIA)
dspu rsrb
dspu rsrb enable-host
dspu rsrb enable-pu

DSPU START

Use the **dspu start** interface configuration command to specify that an attempt will be made to connect to the remote resource defined by host name or PU name. Use the **no** form of this command to cancel the definition.

> **dspu start** {*host-name* | *pu-name*}
> **no dspu start** {*host-name* | *pu-name*}

Syntax	Description
host-name	Name of a host defined in a **dspu host** command.
pu-name	Name of a PU defined in a **dspu pu** command.

Default

There are no default settings.

Command Mode

Interface configuration

Usage Guidelines

This command first appeared in Cisco IOS Release 10.3.

Before issuing this command, you must enable the correct address using the appropriate **dspu enable-host** or **dspu enable-pu** command.

This command is only valid if the target address (RMAC SDLC, DLCI, or X.25 parameter) has been defined for the resource. For a host resource, this is not a problem because the address specification is mandatory, but for a PU resource, specifying the address is optional. The **dspu start** command will fail if the address is missing.

Example

In the following example, the DSPU will initiate a connection with the *ciscopu* downstream PU on Token Ring interface 0:

```
dspu pu ciscopu xid-rcv 05D00001 rmac 1000.5AED.1F53 lsap 20
interface tokenring 0
 dspu enable-pu lsap 20
 dspu start ciscopu
```

Related Commands

dspu enable-host (Ethernet, Frame Relay, Token Ring, FDDI)
dspu enable-host (QLLC)
dspu enable-host (SDLC)
dspu enable-pu (Ethernet, Frame Relay, Token Ring, FDDI)
dspu enable-pu (SDLC)
dspu enable-pu (QLLC)
dspu host (Frame Relay)
dspu host (QLLC)
dspu host (SDLC)
dspu host (Token Ring, Ethernet, FDDI, RSRB, VDLC)
dspu pu (Frame Relay)
dspu pu (QLLC)
dspu pu (SDLC)
dspu pu (Token Ring, Ethernet, FDDI, RSRB, VDLC, NCIA)

DSPU VDLC

Use the **dspu vdlc** global configuration command to identify the local virtual ring and virtual MAC address that will be used to establish DSPU host and downstream connections over DLSw+ using virtual data-link control. Use the **no** form of this command to cancel the definition.

> **dspu vdlc** *ring-group virtual-mac-address*
> **no dspu vdlc** *ring-group virtual-mac-address*

Syntax	Description
ring-group	Local virtual ring number identifying the SRB ring group.
virtual-mac-address	Virtual MAC address that represents the DSPU virtual data-link control.

Default

There are no default settings.

Command Mode

Global configuration

Usage Guidelines

This command first appeared in Cisco IOS Release 11.2.

The virtual data-link control local virtual ring must have been previously configured using the **source-bridge ring-group** command.

The virtual data-link control virtual MAC address must be unique within the DLSw+ network.

To avoid an address conflict on the virtual MAC address, use a locally administered address in the form 4000.*xxxx.xxxx*.

Example

The following example defines DSPU to start a connection to the host using virtual data-link control. The DSPU virtual data-link control is identified by its virtual MAC address 4000.4500.01f0, existing on the SRB virtual ring 99. When the DSPU attempts an outgoing connection to the host HOST-B, the connection will be established across the virtual ring 99.

```
source-bridge ring-group 99
dlsw local-peer peer-id 150.10.16.2
dlsw remote-peer 0 tcp 150.10.16.1

dspu vdlc 99 4000.4500.01f0
dspu vdlc enable-host lsap 12

dspu host HOST-B xid-snd 065bbbb0 rmac 4000.7000.01f1 rsap 4 lsap 12 focalpoint

dspu vdlc start HOST-B

interface serial 3
 description IP connection to dspu7k
 ip address 150.10.16.2 255.255.255.0
 clockrate 4000000
```

Related Commands

dlsw local-peer
dlsw remote-peer
dspu vdlc enable-host
dspu vdlc enable-pu
dspu vdlc start
source-bridge ring-group

DSPU VDLC ENABLE-HOST

Use the **dspu vdlc enable-host** global configuration command to enable a SAP for use by DSPU host connections. Use the **no** form of this command to disable the SAP.

    dspu vdlc enable-host [**lsap** *local-sap*]
    no dspu vdlc enable-host [**lsap** *local-sap*]

Syntax

lsap *local-sap*

Description

(Optional) Specifies that the local SAP address will be activated as an upstream SAP for both receiving incoming connection attempts and for starting outgoing connection attempts. The default is 12.

Default

The default local SAP is 12.

Command Mode

Global configuration

Usage Guidelines

This command first appeared in Cisco IOS Release 11.2.

Example

In the following example, the local SAP address 12 is enabled for use by the host PU HOST-B:

```
source-bridge ring-group 99
dlsw local-peer peer-id 150.10.16.2
dlsw remote-peer 0 tcp 150.10.16.1

dspu vdlc 99 4000.4500.01f0
dspu vdlc enable-pu lsap 8
dspu vdlc enable-host lsap 12

dspu host HOST-B xid-snd 065bbbb0 rmac 4000.7000.01f1 rsap 4 lsap 12 focalpoint
dspu pool pool-b host HOST-B lu 2 254

dspu host HOST3K-A xid-snd 05d0000a rmac 4000.3000.0100 rsap 8 lsap 12
dspu pool pool3k-a host HOST3K-A lu 2 254

dspu pu PU3K-A xid-rcv 05d0000a rmac 4000.3000.0100 rsap 10 lsap 8
dspu lu 2 254 pool pool-b

dspu default-pu
dspu lu 2 5 pool pool3k-a

dspu vdlc start HOST-B
dspu vdlc start HOST3K-A
dspu vdlc start PU3K-A

interface serial 3
 description IP connection to dspu7k
 ip address 150.10.16.2 255.255.255.0
 clockrate 4000000
```

Related Commands

dspu host (Token Ring, Ethernet, FDDI, RSRB, VDLC)
dspu vdlc

DSPU VDLC ENABLE-PU

Use the **dspu vdlc enable-pu** global configuration command to enable a SAP for use by DSPU virtual data-link control downstream connections. Use the **no** form of this command to disable the SAP.

> **dspu vdlc enable-pu** [**lsap** *local-sap*]
> **no dspu vdlc enable-pu** [**lsap** *local-sap*]

Syntax	*Description*
lsap *local-sap*	(Optional) Specifies that the local SAP address will be activated as an upstream SAP for both receiving incoming connection attempts and for starting outgoing connection attempts. The default is 8.

Default

The default local SAP is 8.

Command Mode

Global configuration

Usage Guidelines

This command first appeared in Cisco IOS Release 11.2.

Example

In the following example, the local SAP address 8 is enabled for use by the downstream PU PU3K-A:

```
source-bridge ring-group 99
dlsw local-peer peer-id 150.10.16.2
dlsw remote-peer 0 tcp 150.10.16.1

dspu vdlc 99 4000.4500.01f0
dspu vdlc enable-pu lsap 8
dspu vdlc enable-host lsap 12

dspu host HOST-B xid-snd 065bbbb0 rmac 4000.7000.01f1 rsap 4 lsap 12 focalpoint
dspu pool pool-b host HOST-B lu 2 254

dspu host HOST3K-A xid-snd 05d0000a rmac 4000.3000.0100 rsap 8 lsap 12
dspu pool pool3k-a host HOST3K-A lu 2 254
```

```
dspu pu PU3K-A xid-rcv 05d0000a rmac 4000.3000.0100 rsap 10 lsap 8
dspu lu 2 254 pool pool-b

dspu default-pu
dspu lu 2 5 pool pool3k-a

dspu vdlc start HOST-B
dspu vdlc start HOST3K-A
dspu vdlc start PU3K-A

interface serial 3
 description IP connection to dspu7k
 ip address 150.10.16.2 255.255.255.0
 clockrate 4000000
```

Related Commands

dspu pu (Token Ring, Ethernet, FDDI, RSRB, VDLC, NCIA)
dspu vdlc

DSPU VDLC START

Use the **dspu vdlc start** global configuration command to specify that an attempt will be made to connect to the remote resource defined by host name or PU name through virtual data-link control. Use the **no** form of this command to cancel the definition.

> **dspu vdlc start** {*host-name* | *pu-name*}
> **no dspu vdlc start** {*host-name* | *pu-name*}

Syntax	Description
host-name	Name of a host defined in a **dspu host** (Token Ring, Ethernet, FDDI, RSRB, VDLC) command.
pu-name	Name of a PU defined in a **dspu pu** (Token Ring, Ethernet, FDDI, RSRB, VDLC, NCIA) command.

Default

There are no default settings.

Command Mode

Global configuration

Usage Guidelines

This command first appeared in Cisco IOS Release 11.2.

Before issuing this command, you must enable the correct local SAP with the appropriate enable command (**dspu vdlc enable-host** for a host resource, and **dspu vdlc enable-pu** for a PU resource).

This command is only valid if the target MAC address has been defined in the resource. For a host resource, this is not a problem because the MAC address is mandatory, but for a PU resource, the MAC address is optional. The command will fail if the MAC address is missing.

Example

In the following example, DSPU attempts to initiate connections with host PU HOST-B, host PU HOST3K-A, and downstream PU PU3K-A over DLSw+ using virtual data-link control:

```
source-bridge ring-group 99
dlsw local-peer peer-id 150.10.16.2
dlsw remote-peer 0 tcp 150.10.16.1

dspu vdlc 99 4000.4500.01f0
dspu vdlc enable-pu lsap 8
dspu vdlc enable-host lsap 12

dspu host HOST-B xid-snd 065bbbb0 rmac 4000.7000.01f1 rsap 4 lsap 12 focalpoint
dspu pool pool-b host HOST-B lu 2 254

dspu host HOST3K-A xid-snd 05d0000a rmac 4000.3000.0100 rsap 8 lsap 12
dspu pool pool3k-a host HOST3K-A lu 2 254

dspu pu PU3K-A xid-rcv 05d0000a rmac 4000.3000.0100 rsap 10 lsap 8
dspu lu 2 254 pool pool-b

dspu default-pu
dspu lu 2 5 pool pool3k-a

dspu vdlc start HOST-B
dspu vdlc start HOST3K-A
dspu vdlc start PU3K-A

interface serial 3
 description IP connection to dspu7k
 ip address 150.10.16.2 255.255.255.0
 clockrate 4000000
```

Related Commands

dspu host (Token Ring, Ethernet, FDDI, RSRB, VDLC)
dspu pu (Token Ring, Ethernet, FDDI, RSRB, VDLC, NCIA)
dspu vdlc
dspu vdlc enable-host
dspu vdlc enable-pu

LAN-NAME

Use the **lan-name** interface configuration command to specify a name for the LAN that is attached to the interface. This name is included in any Alert sent to the SNA host when a problem occurs on this interface or LAN. Use the **no** form of this command to revert to the default name.

> **lan-name** *lan-name*

Syntax	Description
lan-name	Name used to identify the LAN when you send Alerts to the SNA host. The default LAN name is the name of the interface.

Default

The default name used for the LAN is the name of the interface, such as tr0.

Command Mode

Interface configuration

Usage Guidelines

This command first appeared in Cisco IOS Release 11.0.

Example

The following example identifies a LAN:

```
lan-name LAN1
```

Related Commands

show sna

LOCATION

Use the **location** global configuration command to specify the physical location of the router or access server. This information is included in the vital product information when this information is requested from an SNA host. Use the **no** form of this command to remove the physical location information.

> **location** *location-description*

Syntax	Description
location-description	A description of the physical location of the device. This can be up to 50 characters long, and can include blanks.

Default

No default is specified.

Command Mode

Global configuration

Usage Guidelines

This command first appeared in Cisco IOS Release 11.0.

Example

The following example describes the location of a router:

```
location Building G, Level 4, Room 45
```

Related Commands

show sna

SHOW DSPU

Use the **show dspu** privileged EXEC command to display the status of the DSPU feature.

> **show dspu** [**pool** *pool-name* | [**pu** {*host-name* | *pu-name*} [**all**]]

Syntax	Description
pool *pool-name*	(Optional) Name of a pool of LUs (as defined by the **dspu pool** command).
pu	(Optional) Name of defined PU (as defined by either the **dspu pu** or the **dspu host** command).
host-name	Name of a host defined in a **dspu host** command.
pu-name	Name of a PU defined in a **dspu pu** command.
all	(Optional) Shows a detailed status.

Command Mode

Privileged EXEC

Usage Guidelines

This command first appeared in Cisco IOS Release 10.3.

Sample Displays

The following is sample output from the **show dspu** command. It shows a summary of the DSPU status.

```
Router# show dspu

dspu host HOST_NAMEA interface PU STATUS ssssssss
FRAMES RECEIVED nnnnnn FRAMES SENT nnnnnn
LUs USED BY DSPU nnn LUs ACTIVE nnn
LUs USED BY API nnn LUs ACTIVE nnn
LUs ACTIVATED BY HOST BUT NOT USED nnn
dspu host HOST_NAMEB interface PU STATUS ssssssss
FRAMES RECEIVED nnnnnn FRAMES SENT nnnnnn
LUs USED BY DSPU nnn LUs ACTIVE nnn
LUs USED BY API nnn LUs ACTIVE nnn
LUs ACTIVATED BY HOST BUT NOT USED nnn
dspu pu PU_NAMEE interface PU STATUS ssssssss
FRAMES RECEIVED nnnnnn FRAMES SENT nnnnnn
LUs USED BY DSPU nnn LUs ACTIVE nnn
LUs USED BY API nnn LUs ACTIVE nnn
LUs ACTIVATED BY HOST BUT NOT USED nnn
dspu pu PU_NAMEF interface PU STATUS ssssssss
FRAMES RECEIVED nnnnnn FRAMES SENT nnnnnn
LUs USED BY DSPU nnn LUs ACTIVE nnn
LUs USED BY API nnn LUs ACTIVE nnn
LUs ACTIVATED BY HOST BUT NOT USED nnn
```

The following is sample output from the **show dspu** command with the **pu** keyword:

```
Router# show dspu pu putest

dspu pu PUTEST interface PU STATUS ssssssss
RMAC remote_mac RSAP remote_sap LSAP local_sap
XID xid RETRIES retry_count RETRY_TIMEOUT retry_timeout
WINDOW window_size MAXIFRAME max_iframe
FRAMES RECEIVED nnnnnn FRAMES SENT nnnnnn
LUs USED BY DSPU nnn LUs ACTIVE nnn
LUs USED BY API nnn LUs ACTIVE nnn
LUs ACTIVATED BY HOST BUT NOT USED nnn
```

The following is sample output from the **show dspu** command with the **all** keyword:

```
Router# show dspu pu putest all

dspu pu PUTEST interface PU STATUS ssssssss
RMAC remote_mac RSAP remote_sap LSAP local_sap
XID xid RETRIES retry_count RETRY_TIMEOUT retry_timeout
WINDOW window_size MAXIFRAME max_iframe
FRAMES RECEIVED nnnnnn FRAMES SENT nnnnnn
LU nnn PEER PU HOST_NAMEA PEER LU nnn STATUS tttttttt
     FRAMES RECEIVED nnnnnn FRAMES SENT nnnnnn
LU nnn PEER PU HOST_NAMEA PEER LU nnn STATUS tttttttt
     FRAMES RECEIVED nnnnnn, FRAMES SENT nnnnnn
LU nnn PEER PU HOST_NAMEB PEER LU nnn STATUS tttttttt
     FRAMES RECEIVED nnnnnn, FRAMES SENT nnnnnn
```

The following shows a summary of the LUs in a pool:

```
Router# show dspu pool poolname

dspu pool poolname host HOST_NAMEA lu start-lu end-lu
```

The following shows the details of all the LUs in a pool:

```
Router# show dspu pool poolname all

dspu pool poolname host HOST_NAMEA lu start-lu end-lu
DSPU POOL poolname INACTIVITY_TIMEOUT timeout-value
lu nnn host HOST_NAMEA peer lu nnn pu PU_NAMEF status tttttttt
lu nnn host HOST_NAMEA peer lu nnn pu PU_NAMEF status tttttttt
lu nnn host HOST_NAMEA peer lu nnn pu PU_NAMEF status tttttttt
```

SHOW SNA

Use the **show sna** privileged EXEC command to display the status of the SNA Service Point feature.

show sna [**pu** *host-name* [**all**]]

Syntax	Description
pu	(Optional) The name of defined PU.
host-name	The name of a host defined in an **sna host** command.
all	(Optional) Shows a detailed status.

Command Mode

Privileged EXEC

Usage Guidelines

This command first appeared in Cisco IOS Release 11.0.

Sample Displays

The following is sample output from the **show sna** command. It shows a summary of the SNA features status.

```
Router# show sna

sna host HOST_NAMEA TokenRing1 PU STATUS active
FRAMES RECEIVED 00450 FRAMES SENT 00010
LUs USED BY DSPU nnn LUs ACTIVE nnn
LUs USED BY API nnn LUs ACTIVE nnn
LUs ACTIVATED BY HOST BUT NOT USED nnn
```

The following is sample output from the **show sna** command with the **pu** keyword:

```
Router# show sna pu putest

sna host PUTEST TokenRing1 PU STATUS active
RMAC 400000000004 RSAP 04 LSAP 04
XID 05d00001 RETRIES 255 RETRY_TIMEOUT 30
WINDOW 7 MAXIFRAME 1472
FRAMES RECEIVED 0450 FRAMES SENT 0010
LUs USED BY DSPU nnn LUs ACTIVE nnn
LUs USED BY API nnn LUs ACTIVE nnn
LUs ACTIVATED BY HOST BUT NOT USED nnn
```

Because the **all** parameter refers to LUs under the PU, this has no significance for the Service Point host.

SNA ENABLE-HOST (QLLC)

Use the **sna enable-host** interface configuration command to enable an X.121 subaddress for use by the SNA Service Point on the interface. Use the **no** form of this command to disable SNA Service Point on the interface.

> **sna enable-host qllc** *x121-subaddress*
> **no sna enable-host qllc** *x121-subaddress*

Syntax	Description
qllc	Required keyword for QLLC data-link control.
x121-subaddress	The X.121 subaddress.

Default

No default X.121 subaddress is specified.

Command Mode

Interface configuration

Usage Guidelines

This command first appeared in Cisco IOS Release 11.0.

Example

In the following example, X.121 subaddress 320108 is enabled for use by host connections:

```
sna enable-host qllc 320108
```

Related Commands

sna host (QLLC)
x25 map qllc

SNA ENABLE-HOST (SDLC)

Use the **sna enable-host** interface configuration command to enable an SDLC address for use by host connections. Use the **no** form of this command to cancel the definition.

> **sna enable-host sdlc** *sdlc-address*
> **no sna enable-host sdlc** *sdlc-address*

Syntax	Description
sdlc	Required keyword for SDLC data-link control.
sdlc-address	The SDLC address.

Default

No default SDLC address is specified.

Command Mode

Interface configuration

Usage Guidelines

This command first appeared in Cisco IOS Release 11.0.

Example

In the following example, SDLC address C1 is enabled for use by host connections:

```
encapsulation sdlc
sdlc role secondary
sdlc address c1
sna enable-host sdlc c1
```

Related Commands

encapsulation sdlc
sna host (SDLC)

SNA ENABLE-HOST (TOKEN RING, ETHERNET, FRAME RELAY, FDDI)

Use the **sna enable-host** interface configuration command to enable SNA on the interface. Use the **no** form of this command to disable SNA on the interface.

> **sna enable-host** [**lsap** *lsap-address*]
> **no sna enable-host** [**lsap** *lsap-address*]

Syntax	Description
lsap	(Optional) Activate a local SAP as an upstream SAP, for both receiving ConnectIn attempts and for starting ConnectOut attempts.
lsap-address	Local SAP. The default is 12.

Default

The default LSAP parameter is 12.

Command Mode

Interface configuration

Usage Guidelines

This command first appeared in Cisco IOS Release 11.0.

Example

The following example enables SNA on the interface and specifies that the local SAP 10 will be activated as an upstream SAP:

```
sna enable-host lsap 10
```

Related Commands

show sna
sna host (Frame Relay)
sna host (Token Ring, Ethernet, FDDI, RSRB, VDLC)

SNA HOST (FRAME RELAY)

Use this form of the **sna host** global configuration command to define a link to an SNA host over a Frame Relay connection. Use the **no** form of this command to cancel the definition.

sna host *host-name* xid-snd *xid* dlci *dlci-number* [rsap *remote-sap*] [lsap *local-sap*]
    [interface *slot/port*] [window *window-size*] [maxiframe *max-iframe*] [retries
    retry-count] [retry-timeout *retry-timeout*] [focalpoint]
no sna host *host-name* xid-snd *xid* dlci *dlci-number* [rsap *remote-sap*] [lsap *local-sap*]
    [interface *slot/port*] [window *window-size*] [maxiframe *max-iframe*] [retries
    retry-count] [retry-timeout *retry-timeout*] [focalpoint]

Syntax	Description
host-name	The specified SNA host.
xid-snd *xid*	The XID that will be sent to the host during connection establishment. The XID value is 8 hexadecimal digits that include both block and ID numbers. For example, if the XID value is 05D00001, the block number is 05D and the ID number is 00001.
dlci *dlci-number*	DLCI number.
rsap *remote-sap*	(Optional) Specifies the SAP address of the remote host PU. The default is 4.
lsap *local-sap*	(Optional) Specifies the local SAP address used by the SNA Service Point to establish connection with the remote host. The default is 12.
interface *slot/port*	(Optional) The slot and port number of the interface.
window *window-size*	(Optional) Specifies the send and receive window sizes used for the host link. The range is 1 to 127. The default is 7.
maxiframe *max-iframe*	(Optional) Specifies the send and receive maximum I-frame sizes used for the host link. The range is 64 to 18432. The default is 1472.
retries *retry-count*	(Optional) Specifies the number of times the SNA Service Point attempts to retry establishing connection with remote host PU. The range is 0 to 255 (0 = no retry attempts, 255 = infinite retry attempts). The default is 255.
retry-timeout *retry-timeout*	(Optional) Specifies the delay (in seconds) between attempts to retry establishing connection with remote host PU. The range is 1 to 600 seconds. The default is 30 seconds.
focalpoint	(Optional) Specifies that the host link will be used for the focal point support.

Default

The default remote SAP is 4.
The default local SAP is 12.
The default window size is 7.
The default maximum I-frame size is 1472.
The default retry count is 255.
The default retry timeout is 30 seconds.

Command Mode

Global configuration

Usage Guidelines

This command first appeared in Cisco IOS Release 11.0.

Example

The following command defines a link to an SNA host:

```
sna host CNM01 xid-snd 05d00001 dlci 200 rsap 4 lsap 4
```

Related Commands

sna enable-host (Token Ring, Ethernet, Frame Relay, FDDI)
sna start

SNA HOST (QLLC)

Use this form of the **sna host** global configuration command to define a link to an SNA host over an X.25/QLLC connection. Use the **no** form of this command to cancel the definition.

> **sna host** *host-name* **xid-snd** *xid* **x25** *remote-x121-addr* [**qllc** *local-x121-subaddr*]
> [**interface** *slot/port*] [**window** *window-size*] [**maxiframe** *max-iframe*] [**retries**
> *retry-count*] [**retry-timeout** *retry-timeout*] [**focalpoint**]
> **no sna host** *host-name* **xid-snd** *xid* **x25** *remote-x121-addr* [**qllc** *local-x121-subaddr*]
> [**interface** *slot/port*] [**window** *window-size*] [**maxiframe** *max-iframe*] [**retries**
> *retry-count*] [**retry-timeout** *retry-timeout*] [**focalpoint**]

Syntax	Description
host-name	The specified SNA host.
xid-snd *xid*	The XID that will be sent to the host during connection establishment. The XID value is 8 hexadecimal digits that include both block and ID numbers. For example, if the XID value is 05D00001, the block number is 05D and the ID number is 00001.
x25 *remote-x121-addr*	The SDLC address.
qllc *local-x121-subaddr*	(Optional) Specifies the SAP address of the remote host PU. The default is 4.
interface *slot/port*	(Optional) The slot and port number of the interface.
window *window-size*	(Optional) Specifies the send and receive window sizes used for the host link. The range is 1 to 127. The default is 7.
maxiframe *max-iframe*	(Optional) Specifies the send and receive maximum I-frame sizes used for the host link. The range is 64 to 18432. The default is 1472.
retries *retry-count*	(Optional) Specifies the number of times the SNA Service Point attempts to retry establishing connection with remote host PU. The range is 0 to 255 (0 = no retry attempts, 255 = infinite retry attempts). The default is 255.

Syntax	Description
retry-timeout *retry-timeout*	(Optional) Specifies the delay (in seconds) between attempts to retry establishing connection with remote host PU. The range is 1 to 600 seconds. The default is 30 seconds.
focalpoint	(Optional) Specifies that the host link will be used for the focal point support.

Default

The default remote SAP is 4.
The default window size is 7.
The default maximum I-frame size is 1472.
The default retry count is 255.
The default retry timeout is 30 seconds.

Command Mode

Global configuration

Usage Guidelines

This command first appeared in Cisco IOS Release 11.0.

Example

The following command defines a link to an SNA host:

```
sna host MLM1 xid-snd 05d00001 x25 320108 qllc 08
```

Related Commands

sna enable-host (QLLC)
sna start

SNA HOST (SDLC)

Use this form of the **sna host** global configuration command to define a link to an SNA host over an SDLC connection. Use the **no** form of this command to cancel the definition.

> **sna host** *host-name* **xid-snd** *xid* **sdlc** *sdlc-addr* [**rsap** *remote-sap*] [**lsap** *local-sap*] [**interface** *slot/port*] [**window** *window-size*] [**maxiframe** *max-iframe*] [**retries** *retry-count*] [**retry-timeout** *retry-timeout*] [**focalpoint**]
> **no sna host** *host-name* **xid-snd** *xid* **rmac** *remote-mac* [**rsap** *remote-sap*] [**lsap** *local-sap*] [**interface** *slot/port*] [**window** *window-size*] [**maxiframe** *max-iframe*] [**retries** *retry-count*] [**retry-timeout** *retry-timeout*] [**focalpoint**]

Syntax	Description
host-name	The specified SNA host.
xid-snd *xid*	The XID that will be sent to the host during connection establishment. The XID value is 8 hexadecimal digits that include both block and ID numbers. For example, if the XID value is 05D00001, the block number is 05D and the ID number is 00001.
sdlc *sdlc-addr*	The SDLC address.
rsap *remote-sap*	(Optional) Specifies the SAP address of the remote host PU. The default is 4.
lsap *local-sap*	(Optional) Specifies the local SAP address used by the SNA Service Point to establish connection with the remote host. The default is 12.
interface *slot/port*	(Optional) The slot and port number of the interface.
window *window-size*	(Optional) Specifies the send and receive window sizes used for the host link. The range is 1 to 127. The default is 7.
maxiframe *max-iframe*	(Optional) Specifies the send and receive maximum I-frame sizes used for the host link. The range is 64 to 18432. The default is 1472.
retries *retry-count*	(Optional) Specifies the number of times the SNA Service Point attempts to retry establishing connection with remote host PU. The range is 0 to 255 (0 = no retry attempts, 255 = infinite retry attempts). The default is 255.
retry-timeout *retry-timeout*	(Optional) Specifies the delay (in seconds) between attempts to retry establishing connection with remote host PU. The range is 1 to 600 seconds. The default is 30 seconds.
focalpoint	(Optional) Specifies that the host link will be used for the focal point support.

Part II

Command Reference

Default

The default remote SAP is 4.
The default local SAP is 12.
The default window size is 7.
The default maximum I-frame size is 1472.
The default retry count is 255.
The default retry timeout is 30 seconds.

Command Mode

Global configuration

Usage Guidelines

This command first appeared in Cisco IOS Release 11.0.

Example

The following command defines a link to an SNA host:

```
sna host CNM01 xid-snd 05d00001 sdlc c1 rsap 4 lsap 4 focalpoint
```

Related Commands

sna enable-host (SDLC)
sna start

SNA HOST (TOKEN RING, ETHERNET, FDDI, RSRB, VDLC)

Use this form of the **sna host** global configuration command to define a link to an SNA host over Token Ring, Ethernet, FDDI, RSRB, or virtual data-link control connections. Use the **no** form of this command to cancel the definition.

> **sna host** *host-name* **xid-snd** *xid* **rmac** *remote-mac* [**rsap** *remote-sap*] [**lsap** *local-sap*]
> [**interface** *slot/port*] [**window** *window-size*] [**maxiframe** *max-iframe*] [**retries**
> *retry-count*] [**retry-timeout** *retry-timeout*] [**focalpoint**]
> **no sna host** *host-name* **xid-snd** *xid* **rmac** *remote-mac* [**rsap** *remote-sap*] [**lsap** *local-sap*]
> [**interface** *slot/port*] [**window** *window-size*] [**maxiframe** *max-iframe*] [**retries**
> *retry-count*] [**retry-timeout** *retry-timeout*] [**focalpoint**]

Syntax	Description
host-name	The specified SNA host.
xid-snd *xid*	The XID that will be sent to the host during connection establishment. The XID value is 8 hexadecimal digits that include both block and ID numbers. For example, if the XID value is 05D00001, the block number is 05D and the ID number is 00001.
rmac *remote-mac*	The MAC address of the remote host PU.
rsap *remote-sap*	(Optional) Specifies the SAP address of the remote host PU. The default is 4.
lsap *local-sap*	(Optional) Specifies the local SAP address used by the SNA Service Point to establish connection with the remote host. The default is 12.
interface *slot/port*	(Optional) The slot and port number of the interface.
window *window-size*	(Optional) Specifies the send and receive window sizes used for the host link. The range is 1 to 127. The default is 7.
maxiframe *max-iframe*	(Optional) Specifies the send and receive maximum I-frame sizes used for the host link. The range is 64 to 18432. The default is 1472.

Syntax	Description
retries *retry-count*	(Optional) Specifies the number of times the SNA Service Point attempts to retry establishing connection with remote host PU. The range is 0 to 255 (0 = no retry attempts, 255 = infinite retry attempts). The default is 255.
retry-timeout *retry-timeout*	(Optional) Specifies the delay (in seconds) between attempts to retry establishing connection with remote host PU. The range is 1 to 600 seconds. The default is 30 seconds.
focalpoint	(Optional) Specifies that the host link will be used for the focal point support.

Defaults

The default remote SAP is 4.
The default local SAP is 12.
The default window size is 7.
The default maximum I-frame size is 1472.
The default retry count is 255.
The default retry timeout is 30 seconds.

Command Mode

Global configuration

Usage Guidelines

This command first appeared in Cisco IOS Release 11.0.

Example

The following command defines a link to an SNA host:

```
sna host CNM01 xid-snd 05d00001 rmac 4001.3745.1088 rsap 4 lsap 4 focalpoint
```

Related Commands

sna enable-host (Token Ring, Ethernet, Frame Relay, FDDI)
sna rsrb enable-host
sna rsrb start
sna start
sna vdlc enable-host
sna vdlc start

SNA RSRB

Use the **sna rsrb** interface configuration command to specify the entities that the SNA feature will simulate at the remote source-route bridge. Use the **no** form of this command to cancel the specification.

> **sna rsrb** *local-virtual-ring bridge-number target-virtual-ring virtual-macaddr*
> **no sna rsrb** *local-virtual-ring bridge-number target-virtual-ring virtual-macaddr*

Syntax	Description
local-virtual-ring	Local virtual ring number.
bridge-number	Virtual bridge number. The valid range is 1 to 15.
target-virtual-ring	Target virtual ring number.
virtual-macaddr	Virtual MAC address.

Default

No defaults are specified.

Command Mode

Interface configuration

Usage Guidelines

This command first appeared in Cisco IOS Release 11.0.

You can specify the bridge number no more than once in any configuration.

Example

The following example identifies a LAN:

```
sna rsrb 88 1 99 4000.FFFF.0001
```

Related Commands

sna rsrb start

SNA RSRB ENABLE-HOST

Use the **sna rsrb enable-host** global configuration command to enable an RSRB SAP for use by SNA Service Point. Use the **no** form of this command to disable the RSRB SAP.

> **sna rsrb enable-host** [**lsap** *local-sap*]
> **no sna rsrb enable-host** [**lsap** *local-sap*]

Syntax	Description
lsap *local-sap*	(Optional) Specifies that the local SAP address will be activated as an upstream SAP for both receiving incoming connections attempts and for starting outgoing connection attempts. The default is 12.

Default

The default local SAP address is 12.

Command Mode

Global configuration

Usage Guidelines

This command first appeared in Cisco IOS Release 11.0.

Example

In the following example, the local SAP address 10 of the RSRB is enabled for use by the *ibm3745* host PU:

```
source-bridge ring-group 99
source-bridge remote-peer 99 tcp 150.10.13.1
source-bridge remote-peer 99 tcp 150.10.13.2

sna rsrb 88 1 99 4000.FFFF.0001
sna rsrb enable-host lsap 10

sna host ibm3745 xid-snd 06500001 rmac 4000.3745.0001 lsap 10

interface serial 0
 ip address 150.10.13.1 255.255.255.0
```

Related Commands

sna host (Token Ring, Ethernet, FDDI, RSRB, VDLC)

SNA RSRB START

Use the **sna rsrb start** global configuration command to specify that an attempt will be made to connect to the remote resource defined by host name through the RSRB. Use the **no** form of this command to cancel the definition.

sna rsrb start *host-name*
no sna rsrb start *host-name*

Syntax	Description
host-name	The name of a host defined in an **sna host** (**Token Ring, Ethernet, FDDI, RSRB, VDLC**) or equivalent command.

Default

There are no default settings.

Command Mode

Global configuration

Usage Guidelines

This command first appeared in Cisco IOS Release 11.0.

Before issuing this command, you must enable the correct local SAP with the appropriate enable command (**sna rsrb enable-host**).

Example

In the following example, the SNA Service Point will initiate a connection with the *ibm3745* host PU across the RSRB link:

```
source-bridge ring-group 99
source-bridge remote-peer 99 tcp 150.10.13.1
source-bridge remote-peer 99 tcp 150.10.13.2

sna rsrb 88 1 99 4000.FFFF.0001
sna rsrb enable-host lsap 10

sna host ibm3745 xid-snd 06500001 rmac 4000.3745.0001 lsap 10
sna rsrb start ibm3745

interface serial 0
 ip address 150.10.13.1 255.255.255.0
```

Related Commands

sna host (**Token Ring, Ethernet, FDDI, RSRB, VDLC**)
sna rsrb

SNA START

Use the **sna start** interface configuration command to initiate a connection to a remote resource. Use the **no** form of this command to cancel the connection attempt.

> **sna start** [*resource-name*]
> **no sna start** [*resource-name*]

Syntax	Description
resource-name	(Optional) Name of a host defined in an **sna host** command.

Default

No default is specified.

Command Mode

Interface configuration

Usage Guidelines

This command first appeared in Cisco IOS Release 11.0.

Before issuing this command, you must enable the correct address using the **sna enable-host** command.

Example

The following example initiates a connection to CNM01:

```
sna start CNM01
```

Related Commands

sna host (Frame Relay)
sna host (QLLC)
sna host (SDLC)
sna host (Token Ring, Ethernet, FDDI, RSRB, VDLC)

SNA VDLC

Use the **sna vdlc** global configuration command to identify the local virtual ring and virtual MAC address that will be used to establish SNA host connections over DLSw+ using virtual data-link control. Use the **no** form of this command to cancel the definition.

> **sna vdlc** *ring-group virtual-mac-address*
> **no sna vdlc** *ring-group virtual-mac-address*

Syntax	Description
ring-group	Local virtual ring number identifying the SRB ring group.
virtual-mac-address	Virtual MAC address that represents the SNA virtual data-link control.

Default

There are no default settings.

Command Mode
Global configuration

Usage Guidelines
This command first appeared in Cisco IOS Release 11.2.

The virtual data-link control local virtual ring must have been previously configured using the **source-bridge ring-group** command.

The virtual data-link control virtual MAC address must be unique within the DLSw+ network.

To avoid an address conflict on the virtual MAC address, use a locally administered address in the form 4000.*xxxx.xxxx*.

Example
The following is an example of an SNA Service Point configuration that uses virtual data-link control over DLSw+:

```
source-bridge ring-group 99
dlsw local-peer peer-id 150.10.16.2
dlsw remote-peer 0 tcp 150.10.16.1

sna vdlc 99 4000.4500.01f0
sna vdlc enable-host lsap 12

sna host HOST-B xid-snd 065bbbb0 rmac 4000.7000.01f1 rsap 4 lsap 12 focalpoint

sna vdlc start HOST-B

interface serial 3
 description IP connection to dspu7k
 ip address 150.10.16.2 255.255.255.0
 clockrate 4000000
```

Related Commands
dlsw local-peer
dlsw remote-peer
sna vdlc start
source-bridge ring-group

SNA VDLC ENABLE-HOST
Use the **sna vdlc enable-host** global configuration command to enable a SAP for use by SNA Service Point. Use the **no** form of this command to disable the SAP.

> **sna vdlc enable-host** [**lsap** *local-sap*]
> **no sna vdlc enable-host** [**lsap** *local-sap*]

Syntax	Description
lsap *local-sap*	(Optional) Specifies that the local SAP address will be activated as an upstream SAP for both receiving incoming connection attempts and for starting outgoing connection attempts. The default is 12.

Default

The default local SAP address is 12.

Command Mode

Global configuration

Usage Guidelines

This command first appeared in Cisco IOS Release 11.2.

Example

In the following example, the local SAP address 12 is enabled for use by the host PU HOST-B:

```
source-bridge ring-group 99
dlsw local-peer peer-id 150.10.16.2
dlsw remote-peer 0 tcp 150.10.16.1

sna vdlc 99 4000.4500.01f0
sna vdlc enable-host lsap 12

sna host HOST-B xid-snd 065bbbb0 rmac 4000.7000.01f1 rsap 4 lsap 12 focalpoint

sna vdlc start HOST-B

interface serial 3
 description IP connection to dspu7k
 ip address 150.10.16.2 255.255.255.0
 clockrate 4000000
```

Related Commands

sna host (Token Ring, Ethernet, FDDI, RSRB, VDLC)

SNA VDLC START

Use the **sna vdlc start** global configuration command to specify that an attempt will be made to connect to the remote resource defined by host name through virtual data-link control. Use the **no** form of this command to cancel the definition.

> **sna vdlc start** *host-name*
> **no sna vdlc start** *host-name*

Syntax	Description
host-name	The name of a host defined in an **sna host** (Token Ring, Ethernet, FDDI, RSRB, VDLC) or equivalent command.

Default

There are no default settings.

Command Mode

Global configuration

Usage Guidelines

This command first appeared in Cisco IOS Release 11.2.

Before issuing this command, you must enable the correct local SAP with the **sna vdlc enable-host** command.

Example

In the following example, SNA Service Point uses virtual data-link control to initiate a connection with the host PU HOST-B:

```
source-bridge ring-group 99
dlsw local-peer peer-id 150.10.16.2
dlsw remote-peer 0 tcp 150.10.16.1

sna vdlc 99 4000.4500.01f0
sna vdlc enable-host lsap 12

sna host HOST-B xid-snd 065bbbb0 rmac 4000.7000.01f1 rsap 4 lsap 12 focalpoint

sna vdlc start HOST-B

interface serial 3
 description IP connection to dspu7k
 ip address 150.10.16.2 255.255.255.0
 clockrate 4000000
```

Related Commands

sna vdlc

CHAPTER 17

Configuring SNA Frame Relay Access Support

This chapter describes Frame Relay Access Support (FRAS) for Systems Network Architecture (SNA) devices and how to use a FRAS host to connect Cisco Frame Relay Access Devices (FRADs) to channel-attached mainframes, LAN-attached FEPs, and LAN-attached AS/400s through a Cisco router.

This chapter describes how to configure FRAS. For a complete description of the commands in this chapter, see Chapter 18, "SNA Frame Relay Access Support Commands."

SNA FRAS CONFIGURATION TASK LIST

To configure FRAS, perform the tasks described in the following sections:

- Configuring FRAS BNN Statically
- Configuring FRAS BNN Dynamically
- Configuring FRAS Boundary Access Node Support
- Configuring SRB over Frame Relay
- Configuring FRAS Congestion Management
- Configuring FRAS DLCI Backup
- Configuring Frame Relay RSRB Dial Backup
- Configuring Frame Relay DLSw+ Dial Backup
- Monitoring and Maintaining FRAS

The "FRAS Configuration Examples" section follows these configuration tasks.

CONFIGURING FRAS BNN STATICALLY

To configure FRAS (Boundary Network Node) BNN statically, perform one of the following tasks in interface configuration mode:

Task	Command
Associate an LLC connection with a Frame Relay DLCI.	**fras map llc** *mac-address lan-lsap lan-rsap* **serial** *port* **frame-relay** *dlci fr-lsap fr-rsap* [**pfid2** | **afid2** | **fid4**]
Associate an SDLC link with a Frame Relay DLCI.	**fras map sdlc** *sdlc-address* **serial** *port* **frame-relay** *dlci fr-lsap fr-rsap* [**pfid2** | **afid2** | **fid4**]

In this implementation, you configure and define each end station MAC and SAP address pair statically.

Because Frame Relay itself does not provide a reliable transport as required by SNA, the RFC 1490 support of SNA uses LLC2 as part of the encapsulation to provide link-level sequencing, acknowledgment, and flow control. The serial interface configured for Internet Engineering Task Force (IETF) encapsulation (RFC 1490) accepts all LLC2 interface configuration commands.

CONFIGURING FRAS BNN DYNAMICALLY

To configure FRAS BNN dynamically, perform one of the the following tasks in interface configuration mode:

Task	Command
Associate an LLC connection with a Frame Relay DLCI.	**fras map llc** *lan-lsap* **serial** *interface* **frame-relay dlci** *dlci fr-rsap*
Associate an SDLC link with a Frame Relay DLCI.	**fras map sdlc** *sdlc-address* **serial** *port* **frame-relay** *dlci fr-lsap fr-rsap* [**pfid2** | **afid2** | **fid4**]

When you associate an LLC connection with a Frame Relay DLCI, the router "learns" the MAC/SAP information as it forwards packets to the host. The FRAS BNN feature provides seamless processing at the router regardless of end-station changes. End stations can be added or deleted without reconfiguring the router.

When you associate an SDLC link with a Frame Relay DLCI, you configure and define each end station MAC and SAP address pair statically.

Because Frame Relay itself does not provide a reliable transport as required by SNA, the RFC 1490 support of SNA uses LLC2 as part of the encapsulation to provide link-level sequencing, acknowledgment, and flow control. The serial interface configured for Internet Engineering Task Force (IETF) encapsulation (RFC 1490) can take all LLC2 interface configuration commands.

CONFIGURING FRAS BOUNDARY ACCESS NODE SUPPORT

To configure Frame Relay boundary access node (BAN), perform the following task in interface configuration mode:

Task	Command
Associate a bridge to the Frame Relay BAN.	fras ban *local-ring bridge-number ring-group ban-dlci-mac* dlci *dlci#1* [*dlci#2 . . . dlci#5*] [bni *mac-addr*]

BAN simplifies router configuration when multiple LLC sessions are multiplexed over the same DLCI. By comparison, SAP multiplexing requires static definitions and maintenance overhead. By using BAN, the Token Ring MAC address is included in every frame to identify uniquely the LLC session. Downstream devices can be added dynamically and deleted with no configuration changes required on the router.

CONFIGURING SRB OVER FRAME RELAY

To configure SRB over Frame Relay, perform the following tasks in interface configuration mode:

Task		Command
Step 1	Specify the serial port.	interface serial *number*
Step 2	Enable Frame Relay encapsulation.	encapsulation frame-relay
Step 3	Configure a Frame Relay point-to-point subinterface.	interface serial *slot/port.subinterface-number* point-to-point
Step 4	Configure a DLCI number for the point-to-point subinterface.	frame-relay interface-dlci *dlci* ietf
Step 5	Assign a ring number to the Frame Relay permanent virtual circuit.	source-bridge *source-ring-number bridge-number target-ring-number* conserve-ring

Cisco IOS software offers the capability to encapsulate source-route bridging traffic using RFC 1490 Bridged 802.5 encapsulation. This provides SRB over Frame Relay functionality. This SRB-over-Frame Relay feature is interoperable with other vendors' implementations of SRB-over-Frame Relay and with some vendors' implementations of FRAS BAN.

SRB-over-Frame Relay does not support the following Cisco IOS software functions:

- Proxy explorer
- Automatic spanning tree
- LAN Network Manager

CONFIGURING FRAS CONGESTION MANAGEMENT

FRAS provides a congestion-control mechanism based on the interaction between congestion notification bits in the Frame Relay packet and the dynamic adjustment of the LLC2 send window. This window shows the number of frames the Cisco IOS software can send before waiting for an acknowledgment. The window size decreases with the occurrence of backward explicit congestion notification (BECN) and increases when no BECN frames are received.

To configure congestion management, perform the following tasks in interface configuration mode:

Task	Command
Step 1 Specify the maximum window size for each logical connection.	**llc2 local-window** *packet-count*
Step 2 Enable the dynamic window flow-control mechanism.	**llc2 dynwind** [**nw** *nw-number*] [**dwc** *dwc-number*]

You can enable the dynamic window mechanism only if you are using Frame Relay IETF encapsulation.

CONFIGURING FRAS DLCI BACKUP

To configure FRAS DLCI backup, perform the following task in interface configuration mode:

Task	Command
Specify an interface to be used for the backup connection and indicate the DLCI number of the session.	**fras ddr-backup interface** *interface dlci-number*

FRAS DLCI backup is an enhancement to Cisco's FRAS implementation that lets you configure a secondary path to the host to be used when the Frame Relay network becomes unavailable. When the primary Frame Relay link to the Frame Relay WAN fails, the FRAS DLCI backup feature causes the router to reroute all sessions from the main Frame Relay interface to the secondary interface. The secondary interface can be either serial or ISDN and must have a data-link connection identifier (DLCI) configured.

Figure 17–1 illustrates Frame Relay backup over an ISDN connection.

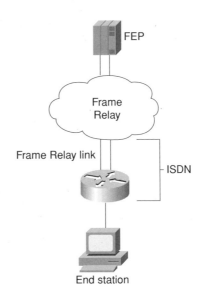

Figure 17–1
FRAS DLCI backup over ISDN.

This feature provides backup for the local end of the Frame Relay connection, not the complete end-to-end connection.

CONFIGURING FRAME RELAY RSRB DIAL BACKUP

When the Frame Relay network is down, the Cisco IOS software checks whether the dial backup feature is configured for the particular DLCI number. If it is configured, the software removes the FRAS to the downstream device connection and establishes the RSRB to this downstream device connection.

To configure RSRB dial backup, perform the following task in interface configuration mode:

Task	Command
Activate Frame Relay RSRB dial backup.	**fras backup rsrb** *vmacaddr local-ring-number target-ring-number host-mac-address*

CONFIGURING FRAME RELAY DLSW+ DIAL BACKUP

The FRAS dial backup-over-DLSw+ feature provides a secondary path that is used when the Frame Relay network becomes unavailable. If preconfigured properly, when the primary link to the Frame

Relay WAN fails, the FRAS dial backup-over-DLSw+ feature moves existing sessions to the alternate link automatically. When the primary link is restored, existing sessions are kept on the backup connection so they can be moved nondisruptively to the primary link at the user's discretion.

To enable FRAS Dial Backup over DLSw+, perform the following task in interface configuration mode:

Task	Command
Configure an auxiliary (backup) route between the end stations and the host for use when the DLCI connection to the Frame Relay network is lost.	**fras backup dlsw** *virtual-mac-address target-ring-number host-mac-address* [**retry** *number*]

Figure 17–2 shows a Frame Relay network with FRAS dial backup over DLSw+ in place.

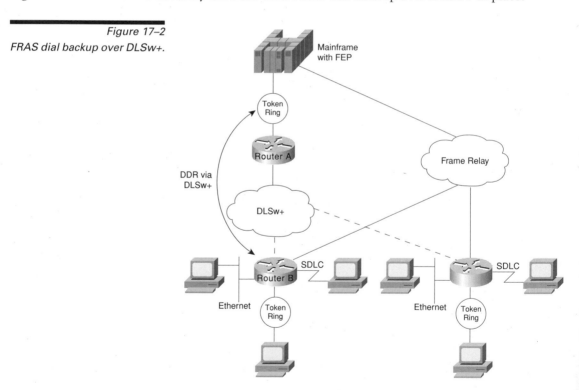

Figure 17–2
FRAS dial backup over DLSw+.

Figure 17–3 shows the active FRAS dial backup over DLSw+ when the Frame Relay connection to the NCP is lost.

Figure 17–3
*FRAS dial backup over
DLSw+ when Frame
Relay is unavailable.*

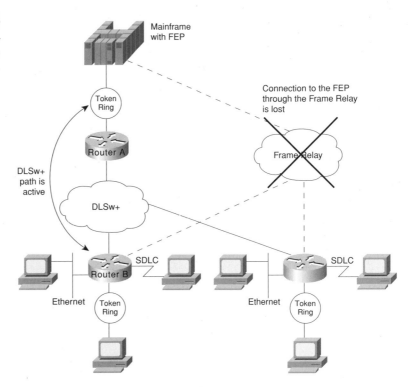

MONITORING AND MAINTAINING FRAS

To display information about the state of FRAS, enter the following command in privileged EXEC mode:

Task	Command
Display the mapping and connection state of the FRAS.	show fras

FRAS CONFIGURATION EXAMPLES

The following sections provide FRAS configuration examples:

- LAN-Attached SNA Devices Example
- SDLC-Attached SNA Devices Example
- FRAS BNN Topology Example
- FRAS BNN Example
- FRAS BAN Example

- SRB over Frame Relay
- FRAS DLCI Backup-over-Serial Interface Example
- FRAS Dial Backup-over-DLSw+ Example

LAN-Attached SNA Devices Example

Figure 17–4 illustrates the configuration of SNA devices attached to a LAN.

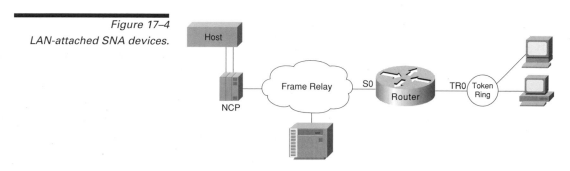

Figure 17–4
LAN-attached SNA devices.

The configuration for the network shown in Figure 17–4 is as follows:

```
interface tokenring 0
 no ip address
 no keepalive
 ring-speed 16
 fras map llc 0800.5a8f.8802 4 4 serial 0 frame-relay 200 4 4
!
interface serial 0
 mtu 2500
 no ip address
 encapsulation frame-relay IETF
 keepalive 12
 frame-relay lmi-type ansi
 frame-relay map llc2 200
```

SDLC-Attached SNA Devices Example

Figure 17–5 illustrates the configuration of SDLC-attached SNA devices.

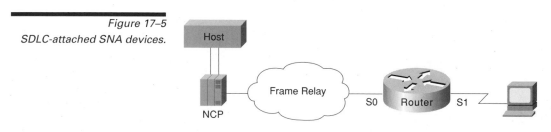

Figure 17–5
SDLC-attached SNA devices.

The configuration file for the network shown in Figure 17–5 is as follows:

```
interface serial 1
 no ip address
 encapsulation sdlc
 no keepalive
 clockrate 56000
 sdlc address C1
 sdlc xid C1 05D01501
 sdlc role primary
 fras map sdlc C1 serial 0 frame-relay 200 4 4
!
interface serial 0
 mtu 2500
 no ip address
 encapsulation frame-relay ietf
 keepalive 12
 frame-relay lmi-type ansi
 frame-relay map llc2 200
```

FRAS BNN Topology Example

FRAS BNN transports SNA traffic across different media through a Cisco router and then through a Frame Relay link to the host. SNA PU 2.0 and PU 2.1 devices may be attached to the remote router through Token Ring, SDLC, or Ethernet to access the Frame Relay network. The FRAS BNN topology is illustrated in Figure 17–6.

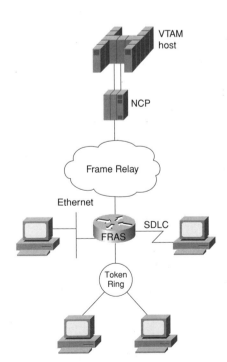

Figure 17–6
FRAS BNN topology.

The original Frame Relay BNN feature transports traffic from multiple PUs over a single DLCI. This function is called SAP multiplexing. The router uses a unique SAP address (fr-lsap) for each downstream PU when communicating with the host. In this implementation, each end station's MAC/SAP address pair must be statically defined to the router. Consequently, the router must be reconfigured each time an end station is moved, added, or deleted. The configuration overhead for this implementation can be high.

The FRAS BNN feature, where the router "learns" the MAC/SAP information as it forwards packets to the host, offers several advantages over the original FRAS BNN implementation. The BNN enhancement alleviates the need to reconfigure the router when end stations are moved, added, or deleted. The configuration is simple: One map definition in the router is sufficient for multiple downstream devices. The router "learns" the addresses of the downstream devices in the normal course of communication (as shown in Figure 17–6).

Figure 17–7 illustrates the Frame Relay BNN configuration for both the original implementation and the enhanced implementation.

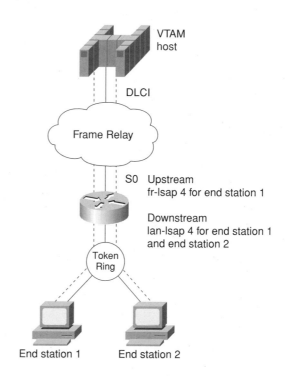

Figure 17–7
Frame Relay BNN support.

If the end station initiates the LLC session, the router acquires the Token Ring address and the SAP value of the end station from the incoming frame. Instead of mapping the end station's MAC/SAP address pair (as was done in the original FRAS BNN implementation), the destination MAC/SAP address pair of the incoming frame is mapped to the Frame Relay DLCI. If the destination SAP specified by the end station is equal to the lan-lsap address, the router associates the LLC (LAN) connection with the Frame Relay DLCI. The MAC address and the SAP address of the end station are no longer required in the router configuration. Thus, in the enhanced FRAS BNN implementation, one configuration command achieves the same result for the end stations as did multiple configuration commands in the original FRAS BNN implementation.

NOTES

The new FRAS BNN feature, which provides seamless processing at the router regardless of end-station changes, is designed to coexist with the original FRAS BNN feature. In Cisco IOS Release 11.2, only LLC2 traffic will be supported. SDLC must be configured using the original BNN implementation.

FRAS BNN Example

The following configuration example enables the FRAS BNN feature. The topology is illustrated in Figure 17–8.

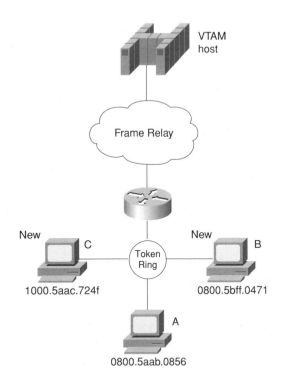

Figure 17–8
FRAS BNN configuration.

```
interface Serial0
 no ip address
 encapsulation frame-relay IETF
 frame-relay lmi-type ansi
 frame-relay map llc2 16
!
interface TokenRing0
 no ip address
 ring-speed 16
 fras map llc 0800.5aab.0856 04 04 Serial 0 frame-relay 16 04 04
 fras map llc 04 Serial 0 frame-relay dlci 16 04
```

— NOTES ───

In this configuration example, the second to last line describes the old configuration for workstation A. The last line describes the configuration for the new workstations B and C.

FRAS BAN Example

The following configuration shows FRAS BAN support for Token Ring and serial interfaces. You must specify the **source-bridge ring-group** global command before you configure the **fras ban** interface command. When Token Ring is configured, the **source-bridge** interface command includes the *local-ring*, *bridge-number*, and the *target-ring* values. The **source-bridge** command enables local source-route bridging on a Token Ring interface.

```
source-bridge ring-group 200
!
interface serial 0
 mtu 4000
 encapsulation frame-relay ietf
 frame-relay lmi-type ansi
 frame-relay map llc2  16
 frame-relay map llc2  17
 fras ban 120 1 200 4000.1000.2000 dlci 16 17
!
interface tokenring 0
 source-bridge 100 5 200
```

For SDLC connections, you must include SDLC configuration commands as follows:

```
!
interface Serial1
 description SDLC line PU2.0
 mtu 265
 no ip address
 encapsulation sdlc
 no keepalive
 clockrate 9600
 sdlc role primary
 sdlc vmac 4000.0000.0000
 sdlc address C2
```

```
    sdlc xid C2 05D01502
    sdlc partner 4000.0000.2345 C2
    sdlc address C8
    sdlc xid C8 05D01508
    sdlc partner 4000.0000.2345 C8
    sdlc address C9
    sdlc xid C9 05D01509
    sdlc partner 4000.0000.2345 C9
    fras ban frame-relay Serial0 4000.0000.2345 dlci 16
    !
interface Serial2
    description SDLC line PU2.1
    no ip address
    encapsulation sdlc
    no keepalive
    clockrate 19200
    sdlc role prim-xid-poll
    sdlc vmac 2000.0000.0000
    sdlc address C6
    sdlc partner 1000.2000.3000 C6
    fras ban frame-relay serial0 1000.2000.3000 dlci 16
```

SRB over Frame Relay

Figure 17–9 illustrates the interoperability provided by SRB over Frame Relay. FRADs B and C forward frames from their locally attached Token Rings over the Frame Relay network using SRB.

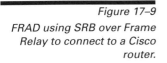

Figure 17–9

FRAD using SRB over Frame Relay to connect to a Cisco router.

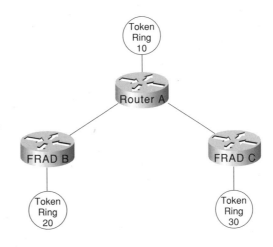

FRAS DLCI Backup-over-Serial Interface Example

The following example shows a configuration for FRAS DLCI backup over a serial interface:

```
    interface serial0
    mtu 3000
    no ip address
```

```
  encapsulation frame-relay IETF
  bandwidth 56
  keepalive 11
  frame-relay map llc2 277
  frame-relay map llc2 278
  frame-relay lmi-type ansi
  fras ddr-backup interface serial1 188
!
interface serial1
  mtu 3000
  no ip address
  encapsulation frame-relay IETF
  no cdp enable
  frame-relay map llc2 188
  frame-relay lmi-type ansi
!
interface serial2
  no ip address
  encapsulation sdlc
  no keepalive
  clock rate 19200
  sdlc role prim-xid-poll
  sdlc address D6
  fras map sdlc D6 s0 frame-relay 277 8 4
!
interface tokenring0
  no ip address
  ring-speed 16
  fras map llc 0000.f63a.2f70 4 4 serial0 frame-relay 277 4 4
```

Figure 17–9 illustrates a network with the following characteristics:

- Virtual ring number of Router A = 100
- Virtual ring number of FRAD B = 200
- Virtual ring number of FRAD C = 300
- DLCI number for the partner's virtual ring (PVC) between Router A and FRAD B = 30
- DLCI number for PVC between Router A and FRAD C = 31

In this example, the Cisco software configures a new option, **conserve-ring,** on the **source-bridge** interface configuration command. When this option is configured, the SRB software does not add the ring number associated with the Frame Relay PVC to outbound explorer frames. This option is permitted for Frame Relay subinterfaces only.

The router configures the partner FRAD's virtual ring number as the ring number for the PVC.

This approach does not require a separate ring number per DLCI. The router configures the partner FRAD's virtual ring number as the ring number for the PVC.

FRAD B configures its virtual ring as 200 and the ring for the PVC as 100. FRAD C configures its virtual ring as 300 and the ring for the PVC as 100.

Configuration of Router A

```
source-bridge ring-group 100
!
interface Serial1
 encapsulation frame-relay
!
interface Serial1.1 point-to-point
 frame-relay interface-dlci 30 ietf
 source-bridge 200 1 100 conserve-ring
 source-bridge spanning
!
interface Serial1.2 point-to-point
 frame-relay interface-dlci 31 ietf
 source-bridge 300 1 100 conserve-ring
 source-bridge spanning
!
interface TokenRing0
 source-bridge 500 1 100
```

FRAS Dial Backup-over-DLSw+ Example

The following examples show configurations for FRAS dial backup over DLSw+:

Configuration for FRAS Dial Backup on a Subinterface

```
source-bridge ring-group 200
dlsw local-peer peer-id 10.8.8.8
dlsw remote-peer 0 tcp 10.8.8.7 dynamic
interface ethernet0
 ip address 10.8.8.8 255.255.255.0
!
interface serial0
 no ip address
 encapsulation frame-relay IETF
 frame-relay lmi-type ansi
!
interface Serial0.1 point-to-point
 description fras backup dlsw+ listening on dlci 16 configuration example
 no ip address
 frame-relay interface-dlci 16
 fras backup dlsw 4000.1000.2000 200 1000.5aed.1f53
!
interface TokenRing0
 no ip address
 ring-speed 16
 fras map llc 0000.f63a.2f50 4 4 Serial0.1 frame-relay 16 4 4
```

Configuration for FRAS Dial Backup on a Main Interface

```
source-bridge ring-group 200
dlsw local-peer peer-id 10.8.8.8
dlsw remote-peer 0 tcp 10.8.8.7 dynamic
```

```
interface ethernet0
 ip address 10.8.8.8 255.255.255.0
 !
interface serial0
 no ip address
 encapsulation frame-relay IETF
 frame-relay lmi-type ansi
frame-relay map llc2 16
fras backup dlsw 4000.1000.2000 200 1000.5aed.1f53
 !
interface Serial1
 ip address 10.8.8.8
 !
interface tokening0
 no ip address
 ring-speed 16
 fras map llc 0000.f63a.2f50 4 4 Serial0 frame-relay 16 4 4
```

FRAS HOST OVERVIEW

The FRAS Host provides a scalable and efficient solution for SNA FRAD access to channel-attached hosts and to LAN-attached hosts. The FRAS Host function operates in two modes, which are documented in the following sections:

- FRAS Host LLC2 Passthru—In this mode, the LLC2 sessions are not locally terminated in the router's LLC2 stack. This is the recommended solution if your scenario includes a Channel Interface Processor (CIP) interface to the mainframe.
- FRAS Host LLC2 Local Termination—In this mode, the LLC2 sessions are locally terminated in the router's LLC2 stack. This is the recommended solution if either of the following is true:
  - Your scenario includes a LAN-attached AS/400 or mainframe
  - Your scenario includes conversion from RFC1490 encapsulation to DLSw+ encapsulation

FRAS Host LLC2 Passthru

The FRAS Host LLC passsthru feature combines with a CIP-attached Cisco router's high-speed channel access to provide FEP-class performance at a fraction of what it would cost to achieve similar functionality using a FEP. If the CIP SNA feature is used to interface with the mainframe, then FRAS Host LLC2 passthru mode is the recommended solution. In this topology, the LLC2 passthru solution to the CIP-SNA LLC2 stack provides better performance, is more robust, and responds well to different types of congestion.

To prevent LLC2 session timeout, LLC2 characteristics (windows and timers) may be tuned on the CIP internal LAN adapter. The CIP/SNA LLC2 stack reacts to congestion by dynamically adjusting its LLC2 transmit window for that LLC2 session in response to dropped frames.

With the FRAS Host LLC passthru feature, you gain performance benefits of a channel attachment without FEP upgrades such as the addition of a Frame Relay interface, an upgrade to NCP (with its associated increase in monthly charges), and a possible increase in system memory.

Figure 17–10 illustrates Cisco FRAD access to a mainframe through a channel-attached Cisco router.

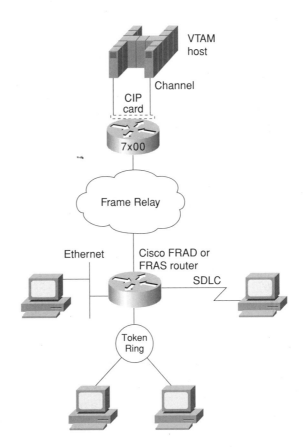

Figure 17–10
Cisco FRAD access to a mainframe through a Cisco 7500.

VTAM host

Channel

CIP card

7x00

Frame Relay

Ethernet

Cisco FRAD or FRAS router

SDLC

Token Ring

FRAS Host LLC2 Local Termination

If the FRAS Host feature is used to allow remote FRADs to communicate with a LAN-attached IBM 3745 or AS/400, then LLC2 termination via DLSw+ local switching is the recommended solution. With this approach, the LLC2 sessions are terminated at the Route Processor. To prevent LLC2 session timeout, LLC2 characteristics (windows and timers) may be tuned on the virtual Token Ring interface. If the dynamic window algorithm is enabled on the virtual Token Ring interface, LLC2 local termination will react to congestion by dynamically adjusting its LLC2 transmit window in response to occurrence of Frame Relay BECN.

When you use the FRAS Host LLC2 local termination feature on a Token Ring-attached FEP, the FRAS Host Cisco router shields the FEP from having to manage the interface to the Frame Relay network. This avoids interface, memory, and NCP upgrades. The FRAS Host Cisco router simply provides LLC2 sessions to the FEP over the LAN.

If used in an environment with AS/400s, FRAS Host LLC2 local termination provides an even more valuable function. The Cisco FRAS Host router offloads the management of the Frame Relay connections from the AS/400. This reduces AS/400 system hardware requirements and frees AS/400 CPU cycles for user applications.

Figure 17–11 illustrates Cisco FRAD access to a LAN-attached SNA host through a Cisco router.

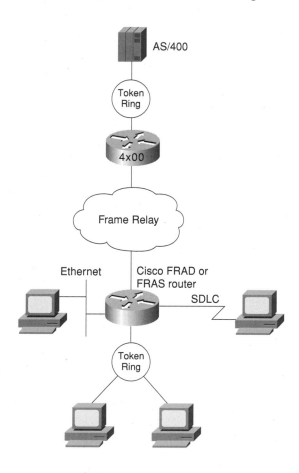

Figure 17–11

Cisco FRAD access to a LAN-attached AS/400 through a Cisco 4500.

Congestion Management

Both passthru and local acknowledgment environments support frame discard eligibility (DE) for additional congestion management. In both environments, you can further tune the interface to the

Frame Relay network by taking advantage of the Cisco IOS Frame Relay features. Taken together, these features increase overall throughput dramatically by comparison to generic FRADs, which typically cannot use the network with the same degree of efficiency.

FRAS HOST CONFIGURATION TASK LIST

To configure the FRAS Host migration feature, perform the tasks in the following sections:

- Creating a Virtual Token Ring Interface
- Configuring Source-Route Bridging on the Virtual Token Ring Interface
- Accepting Default LLC2 passthru or Enabling LLC2 Local Termination
- Enabling the FRAS Host Feature for BAN or BNN
- Monitoring LLC2 Sessions Using FRAS Host

The "FRAS Host Configuration Examples" section follows these configuration tasks.

Creating a Virtual Token Ring Interface

To configure a virtual Token Ring interface, perform the following task in interface configuration mode:

Task	Command
Configure a virtual Token Ring interface.	**interface virtual-tokenring** *number*

Configuring Source-Route Bridging on the Virtual Token Ring Interface

To configure SRB on the Token Ring interface, perform the following tasks beginning in global configuration mode:

Task	Command
Step 1 Enable local source-route bridging.	**source-bridge ring-group** *ring-group virtual-mac-address*
Step 2 Enable FRAS Host traffic to access the SRB domain.	**source-bridge** *local-ring bridge-number target-ring*

— **NOTES** —

If you are using LLC2 passthru with an Ethernet-attached host, you must configure the Cisco source-route translational bridging (SR/TLB) feature.

Accepting Default LLC2 Passthru or Enabling LLC2 Local Termination

LLC2 passthru is the default operational mode for all FRAS Host connections that use a virtual Token Ring interface. You do not need to perform any configuration to accept the default LLC2 passthru mode.

To enable LLC2 local termination for FRAS Host connections using the virtual Token Ring, perform the following tasks, beginning in global configuration mode:

Task	Command
Step 1 Enable data-link local switching.	**dlsw local-peer**
Step 2 Enable LLC2 local termination for FRAS Host connections.	**fras-host dlsw-local-ack**

Enabling the FRAS Host Feature for BAN or BNN

To enable the FRAS Host for BAN or BNN, perform the following tasks in interface configuration mode:

Task	Command
Step 1 Configure the FRAS host for BNN.	**fras-host bnn** (*sub*)*interface* **fr-lsap** *sap* **vmac** *virt-mac* **hmac** *hmac* [**hsap** *hsap*]
Step 2 Configure the FRAS host for BAN.	**fras-host ban** (*sub*)*interface* **hmac** *hmac* [**bni** *bni-mac*]

Monitoring LLC2 Sessions Using FRAS Host

To display the status of LLC2 sessions using FRAS Host, perform the following task in privileged EXEC mode:

Task	Command
Display the status of LLC2 sessions using FRAS Host.	**show fras-host** [(*sub*)*interface*] [**dlci** *dlci-num*] [**detail**]

FRAS HOST CONFIGURATION EXAMPLES

The following sections provide FRAS Host configuration examples:

- Cisco FRAD or FRAS Router A with BNN Configuration Example
- Cisco FRAD or FRAS Router B with BAN Configuration Example

- Cisco FRAD or FRAS Router C with BAN Configuration Example
- FRAS Host CIP Connection to VTAM Configuration Example
- FRAS Host Ethernet Connection to AS/400 Configuration Example

The following examples show the configuration for the network shown in Figure 17–12.

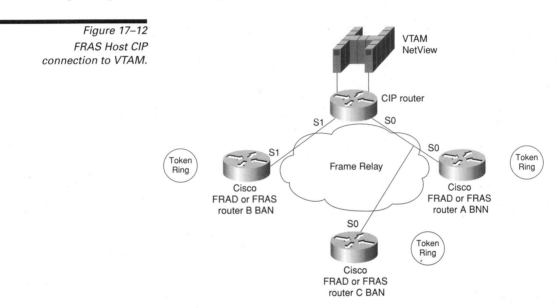

Figure 17–12
FRAS Host CIP
connection to VTAM.

Cisco FRAD or FRAS Router A with BNN Configuration Example

```
interface Serial0
 encapsulation frame-relay IETF
 frame-relay map llc2 16
!
interface TokenRing0
 fras map llc 4001.2222.0000 4 4 Serial0 frame-relay 16 4 4
```

Cisco FRAD or FRAS Router B with BAN Configuration Example

```
source-bridge ring-group 200
!
interface Serial0
 encapsulation frame-relay IETF
 frame-relay map llc2 37
 fras ban 10 1 200 4000.3745.0000 dlci 37
!
interface TokenRing0
 source-bridge 20 1 200
```

Cisco FRAD or FRAS Router C with BAN Configuration Example

```
source-bridge ring-group 400
!
interface Serial0
 encapsulation frame-relay IETF
 frame-relay map llc2 46
 fras ban 50 1 400 4000.3745.0220 dlci 46 bni 4001.3745.1088
!
interface TokenRing0
 source-bridge 60 1 400
```

FRAS Host CIP Connection to VTAM Configuration Example

```
source-bridge ring-group 100
!
interface Serial0/1
 encapsulation frame-relay IETF
 frame-relay map llc2 16
 frame-relay map llc2 46
!
interface Serial0/2
 encapsulation frame-relay IETF
!
interface Serial0/2.37 point-to-point
 frame-relay interface-dlci 37
!
interface Channel4/0
 no keepalive
!
interface Channel4/1
 no keepalive
 lan TokenRing 0
  source-bridge 104 1 100
  adapter 0 4001.3745.1008
!
interface Virtual-TokenRing0
 source-bridge 47 1 100
 source-bridge spanning
 fras-host bnn Serial 0/1 fr-lsap 04 vmac 4005.3003.0000 hmac 4001.3745.1088
 fras-host ban Serial 0/1 hmac 4001.3745.1088 bni 4001.3745.1088
 fras-host ban Serial 0/2.37 hmac 4001.3745.1088
```

The following example shows the configuration for the network shown in Figure 17–13.

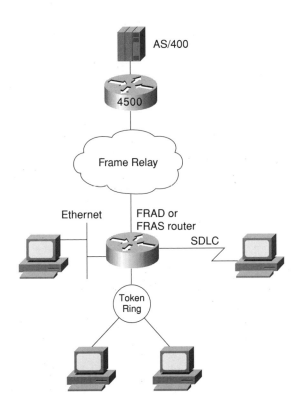

Figure 17–13
FRAS Host Ethernet
connection to AS/400.

AS/400

4500

Frame Relay

Ethernet

FRAD or
FRAS router

SDLC

Token
Ring

FRAS Host Ethernet Connection to AS/400 Configuration Example

```
source-bridge ring-group 226
dlsw local-peer
dlsw bridge-group 1
!
interface Ethernet0
 bridge-group 1
!
interface Serial2
 encapsulation frame-relay IETF
 frame-relay map llc2 502
 frame-relay lmi-type ansi
!
interface Virtual-TokenRing0
 no ip address
 ring-speed 16
 source-bridge 1009 1 226
 fras-host dlsw-local-ack
 fras-host bnn Serial2 fr-lsap 04 vmac 4000.1226.0000 hmac 0800.5ae1.151d
```

FRAS MIB

The FRAS Management Information Base (MIB) CISCO-DLCSW-MIB.MY is a collection of managed objects that can be accessed via a network management protocol such as SNMP. The objects in the MIB support LLC- and SDLC-attached devices for both BNN and BAN formats of RFC 1490. The FRAS MIB user interface is defined by the network manager's SNMP application.

CHAPTER 18

SNA Frame Relay Access Support Commands

This chapter describes the commands to configure Systems Network Architecture (SNA) Frame Relay Access Support (FRAS). For SNA FRAS configuration tasks and examples, see Chapter 17, "Configuring SNA Frame Relay Access Support."

NOTES

Because Frame Relay does not provide the reliable transport required by SNA, the RFC 1490 support of SNA uses Logical-Link Control, type 2 (LLC2) as part of the encapsulation to provide link-level sequencing, acknowledgment, and flow control. The serial interface configured for Internet Engineering Task Force (IETF) encapsulation (RFC 1490) accepts all LLC2 interface configuration commands. For more information about LLC2 interface configuration commands, see Chapter 12, "LLC2 and SDLC Commands."

FRAME-RELAY MAP LLC2

Use the **frame-relay map llc2** interface configuration command to map LLC2 traffic to a data-link connection identifier (DLCI).

> **frame-relay map llc2** *dlci-number*

Syntax	*Description*
dlci-number	Frame Relay DLCI.

Default

No defaults are defined.

Command Mode

Interface configuration

Usage Guidelines

This command first appeared in Cisco IOS Release 10.3.

Example

The following example maps LLC2 traffic to DLCI number 200:

```
frame-relay map llc2 200
```

FRAME-RELAY MAP RSRB

Use the **frame-relay map rsrb** interface configuration command to specify the DLCI number onto which the RSRB traffic is to be mapped.

frame-relay map rsrb *dlci-number*

Syntax	*Description*
dlci-number	Frame Relay DLCI.

Default

No defaults are defined.

Command Mode

Interface configuration

Usage Guidelines

This command first appeared in Cisco IOS Release 10.3.

Example

The following example shows RSRB traffic mapped to DLCI number 30:

```
frame-relay map rsrb 30
```

Related Commands

encapsulation frame-relay

FRAS BACKUP DLSW

Use the **fras backup dlsw** interface configuration command to configure an auxiliary route between the end stations and the host for use as a backup when the DLCI connection to the Frame Relay network is lost. Use the **no** form of this command to cancel the backup configuration.

fras backup dlsw *virtual-mac-address target-ring-number host-mac-address* [**retry** *retry-number*]

no fras backup dlsw *virtual-mac-address target-ring-number host-mac-address* [**retry** *retry-number*]

Syntax	Description
virtual-mac-address	12-digit hexadecimal string used as a source MAC address for all packets going to the host.
target-ring-number	Number configured in the **source-bridge ring-group** command. This is a virtual ring. The valid range is 1 to 4095.
host-mac-address	Destination MAC address of the host.
retry *retry-number*	(Optional) Number of attempts by the end station to reconnect to the primary Frame Relay interface before activating the backup link. The range is 1 to 5 retries. If the **retry** option is not specified, the default number of retries is 5.

Default

FRAS dial backup over DLSw+ is disabled.

Command Mode

Interface configuration

Usage Guidelines

This command first appeared in Cisco IOS Release 11.2 F.

Configure DLSw+ as normally required. Specify the optional keyword **dynamic** at the end of the **dlsw remote-peer** configuration command to enable the peer relationship to be established only when needed (for example, when the **fras backup dlsw** command becomes active).

Example

The following example configures FRAS dial backup over DLSw+:

```
fras backup dlsw 4000.1000.2000 200 1000.5aed.1f53
```

Related Commands

dlsw local-peer
dlsw remote-peer tcp
frame-relay lmi-type
frame-relay map llc2
fras map llc
show fras
source-bridge ring-group

Part II

Command Reference

FRAS BAN

Use the **fras ban** interface configuration command to associate bridging over a Frame Relay network using boundary access node (BAN). Use the **no** form of this command to cancel each association.

> **fras ban** *local-ring bridge-number ring-group ban-dlci-mac* **dlci** *dlci#1* [*dlci#2 ... dlci#5*] [**bni** *mac-addr*]
>
> **no fras ban** *local-ring bridge-number ring-group ban-dlci-mac* **dlci** *dlci#1* [*dlci#2 ... dlci#5*] [**bni** *mac-addr*]

Syntax	Description
local-ring	Decimal number from 1 to 4095 describing the Token Ring interface.
bridge-number	Decimal number from 1 to 15 that uniquely identifies a bridge connecting two rings.
ring-group	Decimal number from 1 to 4095 representing a collection of Token Ring interfaces on one or more routers.
ban-dlci-mac	Frame Relay BAN PVC MAC address.
dlci#1 [*dlci#2 ... dlci#5*]	Frame Relay DLCI. Each DLCI number is unique and is a decimal within the range of 16 to 1007. The keyword **dlci** precedes the list of one or more DLCI numbers. If more than one DLCI number is needed for load balancing in the FRAS BAN configuration command, a maximum of five DLCI numbers are allowed.
bni *mac-addr*	(Optional) Boundary node identifier (BNI) MAC address of the NCP that receives frames from the router.

Default

No defaults are defined.

Command Mode

Interface configuration

Usage Guidelines

This command first appeared in Cisco IOS Release 11.1.

Multipule **fras ban** commands may be configured; however, each **fras ban** command must use a unique DLCI MAC address.

You must configure the **source-bridge ring-group** global configuration command prior to configuring the **fras ban** command.

Example

The following configuration shows FRAS BAN support for Token Ring and serial interfaces:

```
source-bridge ring-group 200
!
interface serial 0
 mtu 4000
 encapsulation frame-relay ietf
 frame-relay lmi-type ansi
 frame-relay map llc2  16
 frame-relay map llc2  17
 fras ban 120 1 200 4000.1000.2000 dlci 16 17
!
interface tokenring 0
 source-bridge 100 5 200
```

Related Commands

source-bridge ring-group

FRAS DDR-BACKUP

Use the **fras ddr-backup** interface configuration command to configure an auxiliary interface for use as a backup when the primary Frame Relay link to the Frame Relay WAN fails. Use the **no** form of this command to cancel the backup configuration.

> **fras ddr-backup interface** *interface dlci-number*
> **no fras ddr-backup**

Syntax	Description
interface *interface*	The interface over which the backup connection is made.
dlci-number	The DLCI number of the session.

Default

FRAS DLCI backup is disabled by default.

Command Mode

Interface configuration

Usage Guidelines

This command first appeared in Cisco IOS Release 11.2 F.

Example

The following example configures FRAS DLCI backup on serial interface 1:

```
fras ddr-backup interface serial1 188
```

Related Commands

show llc2
show fr pvc
show fras

FRAS-HOST BAN

Use the **fras-host ban** interface configuration command to enable the FRAS Host function for BAN.
Use the **no** form of this command to disable the FRAS Host BAN functionality.

> **fras-host ban** *(sub)interface* **hmac** *hmac* [**bni** *bni*]
> **no fras-host ban**

Syntax	Description
(sub)interface	Associated Frame Relay interface or subinterface.
hmac hmac	MAC address of the CIP adapter or LAN-attached host.
bni *bni*	(Optional) Boundary node identifier MAC address. The default *bni* is 4FFF.0000.0000.

Default

The FRAS Host function for BAN is disabled for the Frame Relay subinterface.
The default *bni* is 4FFF.0000.0000.

Command Mode

Interface configuration

Usage Guidelines

This command first appeared in Cisco IOS Release 11.2 F.

Example

The following example enables the FRAS Host function for BAN:

```
fras-host ban Serial0 hmac 4001.3745.0001
```

Related Commands

fras ban
fras-host bnn
fras-host dlsw-local-ack
interface virtual-tokenring

FRAS-HOST BNN

Use the **fras-host bnn** interface configuration command to enable the FRAS Host function for BNN. Use the **no** form of this command to disable the FRAS Host function.

fras-host bnn *(sub)interface* **fr-lsap** *sap* **vmac** *virt-mac* **hmac** *hmac* [**hsap** *hsap*]
no fras-host bnn

Syntax	Description
(sub)interface	Associated Frame Relay interface or subinterface.
fr-lsap *sap*	LLC2 service access point (SAP). The destination SAP on inbound BNN frames received from Frame Relay.
vmac *virt-mac*	Used in combination with the DLCI number to form a unique MAC address. The first four bytes of the MAC address are formed by the VMAC while the last two bytes are formed from the DLCI number. The last two bytes of the VMAC must be configured as zeros.
hmac *hmac*	MAC address of the CIP adaptor or LAN-attached host.
hsap *hsap*	(Optional) Host SAP. If this parameter is not specified, the host SAP value used will match **fr-lsap**.

Default
FRAS Host for BNN is disabled for the Frame Relay subinterface.

Command Mode
Interface configuration

Usage Guidelines
This command first appeared in Cisco IOS Release 11.2 F.

Example
The following example enables the FRAS Host function for BNN:

```
fras-host bnn Serial0 fr-lsap 04 vmac 4005.3003.0000 hmac 4001.3745.0001
```

Related Commands
fras-host ban
fras-host dlsw-local-ack
fras-map
interface virtual-tokenring

Part II

Command Reference

FRAS-HOST DLSW-LOCAL-ACK

Use the **fras-host dlsw-local-ack** interface configuration command to enable LLC2 local termination for FRAS Host connections using the virtual Token Ring. Use the **no** form of this command to disable LLC2 local termination.

> **fras-host dlsw-local-ack**
> **no fras-host dlsw-local-ack**

Syntax   Description

This command has no arguments or keywords.

Default

The default state is FRAS Host LLC2 local termination disabled.

Command Mode

Interface configuration

Usage Guidelines

This command first appeared in Cisco IOS Release 11.2 F.

Example

The following command enables LLC2 local termination for FRAS Host connections using the virtual Token Ring:

```
fras-host dlsw-local-ack
```

Related Commands

dlsw local-peer
fras-host ban
fras-host bnn
interface virtual-tokenring

FRAS MAP LLC

Use the **fras map llc** interface configuration command to associate an LLC connection with a Frame Relay DLCI. Use the **no** form of this command to disable the association.

> **fras map llc** *lan-lsap* **serial** *interface* **frame-relay dlci** *dlci fr-rsap*
> **no fras map llc** *lan-lsap* **serial** *interface* **frame-relay dlci** *dlci fr-rsap*

Syntax	Description
lan-lsap	LLC2 LAN SAP that is the local SAP address of the router.
serial *interface*	Serial interface on which Frame Relay is configured.
frame-relay dlci *dlci*	Frame Relay DLCI.
fr-rsap	LLC2 Frame Relay SAP that is the destination SAP of the router on the Frame Relay side.

Default

The default state is FRAS BNN enhancement disabled.

Command Mode

Interface configuration

Usage Guidelines

This revised version of the **fras map llc** command for the enhanced FRAS BNN functionality first appeared in Cisco IOS Release 11.2 F.

If the destination SAP specified by the end station is equal to *lan-lsap*, the router associates the LLC (LAN) connection with the Frame Relay DLCI.

The MAC address and the SAP address of the end station are no longer required for the BNN enhanced configuration.

Example

In the FRAS BNN enhancement, the revised **fras map llc** command achieves the same result as using multiple **fras map llc** commands in the original FRAS BNN implementation. The following example provides one map definition for both end stations:

```
fras map llc 4 Serial 0 frame-relay dlci 16 04
```

Related Commands

show fras
show llc2

FRAS MAP SDLC

Use the **fras map sdlc** interface configuration command to associate an SDLC link with a Frame Relay DLCI. Use the **no** form of this command to cancel the association.

> **fras map sdlc** *sdlc-address* **serial** *port* **frame-relay** *dlci fr-lsap fr-rsap* [**pfid2** |
>   **afid2** | **fid4**]
> **no fras map sdlc** *sdlc-address* **serial** *port* **frame-relay** *dlci fr-lsap fr-rsap* [**pfid2** |
>   **afid2** | **fid4**]

Syntax	Description
sdlc-address	SDLC address of the downstream SNA device in hexadecimal.
serial *port*	Serial interface on which Frame Relay is configured.
frame-relay *dlci*	Frame Relay DLCI.
fr-lsap	Local SAP address of the logical-link connection on the Cisco Frame Relay Access Device (CFRAD).
fr-rsap	Destination SAP address on the host.
pfid	(Optional) FID2 SNA transmission header for SNA peripheral traffic.
afid2	(Optional) FID2 transmission header for APPN traffic.
fid4	(Optional) Transmission header used on SNA subarea flows.

Default

No defaults are defined.

Command Mode

Interface configuration

Usage Guidelines

This command first appeared in Cisco IOS Release 10.3.

You can map multiple SDLC links to a DLCI.

Example

The following example associates an SDLC link with a Frame Relay DLCI:

```
fras map sdlc c1 serial 0 frame-relay 200 4 4
```

Related Commands

frame-relay map llc2

INTERFACE VIRTUAL-TOKENRING

Use the **interface virtual-tokenring** command to create a virtual Token Ring interface. Use the **no** form of this command to cancel the configuration.

> **interface virtual-tokenring** *number*
> **no interface virtual-tokenring**

Syntax	Description
number	Number of the virtual Token Ring.

Default

No defaults are assigned.

Command Mode

Interface configuration

Usage Guidelines

This command first appeared in Cisco IOS Release 11.2 F.

Example

The following example configures the virtual Token Ring interface:

```
interface virtual-tokenring 0
```

Related Commands

source bridge
fras ban
fras-host bnn

LLC2 DYNWIND

Use the **llc2 dynwind** interface configuration command to enable dynamic window congestion management. Use the **no** form of this command to cancel the configuration.

llc2 dynwind [**nw** *nw-number*] [**dwc** *dwc-number*]
no llc2 dynwind [**nw** *nw-number*] [**dwc** *dwc-number*]

Syntax	Description
nw *nw-number*	(Optional) Specifies a number of frames that must be received to increment the working window value by 1. The default is 4.
dwc *dwc-number*	(Optional) Specifies the number by which the working window value is divided when BECN occurs. Valid numbers are 1, 2, 4, 8, and 16. 1 is a special value that indicates that the working window value should be set to 1 when BECN is indicated. The default is 1.

Defaults

The default *nw-number* value is 4.

The default *dwc-number* value is 1.

Command Mode

Interface configuration

Usage Guidelines

This command first appeared in Cisco IOS Release 10.3.

Example

The following example specifies that to increment the working window, 6 frames must be received, and the working window value should be set to 1 when BECN occurs:

```
llc2 dynwind nw 6 dwc 1
```

SHOW FRAS

Use the **show fras** privileged EXEC command to view notification that the FRAS dial backup-over-DLSw+ feature is active, to display information about the connection state in FRAS, and to display current BNN, BAN, and dial backup information.

    show fras

Syntax   Description

This command has no arguments or keywords.

Command Mode

Privileged EXEC

Usage Guidelines

This command first appeared in Cisco IOS Release 11.1.

Sample Display

The following is sample output from the **show fras** command:

```
Router# show fras

Boundary Network Node (BNN):
DLCI: 66
  Type  Destination     Int   LSap  RSap  Role  State
  fr                          4     4     S     ls_reset (Backup is enabled)
  llc   0000.f63a.2f50  To0   4     4     P     ls_contacted
```

Table 18–1 describes significant fields shown in the display.

Table 18–1 *Show FRAS Field Descriptions*

Field	Description
Type	Connection type. The display example shows LLC and Frame Relay.
Destination	Destination MAC address from the perspective of the Cisco IOS software.

Table 18-1 *Show FRAS Field Descriptions, Continued*

Field	Description
Int	Interface on which the connection resides.
LSap	Local SAP value.
RSap	Remote SAP value.
Role	Local link station role; P means primary and S means secondary.
State	Link station protocol machine state. This value may be one of the following states: • ls_reset—Initial state. • ls_RqOpnStnSent—TEST frame sent; request to open a connection endpoint. • ls_ExchgXid—XID negotiation taking place. • ls_ConnRqSent—SABME sent (connecting side). • ls_SigStnWait—Waiting for signal to clean up the congestion and respond to polling with an RNR. • ls_ConnRspWait—Wait for the other connection end point to bring up the link. • ls_ConnRspSent—A UA has been sent and the router is waiting for a RR to clear up the flow. • ls_Contacted—Everything is connected • ls_DiscWait—Wait for acknowledge to disconnect request.
Backup is enabled	Notification displayed when the FRAS dial backup feature is configured.

SHOW FRAS-HOST

Use the **show fras-host** EXEC command to display the status of LLC2 sessions using FRAS Host.

    show fras-host [*(sub)interface*] [**dlci** *dlci-num*] [**detail**]

Syntax	Description
(sub)interface	Only display LLC2 sessions from a specified Frame Relay interface or subinterface.
dlci *dlci-number*	Only display LLC2 sessions from a specified DLCI.
detail	Display additional information such as the routing information fields (RIFs) and statistics associated with the LLC2 sessions.

Command Mode

EXEC

Usage Guidelines

This command first appeared in Cisco IOS Release 11.2 F.

Sample Display

The following is sample output from the **show fras-host** command:

```
router# show fras-host

Number of Active Control Blocks = 2
Number of Available Control Blocks in Pool = 126

Port  DLCI  Type  FrRsap  FrLSap  HostSap  VMac            HostMac
Se0   16    BNN   04      08      04       4000.ABBA.001E  4000.3000.2000
Se1   37    BAN   04      04      04       4000.0223.0019  4000.3000.2000
```

Table 18–2 describes significant fields shown in the display

Table 18–2   *Show FRAS Host Field Descriptions*

Field	Description
Port	Frame Relay interface or subinterface associated with this LLC2 session.
DLCI	DLCI number associated with this LLC2 session.
Type	FRAS encapsulation type associated with this LLC2 session.
FrRsap	Frame Relay Remote LLC2 Sap associated with this LLC2 session. This SAP is the source sap on LLC2 frames sent by the remote FRAD.
FrLSap	Frame Relay Local LLC2 SAP associated with this LLC2 session. This SAP is the destination SAP on LLC2 frames sent by the remote FRAD.
HostSap	Destination SAP on LLC2 frames sent to the CIP or LAN-attached AS/400. This SAP will be identical to FrLsap unless the **hsap** parameter is configured on the **fras-host bnn** command.
VMac	MAC Address associated with the remote FRAD for this LLC2 session.
HostMac	Mac Address associated with the host for this LLC2 session.

Related Commands

fras-host ban
fras-host bnn
fras-host dlsw-local-ack

SHOW FRAS MAP

Use the **show fras map** privileged EXEC command to display the mapping and connection state of FRAS.

show fras map

Syntax   Description

This command has no arguments or keywords.

Command Mode

Privileged EXEC

Usage Guidelines

This command first appeared in Cisco IOS Release 10.3.

Sample Display

The following is sample output from the **show fras map** command:

```
Router# show fras map

Type Destination    Int  LSap  RSap  Role  State
tr   0800.5a8f.8802 tr0  4     4     P     ls_contacted
fr   200            s0   4     4     S     ls_contacted
```

Table 18–3 describes significant fields shown in the display.

Table 18–3 *Show FRAS Map Field Descriptions*

Field	Description
Type	Interface type.
Destination	Destination address.
Int	Interface.
LSap	Local SAP.
RSap	Remote SAP.
Role	Local link station role; P means primary, S means secondary.
State	Link station protocol machine state.

SOURCE-BRIDGE

Use the **source-bridge** interface configuration command to configure an interface for source-route bridging. Use the **no** form of this command to disable source-route bridging on an interface.

source-bridge *source-ring-number bridge-number target-ring-number* [**conserve-ring**]
no source-bridge *source-ring-number bridge-number target-ring-number* [**conserve-ring**]

Syntax	Description
source-ring-number	Ring number for the interface's Token Ring or FDDI ring. It must be a decimal number in the range 1 to 4095 that uniquely identifies a network segment or ring within the bridged Token Ring or FDDI network
bridge-number	Number that uniquely identifies the bridge connecting the source and target rings. It must be a decimal number in the range 1 to 15.
target-ring-number	Ring number of the destination ring on this router. The number must be unique within the bridged Token Ring or FDDI network. The target ring can also be a ring group. It must be a decimal number.
conserve-ring	(Optional) Keyword to enable SRB over Frame Relay. When this option is configured, the SRB software does not add the ring number associated with the Frame Relay partner's virtual ring (PVC) to outbound explorer frames. This option is permitted for Frame Relay subinterfaces only.

Default
SRB is disabled.

Command Mode
Interface configuration

Usage Guidelines
This revised version of the **source-bridge** command to enable SRB over Frame Relay first appeared in Cisco IOS Release 11.2 F.

The parser automatically displays the word "active" in the **source-bridge** command in configurations that have SRB enabled. You do not need to enter the **source-bridge** command with the **active** keyword.

Examples
In the following example, Token Rings 129 and 130 are connected via a router:

```
interface tokenring 0
 source-bridge 129 1 130
!
interface tokenring 1
 source-bridge active 130 1 129
```

In the following example, an FDDI ring on one router is connected to a Token Ring on a second router across a DLSw+ link:

```
dlsw local-peer peer-id 132.11.11.2
dlsw remote-peer 0 tcp 132.11.11.3
interface fddi 0
 no ip address
 multiring all
 source-bridge active 26 1 10
!
dlsw local-peer peer-id 132.11.11.3
dlsw remote-peer 0 tcp 132.11.11.2
interface tokenring 0
 no ip address
 multiring all
 source-bridge active 25 1 10
```

In the following example, a router forwards frames from a locally attached Token Ring over the Frame Relay using SRB:

```
source-bridge ring-group 200
!
interface Serial0
 encapsulation frame-relay
!
interface Serial0.30 point-to-point
 frame-relay interface-dlci 30 ietf
 source-bridge 100 1 200 conserve-ring
 source-bridge spanning
!
interface TokenRing0
 source-bridge 600 1 200
```

Related Commands

debug frame-relay packet
debug source bridge
debug source error
debug source event
encapsulation frame-relay
frame-relay interface-dlci
source-bridge ring-group
source-bridge transparent

19

Configuring
Advanced Peer-to-Peer
Networking

Many enterprises today maintain two networks: a traditional, hierarchical Systems Network Architecture (SNA) subarea network and an interconnected LAN network, based on connectionless, dynamic protocols. The advantage of the subarea SNA network is that it is manageable and deterministic and provides guaranteed response time. The disadvantages are that it requires extensive system definition and does not take advantage of the capabilities of intelligent devices.

Cisco provides remote source-route bridging (RSRB) and data-link switching plus (DLSw+), which enable encapsulation of SNA traffic and consolidation of SNA with multiprotocol networks.

Advanced Peer-to-Peer Networking (APPN) gives the additional flexibility to route SNA natively, without encapsulation. You can use APPN by itself or in combination with RSRB and DLSw+ to provide the best solution for your networking needs.

High Performance Routing (HPR) is an enhancement to APPN that improves network performance and reliability. Considered the next step in the evolution of SNA networking, HPR provides two new elements: Rapid Transport Protocol (RTP) and Automatic Network Routing (ANR).

This chapter describes how to configure APPN. For a complete description of the APPN commands in this chapter, see Chapter 20, "APPN Configuration Commands."

APPN COMMAND MODES

APPN offers the ability to define attributes of the APPN network that can become quite complex. To easily manage the capability to define the details of APPN, special configuration command modes and conventions have been developed.

Because APPN offers a large number of configuration options, specific configuration dialogues are used for each major APPN configuration task. When you define the major item, you will automatically enter the detailed configuration mode for that item. There are two options to exit the detailed mode. The "complete" command exits the detailed configuration mode and updates the

APPN subsystem with the changes. The **exit** command leaves the definition in **no complete** state and does not update the APPN subsystem.

COMPLETING APPN DEFINITIONS

No APPN definition is usable by the APPN subsystem until the definition is marked as complete. This is accomplished by entering the **complete** command when you have finished defining items in the detailed configuration mode.

CHANGING APPN DEFINITIONS

To update a major definition item that is already known to APPN, enter the major item definition as it was originally defined. Then, to indicate that you wish to modify an existing definition, enter **no complete**. You will then be able to change the items in the detailed configuration mode for that major definition. Remember to enter **complete** when you have finished changing the configuration item to update the APPN subsystem with your changes.

APPN CONFIGURATION TASK LIST

To configure APPN in your network, perform the tasks discussed in the following sections. Because of the hierarchical nature of APPN definitions, you should configure APPN by following the order specified below. Definition of an APPN Control Point and at least one APPN port are required. In addition, you must start the APPN subsystem to activate APPN routing. The other tasks in this list are optional, and might or might not need to be configured, depending on the APPN network configuration you have.

- Defining an APPN Control Point
- Configuring Serial Interface Encapsulation
- Defining an APPN Port
- Defining an APPN Link Station
- Defining an APPN Connection Network
- Defining an APPN Class of Service
- Defining an APPN Mode
- Defining an APPN Partner LU Location
- Starting the APPN Subsystem
- Stopping the APPN Subsystem
- Starting and Stopping APPN Ports and Link Stations
- Tuning the APPN Network
- Monitoring the APPN Network

See the end of this chapter for the "APPN Configuration Examples" section.

DEFINING AN APPN CONTROL POINT

An APPN control-point definition is required to use APPN. This definition adds the fully qualified control-point name for the node, which is a combination of a network identifier and a control-point name. The network identifier must be the same as other network nodes in the APPN subnetwork attached to this node. The control-point name identifies this node uniquely within the particular subnetwork.

To define an APPN control point, perform the following task in global configuration mode:

Task	Command
Define an APPN control point.	**appn control-point** *netid.cpname*

Performing this task takes you from global configuration mode into APPN control-point configuration mode. From this mode, you can perform any of the following optional definition tasks, which identify various capabilities and attributes of the control point.

APPN offers configuration commands that allow you to limit the resources on the router that are consumed for APPN. You may configure both the maximum memory and maximum percentage of system buffers that APPN is permitted to use. APPN cached directory entries and cached topology routing trees can also be limited to a maximum number.

To configure these resources, perform the following tasks in APPN control-point configuration mode:

Task		Command
Step 1	Specify the maximum memory available to APPN.	**maximum-memory** *bytes*
Step 2	Specify the maximum percentage of system buffers available to APPN.	**buffer-percent** *number*
Step 3	Specify the maximum number of cached directory entries.	**max-cached-entries** *number*
Step 4	Specify the maximum number of cached topology routing trees.	**max-cached-trees** *number*

By default, the central resource registration function is enabled in the router so that registration of downstream resources in the central directory server will be attempted by the router when it receives a request from the control point that owns the resource. If there is unpredictable behavior related to the central resource registration function or central directory server, use the **no central-resource-registration** command to disable the central resource registration function. In normal circumstances, there should not be any reason to disable the central resource registration function.

To enable or disable the central resource registration function, perform the following tasks in APPN control-point configuration mode:

Task	Command
Step 1 Enable the central resource registration function.	**central-resource-registration**
Step 2 Disable the central resource registration function.	**no central-resource-registration**

If you plan to use Dependent LU Requestor (DLUR) to provide services for dependent LUs connected to this APPN node, you must indicate that this DLUR function is requested for this control point. In addition, you may configure node-wide defaults for the Dependent LU Server and Backup Dependent LU Server that this node will contact.

To specify DLUR or DLUS services for this control point, perform the following tasks in APPN control-point configuration mode:

Task	Command
Step 1 Specify that the DLUR is supported on the control point.	**dlur**
Step 2 Specify the name of the default DLUS that provides SSCP services to the downstream PU.	**dlus** *netid.cpname*
Step 3 Specify the default backup DLUS to perform SSCP services for downstream PUs if the default DLUS is unavailable.	**backup-dlus** *netid.cpname*

You may configure the relative resistance you want this node to have when being considered for APPN intermediate session routing (ISR). This is a number in the range 0 through 255 that specifies this node's relative resistance. The default resistance is 128.

To configure the relative resistance of the local node, perform the following task in APPN control-point configuration mode:

Task	Command
Specify the resistance of the local node.	**route-additional-resistance** *number*

Cisco's APPN implementation allows you to save the APPN directory on a TFTP host. This feature allows the node to restore previously learned directory information when the node is restored to service or in the event of a failure.

To save the APPN directory, perform the following tasks in APPN control-point configuration mode:

Task	Command
Step 1 Enable directory safe store and specify the IP host address and the file path for safe store.	**safe-store-host ip address** *address* **directory** *path*
Step 2 Specify the number of separate cache instances to save before overwriting previous instances.	**safe-store-cycle** *number*
Step 3 Specify how often the directory database is stored to permanent media.	**safe-store-interval** *interval*

The ID number and ID block combine to form the identifier for this node in the XID that is exchanged when the local node connects to other nodes.

To specify the ID number and ID block, perform the following tasks in APPN control-point configuration mode:

Task	Command
Step 1 Specify the ID block (the first 3 digits of the node identifier for the local node).	**xid-block-number** *number*
Step 2 Specify the ID number (the last 5 digits of the node identifier for the local node).	**xid-id-number** *number*

Configuring HPR Resources

APPN HPR offers configuration commands that allow you to limit the resources on the router that are used for APPN HPR. To configure these resources, perform the following tasks in APPN control-point configuration mode:

Task		Command
Step 1	Enable HPR	**hpr**
Step 2	Specify the maximum number of sessions allowed over an RTP connection.	**hpr max-sessions** *num-sessions*
Step 3	Specify the maximum number of request packets to send before closing the RTP connection.	**hpr retries** *low-retries medium-retries high-retries network-retries*
Step 4	Specify how many seconds to wait for a packet to be received before initiating a path switch.	**hpr timers liveness** *low-time medium-time high-time network-time*
Step 5	Specify the amount of time allowed to attempt a path switch for an RTP connection.	**hpr timers path-switch** *low-time medium-time high-time network-time*

The following commands allow for the addition, removal, or completion of configuration items within the APPN control-point configuration mode.

Task	Command
Negate or restore the default value for a configuration command.	**no** *command*
Complete the APPN control point definition, return to global configuration mode, and update the APPN subsystem.	**complete**
Allow modifications to a previously completed APPN control point definition.	**no complete**
Exit APPN control point definition dialog without completing the definition and without updating the APPN subsystem.	**exit**

CONFIGURING SERIAL INTERFACE ENCAPSULATION

If you plan to use APPN over a serial interface, the interface must be configured as a serial encapsulation type supported by APPN. The following encapsulation types are supported:

- ATM
- Frame Relay
- PPP
- SDLC
- SMDS
- X25
- ISDN (via PPP)

DEFINING AN APPN PORT

An APPN port definition is used to associate APPN capabilities with a specific interface APPN will use. Each interface that will be used for APPN communications requires an APPN port definition statement. A port can be associated with a specific interface by performing the following task in global configuration mode:

Task	Command
Define an APPN port associated with an interface.	**appn port** *portname interface*

A port may also be associated with a source-route bridge ring group to enable APPN to send and receive traffic to any local or remote source-route bridged station. To configure a virtual port that connects to a source-bridge ring-group, perform the following task in global configuration mode:

Task	Command
Define an APPN Port associated with a source-route bridge group.	**appn port** *portname* **rsrb**

A port may also be associated with virtual data-link control to allow link stations using this port to connect over DLSw+ using virtual data-link control. To configure an APPN virtual data-link control port, perform the following task in global configuration mode:

Task	Command
Define an APPN Port associated with virtual data-link control.	**appn port** *portname* **vdlc**

Performing any of these tasks takes you from global configuration mode into APPN-port configuration mode. From this mode, you can perform one or more of the definition tasks that follow. These tasks define various capabilities and attributes of the port. Some tasks are required; others are optional.

Configuring APPN HPR Port Definitions

You can specify the SAP value used for Automatic Network Routing frames. The SAP value is used by all link stations that use the port. To specify the SAP value, perform the following task in APPN-port configuration mode:

Task	Command
Specify the SAP for Automatic Network Routing frames.	**hpr sap** *sap*

HPR is enabled at the control-point configuration mode. To selectively disable HPR on a port definition, perform the following task in APPN-port configuration mode:

Task	Command
Disable support for HPR on a port.	**no hpr**

Each APPN link negotiates a maximum basic transmit unit size during the connection phase with an adjacent node. This value limits the size of an SNA frame that can be sent over the link. On a port, the maximum basic transmit unit that can be received on this port can be configured and will be enforced for every APPN link using this port. In addition, the desired maximum basic transmit unit that can be sent by this node can be specified. The maximum basic transmit unit must be configured to be smaller than the maximum transmission unit (MTU) for the interface associated with this port.

The maximum basic transmit unit for a link can affect APPN ISR performance. Larger maximum basic transmit units allow more data to be placed in each SNA frame, offering higher data throughput for APPN ISR.

To configure the maximum basic transmit unit size, perform the following tasks in APPN-port configuration mode:

Task	Command
Step 1 Specify the desired maximum receive basic transmit unit.	**max-rcv-btu-size** *size*

Task	Command
Step 2 Specify the maximum basic transmit unit size for transmission groups using this port.	**desired-max-send-btu-size** *size*

APPN uses SAP 4 by default. If you want APPN to use a different SAP on this port, perform the following task in APPN-port configuration mode:

Task	Command
Specify the local SAP to activate on the interface.	**local-sap** *sap*

The maximum number of link stations that can use an APPN port at any one time is configurable, as is the number of this maximum that are reserved for link stations connecting in to this port and link stations connecting out from this port.

To specify the maximum number of link stations, perform the following tasks in APPN-port configuration mode:

Task	Command
Step 1 Specify the maximum number of active link stations allowed on this port.	**max-link-stations** *number*
Step 2 Specify the number of link stations to be reserved for inbound links.	**reserved-inbound** *number*
Step 3 Specify the number of link stations to be reserved for outbound links.	**reserved-outbound** *number*

A port is configured, by default, to accept connections from other APPN nodes dynamically without requiring a link station definition for that node. It is possible to configure a port so that it does not accept incoming connection requests unless a link station has been predefined for the partner node.

To configure a port so that it does not accept incoming connection requests, perform the following task in APPN-port configuration mode:

Task	Command
Specify that this port will not create dynamic link stations.	**no service-any**

The **null-xid-poll** command permits PU 2.0 devices that connect in with XID0 to build a dynamic link station. It is no longer necessary to configure a link definition. When this command is used, the router expects its partner to reveal its identity first by responding with either XID3 or XID0.

This feature works in a mixed environment of PU 2.0 and PU 2.1 devices where the same APPN port is shared by both types of devices. By default, XID3 is used to poll the devices. When a PU 2.0 device responds with XID0, the link is created and established dynamically. PU 2.1 devices are not affected by this change, and go through the XID3 negotiation as usual.

To configure **null-xid-poll**, perform the following task in APPN-port configuration mode:

Task	Command
Specify that the null XID should be used to poll the remote node associated with this APPN port.	**null-xid-poll**

Care must be exercised when configuring **null-xid-poll**. If two Cisco APPN network node routers connect across ports configured with **null-xid-poll**, the APPN connection will fail because both routers expect the other to respond first using either XID0 or XID3. Similar behavior might occur when a port configured with **null-xid-poll** attempts communication with a front-end processor configured for XID polling. You only need to configure **null-xid-poll** when dealing with a PU 2.0 device that does not respond gracefully to the XID3 poll.

If the port defined is an RSRB virtual port, the port must be assigned a MAC address and must be associated with a source-route bridge ring group. To assign a MAC address and associate it with a source-route bridge ring group, perform the following task in APPN-port configuration mode:

Task	Command
Assign a MAC address and ring number to an RSRB virtual port, and associate it with a source-route bridge ring group.	**rsrb-virtual-station** *mac-address local-ring bridge-number target-ring*

If the port defined is a virtual data-link control port, the port must be associated with a source-route bridge ring group and assigned a MAC address. To associate the port with a ring group and assign it a MAC address, perform the following task in APPN-port configuration mode:

Task	Command
Associate the virtual data-link control port with a source-route bridge ring group, and assign a MAC address.	**vdlc** *ring-group* [**vmac** *vdlc-mac-address*]

If the port is defined as an SDLC port, the secondary SDLC address can be specified. For X.25, an X.121 address for this port may be configured. To specify the secondary SDLC address or the X.25 subaddress, perform one of the following tasks in APPN-port configuration mode:

Task	Command
Assign a secondary SDLC address to this port.	sdlc-sec-addr *address*
Assign an X.121 address for a port on an X.25 interface.	x25-subaddress {pvc | svc} *address*

Many APPN-port configuration commands are used to assign link station parameters for dynamic links that use this port. These values also can be used to establish default values for defined link stations associated with this port. The following configuration tasks are used to configure default link station values for link stations associated with this port. For more information on these tasks, see the following section, "Defining an APPN Link Station."

Task	Commands
Specify the cost per byte transmission group characteristic for link stations on this port.	cost-per-byte *cost*
Specify the cost per connect time transmission group characteristic for link stations on this port.	cost-per-connect-time *cost*
Specify the effective capacity transmission group characteristic for link stations on this port.	effective-capacity *capacity*
Specify that the link stations on this port should be taken down when no sessions are using the link.	limited-resource
Specify the propagation delay transmission group characteristic for link stations on this port.	propagation-delay {minimum | lan | telephone | packet-switched | satellite | maximum}
Specify how many times a link station will attempt activation and the interval between retries	retry-limit {*retries* | infinite} [*interval*]
Specify the link station role used in XID negotiations.	role {negotiable | primary | secondary}
Specify the security level transmission group characteristic for link stations on this port.	security *security-level*

Task	Commands
Specify the user-defined-1 transmission group characteristic for link stations on this port.	**user-defined-1** *value*
Specify the user-defined-2 transmission group characteristic for link stations on this port.	**user-defined-2** *value*
Specify the user-defined-3 transmission group characteristic for link stations on this port.	**user-defined-3** *value*

The following commands allow for the addition, removal, or completion of configuration items within the APPN-port configuration mode.

Task	Command
Negate or restore the default value for a configuration command.	**no** *command*
Complete the APPN port definition, return to global configuration mode, and update the APPN subsystem.	**complete**
Allow modifications to a previously completed APPN port definition.	**no complete**
Exit APPN port definition dialog without completing the definition and without updating the APPN subsystem.	**exit**

DEFINING AN APPN LINK STATION

A link station is a representation of the connection or potential connection to another node. In many cases, if the partner node is initiating the connection, a link station definition is not necessary. It will be built dynamically when the partner node initiates the connection. You must define a link station if you want this node to initiate APPN connections with other nodes. You also may define a link station to specify attributes of an APPN connection regardless of which node initiates the connection.

To define an APPN logical link, perform the following task in global configuration mode:

Task	Command
Define an APPN logical link.	**appn link-station** *linkname*

Performing this task takes you from global configuration mode into APPN link-station configuration mode. From the APPN link-station configuration mode, you must associate the link station with an APPN port that it will use.

Task	Command
Associate a link station with the APPN port that it will use.	**port** *portname*

The following optional configuration tasks also can be performed in APPN link-station configuration mode.

Configuring APPN HPR Link Definitions

HPR is enabled at the control-point configuration mode. To selectively disable HPR on a link definition, perform the following task in APPN link-station configuration mode:

Task	Command
Disable support for HPR on a link.	**no hpr**

When defining a link that can initiate a connection to a partner node, a destination address must be provided to allow this node to contact the partner. This address is also used for incoming connections to associate the appropriate link station with the incoming call. The following configuration commands for specifying a destination address are dependent upon the media in use.

Task	Command
Configure the remote address of a node across an ATM interface.	**atm-dest-address** *pvc*
Specify the Frame Relay DLCI of the partner node for Frame Relay links.	**fr-dest-address** *dlci* [*sap*]
Specify a destination address and destination SAP for LAN media that use a 6-byte hardware address. This includes Token Ring, Ethernet, FDDI, and connections through RSRB and virtual data-link control.	**lan-dest-address** *mac-addr* [*sap*]
Specify the destination SAP across a PPP interface.	**ppp-dest-address** *sap*
Specify the SDLC address for the partner node for SDLC links.	**sdlc-dest-address** *address*

Task	Command
Specify the remote address of a node across an SMDS interface.	**smds-dest-address** *address sap*
Specify the X.25 address for the partner node for X.25 links.	**x25-dest-address** *address*

For most APPN connections, the adjacent control point name, transmission group number, and link station role can be learned or negotiated dynamically so there is no reason to configure them. If necessary, these items can be configured with the following commands. If the partner node requests values which differ from the values coded, the link activation will fail.

Task	Command
Step 1 Specify the name of the partner node for the link station.	**adjacent-cp-name** *netid.cpname*
Step 2 Specify the transmission group number for the link.	**tg-number** *number*
Step 3 Specify the link station role.	**role** {**negotiable** | **primary** | **secondary**}

A link station defaults to attempt a connection with the adjacent node when the APPN subsystem starts. If you wish to define a link, but not have it automatically attempt to establish a connection with the partner node, perform the following task in APPN link-station configuration mode:

Task	Command
Specify that the link will not attempt to establish an APPN connection when the APPN subsystem is started.	**no connect-at-startup**

APPN attempts to bring up CP-CP sessions on the first active link between network nodes. It is possible to prevent CP-CP session establishment on a link by performing the following task in APPN link-station configuration mode:

Task	Command
Specify that no CP-CP sessions will be established on this link.	**no cp-cp-sessions-supported**

By default, APPN accepts connections and learns the node type of the partner node during XID exchange. If you wish to enforce that only a certain node type is permitted to connect via this link station, perform the following task in APPN link-station configuration mode:

Task	Command
Specify that the adjacent node type must be verified as a requirement of link activation.	**verify-adjacent-node-type** {**learn** | **len** | **nn**}

If you want this link to disconnect when no sessions are using it, you may indicate that the link is a limited resource by performing the following task in APPN link-station configuration mode:

Task	Command
Specify that the link is to be taken down when no sessions are using the link.	**limited-resource**

When this node is attempting to establish a connection with an adjacent node, you can configure the number of times this node will attempt to initiate contact and the time interval between connection attempts. Each time the link station is started, the retry count is reset and the node will attempt connection until the retry limit is reached. To specify the retry limit, perform the following task in APPN link-station configuration mode:

Task	Command
Specify how many times a link station will attempt activation, and the interval between retries.	**retry-limit** {*retries* | **infinite**} [*interval*]

APPN links can be configured to interoperate with priority or custom queuing mechanisms available in the Cisco IOS software. To configure an APPN link for priority or custom queuing, perform one of the following tasks in APPN link-station configuration mode:

Task	Command
Specify the custom queuing queue number for this link station.	**link-queuing custom** *queue-number*
Specify the priority queuing parameter for this link station.	**link-queuing priority** *level*

If you are using dependent LU requestor (DLUR), you may configure the primary and backup dependent LU server (DLUS) for links on which this node is providing SSCP services via the DLUR function. These definitions override the node-wide defaults that might have been configured in APPN control-point configuration mode.

To configure the primary and backup dependent LU server (DLUS), perform the following tasks in APPN link-station configuration mode:

Task	Command
Specify the name of the DLUS node that provides SSCP services to the downstream PUs of the link.	**dlus** *netid.cpname*
Specify the backup DLUS node that will be used in the event the primary DLUS is unreachable.	**backup-dlus** *netid.cpname*

Normally, DLUR will discover the capabilities of the adjacent node and will initiate the proper XID exchange for PU type 2.0 nodes. However, a node that sends null XID but cannot receive XID3 will require configuration as a type 2.0 device to allow the node to connect properly for DLUR services. In addition, if you want to configure this node to establish the link to the downstream PU in cases where the DLUS is initiating the activation of the device, you must configure the downstream PU name as it is known to the DLUS. In most cases, the DLUR initiates activation of the device, so coding the PU name is not necessary.

To configure a node as a type 2.0 device and configure the downstream PU name, perform the following tasks in APPN link-station configuration mode:

Task		Command
Step 1	Specify that the downstream PU whose dependent LU request is propagated through the link is a PU Type 2.0.	**pu-type-20**
Step 2	Specify the downstream PU name.	**dlur-dspu-name** *pu-name*

APPN calculates routes for SNA sessions using a complex algorithm that compares various characteristics of an APPN transmission group with the acceptable range of these characteristics defined in the APPN class of service (COS) requested. Cisco uses defaults for these values that offer basic APPN functionality without the need to customize transmission group characteristics. However, if you wish to configure transmission group characteristics for an APPN connection, use the following configuration commands.

To configure the transmission group characteristics for an APPN connection, perform one or more of the following tasks in APPN link-station configuration mode:

Task	Commands
Specify the cost per byte transmission group characteristic for this link.	cost-per-byte *cost*
Specify the relative cost per connection transmission group characteristic for the link.	cost-per-connect-time *cost*
Specify effective-capacity transmission group characteristic for the link.	effective-capacity *capacity*
Specify the propagation delay transmission group characteristic for the link.	propagation-delay {minimum | lan | telephone | packet-switched | satellite | maximum}
Specify the security level transmission group characteristic for the link.	security *security-level*
Specify the user-defined-1 transmission group characteristic for this link station.	user-defined-1 *value*
Specify the user-defined-2 transmission group characteristic for this link station.	user-defined-2 *value*
Specify the user-defined-3 transmission group characteristic for this link station.	user-defined-3 *value*

The following commands allow for the addition, removal, or completion of configuration items within the APPN link-station configuration mode.

Task	Command
Negate or restore the default value for a configuration command.	no *command*
Complete the APPN link station definition, return to global configuration mode, and update the APPN subsystem.	complete
Allow modifications to a previously completed APPN link station definition.	no complete
Exit APPN link station definition dialog without completing the definition and without updating the APPN subsystem.	exit

DEFINING AN APPN CONNECTION NETWORK

An APPN connection network allows nodes on the same shared media to connect directly, even if there is no APPN link defined between them. Connection networks can be used to provide any-to-any connectivity on shared media without the need to define any-to-any link station connectivity. When a route is calculated through a connection network, a dynamic link station will be built and a connection will be established between the nodes on each side of the connection network. You must configure the same connection network name at each node that will participate in the connection network.

To indicate that this node is a member of a specific connection network, perform the following task in global configuration mode:

Task	Command
Define an APPN connection network.	**appn connection-network** *netid.cnname*

Performing this task takes you from global configuration mode into APPN connection network configuration mode.

From APPN connection network configuration mode, you can specify up to five ports that are visible to the connection network. Usually, only a single port definition is desired for each connection network. However, in some instances it might be desirable to have more than one port as a member of a connection network, especially if two ports are attached to the same physical media. APPN route selection may choose any of the listed ports when calculating routes to or from any other member of this connection network. Therefore, it is important to ensure that each port listed is accessible by means of hardware address from every member of the connection network.

Ensure the port you choose is on an interface type that supports APPN connection networks. Connection network definitions are supported on Token Ring, Ethernet, and FDDI interfaces, as well as RSRB and DLSw+ virtual ports.

To associate a port name with this connection network definition, perform the following task in APPN connection network configuration mode:

Task	Command
Associate a port name with this connection network definition.	**port** *portname*

The following commands allow for the addition, removal, or completion of configuration items within the APPN connection network configuration mode.

Task	Command
Negate or restore the default value for a configuration command.	**no** *command*
Complete the APPN connection network definition, return to global configuration mode, and update the APPN subsystem.	**complete**
Allow modifications to a previously completed APPN connection network definition.	**no complete**
Exit APPN connection network definition dialog without completing the definition and without updating the APPN subsystem.	**exit**

DEFINING AN APPN CLASS OF SERVICE

Cisco provides standard predefined APPN class-of-service definitions that are commonly used in APPN networks. These are #BATCH, #BATCHSC, #CONNECT, #INTER, #INTERSC, SNAS-VCMG, CPSVCMG. You can define an APPN class of service or modify the predefined definitions. Each class-of-service definition must have between one and eight node rows, between one and eight transmission group rows, and a transmission priority to be used for this class of service.

Each node row defines the weight to be assigned to a node used in APPN route calculation that is within the range of values for this row. The first row should have the smallest weight and the most restrictive range of acceptable values. Subsequent rows should have higher weight and be less restrictive than the previous rows in the range of acceptable values. Note that if a node does not fit within the acceptable range for any of the node rows, it will not be considered for inclusion in a route with the class of service.

For each node row defined, specify maximum and minimum values for node congestion and route-additional resistance. Node congestion is either yes or no; route-additional resistance is a value between 0 and 255 with higher numbers indicating higher resistance to intermediate routes.

Similarly, each transmission group row defines the weight to be assigned to a link used in APPN route calculation that is within the acceptable range of values for this row. Like node rows, each subsequent row should increase in weight and be less restrictive than the previous in the range of acceptable values. If the transmission group characteristics do not lie within the acceptable range for any of the transmission group rows, the link will not be considered when calculating a route with this class of service.

Each transmission group row allows you to specify the maximum and minimum values for cost per byte, cost per connect, link capacity, propagation delay, security, and three user-defined characteristics. Each of these values is specified using a relative value between 0 and 255.

To define a class of service, perform the following task in global configuration mode:

Task	Command
Define an APPN class of service.	**appn class-of-service** *cosname*

Performing this task takes you from global configuration mode into APPN class-of-service configuration mode. From the class of service mode, you must perform the following tasks:

Task		Command
Step 1	Specify a node row number, the weight for this row, and the minimum and maximum values that may be assigned this weight.	**node-row** *index* **weight** *weight* **congestion** {yes | no} {yes | no} **route-additional-resistance** *min max*
Step 2	Specify a transmission group row number, the weight for this row, and the minimum and maximum values for transmission groups that may be assigned this weight.	**tg-row** *index* **weight** *weight* **byte** *min max* **time** *min max* **capacity** *min max* **delay** *min max* **security** *min max* **user1** *min max* **user2** *min max* **user3** *min max*
Step 3	Specify the transmission priority for the class of service.	**transmission-priority** *priority*

The following commands allow for the addition, removal, or completion of configuration items within the APPN class-of-service configuration mode:

Task	Command
Negate or restore the default value for a configuration command.	**no** *command*
Complete the APPN class-of-service definition, return to global configuration mode, and update the APPN subsystem.	**complete**

Task	Command
Allow modifications to a previously completed APPN class-of-service definition.	**no complete**
Exit APPN class-of-service definition dialog without completing the definition and without updating the APPN subsystem.	**exit**

DEFINING AN APPN MODE

An APPN mode definition is used by a network node to associate a mode name received on an APPN search or session request with a class of service known to this node. Most APPN nodes will supply the class of service to their network node server, so mode definition may not be required in many APPN networks. However, if this node is providing network node services to an end node that does not supply a class of service, or this node is providing network node services for a LEN node, mode definitions might be required for each mode that is used by the partner node.

Cisco provides standard predefined mode definitions for modes that are commonly used in an APPN network. The predefined mode names are the blank mode, #BATCH, #BATCHSC, #INTER, #INTERSC, CPSVCMG, and SNASVCMG. You can change a predefined mode or define a new mode. To define an APPN mode, perform the following task in global configuration mode:

Task	Command
Define an APPN mode.	**appn mode** *modename*

Performing this task takes you from global configuration mode into APPN mode configuration mode. Within this mode, you must assign a class of service to the mode definition.

Task	Command
Associate a class of service with the defined mode.	**class-of-service** *cosname*

The following commands allow for the addition, removal, or completion of configuration items within the APPN mode configuration mode.

Task	Command
Negate or restore the default value for a configuration command.	**no** *command*
Complete the APPN mode definition, return to global configuration mode, and update the APPN subsystem.	**complete**

Task	Command
Allow modifications to a previously completed APPN mode definition.	**no complete**
Exit APPN class-of-service definition dialog without completing the definition and without updating the APPN subsystem.	**exit**

DEFINING AN APPN PARTNER LU LOCATION

The APPN directory stores names of resources and their owners. Usually this information is learned dynamically via APPN searches. However, you might wish to define manually the location of specific resources. Doing so can improve network performance by allowing directed APPN searches to travel straight to the owning control point, without the need for an initial broadcast search for the resource. However, APPN is known for its dynamic capabilities, not its need for system definition. For this reason, and for easier manageability, it is good practice to define location names only when necessary.

When a LEN node is attached to an APPN network node, all destination resources that reside on the LEN node must be defined on the network node to be reachable via the APPN network.

To define a partner LU location, perform the following task in global configuration mode:

Task	Command
Specify the partner resource name.	**appn partner-lu-location** *netid.luname*

Performing this task takes you from the global configuration mode into the APPN partner LU location configuration mode.

You must configure an owning control point for each partner LU configured. The owning control point is the control point name for the LEN, end node, or network node on which the resource resides. To specify the name of the control point owning the partner LU, perform the following task in APPN partner LU location configuration mode:

Task	Command
Specify the name of the control point owning the partner LU.	**owning-cp** *netid.cpname*

If this node is not the network node server for the resource, you may also configure the network node server name. To reduce APPN searching, the network node server operand must be coded and must be the current server for the resource.

If this node is the network node server for the resource being defined, do not configure a network node server.

To specify the name of the network node server for the resource, perform the following task in APPN partner LU location configuration mode:

Task	Command
Specify the name of the network node server for the resource.	**serving-nn** *netid.cpname*

A partial name wildcard partner LU is a definition that applies to all resources that match a partial name. For example, a definition for location NETA.PE, which is specified as a wildcard definition, serves as a entry for NETA.PEANUT and NETA.PENNY, but not NETA.PUMKIN. Be careful when using partial name wildcards, as they can easily cause network problems if resources that match the partial name do not actually exist in the specified location.

A full wildcard partner LU definition is specified by defining a partner LU location without specifying a resource name and specifying the wildcard option. Full wildcards answer positively to any search for any resource in the network. Only one full wildcard definition can exist in an APPN network. Full wildcards are sometimes used when the APPN subnetwork is small and an attached LEN node is the gateway to a large connected network. Full wildcard definitions reduce APPN performance and can cause a variety of network problems. Hence, use of full wildcard definitions should be avoided.

To specify a partial name or full wildcard partner LU, perform the following task in APPN partner LU location configuration mode:

Task	Command
Specify the entry as a partial-name wildcard or a full wildcard.	**wildcard**

The following commands allow for the addition, removal, or completion of configuration items within the APPN partner LU location configuration mode.

Task	Command
Negate or restore the default value for a configuration command.	**no** *command*

Task	Command
Complete the APPN partner LU definition, return to global configuration mode, and update the APPN subsystem.	complete
Allow modifications to a previously completed APPN partner LU definition.	no complete
Exit APPN partner LU definition dialog without completing the definition and without updating the APPN subsystem.	exit

STARTING THE APPN SUBSYSTEM

As indicated by the following commands, the APPN subsystem may be started via global configuration mode or privileged EXEC mode.

Task	Command
Start the APPN subsystem from global configuration mode. Provided this configuration is saved, the APPN subsystem will start each time the router is booted.	appn routing
Start the APPN subsystem from privileged EXEC mode without affecting the current configuration.	appn start

STOPPING THE APPN SUBSYSTEM

The APPN subsystem may be stopped through global configuration mode or privileged EXEC mode commands.

Task	Command
Deactivate APPN routing from global configuration mode and remove it from the current configuration.	no appn routing
Deactivate APPN routing from privileged EXEC mode without affecting the current configuration.	appn stop

STARTING AND STOPPING APPN PORTS AND LINK STATIONS

APPN port and link station definitions are started automatically when the APPN subsystem starts. However, configuration commands will not take effect on an APPN port or link when it is active.

The following privileged EXEC commands allow an APPN ports and link stations to be stopped and started when making configuration changes or when resetting the APPN port or link is desired:

Task	Command
Deactivate the specified APPN link.	**appn stop link-station** *linkname*
Deactivate the specified APPN port.	**appn stop port** *portname*
Activate the specified APPN link.	**appn start link-station** *linkname*
Activate the specified APPN port.	**appn start port** *portname*

TUNING THE APPN NETWORK

Two new APPN Scalability Enhancement features, Locate Throttling and Negative Caching, allow you to conserve network resources. Locate Throttling reduces multiple network broadcasts for the same target resource when a broadcast request is already pending from the network node server (NNS). Negative Caching prevents excess searches to unreachable resources. These two features significantly reduce network traffic, particularly in the event of an unexpected resource failure.

Locate Throttling

The Locate Throttling feature prevents multiple broadcast locate searches that can occur when more than one resource requests sessions with the same destination LU.

When more than one resource requests sessions with the same destination LU, APPN initiates searches for each request. This can consume large amounts of network resources, particularly if APPN broadcast searches are performed.

The Locate Throttling feature offers a way to regulate, or "throttle," locate searches to the same destination LU. For example, if the response to a locate request is pending, and another search request is issued for the same destination LU that the router has no knowledge of, then the subsequent search request for that LU is queued to wait for the response from the first search. The locate request is withheld only if it is a locate-broadcast search. For a locate-directed search, no queuing is necessary.

Negative Caching

The Negative Caching feature prevents excess searches to unreachable resources.

When a resource becomes unavailable in the network, either temporarily or for an extended period of time, there might be a great number of subsequent requests for that resource. This consumes network resources unnecessarily and quite often adversely affects network performance.

The Negative Caching feature offers a means of reducing the search broadcast by retaining searches to unreachable resources. If a resource is unreachable in the network, the router rejects requests to the resource. A configurable timer allows you to determine the length of time a resource is considered unreachable. During this period, requests for the resource are rejected. When the timer expires, a full search is performed upon receipt of the first search request for that resource. A configurable threshold allows you to determine the number of searches to be rejected before a full APPN search is performed. When either of the two thresholds expires, a full APPN search is performed.

Each APPN network resource must be defined on the node where the resource exists. When the resource is defined, it can be found through network searches. Optionally, the resource location may be defined in other nodes to optimize directory services search logic.

Registered directory entries are created dynamically in the local directory of the network node. These entries represent local LUs of an adjacent end node for which the network node is providing network node server function.

Cached directory entries are added dynamically and are based on the results of previous searches. A cache entry allows the node to attempt a directed search straight to the destination resource. If a cache entry does not exist, or the entry is incorrect, a broadcast search is issued to query each network node in the network for the destination resource. Each cache entry is verified before use to make sure the resource is still available. If the resource is not found, a broadcast search is attempted.

You can configure the APPN search function to conserve network resources by performing either of the following tasks in APPN control-point configuration mode:

Task	Command
Prevent multiple broadcast locate searches to the same destination LU.	**locate-queuing**
Prevent multiple locate broadcast searches to unreachable resources.	**negative-caching [time]** *time* **[threshold]** *threshold-value*

MONITORING THE APPN NETWORK

You can monitor the status and configuration of the APPN subsystem by issuing any of the following commands in EXEC mode:

Task	Command
Display APPN classes of service that are defined to the local node.	**show appn class-of-scrvice [brief	detail]**
Display APPN connection networks that are defined to the local node.	**show appn connection-network [brief	detail]**
Display the contents of the APPN directory database.	**show appn directory [name** *cp-name*] **[brief	detail]**
Display dependent LUs served by the DLUR function.	**show appn dlur-lu [pu** *pu-name*] **[brief	detail]**

Task	Command
Display dependent PUs served by the DLUR function.	**show appn dlur-pu** [**dlus** *dlus-name*] [**brief | detail**]
Display the status of connections to dependent LU servers.	**show appn dlus** [**brief | detail**]
Display information about the SNA sessions that are currently being routed through the local node.	**show appn intermediate-session** [**pcid** *pcid*] [**name** *lu-name*] [**brief | detail**]
Display information about the APPN link stations that are active on or defined to the local node.	**show appn link-station** [**name** *link-station-name*] [**port** *port-name*] [**brief | detail**]
Display information about the APPN modes defined to the local node.	**show appn mode**
Display information about the local APPN control point.	**show appn node**
Display information about the APPN ports that are active on the local node.	**show appn port** [**port** *port-name*] [**brief | detail**]
Display information about RTP connections.	**show appn rtp** [**connection** *connection-id*] [**class-of-service** *cos-name*] [**name** *cp-name*] [**brief | detail**]
Display information about the SNA LU6.2 sessions, such as CP-CP sessions, that originate at the local node.	**show appn session** [**pcid** *pcid*] [**name** *lu-name*] [**brief | detail**]
Display the contents of the APPN topology database.	**show appn topology** [**name** *cp-name*] [**brief | detail**]

APPN CONFIGURATION EXAMPLES

The following sections provide example configurations that show how to configure various aspects of an APPN network:

- Locate Throttling Configuration Example
- Negative Caching Configuration Example
- APPN HPR Configuration Example
- APPN Link-over-Token Ring Configuration Example
- APPN Link-over-FDDI Configuration Example
- APPN Link-over-Frame Relay Configuration Example

- APPN Link-over-SDLC Configuration Example
- APPN Link-over-RSRB Using TCP Local Acknowledgment Configuration Example
- APPN Link-over-DLSw+ Using Virtual Data-Link Control Configuration Example
- APPN Connection Network-over-DLSw+ Using Virtual Data-Link Control Configuration Example
- APPN Link-over-QLLC Configuration Example
- APPN Link-over-ATM Configuration Example
- APPN Link-over-PPP Configuration Example
- APPN Link-over-SMDS Configuration Example
- APPN-over-Ethernet LAN Emulation Example

These examples specify proper configuration between two Cisco routers. If you are defining an APPN connection to a non-Cisco APPN platform, the configuration for the Cisco IOS software will be similar to those shown here.

Locate Throttling Configuration Example

The following example enables the Locate Throttling feature, which is disabled by default:

```
interface tokenring 0
!
appn control-point neta.router1

 appn port tr0 tokenring 0
  complete

 locate-queuing
  complete
```

Negative Caching Configuration Example

The following example configures the Negative Caching feature to specify that requests for unreachable resources will be retained in the directory database for 90 seconds or until 25 locate-search requests have been made:

```
interface tokenring 0
!
appn control-point neta.router1
!
 negative-caching time 90 threshold 25
  complete
```

APPN HPR Configuration Example

The following configuration connects two routers with a Frame Relay link and enables HPR.

Router A

```
    interface Serial0
     encapsulation frame-relay IETF
     no keepalive
     clock rate 1000000
     frame-relay map llc2 141
     frame-relay map hpr 141
    !
    appn control cisco.routera
     hpr
     hpr timers liveness 1200 600 300 60
      complete
    !
    appn port FRAME0 Serial0
     complete
    !
    appn link-station routerb
     port FRAME0
     fr-dest-address 141
     effective-capacity 1000000
      complete
```

Router B

```
    interface Serial0
     encapsulation frame-relay IETF
     no keepalive
     frame-relay map llc2 141
     frame-relay map hpr 141
    !
    appn control cisco.routerb
     hpr
     hpr timers liveness 1200 600 300 60
      complete
    !
    appn port FRAME0 Serial0
      complete
    !
    appn link-station routera
     port FRAME0
     fr-dest-address 141
     effective-capacity 1000000
      complete
```

APPN Link-over-Token Ring Configuration Example

The following example illustrates a basic APPN link over Token Ring media. In this example, Router 1 is configured to establish the connection, while Router 2 will wait for the connection from Router 1 and build a dynamic link station when Router 1 connects.

Configuration for Router 1

```
interface tokenring 0
!
appn control-point neta.router1
  complete
!
appn port tr0 tokenring 0
  complete
!
appn link-station router2
 port tr0
 lan-dest-address 1111.1111.1112
  complete
```

Configuration for Router 2

```
! tokenring 1 mac address is 1111.1111.1112
interface tokenring 1
!
appn control-point neta.router2
  complete
!
appn port tr1 tokenring 0
  complete
```

APPN Link-over-FDDI Configuration Example

The following example illustrates an APPN link-over-FDDI. In this example, each router is configured with a defined link station to the other. Both routers are configured to not accept dynamic APPN connection requests on the FDDI port. Router 1 is configured to attempt to connect to Router 2, retrying every minute if the connection is not established. Router 2 is configured to wait for an incoming call from Router 1 and not attempt to establish the connection.

Configuration for Router 1

```
! FDDI0 mac address is 1111.1111.1111
interface Fddi 0
!
appn control-point neta.router1
  complete
!
appn port fd0 Fddi0
 no service-any
 complete
!
appn link-station router2
 port fd0
 lan-dest-address 1111.1111.1112
 retry-limit infinite 60
  complete
```

Configuration for Router 2

```
! FDDI0 mac address is 1111.1111.1112
interface Fddi0
!
appn control-point neta.router1
  complete
!
appn port fd0 Fddi0
 no service-any
  complete
!
appn link-station router2
 port fd0
 lan-dest-address 1111.1111.1111
 no connect-at-startup
  complete
```

APPN Link-over-Frame Relay Configuration Example

The following example illustrates an APPN link over Frame Relay. Both routers are configured to attempt to establish the connection with the partner.

Configuration for Router 1

```
interface serial 0
 encapsulation frame-relay IETF
 frame-relay map llc2 22
!
appn control-point neta.router1
  complete
!
appn port framerly serial 0
  complete
!
appn link-station router2
 port framerly
 fr-dest-address 22
  complete
```

Configuration for Router 2

```
interface serial 3
 encapsulation frame-relay IETF
 frame-relay map llc2 21
!
appn control-point neta.router2
  complete
!
appn port frame serial 3
  complete
```

```
!
appn link-station router1
 port frame
 fr-dest-address 21
 complete
```

APPN Link-over-SDLC Configuration Example

The following example illustrates an APPN link over Synchronous Data-Link Control (SDLC). In this example, Router 2 is configured without a link station—it will be built dynamically when contacted by Router 1.

Configuration for Router 1

```
interface serial 0
 encapsulation sdlc
 sdlc address c1
!
appn control-point neta.router1
  complete
!
appn port sdlc serial 0
 sdlc-sec-addr c1
  complete
!
appn link-station router2
 port sdlc
 sdlc-dest-address c1
  complete
```

Configuration for Router 2

```
interface serial 3
 encapsulation sdlc
 sdlc address c1
!
appn port sdlc serial 3
 sdlc-sec-addr c1
 complete
```

APPN Link-over-RSRB Using TCP Local Acknowledgment Configuration Example

The following example illustrates an APPN link using an RSRB virtual port. This configuration allows APPN links to span a routed IP multiprotocol network cloud as well as offer transport over interface encapsulation types not supported natively by APPN. In this example, the interface encapsulation is HDLC, the default for serial interfaces. Both routers are configured to attempt to initiate the connection with the other when their respective link stations are activated.

Configuration for Router 1

```
source-bridge ring-group 33
source-bridge remote-peer 33 tcp 1.1.1.1
source-bridge remote-peer 33 tcp 1.1.1.2 local-ack
!
interface serial 0
 ip address 1.1.1.1 255.255.255.0
!
appn control-point neta.router1
  complete
!
appn port rsrbport rsrb
 rsrb-virtual-station 1111.1111.1111 13 1 33
  complete
!
appn link-station router2
 port rsrbport
 lan-dest-address 1111.1111.1112
  complete
```

Configuration for Router 2

```
source-bridge ring-group 33
source-bridge remote-peer 33 tcp 1.1.1.2
source-bridge remote-peer 33 tcp 1.1.1.1 local-ack
!
interface serial 3
 ip address 1.1.1.2 255.255.255.0
!
appn control-point neta.router2
  complete
!
appn port rsrbport rsrb
 rsrb-virtual-station 1111.1111.1112 23 1 33
  complete
!
appn link-station router1
 port rsrbport
 lan-dest-address 1111.1111.1111
  complete
```

APPN Link-over-DLSw+ Using Virtual Data-Link Control Configuration Example

Figure 19–1 illustrates an example of an APPN link-over-DLSw+, where Node 1 has a link defined to Node 3. Node 3 merely has an APPN virtual data-link control port and will create a dynamic link station when Node 1 starts its link station.

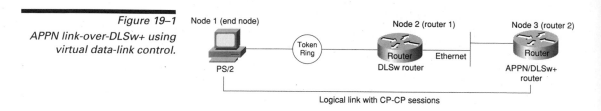

Figure 19–1
APPN link-over-DLSw+ using
virtual data-link control.

Logical link with CP-CP sessions

The relevant portions of the configuration for each node are listed below.

Configuration for Node 3 (Router 2)

```
source-bridge ring-group 100
dlsw local-peer peer-id 172.18.3.111
dlsw remote-peer 0 tcp 172.18.3.133
!
interface ethernet 0
 ip address 172.18.3.111 255.255.255.0
 loopback
 media-type 10BaseT
!
appn control-point NETA.BART
 complete
!
appn port VDLC vdlc
 vdlc 100 vmac 4000.4545.6969
 complete
 !
```

Configuration for Node 2 (Router 1)

```
!
source-bridge ring-group 100
source-bridge ring-group 33
dlsw local-peer peer-id 172.18.3.133
dlsw remote-peer 0 tcp 172.18.3.111
!
interface ethernet 0
 ip address 172.18.3.133 255.255.255.0
 loopback
 media-type 10BaseT
!
interface tokenring 0
 no ip address
 ring-speed 16
 source-bridge 1 1 100
!
```

Configuration for Node 1 (End Node):

```
DEFINE_LOCAL_CP   FQ_CP_NAME(NETA.APU          )
                  CP_ALIAS(APU )
                  NAU_ADDRESS(INDEPENDENT_LU)
                  NODE_TYPE(EN)
                  NODE_ID(X'05D00000')  ·
                  NW_FP_SUPPORT(NONE)
                  HOST_FP_SUPPORT(YES)
                  MAX_COMP_LEVEL(NONE)
                  MAX_COMP_TOKENS(0);

DEFINE_LOGICAL_LINK   LINK_NAME(BART )
                      ADJACENT_NODE_TYPE(NN)
                      PREFERRED_NN_SERVER(NO)
                      DLC_NAME(IBMTRNET)
                      ADAPTER_NUMBER(0)
                      DESTINATION_ADDRESS(X'40004545696904')
                      ETHERNET_FORMAT(NO)
                      CP_CP_SESSION_SUPPORT(YES)
                      ACTIVATE_AT_STARTUP(no)
                      LIMITED_RESOURCE(NO)
                      LINK_STATION_ROLE(use_adapter_definition)
                      SOLICIT_SSCP_SESSION(NO)
                      MAX_ACTIVATION_ATTEMPTS(USE_ADAPTER_DEFINITION)
                      USE_PUNAME_AS_CPNAME(NO)
                      EFFECTIVE_CAPACITY(USE_ADAPTER_DEFINITION)
                      COST_PER_CONNECT_TIME(USE_ADAPTER_DEFINITION)
                      COST_PER_BYTE(USE_ADAPTER_DEFINITION)
                      SECURITY(USE_ADAPTER_DEFINITION)
                      PROPAGATION_DELAY(USE_ADAPTER_DEFINITION)
                      USER_DEFINED_1(USE_ADAPTER_DEFINITION)
                      USER_DEFINED_2(USE_ADAPTER_DEFINITION)
                      USER_DEFINED_3(USE_ADAPTER_DEFINITION);
```

APPN Connection Network-over-DLSw+ Using Virtual Data-Link Control Configuration Example

Figure 19–2 illustrates a connection network, NETA.CONN, over DLSw+ using virtual data-link control on the network nodes.

The relevant portions of the configuration for each network node are listed below.

Configuration for End Node 1

```
DEFINE_LOCAL_CP    FQ_CP_NAME(NETA.EN1)
                   CP_ALIAS(EN1)
                   NAU_ADDRESS(INDEPENDENT_LU)
                   NODE_TYPE(EN)
                   NODE_ID(X'05D00000')
                   NW_FP_SUPPORT(NONE)
                   HOST_FP_SUPPORT(YES)
                   MAX_COMP_LEVEL(NONE)
                   MAX_COMP_TOKENS(0);
DEFINE_LOGICAL_LINK    LINK_NAME(TONN1)
                       ADJACENT_NODE_TYPE(NN)
                       PREFERRED_NN_SERVER(NO)
                       DLC_NAME(IBMTRNET)
                       ADAPTER_NUMBER(0)
                       DESTINATION_ADDRESS(X'40001111222204')
                       ETHERNET_FORMAT(NO)
                       CP_CP_SESSION_SUPPORT(YES)
                       ACTIVATE_AT_STARTUP(NO)
                       LIMITED_RESOURCE(NO)
                       LINK_STATION_ROLE(USE_ADAPTER_DEFINITION)
                       SOLICIT_SSCP_SESSION(NO)
                       MAX_ACTIVATION_ATTEMPTS(USE_ADAPTER_DEFINITION)
                       USE_PUNAME_AS_CPNAME(NO)
                       EFFECTIVE_CAPACITY(USE_ADAPTER_DEFINITION)
                       COST_PER_CONNECT_TIME(USE_ADAPTER_DEFINITION)
                       COST_PER_BYTE(USE_ADAPTER_DEFINITION)
                       SECURITY(USE_ADAPTER_DEFINITION)
                       PROPAGATION_DELAY(USE_ADAPTER_DEFINITION)
```

```
                          USER_DEFINED_1(USE_ADAPTER_DEFINITION)
                          USER_DEFINED_2(USE_ADAPTER_DEFINITION)
                          USER_DEFINED_3(USE_ADAPTER_DEFINITION);
```

Configuration for Router 1

```
source-bridge ring-group 113
dlsw local-peer peer-id 10.2.17.1
dlsw remote-peer 0 tcp 10.2.17.2
!
interface TokenRing0/0
 no ip address
 ring-speed 16
!
interface TokenRing0/1
 ip address 10.2.17.1 255.255.255.0
 no ip address
 ring-speed 16
!
appn control-point NETA.NN1
  complete
!
appn port TR0 TokenRing0/0
  complete
!
appn port VDLC vdlc
 vdlc 113 vmac 4000.2222.3333
 source-bridge 1 1 113
  complete
!
appn connection-network NETA.CONN
 port VDLC
  complete
!
appn link-station T0NN2
 port VDLC
 lan-dest-address 4000.3333.4444
  complete
```

Configuration for Router 2

```
source-bridge ring-group 113
dlsw local-peer peer-id 10.2.17.2
dlsw remote-peer 0 tcp 10.2.17.1
dlsw remote-peer 0 tcp 10.2.17.3
!
interface TokenRing0/0
 ip address 10.2.17.2 255.255.255.0
 no ip address
 ring-speed 16
!
appn control-point NETA.NN2
  complete
```

```
 !
 appn port VDLC vdlc
  vdlc 113 vmac 4000.3333.4444
  source-bridge 1 1 113
   complete
 !
```

Configuration for Router 3

```
 source-bridge ring-group 113
 dlsw local-peer peer-id 10.2.17.3
 dlsw remote-peer 0 tcp 10.2.17.2
 !
 interface TokenRing0/0
  no ip address
  ring-speed 16
 !
 interface TokenRing0/1
  ip address 10.2.17.3 255.255.255.0
  no ip address
  ring-speed 16
 !
 appn control-point NETA.NN3
   complete
 !
 appn port TR0 TokenRing0/0
   complete
 !
 appn port VDLC vdlc
  vdlc 113 vmac 4000.4444.5555
  source-bridge 1 1 113
   complete
 !
 appn connection-network NETA.CONN
  port VDLC
   complete
 !
 appn link-station T0NN2
  port VDLC
  lan-dest-address 4000.3333.4444
   complete
 !
```

Configuration for End Node 2

```
 DEFINE_LOCAL_CP  FQ_CP_NAME(NETA.EN2)
                  CP_ALIAS(EN2)
                  NAU_ADDRESS(INDEPENDENT_LU)
                  NODE_TYPE(EN)
                  NODE_ID(X'05D00000')
                  NW_FP_SUPPORT(NONE)
                  HOST_FP_SUPPORT(YES)
```

```
                    MAX_COMP_LEVEL(NONE)
                    MAX_COMP_TOKENS(0);
DEFINE_LOGICAL_LINK  LINK_NAME(TONN3)
                     ADJACENT_NODE_TYPE(NN)
                     PREFERRED_NN_SERVER(NO)
                     DLC_NAME(IBMTRNET)
                     ADAPTER_NUMBER(0)
                     DESTINATION_ADDRESS(X'40005555666604')
                     ETHERNET_FORMAT(NO)
                     CP_CP_SESSION_SUPPORT(YES)
                     ACTIVATE_AT_STARTUP(NO)
                     LIMITED_RESOURCE(NO)
                     LINK_STATION_ROLE(USE_ADAPTER_DEFINITION)
                     SOLICIT_SSCP_SESSION(NO)
                     MAX_ACTIVATION_ATTEMPTS(USE_ADAPTER_DEFINITION)
                     USE_PUNAME_AS_CPNAME(NO)
                     EFFECTIVE_CAPACITY(USE_ADAPTER_DEFINITION)
                     COST_PER_CONNECT_TIME(USE_ADAPTER_DEFINITION)
                     COST_PER_BYTE(USE_ADAPTER_DEFINITION)
                     SECURITY(USE_ADAPTER_DEFINITION)
                     PROPAGATION_DELAY(USE_ADAPTER_DEFINITION)
                     USER_DEFINED_1(USE_ADAPTER_DEFINITION)
                     USER_DEFINED_2(USE_ADAPTER_DEFINITION)
                     USER_DEFINED_3(USE_ADAPTER_DEFINITION);
```

APPN Link-over-QLLC Configuration Example

The following example illustrates an APPN link over QLLC to an AS400.

```
interface serial 1
 no ip address
 encapsulation x25 dce
 no keepalive
 x25 address 1024
 x25 map qllc 1234
 clockrate 19200
 no cdp enable
!
appn control-point NETA.APPN1
  complete
!
appn port QLLC1 serial 1
  complete
!
appn link-station AS400
 port QLLC1
 x25-dest-address svc 1234
  complete
```

APPN Link-over-ATM Configuration Example

The following example illustrates an APPN link over ATM:

```
interface ATM2/0
 atm pvc 1 1 12 aal5nlpid
 map-group atm-appn2
!
appn control-point NETA.APPN2
  complete
!
appn port ATM ATM2/0
  complete
!
appn link-station ATMLINK
 port ATM
 atm-dest-address 1
  complete
```

APPN Link-over-PPP Configuration Example

The following example illustrates an APPN link over PPP:

```
interface serial 1
 ip address 10.1.1.2 255.255.255.0
 encapsulation ppp
 no keepalive
 no fair-queue

appn control-point NETA.APPN2
  complete

appn port PPP serial 1
  complete

appn link-station PPPLINK
 port PPP
  complete
```

APPN Link-over-SMDS Configuration Example

The following example illustrates and APPN link over SMDS:

```
interface serial 0
 ip address 10.1.1.1 255.255.255.0
 encapsulation smds...

appn control-point NETA.APPN2
  complete

appn port SMDS serial 0
  complete
```

```
appn link-station SMDSLINK
 port SMDS
 smds-dest-address c120.0000.0002
  complete
```

APPN-over-Ethernet LAN Emulation Example

APPN over Ethernet LAN Emulation (LANE) is an enhancement to Cisco's APPN intermediate session routing (ISR) implementation that allows an APPN router to participate in an emulated LAN.

APPN over Ethernet LANE enables the APPN network node on the router to communicate with an end system on a switched LAN environment.

Figure 19–3 shows a typical scenario for the support of APPN over Ethernet LANE. The Catalyst 5000 is defined as the LAN Emulation Configuration Server (LECS), LAN Emulation Server (LES), broadcast and unknown server (BUS) and LEC. The network node router is a LEC using the Catalyst 5000 as the server and it is on the same emulated LAN as the Catalyst 5000. This feature allows a workstation that is attached to a legacy Ethernet segment to connect to the network node server, which is directly attached to an ATM network.

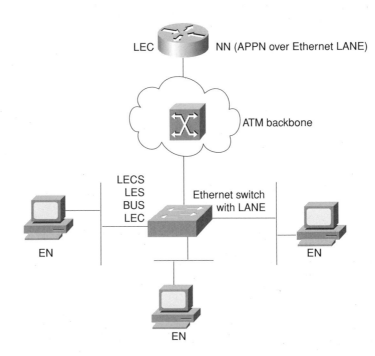

Figure 19–3

Typical topology using APPN over Ethernet LANE.

In the following example, an enterprise is migrating their flat source-route bridged campus network to a switch-based ATM network. The new network has an ATM backbone that consists of ATM

LS1010 switches and Catalyst 5000 switches. The campus network's Token Ring ports are replaced with Ethernet. The backbone protocol is TCP and APPN.

The following configuration reflects the network illustrated in Figure 19–3.

Configuration of the Primary DLUR Router

```
service internal
service udp-small-servers
service tcp-small-servers
!
hostname dlur1
!
!
interface ATM 1/0
 no ip address
 shutdown
!
interface TokenRing 4/0
 ip address 172.22.24.201 255.255.255.0
 ring-speed 16
 multiring all
!
interface ATM 9/0
 mtu 1500
 no ip address
 no ip mroute-cache
 no ip route-cache
 atm clock INTERNAL
 atm pvc 1 0 5 qsaal
 atm pvc 2 0 16 ilmi
 atm pvc 223 1 32 aal5nlpid
 atm pvc 224 1 34 aal5nlpid
!
interface ATM 9/0.1 multipoint
 ip address 10.10.10.1 255.255.255.0
 no ip mroute-cache
 no ip route-cache
 lane client ethernet RED
!
interface ATM 9/0.2 multipoint
 ip address 10.10.50.50 255.255.255.0
 no ip redirects
 no ip mroute-cache
 no ip route-cache
 lane client ethernet BLUE
 standby 1 priority 100
 standby 1 preempt
 standby 1 authentication usaa
 standby 1 ip 10.10.50.70
```

```
!
interface ATM 10/0
 mtu 1500
 no ip address
 atm clock INTERNAL
 atm pvc 1 0 5 qsaal
 atm pvc 2 0 16 ilmi
 atm pvc 60 1 36 aal5nlpid
!
interface ATM 10/0.1 multipoint
 lane client ethernet RED
!
interface ATM 10/0.2 multipoint
 lane client ethernet BLUE
!
!
appn control-point NETA.LATCP3
  dlus NETA.SJMVS1
  dlur
  complete
!
appn port BACK1483 ATM 10/0
  complete
!
appn port BACK1483 ATM 10/0
  complete
!
appn port REDLANE ATM 10/0.1
  complete
!
appn port BLUELANE ATM 10/0.2
  complete
!
appn port BLUELAN9 ATM 9/0.2
  complete
!
appn port REDLAN9 ATM 9/0.1
  complete
!
appn link-station TOCIP190
  port RFC1483
  atm-dest-address 223
  complete
!
appn link-station TOCIP191
  port RFC1483
  atm-dest-address 224
  complete
```

```
!
appn link-station BACKUP
 port BACK1483
 atm-dest-address 60
  complete
!
appn link-station DLUR2
 port BLUELANE
 lan-dest-address 0060.474a.2140
  complete
!
no ip classless
ip route 0.0.0.0 0.0.0.0 172.22.24.1
!
!
line con 0
 exec-timeout 0 0
line aux 0
 transport input all
line vty 0
 password lab
 login
 length 49
 width 126
line vty 1 4
 password lab
 login
!
scheduler heapcheck process
end
```

Configuration of the Secondary DLUR Router

```
!
version 11.2
service udp-small-servers
service tcp-small-servers
!
hostname dlur2
!
!
interface TokenRing 4/0
 ip address 172.22.24.202 255.255.255.0
 no ip mroute-cache
 no ip route-cache
 ring-speed 16
 multiring all
!
interface ATM 9/0
 mtu 1500
 no ip address
 no ip mroute-cache
 no ip route-cache
```

```
 atm clock INTERNAL
 atm pvc 1 0 5 qsaal
 atm pvc 2 0 16 ilmi
 atm pvc 223 1 33 aal5nlpid
 atm pvc 224 1 35 aal5nlpid
!
interface ATM 9/0.1 multipoint
 no ip mroute-cache
 no ip route-cache
 lane client ethernet RED
!
interface ATM 9/0.2 multipoint
 ip address 10.10.50.60 255.255.255.0
 no ip redirects
 no ip mroute-cache
 no ip route-cache
 lane client ethernet BLUE
 standby 1 priority 10
 standby 1 preempt
 standby 1 authentication usaa
 standby 1 ip 10.10.50.70
!
interface ATM 10/0
 mtu 1500
 no ip address
 atm clock INTERNAL
 atm pvc 1 0 5 qsaal
 atm pvc 2 0 16 ilmi
 atm pvc 60 1 36 aal5nlpid
!
interface ATM 10/0.1 multipoint
 lane client ethernet RED
!
interface ATM 10/0.2 multipoint
 lane client ethernet BLUE
!
!
appn control-point NETA.RISCP3
  dlus NETA.SJMVS1
  dlur
  complete
!
appn port RFC1483 ATM9/0
  complete
!
appn port BACK1483 ATM10/0
  complete
```

```
!
appn port REDLANE ATM10/0.1
  complete
!
appn port BLUELANE ATM10/0.2
  complete
!
appn port REDLAN9 ATM9/0.1
  complete
!
appn port BLUELAN9 ATM9/0.2
  complete
!
appn link-station TOCIP190
 port RFC1483
 atm-dest-address 223
  complete
!
appn link-station TOCIP191
 port RFC1483
 atm-dest-address 224
  complete
no ip classless
ip route 0.0.0.0 0.0.0.0 172.22.24.1
!
line con 0
 exec-timeout 0 0
line aux 0
 transport input all
line vty 0
 password lab
 login
 length 49
 width 126
line vty 1 4
 password lab
 login
```

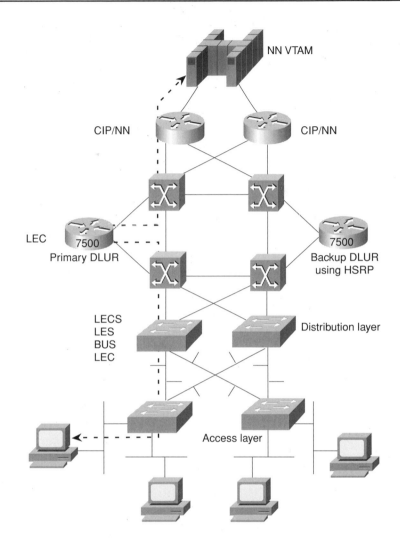

Figure 19–4
Migrating a source-route
bridged network to a
switch-based ATM network.

In Figure 19–4, workstations are attached to an access Catalyst switch. The access Catalyst switch is connected to a distribution-layer Catalyst switch over Fast Ethernet. The distribution Catalyst switch has an ATM link to the LS1010 switch. Using LANE, the Dependent LU Requester (DLUR) router and the distribution Catalyst switch appear to be on the same LAN.

No APPN configuration is required for the primary DLUR router in this example. The following example shows the configuration of the primary DLUR:

Primary DLUR Router Configuration of the Interface

```
interface ATM 9/0.2 multipoint
 ip address 10.10.50.50 255.255.255.0
 no ip redirects
 no ip mroute-cache
 no ip route-cache
 lane client ethernet BLUE
 standby 1 priority 100
 standby 1 preempt
 standby 1 authentication usaa
 standby 1 ip 10.10.50.70
```

Secondary DLUR Configuration of the Interface

```
interface ATM 9/0.2 multipoint
 ip address 10.10.50.60 255.255.255.0
 no ip redirects
 no ip mroute-cache
 no ip route-cache
 lane client ethernet BLUE
 standby 1 priority 10
 standby 1 preempt
 standby 1 authentication usaa
 standby 1 ip 10.10.50.70
```

Priority determines whether the router is primary or secondary. The router that has the higher priority is the primary and the other is the backup.

To access the host, the workstation uses the boundary functions of the DLUR router. The workstations define an Ethernet link to the DLUR router. The DLUR router defines an Ethernet emulated LAN link to the workstation. The advantage of using LANE is that existing LAN-based applications can run over an ATM-switched network without changes.

CHAPTER 20

APPN Configuration Commands

This chapter describes the commands to configure and monitor the Advanced Peer-to-Peer Networking (APPN) feature. For APPN configuration tasks and examples, see Chapter 19, "Configuring Advanced Peer-to-Peer Networking."

ADJACENT-CP-NAME

Use the **adjacent-cp-name** APPN link-station configuration command to specify the name of the partner node for the link station. Use the **no** form of this command to delete the definition.

> **adjacent-cp-name** *netid.cpname*
> **no adjacent-cp-name**

Syntax	Description
netid.cpname	Fully qualified network name of the remote control point. A fully qualified name is a string of 1 to 8 characters, a period, and another string of 1 to 8 characters. The following characters are acceptable: A–Z, a–z 0–9 $ # @ The first character of each string must not be a number. The default is that no partner nodes are specified.

Default

No partner nodes are specified.

Command Mode

APPN link-station configuration

Usage Guidelines

This command first appeared in Cisco IOS Release 11.0.

If the name configured with this command does not match the remote node's control-point (CP) name, the link will not come up. If the **no** form of the command is issued, or the command is not issued at all, no checking is done. This command must be specified if the adjacent node is LEN.

Example

The following example defines a link station that specifies the name of the partner node:

```
appn link-station APPN1
  port TR0
  lan-dest-address 1000.C4C1.E5C5
  adjacent-cp-name CISCO.APPN1
  complete
```

Related Commands

appn link-station
show appn link-station

APPN CLASS-OF-SERVICE

Use the **appn class-of-service** global configuration command to define an APPN class of service that is not an IBM-supplied default. Use the **no** form of this command to delete the definition. This command begins the APPN class-of-service configuration command mode.

> **appn class-of-service** *cosname*
> **no appn class-of-service** *cosname*

Syntax	Description
cosname	Class-of-service (COS) name not among IBM default names. COS names must be a Type A character string. A Type A character string contains 1 to 8 of the following characters: A–Z, a–z 0–9 $ # @

Defaults

There is no default class-of-service name.

If this command is not issued, an IBM default COS can be used. The IBM-supplied default classes of service are #CONNECT, #BATCH, #INTER, #BATCHSC, #INTERSC, CPSVCMG, and SNAS-VCMG.

Command Mode

Global configuration

Usage Guidelines

This command first appeared in Cisco IOS Release 11.0.

COS is a definition of the transport network characteristics that should be used to establish a particular session. The COS definition assigns relative values to factors such as acceptable levels of security, cost per byte, cost-per-connect time, propagation delay, and effective capacity. APPN network nodes use COS to select the best session routes between LUs.

If one of the IBM-default classes of service does not meet the needs of a particular network, the **appn class-of-service** global configuration command can be used to create a user-defined definition.

Part II

Command Reference

Example

The following example defines a COS with one node row and one tg row:

```
appn class-of-service #SECURE
  node-row 1 weight 5 congestion no no route-additional-resistance 0 255
  tg-row 1 weight 30 byte 0 255 time 0 255 capacity 0 255 delay 0 255 security 200 255
  user1 0 255 user2 0 255 user3 0 255
  complete
```

Related Commands

node-row
show appn class-of-service
tg-row
transmission-priority

APPN CONNECTION-NETWORK

Use the **appn connection-network** global configuration command to specify the fully qualified network name for the connection network. Use the **no** form of this command to delete the definition. This command begins the APPN connection-network configuration command mode.

> **appn connection-network** *netid.cnname*
> **no appn connection-network** *netid.cnname*

Syntax	Description
netid.cnname	Fully qualified network name for the connection network. *cnname* is the name of the virtual network node in the connection network. A fully qualified name is a string of 1 to 8 characters, a period, and another string of 1 to 8 characters. The following characters are acceptable: A–Z, a–z 0–9 $ # @ The first character of each string must not be a number.

Default

No default connection-network name is assigned.

Command Mode

Global configuration

Usage Guidelines

This command first appeared in Cisco IOS Release 11.0.

The connection-network name must be the same on all nodes that define the connection network, and must be different from any other connection network, LU, or control point in the total network.

Example

The following example defines a connection network using APPN port TR0:

```
appn connection-network CISCO.CAPPN1
  port TR0
  complete
```

Related Commands

port (APPN connection network)
show appn connection-network

APPN CONTROL-POINT

Use the **appn control-point** global configuration command to specify the fully qualified control-point name for the node. Use the **no** form of this command to delete the name and clear all APPN definitions. This command begins the APPN control-point configuration command mode.

appn control-point *netid.cpname*
no appn control-point *netid.cpname*

Syntax	Description
netid.cpname	Fully qualified control-point name for the local node. A fully qualified name is a string of 1 to 8 characters, a period, and another string of 1 to 8 characters. The following characters are acceptable: A–Z, a–z 0–9 $ # @ The first character of each string must not be a number.

Default

No default control-point name is assigned.

Command Mode

Global configuration

Usage Guidelines

This command first appeared in Cisco IOS Release 11.0.

You must issue the **appn control-point** command to activate APPN routing. There can be only one control-point definition in the system. The control-point name must be unique in the network.

Example

The following example defines a control point named CISCO.APPN1:

```
appn control-point CISCO.APPN1
  complete
```

Related Commands

appn routing
appn start
appn stop
backup-dlus (APPN control point)
buffer-percent
dlur
dlus (APPN control point)
interrupt-switched
max-cached-entries
max-cached-trees
maximum-memory
route-additional-resistance
safe-store-cycle
safe-store-host

safe-store-interval
show appn node
xid-block-number
xid-id-number

APPN LINK-STATION

Use the **appn link-station** global configuration command to assign the name of an adjacent link station. Use the **no** form of this command to delete the link-station name. This command begins the APPN link-station configuration command mode.

> **appn link-station** *linkname*
> **no appn link-station** *linkname*

Syntax	Description
linkname	Name that identifies the link station. The name must be a Type A string. A Type A character string contains 1 to 8 of the following characters: A–Z, a–z 0–9 $ # @

Default

No default link-station name is assigned.

Command Mode

Global configuration

Usage Guidelines

This command first appeared in Cisco IOS Release 11.0.

A link represents a connection between a local link station and a link station in an adjacent node. The link can be considered a direct connection between two distinct Type 2.1 or Type 2.0 nodes. The link station provides a route over which local sessions or intermediate sessions can pass. Two link stations are required to build a link: one on each node.

A link station can be predefined with the **appn link-station** command, or dynamically defined. If you specify **service-any** in the associated **appn port** command, link stations can be dynamically defined when a connect request is received. In this case, the **appn link-station** command would not be required. You must define an APPN link station if you intend this node to initiate the connection to the adjacent node.

Example

The following example defines a link station using port TR0:

```
appn link-station CISCO1
  port TR0
  lan-destination-address 0200.0000.0001
  complete
```

Related Commands

adjacent-cp-name
atm-dest-address
backup-dlus (APPN link station)
connect-at-startup
cost-per-byte (APPN link station)
cost-per-connect-time (APPN link station)
cp-cp-sessions-supported
dlur-dspu-name
dlus (APPN link station)
effective-capacity (APPN link station)
fr-dest-address
lan-dest-address
limited-resource (APPN link station)
link-queuing
port (APPN link station)
ppp-dest-address
propagation-delay (APPN link station)
pu-type-20
retry-limit (APPN link station)
role (APPN link station)
sdlc-dest-address
security (APPN link station)
show appn link-station
smds-dest-address
tg-number
user-defined-1 (APPN link station)
user-defined-2 (APPN link station)
user-defined-3 (APPN link station)
verify-adjacent-node-type
x25-dest-address

APPN MODE

Use the **appn mode** global configuration command to specify a new mode or to change an IBM-defined mode and identify the class of service associated with the mode name. Use the **no** form of this command to delete the previous definition. This command begins the APPN-mode configuration command mode.

> **appn mode** *modename*
> **no appn mode** *modename*

Syntax	Description
modename	Name of the mode. A Type A character string. A Type A character string contains 1 to 8 of the following characters: A–Z, a–z 0–9 $ # @

Default

IBM-defined [blank] mode

Command Mode

Global configuration

Usage Guidelines

This command first appeared in Cisco IOS Release 11.0.

The IBM-defined modes are #BATCH, #BATCHSC, #INTER, #INTERSC, #CPSVCMG, #SNAS-VCMG, #CPSVRMG, and [blank]. These definitions cannot be changed.

This command is required when LEN nodes are using this node for network services. The LEN node will issue a BIND containing this mode name; this command will be used to associate the mode name with a COS name.

Example

The following example changes the IBM-defined mode #BATCH to use the #CONNECT class of service:

```
appn mode #BATCH
 class-of-service #CONNECT
 complete
```

Related Commands

class-of-service
show appn mode

APPN PARTNER-LU-LOCATION

Use the **appn partner-lu-location** global configuration command to specify an LU that would be the destination LU for an LU-LU session request from an LU using this node for network services. Use the **no** form of this command to delete the previous definition. This command begins the APPN partner-LU configuration command mode.

> **appn partner-lu-location** *netid.luname*
> **no appn partner-lu-location** *netid.luname*

Syntax	Description
netid.luname	Fully qualified name of the partner LU. A fully qualified name is a string of 1 to 8 characters, a period, and another string of 1 to 8 characters. The following characters are acceptable: A–Z, a–z 0–9 $ # @ The first character of each string must not be a number.

Default

No default *netid.luname* is specified. You must supply a value; otherwise, the configuration will fail.

Command Mode

Global configuration

Usage Guidelines

This command first appeared in Cisco IOS Release 11.0.

Use this command to define an entry in the directory database. This command improves network performance by allowing directed LOCATE (because the partner name is known) instead of a broadcast. The disadvantage is that definitions must be created. Alternatively, partner names can be discovered dynamically and added to the database as they are learned. This process, however, requires either prior sessions to the node or broadcast traffic (which causes additional network traffic) sent to locate the node.

Example

The following example defines the location of an LU named CISCO.LU21:

```
appn partner-lu-location CISCO.LU21
 owning-cp CISCO.CP2
 complete
```

Part
II

Command Reference

Related Commands

owning-cp
serving-nn
show appn directory
wildcard

APPN PATH-SWITCH CONNECTION

Use the **appn path-switch connection** EXEC command to manually initiate a path switch if a better path exists.

>   **appn path-switch connection** *rtp-connection-id*

Syntax	*Description*
rtp-connection-id	An RTP connection ID is a 16-byte hexadecimal number.

Command Mode

EXEC

Usage Guidelines

This command first appeared in Cisco IOS Release 11.3.

Example

The following example initiates a path switch:

```
appn path-switch connection 8000000000A06278
```

Related Commands

show appn rtp

APPN PORT

Use the **appn port** global configuration command to define an APPN port and relate it to a previously defined interface.

>   **appn port** *portname* {*interface* | **rsrb** | **vdlc**}
>   **no appn port** *portname*

Syntax	*Description*
portname	Port name to be associated with the interface.
interface	Previously defined interface type and number with which the port name is to be associated.

Syntax	Description
rsrb	Specify **rsrb** instead of an interface if this port will utilize RSRB as a transport protocol.
vdlc	Specify **vdlc** to allow link stations using this virtual port to connect over DLSw+, or any other higher-layer protocol that is CLSI-compliant, using virtual data-link control (VDLC).

Defaults

No default port name is specified. No default interface is provided. You must provide the port name and interface or the configuration will fail.

Command Mode

Global configuration

Usage Guidelines

This command first appeared in Cisco IOS Release 11.0.

At least one APPN port must be defined for each interface that will participate in APPN routing. If more that one service access point (SAP) will be used over a particular port, then a port must be defined for each SAP.

If you configure APPN to run over DLSw+, you specify **vdlc** and must also use the **vdlc** APPN-port configuration command to identify which ring group the APPN VDLC port uses and, optionally, which virtual MAC address is used as the local MAC address identifying this APPN port.

Examples

The following example associates an APPN port named FDDI0 with FDDI interface 0:

```
appn port FDDI0 fddi0
  complete
```

In the following example, the **appn port vdlc** command creates an APPN VDLC port named "vdlcport," and the **vdlc** APPN-port configuration command identifies the ring group (100) and VDLC virtual MAC address (4000.3745.000):

```
appn port VDLCPORT vdlc
  vdlc 100 vmac 4000.3745.0000
  complete
```

Related Commands

appn start port
appn stop port
cost-per-byte (APPN port)
cost-per-connect-time (APPN port)

desired-max-send-btu-size
effective-capacity (APPN port)
interface
limited-resource (APPN port)
local-sap
max-link-stations
max-rcv-btu-size
propagation-delay (APPN port)
reserved-inbound
reserved-outbound
retry-limit (APPN port)
role (APPN port)
rsrb-virtual-station
sdlc-sec-addr
security (APPN port)
service-any
show appn port
user-defined-1 (APPN port)
user-defined-2 (APPN port)
user-defined-3 (APPN port)
vdlc
x25-subaddress

APPN ROUTING

Use the **appn routing** global configuration command to indicate that APPN routing should be activated. Use the **no** form to deactivate APPN routing.

> **appn routing**
> **no appn routing**

Syntax   Description

This command has no arguments or keywords.

Default

APPN routing is disabled.

Command Mode

Global configuration

Usage Guidelines

This command first appeared in Cisco IOS Release 11.0.

For **appn routing** to complete successfully, an APPN control point must be configured using the **appn control-point** global configuration command.

Example

The following example activates APPN routing:

```
appn routing
```

Related Commands

appn control-point
appn start
appn stop

APPN START

Use the **appn start** EXEC command to activate the APPN subsystem in this node.

    appn start

Syntax   Description

This command has no arguments or keywords.

Default

The APPN subsystem is disabled.

Command Mode

EXEC

Usage Guidelines

This command first appeared in Cisco IOS Release 11.0.

Example

The following example activates APPN:

```
appn start
```

Related Commands

appn routing
appn stop

APPN START LINK-STATION

Use the **appn start link-station** EXEC command to activate a logical APPN link.

    appn start link-station *linkname*

Syntax	Description
linkname	Name of the link station. Must be a Type A character string. A Type A character string contains 1 to 8 of the following characters: A–Z, a–z 0–9 $ # @

Default

No logical APPN links are activated.

Command Mode

EXEC

Usage Guidelines

This command first appeared in Cisco IOS Release 11.0.

Example

The following example activates an APPN link station:

```
appn start link-station TR0
```

Related Commands

appn link-station
appn stop link-station
show appn link-station

APPN START PORT

Use the **appn start port** EXEC command to activate APPN routing over a particular port.

> **appn start port** *portname*

Syntax	Description
portname	Name of the port. Must be a Type A character string. A Type A character string contains 1 to 8 of the following characters: A–Z, a–z 0–9 $ # @

Default

No APPN routing is activated.

Command Mode

EXEC

Usage Guidelines

This command first appeared in Cisco IOS Release 11.0.

This command is used also when the APPN subsystem is started already and a port is added or a characteristic is changed by subcommand.

Example

The following example activates APPN routing over port TR0:

```
appn start port TR0
```

Related Commands

appn port
appn stop port
show appn port

APPN STOP

Use the **appn stop** EXEC command to deactivate APPN routing without affecting the current configuration.

appn stop

Syntax   Description

This command has no arguments or keywords.

Default

This command has no default state.

Command Mode

EXEC

Usage Guidelines

This command first appeared in Cisco IOS Release 11.0.

Example

The following command deactivates APPN routing:

```
appn stop
```

Related Commands

appn control-point
appn routing
appn start

APPN STOP LINK-STATION

Use the **appn stop link-station** EXEC command to deactivate an APPN connection between the local node and an adjacent node.

    appn stop link-station *linkname*

Syntax	Description
linkname	Name of the link station. The name must be a Type A character string. A Type A character string contains 1 to 8 of the following characters: A–Z, a–z 0–9 $ # @

Default

This command has no default state.

Command Mode

EXEC

Usage Guidelines

This command first appeared in Cisco IOS Release 11.0.

Example

The following command deactivates an APPN link between the local node and an adjacent node:

```
appn stop link-station APPN1
```

Related Commands

appn link-station
appn start link-station

APPN STOP PORT

Use the **appn stop port** EXEC command to deactivate APPN routing over a specified port.

> **appn stop port** *portname*

Syntax	Description
portname	Name of the port. Must be a Type A character string. A Type A character string contains 1 to 8 of the following characters: A–Z, a–z 0–9 $ # @

Default

This command has no default state.

Command Mode

EXEC

Usage Guidelines

This command first appeared in Cisco IOS Release 11.0.

For a port deactivation to be successful, no APPN link station can be active on that port.

Example

The following example deactivates APPN routing over port TR0:

```
appn stop port TR0
```

Related Commands

appn port
appn start port

ATM-DEST-ADDRESS

Use the **atm-dest-address** APPN link-station configuration command to specify the address of the partner node for ATM links. Use the **no** form of this command to delete the definition.

> **atm-dest-address** *pvc*
> **no atm-dest-address**

Syntax	Description
pvc	Permanent virtual circuit (PVC) of the remote node. Valid range is 1 to 4096.

Defaults

No default PVC or SAP is provided.

Command Mode

APPN link-station configuration

Usage Guidelines

This command first appeared in Cisco IOS Release 11.1.

The command should be specified only if the APPN port used by the link station is an ATM port. Note that for the Cisco 4500, the default maximum number of PVCs allowed is 32.

Example

The following example specifies ATM destination address 1:

```
interface ATM2/0
 atm pvc 1 1 12 aal5nlpid
 map-group atm-appn2
 !
appn control-point NETA.APPN2
 complete
!
appn port ATM ATM2/0
 complete
!
appn link-station ATMLINK
 port ATM
 atm-dest-address 1
 complete
```

Related Commands

appn link-station
lan-dest-address
sdlc-dest-address
show appn link-station

BACKUP-DLUS (APPN CONTROL POINT)

Use the **backup dlus** APPN control-point configuration command to specify the name of the default backup DLUS, which performs SSCP services for downstream PUs if the default DLUS is unable to provide the services. Use the **no** form of this command to delete the definition.

> **backup-dlus** *netid.cpname*
> **no backup-dlus**

Syntax	Description
netid.cpname	Fully qualified network name. A fully qualified name is a string of 1 to 8 characters, a period, and another string of 1 to 8 characters. The following characters are acceptable: A–Z, a–z 0–9 $ # @ The first character of each string must not be a number.

Default

No backup DLUS is specified.

Command Mode

APPN control-point configuration

Usage Guidelines

This command first appeared in Cisco IOS Release 11.0.

You must specify **dlur** and **dlus** before you can specify **backup-dlus**. You can use the **backup-dlus** link-station configuration command to override this command for a particular link station.

Example

The following example defines an APPN control point with a backup DLUS:

```
appn control-point CISCO.ROUTER
 dlur
 dlus CISCO.APPN1
 backup-dlus CISCO.APPN2
 complete
```

Related Commands

appn control-point
backup-dlus (APPN link station)

BACKUP-DLUS (APPN LINK STATION)

Use the **backup-dlus** APPN link-station configuration command to specify the default backup DLUS node that provides SSCP services to the downstream PUs of the link in the event that the DLUS is unable to provide the DLUR function. Use the **no** form of this command to delete the definition.

backup-dlus *netid.cpname*
no backup-dlus

Syntax	Description
netid.cpname	Fully qualified network name. A fully qualified name is a string of 1 to 8 characters, a period, and another string of 1 to 8 characters. The following characters are acceptable: A–Z, a–z 0–9 $ # @ The first character of each string must not be a number.

Default

The default state is **no backup-dlus.**

Command Mode

APPN link-station configuration

Usage Guidelines

This command first appeared in Cisco IOS Release 11.0.

You must specify the **dlur** and **dlus** APPN control-point commands before you can specify **backup-dlus.** You can use the **backup-dlus** link-station configuration command on the link station to override this command for that particular link station.

Example

The following example specifies the backup DLUS node for a link station:

```
appn link-station CISCO.HOST
  port FDDI0
  lan-dest-address 0200.0000.1234
  dlus CISCO.APPN1
  backup-dlus CISCO.APPN3
  complete
```

Related Commands

appn link-station
backup-dlus (APPN control point)
dlus (APPN control point)
dlus (APPN link station)

BUFFER-PERCENT

Use the **buffer-percent** APPN control-point configuration command to specify the percent of buffers that are reserved for use by APPN. Use the **no** form of this command to cancel the buffer reservation.

buffer-percent *number*
no buffer-percent

Syntax	*Description*
number	Maximum percentage of I/O memory that APPN is allowed to allocate for buffers. The valid range is 1 to 100 percent. The default is 100 percent.

Default

100 percent

Command Mode

APPN control-point configuration

Usage Guidelines

This command first appeared in Cisco IOS Release 11.0.

Use the **buffer-percent** command to ensure that APPN will not monopolize the buffers. If other protocols are to be routed through the local node, this command can reserve buffers for protocols other than APPN.

Example

The following example limits APPN's buffer usage to 25 percent of the device's buffers:

```
appn control-point CISCO.ROUTER
 buffer-percent 25
 complete
```

Related Commands

appn control-point
show buffers
show memory

CENTRAL-RESOURCE-REGISTRATION

Use the **central-resource-registration** APPN control-point configuration command to enable the central resource registration function. Use the **no** form of this command to disable the central resource registration function.

central-resource-registration
no central-resource-registration

Syntax   Description

This command has no arguments or keywords.

Default

The central resource registration function is enabled.

Command Mode

APPN control-point configuration

Usage Guidelines

This command first appeared in Cisco IOS Release 11.2.

By default, the central resource registration function is enabled in the router so that registration of downstream resources in the central directory server will be attempted by the router when it receives a request from the control point that owns the resource. If there is unpredictable behavior related to the central resource registration or central directory server, use the **no central-resource-registration** command to disable the central resource registration function. In normal circumstances, there should not be any reason to disable the central resource registration function.

Example

The following example disables the central resource registration function:

```
appn control-point neta.router
  no central-resource-registration
  complete
```

Related Commands

show appn directory

CLASS-OF-SERVICE

Use the **class-of-service** APPN-mode configuration command to specify the class of service that maps to a particular mode name. Use the **no** form of this command to delete the definition.

```
class-of-service cosname
no class-of-service
```

Syntax	Description
cosname	Name of the class of service. Must be a Type A character string. A Type A character string contains 1 to 8 of the following characters: A–Z, a–z 0–9 $ # @ The default is #CONNECT.

Default

The default class-of-service name is #CONNECT.

Command Mode

APPN-mode configuration

Usage Guidelines

This command first appeared in Cisco IOS Release 11.0.

LEN nodes use this node for network services. The mode name is passed in the BIND and this command is used to correlate the mode name to a class-of-service name.

Example

The following example defines a mode with class of service #INTER:

```
appn mode MAPPN1
 class-of-service #INTER
 complete
```

Related Commands

appn mode

CONNECT-AT-STARTUP

Use the **connect-at-startup** APPN link-station configuration command to specify that the link will call out to the partner and attempt to bring up the link when the link's definition is complete. Use the **no** form of this command to delete the definition.

connect-at-startup
no connect-at-startup

Syntax   Description

This command has no arguments or keywords.

Default

Connect-at-startup is enabled.

Command Mode

APPN link-station configuration

Usage Guidelines

This command first appeared in Cisco IOS Release 11.0.

Example

The following example deactivates call out for APPN link station ETHER12:

```
appn link-station ETHER12
 appn port ETHER1
 lan-dest-address 0200.0000.4321
 no connect-at-startup
 complete
```

Related Commands

appn link-station

COST-PER-BYTE (APPN LINK STATION)

Use the **cost-per-byte** APPN link-station configuration command to specify the cost per byte of transmitting a byte of data over this connection. Use the **no** form of this command to delete the definition.

> **cost-per-byte** *cost*
> **no cost-per-byte**

Syntax

cost	Number in the range 0 to 255. The default is the value specified in the **appn port** command.

Default

The default value specified in the **appn port** command.

Command Mode

APPN link-station configuration

Usage Guidelines

This command first appeared in Cisco IOS Release 11.0.

Use this command to specify the relative cost to transmit a byte over the link. The relative cost per byte is used in route selection. Cost per byte may be specified at the port level, in which case it applies to all link stations that connect through the port. Cost per byte specified at the link-station level overrides the cost per byte specified at the port level, and relates to the defined link station only. This value is compared to the values specified for a class of service to determine if this link can be used to support the class of service.

Example

The following example sets the cost-per-byte value to 10:

```
appn link-station CISCO1
 port RSRB1
 lan-dest-address 1000.2020.0211
 cost-per-byte 10
 complete
```

Related Commands

appn link-station
cost-per-byte (APPN port)
show appn link-station

COST-PER-BYTE (APPN PORT)

Use the **cost-per-byte** APPN-port configuration command to specify the cost per byte of transmitting a byte of data through this port. Use the **no** form of this command to delete the definition.

> **cost-per-byte** *cost*
> **no cost-per-byte**

Syntax	Description
cost	Number in the range 0 to 255. The default is 0.

Default

The default cost is 0.

Command Mode

APPN-port configuration

Usage Guidelines

This command first appeared in Cisco IOS Release 11.0.

Specifying **cost-per-byte** at the port level applies to all link stations accessed through this port, unless **cost-per-byte** is specified on an individual **appn link-station** command. Specifying this value on the **appn link-station** command overrides the port value. The cost is used in route selection for a particular class of service. Cost per byte specified at the link-station level overrides the cost per byte specified at the port level, and relates to the defined link station only. This value is compared to the values specified for a class of service to determine if this link can be used to support the class of service.

Example

The following example sets the cost-per-byte value to 10:

```
appn port FR0 serial 0
 cost-per-byte 100
 complete
```

Related Commands

appn port
cost-per-byte (APPN link station)
show appn port

COST-PER-CONNECT-TIME (APPN LINK STATION)

Use the **cost-per-connect-time** APPN link-station configuration command to specify the relative cost of the link. Use the **no** form of this command to delete the definition.

> cost-per-connect-time *cost*
> no cost-per-connect-time

Syntax   *Description*

cost   Number in the range 0 to 255. The default is the value specified in the **appn port** command.

Default

The default value specified in the **appn port** command.

Command Mode

APPN link-station configuration

Usage Guidelines

This command first appeared in Cisco IOS Release 11.0.

The relative cost of the link, which typically reflects the tariff of the transmission facility, is used in route selection. Cost-per-connect time may be specified at the port level, in which case it applies to all link stations that connect through the port. Cost-per-connect time specified at the link-station level overrides the cost-per-connect time specified at the port level, and relates to the defined link station only. This value is compared to the values specified for a class of service to determine if this link can be used to support the class of service.

Example

The following example sets the cost-per-connect time to 100:

```
appn link-station CISCO4
  port FDDI0
  cost-per-connect-time 100
  complete
```

Related Commands

appn link-station
cost-per-connect-time (APPN port)
show appn link-station

COST-PER-CONNECT-TIME (APPN PORT)

Use the **cost-per-connect-time** APPN-port configuration command to specify the cost-per-connect time. Use the **no** form of this command to delete the definition.

cost-per-connect-time *cost*
no cost-per-connect-time

Syntax	Description
cost	Number in the range 0 to 255. The default is 0.

Default

The default cost is 0.

Command Mode

APPN-port configuration

Usage Guidelines

This command first appeared in Cisco IOS Release 11.0.

Specifying **cost-per-connect-time** at the port level applies to all link stations accessed through this port, unless **cost-per-connect-time** is specified on an individual **appn link-station** command. Specifying this value on the **appn link-station** command overrides the port value. The cost is used in route selection for a particular class of service. Cost-per-connect time specified at the link station level overrides the cost-per-connect time specified at the port level, and relates to the defined link station only. This value is compared to the values specified for a class of service to determine if this link can be used to support the class of service.

Example

The following example sets the cost-per-connect time to 100:

```
appn port SDLC0 Serial1
 cost-per-connect-time 100
 complete
```

Related Commands

appn port
cost-per-connect-time (APPN link station)
show appn port

CP-CP-SESSIONS-SUPPORTED

Use the **cp-cp-sessions-supported** APPN link-station configuration command to specify that a control point-control point (CP-CP) session can be established over this connection. Use the **no** form of this command to specify that a CP-CP session cannot be established over this link.

> **cp-cp-sessions-supported**
> **no cp-cp-sessions-supported**

Syntax   Description

This command has no arguments or keywords.

Default

CP-CP sessions are supported.

Command Mode

APPN link-station configuration

Usage Guidelines

This command first appeared in Cisco IOS Release 11.0.

The **no** form of this command must be specified for a link to a LEN node.

CP sessions to additional NNs are optional. Having fewer CP-CP sessions reduces the number of topology-update messages and memory required, while increasing convergence time (the time required to update all network nodes).

Example

The following example specifies that no CP-CP sessions are supported:

```
appn link-station FDDI41
 port FDDI1
 lan-dest-address 0400.0000.2323
 no cp-cp-sessions-supported
 complete
```

Related Commands

appn link-station
show appn link-station
verify-adjacent-node-type

DESIRED-MAX-SEND-BTU-SIZE

Use the **desired-max-send-btu-size** APPN-port configuration command to specify the maximum BTU size on this link. Use the **no** form of this command to delete the definition.

desired-max-send-btu-size *size*
no desired-max-send-btu-size

Syntax	*Description*
size	BTU size (in bytes) on this link, in the range 99 to 5107. The default is 1024 bytes.

Default

The default size is 1024 bytes.

Command Mode

APPN-port configuration

Usage Guidelines

This command first appeared in Cisco IOS Release 11.0.

The MTU size must be big enough to accommodate the configured size of the BTU.

Example

The following example sets the maximum BTU size to 4000:

```
appn port TR0 tokenring 0/0
  desired-max-send-btu-size 4000
  complete
```

Related Commands

appn port
mtu
show appn port

DLUR

Use the **dlur** APPN control-point configuration command to specify that the Dependent LU Requestor (DLUR) function is supported on this CP. Use the **no** form of this command to delete the definition.

> **dlur**
> **no dlur**

Syntax   Description

This command has no arguments or keywords.

Default

DLUR is not specified.

Command Mode

APPN control-point configuration

Usage Guidelines

This command first appeared in Cisco IOS Release 11.0.

Example

The following example specifies the DLUR function on the CP:

```
appn control-point CISCO.ROUTER
  dlur
  dlus CISCO.HOST
  complete
```

Related Commands

appn control-point
dlus (APPN control point)
show appn dlur-lu
show appn dlur-pu
show appn dlus

DLUR-DSPU-NAME

Use the **dlur-dspu-name** APPN link-station configuration command to specify the name of the downstream PU connected by this link. Use the **no** form of this command to delete the definition.

> **dlur-dspu-name** *pu-name*
> **no dlur-dspu-name**

Syntax	Description
pu-name	Type A character string. A Type A character string contains 1 to 8 of the following characters: A–Z, a–z 0–9 $ # @

Default

No default name is specified.

Command Mode

APPN link-station configuration

Usage Guidelines

This command first appeared in Cisco IOS Release 11.0.

The DLUR function requires the specification of the DSPU name for a PU 2.0 node. Specification also is required when the DLUR function must activate the link to a PU 2.1 or PU 2.0 node, when driven by a host-initiated PU activation, and when the link to the PU is not active.

Example

The following example specifies the DSPU name of a downstream node:

```
appn link-station LINK4
  port TR1
  lan-dest-address 1000.2020.0211
  dlur-dspu-name PU003334
  pu-type-20
  complete
```

Related Commands

appn link-station
dlur
dlus (APPN link station)

DLUS (APPN CONTROL POINT)

Use the **dlus** APPN control-point configuration command to specify the name of the default Dependent LU Server (DLUS) that provides SSCP services to the downstream PUs. Use the **no** form of this command to delete the definition.

dlus *netid.cpname*
no dlus

Syntax	Description
netid.cpname	Fully qualified CP name. A fully qualified name is a string of 1 to 8 characters, a period, and another string of 1 to 8 characters. The following characters are acceptable: A–Z, a–z 0–9 $ # @ The first character of each string must not be a number.

Default

No default DLUS is defined.

Command Mode

APPN control-point configuration

Usage Guidelines

This command first appeared in Cisco IOS Release 11.0.

The **dlur** command must be specified if **dlus** is specified. The name of the node-default DLUS should be specified when supporting downstream PUs that request or require ACTPUs, when DLUR does not currently have an active session with the DLUS, and when no DLUS or back-up DLUS name has been provided on the APPN link-station definition.

Example

The following example defines the DLUS:

```
appn control-point CISCO.ROUTER1
  dlur
  dlus CISCO.APPN1
  complete
```

Related Commands

appn control-point
dlur
dlus (APPN link station)
show appn dlur-lu

DLUS (APPN LINK STATION)

Use the **dlus** APPN link-station configuration command to specify the name of the default Dependent LU Server (DLUS) node that provides SSCP services to the downstream PUs of this link station. Use the **no** form of this command to delete the definition.

dlus *netid.cpname*
no dlus

Syntax	Description
netid.cpname	Fully qualified CP name. A fully qualified name is a string of 1 to 8 characters, a period, and another a string of 1 to 8 characters. The following characters are acceptable: A–Z, a–z 0–9 $ # @ The first character of each string must not be a number.

Default

No default DLUS is specified.

Command Mode

APPN link-station configuration

Usage Guidelines

This command first appeared in Cisco IOS Release 11.0.

The **dlus** command is used to override the value of **dlus** specified in the control-point definition.

Example

The following example specifies the DLUS for a specific APPN link station:

```
appn link-station LINK5
  port TR1
  lan-dest-address 0200.0000.5678
  dlus CISCO.APPN1
  complete
```

Related Commands

appn control-point
dlur
dlus (APPN control point)
show appn dlus

EFFECTIVE-CAPACITY (APPN LINK STATION)

Use the **effective-capacity** APPN link-station configuration command to specify the bit rate for the connection. Use the **no** form of this command to delete the definition.

effective-capacity *capacity*
no effective-capacity

Syntax	Description
capacity	Number of bits per second in the range 0 to 100000000. The default is the value specified in the **appn port** command.

Default

The value specified in the **appn port** command.

Command Mode

APPN link-station configuration

Usage Guidelines

This command first appeared in Cisco IOS Release 11.0.

The bit rate is compared to the class-of-service requirements when selecting routes. This can be specified on the link-station command to identify the bit rate for this link station only. This value overrides the value specified on the port command. Effective capacity is used by the node to determine the least-cost route for APPN intermediate sessions.

Example

The following example defines the effective capacity:

```
appn link-station FRLINK44
 port FR0
 fr-dest-address 44
 effective-capacity 4000000
 complete
```

Related Commands

appn link-station
effective-capacity (APPN port)
show appn link-station

EFFECTIVE-CAPACITY (APPN PORT)

Use the **effective-capacity** APPN-port configuration command to specify the effective capacity of a link. Use the **no** form of this command to delete the definition.

effective-capacity *capacity*
no effective-capacity

Syntax	Description
capacity	Number of bits per second in the range 0 to 100000000. The default is media-dependent.

Default

The default is media-dependent:

Ethernet—10,000,000 bps
FDDI—100,000,000 bps
Frame Relay—56,000 bps
QLLC—56,000 bps
RSRB—56,000 bps
SDLC—56,000 bps
Token Ring—16,000,000 bps

Command Mode

APPN-port configuration

Usage Guidelines

This command first appeared in Cisco IOS Release 11.0.

Specifying this command at the port level identifies the capacity for all link stations accessed through this port. Specifying this command on the link-station command overrides the port value. This command also specifies the value for dynamically created transmission groups. The cost is used in route selection for a particular class of service.

Example

The following example defines the effective capacity:

```
appn port FR0 serial 1/1
  effective-capacity 2000000
  complete
```

Related Commands

appn port
effective-capacity (APPN link station)
show appn port

FR-DEST-ADDRESS

Use the **fr-dest-address** APPN link-station configuration command to specify the address of the partner node for Frame Relay links. Use the **no** form of this command to delete the definition.

fr-dest-address *dlci* [*sap*]
no fr-dest-address

Syntax	Description
dlci	Number in the range 16 to 1007 that represents the DLCI, or virtual circuit, for a Frame Relay connection.
sap	(Optional) 1-byte hexadecimal number in the range 04 to EC, and divisible by 4.

Defaults

No default DLCI is provided.

The default SAP is 04 (hexadecimal)

Command Mode

APPN link-station configuration

Usage Guidelines

This command first appeared in Cisco IOS Release 11.0.

The command should be specified only if the APPN port used by the link station is a Frame Relay port.

Example

The following example specifies DLCI 100:

```
appn link-station FRLNK100
  port FR0
  fr-dest-address 100
  complete
```

Related Commands

appn link-station
lan-dest-address
sdlc-dest-address
show appn link-station

HPR (APPN CONTROL POINT)

Use the **hpr** APPN control-point configuration command to specify that HPR is supported in this router. Use the **no** form of this command to disable HPR in this router.

hpr
no hpr

Syntax   Description

This command has no arguments or keywords.

Default

HPR is not supported by default.

Command Mode

APPN control-point configuration

Usage Guidelines

This command first appeared in Cisco IOS Release 11.3.

Example

The following example enables HPR support for this router:

    hpr

Related Commands

show appn node
show appn rtp

HPR (APPN LINK STATION)

Use the **hpr** APPN link-station configuration command to specify that HPR is supported over the indicated link station. Use the **no** form of this command to disable HPR over the link station.

hpr
no hpr

Syntax   Description

This command has no arguments or keywords.

Default

If the **hpr** command is not specified at the link station, then the default is the value configured for the corresponding port definition.

Command Mode

APPN link-station configuration

Usage Guidelines

This command first appeared in Cisco IOS Release 11.3.

Example

The following example disables HPR support on the link station:

```
no hpr
```

Related Commands

hpr (APPN control point)
hpr (APPN port)
show appn link-station

HPR (APPN PORT)

Use the **hpr** APPN-port configuration command to specify that HPR is supported over the indicated port. Use the **no** form of this command to disable HPR over the link station.

    hpr
    no hpr

Syntax   Description

This command has no arguments or keywords.

Default

If this command is not specified for a port, the default is the value configured for the control-point definition.

Command Mode

APPN-port configuration

Usage Guidelines

This command first appeared in Cisco IOS Release 11.3.

Example

The following example disables HPR support on port:

```
no hpr
```

Related Commands

hpr (APPN control point)
hpr (APPN port)
show appn link-station

HPR MAX-SESSIONS

Use the **hpr max-sessions** APPN control-point configuration command to specify the maximum number of sessions allowed over an RTP connection. Use the **no** form of this command to cancel the specification.

> **hpr max-sessions** *num-sessions*
> **no hpr max-sessions**

Syntax	Description
num-sessions	Maximum number of sessions allowed over an RTP connection. The valid range is 1 to 65535. The default is 65535.

Default

The default maximum number of sessions allowed is 65535.

Command Mode

APPN control-point configuration

Usage Guidelines

This command first appeared in Cisco IOS Release 11.3.

Example

The following example sets the maximum number of sessions allowed over an RTP session to 32:

```
hpr max-sessions 32
```

Related Commands

show appn node
show appn rtp

HPR RETRIES

Use the **hpr retries** APPN control-point configuration command to specify the number of times to retry sending a packet before initiating a path switch of the RTP connection. Use the **no** form of this command to cancel the specification.

> **hpr retries** *low-retries medium-retries high-retries network-retries*
> **no hpr retries**

Syntax	Description
low-retries	Number of times to retry sending a low-priority packet before initiating a path switch. Valid values are 0 to 10. The default is 6.
medium-retries	Number of times to retry sending a medium-priority packet before initiating a path switch. Valid values are 0 to 10. The default is 6.
high-retries	Number of times to retry sending a high-priority packet before initiating a path switch. Valid values are 0 to 10. The default is 6.
network-retries	Number of times to retry sending a network-priority packet before initiating a path switch. Valid values are 0 to 10. The default is 6.

Default

The default for all four retry values is 6.

Command Mode

APPN control-point configuration

Usage Guidelines

This command first appeared in Cisco IOS Release 11.3.

Example

The following example sets the HPR retry values:

```
hpr retries 10 6 4 2
```

Related Commands

hpr timers liveness
show appn node
show appn rtp

HPR SAP

Use the **hpr sap** APPN-port configuration command to specify the SAP for automatic network routing frames. Use the **no** form of this command to cancel the SAP specification and revert to the default SAP.

> **hpr sap** *sap*
> **no hpr sap**

Syntax	Description
sap	SAP value, in hexadecimal, used for automatic network routing frames. Valid hexadecimal values are even numbers in the range 0x02 to 0xFE. The default SAP value is 0xc8.

Default

The default SAP value is 0xc8.

Command Mode

APPN-port configuration

Usage Guidelines

This command first appeared in Cisco IOS Release 11.3.

The SAP value is configured on the port and is used by all link stations that use that port.

Example

The following example specifies a SAP value of 0x02:

```
hpr sap 0x02
```

Related Commands

show appn port
show appn rtp

HPR TIMERS LIVENESS

Use the **hpr timers liveness** APPN control-point configuration command to specify how many seconds to wait for a packet to be received before initiating a path switch. Use the **no** form of this command to cancel the timers.

> **hpr timers liveness** *low-time medium-time high-time network-time*
> **no hpr timers liveness**

Syntax	Description
low-time	Time, in seconds, for a node to wait to send an HPR status request when no low-priority data traffic is present. The valid range is 1 to 180 seconds. The default time is 45 seconds.
medium-time	Time, in seconds, for a node to wait to send an HPR status request when no medium-priority data traffic is present. The valid range is 1 to 180 seconds. The default time is 45 seconds.
high-time	Time, in seconds, for a node to wait to send an HPR status request when no high-priority data traffic is present. The valid range is 1 to 180 seconds. The default time is 45 seconds.
network-time	Time, in seconds, for a node to wait to send an HPR status request when no network-priority data traffic is present. The valid range is 1 to 180 seconds. The default time is 45 seconds.

Default

The default for each of the four time values is 45 seconds.

Command Mode

APPN control-point configuration

Usage Guidelines

This command first appeared in Cisco IOS Release 11.3.

Example

The following example sets the HPR liveness timers:

```
hpr timers liveness 180 120 60 30
```

Related Commands

hpr retries
show appn node
show appn rtp

HPR TIMERS PATH-SWITCH

Use the **hpr timers path-switch** APPN control-point configuration command to specify the amount of time allowed to attempt a path switch for an RTP connection. Use the **no** form of this command to cancel the specification.

> **hpr timers path-switch** *low-time medium-time high-time network-time*
> **no hpr timers**

Syntax	Description
low-time	Time, in seconds, allowed to perform a path switch for a low-priority RTP connection. The valid range is 0 to 7200 seconds. The default is 480 seconds.
medium-time	Time, in seconds, allowed to perform a path switch for a medium-priority RTP connection. The valid range is 0 to 7200 seconds. The default is 240 seconds.
high-time	Time, in seconds, allowed to perform a path switch for a high-priority RTP connection. The valid range is 0 to 7200 seconds. The default is 120 seconds.
network-time	Time, in seconds, allowed to perform a path switch for a network-priority RTP connection. The valid range is 0 to 7200 seconds. The default is 60 seconds.

Default

The default time allowed to attempt a low-priority RTP connection is 480 seconds.
The default time allowed to attempt a medium-priority RTP connection is 240 seconds.
The default time allowed to attempt a high-priority RTP connection is 120 seconds.
The default time allowed to attempt a network-priority connection is 60 seconds.

Command Mode

APPN control-point configuration

Usage Guidelines

This command first appeared in Cisco IOS Release 11.3.

Part
II

Command Reference

Example

The following example sets the HPR path-switch timers:

```
hpr timers path-switch 1200 600 300 120
```

INTERRUPT-SWITCHED

Use the **interrupt-switched** APPN control-point configuration command to specify that ISR should be processed at the interrupt level. Use the **no** form of this command to cancel the specification.

> **interrupt-switched**
> **no interrupt-switched**

Syntax   Description

This command has no arguments or keywords.

Default

Disabled

Command Mode

APPN control point

Usage Guidelines

This command first appeared in Cisco IOS Release 11.0.

This command improves the performance of ISR routing. The command can be used only if segment size is the same on all nodes in the message path. Resegmenting cannot be accomplished at the interrupt level. Also, this command should be used only when routing between interfaces with similar speeds. This is because no pacing is done in the node when **interrupt-switched** is specified.

Example

The following example specifies that ISR should be processed at the interrupt level:

```
appn control-point CISCO.APPN1
  interrupt-switched
  complete
```

Related Commands

appn control-point
show appn intermediate-session

LAN-DEST-ADDRESS

Use the **lan-dest-address** APPN link-station configuration command to specify the MAC address of the partner node. Use the **no** form of this command to delete the definition.

> **lan-dest-address** *lan-addr* [*sap*]
> **no lan-dest-address**

Syntax	Description
lan-addr	12-byte hexadecimal number in the form *xxxx.xxxx.xxxx*.
sap	(Optional) 1-byte hexadecimal number in the range 04 to EC, and divisible by 4.

Defaults

No default lan-addr is specified.

The default SAP is 04 (hexadecimal).

Command Mode

APPN link-station configuration

Usage Guidelines

This command first appeared in Cisco IOS Release 11.0.

This command is required for interface types Token Ring, Ethernet, or FDDI. It is not allowed for other interface types.

Example

The following example sets the MAC address and SAP for a link to a partner node:

```
appn link-station LINK0001
  port ETHER1
  lan-dest-address 1234.cfe0.9745 08
  complete
```

Related Commands

appn link-station
fr-dest-address
sdlc-dest-address
show appn link-station

LIMITED-RESOURCE (APPN LINK STATION)

Use the **limited-resource** APPN link-station configuration command to specify that the connection be taken down when no sessions are using it. Use the **no** form of this command to specify that the connection will remain active when no sessions are using it.

> limited-resource
> no limited-resource

Syntax   Description

This command has no arguments or keywords.

Default

The value specified in the **appn port** command.

Command Mode

APPN link-station configuration

Usage Guidelines

This command first appeared in Cisco IOS Release 11.0.

This command identifies a link that has a higher cost or is a switched connection and should not remain active if no resource is using the link. The **limited-resource** command issued at the APPN link-station level overrides the same command issued at the APPN-port level.

Example

The following example specifies that the link be taken down when no sessions are active:

```
appn link-station FRLINK34
  port FR1
  fr-dest-address 34
  limited-resource
  complete
```

Related Commands

appn link-station
limited-resource (APPN port)
show appn link-station

LIMITED-RESOURCE (APPN PORT)

Use the **limited-resource** APPN-port configuration command to specify that the link be taken down when no sessions are using the link. Use the **no** form of this command to specify that the link will remain active when no sessions are using the link.

> **limited-resource**
> **no limited-resource**

Syntax   Description

This command has no arguments or keywords.

Default

The default is no limited resource.

Command Mode

APPN-port configuration

Usage Guidelines

This command first appeared in Cisco IOS Release 11.0.

This command identifies a link that has a higher cost or is a switched connection and should not remain active if no resource is using the link. This command applies to all link stations accessed through this port. Specifying limited resource at the link-station level overrides this command.

Example

The following example activates limited resource:

```
appn port FR0 serial 0/2
  limited-resource
  complete
```

Related Commands

appn port
limited-resource (APPN link station)
show appn port

LINK-QUEUING

Use the **link-queuing** APPN link-station configuration command to specify queuing options and parameters for the link station. Use the **no** form of the command to cancel the option.

> **link-queuing** {**priority** *level* | **custom** *queue-number*}
> **no link-queuing**

Syntax	*Description*
priority *level*	Priority level, indicated by one of the following keywords: **high, medium, normal, low.**
custom *queue-number*	Priority number used to specify custom queuing for the link station. The default is that no number is assigned.

Default

No default priority number is assigned.

Command Mode

APPN link-station configuration

Usage Guidelines

This command first appeared in Cisco IOS Release 11.0.

Example

The following example specifies medium-priority level queuing for the link station:

```
link-queuing medium
```

Related Commands

show appn link-station

LOCAL-SAP

Use the **local-sap** APPN-port configuration command to specify the local service access point (SAP) to activate on the interface. Use the **no** form of this command to delete the definition.

> **local-sap** *sap*
> **no local-sap**

Syntax	*Description*
sap	Hexadecimal number in the range 04 to EC, and divisible by 4. The default is 04.

Default

The default local SAP is 04 (hexadecimal).

Command Mode

APPN-port configuration

Usage Guidelines

This command first appeared in Cisco IOS Release 11.0.

Example

The following example specifies the local SAP:

```
appn port TR0 tokenring 0
 local-sap 44
 complete
```

Related Commands

appn port
show appn port

LOCATE-QUEUING

Use the **locate-queuing** APPN control-point configuration command to enable the Locate Throttling function on this control point and prevent multiple broadcast locate-searches to the same destination LU. Use the **no** form of this command to disable the Locate Throttling function.

    locate-queuing
    no locate-queuing

Syntax   Description

This command has no arguments or keywords.

Default

Locate queuing is disabled.

Command Mode

APPN control-point configuration

Usage Guidelines

This command first appeared in Cisco IOS Release 11.3.

When the **locate-queuing** command is enabled, it is applied at the network-node server only for locate-search requests from its end node.

Example

The following example enables the Locate Throttling feature:

```
locate-queuing
```

Related Commands

appn control-point
negative-caching
show appn directory
show appn node

MAX-CACHED-ENTRIES

Use the **max-cached-entries** APPN control-point configuration command to specify the maximum number of cached directory entries. Use the **no** form of this command to delete the definition.

> **max-cached-entries** *number*
> **no max-cached-entries**

Part
II

Command Reference

Syntax	*Description*
number	Maximum number of cached directory entries. The valid range is 0 to 32767. The default is 255.

Default

255 cached directory entries

Command Mode

APPN control-point configuration

Usage Guidelines

This command first appeared in Cisco IOS Release 11.0.

This command enables you to balance memory usage and performance. A large number requires more memory, but reduces the number of network broadcasts. Cached directory entries are created as nodes learn locations of other network resources. This command affects cached entries only. A value of zero still allows location of node, but broadcasts are required.

Example

The following example specifies the maximum number of cached directory entries:

```
appn control-point CISCO.ROUTER
  max-cached-entries 100
  complete
```

Related Commands

appn control-point
show appn node

MAX-CACHED-TREES

Use the **max-cached-trees** APPN control-point configuration command to specify the maximum number of cached class-of-service routing trees. Use the **no** form of this command to delete the definition.

> **max-cached-trees** *number*
> **no max-cached-trees**

Syntax	Description
number	Maximum number of cached class-of-service routing trees. The valid range is 0 to 32767. The default is 20.

Default

20 trees

Command Mode

APPN control-point configuration

Usage Guidelines

This command first appeared in Cisco IOS Release 11.0.

This command allows you to balance memory usage and performance. Each cached tree represents all paths through the network for a class of service. If you specify a lower number, fewer will be cached and longer processing time might be required to calculate the paths through the network and select a route.

Example

The following example specifies the maximum number of cached topology trees:

```
appn control-point CISCO.ROUTER
 max-cached-trees 5
 complete
```

Related Commands

appn control-point
show appn node

MAXIMUM-MEMORY

Use the **maximum-memory** APPN control-point configuration command to specify the maximum amount of memory available to APPN. Use the **no** form of the command to cancel the specification.

> **maximum-memory** *bytes*
> **no maximum-memory**

Syntax	Description
bytes	Maximum amount of memory (in bytes) available to APPN. The valid range is 3000000 to 64000000 bytes. The default is that APPN has access to all memory.

Default

The default is that APPN has access to all memory.

Command Mode

APPN control-point configuration

Usage Guidelines

This command first appeared in Cisco IOS Release 11.0.

This command ensures that APPN will not monopolize the memory of the device and that other protocols being routed will have memory available.

Example

The following example specifies the maximum amount of memory available to APPN as 16000000 bytes (16 MB):

```
appn control-point CISCO.APPN1
  maximum-memory 16000000
  complete
```

Related Commands

appn control-point

MAX-LINK-STATIONS

Use the **max-link-stations** APPN-port configuration command to specify the maximum number of active link stations allowed on this port. Use the **no** form of the command to delete the definition.

max-link-stations *number*
no max-link-stations

Syntax	Description
number	Number in the range 1 to 255. Must be greater than or equal to the sum of **reserved-inbound** and **reserved-outbound**. The default is media-dependent.

Default

The default is media-dependent.

Ethernet—255G
FDDI—255
Frame Relay—255
QLLC—1
RSRB—255
SDLC—1
Token Ring—255

Command Mode

APPN-port configuration

Usage Guidelines

This command first appeared in Cisco IOS Release 11.0.

For leased negotiable lines, the maximum value is 1.

For leased primary lines, not multidrop, the maximum value is 1 and inbound is 0.

For leased secondary lines and switched lines, the maximum value is 1.

Example

The following example sets the maximum link stations:

```
appn port TR01 tokenring 0/1
 max-link-stations 10
 complete
```

Related Commands

appn port
reserved-inbound
reserved-outbound
show appn port

MAX-RCV-BTU-SIZE

Use the **max-rcv-btu-size** APPN-port configuration command to specify the desired maximum receive-BTU. Use the **no** form of this command to delete the definition.

max-rcv-btu-size *size*
no max-rcv-btu-size

Syntax	Description
size	Maximum receive-BTU (in bytes), in the range 99 to 5107. The default is 1024 bytes.

Default
1024 bytes

Command Mode
APPN-port configuration

Usage Guidelines
This command first appeared in Cisco IOS Release 11.0.

The BTU specifies a maximum message size at the physical layer, similar to the MTU in TCP/IP. Do not confuse BTU with MAXRU, which is session related.

Example
The following example sets the maximum BTU value to 500:

```
appn port TR11 tokenring1/1
  max-rcv-btu-size 500
  complete
```

Related Commands
appn port
show appn port

MINIMUM-MEMORY

Use the **minimum-memory** APPN control-point configuration command to specify the minimum amount of memory available to APPN. Use the **no** form of the command to cancel the specification.

> **minimum-memory** *bytes*
> **no minimum-memory**

Syntax	Description
bytes	Maximum amount of memory (in bytes) available to APPN. The valid range is 1000000 to 64000000. The default is 1000000 bytes.

Default
The default is 1000000 bytes.

Command Mode

APPN control-point configuration

Usage Guidelines

This command first appeared in Cisco IOS Release 11.0.

This command ensures that APPN always will have a specified amount of memory. Memory that is dedicated to APPN will not be available for other processing.

Example

The following example reserves 10000000 bytes (10 MB) of memory for APPN:

```
appn control-point CISCO.APPN1
  minimum-memory 10000000
  complete
```

Related Commands

appn control-point
maximum-memory

NEGATIVE-CACHING

Use the **negative-caching** APPN control-point configuration command to specify that the negative-caching function is enabled on this control point. Use the **no** form of this command to disable the negative-caching function.

> **negative-caching** [**time**] *time* [**threshold**] *threshold-value*
> **no negative-caching**

Syntax	Description
time *time*	Length of time, in seconds, that the negative cache entry will remain in the directory database. This timer determines how long a resource is considered unreachable. The range is 0 to 3600 seconds. The default is 60 seconds.
threshold *threshold-value*	Number of locate-searches to be rejected. When this threshold expires, the negative cache entry will be removed from the directory database. The range is 0 to 1000 searches. The default is 20 searches.

Default

Negative caching is disabled.

The default time is 60 seconds.

The default threshold is 20 locate-searches.

Command Mode

APPN control-point configuration

Usage Guidelines

This command first appeared in Cisco IOS Release 11.3.

When negative caching is enabled, it is applied at the network-node server only for locate-search requests from its end node.

Example

The following example configures the negative-caching feature to specify that requests for unreachable resources will be retained in the directory database for 30 seconds or until 10 locate-search requests have been made:

```
negative-caching time 30 threshold 10
```

Related Commands

appn control-point
locate-queuing
show appn directory
show appn node

NODE-ROW

Use the **node-row** APPN class-of-service configuration command to specify a node description or node row, and associated weights defined for this class of service. Use the **no** form of this command to delete a previous node-row description.

> **node-row** *index* **weight** *weight* **congestion** {yes | no} {yes | no} **route-additional-resistance**
> *min max*
> **no node-row** *index*

Syntax	Description
index	Specifies which row is being entered. The valid range is 1 to 8.
weight *weight*	Weight assigned to a node, given the characteristics identified in the remainder of the row. The weight of row n must be less than the weight of row n + 1. The valid range is 0 to 255.
congestion	Minimum and maximum congestion tolerance for the node row.
yes yes	Only yes. Only congested transmission groups match this row.
no yes	Yes or no. Congestion does not affect class-of-service row.

Syntax	Description
no no	Only no. Only noncongested transmission groups match this row. The default is no no.
route-additional-resistance *min max*	Minimum and maximum additional resistance value for the row. The value is compared to the same parameter defined in the CP for each network node and exchanged on the topology database updates. The valid range for minimum and maximum is 0 to 255. The default range for minimum and maximum is 0 0.

Defaults

No default node row is specified.

No default weight is specified.

The default congestion tolerance is no no.

The default route additional resistance is 0 0.

Command Mode

APPN class-of-service configuration

Usage Guidelines

This command first appeared in Cisco IOS Release 11.0.

You can define up to 8 rows. Each row represents the characteristics of a node that meets the requirements for this class of service and defines a weight for the node that will be used in calculating the cost of a total route.

If the congestion maximum is set to "no," the congestion minimum must also be set to "no."

Example

The following example defines an APPN class of service with one node row:

```
appn class-of-service #SECURE
 node-row 1 weight 5 congestion no no route-additional-resistance 0 255
 tg-row 1 weight 30 byte 0 255 time 0 255 capacity 0 255 delay 0 255 security 200 255
 user1 0 255 user2 0 255 user3 0 255
 complete
```

Related Commands

appn class-of-service
show appn class-of-service

NULL-XID-POLL

Use the **null-xid-poll** APPN-port configuration command to specify that the null XID should be used to poll the remote node associated with this APPN port. Use the **no** form of the command to cancel the specification.

    null-xid-poll
    no null-xid-poll

Syntax   Description

This command has no arguments or keywords.

Default

XID3 negotiation is used to poll remote devices.

Command Mode

APPN-port configuration

Usage Guidelines

This command first appeared in Cisco IOS Release 11.2.

The **null-xid-poll** command permits PU 2.0 devices that connect in with XID0 to build a dynamic link station. It is no longer necessary to configure a link definition. When this command is used, the router expects its partner to reveal its identity first by responding with either XID3 or XID0.

This feature works in a mixed environment of PU 2.0 and PU 2.1 devices where the same APPN port is shared by both types of devices. By default, XID3 is used to poll the devices. When a PU 2.0 device responds with XID0, the link is created and established dynamically. PU 2.1 devices are not affected by this change, and go through the XID3 negotiation as usual.

Some care must be exercised when configuring **null-xid-poll**: If two Cisco APPN network-node routers connect across ports configured with **null-xid-poll**, the APPN connection will fail because both routers expect the other to respond first using either XID0 or XID3. Similar behavior might occur when a port configured with **null-xid-poll** attempts communication with a front-end processor configured for XID polling. You only need to configure **null-xid-poll** when dealing with a PU 2.0 device that does not respond gracefully to the XID3 poll.

Example

The following example specifies that null XID should be used to poll the remote nodes associated with the APPN port FDDI0.

```
appn port FDDI0 fddi 0
 null-xid-poll
 complete
```

Related Commands

appn port

OWNING-CP

Use the **owning-cp** APPN partner LU-location configuration command to specify the name of the CP that owns the partner LU. Use the **no** form of this command to delete the definition.

> **owning-cp** *netid.cpname*
> **no owning-cp**

Syntax	Description
netid.cpname	Fully qualified network name. A fully qualified name is a string of 1 to 8 characters, a period, and another string of 1 to 8 characters. The following characters are acceptable: A–Z, a–z 0–9 $ # @ The first character of either string must not be a number.

Default

No default name is assigned.

Command Mode

APPN partner LU-location configuration

Usage Guidelines

This command first appeared in Cisco IOS Release 11.0.

The *netid.cpname* argument must be unique in the network and must match the name specified as control point on the specific node.

Example

The following command sets the owning CP name:

```
appn partner-lu-location CISCO.LU000012
  owning-cp CISCO.CP00001
  complete
```

Related Commands

appn partner-lu-location
show appn directory

PORT (APPN CONNECTION NETWORK)

Use the **port** APPN connection-network configuration command to specify the ports that have visibility to the connection network. Use the **no** form of this command to delete the definition.

> **port** *portname*
> **no port** *portname*

Syntax	Description
portname	Type A name. A Type A character string contains 1 to 8 of the following characters: A–Z, a–z 0–9 $ # @

Default

No default port name is assigned.

Command Mode

APPN connection-network configuration

Usage Guidelines

This command first appeared in Cisco IOS Release 11.0.

Up to five ports can be specified by repeating the command. Port names must be previously defined by the **appn port** command.

Example

The following example specifies an APPN connection-network with one port:

```
appn connection-network CISCO.CN1
  port TR0
  complete
```

Related Commands

appn connection-network
appn port
show appn connection-network

PORT (APPN LINK STATION)

Use the **port** APPN link-station configuration command to specify the port that can be used to access the link station. Use the **no** form of this command to delete the definition.

port *portname*
no port

Syntax	Description
portname	Type A name. (Required when defining a new link station; optional on subsequent changes to the link station.) A Type A character contains 1 to 8 of the following characters: A–Z, a–z 0–9 $ # @

Default

No default port is specified.

Command Mode

APPN link-station configuration

Usage Guidelines

This command first appeared in Cisco IOS Release 11.0.

The *portname* argument must be a value defined in a previous **appn port** command. The **port** command is required to define an APPN link station.

Example

The following example defines the port:

```
appn link-station FDDILINK
  port FDDI0
  lan-dest-address 0200.0000.cfbd
  complete
```

Related Commands

appn link-station
appn port
show appn link-station

PPP-DEST-ADDRESS

Use the **ppp-dest-address** APPN link-station configuration command to specify the remote SAP of a node across a PPP interface. Use the **no** form of this command to delete the definition.

ppp-dest-address *sap*
no ppp-dest-address

Syntax	*Description*
sap	Service access point of the remote node. The default is 04 hexadecimal.

Default

The default SAP is 04 hexadecimal.

Command Mode

APPN link-station configuration

Usage Guidelines

This command first appeared in Cisco IOS Release 11.1.

The command should be specified only if the APPN port used by the link station is a PPP port.

Related Commands

appn link-station
show appn link-station

PROPAGATION-DELAY (APPN LINK STATION)

Use the **propagation-delay** APPN link-station configuration command to specify the amount of inherent delay of the connection. Use the **no** form of this command to delete the definition.

> **propagation-delay {minimum | lan | telephone | packet-switched | satellite | maximum}**
> **no propagation-delay**

Syntax	*Description*
minimum	No delay.
lan	Less than 480 microseconds delay.
telephone	Between 480 and 49152 microseconds delay.
packet-switched	Between 49152 and 245760 microseconds delay.
satellite	Greater than 245760 microseconds delay.
maximum	Maximum delay allowed.

Default

The value specified in the **appn port** command.

Command Mode

APPN link-station configuration

Usage Guidelines

This command first appeared in Cisco IOS Release 11.0.

The inherent delay is used in route selection by comparing this value to the value requested for a particular class of service. This value supersedes any value specified on the **appn port** command. Propagation delay is used by the node to determine the least-cost route for APPN intermediate sessions.

Example

The following example specifies a delay of less than 480 microseconds:

```
appn link-station FRLINK12
   port FR1
   propagation-delay lan
   complete
```

Related Commands

appn link-station
show appn link-station

PROPAGATION-DELAY (APPN PORT)

Use the **propagation-delay** APPN-port configuration command to specify the propagation delay of the link. Use the **no** form of this command to delete the definition.

> **propagation-delay** {**minimum** | **lan** | **telephone** | **packet-switched** | **satellite** | **maximum**}
> **no propagation-delay**

Syntax	Description
minimum	No delay.
lan	Less than 480 microseconds delay.
telephone	Between 480 and 49152 microseconds delay.
packet-switched	Between 49152 and 245760 microseconds delay.
satellite	Greater than 245760 microseconds delay.
maximum	Maximum delay allowed.

Default

Media-dependent:

Ethernet—**lan**
FDDI—**lan**
Frame Relay—**packet-switched**
QLLC—**packet-switched**

RSRB—packet-switched
SDLC—telephone
Token Ring—lan

Command Mode

APPN-port configuration

Usage Guidelines

This command first appeared in Cisco IOS Release 11.0.

This command applies to all link stations accessed through this port. Specifying propagation delay at the link-station level overrides this command. The value of propagation delay is used by the node to determine the least-cost route for APPN intermediate sessions.

Example

The following example specifies a delay of less than 480 microseconds:

```
appn port FR1 Serial1/1
  propagation-delay lan
  complete
```

Related Commands

appn port
show appn port

PU-TYPE-20

Use the **pu-type-20** APPN link-station configuration command to indicate that the downstream PU whose dependent-LU request is propagated through the link is a PU type 2.0. Use the **no** form of this command, or omit this command, to indicate that the downstream PU is a type 2.1.

pu-type-20
no pu-type-20

Syntax   Description

This command has no arguments or keywords.

Default

The downstream PU is defined as a PU type 2.1.

Command Mode

APPN link-station configuration

Usage Guidelines

This command first appeared in Cisco IOS Release 11.0.

This command normally is used in conjunction with the **dlur-dspu-name** link-station configuration command.

Example

The following example indicates that the downstream PU is a PU type 2.0:

```
appn link-station LINK0001
  port TR0
  lan-dest-address 1000.4521.9812
  pu-type-20
  dlur-dspu-name PU009812
  complete
```

Related Commands

appn link-station
dlur-dspu-name
show appn link-station

RESERVED-INBOUND

Use the **reserved-inbound** APPN-port configuration command to specify the number of link stations (out of **max-link-stations**) to be reserved for inbound links (partner initiates). Use the **no** form of this command to delete a previous definition.

     reserved-inbound *number*
     no reserved-inbound

Syntax	*Description*
number	Number in the range 0 to 255. The default is 0.

Default

Zero link stations.

Command Mode

APPN-port configuration

Usage Guidelines

This command first appeared in Cisco IOS Release 11.0.

The total of **reserved-inbound** plus **reserved-outbound** must be less than or equal to the maximum number of link stations allowed on the port. This value is configured using the **max-link-stations** command.

Example

The following example sets the number of link stations reserved for inbound links to 50:

```
appn port TR0 tokenring 0
 reserved-inbound 50
 complete
```

Related Commands

appn port
max-link-stations
reserved-outbound
show appn port

RESERVED-OUTBOUND

Used the **reserved-outbound** APPN-port configuration command to specify the number of link stations (of **max-link-stations**) to be reserved for outbound link stations where this node initiates the connection. Use the **no** form of this command to delete the definition.

> **reserved-outbound** *number*
> **no reserved-outbound**

Syntax	Description
number	Number in the range 0 to 255. The default is 0.

Default

Zero link stations.

Command Mode

APPN-port configuration

Usage Guidelines

This command first appeared in Cisco IOS Release 11.0.

The total of **reserved-inbound** plus **reserved-outbound** must be less than or equal to the maximum number of link stations allowed on the port. This value is configured using the **max-link-stations** command.

Example

The following example sets the number of link stations reserved for outbound links to 50:

```
appn port TR1 tokenring 1
  reserved-outbound 50
  complete
```

Related Commands

appn port
max-link-stations
reserved-inbound
show appn port

RETRY-LIMIT (APPN LINK STATION)

Use the **retry-limit** APPN link-station configuration command to specify the number of times a link station attempts reactivation after failure. Use the **no** form of this command to specify the default.

retry-limit {*retries* | **infinite** [*interval*]}
no retry-limit

Syntax	Description
retries	Number of reactivation attempts. The valid range is 0 to 255 (0 equals infinite retries). The default is 5.
infinite	Infinite retries.
interval	(Optional) Amount of time allowed between reactivation attempts (in seconds). The valid range is 0 to 32767 seconds. The default is 30 seconds.

Defaults

The default number of retries is 5.

The default amount of time is 30 seconds.

Command Mode

APPN link-station configuration

Usage Guidelines

This command first appeared in Cisco IOS Release 11.0.

This value supersedes any value specified in the **appn port** command.

Example

The following example specifies 25 retries for APPN link station LINK12:

```
appn link-station LINK12
  port FDDI1
  lan-dest-address 4000.0211.4567
  retry-limit 25
  complete
```

Related Commands

appn link-station
show appn link-station

RETRY-LIMIT (APPN PORT)

Use the **retry-limit** APPN-port configuration command to specify how many times a line will attempt reactivation after failure. Use the **no** form of this command to delete the previous definition.

> **retry-limit** {*retries* | **infinite**} [*interval*]
> **no retry-limit**

Syntax	Description
retries	Number of reactivation attempts. The valid range is 0 to 255 (0 equals infinite retries). The default is 5.
infinite	Infinite retries.
interval	(Optional) Amount of time allowed between reactivation attempts (in seconds). The default is 30 seconds.

Defaults

The default number of retries is 5.

The default amount of time is 30 seconds.

Command Mode

APPN-port configuration

Usage Guidelines

This command first appeared in Cisco IOS Release 11.0.

This command applies to all link stations accessed through this port. Specifying a retry limit at the link-station level overrides this command.

Example

The following example specifies 25 retries:

```
appn port ETHER0 ethernet 0
 retry-limit 25
 complete
```

Related Commands

appn port
show appn port

ROLE (APPN LINK STATION)

Use the **role** APPN link-station configuration command to specify the link-station role used in XID negotiations. Use the **no** form of this command to delete a previous definition.

> **role** {**negotiable** | **primary** | **secondary**}
> **no role**

Syntax	*Description*
negotiable	The link station can be the primary or secondary end of the link-station connection.
primary	The link station is the primary end of the link-station connection.
secondary	The link station is the secondary end of the link-station connection.

Default

The value specified in the **appn port** command.

Command Mode

APPN link-station configuration

Usage Guidelines

This command first appeared in Cisco IOS Release 11.0.

This command overrides the value specified on the port definition.

Example

The following example sets the role to primary:

```
appn link-station LINK44
 port ETHER1
 lan-dest-address 0200.98ab.de23
 role primary
 complete
```

Related Commands

appn link-station
show appn link-station

ROLE (APPN PORT)

Use the **role** APPN-port configuration command to specify the link-station role used in XID negotiations for all link stations defined through this port. Use the **no** form of this command to delete a previous definition.

>   role {negotiable | primary | secondary}
>   no role

Syntax

Syntax	*Description*
negotiable	The link station can be the primary or secondary end of the link-station connection.
primary	The link station is the primary end of the link-station connection.
secondary	The link station is the secondary end of the link-station connection.

Default

The default role is **negotiable**.

Command Mode

APPN-port configuration

Usage Guidelines

This command first appeared in Cisco IOS Release 11.0.

This command applies to all link stations accessed through this port. Specifying a role at the link station overrides this command.

Example

The following example sets the role to primary:

```
appn port FDDI0 fddi 0
  role primary
  complete
```

Related Commands

appn port
show appn port

ROUTE-ADDITIONAL-RESISTANCE

Use the **route-additional-resistance** APPN control-point configuration command to specify an arbitrary value for the local node. Use the **no** form of this command to delete the definition.

> **route-additional-resistance** *number*
> **no route-additional-resistance**

Syntax	Description
number	Arbitrary value in the range of 0 to 255. The default is 128.

Default

The default resistance value is 128.

Command Mode

APPN control-point configuration

Usage Guidelines

This command first appeared in Cisco IOS Release 11.0.

The route-additional-resistance value is included in topology updates and is used by network nodes to select a least-cost path associated with a particular class of service. You use this command to assign an arbitrary value and to indicate preference or nonpreference for particular nodes in route paths.

Example

The following example specifies a route-additional-resistance value of 200:

```
appn control-point CISCO.ROUTER
  route-additional-resistance 200
  complete
```

Related Commands

appn control-point
show appn node

RSRB-VIRTUAL-STATION

Use the **rsrb-virtual-station** APPN-port configuration command to configure APPN for remote source-route bridging. Use the **no** form of this command to delete the configuration.

> **rsrb-virtual-station** *mac-address local-ring bridge-number target-ring*
> **no rsrb-virtual-station**

Syntax	Description
mac-address	Virtual MAC address on which APPN resides.
local-ring	Virtual ring number on which the APPN station resides. The valid range is 1 to 255.
bridge-number	Bridge number connecting the local virtual ring and the RSRB target virtual ring. The valid range is 1 to 15.
target-ring	Target ring through which the local ring bridges data. The valid range is 1 to 255.

Default

No defaults are defined.

Command Mode

APPN-port configuration

Usage Guidelines

This command first appeared in Cisco IOS Release 11.0.

Example

The following example defines an APPN port that uses RSRB as a transport protocol:

```
appn port rsrb
  rsrb-virtual-station 1234.1234.1234 50 1 60
  complete
```

Related Commands

appn port
show appn port

SAFE-STORE-CYCLE

Use the **safe-store-cycle** APPN control-point configuration command to specify the number of cache instances to be saved. Use the **no** form of this command to delete the previous definition.

safe-store-cycle *number*
no safe-store-cycle

Syntax	Description
number	Number of cache instances to be saved. The valid range is 1 to 99. The default is 2.

Default

The default is 2.

Command Mode

APPN control-point configuration

Usage Guidelines

This command first appeared in Cisco IOS Release 11.0.

The file-naming convention used for the cache instances is

```
control-point-name.dnn
```

where *nn* is a number in the range from 00 to the cycle number specified. The files that will be generated in the example are:

```
APPN1.d00
APPN1.d01
APPN1.d02
APPN1.d03
```

Example

The following example specifies that 3 cache instances will be saved:

```
appn control-point CISCO.APPN1
  safe-store-host ip-address 171.69.44.1 directory appnsafe
  safe-store-cycle 3
  complete
```

Related Commands

appn control-point

SAFE-STORE-HOST

Use the **safe-store-host** APPN control-point configuration command to specify the IP host address and the file path for safe store. Use the **no** form of this command to delete the previous definition.

> **safe-store-host ip-address** *address* **directory** *path*
> **no safe-store-host**

Syntax	*Description*
ip-address *address*	Host IP address.
directory *path*	File path for safe store.

Default

No defaults are assigned.

Command Mode

APPN control-point configuration

Usage Guidelines

This command first appeared in Cisco IOS Release 11.0.

Some TFTP hosts might require you to create the file entries in advance. Refer to the **safe-store-cycle** command reference entry for the file-naming convention.

Example

The following example specifies that the IP host address and the file path where the database will be stored:

```
appn control-point CISCO.APPN1
  safe-store-host ip-address 171.69.44.1 directory appnsafe
  safe-store-cycle 3
  complete
```

Related Commands

appn control-point

SAFE-STORE-INTERVAL

Use the **safe-store-interval** APPN control-point configuration command to specify how often the directory database is stored to permanent media. Use the **no** form of this command to delete the previous definition.

> **safe-store-interval** *interval*
> **no safe-store-interval**

Syntax	Description
interval	Interval in minutes between storage of the directory database to permanent media. The valid range is 0 to 32767 minutes. The default is 20 minutes.

Default

20 minutes

Command Mode

APPN control-point configuration

Usage Guidelines

This command first appeared in Cisco IOS Release 11.0.

This command allows you to balance processor usage with potential performance savings. A longer interval reduces the processor cycles used to save data, but potentially reduces the validity of the data due to less frequent updates.

Example

The following example specifies that the database will be stored to permanent media every 30 minutes:

```
appn control-point CISCO.APPN1
  safe-store-host ip-address 171.69.44.1 directory appnsafe
  safe-store-interval 30
  complete
```

Related Commands

appn control-point

SDLC-DEST-ADDRESS

Use the **sdlc-dest-address** APPN link-station configuration command to specify the local address of the partner node for nonswitched SDLC. Use the **no** form of this command to delete the definition.

> **sdlc-dest-address** *address*
> **no sdlc-dest-address** *address*

Syntax	Description
address	2-digit hexadecimal number in the range of 00 to FE.

Default

No default address is assigned.

Command Mode

APPN link-station configuration

Usage Guidelines

This command first appeared in Cisco IOS Release 11.0.

This command is optional if the interface type is switched SDLC. It is not allowed for other interface types.

Example

The following example assigns address F1:

```
appn link-station LINK12
  port SDLC1
  sdlc-dest-address f1
  complete
```

Related Commands

appn link-station
show appn link-station

SDLC-SEC-ADDR

Use the **sdlc-sec-addr** command to configure APPN for SDLC. Use the **no** form of this command to delete the configuration.

> **sdlc-sec-addr** *sdlc-address*
> **no sdlc-sec-addr**

Syntax	*Description*
sdlc-address	SDLC secondary address. The valid range is 00 to FE (hexadecimal). The default is 00.

Default

The default address is 00.

Command Mode

APPN-port configuration

Usage Guidelines

This command first appeared in Cisco IOS Release 11.0.

Example

The following example defines a port with a local SDLC address of 2.

```
appn port serial 1
  sdlc-sec-addr 2
  complete
```

Related Commands

appn port
show appn port

SECURITY (APPN LINK STATION)

Use the **security** APPN link-station configuration command to specify the security level of the connection. Use the **no** form of this command to delete the previous definition.

> **security** *security-level*
> **no security**

Syntax	Description
security-level	One of the following keywords: **nonsecure, public-switched, underground-cable, secure-conduit, guarded-conduit, encrypted, guarded-radiation**. The default is the value specified in the **appn port** command.

Default

The default value specified in the **appn port** command.

Command Mode

APPN link-station configuration

Usage Guidelines

This command first appeared in Cisco IOS Release 11.0.

The security level is used in route selection.

Example

The following example sets the security level to encrypted:

```
appn link-station LINK12
  security encrypted
  complete
```

Related Commands

appn link-station
show appn link-station

SECURITY (APPN PORT)

Use the **security** APPN-port configuration command to specify security level of the connection. Use the **no** form of this command to delete the previous definition.

```
security security-level
no security
```

Syntax	Description
security-level	One of the following keywords: **nonsecure, public-switched, underground-cable, secure-conduit, guarded-conduit, encrypted, guarded-radiation**. The default is **nonsecure**.

Default

The default security is **nonsecure**.

Command Mode

APPN-port configuration

Usage Guidelines

This command first appeared in Cisco IOS Release 11.0.

The command applies to all link stations accessed through this port. Specifying security at the link-station level overrides this command.

Example

The following command sets the security level to encrypted:

```
appn port TR0 tokenring 0
  security encrypted
  complete
```

Related Commands

appn port
show appn port

SERVICE-ANY

Use the **service-any** APPN-port configuration command to specify that this port will create dynamic transmission groups for outbound or inbound links. Use the **no** form of this command to specify that the link station must be defined through configuration commands.

    service-any
    no service-any

Syntax   Description

This command has no arguments or keywords.

Default

The default state is **service-any**.

Command Mode

APPN-port configuration

Usage Guidelines

This command first appeared in Cisco IOS Release 11.0.

Specifying **no service-any** serves as a security mechanism to control who may or may not connect to the local node.

Example

The following example deactivates service-any:

```
appn port FDDI0 fddi0
  no service-any
  complete
```

Related Commands

appn port
show appn port

SERVING-NN

Use the **serving-nn** APPN partner LU-location configuration command to specify the name of the network-node server servicing the partner LU. Use the **no** form of this command to delete the definition.

> **serving-nn** *netid.cpname*
> **no serving-nn**

Syntax	Description
netid.cpname	Fully qualified network name. A fully qualified name is a string of 1 to 8 characters, a period, and another string of 1 to 8 characters. The following characters are acceptable: A–Z, a–z 0–9 $ # @ The first character of either string must not be a number. The default is the CP name of the local network node.

Default

The CP name of the local network node.

Command Mode

APPN partner LU-location configuration

Usage Guidelines

This command first appeared in Cisco IOS Release 11.0.

The **serving-nn** may be specified as null if the LU name is specified as null. This specification indicates a wildcard definition for all LUs.

Example

The following example specifies the name of the network-node server for the partner LU CISCO.APPN1:

```
appn partner-lu-location CISCO.LU000012
  serving-nn CISCO.APPN1
  complete
```

Related Commands

appn partner-lu-location
show appn directory

SHOW APPN CLASS-OF-SERVICE

Use the **show appn class-of-service** EXEC command to display the APPN classes of service defined to the local node.

show appn class-of-service [brief | detail]

Syntax	Description
brief	(Optional) Short display of APPN classes of service.
detail	(Optional) Long display of APPN classes of service.

Default

The default is **brief**.

Command Mode

EXEC

Usage Guidelines

This command first appeared in Cisco IOS Release 11.0.

Sample Displays

Brief sample display:

```
Number of class of service definitions        7
    APPN Classes of Service
        Name    Trans. Pri.  Node Rows  TG Rows
        -------- -----------  ---------  -------
    1> #CONNECT  Medium          8          8
    2> CPSVCMG   Network         8          8
    3> SNASVCMG  Network         8          8
    4> #INTER    High            8          8
    5> #INTERSC  High            8          8
    6> #BATCH    Low             8          8
    7> #BATCHSC  Low             8          8
```

Detailed sample display:

This example shows just one part of one table. There could be up to 8 node rows and 8 TGs and multiple tables. This shows, however, the correspondence between the configuration commands and **show** commands.

```
Number of class of service definitions      8
1> Class of service name                    #connect
    Transmission priority                   Medium
    Number of node rows                     8
    Number of TG rows                       8
1.1> Node row weight                        5
        Congestion min                      no
        Congestion max                      no
        Route additional resistance min     0
  .     Route additional resistance max     31

  .                                         .
1.1>TG row weight                           30
        cost-per-connect time min           0
        cost-per-connect time max           0
     Cost per byte min                      0
     Cost per byte max                      0
     Security min                           Nonsecure
     Security max                           Maximum security
     Propagation delay min                  0 microseconds (minimum)
     Propagation delay max                  384 microseconds (local area network)
     Effective capacity min                 4 megabits per second
     Effective capacity max                 604 gigabits per second
     User defined parameter 1 min           0
     User defined parameter 1 max           255
     User defined parameter 2 min           0
     User defined parameter 2 max           255
     User defined parameter 3 min           0
     User defined parameter 3 max           255
```

Figure 20–1 describes significant fields shown in the display.

Table 20–1 *Show APPN Class-of-Service Detail Field Descriptions*

Field	Description
Class of service name	Administratively assigned name for this COS.
Transmission priority	Relative priority this COS will receive when transmitting out of this node.
Number of node rows	Number of node rows associated with this COS.
Node of TG rows	Number of TG rows associated with this COS.
Node row weight	Weight assigned to this node given the characteristics identified in the remainder of this row.

Table 20–1 *Show APPN Class-of-Service Detail Field Descriptions, Continued*

Field	Description
Congestion min	If set to "yes," this node row will be chosen only if the node is congested. If set to "no," this node row may be chosen if the node is congested. If the congestion maximum is set to "no," the congestion minimum must also be set to "no."
Congestion max	If set to "yes," this node row may be chosen if the node is congested. If set to "no," this node row never will be chosen for this COS.
Route additional resistance min	Minimum route additional resistance for this node row.
Route additional resistance max	Maximum route additional resistance for this node row.
TG row weight	Weight associated with this TG given the characteristics identified in the remainder of this row.
cost-per-connect time min	Minimum acceptable value for cost-per-connect time for this TG row.
cost-per-connect time max	Maximum acceptable value for cost-per-connect time for this TG row.
Cost per byte min	Minimum acceptable value for cost per byte for this TG row.
Cost per byte max	Maximum acceptable value for cost per byte for this TG row.
Security min	Minimum acceptable value for security for this TG row.
Security max	Maximum acceptable value for security for this TG row.
Propagation delay min	Minimum acceptable value for propagation delay for this TG row.
Propagation delay max	Maximum acceptable value for propagation delay for this TG row.
Effective capacity min	Minimum acceptable value for effective capacity for this TG row.
Effective capacity max	Maximum acceptable value for effective capacity for this TG row.
User-defined parameter 1 min	Minimum value for a network-unique TG characteristic—parameter 1.
User-defined parameter 1 max	Maximum value for a network-unique TG characteristic—parameter 1.

Table 20–1   *Show APPN Class-of-Service Detail Field Descriptions, Continued*

Field	Description
User-defined parameter 2 min	Minimum value for a network-unique TG characteristic—parameter 2.
User-defined parameter 2 max	Maximum value for a network-unique TG characteristic—parameter 2.
User-defined parameter 3 min	Minimum value for a network-unique TG characteristic—parameter 3.
User-defined parameter 3 max	Maximum value for a network-unique TG characteristic—parameter 3.

Related Commands

appn class-of-service
class-of-service

SHOW APPN CONNECTION-NETWORK

Use the **show appn connection-network** EXEC command to display the APPN connection networks defined to the local node.

   show appn connection-network [brief | detail]

Syntax   *Description*
brief   (Optional) Short display of APPN connection networks.
detail   (Optional) Long display of APPN connection networks.

Default
The default is **brief.**

Command Mode
EXEC

Usage Guidelines
This command first appeared in Cisco IOS Release 11.0.

Sample Displays

Brief sample display:

```
Connection network definitions            2
      APPN Connection Networks
         Resource Name    Attached Ports  First Port Name
         ----------------  --------------  ---------------
      1> NETA.CN                 2         TR0
                                           ABCDEFGH
      2> NETADDDD.WWWWEEEE        1         TR0
```

Detailed sample display:

```
Connection network definitions            1

   1>Connection network name            NETA.CONNECT
      Effective capacity                 15974400 bits per second
      cost-per-connect time              0
      Cost per byte                      0
      Propagation delay                  384 microseconds (local area network)
      User defined parameter 1           128
      User defined parameter 2           128
      User defined parameter 3           128
      Security                           Nonsecure
      Attached ports                     1

   1.1>Port name                         TR0
```

Figure 20–2 describes significant fields shown in the display.

Table 20–2 *Show APPN Connection-Network Detail Field Descriptions*

Field	Description
Connection network name	Fully qualified name of the connection network.
Effective capacity	Bit rate for the connection network.
cost-per-connect time	Relative cost of this connection network's TG.
Cost per byte	Cost-per-byte of transmitting a byte over this TG.
Propagation delay	Inherent delay of the connection network.
User-defined parameter 1	Value for a network-unique TG characteristic—parameter 1.
User-defined parameter 2	Value for a network-unique TG characteristic—parameter 2.
User-defined parameter 3	Value for a network-unique TG characteristic—parameter 3.
Security	Security level for this connection network.
Attached ports	Number of ports associated with the connection network.
Port Name	Port supporting this connection network.

Related Commands

appn connection-network

SHOW APPN DIRECTORY

Use the **show appn directory** EXEC command to display negative cache entries and the remaining time and threshold-count values.

> **show appn directory**

Syntax   Description

This command has no arguments or keywords.

Command Mode

Privileged EXEC

Usage Guidelines

This command first appeared in Cisco IOS Release 11.0.

Sample Display

In the following example, two negative cache entry-type entries are found in the directory database table. Notice that the NETA.EN2 resource was entered as a cache entry previously, so its Owning CP Name and NN Server information are known. On the other hand, NETA.EN3 was not found on the APPN network during a previous locate-search, so the corresponding information for that resource is empty.

```
router1# show appn directory

  Total directory entries              4
      APPN Directory Entries
          Resource Name    Owning CP Name      NN Server         Entry Type
          ---------------  ----------------    ----------------  ----------
     1>  NETA.ROUTER1      NETA.ROUTER1        NETA.ROUTER1      Home
     2>  NETA.EN1          NETA.EN1            NETA.ROUTER1      Register
     3>  NETA.EN2          NETA.EN2            NETA.ROUTER2      NCache
     4>  NETA.EN3                                                NCache

router2# show appn directory detail

  Total directory entries              4

1>LU name                             NETA.ROUTER1
   Owning CP name                      NETA.ROUTER1
   Network node CP name                NETA.ROUTER1
   LU entry type                       Home
   Register Resource                   No
```

```
  2>LU name                             NETA.EN1
    Owning CP name                      NETA.EN1
    Network node CP name                NETA.ROUTER1
    LU entry type                       Register
    Register Resource                   No
  3>LU name                             NETA.EN2
    Owning CP name                      NETA.EN2
    Network node CP name                NETA.ROUTER2
    LU entry type                       NCache
    Register Resource                   No
    NCache time Remaining               2
    NCache count Remaining              5
  4>LU name                             NETA.EN3
    Owning CP name
    Network node CP name
    LU entry type                       NCache
    Register Resource                   No
    NCache time Remaining               0
    NCache count Remaining              10
```

Related Commands

appn partner-lu-location
central-resource-registration

SHOW APPN DLUR-LU

Use the **show appn dlur-lu** EXEC command to display all active SSCP dependent LUs known to DLUR.

> show appn dlur-lu [**pu** *pu-name*] [**brief** | **detail**]

Syntax	Description
pu *pu-name*	8-character Type A string of a specific PU.
brief	(Optional) Short display of the APPN directory database.
detail	(Optional) Long display of the APPN directory database.

Default

The default is **brief**.

Command Mode

EXEC

Usage Guidelines

This command first appeared in Cisco IOS Release 11.0.

Sample Displays

Brief sample display:

```
APPN DLUR-LU:
      LU Name    PU Name    DLUS Name    PLU Name
      -------    -------    ---------    ----------
   1> SJDRLU11   BEAGLE     NETA.CPAC    NETA.TSO0005
```

Detailed sample display:

```
LU name                           SJDRLU11
PU name                           BEAGLE
Dependent LU Server Name          NETA.CPAC
LU location                       Remote
NAU address                       2
PLU name                          NETA.TSO0005
```

Figure 20–3 describes significant fields shown in the display.

Table 20–3   *Show APPN DLUR-LU Field Descriptions*

Field	Description
LU name	Logical unit name of the active SSCP-dependent LUs supported by DLUR.
PU name	Physical unit name of the active SSCP-dependent LU.
DLUS name	Fully qualified name of the DLUS providing SSCP services for the SSCP-dependent LU.
LU location	Always identifies the LUs as remote LUs.
NAU address	Network addressable unit of the LU.
PLU name	When the SSCP-dependent LU has an active session, the name of the primary LU name will be displayed.

Related Commands

backup-dlus (APPN control point)
dlur
dlus (APPN control point)
show appn dlur-pu
show appn dlus

SHOW APPN DLUR-PU

Use the **show appn dlur-pu** EXEC command to display all active SSCP-dependent PUs known to DLUR.

> **show appn dlur-pu** [**dlus** *dlus-name*] [**brief** | **detail**]

Syntax	Description
dlus *dlus-name*	(Optional) 17-character Type A string of a specific DLUS.
brief	(Optional) Short display of the APPN directory database.
detail	(Optional) Long display of the APPN directory database.

Default

The default is **brief**.

Command Mode

EXEC

Usage Guidelines

This command first appeared in Cisco IOS Release 11.0.

Sample Displays

Brief sample display:

```
APPN DLUR-PU:
        PU Name  Active DLUS  Defined DLUS  Backup DLUS
        -------  -----------  ------------  -----------
   1> BEAGLE    NETA.CPAC
```

Detailed sample display:

```
PU name                           BEAGLE
Defined DLUS name
Backup DLUS name
Physical unit (PU) Node ID        05D00010
PU location                       Downstream
Active DLUS name                  NETA.CPAC
ANS support                       Continue
PCID                              D6DB11281AF90044
Fully qualified CP name           NETA.WONDER
```

Table 20-4 *Show APPN DLUR-PU Detail Field Descriptions*

Field	Description
PU name	Physical unit name of active SSCP-dependent PUs.
Defined DLUS name	DLUS name specified with the **dlus** (APPN link station) configuration command.
Backup DLUS name	DLUS name specified with the **backup-dlus** (APPN link station) configuration command.
PU Node ID	IDBLK and IDNUM of the PU.

Table 20–4 *Show APPN DLUR-PU Detail Field Descriptions, Continued*

Field	Description
PU Location	Always identifies the PU as downstream.
Active DLUS name	Fully qualified name of the DLUS providing SSCP services for the PU.
ANS support	Identifies whether DLUR will keep active LU-LU sessions (Continue) when the connection to the DLUS is lost or whether DLUR will tear down active LU-LU sessions (Stop).
PCID	Procedure correlation identifier used to distinguish encapsulated traffic associated with this PU.
Fully qualified CP name	Fully qualified CP name of the CP which generated the PCID above.

Related Commands

backup-dlus (APPN control point)
dlur
dlus (APPN control point)
show appn dlur-lu
show appn dlus

SHOW APPN DLUS

Use the **show appn dlus** EXEC command to display all LUs known to DLUR.

  show appn dlus [brief | detail]

Syntax	*Description*
brief	(Optional) Short display of the APPN directory database.
detail	(Optional) Long display of the APPN directory database.

Default
The default is **brief**.

Command Mode
EXEC

Usage Guidelines
This command first appeared in Cisco IOS Release 11.0.

Sample Displays

Brief sample display:

```
APPN DLUS:
      DLUS Name    State   # Active PUs
      ---------    -----   ----------
   1> NETA.CPAC    ACTIVE          1
```

Detailed sample display:

```
      Dependent LU Server Name              NETA.CPAC
      Is this default DLUS?                 Yes
      Is this default backup DLUS?          No
      Pipe State                            Active
      Number of active PUs                  1
      Pipe statistics
      # of REQACTPU requests sent           1
      # of REQACTPU responses received      1
      # of ACTPU requests received          1
      # of ACTPU responses sent             1
      # of REQDACTPU requests sent          0
      # of REQDACTPU responses received     0
      # of DACTPU requests received         0
      # of DACTPU responses sent            0
      # of ACTLU requests received          1
      # of ACTLU responses sent             1
      # of DACTLU requests received         0
      # of DACTLU responses sent            0
      # of SSCP_PU MUs received             0
      # of SSCP_PU MUs sent                 0
      # of SSCP_LU MUs received             4
      # of SSCP_LU MUs sent                 5
```

Figure 20–5 describes significant fields shown in the display.

Table 20–5 *Show APPN DLUS Detail Field Descriptions*

Field	Description
DLUS name	Fully qualified DLUS name.
default DLUS	Identifies the DLUS as the node default DLUS.
default backup DLUS	Identifies the DLUS as the node backup default DLUS.
Pipe State	Identifies the state of the DLUS-DLUR connection.
Number of active PUs	Total number of active PUs.
REQACTPU sent/rcvd	Number of REQACTPU requests sent to the DLUS and the number of REQACTPU responses received from DLUS.
ACTPU rcvd/sent	Number of ACTPU responses sent to the DLUs and the number of ACTPU requests received from the DLUS.

Table 20–5 *Show APPN DLUS Detail Field Descriptions, Continued*

Field	Description
REQDACTPU rcvd/sent	Number of REQDACTPU requests sent to the DLUS and the number of REQDACTPU responses received from the DLUS.
DACTPU sent/rcvd	Number of DACTPU responses sent to the DLUS and the number of DACTPU requests received from the DLUS.
ACTLU rcvd/sent	Number of ACTLU responses sent to the DLUS and the number of ACTLU requests received from the DLUS.
DACTLU rcvd/sent	Number of DACTLU responses sent to the DLUS and the number of DACTLU requests received from the DLUS.
SSCP PU MUs rcvd/sent	Number of SSCP PU MUs sent and received from the DLUS.
SSCP LU MUs rcvd/sent	Number of SSCP LU MUs sent and received from the DLUS.

Related Commands

backup-dlus (APPN control point)
dlur
dlus (APPN control point)

SHOW APPN INTERMEDIATE-SESSION

Use the **show appn intermediate-session** EXEC command to display information about the SNA sessions that are currently being routed through the local node.

> show appn intermediate-session [pcid *pcid*] [name *lu-name*] [brief | detail]

Syntax	*Description*
pcid *pcid*	(Optional) Filter by procedure correlation identifier (PCID). PCID is a 16-byte hexadecimal number.
name *lu-name*	(Optional) Filter by fully qualified LU name.
brief	(Optional) Short display of APPN intermediate session information.
detail	(Optional) Long display of APPN intermediate session information.

Default

The default is **brief**.

Command Mode

EXEC

Usage Guidelines

This command first appeared in Cisco IOS Release 11.0. The following keywords and arguments first appeared in Cisco IOS Release 11.1: **pcid** *pcid*, **name** *lu-name*.

Sample Displays

Brief sample display:

```
Number of intermediate sessions         1
      APPN Intermediate Sessions
        PCID (hex)    Primary LU Name   Secondary LU Name   Mode     COS
      ---------------  ----------------- -----------------  -------- --------
     1> C6D328B0922EE4FF  NETA.MARGE        NETA.APU           #INTER   #INTER
```

Detailed sample display:

```
Number of intermediate sessions         2

   1>Procedure correlator ID (PCID) X'SS3321E8934CF101'
   Primary LU name NETA.LISA
   Secondary LU name NETA.BART
   Mode name #INTER
   Class of service name #INTER
   Primary side adjacent CP name           NETA.PATTY
      Secondary side adjacent CP name         CISCO.MARGE
      Primary side link name                  PATTY
      Secondary side link name                MARGE
   PCID generator CP name                  NETA.PATTY

   2>Procedure correlator ID (PCID) X'DD3321E8944CF101'
   Primary LU Name NETA.LISA
   Secondary LU Name NETA.BART
   Mode name SNASVCMG
   Class of service name SNASVCMG
   Primary side adjacent CP name           NETA.PATTY
      Secondary side adjacent CP name         CISCO.MARGE
      Primary side link name                  PATTY
      Secondary side link name                MARGE
   PCID generator CP name                  NETA.PATTY
```

Figure 20–6 describes significant fields shown in the display.

Table 20–6 *Show APPN Intermediate-Session Detail Field Descriptions*

Field	Description
Procedure correlator ID (PCID)	PCID for this session.
Primary LU name	Primary LU name for this session.
Secondary LU name	Secondary LU name for this session.
Mode name	Mode used by this session.

Table 20–6 *Show APPN Intermediate-Session Detail Field Descriptions, Continued*

Field	Description
Class-of-service name	Class of service used by this session.
Primary side adjacent CP name	Fully qualified name of the adjacent CP on the primary side.
Secondary side adjacent CP name	Fully qualified name of the adjacent CP on the secondary side.
Primary side link name	Link name used on the primary side.
Secondary side link name	Link name used on the secondary side.
PCID generator CP name	Fully qualified CP name that generated the PCID.
Session interrupt switched	Specifies if this session is processed at interrupt-level.

Related Commands

show appn connection-network

SHOW APPN LINK-STATION

Use the **show appn link-station** EXEC command to display information about the APPN link stations active on or defined to the local node.

> **show appn link-station** [**name** *link-station-name*] [**port** *port-name*] [**brief** | **detail**]

Syntax	Description
name *link-station-name*	(Optional) Filter by link-station name.
port *port-name*	(Optional) Filter by port name.
brief	(Optional) Short display of active APPN links. Brief is the default display.
detail	(Optional) Long display of active APPN links with more information.

Default

The default is **brief**.

Command Mode

EXEC

Usage Guidelines

This command first appeared in Cisco IOS Release 11.0. The following keywords and options first appeared in Cisco IOS Release 11.1: **name** *link-station-name*, **port** *port-name*.

Sample Displays

The following is a short display of active APPN links. This display is created by the **show appn link-station** command with the **brief** keyword:

```
Number of active links 1
APPN Logical Links
      Link Name  State     Port Name  Adjacent CP Name  Node Type
      ---------  --------  ---------  ----------------  -----------
   1> ROSEBUD    Active    TOK0       NETA.APU          Learn
   2> HOST       Inactive  FDDI0                        Learn
   3> DOWNSTR    Inactive  RSRB                         Learn
   4> CANE       Inactive  FDDI0                        Learn
```

The following is a long display of active APPN links. This display is created by the **show appn link-station** command with the **detail** keyword:

```
Number of links                   1

1>Link name                           ROSEBUD
     Port name                        TOK0
     Interface name                   TokenRing0
     Destination DLC address (remote SAP)  1111.2222.3333 (04)
     Link state                       Active
     Deactivating link                No
     Max send frame data (BTU) size   0
     Adjacent node CP name            NETA.APU
     Adjacent node type               Learn
     CP-CP session support            Yes
     Link station role                Negotiable
     Line type                        Shared access transport facility
     Transmission group number        0
     Effective capacity               100000000 bits per second
     cost-per-connect time            0
     Cost per byte                    0
     Propagation delay                384 microseconds (local area network)
     User defined parameter 1         128
     User defined parameter 2         128
     User defined parameter 3         128
     Security                         Nonsecure
     HPR supported                    Yes
     HPR RTP support level            (CF¦RTP¦Base)
     HPR local SAP                    0xC8
     HPR remote SAP                   0xC8
     HPR ERP used                     No
     HPR ANR label                    0x8003
     Queuing Type                     Default
     Primary DLUS Name
     Backup DLUS Name
     Downstream PU Name
     Retry link station               No
```

Table 20–7 describes significant fields shown in the display.

Table 20–7   *Show APPN Link-Station Field Descriptions*

Field	Description
Link name	Name of the link station.
Port name	Port this link station is using.
Interface name	Interface used by this link.
Destination DLC address (remote SAP)	Data-Link Control address of the partner node and its SAP.
Link state	State of the link.
Deactivating link	Indicates if the link is deactivating.
Max send frame data (BTU) size	Maximum BTU size this link can support.
Adjacent node CP name	Name of the partner node for the link station.
Adjacent node type	Node type of the partner node of this link.
CP-CP session support	Specifies whether CP-CP sessions can be supported.
Link-station role	Specifies the role the link uses in XID negotiation.
Line type	Specifies the line type.
Transmission group number	Transmission group assigned to this link.
Effective capacity	Bit rate of this link.
cost-per-connect time	Relative cost of this link.
Cost per byte	Cost per byte of transmitting over this link.
Propagation delay	Specifies the inherent delay of the link.
User defined parameter 1	Value for a network-unique transmission group characteristic—parameter 1.
User defined parameter 2	Value for a network-unique transmission group characteristic— parameter 2.
User defined parameter 3	Value for a network-unique transmission group characteristic—parameter 3.
Security	Security level of the link.
HPR supported	Indicates whether or not HPR is supported over the link station.

Table 20–7 *Show APPN Link-Station Field Descriptions, Continued*

Field	Description
HPR RTP support level	Specifies the level of HPR support: CF—Control flows over RTP tower is supported. RTP—RTP tower is supported. Base—Only base HPR is supported.
HPR local SAP	Value for the local SAP used by HPR traffic.
HPR remote SAP	Value for the remote SAP used by HPR traffic.
HPR ERP used	Indicates whether or not the link level error recovery protocol is used.
HPR NCE label	ANR string that represents the network connection end point.
Queuing Type	Indicates if a special queuing algorithm has been configured for this link station. Can be default, priority, custom, or fair.
Primary DLUS Name	If the DLUR feature is configured, this specifies the control-point name of the corresponding DLUS.
Backup DLUS Name	If the DLUR feature is configured, this specifies the control-point name of the corresponding backup DLUS.
Downstream PU Name	If this link is to a PU 2.0 type device, this field specifies the PU name of the remote node.
Retry link station	Indicates if the retry feature has been configured for this link and specifies the number of retries and the retry interval in seconds.

Related Commands

appn link-station

SHOW APPN MODE

Use the **show appn mode** EXEC command to display information about the APPN modes defined to the local node.

  show appn mode

Command Mode
EXEC

Usage Guidelines
This command first appeared in Cisco IOS Release 11.0.

Sample Display
```
Number of modes                8
     APPN Modes
     Name        Associated COS
     --------    --------------
  1>             #CONNECT
  2> #BATCH      #BATCH
  3> #BATCHSC    #BATCHSC
  4> #INTER      #INTER
  5> #INTERSC    #INTERSC
  6> CPSVCMG     CPSVCMG
  7> SNASVCMG    SNASVCMG
  8> CPSVRMGR    SNASVCMG
```
Table 20–8 describes significant fields shown in the display.

Table 20–8 *Show APPN Mode Field Descriptions*

Field	Description
Name	Mode name.
Associated COS	Class of service to this mode maps.

Related Commands
appn mode

SHOW APPN NODE

Use the **show appn node** EXEC command to display information about the local APPN control point.

show appn node

Command Mode
EXEC

Usage Guidelines
This command first appeared in Cisco IOS Release 11.0.

Sample Display

```
Network name                              NETA
   Control point (CP) name                BARNEY
   Node ID (for XID)                      X'07700000'
   Route additional resistance            128
   Maximum directory cache entries        255
   Current directory cache entries        0
   Directory save interval                2
Maximum sessions per RTP connection       65535
hpr timers liveness (low/med/hi/net)       1/1/1/1
Maximum RTP retries (low/med/hi/net)      6/6/6/6
Path switch timer (low/med/hi/net)        480/240/120/60
Locate-queue Enabled                      Yes
Total locate-q found count                2
Negative-caching Enabled                  Yes
Total negative-cache match count          30
```

Table 20–9 describes significant fields shown in the display.

Table 20–9 *Show APPN Node Field Descriptions*

Field	Description
Network name	Network name for this node.
Control point (CP) name	Control-point name for this node.
Node ID (for XID)	8-digit hexadecimal node ID value for this node.
Route additional resistance	Arbitrary value associated with the cost of sessions passing through this node.
Maximum directory cache entries	Maximum number of cached directory entries.
Current directory cache entries	Current number of cached directory entries.
Directory save interval	Time (in minutes) between directory safe stores.
Maximum sessions per HPR connection	Indicates the value configured for **hpr max-sessions**.
HPR timers liveness	Indicates the values configured for **hpr timers liveness**. The four values are for low-, medium-, high-, and network-priority packets.
Maximum HPR retries	Indicates the values configured for **hpr retries**. The four values are for low-, medium-, high-, and network-priority packets.

Table 20–9 *Show APPN Node Field Descriptions, Continued*

Field	Description
Path switch timer	Indicates the values configured for **hpr timers path-switch**. The four values are for low-, medium-, high-, and network-priority packets.
Locate-queue Enabled	Indicates whether the locate queuing feature has been enabled.
Negative-caching Enabled	Indicates whether the directory negative-caching feature has been enabled.

Related Commands

appn control-point

SHOW APPN PORT

Use the **show appn port** EXEC command to display information about the APPN ports active on the local node.

> **show appn port** [**port** *port-name*] [**brief** | **detail**]

Syntax	Description
port *port-name*	(Optional) Filter by port name.
brief	(Optional) Short display of APPN port definitions.
detail	(Optional) Long display of APPN port definitions.

Default

The default is **brief**.

Command Mode

EXEC

Usage Guidelines

This command first appeared in Cisco IOS Release 11.0. The **port** keyword first appeared in Cisco IOS Release 11.1. The output display changed in Release 11.2 to incorporate information about the HPR feature.

Sample Displays

The following is a short display of APPN port definitions. This display is created by the **show appn port** command with the **brief** keyword:

```
Number of ports                           2
      APPN Ports
      Name      State      SAP    HPR-SAP    Interface
      --------  --------   ---    -------    ------------
   1> TOK0      Active     x04    xC8        TokenRing0
   2> TOK1      Active     x04    xC8        TokenRing1
```

The following is a long display of APPN port definitions. This display is created by the **show appn port** command with the **detail** keyword:

```
Number of ports                              2

1>Port name                                  TOK0
   Interface name                            TokenRing0
   Port State                                Active
   SAP                                       X'04'
   Link station role                         Negotiable
   Limited resource                          No
   Max frame send data (BTU) size            2000
   Maximum receive BTU size                  2000
   Effective capacity                        16000000 bits per second
   cost-per-connect time                     0
   Cost per byte                             0
   Propagation delay                         384 microseconds (local area network)
   User defined parameter 1                  128
   User defined parameter 2                  128
   User defined parameter 3                  128
   Security                                     Nonsecure
   Total available link stations                65535
   Number reserved for inbound link stations    0
   Number reserved for outbound link stations   0
   HPR supported                                Yes
   HPR SAP                                      X'C8'
   Allow dynamic link stations (service any)    Yes
   Retry link stations                          No
```

Table 20–10 describes significant fields shown in the display.

Table 20–10 *Show APPN Port Detail Field Descriptions*

Field	Description
Port name	Name of this port.
Interface name	Interface used by this port.
Port State	Current state of this port.
SAP	Default service access point for links on this port.

Part II

Command Reference

Table 20–10   *Show APPN Port Detail Field Descriptions, Continued*

Field	Description
Link station role	Specifies the role link stations used in XID negotiation.
Limited resource	Specifies if links on this port should be taken down when no sessions are using the link.
Max send frame data (BTU) size	The largest size allowed for basic transmission units sent through this port.
Maximum receive BTU size	The largest size allowed for basic transmission units received through this port.
Effective capacity	Bit rate of this port.
cost-per-connect time	Relative cost of the links on this port.
Cost per byte	Cost per byte of transmitting a byte over the links on this port.
Propagation delay	Specifies the inherent delay of the port.
User defined parameter 1	Value for a network-unique transmission group characteristic—parameter 1.
User defined parameter 2	Value for a network-unique transmission group characteristic—parameter 2.
User defined parameter 3	Value for a network-unique transmission group characteristic—parameter 3.
Security	Security level of this port.
Total available link stations	The maximum number of link stations supported for this port.
Number reserved for inbound link stations	Of the total available link stations, the number reserved for inbound connections.
Number reserved for outbound link stations	Of the total available link stations, the number reserved for outbound connections.
HPR supported	Indicates whether or not HPR is supported over the port.
HPR SAP	Service access point for HPR frames on this port.

Table 20-10 *Show APPN Port Detail Field Descriptions, Continued*

Field	Description
Allow dynamic link stations (service any)	Indicates if this port will accept incoming connections from remote nodes without requiring a link-station definition at the local node.
Retry link stations	Specifies the number of times and the time between retries that the node will retry links that have failed before giving up.

Related Commands

appn port

SHOW APPN RTP

Use the **show appn rtp** EXEC command to display information about the RTP connections.

    show appn rtp [brief | detail]

Syntax	Description
brief	(Optional) Short display of APPN RTP connections.
detail	(Optional) Long display of APPN RTP connections.

Default

The default display is **brief.**

Command Mode

EXEC

Usage Guidelines

This command first appeared in Cisco IOS Release 11.2.

Sample Displays

The following is a short display of APPN RTP connections. This display is created by the **show appn rtp** command with the **brief** keyword:

```
TCID                 Partner Node      COS
-----------------    ------------      ------
0000000012345678     NETA.LISA         #BATCH
```

The following is a short display of APPN RTP connections. This display is created by the
show appn rtp command with the **detail** keyword:

```
Number of RTP connections                          1
Local TCID                         X'8000000000EBF6E8'
  Local CP name                      NETA.APPN2
  Remote NCEID                       X'8280'
  Remote TCID                        X'8000000000000000'
  Remote CP name                     NETA.FRANS
  Class of service name              SNASVCMG
  Liveness timer                     60 seconds
  Short request timer              1 milliseconds
  Path switch timer                  60 seconds
  Total bytes sent                   153
  Total bytes received               0
  Minimum send rate                  0
  Current send rate                  2208 Kilobits/second
  Maximum send rate                  9830 Kilobits/second
  Round trip delay time              4000 microseconds
  ANR string                         X'C60080008280FF00'
  Route                              NETA.APPN2          <-tg21->
                                     NETA.FRANS
```

Table 20–11 describes significant fields shown in the display.

Table 20–11   *Show APPN RTP Detail Field Descriptions*

Field	Description
Local TCID	Connection ID that uniquely identifies this connection. It is a 16-digit hexadecimal number.
Local CP name	Control-point name of the local node.
Remote NCEID	ANR label that represents the network connection end point at the remote node.
Remote TCID	Unique connection ID that the remote node uses to identify this connection.
Remote CP name	Control-point name of the remote node.
Class of service name	Name of the class of service used for packets flowing over this connection.
Liveness timer	Value configured for HPR timers liveness.
Short request timer	Calculated value for the timer used to wait for acknowledgment of HPR status request packets.
Path switch timer	Value configured for HPR timers path switch.
Total bytes sent	Running count of the amount of data sent over this connection.

Table 20-11 *Show APPN RTP Detail Field Descriptions, Continued*

Field	Description
Total bytes received	Running count of the amount of data received over this connection.
Minimum send rate	Minimum send rate allowed for this connection.
Current send rate	Calculated value for the current optimal send rate for this connection.
Maximum send rate	Maximum send rate allowed for this connection.
Round trip delay time	Measured round-trip delay for an HPR status request packet.
ANR string	HPR routing string put in the NHDR of each packet sent over this connection.
Route	Control-point name and transmissions group number representing each hop through intermediate nodes for the route taken by packets sent or received over this connection.

Related Commands

hpr max-sessions
hpr retries
hpr timers liveness
hpr timers path-switch

SHOW APPN SESSION

Use the **show appn session** EXEC command to display information about the SNA LU 6.2 sessions, such as CP-CP sessions, that originate from the local node.

    show appn session [pcid *pcid*] [name *lu-name*] [brief | detail]

Syntax	*Description*
pcid *pcid*	(Optional) Filter by procedure correlator identifier (PCID). PCID is a 16-byte hexadecimal number.
name *lu-name*	(Optional) Filter by fully qualified LU name.
brief	(Optional) Short display of APPN session information.
detail	(Optional) Long display of APPN session information.

Default

The default is **brief**.

Command Mode

EXEC

Usage Guidelines

This command first appeared in Cisco IOS Release 11.0. The following keywords and arguments first appeared in Cisco IOS Release 11.1: **pcid** *pcid*, **name** *lu-name*.

Sample Displays

The following is a short display of APPN session information. This display is created by the **show appn session** command with the **brief** keyword:

```
Number of sessions                       4
     APPN Endpoint Sessions
        PCID (hex)        Local LU Name    Partner LU Name    Mode      COS
     ----------------    ---------        ---------------    -------   --------
     1> C6D328B0912EE4FF  NETA.BART        NETA.MARGE         CPSVCMG   CPSVCMG
     2> F1DBABC818AB53AC  NETA.BART        NETA.APU           CPSVCMG   CPSVCMG
     3> F37F3BE237DE7242  NETA.BART        NETA.MARGE         CPSVCMG   CPSVCMG
     4> C21BFDC300ED68DB  NETA.BARNEY      NETA.LISA          #INTER    #INTER
```

The following is a long display of APPN session information. This display is created by the **show appn session** command with the **detail** keyword:

```
Number of sessions                       4

4>LU name                               NETA.BARNEY
   Partner LU name                      NETA.LISA
   Mode name                            #INTER
   Class of service name                #INTER
   Link name                            *OverHPR
   HPR RTP PCID                         X'8877665544332211'
   Send maximum RU size                 1920
   Receive maximum RU size              1920
   Send pacing window                   2
   Receive pacing window                8
   Pacing type                          Adaptive
   Outbound destination address (DAF)
   Outbound origin address (OAF)
   OAF-DAF assignor indicator (ODAI)
   FID5 Session ID                      X'8123456712345678'
   Procedure correlator ID (PCID)       X'C21BFDC300ED68DB'
   PCID generator CP name               NETA.BARNEY
   Session ID                           X'000000000093B198'
   Conversation group ID                133
```

Table 20–12 describes significant fields shown in the display.

Table 20–12 *Show APPN Session Detail Field Descriptions*

Field	Description
LU name	Fully qualified name of the local LU.
Partner LU name	Fully qualified name of the partner LU.
Mode name	Mode used by this session.
Class of service name	Class of service used by this session.
Link name	Link this session traverses.
HPR RTP PCID	Procedure correlator identifier.
Send maximum RU size	Maximum RU size that can be sent on this session.
Receive maximum RU size	Maximum RU size that can be received on this session.
Send pacing window	Current send pacing window size.
Receive pacing window	Current receive pacing window size.
Pacing type	Type of pacing used by this session.
Outbound destination address (DAF)	Session routing destination address.
Outbound origin address (OAF)	Session routing origin address.
OAF-DAF assignor indicator (ODAI)	Defines which session partner chose the addresses (DAF and OAF) for a session. Together with the DAF and OAF values, the ODAI forms the local form session identifier (LFSID). The DAF and OAF values used in the transmission header (TH) in one direction are reversed in the other direction.
FID5 Session ID	If this session is activated using HPR instead of the OAF, DAF, ODAI session identifier, the session is identified by this 8-byte hexadecimal value.
Procedure correlator ID (PCID)	PCID used by this session.
PCID generator CP name	Fully qualified CP name which generated this PCID.
Session ID	Local session ID.
Conversation group ID	Conversation group ID for this session.

SHOW APPN TOPOLOGY

Use the **show appn topology** EXEC command to display the contents of the APPN topology database.

> **show appn topology** [**name** *cp-name*] [**brief** | **detail**]

Syntax	Description
name *cp-name*	(Optional) Filter by fully qualified CP name.
brief	(Optional) Short display of APPN topology information.
detail	(Optional) Long display of APPN topology information.

Default

The default is **brief**.

Command Mode

EXEC

Usage Guidelines

This command first appeared in Cisco IOS Release 11.0.

Sample Displays

The following is a short display of APPN topology information. This display is created by the **show appn topology** command with the **brief** keyword:

```
Number of network nodes                 3
    APPN Topology Entries
    Resource Name      Type         TG#  Dest. Node        TG Type   TG Status
    ------------       -----------  ---  --------------    -------   ---------
 1> NETA.BARNEY        Network Node
    1>                               0   NETA.CN           Intermed  Active
    2>                               0   NETA.CN1          Intermed  Active
    3>                               21  NETA.R2CP0389     Intermed  Active
    4>                               21  NETA.BART         Intermed  Active
```

The following is a long display of APPN topology information. This display is created by the **show appn topology** command with the **detail** keyword:

```
Number of network nodes                  6

 1>Network node CP name                   NETA.MAGGIE
   Node type                              Network Node
   Route additional resistance     128
   Congested?                      No
   Quiescing?                      No
   ISR depleted?                   No
   Time left in topology           15
   Current FRSN                    29
   Resource Sequence Number        4
   Last FRSN sent                  0
   Last FRSN received              0
   Node HPR Level                  RTP
   Number of TGs                   2
```

```
1.1>TG partner CP name              NETA.BARNEY
Transmission group number           21
TG partner node type                Real
Tg Type                             Endpoint
TG Status                           Active
Quiescing?                          No
Topology                            Network
Effective capacity                  16 megabits per second
cost-per-connect time               0
Cost per byte                       0
Propagation delay                   384 microseconds (local area network)
User defined parameter 1            128
User defined parameter 2            128
User defined parameter 3            128
Security                            Nonsecure
Time left in topology               15
Current FRSN                        29
Resource Sequence Number            4
HPR enabled                         Yes
HPR RTP level                       RTP
```

Table 20–13 describes significant fields shown in the display.

Table 20–13 *Show APPN Topology Field Descriptions*

Field	Description
Network node CP name	Fully qualified name of the resource.
Node type	Resource type of this node.
Route additional resistance	Arbitrary number associated with the cost of using this node.
Congested?	Specifies whether the node is capable of processing requests.
Quiescing?	Specifies whether the node is stopping.
ISR depleted?	Specifies whether the node is capable of processing more ISR requests.
Number of TGs	Number of transmission groups associated with the network node.
TG partner CP name	Partner node's fully qualified name.
Transmission group number	Transmission group number.
TG partner node type	Resource type for the partner of this transmission group.
TG Type	Type of transmission group: intermediate or endpoint.
TG Status	Status of the transmission group.

Table 20–13 *Show APPN Topology Field Descriptions, Continued*

Field	Description
Quiescing?	Specifies whether the transmission group is in the process of stopping.
Topology	Topology type: local or network.
Effective capacity	Bit rate of the transmission group.
Cost-per-connect time	Relative cost of the transmission group.
Cost per byte	Cost per byte of transmitting over the transmission group.
Propagation delay	Specifies the inherent delay of the transmission group.
User-defined parameter 1	Value for a network-unique transmission group characteristic—parameter 1.
User-defined parameter 2	Value for a network-unique transmission group characteristic—parameter 2.
User-defined parameter 3	Value for a network-unique transmission group characteristic—parameter 3.
Security	Security level of the transmission group.
Time left in topology	The number of days that APPN will wait before removing this node from the topology database.
Current FRSN	The current flow-reduction sequence number for this resource. This value is used to reduce topology exchange between two NNs if they temporarily lose contact.
Resource Sequence Number	The current resource sequence number for this resource. This number is used by APPN to prevent loops when exchanging topology information.
HPR enabled	Specifies if this node or transmission group support HPR.
HPR RTP level	Specifies the level of HPR support for this node or transmission group: Base—HPR base support only. RTP—Supports the HPR RTP feature tower. CF—Supports the HPR control-flows feature tower.

SMDS-DEST-ADDRESS

Use the **smds-dest-address** APPN link-station configuration command to specify the SMDS address of the partner node. Use the **no** form of this command to delete the definition.

smds-dest-address *smds-addr* [*sap*]
no smds-dest-address

Syntax	Description
smds-addr	8-byte hexadecimal number in the form HD.DD.DD.HH.
sap	1-byte hexadecimal number in the range 04 to EC, and divisible by 4.

Defaults

No default *smds-addr* is specified.

The default SAP is 04 (hexadecimal).

Command Mode

APPN link-station configuration

Usage Guidelines

This command first appeared in Cisco IOS Release 11.1.

This command is required for interface types Token Ring, Ethernet, or FDDI. It is not allowed for other interface types.

Example

The following example sets the MAC address and SAP for a link to a partner node:

```
appn link-station LINK0001
  port ETHER1
  smds-dest-address 11.22.33.44 08
  complete
```

Related Commands

appn link-station
fr-dest-address
sdlc-dest-address
show appn link-station
smds address

TG-NUMBER

Use the **tg-number** APPN link-station configuration command to specify the transmission-group number for the connection. Use the **no** form of this command to delete the previous definition.

tg-number *number*
no tg-number

Syntax	Description
number	Number in the range 0 to 255. The default is 0.

Default

Transmission-group number is 0.

Command Mode

APPN link-station configuration

Usage Guidelines

This command first appeared in Cisco IOS Release 11.0.

If zero, the transmission-group number is negotiable.

Example

The following example sets the transmission-group number to 10:

```
appn link-station LINK4
 port ETHER1
 lan-dest-address 0200.6f8e.1a3b
 tg-number 10
 complete
```

Related Commands

appn link-station
show appn link-station

TG-ROW

Use the **tg-row** APPN class-of-service configuration command to specify a transmission-group description, or transmission-group row, and associated weight for the row. Use the **no** form of this command to delete the previous definition.

tg-row *index* weight *weight* byte *min max* time *min max* capacity *min max* delay *min max*
     security *min max* user1 *min max* user2 *min max* user3 *min max*
no tg-row *index*

Syntax	Description
index	Specifies which row is being entered. The valid range is 1 to 8.
weight *weight*	Weight assigned to a transmission group, given the characteristics defined in the remainder of the row.

Syntax	Description
byte *min max*	Minimum and maximum cost-per-byte values, compared with the **cost-per-byte** command on the port or link-station command.
time *min max*	Minimum and maximum cost-per-connect-time values, compared with the **cost-per-connect-time** command on the port or link-station command.
capacity *min max*	Minimum and maximum capacity values, compared with the **effective-capacity** command on the port or link-station command.
delay *min max*	Two values compared with the **propagation-delay** command.
security *min max*	Value compared with the **security** command. The minimum and maximum are specified with one of the defined values, in ascending order:
user1 *min max*	Number in the range 1 to 255.
user2 *min max*	Number in the range 1 to 255.
user3 *min max*	Number in the range 1 to 255.

Part
II

Default

There is no default provided. A minimum of one transmission-group row must be provided or the configuration will fail.

Command Mode

APPN class-of-service configuration

Usage Guidelines

This command first appeared in Cisco IOS Release 11.0.

The characteristics of transmission groups in the topology database are compared to the characteristics in each row. A weight is assigned, which determines a low-cost route for a session. You can define from one to eight transmission-group rows.

Example

The following example defines an APPN class of service with one transmission-group row:

```
appn class-of-service #SECURE
  node-row 1 weight 5 congestion no no route-additional-resistance 0 255
  tg-row 1 weight 30 byte 0 255 time 0 255 capacity 0 255 delay 0 255 security 200 255
  user1 0 255 user2 0 255 user3 0 255
  complete
```

Related Commands

appn class-of-service
show appn class-of-service

TRANSMISSION-PRIORITY

Use the **transmission-priority** APPN class-of-service configuration command to specify the transmission priority for the class of service. Use the **no** form of this command to delete the previous definition.

> **transmission priority** *priority*
> **no transmission priority**

Syntax	*Description*
priority	One of the following keywords: **network, high, medium, low.**

Default

The default priority is **medium.**

Command Mode

APPN class-of-service configuration

Usage Guidelines

This command first appeared in Cisco IOS Release 11.0.

The value **network** is reserved for control traffic and cannot be specified for LU-LU sessions. High, medium, and low reflect the priority that traffic for an individual application should receive when congestion begins to build and queues form.

Example

The following example defines an APPN class of service with a transmission priority of high:

```
appn class-of-service #SECURE
  transmission-priority high
  node-row 1 weight 5 congestion no no route-additional-resistance 0 255
  tg-row 1 weight 30 byte 0 255 time 0 255 capacity 0 255 delay 0 255 security 200 255
  user1 0 255 user2 0 255 user3 0 255
  complete
```

Related Commands

appn class-of-service
show appn class-of-service

USER-DEFINED-1 (APPN LINK STATION)

Use the **user-defined-1** APPN link-station configuration command to specify the relative value for a network-unique transmission-group characteristic. Use the **no** form of this command to delete the definition.

> **user-defined-1** *value*
> **no user-defined-1**

Syntax	Description
value	Number in the range 0 to 255 used to specify the relative value. The default is the value specified in the **appn port** command.

Part
II

Command Reference

Default

The value specified in the **appn port** command.

Command Mode

APPN link-station configuration

Usage Guidelines

This command first appeared in Cisco IOS Release 11.0.

This command can be used to specify a user-defined characteristic of this link. The value of a network-unique transmission-group characteristic is used in route selection.

Example

The following example defines an APPN link station with a **user-defined-1** value of 200.

```
appn link-station LINK17
  port TOKEN1
  lan-dest-address 1000.4455.abcd
  user-defined-1 200
  complete
```

Related Commands

appn link-station
show appn link-station

USER-DEFINED-1 (APPN PORT)

Use the **user-defined-1** APPN-port configuration command to specify the relative value for a network-unique transmission-group characteristic. Use the **no** form of this command to delete the definition.

> **user-defined-1** *value*
> **no user-defined-1**

Syntax	Description
value	Number in the range 0 to 255 used to specify the relative value. The default is 128.

Default

The default is 128.

Command Mode

APPN-port configuration

Usage Guidelines

This command first appeared in Cisco IOS Release 11.0.

This command is specified for defined transmission groups (with the **appn link-station** command) if the command has not been specified at that level. This command also specifies the value for dynamically created transmission groups. The cost is used in route selection for a particular class of service.

Example

The following example defines a port with a **user-defined-1** value of 50.

```
appn port ETHER1
 user-defined-1 50
 complete
```

Related Commands

appn port
show appn port

USER-DEFINED-2 (APPN LINK STATION)

Use the **user-defined-2** APPN link-station configuration command to specify the relative value for a network-unique transmission-group characteristic. Use the **no** form of this command to delete the definition.

> **user-defined-2** *value*
> **no user-defined-2**

Syntax	Description
value	Number in the range 0 to 255 used to specify the relative value. The default is the value specified in the **appn port** command.

Default

The value specified in the **appn port** command.

Command Mode

APPN link-station configuration

Usage Guidelines

This command first appeared in Cisco IOS Release 11.0.

This command can be used to specify a user-defined characteristic of this link. The value of a network-unique transmission-group characteristic is used in route selection.

Example

The following example defines an APPN link station with a **user-defined-2** value of 200.

```
appn link-station LINK17
 port TOKEN1
 lan-dest-address 1000.4455.abcd
 user-defined-2 200
 complete
```

Related Commands

appn link-station
show appn link-station

USER-DEFINED-2 (APPN PORT)

Use the **user-defined-2** APPN-port configuration command to specify the relative value for a network-unique transmission-group characteristic. Use the **no** form of this command to delete the definition.

> **user-defined-2** *value*
> **no user-defined-2**

Syntax	*Description*
value	Number in the range 0 to 255 used to specify the relative value. The default is 128.

Default

The default is 128.

Command Mode

APPN-port configuration

Usage Guidelines

This command first appeared in Cisco IOS Release 11.0.

This command is specified for defined transmission groups (with the **appn link-station** command) if the command has not been specified at that level. This command also specifies the value for dynamically created transmission groups. The cost is used in route selection for a particular class of service.

Example

The following example defines a port with a **user-defined-2** value of 50.

```
appn port ETHER1
 user-defined-2 50
 complete
```

Related Commands

appn port
show appn port

USER-DEFINED-3 (APPN LINK STATION)

Use the **user-defined-3** APPN link-station configuration command to specify the relative value for a network-unique transmission-group characteristic. Use the **no** form of this command to delete the definition.

> user-defined-3 *value*
> no user-defined-3

Syntax	*Description*
value	Number in the range 0 to 255 used to specify the relative value. The default is the value specified in the **appn port** command.

Default

The value specified in the **appn port** command.

Command Mode

APPN link-station configuration

Usage Guidelines

This command first appeared in Cisco IOS Release 11.0.

This command can be used to specify a user-defined characteristic of this link. The value of a network-unique transmission-group characteristic is used in route selection.

Example

The following example defines an APPN link station with a **user-defined-3** value of 200.

```
appn link-station LINK17
  port TOKEN1
  lan-dest-address 1000.4455.abcd
  user-defined-3 200
  complete
```

Related Commands

appn link-station
show appn link-station

USER-DEFINED-3 (APPN PORT)

Use the **user-defined-3** APPN-port configuration command to specify the relative value for a network-unique transmission-group characteristic. Use the **no** form of this command to delete the definition.

user-defined-3 *value*
no user-defined-3

Syntax	Description
value	Number in the range 0 to 255 used to specify the relative value. The default is 128.

Default

The default is 128.

Command Mode

APPN-port configuration

Usage Guidelines

This command first appeared in Cisco IOS Release 11.0.

This command is specified for defined transmission groups (with the **appn link-station** command) if the command has not been specified at that level. This command also specifies the value for dynamically created transmission groups. The cost is used in route selection for a particular class of service.

Example

The following example defines a port with a **user-defined-3** value of 50.

```
appn port ETHER1
  user-defined-3 50
  complete
```

Related Commands

appn port
show appn port

VDLC

Use the **vdlc** APPN-port configuration command to identify which ring group the APPN VDLC port uses and, optionally, which virtual MAC address is used as the local MAC address identifying this APPN port. Use the **no** form of this command to delete the configuration.

> **vdlc** *ring-group* [**vmac** *vdlc-mac-address*]
> **no vdlc** *ring-group* [**vmac** *vdlc-mac-address*]

Syntax	Description
ring-group	Ring-group number matching the number you specified with the **source-bridge ring-group** command. The valid range is 1 to 4095.
vmac *vdlc-mac-address*	(Optional) Virtual MAC address used as the local MAC address identifying this APPN port.

Default

No defaults are defined.

Command Mode

APPN-port configuration

Usage Guidelines

This command first appeared in Cisco IOS Release 11.2.

Use the **appn port vdlc** command to define a VDLC port before using the **vdlc** command.

The virtual MAC address must be defined in either the **source-bridge ring-group** command or in the **vdlc** command. If a virtual MAC address is defined in the **source-bridge ring-group** command, providing a virtual MAC address in the **vdlc** command is optional.

To avoid an address conflict on the virtual MAC address, use a locally administered address in the form 4000.*xxxx.xxxx*.

Examples

The following example defines an APPN port that uses VDLC. The **vdlc** subcommand specifies both the ring group (100) and the virtual MAC address (4000.3745.0000) to be used as the local MAC address identifying this port.

```
appn port VDLCPORT vdlc
 vdlc 100 vmac 4000.3745.0000
 complete
```

The following example defines an APPN port that uses VDLC. The MAC address to be used as the local MAC address identifying this virtual port is the MAC address specified in the **source-bridge ring-group** command. The **vdlc** subcommand only specifies the ring group.

```
source-bridge ring-group 100 4000.3745.0000
dlsw local-peer peer-id 172.18.3.111
dlsw remote-peer 0 tcp 172.18.3.125
!
interface ethernet 0
 ip address 172.18.3.111 255.255.255.0
 loopback
 media-type 10BaseT
!
interface TokenRing 0
 no ip address
 ring-speed 16
!
appn control-point NETA.BART
 complete
!
appn port VDLC vdlc
 vdlc 100
 complete
!
appn port TR0 TokenRing 0
 complete
```

Related Commands

appn port
show appn port

VERIFY-ADJACENT-NODE-TYPE

Use the **verify-adjacent-node-type** APPN link-station configuration command to specify that the adjacent node type must be verified as a requirement of link activation. Use the **no** form of this command to delete the definition.

> verify-adjacent-node-type {learn | len | nn}
> no verify-adjacent-node-type

Syntax	Description
learn	Any adjacent node type is accepted.
len	Only LEN-adjacent node type is accepted.
nn	Only NN-adjacent node type is accepted.

Default

The default node type is **learn**.

Command Mode

APPN link-station configuration

Usage Guidelines

This command first appeared in Cisco IOS Release 11.0.

If the adjacent node type is LEN, the **cp-cp-sessions-supported** command must specify no.

If the adjacent node type is LEN, the **adjacent-cp-name** must be specified.

There is no verification for type EN.

Example

The following example specifies that any adjacent node type is accepted:

```
appn link-station NN4
 port ETHER1
 lan-dest-address 0200.5672.3212
 verify-adjacent-node-type nn
 complete
```

Related Commands

appn link-station
show appn link-station

WILDCARD

Use the **wildcard** APPN partner LU-location configuration command to specify this entry as a "wildcard." Use the **no** form of this command to delete the previous definition.

> **wildcard**
> **no wildcard**

Syntax   Description

This command has no arguments or keywords.

Default

The default state is **no wildcard**.

Command Mode

APPN partner LU-location configuration

Usage Guidelines

This command first appeared in Cisco IOS Release 11.0.

A wildcard entry serves any LU whose name matches the configured name up to the length of the configured name. Without an LU name and wildcard specified, the entry services all LUs.

Example

The following example defines a wildcard that represents any LU that starts with LU2, such as LU21, LU221, LU234, and so on:

```
appn partner-lu-location LU2
  owning-cp CISCO.CP2
  wildcard
  complete
```

Related Commands

appn partner-lu-location
show appn directory

X25-DEST-ADDRESS

Use the **x25-dest-address** APPN link-station configuration command to specify the local address of the partner node for QLLC. Use the **no** form of this command to delete the specification.

> **x25-dest-address [pvc | svc]** *address*
> **no x25-dest-address**

Syntax	Description
pvc	(Optional) Uses X.25 permanent virtual circuit.
svc	(Optional) Uses X.25 switched virtual circuit.
address	X.25 destination link-station address.

Default

No default address is specified.

Command Mode

APPN link-station configuration

Usage Guidelines

This command first appeared in Cisco IOS Release 11.0.

The *address* argument must be a valid X.121 address. This address must match that assigned by the X.25 network service provider.

Example

The following example configures the X.25 destination address:

```
appn link-station QLLC
  port QLLC1
  x25-dest-address 170090
  complete
```

Related Commands

appn link-station
show appn link-station

X25-SUBADDRESS

Use the **x25-subaddress** APPN-port configuration command to configure APPN over QLLC. Use the **no** form of this command to delete the configuration.

> **x25-subaddress [pvc | svc]** *address*
> **no x25-subaddress**

Syntax	Description
pvc	(Optional) Uses X.25 permanent virtual circuit.
svc	(Optional) Uses X.25 switched virtual circuit.
address	X.25 subaddress from which data is received.

Default

No default address is assigned.

Command Mode

APPN-port configuration

Usage Guidelines

This command first appeared in Cisco IOS Release 11.0.

The *address* argument must be a valid X.121 address. This address must match that assigned by the X.25 network service provider.

Example

The following example configures the X.25 subaddress from which data is received:

```
appn port QLLC1 Serial0/1
  x25-subaddress svc 0001121
  complete
```

Related Commands

appn port
show appn port

XID-BLOCK-NUMBER

Use the **xid-block-number** APPN control-point configuration command to specify the first three digits of the node identifier for the local node. Use the **no** form of this command to delete the definition.

    xid-block-number *number*
    no xid-block-number

Syntax	*Description*
number	Three-digit hexadecimal number in the range 000 to FFF. The default is 077.

Default

The default is 077 (hexadecimal).

Command Mode

APPN control-point configuration

Usage Guidelines

This command first appeared in Cisco IOS Release 11.0.

A unique ID is required for links to older versions of VTAM.

Example

The following example specifies XID block number 456:

```
appn control-point CISCO.ROUTER
  xid-block-number 456
  complete
```

Related Commands

appn control-point
show appn node

XID-ID-NUMBER

Use the **xid-id-number** APPN control-point configuration command to specify the last five digits of the node ID for the local node. Use the **no** form of this command to delete the previous definition.

xid-id-number *number*
no xid-id-number

Syntax   *Description*

number   Five-digit hexadecimal number in the range 00000 to FFFFF.

Default

The default is 00000 (hexadecimal).

Command Mode

APPN control-point configuration

Usage Guidelines

This command first appeared in Cisco IOS Release 11.0.

The XID ID and block numbers are included in XID exchanges and alert information, and are required for communicating with older versions of VTAM.

Example

The following example specifies XID ID number 0cab7:

```
appn control-point CISCO.ROUTER
 xid-id-number 0cab7
 complete
```

Related Commands

appn control-point
show appn node

21

Configuring NCIA Client/Server Topologies

This chapter describes native client interface architecture (NCIA) support for Systems Network Architecture (SNA) devices. NCIA Server and the NCIA client/server model extend the scalability of NCIA I, the earlier NCIA implementation, by minimizing the number of central-site RSRB or DLSw+ peer connections required to support a large number of NCIA clients. For a complete description of the commands mentioned in this chapter, see Chapter 22, "NCIA Server Configuration Commands."

NCIA SERVER SESSION TO LOCAL TOKEN RING USING DLSW+ LOCAL SWITCH

The network configuration shown in Figure 21–1 includes NCIA clients that connect to a front-end processor (FEP) on a Token Ring through a local router (the NCIA server). The virtual ring is used in conjunction with DLSw+ local switch. The routing information field (RIF) of each circuit is terminated on the virtual ring. Figure 21–2 shows a logical view of an NCIA server session using a DLSw+ local switch (connected to a local Token Ring). In addition to Token Ring, an NCIA server also supports Ethernet, SDLC, and QLLC network connections, as well as Channel Interface Processor (CIP) connections through a DLSw+ local switch. For more information on the different media types that a DLSw+ local switch supports, see Chapter 7, "Configuring Data-Link Switching Plus."

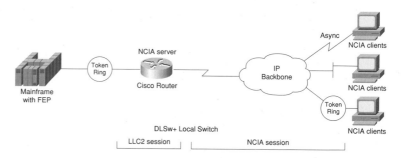

Figure 21–1
NCIA Server session to local Token Ring using DLSw+ local switch.

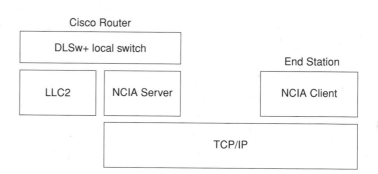

Figure 21–2
Logical view of NCIA Server session to a local Token Ring using DLSw+ local switch.

Configuration Task List

To configure an NCIA session connected to a local Token Ring, perform the tasks in the following sections.

- Defining a Source-Bridge Ring Group for DLSw+
- Defining a DLSw+ Local Peer for the Router
- Configuring an NCIA Server on the Router

For a configuration example, see "NCIA Server Session to Local Token Ring Using DLSw+ Local Switch Example" at the end of this chapter.

Defining a Source-Bridge Ring Group for DLSw+

In DLSw+, the source-bridge ring group specifies the virtual ring that will appear to be the last ring in the RIF. This ring is transparent to the NCIA client. From the host's point of view, all NCIA clients look like stations sitting on the virtual ring. To define a source-bridge ring group for DLSw+, perform the following task in global configuration mode:

Task	Command
Define a ring group.	**source-bridge ring-group** *ring-group* [*virtual-mac-address*]

Defining a DLSw+ Local Peer for the Router

Defining a DLSw+ local peer for a router enables DLSw+ local switch. You specify all local DLSw+ parameters as part of the local peer definition. To define a local peer, perform the following task in global configuration mode:

Task	Command
Define the DLSw+ local peer.	dlsw local-peer [peer-id *ip-address*] [group *group*] [border] [cost *cost*] [lf *size*] [keepalive *seconds*] [passive] [promiscuous] [biu-segment]

Configuring an NCIA Server on the Router

Configuring an NCIA server on a router enables the router to perform two roles:

- Establish TCP/NDLC sessions with clients for the purpose of sending and receiving data.
- Use the standard interface (CLSI) to communicate with other software modules in the router, such as APPN, DLSw+, and DSPU, and act as the data intermediary between them and the clients of the NCIA server.

To configure an NCIA server, perform the following task in global configuration mode:

Task	Command
Configure the NCIA server.	ncia server *server-number server-ip-address server-virtual-mac-address virtual-mac-address virtual-mac-range* [inbound-only] [keepalive *seconds*] [tcp_keepalive *minutes*]

NCIA SERVER SESSION WITH DLSW+

In the network configuration shown in Figure 21–3, the NCIA server uses DLSw+ to connect its clients to the FEP through a remote router. Figure 21–4 shows a logical view of the NCIA Server session with DLSw+.

Figure 21–3
NCIA Server session
with DLSw+.

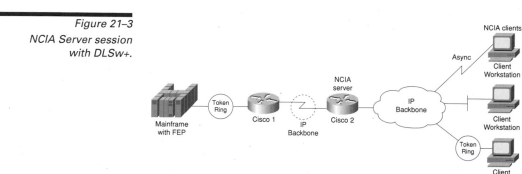

Figure 21–4
Logical view of NCIA
Server with DLSw+.

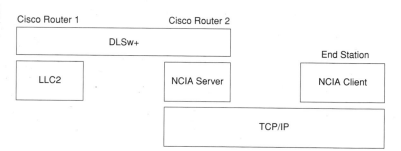

Configuration Task List

To configure an NCIA Server session connected to a remote router using DLSw+, perform the tasks in the following sections.

- Defining a Source-Bridge Ring Group for DLSw+
- Defining a DLSw+ Local Peer for the Router
- Defining a DLSw+ Remote Peer
- Configuring an NCIA Server on the Local Router

For a configuration example, see "NCIA Server Session with DLSw+ Example" at the end of this chapter.

Defining a Source-Bridge Ring Group for DLSw+

The source-bridge ring can be shared between DLSw+ and SRB/RSRB. In DLSw+, the source-bridge ring group specifies the virtual ring that will appear to be the last ring in the RIF. Because RIFs are terminated at the router, there is no correlation between the ring-group number specified in DLSw+ peers. The numbers can be the same for management simplicity, but they do not have to be. To define a source-bridge ring group for DLSw+, perform the following task in global configuration mode:

Task	Command
Define a ring group.	**source-bridge ring-group** *ring-group* [*virtual-mac-address*]

Defining a DLSw+ Local Peer for the Router

Defining a DLSw+ local peer for a router enables DLSw+. You specify all local DLSw+ parameters as part of the local peer definition. To define a local peer, perform the following task in global configuration mode:

Task	Command
Define the DLSw+ local peer.	**dlsw local-peer** [**peer-id** *ip-address*] [**group** *group*] [**border**] [**cost** *cost*] [**lf** *size*] [**keepalive** *seconds*] [**passive**] [**promiscuous**] [**biu-segment**]

Defining a DLSw+ Remote Peer

To configure TCP encapsulation on a remote peer, perform the following task in global configuration mode:

Task	Command
Define a TCP encapsulation remote peer.	**dlsw remote-peer** *list-number* **tcp** *ip-address* [**backup-peer** *ip-address*] [**bytes-netbios-out** *bytes-list-name*] [**cost** *cost*] [**dest-mac** *mac-address*] **dmac-output-list** *access-list-number* [**dynamic**] [**host-netbios-out** *host-list-name*] [**inactivity** *minutes*] [**keepalive** *seconds*] [**lf** *size*] [**linger** *minutes*] [**lsap-output-list** *list*] [**no-llc** *minutes*] [**priority**] [**tcp-queue-max** *size*] [**timeout** *seconds*]

Configuring an NCIA Server on the Local Router

Configuring an NCIA server on the local router enables the router to perform two roles:

- Establish TCP/NDLC sessions with clients to send and receive data.
- Use the standard interface (CLSI) to communicate with other software modules in the router, such as APPN, DLSw+, and DSPU, and act as the data intermediary between them and the NCIA clients.

To configure an NCIA server, perform the following task in global configuration mode:

Task	Command
Configure the NCIA server.	**ncia server** *server-number server-ip-address server-virtual-mac-address virtual-mac-address virtual-mac-range* [**inbound-only**] [**keepalive** *seconds*] [**tcp_keepalive** *minutes*]

NCIA SERVER SESSION WITH DSPU

In the network configuration shown in Figure 21–5, the NCIA server uses DSPU to connect its clients to the FEP through a remote router. Figure 21–6 shows a logical view of the NCIA Server session with RSRB/DLSw+ and DSPU.

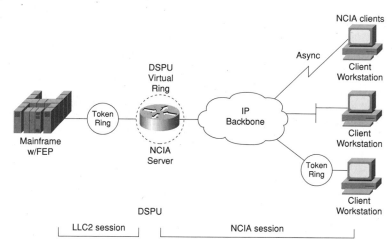

Figure 21–5
NCIA Server session with DSPU.

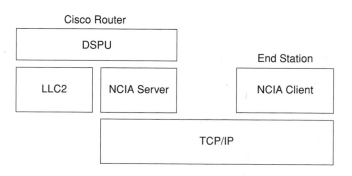

Figure 21–6
Logical view of NCIA Server with DSPU.

Configuration Task List

To configure an NCIA Server session connected to a remote router using DSPU, perform the tasks in the following sections.

- Defining DSPU Upstream Host
- Explicitly Defining Downstream PU
- Defining Dedicated LU
- Configuring the NCIA Server as the Underlying Transport Mechanism

For a configuration example, see "NCIA Server Session with DSPU Example" at the end of this chapter.

Defining DSPU Upstream Host

To define a DSPU host over Token Ring, Ethernet, FDDI, remote source-route bridging (RSRB), or virtual data-link control (VDLC) connections, perform the following task in global configuration mode:

Task	Command
Define a DSPU host over Token Ring, Ethernet, FDDI, RSRB, or virtual data-link control connections.	**dspu host** *host-name* **xid-snd** *xid* **rmac** *remote-mac* [**rsap** *remote-sap*] [**lsap** *local-sap*] [**interface** *slot/port*] [**window** *window-size*] [**maxiframe** *max-iframe*] [**retries** *retry-count*] [**retry-timeout** *retry-timeout*] [**focalpoint**]

Explicitly Defining Downstream PU

To explicitly define a downstream PU over Token Ring, Ethernet, FDDI, RSRB, virtual data-link control, or NCIA connections, perform the following task in global configuration mode:

Task	Command
Explicitly define a downstream PU over Token Ring, Ethernet, FDDI, RSRB, virtual data-link control, or NCIA connections.	**dspu pu** *pu-name* [**rmac** *remote-mac*] [**rsap** *remote-sap*] [**lsap** *local-sap*] [**xid-rcv** *xid*] [**interface** *slot/port*] [**window** *window-size*] [**maxiframe** *max-iframe*] [**retries** *retry-count*] [**retry-timeout** *retry-timeout*]

Defining Dedicated LU

To define a dedicated LU or a range of dedicated LUs for an upstream host and downstream PU, perform the following task in global configuration mode:

Task	Command
Define a dedicated LU or a range of dedicated LUs for a downstream PU.	dspu lu *lu-start* [*lu-end*] {host *host-name host-lu-start* | pool *pool-name*} [pu *pu-name*]

Configuring the NCIA Server as the Underlying Transport Mechanism

To configure the NCIA server as the underlying transport mechanism, perform the following task in global configuration mode:

Task	Command
Configure the NCIA server as the underlying transport mechanism.	dspu ncia [*server-number*]

To enable a local SAP on the NCIA server for use by downstream PUs, perform the following task in global configuration mode:

Task	Command
Enable local SAP for downstream PUs.	dspu ncia enable-pu [lsap *local-sap*]

NCIA SERVER SESSION WITH RSRB

The network configuration shown in Figure 21–7 includes NCIA clients that connect to a FEP on a Token Ring through a remote router. Figure 21–8 shows a logical view of the NCIA Server session with RSRB (to a remote Token Ring). Because DLSw+ is the latest technology provided by Cisco, Cisco does not encourage using the NCIA Server feature with RSRB. If the router on the host side is running DLSw+, RSRB should not be used. Support for the NCIA Server feature with RSRB is provided to encourage RSRB users to migrate to DLSw+.

Figure 21–7
NCIA Server session
with RSRB.

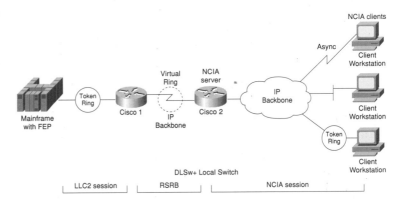

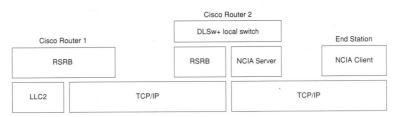

Figure 21–8
Logical view of NCIA Server
session with RSRB (Remote
Token Ring).

Configuration Task List

To configure an NCIA Server session connected to a remote Token Ring using RSRB, perform the tasks in the following sections.

- Defining a Source-Bridge Ring Group for DLSw+ and RSRB
- Identifying the Remote Peer (TCP Connection)
- Defining a DLSw+ Local Peer for the Local Router
- Configuring an NCIA Server on the Router
- Configuring an RSRB Ring for the NCIA Server on the Local Router

For a configuration example, see the "NCIA Server Session with DLSw+ Example" section at the end of this chapter.

Defining a Source-Bridge Ring Group for DLSw+ and RSRB

The source-bridge virtual ring can be shared between DLSw+ and SRB/RSRB. In DLSw+, the source-bridge ring group specifies the virtual ring that will appear to be the last ring in the RIF. Because RIFs are terminated at the router, the ring-group numbers specified in commands to set up DLSw+ peers can be different. The ring-group numbers can be the same for management simplicity, but they do not have to be.

To define a source-bridge ring group for DLSw+, perform the following task in global configuration mode:

Task	Command
Define a ring group.	**source-bridge ring-group** *ring-group* [*virtual-mac-address*]

Identifying the Remote Peer (TCP Connection)

In Cisco's implementation, whenever you connect Token Rings using non-Token Ring media, you must treat that non-Token Ring media as a virtual ring by assigning it to a ring group. Every router with which you want to exchange Token Ring traffic must be a member of this same ring group. For more information about defining a ring group, see "Defining a Ring Group in SRB Context" in Chapter 3, "Configuring Source-Route Bridging."

To identify the remote peers, perform the following task in global configuration mode:

Task	Command
Identify the IP address of a peer in the ring group with which to exchange source-bridge traffic using TCP.	**source-bridge remote-peer** *ring-group* **tcp** *ip-address* [**lf** *size*] [**tcp-receive-window** *wsize*] [**local-ack**] [**priority**]

Specify one **source-bridge remote-peer** command for each peer router that is part of the virtual ring. Also specify one **source-bridge remote-peer** command to identify the IP address of the local router. NCIA Server supports only RSRB pass-through mode. Local acknowledgment is not supported.

Defining a DLSw+ Local Peer for the Local Router

Defining a DLSw+ local peer for the local router enables DLSw+. You specify all local DLSw+ parameters as part of the local peer definition. To define a local peer, perform the following task in global configuration mode:

Task	Command
Define the DLSw+ local peer.	**dlsw local-peer** [**peer-id** *ip-address*] [**group** *group*] [**border**] [**cost** *cost*] [**lf** *size*] [**keepalive** *seconds*] [**passive**] [**promiscuous**] [**biu-segment**]

Configuring an NCIA Server on the Router

Configuring an NCIA server on a router enables the router to perform two roles:

- Establish TCP/NDLC sessions with clients for the purpose of sending and receiving data.
- Use the standard interface (CLSI) to communicate with other software modules in the router, such as APPN, DLSw+, and DSPU, and to act as the data intermediary between them and the NCIA clients.

To configure an NCIA server, perform the following task in global configuration mode:

Task	Command
Configure the NCIA server.	ncia server *server-number server-ip-address* *server-virtual-mac-address virtual-mac-address* *virtual-mac-range* [**inbound-only**] [**keepalive** *seconds*] [**tcp_keepalive** *minutes*]

Configuring an RSRB Ring for the NCIA Server on the Local Router

Configuring an RSRB ring to associate with the NCIA server on the local router provides the virtual ring that connects the DLSw+ ring within the local router and the target ring between the local router and the remote router.

To configure an RSRB ring for the NCIA server on the local router, perform the following task in global configuration mode:

Task	Command
Define the NCIA/RSRB interface.	ncia rsrb *virtual-ring local-bridge local-ring ncia-bridge* *ncia-ring virtual-mac-address*

MONITORING AND MAINTAINING AN NCIA SERVER NETWORK

You can monitor and maintain the operation of an NCIA Server network. To display information about the state of the NCIA Server feature and perform maintenance tasks, perform the following tasks in EXEC mode:

Task		Command
Step 1	Show the status of the NCIA server.	**show ncia server** [*server-number*]
Step 2	Show the status of the NCIA client.	**show ncia client** [sap-list] [*ip-address*]

Task	Command
Step 3 Terminate an NCIA client connection.	**clear ncia client** [*ip-address*]
Step 4 Show the status of an NCIA circuit.	**show ncia circuits** [*id-number*]
Step 5 Drop an NCIA circuit.	**clear ncia circuit** [*id-number*]
Step 6 Terminate the active connection to the specified client and release all control blocks of the registered client.	**clear ncia client registered** [*ip-address*]
Step 7 Stop an NCIA server.	**ncia stop**
Step 8 Restart an NCIA server.	**ncia start**

NCIA Server Configuration Examples

The following sections provide NCIA Server configuration examples:

- NCIA Server Session to Local Token Ring Using DLSw+ Local Switch Example
- NCIA Server Session with DLSw+ Example
- NCIA Server Session with DSPU Example
- NCIA Server Session with RSRB Example

NCIA Server Session to Local Token Ring Using DLSw+ Local Switch Example

Figure 21–9 illustrates the use of DLSw+ local peer with an NCIA Server session to a local Token Ring.

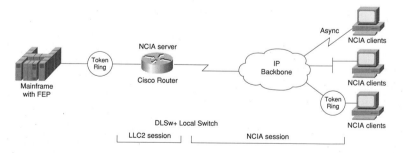

Figure 21–9
NCIA Server session to local Token Ring using DLSw+ local switch.

The following is a configuration file for the network example shown in Figure 21–9:

```
source-bridge ring-group 44
dlsw local-peer
ncia server 1 10.2.20.4 4000.3174.0001 4000.0000.0001 128
!
interface token ring 0
 ring-speed 16
 source-bridge 21 3 44
```

NCIA Server Session with DLSw+ Example

Figure 21–10 illustrates the use of DLSw+ with an NCIA Server session.

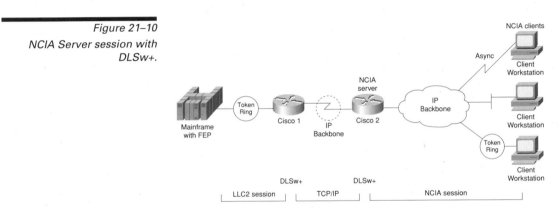

Figure 21–10
NCIA Server session with DLSw+.

The following is a configuration file for the network example shown in Figure 21–10:

```
source-bridge ring-group 44
dlsw local-peer peer-id 10.2.20.4
dlsw remote-peer 0 tcp 10.2.20.3
ncia server 1 10.2.20.4 4000.3174.0001 4000.0000.0001 128
```

NCIA Server Session with DSPU Example

Figure 21–11 illustrates an NCIA Server session with RSRB/DLSw+ and DSPU.

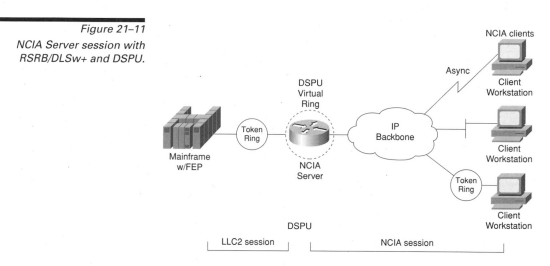

Figure 21–11
NCIA Server session with
RSRB/DLSw+ and DSPU.

The following is a configuration file for the network example shown in Figure 21–11:

```
ncia server 1 10.2.20.4 4000.3745.0001 4000.0000.0001 128
!
dspu ncia 1
dspu ncia enable-pu lsap 8
!
dspu host HOST-9370 xid-snd 11100001 rmac 4000.1060.1000 rsap 4 lsap 4
!
dspu pu CISCOPU-A xid-rcv 01700001
dspu lu 2 6 host HOST-9370 2
!
interface TokenRing 0
 ring-speed 16
 llc2 xid-retry-time 0
 dspu enable-host lsap 4
 dspu start HOST-9370
```

NCIA Server Session with RSRB Example

Figure 21–12 illustrates the use of RSRB with an NCIA Server session.

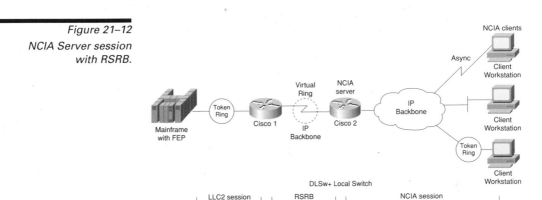

Figure 21–12
NCIA Server session
with RSRB.

The following is a configuration file for router Cisco 2 for the network example shown in Figure 21–12:

```
source-bridge ring-group 44
source-bridge ring-group 22
source-bridge remote-peer 22 tcp 10.2.20.3
source-bridge remote-peer 22 tcp 10.2.20.4
dlsw local-peer
ncia server 1 10.2.20.4 4000.3174.0001 4000.0000.0001 128
ncia rsrb 22 2 33 4 44 1111.1111.2222
```

CHAPTER 22

NCIA Server Configuration Commands

This chapter describes the commands you use to configure Native Client Interface Architecture (NCIA) client/server support for Systems Network Architecture (SNA) devices. For NCIA Server configuration tasks and examples, see Chapter 21, "Configuring NCIA Client/Server Topologies."

CLEAR NCIA CIRCUIT

Use the **clear ncia circuit** privileged EXEC command to drop a specified NCIA circuit.

> **clear ncia circuit** [*id-number*]

Syntax	Description
id-number	(Optional) Number assigned to identify the circuit. If no circuit ID number is specified, the command drops all circuits.

Command Mode

Privileged EXEC

Usage Guidelines

This command first appeared in Cisco IOS Release 11.2.

If no circuit ID number is specified, the command drops all circuits.

Example

The following example clears the active NCIA circuit identified as 791F8C:

```
clear ncia circuit 791F8C
```

Related Commands
show ncia circuits

CLEAR NCIA CLIENT

Use the **clear ncia client** privileged EXEC command to terminate a specified active client connection.

> **clear ncia client** [*ip-address*]

Syntax	*Description*
ip-address	(Optional) IP address of the client. If no IP address is specified in the command, the command terminates all active client connections.

Command Mode
Privileged EXEC

Usage Guidelines
This command first appeared in Cisco IOS Release 11.2.

If no IP address is specified in the command, the command terminates all active client connections.

Example
The following example terminates the active connection to the client identified by the IP address 10.2.20.126:

```
clear ncia client 10.2.20.126
```

Related Commands
show ncia client

CLEAR NCIA CLIENT REGISTERED

Use the **clear ncia client registered** privileged EXEC command to release the control block of a specified registered client after terminating the active connection to it.

> **clear ncia client registered** [*ip-address*]

Syntax	*Description*
ip-address	(Optional) IP address of the registered client. If no IP address is specified in the command, the command releases the control blocks of all registered clients after terminating any active connections to them.

Command Mode

Privileged EXEC

Usage Guidelines

This command first appeared in Cisco IOS Release 11.2.

If no IP address is specified in the command, the command releases the control blocks of all registered clients after terminating any active connections to them.

Example

The following example terminates the active connection to the registered client identified by the IP address 10.2.20.126 and releases its control block:

```
clear ncia client registered 10.2.20.126
```

Related Commands

show ncia client

NCIA

Use the **ncia** privileged EXEC command to stop and start an NCIA server.

> **ncia {start | stop}**

Syntax	Description
start	Starts the NCIA server when it has been stopped using the **ncia stop** command.
stop	Stops the NCIA server. When the server is stopped, all clients are disconnected, all circuits are dropped, and no clients can connect to the server.

Command Mode

Privileged EXEC

Usage Guidelines

This command first appeared in Cisco IOS Release 11.2.

As soon as the NCIA server is configured, it begins running. If an NCIA server is configured and the configuration is stored in the NVRAM of the router, when the router boots up, the server is started automatically. Issuing the **ncia start** command when a server is already running causes the router to output the message:

```
NCIA server is running already!
```

Part
II

Command Reference

Example

The following example stops an active NCIA server:

```
ncia stop
```

Related Commands

ncia server

NCIA CLIENT

Use the **ncia client** global configuration command to configure an NCIA client on a Cisco router. Use the **no** form of this command to remove the configuration.

> **ncia client** *server-number client-ip-address virtual-mac-address* [**sna** | **all**]
> **no ncia client** *server-number client-ip-address virtual-mac-address* [**sna** | **all**]

Syntax	Description
server-number	Number assigned to identify the server. Currently, the server number must be configured with a value of 1.
client-ip-address	IP address of the client.
virtual-mac-address	Virtual MAC address of the client.
sna	(Optional) NCIA client only supports SNA traffic.
all	(Optional) NCIA client supports all types of traffic. If you do not specify **all** as the supported traffic type when you configure an NCIA client, the client only supports SNA traffic.

Default

No NCIA client is configured.

Command Mode

Global configuration

Usage Guidelines

This command first appeared in Cisco IOS Release 11.2.

You must use the **ncia server** command to configure an NCIA server on the router before using the **ncia client** command to configure an NCIA client.

The purpose of configuring a client is so the NCIA server can connect outward to a client. When an end station on the LAN side tries to connect to a client, the end station sends an explorer. When the server receives this explorer, the server tries to match the MAC address in the client database. If it finds a match, the server then connects to that client. If the server's capability to connect outward to clients is not needed, there is no reason to configure any clients.

Each client is assigned a MAC address from the pool created by the **ncia server** command. There are two exceptions to this guideline:

- A MAC address outside the pool created by the **ncia server** command can be defined in the **ncia client** command.

  When a client configured with a MAC address outside the pool connects to the server, the client's configured MAC address is used, rather than allocating a new one from the pool.

- If a client has its own MAC address, it uses that address.

  The MAC address is recognized during the "capability exchange" period when the client establishes a session with the NCIA server. Normally, it is not necessary to configure any client. The server accepts a connection from any unconfigured client. If the unconfigured client does not have its own MAC address, a MAC address from the pool will be assigned to it. If the unconfigured client has its own MAC address, that MAC address is used. If the client has its own MAC address and it is configured using the **ncia client** command, the two MAC addresses must match; otherwise, the connection will not be established.

If you do not specify **all** as the supported traffic type when you configure an NCIA client, the client only supports SNA traffic.

Example

The following example configures an NCIA client on a router:

```
ncia client 1 10.2.20.5 1111.2222.3333
```

Related Commands

ncia server
dlsw local-peer

NCIA RSRB

Use the **ncia rsrb** global configuration command to configure an RSRB ring to associate with an NCIA server on a Cisco router. Use the **no** form of this command to remove the configuration.

ncia rsrb *virtual-ring local-bridge local-ring ncia-bridge ncia-ring virtual-mac-address*
no ncia rsrb

Syntax	Description
virtual-ring	RSRB ring-group number. This number corresponds to the ring-number parameter defined by a **source-bridge ring-group** command.
local-bridge	Number of the bridge connecting the virtual ring and the local ring.
local-ring	Number of the virtual ring connecting the virtual ring and the NCIA ring.
ncia-bridge	Number of the bridge connecting the local ring and the NCIA ring.

Syntax	Description
ncia-ring	NCIA ring-group number. This number corresponds to the ring-number parameter defined by a **source-bridge ring-group** command.
virtual-mac-address	Local ring virtual MAC address.

Default

No RSRB ring is configured.

Command Mode

Global configuration

Usage Guidelines

This command first appeared in Cisco IOS Release 11.2.

You must use the **ncia server** command to configure an NCIA server on the router before using the **ncia rsrb** command to configure an RSRB ring to associate with the server.

Example

The following example configures a virtual ring to associate with an NCIA server on a Cisco router:

```
source-bridge ring-group 22
source-bridge ring-group 44
ncia rsrb 44 4 33 3 22 1111.1111.2222
```

Related Commands

ncia server
source-bridge ring-group

NCIA SERVER

Use the **ncia server** global configuration command to configure an NCIA server on a Cisco router. Use the **no** form of this command to remove the configuration.

> **ncia server** *server-number server-ip-address server-virtual-mac-address virtual-mac-address virtual-mac-range* [**inbound-only**] [**keepalive** *seconds*] [**tcp_keepalive** *minutes*]
> **no ncia server**

Syntax	Description
server-number	Number assigned to identify the server. Currently, the server number must be configured with a value of 1.
server-ip-address	IP address used to accept the incoming connection, or to make an out-going connection.

Syntax	Description
server-virtual-mac-address	MAC address of the server.
virtual-mac-address	The first MAC address of the virtual MAC address pool.
virtual-mac-range	The range of virtual MAC addresses that can be assigned to the client. The valid range is 1 to 4095. This number sets the upper limit on the number of contiguous MAC addresses that make up the MAC address pool.
inbound-only	(Optional) When **inbound-only** is configured, the NCIA server cannot make an out-going connection.
keepalive *seconds*	(Optional) Keepalive interval in seconds. The valid range is 0 to 1200. Setting the value to 0 turns the **keepalive** off.
tcp_keepalive *minutes*	(Optional) TCP keepalive processing interval in minutes. The valid range is 0 to 99 minutes. Setting the value to 0 stops TCP from sending keepalive packets when an NCIA client is idle. If no **tcp_keepalive** value is set, the default waiting period for TCP keepalive packets is 20 minutes.

Default

No NCIA server is configured.

Command Mode

Global configuration

Usage Guidelines

This command first appeared in Cisco IOS Release 11.2.

Before configuring an NCIA server, you must use the **dlsw local-peer** command to configure a DLSw+ local peer on this router. Depending on your network design, you may need to use the **ncia client** command to configure an NCIA client on this router (optional), or use the **ncia rsrb** command to configure an RSRB ring to associate with this router (optional).

If you use the **inbound-only** option, there is no need to configure any NCIA clients (the server does not make out-going connections).

In a DSPU configuration, before a client can establish a connection to a downstream PU, such as a PC or workstation, the MAC address of the server (*server-virtual-mac-address*) must be defined at the PC or workstation as the destination MAC address. This MAC address appears as the server MAC address in the output of the **show ncia circuits** command.

Part II

Command Reference

Example

The following example configures an NCIA server on a Cisco router:

```
ncia server 1 10.2.20.4 4000.3174.0001 4000.0000.0001 128 keepalive 0 tcp_keepalive 0
```

Related Commands

dlsw local-peer
ncia client
ncia rsrb

SHOW NCIA CIRCUITS

Use the **show ncia circuits** privileged EXEC command to display the state of all circuits involving this MAC address as a source and destination.

   show ncia circuits [*id-number*]

Syntax	*Description*
id-number	(Optional) Number assigned to identify the circuit. If no ID number is specified, the command lists information for all circuits.

Default

If no ID number is specified, the command lists information for all circuits.

Command Mode

Privileged EXEC

Usage Guidelines

This command first appeared in Cisco IOS Release 11.2.

Use the **show ncia client** command to list the active circuits by circuit ID number, then use a specific circuit ID number in the **show ncia–circuits** command.

Sample Display

The following is sample output from the **show ncia circuits** command:

```
Router# show ncia circuits

IP             State                    ID        Mac         SAP CW  GP
10.2.20.125    START_DL_RCVD   (Client)10000000  1000.0000.0001  4   0   0
                               (Server)163D04    4000.1060.1000  4   10  0
```

Table 22–1 describes significant fields shown in the display.

Table 22–1 *Show NCIA Circuits Field Descriptions*

Field	Description
IP	IP address of the client.
State	Communication state of the circuit.
ID	Circuit ID number. The server circuit ID is used by the server to identify a circuit. Use this ID in the **show ncia circuits** command. The client circuit ID is for information only.
Mac	Client MAC address is the MAC address used by the client; server MAC address is the MAC address used by the host. In a DSPU configuration, the server MAC address is the one defined in the **dspu ncia** command as *server-virtual-mac-address*.
SAP	Local address (LSAP), specified in the **dspu enable-pu** command.
CW	Current Window, the number of packets that can be increased or decreased for each Increment or Decrement operation.
GP	Granted Packets, the number of packets the client or server is permitted to send to the other.

SHOW NCIA CLIENT

Use the **show ncia client** EXEC command to display the status of the NCIA client.

> **show ncia client** [sap-list] [*ip-address*]

Syntax	*Description*
sap-list	(Optional) Display the SAPs supported by the client. If the **sap-list** option is not specified, the command does not display SAP list information.
ip-address	(Optional) Client IP address. If no IP address is specified, the command lists information for all clients.

Defaults

If the **sap-list** option is not specified, the command does not display SAP list information.

If no IP address is specified, the command lists information for all clients.

Command Mode

EXEC

Usage Guidelines

This command first appeared in Cisco IOS Release 11.2.

Use the **show ncia server** command to list the active clients by IP address, then use a specific IP address in the **show ncia–client** command.

Sample Displays

The following are sample outputs from the **show ncia client** command:

```
Router# show ncia client

IP              State  MacAddr       Flags   Num SAP   PktRxd  PktTxd  Drop
10.2.20.123         4  1000.0000.0011 0x0800    3          27      36    0
   Circuit[1] : 791F8C
10.2.20.126         4  1000.0000.0011 0x0800    1          28      58    0
   Circuit[2] : 793500

Router# show ncia client sap-list 10.2.20.123

IP              Num SAPS  Sap List
10.2.20.123        3       4 8 c
```

Table 22–2 describes significant fields shown in the display.

Table 22–2 *Show NCIA Client Field Descriptions*

Field	Description
IP	IP address of the client.
State	Communication state of the client. Possible values are: 0 CLOSED—Read and write pipe closed 1 OPEN_WAIT—Active open 2 CAP_WAIT—Waiting for a cap exchange request 3 CAP_NEG—Waiting for a cap exchange req/rsp 4 OPENED—Both pipes opened 5 BUSY—WAN transport is congested 6 CLOSE_WAIT—Close connection 7 SHUTDOWN_PENDING—TCP, HOST or router shutdown
MacAddr	MAC address of the client.
Flags	Current operational status of the client. Possible values are: 0×0100—Client is configured 0×0200—Client is registered (a client connects to the server to register itself, and then disconnects) 0×0800—Client is active
Num SAP	The number of SAPs supported by this client. 0 indicates this client supports all SAPs.
PktRxd	Number of packets transmitted downstream from the server toward a client workstation.

Table 22-2 *Show NCIA Client Field Descriptions, Continued*

Field	Description
PktTxd	Number of packets the server received from a downstream client workstation.
Drop	Number of packets that should have been transmitted to a downstream client, but dropped by the server because the TCP connection has failed. Normally, no packets should be dropped.
Circuit[n]	The bracketed decimal indicates the order of the circuit in the list. The hexadecimal circuit ID is used by the server to identify a circuit. The circuit ID can be used to query circuit status in the **show ncia circuits** command.
SAP List	The list of SAPs supported by this client. A client can specify a maximum of 16 SAPs. If the "Num SAP" field is 0, no SAPs are displayed in this field.

SHOW NCIA SERVER

Use the **show ncia server** EXEC command to display the state of the NCIA server.

> **show ncia server** [*server-number*]

Syntax	Description
server-number	(Optional) NCIA server number. If no server number is specified, the command lists information for all servers.

Default

If no server number is specified, the command lists information for all servers.

Command Mode

EXEC

Usage Guidelines

This command first appeared in Cisco IOS Release 11.2.

Sample Display

The following is sample output from the **show ncia server** command:

```
Router# show ncia server

NCIA Server [1]:
    IP address: 10.2.20.4
    Server Virtual MAC address: 4000.3174.0001
    Starting MAC address: 1000.0000.0001
    MAC address range: 128
    Flags: 0x02
    Number of MAC addresses being used: 0
```

Table 22–3 describes significant fields shown in the display.

Table 22–3 *Show NCIA Server Field Descriptions*

Field	Description
NCIA Server	Server number. Currently, only a single NCIA server is supported.
IP Address	Server IP address, used to accept incoming connections.
Server Virtual MAC Address	Virtual MAC address that represents this server.
Starting MAC Address	Virtual MAC address that begins the virtual MAC address pool range.
MAC Address Range	Virtual MAC address range that can be assigned to the NCIA client. This number sets the upper limit on the number of contiguous MAC addresses that make up the MAC address pool.
Flags	Current operational status of the NCIA server: 0×01: NCIA server is configured 0×02: NCIA server is running 0×03: NCIA server is configured and is running
Number of MAC addresses being used	Number of MAC addresses in the MAC address pool that have been assigned to clients. This number reflects connected clients that do not have their own MAC addresses and must be assigned one from the MAC address pool.

CHAPTER 23

Configuring IBM Channel Attach

This chapter describes how to configure the Cisco 7000 with RSP7000 and Cisco 7500 series mainframe Channel Interface Processor (CIP), which supports the IBM channel attach feature.

For hardware technical descriptions and information about installing the router interfaces, refer to the hardware installation and maintenance publication for your product. For command descriptions and usage information, see Chapter 24, "IBM Channel Attach Commands."

CISCO'S IMPLEMENTATION OF THE IBM CHANNEL ATTACH INTERFACE

Support for IBM channel attach is provided on the Cisco 7000 with RSP7000 and Cisco 7500 series routers by the Channel Interface Processor (CIP) and an appropriate interface adapter card. With a CIP and the ESCON Channel Adapter (ECA) or bus-and-tag Parallel Channel Adapter (PCA), a Cisco 7000 with RSP7000 and Cisco 7500 series router can be directly connected to a mainframe, replacing the function of an IBM 3172 interconnect controller. This connectivity enables mainframe applications and peripheral access from LAN-based workstations.

A single CIP can support up to two channel adapter cards in any combination. Because of this flexibility, upgrading from parallel bus-and-tag to ESCON is simplified. The CIP can be configured for ESCON support by replacing a PCA with an ESCON adapter. Note that this upgrade procedure must be done by authorized service personnel.

The CIP provides support for the environments discussed in the following sections:

- TCP/IP Environments Using CLAW
- TCP/IP Offload Environments
- CIP SNA (CSNA) Environments
- TN3270 Server Environments Under CSNA

TCP/IP Environments Using CLAW

TCP/IP mainframe protocol environments for IBM operating systems Multiple Virtual Storage (MVS) and Virtual Machine (VM) are supported. This support includes TCP/IP-based applications such as terminal emulation (Telnet), the File Transfer Protocol (FTP), Simple Mail Transfer Protocol (SMTP), and Network File System (NFS), a distributed file access system. In addition, Internet Control Message Protocol (ICMP) and User Datagram Protocol (UDP) are supported.

A CIP configured with 8 megabytes (MB) of memory can support up to 128 CLAW connections, or 256 devices. Because each CLAW connection requires two devices, that allows a maximum of 128 CLAW connections per interface adapter card. However, a maximum of 32 CLAW connections is recommended.

TCP/IP Offload Environments

TCP/IP mainframe protocol environments for IBM operating systems MVS and VM are supported.

The CIP TCP/IP offload feature delivers the same function as the TCP/IP "offload" function on the 3172 Interconnect Controller (Model 3), but without the performance penalty. This feature implements the 3172 offload protocol for transporting application requests over the IBM ESCON or bus-and-tag channels.

All functionality provided in the CLAW environment is also supported in the TCP/IP offload environment because the function ships TCP/IP application calls over the mainframe channel using the CLAW channel protocol.

CIP SNA (CSNA) Environments

The CSNA feature provides support for SNA protocols over both ESCON and PCA interfaces to the IBM mainframe. As an IBM 3172 replacement, the CIP must support the External Communications Adapter (XCA) feature of VTAM, which allows VTAM to define Token Ring devices attached to the 3172 as switched devices.

In SNA environments, support for the XCA feature of VTAM allows the CIP to provide an alternative to front-end processors (FEPs) at sites where NCP is not required for SNA routing functions.

By providing CLS and the Logical Link Control, type 2 (LLC2) protocol stack on the CIP card, all frames destined to the CIP or from the CIP card can be fast switched by the router. The presentation of multiple "virtual" LAN media types allows the CSNA feature to take advantage of current source-route bridging (SRB), remote source-route bridging (RSRB), data-link switching plus (DLSw+), transparent bridging, SDLC-LLC2 translation (SDLLC), and Qualified Logical Link Control (QLLC) services.

NOTES

In the implementation of CSNA, the multiple virtual LAN media types available are referred to as *internal* LAN types because they exist as internal processes on the CIP card.

The CSNA feature supports the following communication through a Cisco 7000 with RSP7000 and Cisco 7500 series router:

- Communication between a channel-attached mainframe running VTAM and a LAN/WAN-attached PU 2.0 SNA node

- Communication between a channel-attached mainframe running VTAM and a LAN/WAN-attached PU 2.1 SNA node

- Communication between a channel-attached mainframe running VTAM and a LAN/WAN-attached PU 5/4 SNA node

- Communication between two mainframes running VTAM channel-attached to the same CIP card or different CIP cards in a Cisco 7000 with RSP7000 and Cisco 7500 series router

The CSNA feature provides SNA connectivity through the use of MAC addresses configured for internal MAC adapters on the Cisco 7000 with RSP7000 and Cisco 7500 series router. These internal MAC adapters correspond to XCA major node definitions in VTAM, providing access points (LAN gateway) to VTAM for SNA network nodes. The internal MAC adapters are configured to exist on internal LANs located on a CIP card. Each CIP card can be configured with multiple internal LANs where an internal LAN can be a Token Ring, Ethernet, or FDDI LAN. Each internal Token Ring or FDDI LAN must be configured to participate in either source-route or transparent bridging and each internal Ethernet LAN must be configured for transparent bridging. Each internal Token Ring or FDDI LAN can be configured with up to 32 internal MAC adapters. An Ethernet internal LAN can support a single internal MAC adapter. The internal MAC adapter is an emulation of LAN adapters in an IBM 3172 interconnect controller.

TN3270 Server Environments Under CSNA

The TN3270 server feature on a CIP card provides mapping between an SNA 3270 host and a TN3270 client connected to a TCP/IP network as shown in Figure 23–1. Functionally, it is useful to view the TN3270 server from two different perspectives: SNA functions and Telnet Server functions.

- SNA Functions

  From the perspective of an SNA 3270 host connected to the CIP, the TN3270 server is an SNA device that supports multiple physical units (PUs), with each PU supporting up to 255 logical units (LUs). The LU can be Type 1, 2, or 3. The SNA host is unaware of the existence of the TCP/IP extension on the implementation of these LUs.

  The LUs implemented by TN3270 server are dependent LUs. To route these dependent LU sessions to multiple virtual telecommunications access method (VTAM) hosts connected to the server in the CIP card, rather than routing in the VTAM hosts, the TN3270 server implements an SNA session switch with end-node dependent LU requester (DLUR) function. Using the DLUR is optional so that the TN3270 server can be used with VTAM versions prior to version 4.2, which provide no APPN support.

SNA session switch allows you to eliminate SNA subarea routing between hosts of TN3270 traffic by establishing APPN links with the primary LU hosts directly.

* Telnet Server Functions

    From the perspective of a TN3270 client, the TN3270 server is a Telnet server that can support approximately 8000 concurrent Telnet sessions. The server on the CIP card supports Telnet connection negotiation and data format as specified in RFC 1576 (referred to as "traditional TN3270") and RFC 1647 (referred to as "TN3270E").

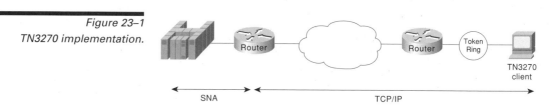

Figure 23–1
TN3270 implementation.

Because the TN3270 server configuration is performed after an interface is configured for CSNA support, TN3270 configuration issues and tasks are addressed separately from the interface configuration tasks. The description of TN3270 configuration issues and tasks begins in the section "Configuring TN3270 on a Channel Interface Processor," later in this chapter.

— **NOTES** —————————————————————————————

To enable the TN3270 server feature, you must have a CIP installed in a Cisco 7000 with RSP7000 or Cisco 7500 series router.

INTERFACE CONFIGURATION TASK LIST

You can perform the tasks in the following sections to configure and maintain IBM channel attach interfaces. In addition, several examples show how host configuration settings correlate to values used in the configuration commands.

— **NOTES** —————————————————————————————

After you select an interface to configure, you can configure that interface for the specific features you prefer: CLAW support, offload support, or CSNA support.

Not all tasks are required. Your CIP image may be preloaded. You must select an interface, after which you configure the features you want supported on that interface.

* Loading the CIP Image
* Selecting the Interface

- Configuring IBM Channel Attach for TCP/IP CLAW Support
- Configuring IBM Channel Attach for TCP/IP Offload Support
- Configuring IBM Channel Attach for CSNA Support
- Selecting Host System Parameters
- Monitoring and Maintaining the Interface

See the end of this chapter for the "IBM Channel Attach Interface Configuration Examples" section.

NOTES

You can configure a CIP interface for any or all of the supported modes. If you want only CSNA support, for example, you need not configure TCP/IP support.

Because the TN3270 server configuration is performed after an interface is configured for CSNA support, TN3270 configuration issues and tasks are addressed separately from the interface configuration tasks. The TN3270 configuration task list begins in the section "TN3270 Configuration Task List" later in this chapter.

LOADING THE CIP IMAGE

Beginning with Cisco IOS Software Release 11.1, the CIP microcode (or CIP *image*) no longer is bundled with the Cisco IOS software. You must have Flash memory installed on the Route Processor (RP) card and 8 MB of RAM installed on your CIP card to use the IBM channel attach features in Cisco IOS Software Release 11.1 and later.

The CIP image is preloaded on Flash cards for all Cisco 7000 with RSP7000 and Cisco 7500 series routers ordered with the CIP option for Cisco IOS Software Release 11.1 and later. Perform the tasks in this section if you are upgrading the CIP image in your router.

To prepare the CIP, perform the following tasks beginning in privileged EXEC command mode:

Task	Command
Copy the CIP image from a server to the Flash memory. Use the appropriate command for your system. You must be running Cisco IOS Release 11.1 or later prior to executing a **copy tftp** command.	**copy tftp flash** *cipxxx-yy* (embedded Flash) **copy tftp slot0:** (Flash card) **copy tftp slot***n***:** (Flash card on 7500 series router) **copy tftp bootflash:** (onboard Flash on 7500 series router)

Task	Command
Configure your router to load the Flash image to the CIP:	
Step 1 Enter global configuration mode and specify that the CIP microcode load from a Flash card in router slot *n* or from embedded Flash.	configure **microcode cip flash slot***n***:***cipxxx-yy* or **microcode cip flash** *cipxxx-yy*
Step 2 Load the image from Flash to the CIP card.	**microcode reload**
Exit configuration mode and display images loaded on the CIP card.	**show controllers cbus**

Rather than as a single image (named *cipxxx-yy*), the CIP image appears as a directory (*cipxxx-yy*) that contains the various image segments to be loaded into the CIP.

The router configuration process takes longer than when using features, because the initial loading of a CIP configuration feature results in the loading of the applicable code and includes any necessary processing.

SELECTING THE INTERFACE

Before you configure your channel attach interface, you must select the interface. Perform the following task in global configuration mode:

Task	Command
Select the channel attach interface and enter interface configuration mode.	**interface channel** *slot/port*

You need not add a space between the interface type (**channel**) and the slot and port number. For example, you can specify **interface channel 3/0** or **interface channel3/0**.

Use the **show extended channel** EXEC command to display current CIP status. This command provides a report for each physical interface configured to support IBM channel attach.

The following section describes how to configure your channel attach interface.

See the section "IBM Channel Attach Interface Configuration Examples" at the end of this chapter for example configuration commands.

CONFIGURING IBM CHANNEL ATTACH FOR TCP/IP CLAW SUPPORT

The following sections describe how to configure the IBM channel attach interface for TCP/IP CLAW support. All tasks, except for configuring other interface support, are required:

- Defining the Routing Process
- Assigning an IP Address
- Configuring the IBM Channel Attach Interface
- Selecting a Data Rate for the Parallel Channel Adapter (PCA)
- Configuring Other Interface Support

See the section "Selecting Host System Parameters" for guidelines on matching interface configuration values with host system values.

Defining the Routing Process

You must configure the routing process that will be used by the Cisco IOS software. Cisco recommends using the Enhanced IGRP routing process to perform IP routing on the IBM channel attach interface. Perform the following steps beginning in global configuration mode:

Task	Command
Step 1 Enter router configuration mode by selecting the routing process, preferably Enhanced IGRP, and the autonomous system the router belongs to.	**router eigrp** *process-id* or **router igrp** *process-id*
Step 2 Define the directly connected networks that are part of the autonomous system.	**network** *network-number*

Assigning an IP Address

You must assign an IP address to the ECA or PCA interface so that it can communicate with other devices (or tasks) on the network. The IP address you assign to the interface must be in the same subnetwork as the hosts with which you wish to communicate. Perform the following task in interface configuration mode:

Task	Command
Assign an IP address and network mask to the selected interface.	**ip address** *address mask*

Configuring the IBM Channel Attach Interface

You must define the devices, or tasks, supported on the interface. Some information you need to perform this task is derived from the following host system configuration files: MVSIOCP, IOCP, and the TCPIP configuration. See the section "Selecting Host System Parameters" for guidelines on matching interface configuration values with host system values.

Perform the following task in interface configuration mode:

Task	Command
Define the CLAW parameters for this device.	**claw** *path device-address ip-address host-name device-name host-app device-app* [**broadcast**]

See the section "IBM Channel Attach Interface Configuration Examples" for samples of **claw** commands for different configurations.

Selecting a Data Rate for the Parallel Channel Adapter (PCA)

When you configure a channel attach interface that supports a PCA card, you must define a data rate of either 3 MBps or 4.5 MBps. Perform the following task in interface configuration mode:

Task	Command
Define the PCA data transfer rate.	**channel-protocol [s	s4]**

Configuring Other Interface Support

To enhance the usefulness of IBM channel attach support, you can further define how the interface and the router interoperate by performing any of the following tasks in interface configuration mode:

Task	Command
Disable fast switching (IP route cache switching). Fast switching is on by default, but access lists can inhibit fast switching. Always include this command when configuring host-to-host communications through the same ECA interface.	**no ip route-cache**
Use access lists to filter connections.	**access-list** access-*list-number* {**permit** | **deny**} *source source-wildcard*

Task	Command
Enable autonomous switching through either the silicon switching engine (SSE) or the CxBus controller.	**ip route-cache [cbus	sse]** or **ip route-cache sse**
Include autonomous switching support for multiple IP datagram applications running on the same CIP, as required. Always include this command when configuring host-to-host communications through the same ECA interface.	**ip route-cache same-interface**

CONFIGURING IBM CHANNEL ATTACH FOR TCP/IP OFFLOAD SUPPORT

The following sections describe how to configure the IBM channel attach interface for TCP/IP offload support. All tasks, except for configuring other interface support, are required:

- Defining the Routing Process
- Assigning an IP Address
- Configuring the IBM Channel Attach Interface
- Selecting a Data Rate for the Parallel Channel Adapter (PCA)
- Configuring Other Interface Support

See the section "Selecting Host System Parameters" for guidelines on matching interface configuration values with host system values.

Defining the Routing Process

You must configure the routing process that will be used by the Cisco IOS software. Cisco recommends using the Enhanced IGRP routing process to perform IP routing on the IBM channel attach interface. Perform the following steps beginning in global configuration mode:

Task	Command
Step 1 Enter router configuration mode by selecting the routing process, preferably Enhanced IGRP, and the autonomous system the router belongs to.	**router eigrp** *process-id*
Step 2 Define the directly connected networks that are part of the autonomous system.	**network** *network-number*

Assigning an IP Address

You must assign an IP address to the ECA or PCA interface so that it can communicate with other devices (or tasks) on the network. The IP address you assign to the interface must be in the same subnetwork as the hosts with which you wish to communicate. Perform the following task in interface configuration mode:

Task	Command
Assign an IP address and network mask to the selected interface.	ip address *address mask*

Configuring the IBM Channel Attach Interface

You must define the devices, or tasks, supported on the interface. Some information you need to perform this task is derived from the following host system configuration files: MVSIOCP, IOCP, and the TCP/IP configuration. See the section "Selecting Host System Parameters" for guidelines on matching interface configuration values with host system values.

Perform the following task in interface configuration mode:

Task	Command
Define the offload parameters for this device.	offload *path device-address ip-address host-name device-name host-app device-app host-link device-link* [broadcast]

See the section "IBM Channel Attach Interface Configuration Examples" for samples of **offload** commands for different configurations.

Selecting a Data Rate for the Parallel Channel Adapter (PCA)

When you configure a channel attach interface that supports a PCA card, you must define a data rate of either 3 MB per second or 4.5 MB per second. Perform the following task in interface configuration mode:

Task	Command
Define the PCA data transfer rate.	channel-protocol [s | s4]

Configuring Other Interface Support

You can further define how the interface and the router interoperate. You can perform any of the following tasks in interface configuration mode to enhance the usefulness of IBM channel attach support:

Task	Command
Disable fast switching (IP route cache switching). Fast switching is on by default, but access lists can inhibit fast switching. Always include this command when configuring host-to-host communications through the same ECA interface.	no ip route-cache
Use access lists to filter connections.	access-list *list* {permit | deny} *source source-wildcard*
Enable autonomous switching through either the silicon switching engine (SSE) or the CxBus controller.	ip route-cache [cbus] or ip route-cache sse
Include autonomous switching support for multiple IP datagram applications running on the same CIP, as required. Always include this command when configuring host-to-host communications through the same ECA interface.	ip route-cache same-interface

CONFIGURING IBM CHANNEL ATTACH FOR CSNA SUPPORT

The following sections describe how to configure the IBM channel attach interface for CSNA support. The last task, "Naming the Internal Adapter," is optional. All other tasks are required.

- Configuring the Channel Information
- Configuring the Internal LAN Interfaces
- Configuring Bridging
- Configuring the Internal Adapter's Link Characteristics
- Naming the Internal Adapter

— **NOTES**

Internal LAN interfaces can be configured only on port 2 of a CIP. Port 0 and port 1 represent physical interface ports; port 2 is always reserved for the internal interface.

Configuring the Channel Information

To define the SNA channels supported by the CSNA feature, perform the following task in interface configuration mode:

Task	Command
Define the CSNA interface.	csna *path device* [**maxpiu** *value*] [**time-delay** *value*] [**length-delay** *value*]

— **NOTES**

The CSNA interface is configured on port 0 or port 1, one of the physical interfaces.

Configuring the Internal LAN Interfaces

To select an internal LAN interface, perform the following tasks beginning in global configuration mode:

Task		Command
Step 1	Select the channel attach interface and enter interface configuration mode.	interface channel *slot*/2
Step 2	Select the maximum number of concurrent LLC2 sessions.	max-llc2-sessions *number*
Step 3	Select the LAN interface and enter internal LAN configuration mode.	lan *type lan-id*

Configuring Bridging

Select the bridging characteristics for Token Ring, FDDI, or Ethernet. Perform either of the following tasks in internal LAN configuration mode:

Task	Command
Select source-route bridging for Token Ring or FDDI.	source-bridge *local-ring bridge-number target-ring*
Select transparent bridging for Ethernet.	bridge-group *bridge-group*

Configuring the Internal Adapter's Link Characteristics

To configure the link characteristics of the internal LAN adapter, perform the following tasks in internal LAN configuration mode:

Task	Command
Step 1 Enter internal adapter configuration mode.	adapter *adapter-number mac-address*
Step 2 Configure the link characteristics.	llc2 ack-delay time *milliseconds* llc2 ack-max *packet-count* llc2 idle-time *milliseconds* llc2 local-window *packet-count* llc2 n2 *retry-count* llc2 t1-time *milliseconds* llc2 tbusy-time *milliseconds* llc2 tpf-time *milliseconds* llc2 trej-time *milliseconds* llc2 xid-neg-val-time *milliseconds* llc2 xid-retry-time *milliseconds*

Naming the Internal Adapter

Select a name for the internal adapter. Perform the following task in internal adapter configuration mode:

Task	Command
Select a name for the internal adapter.	name *name*

SELECTING HOST SYSTEM PARAMETERS

This section describes how to correlate values found in the VM and MVS system I/O configuration program (IOCP) files with the fields in the **claw** interface configuration command and the **offload** interface configuration command. In addition, you will need configuration information from the host TCP/IP application configuration file.

Values from the Host IOCP File

When you define CLAW or offload parameters, you must supply path information and device address information to support routing on an IBM channel. The path information can be simple, in the case of a channel directly attached to a router, or more challenging when the path includes an ESCON director switch or multiple image facility support.

The *path* argument is a concatenation of three hexadecimal numbers that represent the values listed in Table 23–1.

Table 23–1 *CLAW Path Argument Values*

CLAW Path Argument Breakdown	Values	Description
Path	01–FF	For a directly attached ESCON channel or any parallel channel, this value is 01 *unless* the system administrator has configured another value. For a channel attached through an ESCON director switch, this value will be the path that, from the Cisco IOS software point of view, exits the switch and attaches to the host.
Channel logical address	0–F	For a parallel channel, this value is 0. For a directly attached ESCON channel, the value may be non-zero. If the host is running in Logical Partition (LPAR) mode and the CHPID is defined as shared, this is the partition number associated with the devices configured in the IOCP. The default for this part of the path argument is 0. Otherwise, the channel logical address associated with the channel is defined in the IOCP.

Table 23-1 *CLAW Path Argument Values, Continued*

CLAW Path Argument Breakdown	Values	Description
Control unit logical address	0–F	For a parallel channel, this value is 0. For a directly attached ESCON channel, the value may be non-zero. If this value is specified in the IOCP, match that value here. Otherwise, the control unit logical address is specified in the IOCP CNTLUNIT statement for the host channel in the CUADD parameter.

In Figure 23–2, two host systems connect to the ESCON director switch, on paths 23 and 29. The channels both exit the switch on path 1B and attach to Router A.

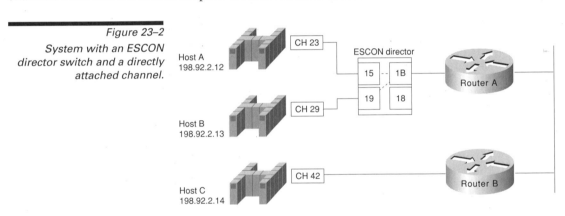

Figure 23–2
System with an ESCON director switch and a directly attached channel.

Note that the path between Host A and Host B is dynamically switched within the ESCON director. A third host is attached directly to Router B through path 42. The IOCP control unit statements would look something like the following examples:

- Host A
  ```
  CNTLUNIT CUNUMBER=0001, PATH=(23), LINK=1B, UNITADD=((00,64)), UNIT=SCTC, CUADD=F
  ```
- Host B
  ```
  CNTLUNIT CUNUMBER=0002, PATH=(29), LINK=1B, UNITADD=((00,64)), UNIT=SCTC, CUADD=A
  ```
- Host C
  ```
  CNTLUNIT CUNUMBER=000A, PATH=(42), UNIT=SCTC, UNITADD=((00,64))
  ```

NOTES

If you use the Hardware Configuration Definition (HCD) program to generate an IOCP and your release of HCD does not support the value RS6K, you might need to set the control unit and device value to SCTC for your ESCON channels. A device mismatch error message will be displayed, but the device will come online and operate correctly.

The system administrator can provide you with the values, for example 15 and 19, for the return channel attachment from the switch to each host. Given these values, the **claw** command *path* argument for the two channel attachments to Router A becomes:

```
claw 150F
claw 190A
```

The **offload** command *path* argument for the two channel attachments to Router A becomes:

```
offload 150F
offload 190A
```

The **claw** command *path* argument for the directly attached channel to Router B is easy to determine:

```
claw 0100
```

Similarly, the **offload** command *path* argument for the directly attached channel to Router B is as follows:

```
offload 0100
```

Next, determine the **claw** or **offload** command *device-address* argument value, which is shown as 00 in the UNITADD parameter for all three devices. This value can be any even value between 00 and 3E, as long as it matches an allowed UNITADD value in IOCP. The **claw** (or **offload**) commands now become:

- Router A (for the **claw** command)

  ```
  claw 150F 00
  claw 190A 00
  ```

- Router A (for the **offload** command)

  ```
  offload 150F 00
  offload 190A 00
  ```

- Router B (for the **claw** command)

  ```
  claw 0100 02
  ```

- Router B (for the **offload** command)

  ```
  offload 0100 02
  ```

Values from the Host TCP/IP File

The remainder of the **claw** and **offload** command arguments are derived from the DEVICE, LINK, and HOME statements in the host TCP/IP configuration files. The statements will be similar to the following:

- Host A

```
DEVICE EVAL CLAW 500 VMSYSTEM C7000 NONE  20  20 4096 4096
LINK EVAL1 IP 0 EVAL
HOME 198.92.2.12    EVAL1
```

- Host B

```
DEVICE EVAL CLAW 600 STSYSTEM C7000 NONE  20  20 4096 4096
LINK EVAL1 IP 0 EVAL
HOME 198.92.2.13    EVAL1
```

- Host C

```
DEVICE EVAL CLAW 700 RDUSYSTM C7000 NONE  20  20 4096 4096
LINK EVAL1 IP 0 EVAL
HOME 198.92.2.14    EVAL1
```

The DEVICE statement lists the *host-name* and *device-name* values to use, which follows the CLAW 500 entry in the DEVICE statement.

The LINK statement links the device name, EVAL, to EVAL1. The IP address for EVAL1 appears in the HOME statement.

Based on this example, you can supply the remainder of the arguments for the sample **claw** commands:

- Router A

```
claw 150F 00 198.92.2.12 VMSYSTEM C7000 TCPIP TCPIP
claw 190A 00 198.92.2.13 STSYSTEM C7000 TCPIP TCPIP
```

- Router B

```
claw 0100 02 198.92.2.14 RDUSYSTM C7000 TCPIP TCPIP
```

Similarly, the sample **offload** commands are as follows:

- Router A

```
offload 150F 00 198.92.2.12 VMSYSTEM C7000 TCPIP API
offload 190A 00 198.92.2.13 STSYSTEM C7000 TCPIP API
```

- Router B

```
offload 0100 02 198.92.2.14 RDUSYSTM C7000 TCPIP API
```

Example of a Derived Value

When you have a directly attached channel, the system administrator may provide you with a system IODEVICE ADDRESS that you can use. In this case, you must work backward through the IOCP file to locate the proper *device-address* argument value for the **claw** command.

In this first example, the IODEVICE ADDRESS value is 800. Using this number, you locate the IODEVICE ADDRESS statement in the IOCP file, which points you to the CNTLUNIT statement that contains the *device-address* argument value for the **claw** or **offload** command:

```
IODEVICE ADDRESS=(0800,256),CUNUMBR=(0012),UNIT=SCTC
**** Address 800 points to CUNUMBR 0012 in the following statement

CNTLUNIT CUNUMBR=0012,PATH=(28),UNIT=SCTC,UNITADD=((00,256))
**** The device-address is the UNITADD value of 00
```

From this example, the **claw** or **offload** command would be similar to the following:

```
claw 0100 00 197.91.2.12 CISCOVM EVAL TCPIP TCPIP
```

In the next example, the system administrator has given you an IODEVICE ADDRESS of 350, which does not correspond exactly to a value in the IOCP file. In this instance, you must calculate an offset *device-address* argument value for the **claw** or **offload** command:

```
IODEVICE ADDRESS=(0340,64),CUNUMBR=(0008),UNIT=SCTC
IODEVICE ADDRESS=(0380,64),CUNUMBR=(0009),UNIT=SCTC
**** Address 350 (340 + 10) is in the range covered by CUNUMBER 0008

CNTLUNIT CUNUMBR=0008,PATH=(24),UNIT=SCTC,UNITADD=((40,64)),SHARED=N, X
**** The device-address is the UNITADD value of 40, offset by 10
**** The device-address to use is 50
```

From this example, the **claw** or **offload** command would be similar to the following:

```
claw 0100 50 197.91.2.12 CISCOVM EVAL TCPIP TCPIP
```

— **NOTES**

In the IOCP examples for the IODEVICE and CNTLUNIT statements, UNIT=SCTC is the usual value for ESCON channels. Parallel channels will have UNIT=3088 in the CNTLUNIT statement and UNIT=CTC in the IODEVICE statement.

— **CAUTION**

When you are running MVS, you must disable the missing interrupt handler (MIH) to avoid introducing errors into the CLAW algorithm.

MONITORING AND MAINTAINING THE INTERFACE

You can perform the tasks in the following sections to monitor and maintain the interfaces:

- Monitoring Interface Status
- Clearing and Resetting an Interface
- Shutting Down and Restarting an Interface
- Running CIP Interface Loopback Diagnostics

Monitoring Interface Status

The software allows you to display information about the interface, including the version of the software and the hardware, the controller status, and statistics about the interfaces. The following table lists some of the interface monitoring tasks. To display the full list of **show** commands, enter **show ?** at the EXEC prompt.

Perform the following commands in privileged EXEC mode:

Task	Command
Step 1 Display information about the CIP interfaces on the Cisco 7000 with RSP7000 and Cisco 7500 series. These commands display information that is specific to the interface hardware.	**show extended channel** *slot/port* **csna** [**admin** | **oper** | **stats**] [*path* [*device-address*]]
	show extended channel *slot/port* **icmp-stack** [*ip-address*]
	show extended channel *slot/port* **ip-stack** [*ip-address*]
	show extended channel *slot/port* **llc2** [**admin** | **oper** | **stats**] [*lmac* [*lsap* [*rmac* [*rsap*]]]]
	show extended channel *slot/port* **statistics** [*path* [*device-address*]]
	show extended channel *slot/port* **subchannel**
	show extended channel *slot/port* **tcp-stack** [*ip-address*]
	show extended channel *slot/port* **udp-listeners** [*ip-address*]
	show extended channel *slot/port* **udp-stack** [*ip-address*]
	show interfaces channel *slot/port* [**accounting**]
Step 2 Display current internal status information for the interface controller cards in the Cisco 7000 with RSP7000 and Cisco 7500 series.	**show controllers** {**cxbus** | **fddi** | **serial** | **t1** | **token**}
Step 3 Display the number of packets for each protocol type that has been sent through the interface for the Cisco 7000 with RSP7000 and Cisco 7500 series.	**show interfaces channel** [*slot/port*]

Task	Command
Step 4 Display the hardware configuration, software version, names and sources of configuration files, and boot images.	show version

Clearing and Resetting an Interface

To clear the interface counters shown with the **show interfaces** command, enter the following command in EXEC mode:

Task	Command
Clear interface counters for router.	**clear counters** [*type slot/port*]

— **NOTES** ——————————————————————————————————

This command will not clear counters retrieved using Simple Network Management Protocol (SNMP). It will clear counters retrieved using only those seen with the EXEC **show interfaces** command.

———————————————————————————————————————

Complete the following task in EXEC mode to clear and reset interfaces. Under normal circumstances, you do not need to clear the hardware logic on interfaces.

Task	Command
Reset the hardware logic on an interface.	**clear interface** *type number*

Shutting Down and Restarting an Interface

You can disable an interface. Doing so disables all functions on the specified interface and marks the interface as unavailable on all monitoring command displays. This information is communicated to other network servers through all dynamic routing protocols. The interface will not be mentioned in any routing updates. On the CIP with an ECA interface adapter, a command is sent to the host to inform it of the impending shutdown. On the CIP with a PCA interface adapter, the **shutdown** command disables the adapter card's transceivers and the PCA stops responding to all commands. A select-out bypass relay must be set manually at the cable connecting to the PCA.

One reason to shut down an interface is if you want to change the interface type of a Cisco 7000 with RSP7000 or Cisco 7500 port online. To ensure that the system recognizes the new interface type, shut down the interface, then reenable it after changing the interface. Refer to your hardware documentation for more details.

To shut down an interface and then restart it, perform the following tasks in interface configuration mode:

Task	Command
Step 1 Shut down an interface.	**shutdown**
Step 2 Reenable an interface.	**no shutdown**

To check whether an interface is disabled, use the EXEC command **show interfaces**. An interface that has been shut down is shown as administratively down in the **show interfaces** command display.

Running CIP Interface Loopback Diagnostics

The CIP does not provide software loopback support. You can use special loopback wrap plugs to perform hardware loopback with the ECA and PCA interface cards. Hardware loopback information is included in the hardware installation notes for the CIP.

CONFIGURING TN3270 ON A CHANNEL INTERFACE PROCESSOR

The following sections describe additional features of TN3270 server support on the CIP. The features discussed include the following:

- Dynamic LU Allocation
- Formation of LU Model Type and Number
- Specific LU Allocation
- SNA Switching—End Node DLUR
- Multiple Hosts Support
- IP Type of Service and Precedence Setting

You also will need to understand the following information before proceeding with TN3270 configuration tasks:

- VTAM Host Configuration Considerations for Dynamic LU Allocation
- LU Address Mapping
- TN3270 Configuration Modes

Dynamic LU Allocation

This is the most common form of request from TN3270 clients emulating a TN3270 terminal. The user typically wants to specify emulating a particular terminal type and normally is not interested in what LOCADDR or LU name is allocated by the host, as long as a network solicitor log-on menu is presented. The server will perform the following on such a session request:

- Form an EBCDIC string based on the model type and number requested by the client (see "Formation of LU Model Type and Number" on the algorithm used). This string is used as a field in a Reply product set ID (PSID) network management vector transport (NMVT).
- Allocate a LOCADDR from the next available LU in the generic LU pool. This LOCADDR is used in the NMVT.
- Send the formatted Reply PSID NMVT to VTAM.

When VTAM receives the NMVT, it will use the EBCDIC model type and number string to look up an LU template under the LUGROUP. For example, the string "327802E" will find a match in the sample configuration shown in Figure 23–3. An ACTLU will be sent and a terminal session with the model and type requested by the client can be established.

Formation of LU Model Type and Number

VTAM requires a model type and number from the Reply PSID NMVT to use as a key to look up in the LU group to find an LU template. The model type is a four-character string; the model number is a two- or three-character string. The server will accept the following formats of terminal type string from the client:

- IBM-<XXXX>-<Y>[-E]: This will be formatted as "XXXX0Y" or "XXXX0YE" in the model type and number field in the Reply PSID NMVT.
- IBM-DYNAMIC: This will result in "DYNAMIC" being put in the model type and number field. The VTAM configuration will need to have "DYNAMIC" defined as a template in the LU group. In fact "IBM-ZZ..Z," where "ZZ..Z" does not match the preceding syntax, will be forwarded as "ZZ..Z."

NOTES

The "E" in the model string refers to 3270 Extended Datastream. It has no connection with the "E" in "TN3270E".

- Any other string is forwarded as is.
- In all cases, the string forwarded is translated from ASCII to EBCDIC and truncated at seven characters.

A complication arises with TN3270E clients that request a copy of the Bind Image. Such clients require SCS data stream on the SSCP-LU flow. All other clients require 3270 data stream on that flow. Therefore, these two kinds of clients must be directed to different LUGROUP entries at the host. To make this as easy as possible, the SCS requirement also is encoded into the model string sent to the host. Following the previously described terminal type string formats accepted by the server, this additional condition is applied:

- If the client has negotiated to receive BIND-IMAGE, the character "S" is overlaid on the fifth character of the string, or appended if the string is less than five characters. See Table 23–2.

Table 23–2 *Examples of Model String Mapping*

String from Client (ASCII)	BIND-IMAGE Requested?	String to Host (EBCDIC)
IBM-3278-4	No	327804
IBM-3279-5E	No	327905E
IBM-3279-3-E	Yes	3279S5E
IBM-DYNAMIC	Yes	DYNASIC
ABC	Yes	ABCS
ABCDEFGH	Yes	ABCDSFG

Specific LU Allocation

A TN3270E client can request a specific LU name by using the TN3270E command CONNECT as documented in RFC 1647. The name requested must match the name by which the TN3270 server knows the LU (see the section "LU Names in the TN3270 Server"), and the host must have activated the LU (with ACTLU).

LU Names in the TN3270 Server

Where SNA session switching is configured (on DLUR PUs), the TN3270 server learns the LU names from the ACTLUs.

For direct PUs, a "seed" name can be configured on the PU. TN3270 server uses this name in conjunction with the LOCADDRS to generate names for the LUs. It is best to use the same naming convention as the host.

SNA Switching—End Node DLUR

An end node DLUR function is implemented as part of the TN3270 server. The purpose of the DLUR is to allow TN3270 LUs to route to multiple VTAM hosts in the CIP card rather than on the VTAM hosts. The need for this feature will increase with the introduction of the new multi-CPU CMOS mainframe, which comprises up to 16 CPUs that appear as separate VTAMs.

The implementation of TN3270 server LUs under DLUR also allows the server to learn about the LU names on the ACTLU, which greatly simplifies the configuration to support specifically requestable LUs such as printers.

Multiple Hosts Support

The TN3270 server supports access to multiple hosts via the configuration on a PU basis (Table 23–3). PUs connected to different hosts/applications can be configured with different IP addresses.

Table 23–3   *Direct PU Configuration in Router*

Command	PU Name	Idblk	IP-address	Type	Adapter number	Lsap	RMAC	RMAC	Lu-seed	Lu-name
PU	X1	05D30001	192.195.80.40	tok	1	4	RMAC	4100.cafe.0001	lu-seed	TN3X1###
PU	X2	05D30002	171.69.176.43	tok	1	8	RMAC	4100.cafe.0002	lu-seed	TN3X2###

From the **pu (direct)** TN3270 configuration command values shown in Table 23–3, PU X2 establishes a link to a host at SAP 4 (the default) on MAC address 4100.cafe.0002. A client connecting to IP address 171.69.176.43 is allocated an LU from that PU and is routed to that host.

Note that by using the DLUR function, all the LUs in the server can be defined and owned by a controlling VTAM. When a client requests an application residing on a different VTAM host, the controlling VTAM will issue the request to the target host which will send a BIND directly to the client. All LU-LU data will then flow directly between the target host and the client without needing to go through the controlling VTAM.

IP Type of Service and Precedence Setting

The TN3270 server supports IP type of service (TOS) precedence setting. TOS is used in router networks to make routing decisions for the generated IP packets. The TN3270 server generates packets that comply to IP TOS and IP precedence values. (Refer to RFC 1349 for a description of IP TOS and IP precedence.)

The Cisco implementation of IP precedence allows values of 0 to 7 while TOS allows values from 0 to 15. You must choose appropriate values for TN3270 screens and printers consistent with your organization's policy.

At the protocol level, IP precedence allows a router network to discriminate between different types of traffic by giving different priorities to them. IP TOS allows router networks to discriminate between different types of traffic by giving different routing characteristics to them. Precedence and TOS values complement one another and provide flexibility in managing your network traffic.

In TN3270 server, two types of TN3270 clients connect: interactive screens or printers. Screens are interactive while printers need bulk data transfer. IP TOS and IP precedence allows you to discriminate between those two types of sessions and assign different precedence values to the interactive connection and the bulk data connection.

IP TOS and IP precedence values can be specified either at the TN3270 server command level or on the individual PU command level. Values can be specified on both levels, in which case siftdown will be used to determine value on individual PU. Siftdown is used when you configure values in

TN3270 server configuration mode that apply to all entities in the server, yet you still can configure individual PUs at the PU configuration mode to alternative values. PU values not specifically changed use the values configured at the TN3270 server configuration mode. This flexibility provides a powerful, yet efficient, way to manage the values.

VTAM Host Configuration Considerations for Dynamic LU Allocation

Other non-Cisco implementations of TN3270 support depend on predefined, static pools of LUs to support different terminal types requested by the TN3270 clients. The CIP TN3270 server implementation removes the static nature of these configurations by using a VTAM release 3.4 feature, dynamic definition of dependent LU (DDDLU). (Refer to the VTAM operating system manuals for your host system, under the descriptions for LUGROUP for more information.) DDDLU dynamically requests LUs using the terminal type provided by TN3270 clients. The dynamic request eliminates the need to define any LU configuration in the server to support TN3270 clients emulating a generic TN3270 terminal.

To support DDDLU, the PUs used by the TN3270 server have to be defined in VTAM with LUSEED and LUGROUP parameters as shown in Figure 23–3.

Figure 23–3

VTAM Host Values Defining LUSEED and LUGROUP.

Example VTAM host values defining LUSEED and LUGROUP name parameters:

TN3270PU PU	.	*	define other PU parameters
	IDBLK=05D,		
	IDNUM=30001,		
	LUSEED=TN3X1###,	*	define the seed component of the LU names created by DDDLU (e.g. LOCADDR 42 will have the name TN3X1042)
	LUGROUP=AGROUP	*	define the LU group name
*			
TN3X1100 LU	LOCADDR=100,	*	define a terminal which requires a specific LU name
	MODETAB=AMODET AB		
*			
TN3X1101 LU	LOCADDR=101,	*	define a printer which requires a specific LU name
	DLOGMODE=M3287C S		

Example VTAM host values defining LUGROUPname, AGROUP:

AGROUP	LUGROU P	*	define LU group to support various terminal types
327802E	LU	USSTAB=USSXXX, LOGAPPL=TPXP001, DLOGMOD=SNX3270 2, SSCPFM=USS3270	*	define template to support IBM 3278 terminal model 2 with Extended Data Stream. Note that the USS messages in USSXXX should be in 3270 datastream.
3278S2E	LU	USSTAB=USSYYY, LOGAPPL=TPXP001, DLOGMOD=SNX3270 2, SSCPFM=USSSCS	*	define template to support IBM 3278 terminal model 2 with Extended Data Stream, for TN3270E clients requesting BIND-IMAGE.
327805	LU	USSTAB=USSXXX, LOGAPPL=TPXP001, DLOGMOD=D4C3278 5, SSCPFM=USS3270	*	define template to support IBM 3279 terminal model 5
@	LU	USSTAB=USSXXX, LOGAPPL=TPXP00 1, DLOGMOD=D4A32 772, SSCPFM=USS3270		this is the default template to match any other terminal types

With the configuration shown in Figure 23–3 defined in the host, the ACTPU sent by VTAM for the PU TN3270PU will have the "Unsolicited NMVT Support" set in the system services control-point (SSCP) capabilities control vector. This allows the PU to dynamically allocate LUs by sending network management vector transport (NMVT) with a "Reply Product Set ID" control vector.

After the TN3270 server sends a positive response to the ACTPU, it will wait for VTAM to send ACTLUs for all specifically defined LUs. In the sample configuration shown in Figure 23–3, ACTLUs will be sent for TN3X1100 and TN3X1101. The server sends a positive response and sets SLU DISABLED. The LOCADDR of these LUs are put into the specific LU cache and reserved for specific LU name requests only.

To allow sufficient time for the VTAM host to send all the ACTLUs, a 30-second timer is started and restarted when an ACTLU is received. When the time expires, it is assumed all ACTLUs defined in VTAM for the PU have been sent. All LUs that have not been activated are available in a generic LU pool to be used for DDDLU unless they have been reserved by the configuration using the **generic-pool deny** TN3270 configuration command.

After the VTAM activation, the server can support session requests from clients using dynamic or specific LU allocation.

LU ADDRESS MAPPING

Logical unit (LU) address mapping allows a client IP address to be mapped, or "nailed," to one or more LU local addresses on one or more physical units (PUs) by means of router configuration commands. You can control the relationship between the TN3270 client and the LU.

Clients from traditional TN3270 (non-TN3270E) devices can connect to specific LUs, which overcomes a limitation of TN3270 devices that cannot specify a "CONNECT LU." LU nailing is useful for TN3270E clients, because you can perform the configuration at the router, providing central control, rather than at the client.

Handling Large Configurations

The largest size nonvolatile random-access memory (NVRAM) planned for the Cisco 7000 and 7500 series routers is 128 KB. The maximum number of nailing commands that can be stored in a 128 KB NVRAM is approximately 4000. However, large configurations may map as many as 10,000 IP addresses to LUs.

To maintain a configuration file that exceeds 128 KB, there are two alternatives. The configuration file can be stored compressed in NVRAM. Or, the configuration file can be stored in Flash memory that is either internal Flash or on a PCMCIA card.

NVRAM Configuration File Compression

The **service compress-config** global command specifies that the configuration file is to be stored compressed in NVRAM. Once the configuration file has been compressed, the router functions normally.

A **show startup-config** EXEC command expands the configuration before displaying it. When the system is booted, it recognizes that the configuration file is compressed and will expand it and proceed normally.

The example below compresses a 129 KB configuration file to 11 KB.

```
router# copy running-config startup-config
Building configuration...
Compressing configuration from 129648 bytes to 11077 bytes
[OK]
```

The size of the configuration must not exceed three times the NVRAM size. For a 128 KB size NVRAM, the largest expanded configuration file size is 384 KB.

NOTES

This compression facility is only available with Cisco IOS Software Release 10 boot ROMs or later.

If the boot ROMs do not recognize a compressed configuration, the following message is displayed:

```
Boot ROMs do not support NVRAM compression Config NOT written to NVRAM
```

Storing Configuration File in Flash

Store the startup configuration file in Flash memory by entering the **boot config slot0:router-config** global command. This command sets the environment variable CONFIG_FILE to load the startup configuration (router-config) from Flash memory, which is PCMCIA slot0 in this case. The buffer that holds the configuration file is usually the size of NVRAM. Larger configurations need larger buffers. To adjust the buffer size, use the **boot buffersize** *bytes* global command.

Note that you must first do a **copy startup-config slot0:router-config** prior to the **boot config slot0:router-config** to create the Flash configuration file. After you have created the Flash configuration file, update the Flash again.

For example, the following commands store the configuration file in Flash memory:

```
copy startup-config slot0:router-config
conf t
  boot buffersize <bytes>
  boot config slot0:router-config
copy running-config startup-config
```

Care must be taken when editing or changing a large configuration. Flash memory space is used every time a **copy running-config startup-config** is issued. Because file management for Flash memory, such as optimizing free space, is not done automatically, you must pay close attention to available Flash memory. Cisco recommends that you use a large-capacity Flash card of at least 20 MB.

LU Nailing and Model Matching

The "model matching" feature of the CIP TN3270 server is designed for efficient use of dynamic LUs. Each client specifies a terminal model type at connection. When a non-nailed client connects and does not request a specific LU, the LU allocation algorithm attempts to allocate an LU that operated with that terminal model the last time it was used. If no such model is available, the next choice is an LU that has not been used since the PU was last activated. Failing that, any available LU is used; however, for dynamic LUs only, there is a short delay in connecting the session.

Where a client or set of clients is nailed to a set of more than one LU, the same logic applies. If the configured LU nailing maps a screen client to a set of LUs, the LU nailing algorithm attempts to match the client to a previously used LU that was most recently used with the same terminal model type as requested by the client for this connection. If a match is found, that LU is used. If a match is not found, any LU in the set that is not currently in use is chosen. If there is no available LU in the set, the connection is rejected.

For example, the following LUs are nailed to clients at address 192.195.80.40, and LUs BAGE1004 and BAGE1005, which were connected but are now disconnected.

```
lu    name     client-ip:tcp      nail state     model     frames in out   idle for
1     BAGE1001 192.195.80.40:3822  Y    P-BIND    327904E   4      4        0:22:35
2     BAGE1002 192.195.80.40:3867  Y    ACT/SESS  327904E   8      7        0:21:20
3     BAGE1003 192.195.80.40:3981  Y    ACT/SESS  327803E   13     14       0:10:13
4     BAGE1004 192.195.80.40:3991  Y    ACT/NA    327803E   8      9        0:0:7
5     BAGE1005 192.195.80.40:3997  Y    ACT/NA    327805    8      9        0:7:8
```

If a client at IP address 192.195.80.40 requests a terminal model of type IBM-3278-5, LU BAGE1005 will be selected over BAGE1004.

```
lu    name     client-ip:tcp      nail state     model     frames in out   idle for
1     BAGE1001 192.195.80.40:3822  Y    P-BIND    327904E   4      4        0:23:29
2     BAGE1002 192.195.80.40:3867  Y    ACT/SESS  327904E   8      7        0:22:14
3     BAGE1003 192.195.80.40:3981  Y    ACT/SESS  327803E   13     14       0:11:7
4     BAGE1004 192.195.80.40:3991  Y    ACT/NA    327803E   8      9        0:1:1
5     BAGE1005 192.195.80.40:4052  Y    ACT/SESS  327805    13     14       0:0:16
```

TN3270 CONFIGURATION MODES

The TN3270 configuration modes and router command prompts are described in the following sections and displayed in Figure 23–4. The TN3270 server can be configured only on Port 2, the internal LAN port, of a CIP card.

Some configuration commands create entities on the CIP. For most of these, the command changes to the mode associated with that entity (for example, a PU). In general, the parameters provided to create the entity come in two sets: those that identify the specific instance of the entity (for example, a PU name) and those that merely set operating parameters. To return to the mode later, the same command is used but with only the first set of parameters. The following example tasks clarify how to return to a command mode without necessarily creating a new entity:

To create a DLUR LSAP and enter DLUR LSAP configuration mode, perform the following task beginning in TN3270 DLUR configuration mode:

Task	Command
Create a DLUR LSAP and enter DLUR LSAP configuration mode.	**lsap token-adapter 1 84**

To return later to the DLUR LSAP configuration mode on the same entity, perform the following task beginning in TN3270 DLUR configuration mode:

Task	Command
Enter DLUR LSAP configuration mode on the same LSAP.	**lsap token-adapter 1**

To remove an entity, the same identification parameters are needed. Perform the following task beginning in TN3270 DLUR configuration mode:

Task	Command
Remove a previously defined DLUR LSAP entity.	**no lsap token-adapter 1**

TN3270 configuration modes described in this section include the following:

- TN3270 Server Configuration Mode
- DLUR Configuration Mode
- DLUR SAP Configuration Mode
- PU Configuration Mode
- Commands Allowed in Multiple Modes

TN3270 Server Configuration Mode

From interface configuration mode, **tn3270-server** command puts you in TN3270 server configuration mode.

The following prompt appears:

```
tn3270-server>
```

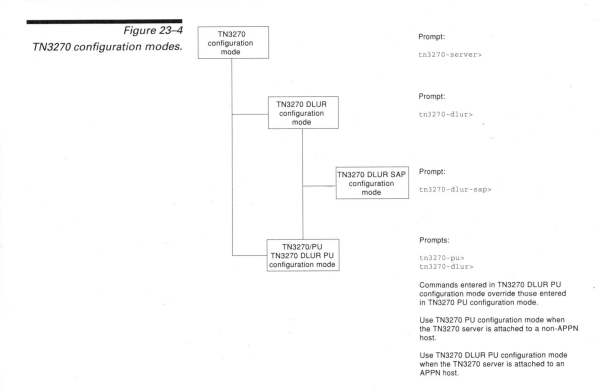

Figure 23–4
TN3270 configuration modes.

DLUR Configuration Mode

From TN3270 server configuration mode, the **dlur** command puts you in DLUR configuration mode.

The following prompt appears:

```
tn3270-dlur>
```

DLUR SAP Configuration Mode

From DLUR server configuration mode, **lsap** command puts you in DLUR SAP configuration mode.

The following prompt appears:

```
tn3270-dlur-lsap>
```

PU Configuration Mode

There are two paths to PU configuration mode: from the TN3270 server configuration mode, or from the DLUR configuration mode. In either mode, the **pu** command puts you in PU configuration mode.

From TN3270 configuration mode, the **pu** command to create a new PU is:

```
pu pu-name idblk-idnum ip-address type adapno lsap [rmac rmac] [rsap rsap] [lu-seed
lu-name-stem]
```

From DLUR configuration mode, the **pu** command to create a new PU is:

```
pu pu-name idblk-idnum ip-address
```

From either mode, to return to PU configuration mode on PU pu-name the command is:

```
pu pu-name
```

The following prompts appear, depending on which mode you are in:

```
tn3270-pu>
tn3270-dlur-pu>
```

Commands Allowed in Multiple Modes

The following commands are valid in TN3270 configuration mode, or in either variation of PU
configuration mode:

- **generic-pool** {permit | deny}
- **idle-time** *seconds*
- **ip precedence** {screen | printer} *value*
- **ip tos** {screen | printer} *value*
- **keepalive** *seconds*
- **shutdown**
- **tcp-port** *port-number*
- **unbind-action** {keep | disconnect}

Values entered in PU configuration mode override settings made in TN3270 configuration mode.
Also, the **no** form of these commands entered in PU configuration mode will restore the command
value entered in TN3270 command mode.

TN3270 CONFIGURATION TASK LIST

The following sections describe how to configure TN3270 server support on the CIP. Not all tasks
are required. See the "TN3270 Configuration Example" section later in this chapter for configuration examples.

NOTES

The TN3270 server is configured on an internal LAN interface in the CIP, which is port 2 of a CIP. Port
0 and port 1 represent physical interface ports; port 2 is a "virtual" port and always reserved for the
internal LAN interface.

Task List for Multiple APPN Hosts

When the host site uses APPN and the TN3270 server can reach multiple hosts, Cisco recommends you use DLUR and configure your PUs under DLUR. In this instance, perform the following tasks:

- Configuring SNA Support
- Configuring TN3270 Server
- Configuring IP Precedence
- Configuring IP TOS
- Configuring DLUR
- Configuring SAPs Under DLUR
- Configuring PUs Under DLUR
- Configuring LU Nailing
- Monitoring the TN3270 Server

NOTES

You can also use DLUR to reach a mix of APPN and non-APPN hosts. The host owning the PUs must be an APPN network node that also supports the subarea (an interchange node). When an SLU starts a session with any of the APPN hosts, it can use session switching to reach that host directly. When it starts a session with a non-APPN host, the traffic will be routed through the owning host.

Task List for non-APPN Hosts

When the host site does not use APPN, you configure your PU parameters for a directly connected host. In this instance, perform the following tasks:

- Configuring SNA Support
- Configuring TN3270 Server
- Configuring IP Precedence
- Configuring IP TOS
- Configuring PU Parameters on the TN3270 Server
- Configuring LU Nailing
- Monitoring the TN3270 Server

Configuring SNA Support

CIP SNA support (CSNA) must be configured prior to configuring TN3270 support. See "Configuring IBM Channel Attach for CSNA Support" earlier in this chapter.

After you have configured CSNA support, you proceed with TN3270 configuration.

Configuring TN3270 Server

This task is required. To establish a TN3270 server on the internal LAN interface on the CIP, perform the following tasks beginning in global configuration mode:

Task		Command
Step 1	Select the channel attach internal LAN interface and enter interface configuration mode.	**interface channel** *slot*/**2**
Step 2	Specify a TN3270 server on the internal LAN interface and enter TN3270 configuration mode.	**tn3270-server**
Step 3	(Optional) Configure maximum number of LUs allowed.	**maximum-lus** *max-number-of-lu-allocated*
Step 4	(Optional) Configure LU session limits for each client IP address or IP subnetwork address.	**client** [*ip* [*ip-mask*]] **lu maximum** *number*
Step 5	(Optional) Configure transmission of a WILL TIMING-MARK.	**timing-mark**
Step 6	(Optional) Assign a TCP port other than the default of 23. This command is also available in PU configuration mode.	**tcp-port** *port-nbr*
Step 7	(Optional) Specify the idle time for server disconnect. This command is also available in PU configuration mode.	**idle-time** *num-of-seconds*
Step 8	(Optional) Specify the maximum time allowed between keepalive marks before the server disconnects. This command is also available in PU configuration mode.	**keepalive** *num-of-seconds*
Step 9	(Optional) Specify whether the TN3270 session will disconnect when an UNBIND command is received. This command is also available in PU configuration mode.	**unbind-action** {keep | disconnect}
Step 10	(Optional) Select whether "leftover" LUs can be used from a generic LU pool. This command is also available in PU configuration mode.	**generic-pool** {permit | deny}

When you use the **tn3270-server** command, you enter TN3270 configuration mode and can use all other commands in the task list. You later can override many configuration values you enter in TN3270 configuration mode from PU configuration mode. On IBM host systems, these types of commands are often referred to as "siftdown" commands because their values can sift down through several levels of configuration and can be altered optionally at each configuration level.

Configuring IP Precedence

To configure IP precedence, perform the following task in TN3270 server or TN3270 PU configuration mode:

Task	Command
Configure the IP level.	**ip precedence** {**screen** | **printer**} *value*

Use the **no ip precedence screen** or the **no ip precedence printer** commands to return the precedence value to a default of 0.

Configuring IP TOS

To configure IP TOS, perform the following task in TN3270 server or TN3270 PU configuration mode:

Task	Command
Configure the IP TOS delay level.	**ip tos** {**screen** | **printer**} *value*

Use the **no ip tos screen** or the **no ip tos printer** commands to return the precedence value to a default of 0.

Configuring PU Parameters on the TN3270 Server

This task is required when configuring PUs that do not use DLUR. To configure PU parameters for the TN3270 server, perform the following tasks beginning in TN3270 configuration mode:

Task	Command
Step 1 Enter PU configuration mode and create or delete PUs with direct host links.	**pu** *pu-name idblk-idnum ip-address type adapno lsap* [**rmac** *rmac*] [**rsap** *rsap*] [**lu-seed** *lu-name-stem*]

Task	Command
Step 2 (Optional) Assign a TCP port other than the default of 23. This command is also available in TN3270 configuration mode.	**tcp-port** *port-nbr*
Step 3 (Optional) Specify the idle time for server disconnect. This command is also available in TN3270 configuration mode.	**idle-time** *num-of-seconds*
Step 4 (Optional) Specify the maximum time allowed between keepalive marks before the server disconnects. This command is also available in TN3270 configuration mode.	**keepalive** *num-of-seconds*
Step 5 (Optional) Specify whether the TN3270 session will disconnect when an UNBIND command is received. This command is also available in TN3270 configuration mode.	**unbind-action** {keep | disconnect}
Step 6 (Optional) Select whether "leftover" LUs can be used from a generic LU pool. This command is also available in TN3270 configuration mode.	**generic-pool** {permit | deny}

When you use the **pu** command, you enter PU configuration mode and can use all other commands in this task list. Configuration values you enter in PU configuration mode will override other values entered while in TN3270 configuration mode. In addition, you can enter PU configuration mode from DLUR configuration mode when configuring PUs that are connected by means of DLUR.

If you are configuring PUs for directly connected hosts, you need not perform any additional configuration tasks.

Configuring DLUR

This task is required when configuring DLUR-connected hosts. To configure DLUR parameters for the TN3270 server, perform the following tasks beginning in TN3270 configuration mode:

Task	Command
Step 1 Create a DLUR function in the TN3270 server and enter DLUR configuration mode.	**dlur** *fq-cpname fq-dlusname*
Step 2 (Optional) Specify the fallback choice for the DLUR DLUS.	**dlus-backup** *dlusname2*
Step 3 (Optional) Specify the preferred network node (NN) server.	**preferred-nnserver** *NNserver*

Configuring SAPs Under DLUR

To configure SAPs under the DLUR function, perform the following tasks beginning in DLUR configuration mode:

Task	Command
Step 1 Create a SAP function under DLUR and enter DLUR SAP configuration mode.	**lsap** *type adapno* [*lsap*]
Step 2 (Optional) Identify an APPN virtual routing node (VRN).	**vrn** *vrn-name*
Step 3 (Optional) Create named links to hosts. A link should be configured to each potential NN server. (The alternative is to configure the NN servers to connect to DLUR.) If VRN is used, it is not necessary to configure links to other hosts. Do not configure multiple links to the same host.	**link** *name* [**rmac** *rmac*] [**rsap** *rsap*]

Configuring PUs Under DLUR

This task is required when configuring DLUR-connected hosts. To configure PUs under the DLUR function, perform the following tasks beginning in DLUR configuration mode:

Task	Command
Step 1 Create a PU function under DLUR and enter PU configuration mode.	**pu** *pu-name idblk-idnum ip-address*
Step 2 Assign a TCP port other than the default of 23.	**tcp-port** *port-nbr*
Step 3 Specify the idle time for server disconnect.	**idle-time** *num-of-seconds*
Step 4 Specify the maximum time allowed between keepalive marks before the server disconnects.	**keepalive** *num-of-seconds*
Step 5 Specify whether the TN3270 session will disconnect when an UNBIND command is received.	**unbind-action** {keep | disconnect}
Step 6 Select whether "leftover" LUs can be used from a generic LU pool.	**generic-pool** {permit | deny}

The **pu** command entered in DLUR configuration mode has different parameters than when it is entered from TN3270 configuration mode.

Configuring LU Nailing

To configure LU nailing, perform the following task in TN3270 PU configuration mode:

Task	Command
Configure the IP address and nail type and specify the locaddr range.	**client** [**printer**] **ip** *ip-address* [*mask*] **lu** *first-locaddr* [*last-locaddr*]

The **client** command allows a client with multiple TN3270 connections from the same IP address to nail their screen connections to LUs that are configured as screen LUs at the host and to nail printer connections to LUs that are configured as printers at the host. When the connection is made, a device type of "328*" is matched to a printer definition, and any other device type is matched to a screen definition.

Monitoring the TN3270 Server

The following table lists some of the monitoring tasks specific to the TN3270 server. To display the full list of **show** commands, enter **show ?** at the EXEC prompt.

Use the following commands in privileged EXEC mode:

Task	Command
Display the current server configuration parameters and the status of the PUs defined in each server.	**show extended channel tn3270-server**
Display the PU configuration parameters, statistics, and all the LUs currently attached to the PU.	**show extended channel tn3270-server** *pu-name*
Display mappings between a nailed client IP address and nailed LUs	**show extended channel tn3270-server nailed-ip** *ip-address*
Display the status of the LU.	**show extended channel tn3270-server** *pu-name* **lu** *lu-number* [**history**]
Display the information about LUs that are defined under an IP address.	**show extended channel tn3270-server client-ip-address** *ip-address*
Display information about the DLUR components.	**show extended channel tn3270-server dlur**

Cisco MultiPath Channel

Cisco MultiPath Channel (CMPC) is Cisco System's implementation of IBM's MultiPath Channel (MPC) feature. CMPC allows the virtual telecommunications access method (VTAM) to establish Advanced-Peer-to-Peer Networking (APPN) connections using both High Performance Routing (HPR) and Intermediate Session Routing (ISR) through a channel-attached Cisco 7000 with RSP7000 and Cisco 7500 series router using the MPC protocols.

An APPN ISR channel connection to a Cisco router also can be established with CSNA. However, an APPN HPR channel connection to a Cisco router is possible only through the use of CMPC.

With CMPC, Cisco 7000 with RSP7000 and Cisco 7500 series routers can be deployed in parallel MVS systems complex (sysplex) configurations.

CMPC can be used to establish an APPN connection between VTAM and the following APPN nodes:

- Another VTAM channel-attached to the same CIP.
- Another VTAM channel-attached to a different CIP in the same router.
- TN3270 server DLUR in the same CIP.

- APPN network node (NN) in the CIP router.
- Other APPN nodes external to the CIP and CIP router: CS/2, AS/400, other LAN or WAN-attached VTAM hosts.

One read subchannel and one write subchannel are supported for each MPC transmission group. The read subchannel and write subchannel may be split over two physical channel connections.

CMPC insulates VTAM from the actual network topology. The MPC protocols are terminated on the CIP and converted to LLC protocols. Once converted to LLC protocols, other Cisco features can be used to connect VTAM to other APPN nodes in the network. CMPC can be used in conjunction with DLSw+, RSRB, SR/TLB, SRB, SDLLC, QLLC, ATM LAN emulation, and FRAS host to provide connectivity to VTAM.

CMPC supports connections to PU 2.1 nodes: APPN NN, APPN EN, and LEN. Subarea connections are not supported.

The CMPC feature coexists on a CIP with the TCP/IP Offload, IP Datagram, TN3270, and CSNA features.

REQUIREMENTS

The following are minimum router requirements to support CMPC:

- CIP version 5.1 (CIP2) with a minimum of 32 MB DRAM
- CIP microcode version cip23-0 or later
- Cisco IOS Release 11.2(6)F or later

The following are minimum host system requirements to support CMPC:

- VTAM V4.2+, for MPC APPN ISR connections
- VTAM V4.3+, for MPC APPN HPR connections

CONFIGURATION OVERVIEW

To configure the CMPC feature, you must configure the host VTAM parameters and the CIP card in the Cisco 7000 with RSP7000 or Cisco 7500 series router. The CMPC Configuration Examples show the VTAM configuration parameters and the router configuration commands for each example.

The following guidelines will help you prepare for CMPC configuration:

- A CMPC link uses two subchannels: one read and one write. Some IBM implementations of MPC allow multiple read and multiple write subchannels. CMPC will not support multiple read and write subchannels. Only one read subchannel and one write subchannel can be configured for each CMPC link. A CMPC link is also referred to as a CMPC transmission group.
- Multiple CMPC links can be configured between the host and the CIP in the Cisco 7500 series router.

- The two subchannels in a CMPC link need not be adjacent devices. Either channel may be the read subchannel and either channel may be the write subchannel. The two subchannels can be on separate channel process IDs in the host.

- The two subchannels must be connected to the same CIP; however, they do not have to be connected to the same CIP port adapter. In other words, it is possible to connect a read subchannel to the CIP's port adapter 0 while the write subchannel is connected to the same CIP's port adapter 1.

- Only APPN connections will be supported across CMPC. For this reason, when TN3270 server is configured with CMPC, it must be configured as an APPN end node with DLUR.

- You must know what device addresses you will be using and the associated channel path statements.

- You must know whether you will use HPR.

- To configure the LLC2 interface for the CIP, you will need to choose a local MAC address and a local SAP address.

- You must know the remote MAC address and remote SAP of the LLC2 peer with which the CMPC communicates.

- You must understand how to configure source-bridge ring groups on the CIP and RSP or RP.

- On the router, the combination of one read subchannel definition, one write subchannel definition, and a transmission-group definition, associated by a unique *tg-name*, makes up a CMPC transmission-group specification.

To help clarify the configuration process, see Figure 23–5, which shows the CMPC link between the VTAM host, the router, and CIP card, and the communication to the LLC2 end point. The read and write addresses defined in the VTAM host correspond to the read and write paths defined for CMPC. CMPC communicates with the LLC2 stack, which communicates to the end point of the connection by means of the IEEE 802.2 link.

Figure 23–5
Logical view of CMPC link.

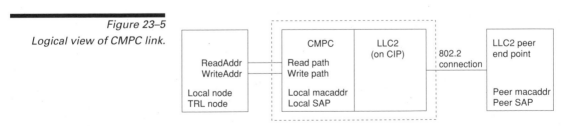

CONFIGURATION TASKS

This section describes the following configuration tasks associated with the CMPC feature. The first two tasks are performed on the VTAM host. The remaining tasks are performed on the router. All tasks are required.

- Configuring the VTAM Transport Resource List Major Node
- Configuring the VTAM Local SNA Major Node
- Configuring the CMPC Subchannels
- Configuring the CMPC Transmission Groups
- Configuring the CIP Internal LAN for CMPC

Configuring the VTAM Transport Resource List Major Node

To configure MPC on the host, define the Transport Resource List (TRL) major node. See the following IBM documents for details on how to configure the TRL major node:

- *VTAM Resource Definition Samples*, SC31-6554
- *VTAM Operation*, SC31-6549
- *VTAM Network Implementation Guide*, SC31-6548

The following is an example of a typical configuration:

```
LAGTRLA   VBUILD TYPE=TRL
LAGTRLEA   TRLE  LNCTL=MPC,MAXBFRU=8,REPLYTO=3.0,                    X
                 READ=(2F0),                                        X
                 WRITE=(2F1)
```

In this example, device 2F0 has been configured for read and 2F1 has been configured for write. The command to activate the TRL should be issued before activating the Local node. If your TRL data set was named LAGTRLA, the activate command would be as follows:

```
v net,act,id=lagtrla,update=add
```

where the ID parameter refers to the name of the data set containing the TRL definition.

Note that "update=add" is preferred. The argument "update=all" can cause inactive TRLEs to be deleted unexpectedly from ISTTRL. However, "update=all" must be used if you change an active TRL data set and wish the changes to become active. The following commands are useful for displaying the current list of TRLEs:

```
d net,trl
d net,id=isttrl,e
d net,trl,trle=trle_name
```

Configuring the VTAM Local SNA Major Node

To configure the MPC channel link on the VTAM host, define the local SNA major node.

The following is an example of a typical configuration:

```
LAGLNA    VBUILD TYPE=LOCAL
  LAGPUA     PU   TRLE=LAGTRLEA,                                    X
                  ISTATUS=ACTIVE,                                   X
                  XID=YES,CONNTYPE=APPN,CPCP=YES,HPR=YES
```

The TRLE parameter in the local node refers to the label on the TRLE statement from the TRL major node LAGTRLA. Also, if you do not want to run HPR, set the HPR parameter to "NO." The local SNA major node must be activated after the TRL node has been activated. If your local node data set was named LAGLNA, the activate command is as follows:

```
v net,act,id=laglna
```

Configuring the CMPC Subchannels

To define a CMPC read subchannel and CMPC write subchannel, perform the following tasks in interface configuration mode on a CIP physical interface:

Task	Command
Step 1 Configure the CMPC read subchannel.	**cmpc** *path device tg-name* {**read** | **write**}
Step 2 Configure the CMPC write subchannel.	**cmpc** *path device tg-name* {**read** | **write**}

These statements define the subchannel addresses that CMPC will use to connect to the host, and correspond to the definitions in the TRL major network node on the host.

Use the **no cmpc** *path* command to remove the definition of a subchannel and to deactivate the CMPC transmission group.

Configuring the CMPC Transmission Groups

To define a CMPC transmission group by name and specify its connection to the LLC2 stack, perform the following task in interface configuration mode on a CIP virtual interface:

Task	Command
Define the CMPC transmission-group name.	**tg** *tg-name* **llc** *type adaptno lsap* [**rmac** *rmac*] [**rsap** *rsap*]

The **tg** command defines an LLC connection with a complete addressing 4-tuple. The *lsap*, *rmac*, and *rsap* are specified explicitly by parameters. The *lmac* is the LMAC of the adapter referred to by the *type* and *adaptno* parameters.

The *tg-name* must match the name given in the **cmpc** command issued in the physical interface(s) on the same CIP.

Use the **no tg** command to remove a CMPC transmission group from the configuration, which will deactivate the named CMPC transmission group.

To change any parameter of the **tg** statement, the statement must be removed by using the **no tg** *tg-name* command.

CONFIGURING THE CIP INTERNAL LAN FOR CMPC

Configuring CMPC support on the CIP internal LAN is similar to configuring CSNA support. Many of the configuration tasks are the same. To configure the internal LAN adapter on the CIP to support CMPC, perform the following tasks:

- Configuring the CIP Internal LANs
- Configuring Source-Route Bridging
- Configuring the Internal Adapter and Its Link Characteristics
- Naming the Internal Adapter

Configuring the CIP Internal LANs

To select a CIP internal LAN interface, perform the following tasks beginning in global configuration mode:

Task		Command
Step 1	Select the channel attach interface and enter interface configuration mode.	**interface channel** *slot*/2
Step 2	Select the maximum number of concurrent LLC2 sessions.	**max-llc2-sessions** *number*
Step 3	Select the LAN interface and enter internal LAN configuration mode.	**lan** *type lan-id*

Use the **no lan** command to disconnect all LLC2 sessions established through all internal LAN interfaces configured on a particular internal LAN.

Up to 18 internal adapters can be configured on an internal LAN.

Configuring Source-Route Bridging

Select the bridging characteristics for Token Ring and FDDI or for Ethernet. Perform either of the following tasks in internal LAN configuration mode:

Task	Command
Select source-route bridging for Token Ring or FDDI.	**source-bridge** *local-ring bridge-number target-ring*

Task	Command
Select transparent bridging for Ethernet.	**bridge-group** *bridge-group*

Configuring the Internal Adapter and Its Link Characteristics

To configure the link characteristics of the internal LAN adapter, perform the following tasks in internal LAN configuration mode:

Task		Command
Step 1	Enter internal adapter configuration mode and configure the adapter.	**adapter** *adapter-number mac-address*
Step 2	Configure the link parameters.	**llc2 ack-delay time** *milliseconds* **llc2 ack-max** *packet-count* **llc2 idle-time** *milliseconds* **llc2 local-window** *packet-count* **llc2 n2** *retry-count* **llc2 t1-time** *milliseconds* **llc2 tbusy-time** *milliseconds* **llc2 tpf-time** *milliseconds* **llc2 trej-time** *milliseconds* **llc2 xid-neg-val-time** *milliseconds* **llc2 xid-retry-time** *milliseconds*

Configuring LLC parameters is optional. Default values are used when no parameters are configured.

Naming the Internal Adapter

To select a name for the internal adapter, perform the following task in internal-adapter configuration mode:

Task	Command
Select a name for the internal adapter.	**name** *name*

Naming an internal adapter is optional.

IBM CHANNEL ATTACH INTERFACE CONFIGURATION EXAMPLES

The following sections include examples to help you understand some aspects of interface configuration:

- Routing Process Configuration Example
- IP Address and Network Mask Configuration Example
- CLAW Configuration Example
- Offload Configuration Example
- CSNA Configuration Example
- Interface Shutdown and Startup Example
- TN3270 Configuration Example
- Configuring Static and Dynamic LUs with LU Nailing Example
- Removing LU Nailing Definitions Example
- Configuring Different Values for Precedence and TOS Example
- Overriding Configured Values Example

Routing Process Configuration Example

The following example configures an Enhanced IGRP routing process in autonomous system 127 and defines two networks to be advertised as originating within that autonomous system:

```
router eigrp 127
 network 197.91.2.0
 network 197.91.0.0
```

IP Address and Network Mask Configuration Example

The following example assigns an IP address and network mask to the IBM channel attach interface on the router:

```
ip address 197.91.2.5 255.255.255.0
```

CLAW Configuration Example

The following example configures the IBM channel attach interface to support a directly connected device:

```
claw 0100 00 197.91.0.21 VMSYSTEM C7000 TCPIP TCPIP
```

Offload Configuration Example

The following example consists of the mainframe host profile statements, buffer poolsize recommendations, and router configuration statements for the network shown in Figure 23–6.

Host Profile Statements

```
; Device statement
DEVICE OFF CLAW 762 CISCOVM CIP1 NONE 20 20 4096 4096
!
; Link Statements (both needed)
LINK OFFL OFFLOADLINK1 1 OFF
LINK MEMD OFFLOADAPIBROAD 162.18.4.59 OFF OFFL
!
; Home Statement
; (No additional home statements are added for offload)
!
!
; Routing information (if you are not using the ROUTED SERVER)
GATEWAY
; NETWORK FIRST HOP  DRIVER   PCKT_SZ   SUBN_MSK      SUBN_VALUE
162.18         =     MEMD     4096      0.0.255.248   0.0.4.56
DEFAULTNET     =     MEMD     1500      0
!
;START statements
START OFF
!
```

Buffer Poolsize Recommendations

See the IBM *TCP/IP Performance Tuning Guide* (SC31-7188-00) for buffer size adjustments.

Router Configuration Statements

The following statements configure the offload feature in the router. When you configure a host-to-host communication through the same ECA adapter, include the **no ip redirects** and **ip route-cache same-interface** commands:

```
!
interface Channel0/0
 ip address 162.18.4.57 255.255.255.248
 no ip redirects
 ip route-cache same-interface
 ip route-cache cbus
 no keepalive
 offload C300 62 162.18.4.59 CISCOVM CIP1 TCPIP TCPIP TCPIP API
!
```

CSNA Configuration Example

The following configuration shows how to configure CSNA in a Cisco 7000 with RSP7000 and Cisco 7500 channel-attached router. This configuration example accommodates the router configuration illustrated in Figure 23–7.

```
source-bridge ring-group 2
source-bridge remote-peer tcp 198.92.0.122
source-bridge remote-peer tcp 198.92.0.123
```

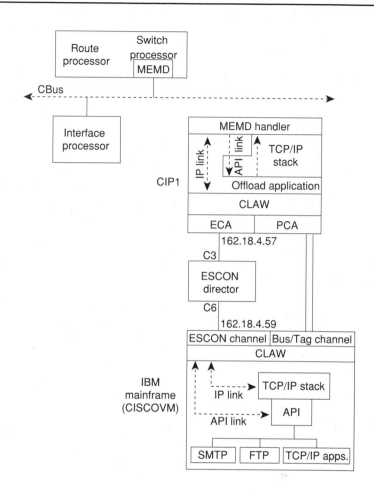

Figure 23–6
Offload network configuration block diagram.

```
!
interface serial 1/0
 ip address 198.92.0.122 255.255.255.0
 clockrate 56000
!
interface tokenring 2/0
 mac-address 400070000411
 no ip address
 ring-speed 16
 source-bridge active 101 1 2
 source-bridge spanning
!
interface ethernet 3/0
 mac-address 020070000412
 no ip address
 bridge-group 1
```

```
!
interface fddi 4/0
 mac-address 400070000413
 no ip address
 source-bridge 102 1 2
!
interface channel 0/0
 csna 0100 80
 csna 0100 81
!
interface channel 0/1
 csna 0100 40
 csna 0100 41 time-delay 30 length-delay 4096
!
interface channel 0/2
!
max-llc2-sessions 2048
!
lan tokenring 0
 source-bridge 1000 1 2
 adapter 0 4000.0000.0401
 adapter 1 4000.0000.0402
 llc2 N2 3
 llc2 t1-time 2000
!
lan tokenring 1
 source-bridge 1001 1 2
 adapter 2 4000.0000.0401
 adapter 3 4000.0000.0403
 llc2 N2 3
 llc2 t1-time 2000
!
lan ethernet 0
 bridge-group 1
 adapter 0 4000.0000.0C01
!
lan fddi 0
 source-bridge 1002 1 2
 adapter 0 4000.0000.0D01
!
bridge 1 protocol ieee
```

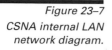

Figure 23–7
CSNA internal LAN
network diagram.

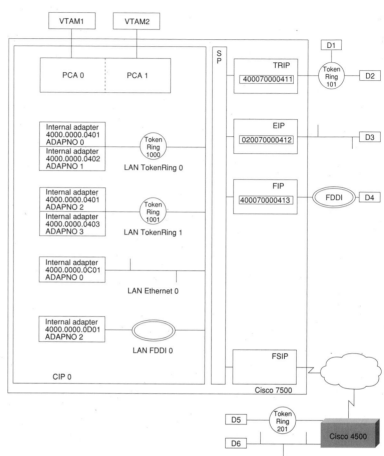

Interface Shutdown and Startup Example

The following example turns off the CIP interface in slot 2 at port 0:

```
interface channel 2/0
  shutdown
```

The following example enables the CIP interface in slot 3 at port 0 that had been previously shut down:

```
interface channel 3/0
  no shutdown
```

TN3270 Configuration Example

The following configuration has three PUs using DLUR and two more with direct connections.

The initial CIP configuration is as follows:

```
interface Channel2/2
 ip address 10.10.20.126 255.255.255.128
 no ip redirects
 no ip directed-broadcast
 ip pim query-interval 0
 ip igmp query-interval 0
 no ip route-cache
 no keepalive
 no clns checksum
 clns congestion-threshold 0
 clns erpdu-interval 0
 clns rdpdu-interval 0
 no clns route-cache
 no clns send-erpdu
 no clns send-rdpdu
 lan TokenRing 0
  source-bridge 223 1 2099
  adapter 0 4100.cafe.0001
   llc2 N1 2057
  adapter 1 4100.cafe.0002
   llc2 N1 2057
```

Configuration dialog to configure the TN3270 function follows:

```
! HOSTA is channel-attached and will open SAP 8 on adapter 0.
! HOSTB is reached via token-ring
! HOSTC is channel-attached non-APPN and will open SAP 4 on adapter 0.

! enter interface configuration mode for the virtual interface in slot 2
router(config)#int channel 2/2

! create TN3270 Server entity
router(config-if)#tn3270-server

! set server-wide defaults for PU parameters
router(cfg-tn3270)#keepalive 0
router(cfg-tn3270)#unbind-action disconnect
router(cfg-tn3270)#generic-pool permit

! define DLUR parameters and enter DLUR configuration mode
router(cfg-tn3270)#dlur SYD.TN3020 SYD.VMG

! create PUs under DLUR
! Note that the first two share an IP address
router(tn3270-dlur)#pu pu0 05d99001 10.10.20.1
router(tn3270-dlur-pu)#pu pu1 05d99002 10.10.20.1
router(tn3270-dlur-pu)#pu pu2 05d99003 10.10.20.2
```

```
! create a DLUR LSAP and enter DLUR LSAP configuration mode
router(tn3270-dlur-pu)#lsap token-adapter 1

! specify the VRN name of the network containing this lsap
router(tn3270-dlur-lsap)#vrn syd.lan4

! create a link from this lsap
router(tn3270-dlur-lsap)#link hosta rmac 4100.cafe.0001 rsap 8
router(tn3270-dlur-lsap)#link hostb rmac 4000.7470.0009 rsap 4
router(tn3270-dlur-lsap)#exit
router(tn3270-dlur)#exit

! create direct pus for the non-APPN Host
! note that they must use different lsaps because they go to the same Host
router(cfg-tn3270)#pu pu3 05d00001 10.10.20.5 tok 1 24 rmac 4100.cafe.0001 lu-seed pu3###
router(tn3270-pu)#pu pu4 05d00002 10.10.20.5 tok 1 28 rmac 4100.cafe.0001 lu-seed pu4###
router(tn3270-pu)#end
```

The resulting configuration from the initial configuration and the configuration dialog follows:

```
interface Channel2/2
 ip address 10.10.20.126 255.255.255.128
 no ip redirects
 no ip directed-broadcast
 ip pim query-interval 0
 ip igmp query-interval 0
 no ip route-cache
 no keepalive
 no clns checksum
 clns congestion-threshold 0
 clns erpdu-interval 0
 clns rdpdu-interval 0
 no clns route-cache
 no clns send-erpdu
 no clns send-rdpdu
 lan TokenRing 0
  source-bridge 223 1 2099
  adapter 0 4100.cafe.0001
  llc2 N1 2057
  adapter 1 4100.cafe.0002
  llc2 N1 2057
 tn3270-server
   pu PU3     05D00001 10.10.20.5     token-adapter 1  24 rmac 4100.cafe.0001 lu-seed PU3###
   pu PU4     05D00002 10.10.20.5     token-adapter 1  28 rmac 4100.cafe.0001 lu-seed PU4###
   dlur SYD.TN3020 SYD.VMG
     lsap token-adapter 1
       vrn SYD.LAN4
       link HOSTB    rmac 4000.7470.0009
       link HOSTA    rmac 4100.cafe.0001 rsap 08
     pu PU0     05D99001 10.10.20.1
     pu PU1     05D99002 10.10.20.1
     pu PU2     05D99003 10.10.20.2
```

Configuring Static and Dynamic LUs with LU Nailing Example

The following example shows a direct PU and a DLUR PU configured with the same listening point. The PUs are configured with the same nailed client IP address.

```
tn3270-server
   pu PU1 05D18081 172.28.1.82 ...
   client ip 192.195.80.40 lu 1 10
dlur
   pu PU2 05D190B3 172.28.1.82
   client ip 192.195.80.40 lu 1 10
```

Assuming each PU has three static LUs, which are ACTLU enabled and not connected, these LUs will be the first to be nailed. That is, the first six connections from client IP address 192.195.80.40 will use the static LUs and subsequent connections will use the remaining dynamic LUs.

Removing LU Nailing Definitions Example

In the following example, locaddrs 1 to 50 are reserved for all remote screen devices in the 171.69.176.0 subnet.

```
interface channel 2/2
   tn3270-server
   pu BAGE4
   client ip 171.69.176.28 255.255.255.0 lu 1 50
```

To remove a nailing definition, the complete range of locaddrs must be specified as configured. So for the example above, the following command would remove the LU nailing definition.

```
no client ip 171.69.176.28 255.255.255.0 lu 1 50
```

If an attempt is made to remove a subset of the range of configured locaddrs, the command is rejected.

```
no client ip 171.69.176.28 255.255.255.0 lu 1 20
% client ip 171.69.176.28 lu not matched with configured lu 1 50
```

Configuring Different Values for Precedence and TOS Example

The following example changes IP precedence and IP TOS to different values under the TN3270 server for both the screen and printer. Note that any PUs defined under this configuration will inherit these values unless the corresponding parameter is specifically changed for that PU.

```
interface channel 3/2
tn3270-server
   ip precedence screen 6
   ip precedence printer 3
   ip tos screen 8
   ip tos printer 4
```

Overriding Configured Values Example

In the following example, the PU PUS1 uses the IP TOS precedence screen and printer values from the values provided in TN3270 server configuration mode. PUS2 uses the IP TOS screen and printer values defined in TN3270 server configuration mode. However, different values for IP precedence are provided for PUS2 under PU configuration mode.

```
interface channel 3/2
tn3270-server
  ip precedence screen 6
  ip precedence printer 3
  ip tos screen 8
  ip tos printer 4
  pu PUS1      05D18009 172.28.1.101    token-adapter 0  AC rsap 08
  pu PUS2      05D18071 172.28.1.99     token-adapter 0  A4 rmac 4000.7470.00e7
   ip precedence screen 7
   ip precedence printer 0
```

CMPC CONFIGURATION EXAMPLES

This section provides sample configurations for the CMPC feature. Throughout these configuration samples, a Cisco 7500 router with an RSP is used to illustrate the configurations. The configurations also apply to a Cisco 7000 router with an RP or an RSP installed. All SAP values are written in hexadecimal form.

Refer to the following configuration examples to see how different networked systems can be configured:

- Connecting VTAM to a Remote PC with Communications Server/2 Example
- Connecting VTAM to the APPN NN on the CIP Example
- Connecting Two VTAM Nodes Using Two CIPs in the Same Router Example
- Connecting VTAM to the APPN NN on a Remote Router with DLUR Example
- TN3270 Server DLUR Running on the Same CIP Example

Connecting VTAM to a Remote PC with Communications Server/2 Example

Figure 23–8 shows the physical components for this example. Figure 23–9 shows the various parameters for each component in the configuration example.

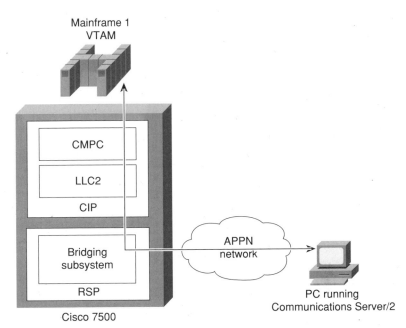

Figure 23–8
Topology for VTAM-to-Remote PC with Communications Server/2.

In Figure 23–8, the following activity occurs:

- VTAM connects to the CMPC driver on the CIP.
- The CMPC driver converts the data to an LLC data stream and passes the data to the LLC2 stack on the CIP.
- The LLC2 stack on the CIP passes the data to the bridging code on the RSP.
- The bridging code on the RSP passes the data to the APPN network.

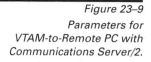

Figure 23–9

Parameters for
VTAM-to-Remote PC with
Communications Server/2.

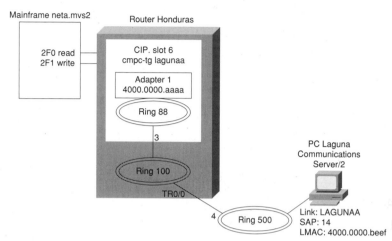

The example in Figure 23–9 shows CMPC running on the CIP and communicating with a PC running Communications Server/2. APPN is not running on the router. It is only running in VTAM and on the PC.

The configuration examples for the VTAM host and the router follow.

Configuration for TRL Node LAGTRLA on MVS2

```
LAGTRA    VBUILD TYPE=TRL
LAGTRLA   TRLE   LNCTL=MPC,MAXBFRU=8,REPLYTO=3.0,              X
                 READ=(2F0),                                   X
                 WRITE=(2F1)
```

Configuration for Local Node LAGLNA on MVS2

```
LAGNNA    VBUILD TYPE=LOCAL
LAGPUA    PU     TRLE=LAGTRLA,                                 X
                 ISTATUS=ACTIVE,                               X
                 XID=YES,CONNTYPE=APPN,CPCP=YES,HPR=YES
```

Configuration for Honduras Router

```
microcode CIP flash slot0:johnchap/cip209-157.mpc
source-bridge ring-group 100
!
interface TokenRing0/0
 no ip address
 ring-speed 16
 source-bridge 500 4 100
!
interface Ethernet1/0
 ip address 172.18.3.24 255.255.255.0
!
```

```
interface Channel6/1
 no ip address
 no keepalive
 cmpc C020 F0 LAGUNAA READ
 cmpc C020 F1 LAGUNAA WRITE
 !
interface Channel6/2
 no ip address
 no keepalive
 lan TokenRing 0
  source-bridge 88 3 100
  adapter 1 4000.aaaa.aaaa
 tg LAGUNAA  llc token-adapter 1  18 rmac 4000.0000.beef rsap 14
```

Activating the Configuration

To activate the configuration, issue the following commands from MVS2:

```
v net,act,id=lagtrla,update=add
v net,act,id=laglna
```

Connecting VTAM to the APPN NN on the CIP Example

Figure 23–10 shows the physical components for this example. Figure 23–11 shows the various parameters for each component in the configuration example.

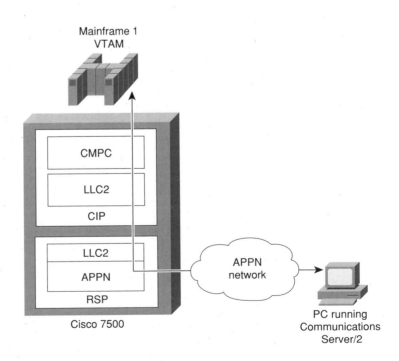

Figure 23–10

Topology for VTAM-to-APPN NN connection on the CIP.

In Figure 23–11, the following activity occurs:

- VTAM connects to the CMPC driver on the CIP.
- The CMPC driver converts the data to an LLC data stream and passes the data to the LLC2 stack on the CIP.
- The LLC2 stack on the CIP passes the data to the LLC2 stack on the RSP.
- The LLC2 stack on the RSP passes the data to APPN on the RSP.
- APPN on the RSP sends the data to the APPN network.

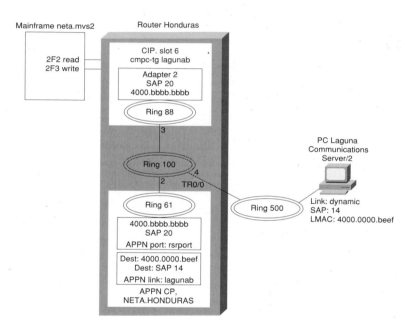

Figure 23–11

Parameters for VTAM-to-APPN
NN connection on the CIP.

The configuration illustrated in Figure 23–11 is more complex because you must configure APPN on the router. There are many different ways to configure APPN. The example is a simple APPN configuration in which SRB is used to connect the APPN NN on the RSP to VTAM and the token ring-attached PC.

It is possible to connect directly to the Token Ring port, an option not shown in the example.

When configuring APPN on the router, you must type the **complete** command before exiting an APPN-configuration subsection. If you need to change an APPN-configuration subsection, you must type the **no complete** command before you can change the subsection. Remember to type **complete** before exiting the subsection. The router ignores the new APPN configuration commands until you type the **complete** command.

Configuration for TRL Node LAGTRLB

```
LAGTRB    VBUILD TYPE=TRL
LAGTRLB   TRLE  LNCTL=MPC,MAXBFRU=8,REPLYTO=3.0,            X
                READ=(2F2),                                 X
                WRITE=(2F3)
```

Configuration for Local SNA Major Node LAGLNB

```
LAGNNB    VBUILD TYPE=LOCAL
LAGPUB    PU    TRLE=LAGTRLB,                               X
                ISTATUS=ACTIVE,                            X
                XID=YES,CONNTYPE=APPN,CPCP=YES
```

Configuration for Honduras Router

```
interface Channel6/1
 no ip address
 no keepalive
 cmpc C020 F2 LAGUNAB READ
 cmpc C020 F3 LAGUNAB WRITE
!
interface Channel6/2
 no ip address
 no keepalive
 lan TokenRing 0
  source-bridge 88 3 100
  adapter 2 4000.bbbb.bbbb
 lan TokenRing 2
 tg LAGUNAB  llc token-adapter 2  20 rmac 4000.0000.bbbb rsap 24
!
!
appn control-point NETA.HONDURAS
    complete
!
appn port RSRBPORT rsrb
  local-sap 24
  desired-max-send-btu-size 4096
  max-rcv-btu-size 4096
  rsrb-virtual-station 4000.0000.bbbb 61 2 100
  complete
!
appn link-station LAGUNAB
  port RSRBPORT
  lan-dest-address 4000.0000.beef 14
  complete
router eigrp 109
 network 172.18.0.0
```

Activating the Configuration

After all configurations are in place, the following commands can be used to start up the links. On the MVS system, enter the following commands:

```
v net,act,id=lagtrlb,update=add
v net,act,id=laglnb
```

On the router, enter the following command from the global configuration mode:

```
appn start
```

Connecting Two VTAM Nodes Using Two CIPs in the Same Router Example

Figure 23–12 shows the physical components for this example. Figure 23–13 shows the various parameters for each component in the configuration example.

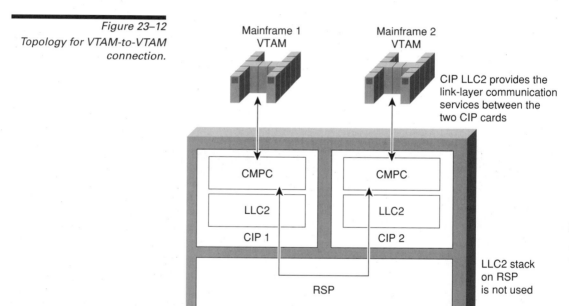

Figure 23–12
Topology for VTAM-to-VTAM connection.

In Figure 23–12, the following activity occurs:

- VTAM on Mainframe 1 passes MPC data to the CMPC driver on CIP 1.
- The CMPC driver on CIP 1 passes the data to the LLC2 stack.
- LLC2 sends the data to CIP 2 in the same router via IEEE 802.2.
- The LLC2 stack on CIP 2 passes the data to the CMPC driver on CIP 2, which passes the data to VTAM on Mainframe 2.

The CIPs could be in different routers or both VTAM connections could be to the same CIP.

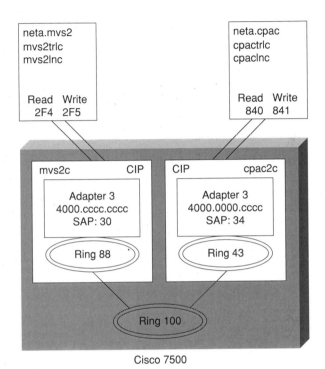

Figure 23–13
Parameters for
VTAM-to-VTAM connection.

```
neta.mvs2
mvs2trlc
mvs2lnc


Read   Write
2F4    2F5
```

```
neta.cpac
cpactrlc
cpaclnc


Read   Write
840    841
```

```
mvs2c              CIP        CIP            cpac2c

    Adapter 3                    Adapter 3
  4000.cccc.cccc              4000.0000.cccc
    SAP: 30                      SAP: 34

    Ring 88                      Ring 43


              Ring 100
```

Cisco 7500

Differing solutions can be configured for the example shown in Figure 23–13. For example, you can have two CIPs in different routers connected via LLC2. You also can configure host connections going into the same CIP card rather than two separate CIP cards.

Configuration for mvs2trlc

```
MVS2TRC  VBUILD TYPE=TRL
MVS2TRLC TRLE  LNCTL=MPC,MAXBFRU=8,REPLYTO=3.0,                  X
               READ=(2F4),                                      X
               WRITE=(2F5)
```

Configuration for mvs2lnc

```
MVS2NNC  VBUILD TYPE=LOCAL
MVS2PUC  PU    TRLE=MVS2TRLC,                                    X
               ISTATUS=ACTIVE,                                  X
               XID=YES,CONNTYPE=APPN,CPCP=YES
```

Configuration for cpactrlc

```
CPACTRC  VBUILD TYPE=TRL
CPACTRLC TRLE  LNCTL=MPC,MAXBFRU=8,REPLYTO=3.0,          X
               READ=(840),                               X
               WRITE=(841)
```

Configuration for cpaclnc

```
CPACNNC  VBUILD TYPE=LOCAL
CPACPUC  PU    TRLE=CPACTRLC,                            X
               ISTATUS=ACTIVE,                           X
               XID=YES,CONNTYPE=APPN,CPCP=YES
```

Configuration for the Router

```
interface Channel4/1
 no ip address
 no keepalive
 cmpc C010 40 CPACC READ
 cmpc C010 41 CPACC WRITE
!
interface Channel4/2
 no ip address
 no keepalive
 lan TokenRing 0
  source-bridge 43 5 100
  adapter 3 4000.0000.cccc
 tg CPACC    llc token-adapter 3  34 rmac 4000.cccc.cccc rsap 30
!
interface Channel6/1
 no ip address
 no keepalive
 cmpc C020 F4 MVS2C READ
 cmpc C020 F5 MVS2C WRITE
!
interface Channel6/2
  lan TokenRing 0
  source-bridge 88 3 100
    adapter 3 4000.cccc.cccc
 tg MVS2C    llc token-adapter 3  30 rmac 4000.0000.cccc rsap 34
```

Activating the Configuration

On the MVS system MVS2, enter the following commands to activate the configuration:

```
v net,act,id=mvs2trlc,update=add
v net,act,id=mvs2lnc
```

On the MVS system CPAC, enter the following commands to activate the configuration:

```
v net,act,id=cpactrlc,update=add
v net,act,id=cpaclnc
```

Connecting VTAM to the APPN NN on a Remote Router with DLUR Example

Figure 23–14 shows the physical components for the DLUS-to-DLUR configuration. Figure 23–15 shows the various parameters for each component in the configuration example.

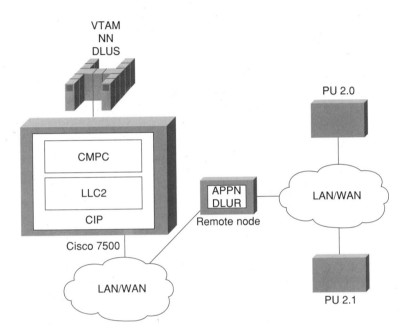

Figure 23–14

Topology for VTAM-to-APPN NN on a remote router with DLUR connection.

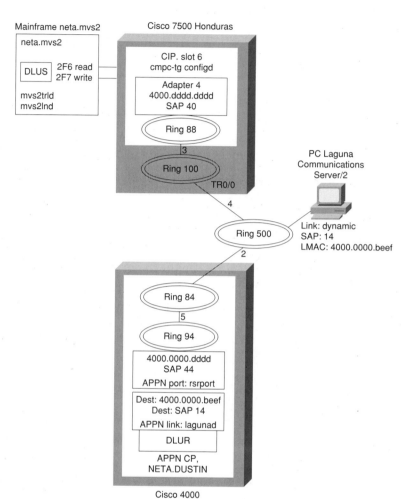

Figure 23–15

Parameters for VTAM-to-APPN NN on a remote router with DLUR connection.

In the example shown in Figure 23–15, DLUS is running on the MVS host. DLUR is running on a remote Cisco 4000 router. The connection from MPC to the APPN stack on the Cisco 4000 is via LLC2. There is no NN on the Cisco 7500. The PC is running Communications Server/2.

Configuration for mvs2trld

```
MVS2TRD  VBUILD TYPE=TRL
MVS2TRLD TRLE  LNCTL=MPC,MAXBFRU=8,REPLYTO=3.0,                    X
               READ=(2F7),                                        X
               WRITE=(2F6)
```

Configuration for mvs2lnd

```
MVS2NND  VBUILD TYPE=LOCAL
MVS2PUD  PU    TRLE=MVS2TRLD,                                    X
               ISTATUS=ACTIVE,                                   X
               XID=YES,CONNTYPE=APPN,CPCP=YES
```

Additional Configuration for Router Honduras

```
interface Channel6/1
 cmpc C020 F6 CONFIGD WRITE
 cmpc C020 F7 CONFIGD READ
!
interface Channel6/2
 lan TokenRing 0
  source-bridge 88 3 100
  adapter 4 4000.dddd.dddd
  tg CONFIGD  llc token-adapter 4  40 rmac 4000.0000.dddd rsap 44
```

Configuration for Router Dustin

```
source-bridge ring-group 84
interface Ethernet0
 ip address 172.18.3.36 255.255.255.0
 media-type 10BaseT
!
interface TokenRing0
 no ip address
 ring-speed 16
 source-bridge 500 2 84
!
appn control-point NETA.DUSTIN
  dlus NETA.MVS2
  dlur
  complete
!
appn port RSRBPORT rsrb
  local-sap 44
  desired-max-send-btu-size 4096
  max-rcv-btu-size 4096
  rsrb-virtual-station 4000.0000.dddd 94 5 84
  complete
!
appn link-station LAGUNAD
  port RSRBPORT
  lan-dest-address 4000.0000.beef 14
  complete
!
appn link-station MVS2D
  port RSRBPORT
  lan-dest-address 4000.dddd.dddd 40
  complete
```

Activating the Configuration

On the MVS2 system, enter the following commands to activate the configuration:

```
v net,act,id=mvs2trld,update=add
v net,act,id=mvs2lnd
```

On the router Dustin, enter the following command from the global configuration mode:

```
appn start
```

TN3270 Server DLUR Running on the Same CIP Example

Figure 23–16 shows the physical components for this example. Figure 23–17 shows the various parameters for each component in the configuration example.

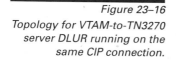

Figure 23–16

Topology for VTAM-to-TN3270 server DLUR running on the same CIP connection.

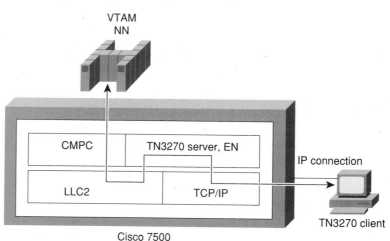

In Figure 23–16, the following activity occurs:

- The TN3270 server on the CIP takes on the role of an APPN EN running DLUR.
- The APPN NN in VTAM communicates with the CMPC driver over the channel.
- The CMPC driver on the CIP passes the data to the LLC2 stack on the CIP via a fast-path loopback driver to the TN3270 server on the CIP.
- The TN3270 server converts the 3270 data stream to a TN3270 data stream and forwards the packets to the IP TN3270 clients in the IP network.

The TN3270 server does not have to be in the same CIP as the CMPC driver.

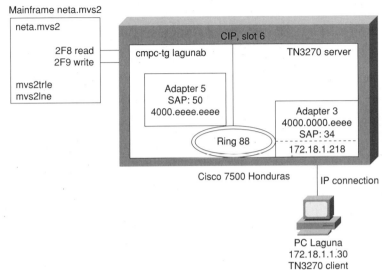

Figure 23–17

Parameters for VTAM-to-TN3270 DLUR running on the same CIP connection.

The following configurations apply to the example shown in Figure 23–17.

Configuration for mvs2trle

```
MVS2TRE   VBUILD TYPE=TRL
 MVS2TRLE TRLE  LNCTL=MPC,MAXBFRU=8,REPLYTO=3.0,
                READ=(2F8),
                WRITE=(2F9)
```

Configuration for mvs2lne

```
MVS2NNE   VBUILD TYPE=LOCAL
MVS2PUE   PU     TRLE=MVS2TRLE,
                 ISTATUS=ACTIVE,
                 XID=YES,CONNTYPE=APPN,CPCP=YES
```

Configuration for swlagtn

```
SWLAGTN   VBUILD TYPE=SWNET,MAXGRP=10,MAXNO=10,MAXDLUR=10
LAGTNPU PU       ADDR=01,                                          X
                 MAXPATH=1,                                        X
                 IDBLK=017,IDNUM=EFEED,                            X
                 PUTYPE=2,                                         X
                 MAXDATA=4096,                                     X
                 LUGROUP=TNGRP1,LUSEED=LAGLU##
```

Configuration for tngrp1

```
TNGRP1E  VBUILD TYPE=LUGROUP
TNGRP1   LUGROUP
DYNAMIC  LU    DLOGMOD=D4C32XX3,                                        X
               MODETAB=ISTINCLM,USSTAB=USSTCPIP,SSCPFM=USS3270
@        LU    DLOGMOD=D4C32784,                                        X
               MODETAB=ISTINCLM,USSTAB=USSTCPIP,SSCPFM=USS3270
```

Additional Router Configuration for Router Honduras

```
interface Channel6/1
 cmpc C020 F8 CONFIGE READ
 cmpc C020 F9 CONFIGE WRITE
!
interface Channel6/2
 lan TokenRing 0
  source-bridge 88 3 100
  adapter 5 4000.eeee.eeee
  adapter 6 4000.0000.eeee
 tn3270-server
  dlur NETA.HOND327S NETA.MVS2
   lsap token-adapter 6  54
    link MVS2TN   rmac 4000.eeee.eeee rsap 50
   pu TNPU       017EFEED 172.18.1.218
  tg CONFIGE  llc token-adapter 5  50 rmac 4000.eeee.eeee rsap 54
```

Activating the Configuration

On the MVS system, enter the following commands to activate the configuration:

```
v net,act,id=mvstrle,update=add
v net,act,id=mvslne
v net,act,id=swhondpu
v net,act,id=swlagtn
v net,act,id=swhondcp
v net,act,id=tngrp1
```

On the router Honduras, enter the following command from TN3270 configuration mode:

```
no shutdown
```

CHAPTER 24

IBM Channel Attach Commands

Use the commands in this chapter to configure IBM channel attach interface features. For hardware technical descriptions and for information about installing the router interfaces, refer to the hardware installation and maintenance publication for your particular product.

For interface configuration information and examples, see Chapter 23, "Configuring IBM Channel Attach."

ADAPTER

Use the **adapter** internal LAN configuration command to configure an internal-adapter interface on an internal LAN. Use the **no** form of this command to remove an internal adapter configuration.

> **adapter** *adapter-number mac-address*
> **no adapter** *adapter-number mac-address*

Syntax	Description
adapter-number	Number in the range 0 to 17 that uniquely identifies the relative adapter number (ADAPNO) on this interface. This value must correspond to the ADAPNO parameter configured in the corresponding virtual telecommunications access method (VTAM) XCA definition.
mac-address	Media access control (MAC) address of this relative adapter. This is a hexadecimal value in the form of *xxxx.xxxx.xxxx*.

Default

This command has no defaults.

Command Mode

Internal LAN configuration

Usage Guidelines

This command first appeared in Cisco IOS Release 11.0.

Before you can configure an internal-adapter interface, you must use the **bridge-group** internal LAN configuration command or the **source-bridge** internal LAN configuration command to configure the bridging type. The only way to get packets to the Channel Interface Processor (CIP) Systems Network Architecture (SNA) feature is through bridging. These two commands are identical to their interface configuration forms.

For transparent bridging, the bridge-group statements identify the interfaces in the same bridge group. Frames are sent only to the interface in the same bridge group.

For source-route bridging, the source-bridge statements identify the interfaces in the same ring group. Frames are sent only to interfaces in the same ring group.

An Ethernet internal LAN can have a **bridge-group** command.

A Token Ring or FDDI internal LAN can have either a **bridge-group** or a **source-bridge** command, but not both.

NOTES ——————————————————————————————————————

If the **source-bridge** command is changed while adapters have active sessions, those sessions will be terminated.

Example

The following example configures an Ethernet internal LAN adapter on relative adapter 12 and MAC address 87AD.0462.3FDE:

```
interface channel 1/2
  lan ethernet 20
    bridge-group 1
    adapter 12 87AD.0462.3FDE
```

Related Commands

bridge-group
llc2
name
source-bridge
lan

CHANNEL-PROTOCOL

Use the **channel-protocol** interface configuration command to define a data rate of either 3 megabytes per second or 4.5 megabytes per second for the Parallel Channel Adapter (PCA) card.

> **channel-protocol** [s | s4]

Syntax	Description
s	(Optional) Specifies a data rate of 3 megabytes per second.
s4	(Optional) Specifies a data rate of 4.5 megabytes per second.

Default

If no value is specified, the default data rate for the PCA is 3 megabytes per second.

Command Mode

Interface configuration

Usage Guidelines

This command first appeared in Cisco IOS Release 10.3.

This command is valid for a PCA adapter card configured on a CIP on the Cisco 7000 with RSP7000 and Cisco 7500 series.

Example

The following command specifies a data rate of 4.5 megabytes per second for the interface:

```
channel-protocol s4
```

CLAW

Use the **claw** interface configuration command to establish the IBM channel attach configuration for an ESCON Channel Adapter (ECA) interface or bus-and-tag Parallel Channel Adapter (PCA) interface on the Cisco 7000 with RSP7000 and Cisco 7500 series.

> **claw** *path device-address ip-address host-name device-name host-app device-app* [**broadcast**]

Part II

Command Reference

Syntax	Description
path	Hexadecimal value in the range 0x0000 to 0xFFFF. This value specifies the data path and consists of two digits for the physical connection (either on the host or on the ESCON director switch); one digit for the control-unit logical address, and one digit for the channel logical address. If not specified in the IOCP, the control-unit logical address and channel logical address default to 0.
device-address	Hexadecimal value in the range 0x00 to 0xFE. This is the unit address associated with the control-unit number and path as specified in the host IOCP file. The device address must have an even value.
ip-address	IP address specified in the HOME statement of the host TCP/IP application configuration file.
host-name	Host name specified in the device statement in the host TCP/IP application configuration file.
device-name	CLAW workstation name specified in the device statement in the host TCP/IP application configuration file.
host-app	Host application name as specified in the host application file. When connected to the IBM TCP host offerings, this value will be **tcpip**, which is the constant specified in the host TCP/IP application file. When attached to other applications, this value must match the value hard coded in the host application.
device-app	CLAW workstation application specified in the host TCP/IP application. When connected to the IBM TCP host offerings, this value will be **tcpip**, which is the constant specified in the host TCP/IP application file. When attached to other applications, this value must match the value hard coded in the host application.
broadcast	(Optional) Enables broadcast processing for this subchannel.

Default

This command has no defaults.

Command Mode

Interface configuration

Usage Guidelines

This command first appeared in Cisco IOS Release 10.3.

This command defines information that is specific to the interface hardware and the IBM channels supported on the interface.

Example

The following example shows how to enable IBM channel attach routing on the CIP port 0, which is supporting a directly connected ESCON channel:

```
interface channel 3/0
 ip address 198.92.0.1 255.255.255.0
 claw 0100 00 198.92.0.21 CISCOVM EVAL TCPIP TCPIP
```

CLIENT (LU LIMIT)

Use the **client** TN3270 configuration command to limit the number of LU sessions that can be established from a client IP address. Use the **no** form of this command to remove a single LU limit associated with a particular IP address.

> **client** [*ip* [*ip-mask*]] **lu maximum** *number*
> **no client** [*ip* [*ip-mask*]] [**lu maximum** *number*]

Syntax	Description
ip	(Optional) IP address of the client. The *ip* value is optional when setting the maximum number of LU sessions. If no IP address is specified, the limit is applied to all clients.
ip-mask	(Optional) IP network mask for the client. The default is 255.255.255.255
number	(Optional and ignored in **no** form of the command) Maximum number of LU sessions. The allowed value is from 0 to 65535.

Default

The default is that there is no limit on the number of concurrent sessions to one client IP address.

In the **no** form of this command, the default *number* is 65535.

Command Mode

TN3270 configuration

Usage Guidelines

This command first appeared in Cisco IOS Release 11.2 BC.

An instance of the **client** (lu limit) command on a given **tn3270-server** is uniquely identified by the *ip-mask* and the logical AND of the *ip* address with that mask. For example, if the command is entered as the following:

```
client 10.1.1.62 255.255.255.192 lu maximum 2
```

then it will be stored (and subsequently displayed by **write term**) as:

```
client 10.1.1.0 255.255.255.192 lu maximum 2
```

The maximum specified on the command can be changed simply by reissuing the command with the new value. It is not necessary to remove the command first.

When you use the **no client** command, only the corresponding **client lu maximum** statement is removed, as identified by the IP address and IP address mask combination. You cannot use **no client** to specify an unlimited number of LU sessions.

For example, if a service bureau has 8000 clients and each client IP address is limited to four LU sessions, you will never need more than 32000 concurrent LU definitions, even when the service is running at 100 percent capacity.

Examples

The following example limits all clients to a maximum of two LU sessions:

```
client lu maximum 2
```

The following example limits a client at IP address 10.1.1.28 to a maximum of three LU sessions:

```
client 10.1.1.28 lu maximum 3
```

The LU limit can be applied to different subnets as shown in the following example. The most exact match to the client IP address is chosen. Clients with IP addresses that reside in the subnet 10.1.1.64 (those with IP addresses in the range of 10.1.1.64 through 10.1.1.127) are limited to a maximum of 5 LU sessions while other clients with IP addresses in the subnet 10.1.1.0 are limited to a maximum of 4 LU sessions.

```
client 10.1.1.0   255.255.255.0 lu maximum 4
client 10.1.1.64 255.255.255.192 lu maximum 5
```

The following example prevents an LU session for the client at IP address 10.1.1.28:

```
client 10.1.1.28 lu maximum 0
```

Related Commands

maximum-lus

CLIENT (LU NAILING)

Use the **client** TN3270 PU configuration mode command to define a range of locaddrs to be reserved for remote devices. Use the **no** form of this command to cancel this definition.

> **client** [printer] **ip** *ip-address* [*mask*] **lu** *first-locaddr* [*last-locaddr*]
> **no client** [printer] **ip** *ip-address* [*mask*] **lu** *first-locaddr* [*last-locaddr*]

Syntax	Description
printer	(Optional) Specifies that a client connection from the nailed IP addresses will be nailed to one of the specified LUs only if the client session negotiates a model type of 328*n*, where *n* is any alphanumeric character. Moreover, it ensures that a printer matching the IP address condition can use only an LU nailed as a printer LU.
	If the **printer** keyword is not specified for any **client** statement that has this IP address set, all model types can use this range of LUs.
ip-address	Specifies remote client IP address.
mask	The mask applied to the remote device address. Multiple client IP addresses in the same subnet can be nailed to the same range of locaddrs.
first-locaddr	Defines a single locaddr to nail.
last-locaddr	(Optional) Defines the end range of inclusive locaddrs to be nailed from *first-locaddr* to *last-locaddr*.

Default
The default is that no LUs are nailed. They are all available to any client.

Command Mode
TN3270 PU configuration mode

Usage Guidelines
This command first appeared in Cisco IOS Release 11.2 BC.

Multiple statements can be configured for one IP address or nail type either on one PU or multiple PUs. But each LU can appear only in one **client** statement.

A client with a nailed IP address can request one of the nailed LUs via the TN3270 device name. If the requested LU is not available, the connection is rejected.

A client with a nailed IP address cannot request an LU outside the range of nailed LUs for its type (screen or printer).

A client with a non-nailed IP address cannot request an LU that is configured as nailed.

The command will be rejected if some of the locaddrs are already nailed. If the locaddrs are currently in use by other remote clients, the nailing statement will take effect only when the locaddr is made available.

To cancel the definition, the **no client** form of the command must be entered exactly as the **client** command was configured originally. If a range of locaddrs was specified, the whole range of locaddrs must be specified to cancel this definition. There is no way to cancel only one locaddr if a whole range of locaddrs was configured.

Examples

In the following example, locaddrs 1 to 50 are reserved for remote devices in the 171.69.176.0 subnet:

```
interface channel 2/2
 tn3270-server
 pu BAGE4
 client ip 171.69.176.28 255.255.255.0 lu 1 50
```

In the following example, locaddrs 1 to 40 are reserved for screen devices in the 171.69.176.0 subnet, while 41 to 50 are reserved for printers in that subnet:

```
interface channel 2/2
 tn3270-server
 pu BAGE4
 client ip 171.69.176.28 255.255.255.0 lu 1 40
 client printer ip 171.69.176.28 255.255.255.0 lu 41 50
```

In the following example, there is an attempt to cancel a definition, but it is rejected because it does not specify the full range of locaddrs and the second attempt fails to specify the correct nail type:

```
interface channel 2/2
 tn3270-server
 pu BAGE4
 client printer ip 171.69.176.50 255.255.255.0 lu 1 100
 no client printer ip 171.69.176.50 255.255.255.0 lu 1
 %Invalid LU range specified
 no client ip 171.69.176.50 255.255.255.0 lu 1 100
 %client ip 171.69.176.50 nail type not matched with configured nail type printer
```

CMPC

Use the **cmpc** interface configuration command to configure a CMPC read subchannel and a CMPC write subchannel. Use the **no** form of this command to remove a subchannel definition and to deactivate the transmission group.

> **cmpc** *path device tg-name* {**read** | **write**}
> **no cmpc** *path device*

Syntax	Description
path	A four-digit hexadecimal value ranging from 0x0000 to 0xFFFF. For PCA (Bus and Tag) use the value 0x0100.
device	A two-digit hexadecimal value that specifies the device address of the CPMC subchannel.
tg-name	The name of the CMPC transmission group. The maximum length of the name is 8 characters.
{**read**	**write**}	The same value, read or write, as specified in the TRL major node.

Default

No default is specified.

Command Mode

Interface configuration

Usage Guidelines

This command first appeared in Cisco IOS Release 11.2 F.

The hexadecimal *path* value specifies the data path and consists of two digits for the physical connection (either on the mainframe or on the ESCON Director Switch), one digit for the channel logical address, and one digit for the control-unit address.

Each **cmpc** configuration command in a given CMPC transmission group specifies the same transmission-group name. The corresponding **tg** command specifies the same transmission-group name. Together, the **cmpc** and **tg** commands make up the transmission-group specification.

The **cmpc** command defines the read/write subchannel addresses that CMPC uses to connect to the host. The command corresponds to the definitions in the TRL major node on the host. Configure the CMPC command on the CIP physical interfaces, *slot*/0 or *slot*/1, and not on the CIP internal LAN interface, *slot*/2. Because CMPC uses read and write subchannel pairs, you can configure the CMPC subchannels on different CIP physical interfaces as long as they are on the same CIP.

The **no cmpc** command deactivates the CMPC transmission group. If the transmission group is used for a non-HPR connection, all sessions using the TG will be terminated immediately. If the transmission group is an HPR connection, all sessions using the transmission group will be terminated if no other HPR connection is available to the host.

Example

The following example configures a read and a write subchannel on path C020 for the CMPC transmission group named CONFIGE:

```
cmpc C020 F8 CONFIGE READ
cmpc C020 F9 CONFIGE WRITE
```

Related Commands

tg

CSNA

Use the **csna** interface configuration command to specify the path and device/subchannel on a physical channel of the Cisco 7000 with RSP7000 and Cisco 7500 series router to communicate with an attached mainframe. Use the **no** form of this command to delete the CIP SNA (CSNA) path.

> **csna** *path device* [**maxpiu** *value*] [**time-delay** *value*] [**length-delay** *value*]
> **no csna** *path device*

Syntax	Description
path	Four-digit hexadecimal value in the range 0x0000 to 0xFFFF. This value specifies the data path and consists of two digits for the physical connection (either on the mainframe or on the ESCON director switch): one digit for the control-unit address, and one digit for the channel logical address. The control-unit address and channel logical address must be specified. For PCA, use the value 0x0100.
device	Device address transmitted on the channel path to select the channel-attached device. For PCA (bus-and-tag), this value refers to the subchannel defined in the XCA major node on the host system.
maxpiu *value*	(Optional) Maximum packet size in bytes that will be transmitted on the interface. The range is 4096 to 65535. The default is 20470 bytes.
time-delay *value*	(Optional) Number of milliseconds to delay before transmitting a received packet on the interface. The range is 0 to 100. The default is 10 ms.
length-delay *value*	(Optional) Amount of data to accumulate, in bytes, before transmitting on the interface. The range is 0 to 65535. The default is 20470 bytes.

Defaults

maxpiu *value*: 20470 (0x4ff6) bytes
time-delay *value*: 10 ms
length-delay *value*: 20470 (0x4ff6) bytes

Command Mode

Interface configuration

Usage Guidelines

This command first appeared in Cisco IOS Release 11.0.

This command is valid for an ESCON or PCA card configured on a CIP on the Cisco 7000 with RSP7000 and Cisco 7500 series. This command is required for CSNA support over a physical channel.

Use the **maxpiu, time-delay,** and **length-delay** keywords to adjust the CIP interface transmission characteristics. You can set the maximum size of packet that the interface will transmit to match the packet size accepted by the host system. You can adjust the delay between the time a packet is received on one of the CIP internal interfaces and transmitted to the host. You also can adjust the transmit-to-host delay by changing the amount of data the CIP accumulates before transmitting to the host.

Changes to the delay values take effect immediately. Any change to the maximum packet size will take effect after the channel is reinitialized. A **length-delay** value of 0 sends the packet as soon as possible.

Using the **no csna** command terminates all subchannels (path and devices) configured on the channel and all Logical Link Control, type 2 (LLC2) sessions established over the subchannels.

Example

The following example shows CSNA, offload, and CLAW configured on the CIP in slot 1, port 0. CSNA can be configured by itself, without dependency on offload or CLAW:

```
interface channel 1/0
 no ip address
 no keepalive
 offload c700 c0 172.18.1.217 TCPIP OS2TCP TCPIP TCPIP TCPIP API
 claw C700 A0 192.18.1.219 EVAL CISCOVM AAA BBB
 csna 0100 10
 csna 0100 11
 csna 0100 12
```

DLUR

Use the **dlur** TN3270 configuration command to enable the Systems Network Architecture (SNA) session switch function on the CIP, or to enter dependent logical unit requester (DLUR) configuration mode. Use the **no** form of this command to disable the SNA session switch function and discard all parameter values associated with the SNA session switch.

> **dlur**
> **dlur** *fq-cpname fq-dlusname*
> **no dlur**

Syntax	Description
fq-cpname	Fully qualified control-point (CP) name used by the SNA session switch and the logical-unit (LU) name for the DLUR function. This name must be unique among APPN nodes in the network including other *fq-cpname* values specified on all other TN3270 servers running under the Cisco IOS software.
fq-dlusname	Fully qualified name of the primary choice for the dependent LU server (DLUS). This is the name of an LU, usually a CP, in an APPN host. The *fq-dlusname* value can be repeated and shared across servers.

Default

No DLUR function is enabled.

Command Mode

TN3270 configuration

Usage Guidelines

This command first appeared in Cisco IOS Release 11.2.

If the SNA session switch function is already enabled, the **dlur** command with no arguments puts you in DLUR configuration mode.

Several parameters in the DLUR configuration mode consist of fully qualified names, as defined by the APPN architecture. Fully qualified names consist of two case-insensitive alphanumeric strings, separated by a period. However, for compatibility with existing APPN products, including VTAM, the characters "#" (pound), "@" (at), and "$" (dollar) are allowed in the fully qualified name strings. Each string is from one to eight characters long; for example, RA12.NODM1PP. The portion of the name before the period is the NETID and is shared between entities in the same logical network.

The **no dlur** command hierarchically deletes all resources defined beneath it.

Example

The following command performs two functions: it enters DLUR configuration mode, and it enables the DLUR function. It defines the LU name for the DLUR as SYD.TN3020 and the primary choice for DLUS as SYD.VMG. Note that the NETID portion of both names is the same:

```
dlur SYD.TN3020 SYD.VMG
```

DLUS-BACKUP

Use the **dlus-backup** DLUR configuration command to specify a backup DLUS for the DLUR function. Use the **no** form of this command to remove a backup DLUS name.

> **dlus-backup** *dlusname2*
> **no dlus-backup**

Syntax	Description
dlusname2	Fully qualified name of the backup DLUS for the DLUR.

Default

No backup DLUS is specified.

Command Mode

DLUR configuration

Usage Guidelines

This command first appeared in Cisco IOS Release 11.2.

Only one backup DLUS can be specified per CIP. If the backup DLUS specified in the **dlus-backup** command is in use when a **no dlus-backup** is issued, the connection is not torn down.

Several parameters in the DLUR configuration mode consist of fully qualified names as defined by the APPN architecture. Fully qualified names consist of two case-insensitive alphanumeric strings, separated by a period. However, for compatibility with existing APPN products, including VTAM, the characters "#" (pound), "@" (at), and "$" (dollar) are allowed in the fully qualified name strings. Each string is from one to eight characters long; for example, RA12.NODM1PP. The portion of the name before the period is the NETID and is shared between entities in the same logical network.

Example

The following command specifies SYD.VMX as the backup DLUS:

```
dlus-backup SYD.VMX
```

GENERIC-POOL

Use the **generic-pool** TN3270 configuration command to specify whether leftover LUs will be made available to TN3270 sessions that do not request a specific LU or LU pool through TN3270E. Use the **no** form of this command to selectively remove the permit or deny condition of generic-pool use.

> **generic-pool {permit | deny}**
> **no generic-pool**

Syntax	Description
permit	Leftover LUs should be made available to TN3270 users wanting generic sessions. This value is the default.
deny	Leftover LUs should not be given to a generic pool. The physical unit (PU) is not automatically fully populated with 255 LOCADDR definitions. The default is the value configured in TN3270 configuration mode.

Defaults

In TN3270 configuration mode, generic-pool use is permitted.

In PU configuration mode, the default is the value currently configured in TN3270 configuration mode.

Command Modes

TN3270 configuration

PU configuration

Usage Guidelines

This command first appeared in Cisco IOS Release 11.2.

A leftover LU is defined as one for which all of the following conditions are true:

- The system services control point (SSCP) did not send an ACTLU during PU start-up.
- The PU controlling the LU is capable of carrying product set ID (PSID) vectors on network management vector transport (NMVT) messages, thus allowing dynamic definition of dependent LU (DDDLU) operation for that LU.

All LUs in the generic pool are, by definition, DDDLU capable.

Values entered for **generic-pool** in TN3270 configuration mode apply to all PUs for that TN3270 server but can be changed in PU configuration mode.

In PU configuration mode, a **no generic-pool** command will restore the **generic-pool** value entered in TN3270 command mode.

In TN3270 configuration mode, the **no generic-pool** command reverts to the default, which permits generic-pool use.

The command takes effect immediately. If **generic-pool deny** is specified on a PU, no further dynamic connections to it will be allowed. Existing sessions are unaffected, but as they terminate, the LUs will not become available for dynamic connections.

Similarly, if **generic-pool permit** is specified, any inactive LUs are immediately available for dynamic connections. Moreover, any active LUs that were dynamic previously (before **generic-pool deny** was issued) return to being dynamic.

Example

The following command permits generic LU-pool use:

```
generic-pool permit
```

IDLE-TIME

Use the **idle-time** TN3270 configuration command to specify how many seconds of LU inactivity, from both host and client, before the TN3270 session is disconnected. Use the **no** form of this command to cancel the idle time period and return to the default.

> **idle-time** *seconds*
> **no idle-time**

Syntax	Description
seconds	Number of seconds, from 0 to 65535. A value of 0 means the session is never disconnected.

Defaults

The default in TN3270 configuration mode is that the session is never disconnected (0).

The default in PU configuration mode is the value currently configured in TN3270 configuration mode.

Command Modes

TN3270 configuration

PU configuration

Usage Guidelines

This command first appeared in Cisco IOS Release 11.2.

The **idle-time** command can be entered in either TN3270 configuration mode or PU configuration mode. A value entered in TN3270 mode applies to all PUs for that TN3270 server, except as overridden by values entered in PU configuration mode.

A **no idle-time** command entered in PU configuration mode will restore the idle-time value entered in TN3270 command mode.

The **idle-time** command affects currently active and future TN3270 sessions. For example, if the **idle-time** value is reduced from 900 seconds to 600 seconds, sessions that have been idle for between 600 and 900 seconds are immediately disconnected.

NOTES

For the purposes of idle-time logic, TIMING-MARKs generated by the keepalive logic do not constitute "activity."

Examples

The following command sets an idle-time disconnect value of 10 minutes:

```
idle-time 600
```

The following command entered in TN3270 configuration mode sets the default idle-time disconnect value to 0, or never disconnect:

```
no idle-time
```

INTERFACE CHANNEL

Use the **interface channel** global configuration command to specify a channel attach interface and enter interface configuration mode.

> **interface channel** *slot/port*

Syntax	Description
slot	Specifies the slot number where the CIP is located. The value is in the range 0 to 5.
port	Specifies the port number where the CIP is located. The value is in the range 0 to 2. Port 0 and 1 are for physical interfaces. Port 2 is for configuring an internal LAN interface on the CIP.

Default

This command has no defaults.

Command Mode

Global configuration

Usage Guidelines

This command first appeared in Cisco IOS Release 11.0. It is used only on the Cisco 7000 with RSP7000 and Cisco 7500 series.

Example

The following example shows how to enter interface configuration mode for a CIP in slot 2 and begin configuring port 0:

```
interface channel 2/0
```

Related Commands

claw
cmpc
csna
lan
max-llc2-sessions
offload
tn3270-server

IP PRECEDENCE

Use the **ip precedence** command to specify the precedence level for IP traffic in the TN3270 server. The **no** form of this command removes the precedence value.

> **ip precedence** {screen | printer} *value*
> **no ip precedence** {screen | printer}

Syntax	Description
screen	Specifies the precedence is for screen devices.
printer	Specifies the precedence is for printer devices.
value	Sets the **precedence** priority. A value between 0 and 7, with 7 being the highest priority. The default is 0.

Default

The default is a precedence value of 0 for both screens and printers.

Command Mode

TN3270 server configuration mode

TN3270 PU configuration mode

Usage Guidelines

This command first appeared in Cisco IOS Release 11.2 BC.

Precedence values applied in TN3270 PU configuration mode override values applied in TN3270 server configuration mode.

You can enter new or different values for IP precedence without first using the **no** form of this command.

During initial Telnet negotiations to establish, or bind, the session, an IP precedence value of 0 and IP TOS value of 0 is used. These values are used until the bind takes place. When the session is a type 2 bind, the TN3270 client is assumed to be a screen; otherwise, the client is assumed to be a printer.

Example

The following example assigns a precedence value of 3 to printers:

```
ip precedence printer 3
```

Related Commands

ip tos

IP TOS

Use the **ip tos** command to specify the TOS level for IP traffic in the TN3270 server. The **no** form of this command removes the TOS value.

> **ip tos** {**screen** | **printer**} *value*
> **no ip tos** {**screen** | **printer**}

Syntax	Description
screen	Specifies the TOS is for screen devices.
printer	Specifies the TOS is for printer devices.
value	Sets the TOS priority. A value between 0 and 15. The default is 0.

Default

The default is a TOS value of 0 for both screens and printers.

Command Mode

TN3270 server configuration mode

TN3270 PU configuration mode

Usage Guidelines

This command first appeared in Cisco IOS Release 11.2 BC.

TOS values applied in TN3270 PU configuration mode override values applied in TN3270 server configuration mode.

The default TOS values for screen and printer are 0. However, RFC 1349 recommends different default values. Specifically, the RFC recommends a default minimize-screen delay value of 8 and a default maximize-printer throughput value of 4. You must configure these values using the **ip tos** command if you want to comply to the defaults as stated in the RFC. Table 24–1 shows the values described in RFC 1349.

Table 24–1   *TOS Defined Values*

Value	Definition	Action
0	All normal.	Use default metric.
8	Minimize delay.	Use delay metric.
4	Maximize throughput.	Use default metric.
2	Maximize reliability.	Use reliability metric.
1	Minimize monetary cost.	Use cost metric.
Other	Not defined.	Reserved for future use.

During initial Telnet negotiations to establish, or bind, the session, an IP precedence value of 0 and IP TOS value of 0 is used. These values are used until the bind takes place. When the session is a type 2 bind, the TN3270 client is assumed to be a screen; otherwise, the client is assumed to be a printer.

When you use the **no** form of the command, the TOS value is either set to 0 for that configuration mode, or the value set at a previous (higher) configuration mode is used. For example, if you are at the TN3270 PU configuration mode and issue a **no ip tos screen** command, any value you configured previously at the TN3270 server configuration mode will take effect.

You can enter new or different values for TOS without first using the **no** form of this command.

Example

In the following example, the TN3270 server TOS screen value is set to 10 and a specific PU TOS screen value is set to 0:

```
interface channel 3/2
  tn3270-server
  ip tos screen 8
  ip tos printer 4
  pu PUS2
   ip tos screen 0
```

Related Commands

ip precedence

KEEPALIVE

Use the **keepalive** TN3270 configuration command to specify how many seconds of inactivity elapse before transmission of a DO TIMING-MARK to the TN3270 client. Use the **no** form of this command to cancel the keepalive period and return to the default.

> **keepalive** *seconds*
> **no keepalive**

Syntax	Description
seconds	Number of seconds, from 0 to 65535. A value of 0 means no keepalive signals are sent. The default is 1800 seconds (30 minutes).

Defaults

The default in TN3270 configuration mode is 1800 seconds (30 minutes).

The default in PU configuration mode is the value currently configured in TN3270 configuration mode.

Command Modes

TN3270 configuration

PU configuration

Usage Guidelines

This command first appeared in Cisco IOS Release 11.2.

The **keepalive** command can be entered in either TN3270 configuration mode or PU configuration mode. A value entered in TN3270 mode applies to all PUs for that TN3270 server, except as overridden by values entered in PU configuration mode. A **no keepalive** command entered in PU configuration mode will restore the **keepalive** value entered in TN3270 command mode.

If the client does not reply within 30 minutes of the transmission of the DO TIMING-MARK, the TN3270 server disconnects the TN3270 session. The DO TIMING-MARK is a Telnet protocol operation that does not affect the client operation.

If the IP path to the client is broken, the TCP layer will detect the failure to acknowledge the DO TIMING-MARK and initiate disconnection. This action will usually take much less than 30 minutes.

The **keepalive** command affects currently active and future TN3270 sessions. For example, reducing the value to a smaller nonzero value will cause an immediate burst of DO TIMING-MARKs on those sessions that have been inactive for a period of time greater than the new, smaller value.

Examples

The following command sets an keepalive disconnect value of 15 minutes (900 seconds):

```
keepalive 900
```

The following command entered in TN3270 configuration mode sets the keepalive disconnect value to 1800 seconds, the default:

```
no keepalive
```

LAN

Use the **lan** interface configuration command to configure an internal LAN on a CIP interface. Use the **no** form of the command to remove an internal LAN interface.

> **lan** *type lan-id*
> **no lan** *type lan-id*

Syntax	Description
type	Interface type for this internal LAN: **ethernet**, **tokenring**, or **fddi**.
lan-id	A number 0 to 31 that uniquely identifies this internal LAN on this CIP. This value must be unique between all internal LANs of the same interface type on a CIP.

Default

This command has no defaults.

Command Mode

Interface configuration

Usage Guidelines

This command first appeared in Cisco IOS Release 11.0.

An internal LAN can be configured only on CIP interface port 2. Interface port 2 represents an internal port on the CIP. You receive an error message if you attempt to configure an internal LAN on any CIP port other than port 2.

Example

The following example shows how to configure an internal LAN Ethernet with a LAN ID of 20 on the CIP in slot 1, port 2:

```
interface channel 1/2
  lan ethernet 20
```

LINK

Use the **link** DLUR SAP configuration command to define and activate a link to a host. Use the **no** form of this command to delete the link definition.

> **link** *name* [**rmac** *rmac*] [**rsap** *rsap*]
> **no link** *name*

Syntax	Description
name	Link name, from one to eight alphanumeric characters. The first character must be alphabetic. The name must be unique within the DLUR function.
rmac	(Optional) Remote MAC address of the form *xxxx.xxxx.xxxx* in hexadecimal. If not specified, a loopback link to another SAP on the same internal LAN adapter is assumed.
name	Link name, from one to eight alphanumeric characters. The first character must be alphabetic. The name must be unique within the DLUR function.
rsap	(Optional) Remote SAP address, 04 to FC in hexadecimal. The *rsap* value must be even and should be a multiple of 4, but this requirement is not enforced. The *rsap* value default is 04.

Defaults

No DLUR link is defined.

The default remote SAP address is 04 (hexadecimal).

Command Mode

DLUR SAP configuration

Usage Guidelines

This command first appeared in Cisco IOS Release 11.2.

The combination of *rmac* and *rsap* must be unique within the DLUR SAP function. These values can only be changed by deleting the link definition, using the **no link** command, and recreating the link definition.

For a link via a channel on this CIP, the TN3270 server and the hosts should open different adapters in the same internal LAN. Using different adapters avoids any contention for SAP numbers, and is also necessary if you configure duplicate MAC addresses for fallback CSNA access to the host. By configuring the adapters in the same internal LAN, you achieve the same performance—bypassing the DLC stacks—as looping back on a single adapter.

Examples

The following command defines a link name and a remote SAP address:

```
link LINK5 rsap 08
```

The following example shows different adapter numbers configured on the same internal LAN to avoid SAP contention. The host uses SAP 4 on token ring adapter 0.

```
lan tokenring 0
 adapter 0 4000.0000.0001
 adapter 1 4000.0000.0002
tn3270-server
 dlur ...
 lsap token-adapter 1
 link HOST rmac 4000.0000.0001 rsap 4
```

LSAP

Use the **lsap** DLUR configuration command to create a SAP in the SNA session switch, or to enter DLUR SAP configuration mode. Use the **no** form of this command to delete a SAP and all SNA session switch links using the internal LAN interface.

> **lsap**
> **lsap** *type adapter-number* [*lsap*]
> **no lsap** *type adapter-number* [*lsap*]

Syntax	Description
type	Internal adapter type on the CIP card, which corresponds to the value specified in the **lan** internal LAN configuration command. The currently supported type is **token-adapter**.
adapter-number	Internal adapter interface on the CIP card, which is the same value specified in the **adapter** internal LAN configuration command.
lsap	(Optional) Local SAP number, 04 to FC, in hex. The value must be even and should normally be a multiple of four. It must be unique within the internal adapter in that no other 802.2 clients of that adapter, in the router or in a host, should be allocated the same SAP. The default value is C0.

Default

The default value for *lsap* is hexadecimal C0.

Command Mode

DLUR configuration

Usage Guidelines

This command first appeared in Cisco IOS Release 11.2.

If the SAP in the SNA session switch function is already created, the **lsap** command with no arguments puts you in DLUR SAP configuration mode.

The **lsap** command can be entered only in DLUR configuration mode.

The **lsap** command uses values that are defined in two other commands: the **lan** internal LAN configuration command and the **adapter** internal LAN configuration command. The **lan** *type* and **adapter** *adapter-number* values configured on the CIP internal LAN interface are used in the **lsap** command.

However, the **lan** *type* keyword is a little different. Where the *type* on the **lan** command is **tokenring**, the corresponding *type* on **lsap** is **token-adapter**. This emphasizes that the number that follows is an **adapter** number, not a **lan** number.

The **no lsap** command hierarchically deletes any links using it. Any sessions using those links are lost.

Example

The following command defines an adapter type, an adapter number, and a local SAP:

```
lsap token 0 B0
```

Related Commands

adapter
lan

MAX-LLC2-SESSIONS

Use the **max-llc2-sessions** internal adapter configuration command to specify the number of concurrent LLC2 sessions that will be supported on the CIP interface. Use the **no** form of this command to remove a value.

> **max-llc2-sessions** *number*
> **no max-llc2-sessions** *number*

Syntax	*Description*
number	A value in the range 0 to 4000. If no value is specified, the default is 256.

Default

The default number of sessions is 256.

Command Mode

Internal adapter configuration

Usage Guidelines

This command first appeared in Cisco IOS Release 11.0.

The maximum number of LLC2 sessions can be configured only on CIP interface port 2. To specify an unlimited number of LLC2 sessions, either omit this command from the adapter configuration on CIP interface port 2, or use a value of 0.

When configured for an unlimited number of LLC2 sessions, the actual number of sessions is determined by the available memory on the CIP.

Example

The following example limits the maximum number of LLC2 sessions to 212:

```
max-llc2-sessions 212
```

MAXIMUM-LUS

Use the **maximum-lus** TN3270 sconfiguration command to limit the number of LU control blocks that will be allocated for TN3270 server use. Use the **no** form of this command to restore the default value.

maximum-lus *number*
no maximum-lus

Syntax   *Description*

number   Maximum number of LU control blocks allowed. The allowed range is
                    0 to 32000. However, the practical upper limit for concurrently
                    operating TN3270 sessions depends on the hardware and usage
                    characteristics. The default is 2100.

Default

Because of the license structure, the default is 2100, which represents the limit of the lower-priced
license (2000) plus a five percent buffer. If you configure a value greater than the default, a license
reminder is displayed.

Command Mode

TN3270 configuration

Usage Guidelines

This command first appeared in Cisco IOS Release 11.2.

Although the value may be varied at any time, reducing it below the current number of LU control
blocks will not release those blocks until a PU is inactivated by DACTPU or by using the **no pu**
command.

If the number of LUs in use reaches 94% of the current setting of maximum-lus, a warning message
is displayed on the console. To prevent annoyance, the threshold for generating such messages is
raised for a period.

The TN3270 server attempts to allocate one LU control block for each LU activated by the hosts.
In the case of dynamic definition of dependent LU (DDDLU), the control block is allocated when
the client requests the LU, in anticipation of an ACTLU from the SSCP host.

By limiting the number of LU control blocks allocated, you can make sure enough memory is available
to support other CIP functions. The control blocks themselves take about 1K bytes per LU.
During session activity, a further 2K per LU might be needed for data. On a CIP, 32 MB of memory
will support 4000 LUs. To support more than 4000 LUs, Cisco recommends 64 MB of memory.

**Part
II**

Command Reference

Example

The following command allows 5000 LU control blocks to be allocated:

```
maximum-lus 5000
```

Related Commands

client (lu limit)
pu (DLUR)
pu (direct)

NAME

Use the **name** internal adapter configuration command to give a name to the internal adapter. Use the **no** form of the command to remove the name assigned to an internal adapter.

> **name** *name*
> **no name** *name*

Syntax   *Description*

name   Name that identifies this internal adapter. Consists of up to 8 characters that do not include blanks.

Default

This command has no defaults.

Command Mode

Internal adapter configuration

Usage Guidelines

This command first appeared in Cisco IOS Release 11.0.

Example

The following example assigns a name to an internal-adapter interface:

```
name VTAM_B14
```

OFFLOAD

Use the **offload** interface configuration command to configure an offload task on the CIP. Use the **no** form of this command to cancel the offload task on the CIP.

> **offload** *path device-address ip-address host-name device-name host-app device-app host-link device-link* [**broadcast**]
> **no offload** *path device-address*

Syntax	Description
path	Hexadecimal value in the range 0x0000 to 0xFFFF. This value specifies the data path and consists of two digits for the physical connection (either on the host or on the ESCON director switch): one digit for the control-unit address, and one digit for the channel logical address. If not specified in the IOCP, the control-unit address and channel logical address default to 0.
device-address	Hexadecimal value in the range 0x00 to 0xFE. This is the unit address associated with the control-unit number and path as specified in the host IOCP file. The device address must have an even value.
ip-address	IP address specified in the host TCP/IP application configuration file.
host-name	Host name specified in the device statement in the host TCP/IP application configuration file.
device-name	CLAW workstation name specified in the device statement in the host TCP/IP application configuration file.
host-app	Host application name as specified in the host application file. When connected to the IBM TCP host offerings, this value will be **tcpip**, which is the constant specified in the host TCP/IP application file. When attached to other applications, this value must match the value hard-coded in the host application.
device-app	CLAW workstation application specified in the host TCP/IP application. When connected to the IBM TCP host offerings, this value will be **tcpip**, which is the constant specified in the host TCP/IP application file. When attached to other applications, this value must match the value hard-coded in the host application.
host-link	Host application name providing the CLAW API link. For IBM-compatible offload software, this always will be **tcpip**.
device-link	CLAW workstation application name providing the CLAW API link. For IBM-compatible offload software, this always will be **api**.
broadcast	(Optional) Enables broadcast processing for this subchannel.

Default

This command has no defaults.

Command Mode

Interface configuration

Usage Guidelines

This command first appeared in Cisco IOS Release 11.0.

The **offload** command uses the same underlying configuration parameters as does the **claw** command.

Example

The following example shows how to enable IBM channel attach offload routing on the CIP port 0, which is supporting a directly connected ESCON channel:

```
interface channel 3/0
 ip address 198.92.0.1 255.255.255.0
 offload 0100 00 198.92.0.21 CISCOVM EVAL TCPIP TCPIP TCPIP API
```

PREFERRED-NNSERVER

Use the **preferred-nnserver** DLUR configuration command to specify a preferred network node (NN) as server. Use the **no** form of this command to remove the preference.

> **preferred-nnserver** *name*
> **no preferred-nnserver**

Syntax	Description
name	A fully qualified name of a NN.

Default

This command has no defaults.

Command Mode

DLUR configuration

Usage Guidelines

This command first appeared in Cisco IOS Release 11.2.

Fully qualified names consist of two case-insensitive alphanumeric strings, separated by a period. However, for compatibility with existing APPN products, including VTAM, the characters "#" (pound), "@" (at), and "$" (dollar) are allowed in the fully qualified name strings. Each string is from one to eight characters long; for example, RA12.NODM1PP. The portion of the name before the period is the NETID and is shared between entities in the same logical network.

When no preferred server is specified, the DLUR will request NN server support from the first suitable node with which it makes contact. If refused, it will try the next one, and so on.

If a preferred server is specified, then DLUR will wait a short time to allow a link to the preferred server to materialize. If the preferred server is not found in that time, any suitable node can be used, as above.

DLUR will not relinquish the current NN server merely because the preferred server becomes available.

Example

The following command selects SYD.VMX as the preferred NN server:

```
preferred-nnserver SYD.VMX
```

PU (DLUR)

Use the **pu** DLUR configuration command to create a PU entity that has no direct link to a host or to enter PU configuration mode. Use the **no** form of this command to remove the PU entity.

> **pu** *pu-name*
> **pu** *pu-name idblk-idnum ip-address*
> **no pu** *pu-name*

Part II

Command Reference

Syntax	Description
pu-name	Name that uniquely identifies this PU.
idblk-idnum	This value must match the *idblk-idnum* value defined at the host. The value must be unique within the subarea. However, the TN3270 server generally cannot tell which remote hosts are in which subareas, so the server only enforces uniqueness within the set of DLUR PUs.
ip-address	IP address that the clients should use as host IP address to map to LU sessions under this PU.

Default

No PU is defined.

Command Mode

DLUR configuration

Usage Guidelines

This command first appeared in Cisco IOS Release 11.2.

If the PU is already created, the **pu** *pu-name* command with no arguments puts you in PU configuration mode. In this mode you can modify an existing PU DLUR entity.

A typical usage for the IP address is to reserve an IP address per host application. For example, clients wanting to connect to TSO specify an IP address that will be defined with PUs that have LOGAPPL=TSO.

Example

The following sequence of commands define three PUs. Two of the PUs share the same IP address, and the third PU has a separate IP address:

```
pu p0  05D99001 192.195.80.40
pu p1  05D99002 192.195.80.40
pu p2  05D99003 192.195.80.41
```

PU (DIRECT)

Use the **pu** TN3270 configuration command to create a PU entity that has its own direct link to a host or to enter PU configuration mode. Use the **no** form of this command to remove the PU entity.

> **pu** *pu-name idblk-idnum ip-address type adapter-number lsap* [**rmac** *rmac*] [**rsap** *rsap*]
> [**lu-seed** *lu-name-stem*]
> **no pu** *pu-name*

Syntax	Description
pu-name	Name that uniquely identifies this PU.
idblk-idnum	This value must match the IDBLK-IDNUM value defined at the host. The value must be unique within the subarea. However, the TN3270 server cannot tell which remote hosts are in which subareas and does not enforce the unique-value requirement.
ip-address	IP address that the clients should use as host IP address to map to LU sessions under this PU.
type	Internal adapter type on the CIP card, which corresponds to the value specified in the **lan** internal LAN configuration command. The currently supported type is **token-adapter**.
adapter-number	Internal adapter interface on the CIP card, which is the same value specified in the **adapter** internal LAN configuration command.
lsap	Local SAP number in hexadecimal, ranging from 04 to FC. The value must be even and must be unique within the internal adapter so that no other 802.2 clients of that adapter, in the router or in a host, should be allocated the same SAP. Other direct links from TN3270 server direct PUs may use the same value on the internal adapter as long as the remote MAC or SAP is different.
rmac *rmac*	(Optional) Remote MAC address. The remote MAC address of the form *xxxx.xxxx.xxxx* hexadecimal, specifying the MAC address of the remote host. If not specified, a loopback link to another SAP on the same internal LAN adapter is assumed.

Syntax	Description
rsap *rsap*	(Optional) Remote SAP address. The remote SAP address is a one- or two-character hexadecimal string, ranging from 04 to FC, specifying the SAP address of the remote host. The default is 04.
lu-seed *lu-name-stem*	(Optional) Provides an LU name that the client can use when a specific LU name request is needed. The format can be *x...x*## or *x...x*### where *x..x* is an alphanumeric string. When ## is specified, it is replaced with the LU LOCADDR in hexadecimal digits to form the complete LU name. When ### is specified, decimal digits are used, padded with leading zeroes to make three characters. The first *x* must be alphabetic and the entire string, including the # symbols, must not exceed 8 characters.

Defaults

No PU is defined.

The default remote SAP address is 04 (hexadecimal).

Command Mode

TN3270 configuration

Usage Guidelines

This command first appeared in Cisco IOS Release 11.2.

If the PU is already created, the **pu** *pu-name* command with no arguments puts you in PU configuration mode, where you can modify an existing PU entity.

The **pu** (direct) command uses values that are defined in two other commands: the **lan** internal LAN configuration command and the **adapter** internal LAN configuration command. The **lan** *type* and **adapter** *adapter-number* values configured on the CIP internal LAN interface are used in the **pu** command.

For a link via a channel on this CIP, the TN3270 server and the hosts should open different adapters in the same internal LAN. Using different adapters avoids any contention for SAP numbers, and is also necessary if you configure duplicate MAC addresses for fallback CSNA access to the host. By configuring the adapters in the same internal LAN, you achieve the same performance—bypassing the DLC stacks—as looping back on a single adapter.

Examples

The following commands configure the TN3270 server to be active, and have one PU, CAPPU1, trying to connect in. An LU seed using hexadecimal digits is defined.

```
tn3270-server
 pu CAPPU1 05D18101 10.14.20.34 token-adapter 3 rmac 4000.0501.0001 lu-seed CAP01L##
```

The following example shows different adapter numbers configured on the same internal LAN to avoid SAP contention. The host uses SAP 4 on token ring adapter 0.

```
lan tokenring 0
 adapter 0 4000.0000.0001
 adapter 1 4000.0000.0002
tn3270-server
 pu PU1 05d00001 10.0.0.1 token-adapter 1 8 rmac 4000.0000.0001 rsap 4
```

Related Commands

adapter
lan

SHOW EXTENDED CHANNEL CMPC

Use the **show extended channel cmpc** privileged EXEC command to display information about each CMPC subchannel configured on the specified CIP interface.

show extended channel *slot/port* **cmpc** [*path* [*device*]]

Syntax	Description
slot	Slot number.
port	Port number, which must be 0 or 1.
path	(Optional) A 4-digit hexadecimal value in the ranging from 0x0000 to 0xFFFF. For PCA (Bus and Tag) use the value 0x0100. If specified, status for all CMPC devices for the specified path will be displayed. If not specified, status for all CMPC devices for all paths under that interface will be displayed.
device	(Optional) A 2-digit hexadecimal value that specifies a device address of the CPMC subchannel. If specified, only status for that CMPC device will be displayed. If not specified, status for all CMPC devices for the specified path will be displayed.

Command Mode

Privileged EXEC

Usage Guidelines

This command first appeared in Cisco IOS Release 11.2 BC.

This command is valid only on the CIP physical interfaces, *slot*/0 or *slot*/1.

Sample Display

The following is sample output on a Cisco 7500 router from the **show extended channel cmpc** command:

```
router# show extended channel 3/0 cmpc c020

          Path Dv  TGName    Dir    Bfrs  Status
CMPC C020 46  MVS2ISRA  READ   10    Active
CMPC C020 47  MVS2ISRA  WRITE  16    Active
CMPC C020 4A  MVS2ISR1  READ   7     Active
CMPC C020 4B  MVS2ISR1  WRITE  16    Active
CMPC C020 4C  MVS2ISR2  READ   7     Active
CMPC C020 4D  MVS2ISR2  WRITE  16    Active
CMPC C020 4E  MVS2TN    READ   0     Inactive
CMPC C020 4F  MVS2TN    WRITE  0     Inactive
```

Table 24–2 describes the fields shown in the display.

Table 24–2 *Show Extended Channel CMPC Field Descriptions*

Field	Description
Path	CMPC channel path configured.
Dv	CMPC subchannel device configured.
TGName	Transmission-group name configured for the CMPC subchannel.
Dir	Identifies this CMPC subchannel as READ or WRITE.
Bfrs	On the read subchannel, this is the number of 4 K-size pages that VTAM has allocated for each Read. This will match the MAXBFRU value configured in the VTAM TRL major node. On the write subchannel, this is the maximum number of 4 K pages VTAM can write to the CIP for a single channel I/O. The value will always be 16 for the write subchannel because the CIP always allows VTAM to write up to 64 KB per channel I/O.
Status	State of the CMPC subchannel. Valid values are: • **Shutdown**—CIP interface for this CMPC subchannel is shut down. In this state, the Bfrs value is not available and will be displayed as zeros. • **Inactive**—CMPC subchannel is not active. • **XID2 Pending**—XID2 handshaking in progress. • **Active**—XID2 exchange completed; CMPC subchannel is active.

SHOW EXTENDED CHANNEL ICMP-STACK

Use the **show extended channel icmp-stack** privileged EXEC command to display information about the Internet Control Message Protocol (ICMP) stack running on the CIP interfaces in a Cisco 7000 with RSP7000 and Cisco 7500 series.

> **show extended channel** *slot/port* **icmp-stack** [*ip-address*]

Syntax	Description
slot	Slot number.
port	Port number.
ip-address	(Optional) Offload IP address.

Command Mode

Privileged EXEC

Usage Guidelines

This command first appeared in Cisco IOS Release 11.0.

Sample Display

The following is sample output on the Cisco 7000 with RSP7000 from the **show extended channel icmp-stack** command:

```
router# show extended channel 4/0 icmp-stack

ICMP Statistics for IP Address 198.92.1.120
  InMsgs         : 200      InErrors       : 201      InDestUnreachs: 202
  InTimeExcds    : 203      InParmProbs    : 204      InSrcQuenchs  : 205
  InRedirects    : 206      InEchos        : 207      OutEchoReps   : 213
  OutTimestamps  : 214      OutTimestampReps: 215     OutAddrMasks  : 216
  OutAddrMaskReps: 217

ICMP Statistics for IP Address 198.92.1.121
  InMsgs         : 201      InErrors       : 202      InDestUnreachs: 203
  InTimeExcds    : 204      InParmProbs    : 205      InSrcQuenchs  : 206
  InRedirects    : 207      InEchos        : 208      OutEchoReps   : 214
  OutTimestamps  : 215      OutTimestampReps: 216     OutAddrMasks  : 217
  OutAddrMaskReps: 218
```

SHOW EXTENDED CHANNEL IP-STACK

Use the **show extended channel ip-stack** privileged EXEC command to display information about the IP stack running on the CIP interfaces in a Cisco 7000 with RSP7000 and Cisco 7500 series.

> **show extended channel** *slot/port* **ip-stack** [*ip-address*]

Syntax	Description
slot	Slot number.
port	Port number.
ip-address	(Optional) IP address specified by the **offload** interface configuration command.

Command Mode

Privileged EXEC

Usage Guidelines

This command first appeared in Cisco IOS Release 11.0.

Sample Display

The following is sample output on the Cisco 7000 with RSP7000 from the **show extended channel ip-stack** command:

```
router# show extended channel ip-stack

IP Statistics for IP Address 198.92.1.120
  Forwarding      : fowarding    DefaultTTL     : 2      InReceives    : 3
  InHdrErrors     : 4            InAddrErrors   : 5      ForwDatagrams : 6
  InUnknownProtos : 7            InDiscards     : 8      InDelivers    : 1313371
  OutRequests     : 10           OutDiscards    : 11     OutNoRoutes   : 12
  ReasmTimeout    : 13           ReasmReqds     : 14     ReasmOKs      : 15
  ReasmFails      : 16           FragOKs        : 17     FragFails     : 18
  FragCreates     : 19           RoutingDiscards: 20

IP Statistics for IP Address 198.92.1.121
  Forwarding      : nofoward     DefaultTTL     : 3      InReceives    : 4
  InHdrErrors     : 5            InAddrErrors   : 6      ForwDatagrams : 7
  InUnknownProtos : 8            InDiscards     : 9      InDelivers    : 1313371
  OutRequests     : 11           OutDiscards    : 12     OutNoRoutes   : 13
  ReasmTimeout    : 14           ReasmReqds     : 15     ReasmOKs      : 16
  ReasmFails      : 17           FragOKs        : 18     FragFails     : 19
  FragCreates     : 20           RoutingDiscards: 21
```

SHOW EXTENDED CHANNEL LLC2

Use the **show extended channel llc2** privileged EXEC command to display information about the LLC2 sessions running on the CIP interfaces in a Cisco 7000 with RSP7000 and Cisco 7500 series.

show extended channel *slot/port* **llc2** [**admin** | **oper** | **stats**] [*lmac* [*lsap* [*rmac* [*rsap*]]]]

Syntax	Description
slot	Slot number.
port	Port number.
admin	(Optional) Shows configured values. This is the default.
oper	(Optional) Shows operational values.
stats	(Optional) Shows statistics.
lmac	(Optional) Local MAC address.
lsap	(Optional) Local service access point (SAP) address, 0 to 256.
rmac	(Optional) Remote MAC address.
rsap	(Optional) Remote SAP address, 0 to 256.

Default

The default is **admin**.

Command Mode

Privileged EXEC

Usage Guidelines

This command first appeared in Cisco IOS Release 11.0.

The default mode of this command is to show the **admin** (configured) values.

Sample Display

The following is sample output on the Cisco 7000 with RSP7000 from the **show extended channel llc2** command:

```
router# show extended channel 2/2 llc2 admin

     Vlan Token  0 vadapter   0 0004.0004.0004
 t1-time   = 1000  tpf-time  = 1000  trej-time = 3200  tbusy-tim = 9600
 idle-time =60000  local-win =    7  recv-wind =    7  N2        =    8
 N1        = 1033  ack-delay =  100  ack-max   =    3  nw        =    0
```

SHOW EXTENDED CHANNEL STATISTICS

Use the **show extended channel statistics** privileged EXEC command to display information about the CIP interfaces on the Cisco 7000 with RSP7000 and Cisco 7500 series. This command displays information that is specific to the interface hardware. The information is generally useful only for diagnostic tasks performed by technical support personnel.

> **show extended channel** *slot/port* **statistics** [*path* [*device-address*]]

Syntax	Description
slot	Slot number.
port	Port number.
path	(Optional) Hexadecimal value in the range 0x0000 to 0xFFFF. This specifies the data path and consists of two digits for the physical connection (either on the host or on the ESCON director switch): one digit for the control-unit address, and one digit for the channel logical address. If not specified, the control-unit address and channel logical address default to 0.
device-address	(Optional) Hexadecimal value in the range 0x00 to 0xFE. This value is the unit address associated with the control-unit number and path as specified in the host IOCP file. For CLAW and offload support, the device address must have an even value.

Default

The data path default for the control-unit address and the channel logical address is 0.

Command Mode

Privileged EXEC

Usage Guidelines

This command first appeared in Cisco IOS Release 10.3.

Sample Display

The following is sample output on the Cisco 7000 with RSP7000 from the **show extended channel statistics** command:

```
router# show extended channel 3/0 statistics

Path: C300 - ESTABLISHED
                     Command            Selective   System    Device      CU
  Dev   Connects    Retries   Cancels     Reset      Reset    Errors     Busy
   60        92         85         5         4          1         0         0
   61        94          0         4         3          1         0         0

             Blocks               Bytes          Dropped Blk   Fail
 Dev-Lnk   Read     Write      Read    Write       Read   Write  memd  Con
  60-00       6         0       192        0          8       0     0    Y
  60-01      82         0      7373        0          0       0     0    Y
  Total:     88         0      7565        0          8       0     0
```

```
    61-00        0         4        0      128         0        0       0    Y
    61-01        0        85        0     9081         0        0       0    Y
    Total:       0        89        0     9209         0        0       0

 Path C300
    Total:      88        89     7565     9209         8        0       0

 Last stats 8 seconds old, next in 2 seconds
```

Table 24–3 describes the fields shown in the display.

Table 24–3   *Show Extended Channel Statistics Field Descriptions*

Field	Description
Path	The path from the CLAW, offload, or CSNA configuration. It tells which port on the switch is used by the channel side of the configuration.
Dev	The device address for each device. For CLAW, you get two device addresses. In the configuration statement, you only specify the even address. Both CLAW and offload get two devices and CSNA gets 1.
Connects	The number of times the channel started a channel program on the device.
Command Retries	The number of times the CIP either had no data to send to the channel (for the read subchannel) or the number of times the CIP had no buffers to hold data from the channel (for the write subchannel). Every command retry that is resumed results in a connect. A command retry may be ended via a cancel.
Cancels	The host requested any outstanding operation to be terminated. It is a measure of the number of times the host program was started.
Selective Reset	Selective reset affects only one device, whereas a system reset affects all devices on the given channel. It is a reset of the device. On VM this will occur whenever you have a device attached and issue a CP IPL command.
System Reset	The number of times the system Initial program load (IPL) command was issued. The command is always issued when the ECA is initialized and when the channel is taken off line.
Device Errors	Errors detected by the ECA or PCA due to problems on the link. This value should always be 0.

Table 24–3   *Show Extended Channel Statistics Field Descriptions, Continued*

Field	Description
CU Busy	The number of times the adapter returned a control-unit busy indication to the host. This occurs after a cancel or reset if the host requests an operation before the CIP has finished processing the cancel or reset.
Dev-Lnk	The first number is the device address. The second number is the logical link. Link 0 is always used for CLAW control messages. For IP datagram mode, link 1 is for actual datagram traffic. For offload, link 2 is for API traffic. For CSNA, the Dev-Lnk is not relevant.
Blocks Read/Blocks Write	CLAW uses the even subchannel for reads and the odd subchannel for writes. Each count is one IP datagram or one control message.
Bytes Read/Bytes Write	Bytes is the sum of the bytes in the blocks.
Dropped Blk Read/Write	If the router switch processor sends data to the CIP faster than it can send it to the channel, then the block is dropped. High values mean the host is not running fast enough. There are drops on write, also. A write drop will occur if the CIP fails to get a MEMD buffer n times for a given block. See Failed memd counter.
Failed memd	The number of times the CIP could not obtain a MEMD buffer on the first try. If this value is high, try allocating more large buffers. The memd information does not apply to CSNA devices.
Con	For link 0, connect of Y means the system validation has completed. For all other links, it means the connection request sequence has completed. Con is an abbreviation for connected. For CSNA devices, a value of Y is displayed when the CSNA device status becomes setupComplete. For all other states, the Con shows a value of N.

SHOW EXTENDED CHANNEL SUBCHANNEL

Use the **show extended channel subchannel** privileged EXEC command to display information about the CIP interfaces on the Cisco 7000 with RSP7000 and Cisco 7500 series. This command displays information that is specific to the interface hardware. The information displayed is generally useful only for diagnostic tasks performed by technical support personnel.

> **show extended channel** *slot/port* **subchannel**

Syntax	Description
slot	Slot number.
port	Port number.

Command Mode

Privileged EXEC

Usage Guidelines

This command first appeared in Cisco IOS Release 10.3.

Sample Display

The following is sample output on the Cisco 7000 with RSP7000 from the **show extended channel subchannel** command:

```
router# show extended channel 3/0 subchannel

Channel3/0: state up
  Flags: VALID ESCON LOADED RQC_PEND MEMD_ENABLED
  Link: C4, Buffers 0, CRC errrors 0, Load count 1
  Link Incident Reports
   implicit 0, bit-error 0, link failed 0,
    NOS 0, sequence timeout 0, invalid sequence 0
  Neighbor Node - VALID
    Class: Switch        Type Number : 009033      Tag: C4
    Model: 001           Manufacturer: IBM
    Plant: 51            Sequence    : 000000010067
  Local Node - VALID
    Class: CTCA-standalone Type Number : C7000      Tag: 30
    Model: 0             Manufacturer: CSC
    Plant: 17            Sequence    : 00000C04953F
                                                                    Last
  Mode    Path Device                                               Sense
  CLAW    C300   60   198.92.1.58 CISCOVM AUBURN TCPIP TCPIP        0000
  CLAW    C300   61   198.92.1.58 CISCOVM AUBURN TCPIP TCPIP        0080

  Last stats 1 seconds old, next in 9 seconds
```

The first line describes the status of the specified CIP and port. The status can be up, down, or administratively down:

```
Channel3/0: state up
```

The next line describes the flags on the CIP:

```
Flags: VALID ESCON LOADED RQC_PEND MEMD_ENABLED
```

- VALID—An adapter is installed. All displays should contain this.

- ESCON—The adapter is an ESCON adapter.

- LOADED—The microcode on the adapter is loaded.

- RQC_PEND—The adapter is attempting to send status to the channel.

- MEMD_ENABLED—The adapter is allowed to send and receive datagrams.

- SIGNAL—The ECA signal light is detected.

The next line displays Link Incident Reports:

```
Link Incident Reports
    implicit 0, bit-error 0, link failed 0,
    NOS 0, sequence timeout 0, invalid sequence 0
```

Link Incidents are errors on an ESCON channel. These errors are reported to the host operating system and are recorded here for more information.

Implicit incidents indicate a recoverable error occurred in the ECA.

Bit errors indicate the bit-error rate threshold was reached. The bit-error rate threshold is 15 error bursts within 5 minutes. An error burst is defined as a time period of 1.5+/-.5 seconds during which one or more code violations occurred. A code violation error is caused by an incorrect sequence of 10 bit characters.

Link failed means a loss of synchronization or light has occurred.

NOS means the channel or switch transmitted the Not Operational Sequence.

Sequence timeout occurs when a connection-recovery timeout occurs or when waiting for the appropriate response while in the transmit off-line sequence (OLS) state.

Invalid Sequence occurs when a UD or UDR is recognized in the wait for offline sequence state. UD is an unconditional disconnect and UDR is an unconditional disconnect response.

The neighbor node describes the channel or switch. The local node describes the router. The VALID flag shows information has been exchanged between the router and channel or switch.

The information displayed under Neighbor Node is as follows:

```
Neighbor Node - VALID
    Class: Switch        Type Number : 009033      Tag: C4
    Model: 001           Manufacturer: IBM
    Plant: 51            Sequence    : 000000010067
```

"Class" will be switch or channel depending on whether the connection is a switched point-to-point connection or a point-to-point connection. "Type number" describes the model of switch or processor. "Tag" describes the physical location of the connector. "Model" is a further classification of type. "Manufacturer" describes who made switch or processor. "Plant" and "sequence" are manufacturer-specific information to define uniquely this one device.

The information displayed under Local Node is as follows:

```
Local Node - VALID
   Class: CTCA-standalone Type Number : C7000        Tag: 30
   Model: 0               Manufacturer: CSC
   Plant: 17              Sequence    : 00000C04953F
```

The class will be CTCA. The type number and model define the router. The tag is the slot and port where the channel interface processor resides. The manufacturer always will be CSC (for Cisco Systems). The plant is the location where the CIP was manufactured. The sequence is the base Ethernet address assigned to the route processor (RP).

The last three lines show currently configured information for the inbound and outbound channel connections:

```
                                                              Last
    Mode     Path Device                                      Sense
    CLAW     C300  60    198.92.1.58 CISCOVM AUBURN TCPIP TCPIP   0000
    CLAW     C300  61    198.92.1.58 CISCOVM AUBURN TCPIP TCPIP   0080
```

The mode can be CLAW, offload, or CSNA. The path, device, IP address, and names are from the CLAW command. Because CLAW and offload commands define two devices, both devices are shown. The last sense are the two bytes of sense data transmitted to the host at the time of the last unit exception. Normally, the value will be 0000 if no unit exception has occurred, or 0080 to indicate that a resetting event has occurred. Resetting events occur whenever an ESCON device starts unless the first command is a 0x02 read command. The CLAW read subchannel always starts with a 0x02 read command, so a resetting event will not occur.

SHOW EXTENDED CHANNEL TCP-STACK

Use the **show extended channel tcp-stack** privileged EXEC command to display information about the TCP stack running on the CIP interfaces in a Cisco 7000 with RSP7000 and Cisco 7500 series.

      show extended channel *slot/port* **tcp-stack** [*ip-address*]

Syntax	Description
slot	Slot number.
port	Port number.
tcp-stack	IP address for the TCP stack on the CIP.
ip-address	(Optional) IP address specified in an **offload** interface configuration command or **tn3270-server** PU configuration command.

Command Mode
Privileged EXEC

Usage Guidelines

This command first appeared in Cisco IOS Release 11.0.

Sample Display

The following is sample output on the Cisco 7000 with RSP7000 from the **show channel tcp-stack** command:

```
router# show extended channel tcp-stack

TCP Statistics for IP Address 198.92.1.120
   RtoAlgorithm: other      RtoMin     : 101     RtoMax      : 102
   MaxConn     : 103        ActiveOpens : 104     PassiveOpens: 105
   AttemptFails: 106        EstabResets : 107     CurrEstab   : 108
   InSegs      : 109        OutSegs    : 110     RetransSegs : 111
   InErrs      : 112        OutRsts    : 113

TCP Statistics for IP Address 198.92.1.121
   RtoAlgorithm: constant   RtoMin     : 102     RtoMax      : 103
   MaxConn     : 104        ActiveOpens : 105     PassiveOpens: 106
   AttemptFails: 107        EstabResets : 108     CurrEstab   : 109
   InSegs      : 110        OutSegs    : 111     RetransSegs : 112
   InErrs      : 113        OutRsts    : 114
```

SHOW EXTENDED CHANNEL TG

Use the **show extended channel tg** privileged EXEC command to display configuration, operational information, and statistics information for CMPC transmission groups configured on the specified CIP internal LAN interface.

show extended channel *slot*/**2 tg** [**oper** | **stats**] [**detailed**] [*tg-name*]

Syntax	Description
slot/2	Slot number.
oper	(Optional) Operational parameters for the CMPC transmission-group values.
stats	(Optional) Statistical values for the CMPC transmission group.
detailed	(Optional) Additional LLC information about the CMPC transmission group.
tg-name	(Optional) Information for the specified *tg-name*.

Command Mode

Privileged EXEC

Usage Guidelines

This command first appeared in Cisco IOS Release 11.2 BC.

If neither the **oper** or **stats** arguments are specified, operational values will be displayed.

Sample Displays

The following is sample output on a Cisco 7500 router from the **show extended channel tg oper** command:

```
router# show extended channel 3/2 tg oper detailed MVS2-TG1

CMPC-TG: MVS2-TG1 Status: ACTIVE
   Adapter:token    1   RMAC:4000.4040.1996      LSAP:04        RSAP:04
   TGN    :21          Local CP: NETA.MVS2       Remote CP: NETA.CALEB
   MaxIn  :4105        MaxOut   :4105
   HPR    :NO          HPR LSAP:04               HPR RSAP :00
   RIF    :0830.1FF1.0041.00A0
Connection LLC2 Information:
   t1-time   = 1000  tpf-time  = 1000  trej-time = 3200  tbusy-tim = 9600
   idle-time =60000  local-win =    7  recv-wind =    7  N2        =    8
   N1-Send   = 1033  N1-Rcv    = 1033  ack-delay =  100  ack-max   =    3
   Nw        =    0  Ww        =    7
   Last Ww Cause = other
   Connection Time: 00:00:00 UTC Jan 1 1970
   Last modified: 00:00:00 UTC Jan 1 1970
```

Table 24–4 describes the fields shown in the display.

Table 24–4 *Show Extended Channel Tg Oper Field Descriptions*

Field	Description
Status	Connection status of the CMPC transmission group. Valid values are: • **Shutdown**—CIP internal LAN interface is shutdown. In this state, all nonconfigurable values will not be displayed and the LLC connection operational values displayed when the detailed argument is specified also are not displayed. • **Inactive**—CMPC transmission group is reset ready to activate. • **LocatingRemoteLinkStation**—Exploring network for configured CMPC transmission-group peer. • **RemoteLinkStationLocated**—CMPC transmission-group network peer found. Waiting for connection negotiation to start. • **XID3Negotiation**—XID negotiation in progress. • **PendingActive**—Connect station pending. • **Active**—CMPC transmission-group connection active.

Table 24–4 *Show Extended Channel Tg Oper Field Descriptions, Continued*

Field	Description
Adapter	Identifies the CIP internal MAC adapter configured for this CMPC transmission group. The MAC address configured for this adapter is the local MAC address for the CMPC transmission-group LLC connection.
RMAC	Remote MAC address configured for the CMPC transmission-group LLC connection.
LSAP	Local SAP configured for the CMPC transmission-group LLC connection.
RSAP	Remote SAP configured for the CMCP transmission-group LLC connection.
TGN	Transmission-group number for this CMPC transmission-group LLC connection. This value is extracted from the XID3 negotiation exchange.
Local CP	Control-point name for VTAM. The name is extracted from XID3s received from VTAM.
Remote CP	Control-point name for the remote node connected by this CMPC transmission group. The name is extracted from XID3 received from the remote node.
MaxIn	Maximum PIU the remote node is allowed to send to VTAM. The value is the max PIU field in the XID3s received from VTAM.
MaxOut	Maximum PIU VTAM is allowed to send to the remote node. The value is the lowest of the max PIU field in the XID3 received from the remote node, the LF (length field) size in the RIF and the CIP virtual interface MTU size.
HPR	Valid values are YES and NO. If HPR is active on this CMPC transmission group, then the value will display YES.
HPR LSAP	Local SAP value used for HPR traffic. This value will be the same as the configured local SAP value.
HPR RSAP	Remote SAP value used for HPR traffic. This value is extracted from the XID3s during the connection negotiation between VTAM and the remote node.
RIF	Routing information field. If the CMPC transmission-group LLC connection is established using source-route bridging, then the RIF used for the connection is displayed here.

Part
II

Command Reference

The following is sample output on a Cisco 7500 router from the **show extended channel tg stats** command:

```
router# show extended channel 3/2 tg stats detail MVS2-TG1

CMPC-TG:MVS2ISR1
    IFramesIn   :51              IFramesOut  :41
    IBytesIn    :4378            IBytesOut   :51803
    UIFramesIn  :0               UIFramesOut :0
    UIBytesIn   :0               UIBytesOut  :0
    TESTRspsIn  :1               TESTCmdsOut :1
    XIDCmdsIn   :3               XIDCmdsOut  :3
    XIDRspsIn   :0               XIDRspsOut  :0
    ConnectReqs :2               ConnectInds :0
    ConnectRsps :2               ConnectCnfms:0
    DISCReqs    :1               DISCInds    :0
    SweepReqsIn :0               SweepReqsOut:0
    SweepRspsIn :0               SweepRspsOut:0
    Wraps       :0
    LastSeqNoIn :9               LastSeqNoOut:7
    LastSeqNoFailureCause        : None
TimeSinceLastSeqNoFailure : never
    LLC2 Connection Statistics:
    LAN Token  0 Adapter   1 4000.cdcd.cdcd
      Local SAP=04 Remote MAC=4000.4040.1996 Remote SAP=04
        LocalBusies     =        0  RemoteBusies    =         0
        IFramesIn       =       51  IFramesOut      =        41
        IOctetsIn       =     4378  IOctetsOut      =     51803
        SFramesIn       =        0  SFramesOut      =         0
        REJsIn          =        0  REJsOut         =         0
        RetransmitsOut  =        0  WwCountChanges  =         0
```

The following is sample output on a Cisco 7500 router from the **show extended channel tg stats** command when the interface is shut down:

```
router# show extended channel 3/2 tg stats detail MVS2-TG1

CIP LLC-TG:MVS2ISR1 -Statistics Not Available
```

Table 24–5 describes the fields shown in the display.

Table 24–5 *Show Extended Channel Tg Stats Field Descriptions*

Field	Description
IFramesIn	Number of connection-oriented PIUs received by this CMPC transmission group from the remote network node.
IFramesOut	Number of connection-oriented PIUs sent by this CMPC transmission group to the remote network node.
UIFramesIn	Number of connectionless PIUs (HPR frames) received by this CMPC transmission group from the remote network node.

Table 24–5 *Show Extended Channel Tg Stats Field Descriptions, Continued*

Field	Description
UIFramesOut	Number of connectionless PIUs (HPR frames) sent by this CMPC transmission group to the remote network node.
TestRspsIn	Number of TEST responses received for this CMPC transmission group.
TestCmdsOut	Number of TEST commands sent by this CMPC transmission group to the configured remote MAC address.
XidCmdsIn	Number of XID commands received for this CMPC transmission group.
XidCmdsOut	Number of XID commands sent by this CMPC transmission group.
XidRspsIn	Number of XID responses received for this CMPC transmission group.
XidRspsOut	Number of XID responses sent by this CMPC transmission group.
SweepReqsIn	Number of CMPC sweep requests received from VTAM on this CMPC transmission group.
SweepReqsOut	Number of CMPC sweep requests sent to VTAM on the CMPC transmission group.
SweepRspsIn	Number of CMPC responses received from VTAM on this CMPC transmission group.
SweepRspsOut	Number of CMPC responses sent to VTAM on this CMPC transmission group.
IBytesIn	Number of bytes for connection-oriented PIUs received by this CMPC transmission group from the remote network node.
IBytesOut	Number of bytes for connection-oriented PIUs sent by this CMPC transmission group to the remote network node.
UIBytesIn	Number of bytes for connectionless PIUs received by this CMPC transmission group from the remote network node.
UIBytesOut	Number of bytes for connectionless PIUs sent by this CMPC transmission group to the remote network node.
ConnectReqs	Number of connect requests received from the host by this CMPC transmission group.

Table 24–5   *Show Extended Channel Tg Stats Field Descriptions, Continued*

Field	Description
ConnectInds	Number of connect indications sent to the host by this CMPC transmission group.
ConnectRsps	Number of connect responses received from the host by this CMPC transmission group.
ConnectCnfms	Number of connect confirms sent to the host by this CMPC transmission group.
DISCReqs	Number of disconnect requests received from the host by this CMPC transmission group.
DISCInds	Number of disconnect indications sent to the host by this CMPC transmission group.
Wraps	The number of times the sequence numbers wrapped for this CMPC transmission group.
LastSeqNoIn	The sequence number on the last CMPC data block sent to the host from this CMPC transmission group.
LastSeqNoOut	The sequence number on the last CMPC data block received from the host for this CMPC transmission group.
LastSeqNoFailureCause	The cause of the last sequence number failure for this CMPC transmission group. Valid values are as follows: • None—No sequence-number failures have occurred on this CMPC transmission group since it was configured or the interface was last "no shut." • Block—The sequence-number failure occurred on a MPC data block received from the host for this CMPC transmission group. • Sweep—The sequence number failure occurred on a sweep command received from the host for this CMPC transmission group.
TimeSinceLastSeqNoFailure	Time since the last CMPC sequence-number failure for this CMPC transmission group. If there have been no failures, "never" is displayed.

SHOW EXTENDED CHANNEL TN3270-SERVER

Use the **show extended channel tn3270-server** privileged EXEC command to display current server configuration parameters and the status of the PUs defined in each TN3270 server.

> **show extended channel** *slot*/**2 tn3270-server**

Syntax	Description
slot/**2**	Specifies a particular CIP in the router where slot is the slot number. The port value for a TN3270 server is always 2.

Command Mode

Privileged EXEC

Usage Guidelines

This command first appeared in Cisco IOS Release 11.2.

Sample Display

The following is sample output on the Cisco 7000 with RSP7000 from the **show extended channel tn3270-server** command:

```
router# show extended channel 3/2 tn3270-server

<current stats> < connection stats >  <response time(ms)>
server-ip:tcp      lu in-use  connect disconn fail   host    tcp
172.28.1.106:23    510   1       12      11    0      54      40
172.28.1.107:23    511   0        0       0    0       0       0
172.28.1.108:23    255   0        0       0    0       0       0
total             1276   1
configured max_lu 20000
idle-time    0          keepalive 1800       unbind-action disconnect
tcp-port    23          generic-pool permit no timing-mark
dlur MPX.GOANCP                          status NOTQRYD   SHUT
dlus MPX.NGMVMPC

name(index)   ip:tcp              xid      state   link  destination     r-lsap
EXT2(1)       172.28.1.106:23     05D18092 ACTIVE  tok 0 4000.7470.00e7 08 04
PUS10(2)      172.28.1.107:23     05D19010 ACTIVE  tok 0 4000.7470.00e7 08 2C
PUS11(3)      172.28.1.107:23     05D19011 ACTIVE  tok 0 4000.7470.00e7 08 28
PUS12(4)      172.28.1.108:23     05D19012 ACTIVE  tok 0 4000.7470.00e7 08 24
PUS9(5)       172.28.1.109:23     05D18509 SHUT    tok 0 4001.3745.1088 04 40
SDTF(7)       172.28.1.107:23     12345678 ACTIVE  tok 0 0800.5a4b.1cbc 04 08
TEST(8)       172.28.1.106:23     05D18091 ACTIVE  tok 0 4000.7470.00e7 08 30
INT1(6)       172.28.1.106:23     05D18091 SHUT    dlur
```

Table 24–6 describes significant fields in the display. Those fields not described correspond to configured values.

Table 24–6 *Show Extended Channel TN3270-server Field Descriptions*

Field	Description
SERVER-IP:TCP	IP address and TCP port number, listening point, configured on one or more PUs.
LU *number*	Total number of LUs available for this listening point.
IN-USE *number*	Number of LUs currently in use.
CONNECT *number*	Total number of connects since the TN3270 feature was started.
DISCONN *number*	Total number of disconnects since the TN3270 feature was started.
FAIL *number*	Total number of failed connects since the TN3270 feature was started.
RESPONSE TIME, HOST *number*	The average response time from the host across all sessions through this server IP address. This is measured from sending CD to the host to receiving the reply.
RESPONSE TIME, TCP *number*	Average response time from the clients on this server IP address. This is measured only when TIMING MARKs are sent. If **no timing-mark** is configured, they are only sent on special occasions, such as Bind.
IDLE-TIME *number*	Configured idle time for this PU.
KEEPALIVE *number*	Configured keepalive for this PU.
UNBIND-ACTION *type*	Configured unbind action for LUs on this PU.
TCP-PORT *number*	Configured TCP port number.
GENERIC-POOL *type*	Configured generic pool for LUs on this PU.
DLUR *fq-cpname*	Configured fully qualified DLUR CP name.

Table 24–6 *Show Extended Channel TN3270-server Field Descriptions, Continued*

Field	Description
STATUS	Possible dlur-dlus-status values and their meanings are: reset—The DLUR-DLUS pipe is reset. pnd-actv—The DLUR-DLUS pipe is pending active. active—The DLUR-DLUS pipe is active. pnd-inac—The DLUR-DLUS pipe is pending inactive.
DLUS *fq-dlusname*	Currently active DLUS.
NAME *pu-name*	This is the name of the PU as configured.
IP:TCP *ip-addr:tcpport*	IP address and TCP port number configured for the PU.
XID *number*	Configured XID - idblk and idnum.
STATE *value*	Possible STATE values and their meanings are: • **shut**—The PU is configured, but in shut state. • **reset**—The link station of this PU is not active. • **test**—PU is sending a TEST to establish link. • **xid**—TEST is responded, XID is sent. • **p-actpu**—The link station is up, but no ACTPU is received. • **active**—ACTPU is received and acknowledged positively. • **act/busy**—Awaiting host to acknowledge the SSCP-PU data. • **wait**—Waiting for PU status from CIP. • **other**—PU in undefined state. • **p-rqactpu-r**—DLUR PU is pending request ACTPU response. • **p-active**—ACTPU received by DLUR but not yet passed to PU. • **p-dactpu**—PU is pending DACTPU.

Table 24–6   *Show Extended Channel TN3270-server Field Descriptions, Continued*

Field	Description
LINK *type*	LINK type is either internal-adapter type and internal-adapter number, or dlur if it is an SNA session switch PU.
DESTINATION *mac-address or PU-name*	If a direct PU, then it is the destination MAC address; otherwise, it is the name of the partner PU.
R-LSAP *number number*	Remote and local SAP values.

SHOW EXTENDED CHANNEL TN3270-SERVER CLIENT-IP-ADDRESS

Use the **show extended channel tn3270-server client-ip-address** privileged EXEC command to display information about all clients at a specific IP address.

> **show extended channel** *slot*/2 **tn3270-server client-ip-address** *ip-address* [**disconnected** | **in-session** | **pending**]

Syntax	Description
slot/2	(Optional) Specifies a particular CIP in the router where slot is the slot number. The port value for a TN3270 server always will be 2.
ip-address	IP address of the client.
disconnected	(Optional) Shows all clients with *ip-address* in disconnected state. Disconnected state refers to an LU session state of ACTIVE or INACTIVE. In this case, the *ip-address* refers to the client that last used the LU.
in-session	(Optional) Shows all clients with *ip-address* in active session state. Active session state refers to an LU session state of ACT/SESS.
pending	(Optional) Shows all clients with *ip-address* in pending state. Pending session state refers to an LU session state of P-SDT, P-ACTLU, P-NTF/AV, P-NTF/UA, P-RESET, P-PSID, P-BIND, P-UNBIND, WT-UNBND, WT-SDT or UNKNOWN.

Command Mode
Privileged EXEC

Usage Guidelines
This command first appeared in Cisco IOS Release 11.2.

Note that this command does not show information about LUs that have never been connected.

Sample Display

The following is sample output on the Cisco 7000 with RSP7000 from the **show extended channel tn3270-server client-ip-address** command. The example shows only active sessions because no other session types exist at this client IP address.

```
router# show extended channel 3/2 tn3270-server client-ip 192.195.80.40

lu    name     client-ip:tcp           nail state     model  frames in out   idle for
1     PUS11001 192.195.80.40:3169       Y   ACT/SESS 327804  5        5       0:5:47


pu is PUS11, lu is DYNAMIC type 2, negotiated TN3270
bytes 155 in, 1758 out; RuSize 1024 in, 3840 out; NegRsp 0 in, 0 out
pacing window 0 in, 1 out; credits 0 in, queue-size 0 in, 0 out
```

The following is sample output using the **disconnected** argument:

```
Router# show extended channel 2/2 tn3270 client-ip 10.14.1.21 disconnected
Total 2 clients found using 10.14.1.21
```

The following is sample output using the **in-session** argument:

```
Router# show extended channel 2/2 tn3270 client-ip 10.14.1.21 in-session
Note: if state is ACT/NA then the client is disconnected

lu    name    client-ip:tcp          nail state     model  frames in out   idle for
3     PU1L03 10.14.1.21:35215         N   ACT/SESS 327804  317      316     0:0:1

pu is PU1, lu is DYNAMIC type 2, negotiated TN3270
bytes 12167 in, 225476 out; RuSize 2048 in, 1536 out; NegRsp 0 in, 0 out
pacing window 0 in, 1 out; credits 0 in, queue-size 0 in, 0 out
Note: if state is ACT/NA then the client is disconnected

lu    name    client-ip:tcp          nail state     model  frames in out   idle for
4     PU1L04 10.14.1.21:35216         N   ACT/SESS 327804  317      316     0:0:1

pu is PU1, lu is DYNAMIC type 2, negotiated TN3270
bytes 12167 in, 225476 out; RuSize 2048 in, 1536 out; NegRsp 0 in, 0 out
pacing window 0 in, 1 out; credits 0 in, queue-size 0 in, 0 out
Note: if state is ACT/NA then the client is disconnected
Total 2 clients found using 10.14.1.21
```

The following is sample output using the **pending** argument:

```
Router# show extended channel 2/2 tn3270 client-ip 10.14.1.21 pending
Total 2 clients found using 10.14.1.21
```

Table 24–7 describes significant fields in the display.

Table 24–7 *Show Extended Channel TN3270-server Client-ip-address Field Descriptions*

Field	Description
lu *locaddr*	LOCADDR of the LU.
name *lu-name*	If the PU is directly connected, then the name shown is the one generated by the seed. If DLUR, then only the unqualified portion is shown. The NETID portion will be the same as the current DLUS.
client-ip:tcp *ip-address:port*	Client's IP address and TCP port number
nail	Status of LU nailing, either Y or N
state *lu-state*	The LU state and their meanings are: • **unknown**—LU in an undefined state. • **inactive**—LU did not receive ACTLU. • **active**—LU received ACTLU and acknowledged positively. • **p-sdt**—LU is bound but there is no SDT yet. • **act/sess**—LU is bound and in session. • **p-actlu**—Telnet connects in and is waiting for ACTLU. • **p-ntf/av**—Awaiting host notify-available response. • **p-ntf/ua**—Awaiting host notify-unavailable response. • **p-reset**—Awaiting a buffer to send DACTLU response. • **p-psid**—Awaiting NMVT Reply PSID response. • **p-bind**—Waiting for host to send bind. • **p-unbind**—Awaiting host unbind response. • **wt-unbnd**—Waiting for client to acknowledge disconnection. • **wt-sdt**—Waiting for client to acknowledge SDT.
MODEL *model*	IBM 3278 model type of client; blank if STATIC LU.
FRAMES IN *number*	Number of frames sent inbound to the host.
FRAMES OUT *number*	Number of frames sent outbound from the host.
IDLE FOR *time*	Time the client has been idle. The time is in HH:MM:SS.
PU IS *pu-name*	Name of the PU.

Table 24–7 *Show Extended Channel TN3270-server Client-ip-address Field Descriptions, Continued*

Field	Description
LU IS *type*	Whether LU is DYNAMIC or STATIC.
NEGOTIATED *type*	Whether client is TN3270 or TN3270E.
BYTES IN / OUT *number/number*	Total number of bytes sent to/received from the host.
RUSIZE IN / OUT *number/number*	RU size as configured in the bind.
NEGRSP IN / OUT *number/number*	Number of SNA negative responses sent to/received from the host.
PACING WINDOW IN / OUT *number/number*	SNA pacing window as configured in the bind.
CREDITS IN *number*	Number of frames that can be sent inbound without requiring an isolated pacing response.
QUEUE SIZE IN *number*	Indicates the number of SNA frames waiting to be sent to the host that are blocked and are waiting for a pacing response.
QUEUE SIZE OUT *number*	SNA frames not yet acknowledged by an isolated pacing response by the TN3270 server.

Part II

Command Reference

SHOW EXTENDED CHANNEL TN3270-SERVER DLUR

Use the **show extended channel tn3270-server dlur** privileged EXEC command to display information about the SNA session switch.

> **show extended channel** *slot*/**2 tn3270-server dlur**

Syntax	Description
slot/2	Specifies a particular CIP in the router where slot is the slot number. The port value for a TN3270 server always will be 2.

Command Mode
Privileged EXEC

Usage Guidelines
This command first appeared in Cisco IOS Release 11.2.

Sample Display

The following is sample output on the Cisco 7000 with RSP7000 from the **show extended channel tn3270-server dlur** command:

```
router# show extended channel 3/2 tn3270-server dlur
dlur MPX.GOANCP
current dlus MPX.NGMVMPC              dlur-dlus status ACTIVE
preferred dlus MPX.NGMVMPC           backup dlus MPX.NGMVMPB
preferred server MPX.NGMVMPA
lsap token-adapter  0 5C      vrn MPX.LAN4           status ACTIVE
    link P390            remote 4000.7470.00e7 08  status ACTIVE
```

Table 24–8 describes significant fields in the display.

Table 24–8 *Show Extended Channel TN3270-server Dlur Field Descriptions*

Field	Description
DLUR *fq-luname*	Fully qualified CP name used by the SNA session switch and the LU name for the DLUR function configured as the *fq-cpname* on the dlur statement.
CURRENT DLUS *fq-luname*	Name of the currently active DLUS, either the primary DLUS or the backup DLUS.
DLUR-DLUS STATUS *dlur-status*	Possible *dlur-dlus-status* values and their meanings are: • **reset**—The DLUR-DLUS pipe is reset. • **pnd-actv**—The DLUR-DLUS pipe is pending active. • **active**—The DLUR-DLUS pipe is active. • **pnd-inac**—The DLUR-DLUS pipe is pending inactive.
PREFERRED-DLUS *fq-luname*	Name of the DLUS as configured on the DLUR statement.
BACKUP-DLUS *fq-luname*	Name of the DLUS that is used if the preferred DLUS is unavailable.
PREFERRED SERVER *fq-luname*	Fully qualified name of the preferred network-node server.
LSAP	Configured value for the local SAP on the configured internal adapter. Token adapter specifies the type of internal adapter used.
VRN *fq-name*	Name of the connection network as configured by the vrn statement for this LSAP and internal adapter pair.

Table 24–8 *Show Extended Channel TN3270-server Dlur Field Descriptions, Continued*

Field	Description
LSAP...STATUS status	Possible *sap-status* values and their meanings are: • **inactive**—Not connected to adapter. • **pnd-actv**—SAP activation in progress. • **active**—SAP open. • **pnd-inac**—SAP deactivation in progress.
LINK *name*	Name of the configured link. If not a configured link, then the name is an invented name, @DLUR*nn*.
REMOTE *mac sap*	Remote MAC and SAP for this link.
LINK...STATUS *status*	Possible *link-status* values and their meanings are: • **inactive**—Not connected to host. • **pnd-actv**—Link activation in progress. • **active**—Link active. • **pnd-inac**—Link deactivation in progress.

SHOW EXTENDED CHANNEL TN3270-SERVER DLURLINK

Use the **show extended channel tn3270-server dlurlink** privileged EXEC command to display information about the DLUR components.

> **show extended channel** *slot*/**2 tn3270-server dlurlink** *name*

Syntax	Description
slot/**2**	Specifies a particular CIP in the router where slot is the slot number. The port value for a TN3270 server always will be 2.
name	Name of the SNA session switch link to be displayed.

Command Mode
Privileged EXEC

Usage Guidelines
This command first appeared in Cisco IOS Release 11.2.

Sample Display

The following is sample output on the Cisco 7000 with RSP7000 from the **show extended channel tn3270-server dlurlink** command:

```
router# show extended channel 3/2 tn3270-server dlurlink P390

lsap token-adapter  0 5C   vrn MPX.LAN4          status ACTIVE
link P390                  remote 4000.7470.00e7 08  status ACTIVE
partner MPX.NGMVMPC        tgn 1                 maxdata   1033
```

Table 24–9 describes significant fields in the display.

Table 24–9   *Show Extended Channel TN3270-server Dlurlink Field Descriptions*

Field	Description
LSAP...VRN...STATUS *status*	Possible *sap-status* values and their meanings are: • **inactive**—Not connected to adapter. • **pnd-actv**—SAP activation in progress. • **active**—SAP open. • **pnd-inac**—SAP deactivation in progress.
LINK *name*	Name is an invented name, @DLUR*nn*, if not a configured link.
LINK ...STATUS *status*	Possible *link-status* values and their meanings are: • **inactive**—Not connected to host. • **pnd-actv**—Link activation in progress. • **active**—Link active. • **pnd-inac**—Link deactivation in progress.
PARTNER *name*	CP name of the remote node for this link.
TGN *tg-number*	Transmission-group number for this link. Because the SNA session switch only supports 1 transmission group per pair of CP names, it is typically 0 or 1.
MAXDATA *maxdata*	Maximum frame size allowed on this link.

SHOW EXTENDED CHANNEL TN3270-SERVER NAILED-IP

Use the **show extended channel tn3270-server nailed-ip** privileged EXEC command to display mappings between a nailed-client IP address and nailed LUs.

show extended channel *slot*/**2 tn3270-server nailed-ip** *ip-address*

Syntax	Description
slot/2	Slot number.
ip-address	Specifies remote client IP address.

Command Mode

Privileged EXEC

Usage Guidelines

This command first appeared in Cisco IOS Release 11.2 BC.

Sample Displays

The following is sample output on the Cisco 7000 with RSP7000 from the **show extended channel tn3270-server nailed-ip** command:

```
router# show extended channel 3/2 tn3270-server nailed-ip 172.28.0.0
172.28.1.0   255.255.255.192    pu BAGE1  lu 1     50
172.28.1.80  255.255.255.248    pu BAGE2  lu 100   200    printer
172.28.1.83                     pu BAGE3  lu 1     60     printer
172.28.1.82                     pu BAGE1  lu 100   200
```

Table 24–10 *Show Extended Channel TN3270-server Nailed-ip Field Descriptions*

Field	Description
172.28.1.0	IP address of the nailed client.
255.255.255.192	Network mask for the range of configured nailed clients.
pu BAGE1	PU name under which the **client** command was configured.
lu 1 50	LU LOCADDR range showing first LOCADDR and last LOCADDR. There need not be a last LOCADDR if only a single LOCADDR rather than a range is configured.
printer	Type of device being nailed to the LOCADDRs. If printer is specified, only clients that are printers are nailed to the LOCADDRs. If screen is specified, only clients that are screens are nailed to the LOCADDRs. If neither is specified, both screens and printers can use the LOCADDRs. A printer client is any client with a device type of "328*". A screen client is a client with any other device type.

SHOW EXTENDED CHANNEL TN3270-SERVER PU

Use the **show extended channel tn3270-server pu** privileged EXEC command to display the PU configuration parameters, statistics and all the LUs currently attached to the PU.

   show extended channel *slot*/**2 tn3270-server pu** *pu-name*

Syntax	Description
extended channel *slot*/**2**	(Optional) Specifies a particular CIP in the router where slot is the slot number. The port value for a TN3270 server always will be 2.
pu-name	PU name that uniquely identifies this PU.

Command Mode

Privileged EXEC

Usage Guidelines

This command first appeared in Cisco IOS Release 11.2.

The display shown depends on whether the PU is a direct PU or a SNA session switch PU.

Sample Displays

The following is sample output on the Cisco 7000 with RSP7000 from the **show extended channel tn3270-server pu** command for a direct PU:

```
router# show extended channel 3/2 tn3270-server pu BAGE1


name(index)    ip:tcp         xid       state     link    destination    r-lsap
BAGE1(1)       172.28.1.82:23    05D18081 ACTIVE    tok 0   4000.7470.00e7 08 10
idle-time   0        keepalive 1800       unbind-act discon   generic-pool perm
bytes 560 in, 3765 out; frames 20 in, 27 out; NegRsp 0 in, 0 out
actlus 12, dactlus 0, binds 2

lu   name      client-ip:tcp     nail    state        model   frames in out   idle for
1    BAGE1001  never connected   Y    ACTIVE                1       1      4:50:44
2    BAGE1002  never connected   Y    ACTIVE                1       1      4:50:44
3    BAGE1003  192.195.80.40:2077  N    ACT/SESS     327804   5       5      5:4:36
4    BAGE1004  192.195.80.40:2644  Y    ACTIVE       327804   5       5      0:36:7

client ip        mask            nail-type  lu first  lu last
192.195.80.40   255.255.255.0     screen       1        2
192.195.80.40   255.255.255.0     printer      4
```

The following is sample output on the Cisco 7000 with RSP7000 from the **show extended channel tn3270-server pu** command for a SNA session switch PU:

```
router# show extended channel 3/2 tn3270-server pu INT1

name(index)    ip:tcp          xid       state     link    destination    r-lsap
INT1(5)        172.28.1.106:23    05D18091 ACTIVE    dlur    MPX.GOAN1
```

```
idle-time   0      keepalive   0      unbind-act discon   generic-pool perm
bytes 50 in, out; frames 87 in, 2 out; NegRsp 3 in, 0 out
actlus 2, dactlus 0, binds 0

lu   name   client-ip:tcp      state   model   frames in out   idle for
1    GOAN1X01 never connected   ACTIVE          1       1       0:32:14
2    GOAN1X02 never connected   ACTIVE          1       1.      0:32:14
```

Table 24–11 describes significant fields in the display.

Table 24–11 *Show Extended Channel TN3270-server PU Field Descriptions*

Field	Description
name (index) *pu-name (index)*	Name and index of the PU as configured.
ip:tcp *ip-addr:tcpport*	IP address and TCP port number configured for the PU.
xid *number*	Configured XID - idblk and idnum.
state *pu-state*	Possible state values and their meanings are as follows: • **SHUT**—PU is configured but in shut state. • **RESET**—Link station of this PU is not active. • **TEST**—PU is sending a TEST to establish link. • **XID**—TEST is responded, XID is sent. • **P-ACTPU**—Link station is up but no ACTPU is received. • **ACTIVE**—ACTPU is received and acknowledged positively. • **ACT/BUSY**—Awaiting host to acknowledge the SSCP-PU data. • **WAIT**—Waiting for PU status from CIP. • **UNKNOWN**—Direct PU in undefined state. • **P-RQACTPU-R**—PU is pending request ACTPU response. • **P-ACTIVE**—DLUR PU and direct PU states disagree. • **P-DACTPU**—PU is pending DACTPU. • **DLUR???**—DLUR PU is in undefined state.
link *type*	LINK type is either internal-adapter type and internal-adapter number or dlur if it is a SNA session switch PU.
destination *mac-address* or *pu-name*	If a direct PU, then it is the destination MAC address; otherwise, it is the name of the partner PU.
r-lsap *number number*	Remote and local SAP values.
idle-time *number*	Configured idle time for this PU.

Table 24-11 *Show Extended Channel TN3270-server PU Field Descriptions, Continued*

Field	Description
keepalive *number*	Configured keepalive for this PU.
unbind-act *type*	Configured unbind action for LUs on this PU.
generic-pool *type*	Configured generic pool for LUs on this PU.
bytes in / out *number/number*	Total number of bytes sent to/received from the host for this PU.
frames in / out *number/number*	Total number of frames sent to/received from the host for this PU.
NegRsp in / out *number/number*	Total number of SNA negative responses sent to/received from the host.
actlus *number*	Total number of ACTLUs received from the host.
dactlus *number*	Total number of DACTLUs received from the host.
binds *number*	Total number of BINDs received from the host.
lu *number*	LOCADDR of the LU.
name *lu-name*	Name of the TN3270 LU.
client-ip:tcp *ip-addr:tcpport*	Client's IP address and TCP port number.
nail	Status of LU nailing, either Y or N

Table 24–11 *Show Extended Channel TN3270-server PU Field Descriptions, Continued*

Field	Description
state *lu-state*	The LU states and their meanings are: • **UNKNOWN**—LU in an undefined state. • **INACTIVE**—LU didn't receive ACTLU. • **ACTIVE**—LU received ACTLU and acknowledged positively. • **P-SDT**—LU is bound but there is no SDT yet. • **ACT/SESS**—LU is bound and in session. • **P-ACTLU**—Telnet connects in and is awaiting ACTLU. • **P-NTF/av**—Awaiting host notify-available response. • **P-NTF/UA**—Awaiting host notify-unavailable response. • **P-RESET**—Waiting for a buffer to send DACTLU response. • **P-PSID**—Waiting for NMVT Reply psid response. • **P-BIND**—Waiting for host to send bind. • **P-UNBIND**—Awaiting host unbind response. • **WT-UNBND**—Waiting for client to acknowledge disconnection. • **WT-SDT**—Waiting for client to acknowledge SDT.
model *model*	IBM 3278 model type of client.
frames in *number*	Number of frames sent inbound to the host.
frames out *number*	Number of frames sent outbound from the host.
idle for *time*	Time the client has been idle. The time is in HH:MM:SS.
client ip	Remote client IP address.
mask	Current network mask.
nail-type	LU nailing type, screen or printer.
lu first	First LU address in the range.
lu last	Last LU address in the range, if one is specified in the **client** configuration command.

Part II

Command Reference

SHOW EXTENDED CHANNEL TN3270-SERVER PU LU

Use the **show extended channel tn3270-server pu lu** privileged EXEC command to display information about the TN3270 server LUs running on CIP interface in a Cisco 7000 with RSP7000 and Cisco 7500 series.

> show extended channel *slot*/2 tn3270-server pu *pu-name* **lu** *locaddr* [**history**]

Syntax	Description
slot/2	Specifies a particular CIP in the router where slot is the slot number. The port value for a TN3270 server always will be 2.
pu-name	PU name that uniquely identifies this PU.
locaddr	LU LOCADDR that uniquely identifies the LU.
history	(Optional) Displays the LU trace history.

Command Mode

Privileged EXEC

Usage Guidelines

This command first appeared in Cisco IOS Release 11.2.

Sample Displays

The following is sample output on the Cisco 7000 with RSP7000 from the **show extended channel tn3270-server pu lu** command for a direct PU:

```
router# show extended channel 3/2 tn3270 pu ext2 lu 3

lu   name    client-ip:tcp        state    model    frames in out   idle for
3    EXT2003 171.69.176.77:3829   ACTIVE   327902E  8       9        0:4:43

pu is EXT2, lu is DYNAMIC type 0, negotiated TN3270
bytes 203 in, 2954 out; RuSize 0 in, 0 out; NegRsp 1 in, 0 out
pacing window 0 in, 1 out; credits 0 in, queue-size 0 in, 0 out
```

The following is sample output on the Cisco 7000 with RSP7000 from the **show extended channel tn3270-server pu lu** command for a SNA session switch PU:

```
router# show extended channel 3/2 tn3270 pu int1 lu 1

lu   name    client-ip:tcp        state    model    frames in out   idle for
1    GOAN1X01 171.69.176.77:3828  ACTIVE            4       4        0:4:51

pu is INT1, lu is STATIC type 0, negotiated TN3270E
bytes 74 in, 1219 out; RuSize 0 in, 0 out; NegRsp 0 in, 0 out
pacing window 0 in, 0 out; credits 0 in, queue-size 0 in, 0 out
```

The following is sample output on the Cisco 7000 with RSP7000 from the **show extended channel tn3270-server pu lu history** command:

```
router# show extended channel 3/2 tn3270 pu pus20 lu 1 history

lu     name    client-ip:tcp          state    model   frames in out   idle for
1    PUS20001  192.195.80.40:2480   ACT/SESS 327804    5        4       0:0:8

pu is PUS20, lu is DYNAMIC type 2, negotiated TN3270
bytes 155 in, 1752 out; RuSize 1024 in, 3840 out; NegRsp 0 in, 0 out>pacing window 0 in,
1 out; credits 0 in, queue-size 0 in, 0 out
traces:
        Client connect req
        Reply PSID pos rsp
        actlu req
        bind req
        sdt req
OUT len=12    2Dxxxxxxxx456B80000D0201
IN  len=25    xxxxxxxxxx45EB80000D0201000000
OUT len=53    2Dxxxxxxxx466B800031010303B1
IN  len=10    2D0001010646EB800031
OUT len=10    2D00010106476B8000A0
IN  len=10    2D0001010647EB8000A0
OUT len=1677  2Cxxxxxxxx010381C07EC7114040
IN  len=9     2C0001010001838100
```

Table 24–12 describes significant fields in the display.

Table 24–12   *Show Extended Channel TN3270-server PU LU Field Descriptions*

Field	Description
LU *locaddr*	LOCADDR of the LU.
NAME *lu-name*	Name of the TN3270 LU.
CLIENT-IP:TCP *ip-addr:tcpport*	Client's IP address and TCP port number.

Table 24–12   *Show Extended Channel TN3270-server PU LU Field Descriptions, Continued*

Field	Description
STATE *lu-state*	The LU state and their meanings are: • **unknown**—LU in an undefined state. • **inactive**—LU didn't receive ACTLU. • **active**—LU received ACTLU and acknowledged positively. • **p-sdt**—LU is bound but there is no SDT yet. • **act/sess**—LU is bound and in session. • **p-actlu**—Telnet connects in and is awaiting ACTLU. • **p-ntf/av**—Awaiting host notify-available response. • **p-ntf/ua**—Awaiting host notify-unavailable response. • **p-reset**—Waiting for a buffer to send DACTLU response. • **p-psid**—Waiting for NMVT Reply psid response. • **p-bind**—Waiting for host to send bind. • **p-unbind**—Awaiting host unbind response. • **wt-unbnd**—Waiting for client to acknowledge disconnection. • **wt-sdt**—Waiting for client to acknowledge SDT.
MODEL *model*	3278 model type of client; blank if STATIC LU.
FRAMES IN *number*	Number of frames sent inbound to the host.
FRAMES OUT number	Number of frames sent outbound from the host.
IDLE FOR time	Time the client has been idle. The time is in HH:MM:SS.
PU IS *pu-name*	Name of the PU.
LU IS *type*	Whether LU is DYNAMIC or STATIC.
NEGOTIATED *type*	Whether client is TN3270 or TN3270E.
BYTES IN / OUT *number/number*	Total number of bytes sent to/received from the host.
RUSIZE IN / OUT *number/number*	RU size as configured in the bind.
NEGRSP IN / OUT *number/number*	Number of SNA negative responses sent to/received from the host.

Table 24–12 *Show Extended Channel TN3270-server PU LU Field Descriptions, Continued*

Field	Description
PACING WINDOW IN / OUT *number/number*	SNA pacing window as configured in the bind.
CREDITS IN *number*	Number of frames that can be sent inbound without requiring an isolated pacing response.
QUEUE SIZE IN *number*	If nonzero, indicates the number of SNA frames waiting to be sent to the host that are blocked, waiting for a pacing response.
QUEUE SIZE OUT *number*	SNA frames not yet acknowledged by an isolated pacing response by the TN3270 server.

SHOW EXTENDED CHANNEL UDP-LISTENERS

Use the **show extended channel udp-listeners** privileged EXEC command to display information about the User Datagram Protocol (UDP) listener sockets running on the CIP interfaces in a Cisco 7000 with RSP7000 and Cisco 7500 series.

> **show extended channel** *slot/port* **udp-listeners** [*ip-address*]

Syntax	Description
slot	Slot number.
port	Port number.
udp-listeners	Specifies UDP listener port display.
slot	Slot number.
ip-address	(Optional) IP address specified in an **offload** interface configuration command.

Command Mode

Privileged EXEC

Usage Guidelines

This command first appeared in Cisco IOS Release 11.0.

Sample Display

The following is sample output on the Cisco 7000 with RSP7000 from the **show channel udp-listeners** command:

```
router# show extended channel 4/0 udp-listeners 198.92.1.120

UDP Listener: IP Address 198.92.1.120      LocalPort 0

UDP Listener: IP Address 198.92.1.120      LocalPort 1

UDP Listener: IP Address 198.92.1.120      LocalPort 2

UDP Listener: IP Address 198.92.1.120      LocalPort 3

UDP Listener: IP Address 198.92.1.120      LocalPort 4

router# show extended channel 4/0 udp-listeners 198.92.1.121

UDP Listener: IP Address 198.92.1.121      LocalPort 0

UDP Listener: IP Address 198.92.1.121      LocalPort 1

UDP Listener: IP Address 198.92.1.121      LocalPort 2

UDP Listener: IP Address 198.92.1.121      LocalPort 3

UDP Listener: IP Address 198.92.1.121      LocalPort 4
```

SHOW EXTENDED CHANNEL UDP-STACK

Use the **show extended channel udp-stack** privileged EXEC command to display information about the UDP stack running on the CIP interfaces in a Cisco 7000 with RSP7000 and Cisco 7500 series.

> **show extended channel** *slot/port* **udp-stack** [*ip-address*]

Syntax	Description
slot	Slot number.
port	Port number.
udp-stack	Selects UDP stack display.
ip-address	(Optional) IP address specified in an **offload** interface configuration command.

Command Mode

Privileged EXEC

Usage Guidelines

This command first appeared in Cisco IOS Release 11.0.

Sample Display

The following is sample output on the Cisco 7000 with RSP7000 from the **show extended channel udp-stack** command:

```
router# show extended channel udp-stack

UDP Statistics for IP Address 198.92.1.120
   InDatagrams : 300        NoPorts     : 301
   InErrors    : 302        OutDatagrams: 303

UDP Statistics for IP Address 198.92.1.121
   InDatagrams : 301        NoPorts     : 302
   InErrors    : 303        OutDatagrams: 304
```

SHOW INTERFACES CHANNEL

Use the **show interfaces channel** privileged EXEC command to display information about the CIP interfaces on the Cisco 7000 with RSP7000 and Cisco 7500 series. This command displays information that is specific to the interface hardware. The information displayed is generally useful for diagnostic tasks performed by technical support personnel only.

show interfaces channel *slot/port* [**accounting**]

Syntax	Description
slot	Slot number.
port	Port number.
accounting	(Optional) Shows interface accounting information.

Command Mode

Privileged EXEC

Usage Guidelines

This command first appeared in Cisco IOS Release 10.3.

Sample Display

The following is sample output on the Cisco 7000 with RSP7000 from the **show interfaces channel** command:

```
Router# show interfaces channel 3/0

Channel3/0 is up, line protocol is up
  Hardware is cxBus IBM Channel
```

```
Internet address is 198.92.1.145, subnet mask is 255.255.255.248
MTU 4096 bytes, BW 0 Kbit, DLY 0 usec, rely 255/255, load 1/255
Encapsulation CHANNEL, loopback not set, keepalive not set
ECA type daughter card
Data transfer rate 12 Mbytes  Number of subchannels 1
Last input never, output never, output hang never
Last clearing of "show interface" counters 0:00:04
Output queue 0/0, 0 drops; input queue 0/75, 0 drops
Five minute input rate 0 bits/sec, 0 packets/sec
Five minute output rate 0 bits/sec, 0 packets/sec
   0 packets input, 0 bytes, 0 no buffer
   Received 0 broadcasts, 0 runts, 0 giants
   0 input errors, 0 CRC, 0 frame, 0 overrun, 0 ignored, 0 abort
   0 packets output, 0 bytes, 0 underruns
   0 output errors, 0 collisions, 0 interface resets, 0 restarts
```

Table 24–13 describes the fields shown in the display.

Table 24–13 *Show Interfaces Channel Field Descriptions*

Field	Description
Channel... is {up | down | administratively down}	Indicates whether the interface hardware is currently active (whether synchronization is achieved on an ESCON channel, or whether operational out is enabled on a parallel channel) and whether it has been taken down by an administrator.
line protocol is {up | down | administratively down}	Indicates whether the software processes that handle the line protocol think the line is usable (that is, whether keepalives are successful).
Hardware is	Hardware type.
Internet address is	IP address and subnet mask.
MTU	Maximum transmission unit of the interface.
BW	Bandwidth of the interface in kilobits per second.
DLY	Delay of the interface in microseconds.
rely	Reliability of the interface as a fraction of 255 (255/255 is 100% reliability), calculated as an exponential average over 5 minutes.
load	Load on the interface as a fraction of 255 (255/255 is completely saturated), calculated as an exponential average over 5 minutes. The calculation uses the value from the **bandwidth** interface configuration command.
Encapsulation	Encapsulation method assigned to interface.
loopback	Indicates whether loopbacks are set.

Table 24–13 *Show Interfaces Channel Field Descriptions, Continued*

Field	Description
keepalive	Indicates whether keepalives are set.
daughter card	Type of adapter card.
Data transfer rate	Rate of data transfer.
Number of subchannels	Number of subchannels.
Last input	Number of hours, minutes, and seconds since the last packet was successfully received by an interface. Useful for knowing when a dead interface failed.
Last output	Number of hours, minutes, and seconds since the last packet was successfully transmitted by an interface.
output hang	Number of hours, minutes, and seconds (or never) since the interface was last reset because of a transmission that took too long. When the number of hours in any of the "last" fields exceeds 24 hours, the number of days and hours is printed. If that field overflows, asterisks are printed.
Last clearing	The time at which the counters that measure cumulative statistics (such as number of bytes transmitted and received) shown in this report were last reset to zero. Note that variables that might affect routing (for example, load and reliability) are not cleared when the counters are cleared. These asterisks (***) indicate the elapsed time is too large to be displayed. 0:00:00 indicates the counters were cleared more than 2^{31}ms (and less than 2^{32}ms) ago.
Output queue, drops input queue, drops	Number of packets in output and input queues. Each number is followed by a slash, the maximum size of the queue, and the number of packets dropped due to a full queue.
Five minute input rate, Five minute output rate	Average number of bits and packets transmitted per second in the last 5 minutes.
packets input	Total number of error-free packets received by the system.
bytes input	Total number of bytes, including data and MAC encapsulation, in the error-free packets received by the system.
no buffer	Number of received packets discarded because there was no buffer space in the main system. Compare with ignored count. Broadcast storms on Ethernets and bursts of noise on serial lines are often responsible for no input buffer events.

Part II

Command Reference

Table 24–13   *Show Interfaces Channel Field Descriptions, Continued*

Field	Description
broadcasts	Total number of broadcast or multicast packets received by the interface.
runts	Number of packets that are discarded because they are smaller than the medium's minimum packet size.
giants	Number of packets that are discarded because they exceed the medium's maximum packet size.
input errors	Total number of no buffer, runts, giants, CRCs, frame, overrun, ignored, and abort counts. Other input-related errors also can increment the count, so that this sum might not balance with the other counts.
CRC	Number of code-violation errors seen on the ESCON interface, where a received transmission character is recognized as invalid. On a parallel interface, the number of parity errors seen.
frame	Number of packets received incorrectly having a CRC error and a noninteger number of octets. This value is always 0.
overrun	Number of times the serial receiver hardware was unable to hand received data to a hardware buffer because the input rate exceeded the receiver's ability to handle the data. This value is always 0.
ignored	Number of received packets ignored by the interface because the interface hardware ran low on internal buffers. These buffers are different than the system buffers mentioned previously in the buffer description. Broadcast storms and bursts of noise can cause the ignored count to be incremented.
abort	Illegal sequence of one bits on a serial interface. This usually indicates a clocking problem between the serial interface and the data-link equipment. This value is always 0.
packets output	Total number of messages transmitted by the system.
bytes	Total number of bytes, including data and MAC encapsulation, transmitted by the system.
underruns	Sum of all errors that prevented the final transmission of datagrams out of the interface being examined. Note that this might not balance with the sum of the enumerated output errors, as some datagrams might have more than one error, and others might have errors that do not fall into any of the specifically tabulated categories.

Table 24-13 *Show Interfaces Channel Field Descriptions, Continued*

Field	Description
output errors	Number of output errors.
collisions	Number of collisions detected. This value is always 0.
interface resets	Number of times an interface has been completely reset. This can happen if packets queued for transmission were not sent within several seconds. On a serial line, this can be caused by a malfunctioning modem that is not supplying the transmit clock signal, or by a cable problem. If the system notices that the carrier-detect line of a serial interface is up, but the line protocol is down, it periodically resets the interface in an effort to restart it. Interface resets also can occur when an interface is looped back or shut down. On the Channel Interface Processor (CIP), this might occur if the host software is not requesting data
restarts	Number of times the controller was restarted because of errors.

SHUTDOWN

Use the **shutdown** interface configuration command to shut down a physical interface or the internal LAN interface on the CIP when you are in interface configuration mode. The **shutdown** command also shuts down TN3270 entities, such as PU, DLUR, and DLUR SAP, depending on which configuration mode you are in when the command is issued. Use the **no** form of this command to restart the interface or entity. The entity affected depends on the mode in which the command is issued.

> shutdown
> no shutdown

Syntax   Description

This command has no arguments or keywords.

Default

The interface or entity is enabled.

Command Modes

CIP interface configuration

TN3270 configuration

PU configuration

DLUR configuration

DLUR SAP configuration

Usage Guidelines

This command first appeared in Cisco IOS Release 11.2.

In CIP interface configuration mode, the command applies to the entire CIP.

In TN3270 configuration mode, the command applies to the whole TN3270 Server.

In PU configuration mode, the command applies to the DLUR or direct PU.

In DLUR configuration mode, the command applies to the whole DLUR subsystem.

In DLUR SAP configuration mode, the command applies to the local SAP.

Example

The following command issued in TN3270 configuration mode shuts down the entire TN3270 server:

```
shutdown
```

TCP-PORT

Use the **tcp-port** TN3270 configuration command to override the default TCP port setting of 23. Use the **no** form of this command to restore the default.

> **tcp-port** *port-number*
> **no tcp-port**

Syntax	Description
port-number	A valid TCP port number in the range of 0 to 65534. The default is 23, which is the IETF standard. The value 65535 is reserved by the TN3270 server.

Defaults

In TN3270 configuration mode, the default is 23.

In PU configuration mode, the default is the value currently configured in TN3270 configuration mode.

Command Modes

TN3270 configuration

PU configuration

Usage Guidelines

This command first appeared in Cisco IOS Release 11.2.

The **tcp-port** command can be entered in either TN3270 configuration mode or PU configuration mode. A value entered in TN3270 mode applies to all PUs for that TN3270 server, except as overridden by values entered in PU configuration mode. The **tcp-port** command affects only future TN3270 sessions.

The **no tcp-port** command entered in PU configuration mode removes the override.

Example

The following command entered in TN3270 configuration mode returns the TCP port value to 23:

```
no tcp-port
```

TG

Use the **tg** interface configuration command to define LLC connection parameters for the CMPC transmission group. Use the **no** form of this command to remove the specified transmission group from the configuration, which also deactivates the transmission group.

tg *name* **llc** *type adapter-number lsap* [**rmac** *rmac*] [**rsap** *rsap*]
no tg *name*

Syntax	Description
name	The name of the CMPC transmission group. The maximum length of the name is eight characters. This must match the name specified on the **cmpc** statements.
llc	Specifies that this TG is connected to the LLC stack on the CIP card.
type	Internal adapter type on the CIP card, which corresponds to the value specified in the **lan** internal LAN configuration command. The currently supported type is **token-adapter**.
adapter-number	Internal-adapter number on the CIP card, which is the same value specified in the **adapter** internal LAN configuration command.
lsap	Local SAP number, 04 to FC, in hexadecimal. The value must be even and normally should be a multiple of four. It must be unique within the internal adapter in that no other IEEE 802.2 clients of that adapter, in the router or in a host, can use the same SAP.

Syntax	Description
rmac *rmac*	(Optional) Remote MAC address of the form *xxxx.xxxx.xxxx* in hexadecimal. If not specified, a loopback link to another SAP on the same internal LAN adapter is assumed.
rsap *rsap*	(Optional) Remote SAP address, 04 to FC in hexadecimal. The *rsap* value must be even and should be a multiple of 4, but this requirement is not enforced. The *rsap* value default is 04.

Default

The *lsap* and *rsap* values default to 04.

Command Mode

Interface configuration

Usage Guidelines

This command first appeared in Cisco IOS Release 11.2 BC.

The **tg** command defines an LLC connection with a complete addressing 4-tuple. The *lsap*, *rmac*, and *rsap* are specified explicitly by parameters. The *lmac* is the local MAC address of the adapter referred to by the *type* and *adapter-number* parameters.

To change any parameter of the **tg** command, the TG must be removed by using **no tg** *name*.

The **no tg** command removes the CMPC transmission group from the configuration. If the transmission group is used for a non-HPR connection, all sessions using the TG will be terminated immediately. If the transmission group is an HPR connection, all sessions using the transmission group will be terminated if no other HPR connection is available to the host.

This command is valid only on the CIP internal interface, *slot*/**2**.

Example

The following example configures a transmission-group name and includes the *rmac* and *rsap* parameters:

```
tg LAGUNAA  llc token-adapter 1  18 rmac 4000.0000.beef rsap 14
```

Related Commands

cmpc

TN3270-SERVER

Use the **tn3270-server** interface configuration command to start the TN3270 server on a CIP or to enter TN3270 configuration mode. Use the **no** form of this command to disable all TN3270 server activity on a CIP.

tn3270-server
no tn3270-server

Syntax Description

This command has no arguments or keywords.

Default

No TN3270 server function is enabled.

Command Mode

Interface configuration

Usage Guidelines

This command first appeared in Cisco IOS Release 11.2.

Only one TN3270 server can run on a CIP. It always will be configured on port 2, which is the internal LAN interface port.

The **no tn3270-server** command shuts down TN3270 server immediately. All active sessions will be disconnected and all DLUR and PU definitions deleted from the router configuration. To restart a TN3270 server, you must reconfigure all parameters.

Example

The following command starts the TN3270 server and enters TN3270 configuration mode:

```
tn3270-server
```

TIMING-MARK

Use the **timing-mark** TN3270 configuration mode command to select whether a WILL TIMING-MARK is transmitted when the host application needs an SNA response (definite or pacing response). Use the **no** form of the command to turn off WILL TIMING-MARK transmission except as used by the keepalive function.

timing-mark
no timing-mark

Syntax Description

This command has no arguments or keywords.

Default

No WILL TIMING-MARKS are transmitted except by keepalive.

Command Mode

TN3270 configuration

Usage Guidelines

This command first appeared in Cisco IOS Release 11.2.

If **timing-mark** is configured, the TN3270 server will send WILL TIMING-MARK as necessary to achieve an end-to-end response protocol. Specifically, TIMING-MARK will be sent if any of the following are true:

- The host application has requested a pacing response.
- The host application has requested a Definite Response, and either the client is not using TN3270E, or the request is not Begin Chain.

The use of the **timing-mark** command can degrade performance. Some clients do not support **timing-mark** used in this way. Therefore, **timing-mark** should only be configured where both of the following are true:

- All clients support this usage.
- The application benefits from end-to-end acknowledgment.

Example

The following command enables TIMING-MARK transmission:

```
timing-mark
```

Related Commands

idle-time
keepalive

UNBIND-ACTION

Use the **unbind-action** TN3270 configuration command to select what action to take when the TN3270 server receives an UNBIND. Use the **no** form of this command to restore the default.

> **unbind-action** {keep | disconnect}
> **no unbind-action**

Syntax	Description
keep	No automatic disconnect will be made by the server upon receipt of an UNBIND.
disconnect	Session will be disconnected upon receipt of an UNBIND.

Defaults

In TN3270 configuration mode, the default is **disconnect**.

In PU configuration mode, the default is the value currently configured in TN3270 configuration mode.

Command Modes

TN3270 configuration

PU configuration

Usage Guidelines

This command first appeared in Cisco IOS Release 11.2.

The **unbind-action** command can be entered in either TN3270 configuration mode or PU configuration mode. A value entered in TN3270 mode applies to all PUs for that TN3270 server, except as overridden by values entered in PU configuration mode. The **unbind-action** command affects currently active and future TN3270 sessions.

The **no unbind-action** command entered in PU configuration mode removes the override.

The **unbind-action** command affects currently active and future TN3270 sessions.

Example

The following command prevents automatic disconnect:

```
unbind-action keep
```

VRN

Use the **vrn** DLUR SAP configuration command to tell the SNA session switch which connection network the internal-adapter interface on the CIP card belongs to. Use the **no** form of this command to remove a network name.

> **vrn** *vrn-name*
> **no vrn**

Syntax	Description
vrn-name	Fully qualified name.

Default

The adapter is not considered to be part of a connection network.

Command Mode

DLUR SAP configuration

Usage Guidelines

This command first appeared in Cisco IOS Release 11.2.

The **vrn** command is used to discover routes without having to configure all possible links.

A connection network is also known as a shared-access transport facility (SATF). This means, at the MAC level, that all nodes in the network can reach each other using the same addressing scheme and without requiring the services of SNA session routing. A bridged LAN (whether source-route or transparent) is an example. Such a network is represented in the APPN topology as a kind of node, termed a virtual routing node (VRN).

To make use of this function, all APPN nodes must use the same VRN name for the SATF.

Refer to the VTAM operating system documentation for your host system for more information regarding the VTAM VNGROUP and VNNAME parameters on the PORT statement of an XCA major node.

Several parameters in the DLUR configuration mode consist of fully qualified names as defined by the APPN architecture. Fully qualified names consist of two case-insensitive alphanumeric strings, separated by a period. However, for compatibility with existing APPN products, including VTAM, the characters "#" (pound), "@" (at), and "$" (dollar) are allowed in the fully qualified name strings. Each string is from one to eight characters long; for example, RA12.NODM1PP. The portion of the name before the period is the NETID and is shared between entities in the same logical network.

Example

The following command sets a VRN name for the TN3270 internal adapter on the CIP:

```
vrn SYD.BLAN25
```

Related Commands

adapter
lan

Ethernet Type Codes

Table A–1 lists known Ethernet type codes. You can use these type codes in transparent bridging and source-route bridging access lists for filtering frames by protocol type. For configuration information on filtering by protocol type, see "Filtering Transparently Bridged Packets" in Chapter 1, "Configuring Transparent Bridging," and "Securing the SRB Network" in Chapter 3, "Configuring Source-Route Bridging."

Table A–1 *Ethernet Type Codes*

Hexadecimal	Description (Notes)
0000-05DC	IEEE 802.3 Length Field
0101-01FF	Experimental; for development (conflicts with 802.3 length fields)
0200	Xerox PARC Universal Protocol (PUP) (conflicts with IEEE 802.3 length fields)
0201	Xerox PUP Address Translation (conflicts with IEEE 802.3 length fields)
0400	Nixdorf Computers (Germany)
0600	Xerox XNS IDP
0660-0661	DLOG (Germany)
0800	DOD Internet Protocol (IP) * * #†
0801	X.75 Internet
0802	NBS Internet
0803	ECMA Internet
0804	CHAOSnet

Table A–1 *Ethernet Type Codes, Continued*

Hexadecimal	Description (Notes)
0805	X.25 Level 3
0806	Address Resolution Protocol (for IP and CHAOS)
0807	XNS Compatibility
081C	Symbolics Private
0888-088A	Xyplex
0900	Ungermann-Bass (UB) Network Debugger
0A00	Xerox IEEE 802.3 PUP
0A01	Xerox IEEE 802.3 PUP Address Translation
0BAD	Banyan VINES IP
0BAE	Banyan VINES Loopback
0BAF	Banyan VINES Echo
1000	Berkeley trailer negotiation
1001-100F	Berkeley trailer encapsulation for IP
1600	VALID system protocol
4242	PCS Basic Block Protocol
5208	BBN Simnet Private
6000	DEC unassigned
6001	DEC Maintenance Operation Protocol (MOP) Dump/Load Assistance
6002	DEC MOP Remote Console
6003	DEC DECnet Phase IV Route
6004	DEC Local Area Transport (LAT)
6005	DEC DECnet Diagnostics
6006	DEC Customer Protocol
6007	DEC Local-Area VAX Cluster (LAVC), SCA
6008	DEC unassigned
6009	DEC unassigned
6010-6014	3Com Corporation

Table A–1 *Ethernet Type Codes, Continued*

Hexadecimal	Description (Notes)
7000	Ungermann-Bass (UB) Download
7001	UB diagnostic/loopback
7002	UB diagnostic/loopback
7020-7029	LRT (England)
7030	Proteon
7034	Cabletron
8003	Cronus VLN
8004	Cronus Direct
8005	HP Probe protocol
8006	Nestar
8008	AT&T
8010	Excelan
8013	Silicon Graphics diagnostic (obsolete)
8014	Silicon Graphics network games (obsolete)
8015	Silicon Graphics reserved type (obsolete)
8016	Silicon Graphics XNS NameServer, bounce server (obsolete)
8019	Apollo Computers
802E	Tymshare
802F	Tigan, Inc.
8035	Reverse Address Resolution Protocol (RARP) (Stanford)
8036	Aeonic Systems
8038	DEC LANBridge Management
8039-803C	DEC unassigned
803D	DEC Ethernet CSMA/CD Encryption Protocol
803E	DEC unassigned
803F	DEC LAN Traffic Monitor Protocol
8040-8042	DEC unassigned

Table A–1 *Ethernet Type Codes, Continued*

Hexadecimal	Description (Notes)
8044	Planning Research Corporation
8046-8047	AT&T
8049	ExperData (France)
805B	Versatile Message Translation Protocol RFC 1045 (Stanford)
805C	Stanford V Kernel, production
805D	Evans & Sutherland
8060	Little Machines
8062	Counterpoint Computers
8065-8066	University of Massachusetts at Amherst
8067	Veeco Integrated Automation
8068	General Dynamics
8069	AT&T
806A	Autophon (Switzerland)
806C	ComDesign
806D	Compugraphic Corporation
806E-8077	Landmark Graphics Corporation
807A	Matra (France)
807B	Dansk Data Elektronik A/S
807C	University of Michigan
807D-807F	Vitalink Communications
8080	Vitalink TransLAN III Management
8081-8083	Counterpoint Computers
809B	Kinetics EtherTalk (AppleTalk over Ethernet)
809C-809E	Datability
809F	Spider Systems, Ltd.
80A3	Nixdorf Computers (Germany)
80A4-80B3	Siemens Gammasonics, Inc.

Table A–1 *Ethernet Type Codes, Continued*

Hexadecimal	Description (Notes)
80C0-80C3	Digital Communications Association (DCA), Inc.
80C1	DCA Data Exchange Cluster
80C4	Banyan VINES IP
80C5	Banyan VINES Echo
80C6	Pacer Software
80C7	Applitek Corporation
80C8-80CC	Intergraph Corporation
80CD-80CE	Harris Corporation
80CF-80D2	Taylor Instrument
80D3-80D4	Rosemount Corporation
80D5	IBM SNA Services over Ethernet
80DD	Varian Associates
80DE	Integrated Solutions Transparent Remote File System (TRFS)
80DF	Integrated Solutions
80E0-80E3	Allen-Bradley
80E4-80F0	Datability
80F2	Retix
80F3	Kinetics AppleTalk Address Resolution Protocol (AARP)
80F4-80F5	Kinetics
80F7	Apollo Computer
80FF-8103	Wellfleet Communications
8107-8109	Symbolics Private
8130	Hayes Microcomputer Products, Ltd. (formerly Waterloo Microsystems, Inc.)
8131	VG Laboratory Systems
8132-8136	Bridge Communications, Inc.
8137	Novell NetWare IPX (old)
8137-8138	Novell, Inc.

Table A–1   *Ethernet Type Codes, Continued*

Hexadecimal	Description (Notes)
8139-813D	KTI
8148	Logicraft, Inc.
8149	Network Computing Devices
814A	Alpha Micro
814C	SNMP
814D-814E	BIIN
814F	Technically Elite Concepts, Inc.
8150	Rational Corporation
8151-8153	Qualcomm, Inc.
815C-815E	Computer Protocol Pty, Ltd.
8164-8166	Charles River Data Systems, Inc.
817D-818C	Protocol Engines, Inc.
818D	Motorola Computer X
819A-81A3	Qualcomm, Inc.
81A4	ARAI Bunkichi
81A5-81AE	RAD Network Devices
81B7-81B9	Xyplex
81CC-81D5	Apricot Computers
81D6-81DD	Artisoft, Inc.
81DE-81E0	Hewlett Packard
81E6-81EF	Polygon, Inc.
81F0-81F2	Comsat Laboratories
81F3-81F5	Science Applications International Corporation (SAIC)
81F6-81F8	VG Analytical, Ltd.
8203-8205	Quantum Software Systems, Ltd.
8221-8222	Ascom Banking Systems, Ltd.
823E-8240	Advanced Encryption Systems, Inc.

Table A–1 *Ethernet Type Codes, Continued*

Hexadecimal	Description (Notes)
827F-8282	Athena Programming, Inc.
8263-826A	Charles River Data Systems
829A-829B	Institute for Industrial Information Technology, Ltd.
829C-82AB	Taurus Controls, Inc.
82AC-838F	Walker Richer & Quinn, Inc.
8390	LANSoft, Inc.
8391-8693	Walker Richer & Quinn, Inc.
8694-869D	Idea Courier
869E-86A1	Computer Network Technology Corporation
86A3-86AC	Gateway Communications, Inc.
86DB	SECTRA - Secure Transmission AB
86DE	Delta Controls, Inc.
86DF	USC-ISI
86E0-86EF	Landis & Gyr Powers, Inc.
8700-8710	Motorola, Inc.
8711-8720	Cray Communications
8725-8728	Phoenix Microsystems
8739-873C	Control Technology, Inc.
8755-8759	LANSoft, Inc.
875A-875C	Norland
875D-8766	University of Utah Dept./Computer Science
8780-8785	Symbol Technologies, Inc.
8A96-8A97	Invisible Software
9000	Loopback (Configuration Test Protocol)
9001	3Com (Bridge) XNS Systems Management
9002	3Com (Bridge) TCP/IP Systems Management
9003	3Com (Bridge) loop detect

Table A-1 *Ethernet Type Codes, Continued*

Hexadecimal	Description (Notes)
FF00	BBN VITAL LANBridge cache wakeups
FF00-FF0F	ISC-Bunker Ramo

[*] An asterisk (*) indicates the current connection in various informational displays.
[†] A pound sign (#) is a delimiting character for configuration commands that contain arbitrary text strings.

Index

Numerics

3174 cluster controller (IBM), reporting frame-copied errors, 229

A

access
  expressions
    combining administrative filters, 220–221
    configuration, 221–222
    modifying, 222–223
    optimizing, 222
    SRB, defining, 252–253
  filters, NetBIOS, configuring for SRB security, 215–217
  access servers, 4, 789–790
  see also access lists
access lists
  assigning
    names to network stations, 275–276
    to input interfaces, 322–323
    to interfaces, 135–136
    to output interfaces, 327–328
  associating with bridge
    group interfaces, 139
  Ethernet type codes (table), 1199, 1206

expressions
  modifying, 222–223
  table, 252–253
extended
  assocating with interfaces, 146
  generating, 117–119
standard, generating, 119–120
type-code, generating, 120–122
vendor code criteria, 253–255
access-expression command, 222
access-list command, 117–122, 218–219, 253–255
acknowledgments
  delay, setting maximum, 592
  require, 592–593
  transmission, criteria, 592
ACSII character sets, specifying, 543–544
activation request units, *see* RUs
active poll lists, specifying cycles, 549–550
adapter command, 1119–1120
adaptive SDLC (Synchronous Data Link Control), enabling T1 connections, 630–631
addresses
  MAC (Media Access Control)
    configuring on Cisco Token Ring, 270–271
    filtering frames, 123–124
    static configuration, 453–454

multicast, forwarding, 81, 154–155
SDLC (Synchronous Data Link Control),
attaching to DLSw+, 626
adjacent-cp-name command, 864, 899
administrative filters
combining, 220–221
configuring for SRB security, 217–220
transparently bridged packets, 81–89
Advanced Peer-to-Peer Networking, *see* APPN
all-route broadcasts,
NetBIOS, enabling, 441
SNA (Systems Network Architecture),
enabling, 441–442
explorer packets, forwarding, 193
see also explorers
any-to-any connectivity, enabling for multiport
bridging, 189–191
Apollo Domain protocol, SRB (source-route
bridging), appending RIF information, 197
AppleTalk protocol, SRB (source-route bridging),
appending RIF information, 197
applications, LNM (LAN Network Manager), SRB
support, 208–214
applying passwords to LRM reporting links, 213
APPN (Advanced Peer-to-Peer Networking),
851, 899
activating
retries, specifying, 964–965
links, 911
ports, 912
routing, 910
startup connection, specifying, 921
subsystem, 911
ATM (Asynchronous Transfer Mode)
configuration (example), 890
destination, 863
links, specifying, 915
BTUs, specifying
maximum receive size, 950
maximum send size, 927
buffers, specifying, 918
capacity, specifying, 931–932
central directory server, 48, 853
central resource registration, 48
disabling, 853, 919
enabling, 854

Cisco's implementation, 40
command modes, 851–852
configuration
examples, 877, 898
services, 44
connections
network, defining, 868
restricting node types, 865
control point, defining, 853–854, 902
COS (class of service)
defining, 869–871, 920
specifying, 900
cost per byte, specifying, 922–923
cost per connection, specifying, 924–925
CP-CP session, permitting, 926
custom queuing, 865
database storage, 969–971
deactivating
links, 914
ports, 915
routing, 913
definitions, completing, 852
destination LU, specifying, 907
directories, saving, 855
directory services, 48
DLUR/DLUS (Dependent Logical Unit
Requestro/Server), 51
backup default, specifying, 916–917
node, specifying, 929–930
permitting function, 928
specifying node, 928
DSPU (Downstream Physical Units), specifying, 961
FDDI configuration (example), 880
Frame Relay
configuration (example), 881
destination, 863
links, specifying, 933
HPR (High-Performance Routing)
enabling, 856
hpr max-sessions command, 856
hpr retries command, 856, 937
hpr sap command, 858, 938
hpr timers liveness command, 856, 939
hpr timers path-switch command, 856,
940

hpr-max-sessions command, 937
link definition configuration, 863
link station configuration, 863
port configuration, 858–860
resources, limiting, 856
ISR (integrated source routing), enabling, 941
limited resources, 875
link stations
active, specifying maximum, 949
default value configuration, 861–862
defining, 862–863
inbound, specifying maximum, 962
name, specifying, 904
outbound, specifying maximum, 963
port, specifying, 957
role, specifying, 966–967
starting and stopping, 874–875
locate throttling, 875
media supported, 41
memory usage, specifying
buffers, 918
cached directory entries, 947
cached routing trees, 948
maximum available, 948
minimum available, 951
mode, defining, 871–872, 905
monitoring
class of service, 977
connection network, 980
dependent LUs, 983
dependent PUs, 984
directory entries, 982
LUs, 986
mode, 993
network, 876–877
node, 994
ports, 996
SNA sessions, 988, 1001
topology, 1003
negative caching, 875–876
networks
monitoring, 876
name, specifying, 901, 976
tuning, 875
node row, specifying, 953

over DLSw+, 22
configuration (example), 883
virtual data link control, 857
over Ethernet LANE, 891
examples, 892
router priority, 898
SRB to switched ATM, network migration
(figure), 897
typical topology (figure), 891
partial name LUs (logical units),
specifying, 873
partner locations, defining, 872–873
partner node, specifying, 899
ATM link, 915
Ethernet link, 942
FDDI link, 942
Frame Relay link, 933
LU-LU session, 907
PPP link, 958
QLLC, 1019
SDLC, 972
SMDS address, 1007
Token Ring link, 942
ports
assigning MAC address, 860–861
defining, 857–858, 908
starting and stopping, 874–875
PPP (Point-to-Point Protocol)
configuration (example), 890
destination, 863
links, specifying, 958
primary servers, configuration, 866
QLLC
example, 889
link, specifying, 1019
X.25 subaddress, configuring, 1020
queuing priority, specifying, 944
route selection, determining
bit rate, specifying, 931–932
cost per byte, 922–923
cost per connection, 924–925
local node, 968
propagation delay, 959–960
routing services, 49

RSRB (Remote Source-Route Bridging)
    configuring, 968
    example, 882
    port, defining, 909
RTP (Rapid Transport Protocol) connection,
    activating, 908
SAP (service access point), activating, 945
scalability enhancements, 875
SDLC (Synchronous Data Link Control)
    configuration example, 882
    link, specifying, 972
    secondary address, configuring, 973
searching resources, 875
security, specifying, 973–974
serial interface encapsulation,
    configuration, 857
session service, 50
SMDS (Switched Multimegabit Data Service)
    configuration (example), 890
    destination, 864
subsystem, starting and stopping, 874
Token Ring configuration (example), 879
transmission, specifying
    groups, 1007–1008
    priority, 1010
virtual data link control
    configuring, 1016
    port, defining, 909
    ring-group, specifying, 1016
    virtual MAC address option, specifying,
        1016
X.25 destination, 864
XID, specifying, 1021
appn class-of-service command, 870, 900
appn connection-network command, 868, 901
appn control-point command, 853, 902
APPN High Performance Routing, *see* APPN, HPR
appn link-station command, 862, 904
appn mode command, 871, 905
appn partner-lu-location command, 872, 907
appn path-switch command, 908
appn port command, 857, 908
appn routing command, 874, 910
appn start command, 874, 911
appn start link-station command, 911
appn start port command, 912

appn stop command, 874, 913
appn stop link station command, 875
appn stop link-station command, 914
appn stop port command, 875, 915
architecture, NCIA (native client interface
    architecture), 1023
AS/400 (application system/400), FRAS (Frame
    Relay Access Support) LLC2 local
    termination, 826
ASP (asynchronous security protocols), Cisco's
    tunneling implementation, 27
asp addr-offset command, 540
asp role command, 541
asp rx-ift command, 542–543
assigning
    access list names to network stations, 275–276
    access lists to input interfaces, 322–323
    access lists to interfaces, 135–136
    access lists to output interfaces, 327–328
    byte offset access list names, 217
    interfaces to bridge groups, 134–135
    interfaces to BSTUN groups, 551
    IP address to local routers (RSRB), 348
    MAC addresses to APPN ports, 860–861
    priority groups to input interfaces, 379–380
    ring groups to Token Ring interfaces
        (multiport bridging), 191
    secondary stations to serial links, 624–625
    STUN-enabled routers primary or secondary
        role, 494
associating
    extended access lists with interfaces, 146
    SAPs with X.25 serial interfaces, 686–687
    virtual MAC addresses with PVC, 716–717
    XIDs with remote X.25 devices, 689–691
asynchronous
    networks, 512–515
    security protocols, *see* ASP, 27
    transfer mode, *see* ATM
ATM (Asynchronous Transfer Mode)
    APPN partner node, specifying, 915
    transparent bridging, configuration, 68
atm-dest-address command, 863, 915
AUTOGEN definition, adjusting for SDLLC, 679
automatic spanning tree, 194–195, 255–256

autonomous
    bridging, enabling, 78–79, 133–134
    switching
        enabling, 334–335
        SRB networks, 224

B

backup
    peers, DLSw+ (Data Link Switching Plus), 408–409
    queue (SRB), modifying, 400–401
backup-dlus command, 854, 866
    APPN control point, 916
    APPN link station, 917
bandwidth, LAT, reducing on serial interfaces, 141
beaconing, 210
Binary Synchronous Communications, see Bisync
Bisync (binary synchronous communication), 27, 510–511
    frame sequencing, 515
    multidrop operation, 512
    point-to-point operation, 511
    routers
        specifying as primary end, 547–548
        specifying as secondary end, 548–549
    statistics, displaying, 570–574
    traffic, encapsulating and routing, 27
block serial tunneling, see BSTUN
blocking
    explorer packets, 193–194
    spanning explorers, 338–339
boards (processor), displaying statistics, 292–297
border peer caching (DLSw+), disabling, 417, 446–447
BPDU (bridge protocol data unit) intervals, configuration, 90–91
bridge acquire command, 122–123
bridge address command, 123
bridge bridge command, 124–125
bridge cmf command, 127–128
bridge command, 62
bridge crb command, 128
bridge domain command, 129–130

bridge forwarding database, viewing classes, 167–169
bridge forward-time command, 130–131
bridge hello-time command, 151–152
bridge irb command, 152–153
bridge lat-service-filtering command, 153
bridge max-age command, 153
bridge multicast-source command, 154–155
bridge priority (spanning-tree) configuration, 90
bridge priority command, 155–156
bridge protocol command, 156–157
bridge protocol ibm command, 255–256
bridge route command, 157–158
bridge-group aging-time command, 132
bridge-group cbus-bridging command, 133–134
bridge-group circuit-group command, 134–135
bridge-group command, 131–132
bridge-group input-lat-service-deny command, 136–137
bridge-group input-lat-service-permit command, 137–138
bridge-group input-lsap-list command, 138–139
bridge-group input-pattern-list command, 139
bridge-group input-type-list command, 140–141
bridge-group lat-compression command, 141
bridge-group output-address-lis command, 141–142
bridge-group output-lat-service-deny command, 142–143
bridge-group output-lat-service-permit command, 143–144
bridge-group output-lsap-list command, 144–145
bridge-group output-pattern-list command, 146
bridge-group output-type-list command, 146–147
bridge-group path-cost command, 147–148
bridge-group priority command, 148–149
bridge-group spanning-disabled command, 149–150
bridge-group sse command, 150–151
bridge-group virtual interface, see BVI
bridging, 68, 202
    autonomous, enabling, 78–79, 133–134
    between dissimilar media, 10
    Frame Relay networks, enabling, 164–165

groups
    assigning interfaces, 131–132, 134–135
    automatic spanning-tree, enabling, 194–195
    BVI (bridge-group virtual interfaces, specifying, 165–166
    DLSw+ (Data Link Switching plus), defining, 406
    group codes, specifying access denial, 136–137, 142–144
    interfaces, associating with access lists, 139
    path costs, 147–148
    permitting access, 137–138, 144–145
    routing, enabling, 157–158
    spanning tree, automatic, 255–256
    specifying protocols for bridging, 124–125, 152–153
    status, displaying, 171–172
IBM 8209, SR/TLB translation compatibility, 202
links, establishing between source-route and transparent bridging, 339–341
logical configuration, displaying, 301–303
numbers (RIF), 196
parameters, displaying, 301
RSRB (Remote Source-Route Bridging), SDLLC configuration, 655–656
    see also RSRB
SR/TLB (source-route translational bridging), 199–201
SRB (source-route bridging), 188, 196
    disabling LNM support, 211–212
    dual-port configuration, 189
    enabling bridging with SRB, 201
    enabling RIFs, 197
    fast-switching FDDI configuration, 192
    FDDI configuration, 191–192
    Frame Relay configuration, 193
    limiting hops, 196
    LNM support, 208–214
    maintenance, 229–230
    multiport, 190–191
    NetBIOS support, 203–208
    over Frame Relay, 811–812
    routed protocol configuration, 196–198
    tuning, 223–227

tables
    aging time (transparent bridging), configuration, 81
    dynamic entries, timout configuration, 132
transit, 7
translational, SDLLC configuration, 657–658
transparent
    configuration, 62–63
    displaying multicast state information, 172–173
    examples, 95–115
    forwarding multicast addresses, 81
    preventing dynamically determined station forwarding, 80
    see also SRT, 62
bsc char-set command, 543
bsc contention command, 543–544
bsc dial-contention command, 544
bsc host-timeout command, 545–546
bsc pause command, 546
bsc poll-timeout command, 546–547
bsc primary command, 547–548
bsc retries command, 548
bsc secondary command, 548–549
bsc servlim command, 549–550
bsc spec-poll command, 550
BSTUN (Block Serial Tunneling), 509, 523
    Cisco's implementation, 27
    enabling, 516, 553–554
    groups, defining, 554–555
    over Frame Relay, enabling passthrough, 560–561
    overview, 23
    peers, removing, 556–558
    protocol groups, defining, 517
    queuing priorities, customizing, 567–569
    serial interface configuration, 558–559
    see also STUN
bstun group command, 519, 551
bstun keepalive-count command, 551–552
bstun lisnsap command, 552–553
bstun peer-name command, 553–554
bstun protocol-group command, 517, 554–555
bstun remote-peer-keepalive command, 555
bstun route address command, 519

bstun route command, 556–558

buffer-percent command, 853, 918

busy stations (LLC2), repolling, 594–595

BVI (bridge-group virtual interface), 8, 165–166

byte

    access list filters, defining for incoming messages, 277–278

    offsets, NetBIOS access filter configuration, 216–217

C

cache

    NetBIOS, clearing dynamically learned entries, 256–257

    RIF (routing information field)

        clearing entries, 257

        enabling synchronization, 291–292

        static entry configuration, 198

    SRB, enabling, 223–224

central directory server, blocking registration attempts, 853

central resource registration, 48

    enabling, 854

    disabling, 853, 919

    feature defined

central routers, configuration, 544–545

central-resource-registration command, 854, 919

channel attach interfaces

    ECA (ESCON channel adapter) interface configuration, 1121–1123

    specifying, 1133–1134

Channel Interface Processor, *see* CIP

channel-protocol command, 1058, 1060, 1121

character sets, specifying, 543–544

CIP (Channel Interface Processor)

    3172 offload function, 1052

    access list, defining, 1058, 1061

    assigning IP address, 1057, 1060

    autonomous switching, 1058, 1061

    channel interfaces, showing, 1056

    CLAW (Common Link Access for Workstations), 1052

        configuration (example), 1096

        device parameters, defining, 1058

        device_address argument, defining, 1066

        path, defining, 1064

CMPC (Cisco Multipath Channel), configuration, 1089

    transmission groups, 1093

    internal LANs, 1094

    local SNA major node, 1092

    read/write subchannels, 1093

    TN3270 server DLUR (example), 1116

    TRL major node, 1092

    VTAM

    VTAMfor two CIP cards (example), 1110

    VTAM local SNA major node, 1092

    VTAM to APPN (example), 1107

    VTAM to APPN on remote router with DLUR (example), 1113

    VTAM to remote PC (example), 1105

    VTAM TRL major node, 1092

configuration

    examples, 1096

    tasks, 1057, 1059

connections, 1052

CSNA (CIP Systems Network Architecture)

    channel information, 1062

    configuration (example), 1097

    LAN support using MAC adapters, 1053

ECA (ESCON Channel Adapter), 1051

ESCON (Enterprise-Systems Connection) director switch, 1064

Flash memory, using, 1055

host system

    configuration files, 1058, 1060

    derived IODEVICE ADDRESS (example), 1067

    DEVICE statement, 1067

    IOCP control unit statements, 1065

    LINK statement, 1067

    TCP/IP configuration file, 1067

    UNITADD parameter, 1066

IBM

    host TCP/IP application, 1064

    operating system file parameters, 1064

IGRP, configuration, 1057, 1059

interfaces

    clearing and resetting, 1070

    configuring, 1058, 1060

    shutting down and restarting, 1070

internal LAN interface configuration, 1063, 1082, 1094

IP (Internet Protocol)
address, assigning, 1057, 1060
route cache, disabling, 1058, 1061
network masks (example), 1096

LLC2 for internal LAN interface, configuration, 1063, 1095

loading Flash image, 1055

loopback support, 1071

memory requirements, 1055

monitor interface status, 1069

offload
configuration (example), 1096
support, 1052, 1059
tasks, configuration, 1144–1146

PCA (Parallel Channel Adapter) data transfer rate, defining, 1058

routing process for CLAW support, configuring, 1057

SNA support, 57

software, loading, 1055

TCP/IP offload support, 57

TN3270 server, 57
APPN, configuring multiple hosts, 1083
configuration modes, 1079, 1082, 1101
DLUR (Dependent Logical Unit Requestor), configuration, 1087
dynamic LU under VTAM, 1075
emulating a terminal, 1071
host values for VTAM, 1076
LU formation, 1072
model type definitions, 1072
monitoring, 1089
non-APPN hosts, configuration, 1083
PU under DLUR, configuration, 1085, 1088
service access point under DLUR, configuration, 1087
SNA support, configuration, 1083
TN3270E clients, 1072–1073
VTAM release 3.4, 1075
VTAM, multiple host support, 1073–1074

VTAM and XCA support, 1052

CIP Systems Network Architecture, *see* CIP, CSNA

circuits
DLSw+ (Data Link Switching Plus)
closing, 417, 439–440
displaying, 478–479
groups
configured interfaces, displaying, 170–171
delay interval, configuration, 125–126
transparent bridging configuration, 92–93

Cisco
7000 series routers, reinitializing SSP, 258–259
MultiPath Channel, *see* CIP, CMPC; CMPC

class-of-service command, 871, 920

CLAW (Common Link Access for Workstations), 1052

claw command, 1058, 1066, 1121–1123

clear bridge command, 158

clear bridge multicast command, 158–159

clear counters command, 1070

clear dlsw circuit command, 439–440

clear dlsw reachability command, 440

clear dlsw statistics command, 440–441

clear interface command, 1070

clear ncia circuit command, 1034, 1039–1040

clear ncia client command, 1034, 1040

clear ncia client registered command, 1034, 1040–1041

clear netbios-cache command, 256–257

clear rif-cache command, 257

clear source-bridge command, 257–258

clear sse command, 159–160, 258–259

clear vlan statistics command, 160

clearing
multicast state information from transparent bridging, 158–159
NetBIOS cache, dynamically learned entries, 256–257
RIF cache, entries, 257
source-bridge counters, 257–258

client command, 1088, 1123–1126

clients
displaying information, 1170–1174
TN3270, specifing keepalive time, 1137–1138

clock rate command, 659

closing DLSw+ circuits, 417

CMPC (Cisco Multipath Channel), displaying subchannel information, 1150–1152
cmpc command, 1126–1127
collecting RIF information, 271–273
coloring transparently bridged packets, 65
combining administrative filters, 220–221
command modes, APPN, 851–852
commands
 DLUR configuration
  dlus-backup, 1130–1131
  link, 1139–1140
  lsap, 1140–1142
  preferred-nnserver, 1146–1147
  pu, 1147–1148
  vrn, 1197–1198
 EXEC
  clear bridge multicast, 158–159
  sdlc test serial, 642–643
  show bridge circuit-group, 170–171
  show bridge multicast, 172
  show controllers token, 361
  show interfaces, 361
  show lnm bridge, 214
  show lnm config, 214
  show lnm interface, 214
  show lnm ring, 215
  show lnm station, 215
  show local-ack, 361
  show ncia client, 1047–1049
  show ncia server, 1049–1050
  show qllc, 700–702
  show span, 313–314
  show sse summary, 180–181, 314–315
  show startup-config, 205
 global configuration
  access-list, 117–122, 218–219, 253–255
  bridge, 62
  bridge acquire, 122–123
  bridge address, 123
  bridge bridge, 124–125
  bridge cmf, 127–128
  bridge crb, 128
  bridge domain, 129–130
  bridge forward-time, 130–131
  bridge hello-time, 151–152
  bridge irb, 152–153

bridge lat-service-filtering, 153
bridge max-age, 153
bridge multicast-source, 154–155
bridge priority, 155–156
bridge protocol, 156–157
bridge protocol ibm, 255–256
bridge route, 157–158
bridge-group aging-time, 132
bstun keepalive-count, 551–552
bstun lisnsap, 552–553
bstun peer-name, 553–554
bstun protocol-group, 517, 554–555
bstun remote-peer-keepalive, 555
dlsw allroute-netbios, 441
dlsw allroute-sna, 441–442
dlsw bgroup-list, 442–443
dlsw bridge-group, 443–445
dlsw disable, 445
dlsw duplicate-path-bias, 446
dlsw group cache disable, 446–447
dlsw group-cache max entries, 447–448
dlsw icannotreach saps, 448–449
dlsw icanreach, 449–450
dlsw llc2 nornr, 450–451
dlsw local-peer, 451–453
dlsw mac-addr, 453–454
dlsw netbios-keepalive-filter, 454–455
dlsw netbios-name, 455–456
dlsw peer-on-demand-defaults, 456–458
dlsw port-list, 458–459
dlsw prom-peer-defaults, 459–460
dlsw remote-peer frame relay, 461–463
dlsw remote-peer fst, 463–465
dlsw remote-peer interface, 465–467
dlsw remote-peer tcp, 467–470
dlsw ring-list, 470–471
dlsw timer, 471–473
dlsw udp-disable, 473–474
dspu activation-window, 751–752
dspu default-pu, 752–753
dspu host, 758–765
dspu lu, 765–766
dspu ncia, 766–767
dspu ncia enable-pu, 767–768
dspu notification-level, 768–769
dspu pool, 769–770

dspu pu, 770–776
dspu rsrb, 777–779
dspu rsrb enable-host, 779–780
dspu rsrb enable-pu, 780–781
dspu rsrb start, 781–782
dspu vdlc, 783–784
dspu vdlc enable-host, 784–786
dspu vdlc enable-pu, 786–787
dspu vdlc start, 787–788
encapsulation frame-relay, 518
interface channel, 1133–1134
interface serial, 518
ip routing, 166
lnm disabled, 212, 263–264
lnm pathtrace-disabled, 212, 266–267
lnm snmp-only, 212, 269
locaddr-priority-list, 360, 380–382
location, 789–790
ncia client, 1042–1043
ncia rsrb, 1043–1044
ncia server, 1044–1046
netbios access-list bytes, 217, 273–275
netbios access-list host, 216, 275–276
netbios name-cache, 207, 279–280
netbios name-cache name-len, 206,
    280–281
netbios name-cache proxy-datagram, 206,
    281–282
netbios name-cache query-timeout, 208,
    282–283
netbios name-cache recognized-timeout,
    208, 283
netbios name-cache timeout, 283–284
nterface fddi, 192
outing, 166
priority-list protocol bstun, 564–565
priority-list protocol ip tcp, 565–566
priority-list stun address, 566–567
queue-list protocol bstun, 567–568
queue-list protocol ip tcp, 568–569
rif, 286–287
rif timeout, 287–288
rif validate-age, 206, 288–289
rif validate-enable, 289–290
rif validate-enable-age, 290–291
rif validate-enable-route-cache, 291–292

rsrb remote-peer lsap-output-list,
    384–385
rsrb remote-peer netbios-output-list,
    385–386
sap-priority-list, 387
sna host, 795–801
sna rsrb enable-host, 802–803
sna rsrb start, 803–804
sna vdlc, 805–806
sna vdlc enable-host, 806–807
sna vdlc start, 807–808
source-bridge, 192
source-bridge connection-timeout, 225
source-bridge cos-enable, 360, 389–390
source-bridge enable-80d5, 318–319
source-bridge explorer-dup-ARE-filter,
    226, 320
source-bridge explorer-fastswitch,
    320–321
source-bridge explorer-maxrate, 226, 321
source-bridge explorerq-depth, 226, 322
source-bridge fst-peername, 390, 704–705
source-bridge largest-frame, 361,
    391–392
source-bridge passthrough, 355, 392–394
source-bridge proxy-netbios-only, 205,
    331
source-bridge qllc-local-ack, 705–706
source-bridge remote-peer frame-relay,
    394–395
source-bridge remote-peer fst, 395–397,
    706–707
source-bridge remote-peer ftcp, 397–398
source-bridge remote-peer interface,
    707–709
source-bridge remote-peer tcp, 398–400,
    709–710
source-bridge ring-group, 191, 332–333,
    710–711
source-bridge route-cache cbus, 192
source-bridge sap-80d5, 336–337
source-bridge sdllc-local-ack, 712
source-bridge tcp-queue-max, 361,
    400–401
source-bridge transparent, 339–341
source-bridge transparent fastswitch,
    341–342

stun keepalive-count, 579, 581
stun protocol-group, 581–582
stun remote-peer-keepalive, 582–583
stun schema offset length format,
    587–588
interface configuration
    access-expression, 222
    asp addr-offset, 540
    asp role, 541
    asp rx-ift, 542–543
    bridge-group, 131–132
    bridge-group cbus-bridging, 133–134
    bridge-group circuit-group, 134–135
    bridge-group input-lat-service-deny,
        136–137
    bridge-group input-lat-service-permit,
        137–138
    bridge-group input-lsap-list, 138–139
    bridge-group input-pattern-list, 139
    bridge-group input-type-list, 140–141
    bridge-group lat-compression, 141
    bridge-group output-address-lis, 141–142
    bridge-group output-lat-service-deny,
        142–143
    bridge-group output-lat-service-permit,
        143–144
    bridge-group output-lsap-list, 144–145
    bridge-group output-pattern-list, 146
    bridge-group output-type-list, 146–147
    bridge-group path-cost, 147–148
    bridge-group priority, 148–149
    bridge-group spanning-disabled, 149–150
    bridge-group sse, 150–151
    bsc char-set, 543
    bsc contention, 543–544
    bsc dial-contention, 544–545
    bsc host-timeout, 545–546
    bsc pause, 546
    bsc poll-timeout, 546–547
    bsc primary, 547–548
    bsc retries, 548
    bsc secondary, 548–549
    bsc servlim, 549–550
    bsc spec-poll, 550
    bstun group, 519, 551
    bstun route, 556–558

bstun route address, 519
channel-protocol, 1121
claw, 1121–1123
cmpc, 1126–1127
csna, 1127–1129
dspu enable-host, 753–755
dspu enable-pu, 756–758
dspu start, 782–783
encapsulation bstun, 558–559
encapsulation sdlc, 610
encapsulation sdlc-primary, 611–612
encapsulation sdlc-secondary, 612–613
encapsulation stun, 559–560
ethernet-transit-oui, 162–164, 259–261
frame-relay map bridge broadcast,
    164–165
frame-relay map bstun, 518, 560–561
frame-relay map llc2, 561
interface bvi, 165–166
lan, 1138–1139
lan-name, 789
llc2 ack-delay-time, 613–614
llc2 ack-max, 614–615
llc2 idle-time, 615–616
llc2 local-window, 616–617
llc2 n2, 617–618
llc2 t1-time, 618–619
llc2 tbusy-time, 619
llc2 tpf-time, 620–621
llc2 trej-time, 621–622
llc2 xid-neg-val-time, 622
llc2 xid-retry-time, 623–624
llc2?tbusy-time, 620
llc2?xid-neg-val-time, 623
lnm alternate, 213, 261–262
lnm crs, 262–263
lnm loss-threshold, 214, 264–265
lnm password, 213, 265–266
lnm rem, 267–268
lnm rps, 268–269
lnm softerr, 214, 269–270
locaddr-priority, 360, 379–380
locaddr-priority-list, 562–563
mac-address, 270–271
multiring, 271–273
netbios enable-name-cache, 277

netbios input-access-filter bytes, 217, 277–278

netbios input-access-filter host, 216, 278–279

netbios output-access-filter bytes, 217, 284–285

netbios output-access-filter host, 216, 285–286

offload, 1144–1146

priority-group, 382–384, 563–564

qllc accept-all-calls, 681–682

qllc dlsw, 474–475

qllc largest-packet, 682–684

qllc npsi-poll, 684–685

qllc partner, 685–686

qllc sap, 686–687

qllc srb, 687–688

qllc xid, 689–690

sap-priority, 386

sdlc address, 624–625

sdlc address ff ack-mode, 625–626

sdlc dlsw, 475–476, 626

sdlc dte-timeout, 626–627

sdlc frmr-disable, 627–628

sdlc holdq, 628–629

sdlc k, 629–630

sdlc line-speed, 630–631

sdlc n1, 631

sdlc n2, 632

sdlc partner, 632–633

sdlc poll-limit-value, 633–634

sdlc poll-pause-timer, 634–635

sdlc poll-wait-timeout, 636–637

sdlc qllc-prtnr, 637

sdlc role, 638–639

sdlc sdlc-largest-frame, 639

sdlc simultaneous, 639–640

sdlc slow-poll, 640–641

sdlc t1, 641–642

sdlc virtual-multidrop, 569–570

sdlc vmac, 644

sdlc xid, 644–645

sdllc partner, 690–691

sdllc ring-largest-frame, 692–693

sdllc sap, 693–694

sdllc sdlc-largest-frame, 694

sdllc traddr, 695–696

sdllc xid, 696–697

sna enable-host, 793–795

sna rsrb, 802

sna start, 804–805

source-bridge, 188–189, 315–318, 355

source-bridge input-address-list, 219, 322–323

source-bridge input-lsap-list, 218, 323–324

source-bridge input-type-list, 219, 324–325

source-bridge keepalive, 391

source-bridge max-hops, 325

source-bridge max-in-hops, 326

source-bridge max-out-hops, 326–327

source-bridge output-address-list, 220, 327–328

source-bridge output-lsap-list, 218, 328–329

source-bridge output-type-list, 219, 329–330

source-bridge proxy-explorer, 330–331

source-bridge route-cache, 223, 333–334

source-bridge route-cache cbus, 334–335

source-bridge route-cache sse, 335

source-bridge spanning, 337–339

stun group, 578–579

stun route address interface dlci, 583–584

stun route address interface serial, 584–585

stun route address tcp, 585–586

stun route all interface serial, 586–587

stun route all tcp, 587

stun sdlc-role primary, 588–589

stun sdlc-role secondary, 589–590

tg, 1193–1194

tn3270-server, 1194–1195

x25 map bridge, 182–185

x25 map qllc, 713–716

x25 pvc qllc, 716–717

internal adapter configuration

max-llc2-sessions, 1142

name, 1144

internal LAN configuration, adapter, 1119–1120

privileged EXEC
    clear bridge, 158
    clear dlsw circuit, 439–440
    clear dlsw reachability, 440
    clear dlsw statistics, 440–441
    clear ncia circuit, 1039–1040
    clear ncia client, 1040
    clear ncia client registered, 1040–1041
    clear netbios-cache, 256–257
    clear rif-cache, 257
    clear source-bridge, 257–258
    clear sse, 159–160, 258–259
    clear vlan statistics, 160
    ncia, 1041–1042
    show bridge, 167–169
    show bridge group, 171–172
    show bridge vlan, 173–174
    show bsc, 570–575
    show bstun, 575–577
    show controllers token, 292–297
    show dlsw capabilities, 476–478
    show dlsw circuits, 478–479
    show dlsw fastcache, 480
    show dlsw peers, 481–483
    show dlsw reachability, 483–486
    show dlsw statistics, 486
    show dspu, 790–792
    show extended channel, 1152–1153
    show extended channel cmpc, 1150–1152
    show extended channel ip-stack,
      1153–1154
    show extended channel llc2, 1154–1155
    show extended channel statistics,
      1155–1158
    show extended channel subchannel,
      1158–1161
    show extended channel tcp-stack, 1161
    show extended channel tg, 1162–1167
    show extended channel tn3270-server,
      1167–1170
    show extended channel tn3270-server
      client-ip-address, 1170–1174
    show extended channel tn3270-server
      dlur, 1174–1176
    show extended channel tn3270-server
      dlurlink, 1176–1177
    show extended channel tn3270-server
      nailed-ip, 1177–1178

    show extended channel tn3270-server pu,
      1178–1182
    show extended channel tn3270-server pu
      lu, 1182–1185
    show extended channel udp-listeners,
      1185–1186
    show extended channel udp-stack,
      1186–1187
    show interfaces, 645–648, 697–700
    show interfaces channel, 1187–1191
    show interfaces crb, 174–176
    show interfaces irb, 177
    show interfaces tokenring, 297–300
    show llc2, 648–651
    show lnm bridge, 301
    show lnm config, 301–303
    show lnm interface, 303–305
    show lnm ring, 305–306
    show lnm station, 306–308
    show local-ack, 388–389
    show ncia circuits, 1046–1047
    show netbios-cache, 308–309
    show rif, 309–310
    show sdllc local-ack, 703–704
    show sna, 792–793
    show source-bridge, 310–313
    show span, 178–180
    show stun, 577–578
    show vlans, 181–182
subinterface configuration
    encapsulation isl, 161
    encapsulation sde, 161–162
TN3270 configuration
    client, 1123–1124
    dlur, 1129–1130
    generic-pool, 1131–1132
    idle-time, 1132–1133
    ip precedence, 1134–1135
    ip tos, 1135–1137
    keepalive TN3270, 1137–1138
    maximum-lus, 1142–1144
    pu, 1148–1150
    shutdown, 1191–1192
    tcp-port, 1192–1193
    timing-mark, 1195–1196
    unbind-action, 1196–1197

TN3270 PU configuration, client, 1124–1126

Common Link Access for Workstations, *see* CIP, CLAW

compatibility, SR/TLB translation with IBM 8209 bridges, 202

complete command, 856

completing APPN definitions, 852

components, DLUR (Dependent Logical Unit Requestor), displaying information, 1176–1177

compression, LAT, enabling, 79

concurrent routing and bridging, 128
    configuration, 73–74
    see also integrated routing and bridging

configuration
    APPN
        connection networks, 868–869
        COS (class of service), 869–871
        custom queuing, 865
        examples, 877, 898
        HPR, 856
        link definitions, 863
        link station default values, 861–862
        local node relative resistance, 854–855
        Locate Throttling, 875
        modes, 871–872
        negative caching, 875–876
        partner location, 872–873
        primary servers (DLUS), 866
        relative resistance, 854–855
        serial interface encapsulation, 857
        subsystem, 874
        transmission group characteristics, 866–867
        type 2.0 nodes, 866
    asynchronous
        links, 512–513
        ports, 540–541
    bridging
        groups, path costs, 147–148
        tables, dynamic entry timeout, 132
        X.25 packets, 182–185
    BSTUN, 509, 516, 523, 538
        defining protocol groups, 517
        on serial interfaces, 558–559
    CIP (Channel Interface Processor), offload tasks, 1144–1146

circuit groups, delay interval, 125–126

CMPC (Cisco Multipath Channel), subchannels, 1126–1127

concurrent routing and bridging, 73–74

DLSw+ (Data Link Switching Plus)
    backup peers, 408–409
    defining bridge groups, 406
    defining local peers, 404–405
    defining remote peers, 406–407
    defining ring lists, 405–406
    defining source-bridge ring groups, 404
    direct encapsulation, 406–407
    duplicate path handling, 416
    examples, 418, 438
    FST encapsulation, 407
    group cache, maximum entry configuration, 415
    peer-on-demand, 415
    promiscuous peer defaults, 415
    reachable resources, 449–450
    ring lists, 470–471
    sessions, 1024–1025
    static paths, 416
    static resources capabilities exchange, 415–416
    TCP encapsulation, 408
    timers, 414

downstream PU connections, 756

explorers
    interface response criteria, 330–331
    maximum byte rate, 321

fast switching SRB over FDDI, 192

Frame Relay
    DLSw+ backup, 813–814
    RSRB backup, 813

FRAS (Frame Relay Access Support)
    examples, 815–823
    BAN (Boundary Access Node), 811
    BNN (Boundary Network Node), 810–811
    DLCI backup, 812–813
    Host, 827–828

FST peer names, 704–705

integrated routing and bridging, 74–77

interfaces
    displaying bridging information, 174–176

priority, 148–149
source-route bridging, 315–317
LLC2
    polling, 594–595
    repolling, 594–595
    setting maximum delay for
        acknowledgments, 592
    transmit-poll-frame timer, 595
    XID transmission, 595–596
NCIA (native client interface architecture),
    1025–1026
NetBIOS name caching, 204–208
    character length configuration, 206
    packet deadtime interval, 207–208
    timeout, 206
QLLC conversion, 660–663
    associating XID with X.25 devices,
        662–663
    customizing, 663–665
    examples, 672–677
REM (Ring-Error VTAM Monitor), 267–268
remote source-bridging peers
    configuration, 391
reporting link passwords (LNM), 265–266
RPS (Ring Parameter Service), 268–269
RSRB
    over FST connection, 347–349
    over FTCP/IP connection, 351–352
    over point-to-point connection, 346–347
    over TCP/IP connection, 350–355
RUs (activation request units), 751–752
SDLC (Synchronous Data Link Control)
    primary stations, 611–612
    secondary stations, 612–613
SDLLC
    associating SAP value, 654
    enabling media translation, 654
    examples, 666–672
    initiating connection to Token Ring
        host, 655
    RSRB, 655–656
    specifying XID value, 654
    with Direct Connection, 653–654
spanning tree, 89–91
SR/TLB (source-route translational bridging),
    199–201

SRB (source-route bridging), 188, 196
    bridging with transparent bridging, 201
    dual-port bridges, 189
    examples, 230, 249
    explorer packet forwarding, 194
    LNM support, 208–214
    multiple dual-port, 189
    multiport, 190–191
    NetBIOS support, 203–208
    over FDDI, 191–192
    over Frame Relay, 193, 811–812
    proxy explorers, 227
    remote peer connections timeout, 225
    RIF static entries (routed protocols), 198
    RIF timeout interval (routed
        protocols), 198
    routed protocols, 196–198
    security, 215–220
STUN (Serial Tunnel)
    assigning routers SDLC primary or sec-
        ondary role, 494
    defining custom protocol, 491
    establishing encapsulation method, 491
    HDLC (High Level Data Link Protocol)
        encapsulation without local
        acknowledgment, 492
    protocol group specification, 489–490
    SDLC broadcast, 488–489
    TCP encapsulation with local
        acknowledgment, 493–495
    TCP encapsulation without local
        acknowledgment, 492
    traffic priorities, 497–499
    with SDLC multilink transmission groups,
        496–497
Token Ring
    monitoring, 262–263
    Cisco implementation, MAC layer
        address, 270–271
transparent bridging, 62–63
    bridge table aging time, 81
    circuit groups, 92–93
    constrained multicast flooding, 93–94
    options, 77–78
    over WANs, 68–73
VLANs (virtual LANs)
    routing between, 65–67

transparently bridged, 63–65

XID (exchange of identification), response time, 623–624

Configuration Report Server, *see* CRS

congestion, FRAS (Frame Relay Access Support), controlling, 812, 826–827

connect-at-startup command, 864, 921

connection networks (APPN), defining, 868–869

connections

APPN

restricting node types, 865

transmission group characteristics, 866–867

DSPU (Downstream Physical Units)

configuration, 756

enabling RSRB SAP, 779–781

hosts, enabling SAP, 784–785

Frame Relay

defining DSPU host, 758–760, 770–772

defining link to SNA host, 795–797

FST (Fast-Sequenced Transport)

RSRB configuration, 347–349

encapsulation, specifying, 395–396, 706–707

FTCP/IP (fast-switched TCP/IP), RSRB configuration, 351–352

LLC2 (logical link control type-2)

displaying active, 648–651

preventing RNR messages, 450–451

local acknowledgments, displaying status, 703–704

peers, retry configuration, 551–552

point-to-point

RSRB configuration, 346–347

direct encapsulation, 394–395, 707–709

QLLC, displaying status, 700–702

SDLC (Synchronous Data Link Control)

defining DSPU host, 761–763, 773–774

defining link to SNA host, 798–800

QLLC correspondence, 637

SRB (source-route bridging), establishing timeout, 317–318

STUN (Serial Tunnel), displaying status, 575–577

TCP/IP (Transport Control Protocol/Internet Protocol), RSRB configuration, 350–355

Token Ring

downstream PU, 774–777

DSPU host, 763–764

link to SNA host, 800–801

X.25

defining downstream PU, 772–773

defining DSPU host, 760–761

defining link to SNA host, 797–798

connectivity

any-to-any

enabling for multiport bridging, 191

multiple dual-port SRBs, 189

QLLC (qualified logical link control), enabling DLSw+, 413

SRB, managing with LNM, 209

Token Ring, SR/TLB (source-route translational bridging), 199–201

constrained multicast flooding

enabling, 127

transparent bridging configuration, 93–94

control points (APPN), defining, 853–854

controlling

all-routes explorer frames on interfaces, 325

dynamic peers (DLSw+), 409–410

FRAS (Frame Relay Access Support), congestion, 812, 826–827

I-frames, transmission, 591–594

information frames, 614–615

spanning tree explorer frames, 326

unacknowledged frame transmission, 617–618

XID (exchange of identification), 622–623

conversion

frames, Token Ring LLC2-to-Ethernet, 202–203

QLLC (qualified logical link control), disabling, 713–716

COS (class of service), defining, 869–871

cost-per-byte command (APPN), 861, 867

link station, 922

port, 923

cost-per-connect-time command (APPN), 861, 867

link station, 924

port, 925

counters, source-bridge, clearing, 257–258

CP-CP (control point-to-control point) sessions, preventing, 864

cp-cp sessions-supported command, 864

cp-cp-sessions-supported command, 926
criteria
  explorer packets, interface response configuration, 330–331
  LLC2 local acknowledgment selection, 356
  sending acknowledgments, 592
CRS (Configuration Report Server), 210
CSNA (CIP Systems Network Architecture)
  see CIP, CSNA
csna command, 1127–1129
customizing
  BSTUN connection queuing priorities, 567–569
  QLLC conversion, 663–665
  SDLLC media translation, 658–659
cycles
  specifying for active poll list, 549–550

D

Data Link Switching Plus, *see* DLSw+
databases (bridge forwarding), viewing classes, 167–169
datagrams (NetBIOS), enabling Cisco IOS transmission, 281–282
DDR (Dial-on-Demand Routing), transparent bridging configuration, 68–70
DE (frame discard eligibility), FRAS Host congestion management, 826
deactivation, detecting in devices, 545–546
DECnet protocol, appending RIF information, 197
dedicated LUs (logical units), 765–766
defining
  APPN
    connection networks, 868–869
    control points, 853–854
    COS (class of service), 869–871
    link stations, 862–863
    modes, 871–872
    partner locations, 872–873
    ports, 857–858
  BSTUN
    protocol groups, 517, 554–555
  byte access list filters for incoming messages, 277–278
  custom STUN protocols, 491

DLSw+ (Data Link Switching Plus)
  local peers, 1025
  source-bridge ring groups, 404
NetBIOS
  hexadecimal pattern offsets, 273–275
  static name cache entries, 280
priority lists, 386–387
ring groups, 332–333
  DLSW+ session configuration, 1024
  multiport bridging, 191
  RSRB over point-to-point connections, 346
SAP (service access point), 358
SDLC (Synchronous Data Link Control), transmission groups, 490
spanning tree protocols, 156–157
SRB (source-route bridging) access expressions, 252–253
station access lists for outgoing messages, 285–287
validation time for explorer frames, 288–289
delay, circuit group transmission interval configuration, 125–126
denying access to bridge groups, 142–144
dependent logical unit requestor, *see* DLUR
dependent logical unit server, *see* DLUS
desired-max-send-btu-size command, 859, 927
destination addresses
  LLC2 sessions, specifying destination address, 632–633
  MAC, filtering, 141–142
detecting device deactivation, 545–546
deterministic load distribution, 6
devices
  bisync (binary synchronous communication), integrating over multiprotocol networks, 512
  deactivation, detecting, 545–546
  routers, concurrent routing and bridging, 128
  X.25
    accepting calls on router, 681–682
    associating with XID, 662–663, 689–691
direct encapsulation
  DLSw+ (Data Link Switching Plus) configuration, 406–407
  Frame Relay, 362, 357
directories, APPN, saving, 855

disabling
    border peer caching, 417
    DLSw+ (Data Link Switching Plus), 445
    fast-switched SR/TLB, 199, 201
    HPR on link definitions (APPN), 863
    LNMs (LAN Network Managers), 263–264
    pathtrace reporting, 266–267
    QLLC conversion, 713–716
    spanning tree on interfaces, 91–92, 149–150
    SRB (Source-Route Bridging), LNM
        functionality, 211–212
    trace, automatic report path, 212
    UDP Unicast, 417
disconnecting TN3270 sessions, 1132–1133
displaying
    bridges
        logical configuration, 301–303
        parameters, 301
    circuit groups, configured interfaces, 170–171
    client information, 1170–1174
    interfaces, bridging configuration information,
        174–176
    LLC2 active connections, 648–651
    local acknowledgment status, 388–389
    network stations, LNM-related information,
        306–308
    processor board statistics, 292–297
    routers, spanning tree topology, 178–180
    spanning tree topology, 313–314
    statistics
        bridge groups, 171–172
        source-bridging, 310–313
        SSP, 180–181, 314–315
        Token Ring interfaces, 297–300
    STUN (Serial Tunnel), connection status,
        575–577
    Token Rings, LNM-related information,
        305–306
    transparent bridging, multicast state
        information, 172–173
    VLANs, subinterfaces, 173–174
dlsw allroute-netbios command, 441
dlsw allroute-sna command, 441–442
dlsw bgroup-list command, 442–443
dlsw bridge-group command, 443–445
dlsw disable command, 445
dlsw duplicate-path-bias command, 446

dlsw group cache disable command, 446–447
dlsw group-cache max entries command, 447–448
dlsw icannotreach saps command, 448–449
dlsw icanreach command, 449–450
dlsw llc2 nornr command, 450–451
dlsw local-peer command, 451–453, 1025,
    1027, 1032
dlsw mac-addr command, 453–454
dlsw netbios-keepalive-filter command, 454–455
dlsw netbios-name command, 455–456
dlsw peer-on-demand-defaults command, 456–458
dlsw port-list command, 458–459
dlsw prom-peer-defaults command, 459–460
dlsw remote-peer frame relay command, 461–463
dlsw remote-peer fst command, 463–465
dlsw remote-peer interface command, 465–467
dlsw remote-peer tcp command, 467–470, 1027
dlsw ring-list command, 470–471
dlsw timer command, 471–473
dlsw udp-disable command, 473–474
DLSw+ (Data Link Switching Plus), 15
    APPN support, 22
    backup peers, 408–409
    Border Peer Caching, 18
        border peers, 17
        disabling, 417, 446–447
    bridge groups, defining, 406
    circuits, displaying, 478–479
    closing circuits, 417, 439–440
    configuration examples, 418, 438
    disabling, 445
    DSPU (Downstream Physical Units), support-
        ing, 22
    duplicate path handling, configuration,
        416, 446
    dynamic peers, controlling, 409–410
    enabling
        Ethernet interfaces, 411
        FDDI interfaces, 411
        Frame Relay, 410–411
        SDLC interfaces, 412
        Token Ring interfaces, 411
    enhancements
        availability, 21
        description, 16, 21
        modes of operation, 16

performance, 19
scalability, 16–18
explorer firewalls, 17
frame processing counter, resetting, 440–441
group cache, limiting entries, 415, 447–448
LLC1 (Logical Link Control Type-1) circuit
support, 18
LNM (LAN Network Manager),
supporting, 22
local peers
defining, 404–405, 1025, 1027, 1032
parameters, 451–453
modes of operation, 16
monitoring, 417–418
Multiple Bridge Groups, 18
NCIA (native client interface architecture)
server sessions, 1025–1026
NetBIOS Dial-on-Demand Routing, 17, 414
on-demand peers, 17
over QLLC, enabling, 474–476
parameters, tuning, 471–473
peer groups, 16, 476–478
peer-on-demand defaults, configuration, 415
performance, 19
port lists, defining, 405–406
promiscuous peer defaults, configuration, 415
QLLC connectivity, enabling, 413
reachability cache
clearing, 417, 440
displaying information, 483–486
reachable resources, configuration, 449–450
remote peers
defining, 406–407
specifying for connection, 461–463
ring lists
configuration, 470–471
defining, 405–406
scalability, 16
sessions, configuration, 1024–1025
SNA (Systems Network Architecture)
host connections, establishing, 805–806
Service Point, supporting, 22
Type of Service, 19
source-bridge ring groups, 404
standard, 13

static
paths, configuration, 416
resources capabilities exchange,
configuration, 415–416
timers, configuration, 414
transport types, description, 19
UDP Unicast,
disabling, 417, 473–474
Enhancement, 17
DLUR (Dependent Logical Unit Requestor)
APPN support, 928
components, displaying information,
1176–1177
configuration commands
dlus-backup, 1130–1131
link, 1139–1140
lsap, 1140–1142
preferred-nnserver, 1146–1147
pu, 1147–1148
vrn, 1197–1198
dlur command, 854, 928, 1129–1130
dlur-dspu-name command, 866, 928
DLUS (Dependent Logical Unit Server)
APPN (Advanced Peer-to-Peer Networks)
support, 929–930
control point, 929
link station, 930
backups, specifying, 1130–1131
dlus command, 854, 866
dlus-backup command, 1130–1131
domains
establishing, 129–130
spanning-tree, establishing multiple, 79–80
transparent, enabling fast switching, 341–342
DSPU (Downstream Physical Units)
configuration, 756
definition of feature, 36
enabling
SDLC addresses, 757–758
X.121 subaddresses, 756–757
Frame Relay data-link control 732–734
over DLSw+ (Data Link Switching Plus), 22
QLLC data-link control 731–732
SNA perspective, 37
status, displaying, 790–792
upstream hosts 719, 720

dspu activation-window command, 751–752

dspu default-pu command, 752–753

dspu enable-host command, 753–755

dspu enable-pu command, 756–758

dspu host command, 758–765

    virtual data link control, 1029

dspu lu command, 765–766, 1030

dspu ncia command, 766–767, 1030

dspu ncia enable-pu command, 767–768

dspu notification-level command, 768–769

dspu pool command, 769–770

dspu pu command, 770–776

    virtual data link control, 1029

dspu rsrb command, 777–779

dspu rsrb enable-host command, 779–780

dspu rsrb enable-pu command, 780–781

dspu rsrb start command, 781–782

dspu start command, 782–783

dspu vdlc command, 783–784

dspu vdlc enable-host command, 784–786

dspu vdlc enable-pu command, 786–787, 1030

dspu vdlc start command, 787–788

dual-port bridges, configuration, 188–189

duplicate path handling (DLSw+),
    configuration, 416

dynamic

    configuration, FRAS BNN, 810–811

    peers (DLSw+), controlling, 409–410

E

EBCDIC character sets, specifying, 543–544

ECA (Escon Channel Adapter), 1051

    channel attach configuration, 1121–1123

effective-capacity command (APPN), 861, 867

    link stations, 931

    ports, 932

enabling

    adaptive SDLC (Synchronous Data Link
        Control) T1, 630–631

    APPN (Advanced Peer-to-Peer Networking)

        central resource registration, 854

        HPR (High Performance Routing), 856

    autonomous

        bridging, 78–79, 133–134

        switching, 334–335

    block serial tunneling, 553–554

bridging on Frame Relay networks, 164–165

BSTUN (Block Serial Tunneling), 516

Cisco IOS NetBIOS datagram transmission,
    281–282

concurrent routing and bridging, 73–74

constrained multicast flooding, 94, 127

DLSw+ (Data Link Switching Plus)

    on Ethernet interfaces, 411

    on Frame Relay, 410–411

    on SDLC interfaces, 412

    over QLLC, 413, 474–476

encapsulation, SDE (Secure Data Exchange),
    161–162

fast switching

    explorers, 320–321

    transparent domains, 341–342

FRAS (Frame Relay Access Support) Dial
    Backup over DLSw+, 814

IP routing, 166

ISL (Inter-Switch Link), 161

local acknowledgment, 352, 357

LRM

    router parameter modification, 213

    servers, 213

LSAPs (Link Service Access Points), 753–754

multiport bridging, any-to-any
    connectivity, 191

NetBIOS

    DDR (Dial-on-Demand Routing), 414,
        454–455

    name caching, 204–208, 277, 283–284

    proxy explorers, 331

packet filtering

    FDDI, 323–324

    SNAP (Subnetwork Access Protocol),
        146–147, 324–325

passthrough, 392–393

peer loss detection, 555, 582–583

primary stations (SDLC), two-way
    simultaneous mode, 639–640

QLLC (Qualified Logical Link Control)

    conversion, 660–663

    conversion on X.25 serial interfaces,
        687–689

    local acknowledgment, 705–706

RIF (Routing Information Field)

    cache synchronization, 291–292

information collection, 271–273
validation, 289–291
routing in bridge groups, 157–158
SDLC (Synchronous Data Link Control)
broadcast, 489
SDLLC, media translation, 654, 695–696
serial interfaces, STUN, 491
SNA (System Network Architecture) session
switch, 1129–1130
spanning explorers, 338–339
SRB (Source-Route Bridging)
automatic spanning-tree, 194–195
fast-switching cache, 223–224
on Token Ring interfaces, 188
RIFs, 197
RSRB configuration, 347–349
SSE, 224, 335
STUN (Serial Tunnel), 488, 580–581
transparent bridging, LAT compression, 79
encapsulation
APPN (Advanced Peer-to-Peer Networks),
serial interface, 857
Ethernet
Token Ring LLC2 frame conversion,
202–203
Type II, selecting, 162–164, 259–261
Frame Relay, SRB configuration, 193
FTCP/IP (fast-switched TCP/IP), RSRB
configuration, 351–352
HDLC (High Level Data Link Protocol)
without local acknowledgment, STUN
configuration, 492
RSRB (Remote Source-Route Bridging)
direct Frame Relay, 357
example, 362
SDE (Secure Data Exchange), enabling,
161–162
STUN (Serial Tunnel)
enabling on serial interfaces, 559–560
establishing method, 491
TCP (Transport Control Protocol)
specifying, 585–586
with local acknowledgment, establishing
for STUN configuration, 493–495
without local acknowledgment,
establishing for STUN
configuration, 492

TCP/IP (Transport Control Protocol/Internet
Protocol)
RSRB configuration, 350–351
RSRB configuration with local
acknowledgment, 352–355
see also direct encapsulation; FST
encapsulation; TCP encapsulation
encapsulation bstun command, 558–559
encapsulation frame-relay command, 518
encapsulation isl command, 161
encapsulation sde command, 161–162
encapsulation sdlc command, 610
encapsulation sdlc-primary command, 611–612
encapsulation sdlc-secondary command, 612–613
encapsulation stun command, 559–560
entities (TN3270), shutting down, 1191–1192
entries
bridge forwarding databases
viewing classes, 167–169
removing, 158
dynamically learned (NetBIOS cache),
clearing, 256–257
error messages
transmission, IOS configuration, 269–270
frame-copied, reporting, 229
ESCON (Enterprise-Systems Connection) director
switch, 1064
establishing
criteria for sending acknowledgments, 592
domains, 129–130
encapsulation method for STUN configuration, 491
FST peer names, 390
links between source-route and transparent
bridging, 339–341
local acknowledgment, 494
SAP priorities, 357–358
SRB interoperability, 227
with IBM PC/3270 emulation software,
228
with TIMAC firmware, 228
STUN connection priorities
queuing, 562–563
traffic, 497–499
transparent bridging, multiple spanning-tree
domains, 79–80

Ethernet
    APPN partner node, specifying, 942
    bridge groups, mapping traffic to remote peers,
        442–443
    connectivity, SR/TLB (source-route transla-
        tional bridging), 199–201
    enabling DLSw+ (Data Link Switching
        Plus), 411
    packet filtering, 140
    type codes, 1199, 1206
    Type II encapsulation
        selecting OUI, 259–261
        selecting OUI code, 162–164
ethernet-transit-oui command, 162–164, 259–261
examples, configuration
    APPN (Advanced Peer-to-Peer Networking),
        877, 898
    DLSw+ (Data Link Switching Plus), 418, 438
    DSPU, 742–749
    FRAS (Frame Relay Access Support), 815–823,
        828–831
    QLLC (Qualified Logical Link Control),
        672–677
    RSRB (Remote Source-Route Bridging)
        direct Frame Relay encapsulation, 362
        over FTCP/IP, 364–365
        over TCP/IP, 362–363
        Token Ring implementation, 375–377
        with IP load sharing example, 374–375
        with LLC2 local acknowledgment,
            372–374
        with local acknowledgment, 366–369
        with local acknowledgment and
            pass-through, 369–372
    SDLLC, 666–672
    SRB (Source-Route Bridging) configuration,
        230, 249
        access expressions, 247–248
        adding static RIF cache entries, 238
        administrative access filters, 246–247
        autonomous-switching, 249
        fast-switching, 249
        filtering bridged Token Ring packets, 245
        LNM for complex networks, 243–244
        LNM for simple networks, 242–243
        multiport, 233–234
        NetBIOS access filters, 244–245

        NetBIOS support, 241–242
        optimized explorer processing, 232
        over FDDI, 235
        over FDDI fast-switching, 236
        over Frame Relay, 236–237
        SR/TLB for simple networks, 238–240
        SR/TLB with access filtering, 240–241
        with automatic spanning-tree, 232
        with multiple virtual ring groups,
            234–235
        with spanning-tree explorers, 231–232
    STUN configuration, 500, 509
    transparent bridging, 95–115
EXEC commands
    clear bridge multicast, 158–159
    sdlc test serial, 642–643
    show bridge circuit-group, 170–171
    show bridge multicast, 172
    show controllers token, 361
    show interfaces, 361
    show lnm bridge, 214
    show lnm config, 214
    show lnm interface, 214
    show lnm ring, 215
    show lnm station, 215
    show local-ack, 361
    show ncia client, 1047–1049
    show ncia server, 1049–1050
    show qllc, 700–702
    show span, 313–314
    show sse summary, 180–181, 314–315
    show startup-config, 205
exit command, 856
explorers
    fast switching, enabling, 320–321
     IOS validation time, defining, 288–289
    maximum byte rate, configuration, 321
    optimizing SRB processing, 225–227
    preventing forwarding in redundant topology
        networks, 320
    proxy, enabling for NetBIOS
        name-caching, 331
    RIF (Routing Information Field), 196
    spanning, 338–339
    see also Token Ring
expressions, see access expressions

extended access lists
    associating with interfaces, 146
    generating, 117–119

F

fast switching, 320–321
    enabling on source-route bridging
        software, 333
    enabling on transparent domains, 341–342
    SRB
        enabling, 223–224
        over FDDI (Fiber Distributed Data
            Interface), configuration, 192
    SR/TLB, disabling, 201
FDDI (Fiber Distributed Data Interface)
    APPN partner node, specifying, 942
    packet filtering, 323–324, 328–329
    SRB configuration, 191–192
    transit bridging, 7
filtering, 1199
    administrative, 220–221
    byte access lists, defining for incoming
        messages, 277–278
    byte offsets (NetBIOS), 216
    Ethernet packets, 140
    frames with MAC address, 123–124
    group-code (LAT), 153
    MAC destination addresses, 141–142
    packets
        FDDI, 328–329
        IEEE 802.2, 138
        SNAP, 146–147
        vendor code criteria, 253–255
    SAP, 358
    station access lists, 278–279
    transparently bridged packets, 81–89
flooding (multicast), enabling, 127
forward delay intervals (spanning-tree),
    configuration, 91
forwarding
    explorers, 193–194
        preventing in redundant topology
            networks, 320
    frames with multicast source addresses,
        154–155

HDLC (High Level Data Link Protocol) traffic
    on serial interfaces, 584–585
multicast addresses, 81
spanning tree explorer frames, 326–327
STUN (Serial Tunnel) traffic, 587
forwarding database, removing entries, 158
frame discard eligibility, see DE
Frame Relay
    APPN partner node, specifying, 933
    bridging, enabling, 164–165
    DLSw+ (Data Link Switching Plus)
        dial backup, configuration, 813–814
        enabling, 410–411
    encapsulation
        RFC 1490, 38
        SNA, 38
    FRAS (Frame Relay Access Support)
        configuration, 827–828
        LLC2 local termination, 825–826
        LLC2 passthru, 824–825
        monitoring, 815
    RSRB (Remote Source-Route Bridging), dial
        backup, configuration, 813
    SRB (Source-Route Bridging),
        configuration, 193
    transparent bridging, configuration, 70–71
frame-relay map bridge broadcast command,
    164–165
frame-relay map bstun command, 518, 560–561
frame-relay map llc2 command, 561, 833
frame-relay map rsrb command, 834
frames
    conversion, Token Ring LLC2-to-Ethernet,
        202–203
    encapsulation, RSRB direct Frame Relay, 357
    explorer, defining validation time, 288–289
    filtering, 123–124
    forwarding, 154–155
    FRAS (Frame Relay Access Support),
        congestion-control, 812
    HDLC (High Level Data Link Protocol),
        encapsulation, 492
    packet filtering, Ethernet type codes, 1199,
        1206
    poll bits, transmit-poll-frame timer
        configuration, 595
    REJ (reject command), sending, 594

sequencing, 514–515
SNAP (Subnetwork Access Protocol), filtering, 330
spanning tree explorer, controlling, 326
TCP, encapsulation, 492–495
X.25, routing configuration, 182–185
XID (exchange of identification), 595–596
see also I-frames
FRAS (Frame Relay Access Support), 37
BAN (boundary access nodes)
configuring, 811, 836
displaying status, 844
enabling, 838
BNN (boundary network nodes)
displaying status, 844
dynamic configuration, 810–811
DLCI connection, 840
enabling, 839
LLC connection, associating, 840
static configuration, 810
configuration examples, 815–823, 828–831
congestion control, 812, 826–827, 843
connection state, displaying status, 844, 847
dial backup over DLSw+
displaying status, 844
enabling, 834
DLCI, 812–813
SDLC (Synchronous Data Link Control) link, associating, 841
backup configuration, 837
host, LLC2 local termination, 840
LLC2 (logical link control type 2)
local termination, 825–826
passthru, 824–825
sessions, displaying status, 845
traffic, mapping, 833
MIB (Management Information Base), 832
monitoring, 815
RSRB (remote source-route bridging), DLCI number, 834
SDLC (Synchronous Data Link Control), link, associating, 841
SRB (source-route bridging) configuration, 847
fras backup dlsw command, 834
fras ban command, 836
fras ddr-backup command, 837

fras map llc command, 840
fras map sdlc command, 841
fras-host ban command, 838
fras-host bnn command, 839
fras-host dlsw-local-ack command, 840
fr-dest-address command, 863, 933
frequency, polling (LLC2)
configuration, 594
controlling, 615–616
FRMRs (Frame Rejects), secondary station support, 627–628
FST (Fast-Sequenced Transport)
encapsulation
DLSw+ (Data Link Switching Plus) configuration, 407
specifying, 395–396
peer names
configuration, 704–705
establishing, 390
performance, 349–350
RSRB configuration, 347–348
assigning IP address, 348
enabling SRB on interfaces, 349
remote peer identification, 348–349
FTCP/IP (Fast-Switched Transport Control Protocol/Internet Protocol)
RSRB configuration, 351
enabling SRB on interfaces, 352
example, 364–365
remote peer identification, 352

G

generating
access lists
extended 117–119
standard, 119–120
type-code, 120–122
bridge groups with automatic spanning tree, 255–256
protocol groups, 581–582
PU entities, 1148–1150
generic-pool command, 1131–1132
global configuration commands
access-list, 117–122, 218–219, 253–255
bridge, 62
bridge acquire, 122–123

bridge address, 123
bridge bridge, 124–125
bridge cmf, 127–128
bridge crb, 128
bridge domain, 129–130
bridge forward-time, 130–131
bridge hello-time, 151–152
bridge irb, 152–153
bridge lat-service-filtering, 153
bridge max-age, 153
bridge multicast-source, 154–155
bridge priority, 155–156
bridge protocol, 156–157
bridge protocol ibm, 255–256
bridge route, 157–158
bridge-group aging-time, 132
bstun keepalive-count, 551–552
bstun lisnsap, 552–553
bstun peer-name, 553–554
bstun protocol-group, 517, 554–555
bstun remote-peer-keepalive, 555
dlsw allroute-netbios, 441
dlsw allroute-sna, 441–442
dlsw bgroup-list, 442–443
dlsw bridge-group, 443–445
dlsw disable, 445
dlsw duplicate-path-bias, 446
dlsw group cache disable, 446–447
dlsw group-cache max entries, 447–448
dlsw icannotreach saps, 448–449
dlsw icanreach, 449–450
dlsw llc2 nornr, 450–451
dlsw local-peer, 451–453
dlsw mac-addr, 453–454
dlsw netbios-keepalive-filter, 454–455
dlsw netbios-name, 455–456
dlsw peer-on-demand-defaults, 456–458
dlsw port-list, 458–459
dlsw prom-peer-defaults, 459–460
dlsw remote-peer frame relay, 461–463
dlsw remote-peer fst, 463–465
dlsw remote-peer interface, 465–467
dlsw remote-peer tcp, 467–470
dlsw ring-list, 470–471
dlsw timer, 471–473
dlsw udp-disable, 473–474

dspu activation-window, 751–752
dspu default-pu, 752–753
dspu host, 758–765
dspu lu, 765–766
dspu ncia, 766–767
dspu ncia enable-pu, 767–768
dspu notification-level, 768–769
dspu pool, 769–770
dspu pu, 770–776
dspu rsrb, 777–779
dspu rsrb enable-host, 779–780
dspu rsrb enable-pu, 780–781
dspu rsrb start, 781–782
dspu vdlc, 783–784
dspu vdlc enable-host, 784–786
dspu vdlc enable-pu, 786–787
dspu vdlc start, 787–788
encapsulation frame-relay, 518
interface channel, 1133–1134
interface serial, 518
ip routing, 166
lnm disabled, 212, 263–264
lnm pathtrace-disabled, 212, 266–267
lnm snmp-only, 212, 269
locaddr-priority-list, 360, 380–382
location, 789–790
ncia client, 1042–1043
ncia rsrb, 1043–1044
ncia server, 1044–1046
netbios access-list bytes, 217, 273–275
netbios access-list host, 216, 275–276
netbios name-cache, 207, 279–280
netbios name-cache name-len, 206, 280–281
netbios name-cache proxy-datagram, 206, 281–282
netbios name-cache query-timeout, 208, 282–283
netbios name-cache recognized-timeout, 208, 283
netbios name-cache timeout, 283–284
nterface fddi, 192
outing, 166
priority-list protocol bstun, 564–565
priority-list protocol ip tcp, 565–566
priority-list stun address, 566–567
queue-list protocol bstun, 567–568

queue-list protocol ip tcp, 568–569
rif, 286–287
rif timeout, 287–288
rif validate-age, 206, 288–289
rif validate-enable, 289–290
rif validate-enable-age, 290–291
rif validate-enable-route-cache, 291–292
rsrb remote-peer lsap-output-list, 384–385
rsrb remote-peer netbios-output-list, 385–386
sap-priority-list, 387
sna host, 795–801
sna rsrb enable-host, 802–803
sna rsrb start, 803–804
sna vdlc, 805–806
sna vdlc enable-host, 806–807
sna vdlc start, 807–808
source-bridge, 192
source-bridge connection-timeout, 225
source-bridge cos-enable, 360, 389–390
source-bridge enable-80d5, 318–319
source-bridge explorer-dup-ARE-filter,
    226, 320
source-bridge explorer-fastswitch, 320–321
source-bridge explorer-maxrate, 226, 321
source-bridge explorerq-depth, 226, 322
source-bridge fst-peername, 390, 704–705
source-bridge largest-frame, 361, 391–392
source-bridge passthrough, 355, 392–394
source-bridge proxy-netbios-only, 205, 331
source-bridge qllc-local-ack, 705–706
source-bridge remote-peer frame-relay,
    394–395
source-bridge remote-peer fst, 395–397,
    706–707
source-bridge remote-peer ftcp, 397–398
source-bridge remote-peer interface, 707–709
source-bridge remote-peer tcp, 398–400,
    709–710
source-bridge ring-group, 191, 332–333,
    710–711
source-bridge route-cache cbus, 192
source-bridge sap-80d5, 336–337
source-bridge sdllc-local-ack, 712
source-bridge tcp-queue-max, 361, 400–401
source-bridge transparent, 339–341
source-bridge transparent fastswitch, 341–342

stun keepalive-count, 579, 581
stun protocol-group, 581–582
stun remote-peer-keepalive, 582–583
stun schema offset length format, 587–588
group cache (DLSw+)
    entries, limiting, 447–448
    maximum entry configuration, 415
group codes
    filtering (LAT), 153
    specifying access to bridge groups, 137–138,
        142–145

H

half-duplex protocols, 514
HDLC (High Level Data Link Protocol),
    encapsulating STUN traffic, 586–587
hexadecimal patterns (NetBIOS), defining,
    273–275
hops, limiting on SRB topologies, 196
host connections
    SDLC (Synchronous Data Link Control)
        addresses, enabling, 794
    non-IBM, enabling Token Ring-to-Ethernet
        LLC2 translation, 336–337

HPR (High Performance Routing)
    enabling, 856
    port definitions, 858–860
hpr command, 858, 863
    APPN control point, 935
    APPN link station, 935
    APPN port, 936
hpr max-sessions command, 856
hpr retries command, 856, 937
hpr sap command, 858, 938
hpr timers liveness command, 856, 939
hpr timers path-switch command, 856, 940
hpr-max-sessions command, 937

I

IBM
    3172, offload support, 57
    8209 bridges, translation compatibility with
        SR/TLB, 202
    channel attach, *see* CIP
    LNM (LAN Network Manager), *see* LNM

PC/3270 emulation software, interoperability with SRB, 228

ibsc dial-contention command, 545

ICMP (Internet Control Message Protocol), displaying stack information, 1152–1153

IDBLK, SDLLC configuration requirements, 679

identifying
    LANs, 789
    remote peers
        RSRB, 347
        FST, 348–349

idle-time command, 1132–1133

IDNUM, SDLLC configuration requirements, 679

IEEE 802.2, 11
    destination address filtering (SRB), 219–220
    packet filtering, 138, 323–324

I-frames (information frames), 639
    acknowledgments, criteria for sending, 592–593
    controlling, 614–615
    largest size for SDLLC, specifying, 659
    maximum size configuration, 639
    REJ (reject command), sending, 594
    transmission control, 591–594
    unacknowledged
        resending, 618–619
        setting T1 time, 593

initiating
    APPN subsystem, 874
    remote resource connections, 804–805

input interfaces, assigning, 322–323

integrated routing, displaying interface configuration information, 177–178

interface bvi command, 165–166

interface channel command, 1056, 1133–1134

interface configuration commands
    access-expression, 222
    asp addr-offset, 540
    asp role, 541
    asp rx-ift, 542–543
    bridge-group, 131–132
    bridge-group cbus-bridging, 133–134
    bridge-group circuit-group, 134–135
    bridge-group input-lat-service-deny, 136–137
    bridge-group input-lat-service-permit, 137–138

bridge-group input-lsap-list, 138–139
bridge-group input-pattern-list, 139
bridge-group input-type-list, 140–141
bridge-group lat-compression, 141
bridge-group output-address-list, 141–142
bridge-group output-lat-service-deny, 142–143
bridge-group output-lat-service-permit, 143–144
bridge-group output-lsap-list, 144–145
bridge-group output-pattern-list, 146
bridge-group output-type-list, 146–147
bridge-group path-cost, 147–148
bridge-group priority, 148–149
bridge-group spanning-disabled, 149–150
bridge-group sse, 150–151
bsc char-set, 543
bsc contention, 543–544
bsc dial-contention, 544–545
bsc host-timeout, 545–546
bsc pause, 546
bsc poll-timeout, 546–547
bsc primary, 547–548
bsc retries, 548
bsc secondary, 548–549
bsc servlim, 549–550
bsc spec-poll, 550
bstun group, 519, 551
bstun route, 556–558
bstun route address, 519
channel-protocol, 1121
claw, 1121–1123
cmpc, 1126–1127
csna, 1127–1129
dspu enable-host, 753–755
dspu enable-pu, 756–758
dspu start, 782–783
encapsulation bstun, 558–559
encapsulation sdlc, 610
encapsulation sdlc-primary, 611–612
encapsulation sdlc-secondary, 612–613
encapsulation stun, 559–560
ethernet-transit-oui, 162–164, 259–261
frame-relay map bridge broadcast, 164–165
frame-relay map bstun, 518, 560–561
frame-relay map llc2, 561
interface bvi, 165–166

lan, 1138–1139
lan-name, 789
llc2 ack-delay-time, 613–614
llc2 ack-max, 614–615
llc2 idle-time, 615–616
llc2 local-window, 616–617
llc2 n2, 617–618
llc2 t1-time, 618–619
llc2 tpf-time, 620–621
llc2 trej-time, 621–622
llc2 xid-retry-time, 623–624
llc2 tbusy-time, 619
llc2 xid-neg-val-time, 622
llc2?tbusy-time, 620
llc2?xid-neg-val-time, 623
lnm alternate, 213, 261–262
lnm crs, 262–263
lnm loss-threshold, 214, 264–265
lnm password, 213, 265–266
lnm rem, 267–268
lnm rps, 268–269
lnm softerr, 214, 269–270
locaddr-priority, 360, 379–380
locaddr-priority-list, 562–563
mac-address, 270–271
multiring, 271–273
netbios enable-name-cache, 277
netbios input-access-filter bytes, 217, 277–278
netbios input-access-filter host, 216, 278–279
netbios output-access-filter bytes, 217, 284–285
netbios output-access-filter host, 216, 285–286
offload, 1144–1146
priority-group, 382–384, 563–564
qllc accept-all-calls, 681–682
qllc dlsw, 474–475
qllc largest-packet, 682–684
qllc npsi-poll, 684–685
qllc partner, 685–686
qllc sap, 686–687
qllc srb, 687–688
qllc xid, 689–690
sap-priority, 386
sdlc address, 624–625
sdlc address ff ack-mode, 625–626
sdlc dlsw, 475–476, 626

sdlc dte-timeout, 626–627
sdlc frmr-disable, 627–628
sdlc holdq, 628–629
sdlc k, 629–630
sdlc line-speed, 630–631
sdlc n1, 631
sdlc n2, 632
sdlc partner, 632–633
sdlc poll-limit-value, 633–634
sdlc poll-pause-timer, 634–635
sdlc poll-wait-timeout, 636–637
sdlc qllc-prtnr, 637
sdlc role, 638–639
sdlc sdlc-largest-frame, 639
sdlc simultaneous, 639–640
sdlc slow-poll, 640–641
sdlc t1, 641–642
sdlc virtual-multidrop, 569–570
sdlc vmac, 644
sdlc xid, 644–645
sdllc partner, 690–691
sdllc ring-largest-frame, 692–693
sdllc sap, 693–694
sdllc sdlc-largest-frame, 694
sdllc traddr, 695–696
sdllc xid, 696–697
sna enable-host, 793–795
sna rsrb, 802
sna start, 804–805
source-bridge, 188–189, 315–318, 355
source-bridge input-address-list, 219, 322–323
source-bridge input-lsap-list, 218, 323–324
source-bridge input-type-list, 219, 324–325
source-bridge keepalive, 391
source-bridge max-hops, 325
source-bridge max-in-hops, 326
source-bridge max-out-hops, 326–327
source-bridge output-address-list, 220, 327–328
source-bridge output-lsap-list, 218, 328–329
source-bridge output-type-list, 219, 329–330
source-bridge proxy-explorer, 330–331
source-bridge route-cache, 223, 333–334
source-bridge route-cache cbus, 334–335
source-bridge route-cache sse, 335
source-bridge spanning, 337–339

stun group, 578–579
stun route address interface dlci, 583–584
stun route address interface serial, 584–585
stun route address tcp, 585–586
stun route all interface serial, 586–587
stun route all tcp, 587
stun sdlc-role primary, 588–589
stun sdlc-role secondary, 589–590
tg, 1193–1194
tn3270-server, 1194–1195
x25 map bridge, 182–185
x25 map qllc, 713–716
x25 pvc qllc, 716–717
interface serial command, 518
interface virtual-tokenring command, 842
interfaces
    all-routes explorer frames,
        controlling, 325
    assigning
        access lists, 135–136
        priority groups, 563–567
        to bridge groups, 131–132, 134–135
        to BSTUN groups, 551
    associating
        with access lists in bridge groups, 139
        with extended access lists, 146
    bisync (binary synchronous communication),
        displaying statistics, 570–574
    bridging configuration, displaying informa-
        tion, 174–176
    BVI (bridge-group virtual interfaces),
        specifying, 165–166
    channel attach, specifying, 1133–1134
    CIP (Channel Interface Processor)
        displaying information, 1187–1191
        displaying IP stack information,
            1153–1154, 1161
        displaying LLC2 session information,
            1154–1155
        displaying UDP listener socket informa-
            tion, 1185–1186
        LAN configuration, 1138–1139
        LLC2 session support, 1142
    FDDI (Fiber Distributed Data Interface)
        enabling DLSw+ (Data Link Switching
            Plus), 411
        fast switching SRB configuration, 192

        SRB configuration, 191–192
    Frame Relay, SRB configuration, 193
    NetBIOS name caching, enabling, 204–208
    priority
        configuration, 148–149
        lists, assigning, 382–384
        spanning-tree, 90
    SDLC (Synchronous Data Link Control)
        displaying information, 697–700
        enabling DLSw+ (Data Link Switching
            Plus), 412
    serial
        enabling QLLC conversion, 661
        reducing LAT traffic, 141
    source-route bridging configuration, 315–317
    spanning tree
        disabling, 91–92, 149–150
    SRB (source-route bridging), defining access
        expressions, 252–253
    STUN (Serial Tunnel)
        enabling, 491
        placing in STUN groups, 578–579
    Token Ring, 842
        assigning ring groups (multiport
            bridging), 191
        displaying statistics, 297–300
        dual port bridging, 189
        enabling DLSw+, 411
        enabling SRB, 188
        multiple dual-port SRB configuration, 189
        multiport bridging, 190–191
        ring groups, 190
        RSRB implementation example, 375–377
interframe timeout, specifying, 542–543
intermediate session routing, see ISR
internal adapter configuration commands
    max-llc2-sessions, 1142
    name, 1144
internal adapters, naming, 1144
internal LAN configuration commands
    adapter, 1119–1120
Internet Control Message Protocol, see ICMP
interoperability, SRB, 227
    with IBM PC/3270 emulation software, 228
    with TIMAC firmware, 228
interrupt-switched command, 941

Inter-Switch Link, *see* ISL
intervals
    BPDUs (bridge protocol data unit), spanning
      tree topology reconfiguration, 153–154
    polling (LLC2)
      configuration, 595
      frequency, 546
IOCP control unit, IBM channel attach
  support, 1065
IOS
    error messages, transmission interval
      configuration, 269–270
    forward delay interval configuration, 130
    NetBIOS proxy configuration, 206–207
IP
    addressing
      enabling STUN (Serial Tunnel), 580–581
      peers, identifying, 398–400
      RSRB, assigning address to local
        router, 348
    routing, enabling, 166
    TOS (type of service precedence), 1074
ip precedence command, 1134–1135
ip route-cache same-interface command, 1061
ip routing command, 166
ip tos command, 1135–1137
IPX (Internet Packet Exchange) protocol,
  appending RIF information, 197
IRB (integrated routing and bridging), 74–77
ISL (Inter-Switch Link), enabling, 161
ISR (intermediate session routing), enabling,
  854, 941

K

keepalive interval, configuration
    remote source-bridging peers, 391
    TN3270 clients, 1137–1138
keepalive TN3270 command, 1137–1138

L

lan command, 1138–1139
lan-dest-address command, 863, 942
lan-name command, 789
LANs (Local-Area Networks)
    configuring on CIP interfaces, 1138–1139

Ethernet, linking DLSw+ to bridge groups,
  443–445
IBM, reporting spurious frame-copied
  errors, 229
identifying, 789
Token Ring, dual-port bridging, 189
LAT
    group-code filtering
      specifying, 153
    service announcements
      filtering, 87–89
Level 3 routers, 196
limited-resource command (APPN), 861, 865
    link station, 943
    port, 944
limiting
    hops on SRB topologies, 196
    LU sessions, 1123–1124
link command, 1139–1140
link stations (APPN)
    default value configuration, 861–862
    defining, 862–863
    starting and stopping, 874–875
link-layer protocol translation, SNA over X.25,
  see QLLC conversion
link-queuing command, 865, 944
links
    APPN, custom queuing, 865
    asynchronous configuration, 512–513
    DLUR (Dependent Logical Unit Requestor),
      defining, 1139–1140
    establishing between source-route and
      transparent bridging, 339–341
listener sockets (UDP), displaying information,
  1185–1186
LLC2 (logical link control type 2)
    acknowledgments, delay configuration, 592
    active connections, displaying, 648–651
    features supported, 28
    I-frames
      largest size for, 658
      T1 time, 593
      transmission control, 591–594
      transmit-poll-frame timer
        configuration, 595
    local acknowledgment, 356–357, 421

RSRB configuration with TCP/IP connections, 352–355

RSRB implementation example, 372–374

polling, 594–595

    frequency configuration, 594

    setting retry limit, 593

primary stations, specifying maximum I-frame size, 692–693

remote stations, resending rejected frames, 621–622

repolling, configuration, 594–595

sessions, 353

    specifying destination address, 632–633

T1 time, 353

LLC2 (Logical Link Control-Type 2), 352

llc2 ack-delay-time command, 613–614

llc2 ack-max command, 614–615

llc2 dynwind command, 843

llc2 idle-time command, 615–616

llc2 local-window command, 616–617

llc2 n2 command, 617–618

llc2 t1-time command, 618–619

llc2 tbusy-time command, 619–620

llc2 tpf-time command, 620–621

llc2 trej-time command, 621–622

llc2 xid-neg-val-time command, 622–623

llc2 xid-retry-time command, 623–624

LNM (LAN Network Manager)

    automatic report path (trace), disabling, 212

    disabling, 211–212, 263–264

    monitoring operation, 214

    over DLSw+, 22

    pathtrace reporting, disabling, 266–267

    reporting links, password configuration, 265–266

    SRB management services, 210

    SRB support, 208–214

    Token Ring management, 210

lnm alternate command, 213, 261–262

lnm crs command, 262–263

lnm disabled command, 212, 263–264

lnm loss-threshold command, 214, 264–265

lnm password command, 213, 265–266

lnm pathtrace-disabled command, 212, 266–267

lnm rem command, 267–268

lnm rps command, 268–269

lnm snmp-only command, 212, 269

lnm softerr command, 214, 269–270

load sharing, IP over RSRB example, 374–375

LOCADD definition, adjusting for SDLLC, 679

locaddr-priority command, 360, 379–380

locaddr-priority-list command, 360, 380–382, 562–563

locaddrs, reserving for remote devices, 1124–1126

local

    acknowledgment, 353

        displaying status, 388–389, 703–704

        establishing, 494

        LLC2, 356–357

        QLLC, enabling, 705–706

        RSRB configuration with TCP/IP connections, 352–355

        SDLC (Synchronous Data Link Control) enabling on STUN routers, 495

        SDLLC (example), 670

    nodes (APPN), relative resistance configuration, 854–855

    peers

        DLSw+ (Data Link Switching Plus) defining, 404–405, 1025

local-sap command, 859, 945

Locate Throttling (APPN), 875

locate-queuing command, 946

location command, 789–790

logical configuration (Token Ring)

    displaying for bridges within routers, 301–303

    monitoring, 262–263

Logical Link Control, type 2, *see* LLC2

logical units, *see* LU, 37

loop-free paths, 150

LRM

    reporting links, 213

    router parameter modification, enabling, 213

    servers, enabling, 213

lsap command, 1140–1142

LSAP (Link Service Access Points), enabling, 753–754

LU nailing, *see* TN3270 server

LUs (logical units), 723

    dedicated, defining, 765–766

    mapping to queuing priorities, 380–382

    partial name, specifying, 873

M

MAC (Media Access Control)
    addresses
        destination, filtering, 141–142
        filtering frames, 123–124
        source, selecting output interface,
            126–127
        static configuration, 453–454
    RIFs (routing information field), SRB
        implementation, 196
MAC layer and source-route bridging, 11
mac-address command, 270–271
maintaining transparently bridged networks, 94–95
maintenance
    RSRB (Remote Source-Route Brigding), 361
    SRB (Source-Route Bridging), 229–230
managing FRAS (Frame Relay Access Support)
    congestion, 812, 826–827
mapping
    LUs (logical units) to queuing priorities,
        380–382
    traffic to remote peers (Ethernet), 442–443
max-cached-entries command, 853, 947
max-cached-trees command, 853, 948
maximum byte rate, configuring on explorers, 321
maximum idle intervals (spanning-tree)
    configuration, 91
maximum-lus command, 1142–1144
maximum-memory command, 853, 948
max-link-stations command, 859, 949
max-llc2-sessions command, 1142
MAXOUT, changing value on host to improve
    SDLLC performance, 659
max-rcv-btu-size command, 858, 950
media translation, SDLLC
    customization, 658–659
    enabling, 654, 695–696
    monitoring, 660
    NTRI (NCP/Token Ring Interconnection),
        677–679
messages, ring error, modifying interval, 214
MIB (Management Information Base)
    APPN (Advanced Peer-to-Peer
        Networking), 41

source-route bridging support, 12
    Token Ring support, 12
MIH (missing interrupt handlers), 1068
minimum-memory command, 951
missing interrupt handler, see MIH
modes (APPN), defining, 871–872
modifying
    access expressions, 222–223
    APPN definitions, 852
    LRM router parameters, 213
monitoring
    APPN network, 876–877
    DLSw+ (Data Link Switching Plus), 417–418
    DSPU (downstream physical units) 742
    FRAS (Frame Relay Access Support), 815
    LNM operation, 214
    QLLC conversion, 665
    RSRB, 361
    SDLLC media translation, 660
    SRB, 229–230
    STUN (Serial Tunnel) network activity, 500
    Token Ring logical configuration, 262–263
    transparently bridged networks, 94–95
multicast flooding, constrained, enabling, 127
multidrop Bisync operation, 512
    SDLLC configuration (example), 669
multilink transmission groups (SDLC), STUN
    (Serial Tunnel) configuration, 496–497
multipoint networks, virtual multidrop
    support, 514
multiport bridging, configuration, 190–191
multiprotocol LAPB, transparent bridging
    configuration, 71–72
multiring command, 271–273

N

name cache (NetBIOS), 203–204
    character length configuration, 206
    enabling, 204–208, 277, 283–284
    entry character length, specifying for
        validation, 280–281
    packet deadtime configuration, 207–208
name command, 1144
naming internal adapters, 1144
Native Client Interface Architecture, see NCIA
NCIA (native client interface architecture), 1023

client/server model, 53, 1023
configuration, 1025–1026
configuration examples, 1034, 1037
DLSw+ (Data Link Switching Plus), 1026
    local switch sessions, 1023–1025, 1034
    configuration (example), 1035
    local peer, defining, 1027
    NCIA server, configuring, 1027
    remote peers, defining, 1027
    source-bridge ring group, defining, 1026
DSPU (Downstream Physical Units) session, 1028
    configuration task list, 1029
    downstream PU, defining, 1029
    configuration, example, 1036
    local SAP for downstream PUs, enabling, 1030
    LU, defining, 1030
    NCIA (native client interface architecture) server, configuring, 1030
    upstream host, defining, 1029
monitoring and maintaining, 1033
NCIA data link control (NDLC), 54
RSRB (Remote Source Route Bridging) session, 1030
    configuration task list, 1031
    DLSw+ local peer, defining, 1032
    example, 1036
    NCIA server, configuring, 1033
    NCIA/RSRB interface, configuring, 1033
    remote peer, defining, 1032
    source-bridge ring group, defining, 1032
    RSRB session configuration
ncia client command, 1042–1043
ncia command, 1041–1042
ncia rsrb command, 1033, 1043–1044
ncia server command, 1044–1046
    DLSw+, 1025, 1028
    RSRB, 1033
ncia start command, 1034
ncia stop command, 1034
NCP, definitions, configuring for SDLLC, 677
Negative Caching (APPN), 875–876
negative-caching command, 952
NetBIOS

access filtering, configuring for SRB security, 215–217
cache, clearing dynamically learned entries, 256–257
datagram transmission,
    specifying dead time, 282–283
    enabling Cisco IOS software transmission, 281–282
DDR (Dial-on-Demand Routing)
    enabling, 414, 454–455
name cache
    character length, 206
    enabling, 204–208, 277, 283–284
    packet deadtime configuration, 207–208
    specifying character length for validation, 280–281
    timeout configuration, 206
packets, defining hexadecimal pattern offsets, 273–275
proxy explorers, enabling, 331
session timeouts, 356–357
single-route explorers
    changing to all-route broadcasts, 441
SRB support, 203–208
static names
    cache entries, defining, 280
    configuration, 455–456
netbios access-list bytes command, 217, 273–275
netbios access-list host command, 216, 275–276
netbios enable-name-cache command, 277
netbios input-access-filter bytes command, 217, 277–278
netbios input-access-filter host command, 216, 278–279
netbios name-cache command, 207, 279–280
netbios name-cache name-len command, 206, 280–281
netbios name-cache proxy-datagram command, 206, 281–282
netbios name-cache query-timeout command, 208, 282–283
netbios name-cache recognized-timeout command, 208, 283
netbios name-cache timeout command, 283–284
netbios output-access-filter bytes command, 217, 284–285

netbios output-access-filter host command, 216, 285–286

networks

APPN (Advanced Peer-to-Peer Networking)

command modes, 851–852

defining control points, 853–854

defining link stations, 862–863

initiating subsystem, 874

Locate Throttling, 875

mode definition, 871–872

monitoring, 876–877

Negative Caching, 875–876

partner location definition, 872–873

port definition, 857–858

tuning, 875

asynchronous, 512–515

ATM (asynchronous transfer mode), transparent bridging, 68

bisync (binary synchronous communication), frame sequencing, 515

DDR (Dial-on-Demand Routing), transparent bridging, 68–70

defining, 869

DLSw+ (Data Link Switching Plus), monitoring, 417–418

Frame Relay

enabling bridging, 164–165

enabling DLSw+, 410–411

transparent bridging, 70–71

interfaces, assigning to bridge groups, 131–132

LNM (LAN Network Manager), SRB support, 208–214

multipoint, virtual multidrop support, 514

multiprotocol

integrating Bisync devices, 512

LAPB, transparent bridging, 71–72

redundant topology, preventing explorer forwarding, 320

RSRB (Remote Source-Route Bridging)

maintenance, 361

tuning, 359–361

SMDS (Switched Multimegabit Data Service) transparent bridging, 72

spanning-trees, blocking and forwarding explorer packets, 193–194

SRB (Source Route-Bridging)

maintenance, 229–230

tuning, 223–227

stations

assigning access list names, 275–276

defining access list filters, 278–279

defining access list filters for outgoing messages, 285–287

displaying LNM-related information, 306–308

STUN (Serial Tunnel), monitoring activity, 500

Token Ring

dual-port bridging, 189

enabling any-to-any connectivity, 191

modifying ring error message interval, 214

transparently bridged

configuration, 62–63

examples, 95–115

monitoring, 94–95

X.25, transparent bridging, 72–73

NNs (network nodes), specifying as server, 1146–1147

no command, 856

no complete command, 856

node-row command, 870, 953

nodes (APPN), type 2.0 configuration, 866

notifications, DSPU (Downstream Physical Units), specifying, 768–769

NTRI (NCP/Token Ring Interconnection), SDLLC media translation, 677–679

null-xid-poll command, 860, 955

O

offload command, 1060, 1144–1146

offload support for TCP/IP, 57

opening connections on Token Ring devices (QLLC conversion), 663

optimizing

access expressions, 222

RSRB (remote source-route bridging) networks, 359–361

SRB (source-route bridging), explorer processing, 225–227

OUI code (Organizational Unique Identifier), selecting for Ethernet Type II encapsulation, 162–164

outing command, 166

output interface, output interfaces,
    assigning access lists, 327–328
    selecting with MAC source address, 126–127
overriding default TCP port setting, 1192–1193
owning-cp command, 872, 956
owning-nn command, 873

P

packet filtering
    access lists, Ethernet type codes, 1199, 1206
    criteria, vendor codes, 253–255
    FDDI (Fiber Distributed Data Interface),
        328–329
        enabling, 323–324
    SNAP (Subnetwork Access Protocol), 324–325
    transparently bridged packets, 81–89
packets
    encapsulation, SDE, enabling, 161–162
    Ethernet, filtering, 140
    explorer
        blocking, 193–194
        forwarding, 193–194
        minimizing on SRB topologies, 194
        RIF (Routing Information Field), 196
        see also explorers
    fast-switching, 201
    IEEE 802.2, filtering, 138
    NetBIOS
        dead-time interval configuration, 207–208
        defining hexadecimal pattern offsets,
            273–275
    SNA (Systems Network Architecture),
        maximum size configuration for X.25,
        682–683
    SNAP (Subnetwork Access Protocol),
        filtering, 146–147
    SR/TLB (source-route translational bridging),
        199–200
    transparently bridged
        coloring, 65
        filtering, 81–89
    X.25, bridging configuration, 182–185
Parallel Channel Adapter (PCA), 1051
parameters
    displaying for bridges, 301

DLSw+ (Data Link Switching Plus),
    configuration, 414, 417
    LLC (logical link control), defining,
        1193–1194
    LNM (LAN Network Manager), SRB support
        configuration, 211
    local peers (DLSw+), defining, 451–453
    router, enabling LRM modification, 213
    spanning-tree, 89–91
partial name LUs (logical units), specifying, 873
partner locations (APPN), defining, 872–873
passthrough, 392–393
    BSTUN over Frame Relay, enabling, 560–561
passwords
    LRM, applying to reporting links, 213
    reporting link (LNM), configuration, 265–266
path costs (bridge groups)
    assigning, 195
    configurations, 147–148
    spanning-tree, 90
paths, loop-free, 150
pathtrace reporting (LNMs), disabling, 266–267
patterns, hexadecimal (NetBIOS), defining,
    273–275
PCA (Parallel Channel Adapter) cards, 1051, 1121
peer-on-demand default configuration, 415,
    456–458
peers
    BSTUN, removing, 556–558
    connections, retry configuration, 551–552
    DLSw+ (Data Link Switching Plus), displaying
        configuration, 476–478
    loss detection, enabling, 555, 582–583
performance, tuning
    APPN (Advanced Peer-to-Peer Networking)
        networks, 875
    FST, 349–350
    RSRB (Remote Source-Route Bridging),
        359–361
permitting access to bridge groups, 137–138,
    144–145
physical unit, see PUs
point-to-point
    Bisync operation, 511
    connections, RSRB configuration, 346
        enabling SRB on interfaces, 347
        remote peer idenitification, 347

ring group definition, 346

direct encapsulation, specifying, 394–395,
465–467

poll bits, transmit-poll-frame timer
configuration, 595

polled asynchronous links, specifying role of
router, 541

polling

cycles

specifying intervals, 546

timeout, specifying, 546–547

frequency, controlling, 615–616

LLC2, 594–595

setting retry limit, 593

pooled LU routing 724

pools, LU, defining host range, 769–770

port command (APPN), 863, 868

connection network, 957

link station, 957

ports

APPN

assigning MAC addresses, 860–861

defining, 857–858

HPR, 858–860

starting and stopping, 874–875

asynchronous

configuration

asynchronous ports
configuration, 540–541

DLSw+, list definition, 405–406

TCP, overriding default, 1192–1193

PPP (Point-to-Point Protocol), 958

ppp-dest-address command, 863, 958

preferred-nnserver command, 1146–1147

preventing

CP-CP sessions, 864

dynamically determined station forwarding, 80

primary

nodes (SDLC), assigning, 588–589

servers (APPN), configuration, 866

stations

LLC2, specifying I-frame maximum size,
27, 692–693

SDLC, 611–612, 639–641

priorities

interfaces, configuration, 148–149

assigning groups, 379–380, 563–567

assigning lists, 382–387

SAP, establishing, 357–358

STUN traffic, establishing, 497–499

priority-group command, 382–384, 563–564

priority-list protocol bstun command, 564–565

priority-list protocol ip tcp command, 565–566

priority-list stun address command, 566–567

privileged EXEC commands

clear bridge, 158

clear dlsw circuit, 439–440

clear dlsw reachability, 440

clear dlsw statistics, 440–441

clear ncia circuit, 1039–1040

clear ncia client, 1040

clear ncia client registered, 1040–1041

clear netbios-cache, 256–257

clear rif-cache, 257

clear source-bridge, 257–258

clear sse, 159–160, 258–259

clear vlan statistics, 160

ncia, 1041–1042

show bridge, 167–169

show bridge group, 171–172

show bridge vlan, 173–174

show bsc, 570–575

show bstun, 575–577

show controllers token, 292–297

show dlsw capabilities, 476–478

show dlsw circuits, 478–479

show dlsw fastcache, 480

show dlsw peers, 481–483

show dlsw reachability, 483–486

show dlsw statistics, 486

show dspu, 790–792

show extended channel, 1152–1153

show extended channel cmpc, 1150–1152

show extended channel ip-stack, 1153–1154

show extended channel llc2, 1154–1155

show extended channel statistics, 1155–1158

show extended channel subchannel,
1158–1161

show extended channel tcp-stack, 1161

show extended channel tg, 1162–1167

show extended channel tn3270-server, 1167–1170

show extended channel tn3270-server client-ip-address, 1170–1174

show extended channel tn3270-server dlur, 1174–1176

show extended channel tn3270-server dlurlink, 1176–1177

show extended channel tn3270-server nailed-ip, 1177–1178

show extended channel tn3270-server pu, 1178–1182

show extended channel tn3270-server pu lu, 1182–1185

show extended channel udp-listeners, 1185–1186

show extended channel udp-stack, 1186–1187

show interfaces, 645–648, 697–700

show interfaces channel, 1187–1191

show interfaces crb, 174–176

show interfaces irb, 177

show interfaces tokenring, 297–300

show llc2, 648–651

show lnm bridge, 301

show lnm config, 301–303

show lnm interface, 303–305

show lnm ring, 305–306

show lnm station, 306–308

show local-ack, 388–389

show ncia circuits, 1046–1047

show netbios-cache, 308–309

show rif, 309–310

show sdllc local-ack, 703–704

show sna, 792–793

show source-bridge, 310–313

show span, 178–180

show stun, 577–578

show vlans, 181–182

processor boards, displaying statistics, 292–297

promiscuous

    peer defaults (DLSw+), configuration, 415

    transport defaults, configuration, 459–460

propagation-delay command (APPN), 861, 867

    link stations, 959

    ports, 960

protocol groups

    BSTUN

        configuration, 489–490

        defining, 517

    generating, 581–582

    SDLC (Synchronous Data Link Control), specifying for STUN configuration, 490

    see also protocols

protocols

    bisync (binary synchronous communication)

        multidrop operation, 512

        point-to-point operation, 511

    Bisync datalink, 510–511

    concurrent routing and bridging, 73–74, 128

    integrated routing and bridging, configuration, 74–77

    NetBIOS

        access filter configuration for SRB security, 215–217

        SRB support, 203–208

    routing

        configuring RIF static cache entries, 198

        configuring RIF timeout interval, 198

        specifying between bridge groups, 152–153

        SRB topology configuration, 196–198

    spanning tree, defining, 156–157

    specifying within bridge groups for bridging, 124–125

    STUN (Serial Tunnel), custom definition, 491

proxy explorers

    enabling for NetBIOS name caching, 205

    SRB configuration, 227

PU (physical units)

    definition, required to configure SDLLC, 679

    devices, defining with DSPU, 36

    type 2 devices, defining, 36

pu command, 1147–1150

pu-type-20 command, 866, 961

Q

QLLC (Qualified Logical Link Control)

    APPN (Advanced Peer-to-Peer Networking)

        configuring, 1020

        partner node, specifying, 1019

    connections, displaying status, 700–702

conversion
    customizing, 663–665
    disabling, 713–716
    enabling, 660–663
    examples, 672–677, 680
    monitoring, 665
    Token Ring devices, opening
        connections, 663
    topology, 33
  enabling DLSw+ (Data Link Switching
    Plus), 413
  local acknowledgment, enabling, 705–706
  upstream host connections, enabling X.121
    subaddresses, 754
qllc accept-all-calls command, 662, 681–682
qllc dlsw command, 474–475
qllc largest-packet command, 682–684
qllc npsi-poll command, 662, 684–685
qllc partner command, 663, 685–686
qllc sap command, 664, 686–687
qllc srb command, 661, 687–688
qllc xid command, 663, 689–690
Qualified Logical Link Control, *see* QLLC
queue-list protocol bstun command, 567–568
queue-list protocol ip tcp command, 568–569
queuing priorities (STUN connections),
  establishing, 562–563

R

reachability cache (DLSW+)
  clearing, 417
  displaying information, 483–486
  removing entries, 440
reducing
  explorer packets on SRB topologies, 194
  explorer traffic for DLSw+, 415–416
  hops on SRB topologies, 196
  LAT traffic on serial interfaces, 141
reinitializing SSP (Silicon Switch Processor) on
  Cisco 7000 series routers, 159–160, 258–259
REJ (reject command), sending, 594
relative resistance (APPN), configuration, 854–855
REM (Ring Error Monitor), 210
  configuration, 267–268
  modifying ring error message reporting
    intervals, 214

remote
  devices, reserving locaddrs, 1124–1126
  peers
    direct encapsulation, displaying
      capabilities, 417
    DLSw+ (Data Link Switching Plus),
      406–408
    mapping traffic to, 458–459
    specifying for connection, 461–463
    transport, FST encapsulation, 463–465
  resources
    connecting, 781–784, 787–788, 803–804
    initiating connections, 804–805
  stations
    LLC2, resending rejected frames, 621–622
    repolling, 619–621
Remote Source-Route Bridging, *see* RSRB
REMOTTO definition, adjusting for SDLLC, 679
removing
  backup DLUS (Dependent Logical Unit Server)
    names, 1130–1131
  BSTUN peers, 556–558
  learned entries from forwarding database, 158
  ring groups, 710–711
  statistics, VLAN, 160
repolling remote stations, 594–595, 619–621
reporting spurious frame-copied errors, 229
reporting links (LNMs), 213, 265–266
reserved-inbound command, 859, 962
reserved-outbound command, 859, 963
resetting frame processing counter (DLSw+),
  440–441
restricting access to bridge groups, 136–137
retry-limit command, 861, 865
  APPN link station, 964
  APPN port, 965
RFCs
  1045, Ethernet type code for Versatile
    Message Translation Protocol, 1202
  1231, IEEE 802.5 Token Ring MIB, 12
  1286, MIB variables for transparent
    bridging, 5
  1434, prestandard DLSw implementation, 16
  1483, ATM fast-path transparent bridging, 6
  1490, BAN support, 38
  multiprotocol encapsulation, 6, 38
  1593, SNMP management via APPN MIB, 41

1795, DLSw standard, 13
RIFs (routing information fields), 11
   bridge numbers, 196
   cache
      clearing entries, 257
      enabling synchronization, 291–292
   collecting information, 271–273
   enabling for SRB, 197
   entry validation, enabling, 289–291
   inactive entries, timeout (in minutes), 287–288
   ring numbers, 196
rif command, 286–287
rif timeout command, 287–288
rif validate-age command, 206, 288–289
rif validate-enable command, 289–290
rif validate-enable-age command, 290–291
rif validate-enable-route-cache command, 291–292
Ring Error Monitor, *see* REM
ring numbers, 196
Ring Parameter Server, *see* RPS
rings
   error detection, modifying intervals, 214
   groups, 190
      assigning to interfaces, 191
      defining, 332–333
      defining for DLSW+ session
         configuration, 1024
      defining for multiport bridging, 191
      peers, identifying IP address, 398–400
   lists
      configuration, 470–471
      DLSw+, defining, 405–406
   removing, 710–711
   RPS (Ring Parameter Service), configuration,
      268–269
role command, 861, 864
   APPN link station, 966
   APPN port, 967
route-additional-resistance command, 854
router-additional-resistance command, 968
routing
   bridges
      displaying logical configuration, 301–303
      see also bridging
   central, configuration, 544–545

Cisco 7000
   displaying CIP interface information,
      1158–1161
   reinitializing SSP, 159–160
concurrent routing and bridging, 128
enabling in bridge groups, 157–158
integrated, displaying interface configuration,
   177–178
IP, enabling, 166
Level 3, 196
multiple dual-port SRBs, any-to-any
   connectivity, 189
NCIA (native client interface architecture)
   configuration, 1025–1026
protocols, 196–198
spanning tree topology, displaying, 178–180
specifying physical location, 789–790
SRB
   dual port bridging, 189
   LNM support, 208–214
   see also SRB
SR/TLB (source-route translational bridging),
   configuration, 199–200
STUN (Serial Tunnel)
   assigning SDLC primary or secondary
      role, 494
   enabling SDLC local
      acknowledgment, 495
routing information field, *see* RIF
RPS (Ring Parameter Server), 210, 268–269
RSRB (Remote Source-Route Bridging), 346
   Cisco's implementation, 12
   direct Frame Relay encapsulation, 357, 362
   FRAS (Frame Relay Access Support), 834
   maintenance, 361
   over FST, 347–348
      assigning IP address, 348
      enabling SRB on interfaces, 349
      remote peer identification, 348–349
   over FTCP/IP, 351
      enabling SRB on interfaces, 352
      example, 364–365
      remote peer identification, 352
   over point-to-point connections, 346
      enabling SRB on interfaces, 347
      remote peer identification, 347
      ring group definition, 346

over TCP/IP, 350
    enabling SRB on interfaces, 351
    example, 362–363
    remote peer identification, 350–351
    with local acknowledgment, 352–355
    SDLLC configuration, 655–656
        over FST, 656
        over TCP, 656
        with Direct Encapsulation, 656
        with local acknowledgment, 657
    Token Ring implementation, example,
       375–377
    tuning, 359–361
    with IP load sharing, 374–375
    with LLC2 local acknowledgment, 366–369,
       372–374
    with local acknowledgment and pass-through
       example, 369–372
rsrb remote-peer lsap-output-list command,
    384–385
rsrb remote-peer netbios-output-list command,
    385–386
rsrb-virtual-station command, 860, 968
RUs (activation request units), transmission,
    751–752

S

safe-store-cycle command, 855, 969
safe-store-host command, 855, 970
safe-store-interval command, 855, 971
SAP (service access point)
    associating value to SDLLC, 654
    filters, defining, 384–385
    prioritization, 357–358
sap-priority command, 386
sap-priority-list command, 387
SAPs
    associating with X.25 serial interfaces,
       686–687
    listening for incoming calls, 552–553
    unreachable, listing, 448–449
saving APPN directories, 855
SDE (Secure Data Exchange), enabling, 161–162
SDLC (Synchronous Data Link Control)
    addresses, attaching to DLSw+, 626
    APPN

        configuring, 973
        partner node, specifying, 972
    enabling DLSw+, 412
    I-frame size, specifying largest, 659
    line speed for, increasing, 659
    local acknowledgment, enabing on STUN
       routers, 495
    multilink transmission groups, STUN
       configuration, 496–497
    primary nodes, assigning, 588–589
    primary stations
        assigning, 638
        configuration, 611–612
    secondary nodes, assigning, 589–590
    secondary stations
        assigning, 638
        configuration, 612–613
        FRMR support, 627–628
        polling limit configuration, 633–634
    sessions, terminating, 632
sdlc address command, 624–625
sdlc address ff ack-mode command, 625–626
sdlc dlsw command, 475–476, 626
sdlc dte-timeout command, 626–627
sdlc frmr-disable command, 627–628
sdlc holdq command, 628–629
sdlc k command, 629–630
sdlc line-speed command, 630–631
SDLC (Synchronous Data Link Control)
sdlc n1 command, 631
sdlc n2 command, 632
sdlc partner command, 632–633
sdlc poll-limit-value command, 633–634
sdlc poll-pause-timer command, 634–635
sdlc poll-wait-timeout command, 636–637
sdlc qllc-prtnr command, 637
sdlc role command, 638–639
sdlc sdlc-largest-frame command, 639, 659
sdlc simultaneous command, 639–640
sdlc slow-poll command, 640–641
sdlc t1 command, 641–642
sdlc test serial command, 642–643
SDLC (Synchronous Data Link Control)
    broadcast configuration, 488–489
    defining, 490

groups, specifying for STUN
     configuration, 490
     local acknowledgment, establishing, 585–586
sdlc virtual-multidrop command, 569–570
sdlc vmac command, 644
sdlc xid command, 644–645
sdlc-dest-address command, 863, 972
sdlc-sec-addr command, 861, 973
SDLLC
     Cisco's implementation, 29
     configuration
          examples, 666–672
          initiating connection to Token Ring
               host, 655
     customizing, 658
     Ethernet and translational bridging,
          configuration, 657
     frame size differences, resolving, 31
     I-frame size, specifying largest, 659
     LLC2 I-frame size, specifying largest, 658
     local acknowledgment state for,
          displaying, 660
     media translation
          customization, 658–659
          enabling, 654, 695–696
          monitoring, 660
          NTRI (NCP/Token Ring Interconnection),
               677–679
     RSRB configuration, 655–656
     SAP (service access point), associating, 654
     serial interfaces, associating with SAP value,
          693–694
     sessions, activating local acknowledgment, 712
     translational bridging, 657–658
     virtual Token Ring implementation, 30
     with Direct Connection, configuration,
          653–654
     XID value, specifying, 654
sdllc partner command, 655, 690–691
sdllc ring-largest-frame command, 658, 692–693
sdllc sap command, 693–694
sdllc sdlc-largest-frame command, 694
sdllc traddr command, 654, 695–696
sdllc xid command, 654, 696–697
secondary nodes (SDLC), assigning, 589–590
secondary stations (SDLC), 28
     configuration, 612–613

FRMR support, 627–628
polling limit, 633–634
Secure Data Exchange, see SDE
security, SRB (source-route bridging)
     administrative filter configuration,
          217–220
     combining administrative filters, 220–221
     NetBIOS access filter configuration,
          215–217
     networks
          multidrop configuration, 512
          multipoint configuration, virtual multi-
               drop support, 514
security association identifiers, 64
security command (APPN), 861, 867
     link station, 973
     port, 974
selecting
     LLC2 local acknowledgment criteria, 356
     OUI code for Ethernet Type II encapsulation,
          162–164
     output interface with MAC source address,
          126–127
sending
     acknowledgments, criteria, 592
     REJ (reject commands), 594
sequencing frames, 514–515
serial interfaces
     BSTUN, configuration, 558–559
     clearing, 1070
     enabling STUN (Serial Tunnel), 491
     encapsulation, configuring, 857
     HDLC (High Level Data Link Protocol) traffic
          forwarding, 584–585
     LAT traffic, reducing, 141
     MAC address, configuration, 644
     QLLC conversion, enabling, 661
     SDLC (Synchronous Data Link Control)
          stations, XID specification, 644–645
     SDLLC
          associating with SAP value, 693–694
          media translation, enabling, 695–696
     STUN (Serial Tunnel), enabling, 559–560
     synchronous, maintaining, 1070

X.25
    associating with SAPs, 686–687
    enabling QLLC conversion, 687–689
servers
    LNM (LAN Network Manager), SRB support, 208–214
    LRM, enabling, 213
    NCIA (native client interface architecture)
        configuration, 1025–1026
        enabling SAP, 767–768
        underlying transport configuration, 766–767
    TN3270
        displaying configuration parameters, 1167–1170, 1178–1182
        limiting LU control blocks, 1142–1144
        specifying IP traffic precedence level, 1134–1135
service announcements (LAT), filtering, 87–89
Service Points (SNA)
    enabling SAP, 806–807
    displaying status, 792–793
    RSRB SAP, enabling, 802–803
    X.121 subaddress, enabling, 793
service-any command, 859, 975
serving-nn command, 976
session switch (SNA), displaying information, 1174–1176
sessions
    CP-CP (control point-to-control point), preventing, 864
    DLSw+ (Data Link Switching Plus), configuration, 1024–1025
    LLC2, 353, 356
        specifying destination address, 632–633
        T1 time, 353
    LU (logical units), limiting, 1123–1124
    NetBIOS, timeouts, 356–357
    passthrough, enabling, 392–393
    SDLC (Synchronous Data Link Control), terminating, 632
    SDLLC, activating local acknowledgment, 712
    TN3270
        disconnecting, 1132–1133
        LU availability, 1131–1132
show appn class-of-service command, 876, 977
show appn connection-network command, 876, 980

show appn directory command, 876–877, 982
show appn dlur-lu command, 983
show appn dlur-pu command, 984
show appn dlus command, 986
show appn intermediate-session command, 877, 988
show appn link-station command, 877, 990
show appn mode command, 877, 993
show appn node command, 877, 994
show appn port command, 877, 996
show appn rtp command, 999
show appn session command, 877, 1001
show appn topology command, 877, 1004
show bridge circuit-group command, 170–171
show bridge command, 167–169
show bridge group command, 171–172
show bridge multicast command, 172
show bridge vlan command, 173–174
show bsc command, 570–575
show bstun command, 575–577
show controllers token command, 292–297, 361
show dlsw capabilities command, 476–478
show dlsw circuits command, 478–479
show dlsw fastcache command, 480
show dlsw peers command, 481–483
show dlsw reachability command, 483–486
show dlsw statistics command, 486
show dspu command, 790–792
show extended channel cmpc command, 1150–1152
show extended channel command, 1056, 1069, 1152–1153
show extended channel ip-stack command, 1153–1154
show extended channel llc2 command, 1154–1155
show extended channel statistics command, 1155–1158
show extended channel subchannel command, 1158–1161
show extended channel tcp-stack command, 1161
show extended channel tg command, 1162–1167
show extended channel tn3270-server client-ip-address command, 1170–1174
show extended channel tn3270-server command, 1167–1170
show extended channel tn3270-server dlur command, 1174–1176

show extended channel tn3270-server dlurlink command, 1176–1177

show extended channel tn3270-server nailed-ip command, 1177–1178

show extended channel tn3270-server pu command, 1178–1182

show extended channel tn3270-server pu lu command, 1182–1185

show extended channel udp-listeners command, 1185–1186

show extended channel udp-stack command, 1186–1187

show fras command, 844

show fras map command, 847

show fras-host command, 845

show interface serial command, 660

show interfaces channel command, 1187–1191

show interfaces command, 361, 645–648, 697–700

show interfaces crb command, 174–176

show interfaces irb command, 177

show interfaces tokenring command, 297–300

show llc2 command, 648–651, 660

show lnm bridge command, 214, 301

show lnm config command, 214, 301–303

show lnm interface command, 214, 303–305

show lnm ring command, 215, 305–306

show lnm station command, 215, 306–308

show local-ack command, 361, 388–389, 660

show ncia circuits command, 1034, 1046–1047

show ncia client command, 1033, 1047–1049

show ncia server command, 1033, 1049–1050

show netbios-cache command, 308–309

show qllc command, 700–702

show rif command, 309–310

show sdllc local-ack command, 703–704

show sna command, 792–793

show source-bridge command, 310–313

show span command, 178–180, 313–314

show sse summary command, 180–181, 314–315

show startup-config command, 205

show stun command, 577–578

show vlans command, 181–182

shutdown command, 1071, 1191–1192

Silicon Switch Processor, *see* SSP

slow-poll capability (SDLC)
    enabling, 640–641

SMDS (Switched Multimegabit Data Service), transparent bridging, configuration, 72

smds-dest-address command, 864, 1007

SNA (System Network Architecture)
    CIP (Channel Interface Processor) support, 57, 1052
    enabling on interfaces, 794–795
    Frame Relay
        DLSw+ dial backup configuration, 813–814
        RSRB dial backup configuration, 813
    FRAS (Frame Relay Access Support), 37
        BAN (boundary access nodes), configuration, 811
        congestion management, 812
        DLCI backup, configuration, 812–813
        dynamic configuration, 810–811
        Host, 824–828
        MIB (Management Information Base), 832
        monitoring, 815
        static configuration, 810
    LAN support using MAC adapters, 1053
    Service Point
        displaying status, 792–793
        over DLSw+, 22
    session switch
        displaying information, 1174–1176
        enabling, 1129–1130
        generating SAP, 1140–1141
    single-route explorers, changing to all-route broadcasts, 441–442
    TOS (Type of Service)
        table, 20
        configuring, 19
    VTAM and XCA support, 1052

sna enable-host command, 793–795

sna host command, 795–801

sna rsrb command, 802

sna rsrb enable-host command, 802–803

sna rsrb start command, 803–804

sna start command, 804–805

sna vdlc command, 805–806

sna vdlc enable-host command, 806–807

sna vdlc start command, 807–808

SNAP (Subnetwork Access Protocol)
    packet filtering, 146–147, 324–325, 330
software, IOS (Internetwork Operating System)
    configuring forward delay interval, 130
    enabling NetBIOS datagram transmission,
      281–282
    NetBIOS proxy configuration, 206–207
source-bridge command, 188–189, 192, 315–318,
    355, 847
source-bridge connection-timeout command, 225
source-bridge cos-enable command, 360, 389–390
source-bridge counters, clearing, 257–258
source-bridge enable-80d5 command, 318–319
source-bridge explorer-dup-ARE-filter command,
    226, 320
source-bridge explorer-fastswitch command,
    320–321
source-bridge explorer-maxrate command,
    226, 321
source-bridge explorerq-depth command, 226, 322
source-bridge fst-peername command, 390, 656,
    704–705
source-bridge input-address-list command, 219,
    322–323
source-bridge input-lsap-list command, 218,
    323–324
source-bridge input-type-list command, 219,
    324–325
source-bridge keepalive command, 391
source-bridge largest-frame command, 361,
    391–392
source-bridge max-hops command, 325
source-bridge max-in-hops command, 326
source-bridge max-out-hops command, 326–327
source-bridge output-address-list command, 220,
    327–328
source-bridge output-lsap-list command, 218,
    328–329
source-bridge output-type-list command, 219,
    329–330
source-bridge passthrough command, 355,
    392–394
source-bridge proxy-explorer command, 330–331
source-bridge proxy-netbios-only command,
    205, 331
source-bridge qllc-local-ack command, 664,
    705–706
source-bridge remote-peer command, 657

source-bridge remote-peer frame-relay command,
    394–395
source-bridge remote-peer fst command, 395–397,
    706–707
source-bridge remote-peer fst-peername
    command, 656
source-bridge remote-peer ftcp command, 397–398
source-bridge remote-peer interface command,
    707–709
source-bridge remote-peer tcp command, 398–400,
    709–710
    NCIA, using DLSw+ and RSRB, 1032
    SDLLC with RSRB over TCP, using, 656
source-bridge ring-group command, 191, 332–333,
    657, 710–711
    NCIA
      DLSw+, 1027
      RSRB, 1032
    SDLLC
      RSRB over FST, 656
      RSRB over TCP, 656
      RSRB using direct encapsulation, 656
source-bridge route-cache cbus command, 192,
    334–335
source-bridge route-cache command, 223, 333–334
source-bridge route-cache sse command, 335
source-bridge sap-80d5 command, 336–337
source-bridge sdllc-local-ack command, 657, 712
source-bridge spanning command, 337–339
source-bridge tcp-queue-max command, 361,
    400–401
source-bridge transparent command, 339–341
source-bridge transparent fastswitch command,
    341–342
source-route bridging, *see* SRB
source-route translational bridging
    see SR/TLB
spanning-tree
    automatic, 194–195, 255–256
    BPDU (bridge protocol data unit) intervals,
      configuration, 90–91
    bridge priority, configuration, 90
    disabling on interfaces, 91–92, 149–150
    explorers
      blocking, 193–194
      controlling, 326
      forwarding, 193–194

forward delay interval, configuration, 91
interface priority, configuration, 90
maximum idle interval, configuration, 91
parameters, configuration, 89
path costs, configuration, 90
protocol definition, 156–157
topology
  displaying, 178–180, 313–314
  reconfiguration, 153–154
specific polls, configuration, 550
specifying
access lists for interfaces, 135–136
APPN, partial name LUs, 873
bridge groups, protocols for bridging, 124–125
channel attach interfaces, 1133–1134
group codes for bridge group access denial, 142–144
interframe timeout, 542–543
name cache (NetBIOS), entry character length for validation, 280–281
routing protocols between bridge groups, 152–153
STUN (Serial Tunnel), protocol group, 489–490
SR/TLB (source-route translational bridging), fast switched, disabling, 201
frame conversion, Token Ring LLC2-to-Ethernet, 202–203
IBM 8209 bridges, translation compatibility, 202
SRB (Source-Route Bridging)
access expressions, defining, 252–253
automatic spanning-tree, enabling, 194–195
autonomous switching, enabling, 224, 334–335
backup queue, modifying, 400–401
bridging routed protocols, 196–198
comparing to Level 3 routing, 196
configuration, examples, 230, 249
connections, establishing timeout, 317–318
definition, 11
displaying statistics, 310–313
dual-port bridges, configuration, 189
enabling fast switching, 333
explorer processing, optimizing, 225–227
fast-switching, enabling, 223–224
hops, limiting, 196

interface configuration, 315–317
interoperability, 227
  with IBM PC/3270 emulation software, 228
  with TIMAC firmware, 228
LNM (LAN Network Manager) support
  beaconing, 210
  configuration, 208–214
  disabling, 211–212
  disabling automatic report path (trace), 212
  monitoring operation, 214
LSAP (link service access point) filters, defining, 384–385
maintenance, 229–230
multiport bridging
  configuration, 190–191
  ring group definition, 191
  ring groups, 190
NetBIOS protocol, 11, 203–208
over FDDI
  configuration, 191–192
  fast-switching configuration, 192
over Frame Relay, configuration, 193, 811–812
proxy explorers, configuration, 227
remote peer connections, timeout, 225
RIFs, 196
  enabling, 197
  static entry configuration, 198
  timeout configuration, 198
ring groups, defining, 332–333
security
  administrative filters, 217–220
  combining administrative filters, 220–221
  NetBIOS access filters, 215–217
spanning tree, explorer packets, 193–194
SR/TLB, fast-switched, disabling, 201
SSE, enabling, 224
ST/TLB, IBM 8209 translation compatibilty, 202
Token Ring, managing with LNM, 210
tuning, 223–227
SRT
compared with SR/TLB, 10
configuration, 62–63

features of Cisco implementation, 9
hardware supporting, 9
SSE (silicone switching engine), enabling, 224, 335
SSP (Silicon Switch Processor)
    reinitializing, 159–160, 258–259
    statistics, displaying, 180–181, 314–315
standard access lists, generating, 119–122
starting APPN ports, 874–875
static configuration
    FRAS BNN, 810
    MAC addresses, 453–454
stations
    access lists, defining for outgoing
        messages, 285–287
        LLC2, repolling, 594–595
        polling, setting retry limit, 593
    assigning access list names, 275–276
    displaying LNM-related information, 306–308
    RIF validation, enabling, 290–291
statistics
    bisync (binary synchronous communication)
        interfaces, displaying, 570–574
    bridge groups, displaying, 171–172
    CIP (Channel Interface Processor) interfaces,
        displaying, 1155–1158
    local acknowledgments, displaying, 388–389
    processor boards, displaying, 292–297
    removing, 160
    SDLC (Synchronous Data Link Control)
        interfaces, displaying, 697–700
    source-bridging, displaying, 310–313
    SSP (Silicon Switch Processor), displaying
        statistics, 180–181, 314–315
    Token ring interfaces, displaying, 297–300
    VLAN, removing, 160
STUN (Serial Tunnel)
    configuration, examples, 500, 509
    defining custom protocol, 491
    Direct Frame Relay connectivity, local
        acknowledgment configuration, 496
    displaying connection status, 575–577
    enabling, 488, 559–560
    encapsulation method, establishing, 491
    features, 24
    modes
        local acknowledgment, 23
        passthrough, 23

    multilink transmission groups, configuration,
        496–497
    network activity, monitoring, 500
    network overview, 23
    overview, 23
    protocol groups, specifying, 489–490
    routers, assigning SDLC primary or secondary
        role, 494
    SDLC
        broadcast configuration, 488–489
        transmission groups, defining, 490
    traffic priorities, configuration, 497–499
stun group command, 578–579
stun keepalive-count command, 579, 581
stun protocol-group command, 581–582
stun remote-peer-keepalive command, 582–583
stun route address interface dlci command,
    583–584
stun route address interface serial command,
    584–585
stun route address tcp command, 585–586
stun route all interface serial command, 586–587
stun route all tcp command, 587
stun schema offset length format command,
    587–588
stun sdlc-role primary command, 588–589
stun sdlc-role secondary command, 589–590
subchannels (CMPC)
    configuration, 1126–1127
    displaying information, 1150–1152
subinterface configuration commands
    encapsulation isl, 161
    encapsulation sde, 161–162
subinterfaces, VLAN, viewing, 173–174
subsystem, APPN
    initiating, 874
    monitoring, 876–877
switching
    autonomous, enabling, 334–335
    SSE (Silicon Switching Engine), enabling, 335
    see also fast switching
synchronization, RIF cache, enabling, 291–292
system generation parameters, configuring for
    SDLLC, 677
Systems Network Architecture, *see* SNA

T

T1 time, 353
TCP (Transport Control Protocol)
    DLSw+ (Data Link Switching Plus),
        configuration, 408
    encapsulation
        with local acknowledgment, 493–495
        without local acknowledgment, 492
    traffic, prioritizing, 389–390
TCP/IP (Transport Control Protocol/Internet
    Protocol), RSRB configuration, 350
    enabling SRB on interfaces, 351
    example, 362–363
    remote peer identification, 350–351
    with local acknowledgment (LLC2), 352–355
tcp-port command, 1192–1193
terminating
    APPN, subsystem, 874
    TN3270 entities, 1191–1192
terms, access expressions (table), 252–253
tg command, 1193–1194
tg-number command, 864, 1007
tg-row command, 870, 1008
timeout
    dynamic entries (bridge tables),
        configuration, 132
    interframe, specifying, 542–543
    NetBIOS name caching configuration, 206,
        356–357
    polling cycles, specifying, 546–547
    remote peer connections, configuration, 225
    RIF, inactive entries, 287–288
    RIF interval, configuring for SRB
        networks, 198
    source route bridge connections
        establishing, 317–318
timers
    DSLw, configuration, 414
    transmit-poll-frame timer (I-frames),
        configuration, 595
timing-mark command, 1195–1196
TN3270 configuration commands
    client, 1123–1124
    dlur, 1129–1130
    generic-pool, 1131–1132
    idle-time, 1132–1133
    ip precedence, 1134–1135

ip tos, 1135–1137
keepalive TN3270, 1137–1138
maximum-lus, 1142–1144
pu, 1148–1150
shutdown, 1191–1192
tcp-port, 1192–1193
timing-mark, 1195–1196
unbind-action, 1196–1197
TN3270 server
    CIP (Channel Interface Processor), 57
    LU nailing
        client command, 1088
        compressing files, 1077
        configuration size limits, 1077
        configuration task, 1088
        defined, 1077
        nailing algorithm, defined, 1078–1079
        storing configuration files in Flash, 1078
    TOS (type of service)
        description, 1074
        IP precedence configuration, 1085
        IP TOS configuration, 1085
        precedence setting, 1074
tn3270-server command, 1085, 1194–1195
Token Ring
    APPN partner node, specifying, 942
    displaying interface statistics, 297–300
    displaying LNM-related information, 305–306
    DSLW+ sessions, configuration, 1024–1025
    dual-port bridging, 189
    extended LAN, 11
    frame format, 11
    LANs, dual port bridges, 188
    LLC2-to-Ethernet
        frame conversion, 202–203
        translation behavior, modifying, 318–319
    logical configuration, monitoring, 262–263
    managing SRB with LNM, 210
    multiport bridging, 190–191
    ring error messages, modifying interval, 214
    ring groups, removing, 710–711
    SRB interoperability, 11, 227
        with IBM PC/3270 emulation
            software, 228
        with TIMAC firmware, 228
    virtual rings, *see* ring groups

Token Ring (Cisco)
    MAC layer address
        configuration, 270–271
topologies
    NCIA (native client interface architecture),
        1023
    redundant network, FST performance,
        349–350
    SR/TLB (source-route translational bridging),
        199–201
    SRB (source-route bridging)
        enabling automatic spanning-tree,
            194–195
        enabling RIFs, 197
        limiting hops, 196
        LNM support, 208–214
        reducing explorer packets, 194
        RIF static entry configuration, 198
        RIF timeout configuration, 198
        security, 215–220
        see also SRB
trace (automatic report path), disabling on
    LNM, 212
traffic
    asynchronous, configuration, 512–513
    Bisync datalink, 510–511
    explorer, reducing, 415–416
    FRAS (Frame Relay Access Support),
        controlling, 812
    HDLC (High Level Data Link Protocol)
        forwarding on serial interfaces, 584–585
    mapping to remote peers, 458–459
    STUN (Serial Tunnel)
        encapsulation, 586–587
        establishing priorities, 497–499
        forwarding, 587
    TCP, prioritizing, 389–390
    Token Ring, administrative filter configuration,
        217–220
transit bridging, 7
translational bridging
    SDLLC configuration, 657–658
    Token Ring-to-Ethernet LLC2, enabling for
        non-IBM hosts, 336–337
    see also SR/TLB

transmission
    error messages, interval configuration,
        269–270
    frames, sequencing, 514–515
    I-frames, controlling, 591–594
    XID (exchange of identification),
        configuration, 595–596
transmission groups
    characteristics, configuration, 866–867
    SDLC (Synchronous Data Link Control),
        defining for STUN configuration, 490
transmission-priority command, 870, 1010
transparent bridging
    bridge table aging time, configuration, 81
    bridging with SRB, 201
    circuit groups, configuration, 92–93
    configuration, 62–63
    constrained multicast flooding, configuration,
        93–94
    examples, 95–115
    features of Cisco implementation, 6
    forwarding dynamically determined stations
        preventing, 80
    integrated routing and bridging, configuring, 7
    LAT compression, enabling, 79
    multicast addresses, forwarding, 81
    multicast state information
        clearing, 158–159
        displaying, 172–173
    multiple spanning-tree domains, establishing,
        79–80
    options, configuration, 77–78
    over WANs, configuration, 68–73
    security association identifiers, 64
    SR/TLB (source-route translational bridging),
        199–201
    VLANs, configuration, 63–65
tuning
    APPN networks, 875
    RSRB, 359–361
    SRB, 223–227
        enabling source-route autonomous
            switching cache, 224
        enabling source-route fast-switching
            cache, 223
        enabling SSE, 224

establishing connection timeout interval,
225
explorer processing optimization,
225–227
proxy explorer configuration, 227
two-way simultaneous mode (SDLC), enabling,
639–640
type 2.0 nodes, configuration, 866
type-code access lists, generating, 120–122

U

UDP (User Datagram Protocol)
disabling, 417, 473–474
listener sockets, displaying information,
1185–1186
unacknowledged frames
resending, 618–619
T1 time configuration, 593
transmission, controlling, 617–618
unbind-action command, 1196–1197
unreachable SAPs, listing, 448–449
updating APPN definitions, 852
upstream host connections, enabling SDLC
addresses, 755
user-defined-1 command, 862, 867
APPN link station, 1011
APPN port, 1011
user-defined-2 command, 862, 867
APPN link station, 1012
APPN port, 1013
user-defined-3 command, 862, 867
APPN link station, 1014
APPN port, 1015

V

validation, RIFs (Routing Information Field),
289–290
vdlc command, 860, 1016
vendor code, packet filtering, 253–255
verify-adjacent-node-type command, 865, 1017
viewing
circuit groups, configured interfaces, 170–171
classes in bridge forwarding database,
167–169
status, bridge groups, 171–172
VLAN subinterfaces, 173–174

VINES protocol (SRB), appending RIF
information, 197
virtual data link control
APPN
over DLSw+, 22–23
port, defining, 909
ring group, specifying, 1016
virtual MAC address option, specifying,
1016
DSPU over DLSw+, supporting, 22
SNA Service Point, over DLSw+,
supporting, 22
virtual
interfaces (Token Ring), creating, 842
LANs, see VLANs
rings, 11
see also ring groups
Token Ring
address (VTRA), using with SDLLC, 30
implementation, 658
VLANs (Virtual LANs), 160
ISL (Inter-Switch Link), enabling, 161
routing between, configuration, 65–67
security association identifiers, 64
subinterfaces, viewing, 173–174
transparently bridged, configuration, 63–65
vrn command, 1197–1198
VTAM (Virtual Telecommunications Access
Method)
definitions, configuring for SDLLC, 678
support on CIP, 1053

W

WANs (Wide Area Networks), transparent
bridging, 68–73
ATM (Asynchronous Transfer Mode), 68
DDR (Dial-on-Demand Routing), 68–70
Frame Relay, 70–71
multiprotocol LAPB, 71–72
SMDS (Switched Multimegabit Data
Service), 72
X.25, transparent bridging, 72–73
wildcard command, 873, 1018
WILL TIMING-MARKs
specifying transmission time, 1195–1196

X

X.25
  bridging configuration, 182–185
  devices, accepting calls on routers, 681–682
  SNA packets, maximum size
    configuration, 682–683
  subaddress, configuring, 1020
  transparent bridging, configuration, 72–73
x25 map bridge command, 182–185
x25 map qllc command, 661, 713–716
x25 pvc qllc command, 661, 716–717
x25 subaddress command, 861
x25-dest-address command, 864, 1019
x25-subaddress command, 1020
XID (exchange of identification)
  associating with X.25 devices, 662–663
  controlling, 622–623
  response time, configuration, 623–624
  specifying value for SDLLC, 654
xid-block-number command, 855, 1021
xid-id-number command, 855, 1021

CISCO CERTIFIED INTERNETWORK EXPERT

Cisco's CCIE certification programs set the professional benchmark for internetworking expertise. CCIEs are recognized throughout the internetworking industry as being the most highly qualified of technical professionals. And, because the CCIE programs certify individuals—not companies— employers are guaranteed any CCIE with whom they work has met the same stringent qualifications as every other CCIE in the industry.

To ensure network performance and reliability in today's dynamic information systems arena, companies need internetworking professionals who have knowledge of both established and newer technologies. Acknowledging this need for specific expertise, Cisco has introduced three CCIE certification programs:

WAN Switching

ISP/Dial

Routing & Switching

CCIE certification requires a solid background in internetworking. The first step in obtaining CCIE certification is to pass a two-hour Qualification exam administered by Sylvan-Prometric. The final step in CCIE certification is a two-day, hands-on lab exam that pits the candidate against difficult build, break, and restore scenarios.

Just as training and instructional programs exist to help individuals prepare for the written exam, Cisco is pleased to announce its first CCIE Preparation Lab. The CCIE Preparation Lab is located at Wichita State University in Wichita Kansas, and is available to help prepare you for the final step toward CCIE status.

Cisco designed the CCIE Preparation Lab to assist CCIE candidates with the lab portion of the actual CCIE lab exam. The Preparation Lab at WSU emulates the conditions under which CCIE candidates are tested for their two-day CCIE Lab Examination. As almost any CCIE will corroborate, the lab exam is the most difficult element to pass for CCIE certification.

Registering for the lab is easy. Simply complete and fax the form located on the reverse side of this letter to WSU. For more information, please visit the WSU Web page at `www.engr.twsu.edu/cisco/` or Cisco's Web page at `www.cisco.com`.

CISCO CCIE PREPARATION LAB

REGISTRATION FORM

Please attach a business card or print the following information:

Name/Title: _____

Company: _____

Company Address: _____

City/State/Zip: _____

Country Code (_____) Area Code (_____) Daytime Phone Number _____

Country Code (_____) Area Code (_____) Evening Phone Number _____

Country Code (_____) Area Code (_____) Fax Number _____

E-mail Address: _____

Circle the number of days you want to reserve lab: 1   2   3   4   5

Week and/or date(s) preferred (3 choices):

_____

_____

_____

Have you taken and passed the written CCIE exam?   Yes   No

List any CISCO courses you have attended:

Registration fee: _____ $500 per day × _____ day(s) = Total _____

Check Enclosed (Payable to WSU Conference Office)

Charge to: _____ MasterCard or Visa exp. Date _____

CC# _____

Name on Card _____

Cardholder Signature _____

Refunds/Cancellations: The full registration fee will be refunded if your cancellation is received at least 15 days prior to the first scheduled lab day.

Wichita State University
University Conferences
1845 Fairmount
Wichita, KS 67260
Attn: Kimberly Moore
Tel: 800-550-1306
Fax: 316-686-6520